T0224354

Lecture Notes in Computer Science 12759

More information about this subseries at http://www.springer.com/series/7407

Alexandra Silva · K. Rustan M. Leino (Eds.)

Computer Aided Verification

33rd International Conference, CAV 2021
Virtual Event, July 20–23, 2021
Proceedings, Part I

 Springer

Editors
Alexandra Silva
University College London
London, UK

K. Rustan M. Leino
Automated Reasoning Group | AWS
Seattle, WA, USA

ISSN 0302-9743   ISSN 1611-3349   (electronic)
Lecture Notes in Computer Science
ISBN 978-3-030-81684-1   ISBN 978-3-030-81685-8   (eBook)
https://doi.org/10.1007/978-3-030-81685-8

LNCS Sublibrary: SL1 – Theoretical Computer Science and General Issues

This Springer imprint is published by the registered company Springer Nature Switzerland AG
The registered company address is: Gewerbestrasse 11, 6330 Cham, Switzerland

Preface

It was our privilege to serve as the program chairs for CAV 2021, the 33rd International Conference on Computer-Aided Verification. CAV 2021 was held as a virtual conference during July 20–23, 2021. The tutorial days were on July 19 and July 24, 2021, and the pre-conference workshops were held during July 18–19, 2021. Due to the COVID-19 outbreak, all events took place online.

CAV is an annual conference dedicated to the advancement of the theory and practice of computer-aided formal analysis methods for hardware and software systems. The primary focus of CAV is to extend the frontiers of verification techniques by expanding to new domains such as security, quantum computing, and machine learning. This puts CAV at the cutting edge of formal methods research, and this year's program is a reflection of this commitment.

CAV 2021 received a very high number of submissions (290). We accepted 16 tool papers, 3 case studies, and 60 regular papers, which amounts to an acceptance rate of roughly 27%. The accepted papers cover a wide spectrum of topics, from theoretical results to applications of formal methods. These papers apply or extend formal methods to a wide range of domains such as concurrency, machine learning, and industrially deployed systems. The program featured keynote talks by Loris D'Antoni (UW-Madison), Corina Pasareanu (NASA), and Anna Slobodova (Centaur Technology, Inc.) as well as invited tutorials by Nate Foster (Cornell University), Zak Kincaid (Princeton) together with Tom Reps (UW-Madison), and Nadia Polikarpova (UC San Diego). Furthermore, we continued the tradition of Logic Lounge, a series of discussions on computer science topics targeting a general audience.

In addition to the main conference, CAV 2021 hosted the following workshops: Formal Approaches to Certifying Compliance (FACC), Formal Methods for ML-Enabled Autonomous Systems (FoMLAS), Formal Methods for Blockchains (FMBC), Numerical Software Verification (NSV), Theory and Practice of String Solving (TPSS), Verifying Probabilistic Programs (VeriProP), Synthesis (SYNT), Satisfiability Modulo Theories (SMT), and Verification Mentoring Workshop (VMW).

Organizing a flagship conference like CAV requires a great deal of effort from the community. The Program Committee for CAV 2021 consisted of 79 members — a committee of this size ensures that each member has to review only a reasonable number of papers in the allotted time. In all, the committee members wrote over 900 reviews while investing significant effort to maintain and ensure the high quality of the conference program. We are grateful to the CAV 2021 Program Committee for their outstanding efforts in evaluating the submissions and making sure that each paper got a fair chance. Like last year's CAV, we made the artifact evaluation mandatory for tool paper submissions and optional, but encouraged, for the rest of the accepted papers. This year saw an unprecedented number of 66 artifact submissions. The Artifact Evaluation Committee consisted of 72 members who put in significant effort to evaluate each artifact. The goal of this process was to provide constructive feedback to tool developers and help make the research published in CAV more reproducible. We are also very grateful to the Artifact Evaluation Committee for their hard work and dedication in evaluating the submitted artifacts.

CAV 2021 would not have been possible without the tremendous help we received from several individuals, and we would like to thank everyone who helped make CAV 2021 a success. First, we would like to thank Clément Pit-Claudel and Maria Schett for chairing the Artifact Evaluation Committee and John Cyphert for putting together the proceedings. We also thank Arie Gurfinkel for chairing the workshop organization, Bor-Yuh Evan Chang for managing sponsorship, Thomas Wies for arranging student fellowships, Norine Coenen for handling publicity, Leopold Haller for organising the Logic Lounge, and Peter Müller for putting together the *Ask me Anything* program. We also thank Jean-Baptiste Jeannin and Arjun Radhakrishna for chairing the Mentoring Committee. Putting together an online conference is a complex task and we are grateful to the virtualization chair Tiago Ferreira, the student volunteer coordinators Tobias Kappé and Tao Gu, the local organizers for the Asia timezone, Ichiro Hasuo and Krishna S, and the team at Slides Live for all their efforts. Last but not least, we would like to thank the members of the CAV Steering Committee (Kenneth McMillan, Aarti Gupta, Orna Grumberg, and Daniel Kroening) for helping us with several important aspects of organizing CAV 2021.

We hope that you will find the proceedings of CAV 2021 scientifically interesting and thought-provoking!

June 2021   Alexandra Silva
                                                                   Rustan Leino

Organization

Steering Committee

Ornal Grumberg	Technion, Israel
Aarti Gupta	Princeton University, USA
Daniel Kroening	Amazon, USA
Kenneth Mcmillan	University of Texas at Austin, USA

Conference Co-chairs

K. Rustan M. Leino	Amazon, USA
Alexandra Silva	University College London, UK

Artifact Co-chairs

Clément Pit-Claudel	Massachusetts Institute of Technology, USA
Maria Schett	University College London, UK

Workshop Chair

Arie Gurfinkel	University of Waterloo, Canada

Verification Mentoring Workshop Organizing Committee

Jean-Baptiste Jeannin (Co-chair)	University of Michigan, USA
Arjun Radhakrishna (Co-chair)	Microsoft Research, USA
Suguman Bansal	University of Pennsylvania, USA
Roopsha Samanta	Purdue University, USA
Caterina Urban	Inria and École Normale Supérieure, France

Logic Lounge Organizer

Leopold Haller	Google Inc., USA

Ask Me Anything Organizer

Peter Müller	ETH Zürich, Switzerland

Publicity Chair

Norine Coenen   CISPA Helmholtz Center for Information Security,
                              Germany

Sponsorship Chair

Bor-Yuh Evan Chang   University of Colorado Boulder, USA

Fellowship Chair

Thomas Wies   New York University, USA

Student Volunteer Coordinators

Tao Gu   University College London, UK
Tobias Kappé   Cornell University, USA

Proceedings and Talks Chair

John Cyphert   University of Wisconsin–Madison, USA

Virtualization Chair

Tiago Ferreira   University College London, UK

Local Organization Chairs

Ichiro Hasuo   National Institute of Informatics, Japan
Krishna S.   IIT Bombay, India

Program Committee

Erika Abraham   RWTH Aachen University, Germany
Elvira Albert   Universidad Complutense de Madrid, Spain
Christel Baier   TU Dresden, Germany
Clark Barrett   Stanford University, USA
Ezio Bartocci   TU Wien, Austria
Josh Berdine   Facebook, UK
Armin Biere   Johannes Kepler University Linz, Austria
Sam Blackshear   Novi, USA
Jasmin Blanchette   Vrije Universiteit Amsterdam, Netherlands
Roderick Bloem   Graz University of Technology, Austria
Borzoo Bonakdarpour   Michigan State University, USA
Ahmed Bouajjani   Université de Paris, France
Tevfik Bultan   University of California, Santa Barbara, USA

Sagar Chaki	Mentor Graphics, USA
Bor-Yuh Evan Chang	University of Colorado Boulder and Amazon, USA
Hana Chockler	King's College London, UK
Cristina David	University of Bristol, UK
Jennifer Davis	Collins Aerospace, USA
Yuxin Deng	East China Normal University, China
Rayna Dimitrova	CISPA Helmholtz Center for Information Security, Germany
Alastair Donaldson	Imperial College London, UK
Constantin Enea	Université de Paris, France
Joao Fernandes	University of Porto, Portugal
Bernd Finkbeiner	CISPA Helmholtz Center for Information Security, Germany
Vijay Ganesh	University of Waterloo, Canada
Pierre Ganty	IMDEA Software Institute, Spain
Aarti Gupta	Princeton University, USA
Arie Gurfinkel	University of Waterloo, Canada
Ichiro Hasuo	National Institute of Informatics, Japan
Marieke Huisman	University of Twente, Netherlands
David N. Jansen	Institute of Software, Chinese Academy of Sciences, China
Jean-Baptiste Jeannin	University of Michigan, USA
Ranjit Jhala	University of California, San Diego, USA
Rajeev Joshi	Amazon, USA
Temesghen Kahsai	The University of Iowa, USA
Benjamin Lucien Kaminski	University College London, UK
Joost-Pieter Katoen	RWTH Aachen University, Germany
Guy Katz	The Hebrew University of Jerusalem, Israel
Laura Kovacs	Vienna University of Technology, Austria
Mitja Kulczynski	Kiel University, Germany
Mohit Kumar Tekriwal	University of Michigan, USA
Orna Kupferman	The Hebrew University of Jerusalem, Israel
Marta Kwiatkowska	University of Oxford, UK
Shuvendu Lahiri	Microsoft Research, USA
Akash Lal	Microsoft Research, India
Kim Larsen	Aalborg University, Denmark
Marijana Lazic	Technical University of Munich, Germany
Owolabi Legunsen	University of Illinois at Urbana-Champaign, USA
K. Rustan M. Leino (Co-chair)	Amazon, USA
Rupak Majumdar	Max Planck Institute for Software Systems, Germany
Ruben Martins	Carnegie Mellon University, USA
Ken McMillan	University of Texas at Austin, USA
Aina Niemetz	Stanford University, USA
Ruzica Piskac	Yale University, USA
Sylvie Putot	Ecole Polytechnique, France

Artifact Evaluation Committee

Isabel Garcia-Contreras	IMDEA Software Institute and Universidad Politecnica de Madrid, Spain
Luke Geeson	Arm, UK
Nick Giannarakis	University of Wisconsin-Madison, USA
Pablo Gordillo	Universidad Complutense de Madrid, Spain
Laura Graves	University of Waterloo, Canada
Zheng Guo	University of California, San Diego, USA
Vedad Hadžić	Graz University of Technology, Austria
Miguel Isabel	Universidad Politécnica de Madrid, Spain
Anastasiia Izycheva	Technical University of Munich, Germany
Chris Jenkins	University of Iowa, USA
Daniela Kaufmann	Johannes Kepler University Linz, Austria
Brian Kempa	Iowa State University, USA
Bettina Könighofer	Graz University of Technology, Austria
Mitja Kulczynski	Kiel University, Germany
Mohit Kumar Tekriwal	University of Michigan, USA
Stella Lau	Massachusetts Institute of Technology, USA
Julien Lepiller	Yale University, USA
Chunxiao Li	University of Waterloo, Canada
Junyi Liu	Institute of Software, Chinese Academy of Sciences, China
Debasmita Lohar	Max Planck Institute for Software Systems, Germany
Makai Mann	Stanford University, USA
Roy Margalit	Tel Aviv University, Israel
Sidi Mohamed Beillahi	Université de Paris and CNRS, France
Marcel Moosbrugger	TU Wien, Austria
Marianela Morales	Inria, France
Jasper Nalbach	RWTH Aachen University, Germany
Andres Noetzli	Stanford University, USA
Mário Pereira	Universidade NOVA de Lisboa, Portugal
Mateo Perez	University of Colorado Boulder, USA
Elizabeth Polgreen	University of California, Berkeley, USA
Mathias Preiner	Stanford University, USA
Tim Quatmann	RWTH Aachen University, Germany
Bob Rubbens	University of Twente, Netherlands
Vimala S.	Indian Institute of Technology, Madras, India
Philipp Schröer	RWTH Aachen University, Germany
Joseph Scott	University of Waterloo, Canada
Amanda Stjerna	Uppsala University, Sweden
Zachary Susag	University of Wisconsin-Madison, USA
Hira Syeda	Chalmers Universityof Technology, Sweden
Martin Tappler	Graz University of Technology, Austria
Michael Tautschnig	Queen Mary University of London, UK
Saeid Tizpaz Niari	University of Texas at El Paso, USA
Hazem Torfah	University of California, Berkeley, USA
Deivid Vale	Radboud University Nijmegen, Netherlands

Masaki Waga	Kyoto University, Japan
Peixin Wang	Shanghai Jiao Tong University, China
Sarah Winkler	Free University of Bozen-Bolzano, Italy
Tobias Winkler	RWTH Aachen University, Germany
Ali Younes	Bauman Moscow State University, Russia
Xiao-Yi Zhang	National Institute of Informatics, Japan
Yuhao Zhang	University of Wisconsin-Madison, USA

Additional Reviewers

Ahmad, Hammad
An, Jie
Armborst, Lukas
Almagor, Shaull
Arenas, Puri
Asadi, Sepideh
Amir, Guy
Arif, Fareed
Asarin, Eugene
Baanen, Anne
Batz, Kevin
Berzish, Murphy
Bacci, Giovanni
Baumeister, Jan
Blicha, Martin
Balasubramanian, A. R.
Belo Lourenço, Cláudio
Boker, Udi
Barbosa, Haniel
Bentkamp, Alexander
Bønneland, Frederik M.
Barwell, Adam
Berger, Jana
Brain, Martin
Castellano, Ezequiel
Chen, Mingshuai
Coenen, Norine
Castro-Pérez, David
Chida, Nariyoshi
Cogumbreiro, Tiago
Cetinkaya, Ahmet
Chipara, Octav
Correas Fernández, Jesús
Cheang, Kevin
Dai, Gaoyang

Defourné, Antoine
Downing, Mara
Darwin, Oscar
Dill, David
Dunn, Isaac
Dave, Vrunda
Dohmen, Taylor
Dureja, Rohit
De Masellis, Riccardo
Doveri, Kyveli
Eberhart, Clovis
Eiers, William
Esen, Zafer
Ebrahimi, Masoud
Farzan, Azadeh
Feng, Yuan
Fleury, Mathias
Fedyukovich, Grigory
Ferraiuolo, Andrew
Gardy, Patrick
Godefroid, Patrice
Graham-Lengrand, Stéphane
Gehani, Ashish
Gomez-Zamalloa, Miguel
Grumberg, Orna
Genaim, Samir
Goorden, Martijn
Guan, Ji
Georgiou, Pamina
Gordillo, Pablo
Guha, Shibashis
Giacobbe, Mirco
Graf, Susanne
Gupta, Ashutosh
Giesl, Jürgen

Habermehl, Peter
Helfrich, Martin
Huang, Chengchao
Hadzic, Vedad
Hofmann, Jana
Huber, Nikolaus
Hark, Marcel
Holík, Lukáš
Hyvärinen, Antti
Hecking-Harbusch, Jesko
Hozzova, Petra
Irfan, Ahmed
Isabel, Miguel
Jaber, Nouraldin
Jha, Susmit
Jovanović, Dejan
Jensen, Mathias Claus
Jiang, Xu
Junges, Sebastian
Jensen, Peter Gjøl
Kadron, Burak
Klikovits, Stefan
Koenighofer, Bettina
Kempa, Brian
Klinkenberg, Lutz
Kremer, Gereon
Kheterpal, Nishant
Klüppelholz, Sascha
Kura, Satoshi
Kim, Edward
La Malfa, Emanuele
Li, Jianlin
Lin, Shaokai
Lachnitt, Hanna
Li, Yangjia
Lorber, Florian
Larraz, Daniel
Li, Yong
Lukina, Anna
Lathouwers, Sophie
Limperg, Jannis
Luppen, Zachary
Lee, Sang-Hwa
Maderbacher, Benedikt
Merayo, Alicia
Mora, Federico

Madnani, Khushraj
Metzger, Niklas
Mueller, Peter
Mallik, Kaushik
Michelmore, Rhiannon
Mundkur, Prashanth
Mann, Makai
Mohaqeqi, Morteza
Murali, Vishnu
Martin-Martin, Enrique
Monti, Raul
Möhle, Sibylle
Mazzucato, Denis
Moosbrugger, Marcel
Nagisetty, Vineel
Nenzi, Laura
Noll, Thomas
Narodytska, Nina
Nikšić, Filip
Nummelin, Visa
Nejati, Saeed
Otoni, Rodrigo
Ozdemir, Alex
Özkan, Burcu
Overbeek, Roy
Pant, Yash Vardhan
Perez, Mateo
Polgreen, Elizabeth
Passing, Noemi
Philipoom, Jade
Poulsen, Danny Bøgsted
Patane, Andrea
Pick, Lauren
Preiner, Mathias
Pereira, Mário
Piribauer, Jakob
Purser, David
Quatmann, Tim
Reynolds, Andrew
Rubbens, Bob
Ryan, Megan
Rowe, Reuben
Sato, Sota
Sebastiani, Roberto
Stanford, Caleb
Schupp, Stefan

Shah, Ameesh
Stankovic, Miroslav
Schurr, Hans-Jörg
Solovyev, Alexey
Stein, Benno
Schwenger, Maximilian
Spel, Jip
Tabar, Asmae
Torfah, Hazem
Tsiskaridze, Nestan
Tekriwal, Mohit
Tschaikowski, Max
Turrini, Andrea
Tibo, Alessandro
Unno, Hiroshi
Vasconcelos, Vasco
Vediramana Krishnan, Hari Govind
Vukmirović, Petar
Vazquez-Chanlatte, Marcell
Venkatesan, Abinaya
Waga, Masaki
Wang, Qisheng

Wilson, Amalee
Wagner, Christopher
Weil-Kennedy, Chana
Winkler, Tobias
Wang, Benjie
Welzel, Christoph
Wu, Haoze
Wang, Fang
Wicker, Matthew
Wu, Min
Wang, Peixin
Xue, Bai
Yu, Emily
Zeljić, Aleksandar
Zhang, Linpeng
Zhou, Mengchu
Zhang, Hanwei
Zhao, Hengjun
Zuleger, Florian
Zhang, Hengjun
Zhou, Li

Contents – Part I

Invited Papers

NNREPAIR: Constraint-Based Repair of Neural Network Classifiers 3
  Muhammad Usman, Divya Gopinath, Youcheng Sun, Yannic Noller,
  and Corina S. Păsăreanu

Balancing Automation and Control for Formal Verification
of Microprocessors 26
  Shilpi Goel, Anna Slobodova, Rob Sumners, and Sol Swords

Algebraic Program Analysis 46
  Zachary Kincaid, Thomas Reps, and John Cyphert

Programmable Program Synthesis 84
  Loris D'Antoni, Qinheping Hu, Jinwoo Kim, and Thomas Reps

Deductive Synthesis of Programs with Pointers: Techniques, Challenges,
Opportunities: (Invited Paper) 110
  Shachar Itzhaky, Hila Peleg, Nadia Polikarpova, Reuben N. S. Rowe,
  and Ilya Sergey

AI Verification

DNNV: A Framework for Deep Neural Network Verification 137
  David Shriver, Sebastian Elbaum, and Matthew B. Dwyer

Robustness Verification of Quantum Classifiers 151
  Ji Guan, Wang Fang, and Mingsheng Ying

BDD4BNN: A BDD-Based Quantitative Analysis Framework
for Binarized Neural Networks 175
  Yedi Zhang, Zhe Zhao, Guangke Chen, Fu Song, and Taolue Chen

Automated Safety Verification of Programs Invoking Neural Networks 201
  Maria Christakis, Hasan Ferit Eniser, Holger Hermanns,
  Jörg Hoffmann, Yugesh Kothari, Jianlin Li, Jorge A. Navas,
  and Valentin Wüstholz

Scalable Polyhedral Verification of Recurrent Neural Networks 225
  Wonryong Ryou, Jiayu Chen, Mislav Balunovic, Gagandeep Singh,
  Andrei Dan, and Martin Vechev

Verisig 2.0: Verification of Neural Network Controllers Using Taylor
Model Preconditioning.   249
   Radoslav Ivanov, Taylor Carpenter, James Weimer, Rajeev Alur,
   George Pappas, and Insup Lee

Robustness Verification of Semantic Segmentation Neural Networks Using
Relaxed Reachability.   263
   Hoang-Dung Tran, Neelanjana Pal, Patrick Musau,
   Diego Manzanas Lopez, Nathaniel Hamilton, Xiaodong Yang,
   Stanley Bak, and Taylor T. Johnson

PEREGRiNN: Penalized-Relaxation Greedy Neural Network Verifier   287
   Haitham Khedr, James Ferlez, and Yasser Shoukry

Concurrency and Blockchain

Isla: Integrating Full-Scale ISA Semantics and Axiomatic
Concurrency Models   303
   Alasdair Armstrong, Brian Campbell, Ben Simner, Christopher Pulte,
   and Peter Sewell

Summing up Smart Transitions.   317
   Neta Elad, Sophie Rain, Neil Immerman, Laura Kovács,
   and Mooly Sagiv

Stateless Model Checking Under a Reads-Value-From Equivalence.   341
   Pratyush Agarwal, Krishnendu Chatterjee, Shreya Pathak,
   Andreas Pavlogiannis, and Viktor Toman

Gobra: Modular Specification and Verification of Go Programs   367
   Felix A. Wolf, Linard Arquint, Martin Clochard, Wytse Oortwijn,
   João C. Pereira, and Peter Müller

Delay-Bounded Scheduling Without Delay!   380
   Andrew Johnson and Thomas Wahl

Checking Data-Race Freedom of GPU Kernels, Compositionally   403
   Tiago Cogumbreiro, Julien Lange, Dennis Liew Zhen Rong,
   and Hannah Zicarelli

GenMC: A Model Checker for Weak Memory Models   427
   Michalis Kokologiannakis and Viktor Vafeiadis

Hybrid and Cyber-Physical Systems

Synthesizing Invariant Barrier Certificates via
Difference-of-Convex Programming.   443
    Qiuye Wang, Mingshuai Chen, Bai Xue, Naijun Zhan,
    and Joost-Pieter Katoen

An Iterative Scheme of Safe Reinforcement Learning for Nonlinear
Systems via Barrier Certificate Generation   467
    Zhengfeng Yang, Yidan Zhang, Wang Lin, Xia Zeng, Xiaochao Tang,
    Zhenbing Zeng, and Zhiming Liu

HYBRIDSYNCHAADL: Modeling and Formal Analysis of Virtually
Synchronous CPSs in AADL   491
    Jaehun Lee, Sharon Kim, Kyungmin Bae, and Peter Csaba Ölveczky

Computing Bottom SCCs Symbolically Using Transition
Guided Reduction   505
    Nikola Beneš, Luboš Brim, Samuel Pastva, and David Šafránek

Implicit Semi-Algebraic Abstraction for Polynomial Dynamical Systems   529
    Sergio Mover, Alessandro Cimatti, Alberto Griggio, Ahmed Irfan,
    and Stefano Tonetta

IMITATOR 3: Synthesis of Timing Parameters Beyond Decidability   552
    Étienne André

Formally Verified Switching Logic for Recoverability
of Aircraft Controller.   566
    Ratan Lal, Aaron McKinnis, Dustin Hauptman, Shawn Keshmiri,
    and Pavithra Prabhakar

SceneChecker: Boosting Scenario Verification Using Symmetry
Abstractions   580
    Hussein Sibai, Yangge Li, and Sayan Mitra

Effective Hybrid System Falsification Using Monte Carlo Tree Search
Guided by QB-Robustness   595
    Zhenya Zhang, Deyun Lyu, Paolo Arcaini, Lei Ma, Ichiro Hasuo,
    and Jianjun Zhao

Fast Zone-Based Algorithms for Reachability in Pushdown
Timed Automata   619
    S. Akshay, Paul Gastin, and Karthik R. Prakash

Security

Verified Cryptographic Code for Everybody   645
  Brett Boston, Samuel Breese, Joey Dodds, Mike Dodds, Brian Huffman,
  Adam Petcher, and Andrei Stefanescu

Not All Bugs Are Created Equal, But Robust Reachability Can
Tell the Difference   669
  Guillaume Girol, Benjamin Farinier, and Sébastien Bardin

A Temporal Logic for Asynchronous Hyperproperties   694
  Jan Baumeister, Norine Coenen, Borzoo Bonakdarpour,
  Bernd Finkbeiner, and César Sánchez

Product Programs in the Wild: Retrofitting Program Verifiers to Check
Information Flow Security   718
  Marco Eilers, Severin Meier, and Peter Müller

Constraint-Based Relational Verification   742
  Hiroshi Unno, Tachio Terauchi, and Eric Koskinen

Pre-deployment Security Assessment for Cloud Services Through
Semantic Reasoning   767
  Claudia Cauli, Meng Li, Nir Piterman, and Oksana Tkachuk

Synthesis

Synthesis with Asymptotic Resource Bounds   783
  Qinheping Hu, John Cyphert, Loris D'Antoni, and Thomas Reps

Program Sketching by Automatically Generating Mocks from Tests   808
  Nate F. F. Bragg, Jeffrey S. Foster, Cody Roux,
  and Armando Solar-Lezama

Counterexample-Guided Partial Bounding for Recursive
Function Synthesis   832
  Azadeh Farzan and Victor Nicolet

PAYNT: A Tool for Inductive Synthesis of Probabilistic Programs   856
  Roman Andriushchenko, Milan Češka, Sebastian Junges,
  Joost-Pieter Katoen, and Šimon Stupinský

Adapting Behaviors via Reactive Synthesis   870
  Gal Amram, Suguman Bansal, Dror Fried, Lucas Martinelli Tabajara,
  Moshe Y. Vardi, and Gera Weiss

Causality-Based Game Solving 894
    Christel Baier, Norine Coenen, Bernd Finkbeiner, Florian Funke,
    Simon Jantsch, and Julian Siber

Author Index 919

Contents – Part II

Complexity and Termination

Learning Probabilistic Termination Proofs 3
   Alessandro Abate, Mirco Giacobbe, and Diptarko Roy

Ghost Signals: Verifying Termination of Busy Waiting 27
   Tobias Reinhard and Bart Jacobs

Reflections on Termination of Linear Loops 51
   Shaowei Zhu and Zachary Kincaid

Decision Tree Learning in CEGIS-Based Termination Analysis 75
   Satoshi Kura, Hiroshi Unno, and Ichiro Hasuo

ATLAS: Automated Amortised Complexity Analysis of Self-adjusting
Data Structures 99
   Lorenz Leutgeb, Georg Moser, and Florian Zuleger

Decision Procedures and Solvers

Theory Exploration Powered by Deductive Synthesis 125
   Eytan Singher and Shachar Itzhaky

CoqQFBV: A Scalable Certified SMT Quantifier-Free Bit-Vector Solver 149
   *Xiaomu Shi, Yu-Fu Fu, Jiaxiang Liu, Ming-Hsien Tsai,
   Bow-Yaw Wang, and Bo-Yin Yang*

Porous Invariants 172
   Engel Lefaucheux, Joël Ouaknine, David Purser, and James Worrell

JavaSMT3: Interacting with SMT Solvers in Java 195
   Daniel Baier, Dirk Beyer, and Karlheinz Friedberger

Efficient SMT-Based Analysis of Failure Propagation 209
   *Marco Bozzano, Alessandro Cimatti, Anthony Fernandes Pires,
   Alberto Griggio, Martin Jonáš, and Greg Kimberly*

ddSMT 2.0: Better Delta Debugging for the SMT-LIBv2 Language
and Friends 231
   Gereon Kremer, Aina Niemetz, and Mathias Preiner

Learning Union of Integer Hypercubes with Queries:
(with Applications to Monadic Decomposition).   243
   Oliver Markgraf, Daniel Stan, and Anthony W. Lin

Interpolation and Model Checking for Nonlinear Arithmetic.   266
   Dejan Jovanović and Bruno Dutertre

An SMT Solver for Regular Expressions and Linear Arithmetic
over String Length   289
   Murphy Berzish, Mitja Kulczynski, Federico Mora, Florin Manea,
   Joel D. Day, Dirk Nowotka, and Vijay Ganesh

Counting Minimal Unsatisfiable Subsets   313
   Jaroslav Bendík and Kuldeep S. Meel

Sound Verification Procedures for Temporal Properties
of Infinite-State Systems   337
   Quentin Peyras, Jean-Paul Bodeveix, Julien Brunel,
   and David Chemouil

Hardware and Model Checking

Progress in Certifying Hardware Model Checking Results   363
   Emily Yu, Armin Biere, and Keijo Heljanko

Model-Checking Structured Context-Free Languages.   387
   Michele Chiari, Dino Mandrioli, and Matteo Pradella

Model Checking ω-Regular Properties with Decoupled Search   411
   Daniel Gnad, Jan Eisenhut, Alberto Lluch Lafuente, and Jörg Hoffmann

AIGEN: Random Generation of Symbolic Transition Systems   435
   Swen Jacobs and Mouhammad Sakr

GPU Acceleration of Bounded Model Checking with ParaFROST.   447
   Muhammad Osama and Anton Wijs

Pono: A Flexible and Extensible SMT-Based Model Checker   461
   Makai Mann, Ahmed Irfan, Florian Lonsing, Yahan Yang,
   Hongce Zhang, Kristopher Brown, Aarti Gupta, and Clark Barrett

Logical Foundations

Towards a Trustworthy Semantics-Based Language Framework via
Proof Generation.   477
   Xiaohong Chen, Zhengyao Lin, Minh-Thai Trinh, and Grigore Roşu

Foundations of Fine-Grained Explainability   500
  Sylvain Hallé and Hugo Tremblay

Latticed k-Induction with an Application to Probabilistic Programs   524
  Kevin Batz, Mingshuai Chen, Benjamin Lucien Kaminski,
  Joost-Pieter Katoen, Christoph Matheja, and Philipp Schröer

Stochastic Systems

Runtime Monitors for Markov Decision Processes.   553
  Sebastian Junges, Hazem Torfah, and Sanjit A. Seshia

Model Checking Finite-Horizon Markov Chains
with Probabilistic Inference   577
  Steven Holtzen, Sebastian Junges, Marcell Vazquez-Chanlatte,
  Todd Millstein, Sanjit A. Seshia, and Guy Van den Broeck

Enforcing Almost-Sure Reachability in POMDPs   602
  Sebastian Junges, Nils Jansen, and Sanjit A. Seshia

Rigorous Roundoff Error Analysis of Probabilistic
Floating-Point Computations.   626
  George Constantinides, Fredrik Dahlqvist, Zvonimir Rakamarić,
  and Rocco Salvia

Model-Free Reinforcement Learning for Branching Markov Decision
Processes   651
  Ernst Moritz Hahn, Mateo Perez, Sven Schewe, Fabio Somenzi,
  Ashutosh Trivedi, and Dominik Wojtczak

Software Verification

Cameleer: A Deductive Verification Tool for OCaml.   677
  Mário Pereira and António Ravara

LLMC: Verifying High-Performance Software   690
  Freark I. van der Berg

Formally Validating a Practical Verification Condition Generator   704
  Gaurav Parthasarathy, Peter Müller, and Alexander J. Summers

Automatic Generation and Validation of Instruction Encoders and Decoders. .   728
  Xiangzhe Xu, Jinhua Wu, Yuting Wang, Zhenguo Yin, and Pengfei Li

An SMT Encoding of LLVM's Memory Model for Bounded
Translation Validation   752
  Juneyoung Lee, Dongjoo Kim, Chung-Kil Hur, and Nuno P. Lopes

Automatically Tailoring Abstract Interpretation to Custom
Usage Scenarios   777
   Muhammad Numair Mansur, Benjamin Mariano, Maria Christakis,
   Jorge A. Navas, and Valentin Wüstholz

Functional Correctness of C Implementations of Dijkstra's, Kruskal's,
and Prim's Algorithms   801
   Anshuman Mohan, Wei Xiang Leow, and Aquinas Hobor

Gillian, Part II: Real-World Verification for JavaScript and C   827
   Petar Maksimović, Sacha-Élie Ayoun, José Fragoso Santos,
   and Philippa Gardner

Debugging Network Reachability with Blocked Paths   851
   S. Bayless, J. Backes, D. DaCosta, B. F. Jones, N. Launchbury,
   P. Trentin, K. Jewell, S. Joshi, M. Q. Zeng, and N. Mathews

Lower-Bound Synthesis Using Loop Specialization and Max-SMT   863
   Elvira Albert, Samir Genaim, Enrique Martin-Martin, Alicia Merayo,
   and Albert Rubio

Fast Computation of Strong Control Dependencies   887
   Marek Chalupa, David Klaška, Jan Strejček, and Lukáš Tomovič

DIFFY: Inductive Reasoning of Array Programs Using
Difference Invariants   911
   Supratik Chakraborty, Ashutosh Gupta, and Divyesh Unadkat

Author Index   937

Invited Papers

NNREPAIR: Constraint-Based Repair
of Neural Network Classifiers

Muhammad Usman[1]($\boxtimes$), Divya Gopinath[2]($\boxtimes$), Youcheng Sun[3]($\boxtimes$),
Yannic Noller[4]($\boxtimes$), and Corina S. Păsăreanu[2]($\boxtimes$)

[1] University of Texas at Austin, Austin, USA
muhammadusman@utexas.edu
[2] KBR Inc., Nasa Ames, Mountain View, USA
{divya.gopinath,corina.s.pasareanu}@nasa.gov
[3] Queen's University Belfast, Belfast, UK
youcheng.sun@qub.ac.uk
[4] National University of Singapore, Singapore, Singapore
yannic.noller@acm.org

Abstract. We present NNREPAIR, a constraint-based technique for
repairing neural network classifiers. The technique aims to fix the logic
of the network at an *intermediate layer* or at the *last layer*. NNREPAIR
first uses *fault localization* to find potentially faulty network parameters
(such as the *weights*) and then performs *repair* using *constraint solving*
to apply small modifications to the parameters to remedy the defects.
We present novel strategies to enable precise yet efficient repair such
as inferring correctness specifications to act as oracles for intermediate
layer repair, and generation of *experts* for each class. We demonstrate
the technique in the context of three different scenarios: (1) Improving the *overall accuracy* of a model, (2) Fixing security vulnerabilities
caused by *poisoning* of training data and (3) Improving the *robustness* of
the network against *adversarial* attacks. Our evaluation on MNIST and
CIFAR-10 models shows that NNREPAIR can improve the accuracy by
45.56% points on poisoned data and 10.40% points on adversarial data.
NNREPAIR also provides small improvement in the overall accuracy of
models, without requiring new data or re-training.

1 Introduction

Neural networks have many applications, being used for example in pattern
analysis, image classification, or sentiment analysis for textual data, and also in
medical diagnosis or perception and control in autonomous driving, which bring
safety and security concerns [10]. These systems learn the network parameters
(weights and biases) through *training* on a set of labeled examples. The performance of the trained networks is independently validated by computing the
accuracy on a held-out labeled test set.

Just like other software systems, trained neural networks can have *defects*
that need *repair*. For example, a trained neural network may have low accuracy

© The Author(s) 2021
A. Silva and K. R. M. Leino (Eds.) CAV 2021, LNCS 12759, pp. 3–25, 2021.
https://doi.org/10.1007/978-3-030-81685-8_1

which may be due to limited training data. One would like to repair the network by modifying its parameters (or a subset of them) to improve its overall accuracy, even in the absence of additional training data. In another scenario, the training data for a neural network has been *poisoned* by an adversary leading to high accuracy on normal data but poor accuracy on poisoned data [6,7,11]. In this case, one would like to repair the network to remedy the defect while still maintaining a high accuracy on non-poisoned data. In yet another scenario, a trained network may have high accuracy on the test set but may be vulnerable to adversarial perturbations, i.e., small modifications to the inputs that lead to unexpected outputs. Recent studies [8,15,20] show that this defect is very common even for highly trained, highly accurate networks. In this case, one would like to repair the network to make it *robust* against adversarial perturbations while at the same time retaining its accuracy on the normal, unperturbed test set.

Retraining could be used to alter the neural network parameters and repair for faults, but it can be very difficult and expensive subject to uncertainties, and may result in a network that is quite different from the original one, thus wasting the effort of the original training.

We present a novel constraint-solving based approach, NNREPAIR, to repair neural networks trained for the task of classification, with respect to all three scenarios described above. Similar to traditional program repair [5,13,22], NNREPAIR first uses *fault localization* to identify the network parameters that are the likely source of defects, followed by *repair*, which uses *constraint solving* to apply small modifications to the network parameters to remedy the defects.

Given a trained neural network model, the potentially faulty components could be the architecture of the model (which is fixed in the design stage) or the learn-able parameters such as the weights and the biases (which are determined during training). In this work, we focus on the learn-able parameters of a neural network model, specifically the weights on the edges connecting neurons. As observed in [9], changing the weights is a common fix for neural networks.

We leverage the organization of a neural network into layers and the natural decomposition of computation that each layer provides, and scope our work to focus the repair on a single layer of the network. Repairs across multiple layers are possible, but they would be less scalable and involve more complex modifications. We propose two types of repairs: *intermediate-layer repair* and *last-layer repair*. Intermediate-layer repair attempts to fix failures by modifying the behavior of neurons at an inner layer of the network. Last-layer repair, on the other hand, attempts to modify the decision constraints at the last layer.

Fault localization is used to mark one or more neurons at a layer as 'suspicious' and to find a sub-set of incoming edges to the suspicious neurons, whose weights will be the target for repair. The repair process involves solving constraints collected from the network, via a simple form of concolic execution [17]. For last-layer repair, the oracle of the repair is the desired label for every failing input and the repair constraints encode this decision. For intermediate-layer repair, we propose a novel use of activation patterns representing specifications of correct behavior at the layer [4] as oracles for repair. This enables us to keep the repair local to the layer and therefore efficient.

Furthermore, to make the *constraint solving* scalable, instead of solving for constraints for all classes at once, we propose to *decompose* the repair into a set of sub-tasks, one for each output class. Specifically, we set-up the constraint solving to correct a subset of the weights with the goal of improving accuracy of the model wrt a specific output class. The result of this repair is a set of *experts*, which are neural networks that improve accuracy of the network wrt specific output classes. We then combine the experts to obtain the final repaired model.

There are a few recent related techniques that propose to use constraint solving for neural network repair. We summarize them in Sect. 6. These techniques tend to focus on last layer repair while we also propose repair at an intermediate layer. Furthermore, we evaluate our initial prototype in three scenarios: improving accuracy, robustness and resilience towards poisoned data. None of the related techniques address all three (albeit potentially possible).

We summarize our contributions as follows.

- We propose and implement a repair technique that applies fault localization and constraint solving to neural networks. Our approach can perform both *last* and *intermediate* layer repair.
- To achieve scalability, our approach decomposes the repair into a set of *experts* which display superior accuracy for specific labels. These are then combined using a set of *strategies* that we propose to obtain the final repair.
- We present a novel technique to make it more efficient to repair inner layers of a neural network by *inferring specifications of correct behavior* (in the terms of the activation patterns) at the output of inner layers, and using them as oracles for repair.
- While previous neural network repair techniques (see Sect. 6) tend to focus solely on improving accuracy, we demonstrate our technique in the context of three different scenarios: (1) Improving the overall accuracy of a model, (2) Fixing security vulnerabilities caused by *poisoning* of training data and (3) Improving the *robustness* of the network against *adversarial* attacks.
- We evaluate the techniques in the context of image classifiers for the MNIST and CIFAR-10 data sets. The results indicate that NNREPAIR can improve the performance of the network by 45.56% points on poisoned data and 10.40% points on adversarial data. NNREPAIR also provides small improvement (+0.20% points), in the overall accuracy of models, without requiring new data or re-training.

2 Background

Neural Networks. In this work we focus on neural network classifiers. These networks take in an input, such as an image, and output a class (or label) specific to the problem they have been trained to solve. Networks are organized in *layers* of different types, including convolutional, activation, and pooling, each of which has a number of nodes. For this paper, we focus on activation layers.

Each node from the previous layer will output into the associated node in the activation layer, which will apply an *activation function*. Common activation functions include linear rectification (a.k.a. ReLU) and sigmoid. For simplicity we discuss here ReLU activations but our work applies to arbitrary activations as discussed below. Let $N(X)$ denote the value of a neuron as a function of the input. $N(X) = \sum_i w_i \cdot N_i(X) + b$ where N_i's denote the values of the neurons in the previous layer of the network and the coefficients w_i and the constant b are referred to as *weights* and *bias*, respectively. If this function evaluates to a non-negative value, the node is *activated* and outputs that value, otherwise it outputs 0. A final decision (logits) layer produces the network decisions based on the real values computed by the network, by applying e.g., a softmax function; in our work we use the max function instead. For a comprehensive introduction to neural networks, see [3].

Activation Patterns. We leverage previous work [4] to infer network properties based on the *activation patterns* of neurons in the network. We will use these activation patterns as oracles for the intermediate layer repair. An activation pattern σ specifies an activation status (*on* or *off*) for some subset of neurons at a layer in the network. All other neurons do not matter. We write $on(\sigma)$ for the set of neurons marked *on*, and $off(\sigma)$ for the set of neurons marked *off* in the pattern σ. Each activation pattern σ defines a predicate $\sigma(X)$ that is satisfied by all inputs X whose evaluation achieves the same activation status for all neurons as prescribed by the pattern.

$$\sigma(X) ::= \bigwedge_{N \in on(\sigma)} N(X) > 0 \; \wedge \; \bigwedge_{N \in off(\sigma)} N(X) \leq 0 \tag{1}$$

A decision pattern σ is a property wrt network F and postcondition P if:

$$\forall X : \sigma(X) \Rightarrow P(F(X)). \tag{2}$$

A postcondition for a classification network is that the top predicted class is C, i.e., $P(Y) := argmax(Y) = C$.

The previous work [4] also describes how to compute activation patterns. The idea is to observe the activation signatures of a large number of inputs and apply decision tree learning over them to infer activation patterns that are thus empirically valid. We adopt the same approach here. The *support* of a pattern is formed by all the inputs that satisfy the pattern. We are interested in computing high-support patterns as they are the most likely to reflect valid properties of the network.

3   Example

This section demonstrates *Intermediate-layer* and *Last-layer* repair on a simple example. Figure 1 shows a simple two-input network with two hidden layers; each containing two ReLU nodes (ReLU(x) = x (on) if x > 0, 0 (off) otherwise), and

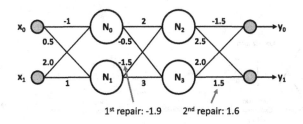

Fig. 1. Example

Table 1. Data for example

	x_0	x_1	N_0	N_1	N_2	N_3	y_0	y_1	class	ideal
X_0	1	1	1	1	0	1	8	6	0	0
X_1	0	1	1	1	1	1	0.25	9.25	1	1
X_2	1	0	0	1	0	1	3	2.25	0	0
X_3	−1	1	1	1	1	0	−7	13.12	1	1
X_4	1.5	2	1	1	1	1	12.68	12.68	1	0
after repair:	1.5	2	1	1	0	1	13.3	10.5	0	0
X_5	0.6	1	1	1	1	1	5.91	5.62	0	1
after repair:	0.6	1	1	1	1	1	5.91	5.95	1	1

two outputs, y_0 and y_1. The weights are depicted on the edges between nodes. For simplicity we assume biases are 0. The input X, which is a two-element array denoted $[x_0, x_1]$, is assigned class 0 if $y_0 > y_1$ and 1 otherwise. Let us assume the model behaves correctly on the first four inputs shown in Table 1. The table also shows the decisions of the ReLU activations for nodes N_0, N_1, N_2, N_3, respectively. Whenever a ReLU node is on, the decision is indicated as a 1 and if it is off, then the decision value is shown as 0.

Consider now the input $X_4 = [1.5, 2.0]$. Assume this input is mis-classified; the output class is 1 but the ideal class is 0. The inaccuracy of the model could be a result of insufficient training. We then aim to build a repair, which in our case focuses on a single layer of the network and modifies the weights feeding into the neurons at that layer.

We keep the repair local to the layer by using activation patterns [4] in lieu of the decision constraints. The insight in [4] is that the logic that every layer implements could be captured as rules in terms of the activation patterns of the neurons. We can observe in the example, that for all inputs correctly classified with label 0, the neuron pair (N_2, N_3) in the second layer has the activation pattern (off, on). For the failing input, this pattern is not satisfied; in fact the activation for (N_2, N_3) for the failing input is (on, on). We use the above observation to fix the failure by performing *intermediate layer* repair. We

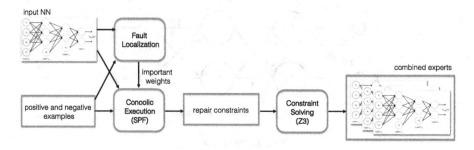

Fig. 2. Overview of the approach

aim to modify the neuron activations of the second layer on the failing input to satisfy the correct-label pattern for class 0 at the layer.

We aim to perform the repair by making minimal changes to the model. We identify the weights to be modified using an attribution-based approach and use constraint solving to compute the values of the new weights (see Sect. 4 for details). Changing the weight of a single edge, connecting N_1 and N_2 from -1.5 to -1.9 changes the activation pattern for (N_2, N_3) to (off, on) on the failing input, while preserving the behavior of the neurons (in terms of their activation pattern) and the output of the model on the passing inputs.

Consider now another input for the above-corrected network, $X_5 = [0.6, 1.0]$. This input is very close to $X_1 = [0.0, 1.0]$ (correctly classified to 1) with a small change to x_0 that makes the model mis-classify the input to 0. This represents a typical adversarial scenario where a correctly classified input is perturbed slightly to create an input that 'jumps' the decision boundary of the network leading to a mis-classification. It can be observed that the activation patterns of the internal layer neurons for X_5 are the same as for the correctly classified input X_1, thus an intermediate-layer repair would not work for this input. Therefore we perform *last-layer repair*. We localize the weights of the edges in the last layer that need repair. Changing the weight on the edge between N_3 and y_1 (from 1.5 to 1.6) corrects the class for the failing test to 1, while retaining the same labels for the other inputs.

4   Approach

Figure 2 gives an overview of our approach. We aim to repair a faulty trained neural network classifier, which is given as input. As in other repair approaches, we consider both positive and negative examples for the repair. The negative examples are used to guide the repair towards correcting the faults while the positive examples are used to constrain the repair to not damage the existing good functionality of the network. We aim for a repair strategy that is scalable and applies small changes to the network. We therefore target the repair on a single layer of the network. Repairs across multiple layers of the network are possible, but they would be less scalable and involve more complex modifications.

Unlike all previous work, which tends to focus the repair at the last layer (see Sect. 6) we propose here techniques for both intermediate and last layer repair. Intuitively, a last layer repair is easier as it aims to modify the weights that impact directly the decisions, and can use the network's output as an *oracle* to guide the repair. However the resulting repair may not generalize well and furthermore the network may be faulty at some intermediate layer. A repair at an intermediate layer can have a higher impact over the network's behavior but it is more difficult as it is not clear what *oracle* to use to guide the repair. One can use the output of the network as the oracle but this may result in an un-manageable large number of constraints to solve. In this work we propose a novel use of neuron activation patterns to act as oracles in intermediate layer repair.

As repairing for all the output classes at the same time can be very difficult, our proposed approach obtains instead a set of *expert networks*, one for each target class, which are easier to compute. These experts are combined to obtain a final repaired classifier. Specifically, our repair strategy has the following steps:

1 *Fault Localization*: The goal of this step is to identify a small set of suspicious neurons and incoming suspicious edges, whose weights we aim to correct.
2 *Concolic Execution*: For the weights of the suspicious edges, we add δ values that are set to 0 in concrete mode, but are designated as symbolic for the symbolic mode. The network is executed concolically along positive and negative examples, to collect the values of suspicious neurons in terms of symbolic expressions.
3 *Constraint Solving*: The symbolic expressions are assembled with a set of repair constraints which are then solved with an off-the-shelf solver. Essentially, the repair constraints need to encode the network decision for the positive examples and modify (i.e., correct) the network decision for the negative examples. For the last layer repair this amounts to adding constraints imposed by the decision layer. For intermediate-layer repair, we use activation patterns instead of decision constraints, allowing us to keep the repair local to the layer.
   The solutions for the symbolic δ's obtained from the solver are used to update the weights of the network, thus obtaining an *expert* for a specific class.
4 *Combining Experts*: Finally the experts obtained for each class are combined to obtain the repaired classifier. This needs to be done carefully, to avoid redundant computations among experts and to not damage the overall accuracy and timing performance of the classification.

In the following we give more details about our approach.

4.1 Intermediate-Layer Repair

Fault Localization. We explore the usage of *activation patterns* of the network (Sect. 2) to act as oracles of correct behavior. We also use these patterns to guide the identification of potentially faulty neurons. Specifically, we use the decision-tree learning approach from [4] to extract *correct-label patterns* corresponding to every output class at an intermediate layer. Each pattern is satisfied by a group of inputs correctly classified to a certain label. Typically multiple correct-label patterns are generated. We select the ones with the highest support, which are mostly likely to hold true on the network for all inputs. Note also that the work in [4] considers ReLU activations but it could be extended to consider arbitrary linear or non-linear activation functions, by comparing the values of neurons with a threshold.

A *correct-label* pattern with high support at a layer indicates that there is a high chance that any input satisfying the pattern at the layer would be classified by the network to the corresponding label. Furthermore, a mis-classified input will not satisfy the *correct-label* pattern for the respective ideal label. For every failing input, we compare the activations of the neurons with those in the respective *correct-label* pattern and consider those *neurons* whose activations differ as the potentially faulty ones. The repair then aims to change the outputs of the neurons for each of the failing inputs, such that they satisfy the correct-label pattern for their ideal labels.

In this work, we select a dense layer (i.e., a fully connected layer which receives input from every neuron in the previous layer) with ReLU activations. Typically such dense layers appear closer to the output and may impact the classification decision more than convolutional layers which process the input. Further, the number of neurons at fully connected layers is typically smaller than at other layers making the pattern-extraction process efficient.

Consider a mis-classified input, X_f with ideal label C. Let σ_C be the *correct-label* pattern with highest support for C. Let L be the layer for this pattern, and let N denote a neuron at layer L. Then the set of suspicious or faulty neurons $\mathcal{N}_{faulty}$ can be defined as follows;

$$N \in \mathcal{N}_{faulty} \iff (N \in on(\sigma_C) \wedge N(X_f) \leq 0) \vee (N \in off(\sigma_C) \wedge N(X_f) > 0) \quad (3)$$

Once the neurons whose outputs need to change are identified, we also need to identify the incoming edges to those neurons whose weights we aim to modify. We use a simple statistical method to identify the *important weights* which impact the respective neuron's output, more for the failing inputs as compared to the passing inputs.

Consider a set *Fail* of failing inputs with the same ideal label C and a set *Pass* of passing inputs. We use $\#(\cdot)$ to denote the cardinality of the sets. The defect score for each edge is determined as follows.

$$Score(E_i) ::= \frac{\sum_{X \in Fail} |N_i(X) \cdot w_i|}{\#Fail} - \frac{\sum_{X \in Pass} |N_i(X) \cdot w_i|}{\#Pass} \quad (4)$$

Here E_i denotes an incoming edge (for a faulty node N), N_i is the corresponding node in the preceding layer and w_i is the weight of the edge.

Thus, we take the average of the absolute values passing through the edge for all the negative examples for C and the average of the absolute values passing through the edge for all the positive examples and subtract them. The intuition is to identify the edges which have more influence on the incorrect decision of the network. We calculate the defect score for each incoming edge to each neuron (N) in $\mathcal{N}_{faulty}$. We then select the edges with top n% of the scores to create the set of faulty edges, for a small n.

Concolic Execution. We perform a simplified form of concolic execution to form symbolic constraints for suspicious neurons. For the weights of the suspicious edges, we add δ values that are set to 0 in concrete mode, but are designated as symbolic in the symbolic mode. The network is executed concolically along both positive and negative examples, to collect the values of neurons as weighted sums in terms of both concrete values and the symbolic δ values. The value of a neuron is computed as constraints of the following form:

$$Sym_{N,X} = \sum_i (w_i + \delta_i) \cdot N_i(X) + \sum_j w_j \cdot N_j(X) + b \qquad (5)$$

Here $Sym_{N,X}$ is a fresh symbolic variable introduced to encode the symbolic value of neuron N for input X, w_i's denote the weights of the suspicious edges (in the suspicious layer) while the w_j's denote the other weights, which do not need modification. Furthermore, $N_i(X)$, $N_j(X)$ represent the concrete values of the neurons coming from the previous layer. Note that no expensive constraint solving is needed in this step.

Repair Constraints and Constraint Solving. For intermediate-layer repair, we add the activation patterns constraints (that imply the decision constraints, see Eq. 1) to the set of constraints. Specifically, for each neuron N in $\mathcal{N}_{faulty}$, and for each (passing or failing) input X we add $Sym_{N,X} > 0$ if $N \in on(\sigma_C)$ and we add $Sym_{N,X} \leq 0$ if $N \in off(\sigma_C)$.

The solutions for the symbolic δ's obtained from the solver guarantee that all the inputs (both passing and failing) satisfy the pattern and are thus likely to be classified as C by the network. These solutions are then used to update the weights of the network, thus obtaining an *expert* for the class C.

Example. Let us consider the example from Sect. 3, the case of the intermediate-layer repair. As already discussed in Sect. 3, let us suppose we consider the activation pattern for class 0 at layer 2. We select N_2 as the target for repair (since its activation along the failing test X_4 is on instead of off) and we want the input to satisfy the pattern {off, on} for {N_2, N_3}. We compute defect scores for the incoming edges to N_2 using the failing input and all passing inputs for classes 0 and 1. The score of the edge between N_0 and N_2 is 2.0 while the score of the edge between N_1 and N_2 is 2.81, we therefore select the second edge as a target for repair. We then build the following constraints from the failing test.

$Sym_{N_2,4} = 2.0 \cdot (-1.0 \cdot 1.5 + 2.0 \cdot 2.0) + (-1.5 + \delta) \cdot (0.5 \cdot 1.5 + 1.0 \cdot 2.0) \wedge Sym_{N_2,4} \leq 0.0$

Similarly, we build constraints from the passing tests that satisfy the pattern for label 0, X_0 and X_2:

$Sym_{N_2,0} = 2.0 \cdot (-1.0 \cdot 1.0 + 2.0 \cdot 1.0) + (-1.5 + \delta) \cdot (0.5 \cdot 1.0 + 1.0 \cdot 1.0) \wedge Sym_{N_2,0} \leq 0.0 \wedge$
$Sym_{N_2,2} = 2.0 \cdot (-1.0 \cdot 1.0 + 2.0 \cdot 0.0) + (-1.5 + \delta) \cdot (0.5 \cdot 1.0 + 1.0 \cdot 0.0) \wedge Sym_{N_2,2} \leq 0.0$

In practice we also add some constraints on δ to keep it small but we omit them here for simplicity. A solution for all the constraints is $\delta = -0.4$ which is used to update the weight for the target repair resulting in an expert for class 0.

4.2   Last-Layer Repair

Fault Localization. In a classifier network the last layer typically contains as many neurons as the number of classes. An input is classified to label C, if the output of the respective neuron is greater than the values of all other output neurons. It is therefore natural to designate this neuron as suspicious for target class C. Let N_C denote the neuron at the last layer corresponding to a class C. We use the same technique as in intermediate layer repair (Eq. 4) to *localize edges* and short-list the important weights which are the target for repair.

Concolic Execution. Similar to the intermediate layer repair, we add symbolic δ values to the important weights and perform concolic execution along passing and failing tests to create the symbolic expression for the node $Sym_{N_C,X}$ (following Eq. 5).

Repair Constraints and Constraint Solving. We then add the decision constraints for the passing and failing inputs:

$$\bigwedge_{C \neq C'} Sym_{N_C,X} > Sym_{N_{C'},X} \tag{6}$$

The obtained solutions guarantee that all the inputs that were used in the repair (both positive and negative) are classified to the correct class. The solutions are used to build the expert for each class. We then combine the experts using the combination strategies outlined in the next section.

Example. Consider now the example from Sect. 3, the case of the last-layer repair. As we aim to repair for class 1 we select for repair the neuron named y_1 in the figure. The score for the edge between N_2 and y_1 is -2.75 and the score for the edge between N_3 and y_1 is 0.45 so we select the latter for repair. We then build the following constraints based on the failed test (note that the expression for the second variable simplifies to a concrete value):

$Sym_{y_1,5} = (2.5 \cdot (2 \cdot (-1 \cdot 0.6 + 2 \cdot 1.0) - 1.9 \cdot (0.5 \cdot 0.6 + 1 \cdot 1.0)) + (1.5 + \delta) \cdot (-0.5 \cdot (-1 \cdot 0.6 + 2 \cdot 1.0) + 3 \cdot (0.5 \cdot 0.6 + 1 \cdot 1.0)))\wedge$

$Sym_{y_0,5} = (-1.5 \cdot (2 \cdot (-1 \cdot 0.6 + 2 \cdot 1.0) - 1.9 \cdot (0.5 \cdot 0.6 + 1 \cdot 1.0)) + 2.0 \cdot (-0.5 \cdot (-1 \cdot 0.6 + 2 \cdot 1.0) + 3 \cdot (0.5 \cdot 0.6 + 1 \cdot 1.0)))\wedge$

$Sym_{y_1,5} > Sym_{y_0,5}$

Similar constraints are added for the positive inputs (we omit them here for brevity). Solving these constraints gives $\delta = 0.1$ which is added to the weight for the edge between N_3 and y_1 to obtain an expert for class 1.

4.3   Combining Experts

We create experts for each label in the dataset. For example, for a neural network trained on the MNIST data set (which is used for the classification of handwritten digits from 0 to 9), we generate 10 experts – one expert per label. We propose three variants of how to combine these experts:

(A) execute the model for all experts and combine the results afterwards,
(B) *merge* all experts into one combined expert before model execution, and
(C) filter strong experts first, then follow variant (A) or (B).

Variant (A) is an instance of *ensemble modeling* [1], which typically involves creating multiple models to predict an outcome. In our case, we start by executing all the experts for each input. This is done in a combined fashion, to avoid repeated execution of same code: before the repaired layer the model is executed with the original weights; starting from the repaired layer the execution is split up for the different experts. At the end of the execution, each expert classifies the input to a certain label. We need to combine the results from all the experts in order to classify the input to a single label.

Each expert can classify the input to any of the labels, however, each expert can be trusted to produce the correct result only for its own respective label. Therefore, we start by generating a set E including the experts that classify the inputs to their respective labels. Note that it could be that multiple experts report that the given input belongs to their respective class or it could be that no expert classifies the given input to the expert's class. If E is empty, then we select the label by the original model. If there is one expert in E, then we select this unique expert. If there are multiple experts in E, then we need to resolve the conflict between experts and choose one label, for which we propose three strategies:

Naive: This strategy simply falls back to the original model.
Confidence: This strategy selects the expert from E with the highest confidence for its own label, i.e., the absolute value of the output node corresponding to the label.
Voting: For the label corresponding to each expert in E, this strategy collects votes from the other experts for the respective label. It then selects the expert from E with the majority of the votes.

In variant (B), we propose to merge the experts before executing the model. For the intermediate-layer repair, for every weight that is considered faulty we update it with the one δ value, which is the *average* of the solutions from all the experts. This creates a single *merged* network. For the last-layer repair, we simply apply all the repairs at once; there is no need for an average as the nodes (and edges) that are targets for repair are disjoint.

In variant (C), instead of using all experts we select a subset of strong experts. Note that each expert is constructed from failing inputs only for the respective label. Therefore, when exposed to data which are supposed to be classified to the expert's label, the expert displays higher accuracy than the original model (higher recall). However, when exposed to data which can belong to different labels, the experts could display lower overall accuracy than the original model (lower precision) due to high false positives. Therefore, we determine which of the experts have both their precision and recall (*F1 score*), computed over all positive/negative inputs, higher than the original model and retain only those while filtering out the rest. The same combination strategies, variant (A), are used to obtain a single classification result for the input.

5   Evaluation

We implemented our approach in the NNREPAIR tool pipeline, which is based on NEUROSPF [21]. It first translates a trained Keras model into Java, uses Symbolic PathFinder (SPF) [16] for concolic execution and z3 [14] for constraint solving. In this section we evaluate NNREPAIR by considering its application to three highly common scenarios; *Scenario 1:* improving accuracy, *Scenario 2:* fixing backdoor attacks, and *Scenario 3:* enhancing adversarial robustness. Our experiments use two commonly used datasets for image classification networks, MNIST and CIFAR-10. We consider two architectures for MNIST with 10 and 7 layers respectively. They are convolutional neural networks (CNNs) and have the typical structure of modern neural networks such as convolutional/dense, max-pooling and softmax layers. The first MNIST model has an accuracy of 96.34% on the standard test set, while the second model has an accuracy of 98.89%. We refer to these models as MNIST-LQ (low-quality) and MNIST-HQ (high-quality) respectively. The CIFAR-10 model is a 15-layer CNN with 890k trainable parameters and has an accuracy of 81.04%. In order to validate our approach, we consider the following research questions:

RQ1 Is NNREPAIR successful in correcting the defects in all three scenarios?
RQ2 How do intermediate-layer repair and last-layer repair compare with each other?
RQ3 What is the inference time overhead introduced by NNREPAIR over the original model?

5.1   Scenarios

(1) The goal of repair in the first scenario is to improve the overall accuracy of a model. We measure the improvement in accuracy on the standard test set, henceforth denoted Test. We use positive and negative examples from the train set, henceforth denoted Train, to generate the repair.

(2) For this scenario, we apply the backdoor attack from [6]. Samples of poisoned data are shown in Fig. 3. The poisoned models have good accuracy on the standard data, but poor accuracy on the poisoned data. The goal of the repair is to improve the accuracy on poisoned data, which we measure on a separate poisoned test set P-Test. At the same time, we expect the repair

Fig. 3. Example poisoned data for MNIST (left) and CIFAR-10 (right). The backdoor is embedded as the white square at the bottom right corner of each image. When the backdoor appears, the poisoned MNIST model will classify the input as "7" and the poisoned CIFAR-10 model will classify it as "horse".

to retain the accuracy on standard, un-poisoned data, which we measure on Test. In this scenario, the first 600 inputs in Train are poisoned (P-Train). We draw from these particular inputs to get the negative examples to focus the repair on the defect. We draw the positive examples from Train.

(3) For the last scenario, we apply adversarial perturbations over Train and Test using FGSM[1], for $\epsilon = 0.05$. This results in four data sets: Train, Adv-Train, Test and Adv-Test. The models have good overall accuracy on Train and Test, but poor accuracy on Adv-Train and Adv-Test. The goal of the repair here is to improve the accuracy on the adversarial data (which we measure on Adv-Test) without damaging too much the accuracy on standard data (which we measure on Test). We draw the negative examples to be used in repair from Adv-Train, while we use positive examples from both Adv-Train and Train. Since we use two separate sets to generate experts, when computing the F1-score for selection of experts, we explored two different options: computing F1 score over Adv-Train only and computing harmonic mean of the F1 scores computed over Train and Adv-Train separately. However, in practice there was no difference as same experts were filtered in both cases.

5.2   Experiment Set-Up

For each of the three scenarios, we experimented with both intermediate-layer and last-layer repairs. We evaluated all the combination strategies (Naive, Confidence, Voting, and Merged) with the F1-filtering option being OFF and ON. When F1-filtering is OFF, the experts for all labels are used in the combination strategies by default, while when it is ON, we only include those experts whose F1 score on Train is greater than the original model.

Intermediate-Layer Repair: We focused on the dense layer just before the output layer for both the MNIST and CIFAR models. The intuition for this selection is that dense layers appearing closer to the output potentially impact the classification decision more than convolutional layers closer to the input (which have the role of feature extraction). The MNIST models have 128 and 100 ReLU nodes and 576 and 400 incoming edges to each neuron at this layer respectively, while the CIFAR model has 512 ReLU neurons and 1,600 incoming edges at this

---

[1] https://www.tensorflow.org/tutorials/generative/adversarial_fgsm.

layer. We extracted high support patterns for correct classification; the average support per label was within 1,013–2,502 across scenarios, out of around 6,000 inputs per label. The neurons short-listed in $\mathcal{N}_{faulty}$ using pattern-based localization varied between 1 and 10 in number. We focused on modifying the weights of the incoming edges having their scores within the top 10%.

We used the patterns extracted at the layer to select a subset of tests for the purpose of constraint solving. As explained in Sect. 4, we used decision-tree learning to extract patterns for correct classification for every label. We also extracted patterns for incorrect classification for each label, which represent neuron activations satisfied by inputs which should ideally be classified to the given label but get mis-classified. From the set of all failing tests for a given label, we select all inputs that satisfy the pattern for incorrect classification for the label. From the set of all passing tests for a given label, we select the subset of inputs that satisfy the pattern for correct classification. We then randomly select # failing tests + 100 inputs from this set. The subset of failing and passing tests selected using the procedure above is used for constraint solving.

Last Layer Repair: At the last layer, the two MNIST models have 10 ReLU nodes and 128 and 100 incoming edges to each neuron respectively, while the CIFAR model has 10 ReLU neurons and 512 incoming edges. For each label, we selected 5 failing and 5 passing inputs randomly from the respective datasets. For the first scenario, both these failing and passing inputs come from the Train set. For the last layer repair top 5 suspicious weights were made symbolic for each expert. We determined empirically that a larger number for symbolic weights and/or passing/failing inputs leads often to unsat constraints while a smaller number may not improve the network.

The poisoned (2) and adversarial (3) scenarios differ from scenario 1, in that they seek to address two challenges. The repaired model needs to have better accuracy than the original model on poisoned and adversarial inputs respectively (evaluated on the P-Test and Adv-Test sets), as well as the accuracy on normal inputs should not be degraded much (evaluated on the normal Test set). For this reason, for the purpose of constraint solving in addition to including passing tests from the respective poisoned and adversarial train sets, we also include passing tests from Train. We performed experiments increasing the number of passing tests included from the normal train set from 0 to 10, 50, and 100.

5.3   Results

Table 2 presents a summary of our results (please refer to the Appendix[2] for more detailed results). The table displays the results for MNIST and CIFAR models for the three scenarios. For each scenario, the results for both intermediate layer and last layer repair are presented in terms of the improvement in accuracy obtained over the original model. This is the best result corresponding to the improvement in accuracy on the respective test sets (normal Test for the first

---

[2] https://arxiv.org/abs/2103.12535.

scenario, P-Test for the second and Adv-Test for the third). The combination strategy and the F1-Filter setting (ON/OFF) used to obtain the best result are also displayed, along with the corresponding improvements in accuracy on the other train and test sets. For the repair, z3 was able to generate solutions for each expert within a minute. The constraint generation using SPF was the bottleneck and SPF generated constraints for each expert within 15–60 min, depending on the number of tests included. However, this could be improved since running SPF on all positive/negative inputs can be performed in parallel. Experiments were performed on a Windows 10.0 machine with Intel Core-i5 and 16 GB RAM. The code, constraint files along with Z3 solution files are available at https://github.com/muhammadusman93/nnrepair.

RQ1: For this research question we seek to investigate if NNREPAIR is successful in correcting defects in all three scenarios. To measure success, we consider the improvement in accuracy provided by the repair in all three scenarios.

The effectiveness of NNREPAIR in improving accuracy (Scenario 1) can be analyzed by considering Table 2 (cases MNIST-LQ, MNIST-HQ and CIFAR10).

We observe that the best results provided by NNREPAIR for the MNIST-LQ model was +0.20, +0.02 for the MNIST-HQ model and +0.16 for the CIFAR10 model. This improvement (albeit small) was achieved without any new inputs or re-training. The quality of the improvement appears to degrade as the quality of the original model increases. We note that achieving improvement in the overall accuracy of an already high-quality model without new data is very challenging. In fact this improvement appears to be in line or better than related repair techniques (see Sect. 6). Note also that the complexity and size of the models do not seem to have an impact on the effectiveness of the repair. The MNIST-HQ architecture is simpler than MNIST-LQ and the CIFAR10 architecture is much bigger and more complex than the MNIST models.

For Scenario 2, on the MNIST-Pois model, NNREPAIR increased the accuracy from 10.38% to 55.94% on poisoned inputs (P-Test). The repair causes a slight decrease (-3.11) in accuracy on non-poisoned inputs (Test) but the repaired model still has a high accuracy ($\geq 95.5\%$) on non-poisoned inputs. On the more challenging CIFAR10-Pois model, the best improvement provided by NNREPAIR is a +3.77 increase on poisoned inputs, and a small decrease in accuracy on non-poisoned inputs (-0.61). For Scenario 3, on the MNIST-Adv model, NNREPAIR increased the accuracy from 28.37% to 38.77% on adversarial inputs, while causing a small decrease (-3.14) in accuracy on non-adversarial inputs. For CIFAR10-Adv, the best result was an increase of +0.34 on adversarial inputs with a minor decrease of -0.07 on non-adversarial inputs.

For the last two scenarios, the primary goal is to improve accuracy on poisoned or adversarial data. Although ideally we would also want to preserve the original accuracy on normal data, this may not always be possible in practice. We experimented with varying number of passing tests from Train for scenarios 2 and 3. The results are presented in the first table in the Appendix. The accuracy of the resulting repair on the poisoned/adversarial test sets tends to decrease as the number of normal passing tests goes up. However, this also reduces the

Table 2. Summary of NNREPAIR performance on all models. Repair column shows the type of repair, i.e., intermediate or last layer. Increase/decrease in accuracy shown in terms of the difference between the accuracy of the repaired model and the original model on the respective datasets. Accuracy of the original model is shown in brackets (in bold) below each data set. The *Strategy* column shows the combination strategy which work best for each scenario. *ALL* means that all strategies performed equally. *F1-Filter* shows if best results were obtained by turning F1-Filter ON or OFF. The number of experts used are shown in brackets.

Model	Repair	Increase/Decrease in accuracy				Strategy	F1-Filter
		Train		**Test**			
		(96.59%)		**(96.34%)**			
MNIST-LQ	Interm	+0.22		+0.20		Votes	ON(3)
MNIST-LQ	Last	+0.00		+0.00		ALL	ON(0
		Train		**Test**			
		(99.81%)		**(98.89%)**			
MNIST-HQ	Interm	+0.01		+0.02		Merged	ON(3)
MNIST-HQ	Last	+0.00		+0.00		ALL	ON(0)
		P-Train		**Test**	**P-Test**		
		(98.99%)		**(98.63%)**	**(10.38%)**		
MNIST-Pois	Interm	+0.00		−0.01	+1.81	Votes	ON(2)
MNIST-Pois.	Last	−2.60		−3.11	+45.56	Confidence	OFF
		Train	**Adv-Train**	**Test**	**Adv-Test**		
		(98.67%)	**(29.92%)**	**(97.87%)**	**(28.37%)**		
MNIST-Adv	Interm	−4.35	+2.75	−4.15	+3.87	Confidence	ON(9)
MNIST-Adv.	Last	−3.99	+11.15	−3.14	+10.40	Merged	ON(10)
		Train		**Test**			
		(87.25%)		**(81.04%)**			
CIFAR10	Interm	+0.03		+0.03		Merged	ON(1)
CIFAR10	Last	+0.12		+0.16		ALL	ON(1)
		P-Train		**Test**	**P-Test**		
		(96.97%)		**(72.26%)**	**(15.89%)**		
CIFAR10-Pois	Interm	+0.03		+0.02	+0.81	Merged	ON(4)
CIFAR10-Pois.	Last	−0.89		−0.61	+3.77	Merged	OFF
		Train	**Adv-Train**	**Test**	**Adv-Test**		
		(87.25%)	**(34.39%)**	**(81.04%)**	**(35.96%)**		
CIFAR10-Adv	Interm	+0.05	+0.22	−0.07	+0.34	Merged	ON(10)
CIFAR10-Adv.	Last	−0.25	+0.37	−0.27	+0.27	Merged	ON(10)

degradation in the accuracy on normal test set. Previous studies in adversarial robustness [23] indicate that one can obtain robust networks but the price to be paid is a significant decrease in accuracy on normal data. Similar considerations apply to the poisoning case. Therefore, we tolerate small decrease in the accuracy on normal Test in our work as well.

The last two columns in Table 2 list the combination strategies and the F1-filtering option which work best for each scenario. The Merged strategy seems to work well for the CIFAR10 model for all the three scenarios. However, there is no clear winner for the MNIST models. In fact, for the last layer repair on CIFAR10, all the strategies gave the same improvement in accuracy. In practice, the users would need to use a separate validation set and try all the strategies to pick the best one for their application domain.

> **Answer RQ1**: NNREPAIR shows benefit in all three scenarios. It can repair a network to make it robust against adversarial perturbations/poisoned inputs while at the same time retain a good accuracy on the normal, unperturbed/non-poisoned test set. NNREPAIR can also improve the overall accuracy of the models, however the effectiveness of the repair tends to decrease when the original accuracy is already high.

RQ2: Table 2 can be used to compare the performance of intermediate-layer and last-layer repair on the different scenarios. For the MNIST models, last-layer repair did not help in improving the overall accuracy. Repairing the dense layer before the output layer using the pattern-based repair helps in increasing the accuracy albeit by a small amount. For the CIFAR10 model, on the other hand, repairing the output layer increases the overall accuracy of the model by 0.16, which is better than intermediate-layer repair (+0.03).

For the poisoned and adversarial scenarios, on the MNIST models, last-layer repair performed better than intermediate layer-repair on the targeted test sets. Intermediate-layer repair increased the accuracy by 1.81 on the poisoned model and 3.87 on the adversarial model while last-layer repair increased the accuracy by 45.56 on the poisoned model and 10.40 on the adversarial model. For CIFAR10-Pois, intermediate layer repair increases the accuracy by 0.81 while last layer repair improves it by 3.77. Note that intermediate-layer repair seems to help better in retaining the accuracy on the standard Test, albeit providing smaller improvements on the target sets (detailed results in the Appendix). Furthermore, for CIFAR10-Adv, intermediate layer repair gives better results than last-layer repair (0.34 vs 0.27 respectively).

To summarize, focusing only on an inner layer of the network or just the output layer may not suffice to correct errors in all models and scenarios. We plan to investigate application of repair at more than one layer. Fault localization approaches may help determine the layer/s to focus on for effective repair for a given application.

> **Answer RQ2:** Intermediate-layer repair helped more in improving the overall accuracy of the models (except for CIFAR10) and last-layer repair was more effective in repairing specific failures such as vulnerabilities to poisoned or adversarial inputs (except on CIFAR10 adversarial model). The take away is that there is not a specific type of repair (last-layer or intermediate layer) that works well consistently and different models and failure scenarios may necessitate repair at different layers.

RQ3: To understand the overhead introduced by running multiple experts and the combination logic, we conducted experiments on one of the models, MNIST-LQ. We executed the original model on the test set and compared the inference time with the model produced by a repair at an intermediate layer (i.e., layer 6) and by a repair at the final layer (i.e., layer 8). Additionally, we measured the inference time for an intermediate layer repair with F1-Filtering (i.e., layer6-F1). We performed this comparison for all 10,000 inputs in the test set.

The *Merge* combination strategy does not require any expert combination after model execution because this strategy merges the repairs in advance. Therefore, there is no change with regard to the original model execution except the weight values used in the calculations, and we did not observe any difference in terms of the inference time. We focus the remaining discussion on the strategies that require the execution of multiple experts. Our experiments show that the time for the expert combination after model execution (as necessary for *Naive*, *Confidence*, and *Voting* combination strategies) is negligible with around 0.0008 ms and also is similar for all these combination strategies. The main overhead is introduced by the additional calculations necessary to compute the multiple expert values at each layer. The box plot in Fig. 4 shows the total time for the model execution for the experts inclusive the time for the *Naive* expert combination.

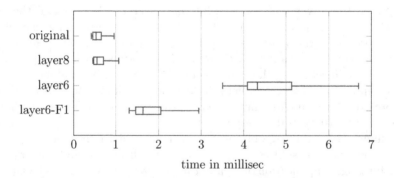

Fig. 4. Inference time comparison (*Naive* Combination Strategy)

The repair at the last layer produces an average slowdown (compared to the original model) of 1.0383x. In contrast, the repair at the intermediate layer produces an average slowdown of 7.7638x. Therefore, it makes sense to apply some filtering of experts, which do not show good performance on the training set (see F1-score filtering in Sect. 4.3). For this experiment we kept 3 experts (see the plot with *layer6-F1*). This reduced model produces an average slowdown of only 3.0742x.

> **Answer RQ3:** The *Merge* combination strategy does not impact the inference time. All other combination strategies introduce a similar overhead. While the inference time for the last-layer repair is comparable with the original model, the inference time for an intermediate-layer repair is expensive. However, it can be significantly reduced with F1 filtering.

5.4 Discussion

The purpose of our evaluation was to showcase the versatility of NNREPAIR in different scenarios. The takeaway from the experiments is that there is not a specific type of repair (last-layer or intermediate layer) that works well consistently and different models and failure scenarios may necessitate repair at different layers. In particular, we believe that the intermediate-layer repair holds the most promise for scaling to large networks and we plan to further experiment with the technique in the future.

Generally, the best repair results are obtained on the poisoning task, where the accuracy can be increased by up to 45% and 3.7% on MNIST and CIFAR10, without a need for retraining, which can be expensive in practice. Furthermore, note that we do not assume knowledge of the poison, as our techniques only use information about correct and incorrect classification. In the future, we plan to perform more experiments with different poisoning scenarios.

We were able to obtain modest accuracy improvements on the high-quality models, while for the low-quality models, re-training can achieve better results (see comparison with MODE in the next section). More experimental comparison with retraining and/or fine-tuning the models is needed to further assess the merits of our constraint-based repair.

The gains in the adversarial setting are not very significant for the larger models. In this work, our goal was to demonstrate the feasibility of using localized constraints solving as a generic technique for addressing a wide range of challenges in deep learning. Adversarial attack is only one potential application scenario that is considered. There is a large body of research work on adversarial attacks and we can not claim in any way that we can cover all attacks.

We also note that the efficacy of NNREPAIR is evaluated statistically (over the test set) as our method does not provide any formal guarantees. In general, it is difficult to guarantee an improvement of the overall accuracy with formalisms, as there are no formal specifications for the image classification domain. Thus, in practice one builds (trains) a model using a statistical measure of accuracy.

6 Related Work

The emphasis of this paper is on neural network repair, where the goal is to "correct" the neural network and improve its performance, robustness and security, by using a small number of labeled inputs. There have been relatively few attempts for repairing a neural network. These neural network repair works can be classified given if re-training is needed and/or if there is a first step to prioritize neuron weights to fix. A number of fix patterns and challenges for neural network repair were collected in [9].

In MODE [12], a neural network is said to be buggy for a specific output label if its test accuracy is lower than the expectation. This is fixed by selecting features that are critical for the misbehavior via differential analysis using a subset of training data and then retraining by selecting inputs from the remaining unused training inputs based on the differential heat map. We ran MODE on the MNIST models from our study. The results are as follows:

Model	Test Acc. (%)
MNIST-LQ	+0.37
MNIST-HQ	−0.40

NNREPAIR has similar performance, i.e., slightly better than MODE on MNIST-HighQuality and slightly worse on MNIST-LowQuality. Meanwhile, the re-training procedure in MODE led to varied performances for the repaired model. The results for MODE are the average outcome after 10 runs, none of which improved the accuracy of MNIST-HighQuality.

Unlike MODE that identifies ill-trained weights or buggy neurons, Apricot [24] first generates a set of models from the original neural network with a reduced set of training data and at each iteration of the training, Apricot adjusts each weight of the repaired model towards the average weight of these reduced models correctly classifying the input while away from the misclassifications. The approach from [19] uses constraint solving for repairing neural networks. It considers a two-dimension slice of the input space of ACAS Xu and uses SMT constraints to achieve weight changes for correct cases that are checked against the specification. We found it non-trivial to extend this approach to typically high-dimensional input space of the image classifiers that we study in this paper.

Typically, a software repair technique (including for neural networks) employs as a first step *fault localization* to determine the code entities that need to be fixed. DeepFault [2] is an approach to spectrum-based fault localization that aims to identify the neurons that are 'more' responsible to adversarial behaviours of a neural network. However, the aim of DeepFault is to generate more adversarial examples, which is the opposite to the repair purpose of our paper. Another related approach, Arachne [18], uses fault localization to identify neural weights (connected to the final output layer) to modify, using Particle Swarm Optimisation (PSO), for better weights to improve the model's accuracy on some particular label. As also noted in [18], increasing the prediction accuracy for a particular label often comes along with the decreasing prediction accuracy of the overall neural network model.

Our NNREPAIR work provides a general repair approach which can be applied for improving accuracy, enhancing robustness against adversarial attacks and fixing the backdoor security problems for neural networks. Although previous techniques could be presumably extended to these scenarios, in practice they were only demonstrated for improving the prediction accuracy of the neural network (in MODE and Apricot) or a particular label (in Arachne).

7   Conclusion and Future Work

We presented NNREPAIR, which uses constraint solving for intermediate-layer and last-layer repair of neural networks. We demonstrated NNREPAIR in three scenarios: improving the *overall accuracy*, fixing security vulnerabilities caused by *data poisoning* and improving the *adversarial robustness* of the networks.

In future work, we plan to experiment with different localization techniques and to evaluate our repair on larger networks and different architectures. Our method can also be applied to multiple layers but we restricted to single-layer for scalability. One avenue for research is to apply single-layer repair repeatedly or compositionally to handle correcting bugs across multiple layers.

References

1. Ensemble learning methods for deep learning neural networks. https://machinelearningmastery.com/ensemble-methods-for-deep-learning-neural-networks
2. Eniser, H.F., Gerasimou, S., Sen, A.: DeepFault: fault localization for deep neural networks. In: Hähnle, R., van der Aalst, W. (eds.) FASE 2019. LNCS, vol. 11424, pp. 171–191. Springer, Cham (2019). https://doi.org/10.1007/978-3-030-16722-6_10
3. Goodfellow, I., Bengio, Y., Courville, A.: Deep Learning. MIT Press, Cambridge (2016)
4. Gopinath, D., Converse, H., Pasareanu, C., Taly, A.: Property inference for deep neural networks. In: 34th International Conference on Automated Software Engineering (ASE), pp. 797–809. IEEE (2019)
5. Goues, C.L., Pradel, M., Roychoudhury, A.: Automated program repair. Commun. ACM **62**(12), 56–65 (2019). https://doi.org/10.1145/3318162
6. Gu, T., Liu, K., Dolan-Gavitt, B., Garg, S.: BadNets: evaluating backdooring attacks on deep neural networks. IEEE Access **7**, 47230–47244 (2019). https://doi.org/10.1109/ACCESS.2019.2909068

7. Huang, L., Joseph, A.D., Nelson, B., Rubinstein, B.I., Tygar, J.D.: Adversarial machine learning. In: 4th Workshop on Security and Artificial Intelligence, pp. 43–58. ACM (2011)
8. Huang, X., et al.: A survey of safety and trustworthiness of deep neural networks: verification, testing, adversarial attack and defence, and interpretability. Comput..Sci. Rev. **37**, 100270 (2020)
9. Islam, M.J., Pan, R., Nguyen, G., Rajan, H.: Repairing deep neural networks: Fix patterns and challenges. In: 42nd International Conference on Software Engineering (ICSE) (2020)
10. Jordan, M.I., Mitchell, T.M.: Machine learning: trends, perspectives, and prospects. Science **349**(6245), 255–260 (2015)
11. Liu, Y., et al.: Trojaning attack on neural networks. In: 25th Annual Network and Distributed System Security Symposium (NDSS) (2018)
12. Ma, S., Liu, Y., Lee, W.C., Zhang, X., Grama, A.: MODE: automated neural network model debugging via state differential analysis and input selection. In: 26th Joint Meeting on European Software Engineering Conference and Symposium on the Foundations of Software Engineering, pp. 175–186. ACM (2018)
13. Monperrus, M.: Automatic software repair: a bibliography. ACM Comput. Surv. **51**(1), 1–24 (2018). https://doi.org/10.1145/3105906
14. de Moura, L., Bjørner, N.: Z3: an efficient SMT solver. In: Ramakrishnan, C.R., Rehof, J. (eds.) TACAS 2008. LNCS, vol. 4963, pp. 337–340. Springer, Heidelberg (2008). https://doi.org/10.1007/978-3-540-78800-3_24
15. Papernot, N., McDaniel, P.D., Jha, S., Fredrikson, M., Celik, Z.B., Swami, A.: The limitations of deep learning in adversarial settings. In: EuroS&P (2016)
16. Păsăreanu, C.S., Visser, W., Bushnell, D.H., Geldenhuys, J., Mehlitz, P.C., Rungta, N.: Symbolic pathfinder: integrating symbolic execution with model checking for java bytecode analysis. Autom. Softw. Eng. **20**(3), 391–425 (2013). https://doi.org/10.1007/s10515-013-0122-2
17. Sen, K., Marinov, D., Agha, G.: CUTE: a concolic unit testing engine for C. In: ESEC/SIGSOFT FSE (2005)
18. Sohn, J., Kang, S., Yoo, S.: Search based repair of deep neural networks. arXiv preprint arXiv:1912.12463 (2019)
19. Sotoudeh, M., Thakur, A.V.: Correcting deep neural networks with small, generalizing patches. In: Workshop on Safety and Robustness in Decision Making (2019)
20. Szegedy, C., et al.: Intriguing properties of neural networks, Technical report (2013). http://arxiv.org/abs/1312.6199
21. Usman, M., Noller, Y., Păsăreanu, C.S., Sun, Y., Gopinath, D.: Neurospf: a tool for the symbolic analysis of neural networks. In: 2021 IEEE/ACM 43rd International Conference on Software Engineering: Companion Proceedings (ICSE-Companion), pp. 25–28 (2021). https://doi.org/10.1109/ICSE-Companion52605.2021.00027
22. Weimer, W., Forrest, S., Le Goues, C., Nguyen, T.: Automatic program repair with evolutionary computation. Commun. ACM **53**, 109–116 (2010). https://doi.org/10.1145/1735223.1735249

23. Wong, E., Kolter, J.Z.: Provable defenses against adversarial examples via the convex outer adversarial polytope. In: 35th International Conference on Machine Learning (ICML), Stockholmsmässan, Stockholm, Sweden, pp. 5283–5292. PMLR (2018). http://proceedings.mlr.press/v80/wong18a.html
24. Zhang, H., Chan, W.: Apricot: a weight-adaptation approach to fixing deep learning models. In: 34th International Conference on Automated Software Engineering (ASE), pp. 376–387. IEEE (2019)

Balancing Automation and Control for Formal Verification of Microprocessors

Shilpi Goel, Anna Slobodova$^{(\boxtimes)}$, Rob Sumners, and Sol Swords

Centaur Technology, Inc., Austin, TX, USA
{shilpi,anna,rsumners,sswords}@centtech.com

Abstract. Formal methods are becoming an indispensable part of the design process in software and hardware industry. It takes robust tools and proofs to make formal validation of large scale projects reliable. In this paper, we will describe the current status of formal verification at Centaur Technology. We will explain our challenges and our methodology—how various proofs and verification artifacts are interconnected and how we keep them consistent over the duration of a project. We also describe our main engine—a powerful symbolic simulator with rewriting capabilities that is integrated in a theorem prover and proven correct.

Keywords: Hardware verification · Microprocessor verification · Microcode verification · Formal methods · ACL2 · Symbolic simulation · Decision procedures

1 Introduction

The discussion of Formal Verification (FV) of software and hardware three decades ago was mostly about case studies or proofs of concept that required a lot of manual effort by researchers. Since then, FV has taken a transformational journey that has resulted in highly automated tools—equivalence checkers, model checkers, SMT solvers, and theorem provers. Large scale formal verification projects were first reported by hardware companies around ten years ago, e.g. Intel [28], IBM [36], ARM [34], and Centaur Technology [18,37]. Success stories of FV at software development companies followed. To name just a few, see Peter O'Hearn's keynote at *PLDI 2020* conference about incorrectness logic and static analysis his group applies at Facebook [30], David Dill's keynote at *CAV 2020* about the Libra project at Facebook [19] and their use of the Move Prover [44], or the invited talk by Byron Cook at *CAV 2018* about the application of formal methods at Amazon Web Services [16]. Formal methods are becoming a reliable and indispensable part of the design process in the commercial software and hardware industries. This newly elevated position of formal verification brings new responsibilities for those that develop tools and methods and those who build proofs. FV teams face various challenges:

© The Author(s) 2021
A. Silva and K. R. M. Leino (Eds.) CAV 2021, LNCS 12759, pp. 26–45, 2021.
https://doi.org/10.1007/978-3-030-81685-8_2

- Tools and libraries used by FV teams are expected to be reliable and maintainable.
- FV teams get involved much sooner in a project cycle, often starting with an incomplete design, and they are expected to give feedback quickly.
- Designs under FV scrutiny are being continuously changed by several designers at a time.
- Specifications change during the process as designers get feedback from back-end tools, or due to the changes in the target market.
- The scope and depth of proofs change as development continues.
- An FV team might be working on several proliferations of a project with overlapping schedules.

These challenges can only be solved by building robust expandable proofs. In this paper, we will describe the approach taken by our FV team at Centaur Technology. Centaur is a relatively small company, of about one hundred employees, that designs x86 compatible microprocessors, focusing on the low cost, low power market. It might surprise many that our formal verification tools are based on a theorem prover. This is only possible because the theorem prover we use, ACL2 [8], has been designed with industrial applications in mind [24]. ACL2 has been successfully used not only at our company but also at many others: e.g. ARM, AMD [35], IBM [36], Rockwell-Collins [22], and Oracle [32]. All our proofs are done within the ACL2 system. ACL2 is used to write specifications, models, tools, and tests, as well as to generate documentation. Two features of ACL2 that are crucial to our work are fast execution and extensibility. Our x86 model [20] is not only one of most complete of its kind, but is capable of executing application programs at a speed of around 3 million instructions per second.

We will start with a brief description of the ACL2 system and the features that make it a good choice for a verification framework (Sect. 2). The reflective features of ACL2 allow us to build verified tools within the system. One such tool is FGL [39], our symbolic simulator equipped with rewriting capabilities. FGL is completely integrated into ACL2 as a verified clause processor. It provides a desirable balance between automation and user guidance. We will describe its mechanism in detail in Sect. 4. We also explain its usability as a highly programmable solver that is capable of proving complex conjectures about Register-Transfer Level (RTL) design and microcode in Sect. 3. FGL and its use within our framework are primary contributions of the work presented in this paper. The challenges enumerated above are illustrated with the process of verification for a single x86 instruction. We explain the complex interconnection of the various parts of the proofs, and describe how they are built and maintained.

2   Our FV Tools

All formal verification at Centaur is done within the framework of ACL2 [8]. ACL2 is an untyped language (a subset of Common Lisp) and a theorem prover that supports first-order logic as expressed in this language. ACL2 also has some limited support for higher-order style definitions [29]. ACL2 is an open source software project that has an active community contributing to an extensive library of proofs and utilities. Centaur has contributed to many libraries that support hardware verification, including support for translating Verilog and System Verilog to ACL2 expressions [7,10] and libraries that support bit operations. ACL2 provides an interface through which it can be connected to trusted tools such as SAT solvers. There is also an integration of Z3 in ACL2 [5] and an interface to the ABC model checker [1,14].

Besides interfaces to trusted tools, ACL2 has a mechanism for extending its reasoning by admitting verified clause-processors [2]. We use this feature in several ways, notably for SVL [43], a routine that automates verification of multipliers, and for FGL, the core tool that provides automation for our microoperation execution and microcode proofs.

FGL, briefly, is a term rewriter geared toward transforming expressions acting on fixed-sized data into Boolean formulas. For example, a specification for an x86 instruction may be written in high-level ACL2. Processing a call of this specification function on variable arguments in FGL yields a result that expresses each of the bits of the writeback data, flags, etc., as a Boolean formula (represented in an and-inverter graph) whose inputs are the symbolic bits of the input variables. Similarly, FGL processing of the ACL2 model of the microcoded implementation for that instruction yields Boolean formula representations of the implementation's outputs. Equivalence checking these two sets of Boolean formulas is then sufficient to show that the implementation result matches the specification. We describe the FGL system in more detail in Sect. 4, showing how it transforms terms into hybrid term/Boolean-function objects and how its behavior may be programmed with rewrite rules.

3 Challenges of Verifying a Single x86 instruction

An intuitive notion of the functional correctness of a microprocessor is that any sequence of bytes decoded as instructions either executes correctly or leads to an exception if byte sequence is illegal. For the x86 instruction set, parsing and decoding a sequence of bytes is a complex process due to the many instruction formats with varying lengths and field types. The Intel 64 and IA-32 Instruction Set Architecture (ISA) is defined by the Software Developer's Manuals [27], which have thousands of pages describing the expected impact of every instruction on the state of the machine. It is a living and growing specification, with new instructions and variants added constantly. The architectural specification does not dictate how the ISA is supposed to be implemented. Various implementation-specific choices, collectively called the *microarchitecture*, include:

- how memory is organized
- how an instruction is decoded into a sequence of microoperations
- the set of microoperations implemented in hardware
- the throughput and latency of microoperations and instructions

and various others features of the microprocessor. In our previous work [21], we described what it means for an x86 instruction to be decoded and executed correctly and how our proofs capture this property. For illustrative purposes, we use the same example that was described in that work. Table 1 describes the x86 double-precision shift right instruction SHRD and Table 2 shows the microoperations that implement it[1]. In this paper, we will recall the individual steps of the verification with a different purpose—to discuss the challenges in each step and how we deal with them. In particular, we will focus on increasing the automation and reducing the time required of engineers to catch and debug problems while maintaining the proofs.

In the process of verification, we refer to two sets of formal specifications: the architectural specification of x86 [20] and a microarchitectural specification, which is a proprietary IP of Centaur and unique to each project. We refer to the former as the *x86 model* and the latter as the *microcode model*. Both of these models are written in ACL2 following an interpreter-style operational semantics approach. The x86 model includes the specification of x86 instructions that operate on the ISA state, and analogously, the microcode model includes the specifications of microoperations that operate on the microarchitectural state. Thanks to the high execution speed of the x86 model, it can be validated by running extensive code. The microcode model is directly compared to the RTL implementation. In addition, for data-intensive operations like floating-point arithmetic, we have the ability to run our models against existing x86 hardware from Intel and AMD. Again, the efficient execution of ACL2 code is crucial for the validation of these models.

Our verification is done on the Register-Transfer Level (RTL) of microprocessor design. We have two goals: to confirm that the RTL behaves as specified by our microarchitectural specification and to show that it implements instructions correctly with respect to our architectural specification.

Table 1. SHRD--Double Precision Shift Right: irrelevant fields elided

Opcode	Instruction	Description
REX.W + 0F AC /r ib	SHRD r/m64, r64, imm8	Shift r/m64 to right imm8 places while shifting bits from r64 in from left

3.1   Front-End and Microcode Verification

The front-end of a microprocessor fetches, decodes, and then translates a sequence of bytes into a sequence of microoperations. For a modern x86 processor, this is one of the more complicated parts of the design. Writing and

---

[1] Note that this is not the actual implementation of SHRD in our current design.

Table 2. SHRD RCX, RDX, imm8: a concrete run

Initial values	RDX := 0x1122_3344_5566_7788 RCX := 0x0123_4567_89AB_CDEF imm8 := 16
Expected values	RDX := 0x1122_3344_5566_7788 RCX := 0x7788_0123_4567_89AB
UOPs from front-end	**Concrete Run & Description**
MOVSX G2, RCX (SSZ: 64; DSZ: 64)	G2 ← 0x0123_4567_89AB_CDEF *Move* RCX *to internal register* G2
MOVZX G3, <imm8> (SSZ: 8; DSZ: 64)	G3 ← 16 *Move immediate to internal register* G3
UOPs in ROM	**Concrete Run & Description**
AND G3, G3, 63 (SSZ: 8; DSZ: 64)	G3 ← 16 *Mask immediate operand*
MOV G10, -1 (SSZ: 64; DSZ: 64)	G10 ← 0xFFFF_FFFF_FFFF_FFFF *Move -1 to internal register* G10
JE G3, 0, ent_nop (SSZ: 16; DSZ: 16)	No jump taken *Jump to routine* ent_nop *if* G3 == 0
SUB G5, 0, G3 (SSZ: 32; DSZ: 32)	G5 ← 0xFFFF_FFF0; ZF ← 0 *Store* -G3 *in internal register* G5; *clear the zero flag because result is non-zero*
SHR<↑ZF> G10, G10, G5 (SSZ: 64; DSZ: 64)	G10 ← 0xFFFF *Shift* G10 *right by* (G5 & 63) *if* ZF == 0
AND<ZF> G10, G10, 0 (SSZ: 64; DSZ: 64)	G10 ← 0xFFFF *Set* G10 *to 0 if* ZF == 1
AND G6, RDX, G10 (SSZ: 64; DSZ: 64)	G6 ← 0x7788 *Store* (RDX & G10) *in internal register* G6
SHR G7, G2, G3 (SSZ: 64; DSZ: 64)	G7 ← 0x0000_0123_4567_89AB *Store* (G2 ≫ G3) *in* G7
SHL G2, G7, G3 (SSZ: 64; DSZ: 64)	G2 ← 0x0123_4567_89AB_0000 *Store* (G7 ≪ G3) *in* G2
OR G2, G2, G6 (SSZ: 64; DSZ: 64)	G2 ← 0x0123_4567_89AB_7788 *Store* (G2 | G6) *in* G2
ROR G7, G2, G3 (SSZ: 64; DSZ: 64)	G7 ← 0x7788_0123_4567_89AB *Rotate* G2 *right by* G3 *and store result in* G7
OR RCX, G7, G7 (SSZ: 64; DSZ: 64)	RCX ← 0x7788_0123_4567_89AB *Store the result of* G7 | G7 *in* RCX

maintaining a formal specification for it would be impractical. The readability and complexity of such a specification would be similar to that of the implementation itself. How, then, do we go about its verification? We have one methodology to verify the decoding of byte sequences into legal/illegal instructions (with appropriate exceptions), and another one to show that legal instructions are implemented correctly via microoperations.

Listing 1.1. SHRD entry in `inst.lst`

```
(xINST "SHRD"
       (OP :OP #xFAC)
       (ARG :OP1 '(:MODR/M.R/M :GPR :MEM)
            :OP2 '(:MODR/M.REG :GPR)
            :OP3 '(:IMM8))
       '(X86-SHLD/SHRD)
       '((:UD (UD-LOCK-USED)))))
```

For illegal instructions, we make sure that all sequences of bytes that do not decode into a sequence of legal instructions are recognized as illegal and we verify that an appropriate exception is signaled. This is done by simulating the front-end on a symbolic sequence of bytes and proving that any input that does not map to a legal opcode (as defined by the decode specification in our x86 model) produces an exception. The decode specification in the x86 model relies heavily on `inst.lst`—a data structure defined by us that captures all the information needed to decode every x86 instruction. The initial version of `inst.lst` was mechanically extracted from the Intel manuals (Chaps. 3–5, Vol. 2) [27] by parsing the tables in the description pages of each instruction and transforming the contents into an ACL2-readable format. For instance, for the implementation in Table 2, the relevant entry in the Intel manuals is in Table 1 and that in `inst.lst` is in Listing 1.1. Since then, `inst.lst` has been inspected, enhanced, and validated against internal and external x86 decoders.

Next we focus on our process for verifying legal instructions. For each instruction, our goal is to prove that for any starting machine state and for any byte sequence representing a legal invocation of that instruction in that state, the front-end produces a sequence of microoperations which, when run on our microcode model, produce the same results as the instruction run on our x86 model[2]. To prove this, we simulate the front-end to generate the corresponding sequence of microoperations. Using FGL, we then prove that the sequence implements the instruction as defined by our x86 specification. FGL symbolically processes the sequence of microoperations as executed on our microcode model, resulting in a symbolic machine state where the bits of the written registers are represented as Boolean formulas in terms of the values read from the initial state. It likewise processes the instruction specification, reducing it to Boolean formulas as well. We can then show by Boolean equivalence checking that the front-end-generated sequence of microoperations has the same effect on the state as the x86 instruction specification. We discuss the process of symbolic simulation of microcode by FGL in Sect. 4. This FGL proof confirms that the front-end's operation is correct for this particular instruction.

This correctness has two caveats. First, it assumes that the individual microoperations are correctly implemented, i.e., in accordance with their specifications in our microcode model. Second, in the case of out-of-order processors, if the microoperations are executed in a different order, that sequence needs to be compared to the sequence generated by the front-end. Currently, we can

---

[2] Note that the microcode model is a proprietary formal model of the microarchitecture implemented by the design. Its validation is discussed later.

ensure only the former—for most microoperations, we have proved that their implementations in the processor's execution units matches their behavior in our microcode model; we discuss this further in Sect. 3.2. However, the latter—the correctness of reordering of the microoperations—is work planned for the future.

There is another part to the verification story. The front-end generates only sequences of microoperations of a limited length. Some instructions are complex and require much longer sequences (e.g. instructions performing transcendental or cryptographic functions). For these instructions, the sequence of microoperations generated by the front-end is just the beginning of the microcode program. The rest is stored in a ROM and the front-end generates the entry-point of this code. That means our verification has to account for those microcode routines.

ROM instructions are more complex than microoperations and they may also be compressed in order to save valuable ROM space. As in the front-end, the specification of this compression and decoding of ROM instructions into sequences of microoperations is complex and also changes during the design process. Even if we could define it formally, the maintenance of such a specification would be very time consuming. Instead, we do the same trick as with the front-end—we symbolically simulate the part of the design that fetches ROM instructions and translates them into a sequence of microoperations. The rest is done similarly as for the sequence of operations generated by the front-end. These proofs implicitly verify the correctness of fetching from ROM and ROM instruction translation. We call this *implicit verification* because we do not have an explicit specification of the translation and fetching. However, we do have formal specifications of the instructions implemented by the microcode. Therefore, the proof of correctness of the instructions implies the correctness of the underlying design, including ROM fetching and translation. In other words, we can verify some parts of the design as black-boxes, without knowing exactly how they work, by reasoning about the overall observable effect on the machine state. The main advantage of this type of verification of both the front-end and microcode translator is that the maintenance of the proofs does not require either deep understanding of the design or writing and maintaining cumbersome specifications.

The microcode sequences generated from x86 instructions that we encountered so far were in the style of straight-line code. We do not expect this to be the case for all of them. In the past, we worked on some microcode stored in ROM that served other purposes [18]. This code had loops and jumps between loops and we were able to do invariant-style proofs. Our main problem at that time was that the proofs were not robust enough and very hard to maintain. Now we are in a much better position, having FGL and a methodology that keeps the microcode model in sync with the design. Hence, we are optimistic about our ability to bring the verification of most, if not all, legal x86 instructions to completion.

Finally, we note that in our previous work [21], we used GL—the predecessor of FGL—as our core verification tool. The benefits of switching to FGL have been considerable. GL had limited support for term rewriting, as a result of which symbolic simulation of the microcode model was difficult and debugging failed proof attempts even more so. As such, instead of programming GL to deal with symbolic machine states, we usually used ACL2's rewriter to "open up" the microcode model and played to GL's strengths by using it for the final equivalence proof that often required non-trivial arithmetic reasoning. In other words, we obtained ACL2 formulas corresponding to the written registers in terms of the values in the initial microcode state, and then used GL to prove that those formulas were equivalent to our specification functions. FGL easily allows us to do these tasks (symbolic simulation and equivalence checking) along with others within a common environment and thereby reduces overhead in our methodology.

3.2 Verification of Execution Units

Everything that was said in Sect. 3.1 relies on the assumption that our microcode model is correct. Parts of that model—front-end decoding and ROM instruction fetch and translate—are implicitly verified. The other part, definitions of micro-operations that form the base of the model, were explicitly defined in ACL2 and need to be validated. A large portion of our work lies in the proofs that confirm that RTL executes the microoperations in compliance with those specifications. In order to achieve that, we build a formal model of the respective RTL module [7], unroll it with respect to the latencies of the microoperations to be verified [6] and check conformance with the specification using FGL.

These microoperations are executed in various units, the number, timing, and organization of which differs based on the specific microarchitecture. We might have separate floating-point add and floating-point multiply units, or one unit that executes both. There might be a unit that implements string operations, another that implements integer operations, and yet another one devoted to SIMD operations, etc. The scope of proofs that confirm correctness of execution of microoperations is dictated by the capacity of the tools we use. During the first years of FV at Centaur, we limited the proof for each microoperation to the specific unit where it was executed [25,26,37]. Since then, improvements to our RTL modeling and symbolic simulation (i.e., FGL) allow us to do the proofs in the scope of the module containing all those units (we refer to that module as the execution module or EXE) [21]. Migration to a higher scope has a huge advantage for the stability of the proofs. First, proofs are robust with respect to the changes of the interfaces of submodules in EXE. For instance, when an interface of a floating-point sub-unit changes to accommodate extra control signals that simplify its logic, very likely the change is transparent to the input-output behavior of EXE and will not effect our proofs. Second, if timing of an internal unit changes, but overall timing of the EXE module does not, that is transparent to the proofs.

Having all microoperation proofs in the same scope has another advantage—we can build just one formal model of the RTL, do one unrolling to the maximum latency, and store it as a constant that can be shared and loaded by individual proofs. A review of the assumptions about the interface and the maintenance of the assumptions is also simplified when all the proofs are done with respect to one module.

3.3   Regressions

Regressions have become an indispensable part of the continuous integration. There are several reasons why we need to re-run our proofs regularly. Since we start to build our proofs early in the design process, design changes occur regularly and can introduce bugs that we need to catch. But proofs can be broken not only due to changes in the design but also because of changes in the specifications, tools, and libraries. While the ISA specification is relatively stable, the microarchitecture specification might change during the project as a result of feedback from back-end tools or better ideas from the designers. Proofs might also change as the design becomes more mature and we add more thorough checks. While the core ACL2 theorem prover is very stable, ACL2 libraries are growing and may be modified by developers outside our team. All of these verification artifacts are tightly interconnected and regressions ensure that we keep them consistent.

When a proof of the correctness of a microoperation fails, there are several possible reasons:

- There is a bug in the RTL design.
- There was a change in the design (interface or timing) that our proofs need to take into account.
- The specification of the microoperation changed; e.g. some flags indicate a new intended use, or a portion of the result became "don't care".

We need to investigate the reason for failure and either report a bug to designers, adjust the proofs, or change the specification of the microoperation.

When we change the specification of a microoperation, the new definition will then be used by our microcode proofs. If those fail, it may indicate that the change affected some instruction implementations in an undesirable way. In other cases, the failure might be a result of missing rewrite rules. Microcode proofs might also fail due to the changes to front-end design or fetch and translate from ROM that introduced a new bug.

Regressions can be scheduled for a specific frequency (daily, weekly, etc.), run manually, or triggered by changes in the design, specification, or tool suite. We use open-source tools like git and Jenkins, and ACL2-specific scripts that compute dependencies on ACL2 files. Regressions also automatically generate a documentation manual from our ACL2 proof scripts [17]. This documentation includes information about which proofs failed and which succeeded and as the result of it, which microoperations and instructions are covered by the successful proofs. This keeps the documentation in sync with the design as well as the proofs. We tag individual documentation topics to indicate their intended audience; e.g., the *General Audience* tag is used when an overview of a verification effort is presented, and the *FV Audience* tag is used when describing proof strategies and verification tools.

4   FGL

Since FGL is the core proof engine used in our microcode and execution unit proofs, we will describe here how it works and how it may be programmed.

FGL [4,39] is part of the ACL2 libraries and publicly available [9]. It is a significant rewrite and extension of GL ("G in the Logic") [38,41,42], which was itself a rewrite and extension of the G System of Boyer and Hunt [13]. The idea behind all of these is to recursively transform ACL2 terms into symbolic objects that represent the values of these terms and that consist mostly of structures containing Boolean function objects. When successful, the result of transforming the body of a conjecture is a single Boolean function, which may be checked for validity. The G System supported Boolean functions represented as binary decision diagrams [15], and operated on symbolic input objects using symbolic counterpart functions derived mechanically from function definitions. GL used an interpreter to capture function behavior rather than translating definitions, and added support for an and-inverter graph (AIG) representation for Boolean functions along with links to external SAT solvers for resolving Boolean function validity. Later changes in GL added preliminary support for rewrite rules and termlike symbolic objects so as to allow for some abstraction.

FGL continues the trend toward user-definable rules displacing built-in behavior. It is a rewriter at its core, so user-defined rewrite rules are the basis of its reasoning system, rather than an add-on. Nevertheless, it comes with an extensive library of rules that replicates the automation provided by GL. Rewrite rules supported by FGL offer powerful capabilities such as programmable binding of free variables and visibility into the syntax of the rewriting targets [39]. FGL also replaces built-in primitive function symbolic counterparts with *meta rules* similar in spirit to ACL2's [23], which similarly allow directly programmable manipulation of the syntax of objects but may also be added by users. FGL adds support for incremental SAT, allowing multiple SAT checks of related formulas to share learned clauses and heuristic information. It also allows global simplification of the entire AIG using combinational circuit simplification methods. Both of these features may be invoked from within rewrite rules; e.g., if the author of a rewrite rule judges that a hypothesis of the rule is unlikely to be solved by rewriting alone, they may specify that incremental SAT should be used to prove it.

Many other projects have also aimed to allow interactive theorem provers to call on automatic decision procedures; too many such efforts exist to list them all. In higher-order logic proof assistants, several tools collectively called *hammers* translate queries into the language of an automated theorem prover

Listing 1.2. Semantics of a machine instruction

```
(defun run-inst (inst st)
  (let* ((instname (first inst))
         (args (rest inst))
         (x (first args))
         (y (second args))
         (ans (case instname
                (const     y)
                (copy      (get-st-reg y st))
                (add       (+ (get-st-reg x st)
                              (get-st-reg y st)))
                (and       (bitwise-and (get-st-reg x st)
                                        (get-st-reg y st)))
                (rshift    (right-shift (get-st-reg y st)
                                        (get-st-reg x st))))))
    (set-st-reg x ans st)))
```

Listing 1.3. Semantics of a straight-line code block

```
(defun run-prog (insts st)
  (if (atom insts)
      st
    (let ((st (run-inst (first insts) st)))
      (run-prog (rest insts) st))))
```

and then translate the emitted proof back into a form acceptable by the original prover [12]. Several decision procedure integrations have also been carried out in ACL2. Reeber and Hunt [33] identified a decidable subclass of ACL2 list formulas and contributed a decision procedure that transforms such a formula into a SAT problem. Peng and Greenstreet [31] process a subclass of ACL2 formulas including integer and rational arithmetic, uninterpreted functions, and algebraic data structures, converting such problems to SMT queries. FGL differs by focusing on the efficient integration of user-extendible term rewriting and Boolean simplification and decision procedures.

4.1   Example

We describe how FGL works at a high level by running through an example, the code of which is publicly available [40]. We define a simple machine model (Listings 1.2, 1.3) that has 16 32-bit registers and a few instructions defined, and use those instructions to implement (in straight-line code) an optimized routine to count the number of bits set in a 32-bit input (Listing 1.4), similar to implementations in *Bit Twiddling Hacks* [11]. We also define a straightforward ACL2 specification count-bits for the bit count operation (Listing 1.5). We prove that for any initial state, if we run this program on the machine, then the resulting state has its register 0 value equal to the count-bits of the value that was in register 0 before running the program (Listing 1.6).

The invocation of def-fgl-thm in Listing 1.6 causes the FGL rewriter to be applied to the conjecture. It begins by descending into the term and applying rewrite rules to subterms from the inside out. In many cases, these rules are just the definitional formulas of the functions we have introduced; for example, the definitions of run-prog, run-inst, and count-bits are used as rewrite rules, so that calls of these functions are replaced by their bodies. Rewriting the term

Listing 1.4. BITCOUNT program listing

```
(defconst *bitcount*
 '((copy 10 0)  ;; copy the operand to regs 10 and 11
   (copy 11 0)
   (const 5 #x55555555) ;; set reg 5 to the mask
   (and 10 5)   ;; bitand the operand with the mask
   (const 0 1)    ;; set reg 0 to 1
   (rshift 11 0) ;; right shift the operand by 1
   (and 11 5)   ;; mask the shifted operand
   ...
   (const 0 #x003f)
   (and 10 0)    ;; mask the relevant bits of the result
   (copy 0 10))) ;; move the result to reg 0.
```

Listing 1.5. count-bits specification function

```
(defun count-bits (x)
  (if (or (not (integerp x)) (<= x 0))
      0
    (+ (nth-bit 0 x)
       (count-bits (right-shift 1 x)))))
```

while opening such definitions effectively conducts a symbolic simulation of the program and its specification. For some functions, it is preferable to avoid opening the definitions and instead use rules that rely on particular properties to simplify combinations of calls; for example, Listing 1.7 shows a rule that simplifies a read of a write of the machine state's register file.[3]

Rather than producing a new term as the result of rewriting each subterm, the FGL rewriter produces hybrid structures we call *symbolic objects* that may (like terms) contain function calls, variable references, and constants, but (unlike terms) also may contain *symbolic Booleans*, represented by a reference into an AIG defining a Boolean function, and *symbolic integers*, represented by a list of references into the AIG giving the two's-complement bits. Table 3 lists the variants of symbolic objects.

In order to prove this conjecture, we aim for the result of rewriting the conjecture to be a symbolic Boolean, which can then be proved valid by encoding its negation as a SAT problem. We therefore want to compute a Boolean formula equivalent to the equal comparison of the specification and implementation results. Working backwards from this goal, we can obtain this if we can represent the specification and implementation results as symbolic integers; the equal

Listing 1.6. Correctness theorem for BITCOUNT

```
(def-fgl-thm bitcount-implements-count-bits
  (let* ((input (get-st-reg 0 st))
         (final-st (run-prog *bitcount* st))
         (result (get-st-reg 0 final-st)))
    (equal result (count-bits input))))
```

---

[3] Since ACL2 is an untyped language, functions have well-defined behavior even on ill-typed inputs. The uses of zero-extend in this rule reflect the choice of the definitions to coerce integers that don't fit in the allotted space into well-typed values by zero-extending them.

Listing 1.7. Read-over-write rule for `get-st-reg`

```
(def-fgl-rewrite get-st-reg-of-set-st-reg
  (equal (get-st-reg i (set-st-reg j v st))
         (if (equal (zero-extend 4 i) (zero-extend 4 j))
             (zero-extend 32 v)
             (get-st-reg i st))))
```

Table 3. Symbolic object variants

– (g-boolean *lit*) represents a Boolean, t or nil, as an AIG literal, *lit*

– (g-integer *lit0* *lit1* ...) represents an integer as a list of AIG literals giving the two's-complement bits, least-significant first

– (g-concrete *obj*) represents the constant *obj* itself

– (g-apply *fn* *args*) represents a function application, where *fn* is a function symbol and *args* is a list of symbolic objects

– (g-var *name*) represents a variable named *name*

– (g-ite *test* *then* *else*) represents an if-then-else, where the three arguments are symbolic objects

– (g-cons *car* *cdr*) represents a cons pair, where the two arguments are symbolic objects

– (g-map *tag* *alist*) represents a table of key/value pairs with constant keys and symbolic values,

supporting fast lookups (see ACL2 documentation on fast alists [3])

comparison of these is the conjunction of the Boolean equivalences between all the corresponding bits. Working further backwards, we'll find that we can similarly compute these values given the bits of the intermediate integer values from which they are computed, etc., back to the original values that are components of the free variables of the conjecture. That is, generally speaking, we wish to represent every intermediate integer value as a symbolic integer. In the next two sections we will describe how to extract Boolean variables from the initial variables of the conjecture (Sect. 4.2) and how to build up Boolean formulas to represent the bits of intermediate values (Sect. 4.3).

4.2   Extracting Boolean Variables

When rewriting a term in a Boolean context such as the test of an `if` expression, FGL will coerce the rewritten result to a symbolic Boolean object. The symbolic Boolean values of symbolic object types other than function calls and variables are easy to determine; for example, integers are non-`nil` and therefore considered true in ACL2. For function call and variable results, this coercion is accomplished by assigning a Boolean variable to the object, either a fresh one—a new primary input node in the underlying AIG— or an existing one when such an assignment has already been recorded for that object. These Boolean variables along with the constants t and `nil` are the base Boolean formulas. More complex formulas are built up from these variables by processing of `if` terms and by low-level meta-routines, introduced below.

The Boolean variables needed for the `bitcount` proof correspond to the bits of the accessed registers of the initial machine state `st`. We introduce rewrite rules that cause FGL to generate 32 Boolean variables for the bits of a 32-bit register when that register is accessed, composing these into a symbolic integer. The two rules involved are shown in Listing 1.8.

Listing 1.8. Rules for generating Boolean variables for initial register values

```
(def-fgl-rewrite get-st-reg-generate-bits
  (implies (syntaxp (fgl-object-case st :g-var))
           (equal (get-st-reg n st)
                  (zero-extend 32 (hide-get-st-reg n st)))))

(def-fgl-rewrite zero-extend-const-width
  (implies (syntaxp (integerp n))
           (equal (zero-extend n x)
                  (if (or (not (integerp n))
                          (<= n 0))
                      0
                    (intcons (intcar x)
                             (zero-extend (1- n) (intcdr x)))))))
```

The FGL rewriter will try to apply the first rule, `get-st-reg-generate-bits`, every time it encounters a call of `get-st-reg`, but due to its `syntaxp` hypothesis it will immediately fail if `st` is not syntactically a variable. In the case of the conjecture we're attempting to prove, this ensures that the rule will only apply to `get-st-reg` calls on the initial state. Such calls will be replaced by the `zero-extend` term of the right-hand side. In that term, `hide-get-st-reg` is an alias for `get-st-reg`; this avoids looping in the application of the rule. The construction of the 32-bit vector of Boolean variables is then accomplished by repeated application of the rule `zero-extend-const-width`. The functions `intcar`, `intcdr`, and `intcons` used here to access or construct bits of an integer as if it were a list of Booleans: `intcar` gets the Boolean value of the least-significant bit (LSB), `intcdr` right-shifts by 1 to remove the LSB, and `intcons` adds a new LSB to an integer, reversing the `intcdr` operation. The first argument to `intcons` is recognized by FGL as a Boolean context, so the rewriter will introduce Boolean variables corresponding to the terms that appear there, namely:

$$\texttt{(intcar (intcdr...(intcdr (hide-st-get k st))...))}$$

The association of each such termlike object with the corresponding Boolean variable is stored in a hash table. Each time a termlike object is found in a Boolean context, it is looked up in the table; if it has an existing entry, the corresponding Boolean variable is returned, and if not, a new Boolean variable is generated and stored.

After generating the new Boolean variable, the `intcons` call becomes a new symbolic integer that now includes that bit. The final value produced by the zero-extend is therefore a symbolic integer consisting of 32 fresh Boolean variables. If the same register were to be accessed again, the same process would occur except that the objects associated with the Boolean variables would be recognized and the same Boolean variables returned again.

4.3   Composing Boolean Functions

The most basic way in which a new Boolean formula is computed from a previous one during FGL's rewriting process is by FGL's built-in handling of `if`. Specifically, if an `if` term occurs in which the two branches are both symbolic

Listing 1.9. Bitwise AND implementation rule

```
(def -fgl -rewrite fgl -bitwise -and
  (equal (bitwise -and x y)
         (if (int -endp -check x -endp x)
             (if (intcar x) (ifix y) 0)
           (if (int -endp -check y -endp y)
               (if (intcar y) (ifix x) 0)
             (intcons (and (intcar x)
                           (intcar y))
                      (bitwise -and (intcdr x) (intcdr y)))))))))
```

Boolean objects, the result is the Boolean if-then-else of the test formula and the two branch formulas. This if-then-else formula is built in the AIG and a reference to the resulting node is returned as the Boolean formula resulting from the `if`. If the two branches are both integer values represented either as symbolic integers or integer constants, then the result is a new symbolic integer, the bits of which are the if-then-elses of the test with the corresponding bits from the two branches.

As a simple example, the rule used to expand calls of `bitwise-and` is shown in Listing 1.9. This rewrites a call of `bitwise-and` on a pair of symbolic integers, producing a new symbolic integer in which each bit's formula is the AND of the corresponding bits of the inputs.

The rule applies to any call of `bitwise-and`. It first checks each of the inputs with `int-endp-check`. This is true if it can be syntactically determined that the input must be either -1 or 0—in particular, if the input's symbolic integer representation has only one bit. (The syntactic check works by binding its result to the free variable `x-endp` introduced within the form. The technical details of this rewriter feature are described elsewhere [39].) If this is true of either input, then the result is based on the one relevant bit of that input (the `intcar`): if it is true, then the input's value is -1 and the result is the other input (coerced to an integer value using `ifix`, which replaces non-integer values with 0); if false, then the input's value is 0 and therefore the result is too. In many cases, the `intcar` value will be a (non-constant) Boolean formula; the result of this `if` is then a new vector of Boolean formulas, each of which is the conjunction of the `intcar` formula with the corresponding bit of the other input.

If the `int-endp-check` test is false on both inputs, then the rule creates the first bit of the result by creating the `and` of the first bits of the two inputs. (In ACL2, `(and x y)` is really shorthand for `(if x y nil)`, so this is actually another `if` merge operation.) It then makes another call of `bitwise-and` on the remaining bits of the two inputs, which will cause another application of this rule; this recurs until the bits of one of the inputs are exhausted.

The `bitwise-and` rule is a particularly simple example of how FGL can be programmed to compute complex Boolean formulas, but designing and proving these sorts of rules for other operations is a straightforward exercise in interactive theorem proving. FGL also includes a library of such rules which the user can safely extend with new rewrite rules as needed.

For some applications, the performance of stepping through iterative rules such as these using the rewriter is insufficient. For these cases, FGL supports creating custom rewriting procedures analogous to ACL2's metafunctions [23] and invoking them via rules similar to ACL2's meta rules. Metafunctions operate directly on the syntactic forms to be rewritten—symbolic objects in FGL, terms in ACL2. They return a resulting term (and substitution in FGL, though not in ACL2) that is equivalent to the input object. To allow a metafunction to be applied during rewriting, a meta rule is admitted, which requires proving a theorem stating that the metafunction produces correct results. It is noteworthy that FGL itself is proven in ACL2 to produce correct results even with user extension via rewrite rules or custom rewriting procedures.

5   Conclusion

Over the past years, formal verification at Centaur has moved beyond its previous focus on data-path proofs for arithmetic modules. Our verification projects have expanded into the areas of front-end decoding and microcode, as well as the implementations of a rich set of microoperations. We engage with the design process in its early stages and maintain and expand our proofs throughout the whole life cycle of the project. Over the years, our tools have been improved and we have learned a few lessons.

We chose to use open-source tools and we are constantly contributing to ACL2 libraries. The ACL2 community has a tested way of collaboration between groups using `git`, peer reviewed commits, and a rich regression suite.

We write specifications that can be expanded and refined in response to design and microarchitectural changes. When the design is incomplete, the specifications are still useful when augmented by relevant assumptions. When a project requires additional flags or features, a modular style of specification allows for appropriate changes. We try to avoid complex specifications like those for the front-end decoder or ROM instruction decoder. These parts of the design are implicitly verified during microcode verification.

Scheduled, triggered, and manual regressions are an important safeguard to avoid breaking consistency among our proofs. They catch undesirable changes in the specifications, tools, and design.

A key to ensuring stability of the proofs is their scope—the bigger the scope, the more stable the proofs, because changes to interfaces of larger modules are less frequent than changes at lower levels. The transition from unit to cluster-level proofs led to substantially higher robustness and easier maintenance. This has been possible due to improvements in the process of building our formal models and enhancements in FGL. We also benefit greatly from enhancements in modern SAT solvers.

We still have considerable work to do towards achieving our verification goals. Some of these goals could be achieved with more man power, whereas for others we do not have the right technology yet. There is a lot of microcode left to be verified. We have not verified the mechanisms of out-of-order microoperation scheduling, but we believe it is possible with our tools. We do not have a complete methodology for verification of memory access instructions yet. Our plan is to work on all these fronts.

References

1. ACL2 Documentation: AIGNET-ABC-INTERFACE Interface to ABC. Accessed April 2021. http://www.cs.utexas.edu/users/moore/acl2/v8-3/combined-manual/?topic=AIGNET_AIGNET-ABC-INTERFACE
2. ACL2 Documentation: CLAUSE-PROCESSOR. Accessed April 2021. http://www.cs.utexas.edu/users/moore/acl2/v8-3/combined-manual/?topic=ACL2_CLAUSE-PROCESSOR
3. ACL2 Documentation: FAST-ALISTS. Accessed April 2021. http://www.cs.utexas.edu/users/moore/acl2/v8-3/combined-manual/?topic=ACL2_FAST-ALISTS
4. ACL2 Documentation: FGL Bit-blasting Prover Framework. Accessed April 2021. https://www.cs.utexas.edu/users/moore/acl2/v8-3/combined-manual/?topic=FGL_FGL
5. ACL2 Documentation: SMTLINK Interface to Z3. Accessed April 2021. http://www.cs.utexas.edu/users/moore/acl2/v8-3/combined-manual/?topic=SMT_SMTLINK
6. ACL2 Documentation: SV Hardware Verification Library. Accessed April 2021. http://www.cs.utexas.edu/users/moore/acl2/v8-3/combined-manual/?topic=ACL2_SV
7. ACL2 Documentation: VL Verilog Toolkit. Accessed April 2021. http://www.cs.utexas.edu/users/moore/acl2/v8-3/combined-manual/?topic=ACL2_VL
8. ACL2 Home Page. Accessed April 2021. http://www.cs.utexas.edu/users/moore/acl2
9. FGL Library in the ACL2 Community Books. Accessed April 2021. https://github.com/acl2/acl2/tree/master/books/centaur/fgl
10. VL Verilog Toolkit. Accessed: April 2021. https://github.com/acl2/acl2/tree/master/books/centaur/vl
11. Anderson, S.E.: Bit twiddling hacks. Accessed: April 2021. https://graphics.stanford.edu/~seander/bithacks.html#CountBitsSetParallel
12. Blanchette, J., Kaliszyk, C., Paulson, L., Urban, J.: Hammering towards QED. J. Formaliz. Reason. **9**(1), 101–148 (2016). https://doi.org/10.6092/issn.1972-5787/4593
13. Boyer, R.S., Hunt, Jr., W.A.: Symbolic simulation in ACL2. In: Proceedings of the Eighth International Workshop on the ACL2 Theorem Prover and Its Applications, ACL2 2009, pp. 20–24. ACM, New York (2009). https://doi.org/10.1145/1637837.1637840
14. Brayton, R., Mishchenko, A.: ABC: an academic industrial-strength verification tool. In: Touili, T., Cook, B., Jackson, P. (eds.) CAV 2010. LNCS, vol. 6174, pp. 24–40. Springer, Heidelberg (2010). https://doi.org/10.1007/978-3-642-14295-6_5
15. Bryant, R.E.: Symbolic Boolean manipulation with ordered binary-decision diagrams. ACM Comput. Surv. **24**(3), 293–318 (1992). https://doi.org/10.1145/136035.136043
16. Cook, B.: Formal reasoning about the security of Amazon web services. In: Chockler, H., Weissenbacher, G. (eds.) CAV 2018, Part I. LNCS, vol. 10981, pp. 38–47. Springer, Cham (2018). https://doi.org/10.1007/978-3-319-96145-3_3
17. Davis, J., Kaufmann, M.: Industrial-strength documentation for ACL2. In: Proceedings of the 12th International Workshop on the ACL2 Theorem Prover and its Applications, ACL2 2014, Vienna, Austria, 12–13 July 2014, pp. 9–25 (2014). https://doi.org/10.4204/EPTCS.152.2

18. Davis, J., Slobodova, A., Swords, S.: Microcode verification – another piece of the microprocessor verification puzzle. In: Klein, G., Gamboa, R. (eds.) ITP 2014. LNCS, vol. 8558, pp. 1–16. Springer, Cham (2014). https://doi.org/10.1007/978-3-319-08970-6_1
19. Dill, D.L.: Formal Verification of Libra Blockchain Smart Contracts. Recording of the keynote (2020). https://www.youtube.com/watch?v=cYxxJU-Wt2U
20. Goel, S.: Formal Verification of Application and System Programs Based on a Validated x86 ISA Model. Ph.D. thesis, Department of Computer Science, The University of Texas at Austin (2016). http://hdl.handle.net/2152/46437
21. Goel, S., Slobodova, A., Sumners, R., Swords, S.: Verifying x86 instruction implementations. In: Proceedings of the 9th ACM SIGPLAN International Conference on Certified Programs and Proofs, CPP 2020, pp. 47–60. Association for Computing Machinery, New York (2020). https://doi.org/10.1145/3372885.3373811
22. Greve, D., Wilding, M.: Evaluatable, high-assurance microprocessors. In: NSA High-Confidence Systems and Software Conference (HCSS), Linthicum, MD, March 2002. http://hokiepokie.org/docs/hcss02/proceedings.pdf
23. Hunt, W.A., Kaufmann, M., Krug, R.B., Moore, J.S., Smith, E.W.: Meta reasoning in ACL2. In: Hurd, J., Melham, T. (eds.) TPHOLs 2005. LNCS, vol. 3603, pp. 163–178. Springer, Heidelberg (2005). https://doi.org/10.1007/11541868_11
24. Hunt, Jr., W.A., Kaufmann, M., Moore, J.S., Slobodova, A.: Industrial hardware and software verification with ACL2. In: Verified Trustworthy Software Systems, vol. 375. The Royal Society (2017). https://doi.org/10.1098/rsta.2015.0399 (Article Number 20150399)
25. Hunt, W.A., Swords, S.: Centaur technology media unit verification. In: Bouajjani, A., Maler, O. (eds.) CAV 2009. LNCS, vol. 5643, pp. 353–367. Springer, Heidelberg (2009). https://doi.org/10.1007/978-3-642-02658-4_28
26. Hunt, Jr., W.A.A., Swords, S., Davis, J., Slobodova, A.: Use of formal verification at centaur technology. In: Hardin, D. (ed.) Design and Verification of Microprocessor Systems for High-Assurance Applications, pp. 65–88. Springer, Boston (2010). https://doi.org/10.1007/978-1-4419-1539-9_3
27. Intel Corporation: Intel 64 and IA-32 Architectures Software Developer's Manual Combined Volumes: 1, 2A, 2B, 2C, 2D, 3A, 3B, 3C, 3D, and 4, November, 2020, Order Number: 325462–070US. https://software.intel.com/en-us/articles/intel-sdm
28. Kaivola, R., et al.: Replacing testing with formal verification in Intel® Core™ i7 processor execution engine validation. In: Bouajjani, A., Maler, O. (eds.) CAV 2009. LNCS, vol. 5643, pp. 414–429. Springer, Heidelberg (2009). https://doi.org/10.1007/978-3-642-02658-4_32
29. Kaufmann, M., Moore, J.S.: Limited second-order functionality in the first-order setting. J. Autom. Reason. **64**, 391–422 (2020). https://doi.org/10.1007/s10817-018-09505-9
30. O'Hearn, P.W.: Formal reasoning and the hacker way (keynote). In: Krishnan, P., Reichenbach, C. (eds.) Proceedings of the 9th ACM SIGPLAN International Workshop on the State Of the Art in Program Analysis, SOAP@PLDI 2020, London, UK, 15 June 2020, p. 1. ACM (2020). https://doi.org/10.1145/3394451.3401953
31. Peng, Y., Greenstreet, M.R.: Smtlink 2.0. In: Electronic Proceedings in Theoretical Computer Science, vol. 280, pp. 143–160, October 2018. https://doi.org/10.4204/eptcs.280.11
32. Rager, D.L., Ebergen, J., Nadezhin, D., Lee, A., Chau, C., Selfridge, B.: Formal Verification of Division and Square Root Implementations, an Oracle Report, pp. 149–160. ACM, IEEE, October 2016

33. Reeber, E., Hunt, W.A.: A SAT-based decision procedure for the subclass of unrollable list formulas in ACL2 (SULFA). In: Furbach, U., Shankar, N. (eds.) IJCAR 2006. LNCS (LNAI), vol. 4130, pp. 453–467. Springer, Heidelberg (2006). https://doi.org/10.1007/11814771_38

34. Reid, A., et al.: End-to-end verification of processors with ISA-formal. In: Chaudhuri, S., Farzan, A. (eds.) CAV 2016, Part II. LNCS, vol. 9780, pp. 42–58. Springer, Cham (2016). https://doi.org/10.1007/978-3-319-41540-6_3

35. Russinoff, D.M.: Formal Verification of Floating-Point Hardware Design: A Mathematical Approach. Springer, Cham (2019). https://doi.org/10.1007/978-3-319-95513-1

36. Sawada, J., Sandon, P., Paruthi, V., Baumgartner, J., Case, M., Mony, H.: Hybrid verification of a hardware modular reduction engine. In: Bjesse, P., Slobodova, A. (eds.) Proceedings of Formal Methods in Computer-Aided Design (FMCAD). ACM/IEEE CEDA (2011). https://www.cs.utexas.edu/users/hunt/FMCAD/FMCAD11/

37. Slobodova, A., Davis, J., Swords, S., Hunt, Jr., W.A.: A flexible formal verification framework for industrial scale validation. In: Proceedings of the 9th IEEE/ACM International Conference on Formal Methods and Models for Codesign (MEMOCODE), pp. 89–97. IEEE/ACM, Cambridge (2011). https://doi.org/10.1109/memcod.2011.5970515

38. Swords, S.: Term-level reasoning in support of bit-blasting. In: Slobodova, A., Hunt, Jr., W.A. (eds.) Proceedings 14th International Workshop on the ACL2 Theorem Prover and its Applications, Austin, Texas, USA, 22–23 May 2017. Electronic Proceedings in Theoretical Computer Science, vol. 249, pp. 95–111. Open Publishing Association (2017). https://doi.org/10.4204/EPTCS.249.7

39. Swords, S.: New rewriter features in FGL. In: Passmore, G., Gamboa, R. (eds.) Proceedings of the Sixteenth International Workshop on the ACL2 Theorem Prover and its Applications, Worldwide, Planet Earth, 28–29 May 2020. Electronic Proceedings in Theoretical Computer Science, vol. 327, pp. 32–46. Open Publishing Association (2020). https://doi.org/10.4204/EPTCS.327.3

40. Swords, S.: FGL example. Accessed April 2021. https://github.com/solswords/fgl-example

41. Swords, S., Davis, J.: Bit-blasting ACL2 theorems. In: Hardin, D., Schmaltz, J. (eds.) Proceedings 10th International Workshop on the ACL2 Theorem Prover and its Applications, Austin, Texas, USA, 3–4 November 2011. Electronic Proceedings in Theoretical Computer Science, vol. 70, pp. 84–102. Open Publishing Association (2011). https://doi.org/10.4204/EPTCS.70.7

42. Swords, S.O.: A Verified Framework for Symbolic Execution in the ACL2 Theorem Prover. Ph.D. thesis, University of Texas at Austin, December 2010. http://hdl.handle.net/2152/ETD-UT-2010-12-2210

43. Temel, M., Slobodova, A., Hunt, W.A.: Automated and scalable verification of integer multipliers. In: Lahiri, S.K., Wang, C. (eds.) CAV 2020. LNCS, vol. 12224, pp. 485–507. Springer, Cham (2020). https://doi.org/10.1007/978-3-030-53288-8_23

44. Zhong, J.E., et al.: The move prover. In: Lahiri, S.K., Wang, C. (eds.) CAV 2020, Part I. LNCS, vol. 12224, pp. 137–150. Springer, Cham (2020). https://doi.org/10.1007/978-3-030-53288-8_7

Algebraic Program Analysis

Zachary Kincaid[1](✉), Thomas Reps[2](✉), and John Cyphert[2](✉)

[1] Princeton University, Princeton, NJ 08540, USA
zkincaid@cs.princeton.edu
[2] University of Wisconsin, Madison, WI 53706, USA
reps@cs.wisc.edu, jcyphert@wisc.edu

Abstract. This paper is a tutorial on algebraic program analysis. It explains the foundations of algebraic program analysis, its strengths and limitations, and gives examples of algebraic program analyses for numerical invariant generation and termination analysis.

1 Introduction

This tutorial provides an introduction to algebraic program analysis, focusing upon techniques for (numerical) invariant generation and termination analysis. By reading this paper, you will learn the answers to the following questions:

- How does one design an algebraic program analysis?
- What new opportunities does algebraic program analysis enable?
- What are the limitations and important open problems in algebraic program analysis?

The origin of algebraic program analysis is the algebraic approach to solving path problems in graphs [1,6,48,59]: (1) compute a regular expression recognizing a set of paths of interest, and (2) interpret that regular expression within an algebraic structure corresponding to the problem at hand. Various path problems (e.g., computing shortest paths, path-finding problems, and dataflow analysis) can be solved by using different algebraic structures to interpret regular expressions.

In the context of program analysis, the graph of interest is a control flow graph for a program, and the algebra defines a space of summaries (approximations of program behavior) and a means for composing them. The algebraic approach amounts to computing a summary for a program in "bottom-up" fashion, building summaries for larger and larger subprograms by applying the operators of the summary algebra.

The general pattern of an algebraic program analysis is: given a system of (recursive) equations defining the semantics of a program, (1) symbolically compute a closed-form solution, and then (2) interpret the closed form within an algebraic structure corresponding to the analysis. The algebraic approach can be contrasted with classical iterative abstract interpretation, which also starts with a system of (recursive) equations defining the semantics of a program. However, the iterative approach is to (a) interpret the operations in the equations in an abstract domain, and then (b) solve the equations over the abstract domain

A. Silva and K. R. M. Leino (Eds.) CAV 2021, LNCS 12759, pp. 46–83, 2021.
https://doi.org/10.1007/978-3-030-81685-8_3

by successive approximation. Thus, the classical approach is one of "interpret and then solve," whereas the algebraic approach is "solve and then interpret."

The algebraic approach can be applied to various kinds of equations and algebraic structures. Three cases we consider in this article, and the corresponding kind of program-analysis problems they can be used to solve, are:

Section 2 (Non-recursive) program summarization: left-linear equations over regular algebras.

Section 4 Linearly-recursive procedure summarization: linear equations over tensor-product domains.

Section 5 Conditional termination analysis: right-linear equations over ω-regular algebras.

Why Algebraic Program Analysis? Algebraic program analysis is a general framework for understanding compositional program analyses. The principle of compositionality states that "the meaning of a complex expression is determined by its structure and the meanings of its constituents" [57]. A program analysis is compositional when the result of analyzing a composite program is a function of the results of analyzing its components. Compositionality enables program analyses to scale to large programs, to be parallelized, to be applied incrementally, and to be applied to incomplete programs [18]. Algebraic program analysis provides a structure in which to think about how to design such an analysis.

Insistence upon compositionality also demands a different perspective on program analysis, which can suggest solutions to problems that may otherwise not be apparent. We demonstrate this principle with a series of examples that illustrate a variety of different ideas that are enabled by thinking of program analysis in compositional terms.

Last, the algebraic framework enables a style of reasoning about the behavior of program analyses themselves. By exploiting compositionality, it is possible to design effective algebraic analyses that satisfy certain laws (e.g., monotonicity— "more information in yields more information out"). Analyses can be classified on the basis of algebraic laws that they satisfy, and we can reason how program transformation affects analysis using these laws.

Why Not Algebraic Program Analysis? While compositionality brings many desirable properties, it comes at the price of losing *context*. Compositionality requires that the analysis of a program component is a function of the source code of that component, and therefore *cannot* depend on the surrounding context in which the component appears in the program. Many program analysis techniques make essential use of context, for example:

- In an iterative abstract interpreter, which propagates information about reachable states from the program entry forwards, the analysis of a component depends on every component that may precede it in an execution.
- In a refinement-based software model checker, which inspects paths that go from entry to an error state, the analysis of a component depends on the whole program.

One of the main challenges of designing a good algebraic program analysis is to overcome this loss of contextual information.

Secondly, algebraic program analysis is less general than iterative program analysis, in the sense that any set of semantic (in)equations can be solved iteratively using the same basic algorithm, whereas each particular type of equation system requires a specialized algorithm. Some problems—e.g., resolving semantic equations of recursive procedures—have no known practical algebraic solutions.

2   Regular Algebraic Program Analysis

This section describes the algebraic approach to solving path problems in graphs [1,6,48,59]. The basic structure of the method is to use regular expressions to capture the set of paths of a graph, and then *interpret* these expressions to obtain a desired result. We illustrate the approach by considering the problem of computing shortest paths, and then show how it can be applied to numerical invariant generation.

First, we establish some basic definitions. The syntax of **regular expressions** over an alphabet Σ is as follows:

$$a \in \Sigma$$
$$R \in \mathsf{RegExp}(\Sigma) ::= a \mid 0 \mid 1 \mid R_1 + R_2 \mid R_1 \cdot R_2 \mid R^*$$

We will sometimes use juxtaposition $R_1 R_2$ (rather than $R_1 \cdot R_2$) to denote concatenation.

The semantics of regular expressions over Σ is given by a Σ-**interpretation** $\mathscr{I} = \langle \mathbf{A}, f \rangle$, which consists of *regular algebra* $\mathbf{A}$ and a *semantic function* f. A **regular algebra** $\mathbf{A} = \left\langle A, 0^A, 1^A, +^A, \cdot^A, *^A \right\rangle$ is an algebraic structure consisting of a set A (called its *universe*) equipped with two distinguished elements $0^A, 1^A \in A$, two binary operations $+^A$ (*choice*) and $\cdot^A$ (*sequencing*), and a unary operation $(-)^{*^A}$ (*iteration*).[1] When the algebra is clear from context, we will drop the superscript. A **semantic function** $f : \Sigma \to A$ maps each letter in Σ to an element of $\mathbf{A}$'s universe.

A Σ-interpretation $\mathscr{I} = \langle \mathbf{A}, f \rangle$ assigns to each regular expression R over Σ to an element $\mathscr{I}[\![R]\!]$ of $\mathbf{A}$ by interpreting each letter according to the semantic function and each regular operator using its counterpart in $\mathbf{A}$:

$$\mathscr{I}[\![0]\!] = 0^A \qquad\qquad \mathscr{I}[\![R_1 \cdot R_2]\!] = \mathscr{I}[\![R_1]\!] \cdot^A \mathscr{I}[\![R_2]\!]$$
$$\mathscr{I}[\![1]\!] = 1^A \qquad\qquad \mathscr{I}[\![R_1 + R_2]\!] = \mathscr{I}[\![R_1]\!] +^A \mathscr{I}[\![R_2]\!]$$
$$\mathscr{I}[\![a]\!] = f(a) \quad \text{For } a \in \Sigma \qquad\qquad \mathscr{I}[\![R^*]\!] = \mathscr{I}[\![R]\!]^{*^A}$$

Notice that the interpretation is compositional: for any expression R, $\mathscr{I}[\![R]\!]$ is a function of the top-level operator in R and the interpretations of its subexpressions.

---

[1] Note that no particular laws are assumed to govern these operations. We will return to this issue in Sect. 3.

Example 1 (Standard interpretation). The *standard* interpretation of regular expressions is the language interpretation, $\mathscr{L} = \langle \mathbf{L}, \ell \rangle$ where $\mathbf{L}$ is the regular algebra of languages. The universe of the interpretation is the set of regular languages over Σ, $0 \triangleq \emptyset$ is the empty language, $1 \triangleq \{\epsilon\}$ is the singleton language containing the empty word, and the operators are

$$X + Y \triangleq X \cup Y \qquad\qquad\qquad \text{Union}$$
$$X \cdot Y \triangleq \{xy : x \in X, y \in Y\} \qquad\qquad \text{Concatenation}$$
$$X^* \triangleq \{x_1 x_2 \ldots x_n : x_1, \ldots, x_n \in X\} \qquad \text{Kleene closure}$$

The semantic function ℓ maps each letter a to the singleton language $\{a\}$. For any regular expression R, $\mathscr{L}[\![R]\!]$ is the (regular) set of words recognized by R. ⌐

We now describe how *non-standard* interpretations can be used to solve problems over directed graphs. A **directed graph** $G = \langle V, E \rangle$ consists of a finite set of vertices V and a finite set of directed edges $E \subseteq V \times V$. A **path** in G is a finite sequence $e_1 e_2 \ldots e_n$ with $e_i \in E$ such that for each i, the destination of e_i matches the source of e_{i+1}. A **path expression** (in G) is a regular expression over the alphabet of edges E that recognizes a set of paths in G. For any pair of vertices $u, v \in V$, there is a path expression $PathExp_G(u, v)$ that recognizes exactly the set of paths in G that begin at u and end at v. There are several ways to compute path expressions. The classical method is Kleene's algorithm [44] for computing a regular expression for a finite state automaton (thinking of G as an automaton over the alphabet E with start state u and final state v). For sparse graphs, there are more efficient alternatives to Kleene's algorithm, in particular Tarjan's algorithm [58]. The insight of the algebraic approach to path problems is that these algorithms can be re-used for multiple purposes: first use a path expression algorithm to find a regular expression recognizing a set of paths of interest, and then compute a problem-dependent (non-standard) interpretation of that expression.

Example 2 (Shortest paths). Consider the integer-weighted graph depicted in Fig. 1a. Suppose that we wish to compute the length of the shortest path from a to c. We begin by computing a path expression recognizing all paths from a to c:

$$\big(\langle a, b \rangle \, \langle b, d \rangle \, (\langle d, e \rangle \, \langle e, d \rangle)^* \, \langle d, a \rangle\big)^* \langle a, b \rangle \, \big(\langle b, c \rangle + \langle b, d \rangle \, (\langle d, e \rangle \, \langle e, d \rangle)^* \, \langle d, c \rangle\big)$$

This path expression can be represented succinctly by the directed acyclic graph (DAG) pictured in Fig. 1b. Define the *distance interpretation* $\mathscr{D}$ where the semantic function maps each edge to its weight, and the algebra's universe consists of the integers along with $\pm\infty$, 0 is interpreted as ∞, 1 as 0, and the operators are as follows:

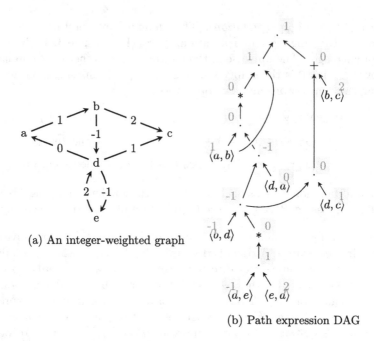

(a) An integer-weighted graph

(b) Path expression DAG

Fig. 1. An integer weighted graph and a path expression DAG representing the paths from a to c

$$d_1 + d_2 \triangleq \min(d_1, d_2) \qquad\qquad \text{Minimum}$$
$$d_1 \cdot d_2 \triangleq d_1 + d_2 \qquad\qquad \text{Addition}$$
$$d^* \triangleq \begin{cases} -\infty & \text{if } d < 0 \\ 0 & \text{otherwise} \end{cases} \qquad\qquad \text{Closure}$$

The weight of the shortest weighted path from a to c is $\mathscr{D}[\![PathExp_G(a,c)]\!] = 1$, which can be calculated efficiently by interpreting the path expression DAG "bottom-up" (see gray labels in Fig. 1b).

Algebraic path-finding can be used to generate invariants by representing a program by a *control flow graph*, and interpreting path expressions within an algebra of program summaries. A **control flow graph** (CFG) $G = \langle V, E, r, C \rangle$ is a directed graph $\langle V, E \rangle$ with a distinguished root (or entry) vertex $r \in V$, and where each edge $e \in E$ is labeled by a command $C(e)$; see Fig. 2a for an example. In the remainder of this section, we give examples of interpretations that can be used to generate (numerical) program summaries.

2.1 Transition-Formula Interpretations

Fix a finite set of variables, X, representing the variables of a program. A **transition formula** is a logical formula $F(X, X')$ whose free variables range over X

and a set of "primed copies" $X' \triangleq \{x' : x \in X\}$. For the purposes of this exposition, we further suppose that variables range over integers, and that transition formulas are expressed in the language of linear integer arithmetic. A transition formula can be interpreted as a binary relation $\rightarrow_F$ over states $\mathsf{State} \triangleq \mathbb{Z}^X$, where $s \rightarrow_F s'$ if and only if F is true when s is used to interpret the un-primed variables and s' is used to interpret the primed variables. For example, if F is the transition formula

$$F \triangleq x' = x + 1 \wedge y = y' \wedge x < y \, ,$$

then we have

$$s \rightarrow_F s' \iff s'(x) = s(x) + 1, s(y) = s'(y), \text{ and } s(x) < s(y) \, .$$

Suppose that $G = \langle V, E, r, C \rangle$ is a control flow graph, where commands range over assignments $x := e$ and assumptions $[c]$, where e is a linear integer term and c is a linear arithmetic formula. (An assumption $[c]$ is a command that does not change the program state, but which can only be executed if the formula c holds.) We define a semantic function tf that maps each control flow edge into the universe of transition formulas by translating the command associated with the edge into logic:

$$\mathit{tf}(e) \triangleq \begin{cases} (x' = e) \wedge \left(\bigwedge_{y \neq x \in X} y' = y \right) & \text{if } C(e) \text{ is } x := e \\ c \wedge \left(\bigwedge_{y \in X} y' = y \right) & \text{if } C(e) \text{ is } [c] \end{cases}$$

We define an algebra of transition formulas as follows:

$$0 \triangleq \mathit{false} \qquad\qquad\qquad\qquad \text{Empty relation}$$

$$1 \triangleq \bigwedge_{x \in X} x' = x \qquad\qquad\qquad \text{Identity relation}$$

$$F + G \triangleq F \vee G \qquad\qquad\qquad\qquad \text{Union}$$

$$F \cdot G \triangleq \exists X''.F(X, X'') \wedge G(X'', X') \qquad \text{Relational composition}$$

Above and elsewhere, we use positional notation for substitution; e.g., $F(X, X'')$ denotes the formula obtained by replacing all the X' symbols with "double primed" symbols in X'' (and leaving the un-primed X symbols as they are). Intuitively, F^* should be interpreted as the reflective transitive closure of F. However, in general it is not possible to compute the reflexive transitive closure of a formula (nor even to *represent* it as a formula). Hence, we must be content with an over-approximate transitive closure operator. There are many different methods for over-approximating transitive closure, so we speak of the *family* of algebras of transition formulas, which have the same basic structure and differ only in the interpretation of the iteration operator. In the remainder of this section, we describe a selection of methods for implementing the iteration operator. *Disclaimer*: for each example, the presentation differs somewhat (sometimes substantially) from the cited source. The examples should be read as "how the cited analysis might be presented in the algebraic framework."

Example 3 (Transitive Predicate Abstraction [47]*).* Fix a set of variables X. Say that a transition formula $p(X, X')$ is

- *reflexive* if $\bigwedge_{x \in X} x = x' \models p(X, X')$
- *transitive* if $p(X, X') \wedge p(X', X'') \models p(X, X'')$

Let P be a finite set of *candidate* reflexive and transitive transition formulas. For example we might choose

$$P \triangleq \begin{array}{l} \{x \bowtie x' : x \in X, \bowtie \in \{\leq, \geq\}\} \\ \cup \{x \bowtie 0 \Rightarrow x' \bowtie 0 : x \in X, \bowtie \in \{\leq, \geq, <, >\}\} \end{array}$$

We can define an iteration operator that over-approximates the reflexive transitive closure of a formula F by the conjunction of the subset of P that is entailed by F:

$$F^* \triangleq \bigwedge \{p \in P : F \models p\} \ . \hspace{3cm} \lrcorner$$

Example 4 (Interval analysis [51]*).* Let $F(X, X')$ be a transition formula. An *inductive interval invariant* for F assigns to each variable $x \in X$ a pair of integers $a_x, b_x \in \mathbb{Z}$ such that if s is a state such that $s(x) \in [a_x, b_x]$ for all $x \in X$ and $s \rightarrow_F s'$, then $s'(x) \in [a_x, b_x]$ for all $x \in X$. Monniaux showed that it is possible to determine optimal inductive interval invariants by posing the inductive-invariance condition symbolically and quantifying over the bounds [51].

Let $P = \{p_x : x \in X\}$ and $Q \triangleq \{q_x : x \in X\}$ be sets of fresh variables, which we use to the lower and upper bounds of intervals, respectively. The set of inductive interval invariants for a formula F can be represented by the formula

$$Inv(F, P, Q) \triangleq \forall X, X'. \left(F \wedge \bigwedge_{x \in X} p_x \leq x \leq q_x \right) \Rightarrow \left(\bigwedge_{x \in X} p_x \leq x' \leq q_x \right)$$

That is, the models of *Inv* (which assign integers to the lower and upper bound variables P and Q) are in one-to-one correspondence with the interval invariants of F. We may universally quantify over all inductive interval invariants to arrive at the following iteration operator:

$$F^* \triangleq \forall P, Q. \left(Inv(F, P, Q) \wedge \bigwedge_{x \in X} p_x \leq x \leq q_x \right) \Rightarrow \left(\bigwedge_{x \in X} p_x \leq x' \leq q_x \right)$$

In contrast to the typical iterative approach with classical widening and narrowing operators, this operator computes a formula that implies *all* (and therefore *most precise*) inductive interval invariants.[2] For example, for the

---

[2] Note that while the formula implies all interval invariants, it does not *itself* take the form of an interval invariant.

loop (**while** $(i \neq n)$ **do** $i := i + 1$), this method yields the following over-approximation of the reflexive transitive closure of F:

$$F^* \equiv n' = n \wedge i \leq i' \wedge (i \leq n \Rightarrow i' \leq n)$$

If we suppose that i is initially 0 and n is initially 100, then this formula implies the loop invariant that n is equal to 100, and i is in the interval $[0, 100]$.   ⌐

Example 5 (Recurrence analysis [4,27]). Let $F(X, X')$ be a transition formula, and let $\mathbf{x}$ and $\mathbf{x}'$ denote vectors containing the variables X and X', respectively. A *linear recurrence inequation of F* is a formula of the form $\mathbf{a}^\mathsf{T}\mathbf{x}' \leq \mathbf{a}^\mathsf{T}\mathbf{x} + b$ that is entailed by F. The idea behind recurrence analysis is to extract a set of linear recurrence inequations for a formula, $\{\mathbf{a}_i^\mathsf{T}\mathbf{x}' \leq \mathbf{a}_i^\mathsf{T}\mathbf{x} + b_i\}_{i \in I}$, and to use the closed form of those recurrences to over-approximate the transitive closure of F:

$$F^* \triangleq \exists k.k \geq 0 \wedge \bigwedge_{i \in I} \mathbf{a}_i^\mathsf{T}\mathbf{x}' \leq \mathbf{a}_i^\mathsf{T}\mathbf{x} + kb_i$$

For instance, consider the following loop:

while $(x > 0)$ **do**
    if $(y < 0)$ { $x := x + y$; $y := y - 1$ }
    else { $x := x - 2$; $y := y - 3$}

The loop exhibits the following recurrences

$$\begin{aligned}(2x' - y') &\leq (2x - y) - 1 \\ y' &\leq y - 1 \\ -y' &\leq -y + 3\end{aligned} \quad \text{or in matrix form,} \quad \begin{bmatrix} 2 & -1 \\ 0 & 1 \\ 0 & -1 \end{bmatrix}\begin{bmatrix} x' \\ y' \end{bmatrix} \leq \begin{bmatrix} 2 & -1 \\ 0 & 1 \\ 0 & -1 \end{bmatrix}\begin{bmatrix} x \\ y \end{bmatrix} + \begin{bmatrix} -1 \\ -1 \\ 3 \end{bmatrix}$$

which yields the following transition formula that summarizes the loop:

$$\exists k.k \geq 0 \wedge (2x' - y') \leq (2x - y') - k \wedge y' \leq y - k \wedge -y' \leq -y + 3k .$$

The loop also exhibits other recurrences (such as $x' \leq x - 1$); however, the three selected recurrences are complete in the sense that all implied recurrences are non-negative linear combinations of these three (e.g., $x' \leq x - 1$ is obtained by adding $1/2$-times the first and second recurrences).

Such a complete set of recurrences exists for any transition formula F, which can be computed as follows. First, observe that the set of linear recurrences of F,

$$Rec(F) \triangleq \{(\mathbf{a}, b) : F \models \mathbf{a}^\mathsf{T}\mathbf{x}' \leq \mathbf{a}^\mathsf{T}\mathbf{x} + b\}$$

is closed under non-negative linear combinations (i.e., it is a *convex cone*). Our goal is to find a (finite) set of generators for $Rec(F)$—a finite set $\{(\mathbf{a}_i, b_i)\}_{i \in B}$ such that

$$Rec(F) = \left\{ (\mathbf{0}, \lambda_0) + \sum_{i \in B} \lambda_i(\mathbf{a}_i, b_i) : \lambda_0 \geq 0, \lambda_i \geq 0 \text{ for all } i \in B \right\} .$$

To compute generators for $Rec(F)$, we first introduce a fresh set of "difference" variables, $\{\delta_x\}_{x \in X}$ and form a formula

$$\Delta(F) \triangleq \exists X, X'.F \wedge \bigwedge_{x \in X} \delta_x = x' - x \ .$$

Observe that $(\mathbf{a}, b) \in Rec(F)$ if and only if $\Delta(F) \models \mathbf{a}^\mathsf{T}\delta \leq b$. Thus, a set of generators for $Rec(F)$ corresponds exactly to a half-space representation for the convex hull of $\Delta(F)$, which can be computed using the algorithm from [27].

The class of linear recurrence inequations considered in this example can be generalized in various ways to yield more powerful invariant generation procedures. In particular,

- [27] computes linear recurrences with polynomial closed forms
- [42] computes polynomial recurrences with polynomial and complex exponential closed forms.
- [41] computes polynomial recurrences with polynomial and rational exponential closed forms.   ⌟

2.2   Weak Interpretations

Transition formulas are an appealing basis for algebraic program analysis, since all the operators (except the iteration operator) are *precise*—they simply encode the meaning of the program into logic. The significance of this is that transition formula algebras delay precision loss *as long as possible*, which helps to overcome loss of contextual information. However, there are algebraic analyses of interest that are defined on weak logical fragments that cannot precisely express union and/or relational composition.

Example 6 (Affine relation analysis [38]). An *affine relation* is a relation that corresponds to the set of models of a transition formula of the form $Ax' = Bx+c$. Define the algebra of affine transition relations to be the regular algebra where the universe is the set of affine transition relations, 0 is interpreted as the empty relation, 1 is interpreted as the identity relation, + is interpreted as the affine hull of $R_1 \cup R_2$ (the smallest affine relation that contains both R_1 and R_2), $\cdot$ is interpreted as relational composition, and $*$ is interpreted as the operation that sends any affine relation R to the limit of the sequence $\{R_i\}_{i=0}^{\infty}$ defined by

$$R_0 = 0 \qquad\qquad R_{i+1} = R_i + (R_i \cdot R) \text{ for } i \geq 0$$

Since we have $R_0 \subseteq R_1 \subseteq \ldots$ and if any R_{i+1} properly contains R_i the dimension of R_{i+1} is strictly greater than that of R_i, this sequence must stabilize in finite time, so the operation R^* is computable.   ⌟

3   Semantic Foundations

This section presents a general view of algebraic program analysis, with the goal of elucidating its underlying principles so that they may be understood outside the setting of graphs and regular expressions. This sets the stage for Sect. 4 and Sect. 5, wherein we will develop program analysis schemes that follow the same general "recipe" that we lay out in this section, but deviate from the instance of this recipe that we saw in Sect. 2.

Following the theory of abstract interpretation [22], we begin with a *concrete semantics* that defines the meaning of a program. The concrete semantics is specified as the least (or greatest) solution to a system of recursive equations. The concrete semantics is not computable—the goal of a program analysis is to *approximate* it. The way that this is accomplished in an algebraic analysis is by symbolically computing a closed-form solution to the semantic equations (i.e., a non-recursive system of equations whose (unique) solution coincides with the concrete semantics), and then interpreting that closed-form solution in an algebraic structure that approximates the algebra of the concrete semantics.

3.1   Semantic Equations

Given a control flow graph G, we can syntactically derive a system of equations $E(G)$—see Fig. 2. For each vertex v, we introduce a variable X_v and an equation $(X_v = R_v)$ that relates that variable to the variables for v's predecessors. Notice that this system of equations can be viewed as a (left-)regular grammar, with each non-terminal symbol X_v recognizing the set of paths from the root r to the vertex v. This is an instance of the more general concept of a solution to a system of equations over an algebraic structure. A *solution* to the system of equations $E(G) = \{X_v = R_v\}_{v \in V}$ over a regular interpretation $\mathscr{I} = \langle \mathbf{A}, f \rangle$ is a function σ that maps each variable to an element of $\mathbf{A}$ such that each equation is satisfied: for each equation $(X_v = R_v)$ in $E(G)$, we have $\sigma(X) = \mathscr{I}_\sigma[\![R]\!]$, where $\mathscr{I}_\sigma$ is the interpretation obtained by extending the semantic function to variables by interpreting them according to σ.

The prototypical concrete semantics of interest in algebraic analysis is the relational semantics. The **relational semantics** of a program associates to every control flow vertex v a reachability relation R_v, which is the set of pairs $\langle s, s' \rangle$ such that if the program begins at r in state s, then it may reach v with state s'. The relational semantics may be obtained as the least solution to the system of semantic equations over the relational interpretation, which is defined as follows. The regular algebra of state relations, $\mathbf{R}$, has binary relations on states as its universe, 0 is interpreted as the empty relation $\emptyset$, 1 is interpreted as the identity relation $\{\langle s, s \rangle : s \in \mathsf{State}\}$, $\cdot$ is interpreted as relational composition, $+$ as union, and $*$ as reflexive, transitive closure. The **relational interpretation** $\mathscr{R}$ is the interpretation over the regular algebra of state relations where the semantic function maps each command to its associated transition relation; e.g., $i := i + 2$ is associated with the set of all pairs $\langle s, s' \rangle$ such that $s'(i) = s(i) + 1$ and $s'(x) = s(x)$ for all $x \neq i$. The relational semantics of a CFG G is the least solution to $E(G)$ over the relational interpretation.

Having formulated the concrete semantics as the solution to a system of equations, we must now solve the system symbolically. The classical algorithm is a variation of Gaussian elimination, given in Algorithm 1. This algorithm is essentially Kleene's algorithm [44] for computing a regular expression for a

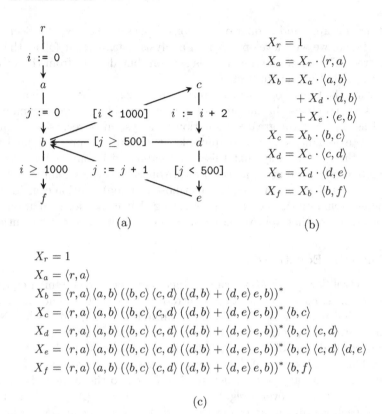

(a)   (b)

$$X_r = 1$$
$$X_a = \langle r, a \rangle$$
$$X_b = \langle r, a \rangle \langle a, b \rangle \left(\langle b, c \rangle \langle c, d \rangle \left(\langle d, b \rangle + \langle d, e \rangle \, e, b \right) \right)^*$$
$$X_c = \langle r, a \rangle \langle a, b \rangle \left(\langle b, c \rangle \langle c, d \rangle \left(\langle d, b \rangle + \langle d, e \rangle \, e, b \right) \right)^* \langle b, c \rangle$$
$$X_d = \langle r, a \rangle \langle a, b \rangle \left(\langle b, c \rangle \langle c, d \rangle \left(\langle d, b \rangle + \langle d, e \rangle \, e, b \right) \right)^* \langle b, c \rangle \langle c, d \rangle$$
$$X_e = \langle r, a \rangle \langle a, b \rangle \left(\langle b, c \rangle \langle c, d \rangle \left(\langle d, b \rangle + \langle d, e \rangle \, e, b \right) \right)^* \langle b, c \rangle \langle c, d \rangle \langle d, e \rangle$$
$$X_f = \langle r, a \rangle \langle a, b \rangle \left(\langle b, c \rangle \langle c, d \rangle \left(\langle d, b \rangle + \langle d, e \rangle \, e, b \right) \right)^* \langle b, f \rangle$$

(c)

Fig. 2. (a) A control flow graph; (b) the corresponding systems of equations; and (c) a closed-form solution.

finite state automaton, recast in the language of equations. The front-solving step eliminates variables one-by-one, at each step i producing a system of equation of equations that is equivalent to the original, but in which the variable X_i does not appear in the right-hand-side of any equations $X_j = R_j$ for $j \geq i$. The back-solving step eliminates all variable occurrences from right-hand-sides, at each step replacing X_i with its closed form R_i in each equation $X_j = R_j$ for $j < i$. An example illustrating the result of solving the system of equations in Fig. 2b symbolically appears in Fig. 2c. The significant difference to the familiar Gaussian elimination algorithm in linear algebra is the "loop-solving" step, which solves a single recursive equation $X_i = R_i$ symbolically by re-arranging R_i into the form $X_i A + B$ and taking BA^* to be the solution. The loop-solving step is justified under the relational interpretation, and more generally for any interpretation over a *Kleene algebra*.[3]

---

[3] The laws of Kleene algebra are not minimal in this regard.

Input   : Left-linear system of equations, $E = \{X_i = R_i\}_{i=1}^n$
Output : Closed-form solution to E
for $i = 1$ **to** n **do**   /* Front-solving */
    Re-arrange R_i in the form $X_iA + B$;
    $R_i \leftarrow BA^*$;   /* "Loop-solving" */
    foreach $j > i$ **do** $R_j \leftarrow R_j[X \mapsto R_i]$;
end
for $i = n$ **to** 2 **do**   /* Back-solving */
    foreach $j < i$ **do** $R_j \leftarrow R_j[X_i \mapsto R_i]$;
end
return E;
Algorithm 1: Gaussian elimination for left-linear systems of equations

Definition 1. *Let* $\mathbf{A} = \langle A, +, \cdot, *, 0, 1 \rangle$ *be a regular algebra. We say that* $\mathbf{A}$ *is an* **idempotent semiring** *if it satisfies the following (for all* $a, b, c, \in A$*):*

$$
\begin{array}{llr}
a + (b + c) = (a + b) + c & a(bc) = (ab)c & \textit{Associativity} \\
a(b + c) = ab + ac & (b + c)a = ba + ca & \textit{Distributivity} \\
a + 0 = a & 1a = a1 = a & \textit{Identity} \\
& a + b = b + a & \textit{Commutativity of } + \\
& a + a = a & \textit{Idempotence} \\
& a0 = 0a = 0 & \textit{Annihilation}
\end{array}
$$

In any idempotent semiring, we may define a **natural order** $\leq$*, where* $a \leq b$ *iff* $a + b = b$*. Note that* $+$ *is the least upper bound with respect to this order.*

We say that $\mathbf{A}$ *is a* **Kleene algebra** *if it is an idempotent semiring and the following hold (for all* $a, x \in A$*):*

$$
\begin{array}{llr}
1 + a(a^*) = a^* & 1 + (a^*)a = a^* & \textit{Unfolding} \\
ax \leq x \Rightarrow a^*x \leq x & xa \leq x \Rightarrow xa^* \leq x & \textit{Induction}
\end{array}
$$

Exercise 1. Show that in any Kleene algebra, the least solution to a (left-)linear recursive equation $X = a + Xb$ exists and is equal to ab^*

The sense in which Gaussian elimination computes a "closed-form solutions" to a system of left-linear equations E is that:

- (*closed form*) the right-hand sides do not refer to variables, and
- (*solution*) for any interpretation $\mathscr{I}$ over a Kleene algebra, for each equation $(X = R) \in E$, we have $\sigma(X) = \mathscr{I}[\![R]\!]$ where σ is the least solution to E over $\mathscr{I}$.

The connection between Gaussian elimination and graph algorithms like Floyd-Warshall inspired Tarjan's path-expression algorithm [58]. In the language of graphs, Tarjan's algorithm computes for each vertex v of a control flow graph G with root r a path expression $PathExp_G(r, v)$ that recognizes the set of paths from r to v; in the language of equations, it solves left-linear systems of equations symbolically. Tarjan's algorithm is preferred to Gaussian elimination in practice: is more efficient (nearly linear time for reducible flow graphs, compared to cubic time for Gaussian elimination) and produces simpler solutions. For expository purposes, we will continue to refer to Gaussian elimination for solving systems of equations, viewing Tarjan's method as an efficient variation.

3.2   Abstract Interpretation

Gaussian elimination can solve a system of left-linear equations over a Kleene algebra (e.g., relational semantics) symbolically. However, the solution cannot be interpreted in the concrete algebra, since operators are not effective (that is, they cannot be implemented by a machine). We approximate the concrete semantics by interpreting the closed-form solution in an effective *abstract* algebra (e.g., one of the transition-formula algebras from Sect. 2).

Following the theory of abstract interpretation [22], the correctness of this approach is justified by establishing a relationship between the "concrete" and "abstract" interpretations. In the algebraic framework, a natural way to express the relationship is via a *soundness relation* [24], which is a binary relation between two algebras that is preserved by the operations of the algebra. Membership of a (concrete, abstract) pair in the relation indicates that the concrete element is approximated by the abstract element.

Definition 2 (Soundness relation).   *Given two Σ-interpretations $\mathscr{I}^\natural = \langle \mathbf{A}^\natural, f^\natural \rangle$ and $\mathscr{I}^\sharp = \langle \mathbf{A}^\sharp, f^\sharp \rangle$, $- \Vdash - \subseteq A^\natural \times A^\sharp$ is a **soundness relation** if $f^\natural(a) \Vdash f^\sharp(a)$ for all $a \in \Sigma$ and $\Vdash$ is a sub-algebra of the product algebra $\mathbf{A}^\natural \times \mathbf{A}^\sharp$; i.e., $0^\natural \Vdash 0^\sharp$, $1^\natural \Vdash 1^\sharp$, and for all $x_1 \Vdash y_1$ and $x_2 \Vdash y_2$ we have*

- $x_1 +^\natural x_2 \Vdash y_1 +^\sharp y_2$
- $x_1 \cdot^\natural x_2 \Vdash y_1 \cdot^\sharp y_2$
- $x_1^{*^\natural} \Vdash y_1^{*^\sharp}$

The definition of soundness relation generalizes to interpretations over other classes of algebraic structures in the natural way: it is a binary relation over two algebras of the same signature that is preserved by every operation in the signature.

Example 7 (Transition formula overapproximation). Let $\mathbf{R}$ denote the algebra of state relations and $\mathbf{TF}$ denote an algebra of transition formulas. The *over-approximation* relation is defined by

$$R \Vdash_O F \iff \forall \langle s, s' \rangle \in R, s \rightarrow_F s'.$$

Preservation of constants and the sequencing and choice operations is easily verified; to show that $\Vdash_O$ is a soundness relation, we need only to show that $R \Vdash_O F$ implies $R^{*^\mathbf{R}} \Vdash_O F^{*^{\mathbf{TF}}}$; i.e., $(-)^{*^{\mathbf{TF}}}$ over-approximates reflexive transitive closure. Of course, this proof depends on the particular implementation of the iteration operator.

The over-approximate soundness relation allows us to *verify* safety properties: if $R \Vdash_O F$ and F entails some property P, then R satisfies P.   ⌐

Example 8 (Transition formula underapproximation). The *under-approximation* relation is defined by

$$R \Vdash_U F \iff \forall s, s'. s \to_F s' \Rightarrow \langle s, s' \rangle \in R,$$

Preservation of constants and the sequencing and choice operations is again easily verified; to show that $\Vdash_U$ is a soundness relation, we need only to show that $R \Vdash_O F$ implies $R^{*^{\mathbf{R}}} \Vdash_O F^{*^{\mathbf{TF}}}$; i.e., $(-)^{*^{\mathbf{TF}}}$ under-approximates reflexive transitive closure. The iteration operators in Sect. 2 are all over-approximate. An example of an under-approximate iteration operator is

$$F^* \triangleq \bigvee_{i=0}^{n} \underbrace{F \circ \cdots \circ F}_{i \ times}$$

(for some fixed choice of n) which corresponds to bounded model checking [9], with an unrolling bound of n.

The under-approximate soundness relation allows us to *refute* safety properties: if $R \Vdash_U F$ and F does not entail some property P, then R does not satisfy P. ⌐

The problem of "approximating the behavior of a program" can be formalized as follows:

Given a system of semantic equations over a set of variables $\mathcal{X}$ describing the concrete semantics of a program (i.e., its least solution $\sigma^\natural$ over some interpretation $\mathscr{I}^\natural$), find some $\sigma^\sharp : \mathcal{X} \to \mathbf{A}^\sharp$ such that for each variable $X \in \mathcal{X}$, we have $\sigma^\natural(X) \Vdash \sigma^\sharp(X)$.

The algebraic approach to this problem is to compute for each variable X a closed form R_X (such that $\sigma^\natural(X) = \mathscr{I}^\natural(R_X)$), and define $\sigma^\sharp(X) \triangleq \mathscr{I}^\sharp(R_X)$. The correctness of this approach is justified by the following soundness lemma, which follows by induction on regular expressions.

Lemma 1 (Soundness). *Let Σ be an alphabet, let $\mathscr{I}^\natural = \langle \mathbf{A}^\natural, f^\natural \rangle$ and $\mathscr{I}^\sharp = \langle \mathbf{A}^\sharp, f^\sharp \rangle$ be Σ-interpretations, and let $\Vdash \subseteq A^\natural \times A^\sharp$ be a soundness relation. Then for any regular expression $R \in \mathsf{RegExp}(\Sigma)$, we have $\mathscr{I}^\natural\llbracket R \rrbracket \Vdash \mathscr{I}^\sharp\llbracket R \rrbracket$*

3.3 Discussion

A subtlety of algebraic program analysis is that most algebras of interest in program analysis are *not* Kleene algebras (for instance, none of the algebras in Sect. 2 are), and so in general, Gaussian elimination does not find solutions to systems of equations over "abstract" interpretations corresponding to program analyses. This technical difficulty is sidestepped by appealing to the concrete semantics (which typically *is* defined over a Kleene algebra, such as the algebra of state relations) to justify the use of path-expression algorithms, and a sound approximating algebra to interpret the resulting expressions. The fact that the abstract interpretation of the closed-form solution to the concrete system of equations does not yield a solution to the abstract system of equations is immaterial: our goal is to *over-approximate* the concrete rather than *solve* the abstract.

Formalizing a program analysis as an algebraic structure allows one to understand the behavior of program analyses in terms of algebraic laws, and use the language of algebra to reason about program analyses. For example, any transition formula algebra (in the family described in Sect. 2.1) is an idempotent semiring, and so any two *-free regular expressions that denote the same language have the same (up to logical equivalence) interpretation as a transition formula. While none of the iteration operators in Sect. 2.1 satisfy the *Unfolding* and *Induction* laws of Kleene algebra, they do satisfy weaker *pre-Kleene algebra* iteration laws:

$$1 \leq a^* \qquad \text{Reflexivity}$$
$$a \leq a^* \qquad \text{Extensivity}$$
$$a^*a^* = a^* \qquad \text{Transitivity}$$
$$a \leq b \Rightarrow a^* \leq b^* \qquad \text{Monotonicity}$$
$$\text{For any } n,\ (a^n)^* \leq a^* \qquad \text{Unrolling}$$

A concrete use-case for these laws appears in [25], which develops regular expression transformation techniques that preserve concrete semantics but are guaranteed to produce (non-strictly) more precise abstract semantics.

Such laws can also be useful for users of program analysis tools. For example, since all operations are monotone (as a consequence of the monotonicity and idempotent-semiring laws), a user can rely on the principle that "more information in yields more information out." If a user alters a program P by adding additional *assume* commands to get a program P' (e.g., expressing invariants that are found by some other automated invariant generation technique, user-provided hints, etc.), monotonicity means that they may rely on the fact that the analysis will produce summaries for P' that are at least as precise as those for P.

A Recipe for Algebraic Program Analysis. We conclude this section by presenting a general view of algebraic program analysis, abstracted from the language of graphs and regular expressions:

1. *(Modeling)* Express the concrete semantics as the least (or greatest) solution to a system of recursive equations (e.g., relational semantics as the least solution to the left-linear system of equations corresponding to a control flow graph).
2. *(Closed forms)* Design a suitable language of "closed-form solutions" and an algorithm for computing them (e.g., regular expressions and path-expression algorithms).
3. *(Interpretation)* Design an abstract interpretation of the language of closed forms and a soundness relation connecting the concrete and abstract interpretations (e.g., transition-formula algebras (Sect. 2.1) and the over-approximate soundness relation (Ex. 7)).

Section 4 and Sect. 5 give two more instances of this generic recipe, generalizing beyond left-linear equations and regular-expressions as closed forms. Section 4 considers linear equations (and an appropriate language of closed forms); Sect. 5 considers another form of equation with ω-regular expressions as closed forms.

4   Interprocedural Analysis

Algebraic program analyses are oriented around computing summaries for program fragments, and are naturally suited to analyzing programs with procedures. Following Cousot & Cousot [23] and Sharir & Pnueli [56], the idea is to structure the analysis in two phases:

Phase I: compute for each procedure X a summary that approximates the behavior of X (including the actions of all procedures called transitively from X).

Phase II: analyze whole-program paths from the start of the main procedure, using the summaries to interpret procedure calls.

An example of a program with procedures is given in Fig. 3(a). The CFGs for its procedures are shown in Fig. 3(b) along with a set of equations corresponding to the CFGs (Fig. 3(c)). For Phase I, it is also useful to consider the following equations in which we have eliminated all variables except for those of the form $X_{s,x}$, which represent the procedure summaries.

$$\begin{aligned}
X_{s_1,x_1} &= (\langle s_1, a \rangle \cdot X_{s_2,x_2} + \langle s_1, b \rangle) \cdot X_{s_2,x_2} \\
X_{s_2,x_2} &= X_{s_3,x_3} \cdot X_{s_3,x_3} \\
X_{s_3,x_3} &= \langle s_3, x_3 \rangle
\end{aligned} \tag{1}$$

This system of equations can be obtained either by a process of successively eliminating variables from Fig. 3(c), or they can be read off directly from each control-flow graph: sequential composition corresponds to $\cdot$, and branching corresponds to $+$.

We can also construct a graph of the dependencies among the variables in the equation system. In this case, we would have

$$X_{s_3,x_3} \longrightarrow X_{s_2,x_2} \longrightarrow X_{s_1,x_1} \tag{2}$$

(which is also isomorphic to the program's call graph). Note that the equations in Eq. (1) are *not* left-linear. However, by eliminating variables in a topological order of Eq. (2), these systems can still be solved using Gaussian elimination (Algorithm 1).

$$\begin{aligned}
X_{s_3,x_3} &= \langle s_3, x_3 \rangle \\
X_{s_2,x_2} &= \langle s_3, x_3 \rangle \cdot \langle s_3, x_3 \rangle \\
X_{s_1,x_1} &= (\langle s_1, a \rangle \cdot \langle s_3, x_3 \rangle \cdot \langle s_3, x_3 \rangle + \langle s_1, b \rangle) \cdot \langle s_3, x_3 \rangle \cdot \langle s_3, x_3 \rangle
\end{aligned} \tag{3}$$

Unfortunately, this strategy breaks down for programs with recursive procedures: the essential difficulty is in computing the summaries of procedures that are directly recursive or part of a set of mutually recursive procedures. We will return to this issue shortly, after a brief discussion of Phase II, which can be addressed via algebraic program analysis, regardless of whether the original equation system contains recursion.

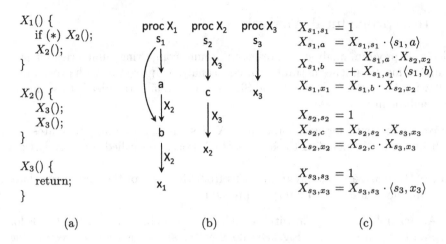

$X_1() \{$
    $\quad$ if $(*) \ X_2();$
    $\quad X_2();$
$\}$

$X_2() \{$
    $\quad X_3();$
    $\quad X_3();$
$\}$

$X_3() \{$
    $\quad$ return;
$\}$

(a)   (b)   (c)

$X_{s_1,s_1} = 1$
$X_{s_1,a} \ = X_{s_1,s_1} \cdot \langle s_1, a \rangle$
$X_{s_1,b} \ = \dfrac{X_{s_1,a} \cdot X_{s_2,x_2}}{+ \ X_{s_1,s_1} \cdot \langle s_1, b \rangle}$
$X_{s_1,x_1} = X_{s_1,b} \cdot X_{s_2,x_2}$

$X_{s_2,s_2} = 1$
$X_{s_2,c} \ = X_{s_2,s_2} \cdot X_{s_3,x_3}$
$X_{s_2,x_2} = X_{s_2,c} \cdot X_{s_3,x_3}$

$X_{s_3,s_3} = 1$
$X_{s_3,x_3} = X_{s_3,s_3} \cdot \langle s_3, x_3 \rangle$

Fig. 3. (a) A three-procedure program scheme. (b) Control-flow graphs for program (a). The edges labeled "X_2" and "X_3" represent calls to the respective procedures. (c) A system of equations corresponding to (b).

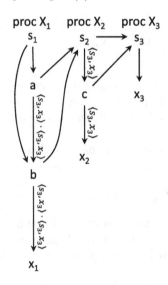

Fig. 4. Graph corresponding to the equation system used for Phase II for the program from Fig. 3.

With closed-form solutions for the procedure summaries in hand, Phase II can be addressed with Gaussian elimination. (Note that for a program with recursive procedures, the transformed Phase II system is still recursive. However, it is *left*-recursive, and so can be handled with regular expressions, and analyzed using the transition-formula interpretations of Sect. 2—the "loops" in Phase II correspond to sequences of recursive calls). Figure 4 shows the equation system

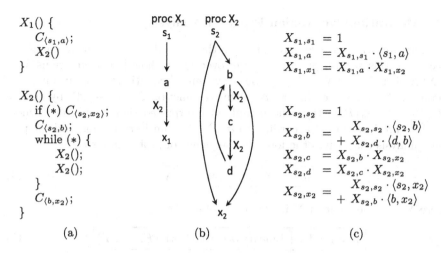

$X_1()$ {
  $C_{\langle s_1,a\rangle}$;
  $X_2()$
}

$X_2()$ {
  if (*) $C_{\langle s_2,x_2\rangle}$;
  $C_{\langle s_2,b\rangle}$;
  while (*) {
    $X_2()$;
    $X_2()$;
  }
  $C_{\langle b,x_2\rangle}$;
}

(a)

proc X_1 proc X_2

(b)

$$X_{s_1,s_1} = 1$$
$$X_{s_1,a} = X_{s_1,s_1} \cdot \langle s_1,a\rangle$$
$$X_{s_1,x_1} = X_{s_1,a} \cdot X_{s_1,x_2}$$

$$X_{s_2,s_2} = 1$$
$$X_{s_2,b} = \begin{aligned} &X_{s_2,s_2} \cdot \langle s_2,b\rangle \\ &+ X_{s_2,d} \cdot \langle d,b\rangle \end{aligned}$$
$$X_{s_2,c} = X_{s_2,b} \cdot X_{s_2,x_2}$$
$$X_{s_2,d} = X_{s_2,c} \cdot X_{s_2,x_2}$$
$$X_{s_2,x_2} = \begin{aligned} &X_{s_2,s_2} \cdot \langle s_2,x_2\rangle \\ &+ X_{s_2,b} \cdot \langle b,x_2\rangle \end{aligned}$$

(c)

Fig. 5. (a) A two-procedure program scheme, where X_1 represents the main procedure, X_2 represents a recursive subroutine, and $C_{\langle s_1,a\rangle}$, $C_{\langle s_2,x_2\rangle}$, $C_{\langle s_2,b\rangle}$, and $C_{\langle b,x_2\rangle}$ represent four program statements. (b) Control-flow graphs for program (a). The three edges labeled "X_2" represent calls to procedure X_2. (c) A system of equations corresponding to (b).

used for Phase II for the program from Fig. 3 in graphical form. The graph is similar to Fig. 3(b) with (i) additional edges from each call-site to the start node of the called procedure, and (ii) the edges previously labeled with "X_2" and "X_3" are now labeled with the values from Eq. (3) for the corresponding procedure summaries: $\langle s_3,x_3\rangle \cdot \langle s_3,x_3\rangle$ and $\langle s_3,x_3\rangle$, respectively.

The remainder of this section focuses on Phase I: computing procedure summaries. Consider the two-procedure program shown in Fig. 5(a). CFGs for its procedures are shown in Fig. 5(b) along with a set of recursive equations corresponding to the interprocedural CFG. Unfortunately, equations like those in Fig. 5(c) do not fit naturally with the recipe given in Sect. 3.3. The essential difficulty is with item 3.3: "Design a suitable language of 'closed-form solutions' and an algorithm for computing them." In particular, we cannot use regular expressions and path-expression algorithms because the equations in Fig. 5(c) are not left-linear (and they cannot be put in left-linear form).

Two ideas are involved in using algebraic program analysis to summarize recursive procedures:

1. The generalization by Esparza et al. [26] of Newton's method—the classical numerical-analysis algorithm for finding roots of real-valued functions—to a method for solving a system of equations over a semiring $\mathcal{S}$, called *Newtonian Program Analysis* (NPA). As in its real-valued counterpart, each iteration of NPA solves a simpler "linearized" problem. (See Sect. 4.1.)
2. The technique of Reps et al. [53] for applying the algebraic-program-analysis recipe to the linearized problems that arise in NPA. (See Sect. 4.2.)

4.1 Motivation: Newtonian Program Analysis

To motivate why we are interested in the special case of linear equations
(Sect. 4.2), this section provides a brief overview of how linear equations arise
in NPA. Let $E = \{X_i = R_i\}_{i=1}^n$ be a system of equations, and fix an inter-
pretation $\mathscr{I}$ over some algebra $\mathbf{A}$. Define a function $\mathbf{f} : A^n \rightarrow A^n$ by $\mathbf{f}(\sigma) =$
$(\mathscr{I}_\sigma[\![R_1]\!], \ldots, \mathscr{I}_\sigma[\![R_n]\!])$ (i.e., the n-tuple of interpreted right-hand-sides, where
variables are interpreted according to σ). NPA is an iterative method for pro-
gram analysis that solves the following sequence of problems for ν:

$$\boxed{\nu^{(0)} = \mathbf{f}(0) \qquad \nu^{(i+1)} = \mathbf{Y}^{(i)}} \tag{4}$$

where $\mathbf{Y}^{(i)}$ is the value of $\mathbf{Y}$ in the least solution of

$$\boxed{\mathbf{Y} = \mathbf{f}(\nu^{(i)}) + \mathrm{LinearCorrectionTerm}(E, \nu^{(i)}, \mathbf{Y})} \tag{5}$$

Thus, NPA is similar to Kleene iteration, except that on each iteration, $\mathbf{f}(\nu^{(i)})$
is "corrected" by an amount controlled by $\mathrm{LinearCorrectionTerm}(E, \nu^{(i)}, \mathbf{Y})$—a
function of $\mathbf{f}$, the current approximation $\nu^{(i)}$, and (vector) variable $\mathbf{Y}$—which
nudges the next approximation $\nu^{(i+1)}$ in the right direction at each step.

The linear correction term is the result of replacing each right-hand side
$R_i = \sum_j R_j$ with a sum $\sum_{i=0}^n R_{i,j,k}$, where each $R_{i,j,k}$ is obtained from $R_{i,j}$ by
replacing all variables, except possibly one, with its interpretation in ν. (The
formal definition can be found elsewhere [26, §3.2].) For example, consider the
system of equations below, a simplified variant of Fig. 5(c) that is obtained by
eliminating all variables except $X_{s_1,x_1}, X_{s_2,b}, X_{s_2,x_2}$:

$$\begin{aligned}
X_{s_1,x_1} &= \langle s_1, a \rangle\, X_{s_1,x_2} \\
X_{s_2,b} &= \langle s_2, b \rangle + X_{s_2,b} \cdot X_{s_2,x_2} \cdot X_{s_2,x_2} \cdot \langle d, b \rangle \\
X_{s_2,x_2} &= \langle s_2, x_2 \rangle + X_{s_2,b}\, \langle b, x_2 \rangle
\end{aligned} \tag{6}$$

The transformation results in the following system (for brevity, we denote
$Y_{s_1,x_1}, Y_{s_2,b}, Y_{s_2,x_2}$ by Y_1, Y_2, Y_3):

$$\begin{aligned}
Y_1 &= \langle s_1, a \rangle \cdot Y_3 \\
Y_2 &= \langle s_2, b \rangle + Y_2 \cdot \nu_3 \cdot \nu_3 \cdot \langle d, b \rangle + \underline{\nu_2 \cdot Y_3 \cdot \nu_3 \cdot \langle d, b \rangle} + \underline{\nu_2 \cdot \nu_3 \cdot Y_3 \cdot \langle d, b \rangle} \\
Y_3 &= \langle s_2, x_2 \rangle + Y_2 \cdot \langle b, x_2 \rangle
\end{aligned} \tag{7}$$

Note that the two underlined summands are both truly *linear*: they are linear,
but not left-linear nor right-linear.

The process of solving Eqs. (4) and (5) for $\nu^{(i+1)}$, given $\nu^{(i)}$, is called
one *Newton round*. On the initial Newton round, we set $\langle \nu_1^{(0)}, \nu_2^{(0)}, \nu_3^{(0)} \rangle \leftarrow$
$\langle 0, \mathscr{I}[\![\langle s_2, x_2 \rangle]\!], \mathscr{I}[\![\langle s_3, x_3 \rangle]\!] \rangle$. On round $i + 1$, we solve Eq. (7) for $\langle Y_1, Y_2, Y_3 \rangle$
with $\langle \nu_1, \nu_2, \nu_3 \rangle$ set to the value $\langle \nu_1^{(i)}, \nu_2^{(i)}, \nu_3^{(i)} \rangle$ obtained on round i, and then
set $\langle \nu_1^{(i+1)}, \nu_2^{(i+1)}, \nu_3^{(i+1)} \rangle \leftarrow \langle Y_1, Y_2, Y_3 \rangle$.

Operationally, the linearization transformation imposes a particular protocol for sampling the program's space of behaviors. For instance, in Fig. 5(b),
the procedure X_2 has two call-sites along the loop through b. In Eq. (7), each
right-hand-side summand in the equation for Y_2 has at most one variable: the
transformation inserted ν_2 or ν_3 at various call-sites (considering $X_{s_2,b}$ as a
pseudo-call-site corresponding to tail recursion), and left at most one variable Y_i
in each summand. In essence, during a given Newton round, the analyzer samples
the behavior of $\mathbf{f}$ by taking the $+$ of various paths through the transformation
of $\mathbf{f}$. Along each path through a (transformed) right-hand side, the summary for
each pseudo-call-site X_i encountered is held fixed at ν_i, except for possibly one
pseudo-call-site on the path, which is explored by visiting (the linearized version
of) the called procedure. The summaries ν_1, ν_2, ν_3 are updated according to the
result of this exploration, and the algorithm performs the next Newton round.

The analogy between NPA and Newton's method in numerical analysis is
that in both cases one creates a linear approximation of $\mathbf{f}(\mathbf{X})$ around the "point"
$(\nu^{(i)}, \mathbf{f}(\nu^{(i)}))$; the solution of the linear system is the next approximation of $\mathbf{X}$.

4.2 Algebraic Program Analysis for Linear Equations

In this section, we instantiate the recipe for algebraic program analysis from
Sect. 3.3 to solve a system of linear equations, such as the linearized problems
that arise as Eq. (5) [53]. This goal may seem out of reach because item 3.3 of
the recipe requires us to "design a suitable language of 'closed-form solutions'
and an algorithm for computing them."

What is a suitable language of closed-form solutions of linear equations?
Clearly the regular expressions and path-expression algorithms used in Sect. 2
and Sect. 3 will not do, because the least solution under the language interpretation to the (truly) linear equation $X = aXb + 1$ is $\{a^i b^i : i \geq 0\}$, which is the
canonical example of a linear-context-free language that is not regular. However,
over fifty years ago, formal-language theorists established that linear-context-
free languages have certain similarities to regular languages [17,34,61], and we
can make use of this property to design a language of closed forms for linear
equations. Intuitively, $\{a^i b^i : i \geq 0\}$ can be obtained by (i) introducing *paired
alphabet symbols*, such as (a, b), (ii) defining *concatenation of paired symbols* as
$(a, b) \cdot (c, d) \stackrel{\text{def}}{=} (ca, bd)$, (iii) defining Kleene-star in the natural way over paired-
symbol concatenation, so $(a, b)^*$ is the language of paired words $\{(a^i, b^i) : i \geq 0\}$,
and (iv) applying an operation that concatenates the left word and right word
of each paired word: $\{(a^i, b^i) : i \geq 0\} \mapsto \{a^i b^i : i \geq 0\}$.

For the purpose of algebraic program analysis, this idea can be formalized by introducing **tensored regular expressions** over an alphabet Σ, whose syntax is defined as follows:[4]

$$a \in \Sigma$$
$$R \in \mathsf{RegExp}(\Sigma) ::= a \mid 0 \mid 1 \mid R_1 + R_2 \mid R_1 \cdot R_2 \mid R^* \mid S^{\natural}$$
$$S \in \mathsf{RegExp}_T(\Sigma) ::= R_1 \otimes R_2 \mid \underline{0} \mid \underline{1} \mid S_1 \oplus S_2 \mid S_1 \odot S_2 \mid S^{\circledast}$$

We can now follow the pattern of Sect. 2, and define algebras suitable for interpreting tensored regular expressions.

Definition 3. *A **tensor-product algebra** $\mathcal{T} = \langle \mathbf{A}, \mathbf{T}, \otimes, \natural \rangle$ consists of two regular algebras $\mathbf{A}$ and $\mathbf{T}$ along with an operation $\otimes : A \times A \to T$, called* tensor product, *and an operation $\natural : T \to A$, called* detensor.

Example 9 (Standard interpretation). The standard interpretation from Example 1 can be extended to tensored regular expressions by defining a universe of languages over word pairs ("tensored words") $T = 2^{\Sigma^* \times \Sigma^*}$, whose operators are given by:

$$X \otimes Y \triangleq \{\langle x, y \rangle : x \in X, y \in Y\}$$
$$Z^{\natural} \triangleq \{\underline{z}\overline{z} : \langle \underline{z}, \overline{z} \rangle \in Z\}$$
$$Z_1 \odot Z_2 \triangleq \{\langle \underline{z_2}\underline{z_1}, \overline{z_1}\overline{z_2} \rangle : \langle \underline{z_1}, \overline{z_1} \rangle \in Z_1, \langle \underline{z_2}, \overline{z_2} \rangle \in Z_2\}$$
$$Z_1 \oplus Z_2 \triangleq Z_1 \cup Z_2$$
$$Z^{\circledast} \triangleq \bigcup_{i \in \mathbb{N}} Z^i$$

Note that this interpretation allows tensored regular expressions to be used to capture linear context-free languages. For instance, the equation $X = aXb + 1$, whose least solution is $\{a^i b^i : i \geq 0\}$ can be written in closed form as $X = ((a \otimes b)^{\circledast})^{\natural}$, and the equation $X = aXa + bXb + 1$, whose least solution is the language of even-length palindromes over $\{a, b\}$, can be written as $X = (((a \otimes a) \oplus (b \otimes b))^{\circledast})^{\natural}$.   ⌟

Example 10 (Relational interpretation). The relational interpretation can be extended to tensored regular expressions by defining an algebra of binary state-pair relations, as follows.[5] The universe is the set of relations on State $\times$ State (i.e., an element of the universe is a subset of State $\times$ State $\times$ State $\times$ State). Comparing with the standard interpretation, (in which an element $\langle p_1, p_2 \rangle$ consists of a "backwards path" p and a "forwards continuation") we may think of

---

[4] A warning about notation: in our previous papers, we used $\oplus$ and $\otimes$ for the two semiring operations, $\odot$ for tensor product, and $\oplus_T$ and $\otimes_T$ for the two tensored-semiring operations. In this paper, we use $+$ and $\cdot$ for the semiring operations, with circles around them for the tensored-semiring versions: $\oplus$ and $\odot$. We use $\otimes$ for tensor product, which is consistent with usual mathematical notation.

[5] That is, an element of the algebra is a pair of pairs of states.

an element $\left\langle \begin{pmatrix} s_1' \\ s_2 \end{pmatrix}, \begin{pmatrix} s_1 \\ s_2' \end{pmatrix} \right\rangle$ of a state-pair relation as consisting of two pre/post state pairs: a "backwards" pair $s_1' \overset{*}{\leftarrow} s_1$ and a "forwards" pair $s_2 \to^* s_2'$. In the algebra of state-pair relations, 0 is interpreted as the empty relation, 1 as the identity relation, and + as union. The remaining operators are given by:

$$R_1 \otimes R_2 = \left\{ \left\langle \begin{pmatrix} s_1' \\ s_2 \end{pmatrix}, \begin{pmatrix} s_1 \\ s_2' \end{pmatrix} \right\rangle : \langle s_1, s_1' \rangle \in R_1, \langle s_2, s_2' \rangle \in R_2 \right\}$$

$$T^{\sharp} = \left\{ \langle s, s' \rangle : \exists s'', s''. \left\langle \begin{pmatrix} s'' \\ s''' \end{pmatrix}, \begin{pmatrix} s \\ s' \end{pmatrix} \right\rangle \in T \wedge s'' = s''' \right\} \tag{8}$$

$$T_1 \odot T_2 = \left\{ \left\langle \begin{pmatrix} s_1 \\ s_2 \end{pmatrix}, \begin{pmatrix} s_1' \\ s_2' \end{pmatrix} \right\rangle : \left\langle \begin{pmatrix} s_1 \\ s_2 \end{pmatrix}, \begin{pmatrix} s_1'' \\ s_2'' \end{pmatrix} \right\rangle \in T_1 \wedge \left\langle \begin{pmatrix} s_1'' \\ s_2'' \end{pmatrix}, \begin{pmatrix} s_1' \\ s_2' \end{pmatrix} \right\rangle \in T_2 \right\}$$

$$T^{\circledast} = \bigcup_{i=0}^{\infty} \underbrace{T \odot \ldots \odot T}_{i \text{ times}}$$

Note that the tensored sequencing operation is just a form of relational composition (over tuples of stacked elements); similarly, tensored iteration is a form of reflexive transitive closure. ⌐

Example 11 (Transition-formula interpretation). Transition formulas can be used to interpret tensored regular expression in a way analogous to the relational interpretation (as one should expect, because there must be a soundness relation between them!). A tensored transition formula T is a formula over four vocabularies, representing the value of the variables before and after a pair of computations. The tensor and detensor operations are essentially the same as those from the relational interpretation, translated into logic:

$$(F_1 \otimes F_2) \left(\begin{pmatrix} X_1' \\ X_2 \end{pmatrix}, \begin{pmatrix} X_1 \\ X_2' \end{pmatrix} \right) \triangleq F_1(X_1, X_1') \wedge F_2(X_2, X_2') \tag{9}$$

$$T^{\sharp}(X, X') \triangleq \exists \begin{pmatrix} Y_1 \\ Y_2 \end{pmatrix} . T \left(\begin{pmatrix} Y_1 \\ Y_2 \end{pmatrix}, \begin{pmatrix} X \\ X' \end{pmatrix} \right) \wedge Y_1 = Y_2$$

In the Eq. (9), the vocabularies X_1, X_1', X_2, and X_2' track the original role of the respective vocabulary in F_1 or F_2. The "stacked" notation is intended to be suggestive of an interpretation of a tensored transition formula over a doubled vocabulary, where the variables are $X_1' \cup X_2$ and their "primed copies" are $X_1 \cup X_2'$. To make the connection with Sect. 2.1 more apparent, we shall define $W_1 = X_1'$, $W_2 = X_2$, $W_1' = X_1$, $W_2' = X_2'$. With this notation, the product operation can be defined as:

$$(T_1 \odot T_2) \left(\begin{pmatrix} W_1 \\ W_2 \end{pmatrix}, \begin{pmatrix} W_1 \\ W_2 \end{pmatrix}' \right) \triangleq \exists \begin{pmatrix} W_1 \\ W_2 \end{pmatrix}'' . T_1 \left(\begin{pmatrix} W_1 \\ W_2 \end{pmatrix}, \begin{pmatrix} W_1 \\ W_2 \end{pmatrix}'' \right) \wedge T_2 \left(\begin{pmatrix} W_1 \\ W_2 \end{pmatrix}'', \begin{pmatrix} W_1 \\ W_2 \end{pmatrix}' \right)$$

As with the relational interpretation, the product operation is just a form of relational composition (over tuples of stacked elements).

Remarkably, the algebra of tensored transition formulas is the same as the algebra of untensored transition formulas, just over an extended set of variables. In particular, the iteration operators from Sect. 3 can be used to implement $\circledast$. For instance, consider the recursive procedure

$foo()$: **if** $(*)$ **then** $a := a + 1$; $foo()$; $b := b + 1$

The path to the recursive call of *foo* and the path from the recursive call to exit can be modeled by the transition formulas F and G, respectively:

$$F \triangleq a' = a + 1 \wedge b' = b$$

$$G \triangleq b' = b + 1 \wedge a' = a$$

A procedure summary for *foo* can be calculated by evaluating $((F \otimes G)^{\circledast})^{\natural}$, using recurrence analysis (Example 5) to implement the $\circledast$ operator:

$$F \otimes G \triangleq a_1 = a_1' - 1 \wedge b_1 = b_1' \wedge b_2' = b_2 + 1 \wedge a_2' = a_2$$

$$(F \otimes G)^{\circledast} \triangleq \exists k.k \geq 0 \wedge a_1 = a_1' - k \wedge b_1 = b_1' \wedge b_2' = b_2 + k \wedge a_2' = a_2$$

$$((F \otimes G)^{\circledast})^{\natural} \triangleq \exists k.k \geq 0 \wedge a' = a + k \wedge b' = b + k$$

We now show how to compute closed forms for linear equations. First, we perform a *regularizing transformation*, which takes a system of linear equations E_{Lin} and converts it into a system of left-linear equations E_{LeftLin}. The transformation takes each right-hand-side term of the form $a \cdot Y \cdot b$ and converts it to $Z \odot (a \otimes b)$, where Y and Z are variables whose values are elements of the regular algebras $\mathbf{A}$ and $\mathbf{T}$ of a tensor-product algebra $\langle \mathbf{A}, \mathbf{T}, \otimes, \natural \rangle$.

Definition 4. *Given a linear equation system E_{Lin} over the regular algebra $\mathbf{A}$ of a tensor-product algebra $\mathcal{T} = \langle \mathbf{A}, \mathbf{T}, \otimes, \natural \rangle$, the **regularizing transformation** τ_{Reg} creates a left-linear equation system $E_{LeftLin} = \tau_{Reg}(E_{Lin})$ over $\mathbf{T}$ by transforming each equation of E_{Lin} as follows:*

$$\frac{Y_j = c_j + \sum_{i,k} (a_{i,j,k} \cdot Y_i \cdot b_{i,j,k})}{Z_j = (1 \otimes c_j) \oplus \bigoplus_{i,k} (Z_i \odot (a_{i,j,k} \otimes b_{i,j,k}))} \tau_{\text{REG}}$$

where Z_i and Z_j are variables that take on values from $\mathbf{T}$.

For instance, if the regularizing transformation is applied to the linear system of equations in Fig. 6a, the result is the system of equations Fig. 6b. Because Fig. 6b is left-linear, we can now use the approach from Sect. 2 and Sect. 3—that is, create a closed-form solution for each variable Z_i by finding a path expression for the variable in the graph Fig. 6c. Finally, one gives a closed-form solution for each variable Y_i for the linear equation system in Fig. 6a by applying $(-)^{\natural}$ to each path expression—see Fig. 6d. This algorithm for computing closed-form solutions to linear equations is justified in the tensored-relational interpretation, and more generally, in any interpretation whose algebra forms what we dub a Kronecker algebra, defined as follows:

$$Y_1 = aY_2b + cY_2d \qquad Z_1 = (Z_2 \odot (a \otimes b)) \oplus (Z_2 \odot (c \otimes d))$$
$$Y_2 = e + fY_1g \qquad Z_2 = (1 \otimes e) \oplus (Z_1 \odot (f \otimes g))$$

(a)

(b)

(c)

$$Y_1 = \begin{pmatrix} (1 \otimes e) \\ \odot \, (((a \otimes b) \oplus (c \otimes d)) \odot (f \otimes g))^{\circledast} \\ \odot \, ((a \otimes b) \oplus (c \otimes d)) \end{pmatrix}^{\natural}$$

$$Y_2 = \big((1 \otimes e) \odot (((a \otimes b) \oplus (c \otimes d)) \odot (f \otimes g))^{\circledast}\big)^{\natural}$$

(d)

Fig. 6. (a) A linear system of equations; (b) its regularization; (c) the graph corresponding to (b); (d) a closed-form solution for (a).

Definition 5. *A **Kronecker algebra** $\mathbf{Kr} = \langle\langle A, +, \cdot, *, 0, 1\rangle, \langle T, \oplus, \odot, \circledast, \underline{0}, \underline{1}\rangle, \otimes, \natural\rangle$ is a tensor-product algebra that consists of two Kleene algebras $\langle A, +, \cdot, *, 0, 1\rangle$ and $\langle T, \oplus, \odot, \circledast, \underline{0}, \underline{1}\rangle$ such that (i) the natural order forms a complete lattice (i.e., both algebras have all infinite sums), and (ii) the following properties hold:*

1. $0 \otimes 0 = \underline{0}$
2. $1 \otimes 1 = \underline{1}$
3. $(a \otimes b)^{\natural} = a \cdot b$, for all $a, b \in A$
4. $(a_1 \otimes b_1) \odot (a_2 \otimes b_2) = (a_2 \cdot a_1) \otimes (b_1 \cdot b_2)$, for all $a_1, a_2, b_1, b_2 \in A$
5. $(t_1 \oplus t_2)^{\natural} = t_1^{\natural} + t_2^{\natural}$, for all $t_1, t_2 \in T$

We assume that all distributivity properties of A and T, as well as item 5, hold for infinite sums. In particular, for item 5, we have

$$\left(\bigoplus_{i \in I} t_i\right)^{\natural} = \sum_{i \in I} t_i^{\natural} \tag{10}$$

4.3 Discussion

The Instantiation of the Recipe. Returning to the recipe from Sect. 3.3, what we have done for a system of linear equations E_{Lin} is to instantiate the recipe as follows:

1. *(Modeling).* The concrete semantics is the least solution of E_{Lin} interpreted in relational semantics.
2. *(Closed forms).* Each variable of E_{Lin} is expressed as the detensor $((-)^{\natural})$ of a tensored regular expression. Closed forms are computed from the closed-forms of the left-linear system of equations $\tau_{\text{Reg}}(E_{\text{Lin}})$ that results from the regularizing transformation (e.g., see Fig. 6).

3. *(Interpretation)*. Tensored regular expressions can be interpreted as tensored transition formulas (Example 11), which are simply transition formulas over a "doubled" vocabulary.

Two Lessons. We would like to mention two lessons that we learned while working on this material over the years.

1. For the problems that arise in NPA, we must solve an equation system that is *truly linear*, not left-linear or right-linear. A reasonable sanity check might go as follows:
   - Algebraic program analysis à la Sect. 2 solves a left-linear (or right-linear) system of equations using methods based on regular expressions.
   - NPA repeatedly creates a system of linear equations that needs to be solved. Such linear equations are related to linear context-free languages, such as the language $\{a^i b^i\}$, which is not regular.
   - Ergo, it is a non-starter to attempt to apply algebraic program analysis to the equations that arise on each round of NPA.

   However, as shown in this section, it was possible to side-step this fundamental mismatch, by extending algebraic program analysis to systems of linear equations using Kronecker algebras, which have additional operations, such as tensor product and detensor.

   Thus, beyond the technical details, perhaps a more important takeaway is "be careful how you apply sanity checks." There is a risk that a plausible-sounding sanity check could cause you to discard an idea that is worth pursuing.

2. In some sense, the solution using Kronecker algebras goes against the grain of what computer scientists typically preach, namely, create appropriate abstractions (in the sense of abstract data-types) for a problem at hand, and then program your solution, thinking of the chosen abstractions as the operations of an abstract machine. This style of thinking is considered central to managing complexity in computer science, and it is generally considered heresy to break an abstraction.

   For algebraic program analysis, the abstraction is regular algebra, used with interpretations that are abstractions (in the sense of abstract interpretation [22]) of a program's concrete transition relations. However, the introduction of tensor product and detensor *breaks* that abstraction! To understand what we mean, consider the definition of $F \cdot G$ for transition relations in Boolean programs, i.e.,

$$(F \cdot G)(W, Z) \triangleq \exists X, Y. F(W, X) \wedge G(Y, Z) \wedge (X = Y),$$

   and the definitions of $F \otimes G$ and $T^{\natural}$,[6] namely,

$$(F \otimes G)(W, X, Y, Z) \triangleq F(W, X) \wedge G(Y, Z)$$
$$T(W, X, Y, Z)^{\natural} \triangleq \exists X, Y. T(W, X, Y, Z) \wedge (X = Y)$$

---

[6] Because we are trying to relate these operations to the untensored product operation $\cdot$, we do not make use of the stacked notation from Sect. 4.2.

The product operation $F \cdot G$ has three distinct steps: (i) conjoin $F(W, X)$ and $G(Y, Z)$; (ii) conjoin the equality $X = Y$; and (iii) project out vocabularies X and Y. In essence, tensor product and detensor break the abstraction of $\cdot$ as an indivisible operation: $\cdot$ is decomposed into two more-granular operations, $\otimes$ and $\oint$. By performing $F \otimes G$, we perform just the first step of $\cdot$, and only later, when $\oint$ is performed, do we "finish up" by applying the second and third steps of $\cdot$. The advantage is that we can operate on tensored values for some number of steps before "finishing" some earlier $\cdot$.

Again, beyond the technical details, the takeaway may be the *process* that we went through, which may be of value as a conceptual tool in other contexts:

- The insight on how to break the abstraction—both as presented here and as occurred during our research seven or eight years ago—came from thinking about one *specific* interpretation of Kleene algebra: transition relations for Boolean programs.
- The algebraic properties of the new, finer-granularity operations allowed us to abstract out a new algebra, dubbed in this paper Kronecker algebra.
- The ideas could now be applied in other contexts by finding other interpretations of Kronecker algebra (or, because we are interested in program analysis, by finding interpretations that over-approximate Kronecker algebra).

5   Termination Analysis

This section describes how algebraic program analysis can be applied to termination analysis, based on the approach of [63]. The goal of termination analysis is to prove that a program has no infinite executions. Our high-level strategy is to exploit compositionality: we prove that a loop terminates by first computing a summary (e.g., a transition formula) for its body, and then finding a termination argument for the summary.

Following Sect. 3, we first formalize a concrete semantics as the (greatest) solution of a system of semantic equations. An appropriate notion of concrete semantics for termination analysis is the set of *non-terminating* states of the program (from which there exists an infinite execution)—the program terminates exactly when none of the program's initial states belong to this set. As in Sect. 3, this system of equations can be derived syntactically from a program's control flow graph—see Fig. 7 for an example. The non-terminating states of the program are the greatest solution to this system of equations over the algebra where the universe is the set of states, $\boxplus$ is interpreted as union (a state is non-terminating if it has at least one infinite execution) and $\boxdot$ is interpreted as preimage (a state is non-terminating iff it can reach a non-terminating state).[7]

---

[7] Despite the fact that this system of equations is right-linear, the method of Sect. 2 does not apply because the system of equations has two sorts instead of one; in particular, $\boxdot$ has type $\boxdot : 2^{\mathsf{State} \times \mathsf{State}} \times 2^{\mathsf{State}} \to 2^{\mathsf{State}}$, and so is not a binary operation on a set.

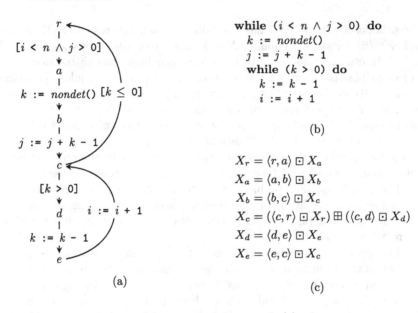

Fig. 7. A program represented by a control flow graph (a), abstract syntax tree (b), and system of equations (c).

A suitable language of "closed-form solutions" for the system of equations that arise in termination analysis is ω-regular expressions. The syntax of ω-**regular expressions** over an alphabet Σ is as follows:

$$a \in \Sigma$$
$$R \in \mathsf{RegExp}(\Sigma) ::= a \mid 0 \mid 1 \mid R_1 + R_2 \mid R_1 \cdot R_2 \mid R^*$$
$$S \in \omega\text{-}\mathsf{RegExp}(\Sigma) ::= R^\omega \mid S_1 \boxplus S_2 \mid R \boxdot S$$

The semantics of a (ω)-regular expressions is given by an interpretation over an ω-algebra and a regular algebra.

Definition 6. *An* ω-**algebra** *over a regular algebra* $\mathbf{A}$ *is 4-tuple* $\mathbf{B} = \left\langle B, \boxdot^B, \boxplus^B, {}^{\omega^B} \right\rangle$ *consisting of a universe* B, *an operation* $\boxdot^B : A \times B \to B$, *an operation* $\boxplus^B : B \times B \to B$, *and an operation* $(-)^{\omega^B} : A \to B$.

Example 12 (Standard interpretation). In the *standard interpretation* of ω-regular expressions, the universe consists of sets of infinite sequences over the alphabet Σ, and the operations are

$$W_1 \boxplus W_2 \triangleq W_1 \cup W_2 \qquad\qquad \text{Union}$$
$$X \boxdot W \triangleq \{xw : x \in X, w \in W\} \qquad\qquad \text{Concatenation}$$
$$X^\omega \triangleq \{x_1 x_2 \cdots : x_1, x_2, \cdots \in X\} \qquad\qquad \text{Infinite repetition}$$

For example, an ω-regular expression that recognizes all infinite paths in Fig. 7a starting at r is:

$$\overbrace{(\langle r,a\rangle\,\langle a,b\rangle\,\langle b,c\rangle\,(\langle c,d\rangle\,\langle d,e\rangle\,\langle e,c\rangle)^*\,\langle c,r\rangle)}^{\text{Outer loop}}{}^{\omega}$$
$$\boxplus((\langle r,a\rangle\,\langle a,b\rangle\,\langle b,c\rangle\,(\langle c,d\rangle\,\langle d,e\rangle\,\langle e,c\rangle)^*\,\langle c,r\rangle)^*\,\langle r,a\rangle\,\langle a,b\rangle\,\langle b,c\rangle)\,\boxdot\,\underbrace{(\langle c,d\rangle\,\langle d,e\rangle\,\langle e,c\rangle)^{\omega}}_{\text{Inner loop}}$$

⌟

Example 13 (Nonterminating state interpretation). The non-terminating state algebra is an ω-algebra over the algebra of state relations. Its universe consists of sets of states. The operators are

$$R \boxdot S \triangleq \{x : \exists y.\,\langle x,y\rangle \in R \wedge y \in S\} \qquad\qquad \text{Preimage}$$

$$S_1 \boxplus S_2 \triangleq S_1 \cup S_2 \qquad\qquad \text{Union}$$

$$R^{\omega} \triangleq \left\{ x_0 \in \textsf{State} : \begin{array}{l}\exists x_1, x_2, \dots \\ \forall i.\,\langle x_i, x_{i+1}\rangle \in R\end{array} \right\} \quad \text{Non-terminating states of } R$$

⌟

Tarjan's path expression algorithm can be adapted to compute an ω-regular expression that recognizes the set of infinite paths in a graph beginning at a particular node [63]. The equational view of this algorithm is that it computes closed-form solutions to right-linear equations over *Büchi algebras* (e.g., the algebra of non-terminating states).

Definition 7 (Büchi algebra). *A Büchi algebra is an ω-algebra over a Kleene algebra satisfying the following:*

$$S_1 \boxplus (S_2 \boxplus S_3) = (S_1 \boxplus S_2) \boxplus S_3 \qquad\qquad \textit{Associativity}$$
$$S_1 \boxplus S_2 = S_2 \boxplus S_1 \qquad\qquad \textit{Commutativity}$$
$$S \boxplus S = S \qquad\qquad \textit{Idempotence}$$
$$((R_1 \cdot R_2) \boxdot S) = R_1 \boxdot (R_2 \boxdot S) \qquad\qquad \textit{Compatibility}$$
$$((R_1 + R_2) \boxdot S) = (R_1 \boxdot S) \boxplus (R_2 \boxdot S) \qquad\qquad \textit{Right-distributivity}$$
$$R \boxdot (S_1 \boxplus S_2) = (R \boxdot S_1) \boxplus (R \boxdot S_2) \qquad\qquad \textit{Left-distributivity}$$
$$R^{\omega} = R \boxdot R^{\omega} \qquad\qquad \textit{Unfold}$$
$$S_1 \preceq (R \boxdot S_1) \boxplus S_2 \Rightarrow S_1 \preceq R^{\omega} \boxplus (R^* \boxdot S_2) \qquad \textit{Coinduction}$$

where $\preceq$ is the order defined by $a \preceq b$ iff $a \boxplus b = b$.

Exercise 2. Show that in any Büchi algebra, the greatest solution to the equation $X = (a \boxdot X) \boxplus z$ exists and is equal to $X = a^{\omega} \boxplus (a^* \boxdot z)$.

Summarizing: we have modeled a program's non-terminating states as the greatest solution to a system of semantic equations, devised a language of "closed form solutions", and identified an algorithm for computing closed form solutions to the equations. It remains only to develop abstract interpretations of the language of closed forms which implements termination analysis.

5.1   Non-terminating State-Formula Interpretations

Just as transition formulas (over variables X and X') can be used to represent state relations, state formulas (over the variables X) can be used to represent sets of (non-terminating) states. We can extend an algebra of transition formulas to an algebra of non-terminating state formulas by defining

$$F \boxdot P \triangleq \exists X'.F(X, X') \wedge P(X') \qquad\qquad \text{Preimage}$$
$$P_1 \boxplus P_2 \triangleq P_1 \vee P_2 \qquad\qquad\qquad\qquad \text{Union}$$

Intuitively, the ω operator should compute the set of non-terminating states of a transition formula. Analogously to the $*$ operator in Sect. 2, this set is uncomputable, and we must be satisfied with an over-approximation (i.e., we aim to compute a state formula that contains all non-terminating states—the soundness relation of interest is the one defined by $N \Vdash S \iff \forall s \in N.s \models S$). There are many ways of doing this, so we speak of the family of non-terminating state formula interpretations. In the remainder of this section, we give examples of ω-operators.

Example 14 (Linear-lexicographic ranking functions [32]*).* Let $F(X, X')$ be a transition formula. A *linear lexicographic ranking function* (LLRF) for F is a sequence of linear terms $t_1, \ldots, t_n$ over X such that for any states s and s' such that $s \rightarrow_F s'$, each t_i evaluates to a non-negative integer in s, and the integer n-tuple decreases in lexicographic order going from s to s'. Since there are no infinite strictly descending chains of non-negative n-tuples of integers with respect to the lexicographic order, if F has an LLRF, then F has no non-terminating states. For example, the inner loop of Fig. 7 has a 1-dimensional LLRF $\langle k \rangle$, and the outer loop has a 2-dimensional LLRF $\langle n - i, j \rangle$.

The problem of determining whether a linear integer arithmetic formula has an LLRF is decidable [32]. If a formula does *not* have an LLRF, then we can use a coarse over-approximation of the non-terminating states of a formula (e.g., the set of states that have at least one outgoing transition). This yields the following interpretation of the ω operator:

$$F^\omega \triangleq \begin{cases} \textit{false} & \text{if there is an LLRF for } F \\ \exists X'.F(X, X') & \text{otherwise} \end{cases}$$

For Fig. 7, using recurrence analysis to implement the $*$ operator (Example 5), we get that every non-terminating state must satisfy *false*—the program terminates from any initial state. ⌐

Example 15 (Unbounded trajectories [63]*).* Let $F(X, X')$ be a transition formula. A necessary (but not sufficient) condition for a state s to be a non-terminating for a transition formula F is that there is a computation of F starting from s for every possible length. This condition is undecidable, but it can be approximated using an approximate transitive-closure operator such as the ones in Sect. 2.1. Suppose that $(-)^*$ is an over-approximate transitive-closure operator. Letting k

and k' be symbols that do not appear in F, we can create a transition formula $\exp(F)$ in one parameter k' such that for any k', if there exists a sequence $s_1 \to_F s_2 \to_F \cdots \to_F s_{k'}$, then $s_1 \to_{\exp(F)} s_{k'}$:

$$\exp(F) \triangleq (F \wedge k' = k + 1)^*[k \mapsto 0]$$

The states s for which there exists a computation $s \to_{\exp(F)} s' \to s''$ for all choices of the parameter k' over-approximates the set of non-terminating states of F:

$$F^\omega \triangleq \forall k' \geq 0. \exists X', X''. \exp(F) \wedge F(X', X'')$$

For example, if $*$ is instantiated to recurrence analysis (Example 5), then on the transition formula

$$F \triangleq i \neq n \wedge i' = i + 2 \wedge n' = n$$

(corresponding to the program **while** $(i \neq n)$ **do** $i := i + 2$), we have

$$F^\omega = i > n \vee (n - i) \bmod 2 = 1 \qquad \lrcorner$$

Additional examples of termination analyses in the algebraic framework appear in [63] and [62].

5.2   The Instantiation of the Recipe

The recipe from Sect. 3.3 is instantiated for termination analysis as follows:

1. *(Modeling).* The concrete semantics is the set of non-terminating states, which is the greatest solution to a system of right-linear equations.
2. *(Closed forms).* The language of closed-forms is given by ω-regular expressions; they can be computed by a variation of Tarjan's algorithm [63].
3. *(Interpretation).* An ω-regular expression can be interpreted as a state formula representing a set of *possibly non-terminating states*, while regular expressions are interpreted as transition formulas (Sect. 2). The soundness relation is over-approximate: we can prove that a program terminates by finding an unsatisfiable pre-condition, but the analysis cannot prove non-termination.

6   Recap

This section contains a few remarks about commonalities among the three kinds of problems and the techniques we have presented for applying algebraic program analysis to them. The paper has been structured around the three-part recipe for algebraic program analysis given in Sect. 3.3. Table 1 recaps how the recipe has been instantiated for the three kinds of problems considered.

Within this paper, all methods for computing closed-form solutions can be understood as some variation of Gaussian elimination, Algorithm 1 (in practice, they are variations of Tarjan's path-expression algorithm). The essential

Table 1. Instantiations of the recipe for algebraic program analysis from Sect. 3.3.

	Section 3.3	Section 4.3	Section 5.2
Analysis type	Intraprocedural	Linear interprocedural	Termination
Modeling	LFP of left-linear equations	LFP of linear equations	GFP of right-linear equations
Closed-form solution	A regular expression (path expression over the CFG)	Detensor of a tensored path expression	An omega-regular expression
Interpretation (concrete)	A Kleene algebra (Definition 1), e.g., transition relations (Sect. 3.1)	A Kronecker algebra (Definition 5), e.g., tensored transition relations (Example 10)	A Büchi algebra (Definition 7), e.g., non-terminating states (Example 13)
Interpretation (abstract)	A regular algebra (Sect. 2), e.g., a transition-formula interpretation (Sect. 2.1)	A tensor-product algebra (Definition 3), e.g., a tensored transition-formula interpretation (Example 11)	An ω algebra (Definition 6), e.g., a non-terminating state-formula interpretation (Sect. 5.1)

Table 2. "Loop-solving" steps.

Equation type	Form of "loop"		Closed form for X
Left-linear	$X = a + Xb$	$\rightsquigarrow$	ab^*
Linear	$X = a + \sum_{i=1}^{m} b_i X c_i$	$\rightsquigarrow$	$((1 \otimes a) \odot (\bigoplus_{i=1}^{m} b_i \otimes c_i)^{\circledast})^{\natural}$
Right-linear	$X = (b \boxdot X) \boxplus z$	$\rightsquigarrow$	$a^{\omega} \boxplus (b^* \boxdot z)$

difference between Sect. 2, Sect. 4, and Sect. 5 is the "loop-solving" step. Each requires the right-hand-side expression R to be in a particular form (left-linear, linear, right-linear), and each requires a different language of expressions in which to express closed forms (regular, tensored regular, ω-regular). Table 2 shows the respective "loop-solving" steps for computing a closed form. Note that in Table 2, the letters a, b_i, c_i, z range over expressions (which may involve variables other than X). For example, to apply the left-linear rule to the equation $X = Xp + Xq + Yr + Z$, we first re-arrange terms on the right-hand side as $X(p + q) + (Yr + Z)$ and then compute the "closed-form" $(Yr + Z)(p + q)^*$.

7   Related Work

Abstracting States Versus State Changes. Classically, invariant generation is conceived as the problem of over-approximating the reachable states of a program. Computing invariants involves solving a system of equations of the form

$$X[r] = v_r \qquad\qquad\qquad r \in Nodes, \text{ the root node}$$
$$X[n] = \sum_{e_{m,n} \in Edges} \mathscr{I}[\![e_{m,n}]\!](X[m]) \qquad n \in Nodes - \{r\} \qquad (11)$$

for the unknowns $X[n]$, $n \in Nodes$, where v_r represents the set of initial states and $\mathscr{I}[\![-]\!]$ provides an interpretation of each CFG edge as a state transformer.

In a solution, $X[n]$ holds a descriptor that represents a superset of the set of program states that can arise at program point n. Note that in Eq. (11), the function $\mathscr{I}[\![e_{m,n}]\!]$ on edge $e_{m,n}$ is *applied* to the value $X[m]$ on node m.

Algebraic program analyses, in contrast, concern dynamics—state *changes*—rather than states. The reason is that algebraic analyses are compositional: states do not compose, but state changes do.

A first step towards abstracting state *changes* was taken by Graham & Wegman [33], who gave a method to solve dataflow equations via *composition* of the state transformers on CFG edges. That is, their basic primitives were (i) composition of functions, and (ii) union of functions. If we adopt this outlook and define $r_1 \cdot r_2$ to be $r_2 \circ r_1$, $r_1 + r_2$ to be the union of r_1 and r_2, and 1 to be the identity function, instead of Eq. (11), the goal would be to solve the following equation system:

$$X[r] = 1 \qquad\qquad r \in \textit{Nodes}, \text{ the root node}$$
$$X[n] = \sum_{e_{m,n} \in \textit{Edges}} X[m] \cdot \mathscr{I}[\![e_{m,n}]\!] \quad n \in \textit{Nodes} - \{r\} \qquad (12)$$

where the unknowns $X[n]$ are now function-valued. Note that the function $\mathscr{I}[\![e_{m,n}]\!]$ on edge $e_{m,n}$ is *composed* with the value $X[m]$ on node m. From here—because one is working over function-valued quantities—it is now natural to formulate interprocedural program-analysis problems by means of equations over unknowns that denote procedure summaries, as was done by Cousot and Cousot [23] and Sharir and Pnueli [56].

"Interpret, Then Solve" Versus "Solve, Then Interpret." The systems in Eqs. (11) and (12) are *interpreted*, in the sense that they are understood as semantic equations valued over a particular abstract domain, say D. Such a system $E = \{X_i = R_i\}_{i \in I}$ can be solved by an iterative method: compute a sequence $\sigma_0, \sigma_1, \cdots \in \{X_i\}_{i \in I} \to D$ of assignments abstract domain values to variables

$$\sigma_0(X_i) \triangleq 0 \qquad\qquad \text{for all } i \in I$$
$$\sigma_{n+1}(X_i) \triangleq \mathscr{I}_{\sigma_n}[\![R_i]\!] \qquad \text{for all } n \geq 0 \text{ and all } i \in I$$

Eventually this process converges—typically with the aid of widening to extrapolate to the limit—upon an assignment that over-approximates the least solution to E.

In algebraic program analysis, we think of a system of equations as an uninterpreted (syntactic) object. Equations are solved symbolically and then the solutions are interpreted in an algebraic structure to obtain an analysis result. The key step in this direction was made by Tarjan [59], who observed that once a solution to the path-expression problem was in hand, multiple dataflow-analysis problems could be solved merely by reinterpreting the alphabet symbols and operators of regular expressions in different algebras—i.e., "solve and then interpret."

Whereas the iterative framework for program analysis has a "built-in" algorithm for analyzing loops and recursive behavior (by computing the limit of a sequence), the algebraic framework does not prescribe any particular method, and it is up to the analysis designer to devise one. This obligation places an additional burden on the analysis designer, but also provides flexibility: the analysis designer may analyze loops in ways that may (Example 6) or may not (Examples 5 and 4) resemble iterative fixpoint computation.

Iteration Operators and Loop Summarization. In the computer-aided-verification community, there is a body of literature on loop summarization (or "loop leaping") and acceleration. Summarization aims to compute or approximate the behavior of (certain) loops, while acceleration aims to approximate the postimage of a set of states under a loop. These techniques have been incorporated into iterative abstract interpretation [28,31], abstraction-refinement-based software model checking [19,37], termination analysis [7,20,60], and resource bound analysis [10,64]. The most closely related techniques to algebraic program analysis are those that build summaries for whole programs in "bottom-up" fashion. Such analyses have been formalized in various ways, including: recursion on the abstract syntax tree (AST) of a program [51], AST rewriting [8], and graph rewriting [47,60]. Algebraic program analysis provides a unifying foundation for such analyses, in the same way that dataflow analysis [39] and (iterative) abstract interpretation [22] provide a unifying foundation for iterative program analyses.

There are several methods for loop summarization, based on finite-monoid affine transformations [11,12,29], difference-bound relations [15,21], octagonal relations [13,14,45], integer vector addition systems [35], fragments of the theory of arrays [2]. For the most part, these summarization methods are non-uniform in the sense that their input language differs from their output language (e.g., [13] takes as input an octagonal relation and produces as output a Presburger formula). This non-uniformity is the essential barrier that must be overcome to use such techniques to implement the iteration operator of an algebraic program analysis (e.g., we can define an iteration operator by using optimization modulo theories [55] to extract the octagonal hull of a Presburger formula, then use [13] to compute a Presburger formula representing its transitive closure).

Elimination-Based Dataflow Analysis. Elimination-based dataflow analysis is a family of dataflow analyses that computes analysis results using methods that resemble Gaussian elimination [3,33,36] (see [54] for a survey). Early methods were specialized to reducible control flow graphs, but operated faster than general Gaussian elimination. Tarjan's algorithm [58] is an elimination method with fast operation on reducible (and "nearly reducible") control flow graphs, but is applicable to arbitrary graphs.

Weighted Graphs. There is a vast literature on solving path problems on weighted graphs where the weights are drawn from a semiring [1,30,50]. Path problems can also be solved on semiring-weighted pushdown systems, which has applications to interprocedural dataflow analysis [52]. This work focuses on *iterative* techniques for solving path problems.

(Non-iterative) algorithms for path problems over algebraic structures with an explicit iteration operator were considered by Aho et al. [1], Backhouse & Carré [5], and Lehmann [48], and was implicit in previous work by Kleene [44], and McNaughton & Yamada [49]. Tarjan connected this line of work with program analysis [58,59].

8 Open Problems

We conclude with a list of challenges suggested by algebraic program analysis.

Scaling SMT-Based Algebraic Program Analysis. The bottom-up interpretation step of a closed-form expression is efficient, in that it operates in linear time and space in the size of the expression DAG in a model where each algebraic operation has unit cost. For logic-based interpretations, however, algebraic operations do *not* have unit cost: operators manipulate formulas, and the size of those formulas may grow as operators are applied. For example, the regular expression a^{2^n} can be represented by an expression DAG with $n+1$ nodes, with the following shape:

$$\cdot \Longrightarrow \cdot \Longrightarrow \cdot \Longrightarrow \cdots \Longrightarrow \cdot \Longrightarrow a$$

If the letter a is interpreted as the transition formula $x' = x + 1$ and $\cdot$ as relational composition, then the transition-formula interpretation of a^{2^n} has size $O(2^n)$. Scaling SMT-based algebraic program analysis to large programs requires techniques for generating *succinct* summaries, and/or efficient reasoning about compact formula representations involving λ-expressions.

Recursive Procedures. Section 4.2 shows how the algebraic approach can be applied to summarize *linearly* recursive procedures. But to compute summaries for generally recursive procedures, current-generation algebraic-program-analysis tools fall back on another non-algebraic scheme (such as hybrid iterative/algebraic, like Kleene or Newton iteration [40,53], or the template-based approach of [16]). This raises the question: is there a practical algebraic method for analyzing general recursion? The essential challenge is in devising a language of "closed forms" that (1) can represent arbitrary context-free languages, and (2) is amenable to an effective interpretation in logic.

Beyond Numerical Domains. To date, all algebraic program analyses have been numerical in nature—they abstract away aspects of program behavior that cannot be captured by integer variables. It remains to be seen whether the algebraic approach can yield practical analyses for reasoning about features like strings, arrays, and the heap. Reasoning about memory manipulation is particularly challenging in a compositional setting, since we cannot rely on the context of a program fragment to resolve aliasing relationships. One possible avenue is to incorporate abductive reasoning to make educated guesses about the shape of memory, as in [18].

Property Refutation. Algebraic program analysis is typically conceived as a method for generating over-approximate summaries. The nature of over-approximation is that the summaries can be used to verify that a program *does* satisfy a property of interest, but not prove that it *doesn't*. An interesting direction for future work is to devise methods by which algebraic program analyses can refute properties, perhaps based on bounded model checking [9], under-approximate loop summarization [46], or symbolic execution [43].

Acknowledgments. Supported, in part, by a gift from Rajiv and Ritu Batra; by a Facebook Research Award; by NSF under grant number 1942537, and by ONR under grants N00014-17-1-2889 and N00014-19-1-2318. Any opinions, findings, and conclusions or recommendations expressed in this publication are those of the authors, and do not necessarily reflect the views of the sponsoring entities.

References

1. Aho, A.V., Hopcroft, J.E., Ullman, J.D.: The Design and Analysis of Computer Algorithms, 1st edn. Addison-Wesley Longman Publishing Co., Inc., Boston (1974)
2. Alberti, F., Ghilardi, S., Sharygina, N.: Definability of accelerated relations in a theory of arrays and its applications. In: Fontaine, P., Ringeissen, C., Schmidt, R.A. (eds.) FroCoS 2013. LNCS (LNAI), vol. 8152, pp. 23–39. Springer, Heidelberg (2013). https://doi.org/10.1007/978-3-642-40885-4_3
3. Allen, F.E., Cocke, J.: A program data flow analysis procedure. Commun. ACM **19**(3), 137 (1976)
4. Ancourt, C., Coelho, F., Irigoin, F.: A modular static analysis approach to affine loop invariants detection. Electr. Notes Theor. Comp. Sci. **267**(1), 3–16 (2010)
5. Backhouse, R., Carré, B.: Regular algebra applied to path-finding problems. J. Inst. Math. Appl. **15**, 161–186 (1975)
6. Backhouse, R.C., Carré, B.A.: Regular algebra applied to path-finding problems. IMA J. Appl. Math. **15**(2), 161–186 (1975)
7. Berdine, J., Chawdhary, A., Cook, B., Distefano, D., O'Hearn, P.: Variance analyses from invariance analyses. In: POPL, pp. 211–224 (2007)
8. Biallas, S., Brauer, J., King, A., Kowalewski, S.: Loop leaping with closures. In: Miné, A., Schmidt, D. (eds.) SAS 2012. LNCS, vol. 7460, pp. 214–230. Springer, Heidelberg (2012). https://doi.org/10.1007/978-3-642-33125-1_16
9. Biere, A., Cimatti, A., Clarke, E., Zhu, Y.: Symbolic model checking without BDDs. In: Cleaveland, W.R. (ed.) TACAS 1999. LNCS, vol. 1579, pp. 193–207. Springer, Heidelberg (1999). https://doi.org/10.1007/3-540-49059-0_14
10. Blanc, R., Henzinger, T.A., Hottelier, T., Kovács, L.: ABC: algebraic bound computation for loops. In: Clarke, E.M., Voronkov, A. (eds.) LPAR 2010. LNCS (LNAI), vol. 6355, pp. 103–118. Springer, Heidelberg (2010). https://doi.org/10.1007/978-3-642-17511-4_7
11. Boigelot, B.: On iterating linear transformations over recognizable sets of integers. Theor. Comput. Sci. **309**(1), 413–468 (2003)
12. Boigelot, B., Wolper, P.: Symbolic verification with periodic sets. In: Dill, D.L. (ed.) CAV 1994. LNCS, vol. 818, pp. 55–67. Springer, Heidelberg (1994). https://doi.org/10.1007/3-540-58179-0_43

13. Bozga, M., Gîrlea, C., Iosif, R.: Iterating octagons. In: Kowalewski, S., Philippou, A. (eds.) TACAS 2009. LNCS, vol. 5505, pp. 337–351. Springer, Heidelberg (2009). https://doi.org/10.1007/978-3-642-00768-2_29
14. Bozga, M., Iosif, R., Konečný, F.: Fast acceleration of ultimately periodic relations. In: Touili, T., Cook, B., Jackson, P. (eds.) CAV 2010. LNCS, vol. 6174, pp. 227–242. Springer, Heidelberg (2010). https://doi.org/10.1007/978-3-642-14295-6_23
15. Bozga, M., Iosif, R., Lakhnech, Y.: Flat parametric counter automata. In: Bugliesi, M., Preneel, B., Sassone, V., Wegener, I. (eds.) ICALP 2006. LNCS, vol. 4052, pp. 577–588. Springer, Heidelberg (2006). https://doi.org/10.1007/11787006_49
16. Breck, J., Cyphert, J., Kincaid, Z., Reps, T.: Templates and recurrences: better together. In: PLDI, pp. 688–702 (2020)
17. Brzozowski, J.A.: Regular-like expressions for some irregular languages. In: SWAT (FOCS), pp. 278–286 (1968)
18. Calcagno, C., Distefano, D., O'Hearn, P.W., Yang, H.: Compositional shape analysis by means of bi-abduction. J. ACM 58(6), 1–66 (2011)
19. Caniart, N., Fleury, E., Leroux, J., Zeitoun, M.: Accelerating interpolation-based model-checking. In: Ramakrishnan, C.R., Rehof, J. (eds.) TACAS 2008. LNCS, vol. 4963, pp. 428–442. Springer, Heidelberg (2008). https://doi.org/10.1007/978-3-540-78800-3_32
20. Chen, H., David, C., Kroening, D., Schrammel, P., Wachter, B.: Bit-precise procedure-modular termination analysis. TOPLAS 40(1), 1:1-1:38 (2018)
21. Comon, H., Jurski, Y.: Multiple counters automata, safety analysis and presburger arithmetic. In: Hu, A.J., Vardi, M.Y. (eds.) CAV 1998. LNCS, vol. 1427, pp. 268–279. Springer, Heidelberg (1998). https://doi.org/10.1007/BFb0028751
22. Cousot, P., Cousot, R.: Abstract interpretation: a unified lattice model for static analysis of programs by construction or approximation of fixpoints. In: POPL, pp. 238–252 (1977)
23. Cousot, P., Cousot, R.: Static determination of dynamic properties of recursive procedures. In: Neuhold, E. (ed.) Formal Descriptions of Programming Concepts, (IFIP WG 2.2, St. Andrews, Canada, August 1977), pp. 237–277. North-Holland (1978)
24. Cousot, P., Cousot, R.: Abstract interpretation frameworks. J. Log. Comput. 2(4), 511–547 (1992)
25. Cyphert, J., Breck, J., Kincaid, Z., Reps, T.W.: Refinement of path expressions for static analysis. Proc. ACM Program. Lang. 3(POPL), 45:1–45:29 (2019)
26. Esparza, J., Kiefer, S., Luttenberger, M.: Newtonian program analysis. J. ACM 57, 6 (2010)
27. Farzan, A., Kincaid, Z.: Compositional recurrence analysis. In: FMCAD, pp. 57–64 (2015)
28. Feautrier, P., Gonnord, L.: Accelerated invariant generation for C programs with aspic and c2fsm. Electr. Notes Theor. Comput. Sci. 267(2), 3–13 (2010)
29. Finkel, A., Leroux, J.: How to compose Presburger-accelerations: applications to broadcast protocols. In: Agrawal, M., Seth, A. (eds.) FSTTCS 2002. LNCS, vol. 2556, pp. 145–156. Springer, Heidelberg (2002). https://doi.org/10.1007/3-540-36206-1_14
30. Gondran, M., Minoux, M.: Graphs, Dioids and Semirings: New Models and Algorithms. ORCS, vol. 41, 1st edn. Springer, Boston (2008). https://doi.org/10.1007/978-0-387-75450-5
31. Gonnord, L., Halbwachs, N.: Combining widening and acceleration in linear relation analysis. In: Yi, K. (ed.) SAS 2006. LNCS, vol. 4134, pp. 144–160. Springer, Heidelberg (2006). https://doi.org/10.1007/11823230_10

32. Gonnord, L., Monniaux, D., Radanne, G.: Synthesis of ranking functions using extremal counterexamples. SIGPLAN Not. **50**(6), 608–618 (2015)
33. Graham, S.L., Wegman, M.N.: A fast and usually linear algorithm for global flow analysis. J. ACM **23**(1), 172–202 (1976)
34. Gruska, J.: Some classifications of context-free languages. Inf. Control **14**(2), 152–179 (1969)
35. Haase, C., Halfon, S.: Integer vector addition systems with states. In: Ouaknine, J., Potapov, I., Worrell, J. (eds.) RP 2014. LNCS, vol. 8762, pp. 112–124. Springer, Cham (2014). https://doi.org/10.1007/978-3-319-11439-2_9
36. Hecht, M.S., Ullman, J.D.: Analysis of a simple algorithm for global data flow problems. In: POPL, pp. 207–217 (1973)
37. Hojjat, H., Iosif, R., Konečný, F., Kuncak, V., Rümmer, P.: Accelerating interpolants. In: Chakraborty, S., Mukund, M. (eds.) ATVA 2012. LNCS, pp. 187–202. Springer, Heidelberg (2012). https://doi.org/10.1007/978-3-642-33386-6_16
38. Karr, M.: Affine relationship among variables of a program. Acta Inf. **6**, 133–151 (1976)
39. Kildall, G.: A unified approach to global program optimization. In: POPL (1973)
40. Kincaid, Z., Breck, J., Boroujeni, A.F., Reps, T.W.: Compositional recurrence analysis revisited. In: PLDI, pp. 248–262 (2017)
41. Kincaid, Z., Breck, J., Cyphert, J., Reps, T.W.: Closed forms for numerical loops. Proc. ACM Program. Lang. **3**(POPL), 55:1–55:29 (2019)
42. Kincaid, Z., Cyphert, J., Breck, J., Reps, T.W.: Non-linear reasoning for invariant synthesis. Proc. ACM Program. Lang. **2**(POPL), 54:1–54:33 (2018)
43. King, J.C.: Symbolic execution and program testing. Commun. ACM **19**(7), 385–394 (1976)
44. Kleene, S.: Representation of events in nerve nets and finite automata. In: Shannon, C., McCarthy, J. (eds.) Automata Stud., pp. 3–40. Princeton University Press, Princeton (1956)
45. Konečný, F.: PTIME computation of transitive closures of octagonal relations. In: Chechik, M., Raskin, J.-F. (eds.) TACAS 2016. LNCS, vol. 9636, pp. 645–661. Springer, Heidelberg (2016). https://doi.org/10.1007/978-3-662-49674-9_42
46. Kroening, D., Lewis, M., Weissenbacher, G.: Under-approximating loops in C programs for fast counterexample detection. In: Sharygina, N., Veith, H. (eds.) CAV 2013. LNCS, vol. 8044, pp. 381–396. Springer, Heidelberg (2013). https://doi.org/10.1007/978-3-642-39799-8_26
47. Kroening, D., Sharygina, N., Tonetta, S., Tsitovich, A., Wintersteiger, C.M.: Loop summarization using abstract transformers. In: Cha, S.S., Choi, J.-Y., Kim, M., Lee, I., Viswanathan, M. (eds.) ATVA 2008. LNCS, vol. 5311, pp. 111–125. Springer, Heidelberg (2008). https://doi.org/10.1007/978-3-540-88387-6_10
48. Lehmann, D.J.: Algebraic structures for transitive closure. Theoret. Comput. Sci. **4**(1), 59–76 (1977)
49. McNaughton, R., Yamada, H.: Regular expressions and state graphs for automata. IRE Trans. Electron. Comput. **9**(1), 39–47 (1960)
50. Mohri, M.: Semiring frameworks and algorithms for shortest-distance problems. J. Autom. Lang. Comb. **7**(3), 321–350 (2002)
51. Monniaux, D.: Automatic modular abstractions for linear constraints. In: POPL, pp. 140–151 (2009)
52. Reps, T., Schwoon, S., Jha, S., Melski, D.: Weighted pushdown systems and their application to interprocedural dataflow analysis. SCP **58**(1–2), 206–263 (2005)
53. Reps, T., Turetsky, E., Prabhu, P.: Newtonian program analysis via tensor product. TOPLAS **39**(2), 9:1–9:72 (2017)

54. Ryder, B.G., Paull, M.C.: Elimination algorithms for data flow analysis. ACM Comput. Surv. (CSUR) **18**(3), 277–316 (1986)
55. Sebastiani, R., Tomasi, S.: Optimization in SMT with $\mathcal{LA}(\mathbb{Q})$ cost functions. In: Gramlich, B., Miller, D., Sattler, U. (eds.) IJCAR 2012. LNCS (LNAI), vol. 7364, pp. 484–498. Springer, Heidelberg (2012). https://doi.org/10.1007/978-3-642-31365-3_38
56. Sharir, M., Pnueli, A.: Two approaches to interprocedural data flow analysis. In: Program Flow Analysis: Theory and Applications. Prentice-Hall (1981)
57. Szabó, Z.: Compositionality (2020). https://plato.stanford.edu/entries/compositionality/
58. Tarjan, R.E.: Fast algorithms for solving path problems. J. ACM **28**(3), 594–614 (1981)
59. Tarjan, R.E.: A unified approach to path problems. J. ACM **28**(3), 577–593 (1981)
60. Tsitovich, A., Sharygina, N., Wintersteiger, C.M., Kroening, D.: Loop summarization and termination analysis. In: Abdulla, P.A., Leino, K.R.M. (eds.) TACAS 2011. LNCS, vol. 6605, pp. 81–95. Springer, Heidelberg (2011). https://doi.org/10.1007/978-3-642-19835-9_9
61. Yntema, M.: Inclusion relations among families of context-free languages. Inf. Control **10**, 572–597 (1967)
62. Zhu, S., Kincaid, Z.: Reflections on termination of linear loops. In: CAV (2021)
63. Zhu, S., Kincaid, Z.: Termination analysis without the tears. In: PLDI (2021)
64. Zuleger, F., Gulwani, S., Sinn, M., Veith, H.: Bound analysis of imperative programs with the size-change abstraction. In: Yahav, E. (ed.) SAS 2011. LNCS, vol. 6887, pp. 280–297. Springer, Heidelberg (2011). https://doi.org/10.1007/978-3-642-23702-7_22

Programmable Program Synthesis

Loris D'Antoni, Qinheping Hu, Jinwoo Kim[✉], and Thomas Reps

University of Wisconsin-Madison, Madison, USA
{ldantoni,qhu28,jkim934,treps}@wisc.edu

Abstract. Program synthesis is now a reality, and we are approaching the point where domain-specific synthesizers can now handle problems of practical sizes. Moreover, some of these tools are finding adoption in industry. However, for synthesis to become a mainstream technique adopted at large by programmers as well as by end-users, we need to design programmable synthesis frameworks that (*i*) are not tailored to specific domains or languages, (*ii*) enable one to specify synthesis problems with a variety of qualitative and quantitative objectives in mind, and (*iii*) come equipped with theoretical as well as practical guarantees. We report on our work on designing such frameworks and on building synthesis engines that can handle program-synthesis problems describable in such frameworks, and describe open challenges and opportunities.

1 Introduction

1.1 A Synthesis Tale

Monica, a software engineer, is trying to write a program for transforming data she has stored in an array of integer numbers. Monica needs to zero-out all the negative entries from the array (they represent irrelevant data points) and add 10 to all the positive entries (this is a normalization step needed in Monica's API). Of course, Monica is a great engineer and she could write this program herself, but since Monica knows that similar problems arise often in her company (i.e., reformatting arrays to match certain APIs), Monica decides to try out this new thing everyone is talking about: *program synthesis*.

Monica wants a tool that takes as input some examples of the desired transformation and a set of operators the program can use, and magically outputs the intended program. In fact, Monica already has an input, a unit test, that she wants to process using her newly synthesized program: $[-1, 2, 3, 10, 31, -14, -11]$, for which the output should be $[0, 12, 13, 20, 41, 0, 0]$.

Monica also knows that the final program will look like a loop that iterates over the input array *arr*, which leads her to develop the grammar in Fig. 1. Monica thinks this grammar is general enough that it will cover a reasonable range of programs for similar tasks but limited enough that it will not result in spurious programs that overfit too much to the examples.

Quickly, Monica discovers that using program synthesis is not so straightforward. There are so many different tools! And they all take different kinds of

© The Author(s) 2021
A. Silva and K. R. M. Leino (Eds.) CAV 2021, LNCS 12759, pp. 84–109, 2021.
https://doi.org/10.1007/978-3-030-81685-8_4

$Start \to x$ = len(arr) - 1; while x>=0 do S
$S \to$ arr[E] = arr[E] + E | arr[E] = E |
$\quad x = E \mid S; S \mid$ if arr[x]>0 then S else S
$E \to 0 \mid 1 \mid x \mid E + E \mid E - E$

Fig. 1. The grammar G_{ex} Monica has in mind for synthesizing programs that iterate over an input array (*Start* is the starting nonterminal). G_{ex} is general enough to cover most programs that iteratively normalize entries in an array.

inputs. After a bit more research, Monica decides to go for one of the many tools, UltraSynth™, and encodes her problem. UltraSynth is written in a C-like language and Monica has mostly programmed in Python for her job. However, Monica decides to give UltraSynth a try and after a few days of learning the ins and outs of UltraSynth, she finally manages to encode her transformation-synthesis problem in UltraSynth. To achieve her goal, Monica had to tweak a bit what the grammar looks like to provide it to UltraSynth, which only accepted grammars without unbounded recursion (i.e., without infinitely many terms) and had to encode the examples in a way that was accepted by the tool.

The time has come and Monica manages to run UltraSynth on an instance of the synthesis problem. UltraSynth outputs the program in Fig. 2b, which is correct on the example. However, this program is needlessly large and contains many unneeded operations.

```
x = len(arr)-1
while x>=0 do
    if arr[x]>0 then
        arr[x] = arr[x]+10
    else
        arr[x] = 0
    x = x-1
```

(a) A possible ideal solution for Monica's problem.

```
x = len(arr)-1
while x>=0 do
    if arr[x]>0 then
        arr[x] = arr[x]+1-1...+1
    else
        arr[x] = 0
    x = x-1
```

(b) A solution for Monica's problem synthesized by UltraSynth. The sequence of ±1s on line 3 adds up to +10.

Fig. 2. Two possible solutions for Monica's synthesis problem.

Monica has already invested a lot of time in learning UltraSynth, so she tries to figure out a way to avoid such problematic programs. Monica astutely realizes that the needless computations in Line 3 of Fig. 2b are due to repeated applications of the minus operator. Monica would like to ask UltraSynth to synthesize the program that contains as few minus operators as possible, but UltraSynth does not support a way to "prefer" one possible program over another. To bypass this limitation, Monica decides to remove the production $E \to E - E$ in order to suppress these programs.

Monica reruns UltraSynth after removing $E \rightarrow E - E$ from the grammar, and to her surprise, UltraSynth continues to run for hours and eventually times out without providing a solution. After investigating the matter, Monica finds out that she has made a mistake and disallowed too many programs—there is no longer a valid solution to the synthesis problem because without subtraction, the variable x cannot be decremented in line 5. UltraSynth was unable to report, or even detect this simple mistake—Why is it so difficult to program a synthesizer and why can't synthesis tools detect the simplest of mistakes?

Monica has finally had enough of synthesis. She goes back to her daily routine and just writes the 7-line piece of code that applies the transformation she intended (Fig. 2a).

1.2   Programmable Synthesis Frameworks

The story of Monica is a common one in program synthesis, where most of the recent focus has been on solving problems rather than building general algorithms, tools, and methodologies. Existing synthesis frameworks are not **programmable** as they lack at least one of the following properties:

Domain-Agnostic. Existing synthesis ideas and algorithms have been introduced with specific domains in mind and are hard to apply to arbitrary synthesis problems. The languages used to specify synthesis problems are therefore domain-specific, and often fail to abstract the logical requirements of the synthesis problem. In our example, Monica had to look for a specific tool that accepted programs of the kind she was interested in. Moreover, she was not permitted to refine the specification to add a quantitative objective she had in mind (minimizing the number of minus operators).

Solver-Agnostic. Different synthesis tools are typically not interchangeable because their underlying solvers solve different types of problems. Even when two solvers can in principle solve the same types of problems, they typically cannot be interchanged or combined because they typically use drastically different formats written in different languages (e.g., Racket [28] vs. C [27]). For example, when Monica found out that UltraSynth was not working as expected, she could not easily try another tool to see if that tool was better.

This state of affairs is unfortunate because synthesis is very general; if synthesis were easier to use, it would benefit many domains. The potential generality, which is currently held back by the need for better support for usability, underscores the need to answer the following question:

Can we make synthesis more programmable?

In this paper, we present the steps we have undertaken in the direction of making synthesis more programmable, including some of the challenges that we faced, and some of the opportunities that the work has opened.

2   An Overview of Programmable Program Synthesis

The goal of enlarging the scope of synthesis has focused our attention on the need to have a framework in which synthesis problems can be addressed. By a *framework*, we mean the conceptual underpinnings that allow one to build tools to automate the creation of solutions for problems in some domain, in this case, program-synthesis problems. The canonical example is how the theory of parsing underlies the `yacc` tool [13], which automates the construction of parsers. For instance, consider the problem that `yacc` addresses:

- An instance of a parsing problem, Parse(L,s), has two parameters: L, a context-free language; and s, a string to be parsed. String s changes more frequently than language L.
- Context-free grammars are a formalism for specifying context-free languages.
- Create a tool that implements the following specification:
  - Input: a context-free grammar that describes language L.
  - Output: a parser, `yyparse()`, such that invoking `yyparse()` on s computes Parse(L,s).

One consideration for building a framework is the existence of a well-defined "engine" (or collection of engines) for performing the desired task—in this case, parsing s with respect to L, once both L and s are at hand. `Yacc` supports just a single engine, which parses a string with respect to a grammar that is LALR(1). In principle, `yacc` could have been a more general tool by having it perform various tests on L to determine what grammar family L belongs to (e.g., LALR(1), LR(1), LL(1), LL(*)), and then emitting a parser that makes use of an appropriate parsing algorithm for that family, falling back on Generalized LR parsing [19] in case L is not in one of the specialized families supported.

Another aspect illustrated by `yacc` is that the parameters to the problem have different "binding times". In this case, string s changes more frequently than language L—i.e., L is bound early, and s is bound late. The framework implementation can exploit the known value of the early-bound parameter to create a more efficient implementation. In the case of `yacc`, it compiles L to tables used by a table-driven LALR(1) parsing algorithm.

2.1   Why Isn't Existing Work in Synthesis Programmable?

There do exist synthesis tools (mostly, solver-aided languages [27, 28]) that allow one to control some aspects of a synthesis problem in a programmable fashion. However, the nature of existing synthesis tools also forces an association between how a synthesis problem is written and how it is solved. For instance, in Sect. 1, the fact that solvers are tightly coupled to some specification language prevented Monica from trying out a different tool after UltraSynth produced an inadequate answer. The current state of program-synthesis tools is depicted in Fig. 3.

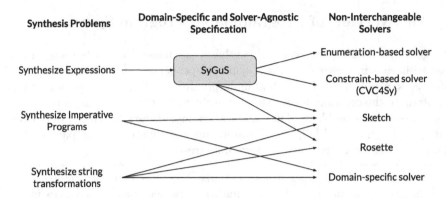

Fig. 3. Program synthesis today, where the lack of separation between specification and solver causes a user to have to encode a problem multiple times to use different tools.

This situation is in direct conflict with the principles articulated at the end of Sect. 1, namely, that a user should be able to program the various aspects of a synthesis problem using a formalism that is both (i) *domain-agnostic* and (ii) *solver-agnostic*. The first property addresses generality: the formalism should be powerful enough to capture a wide variety of synthesis problems (e.g., SQL, regular expressions, and imperative programs). The second property opens the door for synthesis-problem specifications to be fed—possibly after a compilation/translation step—to different specialized solvers, or to multiple solvers with different capabilities.

Another example that one may consider a programmable framework is Syntax-Guided Synthesis (SYGUS) [1], which is a successful synthesis framework targeted at expressions. The defining characteristic of SYGUS, compared to other synthesis approaches such as solver-aided languages, is that it allows one to write synthesis problems in a completely logical format.

Example 1. Consider the simple problem of synthesizing the maximum max of two input variables, x and y. There are two parts to a SYGUS problem: a syntactic part, written as a context free grammar such as the example G_S below:

$$G_S ::= Start \rightarrow \text{x} \mid \text{y} \mid Start + Start \mid \text{if x<y then } Start \text{ else } Start$$

and the specification part, which is written as a Boolean formula ψ_S:

$$\psi_S \equiv \forall x, y. max(x, y) \geq x \wedge max(x, y) \geq y \wedge (max(x, y) = x \vee max(x, y) = y)$$

A SYGUS problem is simply the pair $sy = (G_S, \psi_S)$, where a solution to the SYGUS problem sy is a term $t \in L(G)$ such that ψ_S holds. For example, the following term is a solution for the function max in the problem we just described:

$$\text{if x < y then y else x.}$$

The advantage of such a logic-based formalism is that it achieves a separation from solver and specification, which allows SYGUS to be *solver-agnostic*. Several different SYGUS solvers have been developed (e.g., [4,7,21,26]), many of which use drastically different internal algorithms that have different strengths for solving different kinds of problems. Moreover, a user of SYGUS need not consider the differing input languages or characteristics of these solvers, and instead can encode their problem just once in the SYGUS format to have access to all the different solvers.

While SYGUS achieves—and shows the benefits of—solver-agnosticity, it *fails to achieve domain-agnosticity* because the framework is targeted specifically at expressions. For example, consider the scenario from Sect. 1: Monica would be unable to encode her problem in SYGUS, because the grammar G_{ex} in Fig. 1 contains a production with a while loop, and loops, which require a custom semantics, cannot be expressed in any decidable theory—a key restriction of SYGUS. SYGUS also does not allow one to express intent outside of the behavioral specification ψ, which would have prevented Monica from trying to optimize the program obtained from UltraSynth in Fig. 2b.

All in all, the current state of program synthesis is an unsatisfactory mess, as depicted in Fig. 3. There are multiple non-interoperable solvers with different input languages, targeting different synthesis domains with varying degrees of overlap. SYGUS, by virtue of solver-agnosticity, provides a unified approach to synthesizing expressions, which forms the basis of multiple solvers. However, while SYGUS is a bright spot, it fails to be general: it does not cope with (1) the *variety of domains* used in synthesis, required to deal with arbitrary languages (e.g., SQL, regular expressions, and imperative programs), and (2) the *variety of collateral considerations* that arise for different domains (e.g., types, quantitative objectives, and probabilities).

2.2 What Does a Programmable Synthesis Framework Look Like?

Our vision of programmable synthesis can be summed up as follows:

programmable synthesis

==

easily instantiable, domain-agnostic, solver-agnostic synthesis framework.

In contrast with Fig. 3, what we would like to have is depicted in Fig. 4, where both user and solver work with a unified general format, regardless of domain or solving technique. Such an approach would allow one to specify a synthesis problem once and for all, without having to worry about the underlying solving strategy. To achieve this goal, it is necessary to distill out the essence of many program-synthesis problems into a specification formalism that is ground in formal methods (e.g., automata and logic) and is agnostic to any specific domain of application. This degree of abstraction also opens the opportunity to lift certain synthesis algorithms and ideas to a higher level that makes these algorithms reusable across different tools. Our framework can then interface to

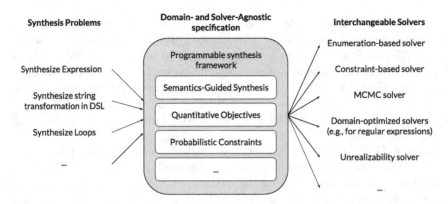

Fig. 4. Programmable program synthesis, where a synthesis problem with arbitrary constraints can be written once and for all in a general format, which can then be dispatched to compatible solvers.

different solving tools (backend solvers) in a way that allows one to easily swap one solver for another, or to use multiple solvers in tandem. If our vision is achieved, the capabilities that would be available to tool designers—discussed in greater detail in Sect. 5—would allow synthesis tools to be created that have the kind of flexibility that Monica expected and needed in Sect. 1.1.

Let us now be more concrete about the requirements for such a framework for synthesis. Following the pattern for `yacc` given above, a framework for synthesis could follow a similar scheme:

- An instance of a synthesis problem $\text{Synthesize}(\mathcal{L}, [\![\cdot]\!]_{\mathcal{L}}, \varphi)$ has three parameters: $\mathcal{L}$, a formal language; $[\![\cdot]\!]_{\mathcal{L}}$, a semantics to ascribe to $\mathcal{L}$; and φ, a behavioral specification for some desired member of $\mathcal{L}$. The behavioral specification φ changes more frequently than $\mathcal{L}$ and $[\![\cdot]\!]_{\mathcal{L}}$.
- Let F_{syntax} and $F_{\text{semantics}}$ be appropriate formalisms for specifying $\mathcal{L}$ and $[\![\cdot]\!]_{\mathcal{L}}$, respectively.
- Create a tool that implements the following specification:
  - Input: an F_{syntax} specification of a language's syntax, and an $F_{\text{semantics}}$ specification of the language's semantics.
  - Output: a function $\text{Synth}_{\mathcal{L},[\![\cdot]\!]_{\mathcal{L}}}(\cdot)$ that takes φ as input and computes $\text{Synthesize}(\mathcal{L}, [\![\cdot]\!]_{\mathcal{L}}, \varphi)$.

To be even more concrete, F_{syntax} could be a regular-tree grammar [5],[1] and $F_{\text{semantics}}$ would be defined over the grammar in a compositional manner, production by production. What we have called collateral considerations (types, quantitative objectives, probabilities, etc.) would be handled as part of the F_{syntax} or $F_{\text{semantics}}$ specifications, depending on the issue at hand. For instance, constraints on program behavior, such as refinement types [24], minimizing/bounding evaluation resources usage [11,15], and probabilistic behavior

---

[1] The grammar would also be equipped with production-by-production pretty-printing rules to specify how to convert a tree to its textual representation.

[22], are semantic concerns that would be part of $F_{semantics}$. Other considerations would be part of F_{syntax}, such as bounds on the use of syntactic constructs [12], or the use of probabilistic generative models of syntactic structures [3,17]. For instance, for these two issues, one could weight the productions of the grammar with values from a semiring, and place a (possibly learned) distribution on the productions, respectively.

The scheme in the box above would allow us to meet the goals of being both domain-agnostic and solver-agnostic,[2] as long as (i) the formalisms for F_{syntax} and $F_{semantics}$ are sufficiently powerful to qualify as "domain-agnostic," and (ii) specifications in these formalisms can be analyzed and broken down into components that can be farmed out to existing solvers (or perhaps to new implementations of the kinds of algorithms used in existing solvers).

Who benefits from such a framework? The existence of a domain- and solver-agnostic framework benefits two parties: (i) users of synthesis tools such as Monica, and (ii) designers of synthesis tools, such as the team behind Ultra-Synth. Both scenarios can be illustrated by making an analogy with LLVM [20]—which provides an intermediate representation for compilation that is similarly both domain- and solver-agnostic. Users of LLVM, which are front-end language designers, benefit from two facts: (i) that the LLVM IR is rich enough to support the range of features their language might have, and (ii) that once their language is compiled down into LLVM IR, the entire library of LLVM IR optimizations is accessible to them. Similarly, a programmable synthesis framework benefits users in two ways: (i) by supporting the full range of features that may be required for a synthesis problem, and (ii) by putting multiple solvers within reach for problems written in the framework. Additionally, a well-defined framework also facilitates *reuse* of problem components: for example, Monica can reuse G_{ex} for synthesizing other array transformations.

On the other hand, backend optimization designers of LLVM benefit from the fact that once their optimization is written in LLVM, all LLVM users may easily access those optimizations if need be. Similarly, tool designers for a programmable synthesis framework rest easy knowing that once their tool supports the framework, those who need it will find it accessible and easy to use—regardless of what internal techniques they decide to use. Note that while the framework intends to be general, tools that interface with the framework can choose to be selective in the problems they support—it is up to the users, or perhaps the framework designers, to match a problem with an appropriate solver (similar to how language designers mix and match backend optimizations for their language in LLVM). In addition, advances at the framework-level—such as

---

[2] We also acknowledge that even the scheme given above, which was modeled on the one for yacc, is open to revision. In particular, the additional degree of parameterization for synthesis ($\mathcal{L}$, $[\![\cdot]\!]_{\mathcal{L}}$, and φ) opens the door for a variety of alternatives, based on different "binding times" for $\mathcal{L}$, $[\![\cdot]\!]_{\mathcal{L}}$, and φ. For instance, a solver that uses different abstract domains as part of a refinement-based search strategy [29] would have $\mathcal{L}$ and φ fixed, but vary $[\![\cdot]\!]_{\mathcal{L}}$. Similarly, when one has quantitative syntactic objectives [12], the solver would carry out its search with φ fixed, $\mathcal{L}$ varying, and $[\![\cdot]\!]_{\mathcal{L}}$ induced as $\mathcal{L}$ changes.

the development of meta-algorithms, as illustrated in Sect. 4.2—instantly benefit all tools that support the framework.

This Paper. New technical challenges, as well as new opportunities, come along with our broader goals. In this paper, we present some of the work that we have done toward building the kind of framework sketched out above.

Specifying Programmable Synthesis Problems (Sect. 3). Semantics-guided synthesis (SEMGUS) is our proposed framework that allows a user to provide both the syntax and semantics for the constructs in the language over which programs are to be synthesized. We show how SEMGUS can easily be extended with quantitative objectives for specifying when a synthesized program is "good" according to a certain metric—e.g., the program should be of minimal size or should maximize a certain outcome.

Solving Programmable Synthesis Problems (Sect. 4). We present solvers that can tackle problems specified in the SEMGUS framework. We also present a meta-solver that can be combined with other SEMGUS solvers to support quantitative objectives. Because our framework does not impose solver-specific restrictions on how synthesis problems are programmed, our solvers can prove unrealizability—i.e., whether a synthesis problem has no solution—of many complex synthesis problems with infinite search spaces.

These steps are just the beginning of what we expect to be a multi-year journey into designing a framework that achieves our goals, and solvers for such a framework. We discuss some of the open challenges and opportunities in Sect. 5.

3 Programmable-Synthesis Specifications

Designing synthesis frameworks that are *programmable* requires one to formally abstract the essence of how one specifies different program-synthesis problems. While we do not claim to have developed a completely unified framework that can capture all synthesis problems yet, in this section we present two ideas for programming many practical synthesis problems: (*i*) SEMGUS, a framework that uses logic and formal methods to make the search space and specifications of all synthesis problems easy to program in arbitrary domains (Sect. 3.1), and (*ii*) an extension of SEMGUS that allows one to specify *quantitative objectives* over the syntactic structure of a synthesized program (Sect. 3.2).

3.1 Semantics-Guided Synthesis

Existing work on program synthesis [1] typically identifies two main components to a synthesis problem: (*i*) a *search space* of candidate programs, which is in essence a small programming language, and (*ii*) a *behavioral specification*, which describes what the synthesized program should do. A programmable synthesis framework must represent (at the very least) these two components in a domain- and solver-agnostic way. Take the syntax-guided synthesis (SYGUS) framework, for example: SYGUS achieves solver-agnosticity by representing the search space as a regular tree grammar, and the specification as a Boolean formula in a decidable background theory.

Then why is SYGUS, and this particular combination of representations, unable to achieve domain-agnosticity? The syntactic component of SYGUS—the grammar—actually does achieve some degree of domain-agnosticity, in the sense that one is free to define a language of one's own. However, SYGUS requires that the specified grammar be contained within a fixed background theory, which are terms with a pre-defined fixed and standardized *semantics*. While this design choice makes the solutions to SYGUS problems easy to verify (using an SMT solver), it limits the *programmability of the search space*.

For example, let us reconsider the example in Sect. 1. If Monica attempted to write her example as a SYGUS problem, she would have been unable to use loops because loops are not part of the supported background theory. What if Monica wanted a solution that operates over a DSL, or had some pre-defined components that she wanted to use (like *len(arr)*)? What if Monica wanted to synthesize regular expressions, or some other programs with relatively non-standard semantics?

One can intuitively understand these scenarios as synthesis problems over different programming languages (search spaces)—a DSL, library functions, regular expressions. To support different programming languages, a synthesis framework needs more than the ability to accept a syntax, it needs the ability to accept a semantics for a language as well. Therefore, developing a programmable synthesis framework capable of supporting all these scenarios requires designing a solver-agnostic way of specifying the semantics of such arbitrary programming languages. SYGUS has shown that regular tree grammars are an effective formalism for programming the syntax of a search space; we extend this with a formalism to program the semantics of the search space as well, which, to achieve true domain-agnosticity, need not be constrained to a fixed background theory.

Semantics as Constrained Horn Clauses. Our solution to this challenge is the Semantics-Guided Synthesis (SEMGUS) framework [14], which allows users to customize the syntax and semantics of the search space. To see how SEMGUS supports programmable semantics, let us consider the production $Start \rightarrow$ while x>=0 do S from Fig. 1 as an example. This production is a while loop, and part of the semantics for a term produced by this production can be expressed using the inference rule below[3] (where Γ represents a state that maps variables to integer values):

$$\frac{[\![x\text{>=}0]\!](\Gamma) = \text{True} \quad [\![s]\!](\Gamma) = \Gamma_1 \quad [\![\text{while } x\text{>=}0 \text{ do } s]\!](\Gamma_1) = \Gamma_2}{[\![\text{while } x\text{>=}0 \text{ do } s]\!](\Gamma) = \Gamma_2} \tag{1}$$

Such semantics are supported in the SEMGUS framework by expressing the inference rule in Eq. (1) as a Constrained Horn Clause (CHC). CHCs are logical formulas, and more precisely, they are implications where one is only allowed

---

[3] A similar rule must be added for the case in which the guard evaluates to false.

to have a single relation in the conclusion, and a conjunction of relations along with one constraint in the premise:

Definition 1 (Constrained Horn Clauses.). *A Constrained Horn Clause is a first-order formula of the form*

$$\forall \overrightarrow{x}, \overrightarrow{x_1}, \ldots, \overrightarrow{x_n}.(\phi \wedge R_1(\overrightarrow{x_1}) \wedge \cdots \wedge R_n(\overrightarrow{x_n}) \implies H(\overrightarrow{x})),$$

where ϕ is a constraint over some background theory that may contain variables from $\overrightarrow{x}, \overrightarrow{x_1}, \ldots, \overrightarrow{x_n}$, and $R_1, \ldots, R_n$ and H are uninterpreted relations.

In SEMGUS, search spaces are represented as regular tree grammars, where productions have associated semantics. In Eq. (1), the semantics of a term x>=0 is represented using the semantic function $[\![\cdot]\!]$. SEMGUS, assumes that each non-terminal N appearing in the grammar has a corresponding logical relation sem$_N$, which we refer to as the *semantic relation*, that represents the behavior of the semantic function $[\![\cdot]\!]$ in Eq. (1). For example, the expression $[\![s]\!](\Gamma) = \Gamma_1$ from Eq. (1) can be translated into the relation sem$_S(\langle s, \Gamma \rangle, \Gamma_1)$.

Example 2 (Semantic Rules as CHCs). The following CHC captures how one would express in SEMGUS the semantics of the production *Start* → while x>=0 do *S* shown in Eq. (1):

$$\frac{\Gamma[\mathsf{x}] \geq 0 \quad \mathsf{sem}_S(\langle s, \Gamma \rangle, \Gamma_1) \quad \mathsf{sem}_{Start}(\langle \texttt{while x>=0 do } s, \Gamma_1 \rangle, \Gamma_2)}{\mathsf{sem}_{Start}(\langle \texttt{while x>=0 do } s, \Gamma \rangle, \Gamma_2)} \tag{2}$$

One can read Eq. (2) as the following implication:

$$\mathsf{sem}_S(\langle s, \Gamma \rangle, \Gamma_1) \wedge \mathsf{sem}_{Start}(\langle \texttt{while x>=0 do } s, \Gamma_1 \rangle, \Gamma_2) \wedge \Gamma[\mathsf{x}] \geq 0 \implies \\ \mathsf{sem}_{Start}(\langle \texttt{while x>=0 do } s, \Gamma \rangle, \Gamma_2) \tag{3}$$

Equation (3) is a CHC where sem$_{Start}$ and sem$_S$ are relations, and $\Gamma[\mathsf{x}] \geq 0$ corresponds to the first-order constraint ϕ.

SEMGUS allows one to specify multiple such CHCs[4] for each *production* in the grammar. CHCs are the logical formalism of choice for expressing these semantics in a language-agnostic way, which are an intuitive and expressive format.
The SEMGUS *Framework.* Once a user has understood how to define a semantics for their grammar, a SEMGUS problem then can be specified simply as a synthesis problem over a grammar equipped with such a semantics.

Definition 2 (SEMGUS). *A* SEMGUS *problem over a theory* T *is a tuple* $sem = (G_{[\![\cdot]\!]}, \psi(x, f(x)))$, *where:*

– *G is a regular tree grammar equipped with the semantics* $[\![\cdot]\!]$,

---

[4] The ability to define multiple semantic rules for a production is useful for productions such as while loops, which are commonly equipped with two rules that describe looping and loop termination.

- $\psi(x, f(x))$ *is a Boolean formula over the theory* $\mathcal{T}$*, that serves as the behavioral specification,*
- f *is a free second-order variable that serves as the function to be synthesized.*

A **solution** *to the* SEMGUS *problem sem is a term* $s \in L(G_{\llbracket . \rrbracket})$ *such that* $\psi(x, \llbracket s \rrbracket(x))$ *holds.*

Example 3 (Monica's Synthesis Problem in SEMGUS*).* Consider the synthesis problem Monica had in Sect. 1. Let $G_{ex\llbracket . \rrbracket}$ be the grammar G_{ex} from Fig. 1, equipped with semantic rules such as the one defined in Eq. (2). Let $\mathsf{E} = \{[-1, 2, 3, 10, 31, -14, -11]\}$, the input array Monica considered for her task. Let $\psi(arr, f(arr))$ be a formula over the theory of arrays and CLIA describing what it means for the program f to be correct on an input arr:

$$\psi(arr, f(arr)) \equiv \bigwedge_{0 \le i < len(arr)} f(arr)[i] = ITE(arr[i] > 0, arr[i] + 10, 0).$$

Then $sem_{ex} = (G_{ex\llbracket . \rrbracket}, \bigwedge_{arr \in E} \psi(arr, f(arr)))$ is a SEMGUS problem defined over a background theory of arrays and CLIA—the behavioral specification requires that the final program satisfies all the examples in E.[5] Moreover, sem_{ex} is written in a completely logical format, and is thus not tied to a specific tool like UltraSynth and can be dispatched to multiple backend solvers (assuming tooling) as Monica pleases.

The ability to customize the semantics for a language in a framework allows that framework to support a plethora of different synthesis problems. One can define synthesis problems over regular expressions, domain-specific languages, imperative languages, or any other language that has a semantics definable as CHCs within the framework, all of which can be tested using different solvers utilizing different strategies.

Example 4 (Regular Expressions Synthesis in SEMGUS*).* Synthesis problems over regular expressions can be expressed succinctly in SEMGUS. The grammar of regular expressions can be captured with the following grammar, where c is a character and ϕ the empty set:

$$R \to c \mid \epsilon \mid \phi \mid R + R \mid R \cdot R \mid R^*$$

Using CHCs, one can also naturally express the semantics of terms $r \in L(R)$. For example, the semantics of Kleene star can be given as the following two CHCs:

$$\frac{}{\mathsf{sem}_R(r^*, \epsilon)} \qquad \frac{\mathsf{sem}_R(r, s_1) \quad \mathsf{sem}_R(r^*, s_2) \quad s = s_1 s_2}{\mathsf{sem}_R(r^*, s)}$$

---

[5] In this example, one could have used a formula simply describing the input/output examples instead of a more complex logical formula. We chose the latter option to illustrate how the behavioral specification can involve terms in interesting theories— e.g., CLIA and arrays.

The rules are based on the expansion $r^* \to \epsilon + r \cdot r^*$: the first rule lets r^* accept ϵ, and the second rule accepts a string s by finding two substrings s_1, s_2, such that s_1 is accepted by r, s_2 is accepted by r^*, and the concatenation $s_1 \cdot s_2$ is equal to s. The specification of the problem can then use expressions of the form $\text{sem}_R(r, s)$ and $\neg\text{sem}_R(r, s)$ to denote whether an example s is positive or negative, respectively.

3.2   Adding Quantitative Syntactic Objectives

In the example discussed in Sect. 1.1, the original synthesis problem Monica posed to the solver was under-constrained and caused the underlying tool to synthesize an undesirable solution that contained unnecessary operations. While the logical-specification mechanism is powerful, it can only capture the functional requirements of the synthesis problem—e.g., the program should perform correctly on a given set of input/output examples. When multiple possible programs can satisfy the specification, a programmable synthesis framework should provide a way to prefer one to the other—i.e., the user of the framework should be able to describe a quantitative objective. In this section, we show how the formal foundations of SEMGuS (i.e., the use of grammars and logic) allow us to easily extend the framework to incorporate quantitative objectives over the syntax of the synthesized program. The ideas we present were originally described in the context of SyGuS [12]; here we show how they can also be applied to SEMGuS.

Adding Quantitative Objectives Using Weighted Grammars. Recall that a SEM-GuS problem is given along with a *regular tree grammar* specifying the search space. In our running example, Monica would like to synthesize a program that has few occurrences of the minus operator. A natural way to express this intent is allowing Monica to tag productions involving such an operator with a cost, let's say 1. Our quantitative extension of SEMGuS builds on this intuition and allows users to add weights/costs to productions in the grammar. This extension leads to a well-studied formalism, weighted tree grammars, keeping the SEMGuS framework general. Intuitively, a *weighted tree grammar* is a grammar in which each production p has an associated weight/cost $\mu(p)$.

Intuitively, the weight of a derivation tree is the *sum* of the weights of all productions.[6] For simplicity, in this paper, we assume that the domain of weights is the natural numbers, and that their sum is the usual application of the $+$-operator. We use $\text{w}_G(t)$ to denote the weight of a term t with respect to the weighted grammar G.

With the weights specified by the weighted grammars, users can specify quantitative objectives as constraint objectives and optimization objectives. A constraint objective is a predicate $\omega(v)$ over a numerical variable v; we say that

---

[6] Weights have to come equipped with operators that tell us how to combine weights of individual productions to obtain the weights of terms. Formally, the weights must be from a semiring; we refer the reader to the original work on this topic [12] for details.

a term t satisfies the constraint objective if $\omega(w_G(t))$ holds. An optimization objective is a flag OPT $\in \{\texttt{True}, \texttt{False}\}$ indicating whether we want to minimize the weight of the solution.

Example 5. Recall that in the example introduced in Sect. 1, Monica wants to avoid redundant occurrences of the minus (-) operator. To express this intent in SEMGUS, Monica can utilize the following weighted grammar.

$$Start \to x \texttt{ = len(arr) - 1; while x>=0 do } S$$
$$S \to \texttt{arr}[E] \texttt{ = arr}[E] + E \mid \texttt{arr}[E] \texttt{ = } E \mid$$
$$x \texttt{ = } E \mid S; \ S \mid \texttt{if arr[x]>0 then } S \texttt{ else } S$$
$$E \to \texttt{0} \mid \texttt{1} \mid \texttt{x} \mid E + E \mid E \texttt{ - } E/1$$

In the weighted grammar, only the rule $E \to E$ - E is assigned the weight 1. All other rules are assigned the weight 0 (omitted for readability). The weight of a term t with respect to this grammar is the number of occurrence of the minus operator in t. If Monica wants to restrict the number of occurrences of the minus operators to be less than 5, she can use the constraint objective $\omega(v) = v < 5$. Furthermore, if she want to minimize the occurrences of the minus operator, she can set the flag OPT to True.

To summarize, a SEMGUS problem with quantitative syntactic objectives is a tuple $sem = (W_{[\![.]\!]}, \psi(x, f(x)), \omega, \text{OPT})$ where $W_{[\![.]\!]}$ is a weighted grammar with a corresponding semantics, ψ is a Boolean formula like before, ω is the constraint objective, and the flag OPT is the optimization objective. The goal is to find a solution that not only satisfies the specification ψ, but also the quantitative objective ω, and is of minimal cost if OPT is set to True.

Quantitative syntactic objectives are useful in applications such as programming by examples [10] and program repair [6], where it is desirable to produce small programs with fewer constants, because such programs are more likely to generalize to examples and test cases outside of the set of examples given by the user. When allowing real-valued weights, syntactic objectives can be also used to find the most likely solution with respect to a given probability distribution. We can assign productions weights that represent their probabilities; the weight of a candidate solution is its likelihood.

4   Programmable-Synthesis Solvers

While a programmable synthesis framework as discussed in Sect. 3 is certainly desirable, it is of little practical use if one is unable to solve the problems that are written in such a framework. In this section, we show that SEMGUS problems can be solved practically. We first describe two general solving techniques for SEMGUS (Sect. 4.1) and then present new algorithmic solving techniques enabled by the SEMGUS framework (Sect. 4.2).

4.1   General Solving Procedures for *SemGuS* Problems

We start off by presenting two solving procedures for general SEMGUS problems we implemented as a tool, rooted in strategies commonly used in existing program synthesizers: enumeration (used in the tool MESSY-Enum) and constraint solving (used in the tool MESSY). Specifically, we will be considering SEMGUS-with-examples problems: SEMGUS problems where the specification is given in terms of a finite set of examples E. An algorithm for solving SEMGUS-with-examples problems can be combined with counterexample-guided inductive synthesis (CEGIS) [27], which generates counterexamples in case a synthesized answer does not meet the general specification, to iteratively increase the example set E and eventually obtain a correct program.

MESSY-Enum: A Basic Enumerator for *SemGuS* Problems. Because SEMGUS also relies on a grammar to specify the syntax of valid terms, like SYGUS, one can employ a simple enumerator that generates terms of increasing size from the grammar and test the enumerated terms against the behavioral specification. With SEMGUS, a term (representing a program) cannot be executed directly, because the semantics to ascribe to it has been specified in the semantic specification. However, because the semantics is specified with CHCs, the term can be executed with a level of interpretation supplied by an off-the-shelf CHC solver. Therefore, MESSY-Enum employs an off-the-shelf CHC solver such as [18] to check if the CHCs are consistent with the specification.[7]

Concretely, given a term t_e to test, one can use the following CHC to check whether t_e meets the specification:

$$\frac{\bigwedge_{e_i \in \mathsf{E}} \mathsf{sem}_{Start}(\langle e_i, t_e \rangle, o_i)}{Realizable} \; \mathsf{Query} \tag{4}$$

The Query rule in Eq. (4) exactly encodes the specification as a CHC: it asks whether the semantics of t_e computed by sem_{Start} is consistent with the set of input-output examples E. If so, the conclusion *Realizable* is provable using the existing set of CHCs—i.e., t_e is a solution to the synthesis problem.

Because we cannot directly execute candidate terms and instead rely on CHC solvers (which may be treated as a blackbox), it is difficult to employ common enumeration optimizations, such as behavioral equivalence caching, or equality saturation. Developing an enumeration-based solver capable of utilizing these ideas would require generating an explicit and efficiently executable interpreter from the given semantics, which is an interesting research challenge and future direction that we discuss in Sect. 5.

---

[7] One can treat CHC solving as akin to a proof search, where the objective is to prove that a specific query holds (in this case, *Realizable* from Eq. (4)) using the provided CHCs.

MESSY: *SemGuS* Problem Solving as CHC-Solving. MESSY-Enum uses a CHC solver to check whether an enumerated term t_e is consistent with the specification or not—however, CHC solvers are also capable of automatically searching for terms that satisfy the specification, as well. Our next solver, MESSY, takes advantage of this fact by expressing *both* the syntax of the search space and the semantics using CHCs. Once the entire search space is modeled this way, one can then slightly modify the Query rule to accommodate this change and directly use a CHC solver to solve the entire SemGuS problem. In essence, Messy reduces solving the SemGuS problem into finding a configuration of variables for which the set of CHC rules (containing syntax, semantics, and specification) is valid—similar to how constraint-based methods in existing synthesizers reduce the synthesis problem to one of solving a set of constraints.

Example 6 (MESSY Encoding). We show how the syntax and semantics used in the production *Start* $\rightarrow$ while x>=0 do S from Fig. 1 can be captured using CHCs. This production states that one can obtain a syntactically valid term while x>=0 do $s \in L(Start)$ for the nonterminal *Start*, given a valid term $s \in L(S)$. Equation (5) encodes this idea as a CHC using the *syntax relations* syn_S, and syn_{Start}, which capture whether the supplied arguments are valid terms that may be derived from the corresponding nonterminals S, and *Start*.

$$\frac{\mathsf{syn}_S(s)}{\mathsf{syn}_{Start}(\text{while x>=0 do } s)} \tag{5}$$

Because the syntax relations provide a way to guarantee that a term t is a valid term in the syntax of a SemGuS problem, one can rewrite the Query rule from Eq. (4) to use this relation instead of an explicitly enumerated term t_e.

$$\frac{\mathsf{syn}_{Start}(t) \quad \bigwedge_{e_i \in \mathsf{E}} \mathsf{sem}_{Start}(\langle e_i, t \rangle, o_i)}{Realizable} \text{ Query} \tag{6}$$

The new Query rule in Eq. (6) has the term t as a free variable—i.e., proving *Realizable* amounts to finding a term $t \in L(Start)$ that is consistent on the input-output examples. A CHC solver presented with this rule, in tandem with the syntax and semantic rules, will then attempt to find a configuration of t such that *Realizable* holds. If the solver can prove that the premises of Equation Eq. (4) hold, then the term t is a solution to the SemGuS problem.

One of the advantages of using such a CHC-based method is when dealing with cases where there is no answer to the synthesis problem, i.e., when there exists no t such that *Realizable* holds. In this case, the SemGuS problem contains *no* answer satisfying the specification within its search space; we say that such a problem is *unrealizable*. Proving unrealizability is something that many existing solvers fail to consider, but is important: for example, Monica would not have had to wait for several hours after modifying the grammar in Sect. 1 if her solver had been able to show that the problem was unrealizable.

4.2   Meta Algorithms for Solving *SEMGUS* Problems

Now that we have shown how to build solvers for general SEMGUS problems (that do not involve quantitative objectives), we turn to 'meta'-algorithms for solving SEMGUS problems, which are 'meta' in the sense that they (i) may be used atop any general SEMGUS solver, (ii) generate modified SEMGUS problems (rather than solutions) that can be easier to solve than the original SEMGUS problem or can be used to solve SEMGUS problems with quantitative objectives. The key component behind these meta-algorithms is the customizability of the search-space description in SEMGUS.

A Meta Solver for Quantitative Objectives. We first present an algorithm for solving SEMGUS problems with quantitative objectives [12]—i.e., where productions in the grammar have weights. We assume, for simplicity, that the only quantitative objective is to find the program of *least cost* that satisfies the specification. The idea of the algorithm is to iteratively reduce the SEMGUS problem with a quantitative objective to a sequence of SEMGUS problems without quantitative objectives, which are used to iteratively find a solution that has least cost—i.e., at each step of the sequence the cost of the solution is improved.

The algorithm operates as follows. Initially, we are given a SEMGUS problem *sem* with a weighted grammar W (we omit the semantic information for brevity) and with the minimization objective OPT set to *true*.[8] The first step of the algorithm is to construct an unweighted grammar G^W by merely erasing all the weights in W. We can now use any SEMGUS solver to solve the resulting SEMGUS problem and obtain a term t_0. This term will have a weight c according to the weighted grammar W, but it might not be the term of least cost that satisfies the specification. Our algorithm therefore tries to find out whether a solution with a lower weight exists, and accordingly constructs an (unweighted) grammar $G^W_{<c}$ such that a term t is accepted by the grammar $G^W_{<c}$ if and only if the weight of t according to W is less than c. When the weights are natural numbers, this construction is always possible [12]. We now have again an unweighted grammar, and we can use a SEMGUS solver to solve the resulting problem. This procedure can be repeated until no better solution exists.

Example 7. Consider the weighted grammar W we presented in Example 5. In particular, let us focus our attention on the following subset of productions that involve non-zero weights:

$$E \rightarrow 0 \mid 1 \mid \texttt{x} \mid E + E \mid E \texttt{ - } E / 1$$

The grammar $G^W_{<3}$, which accepts all terms of weight less than 3 is as follows:

$$
\begin{aligned}
E &\rightarrow E_2 \mid E_1 \mid E_0 \\
E_2 &\rightarrow E_1 \texttt{ - } E_0 \mid E_0 \texttt{ - } E_1 \\
E_1 &\rightarrow E_0 \texttt{ - } E_0 \\
E_0 &\rightarrow 0 \mid 1 \mid \texttt{x} \mid E_0 + E_0
\end{aligned}
$$

---

[8] For simplicity, we assume no further quantitative objectives are present, but the general case can be handled using similar ideas [12].

Intuitively, each non-terminal E_i produces all and only terms with exactly i minus operators.

The meta solver for quantitative objectives shows how using a solver-agnostic specification formalism—i.e., grammars—enables algorithms that operate at the specification level and can be reused across multiple solvers.

Underapproximating Semantics with SEMGUS. The previous section showed how the programmability of the search-space syntax (i.e., the grammar) allows us to design meta-algorithms to solve SEMGUS problems involving quantitative objectives. In this section, we show how the programmability of the search-space *semantics* can be used to build meta-algorithms that can make synthesis faster. The key idea is to generate "simpler" variants of the original SEMGUS problem that use an *underapproximating semantics*, where an underapproximating semantics is defined as a subset of the original semantics that must be precise on the subset on which it is defined.

Definition 3. *For a grammar G equipped with a semantics $\llbracket \cdot \rrbracket$, we say $\llbracket \cdot \rrbracket^\flat$* underapproximates $\llbracket \cdot \rrbracket$ on G, or that $\llbracket \cdot \rrbracket^\flat$ is an underapproximating semantics *for G with respect to $\llbracket \cdot \rrbracket$, if for every term $t \in L(G)$, every state Γ, and every value v on which $\llbracket \cdot \rrbracket^\flat$ is defined, $\llbracket t \rrbracket^\flat(\Gamma, v) = \llbracket t \rrbracket(\Gamma, v)$.*

One easy way to underapproximate a semantics is to simply "eliminate" certain operators from a grammar by not defining semantic rules for them. However, the concept of underapproximation need not be bounded to eliminating operators from a grammar—it may have a fully semantic meaning instead, for example, a bound on the number of possible loop iterations. The key intuition is that underapproximation is sound for use in synthesis—if a term t is the answer to a synthesis problem sy, sy actually does not need to contain any syntax or semantics outside of what is used to define and compute t. (In contrast, overapproximation is sound for proving unrealizability.)

Example 8. Recall, once again, the synthesis problem Monica has in Sect. 1. The grammar G_{ex} of Fig. 1 contains a while loop, which has a complex semantics that can be expensive to compute and, most importantly, allows nonterminating behavior. Most existing synthesizers [27,28] explicitly prohibit nontermination by only considering finitely many unrollings for loops (because most answers to a synthesis problem will indeed terminate).

Fortunately, Monica knows that on her example $[-1, 2, 3, 10, 31, -14, -11]$, the loop should iterate no more than 7 times to process every element of the array. Monica may then choose to supply the synthesizer with an underapproximating semantics that limits the number of loop iterations to 7, which could greatly reduce the amount of computation the synthesizer must perform—for example, a naive enumerator might get stuck on a nonterminating loop when using the precise semantics, while terminating quickly when using the underapproximating semantics. Such a semantics can be expressed easily by adding a loop counter c to the semantics of loops given in Eq. (2), yielding the following CHC:

$$\frac{c \geq 0 \quad \Gamma[\text{x}] \geq 0 \quad \text{sem}_S(\langle s, \Gamma, c-1 \rangle, \Gamma_1) \quad \text{sem}_{Start}(\langle \text{while x>=0 do } s, \Gamma_1, c-1 \rangle, \Gamma_2)}{\text{sem}_{Start}(\langle \text{while x>=0 do } s, \Gamma, c \rangle, \Gamma_2)} \tag{7}$$

Setting $c = 7$ in the Query rule now ensures that loops run at most 7 iterations.

Abstract Semantics with *SEMGUS*. Similar to how we used underapproximating semantics to find solutions to a SEMGUS problem, abstract (overappoximating) semantics can be used to prove that a SEMGUS problem is unrealizable.

Definition 4. *For a grammar G equipped with a semantics $\llbracket \cdot \rrbracket$, we say $\llbracket \cdot \rrbracket^{\#}$ is an abstract semantics for G with respect to $\llbracket \cdot \rrbracket$ if there exists an abstraction function α and a concretization function γ, such that for all $t \in L(G)$, if $\llbracket t \rrbracket(\Gamma, v)$ holds, then $\llbracket t \rrbracket^{\#}(\alpha(\Gamma), \alpha(v))$ holds, and $\Gamma \in \gamma(\alpha(\Gamma))$, $v \in \gamma(\alpha(v))$, i.e., α and γ form a Galois connection.*

In contrast to underapproximating semantics, abstract semantics are sound when used to prove *unrealizability*—i.e., that a synthesis problem has no solution that satisfies its specification within its search space. Consider the use of abstract interpretation in program analysis: abstract interpretation is most often used to prove that a program cannot reach a certain set of bad states, while often being unable to guarantee that a program will produce a specific value, due to lack of precision. Similarly, an abstract semantics will often be unable to guarantee that a synthesized program satisfies the specification, due to lack of precision—but it can guarantee that all programs in the search space will *never* be able to produce a certain set of values, which can be used to prove unrealizability.

Example 9. Consider the scenario from Sect. 1, in which Monica removed subtraction from her grammar in an attempt to simplify the synthesized program. The removal of subtraction made the problem unrealizable—and UltraSynth ran for hours on end because it could not prove that this was the case. While proving unrealizability can be very difficult in general, a solver capable of reasoning about abstract domains and semantics could have utilized an (abstract) semantic rule such as Eq. (8) below:

$$\frac{\text{sem}_E(\langle e_1, \Gamma \rangle, \{pos\}) \quad \text{sem}_E(\langle e_2, \Gamma \rangle, \{pos\})}{\text{sem}_E(\langle e_1 + e_2, \Gamma \rangle, \{pos\})} \tag{8}$$

Equation (8) is defined on the abstract domain $\{pos, zero, neg\}$—corresponding to positive, zero, and negative values—and captures the fact that the sum of two positive numbers will always be positive. This rule will be able to prove that G_{ex} without subtraction will *never* be able to modify x to a negative value, and thus that no program in the search space will terminate (leading to unrealizability).

Unrealizability is a property that is ignored by many current synthesizers, but it is a very important property nonetheless. One practical way to think about unrealizability is as a sanity check, like a type system: the fact that a synthesis problem provided by an end user is unrealizable means that the synthesis problem is malformed in the sense that the user has got some of their specifications wrong. Similar scenarios happen daily with ordinary programming, and we expect them to happen with synthesis as well—thus, it is desirable that synthesizers be able to detect these problems, and report them early on if possible, without running indefinitely, as in Sect. 1. Unrealizability also has applications in computing optimal solutions, as in Sect. 4.2: unrealizability given a grammar with a lower weight bound ensures that the current solution is optimal.

5   The Future of Programmable Synthesis and SEMGUS

We hope we have convinced the reader that synthesis could use more programmability, and that SEMGUS addresses many of the programmability issues of existing synthesis work. But what lies ahead? How can we make programmable synthesis truly practical? In this section, we first outline some of the steps we are undertaking to answer this question (Sect. 5.1).

More importantly, we would also like to emphasize that *the vision of programmable program synthesis can only be realized through a community effort.* We will conclude this section with ideas to involve the synthesis community to help us realize our vision (Sect. 5.2).

5.1   What Are We Working on Next?

In this section, we present some of the directions our group is pursuing in extending SEMGUS to richer objectives and building better solvers for it. We also describe some open problems related to SEMGUS.

Interfacing Existing Program Synthesizers with SEMGUS. The bulk of our discussion in Sect. 3 was about achieving domain-agnosticity by building upon the ideas that SYGUS used in achieving solver-agnosticity. However, there also exist synthesis tools that are already domain-agnostic; most notably, solver-aided languages such as Sketch [27], Rosette [28], MiniKanren [8], and Prose [25]. While these tools are not solver-agnostic, they can in principle be used as SEMGUS solvers by virtue of their domain-agnosticity.

To use such existing tools as SEMGUS solvers, one must develop a compiler of sorts to translate a SEMGUS problem (written in the logical format from Sect. 3) to the specific front-end language of the tool. This task is not trivial for a number of reasons. First, each of these tools implement restrictions on the types of synthesis problems they accept; these restrictions are what enables their fast algorithms. For example, Rosette, Sketch, and MiniKanren only support finite search spaces (i.e., finite grammars), and this fact is encoded in different ways for different tools (e.g., by imposing bounds on the search depth or by imposing syntactic bounds on the search space). Second, some of these solvers implicitly use limited semantics—e.g., Sketch limits how many times a loop can be executed. Third, some of these solvers require special inputs that are useful to guide the synthesis engine—e.g., Prose requires the user to provide a semantics for each operator in the input language as well as an *inverse semantics* that can be executed *backwards*; the inverse semantics is used to perform efficient enumeration.

Soundly compiling SEMGUS problems to these tools requires one to modify the original problems to fit these restrictions. Thankfully, the flexibility of SEMGUS comes to our aid! In Sect. 4.2, we have described ideas for transforming SEMGUS problems using restricted grammars or underapproximating semantics. These transformations are sound for synthesis—i.e., a solution to the transformed synthesis problem, which satisfies the restrictions of a particular external tool, is still a solution to the original problem—and thus can be used to interface with external tools. We are currently working on automating such translations.

The case of Prose is particularly interesting in that it requires inverse semantics, which are not immediately available from a SEMGUS problem. However, because SEMGUS semantics are expressed logically as CHCs, one can automatically invert these semantics starting from the CHCs—we are currently developing a tool that performs this inversion automatically and uses the inverse semantics to interface with Prose.

Other more specialized solvers, such as those for synthesizing regular expressions [23], could also be interfaced with our framework, with the limitation that they will only be able to handle specific problems. The more general question here is: how can we determine whether a specific SEMGUS problem is compatible with a specialized solver? We are working on designing "theories" that describe specific semantics for which specialized solvers exist. For example, if one were to use SEMGUS to work with regular expressions, they could import the regular-expression theory, which by design would enable compatibility with certain solvers. Note that this approach is still solver-agnostic because any general SEMGUS solver would still be able to use this problem definition.

Lifting Existing Synthesis Algorithms to Work with SEMGUS. While interfacing existing synthesizers with SEMGUS is one straightforward way of creating SEMGUS solvers, we envision that higher efficiency can be achieved by designing solvers that take advantage of the structure of SEMGUS problems. Is it possible to lift algorithms (not tools) that have previously been successful with SYGUS or other synthesizers up into SEMGUS?

For example, consider the problem of building an efficient enumeration algorithm for SEMGUS, an algorithmic technique that is now successfully employed in most SYGUS solvers [2,4,21]. The success of enumeration has been driven by a number of clever ideas for efficiently pruning the search space of relevant programs. An example was mentioned in Sect. 4.1, where we discussed the challenges with employing strategies such as behavioral equivalence caching or equality saturation on SEMGUS due to the lack of an executable semantics—i.e., in SEMGUS, evaluating a term on an input requires a costly call to a CHC solver. We are currently building an enumeration algorithm for SEMGUS that addresses this limitation. Our algorithm first synthesizes an executable interpreter from the SEMGUS problem semantics, and then uses this executable interpreter to guide the search. To scale, our approach must handle other challenges, which we are also working on—e.g., discovering which operators have a semantics that is associative or commutative can help us avoid enumerating equivalent terms.

While the generality of SEMGUS is an obstacle to adapting some well-known algorithms, the same generality also helps SEMGUS provide a natural interface to express other algorithms, such as program synthesis using abstraction refinement [29]. The approach taken here is to synthesize programs that work on an abstract domain, and repeatedly refine the abstract domain until a program is found that is correct under the concrete semantics. This approach, in a sense, uses a meta-algorithm that can be expressed naturally in SEMGUS, as discussed in Sect. 4.2. We believe that SEMGUS will naturally be able to express many such meta-algorithms, and further accelerate the development of new meta-algorithms.

Supporting Richer Specifications. Beyond the basic specification mechanisms, SEMGUS already supports syntactic quantitative objectives through weighted grammars (Sect. 3.2). To capture the breadth of specifications appearing in modern synthesis applications, the SEMGUS framework will have to evolve over time. While we are investigating a number of complex objectives that will require extensions to the framework (e.g., probabilistic specifications), in the following paragraph we describe a specification mechanism the current SEMGUS framework can already capture for free: types.

Consider the problem of synthesizing a program that meets a given time complexity (or asymptotic resource usage in general) [11,16]. In existing work, such bounds are specified (and proven correct) using a dependent type system. The solver uses the type system to guide the search, by enumerating only terms that satisfy a certain type. We observe that the SEMGUS framework is already able to capture such type-based specifications! In particular, types are a form of *static* semantics that can be associated with terms and, in most cases, typing rules can be encoded as CHCs, similarly to how one encodes semantic rules. For example, the following dependent type rule can be captured using a CHC where each typing judgment $t : type$ is described using a relation $r(t, type)$.

$$\frac{a : \{\texttt{Int} \mid \varphi_a(v)\} \quad b : \{\texttt{Int} \mid \varphi_b(v)\} \quad + : x : \texttt{Int} \to y : \texttt{Int} \to \{\texttt{Int} \mid v = x + y\}}{a + b : \{\texttt{Int} \mid v = x + y \land \varphi_a(x) \land \varphi_b(y)\}} \tag{9}$$

5.2 What Can the Synthesis Community Do?

As we mentioned at the beginning of this section:

The vision of programmable program synthesis can only be realized through a community effort.

We discuss problems the community can help with in this concluding section.

A Broader Scope for Synthesis. The scope and potential of synthesis is very broad, in fact even broader than what has been discussed in this paper. An invited paper by Gulwani began [9]

> Program Synthesis is the task of discovering an executable program from user intent expressed in the form of some constraints.

However, we feel that this viewpoint is actually somewhat narrow. We believe that insight on many problems can be obtained via the "lens" of synthesis: for many computing tasks, the goal is to produce some artifact to which some semantics is attached, and the process of producing that artifact can be thought of as a synthesis problem. For instance, in an AI planning problem, the artifact is a plan—i.e., Monica from Sect. 1 is a robot, and the sought-for program must navigate her from point A to point B (e.g., minimizing power consumption and time, while avoiding collisions and satisfying other safety guarantees). Closer to home for the CAV community, inside many tools for statically checking assertions in programs (such as SLAM or BLAST), the key component is one that creates an abstracted model of the program that is sufficiently precise to show that an assertion violation is not possible. Among the artifacts that may need to be synthesized are inductive invariants, abstract transformers, function summaries, and interface specifications. Thus, we conclude by offering the following wider definition of synthesis, which connects this broader outlook with the semantics-based perspective that we have presented in this paper:

> Synthesis is the task of discovering a syntactic object—selected from some formalism in which each syntactic object has a rigorously defined semantics—from an "intent" expressed in the form of some kind of constraint.

We believe that the issues discussed in this paper will be increasingly important if synthesis is to be applied successfully to the creation of artifacts that have semantics, but are not programs *per se*.

The generality of our framework can bridge the gap between the many applications of synthesis, and we hope that the community will engage in our work by modeling their synthesis problems in SEMGUS, and by adapting their solvers to work with SEMGUS. Such contributions will result in new benchmarks and solvers, contributing to the programmability and effectiveness of SEMGUS.

Standardization and Competitions. We believe that the idea of a programmable synthesis framework, and SEMGUS, the start of such a framework, represents a step forward in program synthesis. Similarly to what happened with SYGUS, SEMGUS must be standardized, other researchers should build solvers for it, and these solvers should compete annually in SEMGUS competitions.

We hope that this paper will encourage readers to experiment with and advance the ideas presented here, in three ways: First, we hope that the generality of the framework will make it easy for people to use it on various problems, which in turn will make it easy to collect large and diverse sets of benchmarks that will make the design of new solvers focused and effective. Second, we hope that researchers will build new algorithms and techniques that are general and can solve problems built in this framework. Third, we hope to soon create a yearly competition that will foster further interest in building general synthesizers for our framework. More than anything, this paper is a call-to-arms—an invitation to help broaden the scope and abilities of program synthesis, toward an era where Monica uses synthesizers just as much as Python during her daily work.

Acknowledgments. Supported, in part, by a gift from Rajiv and Ritu Batra; by multiple Facebook Research Awards; by a Microsoft Faculty Fellowship; by NSF under grants 1420866, 1763871, and 1750965; by ONR under grants N00014-17-1-2889 and N00014-19-1-2318; and a grant from the Korea Foundation for Advanced Studies. Any opinions, findings, and conclusions or recommendations expressed in this publication are those of the authors, and do not necessarily reflect the views of the sponsoring entities.

References

1. Alur, R., et al.: Syntax-guided synthesis. In: Formal Methods in Computer-Aided Design (FMCAD), pp. 1–8. IEEE (2013)
2. Alur, R., Radhakrishna, A., Udupa, A.: Scaling enumerative program synthesis via divide and conquer. In: Legay, A., Margaria, T. (eds.) TACAS 2017, Part I. LNCS, vol. 10205, pp. 319–336. Springer, Heidelberg (2017). https://doi.org/10.1007/978-3-662-54577-5_18
3. Amodio, M., Chaudhuri, S., Reps, T.W.: Neural attribute machines for program generation. CoRR, abs/1705.09231 (2017)
4. Barke, S., Peleg, H., Polikarpova, N.: Just-in-time learning for bottom-up enumerative synthesis. Proc. ACM Program. Lang. 4(OOPSLA,), 1–29 (2020)
5. Comon, H., et al.: Tree automata techniques and applications (2007). http://www.grappa.univ-lille3.fr/tata. Accessed 12 October 2007
6. D'Antoni, L., Samanta, R., Singh, R.: QLOSE: program repair with quantitative objectives. In: Chaudhuri, S., Farzan, A. (eds.) CAV 2016. LNCS, vol. 9780, pp. 383–401. Springer, Cham (2016). https://doi.org/10.1007/978-3-319-41540-6_21
7. ESolver. https://github.com/abhishekudupa/sygus-comp14
8. Feldman, M.Q., Wang, Y., Byrd, W.E., Guimbretière, F., Andersen, E.: Towards answering "Am I on the right track?" Automatically using program synthesis. In Proceedings of the 2019 ACM SIGPLAN Symposium on SPLASH-E, SPLASH-E 2019, pp. 13–24, New York, NY, USA. Association for Computing Machinery (2019)
9. Gulwani, S.: Dimensions in program synthesis. In: PPDP (2010)
10. Gulwani, S.: Programming by examples: applications, algorithms, and ambiguity resolution. In: Olivetti, N., Tiwari, A. (eds.) IJCAR 2016. LNCS (LNAI), vol. 9706, pp. 9–14. Springer, Cham (2016). https://doi.org/10.1007/978-3-319-40229-1_2
11. Hu, Q., Cyphert, J., D'Antoni, L., Reps, T.: Synthesis with asymptotic resource bounds. In: CAV (2021)
12. Hu, Q., D'Antoni, L.: Syntax-guided synthesis with quantitative syntactic objectives. In: Chockler, H., Weissenbacher, G. (eds.) CAV 2018, Part I. LNCS, vol. 10981, pp. 386–403. Springer, Cham (2018). https://doi.org/10.1007/978-3-319-96145-3_21

13. Johnson, S.: YACC: Yet another compiler-compiler. Technical Report Computer Science Technical report 32, Bell Laboratories (1975)
14. Kim, J., Hu, Q., D'Antoni, L., Reps, T.: Semantics-guided synthesis. Proc. ACM on Program. Lang. **5**(POPL), 1–32 (2021)
15. Knoth, T., Wang, D., Polikarpova, N., Hoffmann, J.:. Resource-guided program synthesis. In: PLDI, pp. 253–268 (2019)
16. Knoth, T., Wang, D., Polikarpova, N., Hoffmann, J.: Resource-guided program synthesis. In: Proceedings of the 40th ACM SIGPLAN Conference on Programming Language Design and Implementation, pp. 253–268 (2019)
17. Kobayashi, N., Sekiyama, T., Sato, I., Unno, H.: Toward neural-network-guided program synthesis and verification. CoRR, abs/2103.09414 (2021)
18. Komuravelli, A., Gurfinkel, A., Chaki, S.: SMT-based model checking for recursive programs. Formal Methods Syst. Des. **48**(3), 175–205 (2016)
19. Lang, B.: Deterministic techniques for efficient non-deterministic parsers. In: Loeckx, J. (ed.) ICALP 1974. LNCS, vol. 14, pp. 255–269. Springer, Heidelberg (1974). https://doi.org/10.1007/978-3-662-21545-6_18
20. Lattner, C., Adve, V.: LLVM: a compilation framework for lifelong program analysis and transformation. In: Proceedings of the 2004 International Symposium on Code Generation and Optimization (CGO 2004), Palo Alto, California, March (2004)
21. Lee, W.: Combining the top-down propagation and bottom-up enumeration for inductive program synthesis. Proc. ACM Program. Lang. **5**(POPL), 1–28 (2021)
22. Nori, A.V., Ozair, S., Rajamani, S.K., Vijaykeerthy, D.: Efficient synthesis of probabilistic programs. In: Proceedings of the 36th ACM SIGPLAN Conference on Programming Language Design and Implementation, pp. 208–217 (2015) Language Design and Implementation, pp. 208–217 (2015)
23. Pan, R., Hu, Q., Xu, G., D'Antoni, L.: Automatic repair of regular expressions. Proc. ACM Program. Lang. **3**(OOPSLA), 1–29 (2019)
24. Polikarpova, N., Kuraj, I., Solar-Lezama, A.: Program synthesis from polymorphic refinement types. In: Proceedings of the 37th ACM SIGPLAN Conference on Programming Language Design and Implementation, pp. 522–538 (2016)
25. Polozov, O., Gulwani, S.: Flashmeta: a framework for inductive program synthesis. In Proceedings of the 2015 ACM SIGPLAN International Conference on Object-Oriented Programming, Systems, Languages, and Applications, OOPSLA 2015, part of SPLASH 2015, Pittsburgh, PA, USA, 25–30 October 2015, pp. 107–126 (2015)
26. Reynolds, A., Deters, M., Kuncak, V., Tinelli, C., Barrett, C.: Counterexample-guided quantifier instantiation for synthesis in SMT. In: Kroening, D., Păsăreanu, C.S. (eds.) CAV 2015, Part II. LNCS, vol. 9207, pp. 198–216. Springer, Cham (2015). https://doi.org/10.1007/978-3-319-21668-3_12
27. Solar-Lezama, A.: Program sketching. Int. J. Softw. Tools Technol. Transf. **15**, 475–495 (2012). https://doi.org/10.1007/s10009-012-0249-7
28. Torlak, E., Bodik, R.: Growing solver-aided languages with Rosette. In: Proceedings of the 2013 ACM International Symposium on New Ideas, New Paradigms, and Reflections on Programming and Software, pp. 135–152 (2013)
29. Wang, X., Dillig, I., Singh, R.: Program synthesis using abstraction refinement. PACMPL **2**(POPL), 63:1-63:30 (2018)

Deductive Synthesis of Programs with Pointers: Techniques, Challenges, Opportunities
(Invited Paper)

Shachar Itzhaky[1], Hila Peleg[1], Nadia Polikarpova[2(✉)], Reuben N. S. Rowe[3], and Ilya Sergey[4,5]

[1] Technion, Haifa, Israel
{shachari,hilap}@cs.technion.ac.il
[2] University of California, San Diego, USA
npolikarpova@eng.ucsd.edu
[3] Royal Holloway, University of London, Egham, UK
reuben.rowe@rhul.ac.uk
[4] Yale-NUS College, Singapore, Singapore
ilya.sergey@yale-nus.edu.sg
[5] National University of Singapore, Singapore, Singapore

Abstract. This paper presents the main ideas behind deductive synthesis of heap-manipulating program and outlines present challenges faced by this approach as well as future opportunities for its applications.

1 Introduction

Just like a journey of a thousand miles begins with a single step, an implementation of a working operating system, cryptographic library, or a compiler begins with writing a single function. This is not quite so for verified software, whose development starts with three "steps": a function *specification* (or, *spec*), followed by its *implementation*, and then by a *proof* that the implementation satisfies the spec. Although recent years have seen an explosion of increasingly diverse and sophisticated verified systems [14,20,26,31,41,48,71,73,96], their cost remains high, owing to the effort required to write formal specifications and proofs in addition to writing the code.

The good news is that in many cases the aforementioned three steps can be replaced by just one of them: writing the spec. The rest can be delegated to *deductive program synthesis* [52]—an emerging approach to automated software development, which takes as input a specifications, and searches for a corresponding program *together with its proof*.

Past approaches to deductive synthesis typically avoided low-level programs with pointers [43,69,83], which are notoriously difficult to reason about, making these approaches inapplicable to automating the development of verified systems code. The few techniques that did handle the heap [47,72] had significant limitations in terms of expressiveness and/or efficiency. Our prior work on the SuSLik

© The Author(s) 2021
A. Silva and K. R. M. Leino (Eds.) CAV 2021, LNCS 12759, pp. 110–134, 2021.
https://doi.org/10.1007/978-3-030-81685-8_5

synthesizer [70], has introduced an alternative approach to synthesis of pointer-manipulating programs, whose key enabling component is the use of Separation Logic (SL) [66,75] as the specification formalism. Due to its proof scalability, Separation Logic enabled modular verification of low-level imperative code and has been implemented in a large number of automated and interactive program verifiers [4,7,18,37,57,62,64,68]. The main novelty of SuSLik was an observation that the structure of SL specifications can be used to efficiently guide the search for a program and its proof. Since then, our follow-up work has explored automatic discovery of recursive auxiliary functions [34], generating independently checkable proof certificates for synthesized programs [93], and giving the user more control over the synthesis using concise mutability annotations [19].

As an appetizer for SL-powered deductive program synthesis consider the problem of flattening a binary tree data structure into a doubly-linked list. Assume also that the programmer would prefer to perform this transformation *in-place*, without allocating new memory, which they conjecture is possible because the nodes of the two data structures have the same size (both are records with a payload and two pointers). With SuSLik, the programmer can describe this transformation using the following Hoare-style SL specification:

$$\{\mathsf{tree}(x, S)\} \; \mathtt{flatten} \; (\mathtt{loc} \; x) \; \{\mathsf{dll}(x, y, S)\} \qquad (1)$$

Here the precondition asserts that initially x points to the root of a tree, whose contents are captured by a set S. The postcondition asserts that after the execution of **flatten**, *the same location* x is a head of a doubly-linked list, with the same elements S as the initial tree (y denotes the existentially quantified back-pointer of the list). The definitions of the two predicates, tree and dll, which constrain the symbolic heaps in the pre- and postcondition are standard for SL [75] and will be shown in Sect. 2.

Given the spec (1), SuSLik takes less than 20 s to generate the program in Fig. 1, written in a core C-like language, as well as a formal proof that the program satisfies the spec. Several things are noteworthy about this program. First, the code indeed does not perform any allocation, and instead accomplishes its goal by switching pointers (in lines 17, 18, 23, and 25); this makes it economical in terms of memory usage as only a low-level program can be: similar code written in a functional language like OCaml would inevitably rely on garbage collection. Second, the main function **flatten** relies on

```
1  flatten(loc x) {
2      if (x == 0) {
3      } else {
4          let l = *(x + 1);
5          let r = *(x + 2);
6          flatten(l);
7          flatten(r);
8          helper (r, l, x);
9      }
10 }
11
12 helper(loc r, loc l,
13                loc x) {
14     if (l == 0) {
15         if (r == 0) {
16         } else {
17             *(r + 2) = x;
18             *(x + 1) = r;
19         }
20     } else {
21         let v = *l;
22         let w = *(l + 1);
23         *(l + 2) = r;
24         helper(r, w, l);
25         *(l + 2) = x;
26     }
27 }
```

Fig. 1. Flattening a tree into a DLL.

an auxiliary recursive function `helper`, which the programmer did not anticipate; in fact the need for this auxiliary—and its specification—is discovered by SuSLik completely automatically. All the programmer has to do to obtain a provably correct implementation of `flatten` is to write the spec (1) and define the two SL predicates it uses, which are, however, reusable across different programs.

At this point, a critical reader might be wondering whether this technology is mature enough to move past hand-crafted benchmarks and assist them in developing the next CompCert [48] or CertiKOS [31]. For one, the program in Fig. 1 does not seem optimal: a closer look reveals that the role of `helper` is to concatenate the lists obtained by flattening the two subtrees, resulting in the overall $O(n^2)$ complexity *wrt.* the size of the original tree.[1] Apart from performance of synthesized programs, the reader might have the following concerns:

- What is the class of programs this approach is fundamentally capable of synthesizing? How picky is it to the exact shape of input specifications?
- Is the proof search predictably fast across a wide range of problems?
- Will the synthesized code be concise and easy to understand?
- Finally, what are the "killer apps" for this technology and in which domains can we hope for its adoption for practical need?

The goal of this manuscript is precisely to illustrate the remaining challenges in SL-based synthesis of heap-manipulating programs and outline some future research directions towards addressing these challenges. In the remainder of this paper we provide the necessary background and a survey of the results to date (Sect. 2); we then zoom in on the promising techniques for improving proof search (Sect. 3); in Sect. 4 we discuss the *completeness* of synthesis, outlining the work that needs to be done in order to formally characterize the class of programs that can and cannot be generated; in Sect. 5 we talk about possible extensions to the synthesis procedure for improving the quality of synthesized programs; finally, in Sect. 6 we discuss possible applications of SL-based synthesis, such as program repair, data migration, and concurrent programming.

2   State of the Art

2.1   Specifications

SuSLik takes as input a Hoare-style specification, *i.e.*, a pair of a pre- and a postcondition. Consider, for example, a specification for a function `swap`,[2] which swaps the values of two pointers:

$$\{x \mapsto a * y \mapsto b\} \; \texttt{swap(loc x, loc y)} \; \{x \mapsto b * y \mapsto a\} \qquad (2)$$

The precondition $x \mapsto a * y \mapsto b$ states that the relevant part of the heap contains two memory locations, x and y, which store values a and b, respectively. We also know that and $x \neq y$, because the semantics of *separating conjunction* ($*$) require that the two heaps it connects be *disjoint*. The postcondition $x \mapsto b * y \mapsto a$ demands that after

---

[1] In Sect. 4 we show what it takes to derive an alternative, linear-time solution.

[2] Our language has no `return` statement, hence all functions have return type `void`, which is omitted from the spec; return values are emulated by writing to the heap.

executing the function, the values stored in x and y be swapped. This specification also implicitly guarantees that swap always terminates and executes without memory errors (*e.g.*, null-pointer dereferencing). Note that x and y also appear as parameters to swap, and hence are *program variables*, *i.e.*, can be mentioned in the synthesized program; the payloads a and b, on the other hand, are *logical variables*, implicitly universally quantified, and must not appear in the program. In the rest of this paper, we distinguish program variables from logical variables by using monotype font for the former.

In general, in a specification $\{\mathcal{P}\}$ f(...) $\{\mathcal{Q}\}$, assertions $\mathcal{P}$, $\mathcal{Q}$ both have the form $\phi; P$, where the *spatial* part P describes the shape of the heap, while the *pure* part ϕ is a plain first-order formula that states the relations between variables (in (2) the pure part in both pre- and postcondition is trivially true, and hence omitted). For the spatial part, SuSLik employs the standard *symbolic heap* fragment of Separation Logic [66,75]. Informally, a symbolic heap is a set of atomic formulas called *heaplets* joined with separating conjunction ($*$). The simplest kind of heaplet is a *points-to* assertion $x \mapsto e$, describing a single memory location with address x and payload e. An empty symbolic heap is represented with emp.

To capture linked data structures, such as lists and trees, SuSLik specifications use *inductive heap predicates*, which are standard in Separation Logic. For instance, the tree predicate used in (1) is inductively defined as follows:

$$
\begin{aligned}
\mathsf{tree}(x, S) \triangleq\ & x = 0 \Rightarrow \{S = \emptyset; \mathsf{emp}\} \\
& \mid\ x \neq 0 \Rightarrow \{S = \{v\} \cup S_l \cup S_r; \\
& \quad [x, 3] * x \mapsto v * \langle x, 1\rangle \mapsto l * \langle x, 2\rangle \mapsto r * \mathsf{tree}(l, S_l) * \mathsf{tree}(r, S_r)\}
\end{aligned}
\tag{3}
$$

The predicate is parametrized by the root pointer x and the set of tree elements S. This definition consists of two guarded *clauses*: the first one describes the empty tree (and applies when the root pointer is null), and the second one describes a non-empty tree. In the second clause, a tree node is represented by a three-element record starting at address x. Records are represented using a generalized form of the points-to assertion with an *offset*: for example, the heaplet $\langle x, 1\rangle \mapsto l$ describes a memory location at the address $x + 1$. The *block* assertion $[x, 3]$ is an artifact of C-style memory management: it represents a memory block of three elements at address x that has been dynamically allocated by malloc (and hence can be de-allocated by free). The first field of the record stores the payload v, while the other two store the addresses l and r of the left and right subtrees, respectively. The two disjoint heaps $\mathsf{tree}(l, S_l)$ and $\mathsf{tree}(r, S_r)$ store the two subtrees. The pure part of the second clause indicates that the payload of the whole tree consists of v and the subtree payloads, S_l and S_r.

2.2   The Basics of Deductive Synthesis

The formal underpinning of SuSLik is a deductive inference system called Synthetic Separation Logic (SSL). Given a pre-/postcondition pair $\mathcal{P}$, $\mathcal{Q}$, deductive synthesis proceeds by constructing a derivation of the SSL *synthesis judgment*, denoted $\{\mathcal{P}\} \rightsquigarrow \{\mathcal{Q}\} \mid c$, for some program c. In this derivation, c is the output program, constructed while searching for the proof of the synthesis goal $\{\mathcal{P}\} \rightsquigarrow \{\mathcal{Q}\}$. Intuitively, the output program c should satisfy the Hoare triple $\{\mathcal{P}\}\, c\, \{\mathcal{Q}\}$. The derivation is constructed by applying inference rules, a subset of which is presented in Fig. 2, and every inference rule "emits" a program fragment corresponding to this deduction.

EMP
$$\frac{\vdash \phi \Rightarrow \psi}{\{\phi; \mathsf{emp}\} \rightsquigarrow \{\psi; \mathsf{emp}\} \mid \mathsf{skip}}$$

FRAME
$$\frac{\{\phi; P\} \rightsquigarrow \{\psi; Q\} \mid c}{\{\phi; P * R\} \rightsquigarrow \{\psi; Q * R\} \mid c}$$

READ
$$\frac{y \text{ is fresh} \quad a \notin \mathsf{PV} \qquad [y/a]\{\phi; \langle x, \iota \rangle \mapsto a * P\} \rightsquigarrow [y/a]\{\mathcal{Q}\} \mid c}{\{\phi; \langle x, \iota \rangle \mapsto a * P\} \rightsquigarrow \{\mathcal{Q}\} \mid \mathsf{let}\ y = *(x + \iota); c}$$

WRITE
$$\frac{\mathsf{Vars}(e) \subseteq \mathsf{PV} \quad e \neq e' \qquad \{\phi; \langle x, \iota \rangle \mapsto e * P\} \rightsquigarrow \{\psi; \langle x, \iota \rangle \mapsto e * Q\} \mid c}{\{\phi; \langle x, \iota \rangle \mapsto e' * P\} \rightsquigarrow \{\psi; \langle x, \iota \rangle \mapsto e * Q\} \mid *(x + \iota) = e; c}$$

Fig. 2. Selected SSL rules (simplified).

EMP
$$\frac{}{\{\mathsf{emp}\} \rightsquigarrow \{\mathsf{emp}\} \mid \mathsf{skip}}$$

FRAME
$$\frac{}{\{x \mapsto b1 * y \mapsto a1\} \rightsquigarrow \{x \mapsto b1 * y \mapsto a1\}} \; \mathsf{skip}$$

WRITE
$$\frac{}{\{x \mapsto b1 * y \mapsto b1\} \rightsquigarrow \{x \mapsto b1 * y \mapsto a1\}} \; *y = a1$$

WRITE
$$\frac{}{\{x \mapsto a1 * y \mapsto b1\} \rightsquigarrow \{x \mapsto b1 * y \mapsto a1\}} \; \begin{array}{l} *x = b1; \\ *y = a1 \end{array}$$

READ
$$\frac{}{\{x \mapsto a1 * y \mapsto b\} \rightsquigarrow \{x \mapsto b * y \mapsto a1\}} \; \begin{array}{l} \mathsf{let}\ b1 = *y; \\ *x = b1; \\ *y = a1 \end{array}$$

READ
$$\frac{}{\{x \mapsto a * y \mapsto b\} \rightsquigarrow \{x \mapsto b * y \mapsto a\}} \; \begin{array}{l} \mathsf{let}\ a1 = *x; \\ \mathsf{let}\ b1 = *y; \\ *x = b1; \\ *y = a1 \end{array}$$

Fig. 3. Derivation of swap.

Figure 3 shows an SSL derivation for swap, using inference rules of Fig. 2. The derivation, read bottom-up, starts with the pre/post pair from (2) as the synthesis goal; each rule application simplifies the goal until both the pre- and the post-heap are empty, and might also prepend a statement (highlighted in grey) to the output program. In the initial goal, the READ rule can be applied to the heaplet $x \mapsto a$ to read the logical variable a from location x into a fresh program variable $a1$; the second application of READ similarly reads from the location y. At this point, the WRITE rule is applicable to the post-heaplet $x \mapsto b1$ because its right-hand side only mentions program variables and can be directly written into the location x; note that this rule equalizes the corresponding heaplets in the pre- and post-condition. After two applications of WRITE, the pre- and the post-heap become equal and can be simply cancelled out by the FRAME rule, leaving emp on either side of the goal; the terminal rule EMP then concludes the derivation. Although very simple, this example demonstrates the secret behind SuSLik's efficiency: the shape of the specification restricts the set of applicable rules and thereby guides program synthesis.

2.3   Synthesis with Recursion and Auxiliary Functions

We now return to our introductory example—flattening a binary tree into a doubly-linked list—whose specification (1) we repeat here for convenience:

$$\{\mathsf{tree}(x, S)\} \; \mathtt{flatten(loc\ x)} \; \{\mathsf{dll}(x, y, S)\}$$

The definition of the tree predicate has been shown above (3); the predicate $\mathsf{dll}(x, y, S)$ describes a doubly-linked list rooted at x with back-pointer y and payload set S:

$$
\begin{aligned}
\mathsf{dll}(x, y, S) \triangleq\ & x = 0 \Rightarrow \{S = \emptyset; \mathsf{emp}\} \\
& \mid x \neq 0 \Rightarrow \{S = \{v\} \cup S'; \\
& \quad [x, 3] * x \mapsto v * \langle x, 1 \rangle \mapsto n * \langle x, 2 \rangle \mapsto y * \mathsf{dll}(n, x, S')\}
\end{aligned}
\tag{4}
$$

Note that in the spec (1) both the set S and the back-pointer y are logical variables, but S is implicitly universally quantified (a so-called *ghost* variable), because it occurs in the precondition, while y is existentially quantified (a so-called *existential* variable), because it only occurs in the postcondition. The reader might be wondering why use an existential here instead of a null pointer: as we show below, such weakening is required

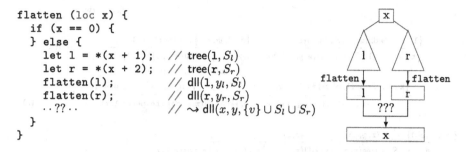

```
flatten (loc x) {
    if (x == 0) {
    } else {
        let l = *(x + 1);      // tree(l, S_l)
        let r = *(x + 2);      // tree(r, S_r)
        flatten(l);            // dll(l, y_l, S_l)
        flatten(r);            // dll(r, y_r, S_r)
        ..??..                 // ↝ dll(x, y, {v} ∪ S_l ∪ S_r)
    }
}
```

Fig. 4. Intermediate synthesis state when deriving `flatten`.

to obtain the solution in Fig. 1; we discuss the alternative spec and corresponding solution in Sect. 4.

At a high level, the synthesis of `flatten` proceeds by eagerly making recursive calls on the left and the right sub-trees, `l` and `r`, as illustrated in Fig. 4, which leads to the following synthesis goal:

$$\{[\mathbf{x}, 3] * \mathbf{x} \mapsto v * \langle \mathbf{x}, 1 \rangle \mapsto 1 * \langle \mathbf{x}, 2 \rangle \mapsto r * \mathsf{dll}(1, y_l, S_l) * \mathsf{dll}(\mathbf{r}, y_r, S_r)\}$$
$$\rightsquigarrow \{\mathsf{dll}(x, y, \{v\} \cup S_l \cup S_r)\} \tag{5}$$

Now the synthesizer must concatenate the two doubly-linked lists, rooted at `l` and `r`, together with the parent node `x` into a single list. Since the spec gives us no access to the last element of either of the two lists, this concatenation requires introducing a *recursive auxiliary function* to traverse one of the lists to the end. We now demonstrate how SuSLik synthesizes recursive calls and discovers the auxiliary using a single mechanism we call *cyclic program synthesis* [34], inspired by cyclic proofs in Separation Logic [11, 76]. The main idea behind cyclic proofs is that, in addition to reaching a terminal rule like EMP, a sub-goal can be "closed off" by forming a cycle to an identical *companion* goal earlier in the derivation; in SSL these cycles give rise to recursive calls.

Figure 5 depicts a cyclic derivation of `flatten`. For now let us ignore the applications of the PROC rule, which do not modify the synthesis goal; their purpose will become clear shortly. Given the initial goal (1), SuSLik first applies the OPEN rule, which unfolds the definition of `tree` in the precondition and emits a conditional with one branch per clause of the predicate. The first branch ($x = 0$) is trivially solved by `skip`, since a null pointer is both an empty tree and an empty list. The second branch is shown in Fig. 5: its precondition contains two predicate instances $\mathsf{tree}(1, S_l)$ and $\mathsf{tree}(\mathbf{r}, S_r)$ for the two sub-trees of `x`.

Now SuSLik detects that either of those instances can be unified with the precondition $\mathsf{tree}(\mathbf{x}, S)$ of the top-level goal, so it fires the CALL rule, which uses cyclic reasoning to synthesize recursive calls. More specifically, CALL has two premises: the first one synthesizes a recursive call and the second one the rest of the program after the call. The spec of the first premise must be identical to some earlier goal, so that it can be closed off by forming a cycle; in our example, the back-link (1) connects the first premise back to the top-level goal. Once a companion goal is identified, SuSLik inserts an application of PROC right above it: its purpose is to delineate procedure boundaries, or, in other words, give a name to the piece of code that the CALL rule is trying to call. To ensure that recursion is terminating, we must prove that $\mathsf{tree}(1, S_l)$ in the precondition of the CALL's premise is strictly smaller than $\mathsf{tree}(\mathbf{x}, S)$ in the pre-

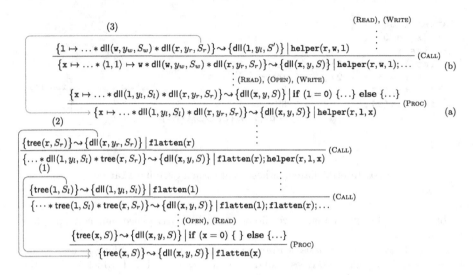

Fig. 5. Derivation of `flatten` and its recursive auxiliary `helper`.

condition of the companion (see [34] for more details about our termination checking mechanism).

After the second application of CALL (to $\mathsf{tree}(r, S_r)$), SuSLik arrives at the goal (5), with two lists in the precondition (marked (a) in Fig. 5). Ignoring again the application of PROC, which will be inserted later, SuSLik proceeds by unfolding the list $\mathsf{dll}(1, y_l, S_l)$ via OPEN, eventually arriving at the goal (b): this goal again has two lists in the precondition but one of them is now *smaller* (it is the tail of $\mathsf{dll}(1, y_l, S_l)$). At this point CALL detects that (a sub-heap of) goal (b) can be unified,[3] with goal (a) thus forming the cycle (3), which this time links to an *internal* goal in the derivation instead of the top-level goal. As before SuSLik inserts an application of the PROC rule just above the companion goal (a), thereby abducing an auxiliary procedure with a fresh name.

2.4   Implementation and Empirical Results

The most up-to-date implementation of SuSLik is publicly available at:

> https://github.com/TyGuS/suslik

Table 1 collects the results of running SuSLik on benchmarks from our prior work [19, 34,70,93] as well as seven new benchmarks, which we added to illustrate various challenges discussed in subsequent sections.[4] Most existing benchmarks had been adapted from the literature on verification and synthesis [24,47,50,72]. In addition to standard textbook data structures, our benchmarks include operations on two less common data structures, which to the best of our knowledge cannot be handled by other synthesizers.

---

[3] This is where we rely on the existential back-pointer in (1): if we replace y_l with 0, then $\mathsf{dll}(1, 0, S_l)$ and $\mathsf{dll}(w, y_w, S_w)$ would not unify.

[4] The code and benchmarks accompanying this paper are available online [35].

Table 1. SuSLik benchmarks and results. We report the number of *Proce*dures generated, total number *Stmt* of statements in those procedures, the ratio *Code/Spec* of code to specification (in AST nodes), and the synthesis time in seconds for standard SuSLik (*Time*), with a simpler cost function (*TimeSC*) and with no bounds on predicate unfolding and calls (*TimeNB*). "-" denotes timeout after 30 minutes. Footnotes indicate the sources of benchmarks.

Data structure	Id	Description	Proc	Stmt	Code/Spec	Time	TimeSC	TimeNB
Integers	1	Swap two	1	4	1.0x	0.2	1.2	0.2
	2	Min of two[1]	1	3	1.1x	0.8	3.0	1.1
Singly linked list	3	Length[2]	1	6	1.4x	0.4	0.5	0.6
	4	Max[2]	1	11	1.9x	3.0	7.0	4.7
	5	Min[2]	1	11	1.9x	2.9	6.7	4.1
	6	Singleton[1]	1	4	0.9x	0.2	0.2	0.2
	7	Deallocate	1	4	5.5x	0.2	0.2	0.2
	8	Initialize	1	4	1.6x	0.4	0.4	0.6
	9	Copy[3]	1	11	2.7x	0.6	1.0	393.3
	10	Append[3]	1	6	1.1x	0.4	0.4	0.6
	11	Delete[3]	1	12	2.6x	1.2	0.9	2.0
	12	Deallocate two	2	9	6.2x	0.2	0.2	0.2
	13	Append three	2	14	2.3x	1.0	2.5	1.7
	14	Non-destructive append	2	21	3.0x	8.0	51.5	-
	15	Union	2	23	5.5x	4.3	20.6	36.0
	16	Intersection[4]	3	32	7.0x	101.1	121.2	-
	17	Difference[4]	2	21	5.1x	4.7	55.0	29.5
	18	Deduplicate[4]	2	22	7.3x	1.8	2.5	5.5
Sorted list	19	Prepend[2]	1	4	0.4x	0.2	0.3	0.3
	20	Insert[2]	1	19	3.1x	1.0	16.2	1.2
	21	Insertion sort[2]	1	7	1.2x	0.7	2.7	42.7
	22	Sort[4]	2	13	4.9x	1.0	1.5	2.9
	23	Reverse[4]	2	11	4.0x	0.7	0.7	1.4
	24	Merge[2]	2	30	4.4x	55.6	10.1	-
Doubly linked list	25	Singleton[1]	1	5	1.1x	0.2	0.2	0.5
	26	Copy	1	22	4.3x	7.2	9.9	-
	27	Append[3]	1	10	1.6x	1.7	27.2	-
	28	Delete[3]	1	19	3.7x	3.4	3.5	-
	29	Single to double	1	23	6.0x	0.7	0.8	4.6
List of lists	30	Deallocate	2	11	10.7x	0.2	0.3	0.3
	31	Flatten[4]	2	17	4.4x	0.6	0.6	1.9
	32	Length[5]	2	21	5.5x	22.8	-	-

(*continued*)

Table 1. (*continued*)

Data structure	Id	Description	Proc	Stmt	Code/Spec	Time	TimeSC	TimeNB
Binary tree	33	Size	1	9	2.5x	0.4	0.6	185.8
	34	Deallocate	1	6	8.0x	0.2	0.2	0.2
	35	Deallocate two	1	16	11.8x	0.4	0.5	0.5
	36	Copy	1	16	3.8x	2.5	42.9	-
	37	Flatten w/append	1	17	4.8x	0.4	0.6	0.7
	38	Flatten w/acc	1	12	2.1x	0.6	0.9	1.9
	39	Flatten	2	23	7.1x	1.5	1.0	5.5
	40	Flatten to dll in place	2	15	9.6x	11.3	-	23.2
	41	Flatten to dll w/null[5]	2	17	11.2x	106.1	1418.3	46.5
BST	42	Insert[2]	1	19	2.8x	14.6	21.7	518.0
	43	Rotate left[2]	1	5	0.2x	6.2	7.0	-
	44	Rotate right[2]	1	5	0.2x	4.9	5.6	-
	45	Find min[5]	1	11	1.4x	66.3	80.2	-
	46	Find max[5]	1	18	2.2x	58.0	80.8	-
	47	Delete root[2]	1	18	1.3x	13.9	-	-
	48	From list[4]	2	27	5.7x	10.0	10.7	-
	49	To sorted list[4]	3	32	7.7x	20.8	11.7	-
Rose tree	50	Deallocate	2	9	12.0x	0.2	0.3	0.2
	51	Flatten	3	25	8.0x	11.0	6.3	-
	52	Copy[5]	2	32	7.9x	-	-	-
Packed tree	53	Pack[5]	1	16	1.6x	-	-	-
	54	Unpack[5]	1	23	2.9x	21.0	-	-

[1] JENNISYS [47]   [2] IMPSYNTH [72]   [3] DRYAD [50]   [4] Eguchi *et al.* [24]   [5] New

A *rose tree* [51] is a variable-arity tree, where child nodes are stored in a linked list; it is described in SL by two mutually recursive predicates (rtree for the tree and children for the list of children), and our synthesized operations on rose trees are also mutually recursive. A *packed tree* is a binary tree serialized into an array; it is interesting because operations on packed trees use non-trivial pointer arithmetic (we discuss them in Sect. 6).

Apart from the size of each program (in statements), we also report the ratio of code size to spec size (both in AST nodes) as a measure of synthesis utility. For the majority of the benchmarks the generated code is larger than the specification, sometimes significantly (up to 12x); the only exceptions are benchmarks with very convoluted specs, such as BST rotations (benchmarks 43 and 44), or extremely simple programs, such as swap from Fig. 3 (benchmark 1) and prepending an element to a sorted list (benchmark 19).

A number of benchmarks generate more than one procedure: those programs require *recursive auxiliaries* [34], such as our running example flatten from Fig. 1 (benchmark 40). It is worth mentioning that benchmarks 37 through 41 encode different versions of flattening a binary tree into a singly or doubly-linked list: 37 and 38 are simplified versions that do not require discovering auxiliaries because they contain additional hints from the user (a library function for appending lists in 37 and an inductive specification for `flatten` with a list accumulator in 38); 39 is similar to 40 but returns a singly-linked list (and hence requires allocation). Finally 41 is a version of 40 that uses 0 instead of y as the back-pointer of the output list; this precludes SuSLik from generating an auxiliary for appending two lists, and instead it discovers a slightly more complex, but *linear-time* solution, which we discuss in Sect. 4.

The missing synthesis times for some benchmarks indicate that they could not be synthesized automatically after 30 min, but were possible to solve in an "interactive" mode, where the search has been given hints on how to proceed in the case of multiple choices. We elaborate on the possibility of generating those programs automatically in subsequent sections. Apart from regular SuSLik time we also report time for two variations discussed in Sect. 3.

3 Proof Search

Similarly to existing deductive program synthesizers [43], SuSLik adopts *best-first* AND/OR *search* [54] to search for a program derivation. The search space is represented as a tree with two types of nodes. An OR-node corresponds to a synthesis goal, whose children are alternative derivations, *any* of which is sufficient to solve the goal. An AND-node corresponds to a rule application, whose children are premises, *all* of which need to be solved in order to build a derivation. Each goal has a *cost*, which is meant to estimate how difficult it is to solve. The search works by maintaining a *worklist* of OR-nodes that are yet to be explored. In each iteration, the node with the least cost is dequeued and expanded by applying all rules enabled according to a *proof strategy*; the node's children are then added back to the worklist.

The proof strategy and the cost function are crucial to the performance of the proof search. In current SuSLik implementation both are ad-hoc and brittle; in the rest of the section we outline possible improvements to their design.

3.1 Pruning via Proof Strategies

A *proof strategy* is a function that takes in a synthesis goal and its ancestors in the search tree, and returns a list of rules enabled to expand that goal. Without strategies, the branching factor of the search would be impractically large. SuSLik's strategies are based on the observation that some orders of rule applications are redundant, and hence can be eliminated from consideration without loss of completeness. Identifying redundant orders is non-trivial and is currently done informally, increasing the risk of introducing incomplete strategies.

For example, SuSLik's proof strategy precludes applying CALL if CLOSE (a rule that unfolds a predicate in the postcondition) has been applied earlier in the derivation. The reasoning is that CALL only operates on the precondition, while CLOSE only operates on the postcondition, hence the two rule applications must be independent, and can always be reordered so that CALL is applied first. But it gets more complicated once we let CALL abduce auxiliaries: now applying CALL after CLOSE could be useful to give it access to more companion goals, whose postconditions differ from that of the top-level goal. Consider for example copying a rose tree with the following spec:

$$\{r \mapsto x * \mathsf{rtree}(x, S)\} \ \texttt{void rtcopy(loc r)} \ \{r \mapsto y * \mathsf{rtree}(y, S) * \mathsf{rtree}(x, S)\} \quad (6)$$

Copying a rose tree seems to require two mutually-recursive procedures: the main one (6) that copies an rtree and an auxiliary one that copies the list of its children, and hence has children instead of rtree in its postcondition. To our surprise, however, our proof strategy does not preclude the derivation of rtcopy (see benchmark 52 in Table 1): in this derivation, the auxiliary returns two rtrees, which are then unfolded after the call to extract the relevant children.

Future Directions. To develop more principled yet efficient strategies, we need to turn to the *proof theory* community, which has accumulated a rich body of work on efficient proof search. One technique of particular interest—*focusing* [53]—defines a *canonical representation* of proofs in linear logic [29] (more precisely, a canonical ordering on the application of proof rules, which can be enforced during the search by tracing local properties). Existing program synthesis work [27,79] has leveraged ideas from focusing, but only in the setting of type inhabitation for pure lambda calculi. SuSLik takes advantage of some of these ideas, too: it designates some rules, such as READ and logical normalization rules, to be *invertible*; these rules can be applied eagerly and need not be backtracked. Beyond focusing, we might explore the applicability of more advanced canonical representations of programs and proofs [1,33,79]. We believe that these techniques will help us formalize and leverage inherent SSL symmetries, such as that two programs operating on disjoint parts of the heap can be executed in any order.

3.2   Prioritization via a Cost Function

When selecting the next goal to expand, SuSLik's best-first search relies on a heuristic cost function of the form (with $p, w > 1$):

$$\text{cost}(\{\phi, P\} \leadsto \{\psi, Q\}) = p * \text{cost}(P) + \text{cost}(Q) \quad \text{cost}(\mathsf{p}(\overline{e})^{u,c}) = w * (1 + u + c)$$
$$\text{cost}(P * Q) = \text{cost}(P) + \text{cost}(Q) \quad \text{cost}(\_) = 1$$

In other words, a cost of a synthesis goal is a (weighted) total cost of all heaplets in its pre- and postcondition. The intuition is that the synthesizer needs to eliminate all these heaplets in order to apply the terminal EMP rule, so each heaplet contributes to the goal being "harder to solve". Predicates are more expensive than other heaplets, because they can be unfolded and produce more heaplets. In addition, for each predicate instance $\mathsf{p}(\overline{e})^{u,c}$ SuSLik keeps track of the number of times it has been unfolded (u) or has gone through a call (c); factoring this into the cost prevents the search from getting stuck in an infinite chain of unfolding or calls. Finally, it can be useful to give a higher weight to the heaplets in the precondition, because many rules that create expensive search branches (most notably CALL) operate on the precondition.

Our implementation currently uses $p = 3, w = 2$, which is a result of manual tuning. Column *TimeSC* in Table 1 shows how synthesis times change if we set $p = 1$. As you can see, SuSLik's performance is quite sensitive even to this small change: four benchmarks, which originally took under 30 s, now time out after 30 minutes, while benchmark 24, on the contrary, is solved five times faster. These results suggest that different synthesis tasks benefit from different search parameters, and that we might need a mechanism to tune SuSLik's search strategy for a given synthesis task.

In addition, because the cost heuristic is not efficient enough at guiding the search, we introduce hard bounds on the number of unfoldings and calls u and c for a predicate instance. Column *TimeNB* in Table 1 shows the results of running SuSLik without these bounds: as you can see, 19 benchmarks time out (compared to only two in the original setup). The requirement to guess sufficient bounds for each benchmark hampers the usability of SuSLik, hence in the future we would like to replace them with a better cost function.

Future Directions. To guide the search in a more intelligent and flexible way, we turn to extensive recent work on using learned models to guide proof search [8,28,49,78,95] and program synthesis [5,15,39,46,55,82]. Guiding *deductive synthesis* would most likely require a non-trivial combination of these two lines of work.

In the area of proof search, existing techniques are used to select the next strategy in a proof assistant script [59,60,78,95], or select a subset of clauses to use in a first-order resolutions proof [9,49]. Although these techniques are not directly applicable to our context, we can likely borrow some high-level insights, such as two-phased search [49], which applies a slow neural heuristic to make important decisions in early stages of search (*e.g.,* which predicate instances to unfold), and then less accurate but much faster hand-coded heuristics take over. Among the many techniques for guiding program synthesis, neural-guided deductive search (NGDS) [39] might be the natural place to start, since it shows how to condition the next synthesis step on the current synthesis sub-goal.

At the same time we also expect the limited size of the available dataset (*i.e.,* the benchmarks from Table 1) would hamper the application of deep learning to SuSLik. An alternative approach is to encode feature extractors [58] and apply machine learning algorithms to the result of such feature extractors. Another approach is to learn a coarse-grained model from available data and then adjust it during search, based on the feedback from incomplete derivations, as in [6,15,82].

4   Completeness

Soundness and completeness are desirable properties of synthesis algorithms. In our case, it is natural to formalize these properties relative to an underlying verification logic, which defines Hoare triples $\{P\}\ c\ \{Q\}$, with the total correctness interpretation "starting from a state satisfying P, program c will execute without memory errors and terminate in a state satisfying Q". This logic can be defined in the style of SMALL-FOOT [7], using a combination of symbolic execution rules and logical rules, with the addition of cyclic proofs to handle recursion [76].

Relative *soundness* means that any solution SuSLik finds can be verified: $\forall P, Q, c.\ P \rightsquigarrow Q \mid c \ \Rightarrow\ \{P\}\ c\ \{Q\}$. Relative *completeness* means that whenever there exists a verifiable program, SuSLik can find one: $\forall P, Q.(\exists c.\{P\}\ c\ \{Q\}) \Rightarrow (\exists c'.\ P \rightsquigarrow Q \mid c')$. Proving relative soundness is rather straightforward, because SSL rules are essentially more restrictive versions of verification rules, hence an SSL derivation can be rewritten by translating every $P \rightsquigarrow Q \mid c$ into $\{P\}\ c\ \{Q\}$.[5] Completeness on the other hand is quite tricky, exactly because SSL rules impose more restrictions on the pre- and postconditions, in order to avoid blind enumeration of programs and instead guide synthesis by the spec. In the rest of this section we look into two major sources of relative incompleteness of SSL: recursive auxiliaries and pure reasoning.

---

[5] In our recent work we have developed an automatic translation from SSL derivations into three Coq-based verification logics [93].

4.1 Recursive Auxiliaries

A common assumption and source of incompleteness in recursive program synthesis [43,67,69] is that (1) synthesis is performed one function f at a time: if auxiliaries are required, their specifications are supplied explicitly; and (2) the specification Φ of f is *inductive*: one can prove that Φ holds of f's body assuming it holds of each recursive call. This restriction hampers the usability of synthesizers, because the user must guess all required auxiliaries and possibly generalize Φ to make it inductive, which in most cases requires knowing the implementation of f. As we have shown in Sect. 2, SuSLik mitigates these limitations to some extent, as it is able to discover auxiliary functions, such as `helper` in Fig. 1, automatically. To make the search tractable, however, cyclic synthesis restricts the space of auxiliary specifications considered by SuSLik to synthesis goals observed earlier in the derivation. Although this restriction is easy to state, we still do not have a formal characterization (or even a firm intuitive understanding) of the class of auxiliaries that SSL fundamentally can and cannot derive. Below we illustrate the intricacies on a series of examples.

```
 1 intersect (loc r, y)          13 insert(int v, loc x, r, y) {
 2 {                             14   let z = *r;
 3   let x = *r;                 15   if (y == 0) { free(x); }
 4   if (x == 0) {               16   else {
 5   } else {                    17     let vy = *y;
 6     let v = *x;               18     let n = *(y + 1);
 7     let n = *(x + 1);         19     if (v == vy) {
 8     *r = n;                   20       *(x + 1) = z;
 9     intersect(r, y);          21       *r = x;
10     insert(v, x, r, y);       22     } else {
11   }                          23       insert(v, x, r, n);
12 }                            24 }}}
```

Fig. 6. Intersection of lists with unique elements. This implementation *cannot be synthesized* from (7), but a slight modification of it can, as explained in the text.

Generalizing Pure Specs. One reason SuSLik might fail to abduce an auxiliary is that the pure part of the companion's goal might be too specific for the recursive call. Let us illustrate this phenomenon using the list intersection problem (benchmark 16 in Table 1) with the following specification, where ulist denotes a singly-linked list with unique elements:

$$\{r \mapsto x * \mathsf{ulist}(x, S_x) * \mathsf{ulist}(y, S_y)\} \rightsquigarrow \{r \mapsto z * \mathsf{ulist}(z, S_x \cap S_y) * \mathsf{ulist}(y, S_y)\} \quad (7)$$

Given this specification, we expected SuSLik to generate the program shown in Fig. 6. To compute the intersection of two input lists rooted in x and y, this program first computes the intersection of y and the tail of x (line 9). The auxiliary `insert` then traverses y to check if it contains v (the head of x), and if so, inserts it into the intermediate result z (line 23), and otherwise, de-allocates the node x (line 15). This program, however, cannot be derived by SSL; to see why let us take a closer look at the synthesis goal after line 9, which serves as the spec for `insert`:

$$\{S_x = \{\mathsf{v}\} \cup S_1 \wedge \mathsf{v} \notin S_1 \wedge S_z = S_1 \cap S_y; \mathsf{r} \mapsto z * \mathsf{ulist}(z, S_z) * \mathsf{ulist}(\mathsf{y}, S_y) *$$
$$\mathsf{x} \mapsto \mathsf{v} * \ldots\} \rightsquigarrow \{S_z' = S_x \cap S_y; \mathsf{r} \mapsto z' * \mathsf{ulist}(z', S_z') * \mathsf{ulist}(\mathsf{y}, S_y)\} \qquad (8)$$

The issue here is that the pure spec is too specific: the precondition $S_z = S_1 \cap S_y$ and the postcondition $S_z' = S_x \cap S_y$ define the behavior of this function in terms of the elements of input lists x and y, but the recursive call in line 23 replaces y with its tail n so these specifications do not hold anymore. The solution is to generalize the pure part of spec (8), so that it does not refer to S_x:

$$\{\mathsf{v} \notin S_z; \mathsf{r} \mapsto z * \mathsf{ulist}(z, S_z) * \mathsf{ulist}(\mathsf{y}, S_y) * \mathsf{x} \mapsto \mathsf{v} * \ldots\}$$
$$\rightsquigarrow \{S_z' = S_z \cup (\{\mathsf{v}\} \cap S_y); \mathsf{r} \mapsto z' * \mathsf{ulist}(z', S_z') * \mathsf{ulist}(\mathsf{y}, S_y)\} \qquad (9)$$

Alas, such a transformation of the pure spec is beyond SuSLik's capabilities.

To our surprise, SuSLik was nevertheless able to generate a solution to this problem by finding an alternative implementation for `insert`, shown on the right. This implementation *appends* v to z instead of *prepending* it; more specifically, `insert` starts by traversing z, and once it reaches the base case, it calls another auxiliary, `intersectOne` (omitted for brevity), which traverses y and returns a list whose elements are $\{\mathsf{v}\} \cap S_y$ (*i.e.*, a list with at most one element), which is then appended to the intersection. At a first glance it is unclear how this superfluous traversal of z can possibly help with generalizing the spec (8); the key to this mystery lies in the recursive call in line 22: note that as the second parameter, instead of the input list x, it actually uses z after replacing its head element with v! This substitution makes the overly restrictive spec of (8) actually hold.

```
13  insert(int v, loc x,
        r, y) {
14    let z = *r;
15    if (z == 0) {
16      intersectOne(v,
          x, r, y)
17    } else {
18      let vz = *z;
19      let n = *(z + 1);
20      *r = n;
21      *z = v;
22      insert(v, z, r,
          y);
23      ...
24  }}
```

Of course this implementation is overly convoluted and inefficient, so in the future we plan equip SuSLik with the capability to generalize pure specs. To this end, we plan to combine deductive synthesis with invariant inference techniques via bi-abduction [86]. For instance, whenever the CALL rule identifies a companion goal, we can replace its pure pre- and post-condition ϕ and ψ with unknown predicates U_ϕ and U_ψ. During synthesis, we would maintain a set of Constrained Horn Clauses over these unknown predicates (starting with: $\phi \Rightarrow U_\phi$ and $U_\psi \Rightarrow \psi$); these constraints can be solved incrementally, like in our prior work [69], pruning the current derivation whenever the constraints have no solution. If synthesis succeeds, the assignment to U_ϕ and U_ψ corresponds to the inductive generalization of the original auxiliary spec. Since only the pure part of the spec is generalized, the spatial part can still be used to guide synthesis.

Accumulator Parameters. It is common practice to introduce an auxiliary recursive function to thread through additional data in the form of "accumulator" inputs or outputs. Cyclic program synthesis has trouble conjuring up arbitrary accumulators, since it constructs auxiliary specifications from the original specification via unfolding and making recursive calls.

Consider linked list reversal (23 in Table 1): SuSLik generates an inefficient, quadratic version of this program, which reverses the tail of the list and then appends its head to the result (hence discovering "append element" as the auxiliary). The canonical linear-time version of reversal requires an auxiliary with *two list arguments*—the already reversed portion and the portion yet to be reversed—and hence is outside of SuSLik's search space: cyclic synthesis cannot encounter a precondition with two lists, as it starts with a single list predicate in the precondition, and neither unfolding nor making a call can duplicate it.

```
1  flatten (loc x) {
2    if (x == 0) {
3    } else {
4      let l = *(x + 1);
5      let r = *(x + 2);
6      flatten(l);
7      helper(r, l, x);
8    }
9  }
10
11 helper (loc r, loc l, loc x) {
12   if (r == 0) {
13     if (l == 0) {} else {
14       *(l + 2) = x;
15     }
16   } else {
17     let rl = *(r + 1);
18     let rr = *(r + 2);
19     *(r + 2) = rl;
20     *(r + 1) = l;
21     helper(rl, l, r);
22     *(x + 2) = rr;
23     *(x + 1) = r;
24     helper(rr, r, x);
25   }
26 }
```

Fig. 7. Flattening a tree into a DLL in linear time.

There are examples, however, where SuSLik surprized us by inventing the necessary accumulator parameters. Consider again our running example, flattening a tree into a doubly-linked list. Recall that given the spec (1), SuSLik synthesizes an inefficient implementation with quadratic complexity. A canonical linear-time solution requires an auxiliary that takes as input a tree and a list accumulator, and simply prepends every traversed tree element to this list; because of the accumulator parameter, discovering this auxiliary seems to be outside of scope of cyclic synthesis. To our surprise, SuSLik is actually able to synthesize a linear-time version of `flatten`, shown in Fig. 7 (and encoded as benchmark 41 in Table 1), given the following specification:

$$\{\mathsf{tree}(\mathtt{x}, S)\}\ \mathtt{flatten\ (loc\ x)}\ \{\mathsf{dll}(\mathtt{x}, 0, S)\} \tag{10}$$

Compared with (1), the existential back-pointer y of the output list is replaced with the null-pointer 0, precluding SuSLik from traversing the output of the recursive call (*cf.* Sect. 2), which in this case comes in handy, since it enforces that every tree element is traversed only once.

The new solution starts the same way as the old one, by flattening the left sub-tree `l`, which leads to the following synthesis goal after line 6:

$$\{\mathsf{dll}(\mathtt{l}, 0, S_l) * \mathsf{tree}(\mathtt{r}, S_r) * [\mathtt{x}, 3] * \mathtt{x} \mapsto v * \ldots\} \rightsquigarrow \{\mathsf{dll}(\mathtt{x}, 0, \{v\} \cup S_l \cup S_r\}) \tag{11}$$

As you can see, the precondition now contains a tree and a list! Since it cannot recurse on the list $\mathsf{dll}(\mathtt{l}, 0, S_l)$, the synthesizer instead proceeds to unfold the tree $\mathsf{tree}(\mathtt{r}, S_r)$ and then use (11) as a companion for two recursive calls on `r`'s sub-trees, turning (11) into a specification for `helper` in Fig. 7.

4.2 Pure Reasoning

To enable synthesis of the wide range of programs demonstrated in Sect. 2, SuSLik must support a sufficiently rich logic of pure formulas. Our implementation currently supports linear integer arithmetic and sets, but the general idea is to make SuSLik parametric *wrt.* the pure logic (as long as it can be translated into an SMT-decidable theory), and outsource all pure reasoning to an SMT solver.

In the context of synthesis, however, outsourcing pure reasoning is trickier than it might seem (or at least trickier than in the context of verification). Consider the following seemingly trivial goal:

$$\{\mathtt{x} \mapsto a + 10\} \rightsquigarrow \{\mathtt{x} \mapsto a + 11\} \tag{12}$$

This goal can be solved by incrementing the value stored in `x`, *i.e.*, by the program `let a1 = *x; *x = a1 + 1`. *Verifying* this program is completely straightforward: a typical SL verifier would use symbolic execution to obtain the final symbolic state $\{\mathtt{x} \mapsto a + 10 + 1\}$, reducing verification to a trivial SMT query $\exists a.a + 10 + 1 \neq a + 11$. *Synthesizing* this program, on the other hand, requires guessing the program expression `a1 + 1`, which does not occur anywhere in the specification.

To avoid blind enumeration of program expressions, SuSLik attempts to reduce the goal (12) to a *syntax-guided synthesis* (SyGuS) query [2]:

$$\exists f.\forall x, a, a_1.a_1 = a + 10 \implies f(x, a_1) = a + 11$$

Queries like this can be outsourced to numerous existing SyGuS solvers [3,32,46,77]; SuSLik uses CVC4 [74] for this purpose. Because SyGuS queries are expensive, the challenge is to design SSL rules to issue these queries sparingly.

$$
\textsc{Read}\;\dfrac{\exists\textsc{-Intro}\;\dfrac{\textsc{Solve-}\exists\;\dfrac{\textsc{Write}\;\dfrac{\textsc{Frame}\;\dfrac{\textsc{Emp}\;\dfrac{}{\{\mathsf{a}_1 = a + 1; \mathsf{emp}\} \rightsquigarrow \{\mathsf{emp}\} \mid \mathbf{skip}}}{\{\mathsf{a}_1 = a + 1;\ \mathtt{x} \mapsto \mathsf{a}_1 + 1\} \rightsquigarrow \{\mathtt{x} \mapsto \mathsf{a}_1 + 1\} \mid \mathbf{skip}}}{\{\mathsf{a}_1 = a + 1; \mathtt{x} \mapsto \mathsf{a}_1\} \rightsquigarrow \{\mathtt{x} \mapsto \mathsf{a}_1 + 1\} \mid *\mathtt{x} = \mathsf{a}_1 + 1}}{\{\mathsf{a}_1 = a + 1; \mathtt{x} \mapsto \mathsf{a}_1\} \rightsquigarrow \{y = a + 2; \mathtt{x} \mapsto y\} \mid *\mathtt{x} = \mathsf{a}_1 + 1}}{\{\mathsf{a}_1 = a + 1; \mathtt{x} \mapsto \mathsf{a}_1\} \rightsquigarrow \{\mathtt{x} \mapsto a + 1\} \mid *\mathtt{x} = \mathsf{a}_1 + 1}}{\{\mathtt{x} \mapsto a + 1\} \rightsquigarrow \{\mathtt{x} \mapsto a + 1\} \mid \mathbf{let}\ \mathsf{a}_1 = *\mathtt{x}; *\mathtt{x} = \mathsf{a}_1 + 1}
$$

Fig. 8. SSL derivation for goal (12).

Figure 8 shows how two pure reasoning rules, ∃-Intro and Solve-∃, work together to solve the goal (12). ∃-Intro is triggered by the postcondition heaplet $\mathtt{x} \mapsto a + 1$, whose right-hand side is a ghost expression, which blocks the application of Write. ∃-Intro replaces the ghost expression with a *program-level* existential variable y (*i.e.*, an existential which can only be instantiated with program expressions). Now Solve-∃ takes over: this rule constructs a SyGuS query using all existentials in the current goal as unknown terms and the pure pre- and post-condition as the SyGuS specification. In this case, the SyGuS query succeeds, replacing the existential y with the program term $\mathtt{a1} + 1$. From here on, the regular Write rule finishes the job.

Note that although the goal (12) is artificially simplified, it is extracted from a real problem: benchmark 32 in Table 1, length of a list of lists. In fact the versions of SuSLik reported in our previous work were incapable of solving this benchmark because they were lacking the ∃-Intro rule, which we only introduced recently. Although the current combination of pure reasoning rules works well for all our benchmarks, it is still incomplete (even modulo the completeness of the pure synthesizer), because, for efficiency reasons, Solve-∃ only returns a single solution to the SyGuS problem, even if the pure specification allows for many. This might be insufficient when Solve-∃ is called before the complete pure postcondition is known (for example, to synthesize actual arguments for a call). Developing an approach to outsourcing pure reasoning that is both complete and efficient is an open challenge for future work.

5 Quality of Synthesized Programs

Should we hope that the output of deductive synthesis will be directly integrated into high-assurance software, we need to make sure that the code it generates is not only correct, but also efficient, concise, readable, and maintainable. The current implementation of SuSLik does not take any of these considerations into account during synthesis; in this section we discuss two of these challenges, and outline some directions towards addressing them.

5.1 Performance

We have already mentioned examples of SuSLik solutions with sub-optimal asymptotic complexity in Sect. 4: for example, SuSLik generates quadratic programs for linked list reversal and tree flattening instead of optimal linear-time versions. Although a linear-time solution to tree flattening from Fig. 7 is actually within SuSLik's search space (even with the more general spec (1)), SuSLik opts for the sub-optimal one simply because it has no ability to reason about performance and hence has no reason to prefer one over the other.

To enable SuSLik to pick the more efficient of the two implementations, we can integrate SSL with a resource logic, such as [56], following the recipe from our prior work on resource-guided synthesis [44]. One option is to annotate each points-to heaplet $x \mapsto^p e$ with non-negative *potential* p, which can be used to pay for execution of statements, according to a user-defined cost model. Predicate definitions can describe how potential is allocated inside the data structure; for example, we can define a tree with p units of potential per node as follows:

$$\mathsf{tree}(x, S, p) \triangleq x = 0 \Rightarrow \{S = \emptyset; \mathsf{emp}\}$$
$$| \quad x \neq 0 \Rightarrow \{S = \{v\} \cup S_l \cup S_r;$$
$$[x, 3] * x \mapsto^p v * \langle x, 1 \rangle \mapsto l * \langle x, 2 \rangle \mapsto r * \mathsf{tree}(l, S_l, p) * \mathsf{tree}(r, S_r, p)\}$$

We can now annotate the specification (1) with potentials as follows:

$$\{\mathsf{tree}(\mathsf{x}, S, 2)\} \; \mathtt{flatten} \; (\mathtt{loc} \; \mathtt{x}) \; \{\mathsf{dll}(\mathsf{x}, y, S, 0)\} \tag{13}$$

If we define the cost of a procedure call to be 1, and the cost of other statements to be 0, this specification guarantees that flatten only makes a number of recursive calls that is linear in the size of the tree (namely, two calls per tree element). With this specification, the inefficient solution in Fig. 1 does not verify: since **helper** traverses the list **r**, it must assign some positive potential to every element of this list in order to pay for the call in line 24, but the specification (13) assigns no potential to the output list. On the other hand, the efficient solution in Fig. 7 verifies: after the recursive call to **flatten** in line 6 we obtain $\{\mathsf{dll}(1, y, S_l, 0) * \mathsf{tree}(r, S_r, 2) * \ldots\}$; **helper** verifies against this specification since it only traverses the tree **r** and hence can use the two units of potential stored in its root to pay for the two calls in lines 21 and 24. In fact, the user need not guess the precise amount of potential $p = 2$ in the spec (13): any constant $p \geq 2$ would work to reject the quadratic solution and admit the linear one.

5.2 Readability

Although readability is hard to quantify, we have noticed several patterns in SuS-Lik-generated code that are obviously unnatural to a human programmer, and hence need to be addressed. Perhaps the most interesting problem arises due to inference of recursive auxiliaries: because SuSLik has no notion of abstraction boundaries, the allocation of work between the different procedures is often sub-optimal. One example is benchmark 39 in Table 1, which flattens a binary tree into a *singly-linked* list. This example is discussed in detail in our prior work [34]; the solution is similar to **flatten** from Fig. 1, except that this transformation cannot be performed in-place: instead, the original tree nodes have to be deallocated, and new list nodes have to be allocated. Importantly, in SuSLik's solution, tree nodes are deallocated inside the **helper** function, whose main purpose is to append two lists. A better design would be to perform deallocation in the main function, so that **helper** has no knowledge of tree nodes whatsoever. To address this issue in the future we might consider different quality metrics when abducing specs for auxiliaries, such as encouraging all heaplets generated by unfolding the same predicate to be processed by the same procedure.

6 Applications

6.1 Program Repair

In our statement of the synthesis problem, complete programs are generated *from scratch* from Hoare-style specifications. But what if the program is already written previously but is buggy—would it be possible to automatically find a fix for it *if* we know what its specification is? This line of research, employing deductive synthesis for automated program repair [30], known as *deductive program repair*, has been explored in the past for functional programs [42] and simple memory safety properties [90], and only recently has been extended to heap-manipulating programs using the approach pioneered by SuSLik [63].

The SL-based deductive repair relies on existing automated deductive verifiers [17] to identify a buggy code fragment (which breaks the verification), followed by the discovery of the correct specification, which is used for the subsequent synthesis of the patch. The main shortcoming of the existing SL-based repair tools is the need to provide the top-level specs for the procedures in order to enable their verification (and potential bug discovery) in the first place. As a way to improve the utility of those tools, a promising direction is to employ existing static analyzers, such as INFER [12], to derive those specifications by *abducing* them from the usages of the corresponding functions [13].

6.2   Data Migration and Serialization

The pay-off of deductive synthesis is especially high for programs like tree flatten-ing, which change the internal representation of a data structure without changing its payload; these programs usually have a simple specification, while their implementa-tions can get much more intricate. One example where such programs can be useful is migration of persistent data: thanks to recent advancements in *non-volatile memory* (NVM) [40,45,84], large amounts of data are now persistently stored in memory, in arbitrary programmer-defined data structures. If the programmer decides to change the data structure, data has to be migrated between the old and the new representations, and writing those migration functions by hand can be tedious. In addition, reallocat-ing large data structures is often prohibitively expensive, so the migration needs to be performed in-place, without reallocation. As we have demonstrated in our running example, this is something that can be easily specified and synthesized in SuSLik.

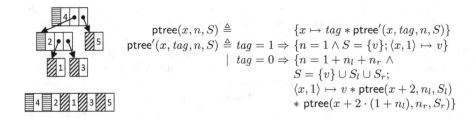

$$\text{ptree}(x, n, S) \triangleq \qquad \{x \mapsto tag * \text{ptree}'(x, tag, n, S)\}$$
$$\text{ptree}'(x, tag, n, S) \triangleq tag = 1 \Rightarrow \{n = 1 \wedge S = \{v\}; \langle x, 1 \rangle \mapsto v\}$$
$$\mid \quad tag = 0 \Rightarrow \{n = 1 + n_l + n_r \wedge$$
$$S = \{v\} \cup S_l \cup S_r;$$
$$\langle x, 1 \rangle \mapsto v * \text{ptree}(x + 2, n_l, S_l)$$
$$* \text{ptree}(x + 2 \cdot (1 + n_l), n_r, S_r)\}$$

Fig. 9. (Left) Pointer-based and packed representations of the same binary tree. (Right) An SL predicate for packed trees.

Another real-world application of this kind of programs is data serialization and de-serialization, where data is transformed back and forth between a standard pointer-based representation and an array so that it can be written to disk or sent over the network [16,91]. For example, Fig. 9 shows a pointer-based full binary tree and its serialized (or *packed*) representation, where the nodes are laid out sequentially in pre-order [92]. The right-hand-side of the figure shows an SL predicate ptree that describes packed trees: every node x starts with a *tag* that indicates whether it is a leaf; if x is not a leaf, its left child starts at the address $x + 2$ and its right child at $x + 2 \cdot (1 + n_l)$, where n_l is the size of the left child, which is typically unknown at the level of the program.

Imagine a programmer wants to synthesize functions that translate between these two representations, *i.e.,* `pack` and `unpack` the tree. The most natural specification for `unpack` would be:

$$\{r \mapsto x * \text{packed}(x, sz, S)\}\text{unpack\_simple(loc r)} \left\{ \begin{matrix} r \mapsto y * \text{packed}(x, sz, S) \\ * \text{tree}(y, sz, S) \end{matrix} \right\} \quad (14)$$

This specification, however, cannot be implemented in SSL: when x is an internal node, we do not know the address of its right subtree, so we have nothing to pass into the second recursive call. Instead `unpack` must traverse the packed tree and discover the address of the right subtree by moving past the end of the left subtree; this can be implemented by returning the address past the end of the ptree together with the root of the newly built tree, as a record:

$$\{r \mapsto x * \langle r, 1 \rangle \mapsto \_ * \ldots\} \text{ unpack(loc r) } \{r \mapsto x + 2 \cdot sz * \langle r, 1 \rangle \mapsto y * \ldots\} \quad (15)$$

With this specification, SuSLik is able to synthesize unpack in 20 s (benchmark 54 in Table 1); as for pack (benchmark 53), it is within the search space (which we confirmed in interactive mode) but automatic search currently times out after 30 minutes. In the future, it would be great if SuSLik could automatically discover an auxiliary with specification (15), given only (14) as inputs; this is similar to the problem of discovering accumulator parameters, which we discussed in Sect. 4, and is outside of capabilities of cyclic synthesis at the moment.

6.3 Fine-Grained Concurrency

Finally, we envision that deductive logic-based synthesis will make it possible to tackle the challenge of synthesizing provably correct concurrent libraries. The most efficient shared-memory concurrent programs implement custom synchronization patterns via fine-grained primitives, such as *compare-and-set* (CAS). Due to sophisticated interference scenarios between threads, reasoning about such programs is particularly challenging and error-prone, and is the reason for the existence of many extensions of *Concurrent* Separation Logic (CSL) [10,65] for verification of fine-grained concurrency [22,23,36,38,61,85,87–89].

For instance, *Fine-Grained* Concurrent Separation Logic (FCSL) [61,80,81], takes a very specific approach to fine-grained concurrency verification, following the tradition of logics such as LRG [25] and CAP [22] and building on the idea of splitting the specification of a concurrent library to a *resource protocol* and Hoare-style pre/post-conditions. State-of-the art automated tools for fine-grained concurrency verification require one to describe *both* the protocol *and* Hoare-style pre/postconditions for the methods to be verified [21,94]. We believe, it should be possible to take those two components and instead synthesize the concurrent method implementations. The resource protocol will provide an extended set of language primitives to compose programs from. Those data structure-specific primitives can be easily specified in FCSL and contribute *derived* inference rules describing when these primitives can be used safely.

Acknowledgements. We thank Andreea Costea and Yutaka Nagashima for their feedback on the drafts of this paper. This research was supported by the National Science Foundation under Grant No. 1911149, by the Israeli Science Foundation (ISF) Grants No. 243/19 and 2740/19, by the United States-Israel Binational Science Foundation (BSF) Grant No. 2018675, by Singapore MoE Tier 1 Grant No. IG18-SG102, and by the Grant of Singapore NRF National Satellite of Excellence in Trustworthy Software Systems (NSoE-TSS).

References

1. Acclavio, M., Straßburger, L.: From syntactic proofs to combinatorial proofs. In: Galmiche, D., Schulz, S., Sebastiani, R. (eds.) IJCAR 2018. LNCS (LNAI), vol. 10900, pp. 481–497. Springer, Cham (2018). https://doi.org/10.1007/978-3-319-94205-6_32

2. Alur, R., et al.: Syntax-guided synthesis. In: FMCAD, pp. 1–8. IEEE (2013)
3. Alur, R., Radhakrishna, A., Udupa, A.: Scaling enumerative program synthesis via divide and conquer. In: Legay, A., Margaria, T. (eds.) TACAS 2017. LNCS, vol. 10205, pp. 319–336. Springer, Heidelberg (2017). https://doi.org/10.1007/978-3-662-54577-5_18
4. Appel, A.W., et al.: Program Logics for Certified Compilers. Cambridge University Press (2014)
5. Balog, M., Gaunt, A.L., Brockschmidt, M., Nowozin, S., Tarlow, D.: Deepcoder: learning to write programs. arXiv preprint arXiv:1611.01989 (2016)
6. Barke, S., Peleg, H., Polikarpova, N.: Just-in-time learning for bottom-up enumerative synthesis. Proc. ACM Program. Lang. 4(OOPSLA), 227:1–227:29 (2020)
7. Berdine, J., Calcagno, C., O'Hearn, P.W.: Symbolic execution with separation logic. In: Yi, K. (ed.) APLAS 2005. LNCS, vol. 3780, pp. 52–68. Springer, Heidelberg (2005). https://doi.org/10.1007/11575467_5
8. Blaauwbroek, L., Urban, J., Geuvers, H.: Tactic learning and proving for the coq proof assistant. In: LPAR. EPiC Series in Computing, vol. 73, pp. 138–150. EasyChair (2020)
9. Blanchette, J.C., Greenaway, D., Kaliszyk, C., Kühlwein, D., Urban, J.: A learning-based fact selector for Isabelle/HOL. J. Autom. Reason. 57(3), 219–244 (2016)
10. Brookes, S., O'Hearn, P.W.: Concurrent separation logic. ACM SIGLOG News 3(3), 47–65 (2016)
11. Brotherston, J., Bornat, R., Calcagno, C.: Cyclic proofs of program termination in separation logic. In: POPL, pp. 101–112. ACM (2008)
12. Calcagno, C., Distefano, D.: Infer: an automatic program verifier for memory safety of C programs. In: Bobaru, M., Havelund, K., Holzmann, G.J., Joshi, R. (eds.) NFM 2011. LNCS, vol. 6617, pp. 459–465. Springer, Heidelberg (2011). https://doi.org/10.1007/978-3-642-20398-5_33
13. Calcagno, C., Distefano, D., O'Hearn, P.W., Yang, H.: Compositional shape analysis by means of bi-abduction. J. ACM 58(6), 26:1–26:66 (2011)
14. Chajed, T., Tassarotti, J., Kaashoek, M.F., Zeldovich, N.: Verifying concurrent, crash-safe systems with perennial. In: SOSP, pp. 243–258. ACM (2019)
15. Chen, Y., Wang, C., Bastani, O., Dillig, I., Feng, Yu.: Program synthesis using deduction-guided reinforcement learning. In: Lahiri, S.K., Wang, C. (eds.) CAV 2020. LNCS, vol. 12225, pp. 587–610. Springer, Cham (2020). https://doi.org/10.1007/978-3-030-53291-8_30
16. Chilimbi, T.M., Hill, M.D., Larus, J.R.: Cache-conscious structure layout. In: PLDI, pp. 1–12. ACM (1999)
17. Chin, W.-N., David, C., Nguyen, H.H., Qin, S.: Automated verification of shape, size and bag properties via user-defined predicates in separation logic. Sci. Comput. Program. 77(9), 1006–1036 (2012)
18. Chlipala, A.: Mostly-automated verification of low-level programs in computational separation logic. In: PLDI, pp. 234–245. ACM (2011)
19. Costea, A., Zhu, A., Polikarpova, N., Sergey, I.: Concise read-only specifications for better synthesis of programs with pointers. In: ESOP 2020. LNCS, vol. 12075, pp. 141–168. Springer, Cham (2020). https://doi.org/10.1007/978-3-030-44914-8_6
20. Delignat-Lavaud, A., et al.: Implementing and proving the tls 1.3 record layer. In: S&P, pp. 463–482. IEEE Computer Society (2017)
21. Dinsdale-Young, T., da Rocha Pinto, P., Andersen, K.J., Birkedal, L.: CAPER: automatic verification for fine-grained concurrency. In: Yang, H. (ed.) ESOP 2017. LNCS, vol. 10201, pp. 420–447. Springer, Heidelberg (2017). https://doi.org/10.1007/978-3-662-54434-1_16

22. Dinsdale-Young, T., Dodds, M., Gardner, P., Parkinson, M.J., Vafeiadis, V.: Concurrent abstract predicates. In: D'Hondt, T. (ed.) ECOOP 2010. LNCS, vol. 6183, pp. 504–528. Springer, Heidelberg (2010). https://doi.org/10.1007/978-3-642-14107-2_24

23. Dodds, M., Feng, X., Parkinson, M., Vafeiadis, V.: Deny-guarantee reasoning. In: Castagna, G. (ed.) ESOP 2009. LNCS, vol. 5502, pp. 363–377. Springer, Heidelberg (2009). https://doi.org/10.1007/978-3-642-00590-9_26

24. Eguchi, S., Kobayashi, N., Tsukada, T.: Automated synthesis of functional programs with auxiliary functions. In: Ryu, S. (ed.) APLAS 2018. LNCS, vol. 11275, pp. 223–241. Springer, Cham (2018). https://doi.org/10.1007/978-3-030-02768-1_13

25. Feng, X.: Local rely-guarantee reasoning. In: POPL, pp. 315–327. ACM (2009)

26. Ferraiuolo, A., Baumann, A., Hawblitzel, C., Parno, B.: Komodo: Using verification to disentangle secure-enclave hardware from software. In: SOSP, pp. 287–305. ACM (2017)

27. Frankle, J., Osera, P.-M., Walker, D., Zdancewic, S.: Example-directed synthesis: a type-theoretic interpretation. In: POPL, pp. 802–815. ACM (2016)

28. Gauthier, T., Kaliszyk, C., Urban, J.: TacticToe: learning to reason with HOL4 tactics. In: LPAR, EPiC Series in Computing, vol. 46, pp. 125–143. EasyChair (2017)

29. Girard, J.-Y.: Linear logic. Theor. Comput. Sci. **50**, 1–102 (1987)

30. Le Goues, C., Pradel, M., Roychoudhury, A.: Automated program repair. Commun. ACM **62**(12), 56–65 (2019)

31. Gu, R., et al.: Certikos: an extensible architecture for building certified concurrent OS kernels. In: OSDI, pp. 653–669. USENIX Association (2016)

32. Huang, K., Qiu, X., Shen, P., Wang, Y.: Reconciling enumerative and deductive program synthesis. In: PLDI, pp. 1159–1174. ACM (2020)

33. Hughes, D.J.D.: Unification nets: Canonical proof net quantifiers. In: LICS, pp. 540–549. ACM (2018)

34. Itzhaky, S., Peleg, H., Polikarpova, N., Rowe, RN.S., Sergey, I.: Cyclic program synthesis. In: PLDI. ACM (2021)

35. Itzhaky, S., Peleg, H., Polikarpova, N., Rowe, R.N.S., Sergey, I.: SuSLik (CAV 2021 Artifact): Code and Benchmarks, May 2021. https://doi.org/10.5281/zenodo.4850342

36. Jacobs, B., Piessens, F.: Expressive modular fine-grained concurrency specification. In: POPL, pp. 271–282. ACM (2011)

37. Jacobs, B., Smans, J., Philippaerts, P., Vogels, F., Penninckx, W., Piessens, F.: VeriFast: a powerful, sound, predictable, fast verifier for C and Java. In: Bobaru, M., Havelund, K., Holzmann, G.J., Joshi, R. (eds.) NFM 2011. LNCS, vol. 6617, pp. 41–55. Springer, Heidelberg (2011). https://doi.org/10.1007/978-3-642-20398-5_4

38. Jung, R., Krebbers, R., Jourdan, J.-H., Bizjak, A., Birkedal, L., Dreyer, D.: Iris from the ground up: a modular foundation for higher-order concurrent separation logic. J. Funct. Program. **28**, E20 (2018)

39. Kalyan, A., Mohta, A., Polozov, O., Batra, D., Jain, P., Gulwani, S.: Neural-guided deductive search for real-time program synthesis from examples. In: ICLR. OpenReview.net (2018)

40. Kawahara, T., Ito, K., Takemura, R., Ohno, H.: Spin-transfer torque RAM technology: review and prospect. Microelectron. Reliab. **52**(4), 613–627 (2012)

41. Klein, G.: SeL4: formal verification of an OS kernel. In: SOSP, pp. 207–220. ACM (2009)

42. Kneuss, E., Koukoutos, M., Kuncak, V.: Deductive program repair. In: Kroening, D., Păsăreanu, C.S. (eds.) CAV 2015. LNCS, vol. 9207, pp. 217–233. Springer, Cham (2015). https://doi.org/10.1007/978-3-319-21668-3_13

43. Kneuss, E., Kuraj, I., Kuncak, V., Suter, P.: Synthesis modulo recursive functions. In: OOPSLA, pp. 407–426. ACM (2013)

44. Knoth, T., Wang, D., Polikarpova, N., Hoffmann, J.: Resource-guided program synthesis. In: PLDI, pp. 253–268. ACM (2019)

45. Lee, B.C., Ipek, E., Mutlu, O., Burger, D.: Architecting phase change memory as a scalable dram alternative. In: ISCA, pp. 2–13. ACM (2009)

46. Lee, W., Heo, K., Alur, R., Naik, M.: Accelerating search-based program synthesis using learned probabilistic models. In: PLDI. ACM (2018)

47. Rustan, K., Leino, M., Milicevic, A.: Program extrapolation with jennisys. In: OOPSLA, pp. 411–430. ACM (2012)

48. Leroy, X.: Formal certification of a compiler back-end or: programming a compiler with a proof assistant. In: POPL, pp. 42–54. ACM (2006)

49. Loos, S.M., Irving, G., Szegedy, C., Kaliszyk, C.: Deep network guided proof search. In: LPAR, EPiC Series in Computing, vol. 46, pp. 85–105. EasyChair (2017)

50. Madhusudan, P., Qiu, X., Stefanescu, A.: Recursive proofs for inductive tree data-structures. In: POPL, pp. 123–136. ACM (2012)

51. Malcolm, G.: Data structures and program transformation. Sci. Comput. Program. **14**(2–3), 255–279 (1990)

52. Manna, Z., Waldinger, R.J.: A deductive approach to program synthesis. ACM Trans. Program. Lang. Syst. **2**(1), 90–121 (1980)

53. Andreoli, J.: Logic programming with focusing proofs in linear logic. J. Logic Comput. **2**, 297–347 (1992)

54. Martelli, A., Montanari, U.: Additive AND/OR graphs. In: IJCAI, pp. 1–11. William Kaufmann (1973)

55. Menon, A., Tamuz, O., Gulwani, S., Lampson, B., Kalai, A.: A machine learning framework for programming by example. In: International Conference on Machine Learning, pp. 187–195 (2013)

56. Mével, G., Jourdan, J.-H., Pottier, F.: Time credits and time receipts in iris. In: Caires, L. (ed.) ESOP 2019. LNCS, vol. 11423, pp. 3–29. Springer, Cham (2019). https://doi.org/10.1007/978-3-030-17184-1_1

57. Müller, P., Schwerhoff, M., Summers, A.J.: Viper: a verification infrastructure for permission-based reasoning. In: Jobstmann, B., Leino, K.R.M. (eds.) VMCAI 2016. LNCS, vol. 9583, pp. 41–62. Springer, Heidelberg (2016). https://doi.org/10.1007/978-3-662-49122-5_2

58. Nagashima, Y.: LiFtEr: language to encode induction heuristics for Isabelle/HOL. In: Lin, A.W. (ed.) APLAS 2019. LNCS, vol. 11893, pp. 266–287. Springer, Cham (2019). https://doi.org/10.1007/978-3-030-34175-6_14

59. Nagashima, Y.: Smart Induction for Isabelle/HOL (Tool Paper). In: FMCAD, pp. 245–254. IEEE (2020)

60. Nagashima, Y., He, Y.: PaMpeR: proof method recommendation system for Isabelle/HOL. In: ASE, pp. 362–372. ACM (2018)

61. Nanevski, A., Ley-Wild, R., Sergey, I., Delbianco, G.A.: Communicating state transition systems for fine-grained concurrent resources. In: Shao, Z. (ed.) ESOP 2014. LNCS, vol. 8410, pp. 290–310. Springer, Heidelberg (2014). https://doi.org/10.1007/978-3-642-54833-8_16

62. Nanevski, A., Vafeiadis, V., Berdine, J.: Structuring the verification of heap-manipulating programs. In: POPL, pp. 261–274. ACM (2010)

63. Nguyen, T.-T., Ta, Q.-T., Sergey, I., Chin, W.-N.: Automated repair of heap-manipulating programs using deductive synthesis. In: Henglein, F., Shoham, S., Vizel, Y. (eds.) VMCAI 2021. LNCS, vol. 12597, pp. 376–400. Springer, Cham (2021). https://doi.org/10.1007/978-3-030-67067-2_17
64. Ni, Z., Shao, Z.: Certified assembly programming with embedded code pointers. In: POPL, pp. 320–333. ACM (2006)
65. O'Hearn, P.W.: Resources, concurrency, and local reasoning. Theor. Comput. Sci. **375**(1–3), 271–307 (2007)
66. O'Hearn, P., Reynolds, J., Yang, H.: Local reasoning about programs that alter data structures. In: Fribourg, L. (ed.) CSL 2001. LNCS, vol. 2142, pp. 1–19. Springer, Heidelberg (2001). https://doi.org/10.1007/3-540-44802-0_1
67. Osera, P.-M., Zdancewic, S.: Type-and-example-directed program synthesis. In: PLDI, pp. 619–630. ACM (2015)
68. Piskac, R., Wies, T., Zufferey, D.: GRASShopper: complete heap verification with mixed specifications. In: Ábrahám, E., Havelund, K. (eds.) TACAS 2014. LNCS, vol. 8413, pp. 124–139. Springer, Heidelberg (2014). https://doi.org/10.1007/978-3-642-54862-8_9
69. Polikarpova, N., Kuraj, I., Solar-Lezama, A.: Program synthesis from polymorphic refinement types. In: PLDI, pp. 522–538. ACM (2016)
70. Polikarpova, N., Sergey, I.: Structuring the synthesis of heap-manipulating programs. Proc. ACM Program. Lang. **3**(POPL), 72:1-72:30 (2019)
71. Protzenko, J., et al.: Evercrypt: a fast, verified, cross-platform cryptographic provider. In: S&P, pp. 983–1002. IEEE Computer Society (2020)
72. Qiu, X., Solar-Lezama, A.: Natural synthesis of provably-correct data-structure manipulations. PACMPL **1**(OOPSLA), 65:1–65:28 (2017)
73. Ramananandro, T., et al.: Everparse: verified secure zero-copy parsers for authenticated message formats. In: USENIX Security Symposium, pp. 1465–1482. USENIX Association (2019)
74. Reynolds, A., Kuncak, V., Tinelli, C., Barrett, C.W., Deters, M.: Refutation-based synthesis in SMT. Formal Meth. Syst. Des. **55**(2), 73–102 (2019)
75. Reynolds, J.C.: Separation logic: a logic for shared mutable data structures. In: LICS, pp. 55–74. IEEE Computer Society (2002)
76. Rowe, R.N.S., Brotherston, J.: Automatic cyclic termination proofs for recursive procedures in separation logic. In: CPP, pp. 53–65. ACM (2017)
77. Saha, S., Garg, P., Madhusudan, P.: Alchemist: learning guarded affine functions. In: Kroening, D., Păsăreanu, C.S. (eds.) CAV 2015. LNCS, vol. 9206, pp. 440–446. Springer, Cham (2015). https://doi.org/10.1007/978-3-319-21690-4_26
78. Sanchez-Stern, A., Alhessi, Y., Saul, L., Lerner, S.: Generating correctness proofs with neural networks. In: Proceedings of the 4th ACM SIGPLAN International Workshop on Machine Learning and Programming Languages, pp. 1–10. ACM (2020)
79. Scherer, G., Rémy, D.: Which simple types have a unique inhabitant? In: ICFP, pp. 243–255. ACM (2015)
80. Sergey, I., Nanevski, A., Banerjee, A.: Mechanized verification of fine-grained concurrent programs. In: PLDI, pp. 77–87. ACM (2015)
81. Sergey, I., Nanevski, A., Banerjee, A., Delbianco, G.A.: Hoare-style specifications as correctness conditions for non-linearizable concurrent objects. In: OOPSLA, pp. 92–110. ACM (2016)
82. Si, X., Yang, Y., Dai, H., Naik, M., Song, L.: Learning a meta-solver for syntax-guided program synthesis. In: International Conference on Learning Representations (2019)

83. Srivastava, S., Gulwani, S., Foster, J.S.: From program verification to program synthesis. In: POPL, pp. 313–326. ACM (2010)
84. Strukov, D.B., Snider, G.S., Stewart, D.R., Williams, R.S.: The missing memristor found. Nature **453**, 80–83 (2008)
85. Svendsen, K., Birkedal, L.: Impredicative concurrent abstract predicates. In: Shao, Z. (ed.) ESOP 2014. LNCS, vol. 8410, pp. 149–168. Springer, Heidelberg (2014). https://doi.org/10.1007/978-3-642-54833-8_9
86. Trinh, M.-T., Le, Q.L., David, C., Chin, W.-N.: Bi-abduction with pure properties for specification inference. In: Shan, C. (ed.) APLAS 2013. LNCS, vol. 8301, pp. 107–123. Springer, Cham (2013). https://doi.org/10.1007/978-3-319-03542-0_8
87. Turon, A.: Understanding and expressing scalable concurrency. Ph.D. thesis, Northeastern University (2013)
88. Turon, A.J., Thamsborg, J., Ahmed, A., Birkedal, L., Dreyer, D.: Logical relations for fine-grained concurrency. In: POPL, pp. 343–356. ACM (2013)
89. Vafeiadis, V., Parkinson, M.: A marriage of rely/guarantee and separation logic. In: Caires, L., Vasconcelos, V.T. (eds.) CONCUR 2007. LNCS, vol. 4703, pp. 256–271. Springer, Heidelberg (2007). https://doi.org/10.1007/978-3-540-74407-8_18
90. van Tonder, R., Le Goues, C.: Static automated program repair for heap properties. In: ICSE, pp. 151–162 ACM (2018)
91. Vollmer, M., Koparkar, C., Rainey, M., Sakka, L., Kulkarni, M., Newton, R.R.: LoCal: a language for programs operating on serialized data. In: PLDI, pp. 48–62. ACM (2019)
92. Vollmer, M., et al.: Compiling tree transforms to operate on packed representations. In: ECOOP. LIPIcs, , vol. 74, pp. 26:1–26:29. Schloss Dagstuhl (2017)
93. Watanabe, Y., Gopinathan, K., Pîrlea, G., Polikarpova, N., Sergey, I.: Certifying the synthesis of heap-manipulating programs (2021). Conditionally accepted at ICFP'21
94. Windsor, M., Dodds, M., Simner, B., Parkinson, M.J.: Starling: lightweight concurrency verification with views. In: Majumdar, R., Kunčak, V. (eds.) CAV 2017. LNCS, vol. 10426, pp. 544–569. Springer, Cham (2017). https://doi.org/10.1007/978-3-319-63387-9_27
95. Yang, K., Deng, J.: Learning to prove theorems via interacting with proof assistants. In: ICML. PMLR, , vol. 97, pp. 6984–6994 (2019)
96. Zinzindohoué, J.-K., Bhargavan, K., Protzenko, J., Beurdouche, B.: HACL*: a verified modern cryptographic library. In: CCS, pp. 1789–1806. ACM (2017)

AI Verification

DNNV: A Framework for Deep Neural Network Verification

David Shriver(✉) ⓘ, Sebastian Elbaum ⓘ,
and Matthew B. Dwyer ⓘ

University of Virginia, Charlottesville, VA, USA
{dls2fc,selbaum,matthewbdwyer}@virginia.edu

Abstract. Despite the large number of sophisticated deep neural network (DNN) verification algorithms, DNN verifier developers, users, and researchers still face several challenges. First, verifier developers must contend with the rapidly changing DNN field to support new DNN operations and property types. Second, verifier users have the burden of selecting a verifier input format to specify their problem. Due to the many input formats, this decision can greatly restrict the verifiers that a user may run. Finally, researchers face difficulties in re-using benchmarks to evaluate and compare verifiers, due to the large number of input formats required to run different verifiers. Existing benchmarks are rarely in formats supported by verifiers other than the one for which the benchmark was introduced. In this work we present DNNV, a framework for reducing the burden on DNN verifier researchers, developers, and users. DNNV standardizes input and output formats, includes a simple yet expressive DSL for specifying DNN properties, and provides powerful simplification and reduction operations to facilitate the application, development, and comparison of DNN verifiers. We show how DNNV increases the support of verifiers for existing benchmarks from 30% to 74%.

Keywords: Deep neural networks · Formal verification · Tool

1 Introduction

Deep neural networks (DNN) are being applied increasingly in complex domains including safety critical systems such as autonomous driving [3, 7]. For such applications, it is often necessary to obtain behavioral guarantees about the safety of the system. To address this need, researchers have been exploring algorithms for verifying that the behavior of a trained DNN meets some correctness property. In the past few years, more than 20 DNN verification algorithms have been introduced [2, 4, 6, 8–11, 15, 21, 22, 24–27, 29–34, 36], and this number continues to grow. Unfortunately, this progress is hindered by several challenges.

First, DNN verifier developers must contend with a rapidly changing field that continually incorporates new DNN operations and property types. While supporting more properties and operations may increase the applicable scope

© The Author(s) 2021
A. Silva and K. R. M. Leino (Eds.) CAV 2021, LNCS 12759, pp. 137–150, 2021.
https://doi.org/10.1007/978-3-030-81685-8_6

Table 1. The network and property formats supported by each verifier. A * indicates that only a subset of the full input format specification is supported.

Verifier	Network format	Property format	Algorithmic approach
Reluplex [16]	Reluplex-NNET	Hard-coded	Search
Planet [10]	RLV	RLV	Search
BaB [6]	RLV	RLV	Search
BaBSB [6]	RLV	RLV	Search
MIPVerify [29]	MIPVerify Julia API	MIPVerify Julia API	Optimization
Neurify [30]	Neurify-NNET	Hard-coded	Search-optimization
DeepZono [25]	ONNX*, ERAN-PYT, ERAN-TF	ERAN Python API	Reachability
DeepPoly [26]	ONNX*, ERAN-PYT, ERAN-TF	ERAN Python API	Reachability
RefineZono [27]	ONNX*, ERAN-PYT, ERAN-TF	ERAN Python API	Reachability
RefinePoly [24]	ONNX*, ERAN-PYT, ERAN-TF	ERAN Python API	Reachability
Marabou [17]	Reluplex-NNET or ONNX*	Marabou Python API	Search
nnenum [1]	ONNX*	nnenum Python API	Search-reachability
VeriNet [14]	ONNX* or Neurify-NNET	VeriNet Python API	Search-optimization

of verifiers to real-world problems, it also increases a verifier's complexity. For example, for a verifier such as *DeepPoly*, supporting additional operations requires non-trivial effort to define and prove correctness of new abstract transformers. For verifiers such as *Reluplex* or *Neurify*, supporting new property types requires implementing a mapping from those properties onto internal verifier structures.

Second, DNN verifier users carry the burden of re-writing property specifications and transforming their models to match a chosen verifier's supported format. That burden is compounded by the diversity of input formats required by each verifier, as illustrated in Table 1. There is little overlap between input formats for verifiers (only *DeepZono* and *DeepPoly* or *BaB* and *BaBSB* which are algorithmically similar), and even when using the same format (as in the case of the popular ONNX format) we find that the underlying operations supported are different. This makes it difficult and costly to run multiple verifiers on a given problem since the user must understand the requirements of each verifier and translate inputs to their formats. While two new formats, VNNLIB [13] and SOCRATES [20], have been introduced in an attempt to standardize DNN verifier input formats, their expressiveness is currently limited and they can require writing new conversion tools for networks, as we discuss at the end of Sect. 3.1.

Finally, DNN verifier researchers face challenges in re-using benchmarks to evaluate and compare verifiers. Most benchmarks exist in the format of the verifier for which they were introduced, and running other verifiers on that benchmark requires writing custom tooling to translate the benchmark to other formats, or writing new input parsers for verifiers to support the given benchmark format. For example, the ACAS Xu benchmark (described in Sect. 5), was originally specified with networks in *Reluplex*-NNET format, and properties hardcoded into the verifier. The benchmark was converted, for example, into RLV format for *BaB* and *BaBSB*, as well as into ONNX with hard-coded properties for *RefineZono*. Other benchmarks, such as the DAVE benchmark used by *Neurify*, has networks specified in *Neurify*-NNET, and properties hard-coded into the verifier. Due to its format, this potentially great benchmark has not been used by other verifiers.

We introduce a framework, DNNV, *to reduce the burden on verifier researchers, developers, and users.* DNNV helps to create and run more re-usable verification benchmarks by standardizing a network and property format, and it increases the applicability of a verifier to richer properties and real-world benchmarks by performing property reductions and simplifying DNN structures.

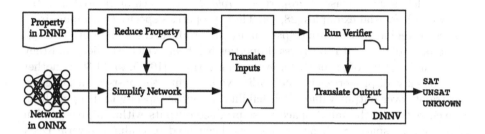

Fig. 1. DNNV architecture

As shown in Fig. 1, DNNV takes as input a network in the common ONNX input format, a property written in an expressive domain-specific language DNNP, and the name of a target verifier. Using the framework and plugins for the target verifier, DNNV transforms the problem by simplifying the network and reducing the property to enable the application of verifiers that otherwise would be unable to run. DNNV then translates the network and property to the input format of the desired verifier, runs that verifier on the transformed problem, and returns the results in a standardized format.

The primary contributions of this work are: (1) the DNNV framework to reduce the burden on DNN verifier researchers, developers, and users; DNNV includes a simple yet expressive DSL for specifying DNN properties, and powerful simplification and reduction operations to increase verifiers' scope of applicability, (2) an open source tool implementing DNNV[1], with support for 13 verifiers, and extensive documentation, and (3) an evaluation demonstrating the cost-effectiveness of DNNV to increase the scope of applicability of verifiers.

2 Background

A deep neural network $\mathcal{N}$ encodes an approximation of a target function $f : \mathbb{R}^n \to \mathbb{R}^m$. A DNN can be represented as a directed graph $G_{\mathcal{N}} = \langle V_{\mathcal{N}}, E_{\mathcal{N}} \rangle$, where nodes, $v \in V_{\mathcal{N}}$, represent operations and edges, $e \in E_{\mathcal{N}}$, represent input

---

[1] https://github.com/dlshriver/DNNV.

arguments to operations. A node without any incoming edges is an input to the DNN. The output of a DNN can be computed by looping over nodes in topological order and computing the value of the node given its inputs. The literature on machine learning has developed a broad range of rich operation types and explored the benefits of different combinations of operations in realizing accurate approximations of different target functions, e.g., [12].

Given a DNN, $\mathcal{N} : \mathbb{R}^n \to \mathbb{R}^m$, a property, $\phi(\mathcal{N})$, defines a set of constraints over the inputs, $\phi_{\mathcal{X}}$ – the pre-condition, and a set of constraints over the outputs, $\phi_{\mathcal{Y}}$ – the post-condition. Verification of $\phi(\mathcal{N})$ seeks to prove or falsify: $\forall x \in \mathbb{R}^n :$ $\phi_{\mathcal{X}}(x) \to \phi_{\mathcal{Y}}(\mathcal{N}(x))$.

A widely studied class of properties is *robustness*, which originated with the study of adversarial examples [28,35]. These properties specify that inputs from a specific region of the input space must all produce the same output class. Detecting violations of robustness properties has been widely studied, and they are a common type of property for evaluating verifiers [10,25,26,29,30]. Another common class of properties is *reachability*, which define the post-condition using constraints over output values. Reachability properties specify that inputs from a given region of the input space must produce outputs within a given region of the output space. Such properties have been used to evaluate several DNN verifiers [16,17,30].

A recent survey on DNN verification [18] classifies these approaches based on their type: reachability, optimization, or search, or a combination of these. Reachability-based methods compute a representation of the reachable set of outputs from an encoding of the set of inputs that satisfy the pre-condition. The computed output set is often an over-approximation of the true reachable output region. The precision of the computed output region depends on the symbolic representation used, e.g., hyper-rectangles, zonotopes, polyhedra. Reachability-based methods include [11,22,24–27,34]. Optimization-based methods formulate property violations as a threshold for an objective function and use optimization algorithms to attempt to satisfy that threshold. Optimization-based methods include [2,9,21,29,33]. Search-based methods explore regions of the input space where they then formulate reachability or optimization sub-problems. Search-based methods include [6,10,15,16,31,32].

3   DNNV Overview

DNNV remedies several key challenges faced by the DNN verification community. A general overview of DNNV is shown in Fig. 1. DNNV takes in a property and network in a standard format, simplifies the network, reduces the property, translates the network and property to the input format of the verifier, runs the verifier, and translates its output. Each of these components can be customized by verifier specific plugins. We explain these components in more detail below.

3.1 Input Formats

As shown in Table 1, existing verifiers do not support a consistent, common input format for networks and properties. DNNV standardizes the input and output formats to aid the community in creating and running verification benchmarks.

ONNX. For specifying general deep neural network architectures, we choose the open source DNN format ONNX [19]. ONNX can represent real-world networks, is supported by many common frameworks (e.g., PyTorch, MXNet) and conversion tools are available for other frameworks (e.g., TensorFlow, Keras). Our current implementation supports a subset of the ONNX specification that subsumes the subsets of ONNX implemented by the supported verifiers. Table 2 shows the number of ONNX operations supported by each of the verifiers included in DNNV. DNNV supports 40% more operations than the verifier with the next highest support. The ONNX subset supported by DNNV is sufficient for almost all existing verification benchmarks, as well as many real-world networks including VGG16 and ResNet34.

Table 2. The number of ONNX operations supported by each verifier.

Verifier	# ONNX operations
DNNV	31
ERAN	22
nnenum	15
marabou	12
VeriNet	12

DNNP. Due to the lack of a standard format for specifying DNN properties, we develop a Python-embedded DSL for DNN properties, which we call DNNP. DNNP is designed to express any property that can be verified by existing DNN verifiers in a form that is independent of the network. DNNP is described in more detail in Appendix A of the extended version of this paper [23].

We demonstrate DNNP with an example of a local robustness property, shown in Fig. 2. The property specifies that, for all inputs, x_ (Lines 14–23), in the input space (Line 18) and within a hyper-rectangle of radius e centered at the given input x (Line 19), the network should predict the same maximum class for both x_ and x (Line 21). For Fashion MNIST, this means that for all images within an L_∞ distance of e (specified on Line 12) from

```
1   from dnnv.properties import *
2   from torchvision.datasets import FashionMNIST
3   from torchvision.transforms import ToTensor
4
5   N = Network("N")
6   data = FashionMNIST("/tmp", download=True,
7                       transform=ToTensor())
8   mean = 0.2860
9   std = 0.3530
10  i = Parameter("data_idx", type=int, default=1)
11  x = (data[i][0][None, :].numpy() - mean) / std
12  e = Parameter("epsilon", type=float) / std
13
14  Forall(
15    x_,
16    Implies(
17      And(
18        (-mean / std) <= x_ <= ((1 - mean) / std),
19        (x - e) < x_ < (x + e),
20      ),
21      argmax(N(x_)) == argmax(N(x)),
22    ),
23  )
```

Fig. 2. Example of a local robustness property specified with DNNP.

image 1 of the dataset (selected on Lines 10–11), the network should classify all of these images the same as it does for image 1. We first import several Python packages that will be useful for specifying the property (Lines 1–3), including the dataset used to train the network, and a method for data manipulation. Because DNNP allows importing arbitrary Python packages, it enables re-use of the same data loading and manipulation methods used to train a network. After importing the necessary utilities, we define several variables that will be used in the final property expression (Lines 5–12). Two of these variables, i on Line 10 and e on Line 12 are declared as parameters, which allows them to be specified on the command line at run time. The value for e must be provided at run time, since no default value is provided. Finally, we define the semantics of the property specification, using methods provided by DNNP, as well as variables defined above (Lines 14–23).

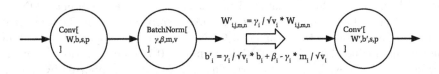

Fig. 3. Batch Normalization Simplification simplifies a batch norm following a convolution operation to an equivalent single convolution operation with modified weights and bias, while maintaining the strides and pads.

Other Input Formats. Since the creation of DNNV, two new input formats, VNNLIB [13] and SOCRATES [20], have emerged in an attempt to standardize the verifier input space. The current draft of VNNLIB also uses ONNX as the DNN input format, however it supports a much smaller set of operations than DNNV, supporting only 17 ONNX operations. The VNNLIB property format is a subset of SMTLIB in which variables of the form X_i are implicitly mapped to network inputs and variables of the form Y_i are implicitly mapped to network outputs. In its current form, this specification only supports DNN models with a single flat input tensor and single flat output tensor, whereas DNNP and ONNX can support DNN models with multiple inputs and output tensors of any shape. SOCRATES proposes a JSON format containing both the property and network specifications. Because DNNV treats networks and properties independently, properties can be re-used for multiple networks, and only a single network must be stored to check multiple properties, resulting in a lower storage cost, especially for large models. Additionally, while the custom JSON format used by SOCRATES requires new DNN translation tools to be written to convert to the required format, the ONNX format used by DNNV is commonly available in most machine learning frameworks. While we believe that ONNX and DNNP are currently the most expressive and easily accessible input formats currently proposed, DNNV can provide benefits to any format through DNN simplification and property reduction to increase the applicability of all verifiers.

3.2 Network Simplification

In order to allow verifiers to be applied to a wider range of real world networks, DNNV provides tools for network simplification. Network simplification takes in an operation graph and applies a set of semantics preserving transformations to the operation graph to remove unsupported structures, or to transform sequences of operations into a single more commonly supported operation.

An operation graph $G_{\mathcal{N}} = \langle V_{\mathcal{N}}, E_{\mathcal{N}} \rangle$ is a directed graph where nodes, $v \in V_{\mathcal{N}}$ represent operations, and edges $e \in E_{\mathcal{N}}$ represent inputs to those operations. Simplification, $simplify : \mathcal{G} \to \mathcal{G}$, transforms an operation graph $G_{\mathcal{N}} \in \mathcal{G}$, to an equivalent DNN with more commonly supported structure, $simplify(G_{\mathcal{N}}) = G_{\mathcal{N}'}$, such that the resulting DNN has the same behavior as the original $\forall x. \mathcal{N}(x) = \mathcal{N}'(x)$, and uses more commonly supported structures.

One such simplification is *batch normalization simplification*, which removes batch normalization operations from a network by combining them with a preceding convolution operation or generalized matrix multiplication (GEMM) operation. This is possible since batch normalization, convolution, and GEMM operations are all affine operations. The simplification of a batch normalization operation following a convolution operation is shown in Fig. 3. If no applicable preceding layer exists, the batch normalization layer is converted into an equivalent convolution operation. This simplification enables the application of verifiers without explicit support for batch normalization operations, such as *Neurify* and *Marabou*, to networks with these operations.

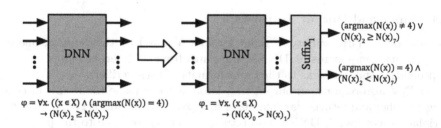

Fig. 4. Property reduction to a local robustness property adds a suffix that classifies outputs as violations or non-violations of the original output constraints, and changing the property to a common form of robustness property.

DNNV currently includes 6 additional DNN simplifications, enumerated and described in more detail in Appendix B of the extended version of this paper [23].

3.3 Property Reduction

In order to allow verifiers to be applied to more general safety properties, DNNV provides tools to reduce properties to a supported form. For instance, properties can be translated to local robustness properties, which are required by *MIPVerify* or reachability properties which are required by *Reluplex*.

Property reduction takes in a verification problem, which is comprised of a property specification and a network, and encodes it as an equivalid set of verification problems with properties in a form supported by a given verifier.

A *verification problem* is a pair, $\psi = \langle \mathcal{N}, \phi \rangle$, of a DNN, $\mathcal{N}$, and a property specification ϕ, formed to determine whether $\mathcal{N} \models \phi$ is *valid*. Reduction, $reduce : \Psi \to P(\Psi)$, aims to transform a verification problem, $\langle \mathcal{N}, \phi \rangle = \psi \in \Psi$, to an equivalid form, $reduce(\psi) = \{\langle \mathcal{N}_1, \phi_1 \rangle, \ldots, \langle \mathcal{N}_k, \phi_k \rangle\}$, in which property specifications are in a common supported form. As defined, reduction has two key properties. The first property is that the set of resulting problems is equivalid with the original verification problem. The second property is that the resulting set of problems all use the same property type. Applying reduction enables verifiers to support a large set of verification problems by implementing support for a single property type.

For example, given a network that classifies images of clothing items, a user may want to specify that, if the network classifies an image as a coat, then the score given to the class of a pullover is not less than the score for the sneaker class. The property is specified in the bottom left of Fig. 4. Such a verification problem can be difficult to specify for many verifiers. For example, *Neurify* would require writing code to specify linear constraints for the property and re-compiling the verifier, and *MIPVerify* cannot support this property as is. DNNV can reduce this verification problem to an equivalent problem with a robustness property.

A high level overview of this reduction is shown in Fig. 4; a more detailed description is provided in Appendix C of the extended version of this paper [23].

3.4 Input and Output Translation

Because of the large variety of input formats required by the verifiers, one of the primary components of DNNV translates from its internal representation of properties and networks to the input formats of each verifier.

DNNV also requires an output translator that can parse the results of running a verifier and returns sat, unsat, or unknown. If the result is sat, indicating a violation was found, DNNV also returns a counter example to the property, and validates that it does violate the property by performing inference with the network and confirming that the input and output do not satisfy the property.

4   Implementation

DNNV is written in 8400 lines of Python code and is available for download and re-use at https://doi.org/10.5281/zenodo.4883626. Python was chosen due to its ubiquitous use for developing deep neural networks. DNNV currently supports 13 verifiers, and was designed to facilitate the integration of new verifiers. The currently supported verifiers are shown in Table 1, along with their original input formats, and algorithmic approach. Around 2000 LOC (of the 8400 total LOC) are used to integrate these 13 verifiers into DNNV, with *Planet* requiring the most effort at 437 lines, and *BaB* and *BaBSB* requiring the least effort with 89 lines of code due to re-use of the *Planet* input translator.

4.1   Supporting Reuse and Extension

DNNV is designed to facilitate the integration of new verifiers. The 5 primary components of DNNV, DNN simplification, property reduction, input translation, verifier execution, and output translation are designed to be re-usable, and to facilitate the implementation of new components by providing utilities for traversing and manipulating operation graphs and properties.

Networks are represented as an operation graph, where nodes represent operations in the DNN and edges represent inputs and outputs to those operations. The operation graph can also be traversed using a visitor pattern. This pattern is particularly useful for the development of DNN simplifications and input translators. It allows developers to easily traverse computation graphs in order to translate operations to the required format. We provide built-in utilities for converting from our internal network representation to ONNX, PyTorch, and TensorFlow models. The implementation also includes utilities for performing pattern matching on operation graphs. We utilize this feature to provide utilities that transform a network from an operation graph representation to a sequential layer representation, which is particularly useful for the network input translator of *Neurify*, which requires DNNs to have a regular structure of a set of convolutional layers followed by fully connected layers, all with relu activations.

4.2   Usage

DNNV can be run from the command line as follows: `python -m dnnv <prop>` `<verifier> --network <name> <path>`, where the arguments correspond to a DNN model in the ONNX format, a property written in DNNP, and the verifier to run. Many additional options can be seen by specifying the `-h` option.

After execution, for each verifier, DNNV reports the verification result as one of `sat` (if the property was falsified), `unsat` (if the property was proven to hold), `unknown` (if the verifier is incomplete and could not prove the property holds), or `error`, along with the reason for error, if an error occurs during DNN and property translation, or during verifier execution. DNNV also reports the time to translate and verify the property.

5   Study

We now examine the applicability of verifiers to existing verification benchmarks with and without DNNV. A verification benchmark consists of a set of verification problems which are used to evaluate the performance of a verifier. A problem is made of a DNN and a property specification and asks whether the property is valid for the given DNN. We consider a verifier to support a benchmark if it can be run on that benchmark out of the box. We consider a verifier to have support for a benchmark through DNNV if DNNV can be run on that benchmark with networks specified using ONNX and properties specified in DNNP, and can reduce, simplify, and translate the problem to work with the target verifier.

Benchmarks. To evaluate benchmark support, we collected the benchmarks used by each of the 13 verifiers supported by DNNV, and determined whether each verifier can run on the benchmark out of the box, and also whether they could be run on the benchmark when DNNV is applied. The verification benchmarks are shown in Table 3 and are also described in more detail in Appendix D of the extended version of this paper [23]. Each row of the table corresponds to a benchmark, to which we assign a short key for identifying the benchmark. For each benchmark, we give the name, some of the verifiers it evaluated, the number of properties (#P) and networks (#$\mathcal{N}$), and features that can make it challenging for verifiers. These features include whether any properties cannot represent their input constraints using hyper-rectangles (¬HR), whether any network in the benchmark contains convolution operations (C), whether any network contains residual structures (R), and whether any network uses any non-ReLU activation functions (¬ReLU).

Results. The support of verifiers for each benchmark is shown in Table 4. Each row of this table corresponds to one of the 13 verifiers supported by DNNV, and each column corresponds to one of the 19 benchmarks identified in Table 3. Each

Table 3. Verifier benchmarks.

Key	Name	Uses	#P	#$\mathcal{N}$	Features ¬HR	C	R	¬ReLU
AX	ACAS Xu	[1,6,16,17,30]	10	45				
CD	Collision Detection	[6,10,17]	500	1				
PM	*Planet* MNIST	[10]	7	1	✓	✓		
TS	TwinStream	[5]	1	81				
PCA	PCAMNIST	[6]	12	17				
MM	*MIPVerify* MNIST	[29]	10000	5	✓			
MC	*MIPVerify* CIFAR10	[29]	10000	2	✓	✓		
NM	*Neurify* MNIST	[14,30]	500	4	✓			
NDв	*Neurify* Drebin	[30]	500	3				
NDv	*Neurify* DAVE	[30]	200	1	✓	✓		
DZM	*DeepZono* MNIST	[25]	1700	10		✓	✓	✓
DZC	*DeepZono* CIFAR10	[25]	1700	5		✓		✓
DPM	*DeepPoly* MNIST	[14,26]	1500	8		✓		✓
DPC	*DeepPoly* CIFAR10	[26]	800	5		✓		
RZM	*RefineZono* MNIST	[27]	800	8		✓		
RZC	*RefineZono* CIFAR10	[27]	200	2		✓		
RPM	*RefinePoly* MNIST	[24]	600	6		✓		
RPC	*RefinePoly* CIFAR10	[24]	300	3		✓	✓	
VC	*VeriNet* CIFAR10	[14]	250	1		✓		

Table 4. Benchmark support by each verifier. The left half of the circle is black if the verifier can support the benchmark out of the box, and is white otherwise. The right half is black if the verifier supports the benchmark through DNNV, and is white otherwise. An absent circle indicates that the verifier can not be made to support some aspect of the benchmark.

Verifier	AX	CD	PM	TS	PCA	MM	MC	NM	NDB	NDv	DZM	DZC	DPM	DPC	RZM	RZC	RPM	RPC	VC
Reluplex	●	◑	○	●	●	○	○	○	◑	○				○	○	○	○	○	○
Planet	●	◑	●	●	●	◑	◑	◑	◑	◑				◑	◑	◑	◑	◑	◑
BaB	●	◑	●	●	●	◑	○	◑	◑	◑				◑	◑	◑	◑	○	◑
BaBSB	●	◑	●	●	●	◑	○	◑	◑	◑				◑	◑	◑	◑	○	◑
MIPVerify	◑	○	○	◑	◑	◑	●	◑	○	◑	○			○	○	○	○	○	○
Neurify	●	○	◑	◑	◑	◑	○	●	●	●				◑	◑	◑	◑	○	◑
DeepZono	●	○	○	◑	◑	◑	◑	◑	◑	◑	○	●	●	●	●	●	●	●	◑
DeepPoly	●	○	○	◑	◑	◑	◑	◑	◑	◑	○	●	●	●	●	●	●	●	◑
RefineZono	●	○	○	◑	◑	◑	◑	◑	◑	◑	○	●	●	●	●	●	●	●	◑
RefinePoly	●	○	○	◑	◑	◑	◑	◑	◑	◑	○	●	●	●	●	●	●	●	◑
Marabou	●	◑	◑	●	●	◑	○	◑	◑	◑				◑	◑	◑	◑	○	◑
nnenum	●	○	◑	◑	◑	◑	○	◑	◑	◑				◑	◑	◑	◑	○	◑
VeriNet	◑	○	○	◑	◑	◑	○	●	◑	○	○	◑	◑	◑	◑	◑	◑	○	●

cell of the table may contain a circle that identifies the support of the verifier for the benchmark. The left half of the circle is black if the verifier can support the benchmark out of the box, and is white otherwise. The right half is black if the verifier supports the benchmark through DNNV, and white otherwise. An absent circle indicates that the verifier can not be made to support some aspect of the benchmark. For the benchmarks shown here, this is always due to the presence of non-ReLU activation functions in some of the networks in the benchmarks.

As shown in Table 4, DNNV can dramatically increase the support of verifiers for benchmarks. For example, the *Planet* verifier could originally be run on 5 of the 19 benchmarks, but could be run on 16 using DNNV. Similarly, the *nnenum* verifier, could originally only be run on 1 of the existing benchmarks, but could be run on 13 using DNNV. **Of the 223 pairs of verifiers and benchmarks for which support may be possible, 166 of them are currently supported by DNNV, an increase of over 2.4 times the 68 pairs supported without DNNV.**

6   Conclusion

We present the DNNV framework for reducing the burden on DNN verifier researchers, developers, and users. DNNV standardizes input and output formats, includes a simple yet expressive DSL for specifying DNN properties, and provides powerful simplification and reduction operations to facilitate the application, development, and comparison of DNN verifiers. Our study showed the potential of DNNV and we made its implementation available, with support for 13 verifiers, and extensive documentation.

Acknowledgment. This material is based in part upon work supported by the National Science Foundation under Grant Number 1900676 and 2019239.

References

1. Bak, S., Tran, H.-D., Hobbs, K., Johnson, T.T.: Improved geometric path enumeration for verifying ReLU neural networks. In: Lahiri, S.K., Wang, C. (eds.) CAV 2020. LNCS, vol. 12224, pp. 66–96. Springer, Cham (2020). https://doi.org/10.1007/978-3-030-53288-8_4
2. Bastani, O., Ioannou, Y., Lampropoulos, L., Vytiniotis, D., Nori, A.V., Criminisi, A.: Measuring neural net robustness with constraints. In: Neural Information Processing Systems, NIPS 2016, pp. 2621–2629. Curran Associates Inc., USA (2016)
3. Bojarski, M., et al.: End to end learning for self-driving cars. In: NIPS 2016 Deep Learning Symposium (2016)
4. Boopathy, A., Weng, T.W., Chen, P.Y., Liu, S., Daniel, L.: CNN-Cert: an efficient framework for certifying robustness of convolutional neural networks. AAAI, January 2019
5. Bunel, R., Turkaslan, I., Torr, P.H.S., Kohli, P., Kumar, M.P.: Piecewise linear neural network verification: a comparative study. CoRR abs/1711.00455v1 (2017). http://arxiv.org/abs/1711.00455v1
6. Bunel, R.R., Turkaslan, I., Torr, P.H.S., Kohli, P., Mudigonda, P.K.: A unified view of piecewise linear neural network verification. In: NeurIPS, pp. 4795–4804 (2018)
7. Codevilla, F., Miiller, M., López, A., Koltun, V., Dosovitskiy, A.: End-to-end driving via conditional imitation learning. In: 2018 IEEE International Conference on Robotics and Automation (ICRA), pp. 1–9, May 2018. https://doi.org/10.1109/ICRA.2018.8460487
8. Dutta, S., Jha, S., Sankaranarayanan, S., Tiwari, A.: Output range analysis for deep feedforward neural networks. In: Dutle, A., Muñoz, C., Narkawicz, A. (eds.) NFM 2018. LNCS, vol. 10811, pp. 121–138. Springer, Cham (2018). https://doi.org/10.1007/978-3-319-77935-5_9
9. Dvijotham, K., Stanforth, R., Gowal, S., Mann, T., Kohli, P.: A dual approach to scalable verification of deep networks. In: Conference on Uncertainty in Artificial Intelligence (UAI 2018), pp. 162–171. AUAI Press, Corvallis (2018)
10. Ehlers, R.: Formal verification of piece-wise linear feed-forward neural networks. In: D'Souza, D., Narayan Kumar, K. (eds.) ATVA 2017. LNCS, vol. 10482, pp. 269–286. Springer, Cham (2017). https://doi.org/10.1007/978-3-319-68167-2_19

11. Gehr, T., Mirman, M., Drachsler-Cohen, D., Tsankov, P., Chaudhuri, S., Vechev, M.: AI2: safety and robustness certification of neural networks with abstract interpretation. In: 2018 IEEE Symposium on Security and Privacy (SP), pp. 3–18, May 2018. https://doi.org/10.1109/SP.2018.00058

12. Goodfellow, I., Bengio, Y., Courville, A.: Deep Learning. MIT Press (2016). http://www.deeplearningbook.org

13. Guidotti, D., Barrett, C., Katz, G., Pulina, L., Narodytska, N., Tacchella, A.: The Verification of Neural Networks Library (VNN-LIB) (2019). www.vnnlib.org

14. Henriksen, P., Lomuscio, A.: Efficient neural network verification via adaptive refinement and adversarial search. In: Giacomo, G.D., et al. (eds.) ECAI 2020. Frontiers in Artificial Intelligence and Applications, vol. 325, pp. 2513–2520. IOS Press (2020). https://doi.org/10.3233/FAIA200385

15. Huang, X., Kwiatkowska, M., Wang, S., Wu, M.: Safety verification of deep neural networks. In: Majumdar, R., Kunčak, V. (eds.) CAV 2017. LNCS, vol. 10426, pp. 3–29. Springer, Cham (2017). https://doi.org/10.1007/978-3-319-63387-9_1

16. Katz, G., Barrett, C., Dill, D.L., Julian, K., Kochenderfer, M.J.: Reluplex: an efficient SMT solver for verifying deep neural networks. In: Majumdar, R., Kunčak, V. (eds.) CAV 2017. LNCS, vol. 10426, pp. 97–117. Springer, Cham (2017). https://doi.org/10.1007/978-3-319-63387-9_5

17. Katz, G., et al.: The Marabou framework for verification and analysis of deep neural networks. In: Dillig, I., Tasiran, S. (eds.) CAV 2019. LNCS, vol. 11561, pp. 443–452. Springer, Cham (2019). https://doi.org/10.1007/978-3-030-25540-4_26

18. Liu, C., Arnon, T., Lazarus, C., Barrett, C., Kochenderfer, M.J.: Algorithms for verifying deep neural networks. CoRR abs/1903.06758 (2019)

19. ONNX: Open Neural Network Exchange (2017). https://github.com/onnx/onnx

20. Pham, L.H., Li, J., Sun, J.: SOCRATES: towards a unified platform for neural network verification. CoRR abs/2007.11206 (2020). https://arxiv.org/abs/2007.11206

21. Raghunathan, A., Steinhardt, J., Liang, P.: Certified defenses against adversarial examples. In: ICLR. OpenReview.net (2018)

22. Ruan, W., Huang, X., Kwiatkowska, M.: Reachability analysis of deep neural networks with provable guarantees. In: IJCAI, pp. 2651–2659. ijcai.org (2018)

23. Shriver, D., Elbaum, S., Dwyer, M.B.: DNNV: A framework for deep neural network verification (2021). http://arxiv.org/abs/2105.12841

24. Singh, G., Ganvir, R., Püschel, M., Vechev, M.T.: Beyond the single neuron convex barrier for neural network certification. In: Wallach, H.M., Larochelle, H., Beygelzimer, A., d'Alché-Buc, F., Fox, E.B., Garnett, R. (eds.) Advances in Neural Information Processing Systems 32: NeurIPS 2019, pp. 15072–15083 (2019)

25. Singh, G., Gehr, T., Mirman, M., Püschel, M., Vechev, M.: Fast and effective robustness certification. In: Bengio, S., Wallach, H., Larochelle, H., Grauman, K., Cesa-Bianchi, N., Garnett, R. (eds.) Advances in Neural Information Processing Systems 31, pp. 10802–10813. Curran Associates, Inc. (2018). http://papers.nips.cc/paper/8278-fast-and-effective-robustness-certification.pdf

26. Singh, G., Gehr, T., Püschel, M., Vechev, M.T.: An abstract domain for certifying neural networks. PACMPL 3(POPL), 41:1–41:30 (2019)

27. Singh, G., Gehr, T., Püschel, M., Vechev, M.T.: Boosting robustness certification of neural networks. In: 7th International Conference on Learning Representations, ICLR 2019, New Orleans, LA, USA, 6–9 May 2019. OpenReview.net (2019). https://openreview.net/forum?id=HJgeEh09KQ

28. Szegedy, C., et al.: Intriguing properties of neural networks. In: Bengio, Y., LeCun, Y. (eds.) 2nd International Conference on Learning Representations, ICLR 2014, Banff, AB, Canada, 14–16 April 2014, Conference Track Proceedings (2014)

29. Tjeng, V., Xiao, K.Y., Tedrake, R.: Evaluating robustness of neural networks with mixed integer programming. In: International Conference on Learning Representations (2019). https://openreview.net/forum?id=HyGIdiRqtm

30. Wang, S., Pei, K., Whitehouse, J., Yang, J., Jana, S.: Efficient formal safety analysis of neural networks. In: NeurIPS, pp. 6369–6379 (2018)

31. Wang, S., Pei, K., Whitehouse, J., Yang, J., Jana, S.: Formal security analysis of neural networks using symbolic intervals. In: USENIX Security Symposium, pp. 1599–1614. USENIX Association (2018)

32. Weng, T., et al.: Towards fast computation of certified robustness for RELU networks. In: ICML, Proceedings of Machine Learning Research, vol. 80, pp. 5273–5282. PMLR (2018)

33. Wong, E., Kolter, J.Z.: Provable defenses against adversarial examples via the convex outer adversarial polytope. In: ICML, Proceedings of Machine Learning Research, vol. 80, pp. 5283–5292. PMLR (2018)

34. Xiang, W., Tran, H., Johnson, T.T.: Output reachable set estimation and verification for multilayer neural networks. IEEE Trans. Neural Netw. Learn. Syst. **29**(11), 5777–5783 (2018). https://doi.org/10.1109/TNNLS.2018.2808470

35. Yuan, X., He, P., Zhu, Q., Li, X.: Adversarial examples: attacks and defenses for deep learning. IEEE Trans. Neural Netw. Learn. Syst. **30**(9), 2805–2824 (2019)

36. Zhang, H., Weng, T., Chen, P., Hsieh, C., Daniel, L.: Efficient neural network robustness certification with general activation functions. Adv. Neural Inf. Process. Syst. **31**, 4944–4953 (2018)

Robustness Verification of Quantum Classifiers

Ji Guan[1]([✉]), Wang Fang[1,2], and Mingsheng Ying[1,3,4]

[1] State Key Laboratory of Computer Science,
Institute of Software, Chinese Academy
of Sciences, Beijing 100190, China
{guanj,fangw}@ios.ac.cn

[2] University of Chinese Academy of Sciences, Beijing 100049, China

[3] Center for Quantum Software and Information, University of Technology Sydney,
Ultimo, NSW 2007, Australia
mingsheng.ying@uts.edu.au

[4] Department of Computer Science and Technology, Tsinghua University,
Beijing 100084, China

Abstract. Several important models of machine learning algorithms have been successfully generalized to the quantum world, with potential speedup to training classical classifiers and applications to data analytics in quantum physics that can be implemented on the near future quantum computers. However, quantum noise is a major obstacle to the practical implementation of quantum machine learning. In this work, we define a formal framework for the robustness verification and analysis of quantum machine learning algorithms against noises. A robust bound is derived and an algorithm is developed to check whether or not a quantum machine learning algorithm is robust with respect to quantum training data. In particular, this algorithm can find adversarial examples during checking. Our approach is implemented on Google's TensorFlow Quantum and can verify the robustness of quantum machine learning algorithms with respect to a small disturbance of noises, derived from the surrounding environment. The effectiveness of our robust bound and algorithm is confirmed by the experimental results, including quantum bits classification as the "Hello World" example, quantum phase recognition and cluster excitation detection from real world intractable physical problems, and the classification of MNIST from the classical world.

Keywords: Quantum machine learning · Robustness verification · Adversarial examples · Robust bound

1 Introduction

In the last few years, the successful interplay between machine learning and quantum physics shed new light on both fields. On the one hand, machine learning has been dramatically developed to satisfy the need of the industry over

© The Author(s) 2021
A. Silva and K. R. M. Leino (Eds.) CAV 2021, LNCS 12759, pp. 151–174, 2021.
https://doi.org/10.1007/978-3-030-81685-8_7

the past two decades. At the same time, many challenging quantum physical problems have been solved by automated learning. Notably, inaccessible quantum many-body problems have been solved by neural networks, one instance of machine learning [1]. On the other hand, as the new model of computation under quantum mechanics, quantum computing has been proved that it can (exponentially) speed up classical algorithms for some important problems [2]. This motivates the development of quantum machine learning and provides the possibility of improving the existing computational power of machine learning to a new level (see the review papers [3,4] for the details). After that, quantum machine learning was integrated into solving real world problems in quantum physics. One essential example is that quantum convolutional neural networks inspired by machine learning were proposed to implement quantum phase recognition [5]. Quantum phase recognition asks whether a given input quantum state belongs to a particular quantum phase of matter. At the same time, more provable advantages of quantum machine learning than the classical counterpart have been reported. For instance, the training complexity of quantum models has an exponential improvement on certain tasks [6]. Stepping into industries, Google recently built up a framework *TensorFlow Quantum* for the design and training of quantum machine learning within its famous classical machine learning platform—TensorFlow [7].

Even though quantum machine learning outperforms the classical counterpart in some way, the difficulties in the classical world are expected to be encountered in the quantum case. Classical machine learning has been found to be vulnerable to intentionally crafted adversarial examples (e.g. [8,9]). Adversarial examples are inputs to a machine learning algorithm that an attacker has crafted to cause the algorithm to make a mistake. One essential mission of machine learning is to prove the absence of or detect adversarial examples used in the defense strategy—adversarial training [10]—appending adversarial examples to the training dataset and retraining the machine learning algorithm to be robust to these examples. However, this goal is not easily achieved [11]. The machine learning community has developed several interesting ideas on designing specific attack algorithms (e.g. [10,12]) to generate adversarial examples, which is far from measuring the robustness against any adversary. Recently, the formal method community has taken initial steps in this direction [13–16], by verifying the robustness of classical machine learning algorithms in a provable way: either a formal guarantee that the algorithms are robust for a given input or a counter-example (adversarial example) is provided if an input is not robust. Some tools have been developed, such as VerifAI [17] and NNV [18]. This phenomenon of vulnerability is more common in the quantum world since quantum noise is inevitable in quantum computation, at least in the current NISQ (Noisy Intermediate-Scale Quantum) era, and thus led to a series of recent works on quantum machine learning robustness against specific noises. For example, Lu et al. [19] studied the robustness to various classical adversarial attacks; Du et al. [20] proved that by appending depolarization noise in quantum circuits for classifications, a robust bound against adversaries can be derived; Liu and Wittek [21] gave a robust bound for the quantum noise coming from a special unitary group. Very recently, Weber et al. [22] formalized a link between binary quantum hypothesis testing [23] and robust quantum machine learning algorithms for classification tasks.

Up to our best knowledge, the existing studies of quantum machine learning robustness only consider the situation of a *known* noise source. However, a fundamental difference between quantum and classical machine learning is that the quantum attacker is usually the surroundings instead of humans in the classical case, and the information of the environment is unknown. To protect against an *unknown* adversary, we need to derive a robust guarantee against a worst-case scenario, from which the commonly-assumed known noise sources (e.g. depolarization noise [20]) are usually far. Yet in the case of unknown noise, several basic issues are still unsolved:

- In theory, it is unclear how to compute a tight and even the optimal bound of the robustness for any given quantum machine learning algorithm.
- In practice, an efficient way to find an adversarial example, which can be used to retraining the algorithm to defense the noise, is lacking. Indeed, we do not even know which metric is a better choice measuring the robustness against noise, the same as the classical case against human attackers [24].

In this work, we define a formal framework for the robustness verification and analysis of quantum machine learning algorithms against noises in which the above problems can be studied in a principled way. More specifically, we choose to use fidelity as the metric measuring the robustness as it is one of the most widely used quantities to quantify the uncertainty of noise in the process of quantum computation, and commonly used in quantum engineering and experimental communities (e.g. [25,26]). Based on this, an analytical robust bound for any quantum machine learning classification algorithm is obtained and can be applied to approximately checking the robustness of quantum machine learning algorithms. Furthermore, we show that computing the optimal robust bound can be reduced to solving a Semidefinite Programming (SDP) problem. These results lead to an algorithm to exactly and efficiently check whether or not a quantum machine learning algorithm is robust with respect to the training data. A special strength of this algorithm is that it can identify useful new training data (adversarial examples) during checking, and these data can be used to implement adversarial training as the same as classical robustness verification. The effectiveness of our robust bound and algorithms is confirmed by the case studies of quantum bits classification as the "Hello World" example of quantum machine learning algorithms, quantum phase recognition and cluster excitation detection from real world intractable physical problems, and the classification of MNIST from the classical world.

In summary, the main technical contributions of the paper are as follows.

- *Computing the optimal robust bound* of quantum machine classification algorithms is reduced to an SDP (Semidefinite Programming) problem;

- *An efficient algorithm* to check the robustness of quantum machine learning algorithms and detect adversarial examples is developed;
- The *implementation* of the robustness verification algorithm on Google's TensorFlow Quantum;
- *Case studies* – Checking the robustness of several popular quantum machine learning algorithms for quantum bits classification, cluster excitation detection and the classification of MNIST (which are all implemented in Google's TensorFlow Quantum), and quantum phase recognition.

2   Quantum Data and Computation Models

For the convenience of the reader, in this section, we recall some basic concepts of quantum data (states) and the quantum computation model.

The basic data of classical computers are bits, represented by two digits 0 and 1. In quantum computing, quantum bits (qubit) play the same role. A qubit is expressed by a normalized complex vector $|\phi\rangle = \begin{pmatrix} a \\ b \end{pmatrix} = a|0\rangle + b|1\rangle$ with complex numbers a and b satisfying the normalization condition $|a|^2 + |b|^2 = 1$. Here, $|0\rangle = \begin{pmatrix} 1 \\ 0 \end{pmatrix}$, $|1\rangle = \begin{pmatrix} 0 \\ 1 \end{pmatrix}$ correspond to bits $0, 1$ respectively, and $\{|0\rangle, |1\rangle\}$ is an orthonormal basis of a 2-dimensional Hilbert (linear) space. In general, for a quantum computer consisting of n qubits, a quantum datum is a normalized complex vector $|\psi\rangle$ in a 2^n-dimensional Hilbert space $\mathcal{H}$. Such a $|\psi\rangle$ is usually called a pure state in the literature of quantum computation.

As a model for computation, a quantum circuit consists of a sequence of, say m quantum logic gates. Each quantum gate can be mathematically represented by a unitary matrix U_i on $\mathcal{H}$, i.e., $U_i^\dagger U_i = U_i U_i^\dagger = I$, where $U_i^\dagger$ is the conjugate transpose of U_i and I is the identity matrix on $\mathcal{H}$. Then the circuit is represented by the unitary matrix $U = U_m \cdots U_1$. If the quantum datum $|\psi\rangle$ is inputted to the circuit, then the output is a quantum datum:

$$|\psi'\rangle = U|\psi\rangle. \tag{1}$$

In practice, a quantum datum may not be completely known and can be thought of as a mixed state or ensemble $\{(p_k, |\psi_k\rangle)\}_k$, meaning that it is at $|\psi_k\rangle$ with probability p_k. Mathematically, it can be described by a density operator ρ (Hermitian positive semidefinite matrix with unit trace[1]) on $\mathcal{H}$:

$$\rho = \sum_k p_k |\psi_k\rangle\langle\psi_k|, \tag{2}$$

where $\langle\psi_k|$ is the conjugate transpose of $|\psi_k\rangle$, i.e., $|\psi_k\rangle = \langle\psi_k|^\dagger$. In this case, the model of quantum computation is tuned to be a super-operator $\mathcal{E}$, i.e. a mapping from matrices to matrices. It can be written as

$$\rho' = \mathcal{E}(\rho). \tag{3}$$

---

[1] ρ has unit trace if $\text{tr}(\rho) = 1$, where trace $\text{tr}(\rho)$ of ρ is defined as the summation of diagonal elements of ρ.

Here, ρ and ρ' are the input and output data (mixed states) of quantum computation $\mathcal{E}$, respectively. Not every super-operator $\mathcal{E}$ is meaningful in physics. It is required to satisfy the following conditions:

- $\mathcal{E}$ is trace-preserving: $\mathrm{tr}(\mathcal{E}(\rho)) = \mathrm{tr}(\rho)$ for all mixed state ρ on $\mathcal{H}$;
- $\mathcal{E}$ is completely positive: for any Hilbert space $\mathcal{H}'$, the trivially extended operator $\mathrm{id}_{\mathcal{H}'} \otimes \mathcal{E}$ maps density operators to density operators on $\mathcal{H}' \otimes \mathcal{H}$, where $\otimes$ denotes the tensor product and $\mathrm{id}_{\mathcal{H}'}$ is the identity map on $\mathcal{H}'$.

Such a super-operator $\mathcal{E}$ admits a Kraus matrix form [2]: there exists a set of matrices $\{E_k\}_k$ on $\mathcal{H}$ such that

$$\mathcal{E}(\rho) = \sum_k E_k \rho E_k^\dagger.$$

Here $\{E_k\}_k$ is called Kraus matrices of $\mathcal{E}$ [2].

The behind dynamics of quantum computers is governed by quantum mechanics, which is applied at the microscopic scale (near or less than 10^{-9} meters). At this level, we cannot directly readout the quantum data as the same as the classical counterpart. The only way to extract information from it is through a quantum measurement, which is mathematically modeled by a set $\{M_k\}_{k=1}^m$ of matrices on its state (Hilbert) space $\mathcal{H}$ with $\sum_k M_k^\dagger M_k = I$. This observing process is probabilistic: if the system is currently in state ρ, then a measurement outcome k is obtained with probability

$$p_k = \mathrm{tr}(M_k^\dagger M_k \rho). \tag{4}$$

After the measurement, the system's state will be collapsed (changed), depending on the measurement outcome k, which is vitally different from the classical computation. If the outcome is k, the post-measurement state becomes

$$\rho_k' = \frac{M_k \rho M_k^\dagger}{\mathrm{tr}(M_k^\dagger M_k \rho)}. \tag{5}$$

This special property makes it hard to accurately estimate the distribution $\{p_k\}_k$ unless enough many copies of ρ are provided.

In summary, quantum data have two different forms—pure state $|\psi\rangle$ and mixed state ρ corresponding to the computation model as a unitary matrix U or a super-operator $\mathcal{E}$, respectively. Not surprisingly, the latter is a generalization of the former by putting:

$$\rho = |\psi\rangle\langle\psi|, \qquad \mathcal{E}(\rho) = U\rho U^\dagger.$$

Because of this, the results obtained for mixed states ρ can also be applied to pure states $|\psi\rangle$. Thus, in this paper, we mainly consider mixed states as the quantum data and super-operators as the model of quantum computation.

3 Quantum Classification Algorithms

In this section, we briefly recall quantum classification algorithms. They are designed for *classification of quantum data*. Essentially, they share the same basic ideas with their classical counterparts but deal with quantum data in the quantum computation model.

3.1 Basic Definitions

In this paper, we focus on a specific learning model called quantum supervised classification. Given a Hilbert space $\mathcal{H}$, we write $\mathcal{D}(\mathcal{H})$ for the set of all (mixed) quantum states on $\mathcal{H}$ (see its definition in Eq. (2)).

Definition 1. *A quantum classification algorithm $\mathcal{A}$ is a mapping $\mathcal{D}(\mathcal{H}) \to \mathcal{C}$, where $\mathcal{C}$ is the set of classes we are interested in.*

Following the training strategy of classical machine learning, the classification $\mathcal{A}$ is learned through a dataset T instead of being pre-defined. This training dataset $T = \{(\rho_i, c_i)\}_{i=1}^{N}$ consists of $N < \infty$ pairs (ρ_i, c_i), meaning that quantum state ρ_i belongs to class c_i. To learn $\mathcal{A}$, we initialize a *quantum learning model*—a parameterized quantum circuit (including measurement control) $\mathcal{E}_\theta$ and a measurement $\{M_k\}_{k \in \mathcal{C}}$. Mathematically, the circuit can be modelled as a quantum super-operator $\mathcal{E}_\theta$ (see its definition in Eq. (3)), and θ is a set of free parameters that can be tuned. Then for each $k \in \mathcal{C}$, we can compute the probability of the measurement outcome being k:

$$f_k(\theta, \rho) = \text{tr}(M_k^\dagger M_k \mathcal{E}_\theta(\rho)). \tag{6}$$

It is worth noting that, as we mentioned before, measuring quantum state ρ is probabilistic and ρ will be changed after measuring. So, in practice, accurately estimating $f_k(\theta, \rho)$ for all $k \in \mathcal{C}$ requires enough many copies of ρ, which is not the same as the classical case, where a single copy of classical data often meets the training process.

The quantum classification algorithm $\mathcal{A}$ outputs the class label c for a quantum state ρ using the following condition:

$$\mathcal{A}(\theta, \rho) = \arg \max_k \text{tr}(M_k^\dagger M_k \mathcal{E}_\theta(\rho)). \tag{7}$$

The learning is carried out as θ is optimized to minimize the empirical risk

$$\min_\theta \frac{1}{N} \sum_{i=1}^{N} \mathcal{L}(f(\theta, \rho_i), c_i), \tag{8}$$

where $\mathcal{L}$ refers to a predefined loss function, $f(\theta, \rho)$ is a probability vector with each $f_k(\theta, \rho), k \in \mathcal{C}$ as its element, and c_i is also seen as a probability vector with the entry corresponding to c_i being 1 and others being 0. The goal is to find the optimized parameters θ^* minimizing the risk in Eq. (8) for the given dataset T.

Mean-squared error (MSE) is the most popular instance of the empirical risk, i.e., the loss function $\mathcal{L}$ is squared error:

$$\mathcal{L}(f(\theta, \rho_i), c_i) = \frac{1}{C}\|f(\theta, \rho_i) - c_i\|_2^2,$$

where C is the number of classes in $\mathcal{C}$, and $\|\cdot\|_2$ is the l_2-norm.

As one can see in the above learning process, the main differences between classical and quantum machine learning algorithms are the learning models and data.

In this paper, we focus on the well-trained quantum classification algorithm $\mathcal{A}$, usually called a quantum classifier. Here, $\mathcal{A}$ is said to be well-trained if training and validation accuracy are both high ($\geq 95\%$). The training (validation) accuracy is the frequency that $\mathcal{A}$ successfully classifies the data in a training (validation) dataset. A validation dataset is mathematically equivalent to a training dataset but only for testing $\mathcal{A}$ rather than learning $\mathcal{A}$. In this context, θ^* is naturally omitted, i.e., $\mathcal{A}(\rho) = \mathcal{A}(\theta^*, \rho)$ and $\mathcal{E}(\rho) = \mathcal{E}_{\theta^*}(\rho)$. Briefly, $\mathcal{A}$ only consists of a super-operator $\mathcal{E}$ and a measurement $\{M_k\}_k$, denoted by $\mathcal{A} = (\mathcal{E}, \{M_k\}_k)$.

3.2   An Illustrative Example

Let us further illustrate the above definitions by a concrete example—Quantum Convolutional Neural Networks (QCNNs) [5], one of the most popular and successful quantum learning models. QCNN extends the main features and structures of the Convolutional Neural Networks (CNNs) to quantum computing.

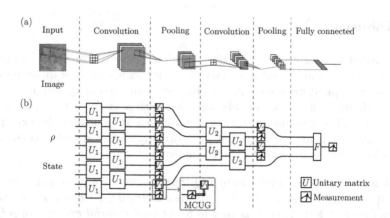

Fig. 1. Simple example of CNN and QCNN. QCNN, like CNN, consists of a convolution layer that finds a new state and a pooling layer that reduces the size of the model. Here, MCUG stands for measurement control unitary gate, i.e., unitary matrix V_1 is applied on the circuit if and only if the measurement outcome is 1.

The model of QCNN applies the convolution layer and the pooling layer from CNNs to quantum systems, as shown in Fig. 1(b). The layout proceeds as follows:

1 The convolution layer (circuit) applies multiple qubit gates U_i between adjacent qubits to find a new state;
2 The pooling layer reduces the size of the quantum system by measuring a fraction of qubits, and the outcomes determine unitary V_i applied to nearby qubits;
3 Repeat the convolution layer and pooling layer defined in 1–2;
4 When the size of the system is sufficiently small, the fully connected layer is applied as a unitary matrix F on the remaining qubits.

The input of QCNNs is an unknown quantum state ρ_{in} and the output is obtained by measuring a fixed number of output qubits. As in the classical case, the learning model (defined as the number of convolution and pooling layers) is fixed, but the involved quantum gates (i.e. unitary matrices) U_i, V_j, F themselves are learned by the above learning process.

Remark 1. Quantum machine learning can also be used to do classical machine learning tasks. Image classification, for example, is one of the most successful applications of Neural Networks (NNs). To explore the possible advantage of quantum computing, Quantum Neural Networks (QNNs) have been used to classify images in [27,28]. It is shown that by encoding images to a quantum state ρ_{in}, QNNs can achieve high accuracy in image classification. We will present a quantum classifier for the classification of MNIST as an example in the evaluation section.

4   Robustness

An important issue in classical machine learning is: how robust is a classification algorithm to adversarial perturbations. A similar issue exists for quantum classifiers against quantum noise. Intuitively, the robustness of quantum classifier $\mathcal{A}$ is the ability to make correct classification with a small perturbation to the input states. Then a quantum state σ is considered as an adversarial example if it is similar to a benign state ρ, but ρ is correctly classified and σ is classified into a class different from that of ρ. Formally,

Definition 2 (Adversarial Example). *Suppose we are given a quantum classifier $\mathcal{A}(\cdot)$, an input example (ρ, c), a distance metric $D(\cdot, \cdot)$ and a small enough threshold value $\varepsilon > 0$. Then σ is said to be an ε-adversarial example of ρ if the following is true*

$$(\mathcal{A}(\rho) = c) \wedge (\mathcal{A}(\sigma) \neq c) \wedge (D(\rho, \sigma) \leq \varepsilon).$$

The leftmost condition $\mathcal{A}(\rho) = c$ asserts that ρ is correctly classified, the middle condition $\mathcal{A}(\sigma) \neq c$ means that σ is incorrectly classified, and the rightmost condition $D(\rho, \sigma) \leq \varepsilon$ indicates that ρ and σ are similar (i.e., their distance is small). Sometimes, without any ambiguity, σ is called an adversarial example of ρ if ε is preset. Notably, by the above definition, if $\mathcal{A}$ incorrectly classifies ρ, then we do not need to consider the corresponding adversarial examples. This is the correctness issue of quantum classifier $\mathcal{A}$ rather than the robustness issue. Hence, in the following discussions, we only consider the set of all correctly recognized states.

The absence of adversarial examples leads to robustness.

Definition 3 (Adversarial Robustness). *Let $\mathcal{A}$ be a quantum classifier. Then ρ is ε-robust for $\mathcal{A}$ if there is no adversarial example of ρ.*

The major problem concerning us in this paper is the following:

Problem 1 (Robustness Verification Problem). Given a quantum classifier $\mathcal{A}(\cdot)$ and an input example (ρ, c). Check whether or not $\mathcal{A}(\sigma) = c$ for all $\sigma \in \mathcal{N}_\varepsilon(\rho)$, where $\mathcal{N}_\varepsilon(\rho)$ is the ε-neighbourhood of ρ as

$$\mathcal{N}_\varepsilon(\rho) = \{\sigma \in \mathcal{D}(\mathcal{H}) : D(\rho, \sigma) \leq \varepsilon)\}.$$

If not, then an adversarial example (counter-example) $\sigma \in \mathcal{N}_\varepsilon(\rho)$ is provided.

Obviously, if δ is a robust bound for an input example (ρ, c) such that $\mathcal{A}(\sigma) = c$ for any state $\sigma \in \mathcal{N}_\delta(\rho)$, then for any $\varepsilon \leq \delta$ (i.e. $\mathcal{N}_\varepsilon(\rho) \subseteq \mathcal{N}_\delta(\rho)$), there is no ε-adversarial example of ρ. It is a challenging problem to compute the optimal robust bound $\delta^* = \max \delta$ so that there is no ε-adversarial example if and only if $\varepsilon \leq \delta^*$.

The above adversarial robustness of quantum states can be generalized to a notion of robustness for quantum classifiers:

Definition 4 (Robust Accuracy). *Let $\mathcal{A}$ be a quantum classifier. The ε-robust accuracy of $\mathcal{A}$ is the proportion of ε-robust states in the training dataset.*

Remark 2. Here, the robust accuracy is defined with respect to the training dataset. In some applications, the dataset can be chosen as another set of quantum states with correct classifications, such as a validation dataset or a combination of it with the training dataset.

The reader should notice that the above definitions of robustness for quantum classifiers are similar to those for classical classifiers. But an intrinsic distinctness between them comes from the choice of distance $D(\cdot, \cdot)$. In the classical case, humans play the role of the adversary, and then such a distance should promise that a small perturbation is imperceptible to humans, and vice versa. Otherwise, we cannot take the advantage of machine learning over human's distinguishability. For instance, in image recognition, the distance should reflect the perceptual similarity in the sense that humans would consider adversarial examples generated by it perceptually similar to benign image [24]. In the quantum case, it is essential to choose a distance D that is meaningful in quantum physics. In this paper, we choose to use the distance:

$$D(\rho, \sigma) = 1 - F(\rho, \sigma)$$

defined by fidelity

$$F(\rho, \sigma) = [\text{tr}(\sqrt{\sqrt{\rho}\sigma\sqrt{\rho}})]^2.$$

Here $\sqrt{\rho} = \sum_k \sqrt{\lambda_k}|\psi_k\rangle\langle\psi_k|$ if ρ admits the spectral decomposition $\sum_k \lambda_k$ $|\psi_k\rangle\langle\psi_k|$. Fidelity is one of the most widely used quantities to quantify such uncertainty of noise by the experimental quantum physics and quantum engineering communities (see e.g. [29, 30]).

Remark 3. The trace distance has been used in recent literature (e.g. [20]) for some issues related to quantum robustness verification:

$$T(\rho, \sigma) = \frac{1}{2}\|\rho - \sigma\|_{tr} = \frac{1}{2}\text{tr}[\sqrt{(\rho - \sigma)^\dagger(\rho - \sigma)}].$$

It is a generalization of the total variation distance, which is a distance measure for probability distributions. So far, to the best of our knowledge, there is no discussion about which distance is better in the literature. Here, we argue that fidelity is better than trace distance in the context of quantum machine learning against quantum noise. As we know, state distinguishability is the basis of measuring the effect of noise on quantum computation. The main difference between trace distance $T(\rho, \sigma)$ and fidelity $F(\rho, \sigma)$ is the number of copies of states ρ and σ as the resource required in the experiments for distinguishing them. More precisely, trace distance quantifies the maximum probability of correctly guessing through a measurement whether ρ or σ was prepared, while fidelity asserts the same quantity whence infinitely many samples of ρ and σ can be supplied (See Appendix A of the extended version of this paper [31] for more details). In quantum machine learning, a large enough number of copies of the states are the precondition of statistics in Eq. (6) for learning and classification. Thus, fidelity is more suitable than trace distance for our purpose.

5   Robust Bound

In this section, we develop a theoretic basis for robustness verification of quantum classifiers. After setting the distance D to be the one defined by fidelity, a robust bound can be derived.

Lemma 1 (Robust Bound). *Given a quantum classifier $\mathcal{A} = (\mathcal{E}, \{M_k\}_{k\in C})$ and a quantum state ρ. Let p_1 and p_2 be the first and second largest elements of $\{\text{tr}(M_k^\dagger M_k \mathcal{E}(\rho))\}_k$, respectively. If $\sqrt{p_1} - \sqrt{p_2} > \sqrt{2\varepsilon}$, then ρ is ε-robust.*

Proof. See Appendix B of the extended version of this paper [31].

The above robust bound gives us a quick robustness verification by the measurement outcomes of ρ without searching any possible adversarial examples. Furthermore, it also can be used to compute an under-approximation of the robust accuracy of $\mathcal{A}$ by one-by-one checking the robustness of quantum states in the training dataset. We will see that the robust bound and the induced robust accuracy scales well in the later experiments. However, $\sqrt{p_1} - \sqrt{p_2} > \sqrt{2\varepsilon}$ is not a necessary condition of ε-robustness. Fortunately, when $\sqrt{p_1} - \sqrt{p_2} \leq \sqrt{2\varepsilon}$, we can compute the optimal robust bound by Semidefinite Programming (SDP). Recall that SDP is a convex optimization concerned with the optimization of a linear objective function over the intersection of the cone of positive semidefinite matrices with an affine space. It has the form

$$
\begin{aligned}
\min \quad & \mathrm{tr}(CX) \\
\text{subject to} \quad & \mathrm{tr}(A_k X) \leq b_k, \quad \text{for } k = 1, \ldots, m \\
& X \geq 0
\end{aligned}
$$

where $C, A_1, \ldots, A_m$ are all Hermitian $n \times n$ matrices (i.e. $A^\dagger = A$), and X is the optimization variable $n \times n$ matrix with $X \geq 0$, i.e., X is positive semidefinite. Many efficient solvers have been developed for solving SDPs—not only compute the minimal value, but also output a corresponding optimal solution X. The following two theorems show that checking ε-robustness and computing optimal robust bound of quantum states can both be reduced to an SDP.

Theorem 1 (ε-robustness Verification). *Let $\mathcal{A} = (\mathcal{E}, \{M_k\}_{k \in \mathcal{C}})$ be a quantum classifier and ρ be a state with $\mathcal{A}(\rho) = l$. Then ρ is ε-robust if and only if for all $k \in \mathcal{C}$ and $k \neq l$, the following problem has no solution (feasibility problem):*

$$
\begin{aligned}
\min_{\sigma \in \mathcal{D}(\mathcal{H})} \quad & 0 \\
\text{subject to} \quad & \sigma \geq 0 \\
& \mathrm{tr}(\sigma) = 1 \\
& \mathrm{tr}[(M_l^\dagger M_l - M_k^\dagger M_k)\mathcal{E}(\sigma)] \leq 0 \\
& 1 - F(\rho, \sigma) \leq \varepsilon
\end{aligned}
$$

Proof. See Appendix C of the extended version of this paper [31].

Actually, the objective function 0 in the above theorem can be chosen as any constant number.

Theorem 2 (Optimal Robust Bound). *Let $\mathcal{A}$ and ρ be as in Theorem 1 with $\mathcal{A}(\rho) = l$, and let δ_k be the solution of the following problem:*

$$
\begin{aligned}
\delta_k = \min_{\sigma \in \mathcal{D}(\mathcal{H})} \quad & 1 - F(\rho, \sigma) \\
\text{subject to} \quad & \sigma \geq 0 \\
& \mathrm{tr}(\sigma) = 1 \\
& \mathrm{tr}[(M_l^\dagger M_l - M_k^\dagger M_k)\mathcal{E}(\sigma)] \leq 0
\end{aligned}
$$

where if the problem is unsolved, then $\delta_k = +\infty$. Then $\delta = \min_{k \neq l} \delta_k$ is the optimal robust bound of ρ.

Proof. The proof is similar to Theorem 1.

Remark 4. One may wonder why checking ε-robustness and computing the optimal robust bound can always be reduced to an SDP. This is indeed implied by the *basic quantum mechanics postulate* of linearity; more specifically, all of the superoperators and measurements used in quantum machine learning algorithms are linear. In contrast, the functions represented by the neural networks in classical machine learning may be nonlinear as the pooling layer is not linear. As a result, the reduced optimization problem for the robustness verification is not convex (e.g. [32]). For overcoming this difficulty, many different methods have been developed to encode the nonlinear activation functions as linear constraints. Examples include NSVerify [33], MIPVerify [34], ILP [35] and ImageStar [13].

Algorithm 1. StateRobustnessVerifier$(\mathcal{A}, \varepsilon, \rho, l)$

Require: $\mathcal{A} = (\mathcal{E}, \{M_k\}_{k \in \mathcal{C}})$ is a well-trained quantum classifier, $\varepsilon < 1$ is a real number, (ρ, l) is an element of the training dataset of $\mathcal{A}$

Ensure: true indicates ρ is ε-robust or **false** with an adversarial example σ indicates ρ is not ε-robust

1: **for each** $k \in \mathcal{C}$ and $k \neq l$ **do**
2:     By an SDP solver, compute δ_k with an optimal state σ_k in the SDP of Theorem 2
3: **end for**
4: Let $\delta = \min_k \delta_k$ and $k^* = \arg\min_k \delta_k$
5: **if** $\delta > \varepsilon$ **then**
6:     **return true**
7: **else**
8:     **return false** and σ_{k*}
9: **end if**

---

6 Robustness Verification Algorithms

In this section, we develop several algorithms for verifying the robustness of quantum classifiers based on the theoretic results presented in the last section.

First, let us consider the robustness of a given quantum state ρ. In many applications (as shown in our experiments in Sect. 7), we are required to check whether ρ is ε-robust for an arbitrarily given threshold ε. Note that once we computed the optimal robust bound δ, checking ε-robustness of ρ is equivalent to compare ε and δ; that is, $\varepsilon \leq \delta$ if and only if ρ is ε-robust. Combining with this simple observation with Theorem 1, we obtain Algorithm 1 for checking the ε-robustness of ρ and finding the minimum adversarial perturbation δ caused by quantum noise. The main cost of Algorithm 1 incurs in solving SDPs in Line 2, which scales as $O(n^{6.5})$ by interior-point methods [36], where n is the number of rows of the semidefinite matrix ρ in SDP, i.e., the dimension of Hilbert space of the quantum states in our case. As we need to apply an SDP solver for $|\mathcal{C}| - 1$ times in Line 1, the total complexity is as follows.

Theorem 3. *The worst case complexity of Algorithm 1 is $O(|\mathcal{C}| \cdot n^{6.5})$, where n is the dimension of input state ρ and $|\mathcal{C}|$ is the number of the set $\mathcal{C}$ of classes we are interested in.*

Now we turn to consider the robustness of a quantum classifier $\mathcal{A}$. Algorithm 2 is designed for checking robustness of $\mathcal{A}$ by combining Algorithm 1 with Lemma 1 (see the discussion in the paragraph after Lemma 1). A major benefit of formal robustness verification for classical classifiers is perhaps that it can be used to detect a counter-example (adversarial example) for a given input (see e.g. [13–16]). This benefit is kept in Algorithm 2 for the robustness verification of quantum classifiers. In particular, we are able to extend the technique of adversarial training in classical machine learning [10] into the quantum case: an adversarial example σ is automatically generated once ε-robustness of ρ fails, and then by appending (σ, l) into the training dataset, we can retrain $\mathcal{A}$ to improve the robustness of the classifier.

Algorithm 2. RobustnessVerifier($\mathcal{A}, \varepsilon, T$)

Require: $\mathcal{A} = (\mathcal{E}, \{M_k\}_{k \in \mathcal{C}})$ is a well-trained quantum classifier, $\varepsilon < 1$ is a real number, $T = \{(\rho_i, l_i)\}$ is the training dataset of $\mathcal{A}$

Ensure: The robust accuracy RA and a set $R = \{< \sigma_j, i_j >\}$, where for each j, ρ_j is an ε-adversarial example of ρ_{i_j}; R can be an empty set if all states in T are ε-robust.

1: $R = \emptyset$ be an empty set.   // *Recording adversarial examples and corresponding indexes of states in training dataset T*

2: **for each** $(\rho_i, l_i) \in T$ **do**

3:     Let p_1 and p_2 be the first and second largest elements of $\{\operatorname{tr}(M_k^\dagger M_k \mathcal{E}(\rho_i))\}_k$, respectively.

4:     **if** $\sqrt{p_1} - \sqrt{p_2} \le \sqrt{2\varepsilon}$ **then**   // *Applying the robust bound in Lemma 1*

5:         **if** StateRobustnessVerifier $(\mathcal{A}, \varepsilon, \rho_i, l_i)$ == **false then**

6:             σ be the output state of StateRobustnessVerifier $(\mathcal{A}, \varepsilon, \rho_i, l_i)$

7:             $R = R \cup \{(\sigma, i)\}$

8:         **end if**

9:     **end if**

10: **end for**

11: **return** $RA = 1 - \frac{|R|}{|T|}$, R // *$|R| = 0$ if R is an empty set*

To analyze the complexity of Algorithm 2, we first see by Theorem 2 that for evaluating the robustness of $\mathcal{A}$—computing its robust accuracy and finding its adversarial examples, one need to call Algorithm 1 for each quantum state in the training dataset, which costs $O(|\mathcal{C}| \cdot n^{6.5})$. Thus, the total complexity of robustness verification is $O(|T| \cdot |\mathcal{C}| \cdot n^{6.5})$, where $|T|$ is the number of elements in the training dataset T. However, the robust bound given in Lemma 1 can help to speed up the process by quickly finding all potential non-robust states, as the complexity of finding the bound is only $O(|\mathcal{C}| \cdot n^3)$, which is the cost of $|\mathcal{C}|$ times of the multiplication of two $n \times n$ matrices. In practice, this bound scales well, as confirmed by our experiments presented in Sect. 7. Therefore, a good strategy for implementing the robustness verification is that we first use robust bound to pick up all potential non-robust states from the given training dataset T and store them in a set T'. Then we check all left candidates in the training dataset T one-by-one using Algorithm 1 and use a set R to record the found adversarial examples and the corresponding indexes of states. This strategy can significantly reduce the complexity to $O(|T'| \cdot |\mathcal{C}| \cdot n^{6.5})$. Indeed, our experiments show that the robust bound given in Lemma 1 scales very well in the sense of $|T'| \ll |T|$.

Remark 5. Thanks to the linearity of the quantum learning model determined by the basic postulate of quantum mechanics, the robustness verification of quantum classifiers can be done in an efficient way (with polynomial time complexity in the size of the input state). It is usually not the case in verifying the robustness of classical machine learning algorithms. For example, DNNs are often non-linear and non-convex, and verifying even some simple properties of them can be an NP-complete problem [37].

Surprisingly, the robustness verification problem for quantum classifiers becomes much harder if we are required to find adversarial examples in *pure states*. Roughly speaking, the reason is that the set of all pure states is not convex, and thus computing the optimal robust bound for pure states is not an SDP, as in Theorem 2. We can prove that it is a Quadratically Constrained Quadratic Program (QCQP), an optimization problem where both the objective function and the constraints are quadratic functions (see Appendix D of the extended version of this paper [31] for the proof), which is NP-hard. Algorithm 1 can be adapted to this pure state robustness verification by calling a QCQP solver instead of an SDP solver in Line 2. Subsequently, Algorithm 2 can use this new version of Algorithm 1 as a subroutine to compute the corresponding robust accuracy and find adversarial examples of pure states. We will evaluate the QCQP-based robustness verification in the case study of MNIST classification in which handwritten digits are encoded in pure states.

7   Evaluation

Algorithm 2 is implemented on *TensorFlow Quantum*—a platform of Google for designing and training quantum machine learning algorithms, by calling an SDP solver—CVXPY: Python Software for Disciplined Convex Programming [38]. This section aims to evaluate our approach with experiments on some concrete examples. This section is arranged as follows. In Subsects. 7.1–7.4, we present several well-trained quantum classifiers. Then the evaluation is carried out in Subsect. 7.5 by applying Algorithm 2 to check the robustness verification of these classifiers and find their adversarial examples if existing.

To demonstrate our method as sufficiently as possible, we check the robustness of four quantum classifiers. We begin with a "Hello World" example—qubits classification, and then we step in two quantum classifiers applied to real world tasks—quantum phase recognition and cluster excitation detection, which are both fundamental and hard problems in quantum physics. At last, to compare with classical robustness verification, we consider the classification of MNIST by encoding handwritten digital images into quantum data. *These experiments cover all illustrated examples of TensorFlow Quantum.*

7.1   Quantum Bits Classification

A "Hello World" example of quantum machine learning is quantum bits classification [7]. The aim is to implement a binary classification for regions on a single qubit, i.e., a perceptron for qubits. Specifically, two random normalized vectors $|a\rangle$ and $|b\rangle$ (pure states) in the X-Z plane of the Bloch sphere are chosen. Around these two vectors, we randomly sample two sets of quantum data points; the objective is to learn a quantum gate to distinguish the two sets. A concrete instance of this type is shown in Fig. 2. In this example, the angles with $|0\rangle$ (Z-axis) of the two states $|a\rangle$ and $|b\rangle$ are $\theta_a = 1$ and $\theta_b = 1.23$, respectively; see the first figure in Fig. 2. Around these two vectors, we randomly sample two sets (one for category "a" and one for category "b") of quantum data points on the sphere, forming a dataset. The dataset consists of 800 samples for the training and 200 samples for the validation. As shown in Fig. 2, we use a parameterized rotation gate $R_y(\theta) = e^{-i\sigma_y\theta/2}$ and a measurement $M = \{M_a = |0\rangle\langle 0|, M_b = |1\rangle\langle 1|\}$ to do the classification. Targeting to minimizing the MSE form of Eq. (8), we use Adam optimizer [39] to update θ. After training, we achieve both 100% training and validation accuracy, and the final parameter θ is 0.4835.

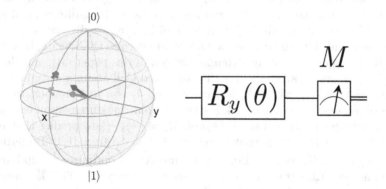

Fig. 2. Training model of quantum bits classification: the left figure shows the samples of the quantum training dataset represented on the Bloch sphere. Samples are divided into two categories, marked by red and yellow, respectively. The vectors are the states around which the samples were taken. The first part of the right figure is a parameterized rotation gate, whose job is to remove the super-positions in the quantum data. The second part is a measurement M along the Z-axis of the Bloch sphere converting the quantum data into classes. (Color figure online)

7.2   Quantum Phase Recognition

Quantum phase recognition (QPR) of one dimensional many-body systems has been attacked by quantum convolutional neural networks (QCNNs) proposed by Cong et al. [5]. Consider a $Z_2 \times Z_2$ symmetry-protected topological (SPT) phase $\mathcal{P}$ and the ground states of a family of Hamiltonians on spin-1/2 chain with open boundary conditions:

$$H = -J \sum_{i=1}^{N-2} Z_i X_{i+1} Z_{i+2} - h_1 \sum_{i=1}^{N} X_i - h_2 \sum_{i=1}^{N-1} X_i X_{i+1}$$

where X_i, Z_i are Pauli matrices [2] for the spin at site i, and the $Z_2 \times Z_2$ symmetry is generated by $X_{\mathrm{even(odd)}} = \prod_{i \in \mathrm{even(odd)}} X_i$. The goal is to identify whether the ground state $|\psi\rangle$ of H belongs to phase $\mathcal{P}$ when H is regarded as a function of $(h_1/J, h_2/J)$. For small N, a numerical simulation can be used to exactly solve this problem [5]; See Fig. 4a in Appendix E of the extended version of this paper [31] for the exact phase boundary points (blue and red diamonds) between SPT phase and non-SPT (paramagnetic or antiferromagnetic) phase for $N = 6$. Thus the 6-qubit instance is an excellent testbed for different new methods and techniques of QPR. Here, we train a QCNN model to implement 6-qubit QPR in this setting.

To generate the dataset for training, we sample a serials of Hamiltonian H with $h_2/J = 0$, uniformly varying h_1/J from 0 to 1.2 and compute their corresponding ground states; see the gray line of Fig. 4a in Appendix E of the extended version of this paper [31]. For the testing, we uniformly sample a set of validation data from two random regions of the 2-dimensional space $(h_1/J, h_2/J)$; see the two dashed rectangles of Fig. 4a. Finally, we obtain 1000 training data and 400 validation data. Our parameterized QCNN circuit is shown in Fig. 4b in Appendix E of the extended version of this paper [31], and the unitaries U_i, V_j, F are parameterized with generalized Gell-Mann matrix basis [40]: $U = \exp(-i \sum_j \theta_j \Lambda_j)$, where Λ_j is a matrix and θ_j is a real number; the total number of parameters θ_j, Λ_j is 114. For the outcome measurement of one qubit, we use measurement $M = \{M_0 = |+\rangle\langle+|, M_1 = |-\rangle\langle-|\}$ to predict that input states belongs to $\mathcal{P}$ with output 0, where $|\pm\rangle = \frac{1}{\sqrt{2}}(|0\rangle \pm |1\rangle)$. Targeting to minimizing the MSE form of Eq. (8), we use Adam optimizer to update the 114 parameters. After training, 97.7% training accuracy and 95.25% validation accuracy are obtained. At the same time, our classifier conducts a phase diagram (the colorful figure in Fig. 4a), where the learned phase boundary almost perfectly matches the exact one gotten by the numerical simulation. All these results indicate that our classifier is well-trained.

7.3   Cluster Excitation Detection

The task of cluster excitation detection is to train a quantum classifier to detect if a prepared cluster state is "excited" or not [7]. Excitations are represented with a X rotation on one qubit. A large enough rotation is deemed to be an excited state and is labeled by 0, while a rotation that isn't large enough is labeled by 1 and is not deemed to be an excited state. Here, we demonstrate this classification task with 6 qubits. We use the circuit shown in Fig. 5a of Appendix E in the extended version of this paper [31] to generate training (840) and validation (360) samples. The circuit generates a cluster state by performing a X rotation (we omit angle θ) on one qubit. The rotation angle θ is ranging from $-\pi$ to π and if $-\pi/2 \leq \theta \leq \pi/2$, the label of the output state is 1; otherwise, the label is 0. The classification circuit model (a quantum convolutional neural network) uses the same structure in TensorFlow Quantum [7], shown in Fig. 5b of Appendix E in the extended version of this paper [31]. The explicit parameterization of C_i, P_j can be found in [7]. The final measurement $M = \{M_0 = |0\rangle\langle 0|, M_1 = |1\rangle\langle 1|\}$. Targeting to minimizing the MSE form of Eq. (8), we use Adam optimizer to update all C_i, P_j. We achieve 99.76% training accuracy and 99.44% validation accuracy.

7.4   The Classification of MNIST

Handwritten digit recognition is one of the most popular tasks in the classical machine learning zoo. The archetypical training and validation data come from the MNIST dataset which consists of 55,000 training samples handwritten digits [41]. These digits have been labeled by humans as representing one of the ten digits from number 0 to 9, and are in the form of gray-scale images that contains 28×28 pixels. Each pixel has a grayscale value ranging from 0 to 255. Quantum machine learning has been used to distinguish a too simplified version of MNIST by downscaling the image sizes to 8×8 pixels. Subsequently, the numbers represented by this version of MNIST can not be perceptually recognized [7]. Here, we build up a quantum classifier to recognize a MNIST version of 16×16 pixels (see second column images of Fig. 3). As demonstrated in [7], we select out 700 images of number 3 and 700 images of number 6 to form our training (1000 images) and validation (400 images) datasets. Then we downscale those 28×28 images to $2^4 \times 2^4$ images (fitting the size of quantum data), and encode them into the pure states of 8 qubits via amplitude encoding. Amplitude encoding uses the amplitude of computational basis to represent vectors with normalization:

$$(x_0, x_2, \ldots, x_{n-1}) \to \sum_{i=0}^{n-1} \frac{x_i}{\sqrt{\sum_{j=0}^{n-1} |x_j|^2}} |i\rangle.$$

where $\{|i\rangle\}$ is a set of orthogonal basis of the 8 qubits state space. The normalization doesn't change the pattern of those images. For learning a quantum classifier, we use the QCNN model in Fig. 6 of Appendix E in the extended version of this paper [31] and use measurement $M = \{M_0 = |+\rangle\langle +|, M_1 = |-\rangle\langle -|\}$. The output of measurement M indicates the numbers: output 1 for number 3 and output 0 for number 6. The explicit parameterization of those C_i, P_j can be found in [7]. Again we use Adam optimizer to update the model parameters minimizing the MSE form of Eq. (8). We finally achieve 98.4% training accuracy and 97.5% validation accuracy.

7.5 Robustness Verification

Now, we start to check the ε-robustness for the above four well-trained classifiers presented in the previous four subsections.

In practical applications, the value of robustness ε in Definition 3 represents the ability of state preparation by quantum controls. For example, the state-of-the-art is that a single qubit can be prepared with fidelity 99.99% (e.g. [29,30]). Here, we choose four different values of ε in each experiment.

To show the scalability of our robust bound given in Lemma 1, we use it to develop an algorithm (Algorithm 3 in Appendix F of the extended version of this paper [31]) to under-approximate the robust accuracy, which is computed by Algorithm 2. Algorithm 3 is a subroutine of Algorithm 2 without calling an SDP solver (whenever a potential non-robust state can be detected by the robust bound in Lemma 1). We compare the verification times by Algorithms 2 and 3.

Table 1. Verification results of quantum bits classification

	Robust accuracy (in percent)			
	$\varepsilon = 0.001$	$\varepsilon = 0.002$	$\varepsilon = 0.003$	$\varepsilon = 0.004$
Robust bound (Lemma 1 - Algorithm 3)	88.13	75.88	58.88	38.25
Robustness algorithm (Theorem 2 - Algorithm 2)	90.00	76.50	59.75	38.88
	Verification times (in seconds)			
Robust bound (Lemma 1 - Algorithm 3)	0.0050	0.0048	0.0047	0.0048
Robustness algorithm (Theorem 2 - Algorithm 2)	1.3260	2.7071	4.6285	6.9095

Table 2. Verification results of quantum phase recognition.

	Robust accuracy (in percent)			
	$\varepsilon = 0.0001$	$\varepsilon = 0.0002$	$\varepsilon = 0.0003$	$\varepsilon = 0.0004$
Robust bound (Lemma 1 - Algorithm 3)	99.20	98.80	98.60	98.30
Robustness Algorithm (Theorem 2 - Algorithm 2)	99.20	98.80	98.60	98.40
	Verification times (in seconds)			
Robust bound (Lemma 1 - Algorithm 3)	1.4892	1.4850	1.4644	1.4789
Robustness algorithm (Theorem 2 - Algorithm 2)	19.531	25.648	28.738	33.537

The experiments are done on a computer with the following configurations: Intel(R) Core(TM) i7-9700 CPU @ 3.00 GHz × 8 Processor, 15.8 GiB Memory, Ubuntu 18.04.5 LTS, with CVXPY: Python Software for Disciplined Convex Programming [38] for solving SDP, and a SciPy solver for finding the minimum of constrained nonlinear multivariable function for solving QCQP.

The experimental results are given in Tables 1, 2, 3 and 4. As an example, we illustrate the details of the result for the case of $\varepsilon = 0.001$ in Table 1. First, we only apply our robust bound in Lemma 1 to pick up all potential non-robust states from the 800 points in the training dataset. Then 95 points are left. Thus, the under-approximation of the robust accuracy computed by Algorithm 3 (in Appendix F of the extended version of this paper [31]) is 88.13%. Next, we check the 0.001-robustness by Algorithm 2. Indeed, only 80 of the points detected by the above robust bound are non-robust and the exact robust accuracy is 90.00%. We also compare the verification time of the two approaches to the robust accuracy. See the second column in Table 1 for the detail, and other experiment results of ε-robustness are also summarized in the same table. Tables 1, 2, 3 and 4 for the verification results show that in all of these experiments, the robust bound obtained in Lemma 1 scales very well, and the robustness verification by Algorithm 3 costs significantly less time (<2 s) than the way of computing the optimal robust bound by Algorithm 2. For example, for quantum phase recog-

Table 3. Verification results of cluster excitation detection

	Robust accuracy (in percent)			
	$\varepsilon = 0.0001$	$\varepsilon = 0.0002$	$\varepsilon = 0.0003$	$\varepsilon = 0.0004$
Robust bound (Lemma 1 - Algorithm 3)	99.05	98.81	98.21	97.86
Robustness algorithm (Theorem 2 - Algorithm 2)	100.0	100.0	100.0	100.0
	Verification times (in seconds)			
Robust bound (Lemma 1 - Algorithm 3)	1.2899	1.2794	1.2544	1.2567
Robustness algorithm (Theorem 2 - Algorithm 2)	209.52	244.79	325.97	365.30

Table 4. Verification results of the classification of MNIST

	Robust accuracy (in percent)			
	$\varepsilon = 0.0001$	$\varepsilon = 0.0002$	$\varepsilon = 0.0003$	$\varepsilon = 0.0004$
Robust bound (Lemma 1 - Algorithm 3)	99.70	99.40	99.30	99.20
Robustness algorithm (Theorem 2 - Algorithm 2)	99.80	99.60	99.30	99.30
	Verification times (in seconds)			
Robust bound (Lemma 1 - Algorithm 3)	0.0803	0.1315	0.0775	0.0811
Robustness algorithm (Theorem 2 - Algorithm 2)	0.3955	0.6751	0.7653	0.8855

nition, for $\varepsilon = 0.0001, 0.0002$ and 0.0003, the under-approximation of the robust accuracy is the same as the real value. Even for the last case of $\varepsilon = 0.0004$, only the 0.1% difference is got. Furthermore, from the tables, the verification time of Algorithm 2 is increasing with the value of ε, while the running time of the method by the robust bound is almost unchanged. This is because the former algorithm uses an SDP or QCQP solver to search all possible adversarial examples for the potential non-robust states picked up by the robust bound, and the number of these states are growing up with the value of ε. These counter-examples detected by the algorithm confirm that our robustness framework is effective. For instance, see Fig. 3 for two visualized adversarial examples generated by Algorithm 2 with a QCQP solver. As we can see, the benign and adversarial images are perceptually similar. This also proves that our robustness verification algorithm can detect not only quantum but also classical adversarial examples.

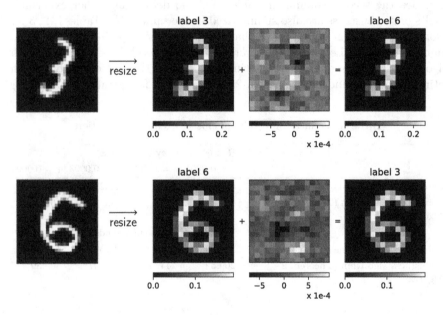

Fig. 3. Two training states and their adversarial examples generated by Algorithm 2 with a QCQP solver: the first column images are 28×28 benign data from MNIST; The second column shows the two downscaled 16×16 grayscale images; The last column images are decoded from adversarial examples founded by Algorithm 2. The third column images are the grayscale difference between benign and adversarial images.

8   Conclusion

In this work, we initiate the research of the formal robustness verification of quantum machine learning algorithms against unknown quantum noise. We found an analytical robustness bound which can be efficiently computed to under-approximate the robust accuracy in practical applications. Furthermore, we developed a robustness verification algorithm that can exactly verify the ε-robustness of quantum machine learning algorithms and provides useful counter-examples for the adversarial training.

For topics for future research, it should be useful in practical applications to find an efficient method that over-approximates the robust accuracy of quantum classifiers. Combined with the under-approximation approach developed in this work, it can help us to more accurately and fast estimate the robust accuracy. In classical machine learning, there exist some works in the literature to achieve this task. For instance, ImageStars, a new set representation, was introduced in [13] to perform efficient set-based analysis by combining operations on concrete images with linear programming, which leads to efficient over-approximative analysis of classical convolutional neural networks.

Tensor networks are one of the best-known data structures for implementing large-scale quantum classifiers (e.g. QCNNs with 45 qubits in [5]). For practical applications, we are going to incorporate tensor networks into our robustness verification algorithm so that it can scale up to achieve the demand of NISQ devices (of ≥ 50 qubits).

More generally, further investigations are required to better understand the role of robustness in quantum machine learning, especially through more experiments on real world applications like learning phases of quantum many-body systems.

Acknowledgment. We would like to thank the anonymous reviewers for their insightful comments. This work was partly supported by the National Key R&D Program of China (Grant No: 2018YFA0306701), the National Natural Science Foundation of China (Grant No: 61832015) and the Australian Research Council (ARC) under grant No.DP210102449.

References

1. Carleo, G., Troyer, M.: Solving the quantum many-body problem with artificial neural networks. Science **355**(6325), 602–606 (2017)
2. Nielsen, M.A., Chuang, I.L.: Quantum Computation and Quantum Information. Cambridge University Press, Cambridge (2010)
3. Biamonte, J., Wittek, P., Pancotti, N., Rebentrost, P., Wiebe, N., Lloyd, S.: Quantum machine learning. Nature **549**(7671), 195–202 (2017)
4. Dunjko, V., Briegel, H.J.: Machine learning & artificial intelligence in the quantum domain: a review of recent progress. Rep. Prog. Phys. **81**(7), 074001 (2018)
5. Cong, I., Choi, S., Lukin, M.D.: Quantum convolutional neural networks. Nat. Phys. **15**(12), 1273–1278 (2019)
6. Huang, H.-Y., Kueng, R., Preskill, J.: Information-theoretic bounds on quantum advantage in machine learning. arXiv preprint arXiv:2101.02464 (2021)
7. Broughton, M., et al.: TensorFlow quantum: a software framework for quantum machine learning. arXiv preprint arXiv:2003.02989 (2020). See https://www.tensorflow.org/quantum for the platform
8. Huang, L., Joseph, A.D., Nelson, B., Rubinstein, B.I.P., Tygar, J.D.: Adversarial machine learning. In: Proceedings of the 4th ACM Workshop on Security and Artificial Intelligence, pp. 43–58 (2011)

9. Goodfellow, I.J., Shlens, J., Szegedy, C.: Explaining and harnessing adversarial examples. In: Bengio, Y., LeCun, Y. (eds.) 3rd International Conference on Learning Representations, ICLR 2015, San Diego, CA, USA, 7–9 May 2015, Conference Track Proceedings (2015)
10. Madry, A., Makelov, A., Schmidt, L., Tsipras, D., Vladu, A.: Towards deep learning models resistant to adversarial attacks. In: 6th International Conference on Learning Representations, ICLR 2018, Vancouver, BC, Canada, 30 April–3 May 2018, Conference Track Proceedings. OpenReview.net (2018)
11. Carlini, N., Wagner, D.: Adversarial examples are not easily detected: bypassing ten detection methods. In: Proceedings of the 10th ACM Workshop on Artificial Intelligence and Security, pp. 3–14 (2017)
12. Brown, T.B., Mané, D., Roy, A., Abadi, M., Gilmer, J.: Adversarial patch. arXiv preprint arXiv:1712.09665 (2017)
13. Tran, H.-D., Bak, S., Xiang, W., Johnson, T.T.: Verification of deep convolutional neural networks using ImageStars. In: Lahiri, S.K., Wang, C. (eds.) CAV 2020. LNCS, vol. 12224, pp. 18–42. Springer, Cham (2020). https://doi.org/10.1007/978-3-030-53288-8_2
14. Elboher, Y.Y., Gottschlich, J., Katz, G.: An abstraction-based framework for neural network verification. In: Lahiri, S.K., Wang, C. (eds.) CAV 2020. LNCS, vol. 12224, pp. 43–65. Springer, Cham (2020). https://doi.org/10.1007/978-3-030-53288-8_3
15. Fremont, D.J., Chiu, J., Margineantu, D.D., Osipychev, D., Seshia, S.A.: Formal analysis and redesign of a neural network-based aircraft taxiing system with VERIFAI. In: Lahiri, S.K., Wang, C. (eds.) CAV 2020. LNCS, vol. 12224, pp. 122–134. Springer, Cham (2020). https://doi.org/10.1007/978-3-030-53288-8_6
16. Kwiatkowska, M.Z.: Safety verification for deep neural networks with provable guarantees (invited paper). In: Fokkink, W.J., van Glabbeek, R. (eds.) 30th International Conference on Concurrency Theory, CONCUR 2019, Amsterdam, the Netherlands, 27–30 August 2019. LIPIcs, vol. 140, pp. 1:1–1:5. Schloss Dagstuhl - Leibniz-Zentrum für Informatik (2019)
17. Dreossi, T., et al.: VERIFAI: a toolkit for the formal design and analysis of artificial intelligence-based systems. In: Dillig, I., Tasiran, S. (eds.) CAV 2019. LNCS, vol. 11561, pp. 432–442. Springer, Cham (2019). https://doi.org/10.1007/978-3-030-25540-4_25
18. Tran, H.-D., et al.: NNV: the neural network verification tool for deep neural networks and learning-enabled cyber-physical systems. In: Lahiri, S.K., Wang, C. (eds.) CAV 2020. LNCS, vol. 12224, pp. 3–17. Springer, Cham (2020). https://doi.org/10.1007/978-3-030-53288-8_1
19. Sirui, L., Duan, L.-M., Deng, D.-L.: Quantum adversarial machine learning. Phys. Rev. Res. **2**, 033212 (2020)
20. Du, Y., Hsieh, M.-H., Liu, T., Tao, D., Liu, N.: Quantum noise protects quantum classifiers against adversaries. arXiv preprint arXiv:2003.09416 (2020)
21. Liu, N., Wittek, P.: Vulnerability of quantum classification to adversarial perturbations. Phys. Rev. A **101**(6), 062331 (2020)
22. Weber, M., Liu, N., Li, B., Zhang, C., Zhao, Z.: Optimal provable robustness of quantum classification via quantum hypothesis testing. npj Quantum Inf. **7**(1), 1–12 (2021)
23. Helstrom, C.W.: Detection theory and quantum mechanics. Inf. Control **10**(3), 254–291 (1967)

24. Sharif, M., Bauer, L., Reiter, M.K.: On the suitability of Lp-norms for creating and preventing adversarial examples. In: Proceedings of the IEEE Conference on Computer Vision and Pattern Recognition Workshops, pp. 1605–1613 (2018)
25. Roque, T.F., Clerk, A.A., Ribeiro, H.: Engineering fast high-fidelity quantum operations with constrained interactions. npj Quantum Inf. **7**(1), 1–17 (2021)
26. Torosov, B.T., Vitanov, N.V.: Smooth composite pulses for high-fidelity quantum information processing. Phys. Rev. A **83**(5), 053420 (2011)
27. Farhi, E., Neven, H., et al.: Classification with quantum neural networks on near term processors. Quantum Rev. Lett. **1**(2), 10–37686 (2020)
28. Oh, S., Choi, J., Kim, J.: A tutorial on quantum convolutional neural networks (QCNN). In: 2020 International Conference on Information and Communication Technology Convergence (ICTC), pp. 236–239. IEEE (2020)
29. Myerson, A.H., et al.: High-fidelity readout of trapped-ion qubits. Phys. Rev. Lett. **100**(20), 200502200502 (2008)
30. Burrell, A.H., Szwer, D.J., Webster, S.C., Lucas, D.M.: Scalable simultaneous multiqubit readout with 99.99% single-shot fidelity. Phys. Rev. A **81**(4), 040302 (2010)
31. Guan, J., Fang, W., Ying, M.: Robustness verification of quantum classifiers. arXiv preprint arXiv:2008.07230 (2020)
32. Ruan, W., Wu, M., Sun, Y., Huang, X., Kroening, D., Kwiatkowska, M.: Global robustness evaluation of deep neural networks with provable guarantees for the hamming distance. In: Kraus, S. (ed.) Proceedings of the Twenty-Eighth International Joint Conference on Artificial Intelligence, IJCAI 2019, Macao, China, 10–16 August 2019, pp. 5944–5952. ijcai.org (2019)
33. Lomuscio, A., Maganti, L.: An approach to reachability analysis for feed-forward ReLU neural networks. arXiv preprint arXiv:1706.07351 (2017)
34. Tjeng, V., Xiao, K.Y., Tedrake, R.: Evaluating robustness of neural networks with mixed integer programming. In: 7th International Conference on Learning Representations, ICLR 2019, New Orleans, LA, USA, 6–9 May 2019. OpenReview.net (2019)
35. Bastani, O., Ioannou, Y., Lampropoulos, L., Vytiniotis, D., Nori, A.V., Criminisi, A.: Measuring neural net robustness with constraints. In: Lee, D.D., Sugiyama, M., von Luxburg, U., Guyon, I., Garnett, R. (eds.) Advances in Neural Information Processing Systems 29: Annual Conference on Neural Information Processing Systems 2016, Barcelona, Spain, 5–10 December 2016, pp. 2613–2621 (2016)
36. Zhang, R.Y., Lavaei, J.: Sparse semidefinite programs with near-linear time complexity. In: 2018 IEEE Conference on Decision and Control (CDC), pp. 1624–1631. IEEE (2018)
37. Katz, G., Barrett, C., Dill, D.L., Julian, K., Kochenderfer, M.J.: Reluplex: an efficient SMT solver for verifying deep neural networks. In: Majumdar, R., Kunčak, V. (eds.) CAV 2017. LNCS, vol. 10426, pp. 97–117. Springer, Cham (2017). https://doi.org/10.1007/978-3-319-63387-9_5
38. Diamond, S., Boyd, S.: CVXPY: a Python-embedded modeling language for convex optimization. J. Mach. Learn. Res. **17**(83), 1–5 (2016)
39. Kingma, D.P., Ba, J.: Adam: a method for stochastic optimization. In: Bengio, Y., LeCun, Y. (eds.) 3rd International Conference on Learning Representations, ICLR 2015, San Diego, CA, USA, 7–9 May 2015, Conference Track Proceedings (2015)
40. Bertlmann, R.A., Krammer, P.: Bloch vectors for qudits. J. Phys. A Math. Theor. **41**(23), 235303 (2008)
41. LeCun, Y., Cortes, C.: MNIST handwritten digit database (2010). http://yann.lecun.com/exdb/mnist/

BDD4BNN: A BDD-Based Quantitative Analysis Framework for Binarized Neural Networks

Yedi Zhang[1], Zhe Zhao[1], Guangke Chen[1], Fu Song[1,2(✉)], and Taolue Chen[3]

[1] ShanghaiTech University, Shanghai, China
songfu@shanghaitech.edu.cn
[2] Shanghai Engineering Research Center of Intelligent Vision and Imaging, Shanghai, China
[3] Birkbeck, University of London, London, UK

Abstract. Verifying and explaining the behavior of neural networks is becoming increasingly important, especially when they are deployed in safety-critical applications. In this paper, we study verification and interpretability problems for Binarized Neural Networks (BNNs), the 1-bit quantization of general real-numbered neural networks. Our approach is to encode BNNs into Binary Decision Diagrams (BDDs), which is done by exploiting the internal structure of the BNNs. In particular, we translate the input-output relation of blocks in BNNs to cardinality constraints which are in turn encoded by BDDs. Based on the encoding, we develop a quantitative framework for BNNs where precise and comprehensive analysis of BNNs can be performed. We demonstrate the application of our framework by providing quantitative robustness analysis and interpretability for BNNs. We implement a prototype tool BDD4BNN and carry out extensive experiments, confirming the effectiveness and efficiency of our approach.

1 Introduction

Deep neural networks (DNNs) have achieved human-level performance in several tasks, and are increasingly being incorporated into various application domains such as autonomous driving [4] and medical diagnostics [53]. Modern DNNs usually contain a great many parameters which are typically stored as 32/64-bit floating-point numbers, and require a massive amount of floating-point operations to compute the output for a single input [60]. As a result, it is often challenging to deploy them on resource-constrained, embedded devices. To mitigate the issue, quantization, which quantizes 32/64-bit floating-points to low bit-width fixed-points (e.g., 4-bits) with little accuracy loss [23], emerges as a promising technique to reduce resource requirements. In particular, binarized neural networks (BNNs) [27] represent the case of 1-bit quantization using the bipolar binaries ±1. BNNs can drastically reduce memory storage and execution time with bit-wise operations, hence substantially improve the time and energy efficiency. BNNs have been demonstrated to achieve a high accuracy for a wide variety of applications [34,41,52].

This work is supported by the National Natural Science Foundation of China (NSFC) under Grants No.: 62072309, and an oversea grant from the State Key Laboratory of Novel Software Technology, Nanjing University (KFKT2018A16).

© The Author(s) 2021
A. Silva and K. R. M. Leino (Eds.) CAV 2021, LNCS 12759, pp. 175–200, 2021.
https://doi.org/10.1007/978-3-030-81685-8_8

DNNs have been shown to lack robustness [11,14,36,49,59] and interpretability of the predictions they make [25,43]. Various formal techniques and heuristics have been proposed to analyze DNNs and interpret their behaviors, most of which focus on *real-numbered* DNNs only. Verification of *quantized* DNNs has not been thoroughly explored so far, although recent results have highlighted its importance: it was shown that a quantized DNN does not necessarily preserve the properties satisfied by the real-numbered DNN before quantization [14,22]. Indeed, the fixed-point number semantics effectively yields a discrete state space for the verification of quantized DNNs whereas real-numbered DNNs feature a continuous state space. The discrepancy could invalidate current verification techniques for real-numbered DNNs when they are directly applied to the quantized counterparts (e.g., both false negative and false positive could occur). Therefore, specialized techniques are required for rigorously verifying quantized DNNs.

Broadly speaking, the existing techniques for quantized DNNs make use of constraint solving which is based on either SAT/SMT or (reduced, ordered) binary decision diagrams (BDDs). A majority of work resorts to SAT/SMT solving. For the 1-bit quantization (i.e., BNNs), typically BNNs are transformed into Boolean formulas where SAT solving is harnessed [12,33,45,46]. Some recent work also studies variants of BNNs [28,48], i.e., BNNs with ternary weights. For quantized DNNs with multiple bits (i.e., fixed-points), it is natural to encode them as quantifier-free SMT formulas, e.g., using bit-vector and fixed-point theories [7,22,24], so that off-the-shelf SMT solvers can be leveraged. In another direction, BDD-based approaches currently can tackle BNNs only [54]. In a nutshell, they encode a BNN and an input region as a BDD, based on which various analyses can be performed via queries on the BDD. The crux of the approach is how to generate the BDD efficiently. In the work [54], the BDD is constructed by BDD learning [44], thus, currently limited to toy BNNs (e.g., 64 input size, 5 hidden neurons, and 2 output size) with relatively small input regions.

On the other hand, existing work mostly focuses on *qualitative* verification, which asks whether there exists an input x (in a specified region) for a neural network such that a property (e.g., local robustness) is violated. In many practical applications, checking only the existence is not sufficient. Indeed, for local robustness, such an (adversarial) input almost surely exists which makes a qualitative answer less meaningful. Instead, *quantitative* verification, which asks how often a property ϕ is satisfied or violated, is far more useful yet more challenging as it could provide a probabilistic guarantee of the behavior of neural networks. Such a quantitative guarantee is essential to certify, for instance, certain implementations of neural network based perceptual components against safety standards of autonomous vehicles [29,32]. Quantitative analysis of general neural networks, however, is challenging, hence received little attention and for which the results are rather limited so far. DeepSRGR [69] presented an abstract interpretation based quantitative robustness verification approach for DNNs which is sound but incomplete. For BNNs, approximate SAT model-counting solvers ($\sharp$SAT) are leveraged [6,47] based on the SAT encoding for the qualitative counterpart. Though probably approximately correct (PAC) style guarantees can be provided, verification cost is usually prohibitively high to achieve higher precision and confidence.

Main Contributions. We propose a BDD-based framework BDD4BNN to support quantitative analysis of BNNs. The main challenge is how to efficiently build BDDs from BNNs [47]. In contrast to previous work [54] which is learning-based and largely treats the BNN as a blackbox, we *directly* encode a BNN and the associated input region into BDDs. In a nutshell, a BNN is a sequential composition of multiple internal blocks and one output block. Each block comprises 3 layers and captures a function $f : \{+1, -1\}^n \to \{+1, -1\}^m$, where n (resp. m) denotes the number of inputs (resp. outputs) of the block. Technically, the function f can be alternatively rewritten as a function over the standard Boolean domain, i.e., $f : \{0, 1\}^n \to \{0, 1\}^m$. A key stepping-stone of our encoding is the observation that the i-th output y_i of the block can be captured by a cardinality constraint of the form $\sum_{j=1}^n \ell_j \geq k$ such that $y_i = +1 \Leftrightarrow \sum_{j=1}^n \ell_j \geq k$, where each literal ℓ_j is either x_j or $\neg x_j$ for the input variable x_j, and k is a constant. We then present an algorithm to encode a cardinality constraint $\sum_{j=1}^n \ell_j \geq k$ as a BDD with $O((n - k) \cdot k)$ nodes in $O((n - k) \cdot k)$ time. As a result, the input-output relation of each block can be encoded as a BDD, the composition of which yields the BDD for the entire BNN. A distinguished advantage of our BDD encoding lies in its support of incremental encoding. In particular, when different input regions are of interest, there is no need to construct the BDD of the entire BNN from scratch.

Encoding BNNs as BDDs enables a wide variety of applications in security analysis and decision explanation of BNNs. In this paper, we highlight two of them within our framework, i.e., robustness analysis and interpretability. It was shown that DNNs have been suffering from poor robustness to adversarial examples [49,50,59]. We consider two quantitative variants of the problem: (1) how many adversarial examples does the BNN have in the input region, and (2) how many of them are misclassified to each class? We further provide an algorithm to incrementally compute the (locally) maximal Hamming distance within which the BNN satisfies the desired robustness properties.

Interpretability is an issue arisen as a result of the blackbox nature of DNNs [25,43]. In application domains such as medical diagnosis, understanding the decisions made by DNNs is a must. We consider two problems: (1) why some inputs are (mis)classified into a class by the BNN and (2) are there any essential features in the input region that are common for all samples classified into a class?

Experimental Results. We implement our framework as a prototype tool BDD4BNN using the CUDD package [58], which scales to BNNs with up to 4 internal blocks, 200 hidden neurons, and 784 input size. To the best of our knowledge, it is the first work to precisely and quantitatively analyze such large BNNs that go significantly beyond the state-of-the-art. The experimental results show that BDD4BNN is significantly more efficient and scalable than the learning-based technique [54]. Furthermore, we demonstrate how BDD4BNN can be used in quantitative robustness analysis and decision explanation of BNNs. For quantitative robustness analysis, our experimental results show that BDD4BNN is considerably ($5\times$ to $1,340\times$) faster and more accurate than the state-of-the-art approximate $\sharp$SAT-based approach [6]. It can also compute precisely the distribution of predicated classes of the images in the input region as well as the locally maximal Hamming distances on several BNNs. For decision explanation, we show the effectiveness of BDD4BNN in computing prime-implicant explanations and essential features of the given input region for some target classes. Note that this work focuses on quantitative verification and interpretability of BNNs and may underperform SAT/SMT-based methods [12,33,45,46] for qualitative verification of BNNs.

In general, our main contributions can be summarized as follows.

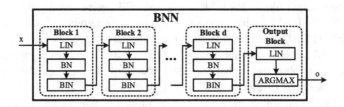

Fig. 1. Architecture of a BNN with $d + 1$ blocks

- We introduce a novel algorithmic approach for encoding BNNs into BDDs that exactly preserves the semantics of BNNs and supports incremental encoding.
- We propose a framework for quantitative verification of BNNs and in particular, we demonstrate the robustness analysis and interpretability of BNNs.
- We implement the framework as an end-to-end tool BDD4BNN and conduct thorough experiments on various BNNs, demonstrating the efficiency and effectiveness of BDD4BNN.

2 Preliminaries

In this section, we briefly introduce binarized neural networks (BNNs) and (reduced, ordered) binary decision diagrams (BDDs).

We denote by $\mathbb{R}$, $\mathbb{N}$, $\mathbb{B}$, and $\mathbb{B}_{\pm 1}$ the set of real numbers, the set of natural numbers, the standard Boolean domain $\{0, 1\}$ and the integer set $\{+1, -1\}$. For $n \in \mathbb{N}$, we denote by $[n]$ the set $\{1, \cdots, n\}$. We will use W, $W', \ldots$ to denote (2-dimensional) matrices, $x, v, \cdots$ to denote (row) vectors, and $x, v, \ldots$ to denote scalars. We denote by $W_{i,:}$ and $W_{:,j}$ the i-th row and j-th column of the matrix W. Similarly, we denote by x_j and $W_{i,j}$ the j-th entry of x and $W_{i,:}$ respectively. In this work, Boolean values $1/0$ will be used as integers $1/0$ in arithmetic computations without typecasting.

2.1 Binarized Neural Networks

A binarized neural network (BNN) [27] is a neural network where weights and activations are predominantly binarized over the domain $\mathbb{B}_{\pm 1}$. In this work, we consider feed-forward BNNs. As shown in Fig. 1, a BNN can be seen as a sequential composition of several internal blocks and one output block. Each internal block comprises 3 layers: a linear layer (LIN), a batch normalization layer (BN), and a binarization layer (BIN). The output block comprises a linear layer and an ARGMAX layer. Note that the input/output of internal blocks and the input of the output block are all vectors over $\mathbb{B}_{\pm 1}$.

Table 1. Definitions of layers in BNNs, where $n_{d+2} = s$ and $\arg\max(\cdot)$ returns the index of the largest entry which occurs first.

Layer	Function	Parameters	Definition
LIN	$t_i^{lin} : \mathbb{B}_{\pm 1}^{n_i} \to \mathbb{R}^{n_{i+1}}$	Weight matrix: $W \in \mathbb{B}_{\pm 1}^{n_i \times n_{i+1}}$ Bias (row) vector: $b \in \mathbb{R}^{n_{i+1}}$	$t_i^{lin}(x) = y$ where $\forall j \in [n_{i+1}]$, $y_j = \langle x, W_{:,j} \rangle + b_j$
BN	$t_i^{bn} : \mathbb{R}^{n_{i+1}} \to \mathbb{R}^{n_{i+1}}$	Weight vectors: $\alpha \in \mathbb{R}^{n_{i+1}}$ Bias vector: $\gamma \in \mathbb{R}^{n_{i+1}}$ Mean vector: $\mu \in \mathbb{R}^{n_{i+1}}$ Std. dev. vector: $\sigma \in \mathbb{R}^{n_{i+1}}$	$t_i^{bn}(x) = y$ where $\forall j \in [n_{i+1}]$, $y_j = \alpha_j \cdot (\frac{x_j - \mu_j}{\sigma_j}) + \gamma_j$
BIN	$t_i^{bin} : \mathbb{R}^{n_{i+1}} \to \mathbb{B}_{\pm 1}^{n_{i+1}}$	–	$t_i^{bin}(x) = y$ where $\forall j \in [n_{i+1}]$, $y_j = \begin{cases} +1, & \text{if } x_j \geq 0; \\ -1, & \text{otherwise.} \end{cases}$
ARGMAX	$t_{d+1}^{am} : \mathbb{R}^s \to \mathbb{B}^s$	–	$t_{d+1}^{am}(x) = y$ where $\forall j \in [s]$, $y_j = 1 \Leftrightarrow j = \arg\max(x)$

Definition 1. *A BNN* $\mathcal{N} : \mathbb{B}_{\pm 1}^{n_1} \to \mathbb{B}^s$ *with s classes is given by a tuple of blocks* $(t_1, \cdots, t_d, t_{d+1})$ *such that* $\mathcal{N} = t_{d+1} \circ t_d \circ \cdots \circ t_1$,

- *for every* $i \in [d]$, $t_i : \mathbb{B}_{\pm 1}^{n_i} \to \mathbb{B}_{\pm 1}^{n_{i+1}}$ *is an internal block comprising a LIN layer* t_i^{lin}, *a BN layer* t_i^{bn} *and a BIN* t_i^{bin} *with* $t_i = t_i^{bin} \circ t_i^{bn} \circ t_i^{lin}$,
- $t_{d+1} : \mathbb{B}_{\pm 1}^{n_{d+1}} \to \mathbb{B}^s$ *is the output block comprising a LIN layer* t_{d+1}^{lin} *and an ARGMAX layer* t_{d+1}^{am} *with* $t_{d+1} = t_{d+1}^{am} \circ t_{d+1}^{lin}$,

where t_i^{bin}, t_i^{bn}, t_i^{lin} *for* $i \in [d]$, t_{d+1}^{lin} *and* t_{d+1}^{am} *are given in Table 1.*

Intuitively, a LIN layer is a linear transformation. A BN layer following a LIN layer is used to standardize and normalize the output of the LIN layer. A BIN layer is used to binarize the real-numbered output vector of the BN layer. In this work, we consider the sign function which is widely used in BNNs to binarize real-numbered vectors. An ARGMAX layer follows a LIN layer and outputs the index of the largest entry as the predicted class which is represented by a one-hot vector. (In case there is more than one such entry, the first one is returned.) Formally, given a BNN $\mathcal{N} = (t_1, \cdots, t_d, t_{d+1})$ and an input $x \in \mathbb{B}_{\pm 1}^{n_1}$, $\mathcal{N}(x) \in \mathbb{B}^s$ is a one-hot vector in which the index of the non-zero entry is the predicated class.

2.2 Binary Decision Diagrams

A BDD [9] is a rooted acyclic directed graph where non-terminal nodes v are labeled by Boolean variables $\mathsf{var}(v)$ and terminal nodes (leaves) v are labeled with values $\mathsf{val}(v) \in \mathbb{B}$, referred to as the 1-leaf and the 0-leaf respectively. Each non-terminal node v has two outgoing edges: $\mathsf{hi}(v)$ meaning $\mathsf{var}(v) = 1$ and $\mathsf{lo}(v)$ meaning $\mathsf{var}(v) = 0$. We will also refer to $\mathsf{hi}(v)$ and $\mathsf{lo}(v)$ as the hi and lo children of v respectively. Moreover, assuming that $x_1, \cdots, x_m$ is the variable ordering, for each node v with $\mathsf{var}(v) = x_i$ and each $v' \in \{\mathsf{hi}(v), \mathsf{lo}(v)\}$ with $\mathsf{var}(v') = x_j$, we have $i < j$. In the graphical representation of BDDs, $\mathsf{hi}(v)$ and $\mathsf{lo}(v)$ are depicted by solid and dashed lines respectively. Multi-Terminal Binary Decision Diagrams (MTBDDs) are a variant of BDDs in which the

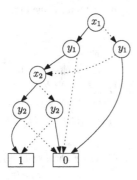

Fig. 2. The reduced BDD for $f(x_1, y_1, x_2, y_2) = (x_1 \Leftrightarrow y_1) \wedge (x_2 \Leftrightarrow y_2)$

Table 2. Some basic BDD operations, where $op \in \{\text{AND}, \text{OR}, \text{XOR}, \text{XNOR}\}$

Operation	Description
$v = \text{VAR}(x)$	$f_v(x) = x$
$v = \text{CONST}(1)$	$f_v = 1$
$v = \text{CONST}(0)$	$f_v = 0$
$\text{NOT}(v)$	$\neg f_v$
$\text{APPLY}(v, v', op)$	$f_v \; op \; f_{v'}$
$\text{EXISTS}(v, X)$	$\exists X. f_v$
$\text{SATALL}(v)$	$\text{SATALL}(f_v)$
$\text{RELPROD}(v, v')$	$f_v \circ f_{v'}$
$\text{ITE}(x, v, v')$	$(x \wedge v) \vee (\neg x \wedge v')$

terminal nodes are not restricted to be 0 or 1. A BDD is *reduced* if it (1) has only one 1-leaf and one 0-leaf, (2) does not contain a node v such that $\text{hi}(v) = \text{lo}(v)$, and (3) does not contain two distinct non-terminal nodes v and v' such that $\text{var}(v) = \text{var}(v')$, $\text{hi}(v) = \text{hi}(v')$ and $\text{lo}(v) = \text{lo}(v')$. For example, Fig. 2 shows the reduced BDD for the Boolean function $f(x_1, y_1, x_2, y_2) = (x_1 \Leftrightarrow y_1) \wedge (x_2 \Leftrightarrow y_2)$. Hereafter, we assume that BDDs are reduced.

Bryant [9] showed that BDDs can serve as a canonical form of Boolean functions. Given a BDD over variables $x_1, \cdots, x_m$, each non-terminal node v with $\text{var}(v) = x_i$ represents a Boolean function $f_v = (x_i \wedge f_{\text{hi}(v)}) \vee (\neg x_i \wedge f_{\text{lo}(v)})$. Operations on Boolean functions can usually be efficiently implemented via manipulating their BDD representations. A good variable ordering is crucial for the performance of BDD manipulations while the problem of finding an optimal ordering for a function is NP-hard. To store and manipulate BDDs efficiently, the nodes are stored in a hash table and the recent computed results are stored in a cache to avoid duplicated computations. In this work, we will use some basic BDD operations such as ITE for If-Then-Else, XOR for exclusive-OR, XNOR for exclusive-NOR (i.e., a XNOR $b = \neg(a$ XOR $b)$) and SATALL(f_v) for the set of all solutions of the Boolean formula f_v. We denote by $\mathcal{L}(v)$ the set SATALL(f_v). For easy reference, more operations are given in Table 2. By $op(v, v')$ we denote the operation APPLY(v, v', op).

3 BDD4BNN Design

3.1 BDD4BNN Overview

An overview of BDD4BNN is depicted in Fig. 3. BDD4BNN comprises four main components: Region2BDD, BNN2CC, BDD Model Builder, and Query Engine. For a fixed BNN $\mathcal{N} = (t_1, \cdots, t_d, t_{d+1})$ and a region R of the input space of $\mathcal{N}$, BDD4BNN constructs the BDDs $(G_i^{out})_{i \in [s]}$ to encode the input-output relation of $\mathcal{N}$ in the region R, where the BDD G_i^{out} corresponds to the class $i \in [s]$. Technically, the region R is partitioned into s parts represented by $(G_i^{out})_{i \in [s]}$. For each property query, BDD4BNN analyzes $(G_i^{out})_{i \in [s]}$ and outputs the query result.

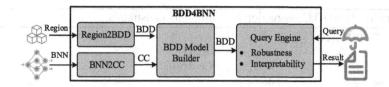

Fig. 3. Overview of BDD4BNN

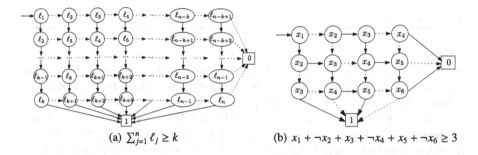

(a) $\sum_{j=1}^{n} \ell_j \geq k$ (b) $x_1 + \neg x_2 + x_3 + \neg x_4 + x_5 + \neg x_6 \geq 3$

Fig. 4. Graphic representation of BDDs using Algorithm 1

The general workflow of our approach is as follows. First, Region2BDD builds up a BDD G_R^{in} from the region R which represents the desired input space of $\mathcal{N}$ for analysis. Second, BNN2CC transforms each block of the BNN $\mathcal{N}$ into a set of cardinality constraints (CCs) similar to [6,46]. Third, BDD Model Builder builds the BDDs $(G_i^{out})_{i \in [s]}$ from all the cardinality constraints and the BDD G_R^{in}. Finally, Query Engine answers queries by analyzing the BDDs $(G_i^{out})_{i \in [s]}$. Our Query Engine currently supports two types of application queries: robustness analysis and interpretability.

In the rest of this section, we first introduce the key sub-component CC2BDD, which provides an encoding of cardinality constraints into BDDs. We then provide details of the components Region2BDD, BNN2CC, and BDD Model Builder. The Query Engine will be described in Sect. 4.

3.2 CC2BDD: Cardinality Constraints to BDDs

A *cardinality constraint* is a constraint of the form $\sum_{j=1}^{n} \ell_j \geq k$ over a vector $\boldsymbol{x}$ of Boolean variables with length n, where the literal ℓ_j is either $\boldsymbol{x}_j$ or $\neg \boldsymbol{x}_j$ for each $j \in [n]$. Note that constraints of the form $\sum_{j=1}^{n} \ell_j > k$, $\sum_{j=1}^{n} \ell_j \leq k$ and $\sum_{j=1}^{n} \ell_j < k$ are equivalent to $\sum_{j=1}^{n} \ell_j \geq k+1$, $\sum_{j=1}^{n} \neg \ell_j \geq n-k$ and $\sum_{j=1}^{n} \neg \ell_j \geq n-k+1$, respectively. We assume that 1 (resp. 0) is a special cardinality constraint that always holds (resp. never holds).

To encode $\sum_{j=1}^{n} \ell_j \geq k$ as a BDD, we observe that all the possible solutions of $\sum_{j=1}^{n} \ell_j \geq k$ can be compactly represented by a BDD-like graph shown in Fig. 4(a), where each node is labeled by a literal, and a solid (resp. dashed) edge from a node labeled by ℓ_j means that the value of the literal ℓ_j is 1 (resp. 0). Thus, each path from the ℓ_1-node to the 1-leaf through the ℓ_j-node (where $1 \leq j \leq n$) captures a set of valuations where ℓ_j followed by a (horizontal) dashed line is set to be 0 while ℓ_j followed by

---

Algorithm 1: BDD Construction for cardinality constraints

---

1 **Proc** CC2BDD(CC : $\sum_{j=1}^{n} \ell_j \geq k$)
2      $G_{k+1,1} = G_{k+1,2} = \cdots = G_{k+1,n-k+1} = \text{CONST}(1)$;
3      $G_{1,n-k+2} = G_{2,n-k+2} = \cdots = G_{k,n-k+2} = \text{CONST}(0)$;
4   **for** ($i = k$; $i \geq 1$; $i - -$) **do**
5   **for** ($j = n - k + 1$; $j \geq 1$; $j - -$) **do**
6   **if** ($\ell_{i+j-1} == x_{i+j-1}$) **then** $G_{i,j} = \text{ITE}(x_{i+j-1}, G_{i+1,j}, G_{i,j+1})$;
7   **else** $G_{i,j} = \text{ITE}(x_{i+j-1}, G_{i,j+1}, G_{i+1,j})$;
8   **return** $G_{1,1}$

---

a (vertical) solid line is set to be 1, and all the other literals which are not along the path can take arbitrary values. Clearly, for each of these valuations, there are at least k positive literals, hence the constraint $\sum_{j=1}^{n} \ell_j \geq k$ holds.

Based on the above observation, we build the BDD for $\sum_{j=1}^{n} \ell_j \geq k$ using Algorithm 1. It builds a BDD for each node in Fig. 4(a), row-by-row (the index i in Algorithm 1) and from right to left (the index j in Algorithm 1). For each node at the i-th row and j-th column, the label of the node must be the literal ℓ_{i+j-1}. We build the BDD $G_{i,j} = \text{ITE}(x_{i+j-1}, G_{i+1,j}, G_{i,j+1})$ if ℓ_{i+j-1} is of the form x_{i+j-1} (Line 6), otherwise we build the BDD $G_{i,j} = \text{ITE}(x_{i+j-1}, G_{i,j+1}, G_{i+1,j})$ (Line 7). Finally, we obtain the BDD $G_{1,1}$ that encodes the solutions of $\sum_{j=1}^{n} \ell_j \geq k$. Consider $x_1 + \neg x_2 + x_3 + \neg x_4 + x_5 + \neg x_6 \geq 3$, Fig. 4(b) shows its BDD by Algorithm 1.

Lemma 1. *For each cardinality constraint $\sum_{j=1}^{n} \ell_j \geq k$, a BDD G with $O((n-k) \cdot k)$ nodes can be computed in $O((n-k) \cdot k)$ time such that $\mathcal{L}(G)$ is the set of all the solutions of $\sum_{j=1}^{n} \ell_j \geq k$.*

Compared with prior works [8,42] which transform general arithmetic constraints into BDDs, we devise a dedicated BDD encoding algorithm for the cardinality constraints without applying reduction, hence it is more efficient.

3.3 Region2BDD: Input Regions to BDDs

In this paper, we consider the following two types of input regions.

- *Input region based on Hamming distance.* For an input $u \in \mathbb{B}_{\pm 1}^{n_1}$ and an integer $r \geq 0$, $R(u, r)$ denotes the set $\{x \in \mathbb{B}_{\pm 1}^{n_1} \mid \text{HD}(x, u) \leq r\}$, where $\text{HD}(x, u)$ denotes the Hamming distance between x and u. Intuitively, $R(u, r)$ includes the input vectors which differ from u by at most r positions.
- *Input region with fixed indices.* For an input $u \in \mathbb{B}_{\pm 1}^{n_1}$ and a set of indices $I \subseteq [n_1]$, $R(u, I)$ denotes the set $\{x \in \mathbb{B}_{\pm 1}^{n_1} \mid \forall i \in [n_1] \setminus I. \, u_i = x_i\}$. Intuitively, $R(u, I)$ includes the input vectors which differ from u only at the indices from I.

Note that both $R(u, n_1)$ and $R(u, [n_1])$ denote the entire input space $\mathbb{B}_{\pm 1}^{n_1}$.

Recall that each input sample is an element from $\mathbb{B}_{\pm 1}^{n_1}$. To represent the region R by a BDD, we transform each value ± 1 into a Boolean value $1/0$. To this end, for each input $u \in \mathbb{B}_{\pm 1}^{n_1}$, we create a new sample $u^{(b)} \in \mathbb{B}^{n_1}$ such that for every $i \in [n_1]$, $u_i =$

$2u_i^{(b)} - 1$. Therefore, $R(u, r)$ and $R(u, I)$ will be represented by $R(u^{(b)}, r)$ and $R(u^{(b)}, I)$, respectively. The transformation functions t_i^{lin}, t_i^{bn}, t_i^{bin} and t_{d+1}^{am} of the LIN, BN, BIN, and ARGMAX layers (cf. Table 1) will be handled accordingly. Note that for convenience, vectors over the Boolean domain $\mathbb{B}$ may be directly given by u or x when it is clear from the context.

Region Encoding Under Hamming Distance. Given an input $u \in \mathbb{B}^{n_1}$ and an integer r, the region $R(u, r)$ can be expressed by a cardinality constraint $\sum_{j=1}^{n_1} \ell_j \leq r$ (which is equivalent to $\sum_{j=1}^{n_1} \neg \ell_j \geq n_1 - r$), where for every $j \in [n_1]$, $\ell_j = x_j$ if $u_j = 0$, otherwise $\ell_j = \neg x_j$. For instance, consider $u = (1, 1, 1, 0, 0)$ and $r = 2$, we have:

$$HD(u, x) = 1 \oplus x_1 + 1 \oplus x_2 + 1 \oplus x_3 + 0 \oplus x_4 + 0 \oplus x_5 = \neg x_1 + \neg x_2 + \neg x_3 + x_4 + x_5.$$

Thus, $R((1, 1, 1, 0, 0), 2)$ can be expressed by the cardinality constraint $\neg x_1 + \neg x_2 + \neg x_3 + x_4 + x_5 \leq 2$, or equivalently $x_1 + x_2 + x_3 + \neg x_4 + \neg x_5 \geq 3$.

By Algorithm 1, the cardinality constraint of $R(u, r)$ can be encoded by the BDD $G_{u,r}^{in}$, such that $\mathcal{L}(G_{u,r}^{in}) = R(u, r)$. Following Lemma 1, we get that:

Lemma 2. *For an input region R given by an input $u \in \mathbb{B}^{n_1}$ and an integer r, a BDD $G_{u,r}^{in}$ with $O(r \cdot (n_1 - r))$ nodes can be computed in $O(r \cdot (n_1 - r))$ time such that $\mathcal{L}(G_{u,r}^{in}) = R(u, r)$.*

Region Encoding Under Fixed Indices. Given an input $u \in \mathbb{B}^{n_1}$ and a set of indices $I \subseteq [n_1]$, the region $R(u, I) = \{x \in \mathbb{B}^{n_1} \mid \forall i \in [n_1] \setminus I. u_i = x_i\}$ can be represented by the BDD $G_{u,I}^{in} \triangleq \text{AND}_{i \in [n_1] \setminus I}\big((u_i == 1)?\text{VAR}(x_i) : \text{NOT}(\text{VAR}(x_i))\big)$. Intuitively, $G_{u,I}^{in}$ states that the value at the index $i \in [n_1] \setminus I$ should be the same as the one in u while the value at the index $i \in I$ is unrestricted. For instance, consider $u = (1, 0, 0, 0)$ and $I = \{3, 4\}$, we have:

$$R((1, 0, 0, 0), \{3, 4\}) = \{(1, 0, 0, 0), (1, 0, 0, 1), (1, 0, 1, 0), (1, 0, 1, 1)\} = x_1 \wedge \neg x_2.$$

Lemma 3. *For an input region R given by an input $u \in \mathbb{B}^{n_1}$ and indices $I \subseteq [n_1]$, a BDD $G_{u,I}^{in}$ with $O(n_1 - |I|)$ nodes can be computed in $O(n_1)$ time such that $\mathcal{L}(G_{u,I}^{in}) = R(u, I)$.*

3.4 BNN2CC: BNNs to Cardinality Constraints

As mentioned before, to encode the BNN $\mathcal{N} = (t_1, \cdots, t_d, t_{d+1})$ as BDDs, we transform the BNN $\mathcal{N}$ into cardinality constraints from which the desired BDDs $(G_i^{out})_{i \in [s]}$ are constructed. To this end, we first transform each internal block $t_i : \mathbb{B}_{\pm 1}^{n_i} \to \mathbb{B}_{\pm 1}^{n_{i+1}}$ into n_{i+1} cardinality constraints, each of which corresponds to one of the outputs of t_i. Then we transform the output block $t_{d+1} : \mathbb{B}_{\pm 1}^{n_{d+1}} \to \mathbb{B}^s$ into $s(s-1)$ cardinality constraints, where one output class yields $(s - 1)$ cardinality constraints.

For each vector-valued function t, we denote by $t_{\downarrow j}$ the (scalar-valued) function returning the j-th entry of the output of t.

Transformation for Internal Blocks. Consider the internal block $t_i : \mathbb{B}_{\pm 1}^{n_i} \to \mathbb{B}_{\pm 1}^{n_{i+1}}$ for $i \in [d]$. Recall that for every $j \in [n_{i+1}]$ and $x \in \mathbb{B}_{\pm 1}^{n_i}$, $t_{i\downarrow j}(x) = t_i^{bin}(t_i^{bn}(\langle x, W_{:,j}\rangle + b_j))$, and each value ± 1 of an input $u \in \mathbb{B}_{\pm 1}^{n_i}$ is replaced by $1/0$ (cf. Sect. 3.3). To be consistent, the function $t_{i\downarrow j} : \mathbb{B}_{\pm 1}^{n_i} \to \mathbb{B}_{\pm 1}$ is reformulated as the function $t_{i\downarrow j}^{(b)} : \mathbb{B}^{n_i} \to \mathbb{B}$ such that for every $x \in \mathbb{B}^{n_i}$, $t_{i\downarrow j}^{(b)}(x) = 0.5 \times (t_i^{bin}(t_i^{bn}(\langle 2x - 1, W_{:,j}\rangle + b_j)) + 1)$, where $\mathbf{1}$ denotes the vector of 1's with the width n_i.

Let $C_{i,j}$ be the following cardinality constraint:

$$
C_{i,j} \triangleq
\begin{cases}
\sum_{k=1}^{n_i} \ell_k \geq \lceil \frac{1}{2} \cdot (n_i + \mu_j - b_j - \frac{\gamma_j \cdot \sigma_j}{\alpha_j}) \rceil, & \text{if } \alpha_j > 0; \\
1, & \text{if } \alpha_j = 0 \wedge \gamma_j \geq 0; \\
0, & \text{if } \alpha_j = 0 \wedge \gamma_j < 0; \\
\sum_{k=1}^{n_i} \neg\ell_k \geq \lceil \frac{1}{2} \cdot (n_i - \mu_j + b_j + \frac{\gamma_j \cdot \sigma_j}{\alpha_j}) \rceil, & \text{if } \alpha_j < 0;
\end{cases}
$$

where for every $k \in [n_i]$, ℓ_k is x_k if $W_{k,j} = +1$, and ℓ_k is $\neg x_k$ if $W_{k,j} = -1$.

Proposition 1. $t_{i\downarrow j}^{(b)} \Leftrightarrow C_{i,j}$.

Proof refers to [71].

Transformation for the Output Block. For the output block $t_{d+1} : \mathbb{B}_{\pm 1}^{n_{d+1}} \to \mathbb{B}^s$, since $t_{d+1} = t_{d+1}^{am} \circ t_{d+1}^{lin}$, then for every $j \in [s]$, we can reformulate $t_{d+1\downarrow j} : \mathbb{B}_{\pm 1}^{n_{d+1}} \to \mathbb{B}$ as the function $t_{d+1\downarrow j}^{(b)} : \mathbb{B}^{n_{d+1}} \to \mathbb{B}$ such that for every $x \in \mathbb{B}^{n_{d+1}}$, $t_{d+1\downarrow j}^{(b)}(x) = t_{d+1\downarrow j}(2x - 1)$.

For every $j' \in [s] \setminus \{j\}$, we define the cardinality constraint $C_{d+1,j'}$ as follows:

$$
C_{d+1,j'} \triangleq
\begin{cases}
\sum_{k=1}^{n_{d+1}} \ell_{d+1,k} \geq \frac{1}{4}(b_{j'} - b_j + \sum_{k=1}^{n_{d+1}}(W_{k,j} - W_{k,j'})) + 1 + \sharp\text{Neg}, \\
\quad \text{if } j' < j \text{ and } \frac{1}{4}(b_{j'} - b_j + \sum_{k=1}^{n_{d+1}}(W_{k,j} - W_{k,j'})) \text{ is an integer}; \\
\\
\sum_{k=1}^{n_{d+1}} \ell_{d+1,k} \geq \lceil \frac{1}{4}(b_{j'} - b_j + \sum_{k=1}^{n_{d+1}}(W_{k,j} - W_{k,j'})) \rceil + \sharp\text{Neg}, \qquad \text{otherwise};
\end{cases}
$$

where $\sharp\text{Neg} = |\{k \in [n_{d+1}] \mid W_{k,j} - W_{k,j'} = -2\}|$, $\ell_{d+1,k}$ is $x_{d+1,k}$ if $W_{k,j} - W_{k,j'} = +2$, $\ell_{d+1,k}$ is $\neg x_{d+1,k}$ if $W_{k,j} - W_{k,j'} = -2$, and $\ell_{d+1,k}$ is 0 if $W_{k,j} - W_{k,j'} = 0$.

Proposition 2. $t_{d+1\downarrow j}^{(b)} \Leftrightarrow \bigwedge_{j' \in [s], j' \neq j} C_{d+1,j'}$.

Proof refers to [71].

For each internal block $t_i : \mathbb{B}_{\pm 1}^{n_i} \to \mathbb{B}_{\pm 1}^{n_{i+1}}$, we denote by $\text{BNN2CC}(t_i)$ the cardinality constraints $\{C_{i,1}, \cdots, C_{i,n_{i+1}}\}$. For each output class $j \in [s]$, we denote by $\text{BNN2CC}^j(t_{d+1})$ the cardinality constraints $\{C_{d+1,1}, \cdots C_{d+1,j-1}, C_{d+1,j+1}, \cdots, C_{d+1,s}\}$. By applying the above transformation to all the blocks of the BNN $\mathcal{N} = (t_1, \cdots, t_d, t_{d+1})$, we obtain its cardinality constraint form $\mathcal{N}^{(b)} = (t_1^{(b)}, \cdots, t_d^{(b)}, t_{d+1}^{(b)})$ such that for each $i \in [d]$, $t_i^{(b)} = \text{BNN2CC}(t_i)$, and $t_{d+1}^{(b)} = (\text{BNN2CC}^1(t_{d+1}), \cdots, \text{BNN2CC}^s(t_{d+1}))$. Given an input $u \in \mathbb{B}^{n_1}$, we denote by $\mathcal{N}^{(b)}(u)$ the index $j \in [s]$ such that all the cardinality constraints in $\text{BNN2CC}^j(t_{d+1})$ hold under the valuation u. It is straightforward to verify:

Theorem 1. $u \in \mathbb{B}_{\pm 1}^{n_1}$ is classified into the class j by the BNN $\mathcal{N}$ iff $\mathcal{N}^{(b)}(u^{(b)}) = j$.

Example 1. Consider the BNN $\mathcal{N} = (t_1, t_2)$ with one internal block t_1 and one output block t_2 as shown in Fig. 5 (left-bottom), where the elements of the Weight matrix W are associated to the edges, and the other parameters are given in the left-up table. The transformation functions of blocks t_1 and t_2 are given in the right-up table, and their cardinality constraints are given in the right-bottom table.

For instance, for each input $x \in \mathbb{B}^3_{\pm 1}$, $y_1 = \text{sign}(-x_1 + x_2 + x_3 + 2.7)$, i.e., $y_1 = +1 \Leftrightarrow -x_1 + x_2 + x_3 + 2.7 \geq 0$. By replacing x_i with $2 \times x_i^{(b)} - 1$ and $x_1^{(b)}$ with $1 - \neg x_1^{(b)}$, we have: $y_1 = +1 \Leftrightarrow (-x_1^{(b)} + x_2^{(b)} + x_3^{(b)} + 0.85 \geq 0) \Leftrightarrow (\neg x_1^{(b)} + x_2^{(b)} + x_3^{(b)} \geq 0.15)$. Thus we get $y_1^{(b)} \Leftrightarrow \neg x_1^{(b)} + x_2^{(b)} + x_3^{(b)} \geq 1$ (note that $y_1^{(b)} = 0 \Leftrightarrow \neg x_1^{(b)} + x_2^{(b)} + x_3^{(b)} < 1$). Similarly, we can deduce that $o_1 \Leftrightarrow y_1 - y_2 \geq 0.7$, and thus $o_1 \Leftrightarrow y_1^{(b)} - y_2^{(b)} \geq 0.35 \Leftrightarrow y_1^{(b)} + \neg y_2^{(b)} \geq 2$.

3.5   BDD Model Builder

The construction of the BDDs $(G_i^{out})_{i \in [s]}$ from the BNN $\mathcal{N}^{(b)}$ and the input region R is done iteratively throughout the blocks. Initially, the BDD for the first block is built, which can be seen as the input-output relation for the first internal block. In the i-th iteration, as the input-output relation of the first $(i-1)$ internal blocks has been encoded into the BDD, we compose this BDD with the BDD for the block t_i which is built from its cardinality constraints $t_i^{(b)}$, resulting in the BDD for the first i internal blocks. Finally, we obtain the BDDs $(G_i^{out})_{i \in [s]}$ of the BNN $\mathcal{N}$, with respect to the input region R.

b_1	α_1	μ_1	γ_1	σ_1	b_2
0.2	0.02	−0.5	0.02	2	−0.8
−0.5	−0.03	1.5	−0.03	3	0.6

$\mathcal{N}(x)$
$y_1 = \text{sign}(-x_1 + x_2 + x_3 + 2.7)$
$y_2 = \text{sign}(-x_1 - x_2 + x_3 - 1)$
$o_1 \Leftrightarrow y_1 - y_2 \geq 0.7$
$o_2 \Leftrightarrow y_1 - y_2 < 0.7$

Cardinality Constraint Encoding
$y_1^{(b)} \Leftrightarrow \neg x_1^{(b)} + x_2^{(b)} + x_3^{(b)} \geq 1$
$y_2^{(b)} \Leftrightarrow \neg x_1^{(b)} + \neg x_2^{(b)} + x_3^{(b)} \geq 2$
$o_1 \Leftrightarrow y_1^{(b)} + \neg y_2^{(b)} \geq 2$
$o_2 \Leftrightarrow y_1^{(b)} + \neg y_2^{(b)} < 2$

Fig. 5. An illustrating example

Design Choice. There are several design choices for efficiency consideration which we discuss as follows. First of all, to encode the input-output relation of an internal block t_i into BDD from its cardinality constraints $t_i^{(b)} = \{C_{i,1}, \cdots, C_{i,n_{i+1}}\}$, we need to compute $\text{AND}_{j \in [n_{i+1}]} \text{CC2BDD}(C_{i,j})$. A simple and straightforward approach is to initially compute a BDD $G = \text{CC2BDD}(C_{i,1})$ and then iteratively compute the conjunction $G = \text{AND}(G, \text{CC2BDD}(C_{i,j}))$ of G and $\text{CC2BDD}(C_{i,j})$ for $2 \leq j \leq n_{i+1}$.

Alternatively, we use a divide-and-conquer strategy to recursively compute the BDDs for the first half and the second half of the cardinality constraints respectively, and then apply the AND-operation. Our preliminary experimental results show that the latter approach often performs better (about 2 times faster) than the former one, although they generate the same BDD.

Second, constructing the BDD directly from the cardinality constraints $t_i^{(b)} = \{C_{i,1}, \cdots, C_{i,n_{i+1}}\}$ becomes prohibitively costly when n_i and n_{i+1} are large, as the BDDs CC2BDD($C_{i,j}$) for $j \in [n_{i+1}]$ need to consider all the inputs in $\mathbb{B}^{n_i}$. To improve efficiency, we apply feasible input propagation. Namely, when we construct the BDD for the block t_{i+1}, we only consider its possible inputs with respect to the output of the block t_i. Our preliminary experimental results show that the optimization could significantly improve the efficiency of the BDD construction.

Third, instead of encoding the input-output relation of the BNN $\mathcal{N}$ as a sole BDD or MTBDD, we opt to use a family of s BDDs $(G_i^{out})_{i \in [s]}$, each of which corresponds to one output class of $\mathcal{N}$. Recall that each output class $i \in [s]$ is represented by $(s-1)$ cardinality constraints. Then, we can build a BDD G_i for the output class i, similar to the BDD construction for internal blocks. By composing G_i with the BDD of the entire internal blocks, we obtain the BDD G_i^{out}. Building a single BDD or MTBDD for the BNN is possible from $(G_i^{out})_{i \in [s]}$, but our approach gives the flexibility especially when a specific target class is interested, which is common for robustness analysis.

Algorithm 2: BDD Construction for BNNs

---

1 **Proc** BNN2BDD(BNN : $\mathcal{N} = (t_1, \cdots, t_d, t_{d+1})$, Region : $R(\boldsymbol{u}, \tau)$)

2      $G^{in} = G_{\boldsymbol{u},\tau}^{in}$ (cf. Section 3.3); $\mathcal{N}^{(b)} = (t_1^{(b)}, \cdots, t_d^{(b)}, t_{d+1}^{(b)})$ (cf. Section 3.4);

3   **for** $(i = 1; i \leq d; i++)$ **do**

4          $G' =$ BLOCK2BDD($t_i^{(b)}, G^{in}, i$);

5          $G^{in} =$ EXISTS($G', \boldsymbol{x}^i$) ;   // $\boldsymbol{x}^i$ denote input variables of $t_i^{(b)}$

6          $G = (i == 1)$? G' : RELPROD(G, G');

7   **for** $(i = 1; i \leq s; i++)$ **do**

8          $G_i =$ BLOCK2BDD($t_{d+1,i}^{(b)}, G^{in}, d+1$);

9          $G_i^{out} =$ RELPROD(G_i, G);

10   **return** $(G_i^{out})_{i \in [s]}$

11 **Proc** BLOCK2BDD(CCs : $\{C_m, \cdots, C_n\}$, InputSpace : G^{in}, BlkIndex : i)

12   **if** $n == m$ **then**

13         $G_1 =$ CC2BDD(C_m) (cf. Algorithm 1);

14         $G =$ AND(G_1, G^{in});

15   **if** $i \neq d+1$ **then** $G =$ XNOR(x_m^{i+1}, G);

16   **else**

17         $G_1 =$ BLOCK2BDD($\{C_m, \cdots, C_{\lfloor \frac{n-m}{2} \rfloor + m}\}, G^{in}, i$);

18         $G_2 =$ BLOCK2BDD($\{C_{\lfloor \frac{n-m}{2} \rfloor + m + 1}, \cdots, C_n\}, G^{in}, i$);

19         $G =$ AND(G_1, G_2);

20   **return** G

Overall Algorithm. The overall BDD construction procedure is shown in Algorithm 2. Given a BNN $\mathcal{N} = (t_1, \cdots, t_d, t_{d+1})$ with s output classes and an input region $R(\boldsymbol{u}, \tau)$, the algorithm outputs the BDDs $(G_i^{out})_{i \in [s]}$, encoding the input-output relation of the BNN $\mathcal{N}$ with respect to the input region $R(\boldsymbol{u}, \tau)$.

The procedure BNN2BDD first builds the BDD representation $G_{\boldsymbol{u}, \tau}^{in}$ of the input region $R(\boldsymbol{u}, \tau)$ and the cardinality constraints from BNN $\mathcal{N}^{(b)}$ (Line 1). The first for-loop builds a BDD encoding the input-output relation of the entire internal blocks w.r.t. $G_{\boldsymbol{u}, \tau}^{in}$. The second for-loop builds the BDDs $(G_i^{out})_{i \in [s]}$, each of which encodes the input-output relation of the entire BNN for a class $i \in [s]$ w.r.t. $G_{\boldsymbol{u}, \tau}^{in}$. The procedure BLOCK2BDD receives the cardinality constraints $\{C_m, \cdots, C_n\}$, a BDD G^{in} representing the feasible inputs of the block and the block index i as inputs, and returns a BDD G. If $i = d+1$, namely, the cardinality constraints $\{C_m, \cdots, C_n\}$ are from the output block, the resulting BDD G encodes the subset of $G_{\boldsymbol{u}, \tau}^{in}$ that satisfy all the cardinality constraints $\{C_m, \cdots, C_n\}$. If $i \neq d+1$, then the BDD G encodes the input-output relation of the Boolean function $f_{m,n}$ such that for every $\boldsymbol{x}^i \in \mathcal{L}(G^{in})$, $f_{m,n}(\boldsymbol{x}^i)$ is the truth vector of the cardinality constraints $\{C_m, \cdots, C_n\}$ under the valuation $\boldsymbol{x}^i$. When $m = 1$ and $n = n_{i+1}$, $f_{m,n}$ is the same as $t_i^{(b)}$, hence $\mathcal{L}(G) = \{\boldsymbol{x}^i \times \boldsymbol{x}^{i+1} \in G^{in} \times \mathbb{B}^{n_{i+1}} \mid t_i^{(b)}(\boldsymbol{x}^i) = \boldsymbol{x}^{i+1}\}$. Detailed explanation refers to [71].

Theorem 2. *Given a BNN $\mathcal{N}$ with s output classes and an input region $R(\boldsymbol{u}, \tau)$, we can compute s BDDs $(G_i^{out})_{i \in [s]}$ such that the BNN $\mathcal{N}$ classifies an input $\boldsymbol{x} \in R(\boldsymbol{u}, \tau)$ into the class $i \in [s]$ iff $\boldsymbol{x}^{(b)} \in \mathcal{L}(G_i^{out})$.*

Algorithm 2 explicitly involves $O(d + s)$ RELPROD-operations, $O(s^2 + \sum_{i \in [d]} n_i)$ AND-operations and $O(d)$ EXISTS-operations.

4 Applications: Robustness Analysis and Interpretability

In this section, we present two applications within BDD4BNN, i.e., robustness analysis and interpretability of BNNs.

4.1 Robustness Analysis

Definition 2. *Given a BNN $\mathcal{N}$ and an input region $R(\boldsymbol{u}, \tau)$, the BNN is (locally) robust w.r.t. the region $R(\boldsymbol{u}, \tau)$ if each sample $\boldsymbol{x} \in R(\boldsymbol{u}, \tau)$ is classified into the same class as the ground-truth class of $\boldsymbol{u}$.*

An adversarial example in the region $R(\boldsymbol{u}, \tau)$ is a sample $\boldsymbol{x} \in R(\boldsymbol{u}, \tau)$ such that $\boldsymbol{x}$ is classified into a class, that differs from the ground-truth class of $\boldsymbol{u}$.

As mentioned in Sect. 1, qualitative verification which checks whether a BNN is robust or not is insufficient in many practical applications. In this paper, we are interested in *quantitative* verification of robustness which asks *how many adversarial examples are there in the input region of the BNN for each class*. To answer this question, given a BNN $\mathcal{N}$ and an input region $R(\boldsymbol{u}, \tau)$, we first obtain the BDDs $(G_i^{out})_{i \in [s]}$ by applying Algorithm 2 and then count the number of adversarial examples for each class in the input region $R(\boldsymbol{u}, \tau)$. Note that counting adversarial examples amounts to computing $|R(\boldsymbol{u}, \tau)| - |\mathcal{L}(G_g^{out})|$, where g denotes the ground-truth class of $\boldsymbol{u}$, and $|\mathcal{L}(G_g^{out})|$ can be computed in time $O(|G_g^{out}|)$.

In some applications, more refined analysis is needed. For instance, it may be acceptable to misclassify a dog as a cat, but unacceptable to misclassify a tree as a car. This suggests that the robustness of BNNs may depend on the classes to which samples are misclassified. To capture this, we consider the notion of targeted robustness.

Definition 3. *Given a BNN $\mathcal{N}$, an input region $R(\boldsymbol{u}, \tau)$, and the class t, the BNN is t-target-robust w.r.t. the region $R(\boldsymbol{u}, \tau)$ if every sample $\boldsymbol{x} \in R(\boldsymbol{u}, \tau)$ is never classified into the class t. (Note that we assume that the ground-truth class of $\boldsymbol{u}$ differs from the class t.)*

The quantitative verification problem of t-target-robustness of a BNN asks *how many adversarial examples in the input region $R(\boldsymbol{u}, \tau)$ are misclassified to the class t by the BNN $\mathcal{N}$*. To answer this question, we first obtain the BDD G_t^{out} by applying Algorithm 2 and then count the number of adversarial examples by computing $|\mathcal{L}(G_t^{out})|$.

Note that, if one wants to compute the (locally) maximal safe Hamming distance that satisfies a robustness property for an input sample (e.g., the proportion of adversarial examples is below a threshold), our framework can incrementally compute such a distance without constructing the BDD models of the entire BNN from scratch.

Definition 4. *Given a BNN $\mathcal{N}$, input region $R(\boldsymbol{u}, r)$ and threshold $\epsilon \geq 0$, r_1 is the (locally) maximal safe Hamming distance of $R(\boldsymbol{u}, \tau)$, if one of the follows holds:*

- *if $Pr(R(\boldsymbol{u}, r)) > \epsilon$, then $Pr(R(\boldsymbol{u}, r_1)) \leq \epsilon$ and $Pr(R(\boldsymbol{u}, r')) > \epsilon$ for $r' : r_1 < r' < r$;*
- *if $Pr(R(\boldsymbol{u}, r)) \leq \epsilon$, then $Pr(R(\boldsymbol{u}, r_1 + 1)) > \epsilon$ and $Pr(R(\boldsymbol{u}, r')) \leq \epsilon$ for $r' : r < r' \leq r_1$;*

where $Pr(R(\boldsymbol{u}, r))$ is the probability $\frac{\sum_{i \in [s], i \neq g} |\mathcal{L}(G_i^{out})|}{|R(\boldsymbol{u}, r)|}$ for g being the ground-truth class of $\boldsymbol{u}$, assuming a uniform distribution of adversarial samples.

Algorithm 3 shows the procedure to incrementally compute the maximal safe Hamming distance for a given threshold $\epsilon \geq 0$, input region $R(\boldsymbol{u}, r)$, and ground-truth class g of $\boldsymbol{u}$. Remark that $Pr(R(\boldsymbol{u}, r))$ may not be monotonic w.r.t. the Hamming distance r.

4.2   Interpretability

In general, interpretability addresses the question of *why some inputs in the input region are (mis)classified by the BNN into a specific class?* We consider the interpretability of BNNs using two complementary explanations, i.e., prime implicant explanations and essential features.

Definition 5. *Given a BNN $\mathcal{N}$, an input region $R(\boldsymbol{u}, \tau)$ and a class g, a prime implicant explanation (PI-explanation) of decisions made by the BNN $\mathcal{N}$ on the inputs $\mathcal{L}(G_g^{out})$ is a minimal set of literals $\{\ell_1, \cdots, \ell_k\}$ such that for every $\boldsymbol{x} \in R(\boldsymbol{u}, \tau)$, if $\boldsymbol{x}$ satisfies $\ell_1 \wedge \cdots \wedge \ell_k$, then $\boldsymbol{x}$ is classified into the class g by the BNN $\mathcal{N}$.*

Algorithm 3: Compute the maximal safe Hamming distance

1   **Proc** MAXHD(BNN : $\mathcal{N} = (t_1, \cdots, t_d, t_{d+1})$, Region : $R(u, r)$, Threshold : ϵ, Class : g)

2      $(G_i^{out})_{i \in [s]}$ =BNN2BDD($\mathcal{N}, R(u, r)$);

3   **if** ($\frac{\sum_{i \in [s], i \neq g} |\mathcal{L}(G_i^{out})|}{|R(u,r)|} > \epsilon$) **then** // decrease r

4   **while** ($r \geq 0$) **do**

5          $r = r - 1$;

6          $(G_i^{out})_{i \in [s]} = (\text{AND}(G_{u,r}^{in}, G_i^{out}))_{i \in [s]}$;

7   **if** ($\frac{\sum_{i \in [s], i \neq g} |\mathcal{L}(G_i^{out})|}{|R(u,r)|} \leq \epsilon$) **then return** r;

8   **else** // increase r

9   **while** ($r \leq n_1$) **do** // n_1 is the input size of the BNN $\mathcal{N}$

10         $r = r + 1$;

11         $(B_i^{out})_{i \in [s]}$ =BNN2BDD($\mathcal{N}, R(u, r) \setminus R(u, r - 1)$);

12         $(G_i^{out})_{i \in [s]} = (\text{OR}(B_i^{out}, G_i^{out}))_{i \in [s]}$;

13   **if** ($\frac{\sum_{i \in [s], i \neq g} |\mathcal{L}(G_i^{out})|}{|R(u,r)|} > \epsilon$) **then return** $r - 1$;

14   **return** r

Intuitively, a PI-explanation $\{\ell_1, \cdots, \ell_k\}$ indicates that $\{\text{var}(\ell_1), \cdots, \text{var}(\ell_k)\}$ are key features, namely, if fixed, the predication is guaranteed no matter how the remaining features change. Remark that there may be more than one PI-explanation for a set of inputs $\mathcal{L}(G_g^{out})$. When g is set to be the class of the benign input u, a PI-explanation on G_g^{out} suggests why these samples are classified into g by the BNN $\mathcal{N}$.

Definition 6. *Given a BNN $\mathcal{N}$, an input region $R(u, \tau)$ and a class g, the essential features for the inputs $\mathcal{L}(G_g^{out})$ are literals $\{\ell_1, \cdots, \ell_k\}$ such that every $x \in R(u, \tau)$, if x is classified into the class g by the BNN $\mathcal{N}$, then x satisfies $\ell_1 \wedge \cdots \wedge \ell_k$.*

Intuitively, the essential features $\{\ell_1, \cdots, \ell_k\}$ denote the key features such that all samples $x \in R(u, \tau)$ that are classified into the class g by the BNN $\mathcal{N}$ must agree on these features. Essential features differ from PI-explanations, where the former can be seen as a necessary condition, while the latter can be seen as a sufficient condition.

BDD libraries (e.g., CUDD [58]) usually provide APIs to identify prime implicants (e.g., Cudd_bddPrintCover and Cudd_FirstPrime) and essential variables (e.g., Cudd_FindEssential). Therefore, prime implicants and essential features can be computed via queries on the BDDs $(G_i^{out})_{i \in [s]}$.

5 Evaluation

We have implemented our framework as a prototype tool **BDD4BNN** based on the CUDD package [58]. BDD4BNN is implemented with Python as the front-end to pre-process BNNs and C++ as the back-end to perform the BDD encoding and analysis. In this section, we report the experimental results, including BDD encoding, robustness analysis based on hamming distance, and interpretability.

Experimental Setup. The experiments were conducted on a machine with Intel Xeon Gold 5118 2.3GHz CPU, 64-bit Ubuntu 20.04 LTS operating systems, 128 G RAM. Each BDD encoding executed on one core limited by 8-h.

Benchmarks. We use the PyTorch (v1.0.1.post2) deep learning platform provided by NPAQ [6] to train and test BNNs. We trained 12 BNN models (P1-P12) with varying sizes using the MNIST dataset [35]. The MNIST dateset contains 70,000 gray-scale 28 × 28 images (60,000 for training and 10,000 for testing) of handwritten digits with 10 classes. In our experiments, we downscale the images (28 × 28) to some selected input size n_1 (i.e., the corresponding image is of the size $\sqrt{n_1} \times \sqrt{n_1}$) and then binarize the normalized pixels of the images.

Details of the BNN models are listed in Table 3, each of which has 10 classes (i.e., $s = 10$). Column 1 shows the name of the BNN model. Column 2 shows the architecture of the BNN model, where $n_1 : \cdots : n_{d+1} : s$ denotes that the BNN model has $d + 1$ blocks, n_1 inputs and s outputs; the i-th block for $i \in [d + 1]$ has n_i inputs and n_{i+1} outputs with $n_{d+2} = s$. Recall that each internal block has 3 layers while the output block has 2 layers. Therefore, the number of layers ranges from 5 to 14, the dimension of inputs ranges from 9 to 784, and the number of hidden neurons per linear layer ranges from 10 to 100. Column 3 shows the accuracy of the BNN model on the test set of the MNIST dataset. (We can observe that the accuracy increases with the size of inputs, the number of layers, and the number of hidden neurons per layer.) We randomly choose 10 images from the training set of the MNIST dataset (one image per class) to evaluate our approach.

5.1 Performance of BDD Encoding

We evaluate BDD4BNN on the BNNs listed in Table 3 using different input regions.

BDD Encoding Using Full Input Space. We evaluate BDD4BNN on the BNNs (P1–P5), where $\mathbb{B}_{\pm 1}^{n_1}$ is used as the input region. The results are shown in Table 4, where $|G|$ denotes the number of BDD nodes in the BDD manager. We can observe that both the execution time and the number of BDD nodes increase with the size of BNNs.

BDD Encoding Under Hamming Distance. We evaluate BDD4BNN on the BNNs (P5–P12). In this case, an input region is given by one of the 10 images and a Hamming distance r ranging from 2 to 6. The average results are shown in Table 5, where $[i]$ (resp. (i)) indicates the number of cases that BDD4BNN runs out of memory (resp. time). Overall, the execution time and the number of BDD nodes increase with r. BDD4BNN succeeded on all the cases when $r \leq 4$, 75 cases out of 80 when $r = 5$, and 48 cases out of 80 when $r = 6$. We observe that the execution time and number of BDD nodes increase with the number of hidden neurons (P6 vs. P7, P8 vs. P9, and P11 vs. P12), while the effect of the number of layers is diverse (P6 vs. P8 vs. P10, and P7 vs. P9). From P9 and P10, we observe that the number of hidden neurons per layer is likely the key impact factor of the efficiency of BDD4BNN. Interestingly, our tool BDD4BNN works well on BNNs with large input sizes (i.e., on P11 and P12).

Table 3. BNN benchmarks

Name	Architecture	Accuracy	Name	Architecture	Accuracy
P1	9:20:10	12.23%	P7	100:100:10	75.16%
P2	16:32:10	28.63%	P8	100:50:20:10	71.1%
P3	16:64:32:10	25.14%	P9	100:100:50:10	77.37%
P4	36:15:10:10	27.12%	P10	100:50:30:30:10	80.63%
P5	64:10:10	49.16%	P11	784:30:50:50:50:10	88.23%
P6	100:50:10	73.25%	P12	784:50:50:50:50:10	86.95%

Table 4. BDD encoding using full input space

Name	P1	P2	P3	P4	P5
Time (s)	≈0	0.78	28.21	10924.51	Timeout
$|G|$	288	18,864	17,636	152,830,875	–

These results demonstrate the efficiency and scalability of **BDD4BNN** on BDD encoding of BNNs. We remark that, compared with the learning-based approach [54], our approach is considerably more efficient and scalable. For instance, the learning-based approach takes 403 s to encode a BNN with 64 input size, 5 hidden neurons, and 2 output size when $r = 6$, while ours takes about 3 s even for a larger network P5.

5.2 Robustness Analysis

We evaluate **BDD4BNN** on the robustness of BNNs, including robustness analysis under different input regions and maximal safe Hamming distance computing.

Robustness Verification with Hamming Distance. We evaluate BDD4BNN on BNNs (P7, P8, P9, and P11) using the 10 images. The input regions are given by the Hamming distance r ranging from 2 to 4, resulting in 120 instances. To the best of our knowledge, NPAQ [6] is the only work that supports quantitative robustness verification of BNNs to which we compare BDD4BNN. Recall that NPAQ only provides PAC-style guarantees. Namely, it sets a tolerable error ε and a confidence parameter δ. The final estimated results of NPAQ have the bounded error ε with confidence of at least $1 - \delta$, i.e.,

$$Pr[(1 + \varepsilon)^{-1}\texttt{RealNum} \leq \texttt{EstimatedNum} \leq (1 + \varepsilon)\texttt{RealNum}] \geq 1 - \delta \quad (1)$$

In our experiments, we set $\varepsilon = 0.8$ and $\delta = 0.2$, as done in [6].

Table 5. BDD encoding under Hamming distance

	r=2		r=3		r=4		r=5		r=6	
	Time(s)	$\|G\|$	Time(s)	$\|G\|$	Time(s)	$\|G\|$	Time(s)	$\|G\|$	Time(s)	$\|G\|$
P5	0.01	1,559	0.03	9,795	0.11	36,796	0.74	176,107	2.94	592,104
P6	0.25	4,670	4.17	84,037	109.26	1,018,571	2,292.5	11,375,842	(5) 17,811	41,883,970
P7	0.65	5,295	22.70	106,754	652.78	1,575,722	(1) 17,399	16,163,078	[10]	-
P8	0.14	6,147	1.95	125,226	44.51	1,668,027	1,146.8	20,519,582	(1) 12,491	172,369,297
P9	1.99	6,139	63.30	136,126	1,428.6	2,005,666	[1](3) 17,039	29,323,244	[10]	-
P10	0.30	4,630	4.87	100,054	101.41	1,603,920	1,909.9	19,844,299	(5) 20,484	173,316,483
P11	5.52	3,128	5.73	22,120	6.60	86,413	11.63	556,774	238.2	2,881,468
P12	12.4	5,693	12.87	49,996	16.92	493,820	403.09	5,739,602	(1) 11,058	16,241,733

Table 6. Robustness verification under Hamming distance

	r	NPAQ [6]			BDD4BNN			Diff	
		#(Adv)	Time(s)	Pr(adv)	#(Adv)	Time(s)	Pr(adv)	#(Adv)	Speed Up
	2	875	271.07	17.32%	1,806	0.65	35.76%	106.4%	416
P7	3	39,587	919.88	23.74%	65,054	22.71	39.01%	64.33%	40
	4	1,023,798	3,862.0	25.04%	1,501,691	661.79	36.73%	46.68%	5
	2	1,601	187.78	31.70%	2,261	0.14	44.76%	41.22%	1,340
P8	3	66,562	396.45	39.92%	64,372	1.96	38.60%	-3.29%	201
	4	1,636,070	1,861.7	40.02%	1,829,103	45.0	44.74%	11.80%	40
	2	1,214	363.44	24.03%	1,406	1.99	27.84%	15.82%	182
P9	3	51,464	3,763.6	30.86%	42,901	63.31	25.73%	-16.64%	58
	4	1,316,181	(1) 9,007.8	32.20%	3,968,609	1,505.0	97.08%	201.5%	5
	2	12,083	3,831.0	3.93%	28,736	5.52	9.34%	137.8%	693
P11	3	0	(2) 4,634.2	0%	0	5.68	0%	-	815
	4	0	(2) 7,979.1	0%	0	6.38	0%	-	1,250

The results on the average of the images are shown in Table 6. NPAQ ran out of time on 5 instances (which occur in P9 with $r = 4$ and P11 with $r = 3$ and $r = 4$), while BDD4BNN successfully verified all the 120 instances. Table 6 only shows the results of 115 instances that can be solved by NPAQ. Columns 3, 4, and 5 (resp. 6, 7, and 8) show the number of adversarial examples, the execution time, and the proportion of adversarial examples in the input region. Column 9 shows the error rate $\frac{\text{RealNum} - \text{EstimatedNum}}{\text{EstimatedNum}}$, where RealNum is from our result, and EstimatedNum is from NPAQ. Column 10 shows the speedup of BDD4BNN compared with NPAQ. Remark that the numbers of adversarial examples are 0 for P11 on input regions with $r = 3$ and $r = 4$ that can be solved by NPAQ. There do exist input regions for P11 that cannot be solved by NPAQ but have adversarial examples (see below). On BNNs that were solved by both NPAQ and BDD4BNN, BDD4BNN is significantly ($5\times$ to $1,340\times$) faster and more accurate than NPAQ. From Table 5 and Table 6, we also found that most of the verification time is spent on BDD encoding while the rest is usually less than 10 s.

Details of Robustness and Targeted Robustness. Figure 6(a) (resp. Fig. 6(b) and Fig. 6(c)) depicts the distributions of classes on P8 with Hamming distance $r = 2$ (resp. P8 with $r = 3$ and P11 with $r = 2$), where on the x-axis $i = 0, \cdots, 9$ denotes the input

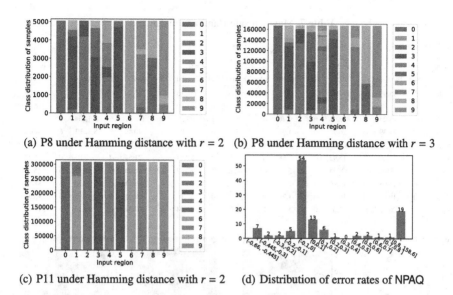

(a) P8 under Hamming distance with $r = 2$ (b) P8 under Hamming distance with $r = 3$

(c) P11 under Hamming distance with $r = 2$ (d) Distribution of error rates of NPAQ

Fig. 6. Details of robustness verification with Hamming distance

region that is within the respective Hamming distance to the image of digit i (called i-region). We can observe that P8 is robust for the 0-region when $r = 2$ and robust for the 6-region when $r = 2$ and $r = 3$, but is not robust for the other regions. (Note P8 is not robust for 0-region when $r = 3$, which is hard to be visualized in Fig. 6(b) due to the small number of adversarial examples.) Most of the adversarial examples in the 1-region and 5-region are misclassified into the digit 3 by P8. P11 is not robust for the 1-region or the 5-region, but is robust for all the other regions. Though P8 and P11 are not robust on some input regions, indeed they are t-target-robust for many target classes t, e.g., P11 is t-target-robust for the 1-region when $t \neq 2$, and the 5-region when $t \neq 3$. (The raw data are given in [71].)

Quality Validation of NPAQ. Figure 6(d) shows the distribution of error rates of NPAQ, where the x-axis is the range of the error rate and the y-axis is the corresponding number of instances. There are 19 instances where the estimated number of adversarial examples exceeds $(1 + \epsilon)$ of the real number of the adversarial examples and 7 instances where the estimated number of adversarial examples is less than $(1 + \epsilon)^{-1}$ of the real number of the adversarial examples. This means that out of 115 instances, only in 89 instances the estimated number is within the allowed range, which is less than $1 - \delta = 0.8$.

Maximal Safe Hamming Distance. As a representative of such an analysis, we evaluate BDD4BNN on 4 BNNs (P7, P8, P9, and P11) with 10 images for 2 robustness thresholds ($\epsilon = 0$ and $\epsilon = 0.03$). The initial Hamming distance r is 3. Intuitively, $\epsilon = 0$ (resp. $\epsilon = 0.03$) means that up to 0% (resp. 3%) samples in the input region can be adversarial.

Table 7 shows the results, where columns SD and Time give the maximal safe Hamming distance and the execution time, respectively. BDD4BNN solved 74 out of 80 instances. (For the remaining 6 instances, BDD4BNN ran out of time or memory, but

Table 7. Maximal safe Hamming distance

Image	P7				P8				P9				P11			
	$\epsilon = 0$		$\epsilon = 0.03$		$\epsilon = 0$		$\epsilon = 0.03$		$\epsilon = 0$		$\epsilon = 0.03$		$\epsilon = 0$		$\epsilon = 0.03$	
	SD	Time(s)	SD	Time(s)	SD	Time(s)	SD	Time(s)	SD	Time(s)	SD	Time(s)	SD	Time(s)	SD	Time(s)
0	1	15.09	4	10,845	2	0.51	6	Timeout	3	746.15	3	737.96	6	29.69	6	29.28
1	-1	19.96	-1	19.13	-1	2.84	-1	2.97	0	155.50	0	155.09	0	6.49	0	6.11
2	2	13.25	3	422.04	0	0.46	0	0.50	1	37.50	4	14,127	6	11,334	6	11,437
3	0	21.39	0	20.94	-1	1.92	-1	2.08	0	41.04	0	40.49	6	8,323.1	6	8,088.3
4	3	426.81	5	OOM	-1	2.41	-1	2.61	2	8.08	5	OOM	6	30.85	6	30.74
5	-1	15.60	-1	15.92	-1	0.68	-1	0.74	-1	22.54	-1	21.54	-1	7.03	-1	6.72
6	4	7,990.6	5	OOM	3	5.69	4	198.26	1	57.37	4	Timeout	6	44.57	6	45.12
7	-1	16.08	-1	15.90	-1	2.49	-1	2.52	1	89.49	4	Timeout	6	89.38	6	88.39
8	-1	19.02	-1	19.28	-1	1.71	-1	1.80	-1	80.16	-1	79.91	6	43.95	6	43.30
9	0	26.82	0	27.69	0	5.09	1	5.39	-1	109.04	-1	107.24	6	338.73	6	327.48

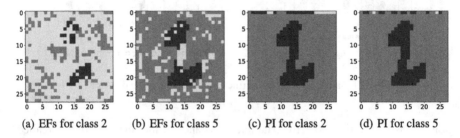

(a) EFs for class 2   (b) EFs for class 5   (c) PI for class 2   (d) PI for class 5

Fig. 7. Graphic representation of essential features and PI-explanations

it was still able to compute a larger safe Hamming distance.) We can observe that the maximal safe Hamming distance increases with the threshold ϵ on several BNNs and input regions. We can also observe that P11 is more robust than others, which is consistent with their accuracies (cf. Table 3). Remark that SD $= -1$ indicates that the input image itself is misclassified.

5.3 Interpretability

To demonstrate the ability of BDD4BNN on interpretability, we consider the analysis of the BNN P12 and the image u of digit 1.

Essential Features. For the input region given by the Hamming distance $r = 4$, we compute two sets of essential features for the inputs $\mathcal{L}(G_2^{out})$ and $\mathcal{L}(G_5^{out})$, i.e., the adversarial examples in the region $R(u, 4)$ that are misclassified into the classes 2 and 5 respectively. The essential features are depicted in Figs. 7(a) and 7(b), where black (resp. blue) color means that the value of the corresponding pixel is 1 (resp. 0), and yellow color means that the value of the corresponding pixel can take arbitrary values. Figure 7(a) (resp. Fig. 7(b)) indicates that the inputs $\mathcal{L}(G_2^{out})$ (resp. $\mathcal{L}(G_5^{out})$) must agree on these black- and blue-colored pixels.

PI-Explanations. For demonstration, we assume that the input region is given by the fixed set of indices $I = \{1, 2, \cdots, 28\}$ which denotes the first row of pixels of 28×28 images. We compute two PI-explanations of the inputs $\mathcal{L}(G_2^{out})$ and $\mathcal{L}(G_5^{out})$. The PI-explanations are depicted in Figs. 7(c) and 7(d). Figure 7(c) (resp. Fig. 7(d)) suggests that, by the definition of the PI-explanation, all the images in the region $R(u, I)$ obtained by assigning arbitrary values to the yellow-colored pixels are always misclassified into the class 2 (resp. class 5), while changing one black-colored or blue-colored pixel would change the predication result since a PI-explanation is a minimal set of literals.

6 Related Work

In this section, we discuss the related work on qualitative/quantitative analysis and interpretability of DNNs. As there is a vast amount of literature regarding these topics, we will only discuss the most related ones to BDD4BNN.

Qualitative Analysis of DNNs. For real-numbered DNNs, various formal verification approaches have been proposed. Typical examples include constraint solving based approaches [17,26,30,31,51], optimization based approaches [10,13,15,16,40,61,67, 68], and program analysis based approaches [2,3,18,20,37–39,55–57,62–64,69].

Existing techniques for quantized DNNs are mostly based on constraint solving, in particular, SAT/SMT solving [12,33,45,46]. Following this line, verification of BNNs with ternary weights [28,48] and quantized DNNs with multiple bits [7,22,24] were also studied. Recently, the SMT-based framework Marabou for real-numbered DNNs [31] has also been extended to support BNNs [1].

Quantitative Analysis of DNNs. Comparing to qualitative analysis, quantitative analysis of neural networks is currently very limited. Two sampling-based approaches were proposed to certify the robustness for both DNNs and BNNs [5,65]. Yang et al. [69] proposed a spurious region-guided refinement approach for real-numbered DNN verification, claiming to be the first work of the quantitative robustness verification of DNNs with soundness guarantees.

Following the SAT-based qualitative analysis of BNNs [45,46], SAT-based quantitative analysis approaches were also proposed [6,21,47]. In particular, approximate SAT model-counting solvers are utilized. Shih et al. [54] also proposed a BDD-based approach to tackle BNNs, similar to our work in spirit. However, our approach is able to handle BNNs of considerably larger sizes than their learning-based method.

Interpretability of DNNs. Though interpretability of DNNs is crucial for explaining predictions, it is very challenging to tackle due to the blackbox nature of DNNs. There is a large body of work on the interpretability of DNNs (cf. [25,43] for a survey). Almost all the existing approaches are heuristic-based and restricted to finding explanations that are local in an input region. Some of them tackle the interpretability of DNNs by learning an interpretable model, such as binary decision trees [19,70] or finite-state automata [66]. In contrast to ours, they target at DNNs and only approximate the original model in the input region. The BDD-based approach [54] mentioned above has been used to compute the PI-explanation, but essential features were not considered therein.

7   Conclusion

In this paper, we have proposed a novel BDD-based framework for quantitative verification of BNNs. We implemented the framework as a prototype tool **BDD4BNN** and conducted extensive experiments on 12 BNN models with varying sizes and input regions. Experimental results demonstrated that **BDD4BNN** is more scalable than the existing BDD-learning based approach, and significantly more efficient and accurate than the existing SAT-based approach **NPAQ**. This work represents the first, but a key, step of the long-term program to develop an efficient and scalable BDD-based quantitative analysis framework for BNNs.

References

1. Amir, G., Wu, H., Barrett, C.W., Katz, G.: An SMT-based approach for verifying binarized neural networks. CoRR abs/2011.02948 (2020)
2. Anderson, G., Pailoor, S., Dillig, I., Chaudhuri, S.: Optimization and abstraction: a synergistic approach for analyzing neural network robustness. In: PLDI, pp. 731–744 (2019)
3. Ashok, P., Hashemi, V., Křetínský, J., Mohr, S.: DeepAbstract: neural network abstraction for accelerating verification. In: Hung, D.V., Sokolsky, O. (eds.) ATVA 2020. LNCS, vol. 12302, pp. 92–107. Springer, Cham (2020). https://doi.org/10.1007/978-3-030-59152-6_5
4. Baidu: Apollo (2021). https://apollo.auto
5. Baluta, T., Chua, Z.L., Meel, K.S., Saxena, P.: Scalable quantitative verification for deep neural networks. CoRR abs/2002.06864 (2020)
6. Baluta, T., Shen, S., Shinde, S., Meel, K.S., Saxena, P.: Quantitative verification of neural networks and its security applications. In: CCS, pp. 1249–1264 (2019)
7. Baranowski, M., He, S., Lechner, M., Nguyen, T.S., Rakamarić, Z.: An SMT theory of fixed-point arithmetic. In: Peltier, N., Sofronie-Stokkermans, V. (eds.) IJCAR 2020. LNCS (LNAI), vol. 12166, pp. 13–31. Springer, Cham (2020). https://doi.org/10.1007/978-3-030-51074-9_2
8. Bartzis, C., Bultan, T.: Construction of efficient BDDs for bounded arithmetic constraints. In: Garavel, H., Hatcliff, J. (eds.) TACAS 2003. LNCS, vol. 2619, pp. 394–408. Springer, Heidelberg (2003). https://doi.org/10.1007/3-540-36577-X_28
9. Bryant, R.E.: Graph-based algorithms for Boolean function manipulation. IEEE Trans. Comput. **35**(8), 677–691 (1986)
10. Bunel, R., Lu, J., Turkaslan, I., Torr, P.H.S., Kohli, P., Kumar, M.P.: Branch and bound for piecewise linear neural network verification. J. Mach. Learn. Res. **21**, 42:1-42:39 (2020)
11. Chen, G., et al.: Who is real Bob? Adversarial attacks on speaker recognition systems. CoRR abs/1911.01840 (2019)
12. Cheng, C.-H., Nührenberg, G., Huang, C.-H., Ruess, H.: Verification of binarized neural networks via inter-neuron factoring. In: Piskac, R., Rümmer, P. (eds.) VSTTE 2018. LNCS, vol. 11294, pp. 279–290. Springer, Cham (2018). https://doi.org/10.1007/978-3-030-03592-1_16

13. Cheng, C.-H., Nührenberg, G., Ruess, H.: Maximum resilience of artificial neural networks. In: D'Souza, D., Narayan Kumar, K. (eds.) ATVA 2017. LNCS, vol. 10482, pp. 251–268. Springer, Cham (2017). https://doi.org/10.1007/978-3-319-68167-2_18

14. Duan, Y., Zhao, Z., Bu, L., Song, F.: Things you may not know about adversarial example: a black-box adversarial image attack. CoRR abs/1905.07672 (2019)

15. Dutta, S., Jha, S., Sankaranarayanan, S., Tiwari, A.: Output range analysis for deep feedforward neural networks. In: Dutle, A., Muñoz, C., Narkawicz, A. (eds.) NFM 2018. LNCS, vol. 10811, pp. 121–138. Springer, Cham (2018). https://doi.org/10.1007/978-3-319-77935-5_9

16. Dvijotham, K., Stanforth, R., Gowal, S., Mann, T.A., Kohli, P.: A dual approach to scalable verification of deep networks. In: UAI, pp. 550–559 (2018)

17. Ehlers, R.: Formal verification of piece-wise linear feed-forward neural networks. In: D'Souza, D., Narayan Kumar, K. (eds.) ATVA 2017. LNCS, vol. 10482, pp. 269–286. Springer, Cham (2017). https://doi.org/10.1007/978-3-319-68167-2_19

18. Elboher, Y.Y., Gottschlich, J., Katz, G.: An abstraction-based framework for neural network verification. In: Lahiri, S.K., Wang, C. (eds.) CAV 2020. LNCS, vol. 12224, pp. 43–65. Springer, Cham (2020). https://doi.org/10.1007/978-3-030-53288-8_3

19. Frosst, N., Hinton, G.E.: Distilling a neural network into a soft decision tree. In: Proceedings of the 1st International Workshop on Comprehensibility and Explanation in AI and ML (2017)

20. Gehr, T., Mirman, M., Drachsler-Cohen, D., Tsankov, P., Chaudhuri, S., Vechev, M.T.: AI^2: safety and robustness certification of neural networks with abstract interpretation. In: S&P, pp. 3–18 (2018)

21. Ghosh, B., Basu, D., Meel, K.S.: Justicia: a stochastic SAT approach to formally verify fairness. CoRR abs/2009.06516 (2020)

22. Giacobbe, M., Henzinger, T.A., Lechner, M.: How many bits does it take to quantize your neural network? In: TACAS 2020. LNCS, vol. 12079, pp. 79–97. Springer, Cham (2020). https://doi.org/10.1007/978-3-030-45237-7_5

23. Gupta, S., Agrawal, A., Gopalakrishnan, K., Narayanan, P.: Deep learning with limited numerical precision. In: ICML, pp. 1737–1746 (2015)

24. Henzinger, T.A., Lechner, M., Žikelić, D.: Scalable verification of quantized neural networks (technical report). arXiv preprint arXiv:2012.08185 (2020)

25. Huang, X., et al.: A survey of safety and trustworthiness of deep neural networks: verification, testing, adversarial attack and defence, and interpretability. Comput. Sci. Rev. **37**, 100270 (2020)

26. Huang, X., Kwiatkowska, M., Wang, S., Wu, M.: Safety verification of deep neural networks. In: Majumdar, R., Kunčak, V. (eds.) CAV 2017. LNCS, vol. 10426, pp. 3–29. Springer, Cham (2017). https://doi.org/10.1007/978-3-319-63387-9_1

27. Hubara, I., Courbariaux, M., Soudry, D., El-Yaniv, R., Bengio, Y.: Binarized neural networks. In: NeurIPS, pp. 4107–4115 (2016)

28. Jia, K., Rinard, M.: Efficient exact verification of binarized neural networks. In: NeurIPS (2020)

29. Kalra, N., Paddock, S.M.: Driving to safety: how many miles of driving would it take to demonstrate autonomous vehicle reliability? Transp. Res. Part A Policy Pract. **94**, 182–193 (2016)

30. Katz, G., Barrett, C., Dill, D.L., Julian, K., Kochenderfer, M.J.: Reluplex: an efficient SMT solver for verifying deep neural networks. In: Majumdar, R., Kunčak, V. (eds.) CAV 2017. LNCS, vol. 10426, pp. 97–117. Springer, Cham (2017). https://doi.org/10.1007/978-3-319-63387-9_5

31. Katz, G., et al.: The Marabou framework for verification and analysis of deep neural networks. In: Dillig, I., Tasiran, S. (eds.) CAV 2019. LNCS, vol. 11561, pp. 443–452. Springer, Cham (2019). https://doi.org/10.1007/978-3-030-25540-4_26

32. Koopman, P., Osyk, B.: Safety argument considerations for public road testing of autonomous vehicles. SAE Int. J. Adv. Curr. Pract. Mobility **1**, 512–523 (2019)

33. Korneev, S., Narodytska, N., Pulina, L., Tacchella, A., Bjorner, N., Sagiv, M.: Constrained image generation using binarized neural networks with decision procedures. In: Beyersdorff, O., Wintersteiger, C.M. (eds.) SAT 2018. LNCS, vol. 10929, pp. 438–449. Springer, Cham (2018). https://doi.org/10.1007/978-3-319-94144-8_27

34. Kung, J., Zhang, D.C., van der Wal, G.S., Chai, S.M., Mukhopadhyay, S.: Efficient object detection using embedded binarized neural networks. J. Signal Process. Syst. **90**(6), 877–890 (2018)

35. LeCun, Y., Cortes, C.: MNIST handwritten digit database (2010)

36. Lei, Y., Chen, S., Fan, L., Song, F., Liu, Y.: Advanced evasion attacks and mitigations on practical ML-based phishing website classifiers. CoRR abs/2004.06954 (2020)

37. Li, J., Liu, J., Yang, P., Chen, L., Huang, X., Zhang, L.: Analyzing deep neural networks with symbolic propagation: towards higher precision and faster verification. In: Chang, B.-Y.E. (ed.) SAS 2019. LNCS, vol. 11822, pp. 296–319. Springer, Cham (2019). https://doi.org/10.1007/978-3-030-32304-2_15

38. Li, R., et al.: PRODeep: a platform for robustness verification of deep neural networks. In: FSE, pp. 1630–1634 (2020)

39. Liu, W., Song, F., Zhang, T., Wang, J.: Verifying ReLU neural networks from a model checking perspective. J. Comput. Sci. Technol. **35**(6), 1365–1381 (2020)

40. Lomuscio, A., Maganti, L.: An approach to reachability analysis for feed-forward ReLU neural networks. CoRR abs/1706.07351 (2017)

41. McDanel, B., Teerapittayanon, S., Kung, H.T.: Embedded binarized neural networks. In: EWSN, pp. 168–173 (2017)

42. Minato, S.I., Somenzi, F.: Arithmetic Boolean expression manipulator using BDDs. Formal Methods Syst. Des. **10**(2), 221–242 (1997). https://doi.org/10.1023/A:1008643722423

43. Molnar, C., Casalicchio, G., Bischl, B.: Interpretable machine learning - A brief history, state-of-the-art and challenges. CoRR abs/2010.09337 (2020)

44. Nakamura, A.: An efficient query learning algorithm for ordered binary decision diagrams. Inf. Comput. **201**(2), 178–198 (2005)

45. Narodytska, N.: Formal analysis of deep binarized neural networks. In: IJCAI, pp. 5692–5696 (2018)

46. Narodytska, N., Kasiviswanathan, S.P., Ryzhyk, L., Sagiv, M., Walsh, T.: Verifying properties of binarized deep neural networks. In: AAAI, pp. 6615–6624 (2018)

47. Narodytska, N., Shrotri, A., Meel, K.S., Ignatiev, A., Marques-Silva, J.: Assessing heuristic machine learning explanations with model counting. In: Janota, M., Lynce, I. (eds.) SAT 2019. LNCS, vol. 11628, pp. 267–278. Springer, Cham (2019). https://doi.org/10.1007/978-3-030-24258-9_19

48. Narodytska, N., Zhang, H., Gupta, A., Walsh, T.: In search for a SAT-friendly binarized neural network architecture. In: ICLR (2020)

49. Papernot, N., McDaniel, P.D., Goodfellow, I.J., Jha, S., Celik, Z.B., Swami, A.: Practical black-box attacks against machine learning. In: CCS, pp. 506–519 (2017)

50. Papernot, N., McDaniel, P.D., Jha, S., Fredrikson, M., Celik, Z.B., Swami, A.: The limitations of deep learning in adversarial settings. In: S&P, pp. 372–387 (2016)

51. Pulina, L., Tacchella, A.: An abstraction-refinement approach to verification of artificial neural networks. In: Touili, T., Cook, B., Jackson, P. (eds.) CAV 2010. LNCS, vol. 6174, pp. 243–257. Springer, Heidelberg (2010). https://doi.org/10.1007/978-3-642-14295-6_24

52. Rastegari, M., Ordonez, V., Redmon, J., Farhadi, A.: XNOR-Net: ImageNet classification using binary convolutional neural networks. In: Leibe, B., Matas, J., Sebe, N., Welling, M. (eds.) ECCV 2016. LNCS, vol. 9908, pp. 525–542. Springer, Cham (2016). https://doi.org/10.1007/978-3-319-46493-0_32

53. Shen, D., Wu, G., Suk, H.I.: Deep learning in medical image analysis. Annu. Rev. Biomed. Eng. **19**, 221–248 (2017)

54. Shih, A., Darwiche, A., Choi, A.: Verifying binarized neural networks by Angluin-style learning. In: Janota, M., Lynce, I. (eds.) SAT 2019. LNCS, vol. 11628, pp. 354–370. Springer, Cham (2019). https://doi.org/10.1007/978-3-030-24258-9_25

55. Singh, G., Ganvir, R., Püschel, M., Vechev, M.T.: Beyond the single neuron convex barrier for neural network certification. In: NeurIPS, pp. 15072–15083 (2019)

56. Singh, G., Gehr, T., Mirman, M., Püschel, M., Vechev, M.T.: Fast and effective robustness certification. In: NeurIPS, pp. 10825–10836 (2018)

57. Singh, G., Gehr, T., Püschel, M., Vechev, M.T.: An abstract domain for certifying neural networks. Proc. ACM Program. Lang. (POPL) **3**, 41:1–41:30 (2019)

58. Somenzi, F.: CUDD: CU decision diagram package (2015)

59. Szegedy, C., et al.: Intriguing properties of neural networks. In: ICLR (2014)

60. Tan, M., Le, Q.V.: EfficientNet: rethinking model scaling for convolutional neural networks. In: ICML, pp. 6105–6114 (2019)

61. Tjeng, V., Xiao, K., Tedrake, R.: Evaluating robustness of neural networks with mixed integer programming. In: ICLR (2019)

62. Tran, H.-D., Bak, S., Xiang, W., Johnson, T.T.: Verification of deep convolutional neural networks using ImageStars. In: Lahiri, S.K., Wang, C. (eds.) CAV 2020. LNCS, vol. 12224, pp. 18–42. Springer, Cham (2020). https://doi.org/10.1007/978-3-030-53288-8_2

63. Tran, H.-D., et al.: Star-based reachability analysis of deep neural networks. In: ter Beek, M.H., McIver, A., Oliveira, J.N. (eds.) FM 2019. LNCS, vol. 11800, pp. 670–686. Springer, Cham (2019). https://doi.org/10.1007/978-3-030-30942-8_39

64. Wan, W., Zhang, Z., Zhu, Y., Zhang, M., Song, F.: Accelerating robustness verification of deep neural networks guided by target labels. CoRR abs/2007.08520 (2020)

65. Webb, S., Rainforth, T., Teh, Y.W., Kumar, M.P.: A statistical approach to assessing neural network robustness. In: ICLR (2019)

66. Weiss, G., Goldberg, Y., Yahav, E.: Extracting automata from recurrent neural networks using queries and counterexamples. In: ICML, pp. 5244–5253 (2018)

67. Wong, E., Kolter, J.Z.: Provable defenses against adversarial examples via the convex outer adversarial polytope. In: ICML, pp. 5283–5292 (2018)

68. Xiang, W., Tran, H., Johnson, T.T.: Output reachable set estimation and verification for multilayer neural networks. TNNLS **29**(11), 5777–5783 (2018)

69. Yang, P., et al.: Improving neural network verification through spurious region guided refinement. CoRR abs/2010.07722 (2020)

70. Zhang, Q., Yang, Y., Ma, H., Wu, Y.N.: Interpreting CNNs via decision trees. In: CVPR, pp. 6261–6270 (2019)

71. Zhang, Y., Zhao, Z., Chen, G., Song, F., Chen, T.: BDD4BNN: a BDD-based quantitative analysis framework for binarized neural networks. CoRR abs/2103.07224 (2021)

Automated Safety Verification of Programs Invoking Neural Networks

Maria Christakis[1], Hasan Ferit Eniser[1]✉, Holger Hermanns[2,6], Jörg Hoffmann[2], Yugesh Kothari[1], Jianlin Li[3,2,7], Jorge A. Navas[4], and Valentin Wüstholz[5]

[1] MPI-SWS, Kaiserslautern and Saarbrücken, Germany
{maria,hfeniser,ykothari}@mpi-sws.org
[2] Saarland University, Saarland Informatics Campus, Saarbrücken, Germany
{hermanns,hoffmann}@cs.uni-saarland.de
[3] SKLCS, Institute of Software, Chinese Academy of Sciences, Beijing, China
ljlin@ios.ac.cn
[4] SRI International, Menlo Park, USA
jorge.navas@sri.com
[5] ConsenSys, Kaiserslautern, Germany
valentin.wustholz@consensys.net
[6] Institute of Intelligent Software, Guangzhou, China
[7] University of Chinese Academy of Sciences, Beijing, China

Abstract. State-of-the-art program-analysis techniques are not yet able to effectively verify safety properties of heterogeneous systems, that is, systems with components implemented using diverse technologies. This shortcoming is pinpointed by programs invoking neural networks despite their acclaimed role as innovation drivers across many application areas. In this paper, we embark on the verification of system-level properties for systems characterized by interaction between programs and neural networks. Our technique provides a tight two-way integration of a program and a neural-network analysis and is formalized in a general framework based on abstract interpretation. We evaluate its effectiveness on 26 variants of a widely used, restricted autonomous-driving benchmark.

1 Introduction

Software is becoming increasingly *heterogeneous*. In other words, it consists of more and more diverse software components, implemented using different technologies such as neural networks, smart contracts, or web services. Here, we focus on programs invoking neural networks, in response to their prominent role in many upcoming application areas. Examples from the forefront of innovation include a controller of a self-driving car that interacts with a neural network identifying street signs [43,48], a banking system that consults a neural network for credit screening [3], or a health-insurance system that relies on a neural network to predict people's health needs [51]. There are growing concerns regarding the effects of integrating such heterogeneous technologies [40].

Despite these software advances, state-of-the-art program-analysis techniques cannot yet effectively reason across heterogeneous components. In fact, program

© The Author(s) 2021
A. Silva and K. R. M. Leino (Eds.): CAV 2021, LNCS 12759, pp. 201–224, 2021.
https://doi.org/10.1007/978-3-030-81685-8_9

analyses today focus on homogeneous units of software in isolation; for instance, to check the robustness of a neural network (e.g., [37,27,36,66,65,64,57,41]), or safety of a program invoking a neural network while—conservatively, but imprecisely—treating the neural network as if it could return arbitrary values. This is a fundamental limitation of prevalent program-analysis techniques, and as a result, we cannot effectively analyze the interaction between diverse components of a heterogeneous system to check system properties.

Many properties of heterogeneous systems depend on components correctly interacting with each other. For instance, consider a program that controls the acceleration of an autonomous vehicle by invoking a neural network with the current direction, speed, and LiDAR image of the vehicle's surroundings. One might want to verify that the vehicle's speed never exceeds a given bound. Even such a seemingly simple property is challenging to verify automatically due to the mutual dependencies between the two components. On the one hand, the current vehicle direction and speed determine the feasible inputs to the neural network. On the other hand, the output of the neural network controls the vehicle acceleration, and thereby, the speed. To infer bounds on the speed (and ultimately prove the property), an automated analysis should therefore analyze how the two components interact.

Our approach. In this paper, we make the first step in verifying safety of heterogeneous systems, and more specifically, of *programs* invoking neural networks. Existing work on verification of neural networks has either focused on the network itself (e.g., with respect to robustness) or on *models* (e.g., expressed using differential equations) that invoke the network, for example as part of a hybrid system [24,59]. In contrast, our approach is designed for verifying safety of a C (or ultimately LLVM) program interacting with the network. In comparison to models, C programs are much more low-level and general, and therefore require an intricate combination of program and neural-network analyses.

More specifically, our approach proposes a symbiotic combination of a program and a neural-network analysis, both of which are based on abstract interpretation [18]. By treating the neural-network analysis as a specialized abstract domain of the program analyzer, we are able to use inferred invariants for the neural network to check system properties in the surrounding program. In other words, the program analysis becomes *aware* of the network's computation. For this reason, we also refer to the overall approach as *neuro-aware program analysis*. In fact, the program and neural-network analyses are co-dependent. The former infers sets of feasible inputs to the neural network, whereas the latter determines its possible outputs given the inferred inputs. Knowing the possible neural-network outputs, in turn, enables proving system safety.

We evaluate our approach on 26 variants of RACETRACK, a benchmark from related work that originates in AI autonomous decision making [4,5,32,46,52,53]. RACETRACK is about the problem of navigating a vehicle on a discrete map to a goal location without crashing into any obstacles. The vehicle acceleration (in discrete directions) is determined by a neural network, which is invoked by a controller responsible for actually moving the vehicle. In Sect. 4, we show the effectiveness of our approach in verifying goal reachability and crash avoidance for 26 RACETRACK variants of varying complexity. These variants constitute a diverse set of verification tasks that differ both in the neural network itself and in how and for what purpose the program invokes the neural network.

Despite our evaluation being focused on this setting, the paper's contribution should not be mistaken as being about RACETRACK verification. Instead, it is about neuro-aware program analysis of heterogeneous systems for autonomous decision making. While RACETRACK is a substantially simplified blueprint for the autonomous-driving context, it features the crucial co-dependent program architecture that is characteristic across the entire domain.

Contributions. Overall, we make the following contributions:

1. We present the first *symbiotic* combination of program and neural-network analyses for verifying safety of heterogeneous systems.
2. We formalize neuro-aware program analysis in a general framework that uses specialized abstract domains.
3. We evaluate the effectiveness of our approach on 26 variants of a widely used, restricted autonomous-driving benchmark.

2   Overview

We now illustrate neuro-aware program analysis on a high level by describing the challenges in verifying safety for a variant of the RACETRACK benchmark. This variant serves as our running example for the class of programs that invoke one or more neural networks to perform a computation affecting program safety.

In general, RACETRACK is a heterogeneous system that simulates the problem of navigating a vehicle to a goal location on a discrete map without crashing into any obstacles. It consists of a neural network, which predicts the vehicle acceleration toward discrete directions, and a controller (implemented in C) that actually moves the vehicle on the map. Alg. 1 shows pseudo-code for our running example, a variant of RACETRACK that incorporates additional non-deterministic noise to make verification harder.

Line 1 non-deterministically selects a state from the map as the *currentState*, and line 2 assumes it is a start state for the vehicle, i.e., it is neither a goal nor an obstacle. On line 3, we initialize the *result* of navigating the vehicle as stuck, i.e., the vehicle neither crashes nor does it reach a goal. The loop on line 5 iterates until either a predefined number of steps N is reached or the vehicle is no longer stuck (i.e., crashed or at a goal state). The if-statement on line 6 adds non-determinism to the controller by either zeroing the vehicle acceleration or invoking the neural network (NN) to make a prediction. Such non-deterministic noise illustrates one type of variant we created to make the verification task more difficult (see Sect. 4.1 for more details on other variants used in our evaluation). Line 10 moves the vehicle to a new *currentState* according to *acceleration*, and the if-statement on line 11 determines whether the vehicle has crashed or reached a goal. The assertion on line 16 denotes the system properties of goal reachability

---

Algorithm 1: An example RACETRACK variant.

1 $currentState \leftarrow \star$
2 **assume** IsStartState($currentState$)
3 $result \leftarrow$ stuck
4 $i \leftarrow 0$
5 **while** $i < N$ **and** $result =$ stuck **do**
6   **if** $\star$ **then**
7      $acceleration \leftarrow 0$
8   **else**
9      $acceleration \leftarrow$ NN($currentState$)
10   $currentState \leftarrow$ Move($currentState, acceleration$)
11   **if** IsCrash($currentState$) **then**
12     $result \leftarrow$ crash
13   **else if** IsGoal($currentState$) **then**
14     $result \leftarrow$ goal
15   $i \leftarrow i + 1$
16 **assert** $result =$ goal

---

and crash avoidance. In case this assertion does not hold but we do prove the *result* to be stuck, then we have only verified crash avoidance.

Note that these are *safety*, and not liveness, properties due to the bounded number of loop iterations (line 5)—N is 50 in our evaluation, thus making bounded model checking [8,15] intractable.

Challenges. Verifying safety of this heterogeneous system with state-of-the-art program-analysis techniques, such as abstract interpretation, is a challenging endeavor.

When considering the controller in isolation, the analysis is sound if it assumes that the neural network may return any output ($\top$). More specifically, the abstract interpreter can ignore the call to the neural network and simply havoc its return value (i.e., consider a non-deterministic value). In our running example, this means that any vehicle acceleration is possible from the perspective of the controller analysis. Therefore, it becomes infeasible to prove a system property such as crash avoidance. In fact, in Sect. 4, we show this to be the case even with the most precise controller analysis.

On the other hand, when considering the neural network in isolation, the analysis must assume that any input is possible ($\top$) even though this is not necessarily the case in the context of the controller. More importantly, without analyzing the controller, it becomes infeasible to prove properties about the entire system; as opposed to properties of the neural network, such as robustness.

Our approach. To address these issues, our approach tightly combines the controller and neural-network analyses in a two-way integration based on abstract interpretation.

In general, an abstract interpreter infers invariants at each program state and verifies safety of an asserted property when it is implied by the invariant inferred in its pre-state. In the presence of loops, as in RACETRACK (line 5 in

Alg. 1), inference is performed for a number of iterations in order to reach a *fixpoint*, that is, infer invariants at each program state that do not change when performing additional loop iterations.

For our running example, to compute the fixpoint of the main loop, the controller analysis invokes the neural-network analysis instead of simply abstracting the call to the neural network by havocking its return value. The invariants inferred by the controller analysis in the pre-state of the call to the network are passed to the neural-network analysis; they are used to restrict the input space of the neural network. In turn, the invariants that are inferred by the neural-network analysis are returned to the controller analysis to restrict the output space. This exchange of verification results at analysis time significantly improves precision. By making the program analysis aware of the network's computation, neuro-aware program analysis is able to prove challenging safety properties of the entire system.

Our implementation combines off-the-shelf, state-of-the-art abstract interpreters, namely, CRAB [34] for the controller analysis and DEEPSYMBOL [41] or ERAN [27,56,57] for the neural-network analysis. CRAB[8] is a state-of-the-art analyzer for checking safety properties of LLVM bitcode programs. Its modular high-level architecture is similar to many other abstract interpreters, such as Astrée [9], Clousot [26], and Infer [11], and it supports a wide range of different abstract domains, such as Intervals [17], Polyhedra [19], and Boxes [33]. Specialized neural-network analyzers, such as DEEPSYMBOL or ERAN, have only very recently been developed to deal with the unique challenges of precisely checking robustness of neural networks; for instance, the challenge of handling the excessive number of "branches" induced by cascades of ReLU activations.

The technical details of this combination are presented in the following section. Note, however, that our technical framework does not prescribe a neural-network analysis that is necessarily based on abstract interpretation. Specifically, it could integrate any sound analysis that, given a set of (symbolic) input states, produces a set of output states over-approximating the return value of the neural network. We also discuss how our approach may integrate reasoning about other complex components, beyond neural networks. Our program analysis is also not inherently tied to CRAB, but could be performed by other abstract interpreters that use the same high-level architecture, such as Astrée [9].

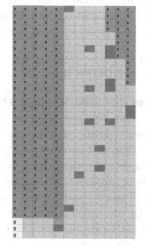

The RACETRACK map on the right, which is borrowed from related work [5,32], shows the verification results achieved by our approach when combining CRAB and DEEPSYMBOL. Gray cells marked with 'x' denote obstacles, and yellow cells

---

[8] https://github.com/seahorn/crab

marked with 'g' denote goal locations. Recall from Alg. 1 that we can consider any cell, which is neither an obstacle nor a goal, as a possible start location.

In our evaluation, we run a separate analysis for each possible start state to identify all start locations from which the vehicle is guaranteed to reach a goal; in other words, the analysis tries to prove that *result* = `goal` holds (line 16 of Alg. 1) for each possible start location. Note that verifying a single start state already constitutes a challenging verification problem since, due to noise, the number of reachable states grows exponentially in the number of loop iterations (the vehicle can navigate to any feasible position). This setting of one start state is common in many reinforcement-learning environments, e.g., Atari games, Procgen [16], OpenAI Gym MiniGrid[9], etc.

Maps like the above are used throughout the paper to display the outcome of a verification process per cell. We color locations for which the process succeeds *green* in all shown maps. Similarly, we color states from which the vehicle might crash into an obstacle *red*; i.e., one or more states reachable from the start state may lead to a crash, and the analysis is not able to show that *result* ≠ `crash` holds before line 16. Finally, states from which the vehicle is guaranteed not to crash but might not reach a goal are colored in *blue*; i.e., the analysis is able to show that *result* ≠ `crash` holds before line 16, but it is not able to show that *result* ≠ `stuck` also holds.

As shown in the map, our approach is effective in verifying goal reachability and crash avoidance for the majority of start locations. Moreover, the verification results are almost identical when combining CRAB with a different neural-network analyzer, namely ERAN (see Sect. 4). Note that, since the analysis considers individual start states, the map may show a red start state that is surrounded by green start states. One explanation for this is that the vehicle never enters the red state from the surrounding green states or that it only enters the red state with a "safe" velocity and direction—imagine that the vehicle velocity when starting from the red state is always 2, whereas when entering it from green states, the velocity is always less. In general, whether a trajectory is safe largely depends on the neural-network behavior, which can be brittle.

3   Approach

As we discussed on a high level, our approach symbiotically combines an existing program analysis (PA) with a neural-network analysis (NNA). The result is a *neuro-aware program analysis* (NPA) that allows for precisely analyzing a program that invokes neural networks (see Fig. 1). In the following, we focus on a single network to keep the presentation simple. As shown in Fig. 1, the two existing analyses are extended to pass information both from PA to NNA (Φ in the diagram) and back (Ψ in the diagram).

In the following, we describe neuro-aware program analysis in more detail and elaborate on how the program analysis drives the neural-network analysis to verify safety properties of the containing heterogeneous system. Since the

---

[9] https://github.com/maximecb/gym-minigrid

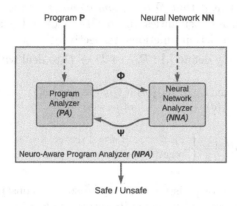

Figure 1: Overview of neuro-aware program analysis.

program analysis drives the neural-network analysis, we will explain the analysis in a top-down fashion by focusing on the program analysis before going into the details of the network analysis. In other words, our description of the program analysis assumes that we have a network analysis that over-approximates the behavior of the neural network.

3.1 Neuro-Aware Program Analysis

For our presentation, we assume imperative programs $\mathcal{P}$ with standard constructs, such as loops, function calls, arithmetic, and pointer operations (our implementation targets LLVM bitcode). In addition, we assume a special function call $o := nn(i_1, \ldots, i_n)$ that calls a neural network with input parameters $i_1, \ldots, i_n$ and returns the result of querying the network in return value o. We also assume that the query does not have side effects on the program state. We denote programs $\mathcal{P}$ augmented with special calls to neural networks as $\mathcal{P}_{nn}$.

We assume an abstract domain D consisting of a set of abstract elements $d \in D$. Domain D is equipped with the usual binary operators $\langle \sqsubseteq, \sqcup, \sqcap, \triangledown \triangle \rangle$, where the ordering between elements is given by $\sqsubseteq$. $\bot_D$ represents the smallest domain element and $\top_D$ the largest (smallest and largest relative to the ordering imposed by $\sqsubseteq$). The least upper bound (greatest lower bound) operator is denoted by $\sqcup$ ($\sqcap$). As usual, if the abstract domain is not finite or the number of elements is too large, then we also assume the domain to be equipped with widening ($\triangledown$) and narrowing ($\triangle$) operators to ensure termination of the fixpoint computation. Moreover, we assume the abstract forget : $D \times \overline{V} \mapsto D$ operation that removes a set of variables from the abstract state, and its dual project : $D \times \overline{V} \mapsto D$ that projects the abstract state onto a set of variables. Finally, we assume the semantics function $[\![.]\!] : \mathcal{P} \mapsto D \mapsto D$ that, given a pre-state, computes the abstract semantics of a program to obtain its post-state; it does so recursively, by induction over the syntax of the program. We do not require that there exists a *Galois connection* [18] between the abstract domain D and the concrete domain

C. The only requirement is that D *over-approximates* C, i.e., $[\![.]\!]^C \subseteq \gamma \circ [\![.]\!] \circ \alpha$ where $[\![.]\!]^C$ is the concrete semantics and $\gamma : D \mapsto C$ and $\alpha : C \mapsto D$ are the concretization and abstraction functions, respectively.

We can then trivially define $\widehat{[\![.]\!]} : \mathcal{P}_{nn} \mapsto D \mapsto D$ to deal with $\mathcal{P}_{nn}$ as follows:

$$\widehat{[\![Cmd]\!]}(d) = \begin{cases} [\![\mathsf{o} := \mathtt{nn}(\mathtt{i_1}, \ldots, \mathtt{i_n})]\!](d) & \text{if } Cmd \equiv \mathsf{o} := \mathtt{nn}(\mathtt{i_1}, \ldots, \mathtt{i_n}) \\ [\![Cmd]\!](d) & \text{otherwise} \end{cases}$$

$$[\![\mathsf{o} := \mathtt{nn}(\mathtt{i_1}, \ldots, \mathtt{i_n})]\!](d) = \begin{cases} \bot_D & \text{if } d = \bot_D \\ \mathsf{forget}(d, \mathsf{o}) & \text{otherwise} \end{cases}$$

However, this definition of $\widehat{[\![.]\!]}$ is not very useful since it conservatively approximates the neural network by havocking its return value o.

To obtain a more precise approximation, we can integrate a designated neural-network analysis. Specifically, we view the neural-network analysis as another abstract domain D_{nn}, where, in practice, we do not require any other operation from D_{nn} except the transfer function for $\mathsf{o} := \mathtt{nn}(\mathtt{i_1}, \ldots, \mathtt{i_n})$ that soundly approximates the semantics of the neural network (see Sect. 3.2 for more details):

$$[\![\mathsf{o} := \mathtt{nn}(\mathtt{i_1}, \ldots, \mathtt{i_n})]\!](d) = \begin{cases} \bot_D & \text{if } d = \bot_D \\ \mathbf{let} \ d_{nn} = \mathsf{convert}(\mathsf{project}(d, i_1, \ldots, i_n)) \ \mathbf{in} \\ \mathbf{let} \ d'_{nn} = [\![\mathsf{o} := \mathtt{nn}(\mathtt{i_1}, \ldots, \mathtt{i_n})]\!]_{D_{nn}}(d_{nn}) \ \mathbf{in} \\ \mathsf{forget}(d, \mathsf{o}) \sqcap \mathsf{convert}^{-1}(d'_{nn}) & \text{otherwise} \end{cases}$$

Intuitively, this more precise transfer function performs the following steps (unless d is $\bot_D$). First, it converts from D to D_{nn} to invoke the transfer function of D_{nn} on the converted value d_{nn}. It then havocs the return value o and conjoins the inferred return value after converting d'_{nn} back to D. In the above definition, functions $\mathsf{convert} : D \mapsto D_{nn}$ and $\mathsf{convert}^{-1} : D_{nn} \mapsto D$ convert from one abstract domain (D) to the other (D_{nn}) and back. We allow for conversions to result in loss of precision, that is, $\forall x \in D \cdot x \sqsubseteq \mathsf{convert}^{-1}(\mathsf{convert}(x))$.

It is important to realize here that the implementation of functions $\mathsf{convert}$ and $\mathsf{convert}^{-1}$, however precise, may still trigger a fatal loss of precision. After all, the abstract domains D and D_{nn} must also be expressive and precise enough to capture the converted values. For example, assume that, in a given program, the function call $\mathsf{o} := \mathtt{nn}(\mathtt{i_1}, \ldots, \mathtt{i_n})$ invokes a neural network to obtain the next move of a vehicle (encoded as a value from 0 to 7). Suppose the abstract return value d'_{nn} is the set of moves $\{1, 7\}$. In this case, given a domain D that cannot express these two moves as *disjuncts*, the implementation of function $\mathsf{convert}^{-1}$ has no choice but to abstract more coarsely; for instance, by expressing the return value as the interval $[1, \ldots, 7]$. Depending on the program, this may be too imprecise to prove safety. This happened to be the case for the RACETRACK variants we analyzed in Sect. 4, which is why we chose to use a disjunctive domain for the analysis; more specifically, we use Boxes [33], which allows us to track Boolean combinations of intervals.

Nevertheless, the considerations and approach described so far are still not precise enough for verifying the safety properties in the variants of RACETRACK that we consider. This is because the controller makes extensive use of (multi-dimensional) arrays, whose accesses are not handled precisely by the analysis. However, we observed that these arrays are initialized at the beginning of the system execution (for instance, to store maps indexed by x-y coordinates), and after initialization, they are no longer modified. Handling such array reads precisely is crucial in our context since over-approximation could conservatively indicate that the vehicle may crash into an obstacle.

Common array domains that summarize multiple elements using one or a small number of abstract elements fail to provide the needed precision. Even a fully expanded array domain [9] that separately tracks each array element loses precision if the index of an array read does not refer to a single array element; in such cases, the join of all overlapping elements will be returned. In addition, the Clang compiler—used to produce the LLVM bitcode that CRAB analyzes—desugars multi-dimensional arrays into single-dimensional arrays. This results in additional arithmetic operations (in particular, multiplications) for indexing the elements; these are also challenging to analyze precisely.

Interestingly, to address these challenges, we follow the same approach as for neural networks, in other words, by introducing a designated and very precise analysis to handle reads from these pre-initialized arrays. More formally, we introduce a new statement to capture such reads, $\mathtt{o} := \mathtt{ar}(\mathtt{i_1}, \ldots, \mathtt{i_n})$, where i_k is the index for the k-th dimension of an n-dimensional array. Note that this avoids index conversions for multi-dimensional arrays since indices of each dimension are provided explicitly. Moreover, it is structurally very similar to the $\mathtt{nn}(\ldots)$ statement we introduced earlier. In particular, the specialized transfer function for D differs only in the two conversion functions and the specialized transfer function $[\![.]\!]_{D_{ar}}$:

$$
[\![\mathtt{o} := \mathtt{ar}(\mathtt{i_1}, \ldots, \mathtt{i_n})]\!](d) =
\begin{cases}
\bot_D & \text{if } d = \bot_D \\
\mathtt{let}\ d_{ar} = \mathsf{convert}_{ar}(\mathsf{project}(d, i_1, \ldots, i_n))\ \mathtt{in} \\
\mathtt{let}\ d'_{ar} = [\![\mathtt{o} := \mathtt{ar}(\mathtt{i_1}, \ldots, \mathtt{i_n})]\!]_{D_{ar}}(d_{ar})\ \mathtt{in} \\
\mathsf{forget}(d, o) \sqcap \mathsf{convert}_{ar}^{-1}(d'_{ar}) & \text{otherwise}
\end{cases}
$$

To keep this transfer function simple, its input is a set of concrete indices and its output a set of concrete values that are retrieved by looking up the indexed elements in the array (after initialization). This makes it necessary for $\mathsf{convert}_{ar}$ to concretize the abstract inputs to a disjunction of (concrete) tuples $(i_1, \ldots, i_n)$ for the read indices. Similarly, $\mathsf{convert}_{ar}^{-1}$ converts the disjunction of (concrete) values back to an element of domain D.

Let us consider the concrete example in Fig. 2 to illustrate this more clearly. Line 1 initializes an array that is never again written to. On line 2, a non-deterministic value is assigned to variable $\mathtt{idx}$, and the subsequent assume-statement constrains its value to be in the interval from 0 to 6. The assertion on line 5 checks that element $\mathtt{elem}$, which is read from the array (on line 4),

```
1  int arr[] = {0, 1, 1, 2, 3, 5, 8, 13};
2  int idx = *;
3  assume(0 <= idx && idx <= 6);
4  int elem = arr[idx];
5  assert(elem < 13);
```

Figure 2: Example illustrating the specialized array domain.

is less than 13. Let us assume that we want to analyze the code by combining the numerical Intervals domain with our array domain D_{ar}; in other words, we assume D is instantiated with Intervals. In the pre-state of the array read, the analysis infers that the abstract value for idx is interval $[0, 6]$. When computing the post-state for the read operation, the analysis converts this interval to the concrete set of indices $\{0, 1, 2, 3, 4, 5, 6\}$ via $convert_{ar}$. The transfer function for the array domain then looks up the (concrete) elements for each index to obtain the (concrete) set $\{0, 1, 2, 3, 5, 8\}$. Before returning this set to the Intervals domain, the analysis applies $convert_{ar}^{-1}$ to obtain the abstract value $[0, 8]$. This post-state allows the numerical domain to prove the assertion.

Note that this array domain is not specific to controllers such as the one used in our RACETRACK variants. In fact, one could consider using it to more precisely analyze other programs with complex arrays that are initialized at runtime; a concrete example would be high-performance hash functions that often rely on fixed lookup tables.

Even more generally, the domains we sketched above suggest that our approach is also applicable to other scenarios; for instance, when a piece of code is too challenging to handle by a generic program analysis, and a simple summary or specification would result in unacceptable loss of precision.

3.2   Neural-Network Analysis

AI^2 [27] was the first tool and technique for verifying robustness of neural networks using abstract interpretation. ERAN is a successor of AI^2; it incorporates specialized transfer functions and abstract domains, such as DeepZ [56] (a variant of Zonotopes [28]) and DeepPoly [57] (a variant of Polyhedra [19]). Meanwhile, DEEPSYMBOL [41] extended AI^2 with a novel *symbolic-propagation* technique. In the following, we first provide an overview of the techniques in ERAN and DEEPSYMBOL. Then, we describe how their domains can be used to implement the specialized transfer function from D_{nn} that was introduced in Sect. 3.1. On a high level, even though we are not concerned with robustness properties in this work, we re-purpose components of these existing tools to effectively check safety properties of heterogeneous systems that use neural networks.

The main goal behind verifying robustness of a neural network is to provide guarantees about whether it is susceptible to adversarial attacks [31,12,50,44]. Such attacks slightly perturb an original input (e.g., an image) that is classified correctly by the network (e.g., as a dog) to obtain an adversarial input that is classified differently (e.g., as a cat). Given a concrete input (e.g., an image), existing tools detect such local-robustness violations by expressing the set of all perturbed inputs (within a bounded distance from the original according to a metric, such as L_∞ [35]) and "executing" the neural network with this set of inputs to obtain a set of outcomes (or labels). The network is considered to be locally robust if there are no more than one possible outcome.

Existing techniques use abstract domains to express sets of inputs and outputs, and define specialized transfer functions to capture the operations (e.g., affine transforms and ReLUs) that are required for executing neural networks. For instance, ERAN uses the DeepPoly [57] domain that captures polyhedral constraints and incorporates custom transfer functions for affine transforms, ReLUs, and other common neural-network operations. DEEPSYMBOL propagates symbolic information on top of abstract domains [65,41] to improve its precision. The key insight is that neural networks make extensive use of operations that apply linear combinations of arguments, and symbolic propagation is able to track linear-equality relations between variables (e.g., activation values of neurons).

Both ERAN and DEEPSYMBOL have the following in common: they define an abstract semantics for reasoning about neural-network operations and for computing an abstract set of outcomes from a set of inputs. We leverage this semantics to implement the specialized transfer function $[\![\mathsf{o} := \mathsf{nn}(\mathsf{i_1}, ..., \mathsf{i_n})]\!]_{D_{nn}}(d_{nn})$ from Sect. 3.1.

4 Experimental Evaluation

To evaluate our technique, we aim to answer the following research questions:

RQ1: How effective is our technique in verifying goal reachability and crash avoidance?

RQ2: How does the quality of the neural network affect the verification results?

RQ3: How does a more complex benchmark affect the verification results?

RQ4: How does the neural-network analyzer affect the verification results?

4.1 Benchmarks

We run our experiments on variants of RACETRACK, which is a popular benchmark in the AI community [4,5,32,46,52,53] and implements the pseudo-code from Alg. 1 in C (see Sect. 2 for a high-level overview of the benchmark).

The RACETRACK code[10] is significantly more complicated than the pseudo-code in Alg. 1 would suggest; more specifically, it consists of around 400 lines of C code and invokes a four-layer fully connected neural network—with 14 inputs, 9 outputs, and 64 neurons per hidden layer (using ReLU activation functions). To name a few sources of complexity, the *currentState* does not just denote a single value, but rather the position of the vehicle on the map, the magnitude and direction of its velocity, its distance to goal locations, and its distance to obstacles. As another example, the MOVE function runs the trajectory of the

---

[10] https://github.com/Practical-Formal-Methods/Racetrack-Benchmark

vehicle from the old to the new state while determining whether there are any obstacles in between.

For simplicity, the code does not use floating-point numbers to represent variables, such as position, velocity, acceleration, and distance. Therefore, the program analyzer does not need to reason about floating-point numbers, which is difficult for CRAB and most other tools. However, this does not semantically affect the neural network or its analysis, both of which do use floats. An interface layer converts the input features, tracked as integers in the controller, to normalized floats for the neural-network analysis. The output from the neural-network analysis is a set of floating-point intervals, which are logically mapped to integers representing discrete possible actions at a particular state.

We evaluate our approach on 26 variants of RACETRACK, which differ in the following aspects of the analyzed program or neural network.

Maps. We adopt three RACETRACK maps of varying complexity from related work [5,32], namely *barto-small* (BS) of size 12 × 35, *barto-big* (BB) of size 30 × 33, and *ring* (R) of size 45 × 50. The size of a map is measured in terms of its dimensions (i.e., width and height). The map affects not only the program behavior, but also the neural network that is invoked. The latter is due to the fact that we train custom networks for different maps.

Neural-network quality. The neural network (line 9 of Alg. 1) is trained, using reinforcement learning [60], to predict an acceleration given a vehicle state, that is, the position of the vehicle on the map, the magnitude and direction of its velocity, its distance to goal locations, and its distance to obstacles. As expected, the quality of the neural-network predictions depends on the amount of training. In our experiments, we use *well* (GOOD), *moderately* (MOD), and *poorly* (POOR) *trained* neural networks. We use the average reward at the end of the training process to control the quality. More details are provided in RQ2.

Noise. We complicate the RACETRACK benchmark by adding two sources of non-determinism, namely *environment* (ENV) and *neural-network* (NN) *noise*. Introducing such noise is common practice in reinforcement learning, for instance, when modeling real-world imperfections, like slippery ground.

When environment noise is enabled, the controller might zero the vehicle acceleration (in practice, with a small probability), instead of applying the acceleration predicted by the neural network for the current vehicle state. This source of non-determinism is implemented by the if-statement on line 6 of Alg. 1. Environment noise may be disabled for states that are too close to obstacles to allow the vehicle to avoid definite crashes by adjusting its course according to the neural-network predictions. The amount of environment noise is, therefore, controlled by the distance to an obstacle (OD) at which we disable it. For example, when OD = 3, environment noise is disabled for all vehicle states that are at most 3 cells away from any obstacle. Consequently, when OD = 1, we have a more noisy environment. Note that we do not consider OD = 0 since the environment would be too noisy to verify safety for any start state.

Note that environment noise is not meant to represent realistic noise, but rather to make the verification task more challenging. However, it is also not entirely unrealistic and can be viewed as "necessarily rectifying steering course close to obstacles". Non-deterministically zeroing acceleration is inspired by related work [32].

For a given vehicle state, the neural network computes confidence values for each possible acceleration; these values sum up to 1. Normally, the predicted acceleration is the one with the largest confidence value, which however might not always be high. When neural-network noise is enabled, the network analyzer considers *any* acceleration for which the inferred upper bound on the confidence value is higher than a threshold ϵ. For example, when $\epsilon = 0.25$, any acceleration whose inferred confidence interval includes values greater than 0.25 might be predicted by the neural network. Consequently, for lower values of ϵ, the neural network becomes more noisy. Such probabilistic action selection is widely used in reinforcement learning [55].

Each of these two sources of noise—ENV and NN noise—renders the verification of a neural-network controller through enumeration of all possible execution paths intractable: due to the non-determinism, the number of execution paths from a given initial state grows exponentially with the number of control iterations (e.g., the main loop on line 5 of Alg. 1). In our RACETRACK experiments, the bound on the number of loop iterations is 50, and as a result, the number of execution paths from any given initial state quickly becomes very large. By statically reasoning about sets of execution paths, our approach is able to more effectively handle challenging verification tasks in comparison to exhaustive enumeration.

Lookahead functionality. We further complicate the benchmark by adding lookahead functionality (not shown in Alg. 1), which aims to counteract incorrect predictions of the neural network and prevent crashes. In particular, when this functionality is enabled, the controller simulates the vehicle trajectory when applying the acceleration predicted by the neural network a bounded number of additional times (denoted LA). For example, when LA = 3, the controller invokes the neural network 3 additional times to check whether the vehicle would crash if we were to consecutively apply the predicted accelerations. If this lookahead functionality indeed foresees a crash, then the controller reverses the direction of the acceleration that is predicted for the current vehicle state on line 9 of Alg. 1. Conceptually, the goal behind our lookahead functionality is similar to the one behind *shields* [2]. While lookahead is explicitly encoded in the program as code, shields provide a more declarative way for expressing such safeguards.

4.2 Implementation

For our implementation[11], we extended CRAB to support specialized abstract domains as described in Sect. 3. To integrate DEEPSYMBOL and ERAN, we implemented a thin wrapper around these tools to enable their analysis to start

---

[11] Our source code can be found at https://github.com/Practical-Formal-Methods/clam-racetrack and an installation at https://hub.docker.com/r/practicalformalmethods/neuro-aware-verification.

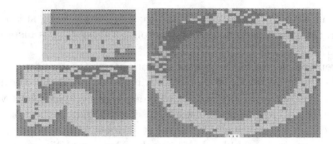

Figure 3: Verification results for RQ1, where ENV(OD = 3). The maps on the left are BS (top) and BB (bottom), and the map on the right is R.

from a set of abstract input states and return a set of abstract output states. Moreover, our wrappers provide control over the amount of neural-network noise (through threshold ϵ).

4.3 Setup

We use deep Q-learning [47] to train a neural network for each RACETRACK variant. We developed all training code in Python using the TensorFlow[12] and Torch[13] deep-learning libraries.

We configure CRAB to use the Boxes abstract domain [33], DEEPSYMBOL to use Intervals [18] with symbolic propagation [41], and ERAN to use DeepPoly [57]. When running the analysis, we did not specify a bound on the available time or memory; consequently, none of our analysis runs led to a time-out or mem-out. Regarding time, we report our results in the following, and regarding memory, our technique never exceeded 13.5GB when analyzing all start states of any map.

We performed all experiments on a 48-core Intel ® Xeon ® E7-8857 v2 CPU @ 3.6GHz machine with 1.5TB of memory, running Debian 10 (buster).

4.4 Results

We now present our experimental results for each research question.

RQ1: How effective is our technique in verifying goal reachability and crash avoidance? To evaluate the effectiveness of our technique in proving these system properties, we run it on the following benchmark variants: BS, BB, and R maps, GOOD neural networks, ENV noise with OD $= 1, 2, 3$, and LA $= 0$ (i.e., no lookahead). The verification results are shown in Figs. 3, 4, and 5 (see Sect. 2 for the semantics of cell colors). These results are achieved when combining CRAB with DEEPSYMBOL, but the combination with ERAN is comparable (see RQ4).

As shown in Fig. 3, for the vast majority of initial vehicle states, our technique is able to verify goal reachability and crash avoidance. This indicates that our integration of the controller and neural-network analyses is highly precise. As

---
[12] https://www.tensorflow.org
[13] http://torch.ch/

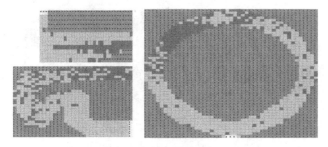

Figure 4: Verification results for RQ1, where ENV(OD = 2).

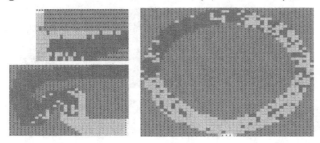

Figure 5: Verification results for RQ1, where ENV(OD = 1).

Table 1: Performance results for RQ1.

MAP	NN	NOISE	LA	NN ANALYZER	TOTAL TIME	AVG TIME	NN AVG TIME
BS	GOOD	ENV(OD = 3)	0	DEEPSYMBOL	1h20m34s	14m53s	30.2%
BB	GOOD	ENV(OD = 3)	0	DEEPSYMBOL	3h52m38s	18m55s	16.1%
R	GOOD	ENV(OD = 3)	0	DEEPSYMBOL	2h58m17s	11m33s	26.6%

expected, the more ENV noise we add (i.e., the smaller the OD values), the fewer states we prove safe (see Figs. 4 and 5).

Tab. 1 shows the performance of our technique. The first four columns of the table define the benchmark settings, the fifth the neural-network analyzer, and the last three show the total running time of our technique for all start states, the average time per state, and the percentage of this time spent on the neural-network analysis. Note that we measure the total time when running the verification tasks (for each start state) in parallel[14]; the average time per state is independent of any parallelization. We do not show performance results for different OD values since environment noise does not seem to have a significant impact on the analysis time.

Recall from Sect. 2 that, without our technique, it is currently only possible to verify properties of a heterogeneous system like RACETRACK by considering the controller in isolation, ignoring the call to the neural network, and havocking its return value. We perform this experiment for all of the above benchmark variants and find that CRAB alone is unable to prove goal reachability or crash

---

[14] https://doi.org/10.5281/zenodo.1146014

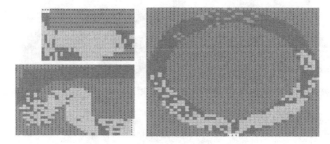

Figure 6: Verification results for RQ2, with MOD neural networks.

Figure 7: Verification results for RQ2, with POOR neural networks.

avoidance for *any* initial vehicle state; in other words, all states are *red*. This is the case even when replacing Boxes with Polyhedra—these two domains perform the most precise analyses in CRAB.

RQ2: How does the quality of the neural network affect the verification results? To evaluate this research question, we run our technique on the following benchmark variants: BS, BB, and R maps, MOD and POOR neural networks, ENV noise with OD = 3, and LA = 0. The verification results are shown in Figs. 6 and 7; they are achieved by combining CRAB with DEEPSYMBOL.

In deep Q-Learning (see Sect. 4.3), a neural network is trained by assigning positive or negative rewards to its predictions. A properly trained network learns to collect higher rewards over a run. Given this, we assess the quality of networks by considering average rewards over 100 runs from randomly selected starting states. If the network collects more than 70% of the maximum achievable reward, we consider it a GOOD agent. If it collects ca. 50% (or respectively, ca. 30%) of the maximum reward, we consider it a MOD (respectively, POOR) agent.

In comparison to Fig. 3, our technique proves safety of fewer states since the quality of the networks is worse. Analogously, more states are verified in Fig. 6 than in Fig. 7. Interestingly, for BB, our technique proves crash avoidance (blue cells) more often when using a POOR neural network (Fig. 7) instead of a MOD one (Fig. 6). We suspect that this is due to the randomness of the training process and the training policy, which penalizes crashes more than getting stuck; so, a POOR neural network might initially only try to avoid crashes.

Regarding performance, the analysis time fluctuates when using MOD and POOR neural networks. There is no pattern even when comparing the time across

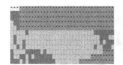 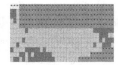 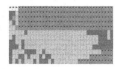

Figure 8: Verification results for RQ3, where LA $= 0, 1, 3$ from left to right.

Table 2: Performance results for RQ3.

MAP	NN	NOISE	LA	NN ANALYZER	TOTAL TIME	AVG TIME	NN AVG TIME
BS	MOD	ENV(OD $= 3$)	0	DEEPSYMBOL	2h27m53s	27m35s	45.0%
BS	MOD	ENV(OD $= 3$)	1	DEEPSYMBOL	8h04m40s	1h12m20s	14.9%
BS	MOD	ENV(OD $= 3$)	3	DEEPSYMBOL	9h30m14s	1h47m05s	11.49%

different map sizes for equally trained networks. This is to be expected as neural networks may behave in unpredictable ways when not trained properly (e.g., the vehicle may drive in circles), which affects the performance of the analysis.

RQ3: How does a more complex benchmark affect the verification results? We complicate the benchmark by adding lookahead functionality, i.e., resulting in LA additional calls to the neural network per vehicle move (see Sect. 4.1 for more details). Since well trained neural networks would benefit less from this functionality, we use MOD networks in these experiments. In particular, we run our technique on the following benchmark variants: BS map, MOD neural networks, ENV noise with OD $= 3$, and LA $= 0, 1, 3$. The verification results are shown in Fig. 8; they are achieved by combining CRAB with DEEPSYMBOL.

As LA increases, the benchmark becomes more robust, yet more complex. We observe that, for larger values of LA, our technique retains its overall precision despite the higher complexity; e.g., there are states that are verified with LA $= 3$ or 1 but not with 0. However, there are also few states that are verified with LA $= 1$ but not with 3. In these cases, the higher complexity does have a negative impact on the precision of our analyses.

Tab. 2 shows the performance of our technique for these experiments. As expected, the analysis time increases as the benchmark complexity increases.

RQ4: How does the neural-network analyzer affect the verification results? We first compare DEEPSYMBOL with ERAN on the following benchmark variants: BS, BB, and R maps, GOOD neural networks, ENV noise with OD $= 3$, and LA $= 0$. The verification results achieved when combining CRAB with ERAN are shown in Fig. 9; compare this with Fig. 3 for DEEPSYMBOL.

We observe the results to be comparable. With DEEPSYMBOL, we color 216 cells green and 1 blue for BS, 455 green for BB, and 499 green and 6 blue for R. With ERAN, the corresponding numbers are 214 cells green and 7 blue for BS, 459 green and 4 blue for BB, and 485 green and 71 blue for R. We observe similar results for other benchmark variants, but we omit them here.

Comparing the two neural-network analyzers becomes more interesting when we enable NN noise. More specifically, we run our technique on the following benchmark variants: BS, BB, and R maps, GOOD networks, NN noise with $\epsilon = 0.25$,

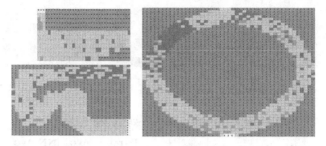

Figure 9: Verification results for RQ4 with ERAN, where ENV(OD = 3).

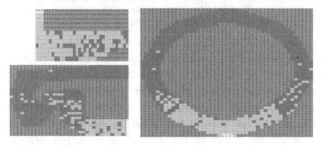

Figure 10: Verification results for RQ4 with DEEPSYMBOL, where NN($\epsilon = 0.25$).

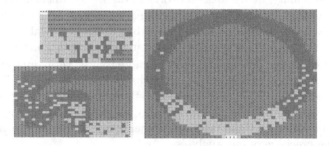

Figure 11: Verification results for RQ4 with ERAN, where NN($\epsilon = 0.25$).

and LA = 0. Fig. 10 shows the verification results when combining CRAB with DEEPSYMBOL, and Fig. 11 when combining CRAB with ERAN.

As shown in the figures, the verification results are slightly better with ERAN. In particular, with DEEPSYMBOL, we color 170 cells green for BS, 109 green for BB, and 195 green for R. With ERAN, the corresponding numbers are 181 cells green for BS, 131 green for BB, and 203 green for R. Despite this, the performance of our technique can differ significantly depending on whether we use DEEPSYMBOL or ERAN, as shown in Tab. 3. One could, consequently, imagine a setup where multiple neural-network analyzers are run in parallel for each verification task. If time is of the essence, we collect the results of the analyzer that terminates first. If it is more critical to prove safety, then we could combine the results of all analyzers once they terminate.

Table 3: Performance results for RQ4.

Map	NN	Noise	LA	NN Analyzer	Total Time	Avg Time	NN Avg Time
BS	Good	env(od = 3)	0	DeepSymbol	1h20m34s	14m53s	30.2%
BS	Good	env(od = 3)	0	Eran	43m21s	8m11s	38.4%
BB	Good	env(od = 3)	0	DeepSymbol	3h52m38s	18m55s	16.1%
BB	Good	env(od = 3)	0	Eran	3h26m17s	16m42s	57.2%
R	Good	env(od = 3)	0	DeepSymbol	2h58m17s	11m33s	26.6%
R	Good	env(od = 3)	0	Eran	4h38m03s	18m18s	53.8%
BS	Good	nn(ϵ = 0.25)	0	DeepSymbol	1h26m09s	15m41s	36.7%
BS	Good	nn(ϵ = 0.25)	0	Eran	45m37s	8m24s	45.0%
BB	Good	nn(ϵ = 0.25)	0	DeepSymbol	2h52m50s	13m24s	20.7%
BB	Good	nn(ϵ = 0.25)	0	Eran	2h59m48s	14m10s	64.7%
R	Good	nn(ϵ = 0.25)	0	DeepSymbol	2h01m18s	7m57s	26.4%
R	Good	nn(ϵ = 0.25)	0	Eran	3h21m32s	13m11s	54.3%

5 Related Work

The program-analysis literature provides countless examples of powerful analysis combinations. To name a few, dynamic symbolic execution [29,10] and hybrid fuzzing [45,58,69] combine random testing and symbolic execution, numerous tools broadly combine static and dynamic analysis [6,20,21,49,30,13,14,22,61], and many tools combine different types of static analysis [7,1,34]. In contrast to neuro-aware program analysis, almost all these tools target homogeneous, instead of heterogeneous, systems. Concerto [61] is a notable exception that targets applications using frameworks such as Spring and Struts. It combines abstract and concrete interpretation, where, on a high level, concrete interpretation is used to analyze framework code, whereas abstract interpretation is used for application code. Instead of building on existing analyzers, as in our work, Concerto introduces a designated technique for analyzing framework code.

There is recent work that focuses specifically on verifying hybrid systems with DNN controllers [24,59]. Unlike in our work, they do not analyze programs that interact with the network, but models; in one case, ordinary differential equations describing the hybrid system [24], and in the other, a mathematical model of a LiDAR image processor [59]. In this context of hybrid systems with DNN controllers, there is also work that takes a falsification approach to the same problem [62,70,23]. They generate corner test cases that cause the system to violate a system-level specification. Moreover, existing reachability analyses for neural networks [25,42,67,68] consider linear or piecewise-linear systems, instead of programs invoking them.

Kazak et al. [39] recently proposed Verily, a technique for verifying systems based on deep reinforcement learning. Such systems have been used in various contexts, such as adaptive video streaming, cloud resource management, and Internet congestion control. Verily builds on Marabou [38], a verification tool for neural networks, and aims to ensure that a system achieves desired service-level objectives (expressed as safety or liveness properties). Other techniques use abstract interpretation to verify robustness [27,57,41] or fairness properties [63] of neural networks. Furthermore, there are several existing techniques for checking properties of neural networks using SMT solvers [37,38,36] and global optimization techniques [54]. In contrast to our approach, they focus on verifying properties of the network in isolation, i.e., without considering a program that queries it. However, we re-purpose two of the above analyzers [57,41] to infer invariants over the neural-network outputs. Gros et al. [32] make use of statistical model checking to obtain quality-assurance reports for a neural network in a noisy environment. Their approach provides probabilistic guarantees about checked properties, instead of definite ones like in our work, and also does not analyze a surrounding system.

6   Conclusion

Many existing software systems are already heterogeneous, and we expect the number of such systems to grow further. In this paper, we present a novel approach to verifying safety properties of such systems that symbiotically combines existing program and neural-network analyzers. Neuro-aware program analysis is able to effectively prove non-trivial system properties of programs invoking neural networks, such as the 26 variants of RACETRACK.

Acknowledgements. We are grateful to the reviewers for their constructive feedback. This work has been supported by DFG Grant 389792660 as part of TRR 248 (see https://perspicuous-computing.science). Jorge Navas has been supported by NSF Grant 1816936. Holger Hermanns and Jianlin Li have been supported by Guangdong Province Science Grant 2018B010107004.

References

1. Albarghouthi, A., Li, Y., Gurfinkel, A., Chechik, M.: UFO: A framework for abstraction- and interpolation-based software verification. In: CAV. LNCS, vol. 7358, pp. 672–678. Springer (2012)
2. Alshiekh, M., Bloem, R., Ehlers, R., Könighofer, B., Niekum, S., Topcu, U.: Safe reinforcement learning via shielding. In: AAAI. pp. 2669–2678. AAAI (2018)
3. Babaev, D., Savchenko, M., Tuzhilin, A., Umerenkov, D.: E.T.-RNN: Applying deep learning to credit loan applications. In: KDD. pp. 2183—2190. ACM (2019)
4. Baier, C., Christakis, M., Gros, T.P., Groß, D., Gumhold, S., Hermanns, H., Hoffmann, J., Klauck, M.: Lab conditions for research on explainable automated decisions. In: TAILOR. LNCS, vol. 12641, pp. 83–90. Springer (2020)
5. Barto, A.G., Bradtke, S.J., Singh, S.P.: Learning to act using real-time dynamic programming. Artif. Intell. **72**, 81–138 (1995)
6. Beyer, D., Chlipala, A.J., Majumdar, R.: Generating tests from counterexamples. In: ICSE. pp. 326–335. IEEE Computer Society (2004)
7. Beyer, D., Henzinger, T.A., Keremoglu, M.E., Wendler, P.: Conditional model checking: A technique to pass information between verifiers. In: FSE. pp. 57–67. ACM (2012)
8. Biere, A., Cimatti, A., Clarke, E.M., Zhu, Y.: Symbolic model checking without BDDs. In: TACAS. LNCS, vol. 1579, pp. 193–207. Springer (1999)

9. Blanchet, B., Cousot, P., Cousot, R., Feret, J., Mauborgne, L., Miné, A., Monniaux, D., Rival, X.: A static analyzer for large safety-critical software. In: PLDI. pp. 196–207. ACM (2003)
10. Cadar, C., Engler, D.R.: Execution generated test cases: How to make systems code crash itself. In: SPIN. LNCS, vol. 3639, pp. 2–23. Springer (2005)
11. Calcagno, C., Distefano, D., Dubreil, J., Gabi, D., Hooimeijer, P., Luca, M., O'Hearn, P.W., Papakonstantinou, I., Purbrick, J., Rodriguez, D.: Moving fast with software verification. In: NFM. LNCS, vol. 9058, pp. 3–11. Springer (2015)
12. Carlini, N., Wagner, D.A.: Defensive distillation is not robust to adversarial examples. CoRR **abs/1607.04311** (2016)
13. Christakis, M., Müller, P., Wüstholz, V.: Collaborative verification and testing with explicit assumptions. In: FM. LNCS, vol. 7436, pp. 132–146. Springer (2012)
14. Christakis, M., Müller, P., Wüstholz, V.: Guiding dynamic symbolic execution toward unverified program executions. In: ICSE. pp. 144–155. ACM (2016)
15. Clarke, E.M., Biere, A., Raimi, R., Zhu, Y.: Bounded model checking using satisfiability solving. FMSD **19**, 7–34 (2001)
16. Cobbe, K., Hesse, C., Hilton, J., Schulman, J.: Leveraging procedural generation to benchmark reinforcement learning. In: ICML. PMLR, vol. 119, pp. 2048–2056. PMLR (2020)
17. Cousot, P., Cousot, R.: Static determination of dynamic properties of programs. In: ISOP. pp. 106–130. Dunod (1976)
18. Cousot, P., Cousot, R.: Abstract interpretation: A unified lattice model for static analysis of programs by construction or approximation of fixpoints. In: POPL. pp. 238–252. ACM (1977)
19. Cousot, P., Halbwachs, N.: Automatic discovery of linear restraints among variables of a program. In: POPL. pp. 84–96. ACM (1978)
20. Csallner, C., Smaragdakis, Y.: Check 'n' Crash: Combining static checking and testing. In: ICSE. pp. 422–431. ACM (2005)
21. Csallner, C., Smaragdakis, Y., Xie, T.: DSD-Crasher: A hybrid analysis tool for bug finding. TOSEM **17**, 1–37 (2008)
22. Czech, M., Jakobs, M.C., Wehrheim, H.: Just test what you cannot verify! In: FASE. LNCS, vol. 9033, pp. 100–114. Springer (2015)
23. Dreossi, T., Donzé, A., Seshia, S.A.: Compositional falsification of cyber-physical systems with machine learning components. In: NFM. LNCS, vol. 10227, pp. 357–372. Springer (2017)
24. Dutta, S., Chen, X., Sankaranarayanan, S.: Reachability analysis for neural feedback systems using regressive polynomial rule inference. In: HSCC. pp. 157–168. ACM (2019)
25. Dutta, S., Jha, S., Sankaranarayanan, S., Tiwari, A.: Learning and verification of feedback control systems using feedforward neural networks. In: ADHS. IFAC-PapersOnLine, vol. 51, pp. 151–156. Elsevier (2018)
26. Fähndrich, M., Logozzo, F.: Static contract checking with abstract interpretation. In: FoVeOOS. LNCS, vol. 6528, pp. 10–30. Springer (2010)
27. Gehr, T., Mirman, M., Drachsler-Cohen, D., Tsankov, P., Chaudhuri, S., Vechev, M.T.: AI2: Safety and robustness certification of neural networks with abstract interpretation. In: S&P. pp. 3–18. IEEE Computer Society (2018)
28. Ghorbal, K., Goubault, E., Putot, S.: The Zonotope abstract domain Taylor1+. In: CAV. LNCS, vol. 5643, pp. 627–633. Springer (2009)
29. Godefroid, P., Klarlund, N., Sen, K.: DART: Directed automated random testing. In: PLDI. pp. 213–223. ACM (2005)

30. Godefroid, P., Nori, A.V., Rajamani, S.K., Tetali, S.: Compositional may-must program analysis: Unleashing the power of alternation. In: POPL. pp. 43–56. ACM (2010)

31. Goodfellow, I.J., Shlens, J., Szegedy, C.: Explaining and harnessing adversarial examples. In: ICLR (2015)

32. Gros, T.P., Hermanns, H., Hoffmann, J., Klauck, M., Steinmetz, M.: Deep statistical model checking. In: FORTE. LNCS, vol. 12136, p. 12136. Springer (2020)

33. Gurfinkel, A., Chaki, S.: Boxes: A symbolic abstract domain of boxes. In: SAS. LNCS, vol. 6337, pp. 287–303. Springer (2010)

34. Gurfinkel, A., Kahsai, T., Komuravelli, A., Navas, J.A.: The SeaHorn verification framework. In: CAV. LNCS, vol. 9206, pp. 343–361. Springer (2015)

35. Horn, R.A., Johnson, C.R.: Matrix Analysis. Cambridge University Press (2012)

36. Huang, X., Kwiatkowska, M., Wang, S., Wu, M.: Safety verification of deep neural networks. In: CAV. LNCS, vol. 10426, pp. 3–29. Springer (2017)

37. Katz, G., Barrett, C.W., Dill, D.L., Julian, K., Kochenderfer, M.J.: Reluplex: An efficient SMT solver for verifying deep neural networks. In: CAV. LNCS, vol. 10426, pp. 97–117. Springer (2017)

38. Katz, G., Huang, D.A., Ibeling, D., Julian, K., Lazarus, C., Lim, R., Shah, P., Thakoor, S., Wu, H., Zeljic, A., Dill, D.L., Kochenderfer, M.J., Barrett, C.W.: The Marabou framework for verification and analysis of deep neural networks. In: CAV. LNCS, vol. 11561, pp. 443–452. Springer (2019)

39. Kazak, Y., Barrett, C.W., Katz, G., Schapira, M.: Verifying deep-RL-driven systems. In: NetAI@SIGCOMM. pp. 83–89. ACM (2019)

40. Larus, J., Hankin, C., Carson, S.G., Christen, M., Crafa, S., Grau, O., Kirchner, C., Knowles, B., McGettrick, A., Tamburri, D.A., Werthner, H.: When computers decide: European recommendations on machine-learned automated decision making. Tech. rep. (2018)

41. Li, J., Liu, J., Yang, P., Chen, L., Huang, X., Zhang, L.: Analyzing deep neural networks with symbolic propagation: Towards higher precision and faster verification. In: SAS. LNCS, vol. 11822, pp. 296–319. Springer (2019)

42. Lomuscio, A., Maganti, L.: An approach to reachability analysis for feed-forward ReLU neural networks. CoRR **abs/1706.07351** (2017)

43. Luo, H., Yang, Y., Tong, B., Wu, F., Fan, B.: Traffic sign recognition using a multi-task convolutional neural network. Trans. Intell. Transp. Syst. **19**, 1100–1111 (2018)

44. Madry, A., Makelov, A., Schmidt, L., Tsipras, D., Vladu, A.: Towards deep learning models resistant to adversarial attacks. In: ICLR. OpenReview.net (2018)

45. Majumdar, R., Sen, K.: Hybrid concolic testing. In: ICSE. pp. 416–426. IEEE Computer Society (2007)

46. McMahan, H.B., Gordon, G.J.: Fast exact planning in Markov decision processes. In: ICAPS. pp. 151–160. AAAI (2005)

47. Mnih, V., Kavukcuoglu, K., Silver, D., Graves, A., Antonoglou, I., Wierstra, D., Riedmiller, M.A.: Playing Atari with deep reinforcement learning. CoRR **abs/1312.5602** (2013)

48. Nassi, B., Mirsky, Y., Nassi, D., Ben-Netanel, R., , Drokin, O., Elovici, Y.: Phantom of the ADAS: Securing advanced driver-assistance systems from split-second phantom attacks. In: CCS. pp. 293–308. ACM (2020)

49. Nori, A.V., Rajamani, S.K., Tetali, S., Thakur, A.V.: The YOGI project: Software property checking via static analysis and testing. In: TACAS. LNCS, vol. 5505, pp. 178–181. Springer (2009)

50. Papernot, N., McDaniel, P.D., Jha, S., Fredrikson, M., Celik, Z.B., Swami, A.: The limitations of deep learning in adversarial settings. In: EuroS&P. pp. 372–387. IEEE Computer Society (2016)
51. Pham, T., Tran, T., Phung, D.Q., Venkatesh, S.: Predicting healthcare trajectories from medical records: A deep learning approach. J. Biomed. Informatics **69**, 218–229 (2017)
52. Pineda, L.E., Lu, Y., Zilberstein, S., Goldman, C.V.: Fault-tolerant planning under uncertainty. In: IJCAI. pp. 2350–2356. IJCAI/AAAI (2013)
53. Pineda, L.E., Zilberstein, S.: Planning under uncertainty using reduced models: Revisiting determinization. In: ICAPS. pp. 217–225. AAAI (2014)
54. Ruan, W., Huang, X., Kwiatkowska, M.: Reachability analysis of deep neural networks with provable guarantees. In: IJCAI. pp. 2651–2659. ijcai.org (2018)
55. Schulman, J., Wolski, F., Dhariwal, P., Radford, A., Klimov, O.: Proximal policy optimization algorithms. CoRR **abs/1707.06347** (2017)
56. Singh, G., Gehr, T., Mirman, M., Püschel, M., Vechev, M.T.: Fast and effective robustness certification. In: NeurIPS. pp. 10825–10836 (2018)
57. Singh, G., Gehr, T., Püschel, M., Vechev, M.T.: An abstract domain for certifying neural networks. PACMPL **3**, 41:1–41:30 (2019)
58. Stephens, N., Grosen, J., Salls, C., Dutcher, A., Wang, R., Corbetta, J., Shoshitaishvili, Y., Kruegel, C., Vigna, G.: Driller: Augmenting fuzzing through selective symbolic execution. In: NDSS. The Internet Society (2016)
59. Sun, X., Khedr, H., Shoukry, Y.: Formal verification of neural network controlled autonomous systems. In: HSCC. pp. 147–156. ACM (2019)
60. Sutton, R.S., Barto, A.G.: Reinforcement Learning: An Introduction. MIT Press (2018)
61. Toman, J., Grossman, D.: CONCERTO: A framework for combined concrete and abstract interpretation. PACMPL **3**(POPL), 43:1–43:29 (2019)
62. Tuncali, C.E., Fainekos, G., Ito, H., Kapinski, J.: Simulation-based adversarial test generation for autonomous vehicles with machine learning components. In: IV. pp. 1555–1562. IEEE Computer Society (2018)
63. Urban, C., Christakis, M., Wüstholz, V., Zhang, F.: Perfectly parallel fairness certification of neural networks. PACMPL **4**, 185:1–185:30 (2020)
64. Wang, S., Pei, K., Whitehouse, J., Yang, J., Jana, S.: Efficient formal safety analysis of neural networks. In: NeurIPS. pp. 6369–6379 (2018)
65. Wang, S., Pei, K., Whitehouse, J., Yang, J., Jana, S.: Formal security analysis of neural networks using symbolic intervals. In: Security. pp. 1599–1614. USENIX (2018)
66. Wicker, M., Huang, X., Kwiatkowska, M.: Feature-guided black-box safety testing of deep neural networks. In: TACAS. LNCS, vol. 10805, pp. 408–426. Springer (2018)
67. Xiang, W., Tran, H., Johnson, T.T.: Output reachable set estimation and verification for multilayer neural networks. TNNLS **29**, 5777–5783 (2018)
68. Xiang, W., Tran, H., Rosenfeld, J.A., Johnson, T.T.: Reachable set estimation and safety verification for piecewise linear systems with neural network controllers. In: ACC. pp. 1574–1579. IEEE Computer Society (2018)
69. Yun, I., Lee, S., Xu, M., Jang, Y., Kim, T.: QSYM: A practical concolic execution engine tailored for hybrid fuzzing. In: Security. pp. 745–761. USENIX (2018)
70. Zhang, Z., Ernst, G., Sedwards, S., Arcaini, P., Hasuo, I.: Two-layered falsification of hybrid systems guided by monte carlo tree search. Trans. Comput. Aided Des. Integr. Circuits Syst. **37**, 2894–2905 (2018)

Scalable Polyhedral Verification
of Recurrent Neural Networks

Wonryong Ryou[1]([✉]), Jiayu Chen[1], Mislav Balunovic[1],
Gagandeep Singh[2], Andrei Dan[3], and Martin Vechev[1]

[1] Department of Computer Science, ETH Zürich, Zurich, Switzerland
wryou@ethz.ch
[2] VMWare Research and Department of Computer Science, UIUC, Champaign, USA
[3] Hitachi Power Grids Research, Zurich, Switzerland

Abstract. We present a scalable and precise verifier for recurrent neural networks, called PROVER based on two novel ideas: (i) a method to compute a set of polyhedral abstractions for the non-convex and non-linear recurrent update functions by combining sampling, optimization, and Fermat's theorem, and (ii) a gradient descent based algorithm for abstraction refinement guided by the certification problem that combines multiple abstractions for each neuron. Using PROVER, we present the first study of certifying a non-trivial use case of recurrent neural networks, namely speech classification. To achieve this, we additionally develop custom abstractions for the non-linear speech preprocessing pipeline. Our evaluation shows that PROVER successfully verifies several challenging recurrent models in computer vision, speech, and motion sensor data classification beyond the reach of prior work.

Keywords: Robustness verification · Polyhedral abstraction ·
Recurrent neural networks · Long short-term memory · Abstraction
refinement · Speech classifier verification

1 Introduction

Recurrent neural networks (RNNs) are widely used to model long-term dependencies in lengthy sequential signals [11,27,43]. Prior work has demonstrated the susceptibility of RNNs to adversarial perturbations of its inputs [28], exposing security vulnerabilities of state-of-the-art RNNs when used in domains such as speech recognition [8,22], malware detection [16], and others. Thus, verifying the robustness of recurrent architectures is critical for their safe deployment. While there has been considerable interest in certifying the robustness of feedforward image classifiers [4,12,13,23,32,37,39,47], less attention has been given to recurrent architectures. As a result, current certification solutions do not scale beyond simple models and datasets, which limits their practical applicability. Further, there has been no work on verifying real-world use cases of RNNs. In this paper, we address both of these challenges and present the first precise and scalable verifier for RNNs based

© The Author(s) 2021
A. Silva and K. R. M. Leino (Eds.) CAV 2021, LNCS 12759, pp. 225–248, 2021.
https://doi.org/10.1007/978-3-030-81685-8_10

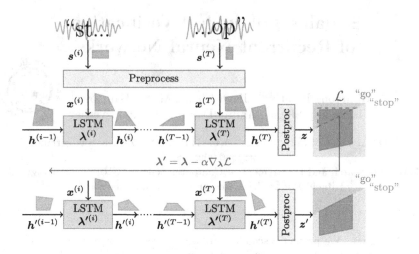

Fig. 1. Certification of recurrent architectures using PROVER: utterance "stop" with perturbations is correctly classified. Possible perturbations are captured and propagated through the system, then refined backward for improved precision. (Color figure online)

on abstract interpretation [10], which enables us to certify robustness of realistic speech recognition systems.

We illustrate the problem setting and overall flow in Fig. 1. Here, a speech recognition model based on the Long Short-Term Memory (LSTM) architecture [15] receives a signal encoding the utterance of "stop" by a human. As such models are usually employed in noisy environments, they must robustly classify variations (e.g., voice changes) to the utterance "stop". However, recent work [8] has shown the model may be fooled into classifying the utterance as "go". It is important to prove such mis-classifications are not possible, thus avoiding a potential exploitation by an adversary, for instance in automated traffic control settings (which can lead to accidents). Our goal is to design a verifier that can formally establish the robustness of such models against noise-induced perturbations. We focus on LSTMs, as they are the most widely used form of RNNs, but our methodology can be easily extended to other architectures (e.g., Gated Recurrent Unit (GRU) [9]). Figure 1 shows how our proposed verifier, called PROVER, (Polyhedral Robustness Verifier of RNNs) automatically verifies the robustness of the model. Here, the labeled rectangles represent operations in the network. The "Preprocess" box captures domain-specific pre-processing operations (typically present when using RNNs, e.g., speech processing). In our method, we first compute a polyhedral abstraction capturing all speech signals given as input to the model under the given perturbation budget. At each timestep i, the pre-processing operation receives a polyhedron $s^{(i)}$ and produces an output polyhedron $x^{(i)}$. This shape is then propagated symbolically through the LSTM and the post-processing stage, resulting in a polyhedral output shape, denoted as z (blue shape in Fig. 1).

Key Challenge: Polyhedral Abstractions for LSTMs. The main challenge in certifying LSTMs is the design of precise and scalable polyhedral abstract transformers for the non-linear operations employed in LSTMs: given a polyhedral shape capturing hidden states $h^{(i-1)}$, to produce the shape capturing the next set of hidden states $h^{(i)}$. A recent method [21] computes this based on gradient-based optimization but suffers from two main limitations. First, the optimization procedure is computationally expensive and does not scale to realistic use cases. Second, the method lacks convergence and optimality guarantees. To address these issues, we introduce a novel technique based on a combination of sampling, linear programming, and Fermat's theorem [1], which significantly improves the precision and scalability compared to prior work [21], while offering asymptotic guarantees of convergence towards the optimal solution.

Refinement via Optimization. To certify robustness, we must verify that each concrete point in the output shape z corresponds to the correct label "stop". However, z can contain, due to over-approximation, spurious incorrect concrete points (it intersects the red region representing incorrect outputs). To address this issue, we form a loss based on the output shape, backpropagate the gradient of this loss through the timesteps and adjust the polyhedral abstractions in each LSTM unit to decrease the loss. The goal is to refine the abstraction, guided by the certification task. We illustrate this process in Fig. 1 using the purple backward arrow with the refined polyhedral abstraction shown in purple. Using the refined abstraction, the new output shape z' (purple polygon) lies completely inside the green region of the output space, meaning it provably contains only correct output vectors (corresponding to "stop"), and hence certification succeeds. Overall, our method significantly increases the precision of end-to-end RNN certification without introducing high runtime costs.

Key Contributions. Our main contributions are:

- A new and efficient method to certify the robustness of RNNs to adversarial perturbations. Our method relies on novel polyhedral abstractions for handling non-linear operations in these architectures.
- A novel method that automatically refines the abstraction for each input example being certified guided by the certification task.
- An implementation of the method in a system called PROVER and evaluation on several benchmarks and datasets. Our results show that PROVER is precise and scales to larger models than prior work. PROVER is also the first verifier able to certify realistic RNN-based speech classifiers. The code is available in https://github.com/eth-sri/prover.

2   Related Work

While the first adversarial examples for neural networks were found in computer vision [6,41], recent work also showed the vulnerability of RNNs [28]. Modern speech recognition systems, based on RNNs, were shown susceptible to small noise crafted by an adversary using white-box attacks [7,8], achieving a 100% success rate against DeepSpeech [14], a state-of-the-art speech-to-text engine. These were later followed by attacks based on universal perturbation [26] and temporal dependency [46]. Recent work [22,31] demonstrates that adversarial examples for audio classifiers are realizable in the real-world. While giving an empirical estimate of the vulnerability of RNNs, these works do not provide any formal guarantees, which is the goal of our work.

There have also been recent works on the verification of RNNs. [2] propose the certification of RNNs based on mixed-integer linear programming, which only works for ReLU-based networks and does not consider LSTMs, which use sigmoid and tanh activations. [45] propose an input discretization method to certify video models that are a combination of CNNs and RNNs. However, discretization does not scale to the perturbations we consider in our work. [18] propose to verify RNNs by automatically inferring temporal homogeneous invariants using binary search. However, their approach is limited to vanilla RNNs and does not apply to the more commonly used LSTM networks considered in this work. [19] propose the statistical variant of Angulin's algorithm [3] for probabilistic verification and counterexample generation for RNNs, however they cannot provide deterministic guarantees as our work. The work most related to ours is POPQORN [21] which uses expensive gradient-based optimizations for every operation in the network. We experimentally show that it does not scale to practical applications such as speech classification.

3 Background

We first define the threat model and then present all operations that are part of the verification procedure, including speech preprocessing and LSTM updates.

3.1 Threat Model

We use a threat model based on the L_∞-norm, where an attacker can change each element of a correctly classified input vector s by an amount $\leq \epsilon \in \mathbb{R}$ [8]. Therefore, our input region can be represented as a conjunction of intervals $[s_i - \epsilon, s_i + \epsilon]$, where s_i is the i-th element of s. The measure of signal distortion in this setting are decibels (dB) defined as:

$$dB(s) = \max_i 20 \cdot \log_{10}(|s_i|); \ dB_s(\delta) = dB(\delta) - dB(s)$$

The quieter the perturbation is, the smaller $dB_s(\delta)$ is. We fix the $dB_s(\delta) =: \epsilon$ as *dB perturbation* and focus on verifying that the model classifies correctly all signals s' possible under our threat model.

3.2 Long Short-Term Memory (LSTM)

LSTM architectures [15] are popular for handling sequential data as they can utilize long-term dependencies. These dependencies are passed through time using two state vectors for the timestep t: cell state $c^{(t)}$ and hidden state $h^{(t)}$. These state vectors are updated using the following formulas:

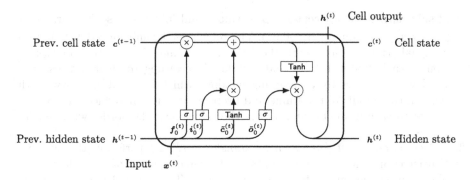

Fig. 2. LSTM cell: $f_0^{(t)}, i_0^{(t)}, o_0^{(t)}$, and $\tilde{c}_0^{(t)}$ represent the pre-activated gates.

$$f_0^{(t)} = [x^{(t)}, h^{(t-1)}]W_f + b_f \qquad\qquad i_0^{(t)} = [x^{(t)}, h^{(t-1)}]W_i + b_i$$

$$o_0^{(t)} = [x^{(t)}, h^{(t-1)}]W_o + b_o \qquad\qquad \tilde{c}_0^{(t)} = [x^{(t)}, h^{(t-1)}]W_{\tilde{c}} + b_{\tilde{c}}$$

$$c^{(t)} = \sigma(f_0^{(t)}) \odot c^{(t-1)} + \sigma(i_0^{(t)}) \odot \tanh(\tilde{c}_0^{(t)}) \qquad h^{(t)} = \sigma(o_0^{(t)}) \odot \tanh(c^{(t)})$$

where $[\cdot, \cdot]$ is the horizontal concatenation of two row vectors, $W_.$ and $b_.$ are the kernel and bias of the cell, respectively, and σ is the sigmoid function. At timestep t, vectors $f_0^{(t)}, i_0^{(t)}, o_0^{(t)}, \tilde{c}_0^{(t)}$ represent pre-activations of the forget gate, input gate, output gate and the candidate gate, respectively. We show an illustration of an LSTM cell in Fig. 2. We treat σ and tanh as forms of activation functions, which is why we define the LSTM using pre-activations.

Intuitively, the *input gate* transforms the input vector, the *forget gate* filters the information from the previous cell state, the *candidate gate* prepares the candidate cell state, and the *output gate* transforms the current hidden state. All of these gates receive as input the hidden state $h^{(t-1)}$ of the previous cell and the input $x^{(t)}$ representing the current frame. This recurrent architecture allows inputs with arbitrary length, enabling LSTMs to handle temporal data, e.g., speech processing.

3.3   Speech Preprocessing

Though there have been various works that operate directly on the raw signal [29,36], speech signals are commonly preprocessed using the *filterbank* or *log Mel-filterbank energy* methods. The result is a vector of coefficients whose elements contain log-scaled values of filtered spectra, one for every Mel-frequency. This method models the non-linear human acoustic perception as power spectrum filters based on Mel-frequencies. The input signal is split into several (possibly overlapping) frames for granular analysis, and the following steps are applied:

1. *Pre-emphasizing and windowing* are preprocessing stages on the raw signals. Speech signals tend to have larger and smoother low-frequency samples and smaller and fluctuating high-frequency samples. *Pre-emphasizing* is a process

of subtracting the adjacent sampled values multiplied by a scalar parameter $(s_j^{(i)} - \alpha s_{j-1}^{(i)},$ commonly $\alpha = 0.97$). This alleviates the unbalanced distribution of signal strength along with the frequency. *Windowing* involves multiplication of each sampled value and 'windows' according to their indices. The window here refers to a Hamming window, which is a bell-like curve with peak in the middle of the frame and drops at the side. It reduces the border effects on each frame by suppressing the values near the border with smaller values.

2. *Power spectrum of Fast Fourier transform (FFT)* performs the discrete Fourier transform (DFT) and obtains the squared norm of each element to obtain intensities in the frequency domain. FFT consists of matrix multiplications with complex entries. We modify it to use only real numbers by: (i) separating real and imaginary parts of the matrix and constructing two separate matrices, (ii) multiplying each matrix with the signal, (iii) squaring the entries, and (iv) adding the resulting matrices entry-wise.

3. *Mel-filter bank log energy:* The Mel-frequency filters are triangular, each emphasizing the power of the selected frequency and suppressing the adjacent ones. In our case, we (i) apply the Mel-filterbank to the power spectrum and (ii) take the log of the entries to adjust the level.

Following [35], each step can be represented as a distinct matrix operation. It allows us to decompose and rearrange the steps into slightly different stages:

1. *Pre-square stage:* $S \to Y = SM_1$. This stage contains pre-emphasizing, windowing (step 1), and FFT (until step 2-(ii)). All operations are representable as matrix multiplications, so we pre-calculate the product matrix.

2. *Square stage:* $Y \to \theta = Y \odot Y$. This is step 2-(iii). Entry-wise square operations cannot be combined with other matrix multiplications.

3. *Pre-log stage:* $\theta \to \tilde{X} = \theta M_2$. From step 2-(iv) through step 3-(i). We combine the operations into a single matrix.

4. *Log stage:* $\tilde{X} \to X = \log \tilde{X}$. Applying entry-wise logarithm (step 3-(ii)).

We use the resulting $X = [x^{(1)} \cdots x^{(T)}]^{\mathsf{T}}$ as the input to the neural network.

3.4   Verification Using DeepPoly Abstract Domain

DeepPoly [39] is a sub-polyhedral abstract domain that associates a lower and an upper polyhedral bound and interval bounds per neuron. It is faster than Polyhedra [40] and more precise than other weakly relational domains such as Octagons [25], Zones [24], and Zonotopes [38] when analyzing neural networks. Previously, it has been succeesfully applied for verifying feedforward networks in [4,39]. Formally, let $\mathcal{X} = \{x_1, x_2, \ldots, x_n\}$ be an ordered set of neurons such that the neurons in layer l appear before the neurons of layer $l' > l$. DeepPoly associates with each neuron x_j, both interval $l_j \leq x_j \leq u_j$ and polyhedral bounds $\sum_{i<j} a_i \cdot x_i + b \leq x_j \leq \sum_{i<j} a_i' \cdot x_i + b'$ where $l_j, u_j, a_i, a_i', b, b' \in \mathbb{R} \cup \{\infty\}$. DeepPoly is exact for affine transformations which are frequently applied both in the speech preprocessing pipeline and the LSTM unit. DeepPoly loses precision

for the non-linear operations in LSTMs. We note that computing polyhedral bounds on their output is more challenging than for feedforward networks.

The precision of the DeepPoly approximation for the non-linear operations depends on the tightness of the interval bounds of the neurons that are input to the non-linear operations. DeepPoly provides a scalable and precise method called *backsubstitution* for optimizing a linear expression within a region defined by the set of DeepPoly constraints. It does so by recursively substituting the bounding linear expressions of target neurons with the polyhedral bounds of previous layers' neurons until reaching the input neurons. It then uses the concrete bounds of the input neurons for computing the result. Backsubstitution is used for computing the interval bounds of neurons input to the non-linear operations as well as for bounding the difference between the neurons in the output layer needed to prove robustness. We refer the reader to [39] for details of the backsubstitution.

4   Overview of *PROVER*

This section illustrates the workings of PROVER on a small example. Our goal is to certify the robustness of a single LSTM cell on the input $x \in [-1.2, 1.2]$. For this example, we assume that there are two output classes and all intermediate LSTM gates $\{i, f, \tilde{c}, o\}$ share the same weights and biases:

$$\{i, f, \tilde{c}, o\} = \begin{bmatrix} 1 \\ 0.5 \end{bmatrix} x + \begin{bmatrix} 0 \\ 1 \end{bmatrix}, \qquad c = \sigma(i) \odot \tanh(\tilde{c}), \qquad h = \sigma(o) \odot \tanh(c).$$

The correct output here is h_2 and to certify robustness we need to prove that $h_2 - h_1 > 0$ holds for all inputs x. In other words, $\min h_2 - h_1 > 0$.

Polyhedral Abstraction. We build our verifier based on the DeepPoly [39] abstraction since DeepPoly outperforms the interval analysis and other competitive domains, as Sect. 3.4 states.

Challenges in Computing Polyhedral Bounds for LSTMs. The composed binary non-linear operations applied in LSTMs such as $\sigma(x) \tanh(y)$ and $\sigma(x)y$ are significantly more complex to handle than the ReLU, Sigmoid, and Tanh activations originally handled by [39]. This is because the non-linear operations in LSTMs mentioned above involve transcendental functions yielding non-linear 3D curves that are neither convex nor concave. The optimal polyhedral bounds for these operations have no closed-form solution and cannot be calculated by simple geometry or algebra. Further, obtaining such bounds is computationally expensive [21]. For example, obtaining the lower linear plane for bounding $\sigma(x) \tanh(y)$ is equivalent to solving a Lagrangian with 6 variables - 3 linear coefficients, 2 interval-bounded coordinates and 1 Lagrange multiplier for the constraint. In contrast, the optimal polyhedral bounds for ReLU, Sigmoid, and Tanh have closed form solutions, easily visualized in 2D.

Precise Polyhedral Bounds via LP. To overcome these challenges, we propose a generic approach based on linear programming (LP) to compute precise polyhedral bounds. We illustrate our approach for calculating a lower polyhedral bound of $h_2 = \sigma(o_2) \tanh(c_2)$. First, we calculate the concrete intervals for the two target variables via *backsubstitution* [39], briefly described in Sect. 3.4. In our case, the target variables are o_2 and c_2 and the backsubstitution yields $o_2 \in [0.4, 1.6]$ and $c_2 \in [-0.79, 0.62]$. Our abstraction can represent the affine transformations exactly. Therefore, we obtain the exact interval for $o_2 = 0.5 \cdot x + 1$ via the backsubstitution whereas the obtained interval for c_2 is an overapproximate one. Then, we uniformly sample a set of points $\{(x_1, y_1), ..., (x_n, y_n)\}$ from the input domain $[0.4, 1.6] \times [-0.79, 0.62]$. We solve the following optimization problem to calculate the lower polyhedral bound of h_2:

$$\min_{A_l, B_l, C_l \in \mathbb{R}} \sum_{i=1}^{n} \left(\sigma(x_i) \tanh(y_i) - (A_l \cdot x_i + B_l \cdot y_i + C_l) \right),$$

subject to the constraint that $A_l \cdot x_i + B_l \cdot y_i + C_l \leq \sigma(x_i) \tanh(y_i)$ for each i. This is a linear program over three variables (A_l, B_l, C_l) that can be solved efficiently in polynomial time. However, the obtained bound may not be sound as the sampled points do not fully cover the continuous input domain. To address this, we shift the plane downwards by an offset (decreasing C_l) equal to the maximum violation between $A_l \cdot x + B_l \cdot y + C_l$ and h_2 based on Fermat's theorem. After solving the linear program and the adjustment, we obtain $A_l = 0.04, B_l = 0.46, C_l = 0.01$ which results in the following lower polyhedral bound to h_2: $h_2 \geq LB_{h_2} = 0.04 \cdot o_2 + 0.46 \cdot c_2 + 0.01$. We compute the upper bound to $h_2 : h_2 \leq UB_{h_2}$ analogously. After computing a polyhedral abstraction of each neuron, we calculate the lower bound of $h_2 - h_1$ via backsubstitution as follows:

$$\min h_2 - h_1 \geq LB_{h_2} - UB_{h_1}$$
$$\geq (0.04 \cdot o_2 + 0.46 \cdot c_2 + 0.01) - (-0.09 \cdot o_1 + 0.66 \cdot c_1 + 0.14)$$
$$\geq 0.04 \cdot o_2 + 0.46 \cdot (0.07 \cdot i_2 + 0.27 \cdot g_2 + 0.09)$$
$$+ 0.09 \cdot o_1 - 0.66 \cdot (-0.04 \cdot i_1 + 0.38 \cdot g_1 + 0.25) - 0.14$$
$$\geq 0.20 \cdot (0.5 \cdot x + 1) - 0.13 \cdot x - 0.10 \geq -0.03 \cdot x - 0.08 \geq -0.11.$$

The precision of the bounds generated by our LP-based method increases with the number of samples yielding optimal bounds (in the sense of small gap) asymptotically. For our example, the computed bounds are optimal.

While our optimal bounds significantly improve precision compared to intervals, they are not sufficient to certify robustness. Prior work for ReLU networks [5,12,23] showed that the greedy approach of always selecting the optimal bounds minimizing the gap can yield less precise results than an adaptive strategy which computes bounds guided by the certification problem. Based on this observation, we introduce a novel approach based on splitting and gradient descent that computes polyhedral abstractions for non-linearities employed in LSTMs informed by the certification problem and proves that $\min h_2 - h_1 > 0$ actually holds.

Abstraction Refinement via Splitting and Gradient Descent. While our method based on LP offers an efficient way to compute polyhedral abstraction of activation functions, its main limitation is that the abstraction cannot be refined based on the certification goal. In this work, we introduce a novel method where we first compute mutiple sound bounds for the neuron using our LP method and then automatically obtain a combination of the computed bounds that improves the lower bound of our certification objective $h_2 - h_1$ for each input example. As before, we use the backsubstitution to obtain the interval bounds for the input variables. Since the output of our LP method is sensitive to the choice of the sampled points, we split the original input region $[l_x, u_x] \times [l_y, u_y]$ to sample more effectively from smaller sub-regions thereby reducing the chances of missing an outlier. We found that splitting along the two diagonals of $[l_x, u_x] \times [l_y, u_y]$ into four triangular zones, denoted as $\mathcal{T}_k$, $k \in \{1, 2, 3, 4\}$, performs the best in our evaluation. We use $\mathcal{T}_0$ to denote the original input region. Next, we calculate four additional planes, for both the upper and lower bounds, by sampling each subregion $\mathcal{T}_k$ and then applying our LP method as before. We refer to each plane as a *candidate bound*:

$$\min_{A_l, B_l, C_l \in \mathbb{R}} \sum_{i=1}^{n} (\sigma(x_i) \tanh(y_i) - (A_l \cdot x_i + B_l \cdot y_i + C_l))$$

$$\text{subject to } \bigwedge_{i=1}^{n} A_l \cdot x_i + B_l \cdot y_i + C_l \leq \sigma(x_i) \tanh(y_i) \text{ where } (x_i, y_i) \sim \mathcal{T}_k$$

Using our LP based method, we obtain the following corresponding candidate polyhedral abstraction for h_2, $LB_{h_2}^k$ for each $\mathcal{T}_k$ in our example:

$$h_2 \geq LB_{h_2}^0 = 0.04 \cdot o_1 + 0.46 \cdot c_1 + 0.01, h_2 \geq LB_{h_2}^1 = 0.04 \cdot o_1 + 0.46 \cdot c_1 + 0.01$$
$$h_2 \geq LB_{h_2}^2 = 0.13 \cdot o_1 + 0.63 \cdot c_1 - 0.17, h_2 \geq LB_{h_2}^3 = 0.04 \cdot o_1 + 0.46 \cdot c_1 + 0.01$$
$$h_2 \geq LB_{h_2}^4 = 0.13 \cdot o_1 + 0.63 \cdot c_1 - 0.17$$

Note that $LB_{h_2}^0$ denotes the polyhedral abstraction calculated for the whole region, and there might be duplicate LB's when the curve in the given subregion is concave. The final bound LB_{h_2} is a linear combination of $LB_{h_2}^k$:

$$LB_{h_2} = \sum_{k=0}^{4} \lambda_i \cdot LB_{h_2}^k, \qquad \sum_{k=0}^{4} \lambda_i = 1.$$

Our optimization algorithm, explained in Sect. 5.2, learns the values of λ_i via gradient descent that maximizes min $h_2 - h_1$. For our example, we obtain $\lambda = (0.09, 0.13, 0.34, 0.09, 0.35)$ as the set of coefficients which results in a new lower bound of $h_2 \geq 0.10 \cdot o_2 + 0.58 \cdot c_2 - 0.11$ for the neuron h_2. We improve the bounds for other neurons in a similar fashion. Using the new bounds, we obtain $h_2 - h_1 \geq 0.01 > 0$ which enables us to correctly certify the predicate of interest. If the certification still fails, it is possible to further refine the abstraction by increasing the number of splits and repeating the procedure above.

Compared to [21], which uses a single bound, our method is more flexible and can tune λ parameters to find a combination of different bounds for each neuron that yields the most precise certification result for each certification instance. Our method is also faster as it performs expensive gradient-based optimization for only the output layer whereas [21] performs this step for each neuron in the LSTM twice. [5,12,23] also suggest a similar idea of bounding ReLU's lower bound using gradient descent, but their approach is limited to unary functions with trivial candidates, not applicable to our setting which requires handling complex binary operations with non-trivial initial bounds.

Generality of Our Method. Our method is generic and can be easily extended to obtain polyhedral bounds for the non-linear operations in other architectures such as transformers [42] and capsule networks [34].

5   Scalable Certification of LSTMs

Next, we formally describe our scalable verifier for LSTM networks. As mentioned in Sect. 4, we build our verifier based on the DeepPoly abstract domain [39] introduced in Sect. 3.4. For simplicity, we focus on computing the polyhedral bounds for the output of non-linear operations. Note that the computed polyhedral bounds contain only the neurons from the previous layers. This restriction is required for backsubstitution used for computing the interval bounds of the inputs, which is an approximate algorithm for solving an LP (e.g. maximize or minimize x_j) within a polyhedral region defined by DeepPoly constraints. In Sect. 5.1, we show how to obtain tight, asymptotically optimal polyhedral bounds on key operations in the LSTM unit: $\sigma(x) \tanh(y)$ and $\sigma(x)y$. Section 5.2 describes a novel method to dynamically choose between different polyhedral bounds for increasing verifier precision.

5.1   Computing Polyhedral Abstractions of LSTM Operations

Our goal is to bound the products of *sigmoid and tanh* and *sigmoid and identity*, using lower and upper polyhedral planes parameterized by coefficients A_l, B_l, C_l and A_u, B_u, C_u, respectively. Let $f(x,y) = \sigma(x)\tanh(y)$ and $g(x,y) = \sigma(x)y$. For $h \in \{f, g\}$ we describe how to obtain the lower and upper bounds of h:

$$A_l \cdot x + B_l \cdot y + C_l \leq h(x,y) \leq A_u \cdot x + B_u \cdot y + C_u$$

We formulate the search for a lower bound of $h(x,y)$ as an optimization problem that minimizes the volume between the bound and the function, subject to the (soundness) constraint that the lower bound is below the function value:

$$\min_{A_l, B_l, C_l} \int_{(x,y) \in B} (h(x,y) - (A_l \cdot x + B_l \cdot y + C_l))$$
$$\text{subject to } A_l \cdot x + B_l \cdot y + C_l \leq h(x,y), \forall (x,y) \in B. \tag{1}$$

We denote $B = [l_x, u_x] \times [l_y, u_y]$ as the boundaries of input neurons x and y obtained using backsubstitution. We next describe our method to solve Eq. (1).

Step 1: Approximation via LP. We solve an approximation of the intractable optimization problem from Eq. (1), obtaining potentially unsound constraints. Unsoundness implies that there can be points in region B which violate the bounds. We build on the approach from [4], which proposes to approximate the objective in Eq. (1) using Monte Carlo sampling. Let $D = \{(x_1, y_1), \ldots, (x_n, y_n)\}$ be a set of points from B sampled uniformly at random. We phrase the following optimization problem:

$$\min_{A_l, B_l, C_l \in \mathbb{R}} \sum_{i=1}^{n} (h(x_i, y_i) - (A_l \cdot x_i + B_l \cdot y_i + C_l))$$

$$\text{subject to} \bigwedge_{i=1}^{n} A_l \cdot x_i + B_l \cdot y_i + C_l \leq h(x_i, y_i). \tag{2}$$

Figure 3 shows an input region with Monte Carlo samples as red circles and summands in the LP objective as vertical lines. As this is a low-dimensional linear program (LP), we can solve it exactly in polynomial time using off-the-shelf LP solvers. We compute a candidate upper bound analogously.

Step 2: Adjusting the Offset to Guarantee Soundness. Since we compute the lower bound from a subset of points in B, there can be a point in B where the value of $h(x, y)$ is less than our computed lower bound. To ensure soundness, we compute $\Delta_l = \min_{(x,y) \in B} h(x, y) - (A_l \cdot x + B_l \cdot y + C_l)$ and then adjust the lower bound by updating the offset $C_l \leftarrow C_l + \Delta_l$, resulting in a sound lower bound plane. While the

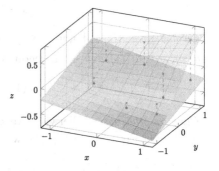

Fig. 3. Visualization of the $z = \sigma(x)\tanh(y)$ curve and the lower bound computed by linear programming. Red crosses represent the sampled points and dashed lines show the difference between the curve and the plane (summands in the optimization). (Color figure online)

method of [4] also performs offset calculation for obtaining sound bounds, they perform certification of image classifiers against geometric perturbations using expensive branch and bound for calculating the offset. In contrast, we exploit the structure of non-linearities used in LSTMs obtaining a closed-form formula for the offset yielding an exact solution. We now provide details of our offset adjustment method for $f(x, y) = \sigma(x)\tanh(y)$ and $g(x, y) = \sigma(x)y$.

Offset Calculation for $f(x, y) = \sigma(x)\tanh(y)$: Let $A_l \cdot x + B_l \cdot y + C_l$ be the initial lower bounding plane obtained from LP in region B. We define $F(x, y)$:

$$F(x, y) = \sigma(x)\tanh(y) - (A_l \cdot x + B_l \cdot y + C_l)$$

To find $\Delta_l = \min_{(x,y) \in B} F(x,y)$, we first find the extreme points by computing partial derivatives.

$$\frac{\partial F}{\partial x} = \sigma(x)\tanh(y)(1 - \sigma(x)) - A_l \tag{3}$$

$$\frac{\partial F}{\partial y} = \sigma(x)(1 - \tanh^2(y)) - B_l \tag{4}$$

We consider three cases:

- *Case 1:* $x \in \{l_x, u_x\}$ and $y \in [l_y, u_y]$ Under this condition, we denote $S_x := \sigma(x)$ as a constant. To ease notation, let $t = \tanh(y)$ where $t \in [\tanh(l_y), \tanh(u_y)]$. Then $\frac{\partial F}{\partial y} \overset{!}{=} 0$ can be rewritten as:

$$1 - t^2 = B_l / S_x \tag{5}$$

- *Case 2:* $y \in \{l_y, u_y\}$ and $x \in [l_x, u_x]$ Here we set $T_y := \tanh(y)$ and $s = \sigma(x)$, $x \in [\sigma(l_x), \sigma(u_x)]$ analogously. $\frac{\partial F}{\partial x} \overset{!}{=} 0$ is rewritten to:

$$s(1 - s) = A_l / T_y \tag{6}$$

- *Case 3: otherwise* Otherwise, we consider both $\frac{\partial F}{\partial x} \overset{!}{=} 0$ and $\frac{\partial F}{\partial y} \overset{!}{=} 0$. By combining Eq. (3) and Eq. (4), we reduce $\tanh(y)$ and obtain:

$$s^4 + (-2 - B_l)s^3 + (1 + 2B_l)s^2 + (-B_l)s - A_l^2 \overset{!}{=} 0 \tag{7}$$

Given that $F(x,y)$ is differentiable and the region B is compact, Fermat's theorem (stationary points) [1] states that F achieves its extremum at either the roots of Eq. (5), Eq. (6), and Eq. (7), or at the 4 corners of B. We evaluate F at these points to get Δ_l. We adjust the offset by replacing $C_l \leftarrow C_l + \Delta_l$. The adjusted F is no less than 0 on any point in B, which means that the plane with adjusted C_l becomes a sound lower bound of the $\sigma(x)\tanh(y)$ curve.

Offset Calculation for $g(x,y) = \sigma(x)y$**:** We next calculate the offset for $\sigma(x)y$. We define the differentiable function $G(x,y) = \sigma(x)y - (A_l \cdot x + B_l \cdot y + C_l)$ over the compact set B and compute:

$$\frac{\partial G}{\partial x} = \sigma(x)y(1 - \sigma(x)) - A_l \tag{8}$$

$$\frac{\partial G}{\partial y} = \sigma(x) - B_l \tag{9}$$

We use Fermat's theorem and consider three cases:

- *Case 1:* $x \in \{l_x, u_x\}$ and $y \in [l_y, u_y]$ When $\sigma(x)$ is fixed, Eq. (9) is constant, which means G is monotonous in this case.

- *Case 2:* $y \in \{l_y, u_y\}$ and $x \in [l_x, u_x]$ Denote $s = \sigma(x)$ where $s \in [\sigma(l_x), \sigma(u_x)]$, then setting Eq. (8) $\overset{!}{=} 0$ becomes

$$s(1 - s) = A_l/y \qquad (10)$$

- *Case 3: otherwise* If there is a local extremum in the region, the Hessian of G must be either positive-definite or negative-definite.

$$\frac{\partial^2 G}{\partial x^2} = \sigma(x)y(1 - \sigma(x))(1 - 2\sigma(x)), \frac{\partial^2 G}{\partial y^2} = 0, \frac{\partial^2 G}{\partial x \partial y} = \sigma(x)(1 - \sigma(x))$$

$$\frac{\partial^2 G}{\partial x^2} \cdot \frac{\partial^2 G}{\partial y^2} - \left(\frac{\partial^2 G}{\partial x \partial y}\right)^2 = -(\sigma(x)(1 - \sigma(x)))^2 < 0$$

Hence, there is no local extremum inside the boundaries.

To summarize, we only need to consider the roots of Eq. (10) to calculate the minimum of G to obtain Δ_l for $\sigma(x)y$. Figure 3 shows the lower bound plane obtained after solving the LP and adjusting the offset. We update the upper bound analogously.

Asymptotic Optimality. We can prove that, similarly to [4], as we increase the number of samples n, the solution of the LP asymptotically approaches the solution of the original problem from Eq. (1). Rephrasing and simplifying the theorem from [4]:

Theorem 1. *Let N be the number of points sampled in the algorithm. Let (ω_l, b_l) be our lower constraint (linear constraints and bias, respectively) and let $L(\omega^*, b^*)$ be the true minimum of function L. For every $\delta > 0$ there exists N_δ such that $|L(\omega_l, b_l) - L(\omega^*, b^*)| < \delta$ for every $N > N_\delta$, with high probability. Analogous result holds for upper constraint (ω_u, b_u) and function U.*

We denote $L = \int_{(x,y)} F(x, y)$ and (ω_l, b_l) are our A_l, B_l, C_l. Following the theorem, our sampling method guarantees the asymptotic optimality of our bounds. The theorem can be extended analogously for the upper bound.

5.2   Abstraction Refinement via Optimization

While our approach based on sampling, linear programming, and Fermat's theorem allows us to obtain (asymptotically) optimal bounds, it still has a fundamental limitation that it produces a *single* bound. Further, this approach is, in a sense, greedy: when considering the *entire* network, it is possible that selecting non-optimal planes for each neuron yields more precise results at the end. Neither the method from [21] nor the method in Sect. 5.1 achieves this. We present the first approach to learn an abstraction refinement that increases the end-to-end precision of certification.

Step 1: Compute a Set of Candidate Bounds. We adapt our approach from Sect. 5.1 to compute a set of candidate planes, instead of a single plane. We run the sampling procedure multiple times, each time on a different subregion of the original region $B = [l_x, u_x] \times [l_y, u_y]$, with the constraints still enforced over the entire region B. We define four different triangular subdomains: $\mathcal{T}_1$ and $\mathcal{T}_2$ are triangles resulting from splitting B along the main diagonal, while $\mathcal{T}_3$ and $\mathcal{T}_4$ are triangles resulting from splitting B along the other diagonal. We additionally define $\mathcal{T}_0 = B$. For each $k \in \{0, 1, 2, 3, 4\}$, we perform sampling and optimization as in Eq. (2), this time sampling from $\mathcal{T}_k$ to obtain candidate lower bounds:

$$\min_{A_l, B_l, C_l \in \mathbb{R}} \sum_{i=1}^{n} (\sigma(x_i) \tanh(y_i) - (A_l \cdot x_i + B_l \cdot y_i + C_l))$$

$$\text{subject to } \bigwedge_{i=1}^{n} A_l \cdot x_i + B_l \cdot y_i + C_l \le \sigma(x_i) \tanh(y_i) \text{ where } (x_i, y_i) \sim \mathcal{T}_k$$

For each neuron i, this yields 5 candidate lower bound and upper bound planes, LB_i^k and UB_i^k for $k \in \{0, 1, 2, 3, 4\}$. These five candidate planes for each of the N neurons are shown in Fig. 4.

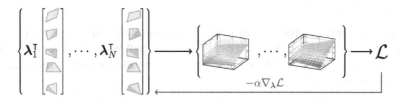

Fig. 4. Learning to combine linear bounds via gradient descent. Here the five candidate planes multiplied by $\boldsymbol{\lambda}$ are depicted either in green or red, or both. Green represents the sampled domain, $\mathcal{T}_k$, and red is the extension of the obtained green plane out of the domain. With the linear combination of the planes, we compute the bound, calculate the loss, and backpropagate. (Color figure online)

Step 2: Find the Optimal Combinations of the Bounds. Next, our goal is to learn a linear combination of the computed candidate bounds which yields the highest end-to-end certification precision for the given input region. To do this, we define the lower and upper bound of neuron i as a linear combination of the proposed five bounds:

$$LB_i = \sum_{k=0}^{4} \lambda_i^{LB} \cdot LB_i^k, \quad \sum_{k=0}^{4} \lambda_i^{LB} = 1, UB_i = \sum_{k=0}^{4} \lambda_i^{UB} \cdot UB_i^k, \quad \sum_{k=0}^{4} \lambda_i^{UB} = 1.$$

Recall that we formulate robustness certification as proving that for all labels i different from the ground truth label t: $z_t - z_i > 0$. The lower bound on $z_t - z_i$ is computed using backsubstitution [39], as shown in our overview example in Sect. 4. However, this lower bound now depends on the coefficients $\boldsymbol{\lambda}$, so we define the function $f(x, \epsilon, i, \boldsymbol{\lambda})$ which computes the lower bound of the expression $z_t - z_i$ when using $\boldsymbol{\lambda}$ to combine the neuron bounds.

We describe our approach to find the best coefficients $\boldsymbol{\lambda}$ in Algorithm 1. Consider the number of possible labels m and the number of binary operations of interest N_{ops}. To find $\boldsymbol{\lambda}$, we solve the optimization problem for each label i:

$$z_t - z_i > \max_{\boldsymbol{\lambda}} f(x, \epsilon, i, \boldsymbol{\lambda})$$

If the solution to the above optimization problem is positive, then we proved robustness with respect to class i. In the algorithm, we initialize $\tilde{\boldsymbol{\lambda}}$, a pre-normalized vector of $\boldsymbol{\lambda}$, for each neuron, uniformly between -1 and 1. Then, in each epoch, we compute the normalized $\boldsymbol{\lambda}$ by applying softmax to $\tilde{\boldsymbol{\lambda}}$ and run certification using $\boldsymbol{\lambda}$, obtaining a loss $\mathcal{L}$ equal to the value $-f(x, \epsilon, i, \boldsymbol{\lambda})$. We perform gradient descent update on $\tilde{\boldsymbol{\lambda}}$ based on the loss. If the loss is negative, we have found $\boldsymbol{\lambda}$ which proves the robustness and the algorithm terminates. The core updating flow is shown in Fig. 4.

Algorithm 1. Learning $\boldsymbol{\lambda}$ via gradient descent

---
Given input $\boldsymbol{x}$, label y, model $\mathcal{M}$, perturbation ϵ
Initialize the polyhedral abstractions and candidate bounds based on $\boldsymbol{x}$, $\mathcal{M}$ and ϵ.
for $i \leftarrow 1$ **to** m **where** $i \neq y$ **do**
    Initialize $\tilde{\boldsymbol{\lambda}} \sim [-1, 1]^{N_{ops} \times 5}$, $epoch \leftarrow 0$
    repeat
        $\boldsymbol{\lambda} \leftarrow \text{SoftMax}(\tilde{\boldsymbol{\lambda}})$, $\mathcal{L} \leftarrow -f(x, \epsilon, i, \boldsymbol{\lambda})$, $\tilde{\boldsymbol{\lambda}} \leftarrow \tilde{\boldsymbol{\lambda}} - \alpha \nabla_{\tilde{\lambda}} \mathcal{L}$, $epoch \leftarrow epoch + 1$
    until $epoch = max\_epoch$ or $\mathcal{L} < 0$
    if $\mathcal{L} \geq 0$ **then**
        return not certified
    end if
end for
return certified

---

6   Certification of Speech Preprocessing

Speech preprocessing transforms the original set of perturbed speech signals, represented via intervals, through complex pipeline operations, into a non-linear and non-convex set. Propagating this set through the network is computationally expensive (infeasible for large models). To address this issue, we define precise overapproximations of key non-linear operations found in the speech preprocessing pipeline, such as Square and Log, expressed in the DeepPoly abstraction. These approximate bounds are computed via constant time closed form formulas based on concrete bounds of the inputs. We note that the first and third stages of the pipeline described in Sect. 3.3 involve an affine transformation, captured exactly using DeepPoly. Overall, when combined with our LSTM verifier, this method yields more precise end-to-end certification results than using intervals for approximating speech preprocessing.

Square. The lower and upper polyhedral bounds of the output of the square function $y = x^2$ where $x \in [l_x, u_x]$ are shown in Fig. 5a. We first consider the bounds for y which minimize the area in the xy-plane. The upper bound UB_y is obtained by computing the chord joining the end points (l_x, l_x^2) and (u_x, u_x^2). The lower bound is a line parallel to UB_y passing through a point $((u_x + l_x)/2, ((u_x + l_x)/2)^2)$ in the middle of the curve.

$$LB_y = (u_x + l_x) \cdot x - ((u_x + l_x)/2)^2 , UB_y = (u_x + l_x) \cdot x - u_x \cdot l_x.$$

While the above bounds would be sufficient in any other domain, they do not work for the speech domain as the subsequent Log requires that the input is strictly non-negative, as it is not defined for negative inputs. Also, we should carefully consider the floating point errors during calculations. Hence, we introduce the additional parameter $\delta \in \mathbb{R}$, a small threshold value to ensure the lower bound stays non-negative. In our experiments, we set $\delta = 1 \times 10^{-5}$. Upper and lower bounds for $y = x^2$ are computed as $UB_y = (u_x + l_x) \cdot x - u_x \cdot l_x$ and $LB_y =$

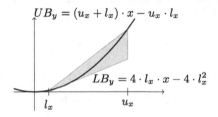

(a) Abstraction for square function with threshold $\delta = 0$

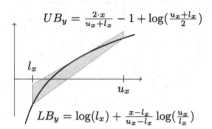

(b) Abstraction for log function.

Fig. 5. Two polyhedral abstractions for the speech preprocessing stage.

$$\begin{cases} 2 \cdot (l_x + \sqrt{l_x^2 - \delta}) \cdot x - (l_x + \sqrt{l_x^2 - \delta})^2 & 3 \cdot l_x^2 + 2 \cdot l_x . u_x - u_x^2 \leq 4 \cdot \delta, \sqrt{\delta} \leq l_x \\ 2 \cdot (u_x - \sqrt{u_x^2 - \delta}) \cdot x - (u_x - \sqrt{u_x^2 - \delta})^2 & 3 \cdot u_x^2 + 2 . u_x . l_x - l_x^2 \leq 4 \cdot \delta, u_x \leq -\delta \\ 0 & l_x \leq \sqrt{\delta}, -\sqrt{\delta} \leq u_x \\ (u_x + l_x) \cdot x - ((u_x + l_x)/2)^2 & o.w. \end{cases}$$

Log. We define the polyhedral abstraction of the output $y = \log(x)$ of the log operation where $x \in [l_x, u_x]$, as shown in Fig. 5b. Our abstractions are optimal and minimize the area in the xy-plane. The lower bound LB_y is the chord joining the end points $(l_x, \log(l_x))$ and $(u_x, \log(u_x))$. The upper bound UB_y is obtained by computing a line parallel to LB_y passing through the middle of the curve at $((u_x + l_x)/2, \log((u_x + l_x)/2))$. Our final abstractions are:

$$LB_y = \log(l_x) + \frac{x - l_x}{u_x - l_x} \log(\frac{u_x}{l_x}), UB_y = \frac{2 \cdot x}{u_x + l_x} - 1 + \log(\frac{u_x + l_x}{2}).$$

7   Experimental Evaluation

We implemented our approach in a verifier called PROVER, using PyTorch [30] and Gurobi 9.0 for solving linear programs. The code is available in https:// github.com/eth-sri/prover. We evaluate PROVER on speech classifiers for FSDD [17] and GSC v2 [44] datasets. Then, we compare PROVER against POPQORN [21] on the MNIST image classification task proposed by it. We note that POPQORN does not scale to the speech classifiers considered in our work. We demonstrate further scalability by verifying large motion sensor sequence classifier trained on HAPT [33] dataset containing 256 hidden dimensional 4 layered LSTM units.

Setup. GSC dataset experiments ran on an Nvidia GeForce RTX 2080, while the rest ran on a single Tesla V100. Following convention from prior work [39], we consider only those inputs that are classified correctly without perturbation. We use the same set of hyperparameters for the experiments unless specifically mentioned. We use 100 sampling points for constructing the linear program and optimize λ parameters using Adam [20] for 100 epochs. During optimization, we initialize the learning rate to 100 and multiply it by 0.98 after every epoch.

7.1   Speech Classification

We certify the robustness of two speech classifiers for the FSDD and GSC v2 datasets. FSDD consists of recordings of digits spoken by six different speakers, recorded at 8 kHz. GSC has 35 distinct labels of single word utterances at 16 kHz. We compare our base method based on sampling and linear programming (Sect. 5.1), denoted as PROVER (LP), and our method using abstraction refinement via optimization (Sect. 5.2), denoted as PROVER (OPT).

Preprocessing. A key challenge in speech classification, not encountered in the image domain, is the complex preprocessing stage before the LSTM network. The preprocessing stage in this experiment consists of FFT and Mel-filter transformations. Preprocessed input then passes through the fully connected layer with ReLU activation followed by the LSTM unit.

FSDD Certification. We used the following parameters for the preprocessing: we slice the raw wave signal with length 256 using a stride of 200 with 10 Mel-frequencies. For this experiment, we trained an LSTM network with two LSTM layers and 32 hidden units each, preceded by a 40 ReLU-activated fully-connected layer. This network achieves an accuracy of 83.6% on the FSDD task. The average number of frames was 14.7. We verify the first 100 correctly classified inputs for each perturbation. Our perturbation metric on speech classification tasks is described in Sect. 3.1. Our results are shown in Fig. 6a and Fig. 6b. We vary the decibel perturbation between –90 dB and –70 dB and evaluate the precision and runtime of PROVER. Figure 6a shows the percentage of certified samples: our method based on optimizing the bounds (OPT) performs best, e.g., certifying twice as many samples compared to LP, for a significant perturbation of –70

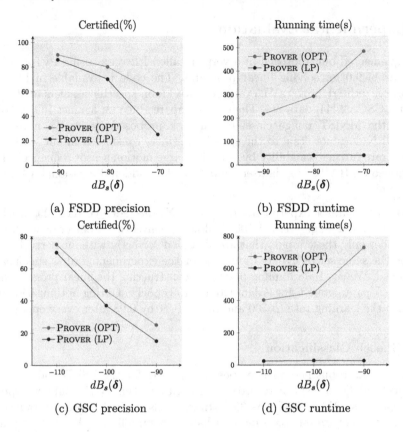

Fig. 6. Performance plots for the FSDD and GSC datasets with different perturbations. All tests are done with the same architecture described in the text.

dB. In terms of runtime, Fig. 6b shows that the OPT runtime increases with the perturbation magnitude, meaning that the optimizer needs more iterations to converge to the resulting bounds.

Interval vs. Polyhedral Abstraction for Speech Preprocessing. We studied experimentally the importance of designing precise polyhedral abstractions of the speech preprocessing pipeline. If we replace the polyhedral bounds for the square and logarithm operations with interval constraints, the precision of PROVER (LP) drops from 86% to 61% on –90 dB and from 70% to 20% on –80 dB. This shows the importance of keeping relational information while overapproximating the speech preprocessing pipeline.

GSC Certification. We used the following parameters for the preprocessing: we downsample the raw input to 8 kHz, sliced the signal in length 1024, followed by 10 Mel-frequency filterbanks. As with the FSDD architecture, we used two layers of LSTM and 50 hidden units each, preceded by a 50 ReLU-activated fully-connected layer. This network achieves accuracy of 80% on the GSC task.

Certifying the GSC classifier is more challenging than FSDD: this dataset has 35 labels, compared to 10 in FSDD. The larger label set size requires PROVER to compare 34 output differences - acquiring the lower bounds of $l_{GT} - l_{FL}$ where each term stands for the final output score for the ground truth and false label, respectively. Figure 6c shows the percentage of certified samples: 75% on –110 dB and 46% on –100 dB with PROVER (OPT), again higher precision than PROVER (LP). Figure 6d shows the longer running time for PROVER (OPT) than on FSDD, due to its larger label set size.

7.2   Image Classification

Based on the setup from [21], we flatten each image into a vector of dimension 784. This vector is partitioned into a sequence of f frames (f depends on the experiment). Next, the LSTM uses this frame as an input.

Comparison with POPQORN. We compare the precision and scalability of PROVER against POPQORN [21]. We trained an LSTM network containing 1 layer with 32 hidden units using standard training, achieving an accuracy of 96.5%. The network receives a sequence of $f = 7$ image slices as input and predicts a digit corresponding to the image.

As POPQORN is slow, we used only ten correctly classified images randomly sampled from the test set. For each frame index i and each method, we compute the maximum perturbation bound ϵ such that the method can certify that the LSTM classifier is robust to perturbations up to ϵ in the L_∞-norm of the i-th slice of the image. We determine the maximum ϵ using the same binary search procedure as in [21].

Table 1. Certification of several LSTM models using PROVER with $\epsilon = 0.01$. F, H, and L denote the number of frames, LSTM hidden units and layers respectively.

F	H	L	Accuracy (%)	Certified (%) by OPT/LP	by OPT Running time (s)
4	**32**	**1**	96.1	91/89	14.5
4	32	2	96.7	92/73	29.1
4	32	3	95.8	95/65	43.1
4	64	1	97.3	93/92	27.0
4	128	1	97.1	95/95	52.4
7	32	1	96.5	63/56	32.1

Figure 7 presents the results of this experiment. We observe that, for all three methods, early frames have smaller ϵ certified perturbation bounds than the later frames. The reason is that the approximation error on frame 1 propagates through the later frames to the classifying layer, while the error on frame 7 only affects the last layer. Across all frames, both our LP and OPT methods significantly outperform POPQORN, meaning that PROVER enables a more precise abstraction than POPQORN. As for speech classifiers, OPT is more precise than LP. We compare running times of the three methods on perturbations in the first frame – most challenging as it requires propagating through all timesteps. Here, PROVER (LP), PROVER (OPT), and POPQORN

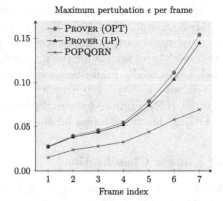

Fig. 7. Results for the comparison between PROVER and POPQORN. Plotted points represent the maximum L_∞ norm perturbation for each frame index 1 through 7.

take 65,348, and 2,160 s respectively per example on average. We conclude that both variants of PROVER are more precise than POPQORN while being 33.2× and 6.21× more scalable for LP and OPT respectively.

Effect of Model Size. We evaluate the scalability of PROVER by certifying several recurrent architectures, with varying number of frames F, hidden units H and LSTM layers L. For each network, we certify the first 100 correctly classified images using the same perturbation $\epsilon = 0.01$ for all frames, with 3 repetitions. While in the previous experiment we certified each frame separately to closely follow the setup from [21], it is more natural to assume the adversary is able to perturb the entire input. The results are shown in Table 1. We observe that the precision of PROVER is affected mostly by the number of frames, as the precision loss accumulates along the frames. Naturally, the running time increases with the number of neurons and frames, as PROVER is optimizing the bounds for each $\sigma(x)\tanh(y)$ operation. However, we also observe a counter-intuitive phenomenon that PROVER (OPT) performs better with multi-layer models than with the single-layer model. The precision from PROVER (LP) drops with the number of LSTM layers unlike those from PROVER (OPT). We hypothesize that an increased number of trainable parameters enhances the flexibility of the bounds for the optimization, allowing us to find more combinations of the bounds that certify the input. PROVER (LP) has non-flexible bounds, so the error propagates.

Effect of Perturbation Budget. We certify the robustness of the MNIST classifier for different ϵ values. We again evaluated 100 correctly classified samples from the test set. Figure 8 shows the experimental results. The OPT version has

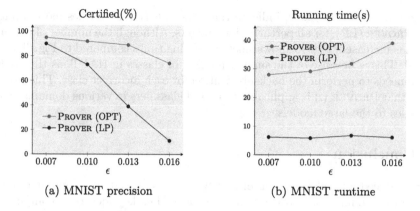

(a) MNIST precision   (b) MNIST runtime

Fig. 8. Results on MNIST with different epsilons and $F = 4, H = 32, L = 2$.

significantly higher precision than LP: i.e., for $\epsilon = 0.013$ in Fig. 8a, LP proves 39% while OPT certifies 89% of samples with a higher runtime in Fig. 8b.

7.3 Motion Sensor Data Classification

We further demonstrate the scalability of PROVER by considering a large classifier containing 4 LSTM layers with 256 hidden units each for the human activity recognition dataset HAPT [33]. Each input in the dataset consists of recorded triaxial linear accelerations and angular velocities, sampled 50 Hz. Here, we restricted HAPT to six activity classes and we trimmed angular velocities to at most 6 s after the point of prediction. Each input sequence is sliced into sliding windows of 0.5 s, which are then passed as an input to the classifier. The trained classifier achieves 88% test accuracy. Identical to the other experiments, we run PROVER on the first 100 correctly classified inputs.

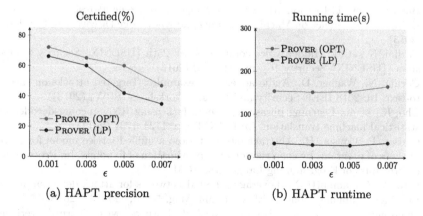

(a) HAPT precision   (b) HAPT runtime

Fig. 9. Results on HAPT with different epsilons and $H = 256, L = 4$.

Results, shown in Fig. 9, indicate that PROVER (OPT) verifies more inputs than PROVER (LP), for all perturbation budgets. Although the number of parameters has increased, Fig. 9b shows smaller running times compared to Fig. 6b and Fig. 6d. This is because of the smaller number of classes in HAPT, as the verification needs to perform the backsubstitution for each incorrect class. This result shows that PROVER (i) is applicable to LSTM classifiers in various domains, and (ii) scales to the large models.

8   Conclusion

We introduced a novel approach for certifying RNNs based on a combination of linear programming and abstraction refinement. The key idea is to compute a polyhedral abstraction of the non-linear operations found in the recurrent cells and to dynamically adjust this abstraction according to each input example being certified. Our experimental results show that PROVER is more precise and scalable than prior work. These advances enable PROVER to certify, for the first time, the robustness of LSTM-based speech classifiers.

References

1. Fermat's theorem. https://planetmath.org/fermatstheoremstationarypoints
2. Akintunde, M.E., Kevorchian, A., Lomuscio, A., Pirovano, E.: Verification of RNN-based neural agent-environment systems. In: Proceedings of the AAAI Conference on Artificial Intelligence (2019)
3. Angluin, D.: Learning regular sets from queries and counterexamples. Inf. Comput. **75**(2), 87–106 (1987)
4. Balunovic, M., Baader, M., Singh, G., Gehr, T., Vechev, M.: Certifying geometric robustness of neural networks. In: Advances in Neural Information Processing Systems (2019)
5. Balunovic, M., Vechev, M.: Adversarial training and provable defenses: Bridging the gap. In: International Conference on Learning Representations (2020)
6. Biggio, B., et al.: Evasion attacks against machine learning at test time. In: Joint European Conference on Machine Learning and Knowledge Discovery in Databases (2013)
7. Carlini, N., et al.: Hidden voice commands. In: 25th {USENIX} Security Symposium ({USENIX} Security 16), pp. 513–530 (2016)
8. Carlini, N., Wagner, D.: Audio adversarial examples: Targeted attacks on speech-to-text. In: 2018 IEEE Security and Privacy Workshops (SPW) (2018)
9. Cho, K., et al.: Learning phrase representations using RNN encoder-decoder for statistical machine translation. In: EMNLP, pp. 1724–1734 (2014)
10. Cousot, P., Cousot, R.: Abstract interpretation: a unified lattice model for static analysis of programs by construction or approximation of fixpoints. In: Proceedings of Principles of Programming Languages, ACM (1977)
11. Diro, A., Chilamkurti, N.: Leveraging LSTM networks for attack detection in fog-to-things communications. IEEE Commun. Mag. **56**(9), 124–130 (2018)
12. Dvijotham, K., et al.: Training verified learners with learned verifiers. arXiv:1805.10265 (2018)

13. Fischer, M., Baader, M., Vechev, M.: Certification of semantic perturbations via randomized smoothing. arXiv:2002.12463 (2020)
14. Hannun, A., et al.: Deep speech: Scaling up end-to-end speech recognition. arXiv:1412.5567 (2014)
15. Hochreiter, S., Schmidhuber, J.: Long short-term memory. Neural Comput. **9**(8), 1735–1780 (1997)
16. Hu, W., Tan, Y.: Black-box attacks against RNN based malware detection algorithms. arXiv:1705.08131 (2017)
17. Jackson, Z.: Free spoken digit dataset (2020). https://github.com/Jakobovski/free-spoken-digit-dataset
18. Jacoby, Y., Barrett, C., Katz, G.: Verifying recurrent neural networks using invariant inference. arXiv:2004.02462 (2020)
19. Khmelnitsky, I., et al.: Property-directed verification of recurrent neural networks. arXiv:2009.10610 (2020)
20. Kingma, D.P., Ba, J.: Adam: A method for stochastic optimization. arXiv:1412.6980 (2014)
21. Ko, C., Lyu, Z., Weng, T., Daniel, L., Wong, N., Lin, D.: Popqorn: Certifying robustness of recurrent neural networks. In: International Conference on Machine Learning (ICML) (2019)
22. Li, J., Qu, S., Li, X., Szurley, J., Kolter, J.Z., Metze, F.: Adversarial music: real world audio adversary against wake-word detection system. In: Advances in Neural Information Processing Systems, pp. 11908–11918 (2019)
23. Lyu, Z., Ko, C.Y., Kong, Z., Wong, N., Lin, D., Daniel, L.: Fastened crown: Tightened neural network robustness certificates. arXiv:1912.00574 (2019)
24. Miné, A.: A new numerical abstract domain based on difference-bound matrices. In: Proceedings of Programs As Data Objects (PADO), pp. 155–172 (2001)
25. Miné, A.: The octagon abstract domain. High. Order Symbolic Comput. **19**(1), 31–100 (2006)
26. Neekhara, P., Hussain, S., Pandey, P., Dubnov, S., McAuley, J., Koushanfar, F.: Universal adversarial perturbations for speech recognition systems. arXiv:1905.03828 (2019)
27. Pachocki, J., et al.: Openai five. https://blog.openai.com/openai-five (2018)
28. Papernot, N., McDaniel, P., Swami, A., Harang, R.: Crafting adversarial input sequences for recurrent neural networks. In: MILCOM 2016–2016 IEEE Military Communications Conference, pp. 49–54. IEEE (2016)
29. Pascual, S., Bonafonte, A., Serra, J.: Segan: Speech enhancement generative adversarial network. arXiv:1703.09452 (2017)
30. Paszke, A., et al.: Automatic differentiation in pytorch (2017)
31. Qin, Y., Carlini, N., Goodfellow, I., Cottrell, G., Raffel, C.: Imperceptible, robust, and targeted adversarial examples for automatic speech recognition. In: International Conference on Machine Learning (ICML) (2019)
32. Raghunathan, A., Steinhardt, J., Liang, P.S.: Semidefinite relaxations for certifying robustness to adversarial examples. In: Advances in Neural Information Processing Systems (NeurIPS), pp. 10877–10887 (2018)
33. Reyes-Ortiz, J.L., Oneto, L., Samà, A., Parra, X., Anguita, D.: Transition-aware human activity recognition using smartphones. Neurocomputing **171**, 754–767 (2016)
34. Sabour, S., Frosst, N., Hinton, G.E.: Dynamic routing between capsules. In: Proceedings of Neural Information Processing Systems (NIPS), pp. 3856–3866 (2017)

35. Sahidullah, M., Saha, G.: Design, analysis and experimental evaluation of block based transformation in MFCC computation for speaker recognition. Speech Commun. **54**(4), 543–565 (2012)
36. Sainath, T.N., Weiss, R.J., Senior, A., Wilson, K.W., Vinyals, O.: Learning the speech front-end with raw waveform CLDNNs. In: Sixteenth Annual Conference of the International Speech Communication Association (2015)
37. Singh, G., Ganvir, R., Püschel, M., Vechev, M.: Beyond the single neuron convex barrier for neural network certification. In: Advances in Neural Information Processing Systems (2019)
38. Singh, G., Gehr, T., Mirman, M., Püschel, M., Vechev, M.: Fast and effective robustness certification. In: Advances in Neural Information Processing Systems (2018)
39. Singh, G., Gehr, T., Püschel, M., Vechev, M.: An abstract domain for certifying neural networks. In: Proceedings of Principles of Programming Languages (POPL) (2019)
40. Singh, G., Püschel, M., Vechev, M.: Fast polyhedra abstract domain. In: Proceedings of Principles of Programming Languages (POPL), pp. 46–59 (2017)
41. Szegedy, C., et al.: Intriguing properties of neural networks. arXiv:1312.6199 (2013)
42. Vaswani, A., et al.: Attention is all you need. In: Proceedings of Neural Information Processing Systems (NIPS) (2017)
43. Vinyals, O., et al.: Alphastar: Mastering the real-time strategy game starcraft ii. DeepMind blog p. 2 (2019)
44. Warden, P.: Speech commands: A dataset for limited-vocabulary speech recognition. arXiv:1804.03209 (2018)
45. Wu, M., Kwiatkowska, M.: Robustness guarantees for deep neural networks on videos. arXiv:1907.00098 (2019)
46. Yang, Z., Li, B., Chen, P.Y., Song, D.: Characterizing audio adversarial examples using temporal dependency (2019)
47. Zhang, H., Weng, T., Chen, P., Hsieh, C., Daniel, L.: Efficient neural network robustness certification with general activation functions. In: Advances in Neural Information Processing Systems, (NeurIPS) (2018)

Verisig 2.0: Verification of Neural Network Controllers Using Taylor Model Preconditioning

Radoslav Ivanov[✉], Taylor Carpenter, James Weimer, Rajeev Alur,
George Pappas, and Insup Lee

University of Pennsylvania,
Philadelphia, PA 19104, USA
{rivanov,carptj,weimerj,alur,
pappasg,lee}@seas.upenn.edu

Abstract. This paper presents Verisig 2.0, a verification tool for closed-loop systems with neural network (NN) controllers. We focus on NNs with tanh/sigmoid activations and develop a Taylor-model-based reachability algorithm through Taylor model preconditioning and shrink wrapping. Furthermore, we provide a parallelized implementation that allows Verisig 2.0 to efficiently handle larger NNs than existing tools can. We provide an extensive evaluation over 10 benchmarks and compare Verisig 2.0 against three state-of-the-art verification tools. We show that Verisig 2.0 is both more accurate and faster, achieving speed-ups of up to 21x and 268x against different tools, respectively.

1 Introduction

Following their increasing popularity, neural networks (NNs) have been recently introduced to various new domains, including safety-critical systems such as autonomous cars [4] and airborne collision avoidance systems [21]. At the same time, NNs have been shown to be greatly susceptible to input perturbations: minor input changes can cause a NN's outputs to vary drastically, as is the case with adversarial examples [26]. Such issues have emphasized the need to formally analyze NN-based systems and assure their safety before they are deployed.

A number of formal verification approaches have been proposed in the last few years to analyze closed-loop systems with NN components. On the one hand, several techniques have been developed for reachability analysis. These works

This work was supported by the Air Force Research Laboratory (AFRL) and the Defense Advanced Research Projects Agency (DARPA) under Contract No. FA8750-18-C-0090, and by the Army Research Office (ARO) under Grant Number W911NF-20-1-0080, and by the Office of Naval Research (ONR) award N00014-20-1-2115. Any opinions, findings and conclusions or recommendations expressed in this material are those of the authors and do not necessarily reflect the views of AFRL, ARO, DARPA, ONR, or the Department of Defense, or the United States Government.

A. Silva and K. R. M. Leino (Eds.) CAV 2021, LNCS 12759, pp. 249–262, 2021.
https://doi.org/10.1007/978-3-030-81685-8_11

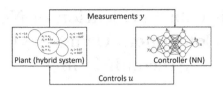

Fig. 1. Overview of the closed-loop system considered in this paper.

handle the NN reachability problem in a variety of ways: by converting the NN into a hybrid system [19]; by casting the problem into a satisfiability modulo convexity problem [25]; by approximating the NN with a Taylor model [8,11,16,20]; or by propagating NN reachable sets using star sets [27,28]. Multiple falsification techniques have been developed as well: these approaches work by adapting existing hybrid-system falsifiers [2,6] to the NN case [7,29,33]; methods for systematic testing through scenario specification languages have been proposed as well [14]. Finally, a number of techniques have been developed to analyze properties of the NN in isolation (e.g., input-output properties) [9,10,12,15,22,30–32], though it is challenging to use these tools in a closed-loop setting as it is unclear what NN specification ensures closed-loop safety in general.

While existing reachability techniques have shown impressive performance, scalability remains an obstacle to applying these tools to realistic systems. In particular, these methods have been evaluated mostly on low-dimensional systems, i.e., systems with several states and at most 41 measurements [18]. The main scalability challenge stems from the fact that reachability is undecidable even for linear hybrid systems [1]. Thus, all approaches overapproximate the true reachable sets using a computationally convenient representation such as polytopes [13] or Taylor models [5]. At the same time, this overapproximation, known as the wrapping effect, leads to quick error accumulation over time, thus making it challenging to verify complex specifications over a longer time horizon.

To address these limitations, we present Verisig 2.0, a scalable tool for verifying safety properties of closed-loop systems with NN controllers. We combine ideas from NN reachability with ideas from hybrid system verification. In particular, we adopt the idea of approximating NNs with Taylor models (TMs) [11,16,20], and we alleviate the wrapping effect through TM preconditioning and shrink wrapping [3,23,24]. Finally, we note that the NN reachability computation can be parallelized since each neuron in a layer can be analyzed independently. We have implemented our tool in conjunction with the hybrid system tool Flow* [5], which enables us to handle general hybrid system models with NN components.

We compare Verisig 2.0 against three tools, namely Verisig [20], NNV [28], and ReachNN* [11]. We use 10 benchmarks that illustrate various challenges, such as hybrid models, non-linear systems and systems with high-dimensional observations. The results indicate that Verisig 2.0 is significantly faster (achieving speed-ups of up to 21x and 268x against Verisig and ReachNN*, respectively) and produces tighter reachable set approximations on all benchmarks.

In summary, this paper has three contributions: 1) a Taylor-model-based NN reachability method using TM preconditioning and shrink wrapping; 2) an efficient implementation that allows for parallel execution; 3) an extensive comparison against existing tools on 10 diverse benchmarks. The source code to reproduce the results is available online (github.com/rivapp/CAV21_repeatability_package) as well as in the main Verisig repository (github.com/Verisig/verisig).

2   Problem Statement

This section outlines the reachability problem addressed in this paper. We consider a closed-loop system, illustrated in Fig. 1, consisting of: a) a plant with states x modeled as a hybrid system; b) measurements y produced as a function of x; c) an NN controller h that takes y as input and produces controls u.

Plant Model. We assume the plant is modeled as a standard hybrid system. In particular, the state space $X = X_D \times X_C$ consists of continuous variables X_C and discrete locations $X_D = \{q_1, \ldots, q_m\}$. When in location $q \in X_D$, the system evolves according to differential equations f_q, i.e., $\dot{x} = f_q(x, u)$, where $x \in X_C$. Each location $q \in X_D$ has an associated invariant $I(q) \subseteq X_C$ that must hold true in that location. Transitions between locations are enabled by guards, which are boolean predicates on the continuous variables. Finally, each continuous variable may be reset to a new value when transitioning to a new location.

Observation Model. The system produces observations $y = g(x)$, where $g : X \to \mathbb{R}^p$. Note that some benchmarks in this paper use state feedback only, i.e., $y = x$.

Controller. The controller h is a fully-connected feedforward NN with sigmoid/tanh activations. Formally, h can be represented as a composition of its L layers:

$$h(y) = h_L \circ h_{L-1} \circ \cdots \circ h_1(y), \tag{1}$$

where each $h_i(y) = a(W_i y + b_i)$ performs a linear function, with parameters W_i and b_i identified during training, followed by a sigmoid/tanh activation a.

Composed System. Although the hybrid system formulation places no restrictions on the controller/plant composition, in the interest of clarity we assume the controller is executed in a time-triggered fashion, with sampling period T, as follows: $u(t) = h(y(t_k))$, for $t \in [t_k, t_k + T)$, where $t_k = kT$ and $k = 0, 1, 2, \ldots$

Closed-Loop Reachability Problem. Let S be a composed system. Given an initial set of states $x(0) \in X_0$, the reachability problem, expressed as property ϕ, is to verify a property ψ of the reachable states of S:

$$\phi(X_0) \equiv (x(0) \in X_0) \Rightarrow \psi(x(t)), \ \forall t \geq 0. \tag{2}$$

3 Background: Neural Networks as Taylor Models

As described in Sect. 1, in this work we adopt a TM-based approach for propagating NN reachable sets. There are two main reasons for this: 1) TMs can approximate any differentiable function over a bounded range given a high enough order; 2) TMs are very effective at approximating hybrid system reachable sets, which allows for a smooth composition between the NN and the rest of the system. The rest of this section formalizes TMs and summarizes the existing approaches to using TMs for NN reachability.

Taylor Model Definition. Intuitively, a TM of a function f is a polynomial approximation p, together with a worst-case error bound I. A j-degree polynomial approximation p of a j times continuously differentiable function f around a point x, written $p(x) \equiv_j f(x)$, is a polynomial p of degree j such that all partial derivatives of f and p coincide at x. Let $\mathbb{I}$ be the set of all intervals $I = [a, b]$ and let $f : D \to \mathbb{R}$ be a function of n variables defined over a domain $D \in \mathbb{I}^n$. Then a Taylor model of f over D of degree j is a pair (p, I) of a polynomial approximation p and an error bound I (also known as a remainder) such that:

$$1)\, f(c) \equiv_j p(c), \text{where } c \text{ is the center of } D,$$
$$2)\, \forall x \in D, \ f(x) \in \{p(x) + e \mid e \in I\}.$$

Taylor Model Arithmetic. Let $TM_1 = (p_1, I_1)$ and $TM_2 = (p_2, I_2)$ be two TMs defined over a domain D. Addition and multiplication are defined as follows [5]:

$$TM_1 + TM_2 = (p_1 + p_2, I_1 + I_2)$$
$$TM_1 \times TM_2 = (p_1 \times p_2, \texttt{Int}(p_1)I_2 + \texttt{Int}(p_2)I_1 + I_1 \times I_2),$$

where $\texttt{Int}(p)$ is an interval bound of p over D.

TMs have shown impressive performance in hybrid system reachability problems due to their ability to approximate any continuously differentiable function given a high enough order [5]. Another appealing feature is that TMs can be used to approximate solutions of differential equations through Picard iteration [5]. Thus, it is natural to try to use TMs to approximate NN reachable sets as well.

Two classes of approaches for approximating NNs with TMs have been developed in the literature. The first one is sampling-based: given a TM TM_y of the inputs y to h, these methods sample points Z from TM_y and corresponding outputs $h(Z)$ to perform polynomial regression [8] or approximation [16]. While these approaches work well for systems with several state variables, they cannot handle higher-dimensional problems due to insufficient sampling.

A second approach to using TMs for NN reachability is to propagate the TMs through each neuron in the NN. Specifically, let $TM_y = (p, I)$ be the TM for y and consider a neuron ν that computes the function $\sigma(wy + b)$, where σ denotes the sigmoid. One can use TM arithmetic [5] to obtain $TM_L = (wp + b, wI)$ for the linear map in ν. For the sigmoid TM, TM_σ, one could obtain a Taylor series expansion of σ around the center of TM_L and get remainder bounds using Taylor's theorem [20]. Thus, the final TM for ν is $TM_\nu = TM_\sigma \circ TM_L$. The benefit of propagating TMs in this fashion is that no sampling is necessary since the NN is approximated directly. On the other hand, scalability challenges manifest in a different way, namely the TM remainders may grow quickly depending on the NN architecture (explained in more detail in Sect. 4).

We adopt the latter approach to approximating NN as TMs due to its improved scalability. The next section describes our approach to reducing the TM remainder size through TM preconditioning and shrink wrapping.

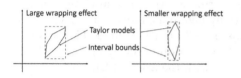

Fig. 2. The wrapping effect for different taylor model orientations.

Fig. 3. Illustration of the shrink wrapping method.

4   Taylor Model Preconditioning and Shrink Wrapping

This section presents our approach to limiting the remainder growth as TMs are propagated through the NN. We explore two complementary techniques, namely TM preconditioning and shrink wrapping. Both of these ideas were originally developed for the purpose of reachability analysis of hybrid systems [3, 23] – in this paper, we adapt them to the NN case.

4.1   Taylor Model Preconditioning

As noted in Sect. 3, although propagating the TM through the NN is preferred since it captures the functional representation of each neuron, it may suffer from quick remainder growth. The following example illustrates this process.

Example 1. Let y_1 and y_2 be inputs to the NN h with corresponding TMs $TM_{y_1} = (p_1, I_1)$ and $TM_{y_2} = (p_2, I_2)$ over domain $D \in \mathbb{I}^n$. Let ν be a neuron in the first layer implementing the function $\nu(y_1, y_2) = \sigma(w_1 y_1 + w_2 y_2 + b)$. The TM for the linear part of ν is

$$TM_L := (p_L, I_L) = (w_1 p_1 + w_2 p_2 + b, w_1 I_1 + w_2 I_2).$$

Let $TM_\sigma = \sigma(a) + \sigma'(a)(TM_L - a) + \sigma''(a)(TM_L - a)^2/2 + I_\sigma$ be a second-order Taylor series expansion of the sigmoid around point a, with remainder I_σ. Using TM arithmetic [5], the TM for ν is $TM_\nu = (p_\nu, I_\nu)$, where

$$p_\nu = \sigma''(a)p_L^2 + (\sigma'(a) - a\sigma''(a))p_L - (\sigma'(a) - 0.5a\sigma''(a))a + \sigma(a)$$
$$I_\nu = \sigma''(a)(2\text{Int}(p_L)I_L + I_L^2) + (\sigma'(a) - a\sigma''(a))I_L + I_\sigma.$$

Remark 1. In order to compute a $TM_\sigma = (p_\sigma, I_\sigma)$ for the sigmoid/tanh, one can follow the procedure described in prior work [20]. In summary, the following three steps need to be performed, assuming the input TM is denoted by TM_L:

1. compute interval bounds, $[a, b]$, for TM_L using interval analysis;
2. obtain a Taylor series approximation, p_σ, of the sigmoid/tanh around the midpoint of $[a, b]$;
3. obtain worst-case error bounds, I_σ, for p_σ using Taylor's theorem.

As shown in Example 1, the remainder is propagated using interval analysis, where a major contributor is the $\mathtt{Int}(p_L)$ term, i.e., the interval bounds of p_L. Since this term approximates the (potentially high-dimensional) input TM with a box, it may introduce significant wrapping effect if the input TM is not a box, as illustrated in Fig. 2. The natural way to address this wrapping effect is through rotating the TM in order to align it with the axes [23,24].

Algorithm 1. NN Verification Using Taylor Model Preconditioning

---

Input: Measurement TM Vector TMV_y, NN h with L layers, and sigmoid activations.
1: $TMV_0 \leftarrow TMV_y$
2: **for each** i in $\{1, \ldots, L\}$ **do**
3:     $TMV_i^L \leftarrow W_i * TMV_{i-1} + b_i$
4:     $(Q + c, \mathbf{0}) \circ (R + Q^\top N, Q^\top \mathbf{I}) \leftarrow TaylorModelPreconditioning(TMV_i^L)$
5:     $TMV_i^\nu \leftarrow TaylorModelForSigmoid((Q, \mathbf{0}))$ //Taylor series approximation
6:     $TMV_i \leftarrow TMV_i^\nu \circ (R + Q^\top(c + N), \mathbf{I})$
7: **end for**
8: **return** TMV_L

Since the set represented by a TM is the image of a polynomial over a given domain, it is challenging to choose an appropriate rotation matrix. However, as discussed in prior work [23,24], if one first normalizes the TM so that the domain is $[-1, 1]^n$, then the linear terms become the largest contributors to interval analysis overapproximation (since higher order terms are less than 1 in magnitude). Thus, a good choice for a rotation matrix is the matrix formed by the linear terms of the (normalized) TM.

To formalize the above concept, let us decompose a TM vector $TMV = (\mathbf{p}, \mathbf{I})$ into $TMV = (c + M + N, \mathbf{I})$, where c denotes the constant terms, M denotes the linear terms and N denotes the higher-order terms. The idea of preconditioning is to decompose $M = QR$, where Q is an orthonormal matrix and R is upper-triangular. This is achieved by splitting TMV into a composition of two TM vectors: $TMV = (Q + c, \mathbf{0}) \circ (R + Q^\top N, Q^\top \mathbf{I})$.[1] Then, each neuron's computation is performed on Q only, which alleviates the wrapping effect introduced by $\mathtt{Int}(p_L)$ in Example 1 since Q is orthonormal.

---

[1] Note that the new remainder may need to be enlarged to also include numerical errors due to the computation of Q.

The algorithm is presented in Algorithm 1. Note that preconditioning is performed in each layer, followed by again composing the two parts into the full TM. While it is possible to represent the final TM as a composition of individual layer TMs, the benefits of preconditioning would decrease after the first layer, since most of the variability is captured in the right-most TM.

4.2 Shrink Wrapping

In systems where verification over a longer time horizon is required, avoiding large remainders may be impossible even with effective preconditioning. In such cases, one could use shrink wrapping in order to refactor the TM into one that results in slower remainder accumulation in the future [3,24].

The high-level idea of shrink wrapping is illustrated in Fig. 3. If the remainder becomes a significant part of the set described by the TM, then TM arithmetic degrades into standard interval analysis. In this case, it helps to transform the TM into a new TM that contains the original one but has no remainder. Thus, even if the new TM is slightly larger, it is propagated symbolically using TM arithmetic, which results in smaller error accumulation in the long run.

The choice of new TM is not obvious and is affected by the system in consideration. The standard approach in related work [3,24] is to focus on the linear terms (assuming the TM is normalized so that $D = [-1, 1]^n$). Specifically, suppose that the system's state x is described by the TM vector $TMV_x = (\mathbf{p}, \mathbf{I}) = (c + M + N, \mathbf{I})$. One option for the new TM vector is to premultiply TMV_x by M^{-1}, thereby reducing the linear terms to the identity matrix, $\mathcal{I}$. Then a shrink wrap factor q is chosen such that the image of the higher-order terms contains the remainder of the initial TM vector, i.e., $TMV_x^{new} = (c + \mathcal{I} + qM^{-1}N, \mathbf{0})$.[2]

While it is possible to choose q by finding bounds on the partial derivatives of the higher-order terms $M^{-1}N$ [3], our initial experiments indicated that a more straightforward approach leads to no loss in precision. In particular, we represent the new TM vector as $TMV_x^{new} = (c + \text{diag}(\mathbf{q}), \mathbf{0})$, where $\mathbf{q} = \text{Int}(TMV_x)$. The last consideration is when to perform the TM conversion: if it is applied too often, more error could be introduced by the frequent elimination of useful information in the TMs. In our experiments, shrink wrapping is triggered when the remainder is larger than $1e^{-6}$ and larger than 1% of the total TM range.

5 Implementation

We implemented our approach in conjunction with the Flow* tool [5], for easy integration with standard hybrid system models. We provide similar TM functions to the ones existing in Flow*, adapted to the case of NNs. In addition to modified data structures, a main difference in our implementation is the option to parallelize the TM vector propagation, i.e., Line 5 in Algorithm 1. This parallelization is possible since each neuron in a layer only depends on the input

---

[2] The new remainder may be greater than 0 due to round-off error during the inversion.

TMs, thus each computation can be done on a separate core. As illustrated in Sect. 7, this implementation brings great benefits, especially in the case of larger NNs, where multiple neuron computations can be performed in parallel.

6 Benchmarks

We use 10 benchmarks to evaluate the proposed approach. These benchmarks were compiled from the related literature [17, 19, 20, 28] and were selected in order to cover a wide variety of systems and controllers: 1) continuous and hybrid systems; 2) systems with state feedback and systems with measurements as a function of the states; 3) low-dimensional systems as well as systems with high-dimensional measurements; 4) controllers with both tanh and sigmoid activations and with a number of neurons varying from 16 to 200 per layer.

Table 1 presents the dynamics and the initial set for each benchmark. For simplicity, all properties are reachability properties (i.e., the problem is to verify whether a goal set is reached from all initial states), though safety properties can be handled as well. In particular, the goal regions are as follows:

- $B_1 : x_1 \in [0, 0.2], x_2 \in [0.05, 0.3]$; $B_2 : x_1 \in [-0.3, 0.1], x_2 \in [-0.35, 0.5]$;

Table 1. List of benchmarks. Benchmarks $B_1 - B_5$ and Tora were introduced by Huang et al. [17]; adaptive cruise control (ACC) was presented by Tran et al. [28]; mountain car (MC), quadrotor with model-predictive control (QMPC) and F1/10 were introduced by Ivanov et al. [20]. We use V to denote the measurement dimension. In F1/10, y is a 21-dimensional LiDAR scan.

Name	Dynamics	V	Initial set
B_1	$\dot{x}_1 = x_2, \dot{x}_2 = ux_2^2 - x_1$	2	$x_1 \in [0.8, 0.9], x_2 \in [0.5, 0.6]$
B_2	$\dot{x}_1 = x_2 - x_1^3, \dot{x}_2 = u$	2	$x_1 \in [0.7, 0.9], x_2 \in [0.7, 0.9]$
B_3	$\dot{x}_1 = -x_1(0.1 + (x_1 + x_2)^2),$	2	$x_1 \in [0.8, 0.9],$
	$\dot{x}_2 = (u + x_1)(0.1 + (x_1 + x_2)^2)$		$x_2 \in [0.4, 0.5]$
B_4	$\dot{x}_1 = -x_1 + x_2 - x_3,$	3	$x_1, x_3 \in [0.25, 0.27],$
	$\dot{x}_2 = -x_1(x_3 + 1) - x_2, \dot{x}_3 = -x_1 + u$		$x_2 \in [0.08, 0.1]$
B_5	$\dot{x}_1 = x_1^3 - x_2,$	3	$x_1 \in [0.38, 0.4], x_2 \in [0.45, 0.47]$
	$\dot{x}_2 = x_3, \dot{x}_3 = u$		$x_3 \in [0.25, 0.27],$
Tora	$\dot{x}_1 = x_2,$	4	$x_1 \in [-0.77, -0.75],$
	$\dot{x}_2 = -x_1 + 0.1\sin(x_3),$		$x_2 \in [-0.45, -0.43],$
	$\dot{x}_3 = x_4,$		$x_3 \in [0.51, 0.54],$
	$\dot{x}_4 = u$		$x_4 \in [-0.3, -0.28]$
ACC	$\dot{x}_1 = x_2, \dot{x}_2 = x_3, \dot{x}_3 = -4 - 2x_3 - \frac{x_3^2}{1000}$	5	$x_1 \in [90, 91], x_2 \in [32, 32.05]$
	$\dot{x}_4 = x_5, \dot{x}_5 = x_6, \dot{x}_6 = 2u - 2x_6 - \frac{x_6^2}{1000}$		$x_4 \in [10, 11], x_5 \in [30, 30.05]$
MC	$x_1^+ = x_1 + x_2,$	2	$x_1 \in [-0.53, -0.5]$
	$x_2^+ = x_2 + 0.0015u - 0.0025\cos(3x_1)$		
QMPC	$\dot{x}_1 = x_4 - 0.25, \dot{x}_2 = x_5 + 0.25, \dot{x}_3 = x_6$	6	$x_1 \in [0.025, 0.05],$
	$\dot{x}_4 = 9.81u_1, \dot{x}_5 = -9.81u_2, \dot{x}_6 = u_3 - 9.81$		$x_2 \in [0, 0.025]$
F1/10	$\dot{x}_1 = x_3\cos(x_4), \dot{x}_2 = x_3\sin(x_4),$	21	$x_1 \in [-0.0025, 0.0025],$
	$\dot{x}_3 = -1.633x_3 + 0.3266(u - 4), \dot{x}_4 = \frac{x_3\tan(u)}{0.225}$		$x_3 \in [-0.0025, 0.0025]$

- $B_3 : x_1 \in [0.2, 0.3], x_2 \in [-0.3, -0.05]$; $B_4 : x_1 \in [-0.05, 0.05], x_2 \in [-0.05, 0]$;
- $B_5(\text{sig}) : x_1 \in [-0.4, -0.28], x_2 \in [0.05, 0.22]$;
- $B_5(\text{tanh}) : x_1 \in [-0.43, -0.38], x_2 \in [0.16, 0.18]$;
- Tora: $x_1 \in [-0.1, 0.2], x_2 \in [-0.9, -0.6]$;
- ACC: $x_1 \in [22.81, 22.87], x_4 \in [29.88, 30.02]$;
- MC: $x_1 \geq 0.45$; QMPC: $x_1, x_2, x_3 \in [-0.32, 0.32]$; F1/10: no crash [18].

7 Experiments

We compare our tool, named Verisig 2.0, against three state-of-the-art tools, namely Verisig [19,20], ReachNN* [11,17], and NNV [27,28]. We selected these tools because they handle NNs with sigmoid/tanh activations. For each benchmark, we record whether each tool could verify the property (or return Unknown due to large approximation error). In addition, we compare the verification times between the different tools. While Verisig and NNV do not support parallel execution,[3] ReachNN* has been optimized for GPU execution, so a comparison in terms of verification times is fair (all experiments were run on an Intel Xeon Gold 6248 running at 2.5 GHz and with an Nvidia GeForce RTX 2080 Ti GPU). Finally, we provide a comparison in terms of reachable sets.

Verification outcomes and times are reported in Table 2. Multiple controllers were used in some benchmarks in order to test a variety of NNs. We present the

Table 2. Verification evaluation. The notation *tanh/sig (n × k)* indicates a NN with tanh/sig activations, n hidden layers and k neurons per layer. For each tool, we provide the verification time in seconds; if a property could not be verified, it is marked as Unknown. If a tool crashed on a benchmark, it is marked as DNF.

Name	NN setup	Verisig 2.0 (40 cores)	Verisig 2.0 (1 core)	Verisig	ReachNN*	NNV
B_1	tanh (2 × 20)	**38 s**	48 s	DNF	Unknown	Unknown
	sig (2 × 20)	**40 s**	49 s	Unknown	69 s	Unknown
B_2	tanh (2 × 20)	Unknown	Unknown	Unknown	Unknown	Unknown
	sig (2 × 20)	**6 s**	8 s	12 s	32 s	Unknown
B_3	tanh (2 × 20)	**32s**	43 s	98 s	128 s	Unknown
	sig (2 × 20)	**36 s**	47 s	98 s	130 s	Unknown
B_4	tanh (2 × 20)	**9 s**	11 s	23 s	20 s	DNF
	sig (2 × 20)	**10 s**	12 s	24 s	20 s	DNF
B_5	tanh (3 × 100)	**48 s**	168 s	Unknown	Unknown	Unknown
	sig (3 × 100)	**51s**	196 s	1063 s	**31 s**	Unknown
Tora	tanh (3 × 20)	**43 s**	70 s	134 s	2524 s	Unknown
	sig (3 × 20)	**50 s**	83 s	136 s	3402 s	Unknown
ACC	tanh (3 × 20)	**529 s**	1512 s	Unknown	DNF	Unknown
MC	sig (2 × 16)	48 s	52 s	**33 s**	N/A	N/A
	sig (2 × 200)	**1241 s**	4311 s	Unknown	N/A	N/A
QMPC	tanh (2 × 20)	**636 s**	697 s	703 s	N/A	N/A
F1/10	tanh (2 × 64)	**3411 s**	3654 s	2021 s	N/A	N/A

---

[3] NNV is parallelized in the case of ReLU activations, but not for smooth activations.

results for Verisig 2.0 as used with one and with 40 cores, in order to illustrate the benefit of parallelization. Note that parallelization helps the most in systems with wider NNs, e.g., the MC benchmark, since a larger part of the computation is devoted to NN computation (relative to plant computation) in these systems.

Comparison with Verisig. Verisig is the closest method to Verisig 2.0, as it also propagates TMs through the NN. Thus, Verisig can be seen as a baseline for our approach, so this comparison illustrates most clearly the benefits of preconditioning and shrink wrapping. Firstly, note that Verisig takes significantly more time to compute reachable sets (21 times slower in the case of the B_5 benchmark) on all but one benchmark – the MC benchmark is peculiar because the NN is very small, hence most of the computation is spent on the plant. Furthermore, Verisig is unable to verify some properties due to increasing error. As shown in Fig. 4, the reachable sets computed by Verisig introduce more approximation error, especially in the challenging ACC benchmark, where preconditioning is particularly useful due to the larger input space.

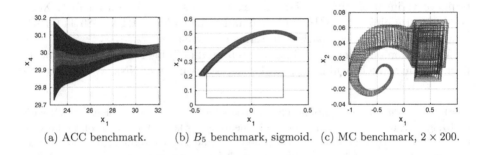

(a) ACC benchmark.   (b) B_5 benchmark, sigmoid.   (c) MC benchmark, 2×200.

Fig. 4. Comparison between the reachable sets produced by Verisig (blue) and Verisig 2.0 (green). Example simulated trajectories are plotted in red. The goal set is shown in magenta. Note that the goal is not reached in the B_5 benchmark. (Color figure online)

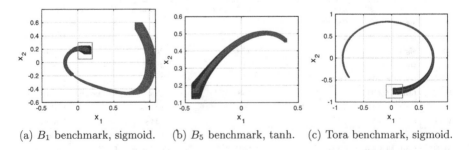

(a) B_1 benchmark, sigmoid.   (b) B_5 benchmark, tanh.   (c) Tora benchmark, sigmoid.

Fig. 5. Comparison between the reachable sets produced by ReachNN* (blue) and Verisig 2.0 (green). Simulated trajectories are plotted in red (not shown in the Tora benchmark to improve visibility). The goal set is shown in magenta. (Color figure online)

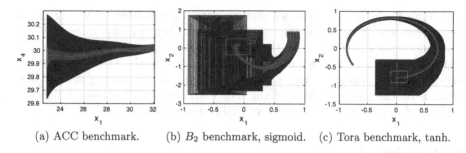

(a) ACC benchmark.   (b) B_2 benchmark, sigmoid.   (c) Tora benchmark, tanh.

Fig. 6. Comparison between the reachable sets produced by NNV (blue) and the Verisig 2.0 approach (green) on three of the benchmarks from Table 2. Example simulated trajectories are plotted in red. The goal set is shown in magenta. (Color figure online)

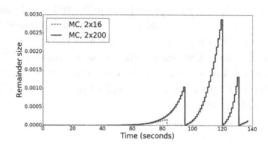

Fig. 7. Verisig 2.0 remainder growth (for position, x_1) on the MC benchmark as we increase the NN size. The remainder is reset to 0 after shrink wrapping.

Comparison with ReachNN*. ReachNN* is a sampling-based approach to NN verification, so it is expected to work well on low-dimensional systems and encounter difficulties as the dimension increases. As can be seen in Table 2, Verisig 2.0 is faster on all but one benchmark, and the difference is especially pronounced on the four-dimensional Tora benchmark, where ReachNN* is 268 times slower. Note that ReachNN* cannot handle hybrid models, so no comparison could be made on those benchmarks. Finally, as shown in Fig. 5, Verisig 2.0 also results in tighter reachable sets – the benefit of shrink wrapping can be observed in Fig. 5a, where the ReachNN* reachable sets eventually start to grow fast whereas Verisig 2.0 is able to maintain low approximation error over time.

Comparison with NNV. Note that NNV is unable to verify any of the properties considered in this paper due to high approximation error. This is mostly due to the fact that NNV is optimized for networks with ReLU activations, where the star set method used in NNV is effective and parallelizable. Figure 6 shows the reachable computed by each tool, where it is clear that Verisig 2.0 maintains tight reachable sets whereas the NNV approximation error grows quickly.

Scalability Evaluation. Finally, we also evaluate the scalability of Verisig 2.0 as we increase the NN size on the MC benchmark. Figure 7 illustrates how the remainder grows over time for the x_1 (position) state. We observe that the larger NN results in significantly larger remainder growth. At the same time, interpreting the remainder growth in isolation may be misleading since it also depends on the size and shape of the true reachable sets. We leave a rigorous analysis of the effect of NN size on scalability for future work.

8   Conclusion

This paper presented Verisig 2.0, a parallelized tool for NN verification. We developed a Taylor-model-based approach in which we reduce the approximation error in reachable sets through Taylor model preconditioning and shrink wrapping. Finally, we provided an extensive evaluation over 10 benchmarks and showed that our method is significantly more accurate and faster than state-of-the-art tools, resulting in 21x and 268x speed-ups on some benchmarks, respectively. For future work, we will investigate which NN architectures are more amenable for verification, both in terms of size and number of layers as well as in terms of weight magnitude and direction.

References

1. Alur, R., et al.: The algorithmic analysis of hybrid systems. Theoret. Comput. Sci. **138**(1), 3–34 (1995)
2. Annpureddy, Y., Liu, C., Fainekos, G., Sankaranarayanan, S.: S-TaLiRo: a tool for temporal logic falsification for hybrid systems. In: Abdulla, P.A., Leino, K.R.M. (eds.) TACAS 2011. LNCS, vol. 6605, pp. 254–257. Springer, Heidelberg (2011). https://doi.org/10.1007/978-3-642-19835-9_21
3. Berz, M., Makino, K.: Suppression of the wrapping effect by taylor model-based verified integrators: long-term stabilization by shrink wrapping. Int. J. Diff. Eq. Appl **10**, 385–403 (2005)
4. Bojarski, M., Del Testa, D., Dworakowski, D., et al.: End to end learning for self-driving cars. arXiv preprint arXiv:1604.07316 (2016)
5. Chen, X., Ábrahám, E., Sankaranarayanan, S.: Flow*: an analyzer for non-linear hybrid systems. In: Sharygina, N., Veith, H. (eds.) CAV 2013. LNCS, vol. 8044, pp. 258–263. Springer, Heidelberg (2013). https://doi.org/10.1007/978-3-642-39799-8_18
6. Donzé, A.: Breach, a toolbox for verification and parameter synthesis of hybrid systems. In: International Conference on Computer Aided Verification (2010)
7. Dreossi, T., Donzé, A., Seshia, S.A.: Compositional falsification of cyber-physical systems with machine learning components. In: Barrett, C., Davies, M., Kahsai, T. (eds.) NFM 2017. LNCS, vol. 10227, pp. 357–372. Springer, Cham (2017). https://doi.org/10.1007/978-3-319-57288-8_26
8. Dutta, S., Chen, X., Sankaranarayanan, S.: Reachability analysis for neural feedback systems using regressive polynomial rule inference. In: 22nd International Conference on Hybrid Systems: Computation and Control, pp. 157–168 (2019)

9. Dutta, S., Jha, S., Sankaranarayanan, S., Tiwari, A.: Output range analysis for deep feedforward neural networks. In: Dutle, A., Muñoz, C., Narkawicz, A. (eds.) NFM 2018. LNCS, vol. 10811, pp. 121–138. Springer, Cham (2018). https://doi. org/10.1007/978-3-319-77935-5_9

10. Ehlers, R.: Formal verification of piece-wise linear feed-forward neural networks. In: D'Souza, D., Narayan Kumar, K. (eds.) ATVA 2017. LNCS, vol. 10482, pp. 269–286. Springer, Cham (2017). https://doi.org/10.1007/978-3-319-68167-2_19

11. Fan, J., Huang, C., Chen, X., Li, W., Zhu, Q.: ReachNN*: a tool for reachability analysis of neural-network controlled systems. In: Hung, D.V., Sokolsky, O. (eds.) ATVA 2020. LNCS, vol. 12302, pp. 537–542. Springer, Cham (2020). https://doi. org/10.1007/978-3-030-59152-6_30

12. Fazlyab, M., Robey, A., Hassani, H., Morari, M., Pappas, G.J.: Efficient and accurate estimation of lipschitz constants for deep neural networks. arXiv preprint arXiv:1906.04893 (2019)

13. Frehse, G., et al.: SpaceEx: scalable verification of hybrid systems. In: Gopalakrishnan, G., Qadeer, S. (eds.) CAV 2011. LNCS, vol. 6806, pp. 379–395. Springer, Heidelberg (2011). https://doi.org/10.1007/978-3-642-22110-1_30

14. Fremont, D.J., Dreossi, T., Ghosh, S., Yue, X., Sangiovanni-Vincentelli, A.L., Seshia, S.A.: Scenic: a language for scenario specification and scene generation. In: Conference on Programming Language Design and Implementation (2019)

15. Gehr, T., Mirman, M., Drachsler-Cohen, D., Tsankov, P., Chaudhuri, S., Vechev, M.: AI2: Safety and robustness certification of neural networks with abstract interpretation. In: 2018 IEEE Symposium on Security and Privacy (SP) (2018)

16. Huang, C., Fan, J., Li, W., Chen, X., Zhu, Q.: Reachnn: reachability analysis of neural-network controlled systems. ACM Trans. Embed. Comput. Syst. (TECS) **18**(5s), 1–22 (2019)

17. Huang, X., Kwiatkowska, M., Wang, S., Wu, M.: Safety verification of deep neural networks. In: International Conference on Computer Aided Verification (2017)

18. Ivanov, R., Carpenter, T., Weimer, J., Alur, R., Pappas, G.J., Lee, I.: Case study: verifying the safety of an autonomous racing car with a neural network controller. In: International Conference on Hybrid Systems: Computation and Control (2020)

19. Ivanov, R., Weimer, J., Alur, R., Pappas, G.J., Lee, I.: Verisig: verifying safety properties of hybrid systems with neural network controllers. In: 22nd ACM International Conference on Hybrid Systems: Computation and Control (2019)

20. Ivanov, R., Carpenter, T.J., Weimer, J., Alur, R., Pappas, G.J., Lee, I.: Verifying the safety of autonomous systems with neural network controllers. ACM Trans. Embed. Comput. Syst. **20**(1) (2020). https://doi.org/10.1145/3419742

21. Julian, K.D., Lopez, J., Brush, J.S., Owen, M.P., Kochenderfer, M.J.: Policy compression for aircraft collision avoidance systems. In: Digital Avionics Systems Conference (DASC), 2016 IEEE/AIAA 35th, pp. 1–10. IEEE (2016)

22. Katz, G., Barrett, C., Dill, D.L., Julian, K., Kochenderfer, M.J.: Reluplex: an efficient SMT solver for verifying deep neural networks. In: Majumdar, R., Kunčak, V. (eds.) CAV 2017. LNCS, vol. 10426, pp. 97–117. Springer, Cham (2017). https:// doi.org/10.1007/978-3-319-63387-9_5

23. Makino, K., Berz, M.: Suppression of the wrapping effect by taylor model-based verified integrators: Long-term stabilization by preconditioning. Int. J. Differ. Equ. Appl. **10**(4) (2011)

24. Neher, M., Jackson, K.R., Nedialkov, N.S.: On taylor model based integration of odes. SIAM J. Numer. Anal. **45**(1), 236–262 (2007)

25. Sun, X., Khedr, H., Shoukry, Y.: Formal verification of neural network controlled autonomous systems. In: Proceedings of the 22nd ACM International Conference on Hybrid Systems: Computation and Control, pp. 147–156. ACM (2019)
26. Szegedy, C., Zaremba, W., Sutskever, I., Bruna, J., Erhan, D., et al.: Intriguing properties of neural networks. arXiv preprint arXiv:1312.6199 (2013)
27. Tran, H.-D., Bak, S., Xiang, W., Johnson, T.T.: Verification of deep convolutional neural networks using ImageStars. In: Lahiri, S.K., Wang, C. (eds.) CAV 2020. LNCS, vol. 12224, pp. 18–42. Springer, Cham (2020). https://doi.org/10.1007/978-3-030-53288-8_2
28. Tran, H., Cai, F., Lopez, D.M., Musau, P., Johnson, T.T., Koutsoukos, X.: Safety verification of cyber-physical systems with reinforcement learning control. ACM Trans. Embed. Comput. Syst. 18(5s), 105 (2019)
29. Tuncali, C.E., Fainekos, G., Ito, H., Kapinski, J.: Simulation-based adversarial test generation for autonomous vehicles with machine learning components. arXiv preprint arXiv:1804.06760 (2018)
30. Wang, S., Pei, K., Whitehouse, J., Yang, J., Jana, S.: Efficient formal safety analysis of neural networks. In: Advances in Neural Information Processing Systems (2018)
31. Weng, T., et al.: Towards fast computation of certified robustness for relu networks. In: International Conference on Machine Learning, pp. 5273–5282 (2018)
32. Xiang, W., Tran, H.D., Johnson, T.T.: Output reachable set estimation and verification for multi-layer neural networks. arXiv preprint arXiv:1708.03322 (2017)
33. Yaghoubi, S., Fainekos, G.: Gray-box adversarial testing for control systems with machine learning components. In: Proceedings of the 22nd ACM International Conference on Hybrid Systems: Computation and Control, pp. 179–184 (2019)

Robustness Verification of Semantic Segmentation Neural Networks Using Relaxed Reachability

Hoang-Dung Tran[1]($\boxtimes$), Neelanjana Pal[2], Patrick Musau[2],
Diego Manzanas Lopez[2], Nathaniel Hamilton[2], Xiaodong Yang[2], Stanley Bak[3],
and Taylor T. Johnson[2]

[1] University of Nebraska-Lincoln, Lincoln, USA
[2] Vanderbilt University, Nashville, USA
[3] Stony Brook University, Stony Brook, USA

Abstract. This paper introduces robustness verification for semantic segmentation neural networks (in short, semantic segmentation networks [SSNs]), building on and extending recent approaches for robustness verification of image classification neural networks. Despite recent progress in developing verification methods for specifications such as local adversarial robustness in deep neural networks (DNNs) in terms of scalability, precision, and applicability to different network architectures, layers, and activation functions, robustness verification of semantic segmentation has not yet been considered. We address this limitation by developing and applying new robustness analysis methods for several segmentation neural network architectures, specifically by addressing reachability analysis of up-sampling layers, such as transposed convolution and dilated convolution. We consider several definitions of robustness for segmentation, such as the percentage of pixels in the output that can be proven robust under different adversarial perturbations, and a robust variant of intersection-over-union (IoU), the typical performance evaluation measure for segmentation tasks. Our approach is based on a new relaxed reachability method, allowing users to select the percentage of a number of linear programming problems (LPs) to solve when constructing the reachable set, through a relaxation factor percentage. The approach is implemented within NNV, then applied and evaluated on segmentation datasets, such as a multi-digit variant of MNIST known as M2NIST. Thorough experiments show that by using transposed convolution for up-sampling and average-pooling for down-sampling, combined with minimizing the number of ReLU layers in the SSNs, we can obtain SSNs with not only high accuracy (IoU), but also that are more robust to adversarial attacks and amenable to verification. Additionally, using our new relaxed reachability method, we can significantly reduce the verification time for neural networks whose ReLU layers dominate the total analysis time, even in classification tasks.

A. Silva and K. R. M. Leino (Eds.) CAV 2021, LNCS 12759, pp. 263–286, 2021.
https://doi.org/10.1007/978-3-030-81685-8_12

1   Introduction

Image segmentation is the process of partitioning an image into multiple portions, or segments, which are sets of pixels, and in short is referred to as segmentation [30]. Segmentation has broad applications, ranging from perception in autonomous cyber-physical systems (e.g., identifying pedestrians, lanes, vehicles, etc. in images) and medical imaging (e.g., identifying tumors, measuring tissue, etc. in X-rays and other medical scans) [31]. *Semantic segmentation* additionally classifies each pixel into a *class* from a set of classes, and hence, can be viewed as a generalization of image classification, the robustness of which has been studied deeply in recent years.

State-of-the-art segmentation approaches typically rely on neural networks, known as *semantic segmentation networks (SSNs)*. Typically SSN architectures take an image as input and are composed of two major portions: a sequence of *down-sampling* layers to extract features from the input image into a latent space, followed by another sequence of *up-sampling* layers, which in essence map the features (roughly corresponding to the classes) from the latent space to the image's pixels, such that each pixel is associated with a class. However, just as neural networks for image classification are well-known to be vulnerable to adversarial perturbations, so too are SSNs [45]. Although deep neural networks (DNN) verification is emerging into an established research area with many tools and techniques proposed to verify safety and robustness specifications of DNNs [22,43] and neural network controlled systems [15,17,34,37], most state-of-art verification techniques for robustness verification of DNNs focus on variants of classification[1], frequently for images [1,5,7,11,19,24,26,29,32,33,46].

To our knowledge, there are no existing methods that can verify robustness of SSNs, which perform a more complex task than image classification, as the output space dimensionality is (typically) of the same order of size as that of the input space (e.g., the output is an image with the width and height of the input image, but with identified classes in the output instead of color bit depth; see Figs. 5 and 7 for examples). We review some existing testing-based robustness evaluation methods in our related work section.

Overview and Contributions. In this paper, we present the first formal approach for verifying SSN robustness using reachability analysis. Our approach's central idea is, if an input image is attacked (perturbed) with some bounded disturbance, we construct a reachable output set that contains all possible classes for each pixel. From the reachable output set, we can formally guarantee an SSN's robustness at the pixel-level, i.e., each pixel is provably classified correctly. Our approach focuses on two effective SSN architectures, including dilated CNNs and transposed CNNs, which to our knowledge, are not supported in any other existing neural network verification approaches. We evaluate our approach on a

---

[1] The ACAS-Xu benchmarks [18] common in neural network verification can be viewed as a form of classifier: the networks produce advisories (weak left, etc.), which in essence are classes, but do not have images as their inputs.

set of SSNs trained with different architectures on the MNIST [21] and M2NIST data sets, the latter of which is a multi-digit variant of MNIST suitable for segmentation evaluation. Additionally, we define and evaluate several metrics for robustness, as the robustness evaluation is more sophisticated for segmentation.

Our reachability-based approach builds on ImageStars, which are an efficient data structure for verifying convolutional neural networks (CNNs) [33], to construct the input set and compute the reachable set layer-by-layer throughout the SSN. The ImageStar approach offers both exact and approximate reachability schemes for analyzing the robustness of CNNs. Although the approximate scheme obtains a tighter reachable set in comparison with the zonotope [28] and new polytope methods [29] by using optimized ranges, in practice, we do not need a tight reachable set in many cases. Indeed, we only need a "tight enough" reachable set to verify a property. Therefore, it is reasonable to let users have the freedom to choose an appropriate level of relaxation in constructing the reachable set for their applications. More relaxation comes with a coarser reachable set and vice versa. To fulfill this need, we also present a new relaxed ImageStar approach to allow users to choose a specific relaxation level defined by a *relaxation factor* (RF) percentage when constructing the reachable set for their applications. This relaxed reachability method can help reduce the verification time of SSNs significantly (up to 99%) in some cases.

In summary, the main contributions of this paper are: 1) the first formal approach for robustness verification of SSNs, 2) a new relaxed ImageStar reachability method, 3) the implementation of the approach in a prototype software tool, 4) thorough assessment of these methods on different network architectures, and 5) insight on how to train robust SSNs that are amenable to verification.

2   Preliminaries and Problem Formulation

2.1   ImageStars

In this section, we review the ImageStar data structure and its properties [33].

Definition 1. *An* ImageStar Θ *is a tuple* $\langle c, V, P, l, u \rangle$ *where* $c \in \mathbb{R}^{h \times w \times nc}$ *is the anchor image,* $V = \{v_1, v_2, \cdots, v_m\}$ *is a set of* m *images in* $\mathbb{R}^{h \times w \times nc}$ *called generator images,* $P : \mathbb{R}^m \to \{\top, \bot\}$ *is a predicate,* l *and* u *are the lower bound and upper bound vectors of the predicate variables, and* h, w, nc *are the height, width, and number of channels of the images, respectively. The generator images are arranged to form the ImageStar's* $h \times w \times nc \times m$ *basis array. The set of images represented by the ImageStar is given as:*

$$\llbracket \Theta \rrbracket = \{x \mid x = c + \Sigma_{i=1}^{m}(\alpha_i v_i) \text{ such that } P(\alpha_1, \cdots, \alpha_m) = \top, l_i \le \alpha_i \le u_i\}.$$

We may refer to both the tuple Θ *and the set of states* $\llbracket \Theta \rrbracket$ *as* Θ. *In this work, we restrict the predicates to be a conjunction of linear constraints,* $P(\alpha) \triangleq C\alpha \le d$ *where, for* p *linear constraints,* $C \in \mathbb{R}^{p \times m}$, α *is the vector of* m-*variables, i.e.,* $\alpha = [\alpha_1, \cdots, \alpha_m]^T$, *and* $d \in \mathbb{R}^{p \times 1}$. *An ImageStar is the empty set if and only if* $P(\alpha)$ *subject to* $l \le \alpha \le u$ *is empty.*

Lemma 1 (Affine mapping of an ImageStar). *An affine mapping of an ImageStar* $\Theta = \langle c, V, P, l, u \rangle$ *with a scale factor* γ *and an offset image* β *is another ImageStar* $\Theta' = \langle c', V', P', l', u' \rangle$ *in which the new anchor, generators and predicate are as follows:*

$$c' = \gamma \cdot c + \beta, \quad V' = \gamma \cdot V, \quad P' \equiv P, \quad l' \equiv l, \quad u'. \equiv u.$$

Note that, the scale factor γ *can be a scalar or a vector containing scalar scale factors in which each factor is used to scale one color channel in the ImageStar.*

2.2   Range of a Specific Input in an ImageStar

We slightly alter the original definition of an ImageStar, [33], by introducing lower bound and upper bound vectors to the predicate variables. Specifically, if we want to find the range of an input $x(i, j, k)$ (where $1 \leq i \leq h$, $1 \leq j \leq w$, $1 \leq k \leq nc$) in an ImageStar Θ, we need to solve the following LP problem.

$$x_{min} = \min(c(i, j, k) + \Sigma_{p=1}^{m} \alpha_i v_p(i, j, k)) \ s.t. \ C\alpha \leq d, l \leq \alpha \leq u, \quad (1)$$

$$x_{max} = \max(c(i, j, k) + \Sigma_{p=1}^{m} \alpha_i v_p(i, j, k)) \ s.t. \ C\alpha \leq d, l \leq \alpha \leq u. \quad (2)$$

However, if we only want to estimate roughly the range of the neuron without solving the LP optimization problem, we can compute the estimated range quickly as follows.

$$x_{min}^{est} = c(i, j, k) + \Sigma_{p=1}^{m} l_p \max(v_p(i, j, k), 0) + \Sigma_{q=1}^{m} u_q \min(v_q(i, j, k), 0), \quad (3)$$

$$x_{max}^{est} = c(i, j, k) + \Sigma_{p=1}^{m} u_p \max(v_p(i, j, k), 0) + \Sigma_{q=1}^{m} l_q \min(v_q(i, j, k), 0). \quad (4)$$

2.3   Semantic Segmentation Networks and Reachability

Definition 2. *A* semantic segmentation network (SSN) *f is a nonlinear function that maps each pixel* $x(i, j)$ *of a multichannel input image x to a target class* $y(i, j)$ *from a set of classes* $\mathcal{L} = \{1, 2, \ldots, L\}$:

$$f : \ x \in \mathbb{R}^{h \times w \times nc} \rightarrow y \in \mathcal{L}^{h \times w}$$
$$x(i, j) \rightarrow y(i, j) \in \mathcal{L}, \quad (5)$$

where h, w, nc *are the height, width, and number of channels of the input image, respectively, and* $(i, j) \in \{1, \ldots, h\} \times \{1, \ldots, w\}$ *are the pixel height and width indices, respectively.*

Definition 3. *Reachability analysis (or shortly, Reach) of a SSN f on an ImageStar input set I is the process of computing all possible classes corresponding to every pixel in all input images x in the ImageStar input set I:*

$$Reach(f, I) : \ I \rightarrow \mathcal{R}_f$$
$$x \rightarrow y = f(x). \quad (6)$$

We call $\mathcal{R}_f(I)$ the pixel-class reachable set *of the SSN corresponding to the input set I (or just $\mathcal{R}_f$ when I is clear from context), in which each pixel-class $pc(i,j) \in \mathcal{R}_f$ at each pixel $(i,j) \in \{1,\ldots,h\} \times \{1,\ldots,w\}$ may contain more than one class, i.e., $pc(i,j) = \{l_1,\ldots,l_m\} \subseteq \mathcal{L}$, for $L \geq m \geq 1$.*

2.4 Adversarial Attacks and Robustness

Definition 4. *An adversarial attack is where a set of n noise images $x_{noise} = [x_1^{noise}, \ldots, x_n^{noise}]$ and corresponding coefficient vector $\epsilon = [\epsilon_1,\ldots,\epsilon_n]^T$ are added to input image x to change the classification result of a network.*

Mathematically, an adversarial attack is a linear parameterized function $g_{\epsilon,x^{noise}}(\cdot)$ that takes an image as an input and produces the corresponding adversarial image.

$$x^{adv} = g_{\epsilon,x^{noise}}(x) = x + \Sigma_{i=1}^n \epsilon_i \cdot x_i^{noise} \tag{7}$$

In this paper, we focus on the robustness analysis of SSNs under adversarial attacks. We refer readers to [45] for a survey of state-of-art attack and defenses approaches, mostly for classification.

Definition 5. *An* unknown, bounded adversarial attack (UBAA) *is an adversarial attack where the value of the coefficient vector ϵ is unknown but bounded in a range $[\underline{\epsilon}, \overline{\epsilon}]$, i.e., $\underline{\epsilon_i} \leq \epsilon_i \leq \overline{\epsilon_i}$. An UBAA can be defined formally as a tuple $\mathcal{A} = \langle \underline{\epsilon}, \overline{\epsilon}, x^{noise} \rangle$.*

Proposition 1 (UBAA as an ImageStar). *Applying an UBAA $\mathcal{A} = \langle \underline{\epsilon}, \overline{\epsilon}, x^{noise} \rangle$ on an image x creates a set of images, which can be represented as an ImageStar $I = \langle c \equiv x, V \equiv x^{noise}, P(\alpha) \equiv P(\epsilon) \equiv \underline{\epsilon} \leq \epsilon \leq \overline{\epsilon} \rangle$.*

Definition 6. *Given a SSN f and an input image x, a pixel $x(i,j) \in x$ is called* robust *to an UBAA $\mathcal{A}$ if and only if: $\forall\, g_{\epsilon,x^{noise}} \in \mathcal{A}$, $f(x^{adv}(i,j)) = f(x(i,j))$, where $x^{adv}(i,j) \in x^{adv} = g_{\epsilon,x^{noise}}(x)$. If $\exists\, g_{\epsilon,x^{noise}} \in \mathcal{A}$ such that $f(x^{adv}(i,j)) \neq f(x(i,j))$, the pixel $x(i,j)$ is called* non-robust.

Definition 7. *The* robustness value (RV) *of a SSN corresponding to an UBAA applied to an input image is defined as $RV = \frac{N_{robust}}{N_{pixels}} \times 100\%$, where N_{robust} is the total number of robust pixels under the attack, and $N_{pixels} = h \cdot w$ is the total number of pixels of the input image.*

Definition 8. *The* robustness sensitivity (RS) *of a SSN corresponding to an UBAA applied to an input image is defined as $RS = \frac{N_{nonrobust} + N_{unknown}}{N_{attackedpixels}}$, where $N_{nonrobust}$ is the total number of non-robust pixels under the attack, $N_{unknown}$ is the total number of pixels whose robustness is unknown (may or may not be robust), and $N_{attackedpixels}$ is the total number of attacked pixels of the input image.*

Definition 9. *The* robust IoU (Intersection-over-Union) (R_{IoU}) *of a SSN corresponding to an UBAA applied to an input image is defined as the average IoU of all labels that are robust under the attack. Let x be a segmentation* *ground-truth image, y be the verified segmentation image under the attack, and IoU_p be the IoU (also known as Jaccard index) of the pth label in the label images x and y, then the robust IoU of the SSN is computed by:*

$$R_{IoU} = \frac{\Sigma_{p=1}^{L} IoU_p}{L}. \tag{8}$$

The robust IoU definition is quite similar to traditional IoU, which is a core metric to evaluate the accuracy in training SSNs. However, instead of assessing the accuracy, we use the robust IoU concept in combination with the robustness value and robustness sensitivity as core metrics to evaluate the robustness of a SSN under adversarial attack in the verification context.

2.5   Robustness Verification Problem Formulation

We consider two robustness verification problems.

Problem 1. Given a SSN f, an image x, and an UBAA $\mathcal{A}$, prove for every pixel $x(i,j) \in x$ that $x(i,j)$ is robust or non-robust to the attack $\mathcal{A}$.

Problem 2. Given a SSN f, a set of N test images $\{x_1, \ldots, x_N\}$, and an UBAA $\mathcal{A}$, compute the average robustness value $\overline{RV}$, the average robustness sensitivity $\overline{RS}$, and the average robust IoU $\overline{R}_{IoU}$ of the SSN (corresponding to $\mathcal{A}$).

The core step in solving these problems is to prove the robustness of a SSN f under an UBAA $\mathcal{A}$ at the pixel-level, i.e., Problem 1, which can be solved using reachability analysis computing the "pixel-class reachable set" $\mathcal{R}_f = Reach(f, I)$ that contains all possible classes of every pixel in the input set I constructed by applying the attack $\mathcal{A}$ on an image x (Proposition 1). Next, we investigate a new relaxed ImageStar reachability method for the ReLU layer, the up-sampling layers, including transposed convolution, dilated convolution, and pixel-classification. We note that the softmax layer can be neglected in the analysis [33].

3   Reachability of SSNs Using Relaxed ImageStars

In this section, we build on the original ImageStar method to develop reachability analysis for the transposed convolution and dilated convolution layers, and propose a new relaxed ImageStar reachability method for the ReLU and pixel-classification layers. The reachability algorithms for other layers can be handled using existing methods, such as those in [33]. Thus, we highlight handling the up-sampling layers, which requires overcoming significant challenges, and has not previously been done. Handling up-sampling layers is necessary for SSN robustness verification.

3.1   Reachability of a Transposed (Dilated) Convolutional Layer

Transposed (dilated) convolutions are frequently used for up-sampling in image segmentation applications to generate an output feature map that has a spatial

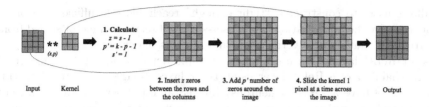

Fig. 1. An example of a transposed convolution operation.

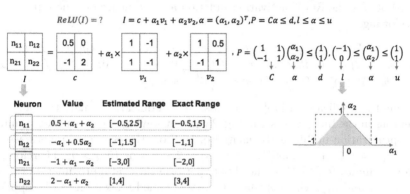

Fig. 2. Example 1.

dimension greater than that of the input feature map. A transposed convolution operation consists of four main steps, depicted in Fig. 1, and is defined by its kernel size k, padding p, and stride s. A dilated convolution operation is defined by its kernel size k, padding p, stride s and dilation factor d.

Lemma 2. *The reachable set of a transposed (dilated) convolutional layer with an ImageStar input set $\mathcal{I} = \langle c, V, P \rangle$ is another ImageStar, specifically $\mathcal{I}' = \langle c', V', P \rangle$ where $c' = TConv(c)$ ($c' = DConv(c)$) is the transposed (dilated) convolution operation applied to the anchor image, $V' = \{v'_1, \ldots, v'_m\}$, $v'_i = TConvZeroBias(v_i)$ ($v'_i = DConvZeroBias(v_i)$) is the transposed (dilated) convolution operation with zero bias applied to the generator images, i.e., using only the weights of the layer. Each of these are affine operations, see [30] for details, and as shown in Lemma 1, ImageStars are closed under affine operations.*[2]

3.2   Relaxed Reachability of a ReLU Layer

In this section, we present the relaxed ImageStar reachability of a ReLU layer. Like the original approximate reachability method [33], the relaxed ImageStar approach computes an overapproximate reachable set of a ReLU layer. However,

---

[2] In most neural network frameworks, transposed and dilated convolution are implemented as convolution with particular choices of padding, stride, and dilation factor as illustrated in Fig. 1 for transposed convolution, which is well-known to be affine.

it allows users to construct a "tight enough" reachable set sufficient to prove properties for their applications via a user-specified relaxation factor scaled from 0% to 100% that reduces verification time. In this paper, we focus on this process for ReLU layers. We use a small example depicted in Fig. 2 to illustrate the reachability of a ReLU layer using the relaxed ImageStar method. In this example, we have a 2×2 (4 neurons) ImageStar input set I with the anchor image c and two generator images v_1 and v_2, and we want to compute an over-approximation of $ReLU(I)$. To do that, we apply the triangle overapproximation rule [10,36] for the ReLU activation function at each neuron of the input set in the following.

Lemma 3. *For any input* $x \in [l, u]$, *the output set* $Y = \{y|\ y = ReLU(x)\}$ *satisfies: (1) If* $l \geq 0$, *then* $y = x$; *(2) If* $u \leq 0$, *then* $y = 0$; *or (3) If* $l < 0$ *and* $u > 0$, *then* $Y \subset \bar{Y} = \{y|\ y \geq 0,\ y \leq \frac{u(x-l)}{u-l},\ y \geq x\}$.

Using the predicate variable's bounds, we can quickly estimate the ranges of all neurons in the ImageStar set in Fig. 2 without solving any linear programming (LP) optimization problems (by using Eq. 3). From the estimated ranges, we see $ReLU(n_{21}) = 0$ $(n_{21} \leq 0)$ and $ReLU(n_{22}) = 2 - \alpha_1 + \alpha_2$ $(n_{22} > 0)$. Therefore, to overapproximate $ReLU(I)$, we need only perform the overapproximation rule on neurons n_{11} and n_{12}, which is where the user-defined relaxation can be applied. In the original approximate reachability approach [33], we use the exact ranges to construct the triangle overapproximation of the ReLU activation function, which requires solving 4 LPs to find the exact ranges for n_{11} and n_{12}, which are $[-0.5, 1.5]$ and $[-1, 1]$ respectively in this example. Now, if users want to *reduce the number of LPs* solved in constructing the overapproximate reachable set to speed up verification, which LPs should be chosen to solve to construct a sufficiently tight overapproximate reachable set? For example, if the users want to relax 50% number of LPs for Example 1, then only $4 - (50\% \times 4) = 2$ LPs are solved to construct an overapproximate reachable set. So, which two LPs should be chosen?

The answer is found by combining the exact ranges obtained by solving LPs and the estimated ranges to construct the overapproximate reachable set. This can be done using on of the following heuristic approaches. These approaches select which neurons and their corresponding lower (upper) bounds should be obtained exactly to construct an as-tight-as-possible overapproximate reachable set with a given allowable number of LPs. Some of these heuristic approaches are based on the estimated ranges information.

3.2.1   Randomly Relaxed Reachability

This approach randomly selects some LPs in the LPs pool to solve to obtain the lower (upper) bounds for some (random) neurons. For Example 1, the LPs pool is as follows.

$$LP_{pool} = \{\min(n_{11}), \max(n_{11}), \min(n_{22}), \max(n_{22}),$$
$$subject\ to: P = C\alpha \leq d, l \leq \alpha \leq u\}.$$

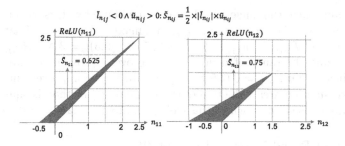

Fig. 3. Overapproximation areas at neurons n_{11} and n_{12} using estimated ranges.

If users relax 50% of the LPs, then the randomly relaxed reachability algorithm selects aimlessly two LPs in the LP pool to solve, and then combines the obtained lower (upper) ranges with the estimated ranges to construct an overapproximate reachable set using the triangle overapproximation rule, i.e., Lemma 3.

From Fig. 2, we can see that the estimated lower ranges of neurons n_{11} and n_{12} are the same as the exact ones. Therefore, if the randomly relaxed reachability algorithm selects $\min(n_{11})$ and $\min(n_{12})$ to solve, the final ranges used for constructing the reachable set exactly match the estimated ranges. This means solving $\min(n_{11})$ and $\min(n_{12})$ wastes time and does not reduce the conservativeness of the overapproximate reachable set, as no tighter ranges are obtained. In another case, if the algorithm selects $\max(n_{11})$ and $\max(n_{12})$, then we can obtain the exact ranges of two neurons by solving only two LPs (instead of four LPs), when combining the estimated lower ranges, i.e., -0.5 for n_{11} and -1 for n_{12} with the optimized upper ranges, i.e., 1.5 for n_{11} and 1 for n_{12}. In this case, the randomly relaxed algorithm can obtain the tightest overapproximate reachable set by solving only 50% of the LPs.

3.2.2 Area-Based Relaxed Reachability

The area-based relaxed reachability approach finds and optimizes the ranges of neurons with the potentially largest triangle overapproximation areas. Figure 3 illustrates the areas of the triangle overapproximation at neurons n_{11} and n_{12} using the estimated ranges. We see the overapproximation area of n_{12} ($\tilde{S}_{n_{12}} = 0.75$) is larger than that of n_{11} ($\tilde{S}_{n_{11}} = 0.625$). Therefore, if users relax 50% of the LPs, the area-based relaxed reachability algorithm will use two LPs to optimize the range of neuron n_{12}, i.e., solving $\min(n_{12})$ and $\max(n_{12})$. With this optimized range, the overapproximation area of the neuron n_{12} reduces from $\tilde{S}_{n_{12}} = 0.75$ to $S_{n_{12}} = 0.5$. If users relax 75% of the LPs, then the algorithm will use two LPs to optimize the range of the neuron n_{12} and one LP to optimize the upper bound of the neuron n_{11}, because $\tilde{u}_{11} = 2.5 > |\tilde{l}_{11}| = 0.5$.

3.2.3 Range-Based Relaxed Reachability

The range-based relaxed reachability approach finds the neurons with the potentially widest ranges to optimize their ranges. For Example 1, unlike the area-based approach, the range-based approach will use two LPs to optimize the range of neuron n_{11}, i.e., solving $\min(n_{11})$ and $\max(n_{11})$, whose estimated range (ER) is widest ($ER_{n_{11}} = |\tilde{u}_{n_{11}} - \tilde{l}_{n_{11}}| = |2.5 - (-0.5)| = 3 > ER_{n_{12}} = 2.5$). After optimizing the range of neuron n_{11}, the overapproximation area at this neuron reduces from $\tilde{S}_{n_{11}} = 0.625$ to $S_{n_{11}} = 0.375$. The improvement in terms of overapproximation area reduction of the range-based method is equivalent to the above area-based approach in this case, i.e., $\Delta S_{n_{11}} = \Delta S_{n_{12}} = 0.25$.

3.2.4   Bound-Based Relaxed Reachability

The bound-based relaxed reachability approach finds neurons with the potentially largest (lower or upper) bounds to optimize their bounds. For Example 1, the algorithm will use two LPs to optimize the upper bounds of the neurons n_{11} and n_{12}, i.e., solving $\max(n_{11})$ and $\max(n_{12})$, because their estimated upper bounds are the ones with largest absolute values. Thus, $|\tilde{u}_{n_{11}}| = 2.5 > |\tilde{u}_{n_{12}}| = 1.5 > |\tilde{l}_{n_{12}}| = 1 > |\tilde{l}_{n_{11}}| = 0.5$. After optimizing these upper bounds, the overapproximation areas at neurons n_{11} and n_{12} reduces to 0.375 and 0.5 respectively. In this case, we can see that the bound-based relaxed approach is the best approach compared to the others since it reduces the overapproximation errors at both neurons n_{11} and n_{12}, effectively reducing the overapproximation areas by $\Delta S_{n_{11}} = \Delta S_{n_{12}} = 0.25$. It is worth noting the obtained overapproximate reachable set is the same as the one obtained by the original approximate ImageStar reachability because the estimated and optimized lower bounds are the same.

3.3   Reachability of a Pixel-Classification Layer

The last layer in an SSN is a pixel-classification layer, which assigns a specific class (label) to each pixel of an input image. Given an $h \times w \times nc$ input image, the size of the input x to the pixel-classification layer is $h \times w \times L$, where L is the number of classes (labels) of the network (we neglect the softmax layer in the analysis). To assign a specific class l, $1 \leq l \leq L$ to a pixel $x(i,j) \in x$, $1 \leq i \leq h, 1 \leq j \leq w$, the value of the pixel $x(i,j)$ at channel l, i.e., $x(i,j,l)$, needs to be the maximum one among L channels. When the input to the network is an ImageStar set instead of a single image, the input to the pixel-classification layer is a $h \times w \times L$ ImageStar set. Depending on the value of the predicate variables in the input set, a pixel $x(i,j)$ in the set may be assigned to more than one class. For example, if $l_1, \ldots, l_m$ are the cross-channel max-point candidates of the pixel $x(i,j)$ in L channels, the pixel-class reachable set of the layer at the considered pixel is $pc(i,j) = \{l_1, \ldots, l_m\}$. By determining all cross-channel max-point candidates of all pixels in the input set, we can obtain the pixel-class reachable set of the layer, which is also the reachable set of the SSN, $\mathcal{R}_f = [pc(i,j)]_{h \times w}$, i.e., the collection of pixel classes at every index (i,j).

Similar to the max-pooling layer [33], determining all cross-channel max-point candidates of all pixels in the input set can be done via solving linear programming (LP) optimization problems, which is time-consuming due to the number of LPs required (or equivalently the size of the LP). To reduce computation time, we estimate the lower and upper bounds of the ImageStar input to the layer using only the ranges of the predicate variables. These bounds are then used to predict all possible cross-channel max-point candidates of all pixels.

4   Verification Algorithm

Our reachability-based verification algorithm for SSNs is presented in Algorithm 4.1. The algorithm takes an SSN f, an input image x, an UBAA $\mathcal{A}$, and a reachability method (exact or approximate) as inputs, then returns the pixel-class reachable set $\mathcal{R}_f$, the robustness value RV, sensitivity RS, and robust IoU R_{IoU} of the SSN. The algorithm works as follows. First, it constructs the input set corresponding to the attack using Proposition 1 (line 2). Then, it computes the pixel-class reachable set of the SSN using reachability analysis layer-by-layer (line 3). Using the pixel-class reachable set, it verifies the robustness of each pixel in the reachable set by comparing its classes with the non-attacked (ground truth) output segmentation image, i.e., $y = f(x)$. If $\mathcal{R}_f(i,j) = y(i,j)$, the pixel $x(i,j)$ is robust under the attack (line 10). If $\mathcal{R}_f(i,j) \neq y(i,j) \wedge y(i,j) \not\subseteq \mathcal{R}_f(i,j)$, the pixel $x(i,j)$ is non-robust under the attack (line 12). Otherwise, the robustness of the pixel $x(i,j)$ is *unknown* (may be robust or non-robust), due to overapproximation. Beyond verifying the robustness of each pixel in the reachable set, it also counts the numbers of 1) robust pixels N_{robust} (line 10), 2) non-robust pixels $N_{nonrobust}$ (line 12), and 3) pixels with unknown robustness $N_{unknown}$ (line 13). Finally, it computes the robustness value, sensitivity and robust IoU of the SSN (lines 12, 13 and 14). The robustness of a SSN under an UBAA should be evaluated on a set of test images (Problem 2).

Algorithm 4.1. Robustness verification of a semantic segmentation network.

Input: $f, x, \mathcal{A}, RF, method$ ▷ SSN, input image, attack, relaxation factor, relaxation method
Output: $\mathcal{R}_f, RV, RS$ ▷ pixel-class reachable set, robustness value, robustness sensitivity
 1: **procedure** $[\mathcal{R}_f, RV, RS]$ = VERIFY$(f, x, \mathcal{A}, RF, method)$
 2:     $I = constructInputSet(x, \mathcal{A})$ ▷ construct an ImageStar input set
 3:     $\mathcal{R}_f = Reach(f, I, method)$ ▷ compute the pixel-class reachable set
 4:     $y = f(x)$ ▷ compute non-attacked output segmentation image
 5:     $h = x.Height, \ w = x.Width$
 6:     $N_{robust} = 0, \ N_{nonrobust} = 0, \ N_{unknown} = 0, \ N_{attackedpixels} = 0$
 7:     **for** $i = 1 : h$ **do**
 8:         **for** $j = 1 : w$ **do**
 9:             **if** $\mathcal{A}.x^{noise}(i,j) \neq 0$ **then** $N_{attackedpixels} = N_{attackedpixels} + 1$
10:             **if** $\mathcal{R}_f(i,j) = y(i,j)$ **then** $N_{robust} = N_{robust} + 1$ ▷ pixel $x(i,j)$ is robust
11:             **else**
12:                 **if** $y(i,j) \not\subseteq \mathcal{R}_f(i,j)$ **then** $N_{nonrobust} = N_{nonrobust} + 1$ ▷ pixel $x(i,j)$
     is non-robust
13:                 **else** $N_{unknown} = N_{unknown} + 1$ ▷ pixel $x(i,j)$ robustness is unknown
14:     $RV = (N_{robust}/(h \cdot w)) \cdot 100\%)$ ▷ robustness value
15:     $RS = (N_{nonrobust} + N_{unknown})/N_{attackedpixels}$ ▷ robustness sensitivity
16:     $R_{IoU} = getAverageIoU(y, \mathcal{R}_f)$ ▷ robust IoU

---

5 Evaluation

Experimental Setup. The approach is implemented in the NNV software tool for verification of deep neural networks[3]. We evaluate our approach by verifying the robustness of a set of SSNs trained on the MNIST [21] and M2NIST datasets shown in Table 1, where class "ten" corresponds to the background, and the other classes to the corresponding digits. The experiments were performed on a computer with an Intel Core i7-6700 CPU at 3.4 GHz with 8 cores and 64 GB Memory running Windows 10. The over-approximating reachability method and 6 cores are used for computing the pixel-class reachable sets.

We randomly selected 100 MNIST images (of size 28×28) and 100 M2NIST images (of size 64×84) to evaluate the robustness of the trained SSNs. We attack each image x in these two test sets using an UBAA brightening attack. Particularly, we darken a pixel $x(i, j)$ in the image if its value is larger than a threshold d, i.e. if $x(i, j) > d \rightarrow x^{adv}(i, j) = a \ll d$. Mathematically, the adversarial darkening attack on an image x can be described as:

$$x^{adv} = x + \epsilon \cdot x^{noise}, \ 1 - \Delta_\epsilon \leq \epsilon \leq 1,$$

$$x^{noise}(i, j) = -x(i, j), \text{ if } x(i, j) > d, \text{ otherwise } x^{noise}(i, j) = 0.$$

For $\epsilon = 1$, we completely darken all the pixels whose values are larger than d (=150 in our experiments), i.e., $x^{adv}(i, j) = 0$. The size of the input set caused by the attack is defined by Δ_ϵ. Generally, we have a large input set when Δ_ϵ is large. To evaluate the average robustness values $(\overline{RV})$ and sensitivities $(\overline{RS})$ of the SSNs (on the test sets) in the connection with the number of attacked pixels, we further restrict the maximum allowable number of attacked pixels by N_{max}.

We focus our evaluation and discussion on three aspects: 1) the robustness and sensitivity of different SSN architectures under adversarial attacks, 2) the effect of SSN architectures and input size on verification performance, and 3) the improvement of the new relaxed reachability method in terms of verification results and performance. For the first two aspects, we use the relaxed reachability method with relaxation factor $RF = 0\%$, i.e., no relaxation, to construct the reachable sets of the SSNs.

---

[3] The examples and tool are available: https://github.com/verivital/nnv/tree/cav2021/code/nnv/examples/Submission/CAV2021. An archival version is available on Zenodo: https://doi.org/10.5281/zenodo.4726346.

Table 1. Semantic Segmentation Network Benchmarks. Notation: 'I': input, 'C': convolution, 'TC': transposed convolution, 'DC': dilated convolution, 'R': ReLU, 'B': batch normalization, 'AP': average-pooling, 'MP': max-pooling, 'S': softmax, 'L': label (pixel classification).

ID	Name	Accuracy(IoU)	Down-sampling	Up-sampling	Input size	Layers
N_1	$mnist\_ap\_tc$	0.87	C+AP	TC	28×28	21 (1I, 7C, 3R, 4B, **2AP, 2TC**, 1S, 1L)
N_2	$mnist\_mp\_tc$	0.85	C+MP	TC	28×28	21 (1I, 7C, 3R, 4B, **2MP, 2TC**, 1S, 1L)
N_3	$mnist\_dc$	0.83	C	DC	28×28	21 (1I, 3C, 3R, 3B, **9DC**, 1S, 1L)
N_4	$m2nist\_ap\_dc$	0.62	C+AP	DC	64×84	16 (1I, 4C, 3R, **3AP, 3DC**, 1S, 1L)
N_5	$m2nist\_ap\_tc$	0.75	C+AP	TC	64×84	22 (1I, 7C, 8R, **2AP, 2TC**, 1S, 1L)
N_6	$m2nist\_dc$	0.72	C	DC	64×84	24 (1I, 1C, 5R, 5B, **10DC**, 1S, 1L)

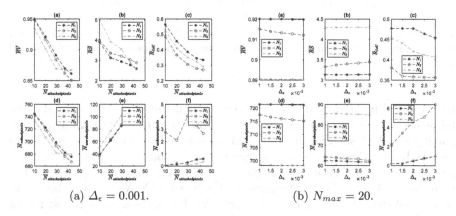

(a) $\Delta_\epsilon = 0.001$.   (b) $N_{max} = 20$.

Fig. 4. The average robustness value, sensitivity, and IoU of MNIST SSNs.

5.1 Robustness and Sensitivity of Different Network Architectures

Max-Pooling vs. Average-Pooling. Max-pooling is the preferred choice over average-pooling for training SSNs because of its nonlinear characteristics. We investigate whether max-pooling is actually better than average-pooling in terms of accuracy and robustness of deep SSN. Figure 4 illustrates the average robustness and sensitivities of MNIST SSNs under different numbers of attacked pixels (Fig. 4a, 20 images are used) and input sizes (Fig. 4b, 10 images are used). We focus on the first two SSNs, i.e. N_1 and N_2. These SSNs have the same architectures (with 21 layers). The only difference is N_1 uses average-pooling for down-sampling while N_2 uses max-pooling for the same task (both SSNs use two transposed convolutional layers for up-sampling). With training, we experienced that N_1 is more accurate than N_2, (0.87 IoU vs. 0.85 IoU, see Table 1). Interestingly, N_1 is also more robust than N_2 since it has a larger average robustness value (Figs. 4a-a, 4b-a), a higher average robust IoU (Figs. 4a-c, 4b-c), and more robust pixels (Figs. 4a-d, 4b-d). One can also see that the average-pooling-based SSN is less sensitive to the attack than the max-pooling-based SSN (Figs. 4a-(b, e, f), 4b-(b, e, f)). Notably, when more pixels are attacked or larger input sizes are used, the max-pooling-based SSN (i.e., N_2) produces more pixels with unknown

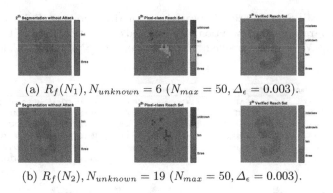

(a) $R_f(N_1)$, $N_{unknown} = 6$ ($N_{max} = 50$, $\Delta_\epsilon = 0.003$).

(b) $R_f(N_2)$, $N_{unknown} = 19$ ($N_{max} = 50$, $\Delta_\epsilon = 0.003$).

Fig. 5. Example pixel-class reachable sets of MNIST SSNs. The max-pooling-based SSN N_2 produces more unknown pixels than the average-pooling-based SSN N_1 (19 vs. 6).

robustness (Figs. 4a-f, 4b-f, and 5). Lastly, when the input size increases, the robustness of the max-pooling-based SSN drops more quickly than the average-pooling-based SSNs (Fig. 4b (a,d)) and its sensitivity increases faster (Fig. 4b -b). We believe the main reason causing the max-pooling-based SSN to be more sensitive to the attack is its high nonlinearity using max-pooling layers. It is quite interesting that even the max-pooling-based SSN N_2 has a higher accuracy (0.85) than the non-max-pooling SSN N_3 (0.83), the average robust IoU of the SSN N_2 is smaller than the one of N_3 (Figs. 4a-c, 4b-c).

Accuracy vs. Robustness; Deeper Networks and ReLU Layer Robustness. Accuracy (and for segmentation, IoU) is one of the most important factors for evaluating deep neural networks. We investigate whether more accurate and deeper SSNs are more robust compared to other architectures. To determine this, we analyze the robustness of two SSNs with different architectures and accuracy trained on the M2NIST data set. The first SSN N_4 is based on dilated convolution with 16 layers and 0.62 (IoU) accuracy (Table 1). The second SSN N_5 is based on transposed convolution with 22 layers and 0.75 (IoU) accuracy. Here, the second SSN is deeper and more accurate than the first SSN. We run the robustness analysis on these two SSNs on a set of 20 M2NIST images. The results are depicted in Fig. 6. In terms of robustness, the more accurate and deeper SSN N_5 is worse than the less accurate one N_4 as it has a smaller average robustness value and IoU (Figs. 6-(a,c), 7). Additionally, N_5 is also more sensitive to the attack than N_4 (Fig. 6-(b,e)) when we increase the number of attacked pixels. The main reason for this result is, the more accurate SSN contains many ReLU layers (8 ReLU layers) compared with the less accurate one (3 ReLU layers). Similar to the max-pooling layer, using many ReLU layers increases the nonlinearity of the SSN to capture complex features of images. Unfortunately, it also makes the SSN more sensitive to the attack.

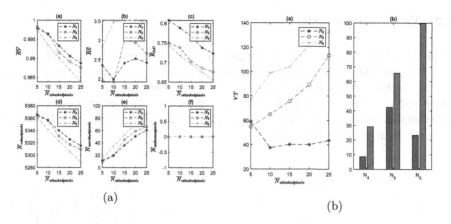

(a)

(b)

Fig. 6. The average robustness value, sensitivities, IoU, verification time ($\Delta_\epsilon = 10^{-5}$) and reachability times (blue for ReLU layers and orange for others, $\Delta_\epsilon = 6 \times 10^{-5}$) of M2NIST SSNs. (Color figure online)

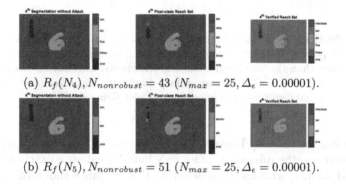

(a) $R_f(N_4)$, $N_{nonrobust} = 43$ ($N_{max} = 25$, $\Delta_\epsilon = 0.00001$).

(b) $R_f(N_5)$, $N_{nonrobust} = 51$ ($N_{max} = 25$, $\Delta_\epsilon = 0.00001$).

Fig. 7. Example pixel-class reachable sets of M2NIST SSNs. The more accurate and deeper SSN N_5 produces more non-robust pixels than the less accurate SSN N_4 (51 vs. 43).

Dilated Convolution vs. Transposed Convolution. Dilated convolution and transposed convolution are typical choices for semantic segmentation tasks. We compare these techniques in terms of accuracy and robustness. On MNIST SSNs, although the transposed-convolution SSNs N_1 and the dilated-convolution SSN N_3 have the same number of layers (21 layers with 3 ReLU), N_3 is less accurate than N_1 (0.83 vs. 0.87 IoU, see Table 1). In terms of robustness, N_3 is also less robust and more sensitive to the attack than N_1, as it has smaller average RV and IoU, and larger sensitivities (Fig. 4). On M2NIST SSNs, by considering 21-layer (8 ReLU) transposed-convolution SSN N_5 and 24-layer (4 ReLU) dilated-convolution SSN N_6, one can see that even with more layers, N_6 is less accurate than N_5 (0.72 vs. 0.75 IoU, see Table 1). Also, N_6 is less robust and more sensitive to the attack than N_5, since it has smaller average RV and IoU, and larger sensitivities (Fig. 6).

5.2   Verification Performance

Dilated Convolution vs. Transposed Convolution. In general, more attacked pixels and larger input size leads to greater verification time, as depicted in Figs. 8a, 8b and 6b-(a). Interestingly, these show that the dilated-convolution-based SSNs require greater verification time than the ones using transposed convolution. For example, the verification time of N_3 is larger than N_2 when they have the same number of layers.

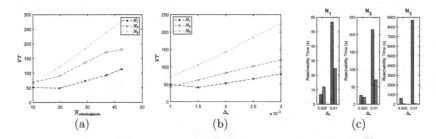

Fig. 8. Verification time is proportional to the number of attacked pixels and input size. The max-pooling-based N_2 and dilated convolution-based N_3 SSNs require more verification time than the average-pooling and transposed convolution-based SSN N_1. The reachability times of ReLU layers (blue) dominates the total reachability time (other layers reachability times are in orange). (Color figure online)

Max-Pooling and ReLU Layers. Using max-pooling layer for down sampling not only decreases the robustness of an SSN but also causes a dramatic increase in time and memory consumption in verification. Figure 8 shows that the verification time (in seconds) of the max-pooling-based SSN N_2 grows significantly compared with the average-pooling-based SSN N_1 when increasing the number of attacked pixels $N_{attackedpixels}$ or the input size Δ_ϵ. When dealing with more number of attacked pixels or larger input size, the max-pooling layer introduces more predicate variables to overapproximate the reachable set, which causes the increase both in computation time and memory usage [33]. Similar to the max-pooling layer, the ReLU layer is also the main source of robustness degradation. Additionally, it may also dominate the reachability time of a SSN, as shown in Fig. 8c. This leads to an increase in the verification time for SSNs with many ReLU layers.

5.3   Reducing Verification Time with Relaxation

When ReLU layer analysis dominates the total verification time significantly, as in the case of MNIST SSNs shown in Fig. 8c and not in the case of M2NIST SSNs depicted in Fig. 6b-(b), we can use the relaxed ImageStar reachability methods to speed up the verification process. Table 2 presents the decrease in the verification times in percentage when applying different relaxation heuristics for ReLU layers. We note that due to the small input size and a small number of attacked pixels, we do not see any changes in the robustness value, sensitivity, and IoU compared with the non-relaxation method, i.e., the original approximate ImageStar method. However, there is a significant improvement in verification time when we apply the relaxed ImageStar reachability for non-max-pooling SSNs N_1 and N_3. More relaxation leads to a higher reduction in the verification time: up to 99% of the verification time can be reduced with 100% relaxation in the reachability of ReLU layers.

Interestingly, using relaxation for the max-pooling-based SSN N_2 decreases the verification performance, i.e., leading to higher verification time. The main reason is that the relaxed reachable sets after ReLU layers become increasingly conservative. At the max-pooling layer, a more conservative reachable set leads to more local max-point candidates that need to be determined via solving more LPs, which causes an increase in the verification time. Additionally, if a local region has more than one max-point candidate, a new predicate variable and its corresponding generator image are introduced [33]. The increase in the number of predicate variables and generator images causes the explosion in the memory

Table 2. The relaxed ImageStar reachability methods can reduce significantly the verification time (in seconds) of MNIST SSN networks except for the one containing max-pooling layers, i.e., N_2. The maximum allowable number of attacked pixels is $N_{max} = 50$ for N_1 and N_2 and $N_{max} = 20$ for N_3.

ID	RF	$\Delta_\epsilon = 0.005$				$\Delta_\epsilon = 0.01$				$\Delta_\epsilon = 0.02$			
		Rand	Area	Range	Bound	Rand	Area	Range	Bound	Rand	Area	Range	Bound
N_1	0.00	20.56	20.23	19.43	19.05	82.57	81.04	76.48	83.51	860.86	861.69	734.99	862.03
	0.25	19.5(↓ 5%)	20.7(↓ −2%)	18.8(↓ 3%)	20.7(↓ −9%)	72.2(↓ 13%)	75.8(↓ 7%)	69.5(↓ 9%)	84.4(↓ −1%)	734.1(↓ 15%)	770.2(↓ 11%)	665.0(↓ 10%)	978.1(↓ −13%)
	0.50	17.7(↓ 14%)	18.6(↓ 8%)	18.3(↓ 6%)	19.0(↓ 0%)	58.3(↓ 29%)	67.0(↓ 17%)	62.1(↓ 19%)	69.5(↓ 17%)	587.8(↓ 32%)	613.6(↓ 29%)	530.7(↓ 28%)	779.5(↓ 10%)
	0.75	17.0(↓ 17%)	17.7(↓ 13%)	16.7(↓ 14%)	16.9(↓ 11%)	47.4(↓ 43%)	49.9(↓ 38%)	51.0(↓ 33%)	53.0(↓ 37%)	347.6(↓ 60%)	389.2(↓ 55%)	361.1(↓ 51%)	439.0(↓ 49%)
	1.00	15.2(↓ 26%)	16.4(↓ 19%)	16.2(↓ 17%)	15.2(↓ 20%)	34.4(↓ 58%)	34.4(↓ 58%)	36.0(↓ 53%)	36.0(↓ 57%)	90.5(↓ 89%)	90.1(↓ 90%)	94.4(↓ 87%)	92.9(↓ 89%)
N_2	0.00	45.13	44.38	43.72	45.19	281.30	285.60	254.02	281.31	MemErr	MemErr	MemErr	MemErr
	0.25	53.1(↓ −18%)	53.5(↓ −21%)	51.8(↓ −19%)	69.9(↓ −55%)	308.0(↓ −9%)	294.7(↓ −3%)	255.6(↓ −1%)	378.1(↓ −34%)	MemErr	MemErr	MemErr	MemErr
	0.50	64.3(↓ −42%)	66.4(↓ −50%)	62.9(↓ −44%)	86.5(↓ −91%)	302.2(↓ −7%)	312.7(↓ −10%)	295.2(↓ −16%)	481.0(↓ −71%)	MemErr	MemErr	MemErr	MemErr
	0.75	72.9(↓ −62%)	75.8(↓ −71%)	72.5(↓ −66%)	93.0(↓ −106%)	306.0(↓ −9%)	309.0(↓ −8%)	344.4(↓ −36%)	448.5(↓ −59%)	MemErr	MemErr	MemErr	MemErr
	1.00	79.6(↓ −76%)	79.5(↓ −79%)	79.8(↓ −83%)	79.9(↓ −77%)	364.4(↓ −30%)	325.4(↓ −14%)	322.1(↓ −27%)	318.5(↓ −13%)	MemErr	MemErr	MemErr	MemErr
N_3	0.00	119.63	118.74	112.48	120.66	1119.16	1116.85	996.56	1116.66	17699.81	17651.30	17260.00	17780.00
	0.25	95.9(↓ 20%)	100.4(↓ 15%)	95.3(↓ 15%)	107.9(↓ 11%)	920.7(↓ 18%)	1020.7(↓ 9%)	874.9(↓ 12%)	1157.0(↓ −4%)	15474.4(↓ 13%)	17222.3(↓ 2%)	14700.0(↓ 15%)	17201.0(↓ 3%)
	0.50	72.7(↓ 39%)	77.8(↓ 35%)	72.2(↓ 36%)	78.5(↓ 35%)	648.4(↓ 42%)	759.4(↓ 32%)	644.2(↓ 35%)	797.8(↓ 29%)	11976.3(↓ 32%)	14566.7(↓ 17%)	11902.0(↓ 31%)	14729.0(↓ 17%)
	0.75	45.5(↓ 62%)	50.2(↓ 58%)	48.5(↓ 57%)	49.6(↓ 59%)	352.6(↓ 68%)	424.9(↓ 62%)	378.1(↓ 62%)	416.8(↓ 63%)	6720.0(↓ 62%)	8556.8(↓ 52%)	7217.0(↓ 58%)	7942.0(↓ 55%)
	1.00	22.0(↓ 82%)	23.0(↓ 81%)	22.9(↓ 80%)	22.3(↓ 81%)	47.6(↓ 96%)	45.7(↓ 96%)	45.7(↓ 95%)	45.2(↓ 96%)	116.1(↓ 99%)	115.7(↓ 99%)	115.4(↓ 99%)	115.2(↓ 99%)

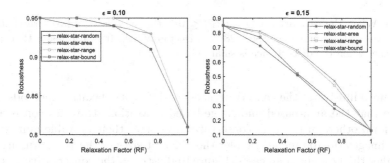

Fig. 9. The conservativeness of different relaxation heuristics. The area-based and range-based relaxation strategies outperform others in terms of conservativeness.

usage for the analysis. In the worst case, it can lead to a memory error as shown in Table 2. Therefore, it is important to have relaxation strategies for max-pooling layers, which will be investigated in our future work.

5.4 Conservativeness of Different Relaxation Heuristics

We have four relaxation heuristics that can be used in the reachability analysis of ReLU layers. The verification time improvement of these methods is quite similar, as shown in Table 2. It is interesting to see how good they are in terms of conservativeness. Unfortunately, we cannot see it clearly via verification of SSNs. Although increasing the number of attacked pixels and input size can eventually show the difference in conservativeness of these methods, it requires a more powerful computer with massive memory for verification. Therefore, to determine the best relaxation heuristic in terms of conservativeness, we evaluate image classification robustness that has been studied extensively recently, and illustrates the benefits of the relaxation method beyond SSN verification. We apply our four relaxation heuristics to verify robustness of an MNIST classification network [29] that is trained by the DiffAI robust training framework under the L_∞-norm attack, where all pixels of an input image are attacked independently by a bounded disturbance defined by ϵ^4. The robustness of the network is quantified in percentage stating how many images of 100 randomly selected images are provably robust under the attack, i.e., classified correctly.

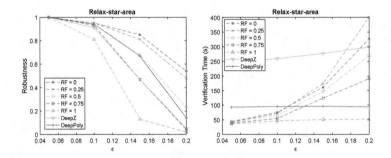

Fig. 10. When the relaxation factor (RF) ≤ 0.5, the area-based relaxed reachability is less conservative than DeepZono [28] and DeepPoly [29]. It is also faster than these approaches when the disturbance is small, i.e., $\epsilon \leq 0.11$.

Figure 9 illustrates the conservativeness of different relaxation methods. One can see that the area-based and range-based relaxation strategies consistently outperform others in terms of conservativeness since their provable numbers of robust images (in 100 images) under the different sizes of the L_∞ norm attacks are higher than others in all cases. Figure 10 illustrates the conservativeness and verification time of our area-based relaxed reachability (with different relaxation

---

4 These benchmarks were used in VNN-COMP'20.

factors (RF)) in comparison with DeepZono [28] and DeepPoly [29]. In terms of conservativeness, the area-based relaxed reachability is better than DeepZono and DeepPoly when we choose a relaxation factor $RF \leq 0.5$. When the disturbance is large, DeepZono and DeepPoly may become very conservative. For example, when the disturbance bound $\epsilon = 0.2$, the only 5 and 14 (over 100) images are proved robust by DeepZono and DeepPoly, respectively. Meanwhile, without relaxation, i.e., relaxation factor $RF = 0$, the area-based relaxed reachability can prove 54 images are robust under the attack. It can prove robustness of 48 and 23 images when the relaxation factors are 0.25 and 0.5, respectively. In terms of verification time, when the disturbance is small, i.e., $\epsilon \leq 0.11$, the area-based relaxed reachability is faster than DeepZono and DeepPoly. It is slower than DeepPoly for larger disturbance (except for the case when the relaxation factor is 1). This increase in the verification time is apparent since DeepZono and DeepPoly do not solve any LPs for constructing the overapproximate reachable set of the network while our approach does. Due to using only estimated ranges of the neurons in constructing the reachable set, DeepZono and DeepPoly are overly conservative for a large disturbance, proving only a few images are robust. This reflects the fact that more computation time for optimization is needed to prove more images robust.

6   Related Work

To enable neural networks use in safety-critical scenarios, many methods have recently been proposed to improve their robustness and temper their susceptibility to adversarial attacks. The following section surveys the landscape of these approaches in order to better contextualize our work.

SSN Robustness. SSNs are used in visual understanding systems in numerous contexts, recent works aim to improve the robustness of these models [13,20,23,25], albeit none that provide worst-case guarantees, as our approach does. For instance, recent work develops rigorous testing-based approaches to evaluate the robustness of SSNs, considering a wide range of architectures, and offering an insightful discussion about the comparative robustness of these modalities against various adversarial attacks [2]. Kamann et al. conducted an extensive evaluation of a state-of-the-art SSN using over 400,000 images and issued a series of recommendations aimed at improving robustness to common perturbations. Zhou et al. presented an automated method for evaluating robustness of SSNs within visual systems for autonomous vehicles, which leverages an additional sensor to generate ground truth labels so that an examination of the classification accuracy of an SSN can be evaluated at runtime[47]. Robust training techniques that incorporate image corruptions and architecture modalities have also been developed for SSNs [20]. Even though such works provide better understanding, potential defenses against adversarial perturbations, run-time evaluation, and comparative robustness measures, they cannot provide formal verification guarantees for SSN robustness as our work does.

Neural Network Verification and Falsification. The bulk of neural network verification approaches have been aimed at verifying input-output properties of DNNs. These methods include SMT [18,19], polyhedral [35,44], mixed integer linear programming (MILP) [9], interval arithmetic [38], zonotope [28], linearization[39], and abstract-domain [29] approaches. There have also been a number of works aimed at testing the robustness of networks with respect to bounded input perturbations such as feature-guided search, global optimization, and game theory [16,42]. One such example is the work of Dreossi et al. where the authors proposed a general definition of robustness for DNNs [8]. Their work categorizes the existing literature into approaches that consider local robustness properties [6], and those that focus on verifying the global robustness of the networks [14]. Most of the existing research in this area focuses on robustness of classification neural networks, specifically image classification. While many approaches aim at verification, methods also exist for falsification of system specifications, in which robustness properties are included [12]. However, to the best of our knowledge, no existing approaches consider verification for SSNs, as we do in this paper.

Sequence Model Verification and Robustness Analysis. Aside from classification tasks, there are several verification approaches for sequence models. Unlike SSN and classification networks, the output of sequence models such as recurrent neural networks (RNNs) depends on spatially or temporally ordered data [4,41]. While some of these efforts are similar in spirit to our work in expanding the classes of problems and models for verification, the verification tasks and approaches differ.

Scalability and Specifications. Finally, verification of DNNs is challenging, and presently the most complex networks remain inaccessible to the majority of methods. However, several recent approaches have focused on improving the efficiency of existing methods via parallelization and other techniques [3,35,40]. As verification work is only meaningful when paired with high-quality specifications, there has been significant work on the importance of semantics when defining system specifications against adversarial attacks [27], and our paper contributes to this direction through our formulation of robustness specifications and metrics for segmentation tasks.

7   Conclusion

We present the first formal approach to verify robustness of SSNs using relaxed reachability analysis. Our evaluation has analyzed the robustness and sensitivity under adversarial attacks on a set of SSNs with typical architectures. From our experiments, we show that while max-pooling and ReLU layers are useful in training highly accurate SSNs, they are also the main sources of robustness and verification performance degradation. SSNs using average-pooling for downsampling and transposed convolution for up-sampling seem to be an optimal choice for achieving high accuracy, robustness, and verification performance.

Additionally, our relaxed reachability approach can help to reduce significantly the total verification time for networks where the reachability time of ReLU layers dominates the network's reachability time, and are applicable to other networks, such as CNNs used for classification. In the future, we will investigate new relaxation heuristics for the max-pooling layer and extend this work to cope with the encoder-decoder SSN architecture where max-unpooling layers are used for up-sampling operations, instead of dilated/transposed convolution as we considered in this paper.

Acknowledgments. The material presented in this paper is based upon work supported the Defense Advanced Research Projects Agency (DARPA) through contract number FA8750-18-C-0089, the Air Force Office of Scientific Research (AFOSR) award FA9550-19-1-0288, and the National Science Foundation (NSF) through grant numbers 1910017 and 2028001. Any opinions, findings, and conclusions or recommendations expressed in this publication are those of the authors and do not necessarily reflect the views of DARPA, AFOSR or NSF.

References

1. Anderson, G., Pailoor, S., Dillig, I., Chaudhuri, S.: Optimization and abstraction: A synergistic approach for analyzing neural network robustness. In: Proceedings of the 40th ACM SIGPLAN Conference on Programming Language Design and Implementation, PLDI 2019, pp. 731–744. Association for Computing Machinery, New York (2019)
2. Arnab, A., Miksik, O., Torr, P.H.: On the robustness of semantic segmentation models to adversarial attacks. In: Proceedings of the IEEE Conference on Computer Vision and Pattern Recognition, pp. 888–897 (2018)
3. Bak, S., Tran, H.-D., Hobbs, K., Johnson, T.T.: Improved geometric path enumeration for verifying ReLU neural networks. In: Lahiri, S.K., Wang, C. (eds.) CAV 2020. LNCS, vol. 12224, pp. 66–96. Springer, Cham (2020). https://doi.org/10.1007/978-3-030-53288-8_4
4. Baluta, T., Shen, S., Shinde, S., Meel, K.S., Saxena, P.: Quantitative verification of neural networks and its security applications. CoRR arXiv:1906.10395 (2019)
5. Botoeva, E., Kouvaros, P., Kronqvist, J., Lomuscio, A., Misener, R.: Efficient verification of relu-based neural networks via dependency analysis. In: Proceedings of the AAAI Conference on Artificial Intelligence, vol. 34, no. 04, pp. 3291–3299 (2020)
6. Carlini, N., Wagner, D.: Towards evaluating the robustness of neural networks. In: 2017 IEEE Symposium on Security and Privacy (SP), pp. 39–57 (2017)
7. Dathathri, S., et al.: Enabling certification of verification-agnostic networks via memory-efficient semidefinite programming (2020)
8. Dreossi, T., et al.: VERIFAI: a toolkit for the formal design and analysis of artificial intelligence-based systems. In: Dillig, I., Tasiran, S. (eds.) CAV 2019. LNCS, vol. 11561, pp. 432–442. Springer, Cham (2019). https://doi.org/10.1007/978-3-030-25540-4_25
9. Dutta, S., Jha, S., Sanakaranarayanan, S., Tiwari, A.: Output range analysis for deep neural networks. arXiv preprint arXiv:1709.09130 (2017)

10. Ehlers, R.: Formal verification of piece-wise linear feed-forward neural networks. In: D'Souza, D., Narayan Kumar, K. (eds.) ATVA 2017. LNCS, vol. 10482, pp. 269–286. Springer, Cham (2017). https://doi.org/10.1007/978-3-319-68167-2_19

11. Fazlyab, M., Morari, M., Pappas, G.J.: Safety verification and robustness analysis of neural networks via quadratic constraints and semidefinite programming. IEEE Trans. Autom. Control 1 (2020)

12. Fremont, D.J., Chiu, J., Margineantu, D.D., Osipychev, D., Seshia, S.A.: Formal analysis and redesign of a neural network-based aircraft taxiing system with VerifAI. In: 32nd International Conference on Computer Aided Verification (CAV) (July 2020)

13. Full, P.M., Isensee, F., Jäger, P.F., Maier-Hein, K.: Studying robustness of semantic segmentation under domain shift in cardiac MRI (2020)

14. Gopinath, D., Katz, G., Păsăreanu, C.S., Barrett, C.: DeepSafe: a data-driven approach for assessing robustness of neural networks. In: Lahiri, S.K., Wang, C. (eds.) ATVA 2018. LNCS, vol. 11138, pp. 3–19. Springer, Cham (2018). https://doi.org/10.1007/978-3-030-01090-4_1

15. Huang, C., Fan, J., Li, W., Chen, X., Zhu, Q.: Reachnn: reachability analysis of neural-network controlled systems. ACM Trans. Embed. Comput. Syst. (TECS) **18**(5s), 1–22 (2019)

16. Huang, X., Kwiatkowska, M., Wang, S., Wu, M.: Safety verification of deep neural networks. In: Majumdar, R., Kunčak, V. (eds.) CAV 2017. LNCS, vol. 10426, pp. 3–29. Springer, Cham (2017). https://doi.org/10.1007/978-3-319-63387-9_1

17. Ivanov, R., Weimer, J., Alur, R., Pappas, G.J., Lee, I.: Verisig: verifying safety properties of hybrid systems with neural network controllers. In: Hybrid Systems: Computation and Control (HSCC) (2019)

18. Katz, G., Barrett, C., Dill, D.L., Julian, K., Kochenderfer, M.J.: Reluplex: an efficient SMT solver for verifying deep neural networks. In: Majumdar, R., Kunčak, V. (eds.) CAV 2017. LNCS, vol. 10426, pp. 97–117. Springer, Cham (2017). https://doi.org/10.1007/978-3-319-63387-9_5

19. Katz, G., et al.: The marabou framework for verification and analysis of deep neural networks. In: Dillig, I., Tasiran, S. (eds.) CAV 2019. LNCS, vol. 11561, pp. 443–452. Springer, Cham (2019). https://doi.org/10.1007/978-3-030-25540-4_26

20. Klingner, M., Bar, A., Fingscheidt, T.: Improved noise and attack robustness for semantic segmentation by using multi-task training with self-supervised depth estimation. In: Proceedings of the IEEE/CVF Conference on Computer Vision and Pattern Recognition (CVPR) Workshops (June 2020)

21. LeCun, Y.: The mnist database of handwritten digits. http://yann.lecun.com/exdb/mnist/ (1998)

22. Liu, C., Arnon, T., Lazarus, C., Barrett, C., Kochenderfer, M.J.: Algorithms for verifying deep neural networks. arXiv preprint arXiv:1903.06758 (2019)

23. Minaee, S., Boykov, Y., Porikli, F., Plaza, A., Kehtarnavaz, N., Terzopoulos, D.: Image segmentation using deep learning: A survey (2020)

24. Mohapatra, J., Weng, T.W., Chen, P.Y., Liu, S., Daniel, L.: Towards verifying robustness of neural networks against a family of semantic perturbations. In: Proceedings of the IEEE/CVF Conference on Computer Vision and Pattern Recognition (CVPR) (June 2020)

25. Oliveira, G., Bollen, C., Burgard, W., Brox, T.: Efficient and robust deep networks for semantic segmentation. Int. J. Rob. Res. **37**, 027836491771054 (2017)

26. Ruan, W., Wu, M., Sun, Y., Huang, X., Kroening, D., Kwiatkowska, M.: Global robustness evaluation of deep neural networks with provable guarantees for the l_0 norm. arXiv preprint arXiv:1804.05805 (2018)

27. Seshia, S.A., et al.: Formal specification for deep neural networks. In: Lahiri, S.K., Wang, C. (eds.) ATVA 2018. LNCS, vol. 11138, pp. 20–34. Springer, Cham (2018). https://doi.org/10.1007/978-3-030-01090-4_2

28. Singh, G., Gehr, T., Mirman, M., Püschel, M., Vechev, M.: Fast and effective robustness certification. In: Advances in Neural Information Processing Systems, pp. 10825–10836 (2018)

29. Singh, G., Gehr, T., Püschel, M., Vechev, M.: An abstract domain for certifying neural networks. Proc. ACM Program. Lang. vol. 3(POPL), p. 41 (2019)

30. Szeliski, R.: Computer Vision: Algorithms and Applications. 2nd edn. Springer, New York (2021) https://doi.org/10.1007/978-1-84882-935-0

31. Thoma, M.: A survey of semantic segmentation. arXiv preprint arXiv:1602.06541 (2016)

32. Tjeng, V., Xiao, K.Y., Tedrake, R.: Evaluating robustness of neural networks with mixed integer programming. In: International Conference on Learning Representations (2019)

33. Tran, H.-D., Bak, S., Xiang, W., Johnson, T.T.: Verification of deep convolutional neural networks using ImageStars. In: Lahiri, S.K., Wang, C. (eds.) CAV 2020. LNCS, vol. 12224, pp. 18–42. Springer, Cham (2020). https://doi.org/10.1007/978-3-030-53288-8_2

34. Tran, H.D., Cei, F., Lopez, D.M., Johnson, T.T., Koutsoukos, X.: Safety verification of cyber-physical systems with reinforcement learning control. In: ACM SIGBED International Conference on Embedded Software (EMSOFT 2019), ACM (October 2019)

35. Tran, H.D., et al.: Parallelizable reachability analysis algorithms for feed-forward neural networks. In: 7th International Conference on Formal Methods in Software Engineering (FormaliSE2019), Montreal, Canada (2019)

36. Tran, H.-D., et al.: Star-based reachability analysis of deep neural networks. In: ter Beek, M.H., McIver, A., Oliveira, J.N. (eds.) FM 2019. LNCS, vol. 11800, pp. 670–686. Springer, Cham (2019). https://doi.org/10.1007/978-3-030-30942-8_39

37. Tran, H.D., Xiang, W., Johnson, T.T.: Verification approaches for learning-enabled autonomous cyber-physical systems. IEEE Design & Test (2020)

38. Wang, S., Pei, K., Whitehouse, J., Yang, J., Jana, S.: Efficient formal safety analysis of neural networks. In: Advances in Neural Information Processing Systems, pp. 6369–6379 (2018)

39. Weng, T.W., et al.: Towards fast computation of certified robustness for relu networks. arXiv preprint arXiv:1804.09699 (2018)

40. Wu, H., et al.: Parallelization techniques for verifying neural networks. In: 2020 Formal Methods in Computer Aided Design (FMCAD), pp. 128–137 (2020)

41. Wu, J., Li, X., Ao, X., Meng, Y., Wu, F., Li, J.: Improving robustness and generality of nlp models using disentangled representations (2020)

42. Wu, M., Wicker, M., Ruan, W., Huang, X., Kwiatkowska, M.: A game-based approximate verification of deep neural networks with provable guarantees. Theor. Comput. Sci. **807**, 298–329 (2020)

43. Xiang, W., et al.: Verification for machine learning, autonomy, and neural networks survey. arXiv preprint arXiv:1810.01989 (2018)

44. Xiang, W., Tran, H.D., Johnson, T.T.: Reachable set computation and safety verification for neural networks with relu activations. arXiv preprint arXiv:1712.08163 (2017)

45. Yuan, X., He, P., Zhu, Q., Li, X.: Adversarial examples: attacks and defenses for deep learning. IEEE Trans. Neural Netw. Learn. Syst. **30**(9), 2805–2824 (2019)

46. Zhang, H., Weng, T.W., Chen, P.Y., Hsieh, C.J., Daniel, L.: Efficient neural network robustness certification with general activation functions. In: Bengio, S., Wallach, H., Larochelle, H., Grauman, K., Cesa-Bianchi, N., Garnett, R. (eds.) Advances in Neural Information Processing Systems. vol. 31, pp. 4939–4948. Curran Associates, Inc. (2018)
47. Zhou, W., Berrio, J., Worrall, S., Nebot, E.M.: Automated evaluation of semantic segmentation robustness for autonomous driving. IEEE Trans. Intell. Transp. Syst. **21**, 1951–1963 (2020)

PEREGRiNN: Penalized-Relaxation Greedy Neural Network Verifier

Haitham Khedr[✉], James Ferlez, and Yasser Shoukry

University of California, Irvine, USA
{hkhedr,jferlez,yshoukry}@uci.edu

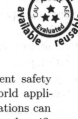

Abstract. Neural Networks (NNs) have increasingly apparent safety implications commensurate with their proliferation in real-world applications: both unanticipated as well as adversarial misclassifications can result in fatal outcomes. As a consequence, techniques of formal verification have been recognized as crucial to the design and deployment of safe NNs. In this paper, we introduce a new approach to formally verify the most commonly considered safety specifications for ReLU NNs – i.e. polytopic specifications on the input and output of the network. Like some other approaches, ours uses a relaxed convex program to mitigate the combinatorial complexity of the problem. However, unique in our approach is the way we use a convex solver not only as a linear feasibility checker, but also as a means of penalizing the amount of relaxation allowed in solutions. In particular, we encode each ReLU by means of the usual linear constraints, and combine this with a convex objective function that penalizes the discrepancy between the output of each neuron and its relaxation. This convex function is further structured to force the largest relaxations to appear closest to the input layer; this provides the further benefit that the most "problematic" neurons are conditioned as early as possible, when conditioning layer by layer. This paradigm can be leveraged to create a verification algorithm that is not only faster in general than competing approaches, but is also able to verify considerably more safety properties; we evaluated PEREGRiNN on a standard MNIST robustness verification suite to substantiate these claims.

Keywords: Machine learning/AI · Decision procedures and solvers

1 Introduction

Neural Networks have become an increasingly central component of modern machine learning systems, including those that are used in safety-critical cyber-physical systems such as autonomous vehicles. The rate of this adoption has exceeded the ability to reliably verify the safe and correct functioning of these components, especially when they are integrated with other components such as

This work was sponsored by the NSF awards #CNS-2002405 and #CNS-2013824.

A. Silva and K. R. M. Leino (Eds.) CAV 2021, LNCS 12759, pp. 287–300, 2021.
https://doi.org/10.1007/978-3-030-81685-8_13

controllers. Thus, there is an increasing need to verify that NNs reliably produce safe outputs, especially subject to malicious adversarial inputs [16,20,27,28].

In this paper, we propose PEREGRiNN, an algorithm for efficiently and formally verifying the input/output behavior of ReLU NNs. In this context, PEREGRiNN falls into the broad category of sound and complete *search and optimization* NN verifiers [22]. The *search* aspect of PEREGRiNN involves iterating over different combinations of neuron activation patterns to verify that each is compatible with the specified safety constraints (on the input and output of the network). Like other algorithms in this category, PEREGRiNN combines this search with *optimization* techniques to make inferences about the feasibility of full-network activation patterns on the basis of activation patterns of only a subset of neurons. The optimization in question reformulates the original NN feasibility problem into a relaxed convex feasibility problem to allow sound inferences: i.e. if the convex relaxation is infeasible, then the original NN problem may soundly be concluded to be infeasible. In this relaxed feasibility problem, the output of each individual neuron is assigned a relaxation variable that is decoupled from the actual output of that neuron. PEREGRiNN also uses a type of reachability analysis (symbolic interval analysis) both to enhance the optimization-based inference described above and as a source of additional sound inference itself. For this reason, PEREGRiNN's search procedure searches neurons in a layer-by-layer fashion, preferring to fix the phases of neurons closest to the input layer first.

In contrast to other search and optimization algorithms, however, PEREGRiNN *augments* each convex feasibility query with a (convex) penalty function in order to obtain better guidance on which activation patterns to search next. In particular, we note that the amount of relaxation needed on a neuron can be regarded as a *quasi-measure* of how close the convex solver came to operating the associated neuron in a valid regime – i.e. at a valid evaluation of that neuron on a particular input. In this sense, the amount of relaxation in aggregate can be regarded as a quasi-measure of how close the solver came to finding a valid evaluation of the network as a whole. Inversely, the largest distance between a relaxation variable and its neuron's closest ReLU constraint intuitively corresponds in some sense to how "problematic" that neuron is with regard to obtaining such a valid evaluation. These distances we refer to as the *"slacks"* for each neuron. Thus, PEREGRiNN may be regarded as *greedily* minimizing a *slack-based penalty*.

Finally, we evaluated the performance of PEREGRiNN by using it to verify the adversarial robustness of networks trained on the MNIST [21] dataset. Our experiments show that PEREGRiNN is on average 1.27× faster than Neurify [31], 1.24× faster than Venus [6], 1.15× faster than nnenum [4], and 1.65× faster than Marabou [19]. It also proves 27%, 19%, 10%, and 51% more properties than the other solvers, respectively. PEREGRiNN's unique convex penalty augmentations are also considered in ablation experiments to validate their benefits.

Related Work. Since PEREGRiNN is a sound and complete verification algorithm, we restrict our comparison to other sound and complete algorithms. NN verifiers can be grouped into roughly three categories: (i) SMT-based methods, which encode the problem into a Satisfiability Modulo Theory problem [11,18,19]; (ii) MILP-based solvers, which directly encode the verification

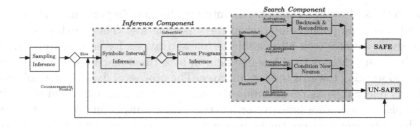

Fig. 1. Block diagram of the PEREGRiNN algorithm

problem as a Mixed Integer Linear Program [3,5–8,14,23,29]; (iii) Reachability based methods, which perform layer-by-layer reachability analysis to compute the reachable set [4,13,15,17,30,32,34,35]; and (iv) convex relaxations methods [10,31,33]. In general, (i), (ii) and (iii) suffer from poor scalability. On the other hand, convex relaxation methods depend heavily on pruning the search space of indeterminate neuron activations; thus, they generally depend on obtaining good approximate bounds for each of the neurons in order to reduce the search space (the exact bounds are computationally intensive to compute [9]). These methods are most similar to PEREGRiNN: for example, [7,25,32] recursively refine the problem using input splitting, and [31] does so via neuron splitting. Other search and optimization methods include: Planet [11], which combines a relaxed convex optimization problem with a SAT solver to search over neurons' phases; and Marabou [19], which uses a modified simplex algorithm.

2 Problem Formulation

In this paper, we will consider Rectified Linear Unit (ReLU) NNs. An n-layer ReLU network, is a composition of n ReLU layer functions: i.e. $\mathcal{NN} = f_n \circ f_{n-1} \circ \cdots \circ f_1$ where the ith ReLU layer function is defined as $f_i : y \in \mathbb{R}^{k_{i-1}} \mapsto \max\{W_i y + b_i, 0\} \in \mathbb{R}^{k_i}$. We refer to f_1 as the *input layer*. Finally, to refer to individual neurons, we use the notation $(z)_j$ to indicate the jth element of z.

Verification Problem. Let $\mathcal{NN}$ be an n-layer NN as defined above. Furthermore, let $P_{y_0} \subset \mathbb{R}^{k_0}$ be a convex polytope in the input space of $\mathcal{NN}$, and let $P_{y_n} \subset \mathbb{R}^{k_n}$ be a convex polytope in the output space of $\mathcal{NN}$. Finally, let $h_\ell : \mathbb{R}^{k_0} \times \mathbb{R}^{k_n} \to \mathbb{R}, \ell = 1, \ldots, m$ be convex functions defining joint input/output constraints on $\mathcal{NN}$. Then the verification problem is to decide whether

$$\left\{ x \in \mathbb{R}^{k_0} \mid x \in P_{y_0} \wedge \mathcal{NN}(x) \in P_{y_n} \wedge \left(\bigwedge_{\ell=1}^{m} h_\ell(x, \mathcal{NN}(x)) \leq 0 \right) \right\} = \emptyset. \quad (1)$$

3 PEREGRiNN Overview

The general structure of PEREGRiNN is depicted in Fig. 1. Like other search and optimization based NN verifiers it has two main components: a *search component* and an *inference component*, and PEREGRiNN iterates back and forth between these these two components until termination. In particular, the search and inference components interact in the following way. The search component successively iterates over all possible on/off activations for each neuron; this is done by fixing these activations one neuron at a time, starting from the input layer and working towards the output layer. The process of fixing a neuron's activation is referred to as *conditioning its phase*: each neuron can be in either its active phase (operating linearly) or inactive phase (outputting zero). Thus, the search component provides the inference component a subset of neurons, each of which has been conditioned; the inference component then attempts to soundly reason about whether the remaining, unconditioned neurons can be operated in such a way as to violate the safety constraint. If the inference component soundly concludes safety for all possible activations of the remaining unconditioned neurons, then the search component backtracks, oppositely reconditioning one of the neurons that was already conditioned. Otherwise, if a sound safe conclusion is not made, then the search component uses information from the inference component to decide on a new neuron to condition, and the process repeats. The algorithm terminates if either a counterexample to safety is found, or else all possible neuron activations are considered without finding such a counterexample.

The convex program inference block is at the heart of the inference component and PEREGRiNN itself. In this block, PEREGRiNN, like other search and optimization solvers, uses a relaxed linear feasibility program where the output of each individual neuron is assigned a relaxation variable that is decoupled from the actual output of that neuron. In the notation of Sect. 2, such a linear feasibility program can be written as follows, where the vector variables $y_i, i \neq 0$ are the relaxation variables.

$$\begin{cases} y_i \geq 0, \ y_i \geq W_i y_{i-1} + b_i & \forall i = 1, \ldots, n \\ y_0 \in P_{y_0}, \ y_n \in P_{y_n}^{\mathsf{c}}, \ \overset{m}{\underset{\ell=1}{\wedge}} h_\ell(y_0, y_n) \leq 0 \end{cases} \quad (2)$$

Importantly, if (2) is infeasible, then the original NN problem in (1) may be soundly concluded to be infeasible as well – and hence, safe. However, as described above, the primary function of the convex feasibility program is to use a set of conditioned neurons supplied by the search component in order to soundly reason about the remaining neurons. To do this, the conditioned neurons supplied by the search component are incorporated into the feasibility program (2) as *equality* constraints in the following way:

$$\text{Neuron } (y_i)_j \text{ ON:} \quad (y_i)_j = (W_i y_{i-1} + b_i)_j \wedge (y_i)_j \geq 0 \quad (3)$$
$$\text{Neuron } (y_i)_j \text{ OFF:} \quad (y_i)_j = 0 \wedge (W_i y_{i-1} + b_i)_j \leq 0. \quad (4)$$

Inferences created by the symbolic interval inference block using Symbolic Interval Analysis [32] are also incorporated using equality constraints like (3) and (4).

Of the remaining blocks, the "Backtracking & Reconditioning" block is essentially described above. The "Condition New Neuron" and "Sampling Inference" blocks have features unique to PEREGRiNN that are described in Sect. 4; the former implements a novel neuron prioritization, and the latter is a unique approach to quickly obtaining initial safety counterexamples.

4 PEREGRiNN Enhancements

4.1 Sum-of-Slacks Penalty

The core enhancement in PEREGRiNN is the inclusion of a specific objective function in the convex program used by the inference component. As per the discussion above, this objective function is interpreted as a *penalty* on how far away a particular solution is from a valid input/output response of the network (and activation pattern on all hidden neurons). Specifically, this penalty function penalizes the sum of all of the "slack" variables for the entire network, where each neuron's slack variable is defined as $s_i \triangleq y_i - (W_i \cdot y_{i-1} + b_i)$. That is the distance between a relaxation variable y_i and the linear response of its associated neuron. During each feasibility/inference call, this has the obvious effect of incentivizing the convex solver to choose an actual input/output response of the network.

In addition, this penalty is effectively the L_1-norm of the *vector* of all the slack variables, since the slack variables are non-negative. The L_1-norm of a vector, used as a penalty function, is well known to effectively encourage *sparsity* on the resulting optimal solution. Thus, the sum-of-slacks effectively incentivizes the convex solver to leave as *few* neurons as possible indeterminate in the solution. That is a sum-of-slacks penalty effectively encourages the convex solver to fix the phases of as many neurons as possible.

4.2 Max-Slack Conditioning Priority

As noted above, the search component of PEREGRiNN operates layer-wise from input layer to output layer in order to leverage Symbolic Interval Analysis for additional inference. Hence, the search component always chooses the next neuron to be searched (i.e. conditioned) from among those as-yet-unconditioned neurons that are closest to the input layer. It further makes sense to only consider conditioning neurons that the convex solver was unable to operate at valid inputs/output. However, the convex solver typically returns several neurons to choose from with this property, and it is necessary to choose which of them to search next. Given the interpretation of a neuron's "slack" variable as a measure of how "problematic" that neuron was for the solver to obtain a valid evaluation of the network, PEREGRiNN's search component chooses the next neuron to condition based on slack-order ranking of those neurons that are not being operated at valid input/output points. This "max-slack" heuristic choice is unique to PEREGRiNN; compare to the output gradient heuristic employed in [31].

4.3 Layer-wise-Weighted Penalty

PEREGRiNN takes the "max-slack" neuron search priority one step further, though. Using techniques similar to those in [26], it is possible to show that there exists weights $q_1, \ldots, q_n$ such that solving (2) with the penalty

$$\min_{y_0,..,y_n} \sum_{i=0}^{n} \sum_{j=1}^{k_i} q_i s_{ij} \tag{5}$$

will result in a solution that is guaranteed to concentrate the most total slack in the earliest (unconditioned) layer. Thus, by using the layer-wise weighted sum-of-slacks penalty in (5), PEREGRiNN is uniquely able to force the (unconditioned) layer closest to the input layer to have the *largest* total slack among all the layers. As a consequence, PEREGRiNN effectively concentrates the most "problematic" neurons in the layer where the next conditioning choice will be made. This scheme makes it much more likely that the neuron with the highest slack among *all* of the neurons will be among the next neurons considered for conditioning – in effect, often guiding the search component to condition on the most problematic neuron in the whole network (although this is not guaranteed).

As noted above, SMC [26] can be used to obtain layer-wise weights that guarantee concentration of slack in the earliest (shallowest) layer. However, these weights are often very large, since they depend on bounding the slack variables (most readily by over-approximation); the effect of this is possible computational instability in the convex program. Thus, as an *implementation* matter, we instead select these weights using a heuristic scheme characterized by two real-valued hyperparameters, λ_0 and γ. In particular, the weight of the ith layer, q_i, is selected as $q_i = \lambda_0 \cdot \gamma^i$. In our experiments, we found the values $\lambda_0 = 10^{-7}$ and $\gamma = 10^3$ to effectively achieve the maximum slack concentration in the earliest layers.

4.4 Initial Counterexample Search by Sampling

Finally, PEREGRiNN extends a simple idea first introduced in [32] to rapidly identify counterexamples by means of sampling. The basic idea is to sample within a known region of the input to the NN (or the input to some deeper layer), and evaluate the NN (sub-NN) exactly on those samples in order to rapidly identify a counterexample; this approach help identify un-safe networks/properties early on. However, whereas [32] samples from within hyper-rectangle sets derived by symbolic interval analysis, PEREGRiNN uses the Volesti [12] Python library to uniformly sample points within the *polytopic* input constraint set, P_{y_0}, and thus applies to be more general input constraint sets in (1).

5 Experiments

We evaluated the performance and effectiveness of PEREGRiNN at verifying the adversarial robustness of NNs trained to recognize digits using the standard MNIST dataset. This verification problem fits into the general NN verification problem described in Sect. 2, and it is described subsequently in detail. In this context, we evaluated PEREGRiNN with two objectives described as follows.

Table 1. Architecture of the NN models used in the experiments

Models	# ReLUs	Architecture
MNIST_FC1	512	$< 784, 256, 256, 10 >$
MNIST_FC2	1024	$< 784, 256, 256, 256, 256, 10 >$
MNIST_FC3	1536	$< 784, 256, 256, 256, 256, 256, 256, 10 >$

1. We conducted ablation experiments for all of PEREGRiNN's novel features as described in Sect. 4. In particular, we compared the performance of a full implementation of PEREGRiNN – i.e. *exactly* as described in Sect. 4 – with implementations that are otherwise the same except for changing one and only one of the following: the penalty function used in the convex program inference block; the neuron prioritization used by the search component.
2. We compared PEREGRiNN against other state-of-the-art NN verifiers, both in terms of the time required to verify individual networks and properties and in terms of the number of properties proved with a common, fixed timeout.

Implementation. We implemented PEREGRiNN in Python, and used an off-the-shelf Gurobi 9.1 [1] convex optimizer for solving linear programs; the Volesti [12] Python interface was used to sample from the input polytope for the sampling inference block. For the other NN verifiers, we used publicly available implementations that were published by their creators (citations are included below). Each instance of of any verifier was run within its own single-core Virtual Box VM with 30 GB of memory; no more than 4 VMs were run concurrently on a host machine with 48 hyperthreaded cores and 256 GB of memory.

5.1   Adversarial Robustness Verification Task

Subsequent experiments used the testbench we describe in this section; it is largely identical to the PAT-FCN test in the VNN-COMP 2020 competition [2].

Neural Networks. We used three ReLU NNs to recognize digits using the standard MNIST training database; these NNs are exactly as in the PAT-FCN portion of [2]. The sizes of these fully-connected networks are described in Table 1. Each entry in the "Architecture" column of Table 1 is the number of number of neurons in a layer, from input layer on the left to output layer on the right.

Verification Properties. We created a number of NN verification tasks based on proving whether the above described networks were robust against max-norm perturbations of their inputs. In particular, each verification task involves proving whether a particular input image, x', always results in the same classification when it is subjected to a max-norm perturbation of at most some fixed size, $\epsilon > 0$. Thus, each such verification problem is parameterized by both the specified input image, x', and the maximum amount of perturbation, ϵ.

Formally, let x' be a given image in category $t \in \{1, \ldots, M\}$, and let $\epsilon > 0$ be a specified maximum amount of max-norm perturbation of x'. Then we say that a NN with M classification outputs, $\mathcal{NN}$, is robust if for each classification category $m \in \{1, \ldots, M\} \setminus \{t\}$ the set of inputs yielding classification of x' as m

$$\phi_m \triangleq \{x \mid x \in \mathbb{R}^{k_0}, \|x - x'\|_\infty \le \epsilon, z \in \mathbb{R}^{k_n}, \max_{i=1,\ldots,n} \mathcal{NN}(x)_i = \mathcal{NN}(x)_m\} \quad (6)$$

is empty. Note that each instance of (6) is compatible with the problem in (1).

Adversarial Robustness Verifier Testbench. Our verification testbench was then constructed by selecting 50 test images from the MNIST test dataset; this set of test images includes the 25 used in the PAT-FCN portion of [2]. Each test instance was then a combination of one of those images, one of the networks from Table 1 and one the following two max-norm perturbations, $\epsilon = 0.02$ or $\epsilon = 0.05$; these perturbations are same ones used in PAT-FCN [2]. Thus, each verification test in our testbench can be identified by one of 300 tuples of the form: $(net, image, perturb.) \in \mathcal{TB} \triangleq \{\texttt{FC1}, \texttt{FC2}, \texttt{FC2}\} \times \{1, \ldots, 50\} \times \{0.02, 0.05\}$.

5.2 Ablation Experiments

In this series of experiments we evaluated the contribution that each of the primary PEREGRiNN enhancements made to its overall performance. This was done by comparing the full PEREGRiNN algorithm – as described in Sect. 4 – with altered versions that replace exactly one of those enhancements at a time. *Note:* removing core features of PEREGRiNN often resulted in much longer run times, so the experiments in this section use a testbench $\mathcal{TB}' \subset \mathcal{TB}$ that excludes all tests with one of the larger networks FC2 or FC3 *and* $\epsilon = 0.05$.

Penalty Function Ablation. Our first ablation experiment evaluated the contribution of PEREGRiNN's unique penalty function features; see Sect. 4.1 and Sect. 4.3. In particular, we ran different variants of PEREGRiNN with the following penalty functions used inside the convex program inference block:

1. *"Weighted sum of slacks"*: PEREGRiNN's own weighted sum of slacks penalty;
2. *"Sum of slacks"*: A sum-of-slacks penalty with equal weighting on all layers;
3. *"Feasibility"*: A feasibility-only convex program such as the one used in other tools, e.g. [31] (i.e. simply using a constant penalty function of 1);
4. *"Inverted weighted sum of slacks"*: PEREGRiNN's own weighted sum of slacks penalty, except with the layer-wise weights applied in reverse order to force slack towards deeper layers rather than shallower ones (see also Sect. 4.3).

Figure 2a shows a cactus plot of the number of proved cases vs. the timeout permitted to the algorithm: i.e. to prove at least a specified number of the test cases, each algorithm must have its timeout set at to the value of its curve in

Fig. 2a. Figure 2b shows a histogram of the number of times each of the algorithm variants needed to call the convex solver in order to terminate; this quantifies each algorithm's cost in a well-known unit of computation, also the single most computationally costly part of PEREGRiNN. Figure 2b plots the number of convex solver calls required for evenly spaced bins of convex solver calls.

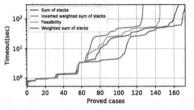   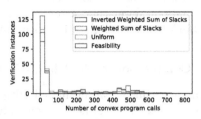

(a) Cactus plot; proved cases vs. timeout   (b) Histogram; number convex calls used

Fig. 2. Performance of PEREGRiNN variants with different objective functions

Conclusions: Figure 2a demonstrates that PEREGRiNN's weighted sum of slacks has a clear benefit over both a uniformly weighted sum-of-slacks penalty and a plain feasibility convex program. For timeouts of longer than ≈ 1.2 seconds, PEREGRiNN overtakes the other two in terms of number of properties proved; even the uniform sum-of-slacks penalty considerably outperforms the feasibility convex program at similar timeouts. Note that _reversing_ the layer-wise weights of PEREGRiNN's penalty function incurs a _performance hit_, especially for timeouts > 1.2 s. This suggests that driving slacks toward shallower layers, where the next neuron is conditioned, is the correct heuristic to apply. Figure 2b also shows that going from feasibility to sum-of-slacks to weighted sum-of-slacks significantly reduces the number of test cases that require between 425 and 525 calls to the convex solver. This order of comparison shows a concomitant net influx of tests into the lowest bin of < 25 convex calls; PEREGRiNN has the most test cases in this category, with ≈ 130 test cases proved in < 25 convex solver calls.

Neuron Conditioning Priority Ablation. In the second ablation experiment, we evaluated the contribution of PEREGRiNN's maximum-slack neuron conditioning priority (see Sect. 4.2). To that end, we ran variants of PERE-GRiNN with three different neuron conditioning priorities for the search component:

1. _"Maximum slack"_: PEREGRiNN's max-slack neuron conditioning priority;
2. _"Minimum slack"_: This variant conditions the neuron with the smallest slack;
3. _"Random choice"_: This variant conditions on a random indeterminate neuron.

The performance of these algorithm variants is shown in Fig. 3a and Fig. 3b. As in the previous ablation experiment, Fig. 3a shows a cactus plot of the number of proved cases vs. the timeout, and Fig. 3b shows a histogram of the number of calls to the convex solver required under each of the conditioning priorities.

Conclusions: Figure 3a shows that PEREGRiNN's max-slack neuron priority allows it to prove slightly more properties than either a random neuron choice priority or the minimum-slack priority. The maximum slack priority also required the fewest total convex calls across all instances: it used 178 fewer than minimum slack and 686 fewer than a random choice. Thus, we conclude PEREGRiNN's max-slack heuristic slightly improves performance on this testbench.

5.3 Comparison with Other NN Verifiers

In this experiment, we evaluated PEREGRiNN with respect to a number of state-of-the-art NN verifiers on our adversarial robustness testbench, $\mathcal{TB}$. In particular, we ran the following tools on $\mathcal{TB}$: Venus [6]; Marabou [19]; Neurify [31]; and nnenum [4]. Venus was run with st_ratio=0.4, depth_power=4, offline_deps = True, online_deps = True, and ideal_cuts = True; Marabou and Neurify were used with default parameters but THREADS = 1; and nnenum had ADVERSARIAL_SEARCH turned off. Each algorithm had its own one-core VM.

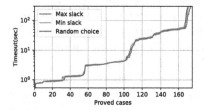
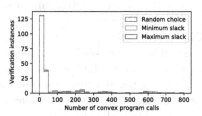

(a) Cactus plot; proved cases vs. timeout   (b) Histogram; number convex calls used

Fig. 3. Performance of PEREGRiNN variants with different conditioning priorities

Figure 4 contains a cactus plot showing the results for each of these algorithms, including PEREGRiNN. For a given number of test cases to be proved, Fig. 4 depicts the corresponding timeout required for each of the algorithm to prove that many cases. Of all the algorithms, PEREGRiNN was able to prove the most properties within the timeout limit of 600 s: PEREGRiNN was able to prove 190 properties; it was followed by nnenum, which proved 172; Venus, which proved 159; Neurify, which proved 149; and Marabou, which proved 125. Marabou consistently performed the worst, proving fewer cases than any other algorithm at every timeout. By contrast, Neurify was able to prove significantly more test cases than any other algorithm for extremely short timeouts, but it failed to prove more than 150 out of 300 test cases across the whole experiment. nnenum performed worse than Neurify on the way to proving 150 test cases, but it fared significantly better than either PEREGRiNN or Venus, which had more or less similar performance below this threshold. However, after ≈150 test cases,

PEREGRiNN significantly outperformed all other algorithms: as the timeout was increased, PEREGRiNN proved additional properties at a rate significantly outpacing its closest competitor in this regime, nnenum. We further note that all algorithms proved a mixture of SAT and UNSAT properties.

This data, taken as a whole, suggests that PEREGRiNN suffers from a worse "best-case" performance than several other algorithms, especially nnenum and Neurify. However, PEREGRiNN's performance seems to be much more consistent across different test cases. This allows it to prove more properties in aggregate at the expense of being slower on a smaller subset of them. This further suggests that PEREGRiNN is significantly less sensitive to peculiarities of particular test cases on the $\mathscr{TB}$ testbench. This will likely be a considerable advantage, on average, when faced with verifying unknown networks and properties of this type.

6 Discussion: Analogy to SAT Solvers

It is possible to draw a loose analogy between SAT solvers and search-and-optimization NN verifiers such as PEREGRiNN. Indeed, since each neuron has two phases, the operational phase of each neuron can be captured by a binary variable; then any valuation of *all* these variables can be interpreted as SAT or UNSAT based on the Input/Output properties to be verified on the network (subject to that conditioning). Thus, the neuron conditioning step in PERE-GRiNN is analogous to variable splitting in a SAT solver, and the *backtrack and re-condition* block (see Fig. 1) functions analogously to backtracking. In this analogy, infeasibility of the convex program and symbolic interval analysis function roughly like unit resolution in a SAT solver: they soundly reason about the overall property before all neurons have been conditioned (i.e. variables split).

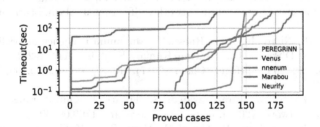

Fig. 4. Cactus plot of various solvers on 300-case testbench, $\mathscr{TB}$

However, the main contribution of PEREGRiNN is a heuristic for deciding which neuron to condition next: it is thus analogous to a heuristic for choosing the next variable to split in a SAT solver. Specifically, PEREGRiNN's heuristic provides a numerical ranking of the as-yet-unconditioned neurons, and therefore has a functional similarity to variable-ranking heuristics in SAT solvers (e.g. VSIDS [24]). On the other hand, PEREGRiNN's neuron ranking comes directly from the output of the convex solver, which we argued reveals some information about the underlying verification problem – this has no direct SAT-solver analog.

7 Conclusion

In this paper, we introduced PEREGRiNN, a new tool for formally verifying input/output properties for ReLU NNs. PEREGRiNN compares favorably with other state-of-the-art NN verifiers, thanks to a number of unique algorithmic features. The benefits of these features were established with ablation experiments.

References

1. Gurobi optimizer 9.1. http://www.gurobi.com
2. International Verification of Neural Networks Competition 2020 (VNN-COMP 2020). https://sites.google.com/view/vnn20
3. Anderson, R., Huchette, J., Ma, W., Tjandraatmadja, C., Vielma, J.P.: Strong mixed-integer programming formulations for trained neural networks. Math. Program. **183**(1), 3–39 (2020). https://doi.org/10.1007/s10107-020-01474-5
4. Bak, S., Tran, H.-D., Hobbs, K., Johnson, T.T.: Improved geometric path enumeration for verifying ReLU neural networks. In: Lahiri, S.K., Wang, C. (eds.) CAV 2020. LNCS, vol. 12224, pp. 66–96. Springer, Cham (2020). https://doi.org/10.1007/978-3-030-53288-8_4
5. Bastani, O., Ioannou, Y., Lampropoulos, L., Vytiniotis, D., Nori, A., Criminisi, A.: Measuring neural net robustness with constraints. Adv. Neural Inf. Process. Syst. **29**, 2613–2621 (2016)
6. Botoeva, E., Kouvaros, P., Kronqvist, J., Lomuscio, A., Misener, R.: Efficient verification of ReLU-based neural networks via dependency analysis. Proc. AAAI Conf. Artif. Intell. **34**, 3291–3299 (2020). https://doi.org/10.1609/aaai.v34i04.5729
7. Bunel, R., Lu, J., Turkaslan, I., Kohli, P., Torr, P., Mudigonda, P.: Branch and bound for piecewise linear neural network verification. J. Mach. Learn. Res. **21**(42), 1–39 (2020)
8. Cheng, C.-H., Nührenberg, G., Ruess, H.: Maximum resilience of artificial neural networks. In: D'Souza, D., Narayan Kumar, K. (eds.) ATVA 2017. LNCS, vol. 10482, pp. 251–268. Springer, Cham (2017). https://doi.org/10.1007/978-3-319-68167-2_18
9. Dutta, S., Jha, S., Sanakaranarayanan, S., Tiwari, A.: Output range analysis for deep neural networks (2017). https://arxiv.org/abs/1709.09130
10. Dvijotham, K., Stanforth, R., Gowal, S., Mann, T.A., Kohli, P.: A dual approach to scalable verification of deep networks. In: Globerson, A., Silva, R. (eds.) Uncertainty in Artificial Intelligence, vol. 1, pp. 550–559 (2018)
11. Ehlers, R.: Formal verification of piece-wise linear feed-forward neural networks. In: D'Souza, D., Narayan Kumar, K. (eds.) ATVA 2017. LNCS, vol. 10482, pp. 269–286. Springer, Cham (2017). https://doi.org/10.1007/978-3-319-68167-2_19
12. Emiris, I.Z., Fisikopoulos, V.: Practical Polytope Volume Approximation. ACM Trans. Math. Softw. **44**(4), 38:1–38:21 (2018). https://doi.org/10.1145/3194656

13. Fazlyab, M., Robey, A., Hassani, H., Morari, M., Pappas, G.: Efficient and accurate estimation of lipschitz constants for deep neural networks. In: Wallach, H., Larochelle, H., Beygelzimer, A., d'Alché-Buc, F., Fox, E., Garnett, R. (eds.) Advances in Neural Information Processing Systems, vol. 32, pp. 11423–11434. Curran Associates, Inc. (2019)
14. Fischetti, M., Jo, J.: Deep neural networks and mixed integer linear optimization. Constraints **23**(3), 296–309 (2018). https://doi.org/10.1007/s10601-018-9285-6
15. Gehr, T., Mirman, M., Drachsler-Cohen, D., Tsankov, P., Chaudhuri, S., Vechev, M.: AI2: Safety and robustness certification of neural networks with abstract interpretation. In: 2018 IEEE Symposium on Security and Privacy (SP), pp. 3–18. IEEE (2018). https://doi.org/10.1109/SP.2018.00058
16. Goodfellow, I.J., Shlens, J., Szegedy, C.S.: Explaining and harnessing adversarial examples (2014). https://arxiv.org/abs/1412.6572
17. Ivanov, R., Weimer, J., Alur, R., Pappas, G.J., Lee, I.: Verisig: verifying safety properties of hybrid systems with neural network controllers. In: Proceedings of the 22nd ACM International Conference on Hybrid Systems: Computation and Control, HSCC 2019, pp. 169–178. Association for Computing Machinery, New York (2019). https://doi.org/10.1145/3302504.3311806
18. Katz, G., Barrett, C., Dill, D.L., Julian, K., Kochenderfer, M.J.: Reluplex: an efficient SMT solver for verifying deep neural networks. In: Majumdar, R., Kunčak, V. (eds.) CAV 2017. LNCS, vol. 10426, pp. 97–117. Springer, Cham (2017). https://doi.org/10.1007/978-3-319-63387-9_5
19. Katz, G., et al.: The marabou framework for verification and analysis of deep neural networks. In: Dillig, I., Tasiran, S. (eds.) CAV 2019. LNCS, vol. 11561, pp. 443–452. Springer, Cham (2019). https://doi.org/10.1007/978-3-030-25540-4_26
20. Kurakin, A., Goodfellow, I., Bengio, S.: Adversarial examples in the physical world (2016). https://arxiv.org/abs/1607.02533
21. LeCun, Y.: The MNIST database of handwritten digits (1998). http://yann.lecun.com/exdb/mnist/
22. Liu, C., Arnon, T., Lazarus, C., Barrett, C., Kochenderfer, M.J.: Algorithms for Verifying Deep Neural Networks (2019). http://arxiv.org/abs/1903.06758
23. Lomuscio, A., Maganti, L.: An approach to reachability analysis for feed-forward relu neural networks (2017). https://arxiv.org/abs/1706.07351
24. Moskewicz, M., Madigan, C., Zhao, Y., Zhang, L., Malik, S.: Chaff: engineering an efficient SAT solver. In: Proceedings of the 38th Design Automation Conference, pp. 530–535 (2001). https://doi.org/10.1145/378239.379017
25. Royo, V.R., Calandra, R., Stipanovic, D.M., Tomlin, C.: Fast neural network verification via shadow prices (2019). https://arxiv.org/abs/1902.07247
26. Shoukry, Y., Nuzzo, P., Sangiovanni-Vincentelli, A.L., Seshia, S.A., Pappas, G.J., Tabuada, P.: SMC: satisfiability modulo convex programming. Proc. IEEE **106**(9), 1655–1679 (2018). https://doi.org/10.1109/JPROC.2018.2849003
27. Song, D., et al.: Physical adversarial examples for object detectors. In: Proceedings of the 12th USENIX Conference on Offensive Technologies. WOOT 2018, USENIX Association (2018)
28. Szegedy, C., et al.: Intriguing properties of neural networks (2013). https://arxiv.org/abs/1312.6199
29. Tjeng, V., Xiao, K., Tedrake, R.: Evaluating robustness of neural networks with mixed integer programming (2017). https://arxiv.org/abs/1711.07356

30. Tran, H.-D., et al.: NNV: the neural network verification tool for deep neural networks and learning-enabled cyber-physical systems. In: Lahiri, S.K., Wang, C. (eds.) CAV 2020. LNCS, vol. 12224, pp. 3–17. Springer, Cham (2020). https://doi.org/10.1007/978-3-030-53288-8_1

31. Wang, S., Pei, K., Whitehouse, J., Yang, J., Jana, S.: Efficient formal safety analysis of neural networks. In: Bengio, S., Wallach, H., Larochelle, H., Grauman, K., Cesa-Bianchi, N., Garnett, R. (eds.) Advances in Neural Information Processing Systems, vol. 31, pp. 6367–6377 (2018)

32. Wang, S., Pei, K., Whitehouse, J., Yang, J., Jana, S.: Formal security analysis of neural networks using symbolic intervals. In: Proceedings of the 27th USENIX Conference on Security Symposium, SEC 2018, pp. 1599–1614. USENIX Association (2018). https://doi.org/10.5555/3277203.3277323

33. Wong, E., Kolter, J.Z.: Provable defenses against adversarial examples via the convex outer adversarial polytope (2017). https://arxiv.org/abs/1711.00851

34. Xiang, W., Tran, H.D., Johnson, T.T.: Reachable set computation and safety verification for neural networks with relu activations (2017). https://arxiv.org/abs/1712.08163

35. Xiang, W., Tran, H.D., Johnson, T.T.: Output reachable set estimation and verification for multilayer neural networks. IEEE Trans. Neural Netw. Learn. Syst. **29**(11), 5777–5783 (2018). https://doi.org/10.1109/TNNLS.2018.2808470

Concurrency and Blockchain

Isla: Integrating Full-Scale ISA Semantics and Axiomatic Concurrency Models

Alasdair Armstrong[1]([✉]), Brian Campbell[2], Ben Simner[1], Christopher Pulte[1], and Peter Sewell[1]

[1] University of Cambridge, Cambridge, UK
alasdair.armstrong@cl.cam.ac.uk
[2] University of Edinburgh, Edinburgh, UK

Abstract. Architecture specifications such as Armv8-A and RISC-V are the ultimate foundation for software verification and the correctness criteria for hardware verification. They should define the allowed sequential and relaxed-memory concurrency behaviour of programs, but hitherto there has been no integration of full-scale instruction-set architecture (ISA) semantics with axiomatic concurrency models, either in mathematics or in tools. These ISA semantics can be surprisingly large and intricate, e.g. 100k+ lines for Armv8-A.

In this paper we present a tool, Isla, for computing the allowed behaviours of concurrent litmus tests with respect to full-scale ISA definitions, in Sail, and arbitrary axiomatic relaxed-memory concurrency models, in the Cat language. It is based on a generic symbolic engine for Sail ISA specifications, which should be valuable also for other verification tasks. We equip the tool with a web interface to make it widely accessible, and illustrate and evaluate it for Armv8-A and RISC-V.

By using full-scale and authoritative ISA semantics, this lets one evaluate litmus tests using arbitrary user instructions with high confidence. Moreover, because these ISA specifications give detailed and validated definitions of the sequential aspects of *systems* functionality, as used by hypervisors and operating systems, e.g. instruction fetch, exceptions, and address translation, our tool provides a basis for developing concurrency semantics for these. We demonstrate this for the Armv8-A instruction-fetch model and self-modifying code examples of Simner et al.

1 Introduction

A processor architecture should define, for any initial machine state, the set of all architecturally allowed observable executions—thus specifying the basic assumptions for programming and for software verification, and the correctness criterion for hardware verification. Architecture specifications have two main parts: the sequential and relaxed-memory concurrent aspects of instruction behaviour, each of which have been studied in previous work. For Armv8-A and RISC-V, Armstrong et al. have established full-scale sequential models in Sail [10,15], a domain-specific language for instruction-set architecture

© The Author(s) 2021
A. Silva and K. R. M. Leino (Eds.) CAV 2021, LNCS 12759, pp. 303–316, 2021.
https://doi.org/10.1007/978-3-030-81685-8_14

(ISA) specification, that are complete enough to boot real-world operating systems such as Linux. For Armv8-A this model is automatically derived from the authoritative Arm-internal specification [24], while for RISC-V it has been hand-written and adopted by RISC-V International. On the concurrency side, relaxed-memory semantics can be specified in two main styles: either as *abstract-microarchitectural operational* models, characterising observable behaviour with explicit out-of-order execution and buffering, or as *axiomatic* models, expressed as a predicate over complete candidate executions represented as graphs of memory events. For Armv8-A and RISC-V "user" concurrency, both exist [1,7,8,22], along with a "Promising ARM" variant [23]. For Armv8-A they have been proved equivalent [21,22]; the authoritative vendor definition is the axiomatic one.

However, while an architecture *should* define the set of allowed executions for arbitrary programs, hitherto there has been no integration of full-scale ISA definitions with axiomatic concurrency models, either in mathematics or in tools (for operational models, this has only been done for RISC-V; other operational models have used small ISA fragments). Research and industry practice for relaxed memory semantics rely on making the semantics *executable as a test oracle*: not just a paper definition (in prose or mathematics), but tool-supported definitions that for small litmus-test examples can *compute* the set of all allowed executions, that can then be compared against experimental data. Many tools have been developed for operational and axiomatic architectural concurrency models [4,6,8,12,14,17–20,25,26,28–32], with axiomatic tools notably including the Herd tool of Alglave and Maranget [4,6,8], that can evaluate litmus tests w.r.t. axiomatic memory models specified in a relational-algebra style in the Cat language [2]. However, all of these previous tools for axiomatic models have (at best) used hard-coded ISA semantics that cover only small fragments of the complete architecture. For example, Zhang et al. [32] use a SMT solver based approach for SoC verification, with a user-specified memory model (TSO or SC), however the instruction level abstractions (ILAs) they use are much more abstract than the ISA semantics we consider.

In this paper we describe a tool, Isla, that integrates full-scale ISA specifications, in Sail, with arbitrary axiomatic models, in the Cat language. We first build a generic symbolic execution library for Sail specifications—which should also be valuable for other verification tasks. We use this to construct a tool for symbolically running binary litmus tests for any Sail ISA under any (non-recursive) Cat axiomatic memory model, using an SMT solver. We equip it with a web interface to make it widely accessible, and illustrate and evaluate all this for Armv8-A and RISC-V. Isla is available at https://isla-axiomatic.cl.cam.ac.uk and https://github.com/rems-project/isla. An extended version of the paper [11], available at https://www.cl.cam.ac.uk/~pes20/isla/, includes appendices showing the main parts of the full Sail/ASL semantics of a sample Armv8-A instruction (add x4, x3, #1); the Armv8-A axiomatic concurrency model (combining the official Arm specification for user concurrency [9,13] with the additions for instruction fetch semantics by Simner et al. [27]); and examples of the latter.

Our approach has several key advantages, which all follow from the fact that mainstream industry ISAs are surprisingly large and intricate. The Armv8-A ISA specification is around 100k lines. It defines the sequential behaviour of the full instruction set in all its detail, including e.g. instruction decoding, behaviour at each exception level, register banking, floating-point, vector instructions, system registers, exceptions, address translation, virtualisation, security extensions, and a host of optional architectural features. Simple litmus tests developed to investigate user concurrency have historically used only very few instructions and very little of this, and hand-written ISA models have sufficed, but even a 'simple' ADD instruction can, in reality, involve surprisingly much of the specification. If one wants to examine arbitrary compiler-generated code one needs many more instructions; and to develop systems concurrency semantics, e.g. covering the concurrency behaviour of instruction fetch, exceptions, or address translation, one might need any of the specification—and it would be exceedingly laborious and error-prone to reproduce it by hand in a hard-coded semantics. By handling the full authoritative Armv8-A ISA, we automatically support litmus tests that use arbitrary instructions, and we enable research on systems concurrency, with high confidence that the ISA follows the vendor specification. We demonstrate this by applying our tool to the model and examples for self-modifying code by Simner et al. [27], and our integration has also identified several places where the ISA specification needs modifications to correctly give the intended behaviour in a concurrent setting, e.g. to remove or enforce additional ordering. Because this is based on authoritative Arm and RISC-V ISA specifications, the work should enable relaxed-memory behaviour to be included in the standard test-edit-debug cycle used in the development of such large and critical specifications.

2   Implementation

Axiomatic relaxed-memory concurrency models, being expressed as logical constraints over candidate execution graphs, lend themselves to solver-based tool implementations. For the instruction-semantics part of such a tool, the most direct approach would be to translate the ISA semantics (for the instructions that occur in a litmus test) directly into SMT and combine that with the axiomatic-model constraints, roughly along the lines of Alglave et al. [3]. That approach was followed by Simner et al. [27], who compiled Sail directly into SMT to test an axiomatic model for instruction-fetch tests, but using a small handwritten Arm fragment, rather than the full Sail model derived from the Arm-internal model. The problem with this direct approach is one of scale: as one covers more of the Arm semantics, the resulting SMT problem simply becomes too large to be practicable. For example, for a load instruction, the virtual address must be translated into a physical address, which is a complex process with a great deal of configurability—there may be zero, one, or two stages of address translation, the page size may vary, the number of levels used in the page table may differ, etc. This approach also required the top level fetch-execute-decode loop to be handled specially, as one cannot translate such an unbounded loop directly into SMT, which imposes significant constraints on the shape of allowable tests.

In contrast, here we build and use a generic symbolic evaluation for Sail definitions using the Z3 SMT solver, which lets us compute the possible symbolic thread-local traces of each instruction, and hence of each thread (treating memory read values as unknowns, left to the concurrency model constraints). It also lets us use the same fetch-decode-execute loop that is used for emulation and co-simulation (which embodies various architecture-specific subtleties).

2.1   Symbolic Execution for Sail

Sail is attractive for symbolic execution for several reasons. First, it is an intentionally simple language, lacking many of the features found in general-purpose languages. Second, it has to support very few programs, just the specifications of major ISAs, so (unlike tools for conventional programming languages) we can tune the execution to them. Third, almost all of the loops in these programs are bounded. Our starting point is the translation of Sail to C, for emulation, by Armstrong et al. [10]. This goes via a simple goto-language intermediate representation which is already well-suited for this task.

Static Function Linearisation. Our symbolic execution always creates a new task when we hit a branch, and we do not ever merge these tasks at join points. This is a good strategy for instruction semantics, as it simplifies the symbolic execution engine significantly, but it does mean some code can cause unnecessary branching. To avoid this we have a static rewrite that can take a function with if statements and rewrite it into a 'linear' form, e.g. as below:

```
var x = 2;
if undefined {
    x = x + 1
} else {
    x = x + 2
};
return x
```
$$\Longrightarrow$$
```
let x0 = 2;
let b = undefined;
let x1 = x0 + 1;
let x2 = x0 + 2;
let x3 = ite(b, x1, x2);
return x3
```

This works by translating the body of the function into SSA form, then replacing the ϕ-functions with if-then-else (ite) functions that translate into the SMT ite. This results in a more complex SMT expression, but less branching in the symbolic execution, so it is a trade-off, but often worthwhile.

Per-Thread Candidate Executions. For each litmus-test thread this symbolic execution will produce a number of *candidate executions*, each of which is a sequence of memory events (memory reads and writes, fences, register accesses, and so on) with the symbolic values of these events potentially being constrained by some SMT formula for the overall execution. For example, consider the Armv8-A instruction add x4, x3, #1. For this instruction, our symbolic evaluator generates an execution:

```
(declare-const input (_ BitVec 64))
(read-reg |R3| nil input)
(define-const output (bvadd input #x0000000000000001))
(write-reg |R4| nil output)
```

where the SMTLIB formula is defined by the declare-const and define-const statements, with read-reg and write-reg effects indicating which variables in the SMT formula correspond to the values read and written to registers (which are otherwise just global variables) by the instruction. We simplify here for brevity, omitting the negative, zero, carry and overflow flags that the model computes. For more complex instructions, there are additional effects for memory accesses, cache maintenance events, barriers, and so on.

2.2   Checking a Litmus Test

Figure 1 shows the overall process of checking a litmus test. Tests can be supplied either in the .litmus format of previous axiomatic and operational tools [4,5, 14], reusing the parser from [4], or as a TOML file (a standard configuration file format, with libraries available for most languages). We first assemble the test with a conventional assembler into an ELF binary and load it into the representation of memory that will be used, before initialising the model with the program counter set to the entry point for each thread, then we symbolically execute the instructions in each thread separately, using the Sail semantics for each instruction, plus the same fetch-execute-decode loop in Sail we would use for emulation, to produce sets of per-thread traces as above. Treating litmus tests essentially as binaries, rather than the more-or-less ad hoc fragments of assembly abstract syntax used by earlier tools, accommodates the fact that the Armv8-A model does not define an abstract syntax, and reduces the gap between what the tool evaluates and what is run in experimental testing. Note that the Arm assembly in Fig. 1, as well as subsequent assembly snippets in this paper, use the standard Arm convention that x0 and w0 refer to the same register, where w0 refers to the lower 32-bits of the register, and x0 refers to the full 64-bit width.

We then generate an SMT problem for every combination of the candidate executions of each thread. This problem consists of the per-thread SMT formulae concatenated together (renaming variables as necessary to avoid name-clashes), combined with the axiomatic memory model (described in more detail below).

Finally, we need to generate some 'glue' SMT that connects the per-thread semantics with the memory model. For every effect in the per-thread SMT semantics we generate an enumeration of *events*, e.g. for an execution with two reads and two writes:

```
(declare-datatypes ((Event 0)) (((R1) (R2) (W1) (W2) (IW))))
```

The event IW is a special write event that represents the initial state. We generate relations such as value-of that relate events to their values as determined by the effects in the per-thread semantics, so if the second read event R2 read the value #xABCD, (value-of R2 #xABCD) would be true. We generate *syntactic dependency*

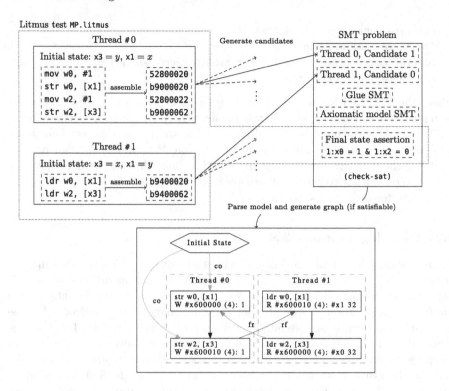

Fig. 1. Overview of process for checking the allowed executions of a litmus test

relations for address, data, and control dependencies, discussed in more detail in Sect. 2.3. Finally, there is a constraint on the final state of each test which specifies values expected in registers and memory after all threads have executed.

The Cat language represents axiomatic memory models as definitions of relations over the above events, and constraints over those relations, e.g. that specific relations are irreflexive, acyclic, or empty (or the negation of any of these). Relations are defined in a point-free relation-algebraic style, in terms of standard relational operators such as composition, intersection and union. The memory models we consider are all multi-copy-atomic, and all recursion in their definitions can trivially be replaced with (reflexive)-transitive closure. Herd's let rec construct computes the least solution to a set of equations [2], which is tricky to represent in SMT, so we do not support it. We believe even relations such as Power's (mutually recursive) preserved program order are nevertheless representable as SMT, so this limitation is mostly in our translation from Cat—we would likely want to use a different syntax to represent these relations for Isla.

A satisfiable solution to the overall SMT problem described above thus represents an execution permitted by the architecture. Parsing the model generated by the SMT solver allows us to generate a graph of the execution by instantiating each relation in the model with the various events. If all generated SMT problems are unsatisfiable for every combination of per-thread candidate executions then there are no permitted executions. If desired we can repeatedly ask the SMT solver for additional distinct models until we have all permitted executions.

2.3 Syntactic Dependency Analysis

Axiomatic memory models for relaxed hardware architectures rely heavily on notions of address, data, and control dependencies between instructions. For example, consider the following assembly:

```
ldr  w0, [x1]   // load 32 bits from address in x1 into x0
cbnz w0, LC01   // compare and branch if non-zero to LC01
LC01:
 mov  w2, #1    // load 1 into x2
 str  w2, [x3]  // store 32 bit-value in x2 to the address in x3
```

Here there is a control dependency between the load (ldr) and the store (str), as the value read by the load is used to determine whether the branch instruction cbnz that precedes the store is taken or not. This control dependency exists irregardless of whether the branch is taken or not—its existence is purely determined by the syntactic structure of the above code.

In general, existing ISA descriptions do not cover this aspect of the architecture well, as they are principally developed only to describe the sequential behaviour. Previous tools have either hand-coded dependency information, which is acceptable for cut-down ISA models but too laborious and error-prone at the scale of the ISA models we use, or used a heavyweight taint-tracking interpreter [15]. Our approach avoids both of these. It is similar to the latter, computing dependencies from the ISA specification, but building the footprint analysis atop our symbolic execution library requires only around 500 LoC.

To express dependencies, we need to associate each event in our candidate executions with the syntactic instruction/opcode that generated them. To do this we use a Sail function __instr_announce(opcode), called in each architecture's fetch-decode-execute loop just after fetching an instruction; this adds a special effect to the candidate execution recording the instruction opcode. We also have another special effect that delimits each fetch-decode-execute cycle, so each effect such as read-mem and write-mem that would give rise to an event can be associated with an opcode, as well as an index in the program order relation for its thread.

For each instruction we also need to know its *footprint*: data about the instruction including which input registers it reads, which output registers it writes, whether it is a branch instruction, and so on. It also contains *taint* information—we need to know which registers writes may contain data 'tainted' by a memory read performed by a load, or which input registers 'taint' data written to memory. The Sail ISA specifications do not explicitly describe this footprint, so we are forced to derive it from the specification.

To do this we symbolically evaluate each opcode independently in a suitably unconstrained environment so as to capture all its possible behaviours. This can be computationally expensive due to the number of possible behaviours some instructions have, so we build a footprint cache to avoid re-computing this where possible. It turns out to be hard to distinguish ordinary branches from instructions that can cause an exception to occur, so we add a special branch address announce effect, created by a Sail function __branch_address_announce that we call in branch instructions. This also enables the taint tracking for branch addresses we need for control dependencies as described above. The taint tracking is achieved simply by looking at what sub-expressions in the generated SMT problem contain variables that also appear in the various effects in each trace.

Once we have this footprint information we can analyse it for the opcodes between each read and write effect and derive the necessary dependency relations over their events. Note that this dependency relation must be exact. If we under-approximate, we will allow executions that should be forbidden, and if we over-approximate we will forbid executions that should be allowed.

In some cases the current Arm-provided ISA specification does not include enough information to identify the architecturally respected dependencies, and our dependency analysis would identify a dependency when there should not be one. To solve this we add some special Sail functions that give fine-grained control of the dependency calculation. For example, in indirect branches we ignore any dependency between the target register Xn and the link register $X30$ by including a function in the Sail definition that tells the footprint analysis to ignore any relation it finds between the two registers.

```
if branch_type == BranchType_INDCALL then {
    ignore_dependency_edge(n, 30);
    X(30) = PC() + 4
};
```

This works by adding a special annotation in the candidate execution trace which can be used by the footprint analysis—for all other purposes it is a no-op. This information should properly become part of the architecture specification, as mistakes in the dependency calculations could be a source of soundness bugs. The lack of support for this information in existing ISA specifications can partly be explained by the lack of tooling to properly explore the integration of ISA specifications with concurrency, something we hope a tool such as ours can address.

2.4 Web Interface

Figure 2 shows the web interface we have developed for our tool, based on the web interface for the C memory model tool Cerberus-BMC by Lau et al. [16]. This can either be run locally, or via a website, https://isla-axiomatic.cl.cam.ac.uk.

3   System Litmus Tests

As mentioned previously, one advantage of our tool is that, because it supports the full sequential ISA, it enables easy experimentation with tests and models

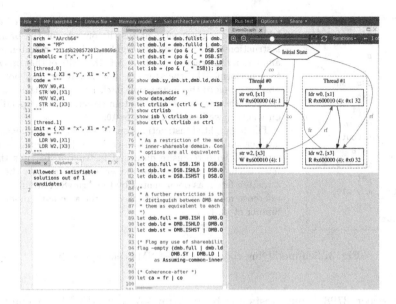

Fig. 2. Web interface for the tool

outside the scope of previous tools, e.g. involving new systems features. For example, Simner et al. developed semantics for Arm instruction fetch and I/D cache maintenance [27]. Consider the litmus test in Fig. 3 [27, §3.3], a simple test involving self-modifying code. In order to run this test and the others in [27] our tool required only minimal changes: we had to add support for data-cache and instruction-cache maintenance events and relations for them in our Cat to SMT translation. Additionally we needed to generalise how we generated the rf (reads-from) relation to generate both the regular rf relation and the new irf (instruction-reads-from) relation. Because our tool already runs tests using a fetch-execute-decode loop, all the instruction fetch events were already available—we in fact filter them out when running user-mode tests.

When generating candidate executions for a thread we normally do not assume anything about what other threads may be doing, but for self-modifying code this would clearly be problematic, as it would imply that any other thread could modify any of this thread's instructions arbitrarily. We therefore mark the memory locations that contain instructions that can be modified and provide in advance all the possible values they might take.

4 Results and Comparisons

We evaluate our tool for correctness and performance with respect to Herd using previous corpora of tests.

```
1     str w0, [x1]
2     dc cvau, x1
3     dsb ish
4     ic ivau, x1
5     dsb ish
6     isb
7     bl f
8     mov w2, w10
9     b Lout
10  f:    b l0
11  l1:   mov w10, #2
12    ret
13  l0:   mov w10, #1
14    ret
15  Lout:
```

In the initial state register x1 contains the address of the label f, and register w0 contains the opcode for the branch instruction b l1. Without the highlighted cache-maintenance and barrier instructions on lines 2–6, the write of that opcode to f performed by the store on line 1 may or may not be observed before the instruction fetch for f, so at the end of the test the register w2 can contain either 1 or 2, depending on whether we branched to l1 or l0.

The highlighted instructions on lines 2–6 are a sequence of data-cache (dc) and instruction-cache (ic) maintenance instructions with requisite data and instruction barriers that must occur to guarantee that the write is observed by the instruction fetch, as documented by the Armv8-A architecture reference manual [7] and captured by the axiomatic model of Simner et al. [27]

Fig. 3. Self-modifying code litmus test SM+cachesync-isb

We select 3798 litmus tests for both Armv8-A and RISC-V to compare between our tool and Herd—these tests include a representative set of features such as barriers and atomics, while exercising all of the basic litmus test shapes. All tests were run on a 2.6GHz Intel Xeon Gold 6240 CPU with 36 physical cores and 400GB of RAM. The tests are split into rough categories based on the contents of the tests. We ran 36 concurrent instances of both our tool and Herd across each set of tests, running Herd with the -speedcheck fast flag which causes it to stop enumerating executions when it resolves the final assertion in each test, which is the closest behaviour to how our tool behaves by default.

To assess correctness, we use a set of golden references for these above tests, for all of which the previous operational RMEM [14] and axiomatic Herd models and tools agree, and which have been extensively validated against hardware implementations. We confirm that our tool produces the same expected results as those models for all the litmus tests, including when run in exhaustive mode.

To assess performance, the table below gives the total real execution time for each batch of tests.

Test set	Number of tests	Isla	Herd
Armv8-A basic 2-thread	1377	49 s	11 s
Armv8-A basic 3-thread	161	11.7 s	1.2 s
Armv8-A exclusives	23	20.2 s	1.5 s
Armv8-A DMB/LD	70	7.4 s	0.7 s
Armv8-A PPO	2020	3 m 29.3 s	16.2 s
RISC-V basic 2-thread	36	0.7 s	0.2 s
RISC-V AMOs	111	2 s	0.7 s

In general Herd is faster for nearly all tests, but this is not surprising given the amount of detail in the full-scale instruction semantics that we are using, particularly for Armv8-A. Our goal is not to be faster, but to support those full-scale ISA semantics while remaining fast enough for practical purposes. We achieve this: most tests take only a second or so to run, which is perfectly usable interactively. For example, given the Armv8-A basic 3-thread tests, for a single sequential run of the tests, the shortest took 872 ms to run, while the longest took 1231 ms. The above batch times are similarly perfectly usable for (e.g.) regression testing while editing a model.

We also evaluate our tool with respect to that of Simner et al., for the instruction-fetch tests (which are currently not supported by Herd) in Sect. 6 of their paper. Our tool returns the expected results for all these tests, including the two tests (FOW and SM.F+ic) that were unsupported by their tool. In terms of performance, we note that their tool took 30 min to run just 90 of the 1377 basic 2-thread tests above, which is awkwardly slow for using a tool in practice, whereas when limiting our tool to 8 cores (to more closely match their experimental setup) our tool will execute all 1377 in under 3 min. We were additionally able to provide further validation that the Simner et al. model behaves as the standard Armv8-A model for non-self-modifying tests by showing that it behaves identically for all 3798 of the non-self-modifying tests above.

Acknowledgement. This work was partially supported by the UK Government Industrial Strategy Challenge Fund (ISCF) under the Digital Security by Design (DSbD) Programme, to deliver a DSbDtech enabled digital platform (grant 105694), ERC AdG 789108 ELVER, EPSRC programme grant EP/K008528/1 REMS, an Arm iCASE award, Arm, and Google. Approved for public release; distribution is unlimited. This work was supported by the Defense Advanced Research Projects Agency (DARPA) and the Air Force Research Laboratory (AFRL), under contract FA8650-18-C-7809 ("CIFV"). The views, opinions, and/or findings contained in this report are those of the authors and should not be interpreted as representing the official views or policies of the Department of Defense or the U.S. Government.

References

1. The RISC-V Instruction Set Manual, Volume I: Unprivileged ISA, Document Version 20191214-draft, 238 pages (2020). https://riscv.org/technical/specifications/. Accessed 23 Sept 2020
2. Alglave, J., Cousot, P., Maranget, L.: Syntax and semantics of the weak consistency model specification language cat. CoRR abs/1608.07531 (2016)
3. Alglave, J., Kroening, D., Tautschnig, M.: Partial orders for efficient bounded model checking of concurrent software. In: Computer Aided Verification - 25th International Conference, CAV, pp. 141–157 (2013). https://doi.org/10.1007/978-3-642-39799-8_9
4. Alglave, J., Maranget, L.: The diy7 tool. http://diy.inria.fr/. Accessed 28 Jan 2021
5. Alglave, J., Maranget, L., Sarkar, S., Sewell, P.: Litmus: running tests against hardware. In: Abdulla, P.A., Leino, K.R.M. (eds.) TACAS 2011. LNCS, vol. 6605, pp. 41–44. Springer, Heidelberg (2011). https://doi.org/10.1007/978-3-642-19835-9_5

6. Alglave, J., Maranget, L., Tautschnig, M.: Herding cats: modelling, simulation, testing, and data mining for weak memory. ACM TOPLAS **36**(2), 7:1–7:74 (2014). https://doi.org/10.1145/2627752

7. Arm: Arm Architecture Reference Manual: Armv8, for Armv8-A architecture profile, 8248 pages (2020). https://developer.arm.com/documentation/ddi0487/fc. Accessed 23 Sept 2020

8. Arm: Memory model tool (2020). https://developer.arm.com/architectures/cpu-architecture/a-profile/memory-model-tool Accessed 26 Jan 2021

9. ARM Ltd.: ARM Architecture Reference Manual (ARMv8, for ARMv8-A architecture profile) (2017). ARM DDI 0487B.a (ID033117). https://developer.arm.com/documentation/ddi0487/b/?lang=en

10. Armstrong, A., et al.: ISA semantics for ARMv8-A, RISC-V, and CHERI-MIPS (2019). http://www.cl.cam.ac.uk/~pes20/sail/

11. Armstrong, A., Campbell, B., Simner, B., Pulte, C., Sewell, P.: Isla: integrating full-scale ISA semantics and axiomatic concurrency models (extended version). In: Extended version of a paper in Proceedings of CAV 2021: 33rd International Conference on Computer-Aided Verification (2021). https://www.cl.cam.ac.uk/~pes20/isla/

12. Bornholt, J., Torlak, E.: Synthesizing memory models from framework sketches and litmus tests. In: Cohen, A., Vechev, M.T. (eds.) Proceedings of the 38th ACM SIGPLAN Conference on Programming Language Design and Implementation, PLDI 2017, Barcelona, Spain, 18–23 June, 2017, pp. 467–481. ACM (2017). https://doi.org/10.1145/3062341.3062353

13. Deacon, W.: The ARMv8 application level memory model. https://github.com/herd/herdtools7/blob/master/herd/libdir/aarch64.cat (2016)

14. Flur, S., French, J., Gray, K., Pulte, C., Sarkar, S., Sewell, P.: RMEM (2020). www.cl.cam.ac.uk/~pes20/rmem/. Accessed 28 Jan 2021

15. Gray, K.E., Kerneis, G., Mulligan, D., Pulte, C., Sarkar, S., Sewell, P.: An integrated concurrency and core-ISA architectural envelope definition, and test oracle, for IBM POWER multiprocessors. In: Proceedings of MICRO-48, the 48th Annual IEEE/ACM International Symposium on Microarchitecture (2015). https://doi.org/10.1145/2830772.2830775

16. Lau, S., Gomes, V.B.F., Memarian, K., Pichon-Pharabod, J., Sewell, P.: Cerberus-BMC: a principled reference semantics and exploration tool for concurrent and sequential C. In: Dillig, I., Tasiran, S. (eds.) Computer Aided Verification. LNCS, vol. 11561, pp. 387–397. Springer, Cham (2019). https://doi.org/10.1007/978-3-030-25540-4_22

17. Mador-Haim, S., et al.: An axiomatic memory model for POWER multiprocessors. In: Proceedings of the 24th International Conference on Computer Aided Verification, pp. 495–512 (2012). https://doi.org/10.1007/978-3-642-31424-7_36

18. Martonosi Research Group: Check research tools and papers. https://check.cs.princeton.edu/. Accessed 28 Jan 2021

19. Owens, S., Sarkar, S., Sewell, P.: A better x86 memory model: x86-TSO. In: Proceedings of TPHOLs 2009: Theorem Proving in Higher Order Logics, LNCS 5674, pp. 391–407 (2009). https://doi.org/10.1007/978-3-642-03359-9_27

20. Park, S., Dill, D.L.: An executable specification and verifier for relaxed memory order. IEEE Trans. Comput. **48**(2), 227–235 (1999)

21. Pulte, C.: The semantics of multicopy atomic ARMv8 and RISC-V. Ph.D. thesis, University of Cambridge (2018). https://www.repository.cam.ac.uk/handle/1810/292229

22. Pulte, C., Flur, S., Deacon, W., French, J., Sarkar, S., Sewell, P.: Simplifying ARM concurrency: multicopy-atomic axiomatic and operational models for ARMv8. In: POPL 2018: Proceedings of the 45th ACM SIGPLAN Symposium on Principles of Programming Languages (2018). https://doi.org/10.1145/3158107
23. Pulte, C., Pichon-Pharabod, J., Kang, J., Lee, S.H., Hur, C.K.: Promising-ARM/RISC-V: a simpler and faster operational concurrency model. In: PLDI 2019: Proceedings of the 40th ACM SIGPLAN Conference on Programming Language Design and Implementation (2019). https://doi.org/10.1145/3314221.3314624
24. Reid, A.: Trustworthy specifications of ARM v8-A and v8-M system level architecture. In: FMCAD 2016, pp. 161–168 (2016). https://alastairreid.github.io/papers/fmcad2016-trustworthy.pdf
25. Sarkar, S., Sewell, P., Alglave, J., Maranget, L., Williams, D.: Understanding POWER multiprocessors. In: Proceedings of PLDI 2011: the 32nd ACM SIGPLAN Conference on Programming Language Design and Implementation, pp. 175–186 (2011). https://doi.org/10.1145/1993498.1993520
26. Sarkar, S., et al.: The semantics of x86-CC multiprocessor machine code. In: Proceedings of POPL 2009: the 36th Annual ACM SIGPLAN-SIGACT Symposium on Principles of Programming Languages, pp. 379–391 (2009). https://doi.org/10.1145/1594834.1480929
27. Simner, B., et al.: Armv8-a system semantics: instruction fetch in relaxed architectures. In: ESOP 2020: Proceedings of the 29th European Symposium on Programming (2020). http://www.cl.cam.ac.uk/~pes20/iflat/top-extended.pdf
28. Trippel, C., Manerkar, Y.A., Lustig, D., Pellauer, M., Martonosi, M.: Full-stack memory model verification with tricheck. IEEE Micro **38**(3), 58–68 (2018)
29. Wickerson, J., Batty, M., Sorensen, T., Constantinides, G.A.: Automatically comparing memory consistency models. In: Castagna, G., Gordon, A.D. (eds.) Proceedings of the 44th ACM SIGPLAN Symposium on Principles of Programming Languages, POPL 2017, Paris, France, 18–20 January 2017, pp. 190–204. ACM (2017). http://dl.acm.org/citation.cfm?id=3009838
30. Yang, Y., Gopalakrishnan, G., Lindstrom, G., Slind, K.: Analyzing the intel Itanium memory ordering rules using logic programming and SAT. In: Geist, D., Tronci, E. (eds.) CHARME 2003. LNCS, vol. 2860, pp. 81–95. Springer, Heidelberg (2003). https://doi.org/10.1007/978-3-540-39724-3_9
31. Yang, Y., Gopalakrishnan, G., Lindstrom, G., Slind, K.: Nemos: a framework for axiomatic and executable specifications of memory consistency models. In: 18th International Parallel and Distributed Processing Symposium (IPDPS 2004), Santa Fe, New Mexico, USA (2004). https://doi.org/10.1109/IPDPS.2004.1302944
32. Zhang, H., Trippel, C., Manerkar, Y.A., Gupta, A., Martonosi, M., Malik, S.: ILA-MCM: integrating memory consistency models with instruction-level abstractions for heterogeneous system-on-chip verification. In: 2018 Formal Methods in Computer Aided Design (FMCAD), pp. 1–10 (2018). https://doi.org/10.23919/FMCAD.2018.8603015

Summing up Smart Transitions

Neta Elad[1], Sophie Rain[2(✉)], Neil Immerman[3], Laura Kovács[2],
and Mooly Sagiv[1]

[1] Tel Aviv University, Tel Aviv, Israel
[2] TU Wien, Vienna, Austria
[3] UMass Amherst, Amherst, USA

Abstract. Some of the most significant high-level properties of currencies are the sums of certain account balances. Properties of such sums can ensure the integrity of currencies and transactions. For example, the sum of balances should not be changed by a transfer operation. Currencies manipulated by code present a verification challenge to mathematically prove their integrity by reasoning about computer programs that operate over them, e.g., in Solidity. The ability to reason about sums is essential: even the simplest ERC-20 token standard of the Ethereum community provides a way to access the total supply of balances.

Unfortunately, reasoning about code written against this interface is non-trivial: the number of addresses is unbounded, and establishing global invariants like the preservation of the sum of the balances by operations like transfer requires higher-order reasoning. In particular, automated reasoners do not provide ways to specify summations of arbitrary length.

In this paper, we present a generalization of first-order logic which can express the unbounded sum of balances. We prove the decidablity of one of our extensions and the undecidability of a slightly richer one. We introduce first-order encodings to automate reasoning over software transitions with summations. We demonstrate the applicability of our results by using SMT solvers and first-order provers for validating the correctness of common transitions in smart contracts.

1 Introduction

A basic challenge in smart contract verification is how to express the functional correctness of transactions, such as currency minting or transferring between accounts. Typically, the correctness of such a transaction can be verified by proving that the transaction leaves the sum of certain account balances unchanged.

Consider for example the task of minting an unbounded number of tokens in the simplified ERC-20 token standard of the Ethereum community [32], as illustrated in Fig. 1[1]. This example deposits the minted amount (n) into the receiver's address (a) and we need to ensure that the mint operation *only* changed the bal-

---

[1] The old- prefix denotes the value of a function before the mint transition, and the new- prefix denotes the value afterwards.

A. Silva and K. R. M. Leino (Eds.) CAV 2021, LNCS 12759, pp. 317–340, 2021.
https://doi.org/10.1007/978-3-030-81685-8_15

```
a:  Address
n:  Nat
────────────────────────────────────────────────────────
mint(a,n)
────────────────────────────────────────────────────────
# Post-conditions
assert new-bal(a) = old-bal(a) + n                    #(i)
for each Address a' ≠ a:                              #(ii)
    assert new-bal(a') = old-bal(a')
assert new-sum() = old-sum() + n                     #(iii)
```

Fig. 1. Minting n tokens in ERC-20.

ance of the receiver. To do so, in addition to (i) proving that the balance of the receiver has been increased by n, we also need to verify that (ii) the account balance of every user address a' different than a has not been changed during the **mint** operation and that (iii) the **sum** of all balances changed exactly by the amount that was minted. The validity of these three requirements (i)-(iii), formulated as the post-conditions of Fig. 1, imply its functional correctness.

Surprisingly, proving formulas similar to the post-conditions of Fig. 1 is challenging for state-of-the-art automated reasoners, such as SMT solvers [6,7,9] and first-order provers [11,19,34]: it requires reasoning that links local changes of the receiver (a) with a global state capturing the **sum** of all balances, as well as constructing that global state as an aggregate of an unbounded but finite number of **Address** balances. Moreover, our encoding of the problem uses discrete coins that are minted and deposited, whose number is unbounded but finite as well.

In this paper we address verification challenges of software transactions with aggregate properties, such as preservation of sums by transitions that manipulate low-level, individual entities. Such properties are best expressed in higher-order logic, hindering the use of existing automated reasoners for proving them. To overcome such a reasoning limitation, we introduce *Sum Logic* (SL) as a generalization of first-order logic, in particular of Presburger arithmetic. Previous works [12,21,31] have also introduced extensions of first-order logic with aggregates by counting quantifiers or generalized quantifiers. In Sum Logic (SL) we only consider the special case of integer sums over uninterpreted functions, allowing us to formalize SL properties with and about unbounded sums, in particular sums of account balances, without higher-order operations (Sect. 3). We prove the decidability of one of our SL extensions and the undecidability of a slightly richer one (Sect. 4). Given previous results [21], our undecidability result is not surprising. In contrast, what may be unexpected is our decidability result and the fact that we can use our first-order fragment for a convenient and practical new way to verify the correctness of smart contracts.

We further introduce first-order encodings which enable automated reasoning over software transactions with summations in SL (Sect. 5). Unlike [5], where SMT-specific extensions supporting higher-order reasoning have been introduced, the logical encodings we propose allow one to use existing reasoners without any modification. We are not restricted to SMT reasoning, but can also leverage generic automated reasoners, such as first-order theorem provers, supporting first-order logic. We believe our results ease applying automated reasoning to smart contract verification even for non-experts.

We demonstrate the practical applicability of our results by using SMT solvers and first-order provers for validating the correctness of common financial transitions appearing in *smart contracts* (Sect. 6). We refer to these transitions as *smart transitions*. We encode SL into pure first-order logic by adding another sort that represents the tokens of the crypto-currency themselves (which we dub "coins").

Although the encodings of Sect. 5 do not translate to our decidable SL fragment from Sect. 4, our experimental results show that automated reasoning engines can handle them consistently and fast. The decidability results of Sect. 5 set the boundaries for what one can expect to achieve, while our experiments from Sect. 5 demonstrate that the unknown middle-ground can still be automated.

While our work is mainly motivated by smart contract verification, our results can be used for arbitrary software transactions implementing sum/aggregate properties. Further, when compared to the smart contract verification framework of [33], we note that we are not restricted to proving the correctness of smart contracts as finite-state machines, but can deal with semantic properties expressing financial transactions in smart contracts, such as currency minting/-transfers.

While ghost variable approaches [14] can reason about changes to the global state (the sum), our approach allows the verifier to specify only the local changes and automatically prove the impact on the global state.

Contributions. In summary, this paper makes the following contributions:

- We present a generalization to Presburger arithmetic (SL, in Sect. 3) that allows expressing properties about summations. We show how we can formalize verification problems of smart contracts in SL.
- We discuss the decidability problem of checking validity of SL formulas (Sect. 4): we prove that it is undecidable in the general case, but also that there exists a small decidable fragment.
- We show different encodings of SL to first-order logic (Sect. 5). To this end, we consider theory-specific reasoning and variations of SL, for example by replacing non-negative integer reasoning with term algebra properties.
- We evaluate our results with SMT solvers and first-order theorem provers, by using 31 new benchmarks encoding smart transitions and their properties (Sect. 6). Our experiments demonstrate the applicability of our results within automated reasoning, in a fully automated manner, without any user guidance.

2   Preliminaries

We consider many-sorted first-order logic (FOL) with equality, defined in the standard way. The equality symbol is denoted by $\approx$.

We denote by STRUCT $[\Sigma]$ the *set of all structures* for the vocabulary Σ. A structure $\mathcal{A} \in$ STRUCT $[\Sigma]$ is a pair $(\mathcal{D}, \mathcal{I})$, where for each sort s, its domain in $\mathcal{A}$ is $\mathcal{D}(s)$, and for each symbol S, its interpretation in $\mathcal{A}$ is $\mathcal{I}(S)$. Note that *models* of a formula φ over a vocabulary Σ are structures $\mathcal{A} \in$ STRUCT $[\Sigma]$.

A *first-order theory* is a set of first-order formulas closed under logical consequence. We will consider, the first-order theory of the natural numbers with addition. This is Presburger arithmetic (PA) which is of course decidable [27]. We write $\mathbb{N}$ to denote the set of natural numbers. We consider $0 \in \mathbb{N}$ and write $\mathbb{N}^+$ to explicitly exclude 0 from $\mathbb{N}$. The vocabulary of PA is $\Sigma_{\text{Presburger}} = (0, 1, c_1, \ldots, c_l, +^2)$, with all constants $0, 1, c_i$ of sort Nat. A structure $\mathcal{A} = (\mathcal{D}, \mathcal{I}) \in$ STRUCT $[\Sigma_{\text{Presburger}}]$ is called a *Standard Model of Arithmetic* when $\mathcal{D}(\text{Nat}) = \mathbb{N}$ and $+^2$ is interpreted as the standard binary addition $+$ function over the naturals. The vocabulary $\Sigma_{\text{Presburger}}$ can be extended with a total order relation, yielding $\Sigma^*_{\text{Presburger}} = (0, 1, +^2, \leq^2)$, where $\leq^2$ is interpreted as the binary relation $\leq$ in Standard Models of Arithmetic.

3   Sum Logic (*SL*)

We now define *Sum Logic (*SL*)* as a generalization of Presburger arithmetic, extending Presburger arithmetic with unbounded sums. SL is motivated by applications of financial transactions over cryptocurrencies in smart contracts. Smart contracts are decentralized computer programs executed on a blockchain-based system, as explained in [28]. Among other tasks, they automate financial transactions such as transferring and minting money. We refer to these transactions as *smart transitions*. The aim of this paper and SL in particular is to express and reason about the post-conditions of smart transitions similar to Fig. 1.

SL expresses smart transition relations among sums of accounts of various kinds, e.g., at different banks, times, etc. Each such kind, j, is modeled by an uninterpreted function symbol, b_j, where $b_j(a)$ denotes the balance of a's account of kind j, and a constant symbol s_j, which denotes the sum of all outputs of b_j. As such, our SL generalizes Presburger arithmetic with (i) a sort Address corresponding to the (unbounded) set of account *addresses*; (ii) *balance* functions b_j mapping account addresses from Address to account values of sort Nat; and (iii) *sum constants* s_j of sort Nat capturing the total sum of all account balances represented by b_j. Formally, the vocabulary of SL is defined as follows.

Definition 1 (SL Vocabulary). *Let*

$$\Sigma^{l,m,d}_{+,\leq} = (a_1, \ldots, a_l, b_1^1, \ldots, b_m^1, c_1, \ldots, c_d, s_1, \ldots, s_m, 0, 1, +^2, \leq^2)$$

be a sorted first-order vocabulary of SL *over sorts* {Address, Nat}, *where*

- *(Addresses) The constants* $a_1, \ldots, a_l$ *are of sort* Address;
- *(Balance functions)* $b_1^1, \ldots, b_m^1$ *are unary function symbols from* Address *to* Nat;

Table 1. ERC-20 token standard

Function	Encoding in SL	Reference in ERC-20
sum	s or s'	totalSupply
bal(a)	$b(a)$ or $b'(a)$	balanceOf
mint(a, v)	$b'(a) \approx b(a) + v$	transfer
transferFrom(f, t, v)	$b'(t) \approx b(t) + v \wedge b(f) \approx b'(f) + v$	transferFrom

- *(Constants and Sums) The constants $c_1, \ldots, c_d, s_1, \ldots, s_m$ and $0, 1$ are of sort* Nat;
- $+^2$ *is a binary function* Nat $\times$ Nat $\rightarrow$ Nat;
- $\leq^2$ *is a binary relation over* Nat $\times$ Nat.

In what follows, when the cardinalities in an SL vocabulary are clear from context, we simply write Σ instead of $\Sigma^{l,m,d}_{+,\leq}$. Further, by $\Sigma^{l,m,d}_{\cancel{+},\cancel{\leq}}$ we denote the sub-vocabulary where the crossed-out symbols are not available. Note that even when addition is not available, we still allow writing numerals larger than 1.

We restrict ourselves to *universal sentences* over an SL vocabulary, with quantification only over the Address sort.

We now extend the Tarskian semantics of first-order logic to ensure that the sum constants of an SL vocabulary $(s_1, \ldots, s_m)$ are equal to the sum of outputs of their associated balance functions (b_j for each s_j) over the respective entire domains of sort Address.

Let Σ be an SL vocabulary. An SL structure $\mathcal{A} = (\mathcal{D}, \mathcal{I}) \in \text{STRUCT}\,[\Sigma]$ representing a model for an SL formula φ is called an SL *model* iff

$$\mathcal{I}(s_j) = \sum_{a \in \mathcal{D}(\text{Address})} [\mathcal{I}(b_j)]\,(a), \quad \text{for each } 1 \leq j \leq m. \qquad \text{(Sum Property)}$$

We write $\mathcal{A} \vDash_{\text{SL}} \varphi$ to mean that $\mathcal{A}$ is an SL model of φ. When it is clear from context, we simply write $\mathcal{A} \vDash \varphi$.

Example 1 (Encoding ERC-20 in SL). As a use case of SL, we showcase the encoding of the ERC-20 token standard of the Ethereum community [32] in SL. To this end, we consider an SL vocabulary $\Sigma^{l,2,d}$. We respectively denote the balance functions and their associated sums as b, b', s, s' in the SL structure over $\Sigma^{l,2,d}$. The resulting instance of SL can then be used to encode ERC-20 operations/smart transitions as SL formulas, as shown in Table 1. Using this encoding, the post-condition of Fig. 1 is expressed as the SL formula

$$b'(a) \approx b(a) + n \;\wedge\; \forall a' \not\approx a.b'(a') \approx b(a') \;\wedge\; s' \approx s + n \qquad (1)$$

formalizing the correctness of the smart transition of minting n tokens in Fig. 1. In the applied verification examples in Sect. 6, rather than verifying the low-level implementation of built-in functions such as mint$_n$, we assume their correctness by including suitable axioms.

4   Decidability of *SL*

We consider the decidability problem of verifying formulas in SL. We show that when there are several function symbols b_j to sum over, the satisfiability problem for SL becomes undecidable[2]. We first present, however, a useful decidable fragment of SL.

4.1   A Decidable Fragment of *SL*

We prove decidability for a fragment of SL, which we call the $(l, 1, d)$-FRAG fragment of SL (Theorem 4). For doing so, we reduce the fragment to Presburger arithmetic, by using regular Presburger constructs to encode SL extensions, that is the uninterpreted functions and sum constants of SL.

The first step of our reduction proof is to consider distinct models, which are models where the Address constants a_i represent distinct elements in the domain $\mathcal{D}(\text{Address})$. While this restriction is somewhat unnatural, we show that for each vocabulary and formula that has a model, there exists an equisatisfiable formula over a different vocabulary that has a *distinct* model (Theorem 1). The crux of our decidability proof is then proving that $(l, 1, d)$-FRAG has *small* Address *space*: given a formula φ, if it is satisfiable, then there exists a model where $|\mathcal{D}(\text{Address})| \leq \kappa(|\varphi|)$, $|\varphi|$ is the length of φ, and $\kappa(.)$ is some computable function (Theorem 3)[3].

Distinct Models. An SL structure $\mathcal{A}$ is considered *distinct* when the l Address constants represent l distinct elements in $\mathcal{D}(\text{Address})$. I.e.,

$$|\{\mathcal{I}(a_1), \ldots, \mathcal{I}(a_l)\}| = l.$$

Since each SL model induces an equivalence relation over the Address constants, we consider partitions P over $\{a_1, \ldots, a_l\}$. For each possible partition P we define a transformation of terms and formulas $\mathcal{T}_P$ that substitutes equivalent Address constants with a single Address constant. The resulting formulas are defined over a vocabulary that has $|P|$ Address constants. We show that given an SL formula φ, if φ has a model, we can always find a partition P such that each of its classes corresponds to an equivalence class induced by that model.

Theorem 1 (Distinct Models). *Let φ be an SL formula over Σ, then φ has a model iff there exists a partition P of $\{a_1, \ldots, a_l\}$ such that $\mathcal{T}_P(\varphi)$ has a distinct model.*   □

Small Address Space. In order to construct a reduction to Presburger arithmetic, we bound the size of the Address sort. For a fragment of SL to be decidable, we therefore need a way to bound its models upfront. We formalize this requirement as follows.

---

[2] Proofs of our results are given in the appendix of [10].

[3] The function $\kappa(.)$ is defined per decidable fragment of SL, and not per formula.

Definition 2 (Small Address Space). *Let* FRAG *be some fragment of SL over vocabulary* $\Sigma = \Sigma_{+,\leq}^{l,m,d}$. FRAG *is said to have* small Address *space if there exists a computable function* $\kappa_\Sigma(.)$, *such that for any* SL *formula* $\varphi \in$ FRAG, φ *has a distinct model iff* φ *has a distinct model* $\mathcal{A} = (\mathcal{D}, \mathcal{I})$ *with small* Address *space, where* $|\mathcal{D}(\text{Address})| \leq \kappa_\Sigma(|\varphi|)$.

We call $\kappa_\Sigma(.)$ *the* bound function *of* FRAG; *when the vocabulary is clear from context we simply write* $\kappa(.)$.

One instance of a fragment (or rather, family of fragments) that satisfies this property is the $(l, 1, d)$-FRAG fragment: the simple case of a *single* uninterpreted "balance" function (and its associated sum constant), further restricted by removing the binary function $+$ and the binary relation $\leq$. Therefore, we derive the following theorem:

Theorem 2 (Small Address Space of $(l, 1, d)$-FRAG).
For any l, d, *it holds* $(l, 1, d)$-FRAG, *the fragment of* SL *formulas over the* SL *vocabulary*

$$\Sigma_{\cancel{+},\cancel{\leq}}^{l,1,d} = (a_1, \ldots, a_l, b^1, c_1, \ldots, c_d, s, 0, 1) \ ,$$

has small Address *space with bound function* $\kappa(x) = l + x + 1$. $\square$

An attempt to trivially extend Theorem 2 for a fragment of SL with two balance functions falls apart in a few places, but most importantly when comparing balances to the sum of a different balance function. In Sect. 4.2 we show that these comparisons are essential for proving our undecidability result in SL.

Presburger Reduction. For showing decidability of some FRAG fragment of SL, we describe a Turing reduction to pure Presburger arithmetic. We introduce a transformation $\tau(.)$ of formulas in SL into formulas in Presburger arithmetic. It maps universal quantifiers to disjunctions, and sums to explicit addition of all balances. In addition, we define an auxiliary formula $\eta(\varphi)$, which ensures only valid addresses are considered, and that invalid addresses have zero balances. The formal definitions of $\tau(.)$ and $\eta(\varphi)$ can be found in [10].

By relying on the properties of *distinctness* and *small* Address *space* we get the following results.

Theorem 3 (Presburger Reduction). *An* SL *formula* φ *has a distinct,* SL *model with small* Address *space iff* $\tau(\varphi) \wedge \eta(\varphi)$ *has a Standard Model of Arithmetic.* $\square$

Theorem 4 (SL Decidability). *Let* FRAG *be a fragment of* SL *that has* small Address *space, as defined in Definition 2. Then,* FRAG *is decidable.*

Proof (Theorem 4). Let φ be a formula in FRAG. Then φ has an SL model iff for some partition P of $\{a_1, \ldots, a_l\}$, $\mathcal{T}_P(\varphi)$ has a *distinct* SL model. For any P, the formula $\mathcal{T}_P(\varphi)$ is in FRAG, therefore $\mathcal{T}_P(\varphi)$ has a *distinct* SL model iff it has a *distinct* SL model with *small* Address *space*.

From Theorem 3, we get that for any P, $\varphi_P \triangleq \mathcal{T}_P(\varphi)$ has a *distinct* SL model iff $\tau(\varphi_P) \wedge \eta(\varphi_P)$ has a Standard Model of Arithmetic. By using the PA decision procedure as an oracle, we obtain the following *decision procedure for a* FRAG *formula* φ:

– For each possible partition P of $\{a_1, \ldots, a_l\}$, let $\varphi_P = \mathcal{T}_P(\varphi)$;
– Using a PA decision procedure, check whether $\tau(\varphi_P) \wedge \eta(\varphi_P)$ has a model, for each P;
– If a model for some partition P was found, the formula φ_P has a *distinct* SL model, and therefore φ has SL model;
– Otherwise, there is no *distinct* SL model for any partition P, and therefore there is no SL model for φ.

Remark 1. Our decision procedure for Theorem 4 requires B_l Presburger queries, where B_l is Bell's number for all possible partitions of a set of size l.

Using Theorem 4 and Theorem 2, we then obtain the following result.

Corollary 1. $(l, 1, d)$-FRAG *is decidable.*   □

4.2   *SL* Undecidability

We now show that simple extensions of our decidable $(l, 1, d)$-FRAG fragment lose its decidability (Theorem 5). For doing so, we encode the halting problem of a two-counter machine using SL with 3 balance functions, thereby proving that the resulting SL fragment is undecidable.

Consider a two-counter machine, whose transitions are encoded by the Presburger formula $\pi(c_1, c_2, p, c_1', c_2', p')$ with 6 free variables: 2 for each of the three registers, one of which being the program counter (PC). We assume w.l.o.g. that all three registers are within $\mathbb{N}^+$, allowing us to use addresses with a zero balance as a special "separator". In addition, we assume that the program counter is 1 at the start of the execution, and that there exists a single halting statement at line H. That is, the two-counter machine halts iff the PC is equal to H.

Reduction Setting. We have 4 `Address` elements for each time-step, 3 of them hold one register each, and one is used to separate between each group of `Address` elements (see Table 2). We have 3 uninterpreted functions from `Address` to `Nat` ("balances"). For readability we denote these functions as c, l, g (instead of b_1, b_2, b_3) and their respective sums as s_c, s_l, s_g:

1. Function c: Cardinality function, used to force size constraints. We set its value for all addresses to be 1, and therefore the number of addresses is s_c.
2. Function l: Labeling function, to order the time-steps. We choose one element to have a maximal value of $s_c - 1$ and ensure that l is injective. This means that the values of l are distinctly $[0, s_c - 1]$.
3. Function g: General purpose function, which holds either one of the registers or 0 to mark the `Address` element as a separating one.

Table 2. Transition system of a 2-counter machine, array view.

Address	l(Address)	c(Address)	g(Address)
	0	1	0
	1	1	c_1 at #0
	2	1	c_2 at #0
a_0	3	1	PC at #0 = 1
$\vdots$	$\vdots$	$\vdots$	$\vdots$
x_1	$4i$	1	0
x_2	$4i+1$	1	c_1 at #i
x_3	$4i+2$	1	c_2 at #i
x_4	$4i+3$	1	PC at #i
x_5	$4i+4$	1	0
x_6	$4i+5$	1	c_1 at #$(i+1)$
x_7	$4i+6$	1	c_2 at #$(i+1)$
x_8	$4i+7$	1	PC at #$(i+1)$
$\vdots$	$\vdots$	$\vdots$	$\vdots$
	s_c-4	1	0
	s_c-3	1	c_1 at #n
	s_c-2	1	c_2 at #n
a_1	s_c-1	1	PC at #$n = H$

Time-step #0 spans the first group. Time-step #i and Time-step #$(i+1)$ span the middle groups. Time-step #$n = \frac{s_c}{4} - 1$ spans the last group.

Each group representing a time-step is a 4 **Address** element, ordered as follows:

1. First, a separating **Address** element x (where $g(x)$ is 0).
2. Then, the two general-purpose counters.
3. Lastly, the program counter.

In addition we have 2 **Address** constants, a_0 and a_1 which represent the PC value at the start and at the end of the execution. The element a_1 also holds the maximal value of l, that is, $l(a_1) + 1 \approx s_c$. Further, a_0 holds the fourth-minimal value, since its the last element of the first group, and each group has four elements.

Formalization Using a Two-Counter Machine. We now formalize our reduction, proving undecidability of SL.
(i) We impose an injective labeling

$$\varphi_1 = \forall x, y.\, (l(x) \approx l(y)) \rightarrow (x \approx y)$$

(ii) We next formalize properties over the program counter PC. The **Address** constant that represents the program counter PC value of the last time-step is set to have the maximal labeling, that is

$$\varphi_2 = \forall x.l(x) \leq l(a_1)$$

Further, the **Address** constant that represents the PC value of the first time-step has the fourth labeling, hence

$$\varphi_3 = l(a_0) \approx 3$$

Finally, the first and last values of the program counter are respectively 1 and H, that is

$$\varphi_4 = g(a_0) \approx 1 \wedge g(a_1) \approx H$$

(iii) We express *cardinality constraints* ensuring that there are as many Address elements as the labeling of the last Address constant $(a_1) + 1$. We assert

$$\varphi_5 = (s_c \approx l(a_1) + 1) \wedge \forall x.\, (c(x) \approx 1)$$

(iv) We encode the transitions of the two-counter machine, as follows. For every 8 Address elements, if they represent two sequential time-steps, then the formula for the transitions of the two-counter machine is valid for the registers it holds. As such, we have

$$\varphi_6 = \forall x_1, \ldots, x_8.\, (F1 \wedge F2 \wedge F3)$$
$$\rightarrow \pi\, (g(x_2), g(x_3), g(x_4), g(x_6), g(x_7), g(x_8))$$

where the conjunction $F1 \wedge F2 \wedge F3$ expresses that $x_1, \ldots, x_8$ are two sequential time-steps, with $F1$, $F2$ and $F3$ defined as below. In particular, $F1$, $F2$ and $F3$ formalize that $x_1, \ldots, x_8$ have sequential labeling, starting with one zero-valued Address element ("separator") and continuing with 3 non-zero elements, as follows:

– Sequential:

$$l(x_2) \approx l(x_1) + 1 \wedge \cdots \wedge l(x_8) \approx l(x_7) + 1 \tag{F1}$$

– Time-steps:

$$g(x_1) \approx 0 \wedge g(x_2) > 0 \wedge g(x_3) > 0 \wedge g(x_4) > 0\,, \tag{F2}$$
$$g(x_5) \approx 0 \wedge g(x_6) > 0 \wedge g(x_7) > 0 \wedge g(x_8) > 0 \tag{F3}$$

Based on the above formalization, the formula $\varphi = \varphi_1 \wedge \cdots \wedge \varphi_6$ is satisfiable iff the two-counter machine halts within a finite amount of time-steps (and the exact amount would be given by $\frac{s_c}{4}$). Since the halting problem for two-counter machines is undecidable, our SL, already with 3 uninterpreted functions and their associated sums, is also undecidable.

Theorem 5. *For any $l \geq 2, m \geq 3$ and d, any fragment of SL over $\Sigma_{+,\leq}^{l,m,d}$ is undecidable.* □

Remark 2. Note that in the above formalization the only use of associated sums comes from expressing the size of the set of Address elements. As for our uninterpreted function $c(.)$ we have $\forall x.c(x) \approx 1$, its sum s_c is thus the amount of addresses. Hence, we can encode the halting problem for two-counter machines in an almost identical way to the encoding presented here, using a generalization of PA with two uninterpreted functions for $l(.)$ and $g(.)$, and a *size operation* replacing $c(.)$ and its associated sum.

5 *SL* Encodings of Smart Transitions

The definition of SL models in Sects. 3 and 4 ensured that the summation constants s_j were respectively equal to the actual summation of all balances $b_j(.)$. In this section, we address the challenge to formalize relations between s_j and $b_j(.)$ in a way that the resulting encodings can be expressed in the logical frameworks of automated reasoners, in particular of SMT solvers and first-order theorem provers.

In what follows, we consider a single transaction or one time-step of multiple transactions over $s_j, b_j(.)$. We refer to such transitions as *smart transitions*. Smart transitions are common in smart contracts, expressing for example the minting and/or transferring of some coins, as evidenced in Fig. 1 and discussed later.

Based on Sect. 3, our smart transitions are encoded in the $\Sigma^{l,2,d}$ fragment of SL. Note however, that neither decidability nor undecidability of this fragment is implied by Theorem 4, nor Theorem 5. In this section, we show that our SL encoding of smart transitions is expressible in first-order logic. We first introduce a sound, *implicit SL encoding*, by "hiding" away sum semantics and using invariant relations over smart transitions (Sect. 5.1). This encoding does not allow us to directly assert the values of any balance or sum, but we can prove that this implicit encoding is complete, relative to a translation function (Sect. 5.2).

By further restricting our implicit SL encoding to this relative complete setting, we consider counting properties to explicitly reason with balances and directly express verification conditions with unbounded sums on s_j and $b_j(.)$. This is shown in Sect. 5.3, and we evaluate different variants of the *explicit SL encoding* in Sect. 6, showcasing their practical use and relevance within automated reasoning.

To directly present our SL encodings and results in the smart contract domain, in what follows we rely on the notation of Table 1. As such, we respectively denote b, b' by old-bal, new-bal and write old-sum, new-sum for s, s'. As already discussed in Fig. 1, the prefixes old- and new- refer to the entire state expressed in the encoding before and after the smart transition. We explicitly indicate this state using old-world, new-world respectively. The non-prefixed versions bal and sum are stand-ins for *both* the old- and new- versions—Fig. 2 illustrates our setting for the smart transition of minting one coin.

With this SL notation at hand, we are thus interested in finding first-order formulas that verify smart transition relations between old-sum and new-sum, given the relation between old-bal and new-bal. In this paper, we mainly focus on the smart transitions of minting and transferring money, yet our results could be used in the context of other financial transactions/software transitions over unbounded sums.

Example 2. In the case of minting n coins in Fig. 1, we require formulas that (a) describe the state before the transition (the old-world, thus pre-condition), (b) formalize the transition (the relation between old-bal and new-bal; (i)-(ii) in

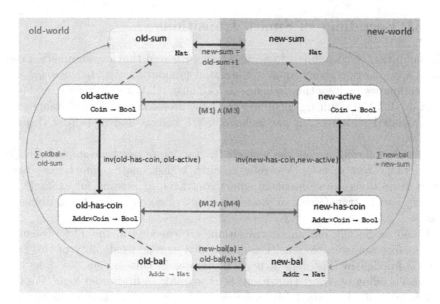

Fig. 2. Implicit SL encoding of $mint_1$, where `Addr` is short for `Address`.

Fig. 1) and (c) imply the consequences for the `new-world` ((iii) in Fig. 1). These formulas verify that minting and depositing n coins into some address result in an increase of the sum by n, that is `new-sum = old-sum + n`, as expressed in the functional correctness formula (1) of Fig. 1.

5.1 *SL* Encoding Using Implicit Balances and Sums

The first encoding we present is a set of first-order formulas with equality over sorts {`Coin, Address`}. No additional theories are considered. The `Coin` sort represents money, where one coin is one unit of money. The `Address` sort represents the account addresses as before. As a consequence, balance functions and sum constants only exist implicitly in this encoding. As such, the property $\text{sum} = \sum_{a \in \text{Address}} \text{bal}(a)$ *cannot be directly expressed in this encoding*. Instead, we formalize this property by using so-called *smart invariant* relations between two predicates `has-coin` and `active` over coins $c \in$ `Coin` and $a \in$ `Address`, as follows.

Definition 3 (Smart Invariants). *Let* `has-coin` $\subseteq$ `Address` $\times$ `Coin` *and consider* `active` $\subseteq$ `Coin`. *A smart invariant of the pair* (`has-coin`, `active`) *is the conjunction of the following three formulas*

1. Only active coins c can be owned by an address a:

$$\forall c : \text{Coin}. \, \exists a : \text{Address}. \, \text{has-coin}(a,c) \to \text{active}(c) . \tag{I1}$$

2. *Every active coin c belongs to some address a:*

$$\forall c : \texttt{Coin}.\ \texttt{active}(c) \rightarrow \exists a : \texttt{Address}.\ \texttt{has-coin}(a, c)\ . \qquad \text{(I2)}$$

3. *Every coin c belongs to at most one address a:*

$$\forall c : \texttt{Coin}.\forall a, a' : \texttt{Address}.$$
$$(\texttt{has-coin}(a, c) \wedge \texttt{has-coin}(a', c) \rightarrow a \approx a')\ . \qquad \text{(I3)}$$

We write $\texttt{inv}(\texttt{has-coin}, \texttt{active})$ *to denote the smart invariant (I1)$\wedge$ (I2)$\wedge$ (I3) of* $(\texttt{has-coin}, \texttt{active})$.

Intuitively, our *smart invariants* ensure that a coin c is *active* iff it is *owned* by precisely one address a. Our smart invariants imply the soundness of our implicit SL encoding, as follows.

Theorem 6 (Soundness of SL **Encoding).** *Given that* $\texttt{sum} = |\texttt{active}|$ *and for every* $a \in \texttt{Address}$ *it holds* $\texttt{bal}(a) = |\{c \in \texttt{Coin} \mid (a, c) \in \texttt{has-coin}\}|$, *then* $\texttt{inv}(\texttt{has-coin}, \texttt{active}) \implies \texttt{sum} = \sum_{a \in \texttt{Address}} \texttt{bal}(a)$. $\qquad \square$

We say that a *smart transition preserves smart invariants*, when

$$\texttt{inv}(\texttt{old-has-coin}, \texttt{old-active})$$
$$\iff \texttt{inv}(\texttt{new-has-coin}, \texttt{new-active}),$$

where $\texttt{old-has-coin}, \texttt{old-active}$ and $\texttt{new-has-coin}, \texttt{new-active}$ respectively denote the functions $\texttt{has-coin}, \texttt{active}$ in the states before and after the smart transition. Based on the soundness of our implicit SL encoding, we formalize smart transitions preserving smart invariants as first-order formulas. We only discuss smart transitions implementing minting n coins here, but other transitions, such as transferring coins, can be handled in a similar manner. We first focus on miniting a single coin, as follows.

Definition 4 (Transition $\texttt{mint}_1(a, c)$**).** *Let there be* $c \in \texttt{Coin}, a \in \texttt{Address}$. *The transition* $\texttt{mint}_1(a, c)$ *activates coin c and deposits it into address a.*

1. *The coin c was inactive before and is active now:*

$$\neg\texttt{old-active}(c) \wedge \texttt{new-active}(c)\ . \qquad \text{(M1)}$$

2. *The address a owns the new coin c:*

$$\texttt{new-has-coin}(a, c) \wedge \forall a' : \texttt{Address}.\ \neg\texttt{old-has-coin}(a', c)\ . \qquad \text{(M2)}$$

3. *Everything else stays the same:*

$$\forall c' : \texttt{Coin}.\ c' \not\approx c \rightarrow (\texttt{new-active}(c') \leftrightarrow \texttt{old-active}(c'))\ , \qquad \text{(M3)}$$
$$\forall c' : \texttt{Coin}.\ \forall a' : \texttt{Address}.\ (c' \not\approx c \vee a' \not\approx a) \rightarrow \qquad \text{(M4)}$$
$$(\texttt{new-has-coin}(a', c') \leftrightarrow \texttt{old-has-coin}(a', c'))\ .$$

The transition $\texttt{mint}_1(a, c)$ *is defined as (M1) $\wedge$ (M2) $\wedge$ (M3) $\wedge$ (M4).*

By minting one coin, the balance of precisely one address, that is of the receiver's address, increases by one, whereas all other balances remain unchanged. Thus, the expected impact on the sum of account balances is also increased by one, as illustrated in Fig. 2. The following theorem proves that the definition of $mint_1$ is *sound*. That is, $mint_1$ affects the implicit balances and sums as expected and hence $mint_1$ preserves smart invariants.

Theorem 7 (Soundness of $mint_1(a, c)$). *Let $c \in$ Coin, $a \in$ Address such that $mint_1(a, c)$. Consider balance functions* old-bal, new-bal : Address $\rightarrow \mathbb{N}$, *non-negative integer constants* old-sum, new-sum, *unary predicates* old-active, new-active $\subseteq$ Coin *and binary predicates* old-has-coin, new-has-coin $\subseteq$ Address $\times$ Coin *such that*

$$|\text{old-active}| = \text{old-sum}, \quad |\text{new-active}| = \text{new-sum},$$

and for every address a', we have

$$\text{old-bal}(a') = |\{c' \in \text{Coin} \mid (a', c') \in \text{old-has-coin}\}|,$$
$$\text{new-bal}(a') = |\{c' \in \text{Coin} \mid (a', c') \in \text{new-has-coin}\}|.$$

Then, new-sum $=$ old-sum $+ 1$, new-bal$(a) =$ old-bal$(a) + 1$. *Moreover, for all other addresses $a' \neq a$, it holds* new-bal$(a') =$ old-bal(a'). ☐

Smart transitions minting an arbitrary number of n coins, as in our Fig. 1, is then realized by repeating the $mint_1$ transition n times. Based on the soundness of $mint_1$, ensuring that $mint_1$ preserves smart invariants, we conclude by induction that n repetitions of $mint_1$, that is *minting n coins, also preserves smart invariants*. The precise definition of $mint_n$ together with the soundness result is stated in [10].

5.2   Completeness Relative to a Translation Function

Smart invariants provide sufficient conditions for ensuring soundness of our SL encodings (Theorem 6). We next show that, under additional constraints, smart invariants are also necessary conditions, establishing thus *(relative) completeness of our encodings*.

A straightforward extension of Theorem 6 however does not hold. Namely, only under the assumptions of Theorem 6, the following formula is not valid:

$$\text{sum} = \sum_{a \in \text{Address}} \text{bal}(a) \quad \Longleftrightarrow \quad \text{inv}(\text{has-coin}, \text{active}).$$

As a counterexample, assume (i) sum $= |\text{active}|$, (ii) for every $a \in$ Address it holds that bal$(a) = |\{c \in \text{Coin} \mid (a, c) \in \text{has-coin}\}|$, that is the assumptions of Theorem 6. Further, let (iii) the smart invariants inv(has-coin, active) hold for all but the coins $c_1, c_2 \in$ Coin and all but the addresses $a_1, a_2 \in$ Address. We also assume that (iv) c_1 is active but not owned by any address and (v) c_2

is active and owned by the two distinct addresses a_1, a_2. We thus have $\mathrm{sum} = \sum_{a \in \mathrm{Address}} \mathrm{bal}(a)$, yet $\mathrm{inv}(\mathrm{has\text{-}coin}, \mathrm{active})$ does not hold.

To ensure completeness of our encodings, we therefore introduce a translation function f that restricts the set $\mathcal{F} \triangleq 2^{\mathrm{Address} \times \mathrm{Coin}} \times 2^{\mathrm{Coin}}$ of $(\mathrm{has\text{-}coin}, \mathrm{active})$ pairs, as follows. We exclude from $\mathcal{F}$ those pairs $(\mathrm{has\text{-}coin}, \mathrm{active})$ that violate smart invariants by both (i) not satisfying (I2), as (I2) ensures that there are not too many active coins, and by (ii) not satisfying at least one of (I1) and (I3), as (I1) and (I3) ensure that there are not too few active coins. The required translation function f (as in [10]) now assigns every pair $(\mathrm{bal}, \mathrm{sum})$ the set of all $(\mathrm{has\text{-}coin}, \mathrm{active}) \in \mathcal{F}$ that satisfy $\mathrm{sum} = |\mathrm{active}|$, $\mathrm{bal}(a) = |\{c \in \mathrm{Coin} \mid \mathrm{has\text{-}coin}(a, c)\}|$ for every address a and have not been excluded.

Theorem 8 (Relative Completeness of SL Encoding). *Let* $(\mathrm{bal}, \mathrm{sum}) \in \mathbb{N}^{\mathrm{Address}} \times \mathbb{N}$ *and let* $(\mathrm{has\text{-}coin}, \mathrm{active}) \in f(\mathrm{bal}, \mathrm{sum})$ *be arbitrary. Then,*

$$\mathrm{sum} = \sum_{a \in \mathrm{Address}} \mathrm{bal}(a) \quad \Longleftrightarrow \quad \mathrm{inv}\,(\mathrm{has\text{-}coin}, \mathrm{active})\,.$$

□

5.3 *SL* Encodings Using Explicit Balances and Sums

We now restrict our SL encoding from Sect. 5.1 to explicitly reason with balance functions during smart transitions. We do so by expressing our translation function f from Sect. 5.2 in first-order logic. We now use the summation constant $\mathrm{sum} \in \mathbb{N}$ and the balance function $\mathrm{bal} : \mathrm{Address} \to \mathbb{N}$ in our SL encoding. In particular, we use our smart invariants $\mathrm{inv}(\mathrm{has\text{-}coin}, \mathrm{active})$ in this explicit SL encoding together with two additional axioms (Ax1, Ax2), ensuring that $\mathrm{sum} = |\mathrm{active}|$ and $\mathrm{bal}(a) = |\{c \in \mathrm{Coin} \mid \mathrm{has\text{-}coin}(a, c)\}|$ for all $a \in \mathrm{Address}$.

To formalize the additional properties, we introduce two counting mechanisms in our SL encoding. The first one is a bijective function $\mathrm{count} : \mathrm{Coin} \to \mathbb{N}^+$ and the second one is a function $\mathrm{idx} : \mathrm{Address} \times \mathrm{Coin} \to \mathbb{N}^+$, where $\mathrm{idx}(a, .) : \mathrm{Coin} \to \mathbb{N}^+$ is bijective for every $a \in \mathrm{Address}$. To ensure that count and $\mathrm{idx}(a, .)$ count coins, we impose the following two properties:

$$\forall c : \mathrm{Coin}.\ \mathrm{active}(c) \iff \mathrm{count}(c) \leq \mathrm{sum}\,, \tag{Ax1}$$

$$\forall c : \mathrm{Coin}.\ \forall a : \mathrm{Address}.\ \mathrm{has\text{-}coin}(a, c) \iff \mathrm{idx}(a, c) \leq \mathrm{bal}(a)\,. \tag{Ax2}$$

Figure 3 illustrates our revised SL encoding for our smart transition mint_1. We next ensure soundness of our resulting explicit encoding for summation, as follows.

Theorem 9 (Soundness of Explicit SL Encodings). *Let there be a pair* $(\mathrm{bal}, \mathrm{sum}) \in \mathbb{N}^{\mathrm{Address}} \times \mathbb{N}$, *a pair* $(\mathrm{has\text{-}coin}, \mathrm{active}) \in \mathcal{F}$, *and functions* $\mathrm{count} : \mathrm{Coin} \to \mathbb{N}^+$ *and* $\mathrm{idx} : \mathrm{Address} \times \mathrm{Coin} \to \mathbb{N}^+$.

Given that count *is bijective,* $\text{idx}(a, .) : \text{Coin} \to \mathbb{N}^+$ *is bijective for every* $a \in$ Address, *and that (Ax1), (Ax2) and* inv(has-coin, active) *hold, then,* sum = |active| *and* $\text{bal}(a) = |\{c \in \text{Coin} : \text{has-coin}(a, c)\}|$, *for every* $a \in$ Address.
In particular, we have $\text{sum} = \sum_{a \in \text{Address}} \text{bal}(a)$.   □

When compared to Sect. 5.1, our explicit SL encoding introduced above uses our smart invariants as axioms of our encoding, together with (Ax1) and (Ax2). In our explicit SL encoding, the post-conditions asserting functional correctness of smart transitions express thus relations among old-sum to new-sum. For example, for mint_n we are interested in ensuring

$$\text{mint}_n \Rightarrow \text{new-sum} = \text{old-sum} + n. \tag{2}$$

By using two new constants old-total, new-total $\in \mathbb{N}$, we can use sum = total as smart invariant for mint_n. As a result, the property to be ensured is then

$$\begin{aligned}(\text{old-sum} = \text{old-total} \wedge \text{new-total} = \text{old-total} + n \wedge \text{mint}_n) \\ \Rightarrow (\text{new-sum} = \text{new-total}).\end{aligned} \tag{3}$$

It is easy to see that the negations of (2) and (3) are equisatisfiable. We note however that the additional constants old-total, new-total used in (3) lead to unstable results within automated reasoners, as discussed in Sect. 6.

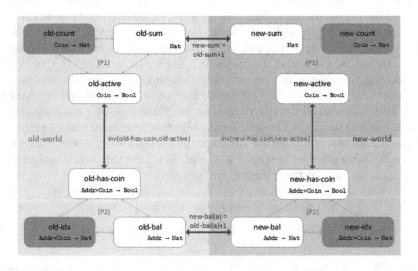

Fig. 3. Explicit SL encoding of mint_1, where Addr is short for Address.

6   Experiments

From Theory to Practice. To make our explicit SL encodings handier for automated reasoners, we improved the setting illustrated in Fig. 3 by applying the following restrictions without losing any generality.

(i) The predicates `has-coin` and `active` were removed from the explicit SL encodings, by replacing them by their equivalent expressions (Ax1)-(Ax2).

(ii) The surjectivity assertions of `count` and `idx` were restricted to the relevant intervals $[1, \text{sum}]$, $[1, \text{bal}(a)]$ respectively.

(iii) Compared to Fig. 3, only one mutual `count` and one mutual `idx` functions were used. We however conclude that we do not lose expressivity of our resulting SL encoding, as shown in [10].

(iv) When our SL encoding contains expressions such as $\forall c : \text{Coin}. \ \text{idx}(a_0, c) \in [l_0, u_0] \iff \text{idx}(a_1, c) \in [l_1, u_1]$, with a_0, a_1 being distinct addresses such that either $u_i \leq \text{bal}(a_i)$ or $l_i > \text{bal}(a_i)$, $i \in \{0, 1\}$, then it can be assumed that the coins in those intervals are in the same order for both functions [10].

Based on the above, we derive three different explicit SL encodings to be used in automated reasoning about smart transitions. We respectively denote these explicit SL encodings by `int`, `nat` and `id`, and describe them next.

Benchmarks. In our experiments, we consider four smart transitions mint_1, mint_n, transferFrom_1 and transferFrom_n, respectively denoting minting and transferring one and n coins. These transitions capture the main operations of linear integer arithmetic. In particular, mint_n implements the smart transition of our running example from Fig. 1.

For each of the four smart transitions, we implement four SL encodings: the implicit SL encoding `uf` from Sect. 5.1 using only uninterpreted functions and three explicit encodings `int`, `nat` and `id` as variants of Sect. 5.3. We also consider three additional arithmetic benchmarks using `int`, which are not directly motivated by smart contracts. Together with variants of `int` and `nat` presented in the sequel, our benchmark set contains 31 examples altogether, with each example being formalized in the SMT-LIB input syntax [1]. In addition to our encodings, we also proved consistency of the axioms used in our encodings.

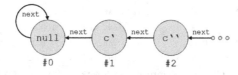

Fig. 4. Linked lists in `id`.

SL Encodings and Relaxations. Our explicit SL encoding `int` uses linear integer arithmetic, whereas `nat` and `id` are based on natural numbers. As naturals are not a built-in theory in SMT-LIB, we assert the axioms of Presburger arithmetic directly in the encodings of `nat` and `id`.

In our id encodings, inductive datatypes are additionally used to order coins. There exists one linked list of all coins for count and one for each $idx(a, .)$, $a \in$ Address. Additionally, there exists a "null" coin, which is the first element of every list and is not owned by any address. As shown in Fig. 4, the numbering of each coin is defined by its position in the respective list. This way surjectivity for count and idx can respectively be asserted by the formulas $\exists c :$ Coin. $count(c) \approx$ sum and $\forall a :$ Address. $\exists c :$ Coin. $idx(a, c) \approx bal(a)$. However, asserting surjectivity for int and nat cannot be achieved without quantifying over $\mathbb{N}^+$. Such quantification would drastically effect the performance of automated reasoners in (fragments of) first-order logics. As a remedy, within the default encodings of int and nat, we only consider relevant instances of surjectivity.

Further, we consider variations of int and nat by asserting proper surjectivity to the relevant intervals of idx and count (denoted as *surj*) and/or adding the total constants mentioned in Sect. 5.3 (denoted as *with* total, *no* total) . These variations of int and nat are implemented for $mint_1$ and $transferFrom_1$.

Experimental Setting. We evaluated our benchmark set of 31 examples using SMT solvers Z3 [7] and CVC4 [6], as well as the first-order theorem prover Vampire [19]. Our experiments were run on a standard machine with an Intel Core i5-6200U CPU (2.30 GHz, 2.40 GHz) and 8 GB RAM. The time is given in seconds and we ran all experiments with a time limit of 300 s. Time out is indicated by the symbol ×. The default parameters were used for each solver, unless stated otherwise in the corresponding tables[4].

Experimental Analysis. We first report on our experiments using different variations of int and nat. Table 3 shows that asserting complete surjectivity for int and nat is computationally hard and indeed significantly effects the performance of automated reasoners. Thus, for the following experiments only

Table 3. Results of $mint_1$ and $transferFrom_1$ using nat and int, with/without the total constants and with/without surjectivity.

mint$_1$				transferFrom$_1$			
no total	Z3	CVC4	Vampire	no total	Z3	CVC4	Vampire
nat	0.02	×	0.92	nat	×	×	15.35
nat surj.	×	×	×	nat surj.	100.03	×	×
int	0.02	0.03	×	int	0.02	0.07	×
int surj.	×	5.96	×	int surj.	1.02	×	×
with total	Z3	CVC4	Vampire	with total	Z3	CVC4	Vampire
nat	0.03	×	2.92	nat	0.28	×	22.54
nat surj.	0.11	×	×	nat surj.	38.24	×	×
int	0.02	0.03	×	int	0.02	0.10	×
int surj.	3.81	5.95	×	int surj.	×	6.56	×

---

[4] The precise calls and encodings are available at github.com/SoRaTu/SmartSums.

Table 4. Smart transitions using implicit/explicit SL encodings.

Encoding	Task			
	$mint_1$	$transferFrom_1$	$mint_n$	$transferFrom_n$
uf	Z3: 0.01	Z3: 0.02	Z3: ×	Z3: ×
	CVC4: 0.02	CVC4: 0.03	CVC4: ×	CVC4: ×
	Vampire: 0.18	Vampire: 0.19	Vampire: 0.35*	Vampire: 0.44*
nat	Z3: 0.02	Z3: ×	Z3: ×	Z3: ×
	CVC4: ×	CVC4: ×	CVC4: ×	CVC4: ×
	Vampire: 0.92	Vampire: 15.35	Vampire: 23.23†	Vampire: 228.22†
int	Z3: 0.02	Z3: 0.02	Z3: 0.03	Z3: 0.11
	CVC4: 0.03	CVC4: 0.07	CVC4: 0.05	CVC4: 0.35
	Vampire: ×	Vampire: ×	Vampire: ×	Vampire: ×
id	Z3: ×	Z3: ×	Z3: ×	Z3: ×
	CVC4: ×	CVC4: ×	CVC4: ×	CVC4: ×
	Vampire: 7.36‡	Vampire: 17.16‡	Vampire: 23.52‡	Vampire: ×

relevant instances of surjectivity, such as $\exists c : \mathtt{Coin.count}(c) = \mathtt{sum}$ were asserted in $\mathtt{int}$ and $\mathtt{nat}$. Table 3 also illustrates the instability of using the $\mathtt{total}$ constant. Some tasks seem to be easier even though their reasoning difficulty increased strictly by adding additional constants.

Our most important experimental findings are shown in Table 4, demonstrating that *our SL encodings are suitable for automated reasoners. Thanks to our explicit SL encodings, each solver can certify every smart transition in at least one encoding.* Our explicit SL encodings are more relevant than the implicit encoding $\mathtt{uf}$ as we can express and compare any two non-negative integer sums, whereas for $\mathtt{uf}$ handling arbitrary values n can only be done by iterating over the $mint_1$ (or $transferFrom_1$) transition. This iteration requires inductive reasoning, which currently only Vampire could do [15], as indicated by the superscript *. Nevertheless, the transactions $mint_1$, $transferFrom_1$, which involve only one coin in $\mathtt{uf}$, require no inductive reasoning as the actual sum is not considered; each of our solvers can certify these examples.

We note that the tasks $mint_n$ and $transferFrom_n$ from Table 4 yield a huge search space when using their explicit SL encodings within automated reasoners. We split these tasks into proving intermediate lemmas and proved each of these lemmas independently, by the respective solver. In particular, we used one lemma for $mint_n$ and four lemmas for $transferFrom_n$. In our experiments, we only used the recent theory reasoning framework of Vampire with split queues [13] and indicate our results in by superscript †.

We further remark that our explicit SL encoding $\mathtt{id}$ using inductive datatypes also requires inductive reasoning about smart transitions and beyond. The need of induction explains why SMT solvers failed proving our $\mathtt{id}$ benchmarks, as shown in Table 4. We note that Vampire found a proof using built-in induction [15] and theory-specific reasoning [13], as indicated by superscript ‡.

We conclude by showing the generality of our approach beyond smart transitions. It in fact enables fully automated reasoning about any two summations

Table 5. Arithmetic reasoning in the explicit SL encoding `int`.

Task		Time		
Transition	Impact			
$\texttt{new-bal}(a_0) = \texttt{old-bal}(a_0) + 3$ $\texttt{new-bal}(a_1) = \texttt{old-bal}(a_1) - 3$	$\texttt{new-sum} = \texttt{old-sum}$	Z3:		0.20
		CVC4:		1.28
		Vampire:		$\times$
$\texttt{new-bal}(a_0) = \texttt{old-bal}(a_0) + 4$ $\texttt{new-bal}(a_1) = \texttt{old-bal}(a_1) - 2$	$\texttt{new-sum} = \texttt{old-sum} + 2$	Z3:		0.58
		CVC4:		7.14
		Vampire:		$\times$
$\texttt{new-bal}(a_0) = \texttt{old-bal}(a_0) + 5$ $\texttt{new-bal}(a_1) = \texttt{old-bal}(a_1) - 3$ $\texttt{new-bal}(a_2) = \texttt{old-bal}(a_2) - 1$	$\texttt{new-sum} = \texttt{old-sum} + 1$	Z3:		1.52
		CVC4:		155.20
		Vampire:		$\times$

$\sum_{i \in I} g(i)$, $\sum_{i \in I} h(i)$ of non-negative integer values $g(i)$, $h(i)$ ($i \in I$) over a mutual finite set I. The examples of Table 5 affirm this claim.

7   Related Work

Smart Contract Safety. Formal verification of smart contracts is an emerging hot topic because of the value of the assets stored in smart contracts, e.g. the DeFi software [3]. Due to the nature of the blockchain, bugs in smart contracts are irreversible and thus the demand for provably bug-free smart contracts is high.

The K interactive framework has been used to verify safety of a smart contract, e.g. in [23]. Isabelle [22] was also shown to be useful in manual, interactive verification of smart contracts [17]. We, however, focus on automated approaches.

There are also efforts to perform deductive verification of smart contracts both on the source level in languages such as Solidity [4,14,33] and Move [35], as well as on the the Ethereum virtual machine (EVM) level [2,29]. This paper improves the effectiveness of these approaches by developing techniques for automatically reasoning about unbounded sums. This way, we believe we support a more semantic-based verification of smart contracts.

Our approach differs from works using ghost variables [14], since we do not manually update the "ghost state". Instead, the verifier needs only to reason about the local changes, and the aggregate state is maintained by the axioms. That means other approaches assume (a) the local changes and (b) the impact on ghost variables (sum), whereas we only assume (a) and automatically prove $a \Rightarrow b$. This way, we reduce the user-guidance in providing and proving (b).

Our work complements approaches that verify smart contracts as finite state machines [33] and methods, like ZEUS [18], using symbolic model checking and abstract interpretation to verify generic safety properties for smart contracts.

The work in [30] provides an extensive evaluation of ERC-20 and ERC-721 tokens. ERC-721 extends ERC-20 with ownership functions, one of which being "approve". It enables transactions on another party's behalf. This is independent of our ability to express sums in first-order logic, as the transaction's initiator is irrelevant to its effect.

Reasoning about Financial Applications. Recently, the Imandra prover introduced an automated reasoning framework for financial applications [24–26]. Similarly to our approach, these works use SMT procedures to verify and/or generate counter-examples to safety properties of low- and high-level algorithms. In particular, results of [24–26] include examples of verifying ranking orders in matching logics of exchanges, proving high-level properties such as transitivity and anti-symmetry of such orders. In contrast, we focus on verifying properties relating local changes in balances to changes of the global state (the sum). Moreover, our encodings enable automated reasoning both in SMT solving and first-order theorem proving.

Automated Aggregate Reasoning. The theory of first-order logic with aggregate operators has been thoroughly studied in [16,21]. Though proven to be strictly more expressive than first-order logic, both in the case of general aggregates as well as simple counting logics, in this paper we present a practical way to encode a weakened version of aggregates (specifically sums) in first-order logic. Our encoding (as in Sect. 5) works by expressing particular sums of interest, harnessing domain knowledge to avoid the need of general aggregate operators.

Previous works [5,20] in the field of higher-order reasoning do not directly discuss aggregates. The work of [20] extends Presburger arithmetic with Boolean algebra for finite, unbounded sets of uninterpreted elements. This includes a way to express the set cardinalities and to compare them against integer variables, but does not support uninterpreted functions, such as the balance functions we use throughout our approach.

The SMT-based framework of [5] takes a different, white-box approach, modifying the inner workings of SMT solvers to support higher-order logic. We on the other hand treat theorem provers and SMT solvers as black-boxes, constructing first-order formulas that are tailored to their capabilities. This allows us to use any off-the-shelf SMT solver.

In [8], an SMT module for the theory of FO(Agg) is presented, which can be used in all DPLL-based SAT, SMT and ASP solvers. However, FO(Agg) only provides a way to express functions that have sets or similar constructs as inputs, but not to verify their semantic behavior.

8   Conclusions

We present a methodology for reasoning about unbounded sums in the context of *smart transitions*, that is transitions that occur in smart contracts modeling transactions. Our sum logic SL and its usage of sum constants, instead of fully-fledged sum operators, turns out to be most appropriate for the setting of smart contracts. We show that SL has decidable fragments (Sect. 4.1), as well as undecidable ones (Sect. 4.2). Using two phases to first implicitly encode SL in first-order logic (Sect. 5.1), and then explicitly encode it (Sect. 5.3), allows us to use off-the-shelf automated reasoners in new ways, and automatically verify the semantic correctness of smart transitions.

Showing the (un)decidability of the SL fragment with two sets of uninterpreted functions and sums is an interesting step for further work, as this fragment supports encoding smart transition systems. Another interesting direction of future work is to apply our approach to different aggregates, such as minimum and maximum and to reason about under which conditions these values stay above /below certain thresholds. A slightly modified setting of our SL axioms can already handle min/max aggregates in a basic way, namely by using $\geq$ and $\leq$ instead of equality and dropping the injectivity/surjectivity (respectively) axioms of the counting mechanisms.

Summing upon multidimensional arrays in various ways is yet another direction of future research. Our approach supports the summation over all values in all dimensions by adding the required number of parameters to the predicate idx and by adapting the axioms accordingly.

Acknowledgement. We thank Petra Hozzová for fruitful discussions on our encodings and Sharon Shoham-Buchbinder for her insights and contributions to this paper. This work was partially funded by the ERC CoG ARTIST 101002685, the ERC StG SYMCAR 639270, the United States-Israel Binational Science Foundation (BSF) grant No. 2016260, Grant No. 1810/18 from the Israeli Science Foundation, Len Blavatnik and the Blavatnik Family foundation, the FWF grant LogiCS W1255-N23, the TU Wien DK SecInt and the Amazon ARA 2020 award FOREST.

References

1. SMTLIB: Satisfiability Modulo Theories Library. https://smtlib.cs.uiowa.edu/papers/smt-lib-reference-v2.6-r2017-07-18.pdf
2. Certora Ltd: The Certora Verifier (2020). www.certora.com
3. Concourse Open Community: DeFi Pulse (2020). https://defipulse.com/
4. Alt, L.: Solidity's SMTChecker can Automatically find Real Bugs (2019). https://medium.com/@leonardoalt/soliditys-smtchecker-can-automatically-find-real-bugs-beb566c24dea
5. Barbosa, H., Reynolds, A., El Ouraoui, D., Tinelli, C., Barrett, C.: Extending SMT solvers to higher-order logic. In: CADE, pp. 35–54 (2019)
6. Barrett, C., et al.: CVC4. In: CAV, pp. 171–177 (2011)
7. De Moura, L., Bjørner, N.: Z3: An efficient SMT solver. In: TACAS, pp. 337–340 (2008)
8. Denecker, M., De Cat, B.: DPLL (Agg): an efficient SMT module for aggregates. In: Logic and Search (2010)
9. Dutertre, B., De Moura, L.: The Yices SMT Solver. Tool paper at http://yices.csl.sri.com/tool-paper.pdf, pp. 1–2 (2006)
10. Elad, N., Rain, S., Immerman, N., Kovács, L., Sagiv, M.: Summing up smart transitions (2021). https://arxiv.org/abs/2105.07663
11. Emerson, A.: Modal and temporal logics. In: Handbook of Theoretical Computer Science, vol. B, pp. 995–1072 (1990)
12. Etessami, K.: Counting quantifiers, successor relations, and logarithmic space. In: JCSS, pp. 400–411 (1997)

13. Gleiss, B., Suda, M.: Layered clause selection for saturation-based theorem proving. In: IJCAR, pp. 34–52 (2020)
14. Hajdu, Á., Jovanovic, D.: Solc-verify: a modular verifier for solidity smart contracts. In: VSTTE, pp. 161–179 (2019)
15. Hajdú, M., Hozzová, P., Kovács, L., Schoisswohl, J., Voronkov, A.: Induction with generalization in superposition reasoning. In: CICM, pp. 123–137 (2020)
16. Hella, L., Libkin, L., Nurmonen, J., Wong, L.: Logics with aggregate operators. J. ACM. **48**(8), 880–907 (2001)
17. Hirai, Y.: Defining the Ethereum virtual machine for interactive theorem provers. In: FC, pp. 520–535 (2017)
18. Kalra, S., Goel, S., Dhawan, M., Sharma, S.: ZEUS: analyzing safety of smart contracts. In: NDSS (2018)
19. Kovács, L., Voronkov, A.: First-order theorem proving and vampire. In: CAV, pp. 1–35 (2013)
20. Kuncak, V., Nguyen, H.H., Rinard, M.: An algorithm for deciding BAPA: Boolean algebra with Presburger arithmetic. In: CADE, pp. 260–277 (2005)
21. Libkin, L.: Logics with counting, auxiliary relations, and lower bounds for invariant queries. In: LICS, pp. 316–325 (1999)
22. Nipkow, T.: Interactive proof: introduction to Isabelle/HOL. In: Software Safety and Security, pp. 254–285 (2012)
23. Park, D., Zhang, Y., Rosu, G.: End-to-end formal verification of Ethereum 2.0 deposit smart contract. In: CAV, pp. 151–164 (2020)
24. Passmore, G.O., et al.: The Imandra automated reasoning system (system description). In: IJCAR, pp. 464–471 (2020)
25. Passmore, G.O.: Formal verification of financial algorithms with Imandra. In: FMCAD, pp. i–i (2018)
26. Passmore, G.O., Ignatovich, D.: Formal verification of financial algorithms. In: CADE, pp. 26–41 (2017)
27. Presburger, M.: Über die Vollständigkeit eines gewissen Systems der Arithmetik ganzer Zahlen, in welchem die Addition als einzige Operation hervortritt. In: Comptes Rendus du I congres de Mathématiciens des Pays Slaves, pp. 92–101 (1929)
28. Sadiku, M., Eze, K., Musa, S.: Smart contracts: a primer (2018)
29. Schneidewind, C., Grishchenko, I., Scherer, M., Maffei, M.: eThor: practical and provably sound static analysis of Ethereum smart contracts. In: CCS, pp. 621–640 (2020)
30. Stephens, J., Ferles, K., Mariano, B., Lahiri, S., Dillig, I.: SmartPulse: automated checking of temporal properties in smart contracts. In: IEEE S&P (2021)
31. Väänänen, J.A.: Generalized quantifiers. In: Bull. EATCS (1997)
32. Vogelsteller, F., Buterin, V.: EIP-20: ERC-20 token standard. In: EIP no. 20 (2015)
33. Wang, Y., et al.: Formal verification of workflow policies for smart contracts in azure blockchain. In: VSTTE, pp. 87–106 (2019)
34. Weidenbach, C., Dimova, D., Fietzke, A., Kumar, R., Suda, M., Wischnewski, P.: SPASS Version 3.5. In: CADE, pp. 140–145 (2009)
35. Zhong, J.E., et al.: The move prover. In: CAV, pp. 137–150 (2020)

Stateless Model Checking Under a Reads-Value-From Equivalence

Pratyush Agarwal[1], Krishnendu Chatterjee[2], Shreya Pathak[1],
Andreas Pavlogiannis[3], and Viktor Toman[2(✉)]

[1] IIT Bombay, Mumbai, India
[2] IST Austria, Klosterneuburg, Austria
viktor.toman@ist.ac.at
[3] Aarhus University, Aarhus, Denmark

Abstract. Stateless model checking (SMC) is one of the standard approaches to the verification of concurrent programs. As scheduling non-determinism creates exponentially large spaces of thread interleavings, SMC attempts to partition this space into equivalence classes and explore only a few representatives from each class. The efficiency of this approach depends on two factors: (a) the coarseness of the partitioning, and (b) the time to generate representatives in each class. For this reason, the search for coarse partitionings that are efficiently explorable is an active research challenge.

In this work we present RVF-SMC, a new SMC algorithm that uses a novel *reads-value-from (RVF)* partitioning. Intuitively, two interleavings are deemed equivalent if they agree on the value obtained in each read event, and read events induce consistent causal orderings between them. The RVF partitioning is provably coarser than recent approaches based on Mazurkiewicz and "reads-from" partitionings. Our experimental evaluation reveals that RVF is quite often a very effective equivalence, as the underlying partitioning is exponentially coarser than other approaches. Moreover, RVF-SMC generates representatives very efficiently, as the reduction in the partitioning is often met with significant speed-ups in the model checking task.

1 Introduction

The verification of concurrent programs is one of the key challenges in formal methods. Interprocess communication adds a new dimension of non-determinism in program behavior, which is resolved by a scheduler. As the programmer has no control over the scheduler, program correctness has to be guaranteed under all possible schedulers, i.e., the scheduler is adversarial to the program and can generate erroneous behavior if one can arise out of scheduling decisions. On the other hand, during program testing, the adversarial nature of the scheduler is to hide erroneous runs, making bugs extremely difficult to reproduce by testing alone (aka Heisenbugs [1]). Consequently, the verification of concurrent programs rests on rigorous model checking techniques [2] that cover all possible program

© The Author(s) 2021
A. Silva and K. R. M. Leino (Eds.) CAV 2021, LNCS 12759, pp. 341–366, 2021.
https://doi.org/10.1007/978-3-030-81685-8_16

behaviors that can arise out of scheduling non-determinism, leading to early tools such as VeriSoft [3,4] and CHESS [5].

To battle with the state-space explosion problem, effective model checking for concurrency is stateless. A stateless model checker (SMC) explores the behavior of the concurrent program by manipulating traces instead of states, where each (concurrent) trace is an interleaving of event sequences of the corresponding threads [6]. To further improve performance, various techniques try to reduce the number of explored traces, such as context bounded techniques [7–10] As many interleavings induce the same program behavior, SMC partitions the interleaving space into equivalence classes and attempts to sample a few representative traces from each class. The most popular approach in this domain is partial-order reduction techniques [6,11,12], which deems interleavings as equivalent based on the way that conflicting memory accesses are ordered, also known as the Mazurkiewicz equivalence [13]. Dynamic partial order reduction [14] constructs this equivalence dynamically, when all memory accesses are known, and thus does not suffer from the imprecision of earlier approaches based on static information. Subsequent works managed to explore the Mazurkiewicz partitioning optimally [15,16], while spending only polynomial time per class.

The performance of an SMC algorithm is generally a product of two factors: (a) the size of the underlying partitioning that is explored, and (b) the total time spent in exploring each class of the partitioning. Typically, the task of visiting a class requires solving a consistency-checking problem, where the algorithm checks whether a semantic abstraction, used to represent the class, has a consistent concrete interleaving that witnesses the class. For this reason, the search for effective SMC is reduced to the search of coarse partitionings for which the consistency problem is tractable, and has become a very active research direction in recent years. In [17], the Mazurkiewicz partitioning was further reduced by ignoring the order of conflicting write events that are not observed, while retaining polynomial-time consistency checking. Various other works refine the notion of dependencies between events, yielding coarser abstractions [18–20]. The work of [21] used a reads-from abstraction and showed that the consistency problem admits a fully polynomial solution in acyclic communication topologies. Recently, this approach was generalized to arbitrary topologies, with an algorithm that remains polynomial for a bounded number of threads [22]. Finally, recent approaches define value-centric partitionings [23], as well as partitionings based on maximal causal models [24]. These partitionings are very coarse, as they attempt to distinguish only between traces which differ in the values read by their corresponding read events. We illustrate the benefits of value-based partitionings with a motivating example.

1.1   Motivating Example

Consider a simple concurrent program shown in Fig. 1. The program has 98 different orderings of the conflicting memory accesses, and each ordering corresponds to a separate class of the Mazurkiewicz partitioning. Utilizing the reads-from abstraction reduces the number of partitioning classes to 9. However, when taking into consideration the values that the events can read and write, the number of cases to consider can be reduced even further. In this specific example, there is only a single behaviour the program may exhibit, in which both read events read the only observable value.

Thread$_1$	Thread$_2$	Thread$_3$
1. $w(x,1)$	1. $w(x,1)$	1. $w(x,1)$
2. $w(y,1)$	2. $w(y,1)$	2. $w(y,1)$
	3. $r(x)$	3. $r(y)$

Equivalence classes:	
Mazurkiewicz [15]	98
reads-from [22]	9
value-centric [23]	7
this work	1

Fig. 1. Concurrent program and its underlying partitioning classes.

The above benefits have led to recent attempts in performing SMC using a value-based equivalence [23,24]. However, as the realizability problem is NP-hard in general [25], both approaches suffer significant drawbacks. In particular, the work of [23] combines the value-centric approach with the Mazurkiewicz partitioning, which creates a refinement with exponentially many more classes than potentially necessary. The example program in Fig. 1 illustrates this, where while both read events can only observe one possible value, the work of [23] further enumerates all Mazurkiewicz orderings of all-but-one threads, resulting in 7 partitioning classes. Separately, the work of [24] relies on SMT solvers, thus spending exponential time to solve the realizability problem. Hence, each approach suffers an exponential blow-up a-priori, which motivates the following question: is there an efficient *parameterized* algorithm for the consistency problem? That is, we are interested in an algorithm that is exponential-time in the worst case (as the problem is NP-hard in general), but efficient when certain natural parameters of the input are small, and thus only becomes slow in extreme cases.

Another disadvantage of these works is that each of the exploration algorithms can end up to the same class of the partitioning many times, further hindering performance. To see an example, consider the program in Fig. 1 again. The work of [23] assigns values to reads one by one, and in this example, it needs to consider as separate cases both permutations of the two reads as the orders for assigning the values. This is to ensure completeness in cases where there are write events causally dependent on some read events (e.g., a write event appearing only if its thread-predecessor reads a certain value). However, no causally dependent write events are present in this program, and our work uses a principled approach to detect this and avoid the redundant exploration. While an example to demonstrate [24] revisiting partitioning classes is a bit more involved one, this property follows from the lack of information sharing between spawned subroutines, enabling the approach to be massively parallelized, which has been discussed already in prior works [21,23,26].

1.2 Our Contributions

In this work we tackle the two challenges illustrated in the motivating example in a principled, algorithmic way. In particular, our contributions are as follows.

(1) We study the problem of verifying the sequentially consistent executions. The problem is known to be NP-hard [25] in general, already for 3 threads. We show that the problem can be solved in $O(k^{d+1} \cdot n^{k+1})$ time for an input of n events, k threads and d variables. Thus, although the problem NP-hard in general, it can be solved in polynomial time when the number of threads and number of variables is bounded. Moreover, our bound reduces to $O(n^{k+1})$ in the class of programs where every variable is written by only one thread (while read by many threads). Hence, in this case the bound is polynomial for a fixed number of threads and without any dependence on the number of variables.

(2) We define a new equivalence between concurrent traces, called the *reads-value-from (RVF)* equivalence. Intuitively, two traces are RVF-equivalent if they agree on the value obtained in each read event, and read events induce consistent causal orderings between them. We show that RVF induces a coarser partitioning than the partitionings explored by recent well-studied SMC algorithms [15,21,23], and thus reduces the search space of the model checker.

(3) We develop a novel SMC algorithm called RVF-SMC, and show that it is sound and complete for local safety properties such as assertion violations. Moreover, RVF-SMC has complexity $k^d \cdot n^{O(k)} \cdot \beta$, where β is the size of the underlying RVF partitioning. Under the hood, RVF-SMC uses our consistency-checking algorithm of Item 1 to visit each RVF class during the exploration. Moreover, RVF-SMC uses a novel heuristic to significantly reduce the number of revisits in any given RVF class, compared to the value-based explorations of [23,24].

(4) We implement RVF-SMC in the stateless model checker Nidhugg [27]. Our experimental evaluation reveals that RVF is quite often a very effective equivalence, as the underlying partitioning is exponentially coarser than other approaches. Moreover, RVF-SMC generates representatives very efficiently, as the reduction in the partitioning is often met with significant speed-ups in the model checking task.

2 Preliminaries

General Notation. Given a natural number $i \geq 1$, we let $[i]$ be the set $\{1, 2, \ldots, i\}$. Given a map $f \colon X \to Y$, we let $\mathsf{dom}(f) = X$ denote the domain of f. We represent maps f as sets of tuples $\{(x, f(x))\}_x$. Given two maps f_1, f_2 over the same domain X, we write $f_1 = f_2$ if for every $x \in X$ we have $f_1(x) = f_2(x)$. Given a set $X' \subset X$, we denote by $f|X'$ the restriction of f to X'. A binary relation $\sim$ on a set X is an *equivalence* iff $\sim$ is reflexive, symmetric and transitive.

2.1 Concurrent Model

Here we describe the computational model of concurrent programs with shared memory under the Sequential Consistency (SC) memory model. We follow a standard exposition of stateless model checking, similarly to [14,15,21–23,28],

Concurrent Program. We consider a concurrent program $\mathcal{H} = \{\text{thr}_i\}_{i=1}^k$ of k deterministic threads. The threads communicate over a shared memory $\mathcal{G}$ of global variables with a finite value domain $\mathcal{D}$. Threads execute *events* of the following types.

(1) A *write event* w writes a value $v \in \mathcal{D}$ to a global variable $x \in \mathcal{G}$.
(2) A *read event* r reads the value $v \in \mathcal{D}$ of a global variable $x \in \mathcal{G}$.

Additionally, threads can execute local events which do not access global variables and thus are not modeled explicitly.

Given an event e, we denote by $\text{thr}(e)$ its thread and by $\text{var}(e)$ its global variable. We denote by $\mathcal{E}$ the set of all events, and by $\mathcal{R}$ ($\mathcal{W}$) the set of read (write) events. Given two events $e_1, e_2 \in \mathcal{E}$, we say that they *conflict*, denoted $e_1 \bowtie e_2$, if they access the same global variable and at least one of them is a write event.

Concurrent Program Semantics. The semantics of $\mathcal{H}$ are defined by means of a transition system over a state space of global states. A global state consists of (i) a memory function that maps every global variable to a value, and (ii) a local state for each thread, which contains the values of the local variables and the program counter of the thread. We consider the standard setting of Sequential Consistency (SC), and refer to [14] for formal details. As usual, $\mathcal{H}$ is execution-bounded, which means that the state space is finite and acyclic.

Event Sets. Given a set of events $X \subseteq \mathcal{E}$, we write $\mathcal{R}(X) = X \cap \mathcal{R}$ for the set of read events of X, and $\mathcal{W}(X) = X \cap \mathcal{W}$ for the set of write events of X. Given a set of events $X \subseteq \mathcal{E}$ and a thread thr, we denote by X_{thr} and $X_{\neq\text{thr}}$ the events of thr, and the events of all other threads in X, respectively.

Sequences and Traces. Given a sequence of events $\tau = e_1, \ldots, e_j$, we denote by $\mathcal{E}(\tau)$ the set of events that appear in τ. We further denote $\mathcal{R}(\tau) = \mathcal{R}(\mathcal{E}(\tau))$ and $\mathcal{W}(\tau) = \mathcal{W}(\mathcal{E}(\tau))$.

Given a sequence τ and two events $e_1, e_2 \in \mathcal{E}(\tau)$, we write $e_1 <_\tau e_2$ when e_1 appears before e_2 in τ, and $e_1 \leq_\tau e_2$ to denote that $e_1 <_\tau e_2$ or $e_1 = e_2$. Given a sequence τ and a set of events A, we denote by $\tau|A$ the *projection* of τ on A, which is the unique subsequence of τ that contains all events of $A \cap \mathcal{E}(\tau)$, and only those events. Given a sequence τ and a thread thr, let τ_{thr} be the subsequence of τ with events of thr, i.e., $\tau|\mathcal{E}(\tau)_{\text{thr}}$. Given two sequences τ_1 and τ_2, we denote by $\tau_1 \circ \tau_2$ the sequence that results in appending τ_2 after τ_1.

A (concrete, concurrent) *trace* is a sequence of events σ that corresponds to a concrete valid execution of $\mathcal{H}$. We let $\text{enabled}(\sigma)$ be the set of enabled events after σ is executed, and call σ *maximal* if $\text{enabled}(\sigma) = \emptyset$. As $\mathcal{H}$ is bounded, all executions of $\mathcal{H}$ are finite and the length of the longest execution in $\mathcal{H}$ is a parameter of the input.

Reads-From and Value Functions. Given a sequence of events τ, we define the *reads-from function* of τ, denoted $\mathsf{RF}_\tau \colon \mathcal{R}(\tau) \to \mathcal{W}(\tau)$, as follows. Given a read event $r \in \mathcal{R}(\tau)$, we have that $\mathsf{RF}_\tau(r)$ is the latest write (of any thread) conflicting with r and occurring before r in τ, i.e., (i) $\mathsf{RF}_\tau(r) \bowtie r$, (ii) $\mathsf{RF}_\tau(r) <_\tau r$, and (iii) for each $\overline{w} \in \mathcal{W}(\tau)$ such that $\overline{w} \bowtie r$ and $\overline{w} <_\tau r$, we have $\overline{w} \le_\tau \mathsf{RF}_\tau(r)$. We say that r reads-from $\mathsf{RF}_\tau(r)$ in τ. For simplicity, we assume that $\mathcal{H}$ has an initial salient write event on each variable.

Further, given a trace σ, we define the *value function* of σ, denoted $\mathsf{val}_\sigma \colon \mathcal{E}(\sigma) \to \mathcal{D}$, such that $\mathsf{val}_\sigma(e)$ is the value of the global variable $\mathsf{var}(e)$ after the prefix of σ up to and including e has been executed. Intuitively, $\mathsf{val}_\sigma(e)$ captures the value that a read (resp. write) event e shall read (resp. write) in σ. The value function val_σ is well-defined as σ is a valid trace and the threads of $\mathcal{H}$ are deterministic.

2.2   Partial Orders

In this section we present relevant notation around partial orders, which are a central object in this work.

Partial Orders. Given a set of events $X \subseteq \mathcal{E}$, a *(strict) partial order* P over X is an irreflexive, antisymmetric and transitive relation over X (i.e., $<_P \subseteq X \times X$). Given two events $e_1, e_2 \in X$, we write $e_1 \le_P e_2$ to denote that $e_1 <_P e_2$ or $e_1 = e_2$. Two distinct events $e_1, e_2 \in X$ are *unordered* by P, denoted $e_1 \parallel_P e_2$, if neither $e_1 <_P e_2$ nor $e_2 <_P e_1$, and *ordered* (denoted $e_1 \nparallel_P e_2$) otherwise. Given a set $Y \subseteq X$, we denote by $P|Y$ the *projection* of P on the set Y, where for every pair of events $e_1, e_2 \in Y$, we have that $e_1 <_{P|Y} e_2$ iff $e_1 <_P e_2$. Given two partial orders P and Q over a common set X, we say that Q *refines* P, denoted by $Q \sqsubseteq P$, if for every pair of events $e_1, e_2 \in X$, if $e_1 <_P e_2$ then $e_1 <_Q e_2$. A *linearization* of P is a total order that refines P.

Lower Sets. Given a pair (X, P), where X is a set of events and P is a partial order over X, a *lower set* of (X, P) is a set $Y \subseteq X$ such that for every event $e_1 \in Y$ and event $e_2 \in X$ with $e_2 \le_P e_1$, we have $e_2 \in Y$.

Visible Writes. Given a partial order P over a set X, and a read event $r \in \mathcal{R}(X)$, the set of *visible writes* of r is defined as

$$\mathsf{VisibleW}_P(r) = \{\, w \in \mathcal{W}(X) : \text{(i) } r \bowtie w \text{ and (ii) } r \nless_P w \text{ and (iii) for each}$$
$$w' \in \mathcal{W}(X) \text{ with } r \bowtie w', \text{ if } w <_P w' \text{ then } w' \nless_P r \,\}$$

i.e., the set of write events w conflicting with r that are not "hidden" to r by P.

The Program Order PO. The *program order* PO of $\mathcal{H}$ is a partial order $<_{\mathsf{PO}} \subseteq \mathcal{E} \times \mathcal{E}$ that defines a fixed order between some pairs of events of the same thread, reflecting the semantics of $\mathcal{H}$.

A set of events $X \subseteq \mathcal{E}$ is *proper* if (i) it is a lower set of $(\mathcal{E}, \mathsf{PO})$, and (ii) for each thread thr, the events X_{thr} are totally ordered in PO (i.e., for each distinct $e_1, e_2 \in X_{\mathsf{thr}}$ we have $e_1 \nparallel_{\mathsf{PO}} e_2$). A sequence τ is *well-formed* if (i) its set of events $\mathcal{E}(\tau)$ is proper, and (ii) τ respects the program order (formally, $\tau \sqsubseteq \mathsf{PO}|\mathcal{E}(\tau)$).

Every trace σ of $\mathcal{H}$ is well-formed, as it corresponds to a concrete valid execution of $\mathcal{H}$. Each event of $\mathcal{H}$ is then uniquely identified by its PO predecessors, and by the values its PO predecessor reads have read.

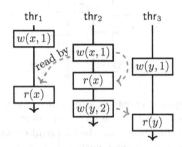

Fig. 2. A trace σ, the displayed events $\mathcal{E}(\sigma)$ are vertically ordered as they appear in σ. The solid black edges represent the program order PO. The dashed red edges represent the reads-from function RF_σ. The transitive closure of all the edges then gives us the causally-happens-before partial order $\mapsto_\sigma$.

Causally-Happens-Before Partial Orders. A trace σ induces a *causally-happens-before* partial order $\mapsto_\sigma \subseteq \mathcal{E}(\sigma) \times \mathcal{E}(\sigma)$, which is the weakest partial order such that (i) it refines the program order (i.e., $\mapsto_\sigma \sqsubseteq \mathsf{PO}|\mathcal{E}(\sigma))$, and (ii) for every read event $r \in \mathcal{R}(\sigma)$, its reads-from $\mathsf{RF}_\sigma(r)$ is ordered before it (i.e., $\mathsf{RF}_\sigma(r) \mapsto_\sigma r$). Intuitively, $\mapsto_\sigma$ contains the causal orderings in σ, i.e., it captures the flow of write events into read events in σ together with the program order. Figure 2 presents an example of a trace and its causal orderings.

3   Reads-Value-From Equivalence

In this section we present our new equivalence on traces, called the *reads-value-from* equivalence (RVF equivalence, or $\sim_{\mathsf{RVF}}$, for short). Then we illustrate that $\sim_{\mathsf{RVF}}$ has some desirable properties for stateless model checking.

Reads-Value-From Equivalence. Given two traces σ_1 and σ_2, we say that they are *reads-value-from-equivalent*, written $\sigma_1 \sim_{\mathsf{RVF}} \sigma_2$, if the following hold.

(1) $\mathcal{E}(\sigma_1) = \mathcal{E}(\sigma_2)$, i.e., they consist of the same set of events.
(2) $\mathsf{val}_{\sigma_1} = \mathsf{val}_{\sigma_2}$, i.e., each event reads resp. writes the same value in both.
(3) $\mapsto_{\sigma_1}|\mathcal{R} = \mapsto_{\sigma_2}|\mathcal{R}$, i.e., their causal orderings agree on the read events.

Figure 3 presents an intuitive example of RVF-(in)equivalent traces.

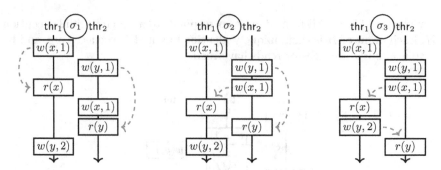

Fig. 3. Three traces σ_1, σ_2, σ_3, events of each trace are vertically ordered as they appear in the trace. Traces σ_1 and σ_2 are RVF-equivalent ($\sigma_1 \sim_{\mathsf{RVF}} \sigma_2$), as they have the same events, same value function, and the two read events are causally unordered in both. Trace σ_3 is not RVF-equivalent with either of σ_1 and σ_2. Compared to σ_1 resp. σ_2, the value function of σ_3 differs ($r(y)$ reads a different value), and the causal orderings of the reads differ ($r(x) \mapsto_{\sigma_3} r(y)$).

Soundness. The RVF equivalence induces a partitioning on the maximal traces of $\mathcal{H}$. Any algorithm that explores each class of this partitioning provably discovers every reachable local state of every thread, and thus RVF is a sound equivalence for local safety properties, such as assertion violations, in the same spirit as in other recent works [21–24]. This follows from the fact that for any two traces σ_1 and σ_2 with $\mathcal{E}(\sigma_1) = \mathcal{E}(\sigma_2)$ and $\mathsf{val}_{\sigma_1} = \mathsf{val}_{\sigma_2}$, the local states of each thread are equal after executing σ_1 and σ_2.

$$
\begin{array}{c}
\text{reads-from[22,28]} \\
\text{reads-value-from} \qquad\qquad \text{data-centric[21]} \quad \text{Mazurkiewicz[14,15,29]} \\
\text{value-centric[23]}
\end{array}
$$

Fig. 4. SMC trace equivalences. An edge from X to Y signifies that Y is always at least as coarse, and sometimes coarser, than X.

Coarseness. Here we describe the coarseness properties of the RVF equivalence, as compared to other equivalences used by state-of-the-art approaches in stateless model checking. Figure 4 summarizes the comparison.

The SMC algorithms of [22] and [28] operate on a *reads-from equivalence*, which deems two traces σ_1 and σ_2 equivalent if

(1) they consist of the same events ($\mathcal{E}(\sigma_1) = \mathcal{E}(\sigma_2)$), and
(2) their reads-from functions coincide ($\mathsf{RF}_{\sigma_1} = \mathsf{RF}_{\sigma_2}$).

The above two conditions imply that the induced causally-happens-before partial orders are equal, i.e., $\mapsto_{\sigma_1} = \mapsto_{\sigma_2}$, and thus trivially also $\mapsto_{\sigma_1}\!|\mathcal{R} = \mapsto_{\sigma_2}\!|\mathcal{R}$.

Further, by a simple inductive argument the value functions of the two traces are also equal, i.e., $\mathsf{val}_{\sigma_1} = \mathsf{val}_{\sigma_2}$. Hence any two reads-from-equivalent traces are also RVF-equivalent, which makes the RVF equivalence always at least as coarse as the reads-from equivalence.

The work of [23] utilizes a *value-centric equivalence*, which deems two traces equivalent if they satisfy all the conditions of our RVF equivalence, and also some further conditions (note that these conditions are necessary for correctness of the SMC algorithm in [23]). Thus the RVF equivalence is trivially always at least as coarse. The value-centric equivalence preselects a single thread thr, and then requires two extra conditions for the traces to be equivalent, namely:

(1) For each read of thr, either the read reads-from a write of thr in both traces, or it does not read-from a write of thr in either of the two traces.
(2) For each conflicting pair of events not belonging to thr, the ordering of the pair is equal in the two traces.

Both the reads-from equivalence and the value-centric equivalence are in turn as coarse as the *data-centric equivalence* of [21]. Given two traces, the data-centric equivalence has the equivalence conditions of the reads-from equivalence, and additionally, it preselects a single thread thr (just like the value-centric equivalence) and requires the second extra condition of the value-centric equivalence, i.e., equality of orderings for each conflicting pair of events outside of thr.

Finally, the data-centric equivalence is as coarse as the classical *Mazurkiewicz equivalence* [13], the baseline equivalence for stateless model checking [14,15,29]. Mazurkiewicz equivalence deems two traces equivalent if they consist of the same set of events and they agree on their ordering of conflicting events.

While RVF is always at least as coarse, it can be (even exponentially) coarser, than each of the other above-mentioned equivalences. We illustrate this in Appendix B of [30]. We summarize these observations in the following proposition.

Proposition 1. RVF *is at least as coarse as each of the Mazurkiewicz equivalence* [15], *the data-centric equivalence* [21], *the reads-from equivalence* [22], *and the value-centric equivalence* [23]. *Moreover,* RVF *can be exponentially coarser than each of these equivalences.*

In this work we develop our SMC algorithm RVF-SMC around the RVF equivalence, with the guarantee that the algorithm explores at most one maximal trace per class of the RVF partitioning, and thus can perform significantly fewer steps than algorithms based on the above equivalences. To utilize RVF, the algorithm in each step solves an instance of the verification of sequential consistency problem, which we tackle in the next section. Afterwards, we present RVF-SMC.

4   Verifying Sequential Consistency

In this section we present our contributions towards the problem of verifying sequential consistency (VSC). We present an algorithm VerifySC for VSC, and we show how it can be efficiently used in stateless model checking.

The VSC Problem. Consider an input pair (X, GoodW) where

(1) $X \subseteq \mathcal{E}$ is a proper set of events, and
(2) $\mathsf{GoodW} \colon \mathcal{R}(X) \to 2^{\mathcal{W}(X)}$ is a good-writes function such that $w \in \mathsf{GoodW}(r)$ only if $r \bowtie w$.

A *witness* of (X, GoodW) is a linearization τ of X (i.e., $\mathcal{E}(\tau) = X$) respecting the program order (i.e., $\tau \sqsubseteq \mathsf{PO}|X$), such that each read $r \in \mathcal{R}(\tau)$ reads-from one of its good-writes in τ, formally $\mathsf{RF}_\tau(r) \in \mathsf{GoodW}(r)$ (we then say that τ *satisfies* the good-writes function GoodW). The task is to decide whether (X, GoodW) has a witness, and to construct one in case it exists.

VSC in Stateless Model Checking. The VSC problem naturally ties in with our SMC approach enumerating the equivalence classes of the RVF trace partitioning. In our approach, we shall generate instances (X, GoodW) such that (i) each witness σ of (X, GoodW) is a valid program trace, and (ii) all witnesses σ_1, σ_2 of (X, GoodW) are pairwise RVF-equivalent ($\sigma_1 \sim_{\mathsf{RVF}} \sigma_2$).

Hardness of VSC. Given an input (X, GoodW) to the VSC problem, let $n = |X|$, let k be the number of threads appearing in X, and let d be the number of variables accessed in X. The classic work of [25] establishes two important lower bounds on the complexity of VSC:

(1) VSC is NP-hard even when restricted only to inputs with $k = 3$.
(2) VSC is NP-hard even when restricted only to inputs with $d = 2$.

The first bound eliminates the possibility of any algorithm with time complexity $O(n^{f(k)})$, where f is an arbitrary computable function. Similarly, the second bound eliminates algorithms with complexity $O(n^{f(d)})$ for any computable f.

In this work we show that the problem is parameterizable in $k + d$, and thus admits efficient (polynomial-time) solutions when both variables are bounded.

4.1   Algorithm for VSC

In this section we present our algorithm VerifySC for the problem VSC. First we define some relevant notation. In our definitions we consider a fixed input pair (X, GoodW) to the VSC problem, and a fixed sequence τ with $\mathcal{E}(\tau) \subseteq X$.

Active Writes. A write $w \in \mathcal{W}(\tau)$ is *active* in τ if it is the last write of its variable in τ. Formally, for each $w' \in \mathcal{W}(\tau)$ with $\mathsf{var}(w') = \mathsf{var}(w)$ we have $w' \leq_\tau w$. We can then say that w is the active write of the variable $\mathsf{var}(w)$ in τ.

Held Variables. A variable $x \in \mathcal{G}$ is *held* in τ if there exists a read $r \in \mathcal{R}(X) \setminus \mathcal{E}(\tau)$ with $\mathsf{var}(r) = x$ such that for each its good-write $w \in \mathsf{GoodW}(r)$ we have $w \in \tau$. In such a case we say that r *holds* x in τ. Note that several distinct reads may hold a single variable in τ.

Executable Events. An event $e \in \mathcal{E}(X) \setminus \mathcal{E}(\tau)$ is *executable* in τ if $\mathcal{E}(\tau) \cup \{e\}$ is a lower set of (X, PO) and the following hold.

(1) If e is a read, it has an active good-write $w \in \mathsf{GoodW}(e)$ in τ.
(2) If e is a write, its variable $\mathsf{var}(e)$ is not held in τ.

Memory Maps. A *memory map* of τ is a function from global variables to thread indices $\mathrm{MMap}_\tau \colon \mathcal{G} \rightarrow [k]$ where for each variable $x \in \mathcal{G}$, the map $\mathrm{MMap}_\tau(x)$ captures the thread of the active write of x in τ.

Witness States. The sequence τ is a *witness prefix* if the following hold.

(1) τ is a witness of $(\mathcal{E}(\tau), \mathsf{GoodW}|\mathcal{R}(\tau))$.
(2) For each $r \in X \setminus \mathcal{R}(\tau)$ that holds its variable $\mathsf{var}(r)$ in τ, one of its good-writes $w \in \mathsf{GoodW}(r)$ is active in τ.

Intuitively, τ is a witness prefix if it satisfies all VSC requirements modulo its events, and if each read not in τ has at least one good-write still available to read-from in potential extensions of τ. For a witness prefix τ we call its corresponding event set and memory map a *witness state*.

Figure 5 provides an example illustrating the above concepts, where for brevity of presentation, the variables are subscripted and the values are not displayed.

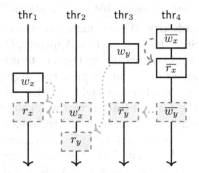

Fig. 5. Event set X, and the good-writes function GoodW denoted by the green dotted edges. The solid nodes are ordered vertically as they appear in τ. The grey dashed nodes are in $X \setminus \mathcal{E}(\tau)$. Events r_x and w'_x are executable in τ. Event $\overline{r_y}$ is not, its good-write is not active in τ. Event $\overline{w_y}$ is also not executable, as its variable y is held by r_y. The memory map of τ is $\mathrm{MMap}_\tau(x) = 1$ and $\mathrm{MMap}_\tau(y) = 3$. τ is a witness prefix, and $\mathcal{E}(\tau)$ with MMap_τ together form its witness state.

Algorithm 1: VerifySC

Input: Proper event set X and good-writes function $\mathsf{GoodW} \colon \mathcal{R}(X) \to 2^{\mathcal{W}(X)}$

Output: A witness τ of (X, GoodW) if (X, GoodW) has a witness, else $\tau = \bot$

1 $\mathcal{S} \leftarrow \{\epsilon\}$; $\mathsf{Done} \leftarrow \{\epsilon\}$

2 **while** $\mathcal{S} \neq \emptyset$ **do**

3   Extract a sequence τ from $\mathcal{S}$

4   **if** $\mathcal{E}(\tau) = X$ **then return** τ ;   `// All events executed, witness found`

5   **foreach** *event e executable in* τ **do**

6   Let $\tau_e \leftarrow \tau \circ e$ `// Execute e`

7   **if** $\not\exists \tau' \in \mathsf{Done}$ *s.t.* $\mathcal{E}(\tau_e) = \mathcal{E}(\tau')$ *and* $\mathrm{MMap}_{\tau_e} = \mathrm{MMap}_{\tau'}$ **then**

8   Insert τ_e in $\mathcal{S}$ and in Done `// New witness state reached`

9 **return** $\bot$ `// No witness exists`

Algorithm. We are now ready to describe our algorithm VerifySC, in Algorithm 1 we present the pseudocode. We attempt to construct a witness of (X, GoodW) by enumerating the witness states reachable by the following process. We start (Line 1) with an empty sequence ϵ as the first witness prefix (and state). We maintain a worklist $\mathcal{S}$ of so-far unprocessed witness prefixes, and a set Done of reached witness states. Then we iteratively obtain new witness prefixes (and states) by considering an already obtained prefix (Line 3) and extending it with each possible executable event (Line 6). Crucially, when we arrive at a sequence τ_e, we include it only if no sequence τ' with equal corresponding witness state has been reached yet (Line 7). We stop when we successfully create a witness (Line 4) or when we process all reachable witness states (Line 9).

Correctness and Complexity. We now highlight the correctness and complexity properties of VerifySC, while we refer to Appendix C of [30] for the proofs. The soundness follows straightforwardly by the fact that each sequence in $\mathcal{S}$ is a witness prefix. This follows from a simple inductive argument that extending a witness prefix with an executable event yields another witness prefix. The completeness follows from the fact that given two witness prefixes τ_1 and τ_2 with equal induced witness state, these prefixes are "equi-extendable" to a witness. Indeed, if a suffix τ^* exists such that $\tau_1 \circ \tau^*$ is a witness of (X, GoodW), then $\tau_2 \circ \tau^*$ is also a witness of (X, GoodW). The time complexity of VerifySC is bounded by $O(n^{k+1} \cdot k^{d+1})$, for n events, k threads and d variables. The bound follows from the fact that there are at most $n^k \cdot k^d$ pairwise distinct witness states. We thus have the following theorem.

Theorem 1. VSC *for n events, k threads and d variables is solvable in $O(n^{k+1} \cdot k^{d+1})$ time. Moreover, if each variable is written by only one thread, VSC is solvable in $O(n^{k+1})$ time.*

Implications. We now highlight some important implications of Theorem 1. Although VSC is NP-hard [25], the theorem shows that the problem is parameterizable in $k + d$, and thus in polynomial time when both parameters are bounded. Moreover, even when only k is bounded, the problem is fixed-parameter tractable in d, meaning that d only exponentiates a constant as opposed to n (e.g., we have a polynomial bound even when $d = \log n$). Finally, the algorithm is polynomial for a fixed number of threads regardless of d, when every memory location is written by only one thread (e.g., in producer-consumer settings, or in the concurrent-read-exclusive-write (CREW) concurrency model). These important facts brought forward by Theorem 1 indicate that VSC is likely to be efficiently solvable in many practical settings, which in turn makes RVF a good equivalence for SMC.

4.2 Practical Heuristics for VerifySC in SMC

We now turn our attention to some practical heuristics that are expected to further improve the performance of VerifySC in the context of SMC.

1. Limiting the Search Space. We employ two straightforward improvements to VerifySC that significantly reduce the search space in practice. Consider the for-loop in Line 5 of Algorithm 1 enumerating the possible extensions of τ. This enumeration can be sidestepped by the following two greedy approaches.

(1) If there is a read r executable in τ, then extend τ with r and do not enumerate other options.
(2) Let $\overline{w}$ be an active write in τ such that $\overline{w}$ is not a good-write of any $r \in \mathcal{R}(X) \backslash \mathcal{E}(\tau)$. Let $w \in \mathcal{W}(X) \backslash \mathcal{E}(\tau)$ be a write of the same variable ($\mathsf{var}(w) = \mathsf{var}(\overline{w})$), note that w is executable in τ. If w is also not a good-write of any $r \in \mathcal{R}(X) \backslash \mathcal{E}(\tau)$, then extend τ with w and do not enumerate other options.

The enumeration of Line 5 then proceeds only if neither of the above two techniques can be applied for τ. This extension of VerifySC preserves completeness (not only when used during SMC, but in general), and it can be significantly faster in practice. For clarity of presentation we do not fully formalize this extended version, as its worst-case complexity remains the same.

2. Closure. We introduce *closure*, a low-cost filter for early detection of VSC instances (X, GoodW) with no witness. The notion of closure, its beneficial properties and construction algorithms are well-studied for the *reads-from consistency verification* problems [21,22,31], i.e., problems where a desired reads-from function is provided as input instead of a desired good-writes function GoodW. Further, the work of [23] studies closure with respect to a good-writes function, but only for partial orders of Mazurkiewicz width 2 (i.e., for partial orders with no triplet of pairwise conflicting and pairwise unordered events). Here we define closure for all good-writes instances (X, GoodW), with the underlying partial order (in our case, the program order PO) of arbitrary Mazurkiewicz width.

   Given a VSC instance (X, GoodW), its closure $P(X)$ is the weakest partial order that refines the program order ($P \sqsubseteq \mathsf{PO}|X$) and further satisfies the following conditions. Given a read $r \in \mathcal{R}(X)$, let $Cl(r) = \mathsf{GoodW}(r) \cap \mathsf{VisibleW}_P(r)$. The following must hold.

(1) $Cl(r) \neq \emptyset$.
(2) If $(Cl(r), P|Cl(r))$ has a least element w, then $w <_P r$.
(3) If $(Cl(r), P|Cl(r))$ has a greatest element w, then for each $\overline{w} \in \mathcal{W}(X) \setminus$ GoodW(r) with $r \bowtie \overline{w}$, if $\overline{w} <_P r$ then $\overline{w} <_P w$.
(4) For each $\overline{w} \in \mathcal{W}(X) \setminus$ GoodW(r) with $r \bowtie \overline{w}$, if each $w \in Cl(r)$ satisfies $w <_P \overline{w}$, then we have $r <_P \overline{w}$.

If (X, GoodW) has no closure (i.e., there is no P with the above conditions), then (X, GoodW) provably has no witness. If (X, GoodW) has closure P, then each witness τ of VSC(X, GoodW) provably refines P (i.e., $\tau \sqsubseteq P$).

Finally, we explain how closure can be used by VerifySC. Given an input (X, GoodW), the closure procedure is carried out before VerifySC is called. Once the closure P of (X, GoodW) is constructed, since each solution of VSC(X, GoodW) has to refine P, we restrict VerifySC to only consider sequences refining P. This is ensured by an extra condition in Line 5 of Algorithm 1, where we proceed with an event e only if it is minimal in P restricted to events not yet in the sequence. This preserves completeness, while further reducing the search space to consider for VerifySC.

3. VerifySC Guided by Auxiliary Trace. In our SMC approach, each time we generate a VSC instance (X, GoodW), we further have available an auxiliary trace $\widetilde{\sigma}$. In $\widetilde{\sigma}$, either all-but-one, or all, good-writes conditions of GoodW are satisfied. If all good writes in GoodW are satisfied, we already have $\widetilde{\sigma}$ as a witness of (X, GoodW) and hence we do not need to run VerifySC at all. On the other hand, if case all-but-one are satisfied, we use $\widetilde{\sigma}$ to guide the search of VerifySC, as described below.

We guide the search by deciding the order in which we process the sequences of the worklist S in Algorithm 1. We use the auxiliary trace $\widetilde{\sigma}$ with $\mathcal{E}(\widetilde{\sigma}) = X$. We use S as a last-in-first-out stack, that way we search for a witness in a depth-first fashion. Then, in Line 5 of Algorithm 1 we enumerate the extension events in the reverse order of how they appear in $\widetilde{\sigma}$. We enumerate in reverse order, as each resulting extension is pushed into our worklist S, which is a stack (last-in-first-out). As a result, in Line 3 of the subsequent iterations of the main while loop, we pop extensions from S in order induced by $\widetilde{\sigma}$.

5 Stateless Model Checking

We are now ready to present our SMC algorithm RVF-SMC that uses RVF to model check a concurrent program. RVF-SMC is a sound and complete algorithm for local safety properties, i.e., it is guaranteed to discover all local states that each thread visits.

RVF-SMC is a recursive algorithm. Each recursive call of RVF-SMC is argumented by a tuple $(X, \text{GoodW}, \sigma, \mathcal{C})$ where:

(1) X is a proper set of events.
(2) GoodW: $\mathcal{R}(X) \to 2^{\mathcal{W}(X)}$ is a desired good-writes function.
(3) σ is a valid trace that is a witness of (X, GoodW).

(4) $\mathcal{C}\colon \mathcal{R} \to$ Threads $\to \mathbb{N}$ is a partial function called *causal map* that tracks implicitly, for each read r, the writes that have already been considered as reads-from sources of r.

Further, we maintain a function $\mathsf{ancestors}\colon \mathcal{R}(X) \to \{\mathsf{true}, \mathsf{false}\}$, where for each read $r \in \mathcal{R}(X)$, $\mathsf{ancestors}(r)$ stores a boolean *backtrack signal* for r. We now provide details on the notions of causal maps and backtrack signals.

Causal Maps. The causal map $\mathcal{C}$ serves to ensure that no more than one maximal trace is explored per RVF partitioning class. Given a read $r \in \mathsf{enabled}(\sigma)$ enabled in a trace σ, we define $\mathsf{forbids}_\sigma^{\mathcal{C}}(r)$ as the set of writes in σ such that $\mathcal{C}$ forbids r to read-from them. Formally, $\mathsf{forbids}_\sigma^{\mathcal{C}}(r) = \emptyset$ if $r \notin \mathsf{dom}(\mathcal{C})$, otherwise $\mathsf{forbids}_\sigma^{\mathcal{C}}(r) = \{w \in \mathcal{W}(\sigma) \mid w \text{ is within first } \mathcal{C}(r)(\mathsf{thr}(w)) \text{ events of } \sigma_{\mathsf{thr}}\}$. We say that a trace σ *satisfies* $\mathcal{C}$ if for each $r \in \mathcal{R}(\sigma)$ we have $\mathsf{RF}_\sigma(r) \notin \mathsf{forbids}_\sigma^{\mathcal{C}}(r)$.

Backtrack Signals. Each call of RVF-SMC (with its GoodW) operates with a trace $\widetilde{\sigma}$ satisfying GoodW that has only reads as enabled events. Consider one of those enabled reads $r \in \mathsf{enabled}(\widetilde{\sigma})$. Each maximal trace satisfying GoodW shall contain r, and further, one of the following two cases is true:

(1) In all maximal traces σ' satisfying GoodW, we have that r reads-from some write of $\mathcal{W}(\widetilde{\sigma})$ in σ'.
(2) There exists a maximal trace σ' satisfying GoodW, such that r reads-from a write not in $\mathcal{W}(\widetilde{\sigma})$ in σ'.

Whenever we can prove that the first above case is true for r, we can use this fact to prune away some recursive calls of RVF-SMC while maintaining completeness. Specifically, we leverage the following crucial lemma, and present the proof in Appendix D of [30].

Lemma 1. *Consider a call* RVF-SMC$(X, \mathsf{GoodW}, \sigma, \mathcal{C})$ *and a trace* $\widetilde{\sigma}$ *extending* σ *maximally such that no event of the extension is a read. Let* $r \in \mathsf{enabled}(\widetilde{\sigma})$ *such that* $r \notin \mathsf{dom}(\mathcal{C})$. *If there exists a trace* σ' *that (i) satisfies* GoodW *and* $\mathcal{C}$, *and (ii) contains* r *with* $\mathsf{RF}_{\sigma'}(r) \notin \mathcal{W}(\widetilde{\sigma})$, *then there exists a trace* $\bar{\sigma}$ *that (i) satisfies* GoodW *and* $\mathcal{C}$, *(ii) contains* r *with* $\mathsf{RF}_{\bar{\sigma}}(r) \in \mathcal{W}(\widetilde{\sigma})$, *and (iii) contains a write* $w \notin \mathcal{W}(\widetilde{\sigma})$ *with* $r \bowtie w$ *and* $\mathsf{thr}(r) \neq \mathsf{thr}(w)$.

We then compute a boolean *backtrack signal* for a given RVF-SMC call and read $r \in \mathsf{enabled}(\widetilde{\sigma})$ to capture satisfaction of the consequent of Lemma 1. If the computed backtrack signal is false, we can safely stop the RVF-SMC exploration of this specific call and backtrack to its recursion parent.

Algorithm. We are now ready to describe our algorithm RVF-SMC in detail, Algorithm 2 captures the pseudocode of RVF-SMC$(X, \mathsf{GoodW}, \sigma, \mathcal{C})$. First, in Line 1 we extend σ to $\widetilde{\sigma}$ maximally such that no event of the extension is a read. Then in Lines 2–5 we update the backtrack signals for ancestors of our current recursion call. After this, in Lines 6–11 we construct a sequence of reads enabled in $\widetilde{\sigma}$. Finally, we proceed with the main while-loop in Line 13. In each while-loop iteration we process an enabled read r (Line 14), and we perform no more while-loop iterations in case we receive a false backtrack signal for r.

Algorithm 2: RVF-SMC(X, GoodW, σ, $\mathcal{C}$)

Input: Proper set of events X, good-writes function GoodW, valid trace σ that
          is a witness of (X, GoodW), causal map $\mathcal{C}$.

1 $\widetilde{\sigma} \leftarrow \sigma \circ \widehat{\sigma}$ where $\widehat{\sigma}$ extends σ maximally such that no event of $\widehat{\sigma}$ is a read

2 **foreach** $w \in \mathcal{E}(\widehat{\sigma})$ **do**   // All extension events are writes

3   **foreach** $r \in \mathrm{dom}(\mathrm{ancestors})$ **do**   // All ancestor mutations are reads

4   **if** $r \bowtie w$ *and* $\mathrm{thr}(r) \neq \mathrm{thr}(w)$ **then**   // Potential new source for r to read-from

5 | $\mathrm{ancestors}(r) \leftarrow$ true   // Set backtrack signal to true

6 $\mathrm{mutate} \leftarrow \epsilon$ // Construct a sequence of enabled reads

7 **foreach** $r \in \mathrm{enabled}(\widetilde{\sigma})$ **do**   // Enabled events in $\widetilde{\sigma}$ are reads

8   **if** $r \in \mathrm{dom}(\mathcal{C})$ **then**   // Causal map $\mathcal{C}$ is defined for r

9 | $\mathrm{mutate} \leftarrow \mathrm{mutate} \circ r$ // Insert r to the end of mutate

10   **else**

11 | $\mathrm{mutate} \leftarrow r \circ \mathrm{mutate}$ // Insert r to the beginning of mutate

12 $\mathrm{backtrack} \leftarrow$ true

13 **while** $\mathrm{backtrack} = $ true *and* $\mathrm{mutate} \neq \epsilon$ **do**

14    $r \leftarrow$ pop front of mutate   // Process next read of mutate

15   **if** $r \notin \mathrm{dom}(\mathcal{C})$ **then**

16 | $\mathrm{backtrack} \leftarrow$ false

17    $F_r \leftarrow \mathrm{VisibleW}_{\mathsf{PO}|\mathcal{E}(\widetilde{\sigma})}(r) \setminus \mathrm{forbids}_{\widetilde{\sigma}}^{\mathcal{C}}(r)$ // Visible writes not forbidden by $\mathcal{C}$

18    $\mathcal{D}_r \leftarrow \{\mathrm{val}_{\widetilde{\sigma}}(w) : w \in F_r\}$ // The set of values that r may read

19   **foreach** $v \in \mathcal{D}_r$ **do**   // Process each value

20      $X' \leftarrow X \cup \mathcal{E}(\widetilde{\sigma}) \cup \{r\}$ // New event set

21      $\mathsf{GoodW'} \leftarrow \mathsf{GoodW} \cup \{(r, \{w \in F_r \mid \mathrm{val}_{\widetilde{\sigma}}(w) = v\})\}$ // New good-writes

22      $\sigma' \leftarrow \mathrm{VerifySC}(X', \mathsf{GoodW'})$ // VerifySC guided by $\widetilde{\sigma}$ or r

23   **if** $\sigma' \neq \bot$ **then**   // $(X', \mathsf{GoodW'})$ has a witness

24 | $\mathcal{C}' \leftarrow \mathcal{C}$

25        $\mathrm{ancestors}(r) \leftarrow \mathrm{backtrack}$ // Record ancestor

26   RVF-SMC(X', $\mathsf{GoodW'}$, σ', $\mathcal{C}'$)

27        $\mathrm{backtrack} \leftarrow \mathrm{ancestors}(r)$ // Retrieve backtrack signal

28   delete r from ancestors   // Unrecord ancestor

29   **foreach** $\mathrm{thr} \in \mathrm{Threads}$ **do**   // Update causal map $\mathcal{C}(r)$ for each thread

30 | $\mathcal{C}(r)(\mathrm{thr}) \leftarrow |\mathcal{E}(\widetilde{\sigma})_{\mathrm{thr}}|$ // Number of events of thr in $\widetilde{\sigma}$

When processing r, first we collect its viable reads-from sources in Line 17, then we group the sources by value they write in Line 18, and then in iterations of the for-loop in Line 19 we consider each value-group. In Line 20 we form the event set, and in Line 21 we form the good-write function that designates the value-group as the good-writes of r. In Line 22 we use VerifySC to generate a witness, and in case it exists, we recursively call RVF-SMC in Line 26 with the newly obtained events, good-write constraint for r, and witness.

To preserve completeness of RVF-SMC, the backtrack-signals technique can be utilized only for reads r with undefined causal map $r \notin \mathrm{dom}(\mathcal{C})$ (cf. Lemma 1). The order of the enabled reads imposed by Lines 6–11 ensures that subsequently, in iterations of the loop in Line 13 we first consider all the reads where we can utilize the backtrack signals. This is an insightful heuristic that often helps in practice, though it does not improve the worst-case complexity.

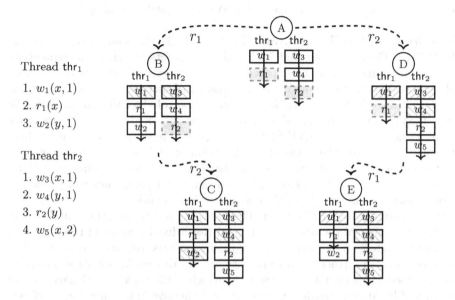

Fig. 6. RVF-SMC (Algorithm 2). Circles represent nodes of the recursion tree. Below each circle is its corresponding event set $\mathcal{E}(\widetilde{\sigma})$ and the enabled reads (dashed grey). Writes with green background are good-writes (GoodW) of its corresponding-variable read. Writes with red background are forbidden by $\mathcal{C}$ for its corresponding-variable read. Dashed arrows represent recursive calls. (Color figure online)

Example. Figure 6 displays a simple concurrent program on the left, and its corresponding RVF-SMC (Algorithm 2) run on the right. We start with RVF-SMC($\emptyset, \emptyset, \epsilon, \emptyset$) (A). By performing the extension (Line 1) we obtain the events and enabled reads as shown below (A). First we process read r_1 (Line 14). The read can read-from w_1 and w_3, both write the same value so they are grouped together as good-writes of r_1. A witness is found and a recursive call to (B) is performed. In (B), the only enabled event is r_2. It can read-from w_2 and w_4, both write the same value so they are grouped for r_2. A witness is found, a recursive call to (C) is performed, and (C) concludes with a maximal trace. Crucially, in (C) the event w_5 is discovered, and since it is a potential new reads-from source for r_1, a backtrack signal is sent to (A). Hence after RVF-SMC backtracks to (A), in (A) it needs to perform another iteration of Line 13 while-loop. In (A), first the causal map $\mathcal{C}$ is updated to forbid w_1 and w_3 for r_1. Then, read r_2 is processed from (A), creating (D). In (D), r_1 is the only enabled event, and w_5 is its only $\mathcal{C}$-allowed write. This results in (E) which reports a maximal trace. The algorithm backtracks and concludes, reporting two maximal traces in total.

Theorem 2. *Consider a concurrent program $\mathcal{H}$ of k threads and d variables, with n the length of the longest trace in $\mathcal{H}$. RVF-SMC is a sound and complete algorithm for local safety properties in $\mathcal{H}$. The time complexity of RVF-SMC is $k^d \cdot n^{O(k)} \cdot \beta$, where β is the size of the RVF trace partitioning of $\mathcal{H}$.*

Novelties of the Exploration. Here we highlight some key aspects of RVF-SMC. First, we note that RVF-SMC constructs the traces incrementally with each recursion step, as opposed to other approaches such as [15,22] that always work with maximal traces. The reason of incremental traces is technical and has to do with the value-based treatment of the RVF partitioning. We note that the other two value-based approaches [23,24] also operate with incremental traces. However, RVF-SMC brings certain novelties compared to these two methods. First, the exploration algorithm of [24] can visit the same class of the partitioning (and even the same trace) an exponential number of times by different recursion branches, leading to significant performance degradation. The exploration algorithm of [23] alleviates this issue using the causal map data structure, similar to our algorithm. The causal map data structure can provably limit the number of revisits to polynomial (for a fixed number of threads), and although it offers an improvement over the exponential revisits, it can still affect performance. To further improve performance in this work, our algorithm combines causal maps with a new technique, which is the backtrack signals. Causal maps and backtrack signals together are very effective in avoiding having different branches of the recursion visit the same RVF class.

Beyond RVF Partitioning. While RVF-SMC explores the RVF partitioning in the worst case, in practice it often operates on a partitioning coarser than the one induced by the RVF equivalence. Specifically, RVF-SMC may treat two traces σ_1 and σ_2 with same events ($\mathcal{E}(\sigma_1) = \mathcal{E}(\sigma_2)$) and value function ($\mathsf{val}_{\sigma_1} = \mathsf{val}_{\sigma_2}$) as equivalent even when they differ in some causal orderings ($\mapsto_{\sigma_1}|\mathcal{R} \neq \mapsto_{\sigma_2}|\mathcal{R}$). To see an example of this, consider the program and the RVF-SMC run in Fig. 6. The recursion node (C) spans all traces where (i) r_1 reads-from either w_1 or w_3, and (ii) r_2 reads-from either w_2 or w_4. Consider two such traces σ_1 and σ_2, with $\mathsf{RF}_{\sigma_1}(r_2) = w_2$ and $\mathsf{RF}_{\sigma_2}(r_2) = w_4$. We have $r_1 \mapsto_{\sigma_1} r_2$ and $r_1 \not\mapsto_{\sigma_2} r_2$, and yet σ_1 and σ_2 are (soundly) considered equivalent by RVF-SMC. Hence the RVF partitioning is used to upper-bound the time complexity of RVF-SMC. We remark that the algorithm is always sound, i.e., it is guaranteed to discover all thread states even when it does not explore the RVF partitioning in full.

6   Experiments

In this section we describe the experimental evaluation of our SMC approach RVF-SMC. We have implemented RVF-SMC as an extension in Nidhugg [27], a state-of-the-art stateless model checker for multithreaded C/C++ programs that operates on LLVM Intermediate Representation. First we assess the advantages of utilizing the RVF equivalence in SMC as compared to other trace equivalences.

Then we perform ablation studies to demonstrate the impact of the backtrack signals technique (cf. Sect. 5) and the VerifySC heuristics (cf. Sect. 4.2).

In our experiments we compare RVF-SMC with several state-of-the-art SMC tools utilizing different trace equivalences. First we consider VC-DPOR [23], the SMC approach operating on the value-centric equivalence. Then we consider Nidhugg/rfsc [22], the SMC algorithm utilizing the reads-from equivalence. Further we consider DC-DPOR [21] that operates on the data-centric equivalence, and finally we compare with Nidhugg/source [15] utilizing the Mazurkiewicz equivalence.[1] The works of [22] and [32] in turn compare the Nidhugg/rfsc algorithm with additional SMC tools, namely GenMC [28] (with reads-from equivalence), RCMC [29] (with Mazurkiewicz equivalence), and CDSChecker [33] (with Mazurkiewicz equivalence), and thus we omit those tools from our evaluation.

There are two main objectives to our evaluation. First, from Sect. 3 we know that the RVF equivalence can be up to exponentially coarser than the other equivalences, and we want to discover how often this happens in practice. Second, in cases where RVF does provide reduction in the trace-partitioning size, we aim to see whether this reduction is accompanied by the reduction in the runtime of RVF-SMC operating on RVF equivalence.

Setup. We consider 119 benchmarks in total in our evaluation. Each benchmark comes with a scaling parameter, called the *unroll* bound. The parameter controls the bound on the number of iterations in all loops of the benchmark. For each benchmark and unroll bound, we capture the number of explored maximal traces, and the total running time, subject to a timeout of one hour. In Appendix E of [30] we provide further details on our setup.

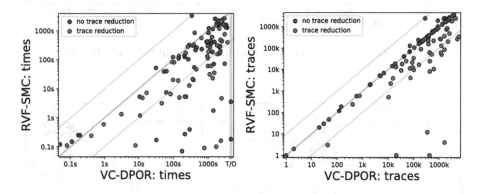

Fig. 7. Runtime and traces comparison of RVF-SMC with VC-DPOR.

---

[1] The MCR algorithm [24] is beyond the experimental scope of this work, as that tool handles Java programs and uses heavyweight SMT solvers that require fine-tuning.

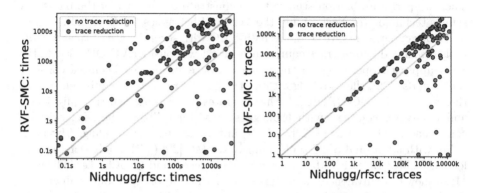

Fig. 8. Runtime and traces comparison of RVF-SMC with Nidhugg/rfsc.

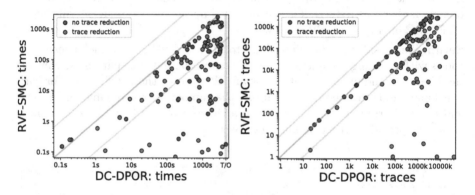

Fig. 9. Runtime and traces comparison of RVF-SMC with DC-DPOR.

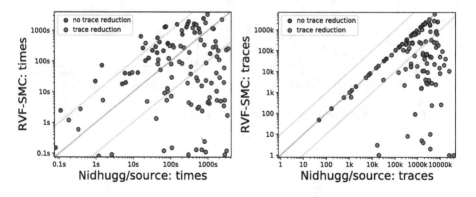

Fig. 10. Runtime and traces comparison of RVF-SMC with Nidhugg/source.

Results. We provide a number of scatter plots summarizing the comparison of RVF-SMC with other state-of-the-art tools. In Fig. 7, Fig. 8, Fig. 9 and Fig. 10 we provide comparison both in runtimes and explored traces, for VC-DPOR, Nidhugg/rfsc, DC-DPOR, and Nidhugg/source, respectively. In each scatter plot, both its axes are log-scaled, the opaque red line represents equality, and the two semi-transparent lines represent an order-of-magnitude difference. The points are colored green when RVF-SMC achieves trace reduction in the underlying benchmark, and blue otherwise.

Discussion: Significant Trace Reduction. In Table 1 we provide the results for several benchmarks where RVF achieves significant reduction in the trace-partitioning size. This is typically accompanied by significant runtime reduction, allowing is to scale the benchmarks to unroll bounds that other tools cannot handle. Examples of this are 27_Boop4 and scull_loop, two toy Linux kernel drivers.

In several benchmarks the number of explored traces remains the same for RVF-SMC even when scaling up the unroll bound, see 45_monabsex1, reorder_5 and singleton in Table 1. The singleton example is further interesting, in that while VC-DPOR and DC-DPOR also explore few traces, they still suffer in runtime due to additional redundant exploration, as described in Sects. 1 and 5.

Table 1. Benchmarks with trace reduction achieved by RVF-SMC. The unroll bound is shown in the column **U**. Symbol "–" indicates one-hour timeout. Bold-font entries indicate the smallest numbers for respective benchmark and unroll.

Benchmark		U	RVF-SMC	VC-DPOR	Nidh/rfsc	DC-DPOR	Nidh/source
27_Boop4 threads: 4	Traces	10	**1337215**	1574287	11610040	–	–
		12	**2893039**	–	–	–	–
	Times	10	**837 s**	1946 s	2616 s	–	–
		12	**2017 s**	–	–	–	–
45_monabsex1 threads: U	Traces	7	**1**	423360	262144	7073803	25401600
		8	**1**	–	4782969	–	–
	Times	7	**0.09 s**	784 s	33 s	3239 s	2819 s
		8	**0.09 s**	–	677 s	–	–
reorder_5 threads: U+1	Traces	9	**4**	1644716	1540	1792290	–
		30	**4**	–	54901	–	–
	Times	9	**0.10 s**	1711 s	0.44 s	974 s	–
		30	**0.09 s**	–	49 s	–	–
scull_loop threads: 3	Traces	2	**3908**	15394	749811	884443	3157281
		3	**115032**	–	–	–	–
	Times	2	**6.55 s**	83 s	403 s	1659 s	1116 s
		3	**266 s**	–	–	–	–
singleton threads: U+1	Traces	20	**2**	**2**	20	20	–
		30	**2**	–	30	–	–
	Times	20	**0.07 s**	179 s	0.08 s	171 s	–
		30	**0.08 s**	–	0.10 s	–	–

Table 2. Benchmarks with little-to-no trace reduction by RVF-SMC. Symbol † indicates that a particular benchmark operation is not handled by the tool.

Benchmark		U	RVF-SMC	VC-DPOR	Nidh/rfsc	DC-DPOR	Nidh/source
13_unverif threads: U	Traces	5	**14400**	14400	**14400**	14400	**14400**
		6	**518400**	–	**518400**	–	**518400**
	Times	5	7.45 s	63 s	3.33 s	68 s	**2.72 s**
		6	376 s	–	134 s	–	**84 s**
approxds_append threads: U	Traces	6	**50897**	1256381	198936	1114746	9847080
		7	**923526**	–	4645207	–	–
	Times	6	**60 s**	995 s	67 s	944 s	2733 s
		7	2078 s	–	**2003 s**	–	–
chase-lev-dq threads: 3	Traces	4	**87807**	†	175331	†	175331
		5	**227654**	†	448905	†	448905
	Times	4	289 s	†	**71 s**	†	**71 s**
		5	995 s	†	210 s	†	**200 s**
linuxrwlocks threads: U+1	Traces	1	**56**	†	59	†	59
		2	**62018**	†	70026	†	70026
	Times	1	0.12 s	†	**0.09 s**	†	0.13 s
		2	42 s	†	15 s	†	**9.50 s**
pgsql threads: 2	Traces	3	**3906**	3906	**3906**	3906	**3906**
		4	**335923**	335923	**335923**	335923	**335923**
	Times	3	3.30 s	5.98 s	1.01 s	4.00 s	**0.51 s**
		4	412 s	911 s	107 s	616 s	**51 s**

Discussion: Little-to-no Trace Reduction. Table 2 presents several benchmarks where the RVF partitioning achieves little-to-no reduction. In these cases the well-engineered Nidhugg/rfsc and Nidhugg/source dominate the runtime.

RVF-SMC Ablation Studies. Here we demonstrate the effect that follows from our RVF-SMC algorithm utilizing the approach of backtrack signals (see Sect. 5) and the heuristics of VerifySC (see Sect. 4.2). These techniques have no effect on the number of the explored traces, thus we focus on the runtime. The left plot of Fig. 11 compares RVF-SMC as is with a RVF-SMC version that does not utilize the backtrack signals (achieved by simply keeping the backtrack flag in Algorithm 2 always true). The right plot of Fig. 11 compares RVF-SMC as is with a RVF-SMC version that employs VerifySC without the closure and auxiliary-trace heuristics. We can see that the techniques almost always result in improved runtime. The improvement is mostly within an order of magnitude, and in a few cases there is several-orders-of-magnitude improvement.

Finally, in Fig. 12 we illustrate how much time during RVF-SMC is typically spent on VerifySC (i.e., on solving VSC instances generated during RVF-SMC).

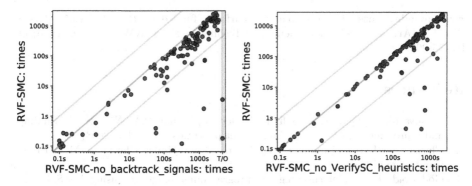

Fig. 11. Ablation studies of RVF-SMC. The left plot compares RVF-SMC with and without backtrack signals. The right plots compares RVF-SMC with and without the closure and auxiliary-trace heuristics of Sect. 4.2.

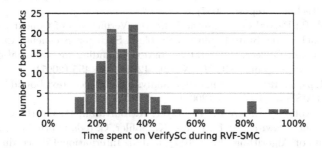

Fig. 12. Histogram that illustrates the percentage of time spent solving VSC instances during RVF-SMC.

7 Conclusions

In this work we developed RVF-SMC, a new SMC algorithm for the verification of concurrent programs using a novel equivalence called *reads-value-from (RVF)*. On our way to RVF-SMC, we have revisited the famous VSC problem [25]. Despite its NP-hardness, we have shown that the problem is parameterizable in $k+d$ (for k threads and d variables), and becomes even fixed-parameter tractable in d when k is constant. Moreover we have developed practical heuristics that solve the problem efficiently in many practical settings.

Our RVF-SMC algorithm couples our solution for VSC to a novel exploration of the underlying RVF partitioning, and is able to model check many concurrent programs where previous approaches time-out. Our experimental evaluation reveals that RVF is very often the most effective equivalence, as the underlying partitioning is exponentially coarser than other approaches. Moreover, RVF-SMC generates representatives very efficiently, as the reduction in the partitioning is often met with significant speed-ups in the model checking task. Interesting future work includes further improvements over the VSC, as well as extensions of RVF-SMC to relaxed memory models.

Acknowledgments. The research was partially funded by the ERC CoG 863818 (ForM-SMArt) and the Vienna Science and Technology Fund (WWTF) through project ICT15-003.

References

1. Musuvathi, M., Qadeer, S., Ball, T., Basler, G., Nainar, P.A., Neamtiu, I.: Finding and reproducing heisenbugs in concurrent programs. In: OSDI (2008)
2. Clarke Jr., E.M., Grumberg, O., Peled, D.A.: Model Checking. MIT Press, Cambridge (1999)
3. Godefroid, P.: Model checking for programming languages using VeriSoft. In: POPL (1997)
4. Godefroid, P.: Software model checking: the VeriSoft approach. FMSD **26**(2), 77–101 (2005)
5. Ball, T., Musuvathi, M., Qadeer, S.: Chess: a systematic testing tool for concurrent software. Technical report (2007)
6. Godefroid, P.: Partial-Order Methods for the Verification of Concurrent Systems: An Approach to the State-Explosion Problem. Springer, Secaucus (1996)
7. Musuvathi, M., Qadeer, S.: Iterative context bounding for systematic testing of multithreaded programs. SIGPLAN Not. **42**(6), 446–455 (2007)
8. Lal, A., Reps, T.: Reducing concurrent analysis under a context bound to sequential analysis. FMSD **35**(1), 73–97 (2009)
9. Chini, P., Kolberg, J., Krebs, A., Meyer, R., Saivasan, P.: On the complexity of bounded context switching. In: Pruhs, K., Sohler, C. (eds.) 25th Annual European Symposium on Algorithms (ESA 2017), Leibniz International Proceedings in Informatics (LIPIcs), Dagstuhl, Germany, vol. 87, pp. 27:1–27:15. Schloss Dagstuhl-Leibniz-Zentrum fuer Informatik. (2017)
10. Baumann, P., Majumdar, R., Thinniyam, R.S., Zetzsche, G.: Context-bounded verification of liveness properties for multithreaded shared-memory programs. In: Proceedings of ACM Programming Language, vol. 5, no. POPL, pp. 1–31 (2021)
11. Clarke, E.M., Grumberg, O., Minea, M., Peled, D.: State space reduction using partial order techniques. STTT **2**(3), 279–287 (1999)
12. Peled, D.: All from one, one for all: on model checking using representatives. In: CAV (1993)
13. Mazurkiewicz, A.: Trace theory. In: Brauer, W., Reisig, W., Rozenberg, G. (eds.) ACPN 1986. LNCS, vol. 255, pp. 278–324. Springer, Heidelberg (1987). https://doi.org/10.1007/3-540-17906-2_30
14. Flanagan, C., Godefroid, P.: Dynamic partial-order reduction for model checking software. In: POPL (2005)
15. Abdulla, P., Aronis, S., Jonsson, B., Sagonas, K.: Optimal dynamic partial order reduction. In: POPL (2014)
16. Nguyen, H.T.T., Rodríguez, C., Sousa, M., Coti, C., Petrucci, L.: Quasi-optimal partial order reduction. In: Computer Aided Verification - 30th International Conference, CAV 2018, Held as Part of the Federated Logic Conference, FloC 2018, Oxford, UK, 14–17 July, 2018, Proceedings, Part II, pp. 354–371 (2018)
17. Aronis, S., Jonsson, B., Lång, M., Sagonas, K.: Optimal dynamic partial order reduction with observers. In: Beyer, D., Huisman, M. (eds.) Tools and Algorithms for the Construction and Analysis of Systems, pp. 229–248. Springer, Cham (2018). https://doi.org/10.1007/978-3-319-89963-3_14

18. Godefroid, P., Pirottin, D.: Refining dependencies improves partial-order verification methods (extended abstract). In: CAV (1993)
19. Albert, E., Arenas, P., de la Banda, M.G., Gómez-Zamalloa, M., Stuckey, P.J.: Context-sensitive dynamic partial order reduction. In: Majumdar, R., Kunčak, V. (eds.) CAV 2017. LNCS, vol. 10426, pp. 526–543. Springer, Cham (2017). https://doi.org/10.1007/978-3-319-63387-9_26
20. Kokologiannakis, M., Raad, A., Vafeiadis, V.: Effective lock handling in stateless model checking. In: Proceedings of ACM Programming Language, vol. 3, no. OOP-SLA, pp. 1–26 (2019)
21. Chalupa, M., Chatterjee, K., Pavlogiannis, A., Sinha, N., Vaidya, K.: Data-centric dynamic partial order reduction. In: Proceedings of ACM Programming Language, vol. 2, no. POPL, pp. 31:1–31:30 (2017)
22. Abdulla, P.A., Atig, M.F., Jonsson, B., Lång, M., Ngo, T.P., Sagonas, K.: Optimal stateless model checking for reads-from equivalence under sequential consistency. In: Proceedings of ACM Programming Language, vol. 3, no. OOPSLA, pp. 1–29 (2019)
23. Chatterjee, K., Pavlogiannis, A., Toman, V.: Value-centric dynamic partial order reduction. In: Proceedings of ACM Programming Language, vol. 3, no. OOPSLA, pp. 1–29 (2019)
24. Huang, J.: Stateless model checking concurrent programs with maximal causality reduction. In: PLDI (2015)
25. Gibbons, P.B., Korach, E.: Testing shared memories. SIAM J. Comput. **26**(4), 1208–1244 (1997)
26. Abdulla, P.A., Atig, M.F., Jonsson, B., Ngo, T.P.: Optimal stateless model checking under the release-acquire semantics. In: Proceedings of ACM Programming Language, vol. 2, no. OOPSLA, pp. 135:1–135:29 (2018)
27. Abdulla, P.A., Aronis, S., Atig, M.F., Jonsson, B., Leonardsson, C., Sagonas, K.: Stateless model checking for TSO and PSO. Acta Informatica **54**(8), 789–818 (2016). https://doi.org/10.1007/s00236-016-0275-0
28. Kokologiannakis, M., Raad, A., Vafeiadis, V.: Model checking for weakly consistent libraries. In: Proceedings of the 40th ACM SIGPLAN Conference on Programming Language Design and Implementation, PLDI 2019, New York, NY, USA, pp. 96–110. ACM (2019)
29. Kokologiannakis, M., Lahav, O., Sagonas, K., Vafeiadis, V.: Effective stateless model checking for c/c++ concurrency. In: Proceedings of ACM Programming Language, 2, no. POPL, pp. 17:1–17:32 (2017)
30. Agarwal, P., Chatterjee, K., Pathak, S., Pavlogiannis, A., Toman, V.: Stateless model checking under a reads-value-from equivalence. CoRR/arXiv abs/2105.06424 (2021)
31. Pavlogiannis, A.: Fast, sound, and effectively complete dynamic race prediction. In: Proceedings ACM Programming Language, vol. 4, no. POPL, pp. 1–29 (2019)
32. Lång, M., Sagonas, K.: Parallel graph-based stateless model checking. In: Hung, D.V., Sokolsky, O. (eds.) ATVA 2020. LNCS, vol. 12302, pp. 377–393. Springer, Cham (2020). https://doi.org/10.1007/978-3-030-59152-6_21
33. Norris, B., Demsky, B.: A practical approach for model checking C/C++11 code. ACM Trans. Program. Lang. Syst. **38**(3), 10:1–10:51 (2016)

Gobra: Modular Specification and Verification of Go Programs

Felix A. Wolf[1], Linard Arquint[1], Martin Clochard[1], Wytse Oortwijn[2],
João C. Pereira[1(✉)], and Peter Müller[1]

[1] Department of Computer Science, ETH Zurich,
Zurich, Switzerland
{felix.wolf,linard.arquint,martin.clochard,
joao.pereira,peter.mueller}@inf.ethz.ch
[2] ESI (TNO), Eindhoven, The Netherlands
wytse.oortwijn@tno.nl

Abstract. Go is an increasingly-popular systems programming language targeting, especially, concurrent and distributed systems. Go differentiates itself from other imperative languages by offering structural subtyping and lightweight concurrency through goroutines with message-passing communication. This combination of features poses interesting challenges for static verification, most prominently the combination of a mutable heap and advanced concurrency primitives.

We present Gobra, a modular, deductive program verifier for Go that proves memory safety, crash safety, data-race freedom, and user-provided specifications. Gobra is based on separation logic and supports a large subset of Go. Its implementation translates an annotated Go program into the Viper intermediate verification language and uses an existing SMT-based verification backend to compute and discharge proof obligations.

Keywords: Separation logic · Program logics · Channel-based concurrency · Interfaces · Deductive verification · Automated verification

1 Introduction

Go is an increasingly popular systems programming language targeting, especially, concurrent and distributed systems such as web applications. It combines standard features of imperative languages, such as mutable heap data structures, with less common concepts, such as structural subtyping and lightweight concurrency through goroutines with message-passing communication.

This combination of features poses interesting challenges for static verification, most prominently the combination of a mutable heap and advanced concurrency primitives. Prior research on Go verification handles some of these features, but not their combination. For instance, Lange et al. [14,15] verify safety and

© The Author(s) 2021
A. Silva and K. R. M. Leino (Eds.) CAV 2021, LNCS 12759, pp. 367–379, 2021.
https://doi.org/10.1007/978-3-030-81685-8_17

liveness of Go's message-passing, but do not consider functional properties about the heap state, whereas Perennial [4] supports heap data structures, but neither channels nor interfaces.

We present Gobra, an automated, modular verifier for heap-manipulating, concurrent Go programs. Gobra supports a large subset of Go, including Go's interfaces and primitive data structures, both of which have not been fully supported in previous work. Gobra verifies memory safety, crash safety, data-race freedom, and user-provided specifications. It takes as input a Go program annotated with assertions such as pre and postconditions and loop invariants. Verification proceeds by encoding the annotated programs into the intermediate verification language Viper [17] and then applying an existing SMT-based verifier. In case verification fails, Gobra reports at the level of the Go program which assertions it could not verify.

Gobra's assertion language builds on established concepts: Gobra uses separation logic style permissions [19] to reason locally about heap data structures. It supports recursive predicates and specification methods to abstract over (possibly unbounded) data structures and their contents. In particular, Gobra has first-class predicates that enable a natural specification of concurrency primitives, for instance, to parameterize a lock by an invariant.

Gobra is intended for the verification of substantial, real-world code, and is currently used to verify the Go implementation of the SCION internet architecture [23]. Our tool paper makes the following technical contributions:

(1) We present the Gobra tool, an automated modular verifier for annotated Go programs. Our evaluation demonstrates that Gobra can verify non-trivial examples with good performance. Our artifact is available online [21].
(2) We define a specification language for functional properties of Go programs. Our specification language provides a consistent abstraction at the level of Go and does not leak details of the underlying encoding.
(3) We present the first specification and verification technique for structural subtyping via Go interfaces.
(4) Our Viper encoding supports, among other features, Go's broad range of built-in data types, such as slices and channels. A lightweight annotation allows it to apply separation logic to reason soundly about addressable memory locations, but use a more efficient encoding for others.

Outline. We demonstrate key features of Gobra on examples (Sect. 2), give an overview of the encoding into Viper (Sect. 3), and provide an experimental evaluation of Gobra (Sect. 4). Lastly, Sect. 5 discusses related work and concludes.

2   Gobra in a Nutshell

This section illustrates Gobra's specification language on simple examples and shows how we handle interfaces and concurrency.

2.1 Basics

Gobra uses a variant of separation logic [19] in order to reason about mutable heap data structures and concurrency. Separation logics associate an access permission with each heap location. Access permissions are held by method executions and transferred between methods upon call and return. A method may access a location only if it holds the associated permission. Permission to a shared location v is denoted in Gobra by acc(&v), which is analogous to separation logic's v ↦ _. Gobra provides an expressive permission model supporting fractional permissions [3] to allow concurrent read accesses while still ensuring exclusive writes, (recursive) predicates to denote access to unbounded data structures, and quantified permissions (also called iterated separating conjunction) to express permissions to random-access data structures such as arrays and slices.

```
1    requires ∀ k int :: 0 ≤ k < len(s)  ⟹  acc(&s[k])
2    ensures  ∀ k int :: 0 ≤ k < len(s)  ⟹  acc(&s[k])
3    ensures  ∀ k int :: 0 ≤ k < len(s)  ⟹  s[k] == old(s[k]) + n
4    func incr (s []int, n int) {
5        invariant 0 ≤ i ≤ len(s)
6        invariant ∀ k int :: 0 ≤ k < len(s)  ⟹  acc(&s[k])
7        invariant ∀ k int :: i ≤ k < len(s)  ⟹  s[k] == old(s[k])
8        invariant ∀ k int :: 0 ≤ k < i  ⟹  s[k] == old(s[k]) + n
9        for i := 0; i < len(s); i += 1 {
10           s[i] = s[i] + n
11       }
12   }
```

Fig. 1. A simple Gobra example showing method and loop contracts.

The example in Fig. 1 illustrates the use of permissions. Method incr increases all elements of a given slice s by an amount n. (Slices are data types that can intuitively be seen as shared arrays of variable length.) The method requires permission to all slice elements (via its precondition) and returns them to the caller (via its first postcondition).

Functional properties are expressed via standard assertions, which include side-effect free Go expressions (including calls to pure methods, as we explain below) as well as universal quantification and old-expressions to refer to the value an expression had in the pre-state of a method. In our example, the second postcondition uses these assertions to express the functional behavior of the method. The loop invariants are analogous to the method contracts and are needed for verification.

In Go, any memory location can either be *shared* or *exclusive*. Shared locations reside on the heap and can, thus, be accessed by multiple methods and threads; reasoning about shared locations requires permissions to ensure race freedom and to enable framing, i.e., preserving information across heap changes. On the other hand, exclusive locations are accessed exclusively by one method execution and may be allocated on the stack; they can be reasoned about as local variables. The Go compiler determines automatically whether a location is shared or exclusive, for instance by determining whether its address is taken at some point of the execution. To make verification independent of a particular compiler analysis, Gobra requires shared locations to be decorated with an extra annotation @ at the declaration point, as illustrated by the following client of incr:

```
1   a@ := [4]int { 1, 2, 4, 8 }
2   incr(a[2:], 2)
3   assert a == [4]int { 1, 2, 6, 10 }
```

The first line declares a Go array a of fixed length 4, with values 1, 2, 4, and 8. This array is sliced on line 2 using the syntax a[2:], thereby omitting the first two elements of a from the created slice. Since a is used in a context in which it is sliced, it is a shared location, which is made explicit via the @ annotation. Consequently, the array creation will produce permissions to the array elements, which are required by incr's precondition. Omitting the @ annotation will cause a verification error.

2.2   Interfaces

Go supports polymorphism through *interfaces*, named sets of method signatures. Subtyping for interfaces is structural: a type implements an interface iff every method of the interface is implemented by the type. The subtype relationship is determined by the type checker, without any declarations from the programmer[1].

Calls on an interface value are dynamically dispatched. In settings with nominal subtyping, dynamic dispatch is handled by proving behavioral subtyping [16]: each subtype declaration requires a proof that the specifications of subtype methods refine the specifications of the corresponding supertype methods. Since structural subtypes are not declared explicitly, we adapt this approach as follows.

Whenever a Go program assigns a value to a variable of an interface type, Gobra requires an *implementation proof*, that is, a proof that each method of the subtype satisfies the specification of the corresponding method in the interface. Implementation proofs are inferred automatically by Gobra in simple cases; user-provided implementation proofs are required especially when they include ghost operations, for instance, to manipulate predicates.

The example in Fig. 2 illustrates this approach. Interface stream (lines 1–8) declares an interface with two methods, hasNext and next. The latter may return values of an arbitrary type, which is denoted by an empty interface. Since interfaces do not contain an implementation, their specification must be fully abstract. To this end, stream introduces an abstract predicate memory, whose definition is provided by the subtypes of the interface. The functional behavior of interface methods can be expressed in terms of pure (that is, side-effect free) abstract methods, here, hasNext, which will also be defined in subtypes.

Next, lines 10–16 show an implementation of the interface in the form of a counter. The counter has a current f and maximum max value. As long as the

---

[1] For the sake of simplicity, we omit *embeddings*, Go's construct for delegation; an extension is straightforward.

```
1    type stream interface{
2      pred memory()
3      requires acc(memory(), _) // arbitrary fraction of memory()
4      pure hasNext() bool
5      requires memory() && hasNext()
6      ensures  memory()
7      next() interface{}
8    }
9
10   type counter struct{ f int; max int }
11   requires acc(&x.f, _) && acc(&x.max, _)
12   pure func (x *counter) hasNext() bool { return x.f < x.max }
13   requires acc(&x.f) && acc(&x.max, 1/2) && x.hasNext()
14   ensures  acc(&x.f) && acc(&x.max, 1/2) && x.f == old(x.f)+1
15   ensures  typeOf(y) == int && y.(int) == old(x.f)
16   func (x *counter) next() (y interface{}) { x.f++;return x.f-1 }
17
18   pred (x *counter) memory() { acc(&x.f) && acc(&x.max) }
19   (*counter) implements stream {
20     pure (x *counter) hasNext_PROOF() bool {
21       return unfolding acc(x.memory(), _) in x.hasNext()
22     }
23     (x *counter) next_PROOF() (res interface{}) { ... }
24   }
```

Fig. 2. An interface specification for a stream (lines 1–8) together with an implementation (lines 10–16) and an implementation proof (lines 18–24). We write `acc(p, _)` to denote an arbitrary, positive amount of predicate p, and simply p for `acc(p, 1/1)`. At line 14, the fractional permission to `&x.max` entails that `x.max` is not modified.

maximum value is not reached, `next` will increase the current value. At line 16, an integer can be assigned to the empty interface since behavioral subtyping holds trivially. The specification at line 15 expresses that the returned interface value contains an integer with the old value of the `f` field.

The counter implementation is completely independent of the `stream` interface. Their connection is established only in the implementation proof (lines 18–24). This proof defines the `memory` predicate from the `stream` interface for receivers of type `counter` (line 18). Moreover, an implementation proof verifies that the specification of each method implementation refines the specification of the corresponding interface method. This proof checks that, assuming the precondition of an interface method, a call to the implementation method with identical arguments establishes the postcondition of the interface method. This format is enforced syntactically and permits ghost operations before and after the call to manipulate predicates. For instance, the proof on line 21 for `hasNext` temporarily unfolds the `memory` predicate to obtain permission to x, which is required by the implementation method, and conversely after the call.

Implementation proofs can be written explicitly, imported from other packages, and also inferred automatically when no explicit proof exists in the current scope. Currently, Gobra does not infer ghost operations such as the `unfolding` on line 21; our experiments suggest that already simple heuristics can deal with many cases occurring in practice. For instance, many implementation proofs we have encountered follow the same pattern: First, the interface predicate instances of the precondition are unfolded. Second, the implementation method is called. Lastly, the interface predicate instances of the postcondition are folded. This pattern can be generated automatically to alleviate the annotation burden.

Gobra's implementation proofs enable one to reason about interfaces without enforcing subtype declarations in either the interface or the declaration, which would defeat the purpose of structural subtyping. This solution allows one to reason about dynamically-dispatched calls. For instance, the following code snippet verifies in Gobra:

```
1  x := &counter{0, 50}
2  var y stream = x
3  fold y.memory()
4  var z interface{} = y.next()
```

In particular, Gobra is able to determine that `next`'s precondition `hasNext()` holds because `y.hasNext()` is equal to `x.hasNext()`, and the latter follows from the definition of `hasNext` (line 12) and the initial value of `x.f`. This intuitive reasoning is enabled by an intricate underlying encoding, which is not exposed to users. Users do not have to know how interface predicates are encoded and can treat interface predicates the same as any other separation-logic predicate.

2.3 Concurrency

Go supports concurrency through *goroutines*, lightweight threads started by prefixing a method call with the `go` keyword. Go offers the usual synchronization primitives, but goroutines idiomatically synchronize via *channels*. Buffered channels provide asynchronous communication, where sending a message blocks only when the buffer is full. Unbuffered channels offer rendez-vouz communication.

Gobra enables verification of concurrent programs by associating Go's synchronization primitives with predicates that do not only express properties of data but also express how permissions to shared memory get transferred between threads. For instance, lock invariants may include properties as well as permissions to the data protected by the lock, and channel invariants include properties and permissions of the data sent over a channel. These invariants are specified via ghost operations when the synchronization primitive is initialized.

Figure 3 illustrates Gobra's concurrency support using an excerpt from a parallel search-and-replace algorithm (see the full paper [22] for the complete example). Method `searchAndReplace` spawns a series of worker threads and then sends each of them a chunk of the input slice to process. The worker threads are joined via a wait group `wg`. Method `worker` implements the worker threads.

Gobra associates channels (like `c` in the example) with a predicate to specify properties and permissions of the sent data. The call `c.Init(...)` on line 10 takes this predicate as an argument. As expressed on line 2, it includes permissions to the chunk a worker operates on. For synchronous channels, an additional predicate can specify permissions transferred in the opposite direction, from the

```
1   pred messagePerm(wg *sync.WaitGroup, chunk []int, x, y int) {
2     ( ∀ i int :: 0 ≤ i < len(chunk) ⟹ acc(&chunk[i]) ) && ...
3   }

4   requires ∀ i int :: 0 ≤ i < len(s) ⟹ acc(&s[i])
5   func searchAndReplace(s []int, x, y int) {
6     var wg@ sync.WaitGroup
7     ghost wg.Init()
8     c := make(chan []int,4)
9     // predicate-name{..., _, ...} is syntax for partial application
10    ghost c.Init(messagePerm{&wg, _, x, y})
11    // Spawn workers
12    invariant acc(c.RecvChannel(), _)
13    invariant c.RecvGotPerm() == messagePerm{&wg, _, x, y}
14    for i := 0; i < numOfWorkers; i++ { go worker(c, wg, x, y) }
15    // Split slice into chunks, which are sent to workers
16    invariant c.SendChannel()
17    invariant c.SendGivenPerm() == messagePerm{&wg, _, x, y}
18    invariant ∀ i int :: offset ≤ i < len(s) ⟹ acc(&s[i])
19    invariant ... // constraints on offset and nextOffset
20    for offset := 0; offset != len(s); offset = nextOffset {
21      nextOffset = ...
22      wg.Add(1)
23      fold messagePerm{&wg, _, x, y}(s[offset:nextOffset])
24      c <- s[offset:nextOffset]
25    }
26    wg.Wait()
27  }

28  requires acc(c.RecvChannel(), _)
29  requires c.RecvGotPerm() == messagePerm{wg, _, x, y};
30  func worker(c <- chan []int, wg *sync.WaitGroup, x, y int) {
31    invariant acc(c.RecvChannel(), _)
32    invariant c.RecvGotPerm() == messagePerm{wg, _, x, y};
33    invariant ok ⟹ messagePerm{wg, _, x, y}(chunk)
34    for chunk, ok := <- c; ok; chunk, ok = <-c {
35      unfold messagePerm{wg, _, x, y}(chunk)
36      ... // replace x with y in chunk
37      wg.Done() // same as wg.Add(-1)
38    }
39  }
```

Fig. 3. Excerpt showing goroutines, channels, and wait groups. The code spawns workers (line 14), sends slice chunks through a channel to the workers (line 24), and then waits on a wait group (line 26). A worker receives a chunk (line 34), processes it, and then notifies the wait group (line 37). For the sake of simplicity, some details were omitted.

receiver to the sender. Initializing a channel also creates send and receive permissions for the channel, which are used to control which threads may access it. In our example, we transfer a fraction of the receive permission to each worker (line 28).

The workers receive permission to the chunk they operate on via a message sent on line 24 and received on line 34. The transfer back is orchestrated through a wait group, which implements an abstract shared counter. Wait groups are used as follows: The main thread adds to the counter the number of units of work to be done in spawned goroutines (line 22). Each spawned goroutine decreases the counter each time a unit of work is done (via a call to Done, line 37). The master can await the counter to reach 0 via a call to `Wait` (line 26). Gobra uses dedicated permissions to express the obligation of a thread to perform units of work before decreasing the counter; each time this happens, permissions are transferred to the wait group and, eventually to the main thread calling `Wait`. We omit the details here for brevity.

In our example, this mechanism allows the main thread to recover the permissions to the entire slice once the workers have terminated. The example in Fig. 3 illustrates only the permission aspect of the verification. Functional correctness can be verified easily based on the explained machinery, by specifying a stronger channel invariant that includes the work obligation for each worker. We omit the details here, but see the full paper [22] for the complete example.

3   Encoding

Gobra encodes an annotated Go program into a Viper program verifying only if the input program is correct. Many features of Gobra are also present in Viper, making parts of the encoding straightforward. For instance, methods, pure methods, and predicates are encoded to their Viper counterpart. Viper's permission model (including fractions, wildcards, and quantifiers) is similar to Gobra's, but memory is represented differently; Viper's heap is object-based, where each object contains all declared fields. Viper's fields store primitive values (including references). To encode Go's compound values such as structs, arrays, slices, and interface values, we use Viper's mechanism to declare mathematical types (such as tuples) using uninterpreted types, uninterpreted functions, and appropriate axioms. Exclusive Go values are directly represented using these mathematical types. For shared values, there is an indirection via the Viper heap to permit aliasing and apply permission-based reasoning.

Interfaces. As explained in Sect. 2.2, our treatment of Go interfaces relies on interface predicates, specification methods, and implementation proofs. We explain how we handle the former two here; based on this encoding, the encoding of implementation proofs is analogous to methods.

Intuitively, we encode interface predicates as a case split over all possible implementations. All implementations not present in the current scope are subsumed by an abstract default case. Consequently, adding an implementation does not invalidate existing proofs, which enables modular reasoning. The predicate for the `stream` example (Fig. 2) is encoded as follows:

```
predicate memory(x: ⟦interface{}⟧) {
    ⟦typeOf(x) == *counter⟧ ? ⟦acc(x.(*counter))⟧ : unknownMemory(x)
}
predicate unknownMemory(x: ⟦interface{}⟧)

function hasNext(x: ⟦interface{}⟧) returns (y: ⟦bool⟧)
    req ⟦acc(x.memory(), _)⟧
    ens ⟦typeOf(x) == *counter⟧ ⟹ y == hasNext_PROOF(⟦x.(*counter)⟧)
```

The body of the predicate branches on the dynamic type of x, with a single case for the (only) given implementation. The abstract predicate `unknownMemory` encodes the default case. The encoding of pure methods such as `hasNext` uses an analogous case split, but uses `hasNext`$_{PROOF}$, which is part of the implementation proof (Fig. 2 line 20) and couples the interface and implementation method. Our encoding of interface predicates is an instance of an *abstract predicate family* [18]. For Go, we have crafted a variant that is well-suited for implementation proofs, pure interface methods, and structural subtyping.

First-Class Predicates. Our support for concurrency uses first-class predicates, for instance, to specify channel invariants (see Sect. 2.3). We encode first-class predicate values as mathematical types, using defunctionalization. Predicate instances are represented by abstract predicates that take the predicate value as an argument. First-class predicates enable us to use library stubs to support concurrency primitives such as mutexes and wait groups. These stubs allow us to encode the use of these concurrency primitives via standard method calls. Go's native channel operations are represented analogously.

4   Implementation and Evaluation

The Gobra implementation consists of a parser and type checker for annotated Go programs and a translation of those programs into the Viper intermediate verification language. The resulting Viper program is verified using Viper's symbolic execution backend, which in turn uses the Z3 SMT solver [7]. Verification errors are translated back to the Go level, such that users are not exposed to the internal encodings. Users never have to inspect the encoding. Error messages contain the failing assertion and a reason describing why the assertion failed. Gobra's test suite contains 407 verification tests (with and without errors) with a total of 10'030 LOCs (Go code and annotations) that take 14.9 min to verify.

We evaluated Gobra on 14 interesting verification problems, which include well-known algorithms and data structures, and cover Go's main features, such as interfaces (Examples 7–9) and concurrency primitives (Examples 13 and 14), including goroutines, mutexes, wait groups, and channels. For each example, Gobra verifies memory safety and functional correctness properties. To assess Gobra's performance on failing verifications, we have additionally constructed two incorrect variations of each example, one with a seeded error in the specification and one in the implementation.

All experiments were executed on a warmed-up JVM on a MacBook Pro with a 2.3 GHz 8-Core Intel Core i9 CPU and 32 GB of RAM, running macOS 11.1 and OpenJDK 11. For each experiment, we measured its verification time using Viper's symbolic execution backend and averaged the duration of twelve executions, excluding the slowest and fastest outlier.

Figure 4 summarizes the results, including the required annotations and verification times for the three variants of each example. The annotation overhead

#	Example	LOC / Spec.	Viper LOC	T [s]	$T_{\text{spec error}}$ [s]	$T_{\text{impl error}}$ [s]
1	binary search tree	125 / 140	632	10.88	10.50	11.67
2	dutchflag	22 / 16	142	2.02	1.78	1.88
3	heapsort	47 / 93	271	16.72	19.30	15.23
4	dense and sparse matrix	69 / 62	326	10.46	10.55	10.06
5	binary tree	59 / 20	217	2.09	2.08	2.11
6	running ex. (Fig. 1)	10 / 11	164	1.71	1.70	1.70
7	running ex. (Fig. 2)	24 / 16	186	1.04	0.98	1.01
8	list of interfaces	46 / 27	219	1.45	1.41	1.54
9	visitor pattern	76 / 30	475	4.38	4.22	5.45
10	zune	31 / 12	141	1.08	1.07	1.06
11	relaxed prefix	25 / 36	158	7.08	5.36	4.19
12	pair insertion sort	50 / 105	353	15.55	12.64	13.96
13	parallel search replace	35 / 94	565	53.18	51.97	61.54
14	parallel sum	31 / 98	527	58.39	50.25	57.69

Fig. 4. Experimental results. For each experiment, we list the number of lines of Go code (LOC), number of lines of specification and proof annotations (Spec), and the average verification time in seconds for correct examples (T), errors in the specification ($T_{\text{spec error}}$), and errors in the implementation ($T_{\text{impl error}}$). A line containing both, code and annotations, is counted as one line of Go code and one line of annotation.

ranges between 0.3 and 3.1 lines of annotations per line of code, which is typical for SMT-based deductive verifiers. Verification times range between a second and a minute per example. The verification times are significantly higher when the verified code uses concurrency features; these examples require quantitatively more and more-complex specifications, which complicates reasoning. Lastly, there is hardly any difference between successful and failed verification attempts. Consistent performance is crucial when verifiers are used interactively, where users run them frequently, especially on programs that do not yet verify.

5   Related Work and Conclusion

Besides Gobra, we are aware of two other verification approaches for Go. Perennial [4] reasons about concurrent, crash-safe systems. Their core techniques are an extension to the Iris framework [13] and independent of Go. They connect their theory to Go programs with Goose, a shallow embedding of Go into Coq [5], which proves that Go code complies with a given transition system. In contrast to Gobra, Perennial does not support core Go features such as channels and interfaces.

Several prior works [9,14,15] infer behavioral types [12] to reason about Go's channel-based message passing. After they infer behavioral types for a given program, they check safety and liveness properties on the inferred types, using model checkers such as mCRL2 [6]. Some works use additional analyses to strengthen the provided guarantees. Lange et al. [15] add a termination analysis to enable one to verify unbounded properties under certain conditions. Gabet and Yoshida [9] extend this work by inferring behavioral types on shared variables and locks to additionally reason about data-race freedom, lock safety, and lock liveness. The approaches by Lange et al. [15] and Gabet and Yoshida [9] are vastly different from Gobra. They do not verify code contracts, but instead verify global properties such as deadlock and data-race freedom. Their automation is high and annotation overhead minimal, but their analyses are not modular and do not verify functional properties of code. Furthermore, they do not verify properties about the state of the heap.

There are some prior works that can handle channel-based concurrency and heap-manipulating programs, but these do not apply directly to Go. Villard et al. [20] introduce a powerful contract mechanism to specify protocols that channels must adhere to. Their channel specification language is more expressive than the one presented in this paper. Their contracts are finite state machines and thus can have multiple phases. However, their channels are always shared between two peers whereas Go supports more advanced concurrency patterns where both channel endpoints are shared between an unbounded number of peers. Actris [10,11] is a concurrent separation logic built on top of the Iris framework to reason about session types in an interactive theorem prover. Actris can go beyond two peers, but to do so, it requires a memory model that is incompatible with Go's memory model. Actris models the sharing of channel endpoints via Iris' ghost locks, which to our knowledge, implies sequentialization of sends, and dually receives, which is not guaranteed by Go's memory model.

Gobra's verification logic and encoding into Viper have been inspired by several other Viper-based verifiers, such as Nagini [8] for Python, Prusti [1] for Rust, and VerCors [2] for Java. None of these verifiers address the Go-specific features that Gobra supports.

Conclusion. We introduced Gobra, the first modular verifier for Go that supports reasoning about a crucial aspect of the language: the combination of channel-based concurrency and heap-manipulating constructs. Moreover, Gobra is the first verifier to support Go's version of interfaces and structural subtyping. In future work, we will expand the properties that can be verified with Gobra, in particular to liveness and hyper-properties. Furthermore, we are applying Gobra to verify the implementation of a full-fledged network router [23]. Gobra is hosted on Github at https://github.com/viperproject/gobra.

Acknowledgements. This project has received funding from the European Union's Horizon 2020 research and innovation program within the framework of the NGI-POINTER Project funded under grant agreement No. 871528.

References

1. Astrauskas, V., Müller, P., Poli, F., Summers, A.J.: Leveraging rust types for modular specification and verification. In: Object-Oriented Programming Systems, Languages, and Applications (OOPSLA), vol. 3, pp. 147:1–147:30. ACM (2019)

2. Blom, S., Huisman, M.: The VerCors tool for verification of concurrent programs. In: Jones, C., Pihlajasaari, P., Sun, J. (eds.) FM 2014. LNCS, vol. 8442, pp. 127–131. Springer, Cham (2014). https://doi.org/10.1007/978-3-319-06410-9_9

3. Boyland, J.: Checking interference with fractional permissions. In: Cousot, R. (ed.) SAS 2003. LNCS, vol. 2694, pp. 55–72. Springer, Heidelberg (2003). https://doi.org/10.1007/3-540-44898-5_4

4. Chajed, T., Tassarotti, J., Kaashoek, M.F., Zeldovich, N.: Verifying concurrent, crash-safe systems with Perennial. In: SOSP, pp. 243–258. ACM (2019)

5. Coq consortium, T.: The Coq proof assistant. https://coq.inria.fr/

6. Cranen, S., et al.: An overview of the mCRL2 toolset and its recent advances. In: Piterman, N., Smolka, S.A. (eds.) TACAS 2013. LNCS, vol. 7795, pp. 199–213. Springer, Heidelberg (2013). https://doi.org/10.1007/978-3-642-36742-7_15

7. de Moura, L., Bjørner, N.: Z3: an efficient SMT solver. In: Ramakrishnan, C.R., Rehof, J. (eds.) TACAS 2008. LNCS, vol. 4963, pp. 337–340. Springer, Heidelberg (2008). https://doi.org/10.1007/978-3-540-78800-3_24

8. Eilers, M., Müller, P.: Nagini: a static verifier for Python. In: Chockler, H., Weissenbacher, G. (eds.) CAV 2018, Part I. LNCS, vol. 10981, pp. 596–603. Springer, Cham (2018). https://doi.org/10.1007/978-3-319-96145-3_33

9. Gabet, J., Yoshida, N.: Static race detection and mutex safety and liveness for go programs (extended version) (2020)

10. Hinrichsen, J.K., Bengtson, J., Krebbers, R.: Actris: session-type based reasoning in separation logic. Proc. ACM Program. Lang. 4(POPL), 1–30 (2019)

11. Hinrichsen, J.K., Bengtson, J., Krebbers, R.: Actris 2.0: Asynchronous session-type based reasoning in separation logic. arXiv preprint arXiv:2010.15030 (2020)

12. Hüttel, H., et al.: Foundations of session types and behavioural contracts. ACM Comput. Surv. 49(1), 1–36 (2016)

13. Jung, R., Krebbers, R., Jourdan, J., Bizjak, A., Birkedal, L., Dreyer, D.: Iris from the ground up: a modular foundation for higher-order concurrent separation logic. J. Funct. Program. 28, e20 (2018)

14. Lange, J., Ng, N., Toninho, B., Yoshida, N.: Fencing off Go: liveness and safety for channel-based programming, pp. 748–761 (2017)

15. Lange, J., Ng, N., Toninho, B., Yoshida, N.: A static verification framework for message passing in Go using behavioural types. In: ICSE, pp. 1137–1148. ACM (2018)

16. Liskov, B., Wing, J.M.: A behavioral notion of subtyping. ACM Trans. Program. Lang. Syst. 16(6), 1811–1841 (1994)

17. Müller, P., Schwerhoff, M., Summers, A.J.: Viper: a verification infrastructure for permission-based reasoning. In: Jobstmann, B., Leino, K.R.M. (eds.) VMCAI 2016. LNCS, vol. 9583, pp. 41–62. Springer, Heidelberg (2016). https://doi.org/10.1007/978-3-662-49122-5_2

18. Parkinson, M., Bierman, G.: Separation logic and abstraction. ACM SIGPLAN Not. 40(1), 247–258 (2005)

19. Reynolds, J.C.: Separation logic: a logic for shared mutable data structures. In: LICS, pp. 55–74. IEEE Computer Society (2002)

20. Villard, J., Lozes, É., Calcagno, C.: Proving copyless message passing. In: Hu, Z. (ed.) APLAS 2009. LNCS, vol. 5904, pp. 194–209. Springer, Heidelberg (2009). https://doi.org/10.1007/978-3-642-10672-9_15

21. Wolf, F.A., Arquint, L., Clochard, M., Oortwijn, W., Pereira, J.C., Müller, P.: Gobra: Modular Specification and Verification of Go Programs (2021). https://doi.org/10.5281/zenodo.4716664

22. Wolf, F.A., Arquint, L., Clochard, M., Oortwijn, W., Pereira, J.C., Müller, P.: Gobra: Modular specification and verification of go programs (extended version). CoRR arXiv:2105.13840 (2021)
23. Zhang, X., Hsiao, H.C., Hasker, G., Chan, H., Perrig, A., Andersen, D.G.: Scion: scalability, control, and isolation on next-generation networks. In: IEEE Symposium on Security and Privacy, pp. 212–227. IEEE (2011)

Delay-Bounded Scheduling Without Delay!

Andrew Johnson[1]([✉]) and Thomas Wahl[1,2]([✉])

[1] Northeastern University, Boston, MA 02115, USA
aj3189@princeton.edu
[2] GrammaTech Inc., Bethesda, USA

Abstract. We consider the broad problem of analyzing safety properties of asynchronous concurrent programs under arbitrary thread interleavings. *Delay-bounded deterministic scheduling*, introduced in prior work, is an efficient bug-finding technique to curb the large cost associated with full scheduling nondeterminism. In this paper we first present a technique to *lift the delay bound* for the case of finite-domain variable programs, thus adding to the efficiency of bug detection the ability to prove safety of programs under arbitrary thread interleavings. Second, we demonstrate how, combined with predicate abstraction, our technique can both refute and verify safety properties of programs with unbounded variable domains, even for unbounded thread counts. Previous work has established that, for non-trivial concurrency routines, predicate abstraction induces a highly complex abstract program semantics. Our technique, however, never statically constructs an abstract parametric program; it only requires some abstract-states set to be closed under certain actions, thus eliminating the dependence on the existence of verification algorithms for abstract programs. We demonstrate the efficiency of our technique on many examples used in prior work, and showcase its simplicity compared to earlier approaches on the unbounded-thread Ticket Lock protocol.

1 Introduction

Asynchronous concurrent programs consist of a number of threads executing in an interleaved fashion and communicating through shared variables, message passing, or other means. In such programs, the set of states reachable by one thread depends both on the behaviors of the other threads, and on the order in which the threads are interleaved to create a global execution. Since the thread interleaving is unknown to the program designer, analysis techniques for asynchronous programs typically assume the worst case, i.e., that threads can interleave arbitrarily; we refer to this assumption as *full scheduling nondeterminism*. In order to prove safety properties of such programs, we must therefore ultimately investigate all possible interleavings.

Partially supported by the US National Science Foundation under grant #1718235.

A. Silva and K. R. M. Leino (Eds.) CAV 2021, LNCS 12759, pp. 380–402, 2021.
https://doi.org/10.1007/978-3-030-81685-8_18

Proposed about a decade ago, *delay-bounded deterministic scheduling* [10] is an effective technique to curb the large cost associated with exploring arbitrary thread interleavings. The idea is that permitting a limited number of scheduling *delays*—skipping a thread when it is normally scheduled to execute— in an otherwise deterministic scheduler approximates a fully nondeterministic scheduler from below. Delaying gives rise to a new thread interleaving, potentially reaching states unreachable to the deterministic scheduler. In the limit, i.e., with unbounded delays, the delaying and the fully nondeterministic scheduler permit the same set of executions and, thus, reach the same states.

Prior work has demonstrated that delay-bounded scheduling can "discover concurrency bugs efficiently" [10], in the sense that such errors are often detected for a small number of permitted delays. The key is that few delays means to explore only few interleavings. Thus, under moderate delay bounds, the reachable state space can often be explored exhaustively, resulting—if no errors are found— in a delay-bounded verification result.

We build on the empirical insight of efficient delay-*bounded* bug detection (testing) or verification, and make the following contributions.

1. Delay-bounded scheduling without delay. If no bug is found while exhaustively exploring the given program for a given delay budget, we "feel good" but are left with an uncertainty as to whether the program is indeed bug-free. We present a technique to remove this uncertainty, as follows. We prove that the set $R(d)$ of states reached under a delay bound d equals the set R of reachable states under *arbitrary* thread interleavings if two conditions are met:

– increasing the delay bound by a number roughly equal to the number of executing threads produces no additional reachable states, and
– set $R(d)$ is closed under a certain set of critical program actions.

In some cases, the set of "critical program actions" may be definable statically at the language level; in others, this must be determined per individual action. To increase the chance that the above two conditions eventually hold, we typically work with conservative abstractions of R; the (precisely computed) abstract reachability set $\overline{R}$ is then used to decide whether the program is safe.

2. Efficient delay-unbounded analysis. We translate the above foundational result into an efficient delay-unbounded analysis algorithm. It starts with a deterministic Round-Robin scheduler, parameterized by the number of rounds r it runs and of delays d it permits, and increases r and d in a delicate schedule *weak-until* the two conditions above hold (it is not guaranteed that they ever will). The key for efficiency is that the reachability sets under increasing r and d are *monotone*. We therefore can determine reachability under parameters $r' \geq r$ and $d' \geq d$ starting from a *frontier* of the states reached under bounds r and d. We present this algorithm and prove it correct. We also prove its termination (either finding a bug or proving correctness), under certain conditions.

3. Delay-unbounded analysis for general infinite-state systems. We demonstrate the power of our technique on programs with unbounded-domain variables and unbounded thread counts. The existence of integer-like variables suggests the use of a form of predicate abstraction. Prior work has shown that predicate abstraction for unbounded-thread concurrent programs leads to complex abstract program semantics [8,15], going beyond even the rich class of well-quasiordered systems [1]. Our delay-unbounded analysis technique does not require an abstract program. Instead, we add to the idea of reachability analysis under increasing r and d a third dimension n, representing increasing thread counts, enjoying a similar convergence property. Circumventing the static construction of the abstract program simplifies the verification process dramatically.

In summary, this paper presents a technique to lift the bound used in delay-bounded scheduling, while (empirically) avoiding the combinatorial explosion of arbitrary thread interleavings. Our technique can therefore find bugs as well as prove programs bug-free. We demonstrate its efficiency using concurrent pushdown system benchmarks, as well as known-to-be-hard infinite-state protocols such as the Ticket Lock [3]. We offer a detailed analysis of internal performance aspects of our algorithm, as well as a comparison with several alternative techniques. We attribute the superiority of our method to the retained parsimony of limited-delay deterministic-schedule exploration.

A full version of this paper, with proofs omitted here and other supplementary information, can be found in an accompanying Technical Report [14].

2   Delay-Bounded Scheduling

2.1   Basic Computational Model

For the purposes of introducing the idea behind delay-bounded scheduling, we define a deliberately broad asynchronous program model. Consider a multi-threaded program $\mathcal{P}$ consisting of n threads. We fix this number throughout the paper up to and including Sect. 5.1, after which we consider parameterized scenarios. Each thread runs its own procedure and communicates with others via shared program variables. A "procedure" is a collection of *actions* (such as those defined by program statements). We define a shared-states set G and, for each thread, a local-states set L_i ($0 \le i < n$). A global program state is therefore an element of $G \times \prod_{i=0}^{n-1} L_i$. In addition, a finite number of states are designated as *initial*. (Finiteness is required in Sect. 4 for a termination argument [Lemma 11].)

The execution model we assume in this paper is asynchronous. A *step* is a pair (s, s') of states such that there exists a thread i ($0 \le i < n$) such that s and s' agree on the local states of all threads $j \ne i$; the local state of thread i may have changed, as well as the shared state. We say thread i *executes* during the step, by executing some action of its procedure.[1] The execution semantics within the procedure is left to the thread (e.g., there may be multiple enabled actions in a state, an action may itself be nondeterministic, etc.). Without loss of generality for safety properties, we assume that the transition relation induced

---

[1] If only the shared state changes, it is possible that the identity of the executing thread is not unique. This small ambiguity is inconsequential for this paper.

by each thread's possible actions be total. That is, instead of an action x being disabled for a thread in state s, we stipulate that firing x from s results in s.

A *path* is a sequence $p = (s_0, \ldots, s_l)$ of states such that, for $0 \leq i < l$, (s_i, s_{i+1}) is a step. This path has length l (= number of steps taken). A state s is *reachable* if there exists a path from some initial state to s. We denote by R the (possibly infinite) set of states reachable in $\mathcal{P}$. Note that these definitions permit arbitrary asynchronous thread interleavings.

2.2 Free and Round-Robin Scheduling

We formalize the notion of a scheduling policy indirectly, by parameterizing the concept of reachability by the chosen scheduler. A state s is *reachable under free scheduling* if there exists a path $p = (s_0, \ldots, s_l)$ from some initial state s_0 to $s_l = s$. A free scheduler is simulated in state space explorers using full nondeterminism. State s is *reachable under n-thread Round-Robin scheduling with round bound* r if there exists a path $p = (s_0, \ldots, s_l)$ from some initial state s_0 to $s_l = s$ such that

1. $\lceil l/n \rceil \leq r$, and
2. for $0 \leq i < l$, thread i (mod n) executes during step (s_i, s_{i+1}).

2.3 Delay-Bounded Round-Robin Scheduling

We approximate the set of states reachable under free scheduling from below, using a relaxed Round-Robin scheduler. The scheduler introduced so far is, however, deterministic and thus *vastly* underapproximates the free scheduler, even for unbounded r. The solution proposed in earlier work is to introduce a limited number d of scheduling *delays* [10]. A delayed thread is skipped in the current round and must wait until the next round.

Definition 1. *State* s *is reachable under Round-Robin scheduling with round bound* r *and delay bound* d *("reachable under $RR(r, d)$ scheduling" for short) if there exists a path* $p = (s_0, \ldots, s_l)$ *from some initial state* s_0 *to* $s_l = s$ *and a function* $f : \{0, \ldots, l-1\} \rightarrow \{0, \ldots, n-1\}$, *called* scheduling function, *such that*

1. *for* $d_p := f(0) + \sum_{i=1}^{l-1} \left((f(i) - f(i-1) - 1) \bmod n \right)$, *we have* $d_p \leq d$,
2. $\lceil \frac{l+d_p}{n} \rceil \leq r$ *(d_p as defined in 1.), and*
3. *for* $0 \leq i < l$, *thread* $f(i)$ *executes during step* (s_i, s_{i+1}).

Variable d_p from 1. quantifies the total delay, compared to a perfect Round-Robin scheduler, that the scheduling along path p has accumulated. Consider the case of $n = 4$ threads T0,...,T3. Then the scheduling sequence $(f(0), \ldots, f(11))$ below on the left, of $l = 12$ steps and involving 13 states, follows a perfect Round-Robin schedule of $r = 3$ rounds (separated by $|$):

0 1 2 3 | 0 1 2 3 | 0 1 2 3   0 1 $\cancel{2}$ 3 | 0 1 2 $\cancel{3}$ | $\cancel{0}$ 1 2 3

The sequence on the right of $l = 9$ steps follows a Round-Robin scheduling of $r = 3$ rounds and a total of $d_p = 3$ delays: one after the second step (T2 is delayed: $3 - 1 - 1 \bmod 4 = 1$), another two delays after the sixth step (T3 and T0 are delayed: $1 - 2 - 1 \bmod 4 = 2$). The final state of this path is reachable under $RR(3,3)$ scheduling. Note that delays effectively shorten rounds.

We denote by $R(r, d)$ the set of states reachable in $\mathcal{P}$ under $RR(r, d)$ scheduling. (Note that this set is finite, for any program $\mathcal{P}$.) It is easy to see that, given sufficiently large r and d, *any* schedule can be realized under $RR(r, d)$ scheduling:

Theorem 2. *State s is reachable under free scheduling iff there exist r, d such that s is reachable under $RR(r, d)$ scheduling: $R = \bigcup_{r,d \in \mathbb{N}} R(r, d)$.*

State-space exploration under free scheduling can therefore be reduced to enumerating the two-dimensional parameter space (r, d) and computing states reachable under $RR(r, d)$ scheduling. This can be used to turn a Round Robin-based state explorer into a semi-algorithm, dubbed *delay-bounded tester* in [10].

An important property of the round and delay bounds is that increasing them can only increase the reachability sets:

Property 3 (Monotonicity in r & d). *For any round and delay bounds r and d:*
$$R(r, d) \subseteq R(r+1, d) \quad , \quad R(r, d) \subseteq R(r, d+1) . \tag{1}$$

This follows from the $\ldots \leq r$ and $\ldots \leq d$ constraints in Definition 1. The property relies on r and d being external to the program, not accessible inside it. Under this provision, monotonicity in any kind of resource bound is a fairly natural *yet not always guaranteed* property; we give a counterexample in Sect. 5.2.

3   Abstract Closure for Delay-Bounded Analysis

The goal of this paper is a technique to prove safety properties of asynchronous programs under arbitrary thread schedules. Theorem 2 affords us the possibility to reduce the exploration of such arbitrary schedules to certain bounded Round-Robin schedules, but we still need to deal with those bounds. In this section we present a closure property for bounded Round-Robin explorations.

3.1   Respectful Actions

Let $\mathcal{S}$ be the set of global program states of $\mathcal{P}$, and let $\alpha \colon \mathcal{S} \to \mathcal{A}$ be an *abstraction function*, i.e., a function that maps program states to elements of some abstract domain $\mathcal{A}$. Function α typically hides certain parts of the information contained in a state, but the exact definition is immaterial for this subsection.

A key ingredient of the technique proposed in this paper is to identify actions of the program executed by a thread with the property that the abstract successor of an abstract state under such an action does not depend on concrete-state information hidden by the abstraction.

Definition 4. *Let x be a program action, and let the relation $s \xrightarrow{i\,:\,x} s'$ denote that $s \to s'$ is a step during which thread i executes x. Action x **respects** α if, for all states $s_1, s_2, s'_1, s'_2 \in \mathcal{S}$ and all $i : 0 \le i < n$:*

$$\alpha(s_1) = \alpha(s_2) \ \wedge \ s_1 \xrightarrow{i,\,x} s'_1 \ \wedge \ s_2 \xrightarrow{i,\,x} s'_2 \ \Rightarrow \ \alpha(s'_1) = \alpha(s'_2) \ . \tag{2}$$

Intuitively, "x respects α" means that successors under action x of α-equivalent states all have the same unique abstraction. Note the special case $s_1 = s_2$, $s'_1 \ne s'_2$: for nondeterministic actions x to respect α, multiple successors s'_1, s'_2 of the same concrete state $s_1 = s_2$ under x also must have the same abstraction.

Example 5. *Consider n-thread concurrent pushdown systems (CPDS), an instance of the asynchronous computational model presented in Sect. 2.1. We have a finite set of shared states readable and writeable by each thread. Each thread also has a finite-alphabet stack, which it can operate on by (i) overwriting the top-of-the-stack element, (ii) pushing an element onto the stack, or (iii) popping an element off the top of the non-empty stack. The classic pointwise top-of-the-stack abstraction function is defined by*

$$\alpha(g, w_0, \ldots, w_{n-1}) = (g, \sigma_0, \ldots, \sigma_{n-1}) \ , \tag{3}$$

where g is the shared state (unchanged by α), w_i is the contents of the stack of thread i, and σ_i is the top of w_i if w_i is non-empty, and empty otherwise [18]. Note that the domain into which α maps is a finite set.

Push and overwrite actions respect α, while pop actions disrespect it: consider the case $n = 1$ and $s_1 = (g, w_0) = (0, 10)$ and $s_2 = (0, 11)$, with stack contents 10 and 11, resp. (left = top). While $\alpha(s_1) = \alpha(s_2) = (0, 1)$, the (unique) successor states of s_1 and s_2 after a pop are not α-equivalent: the elements 0 and 1 emerge as the new top-of-the-stack symbols, respectively, which α can distinguish.

The notion of respectful actions gives rise to a condition on sets of abstract states that we will later use for convergence proofs:

Definition 6. *An abstract-state set A is **closed under actions disrespecting** α if, for every $\mathbf{a} \in A$ and every successor $\mathbf{a'}$ of $\mathbf{a}$ under a disrespectful action, $\mathbf{a'} \in A$.*

For maximum precision: a' is said to be a successor of a under a disrespectful action if there exist concrete states s and s', a thread id i and an action x such that $\alpha(s) = a$, $\alpha(s') = a'$, x disrespects α, and $s \xrightarrow{i\,:\,x} s'$. If abstraction α is clear from the context, we may just say "closed under disrespectful actions".

3.2 From Delay-Bounded to Delay-Unbounded Analysis

We now present our idea to turn a round- and delay-bounded tester into a (partial) verifier, namely by exploring the given asynchronous program for a number of round and delay bounds until we have "seen enough". Recall the notations R and $R(r, d)$ defined in Sect. 2. We also use $\overline{R}$ and $\overline{R}(r, d)$ short for

$\alpha(R)$ and $\alpha(R(r,d))$, i.e. the respective abstract reachability sets. (Note that $\overline{R}$ is *not* an abstract fixed point—instead, it is the result of applying α to the concrete reachability set R; see discussion in Sect. 7.)

Theorem 7. *For any $r, d \in \mathbb{N}$, if $\overline{R}(r,d) = \overline{R}(r+1, d+n-1)$ and $\overline{R}(r,d)$ is closed under actions disrespecting α, then $\overline{R}(r,d) = \overline{R}$.*

The theorem states: if the set of *abstract* states reachable under $RR(r,d)$ scheduling does not change after increasing the round bound by 1 and the delay bound by $n-1$, and it is closed under disrespectful actions, then $\overline{R}(r,d)$ is in fact the *exact* set $\overline{R}$ of abstract states reachable under a *free* scheduler: no approximation, no rounds, no delays, no Round-Robin.

Proof. of Theorem 7: we have to show that $\overline{R}(r,d)$ is closed under the abstract image function $\overline{Im}$ induced by α, defined as

$$\overline{Im}(a) = \{a' : \exists s, s' : \alpha(s) = a, \ \alpha(s') = a', \ s \to s'\} \ .$$

That is, we wish to show $\overline{Im}(\overline{R}(r,d)) \subseteq \overline{R}(r,d)$, which proves that no more abstract states are reachable. Consider $a \in \overline{R}(r,d)$ and $a' \in \overline{Im}(a)$, i.e. we have states s, s' such that $\alpha(s) = a$, $\alpha(s') = a'$, and $s \xrightarrow{i\,:\,x} s'$ for some thread i and some action x. The goal is to show that $a' \in \overline{R}(r,d)$.

To this end, we distinguish flavors of x. If x disrespects α, then $a' \in \overline{R}(r,d)$, since the set is closed under disrespectful actions.

So x respects α. Since $a \in \overline{R}(r,d)$, there exists a state $s_0 \in R(r,d)$ with $\alpha(s_0) = a$. Suppose for a moment that thread i is scheduled to run in state s_0. Then it can execute action x; any successor state s_0' satisfies $s_0' \in R(r,d)$, and:

$$a' \stackrel{(\text{def } a')}{=} \alpha(s') \stackrel{(x \text{ resp. } \alpha)}{=} \alpha(s_0') \stackrel{(\text{def } s_0')}{\in} \alpha(R(r,d)) = \overline{R}(r,d) \ .$$

But what if the thread scheduled to run in state s_0 under $RR(r,d)$ scheduling, call it j, **is not thread** i? Then we *delay* any threads that are scheduled before thread i's next turn; if $i < j$, this "wraps around", and we need to advance to the next round. The program state has not changed—we are still in s_0. Let s_0' be the successor state obtained when thread i now executes action x, and $\lambda(i,j) = 1$ if $i < j$, 0 otherwise. Then we have $s_0' \in R(r + \lambda(i,j), d + (j-i) \bmod n)$, and:

$$a' \stackrel{(\text{def } a')}{=} \alpha(s') \stackrel{(x \text{ resp. } \alpha)}{=} \alpha(s_0') \stackrel{(\text{def } s_0', \alpha)}{\in} \overline{R}(r + \lambda(i,j), d + (j-i) \bmod n)$$
$$\stackrel{(\text{monot. } r, d)}{\subseteq} \overline{R}(r+1, d+n-1) \stackrel{(\text{Thm. 7})}{=} \overline{R}(r,d) \ .$$

This concludes the proof of Theorem 7. $\qquad\qquad\qquad\qquad\qquad\qquad\qquad\qquad\square$

Example 8. *Consider a simple 3-thread system with a shared-states set $G = \{0, 1, 2\}$. The local state of each thread is immaterial; function α just returns the shared state: $\alpha(g, l_0, l_1, l_2) = g$. The threads' procedures consist of the following actions, which update only the shared state:*

Thread T0: $0 \rightarrow 1$ *Thread T1:* $0 \rightarrow 1$ *Thread T2:* $0 \rightarrow 2$.

Table 1 shows the set of reachable states for different round and delay bounds. For example, with one round and zero delays, the only feasible action is T0's. The reachable states are 0 (initial) and 1 (found by T0). The table shows a path to a pair (r, d) that meets the conditions of Theorem 7. From $(r, d) = (1, 0)$ we increment r to find a plateau in r of length 1. We then increase d to try to find a plateau in d of length $n - 1 = 2$. This example shows that a delay plateau of length 1 is not enough, as 2 is only reachable at least 2 delays. At $(2, 2)$ we find a new state (2), so we restart the search for plateaus in r and d. At $(3, 4)$, the plateau conditions for Theorem 7 are met. There are no disrespectful transitions, so by Theorem 7, we know that $\overline{R}(3, 4) = \overline{R}$.

Table 1. Reachable states in Example 8 under various round and delay bounds. The boxed set passes the convergence test suggested by Theorem 7

	$d = 0$	$d = 1$	$d = 2$	$d = 3$	$d = 4$
$r = 1$	$\{0,1\}$	$\{0,1\}$	$\{0,1,2\}$	$\{0,1,2\}$	$\{0,1,2\}$
$r = 2$	$\{0,1\} \longrightarrow$	$\{0,1\} \longrightarrow$	$\{0,1,2\}$	$\{0,1,2\}$	$\{0,1,2\}$
$r = 3$	$\{0,1\}$	$\{0,1\}$	$\{0,1,2\} \rightarrow$	$\{0,1,2\} \rightarrow$	$\boxed{\{0,1,2\}}$

4 Efficient Delay-Unbounded Analysis

Turning Theorem 7 into a reachability algorithm requires efficient computation of the sets $R(r, d)$. This section presents an approach to achieve this, by expanding only *frontier* states when either the round or the delay parameter is increased.

To this end, let C be a state property (such as an assertion) that respects α, in the sense that, for any states s_1, s_2, if $\alpha(s_1) = \alpha(s_2)$, then $s_1 \models C$ iff $s_2 \models C$. From now on, we further assume the domain $\mathcal{A}$ of abstraction function α to be finite, which will ensure termination of our algorithm (see Lemma 11 later).

Our verification scheme for C is shown in Algorithm 1, which uses Algorithm 2 as a subroutine. In the rest of this paper, we also refer to Algorithm 1 as *Delay- (and round-) UnBounded Analysis*, DrUBA for short.

The main data structure used in the algorithms is that of a `State`, which stores both program variables and scheduling information, in the attributes *finder*, *rounds_taken*, and *delays_taken*. For a state s, variables $s.rounds\_taken$ and $s.delays\_taken$ represent the number of times the scheduler started a round and delayed a thread, resp., to get to s. Variable $s.finder$ contains the index of the thread whose action produced s. This is enough information to continue

---

Algorithm 1. Verifying property C against all reachable states of program $\mathcal{P}$

Input: n-thread asynchronous program, property C
Output: "safe", "violation of C", or "unknown"
1: *Reached* := (finite) set of initial states   ▷ *Reached*: states reached so far
2: r := 0; d := 0
3: **repeat**
4:    *Frontier* := $\{s \in \text{Reached} : s.\text{rounds\_taken} = r\}$
5:    r++
6:    **for** $s \in \text{Frontier}$ **do**
7:        *Reached* := $\text{Reached} \cup \text{FinishRounds}(s, r + 1, C)$
8:    r++
9: **until** round plateau of length 1
10: **repeat**
11:    *Frontier* := $\{s \in \text{Reached} : s.\text{delays\_taken} = d\}$
12:    d++
13:    **for** $s \in \text{Frontier}$ **do**
14:        s' := s ▷ copy of state s
15:        $s'.\text{delays\_taken}$++
16:        $s'.\text{finder}$:= $(s'.\text{finder} + 1) \bmod n$
17:        **if** $s'.\text{finder} \bmod n = 0$ **then**
18:            $s'.\text{rounds\_taken}$++
19:        *Reached* := $\text{Reached} \cup \text{FinishRounds}(s', r, C)$
20:    **if** new abstract state found during **for** loop in Line 13 **then**
21:        **goto** 3   ▷ abort second **repeat** loop; go back to first
22: **until** delay plateau of length $n - 1$
23: **if** $\alpha(\text{Reached})$ is closed under disrespectful actions **then**
24:    **return** "safe"
25: **else**
26:    **return** "unknown"

Algorithm 2. $\text{FinishRounds}(s, r, C)$

Input: s: state, r: round bound, C: state property
Output: states reachable from s up to round bound r, without delaying
1: Set<State> *Unexplored* := $\{s\}$, *Reached* := $\{\}$
2: **while** *Unexplored* != $\{\}$ **do**
3:    select and remove some state u from *Unexplored*
4:    **if** u violates C **then**
5:        **throw** "violation of C (witnessed by reaching state u)"
6:    *Reached* := $\text{Reached} \cup \{u\}$
7:    **if** $u.\text{finder} < n - 1$ **or** $u.\text{rounds\_taken} < r$ **then**   ▷ if u schedulable
8:        *Unexplored* := $\text{Unexplored} \cup (\text{Image}(u) \setminus \text{Reached})$
9: **return** *Reached*

the execution from s later, starting with the thread after *finder*. For the initial states, *rounds_taken* and *delays_taken* are zero, and *finder* is $n-1$ (the latter so that expanding the initial states starts with thread $(n-1)+1 \bmod n = 0$). For set membership testing, two states are considered equal when they agree on their finders and on program variables. The *rounds_taken* and *delays_taken* variables are for scheduling purposes only and ignored when checking for equality.

As mentioned in Prop. 3, the sequence of reachability sets is monotone with respect to both rounds and delays, for any program. This entails two useful properties for Algorithm 1. First, we can increase the bounds in any order and at individual rates. Second, it suffices to expand states at the frontier of the exploration, without missing new schedules. When adding a new delay, we only need to delay those states that were (first) found in schedules using the maximum delays. When adding a round, we only need to expand states that were (first) found in the last round of a schedule.

Algorithm 1 first advances the round parameter r until a round plateau has been reached (Lines 3–9). It does so by running the *FinishRounds* function on *frontier states* s: those that were reached in the final round r of the previous round iteration. *FinishRounds* (Algorithm 2) explores from the given state s, Round-Robin style, up to the given round, without delaying any thread. The actual expansion of a state happens in function *Image* (Line 8 of Algorithm 2), which computes a state's successors and initializes their scheduling variables: *rounds_taken* and *delays_taken* are copied from u, the *finder* of the successor is the next thread ($+1 \bmod n$). If this wraps around, *rounds_taken* is incremented as well.

Back to the main Algorithm 1: we have reached a round plateau of length 1 if the entire **for** loop in Line 6 sees no new *abstract* states (no new elements in $\alpha(Reached)$). If so, we are not ready yet to perform the convergence test (recall Example 8). Instead, Algorithm 1 now similarly advances the delay parameter d (Lines 10–22). For each frontier state (*delays_taken* $= d$), we delay the thread scheduled to execute from this state (by incrementing (mod n) the *finder* variable), and record the taken delay (Line 15). Then we again call the *FinishRounds* function and merge in the states found. Importantly, these merges preserve states already in *Reached*, meaning that the algorithm will keep states found earlier in the exploration (with smaller r, d).

The loop beginning in Line 10 repeats until a delay plateau of length $n-1$ is encountered (as required by Theorem 7). This means that during $n-1$ consecutive **repeat** iterations, the **for** loop in 13 did not find any new abstract states. When the round and delay plateaus have the required lengths (1 and $n-1$, resp.), we invoke the convergence test (Line 23), which amounts to applying Theorem 7. If the test fails, Algorithm 1 returns "unknown".

Towards proving partial correctness of Algorithm 1, we first show that the states eventually collected in set *Reached* by the algorithm correspond exactly to the round- and delay-bounded reachability sets $R(r, d)$, and that—after the two main **repeat** loops—a plateau of sufficient length has been generated. As a corollary, the algorithm is partially correct, i.e. it returns correct answers if it terminates.

Lemma 9. *If Algorithm 1 reaches Line 23, the current values of r and d satisfy:* *(i) Reached = $R(r, d)$, and (ii) $\overline{R}(r - 1, d - (n - 1)) = \overline{R}(r, d)$.*

Corollary 10. *The answers "safe" and "violation of C" returned by Algorithm 1 are correct.*

The algorithm won't return either "safe" or "violation of C" in one of two situations: when the convergence test fails in Line 23 (it gives up), and when it fails to ever reach this line. The latter can be prevented using a finite-domain α:

Lemma 11. *If the domain $\mathcal{A}$ of abstraction function α is finite, Algorithm 1 terminates on every input.*

Since abstraction α approximates the information contained in a state, a plateau may be *intermediate*, e.g. $\overline{R}(1,0) \subsetneq \overline{R}(1,1) = \overline{R}(2,2) \subsetneq \overline{R}(2,3)$. Thus, stopping the exploration simply on account of encountering a plateau—even of lengths $(1, n-1)$—is unsound. Intermediate plateaus make our algorithm (unavoidably) incomplete: if the test in Line 23 fails, then there are known-to-be-reachable abstract states with abstract successors whose reachability cannot be decided at that moment. If we knew the plateau to be intermediate, we could keep exploring the sets $R(r, d)$ for larger values of r and d until the next plateau emerges, hoping that the convergence test succeeds at that time. In general, however, we cannot distinguish intermediate from final plateaus.

5   DrUBA with Unbounded-Domain Variables

In addition to unbounded control structures like stacks, which come up in push-down systems and were discussed in Ex 5, infinite state spaces in programs are often due to (nominally) unbounded-domain program variables. This presents no problem for the computation of the concrete reachability sets *Reached* in Algorithm 1: for any round and delay bounds (r, d), the set of concrete reachable states $RR(r, d)$ is finite and thus explicitly computable (no symbolic data structures are needed).[2] On the other hand, termination of the same algorithm requires that it eventually reach a plateau in r and d of sufficient length. This is guaranteed by an abstraction function α that maps concrete states into a finite abstract space. A finite abstract domain is therefore highly desirable.

A generic abstraction that reduces an unbounded data domain to a finite one is predicate abstraction [4,13, see [14] for a short primer]. The goal in this section is to demonstrate how the simple scheme of delay-unbounded analysis can be combined with predicate abstraction to verify unbounded-thread programs.

---

[2] Contrast this to a *context-switch* bound, under which reachability sets can be infinite.

5.1 The Fixed-Thread Case

Consider program $\mathbb{P}$ in Fig. 1 on the left [8, page 4: program $\mathbb{P}''$]. Intuitively, variable m counts the number of threads spawned to execute $\mathbb{P}$ concurrently. It is easy to see that "the assertion in [$\mathbb{P}$] cannot be violated, no matter how many threads execute [$\mathbb{P}$], since no thread but the first will manage to" [8] enter the *true* branch of the **if** statement and reach the assertion.

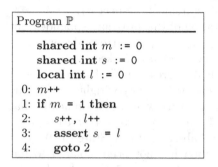
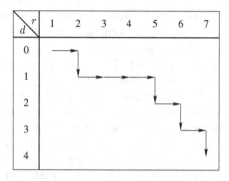

Fig. 1. Left: program $\mathbb{P}$; **Right:** how Algorithm 1 operates on (an abstraction of) it

Previous work has shown that even the 1-thread version of this program cannot be proved correct using predicate abstraction **unless** we permit predicates that depend on both shared and local variables [9, for the unprovability result], which have been referred to as *mixed* [8]. An example is the predicate $p :: (s = l)$, which comes up in the assertion. The dependence of p on both shared and thread-local data causes standard solutions that track the truth value of p in a shared or local Boolean variable to be unsound. The solution proposed in [8] is to use *broadcast* instructions to have the executing thread notify all other threads whenever the truth value of p changes. This solution comes with two disadvantages: (i) the resulting Boolean broadcast programs are more expensive to analyze than strictly asynchronous Boolean programs, and (ii) the solution cannot be extended to the unbounded-thread case.

Let us consider how we can verify this program using Algorithm 1, for the fixed-thread case; we consider $n = 2$ threads. We will have to use mixed predicates as in [8], but since we never execute the abstract Boolean program, there is no need for constructing it. As a result, there is no need for broadcast instructions.

The program generates an unbounded number of reachable concrete states, but we explore it only under round and delay bounds r and d. As per Algorithm 1, we increase these bounds until we have reached plateaus of lengths 1 and $n - 1 = 1$, resp. Plateaus are determined over the abstract-state set, so we need a function α.

First attempt: a single predicate. We define α as follows, for a concrete state c:

$$\alpha_1(c) \quad = \quad (c.pc_0, \, c.s = c.l_0) \in 0, \ldots, 4 \times \{0, 1\} \,,$$

where $c.pc_0$, $c.l_0$, and $c.s$ are the values of thread 0's pc and local variable l, and of shared variable s, in state c, respectively. The function extracts from a concrete state the current program location of thread 0 and the value of predicate $p :: (s = l)$ for thread 0.[3] The only statement *not* respecting α_1 is the **if** statement in Line 1: here, the new value of the pc cannot be determined from the current values of pc and predicate p alone. All other statements respect α_1.

We can now perform an iterative exploration of this program—bounded but exhaustive within each bound. In Fig. 1 on the right, red arrows denote "new abstract state reached". A red horizontal arrow $(r\text{++})$ means: "keep increasing r". A red vertical arrow $(d\text{++})$ means: "switch to increasing r". In other words, following a red arrow—no matter the direction—we always go "right" $(r\text{++})$. The green horizontal arrow followed by a green vertical arrow at the end indicates that we have reached the first plateaus of length 1 in *both* directions: at $(r, d) = (7, 4)$.

At this point we have reached a total of 7 abstract states. State $(3, 0)$ ($pc = 3$, $s \neq l$) is not among them, so the assertion has not been violated so far. We run the convergence test, to determine whether set $\overline{R}(7, 4)$ is closed under disrespectful actions. Since the **if** in Line 1 is the only disrespectful statement, we only need to check successors of abstract states of the form $(1, ?)$ (i.e., with $pc = 1$). Unfortunately, $\overline{R}(7, 4)$ contains abstract state $(1, 0)$ (a reachable abstract state) but not its abstract successor $(2, 0)$. This state is unreachable, but we do not know that at this point. This causes Algorithm 1 to return "unknown".

Second attempt: two predicates. The disrespectful action causing the failure suggests that we need to keep track of whether the branch in Line 1 can be taken, i.e. whether $m = 1$. We refine our abstraction using this (non-mixed) predicate:

$$\alpha_2(c) \quad = \quad (c.pc_0, \, c.s = c.l_0, \, c.m = 1) \in 0, \ldots, 4 \times \{0, 1\}^2 \,. \tag{4}$$

The abstract successors of the **if** statement can now be decided based only on knowledge provided by α_2, i.e. the statement respects α_2. There is, however, another statement disrespecting α_2, and only one: the increment $m\text{++}$ in Line 0. If $m \neq 1$, we cannot decide whether $m = 1$ will be true after the increment.

We again perform our iterative exploration of this program, and find the first suitable plateau at the same point $(r, d) = (7, 4)$. This time, however, we have reached a total of 12 abstract states (all of them "safe"). We run the convergence test: we only need to check already reached abstract states of the form $(0, ?, 0)$ ($pc = 0$, $m \neq 1$). Set $\overline{R}(7, 4)$ contains exactly one state of this form: $(0, 1, 0)$, which $m\text{++}$ can turn into $(1, 1, 0)$ and $(1, 1, 1)$—note that the next pc value is unambiguous (1), and predicate $s = l$ is not affected. **The good news** is now that both abstract states $(1, 1, 0)$ and $(1, 1, 1)$ are contained in $\overline{R}(7, 4)$. This proves this set closed under disrespectful actions; Algorithm 1 terminates: the assertion is safe for any execution schedule, for the case of $n = 2$ threads.

---

[3] Tracking these values for thread 0 suffices: the multi-threaded program is symmetric.

We summarize that, in our solution above, we assumed a lucky hand in picking predicates—the question of predicate discovery is orthogonal to the delay-unbounded analysis scheme. However, the proof obtained using Algorithm 1 does not involve costly broadcast operations, previously proposed as an ingredient to extend predicate abstraction to concurrent programs. A second, more powerful advantage is that, unlike the earlier broadcast solution, Algorithm 1 extends gracefully to the unbounded-thread case. This is the topic of the rest of this section.

5.2   The Unbounded-Thread Case

The goal now is to investigate whether an asynchronous unbounded-domain variable program is safe for *arbitrary* thread counts (and thread interleavings).

Existing solutions. We are aware of only one general technique that combines predicate abstraction with unbounded-thread concurrency [15]. That technique can achieve the above goal, roughly as follows. In addition to standard and mixed predicates used also in the fixed-thread case, we now permit *inter-thread* predicates, which quantify over all threads other than the executing one. Such predicates allow us to express, for example, that a thread's local variable l's value is larger than that of any other thread: $\forall i : i \neq self : l > l_i$. Predicates of this type are provably required during predicate abstraction to verify the safety of the Ticket Lock algorithm [3,15].

Abstraction against inter-thread predicates leads to a *dual-reference program* [15], a process that is already far more complex than standard sequential or even fixed-thread predicate abstraction. But we pay another price for using these predicates: namely, the loss of *monotonicity* of the transition relation w.r.t. a standard well-quasiordering $\preccurlyeq$ on infinite state sets of unbounded-thread Boolean programs. In this context, monotonicity states, roughly, that adding passive threads to a valid transition keeps the transition intact.

This price is heavy, since monotonicity w.r.t. $\preccurlyeq$ would have given us a well-quasiordered infinite-state transition system, for which local-state reachability properties are decidable [1]; working implementations exist. The above-mentioned prior work attempts to salvage the situation, by adding a set of transitions (the *non-monotone fragment*) to the dual-reference program that restore monotonicity and further overapproximate but without affecting the reachability of unsafe states [15].

Alternative solution. We now propose a solution that uses the same type of inter-thread predicates (this is inevitable), but renders dual-reference programs, the monotone closure of the transition relation and all other "overhead" introduced in [15] unnecessary. We will use Algorithm 1 as a sub-routine.

The idea is as follows. Sect. 5.1 suggests a way to verify fixed-thread asynchronous programs, using a combination of predicate abstraction and Algorithm 1 . To handle the unbounded-thread case, we wrap another layer of incremental resource bounding around this combined algorithm—the "resource" this time is the number n of threads executing the program. For each member of a sequence of increasing fixed thread counts we compute the set of abstract states reachable under arbitrary thread interleavings. This is purely a sub-routine; we will use the method proposed in Sect. 5.1 (others are possible, e.g. [8]).

The incremental (in n) analysis proceeds until we have reached a thread plateau *of length 1*, and then run the convergence test: we check the current abstract reachability set for closure under disrespectful actions. This time, the abstract transitions must take into account that the number of executing threads is unknown. It is easy to see that a plateau of length 1 is sufficient: we compute the set of abstract states reachable under *arbitrary* thread schedules; thus, the obstacle of non-schedulability of thread i in the proof of Theorem 7 that forced us to wait for a (delay) plateau of length $n - 1$ does not apply here.

A non-monotone resource parameterization

Before we demonstrate this idea on program $\mathbb{P}$, we justify our strategy of combining resource bounds. The idea presented above can be viewed as a multi-resource analysis problem where we increment r and d in an "inner loop" (represented by Algorithm 1 as a sub-routine to compute fixed-thread reachability sets), and n in an outer loop. Both loops compute monotonously increasing reachability sequences: for "inner" this is Prop. 3; for "outer" this is easy to see. Theorem 7 relies upon the monotonicity: without it, the test $\overline{R}(r, d) = \overline{R}(r + 1, d + n - 1)$ makes the algorithm unsound.

The way we nest the three involved resource parameters is not arbitrary: Round-Robin reachability under an increasing thread count is not monotone. More precisely, making the thread-count parameter n explicit, let $R(r, d, n)$ denote the set of states reachable in the n-thread program $\mathcal{P}$ under $RR(r, d)$ scheduling. Then $R(r, d, n) \subseteq R(r, d, n + 1)$ is **not** valid. The following example illustrates this (at first counter-intuitive) monotonicity violation:

Example 12. *Consider the asynchronous Boolean program over shared variables s and t on the right. Here we have $R(3, 0, 1) \not\subseteq R(3, 0, 2)$: given 1 thread (sequential execution), a state with*

shared bool $s := 0$, $t := 0$
0: $t := !t$
1: **if** t **then**
2:      $s := 1$

$s = 1$ *is reachable. With 2 symmetric threads, under delay-free Round-Robin scheduling ($d = 0$), the first and second thread will repeatedly flip t to 1 and back to 0, resp., before either one has a chance to get past the guard in Line 1.*

A stronger result is: for all $r \in \mathbb{N}$, $R(3, 0, 1) \not\subseteq R(r, 0, 2)$, i.e. we cannot make up for the poor scheduling of the second thread by adding more rounds.

The consequence for us is that we cannot compute, for fixed r, d, the sets $R(r, d, \infty)$, using the closure-under-disrespectful-actions paradigm. Instead we must, for each n, compute $R(\infty, \infty, n)$ (using Algorithm 1 or otherwise) and increase n in the outer loop.

Verifying program $\mathbb{P}$ for unbounded thread count

We recall that, given the two predicates shown in Eq. (4) and the pc, we were able to verify program $\mathbb{P}$ correct (under arbitrary thread interleavings) for $n = 2$

threads; a total of 12 abstract states were reached (out of $5 \cdot 2^2 = 20$ possible). Advancing the outer loop, we invoke Algorithm 1 for $n = 3$ threads. This reveals another reachable abstract state, namely $pc = 0$, $s \neq l$, $m \neq 1$. Unfortunately, this state causes Algorithm 1 to return "unknown": under α_2, one currently unreached abstract successor is $pc = 1$, $s \neq l$, $m = 1$, violating closure. Observing that a thread executing Line 1 with $m = 1$ must be the first thread executing, we try tracking the initial value of m:

$$\alpha_3(c) \quad = \quad (c.pc_0, \ c.s = c.l_0, \ c.m = 1, \ c.m = 0) \in 0, \ldots, 4 \times \{0,1\}^3 \ . \quad (5)$$

Interestingly, *all actions (statements) of program* $\mathbb{P}$ *respect abstraction* α_3. This means that the test for closure under disrespectful actions is *vacuously true*—we can stop as soon as we have reached a plateau in n of length 1. We don't have to wait long for this plateau: we invoke Algorithm 1 for $n = 3$ and $n = 4$ under abstraction α_3. (Note that $n = 4$ requires a longer plateau than $n = 3$.) The abstract reachability sets consist of the same 14 abstract states in both cases. We report the program safe, for arbitrary interleavings and arbitrary thread counts. We can also report the exact set of 14 reachable abstract states.

We again summarize that, while we still (and unavoidably) use mixed predicates, we do not construct a thread-parameterized abstract program, which would require broadcast statements [8] and a rather involved dual-reference transition semantics [15]. In fact, we did not even need to test for closure under any abstract images, since the chosen abstraction enjoys respect from all actions.

6 Evaluation

Our goal for the evaluation of DrUBA was to answer the following questions:

1. How does DrUBA compare to abstract fixed-point computation ("AI")?
2. How does DrUBA compare to the approach from [18] ("CUBA")?
3. How expensive is the state exploration along a plateau in Algorithm 1?
4. What is the performance benefit of the frontier optimization in Algorithm 1?

Questions 1 and 2 serve to compare DrUBA against other techniques; Questions 3 and 4 investigate features of Algorithm 1.

To this end we implemented, in Java 11, a verifier using Algorithm 1 that takes concurrent pushdown systems as input; we refer to this verifier as DrUBA in this section.[4] We also implemented the AI approach in Java 11. For the comparison with the context-unbounded approach, we used a publicly available tool[5]. Our experiments are based on the concurrent benchmark programs also used in [18]. The experiments are performed on a 3.20GHz Intel i5 PC. The memory limit was 8GB, with a timeout of 1 h.

---

[4] DrUBA implementation available at https://doi.org/10.5281/zenodo.4726301.
[5] https://github.com/lpzun/cuba.

6.1   Results

Table 2 reports the benchmark names, the thread counts, and the size of the reachable abstract state space (columns 1–3). The second part of the table shows the time it took each verifier to fully explore the state space and confirm convergence. For the AI approach, we check whether the abstract state space is closed under *all* operations each time either r or d is incremented. Algorithm 1 was faster than "AI" on every example except Stefan-4,5. Stefan is the only program that actually does not require any delays to discover all reachable abstract states. The results indicate that the AI approach spends approximately half of its computation time doing repeated convergence tests after each bound increment. Furthermore, as state sets increase in size, AI seems to take even longer, as with the Bluetooth3 (2+3) example. The convergence test needed for "AI" includes checking closure under both respectful and disrespectful actions, making it more costly than the one used in Algorithm 1.

Algorithm 1 also improved on the results with "CUBA". For examples that took longer than a few seconds, DrUBA was able to run in less time on the same benchmark. The difference on small examples is likely due to a different implementation language (C++ vs. Java). DrUBA does not explore as many schedules, and explores fewer as the delay and round bounds approach their cutoff values (as noted below). Additionally, DrUBA was less memory-intensive for large examples for which the CUBA approach cannot prove that the set of reachable states per context bound is finite. In this case, "CUBA" requires the use of more expensive symbolic representations of states sets. Algorithm 1 does not suffer from this problem—the reachability sets in each iteration are finite. For the Stefan-5 example, "CUBA" ran out of memory after 23 min. DrUBA was able to prove convergence for this example (as was "AI").

Table 3 reports the number of times Algorithm 1 computed the image (successors) of a state until reaching the final r-d-plateau (Col. 3) and during the final plateau (Col. 4), as well as the total number of image computations without the *frontier* optimization (Col. 5). The table offers convincing evidence to support our heuristic that waiting for a long d-plateau at the end of exploration is not costly, answering Question 3.. On most benchmarks, the amount of computation done during the plateau (Col. 4) was negligible. This included our largest example, Bluetooth3 (2+3). The exception to this is the Stefan examples, which—as mentioned earlier—do not require any delays to reach the full abstract state set (the d-plateau starts at $(r_{\max},0)$). Finally, a naive implementation that does not take advantage of monotonicity, forgoing the frontier approach to expanding the state set, was orders of magnitude worse. This is because it has to recompute the whole set for every iteration of r or d. This answers Question 4..

Comparing Col. 7 in Table 2 to the cutoff context-switch bounds from [18], we find that, while the r and d bounds were large, not all programs that needed large bounds took a long time to verify. For example, the Bluetooth3 (2+1) example took much less time than Stefan-5, despite requiring 21 more delays (with similar rounds). A hint for the reason can be found in Table 3. Once the set of abstract states is close to the $\overline{R}$, there are very few new states on the

Table 2. Benchmark description and running times for different algorithms. Threads: # of threads ($a + b$: the respective numbers of threads from two different templates); $\overline{R}$: number of reachable abstract states; Time: running time (sec) for each algorithm ("—": timeout or memory-out); r_{max}, d_{max}: round and delay counts at the *end* of each plateau when convergence was detected.

1	2	3	4	5	6	7
Benchmark	Threads	$|\overline{R}|$	Time: Algorithm 1	Time: "AI"	Time: "CUBA"	r_{max}, d_{max} Algorithm 1
1 Bluetooth1	1+1	1010	.69	.92	.32	23, 15
	1+2	5468	3.32	6.79	2.25	32, 29
	2+1	18972	8.52	16.69	13.60	35, 26
2 Bluetooth2	1+1	1018	.71	.98	.29	23, 15
	1+2	5468	3.60	6.68	2.62	32, 29
	2+1	18972	8.81	16.68	13.97	35, 26
3 Bluetooth3	1+1	1018	.72	1.23	.41	23, 15
	1+2	5468	3.61	6.40	2.79	32, 29
	2+1	19002	9.97	16.27	14.50	35, 26
	2+2	94335	70.71	136.31	343.05	44, 40
	2+3	460684	654.47	2084.76	TO	56, 56
4 BST-Insert	1+1	272	.36	.49	.14	31, 16
	2+1	6644	3.62	5.25	10.09	49, 32
	2+2	14256	8.12	14.87	99.94	50, 38
5 Filecrawler	1+2	246	.37	.54	.05	20, 12
6 K-Induction	1+1	130	.51	.74	.48	20, 09
7 Proc-2	2+2	352	.56	.77	2.05	19, 20
8 Stefan	2	31	.24	.36	.04	13, 02
	4	687	13.99	13.82	20.33	32, 04
	5	3085	428.22	295.02	OOM	35, 05
	8	—	OOM	OOM	OOM	—
9 Dekker	2	1507	.82	1.62	.39	37, 16

frontier. We can see this in the small numbers in Col. 4, but it also applies to the round bound. If a state is rediscovered, it is not expanded in further round increments. Once the round bound is large enough, there are few deep schedules of maximum possible length (nr) that produce new concrete states.

6.2 Unbounded-Thread Experiments

We implemented Algorithm 1 in combination with predicate abstraction as detailed in Sect. 5.2 to check the effectiveness of our technique on a tricky concurrent program that requires unbounded variable domains. The Ticket Lock

Table 3. Detailed analysis of Algorithm 1, measuring the number of times the program computed the successors of a state. Col. 3 reports the image operations Algorithm 1 performed before reaching the FP (final plateau), Col. 4—the number of additional image operations computed until the program ended. Col. 5 shows the image operations without the *frontier* improvement, requiring recomputing each $\overline{R}(r, d)$ from the initial states.

	1	2	3	4	5
	Benchmark	Threads	Calls to *Image* $\rightarrow$ begin FP	Calls to *Image* Begin $\rightarrow$ end FP	Calls to *Image* w/o frontier
1	Bluetooth1	1+1	4,034	1	339,261
		1+2	23,441	3	4,758,084
		2+1	80,283	19	23,199,458
2	Bluetooth2	1+1	4,103	1	350,587
		1+2	23,493	3	4,780,778
		2+1	80,714	19	23,290,556
3	Bluetooth3	1+1	4,096	8	348,851
		1+2	23,493	3	4,786,950
		2+1	80,834	19	23,467,470
		2+2	478,426	2	283,910,446
		2+3	2,766,625	6	—
4	BST-Insert	1+1	780	1	82,130
		2+1	29,802	6	17,785,065
		2+2	62,190	25	34,335,106
5	Filecrawler	1+2	1,056	4	202,074
6	K-Induction	1+1	5,636	974	218,715
7	Proc-2	2+2	2,501	1,298	578,099
8	Stefan	2	367	59	500,494
		4	658,696	261,881	—
		5	10,299,293	6,621,157	—
		8	—	—	—
9	Dekker	2	3,636	2	688,836

protocol [3] and the predicates used to prove its correctness are shown in Fig. 2. In Line 0, threads wait to enter the Critical Section, whose code is at the beginning of Line 1; the rest of Line 1 is exit code to prepare the thread for re-entry. In the predicates on the right, subscript i denotes thread i's copy of a local variable.

This example has been shown to require significant adjustments to predicate abstraction to accommodate fixed-thread concurrency [8], and has been claimed to require an entirely new theory to cope with the unbounded-thread case [15]. We rely on the same predicates used in earlier work, and it is clear what motivates each predicate. P1 ensures t is a"new" ticket larger than previous ones, P2 is

```
shared int s := 0, t := 0
local int l := fetch_and_add(t)
0: while s ≠ l do;        ▷ wait for s = l
1: critical-section code here
   inc(s)
   l := fetch_and_add(t)
   goto 0
```

P1: $\forall i : t > l_i$
P2: $|\{i : pc_i = 1\}| \geq 2$
P3: $s = l$
P4: $\forall i : i \neq self : l \neq l_i$

Fig. 2. Left: the Ticket Lock protocol; **Right:** four predicates used to prove it correct

used to check the safety property, P3 tracks the condition in Line 0, and P4 means that the operating thread's l is unique. DrUBA finds four abstract states for both 2 threads and 3 threads using Algorithm 1. This is an n-plateau of length 1.

To prove convergence for both Algorithm 1 and the "outer loop" incrementing n, we used the ACL2s theorem prover [7]. We specified the data in a concrete state, and the four abstract states that were found. Only the second statement disrespects this abstraction w.r.t. r, d and n, as we know the value of the test in the first statement for an abstract state. Given these, ACL2s was able to verify that the set of abstract states is closed under the semantics of statement 1. As a result, we can report that Ticket Lock is safe (P2 is invariantly false), for an arbitrary number of threads and arbitrary thread interleavings.

7   Discussion of Related Work

This work is inspired from two angles. The first is clearly the delay-bounded scheduling (DBS) technique [10]. The authors formalize this concept and show its effectiveness as a testing scheme. Their computational model of a dynamic task buffer is somewhat different from ours. We have not discussed dynamic thread creation here; it can be simulated by creating threads up-front and delaying them until such time as they are supposed to come into existence. The DBS paper also presents a sequentialization technique that can be turned into a symbolic verifier via verification-condition generation and SMT solving. This, however, requires bounding loops and recursion. Our approach combines exhaustive finite-state model exploration with convergence detection and thus does not suffer from these restrictions.

The second inspiration comes from an earlier context-unbounded analysis technique [18]. Similar in spirit to the present work, [18] started from a yet earlier context-bounded analysis technique and describes a condition under which a chosen context bound is sufficient to reach all states reachable under some abstraction. For the case of concurrent pushdown systems (CPDS)—the verification target of [18]—, the pop operation plays a crucial role in establishing this condition; note that, in our work, pop actions disrespect the top-of-the-stack abstraction commonly used for CPDS.

Our work has a number of advantages over [18]. First, and crucially, the set of states reachable under a context bound can be infinite (a single context can already generate infinitely many states); its determination thus requires more expensive symbolic reachability methods. In contrast, the reachability set under Round-Robin scheduling with a round- and a delay bound *is always finite*; moreover, it can be computed very easily, even for complex programs. This makes our technique a prime choice for lifting existing testing schemes to verifiers. A second advantage over [18] is that we retain much of the efficiency of the "almost deterministic" exploration delay-bounded scheduling, as demonstrated in Sect. 6. A downside of our work is that our convergence condition is sound only after a plateau has emerged of length roughly equal to the number of running threads; this is not required in [18]. However, as also demonstrated in Sect. 6, our efforts to compute reachable states for increasing r, d in a *frontier-driven* way nearly annihilates this drawback: in most cases, only a small number of image computations happen along the plateau.

An alternative to our verification approach is a classical analysis based on abstract interpretation [6]. Given function α, such analysis interprets the entire program abstractly, and then computes a fixed point under the abstract program's transition relation. This fixed point, if it exists, overapproximates the set of reachable abstract states. Hence, the absence of error states in the fixed point implies safety, but the presence of errors does not immediately permit a conclusion. In contrast, our technique interleaves *concrete* state space exploration (enabling genuine testing) with *abstraction-based* convergence detection. We believe this to be a useful approach in practical programming environments, where abstract proof engines with poorly understood bug-finding capabilities may be met with skepticism. A more detailed discussion of DrUBA vs. Abstract Interpretation can be found in the Appendix of [14].

Underapproximating program behaviors using bounding techniques is a widespread solution to address undecidability of safety verification problems. Examples include depth- [12] and context-bounding [16,17,20], delay-bounding [10], bounded asynchrony [11], preemption-bounding [19], and phase-bounded analysis [2,5]. Many of these bounding techniques admit decidable analysis problems [16,17,20] and thus have been successfully used in practice for bug finding. Round- and delay-bounded Round-Robin scheduling trivially renders safety decidable, since the delay-program is finite-state. In addition, it is very easy to implement, avoiding, for example, the need for symbolic data structures and algorithms to represent and process intermediate reachability sets.

8   Conclusion

We have presented an approach to enhancing delay-bounded scheduling in asynchronous programs with a convergence test that, if successful, certifies that all states from some chosen abstract domain have been reached. The resulting algorithm inherits from earlier work the capability to detect bugs efficiently, but can also prove safety properties, under arbitrary thread interleavings. It exploits the monotonicity of delay-bounded reachability sets to expand states and test for convergence only when needed. We have further demonstrated that, combined with predicate abstraction using powerful predicates, tricky unbounded-thread routines over unbounded data, such as the Ticket Lock, can be verified using substantially less machinery than proposed in earlier work. We have shown the experimental competitiveness of our approach against several related techniques.

References

1. Abdulla, P.A.: Well (and better) quasi-ordered transition systems. Bull. Symb. Logic **16**(4), 457–515 (2010)
2. Abdulla, P.A., Atig, M.F., Cederberg, J.: Analysis of message passing programs using smt-solvers. In ATVA, pp. 272–286 (2013)
3. Andrews, G.R.: Concurrent programming: Principles and practice. Benjamin-Cummings Publishing Co. (1991)
4. Ball, T., Majumdar, R., Millstein, T.D., Rajamani, S.K.: Automatic predicate abstraction of C programs. In PLDI, pp. 203–213 (2001)
5. Bouajjani, A., Emmi, M.: Bounded phase analysis of message-passing programs. Int. J. Softw. Tools Technol. Transf. **16**(2), 127–146 (2013). https://doi.org/10.1007/s10009-013-0276-z
6. Cousot, P., Cousot, R.: Abstract interpretation: a unified lattice model for static analysis of programs by construction or approximation of fixpoints. In POPL, pp. 238–252 (1977)
7. Dillinger, P.C., Manolios, P., Vroon, D., Moore, J.S.: ACL2s: "the ACL2 Sedan". Electron. Notes Theor. Comput. Sci. **174**(2), 3–18 (2007)
8. Donaldson, A., Kaiser, A., Kroening, D., Wahl, T.: Symmetry-aware predicate abstraction for shared-variable concurrent programs. In: Computer Aided Verification (CAV), pp. 356–371 (2011)
9. Donaldson, A.F., Kaiser, A., Kroening, D., Wahl, T.: Symmetry-aware predicate abstraction for shared-variable concurrent programs (Extended Technical Report). CoRR, abs/1102.2330 (2011)
10. Emmi, M., Qadeer, S., Rakamaric, Z.: Delay-bounded scheduling. In: Principles of Programming Languages (POPL), pp. 411–422 (2011)
11. Fisher, J., Henzinger, T.A., Mateescu, M., Piterman, N.: Bounded asynchrony: Concurrency for modeling cell-cell interactions. In: Formal Methods in Systems Biology, pp. 17–32 (2008)
12. Godefroid, P.: Model checking for programming languages using VeriSoft. In: POPL, pp. 174–186 (1997)
13. Graf, S., Saïdi, H.: Construction of abstract state graphs with PVS. In: CAV, pp. 72–83 (1997)
14. Johnson, A., Wahl, T.:Delay-bounded scheduling without delay! (Extended Technical Report). CoRR, abs/2105.07277 (2021)
15. Kaiser, A., Kroening, D., Wahl, T.: Lost in abstraction: monotonicity in multi-threaded programs. Inf. Comput. (IaC) **252**, 30–47 (2017)
16. La Torre, S., Parthasarathy, M., Parlato, G.: Analyzing recursive programs using a fixed-point calculus. In: PLDI, pp. 211–222 (2009)
17. Lal, A., Reps, T.: Reducing concurrent analysis under a context bound to sequential analysis. Form. Methods Syst. Des. **35**(1), 73–97 (2009)

18. Liu, P., Wahl, T.: CUBA: interprocedural context-unbounded analysis of concurrent programs. In: Programming Languages Design and Implementation (PLDI), pp. 105–119 (2018)
19. Musuvathi, M., Qadeer, S.: Iterative context bounding for systematic testing of multithreaded programs. In: PLDI, pp. 446–455 (2007)
20. Qadeer, S., Rehof, J.: Context-bounded model checking of concurrent software. In: TACAS, pp. 93–107 (2005)

Checking Data-Race Freedom of GPU Kernels, Compositionally

Tiago Cogumbreiro[1]([✉]) [iD], Julien Lange[2] [iD],
Dennis Liew Zhen Rong[1] [iD], and Hannah Zicarelli[1] [iD]

[1] University of Massachusetts Boston, Boston, USA
{tiago.cogumbreiro,zhenrong.liew001,hannah.zicarelli001}@umb.edu
[2] Royal Holloway, University of London, Egham, UK
julien.lange@rhul.ac.uk

Abstract. GPUs offer parallelism as a commodity, but they are difficult to program correctly. Static analyzers that guarantee data-race freedom (DRF) are essential to help programmers establish the correctness of their programs (kernels). However, existing approaches produce too many false alarms and struggle to handle larger programs. To address these limitations we formalize a novel compositional analysis for DRF, based on access memory protocols. These protocols are behavioral types that codify the way threads interact over shared memory.

Our work includes fully mechanized proofs of our theoretical results, the first mechanized proofs in the field of DRF analysis for GPU kernels. Our theory is implemented in Faial, a tool that outperforms the state-of-the-art. Notably, it can correctly verify at least 1.42× more real-world kernels, and it exhibits a linear growth in 4 out of 5 experiments, while others grow exponentially in all 5 experiments.

Keywords: GPU · Data-race · Static analysis · Behavioural types

1 Introduction

GPUs are massively parallel devices that promise a great return on investment at a cost: they are notably difficult to program. In GPU programming, hundreds of lightweight threads share portions of arrays in parallel (without locks)—very different from the programming model of multithreaded programs written in C or Java with heavy-weight heterogeneous threads. Data-race freedom (DRF) analysis aims to guarantee that for all possible executions, every array cell being written by one thread cannot be concurrently accessed by another thread.

In the field of static analysis of DRF in GPU programs, there is a tension between efficiency and correctness (no missed data-races and no false alarms) that thus far is unresolved. Bug finding tools [26,27,33] favor correctness over efficiency: they provide correct results at small scales, by simulating the program execution. Such tools are incapable of handling certain parameters symbolically (*e.g.*, array size) and can easily exhaust users' resources (*e.g.*, loops with long iteration spaces or unknown bounds). Approaches based on Hoare logic [5,7,22]

© The Author(s) 2021
A. Silva and K. R. M. Leino (Eds.) CAV 2021, LNCS 12759, pp. 403–426, 2021.
https://doi.org/10.1007/978-3-030-81685-8_19

Fig. 1. Work-flow of the verification.

can cope with medium-sized programs, do not miss data-races, and do not require array size information; however, they suffer from a high-rate of false alarms and require code annotations written by concurrency experts. Finally, tools that can cope with larger programs and do not require array size information either miss data-races [24] or overwhelm the user with false alarms [37].

To appease this tension, we introduce a novel static DRF analysis that can handle larger programs and produce fewer false alarms than related work, without missing data-races. Additionally our analysis does not require code annotations or array size information. Our verification framework hinges on *access memory protocols*, a new family of behavioral types [1] that codify the way threads interact through shared memory. Our behavioral types also make evident two aspects of the analysis that can be made separate: concurrency analysis (*i.e.*, could these two expressions run in parallel?) and data-race conflict detection (*i.e.*, do these array indices match?).

Contributions and Synopsis. This paper includes the following contributions.

(1) In Sect. 3, we formalize the syntax, semantics, and well-formedness conditions for access memory protocols, which are behavioral types for GPU programs. This behavioral abstraction results in a simpler yet more expressive theory than previous works, *e.g.*, it does not require user-provided loop invariants.
(2) In Sect. 4, we show that our DRF analysis of access memory protocols can be soundly and completely reduced to the satisfiability of an SMT formula, see Theorems 1 and 3. Our theory and results on access memory protocols are fully mechanized in Coq. To the best of our knowledge, this is the first mechanized proof of correctness of a DRF analysis for GPU programs.
(3) We show that our DRF analysis of access memory protocols is compositional when protocols satisfy a structural property, see Theorem 2. Additionally, we show how to transform protocols when they do not meet this property.
(4) In Sect. 5 we present Faial, which infers access memory protocols from CUDA kernels and implements our theory. Our experiments show that Faial is more precise and scales better than existing tools.
(5) In Sect. 6, we present a thorough experimental evaluation of Faial against related work [5,24,26,27], the largest comparative study of GPU verification (5 tools in 260 kernels, 3 tools compared in 487 kernels). Faial verified 218 out of 227 real-world kernels (at least 1.42× more than other tools) and correctly verified more handcrafted tests than other tools (4 out of 5). In a synthetic benchmark suite (250 kernels), Faial is the only tool to exhibit linear growth in 4 out of 5 experiments, while others grow exponentially in all 5 experiments.

Listing 2.1 Examples of racy kernels, l.h.s. is from [34] and r.h.s. simplifies l.h.s. for clarity, with one-dimensional array and thread identifier, and 1-stride loops.

```
1  for ( int  r = 0;  r < N; r++) {
2    for ( int  i = 0;  i<TILE_DIM; i+=BLOCK_ROWS)
3      { tile [ tid .y+i ][ tid .x] = idata [index_ in+i*width];}
4      __syncthreads();
5    for ( int  j = 0;  j<TILE_DIM; j+=BLOCK_ROWS)
6      { odata[index_ out+j*height] = tile [ tid .x][ tid .y+j ];}}
```

```
1  for ( int  r = 0;  r < N; r++) {
2    for ( int  i = 0;  i<M; i++)
3      { tile [ tid ] = ...;}
4      __syncthreads();
5    for ( int  j = 0;  j<M; j++)
6      {... = tile [ tid+j ];}}
```

Our paper is accompanied by an implementation (Faial), an evaluation framework (inc. datasets), and proof scripts (in Coq) for each theorem. All of these are available in our artifact [9].

2   Overview

This section gives an overview of our approach by examining a data-race we found in published work [17,34]. We discuss the challenges that such examples pose to the state-of-the-art of DRF analysis. Then we introduce a verification framework based on *access memory protocols*: behavioral types [1] that codify the way threads interact via shared memory. Figure 1 gives an overview of the verification pipeline. We start from CUDA kernels, from which we infer access memory protocols. Protocols are then checked for well-formedness and transformed in three steps into formulas that are verified by an SMT solver.

2.1   Challenges of GPU Programming

GPU Programming Model. The key component of GPU programming is the *kernel* program, or just kernel, that runs according to the Single-Instruction-Multiple-Thread (SIMT) execution model, where multiple threads run a single instruction concurrently. A kernel is parameterized by a special variable that holds a thread identifier, henceforth named tid. In parallel, each member of a group of threads runs an instantiated copy of the kernel by supplying its identifier as an argument. Threads communicate via shared memory (arrays) and mediate communication via barrier synchronization (an execution point where all threads must wait for each other before advancing further). Writes are only guaranteed to be visible to other threads after a barrier synchronization.

GPU programming platforms usually group threads hierarchically in multiple levels, across which no inter-groups synchronization is possible. In both the literature [6,24] and this work, the focus is on intra-group communication.

Challenges. We motivate the difficulty of analyzing data-races by studying a programming error found in the wild, reported in Listing 2.1 (left). This excerpt comes from a tutorial [34] on optimizing numeric algorithms for GPUs. The code listing transposes a matrix N-times with an outer loop indexed by variable r.

Remarkably, the tutorial [34] does not inform the readers that Listing 2.1 contains a subtle *data-race*: one transpose-operation starts (the writes to tile

Listing 2.2 Minimal representative example of an access memory protocol highlighting the data-race in Listing 2.1.

```
1  // r = 0
2  for^U j in 0..M    // for (int j = 0; j<M; j++)
3    {rd[tid+j]};     //  _ = tile [tid+i];
4  // r = 1
5  for^U i in 0..M    // for (int i = 0; i<M; i++)
6    {wr[tid]}        //  tile [tid] = _;
```

in line 3) without awaiting the termination of the previous transpose-operation (the reads from tile in line 6), thus corrupting the data over time and possibly skewing the timing of the optimization to appear faster than it should be. We found a related data-race in [17], which reuses code from [34].

Our tool, Faial, successfully identifies the program state that triggers the data-race in Listing 2.1: when r=1 and N=2. However, state-of-the-art tools struggle to accurately analyze Listing 2.1, as evaluated in Sect. 6 (Claim 1: Test 1). Symbolic execution tools, such as [26,27], timeout for N>1, and, in general, cannot handle symbolic (unknown) bounds. GPUVerify [6], a tool based on Hoare logic, reports a false alarm: a spurious data-race when r=0 and N=1. PUG [24] incorrectly identifies the example as DRF, as its analysis appears to ignore data-races originating from different iterations of a loop.

2.2   Memory Access Protocols by Example

We now investigate the data-race in Listing 2.1 with an access memory protocol. For presentation purposes, we focus our discussion on Listing 2.1 (r.h.s.), that simplifies the l.h.s. whilst retaining the root cause of its data-race, which stems from the interaction between both loops. We discuss how we support multi-dimensional arrays, multi-dimensional thread identifiers, and arbitrary loop strides in Sect. 5. In our Coq formalism the notion of "accesses" (and their dimensions) is a parameter of the theory, thus orthogonal to the theory presented here.

Consider the execution of the end of the first iteration (r=0) and the beginning of the second (r=1) iteration of the outer-loop. In this case, the execution of the j-loop when r=0 is not synchronized with the execution of the i-loop when r=1 as there is no call to __syncthreads() in between.

The access memory protocol in Listing 2.2 captures this *partial* execution from the viewpoint of array tile. By design access memory protocols over approximate kernels by abstracting away *what* data is being written to/read from an array, to focus on *where* data is being written. The protocol models the two problematic loops of Listing 2.1, *i.e.*, the j-loop when r=0 and the i-loop when r=1. The first loop reads (rd[tid+j]) from the array, while the second writes (wr[tid]) to it. Evaluation of a protocol follows the SIMT model: each thread evaluates wr[tid] by instantiating tid with their unique identifier (hereafter, an integer), *e.g.*, thread 0 yields wr[0] and thread 1 yields wr[1].

Analysis of Unsynchronized Protocols. We say that a protocol is DRF when all concurrent accesses are pair-wise DRF, *i.e.*, when issued by different threads on the same index, then neither access is a write. For instance the respective sets of concurrent accesses of threads 0 and 1 in Listing 2.2 is given below

$$\text{tid} = 0 \qquad\qquad\qquad\qquad\qquad \text{tid} = 1$$
$$\{\text{rd}[j] \mid 0 \leq j < M\} \cup \{\text{wr}[0]\} \quad DRF\ with?\quad \{\text{rd}[1{+}j] \mid 0 \leq j < M\} \cup \{\text{wr}[1]\}$$

When M>1, thread 0 (l.h.s) accesses $\text{rd}[1]$ and thread 1 (r.h.s) accesses $\text{wr}[1]$. Thus, there is a data-race on index 1 of the array.

A fundamental challenge of static DRF verification is how to handle loops. Symbolic execution approaches that unroll loops, *e.g.*, [26,27], cannot handle large nor symbolic iteration spaces. Static approaches that use Hoare logic, *e.g.*, [5,7,22], require user-provided loop invariants. Another approach is to reduce loops to verifying the satisfiability of a corresponding universally quantified formula, *e.g.*, [25,30]. This has the advantage of being fast and not requiring invariants. However, its previous application to GPU programming, *i.e.*, PUG, is unsound due to the interaction between barrier synchronizations and loops, *e.g.*, PUG misses the data-race in Listing 2.1. We give more details in Sect. 6.

Our Approach. A key contribution of our work is to identify conditions that allow a kernel to be reduced to a first-order logic formula, by precisely characterizing the effect of barrier synchronization in loops. To this end, the language of access memory protocols distinguishes syntactically between protocol fragments that synchronize from those that do not. For instance, the protocol in Listing 2.2 is identified as *unsynchronized*, as it does not include any synchronization.

In Sect. 4, we show that the DRF analysis of unsynchronized protocols can be precisely reduced to a first-order logic formula, where universally quantified formulae represent loops, thus obviating the need to unroll them explicitly. For instance, we reduce the verification of Listing 2.2 to asking whether for all M, t_1, and t_2, where $t_1 \neq t_2$ are thread identifiers, the following holds:

$$\forall j_1, i_1, j_2, i_2 \colon 0 \leq j_1 < M \wedge 0 \leq i_1 < M \wedge 0 \leq j_2 < M \wedge 0 \leq i_2 < M \implies$$
$$\{\text{rd}[t_1 + j_1]\} \cup \{\text{wr}[t_1]\} \quad DRF\ with?\quad \{\text{rd}[t_2 + j_2]\} \cup \{\text{wr}[t_2]\}$$

This formula is *unprovable* since $\text{rd}[t_1 + j_1]$ races with $\text{wr}[t_2]$ when, *e.g.*, $t_1 = 0$, $t_2 = 1$, $j_1 = 1$, and $M > 1$. Hence, our technique flags Listing 2.2 as racy.

Analysis of Synchronized Protocols. The protocol in Listing 2.3 (left) models *all* the interactions over the shared array tile from Listing 2.1. This protocol consists of one outer loop r that contains two inner loops separated by a barrier synchronization (sync). The first inner loop writes ($\text{wr}[\text{tid}]$) to the array, while the second reads ($\text{rd}[\text{tid} + \text{j}]$) from the array.

Listing 2.3 access memory protocols (left) of array tile from Listing 2.1 and its aligned version (right).

```
                                            1  forᵁ i in 0..M { wr[tid] }
                                            2  sync;
1  forˢ r in 0..N {                         3  forˢ r in 1..N {
2    forᵁ i in 0..M { wr[tid] }             4    forᵁ j in 0..M { rd[tid + j] }
3    sync;                  aligns to       5    forᵁ i in 0..M { wr[tid] }
4    forᵁ j in 0..M { rd[tid + j] }         6    sync; }
5  }                                        7  forᵁ j in 0..M { rd[tid + j] }
```

This protocol illustrates how our language syntactically differentiates between protocols fragments that synchronize from those that do not. Concretely, our language precludes an unsynchronized loop (for^U $x \in n..m$ $\{u\}$) from calling sync anywhere in u, and it requires that a synchronized loop (for^S $x \in n..m$ $\{p\}$) includes at least one occurrence of sync. The superscript U (resp. S) stands for synchronized (resp. unsynchronized). This distinction can be inferred automatically and yields a compositional analysis, as we explain below.

The behavior of synchronized loops is difficult to analyse because they may contain data-races that span more than one iteration. For instance an instruction of iteration r in Listing 2.3 may race with an instruction of iteration r+1.

Our Approach. In this work we show that the DRF analysis of synchronized protocols can safely be reduced to a first-order logic formula when such loops are *aligned*, *i.e.*, when there is at least one synchronization exactly before the loop and one at the end of its body. In Sect. 4.1 we show how to transform an arbitrary access memory protocol into an aligned protocol using a syntax-driven transformation technique called *barrier aligning*. Intuitively, barrier aligning normalizes loops so that they do not "leak" accesses between iterations. The right-hand side of Listing 2.3 shows the result of applying *barrier aligning* on the protocol from Listing 2.3 (left). Observe that the fragment before the aligned loop (line 1) corresponds to the unsynchronized part of the original loop (before sync). The original loop itself is rearranged so that the part succeeding sync is moved to the beginning of the aligned loop (lines 3–6). The fragment following the aligned loop (line 7) corresponds to the unsynchronized loop that appears after the sync in the original protocol.

In Sect. 4.1 we show that aligned protocols enable *compositional* verification: protocol fragments between two barriers can be analyzed independently. This compositional analysis is possible because (*i*) there is no causality between instructions, except through sync and (*ii*) aligned protocols syntactically delimit the causality induced by sync. For instance, the aligned protocol in Listing 2.3 can be reduced to analyzing the following three protocol fragments independently:

$$\text{for}^U\ i \in 0..M\ \{\text{wr}[\text{tid}]\} \qquad \text{for}^U\ j \in 0..M\ \{\text{rd}[\text{tid} + j]\}$$
$$\text{for}^S\ r \in 1..N\ \{\text{for}^U\ j \in 0..M\ \{\text{rd}[\text{tid} + j]\}; \text{for}^U\ i \in 0..M\ \{\text{wr}[\text{tid}]\}; \text{sync}\}$$

The first two protocols are handled like Listing 2.2 because they are unsynchronized. Representing a synchronized loop as a formula becomes possible when the protocol is *aligned*: both threads must share the same value for r at each iteration. Hence, we reduce the verification to asking whether for all N, M, t_1, and t_2 where $t_1 \neq t_2$ and the following holds:

$$\forall r, j_1, i_1, j_2, i_2 \colon 1 \leq r < N \land 0 \leq j_1 < M \land 0 \leq i_1 < M \land 0 \leq j_2 < M \land 0 \leq i_2 < M$$
$$\implies \{\mathsf{rd}[t_1 + j_1]\} \cup \{\mathsf{wr}[t_1]\} \quad DRF \ with? \quad \{\mathsf{rd}[t_2 + j_2]\} \cup \{\mathsf{wr}[t_2]\}$$

Our technique identifies Listing 2.3 as racy since this formula is *unprovable*, *i.e.*, $\mathsf{rd}[t_1+j_1]$ races with $\mathsf{wr}[t_2]$ when $r = 1$, $t_1 = 0$, $t_2 = 1$, $j_1 = 1$, $N > 1$ and $M > 1$.

3   Access Memory Protocols

An access memory protocol describes the interaction between a group of threads and a single shared-memory location. A protocol records *where* in memory accesses take place, but abstracts away from *what* data is read from/written to memory. The language of protocols distinguishes between an unsynchronized protocol fragment $u \in \mathcal{U}$, that disallows synchronization, from a synchronized fragment $p \in \mathcal{S}$ that must include a synchronization. The syntax and semantics of access memory protocols is given in Figure 2. Our operational semantics is inspired by the synchronous, delayed semantics (SDV) from Betts et al. [6], where threads execute independently and communicate upon reaching a barrier.

Hereafter, i, j, k are metavariables over non-negative integers picked from the set $\mathbb{N}$. An arithmetic expression n is either: an integer variable x, an integer i, or a binary operation on integers that yields an integer. A boolean expression b is either a boolean literal, an arithmetic comparison $\diamond$, or a propositional logic connective $\circ$. We write $n \downarrow i$ when expression n evaluates to integer i, where evaluation is defined in the natural way. We overload the notation for Boolean expressions, *e.g.*, $b \downarrow \mathtt{true}$ means that expression b evaluates to $\mathtt{true}$.

Unsynchronized Fragment. A protocol $u \in \mathcal{U}$ either does nothing (skip), accesses a shared memory location $o[i]$ (reads from/writes to index i), performs sequential composition, or loops. Figure 2 gives the semantics of unsynchronized protocols, which is parameterized by a set of thread identifiers $\mathcal{T} \subseteq \mathbb{N}$, where $|\mathcal{T}| \geq 2$.

Evaluation of an unsynchronized protocol u by a thread identifier i, written $u \downarrow_i P$, yields a *phase*, *i.e.*, a set $P \in \mathcal{P}$ of *access values* $\alpha \in \mathbb{A}$. Each access value, or just access, notation $i{:}o[j]$, consists of its issuing thread identifier i, an access mode o (read/write), and an index j. Protocol skip produces no accesses. A memory access $o[n]$ evaluates the index and creates a singleton phase. Sequencing and looping are standard. Loop ranges include the lower bound and exclude the upper bound. Similarly to SDV, Rule $\mathcal{U}$-par executes a copy of the unsynchronized code u for each thread $i \in \mathcal{T}$ by replacing the special variable tid by the thread identifier, $u[\mathsf{tid} := i]$, which results in the union of the accesses of all threads. To simplify the presentation we omit the unsynchronized conditionals, however they are included in our Coq formalism and are fully supported by Faial, see Sect. 5.

Syntax

$$\mathbb{N} \ni i \quad ::= \quad 0 \mid 1 \mid \cdots$$
$$n \quad ::= \quad x \mid i \mid n \star n$$
$$\mathcal{B} \ni b \quad ::= \quad \texttt{true} \mid \texttt{false} \mid n \diamond n \mid b \circ b$$
$$\mathcal{U} \ni u \quad ::= \quad \texttt{skip} \mid o[n] \mid u\,;u \mid \texttt{for}^\mathsf{U} \; x \in n..m \; \{u\}$$
$$\mathcal{S} \ni p \quad ::= \quad \texttt{sync} \mid u \mid p\,;p \mid \texttt{for}^\mathsf{S} \; x \in n..m \; \{p\}$$

$$o \quad ::= \quad \texttt{wr} \mid \texttt{rd}$$
$$\mathbb{A} \ni \alpha \quad ::= \quad i{:}o[i]$$
$$\mathcal{P} \ni P \quad ::= \quad \{\alpha_1, \ldots, \alpha_n\}$$
$$H \quad ::= \quad [] \mid P {::} H$$

Big-step semantics for $\mathcal{U}$ $\qquad$ $\boxed{u \downarrow_i P}$ $\quad$ $\boxed{u \downarrow_\mathcal{T} S}$

$\mathcal{U}$-SKIP
$$\frac{}{\texttt{skip} \downarrow_i \emptyset}$$

$\mathcal{U}$-ACC
$$\frac{n \downarrow j}{o[n] \downarrow_i \{i{:}o[j]\}}$$

$\mathcal{U}$-SEQ
$$\frac{u_1 \downarrow_i P_1 \qquad u_2 \downarrow_i P_2}{u_1\,;u_2 \downarrow_i P_1 \cup P_2}$$

$\mathcal{U}$-FOR-1
$$\frac{(n \geq m) \downarrow \texttt{true}}{\texttt{for}^\mathsf{U} \; x \in n..m \; \{u\} \downarrow_i \emptyset}$$

$\mathcal{U}$-FOR-2
$$\frac{(n < m) \downarrow \texttt{true} \qquad u[x := n] \downarrow_i P_1 \qquad \texttt{for}^\mathsf{U} \; x \in n+1..m \; \{u\} \downarrow_i P_2}{\texttt{for}^\mathsf{U} \; x \in n..m \; \{u\} \downarrow_i P_1 \cup P_2}$$

$\mathcal{U}$-PAR
$$\frac{S = \bigcup \{u[\mathsf{tid} := i] \downarrow_i P_i \mid i \in \mathcal{T}\}}{u \downarrow_\mathcal{T} S}$$

History concatenation and merging $\qquad$ $\boxed{H \cdot H}$ $\quad$ $\boxed{H \odot H}$

$$[P_1 \ldots P_n] \cdot [P_{n+1} \ldots P_{n+k}] = [P_1 \ldots P_{n+k}] \quad (H \cdot [P]) \odot ([P'] \cdot H') = H \cdot [P \cup P'] \cdot H'$$

Big-step semantics for $\mathcal{S}$ $\qquad$ $\boxed{p \downarrow H}$

$\mathcal{S}$-SYNC
$$\frac{}{\texttt{sync} \downarrow [\emptyset, \emptyset]}$$

$\mathcal{S}$-PAR
$$\frac{u \downarrow_\mathcal{T} P}{u \downarrow [P]}$$

$\mathcal{S}$-SEQ
$$\frac{p \downarrow H \qquad q \downarrow H'}{p\,;q \downarrow H \odot H'}$$

$\mathcal{S}$-FOR-1
$$\frac{(n \geq m) \downarrow \texttt{true}}{\texttt{for}^\mathsf{S} \; x \in n..m \; \{p\} \downarrow [\emptyset]}$$

$\mathcal{S}$-FOR-2
$$\frac{(n < m) \downarrow \texttt{true} \qquad p[x := n] \downarrow H \qquad \texttt{for}^\mathsf{S} \; x \in n+1..m \; \{p\} \downarrow H'}{\texttt{for}^\mathsf{S} \; x \in n..m \; \{p\} \downarrow H \odot H'}$$

Structurally well-formed protocols $\qquad$ $\boxed{swf(p)}$

$$swf(u\,;\texttt{sync})$$

$$\frac{swf(p) \qquad swf(q)}{swf(p\,;q)}$$

$$\frac{swf(p) \qquad \mathsf{tid} \notin fv(n) \cup fv(m)}{swf(u_1\,;\texttt{for}^\mathsf{S} \; x \in n..m \; \{p\,;u_2\})}$$

Data-race, safe phase, and safe history $\qquad$ $\boxed{\alpha \# \beta}$ $\quad$ $\boxed{safe(P)}$ $\quad$ $\boxed{safe(H)}$

$$\frac{\texttt{wr} \in \{o, o'\} \qquad i \neq j}{i{:}o[k] \# j{:}o'[k]}$$

$$\frac{\forall \alpha, \beta \in P : \neg(\alpha \# \beta)}{safe(P)}$$

$$\frac{\forall P \in H : safe(P)}{safe(H)}$$

Fig. 2. Syntax, semantics, and properties of access memory protocols.

Synchronized Fragment. A protocol $p \in \mathcal{S}$ may perform barrier synchronization sync, run unsynchronized code u, perform sequential composition, and loop. Figure 2 gives the semantics of a protocol, notation $p \downarrow H$. Evaluation of a protocol p yields a *history* (ranged over by H), *i.e.*, a list of phases (P) that records how memory was accessed. We use :: as list constructor and · for the usual list concatenation operator. Histories are merged using the special ⊙-operator.

A barrier synchronization creates two empty phases, corresponding to phases before and after synchronization. Running an unsynchronized protocol yields a single phase containing all accesses performed by that protocol. Sequencing two synchronized protocols p with q merges the last phase of the former with the first phase of the latter, as these two phases run concurrently. The base case of a synchronized loop produces a singleton history containing the empty phase. Running one iteration of a synchronized loop sequences the history of the first iteration with the rest of the loop, by merging the two histories.

Next, we introduce the notion of well-formed protocols, a restriction of structurally well-formed protocols, see $swf(p)$ in Figure 2. We discuss how well-formedness is enforced in Sect. 5. We write $fv(p)$ (resp. $fv(n)$) for the free variables of p (resp. n).

Definition 1 (Well-formed protocol, $p \in \mathcal{W}$). *We say that a protocol is well-formed, notation $p \in \mathcal{W}$, when $swf(p)$, $fv(p) \subseteq \{\mathsf{tid}\}$, and every synchronized loop executes at least one iteration.*

DRF is formalized at the bottom of Figure 2. Two accesses are in a data-race (or racy) when there exist two different threads that access the same index k, and one of these accesses is a write. Our definition does not distinguish between harmful and *benign* data races, a data-race in which both threads write the same value. Phase P is *safe* iff each pair of accesses it contains is not racy. History P is *safe* when all of its phases are safe. We say that p is DRF iff $p \downarrow H$ and $safe(H)$.

4 DRF-Preserving Transformations of Protocols

This section presents the main steps of the DRF analysis summarized in Figure 1: barrier aligning (Sect. 4.1) and splitting (Sect. 4.2).

This section also includes our key theoretical results. We establish that these steps preserve and reflect data-races (*i.e.*, any and all data-races are found), see Theorem 1 and Theorem 3. We make precise the notion of compositionality that makes our approach scalable in Theorem 2.

4.1 Aligning Protocols

The first transformation step normalizes protocols by aligning synchronized loops, which in turn enables a form of compositional verification. The goal of the transformation is to produce protocols which belong to $\mathcal{A}$, see top of Figure 3.

Barrier aligning (or just aligning) is performed by function *align*, given in the bottom half of Figure 3. The function returns a pair whose first element is an

---

Aligned protocols $\boxed{p \in \mathcal{A}}$

$$u\,;\mathsf{sync} \in \mathcal{A} \qquad \frac{p \in \mathcal{A} \quad q \in \mathcal{A}}{p\,;q \in \mathcal{A}} \qquad \frac{p \in \mathcal{A} \quad q \in \mathcal{A}}{p\,;\mathsf{for}^{\mathsf{s}}\,x \in n..m\,\{q\} \in \mathcal{A}}$$

Sequencing aligned protocols $\boxed{\,\substack{\circ\\\circ}: \mathcal{U} \to \mathcal{A} \to \mathcal{A}\,}$ $\boxed{\,\substack{\circ\\\circ}: (\mathcal{A} \times \mathcal{U}) \to (\mathcal{A} \times \mathcal{U}) \to \mathcal{A} \times \mathcal{U}\,}$

$$u\,\substack{\circ\\\circ}\,(u'\,;\mathsf{sync}) = (u\,;u')\,;\mathsf{sync} \qquad u\,\substack{\circ\\\circ}\,(p\,;q) = (u\,\substack{\circ\\\circ}\,p)\,;q \qquad (p,\,u)\,\substack{\circ\\\circ}\,(q,\,u') = (p\,;(u\,\substack{\circ\\\circ}\,q),\,u')$$

Aligning protocols $\boxed{align: \mathcal{W} \to \mathcal{A} \times \mathcal{U}}$

$$align(u\,;\mathsf{sync}) = (u\,;\mathsf{sync},\,\mathsf{skip}) \qquad align(p\,;q) = align(p)\,\substack{\circ\\\circ}\,align(q)$$

$$\frac{align(p) = (q,\,u_3) \qquad q_1 = u_1\,\substack{\circ\\\circ}\,q[x := n] \qquad u = u_3\,;u_2}{align(u_1\,;\mathsf{for}^{\mathsf{s}}\,x \in n..m\,\{p\,;u_2\}) = (q_1\,;\mathsf{for}^{\mathsf{s}}\,x \in n+1..m\,\{u[x := x-1]\,\substack{\circ\\\circ}\,q\},\,u[x := m-1])}$$

Fig. 3. Aligning protocols.

aligned and synchronized protocol, and whose second element is an unsynchronized protocol. Intuitively, the pair represents a sequence which we delimitate syntactically. We note that the output of *align*, say (q, u), can be trivially made into an aligned protocol: $q; u; \mathsf{sync}$. The case for synchronization is simple, *align* returns the input protocol as the first component of the pair and skip as the second component (the input protocol is already fully aligned). The case for sequence consists of the sequential composition of the pair aligned with unsynchronized code using operator ($\substack{\circ\\\circ}$). Sequencing two pairs $(p, u) \substack{\circ\\\circ} (q, u')$ amounts to sequencing u to the outer-most piece of unsynchronized code present in q.

Dealing with synchronized loops is more involved. Given a loop $u_1; \mathsf{for}^{\mathsf{s}}\,x \in n..m\,\{p; u_2\}$, we produce a protocol consisting of the fragment preceding the loop and the synchronized part of its first iteration (q_1), an aligned loop starting at $n+1$, and the unsynchronized part of its last iteration ($u[x := m-1]$). See Listing 2.3 for an example of protocol aligning. We note that we can always unroll the loop because the analysis only considers non-empty synchronized loops; we discuss how to enforce this assumption in Sect. 5.

We now state two fundamental properties of barrier aligning: preserving and reflecting DRF (Theorem 1), and enabling compositional verification (Theorem 2). Theorem 1 states that verifying DRF of a well-formed protocol p is equivalent to verifying DRF of its aligned counterpart.

Theorem 1 (Correctness of Align). *If $p \in \mathcal{W}$ and $align(p) = (q, u)$, then p is DRF if and only if $q; u$ is DRF.*

To state our compositionality result, we introduce a language of contexts:

$$\mathcal{C} ::= [\_] \mid u;\mathsf{sync} \mid p;\mathcal{C} \mid \mathcal{C};p \mid \mathcal{C};\mathsf{for}^{\mathsf{s}}\,x \in n..m\,\{p\} \mid p;\mathsf{for}^{\mathsf{s}}\,x \in n..m\,\{\mathcal{C}\}$$

Syntax

$$\mathcal{L} \ni h ::= \textsf{skip} \mid n{:}o[m] \mid h\,;h \mid \textsf{var}\ x\ \textsf{in}\ n..m; h$$

Product of histories $\boxed{H \otimes H}$

$$H_1 \otimes H_2 = [P_1 \cup P_2 \mid (P_1, P_2) \in H_1 \times H_2]$$

Big-step semantics $\boxed{h \Downarrow H}$

$$\frac{}{\textsf{skip} \Downarrow [\emptyset]} \qquad \frac{n \downarrow i \quad m \downarrow j}{n{:}o[m] \Downarrow [\{i{:}o[j]\}]} \qquad \frac{h_1 \Downarrow H_1 \quad h_2 \Downarrow H_2}{h_1\,;h_2 \Downarrow H_1 \otimes H_2} \qquad \frac{(n \geq m) \downarrow \textsf{true}}{\textsf{var}\ x\ \textsf{in}\ n..m; h \Downarrow [\emptyset]}$$

$$\frac{(n < m) \downarrow \textsf{true} \quad h[x := n] \Downarrow H_1 \quad \textsf{var}\ x\ \textsf{in}\ n+1..m; h \Downarrow H_2}{\textsf{var}\ x\ \textsf{in}\ n..m; h \Downarrow H_1 \cdot H_2}$$

Projection $\boxed{trace : \mathcal{U} \to \mathcal{L}}$

$$trace(o[n]) = \textsf{tid}{:}o[n] \qquad trace(\textsf{for}^{\textsf{u}}\ x \in n..m\ \{u\}) = \textsf{var}\ x\ \textsf{in}\ n..m; trace(u)$$

$$trace(u_1\,;u_2) = trace(u_1)\,;trace(u_2) \qquad trace(\textsf{skip}) = \textsf{skip}$$

Splitting protocols $\boxed{split : \mathcal{A} \to [\mathcal{L}]}$

$$split(p\,;q) = split(p) \cdot split(q)$$

$$\frac{t_1, t_2\ \textsf{fresh} \quad h_1 = trace(u)[\textsf{tid} := t_1] \quad h_2 = trace(u)[\textsf{tid} := t_2]}{split(u\,;\textsf{sync}) = [\textsf{var}\ t_1\ \textsf{in}\ 1..|\mathcal{T}|; \textsf{var}\ t_2\ \textsf{in}\ 0..t_1; h_1\,;h_2]}$$

$$split(p\,;\textsf{for}^{\textsf{s}}\ x \in n..m\ \{q\}) = split(p) \cdot [\textsf{var}\ x\ \textsf{in}\ n..m; h \mid h \in split(q)]$$

Fig. 4. Syntax and semantics of symbolic traces, and splitting of protocols.

The base cases correspond to a hole [_] or an unsynchronized protocol (followed by sync). The other cases follow the structure of access memory protocols.

Theorem 2 (Compositionality). *Let $\mathcal{C}$ be a context, s.t. $\mathcal{C}[\textsf{skip}; \textsf{sync}]$ is DRF. For all $p \in \mathcal{A}$, if p is DRF, $fv(p) \subseteq \{\textsf{tid}\}$, then $\mathcal{C}[p] \in \mathcal{A}$ and $\mathcal{C}[p]$ is also DRF.*

Compositionality allows Faial to analyze each fragment of an aligned protocol independently, by splitting the given protocol into multiple symbolic traces.

4.2   Splitting Protocols into Symbolic Traces

The second verification step, *splitting*, consists in transforming an aligned protocol into *symbolic traces*, *i.e.*, symbolic representations of sets of memory accesses which occur between two synchronizations.

Symbolic Traces. Intuitively, symbolic traces are a thin abstraction over an SMT formula. We describe how to translate a symbolic trace to a formula in Sect. 5.

We give the syntax and semantics of symbolic traces in Figure 4. Expression skip terminates a trace. Expression $n{:}o[m]$ states that thread n accesses index m with mode o. Expression $h_1; h_2$ composes two symbolic traces using operator $\otimes$, also given in Figure 4. Expression var x in $n..m; h$ binds variable x in h, where variable x is an integer in the range induced from n and m. The semantics of a symbolic trace yields a history with a phase for each possible variable assignment. Expression skip yields a single empty phase. Expression $n{:}o[m]$ evaluates to a singleton set that contains the access value that results from evaluating the thread-identifier expression n and the index expression m. Sequencing histories $h_1; h_1$ consists of performing the product of phases (operator $\otimes$), which consists of merging every phase of H_1 with every phase of H_2. A variable binder behaves like a skip when the range of values is empty. Otherwise, we fork two histories H_1 and H_2. We assign the lower bound of the set in H_1, and we recursively evaluate a variable binder where we increment its lower bound in H_2.

Barrier splitting is the transformation from aligned protocols to symbolic traces, performed via functions *trace* and *split*, defined in Figure 4. Function *trace* extracts the symbolic trace of an unsynchronized program for a single thread. Memory accesses are tagged with the owner thread tid, and unsynchronized loops are converted into variable bindings. Function *split* returns a list of symbolic traces. The case for $p; q$ is trivial (operator $\cdot$ stands for list concatenation). The base case of *split* is for unsynchronized protocol fragment u, which produces a list containing a single symbolic trace. It introduces fresh variables t_1 and t_2 that represent two (distinct) symbolic thread identifiers. The rest of the trace consists of the trace of u instantiated to the first thread identifier t_1 followed by its instantiation to the second thread identifier t_2. The case for synchronized loops simply reinterprets the loop as a variable binder. Function *split* leads to an exponential blow up wrt. nesting of synchronized loops, but this has not posed problems in practice, *c.f.*, Claim 2.

Example 1. Let $\hat{p} = \text{wr}[\text{tid} + 1]; \text{rd}[\text{tid} + 2]; \text{sync}$. We have that $split(\hat{p})$ returns:

$$\text{var } t_1 \text{ in } 1..|\mathcal{T}|; \text{var } t_2 \text{ in } 0..t_1; t_1{:}\text{wr}[t_1{+}1]; t_1{:}\text{rd}[t_1{+}2]; t_2{:}\text{wr}[t_2{+}1]; t_2{:}\text{rd}[t_2{+}2]$$

We show that barrier splitting preserves and reflects DRF.

Theorem 3. *Let $p \in \mathcal{A}$, such that $p \downarrow H_1$, and $H_2 = [H \mid h \in split(p) \wedge h \Downarrow H]$, then $safe(H_1)$ if and only if $safe(H_2)$.*

Hence we have established that aligning (Theorem 1) and splitting (Theorem 3) preserve and reflect data-races, *i.e.*, any and all data-races are found. Thus, the only source of approximation in our analysis stems from the inference of protocols from CUDA kernels, which we discuss in the next section. Theorem 3 highlights the compositionality of our analysis, as each symbolic trace resulting from function *split* can be analyzed independently.

5   Implementation

In this section we present our tool, Faial, that implements the steps described in Figure 1. Faial takes a CUDA kernel as input and produces results that either identify the kernel as DRF or list specific data-races. In this section, we describe the implementation of the protocol inference, well-formedness checks, and transformation to SMT.

Inference. This step transforms a CUDA kernel into access memory protocols (one for each shared array). It uses `libclang` [23] to parse the kernel, a standard single static assignment (SSA) transformation to simplify the analysis of indices and arrays, and code slicing to only retain code related to *shared* array accesses. We note that Faial supports constructs of the CUDA programming model that are not directly modeled by access memory protocols, *e.g.*, unstructured loops, conditionals, function calls, and multi-dimensional arrays. To support multi-dimensional thread identifiers, we extend the language of protocols to support multiple thread identifiers, and adapt function *split* accordingly. The main challenges are related to loops and function calls.

Whenever possible loops are transformed to loops with a stride of 1 following ideas from loop normalization [24] and abstraction [30]. For instance, in **for**(int i=lb;i<ub;i+=s){S} we change the stride from s into 1 by executing the loop body S when the loop variable i is divisible by stride, *i.e.*, the loop becomes **for**(int i=lb;i<ub;i++) **if**((i+lb)%s==0){S}. Similarly, a loop ranging over powers of n, *e.g.*, **for**(int i=lb;i<ub;i*=s), becomes **for**(int i=lb;i<ub;i++) **if**(powerof(i,s)){S}, where function powerof(i,s) tests whether i is a power of base s. We approximate **while**s as a structured loop with an unknown upper bound.

Function calls that manipulate shared memory are uncommon in GPU programming. Additionally auxiliary functions that manipulate shared memory have a compiler annotation to inline their bodies, hence we can inline such calls easily. Faial cannot handle recursive functions, but these rarely occur in practice. Function calls that do not access shared memory are simply discarded.

Well-Formedness. This step ensures that kernels Faial analyzes meet the well-formedness conditions, *i.e.*, $p \in \mathcal{W}$, including the assumptions that synchronized loops iterate at least once, see Definition 1. First, Faial annotates loops with a synchronized/unsynchronized tag according to the presence of sync in the loop body, then adjusts the precedence of sequencing to group all unsynchronized code preceding a sync or a synchronized loops. Synchronized loops of well-formed protocols cannot manipulate thread-local variables (*i.e.*, tid), an assumption shared by the CUDA programming model. Hence, Faial flags such kernels as erroneous. Next, Faial adds assertions before/after synchronized loops to check that the loop range is non-empty, *i.e.*, loops execute at least once. Similarly to loops, conditionals are tagged as synchronized or unsynchronized. Then, Faial inlines synchronized conditionals, *i.e.*, when a synchronized conditional is found, two copies of the input program are created and each copy is prefixed by a global assertion corresponding to the condition. Faial does not support synchronized conditionals that appear within synchronized loops. We have not found real-world kernels that include such a construction.

Quantification. This step transforms each symbolic trace (Figure 4) into an SMT formula, to check for *safety, c.f.,* Figure 2. The presented formalism assumes a decidable fragment. However, as CUDA programs may include multiplication in index expressions, Faial uses an undecidable logic (SMTLib's QF_LIA). Essentially, the generated formula guarantees that the indices of array accesses are distinct when there is at least one write. We illustrate this straightforward transformation with Example 2.

Example 2. The formula generated from the trace in Example 1 is given below:

$$\forall t_1, t_2 : 1 \leq t_1 < |\mathcal{T}| \wedge 0 \leq t_2 < t_1 \wedge (\mathsf{m}_1 = \mathsf{wr} \vee \mathsf{m}_2 = \mathsf{wr}) \implies$$
$$((\mathsf{idx}_1 = t_1 + 1 \wedge \mathsf{m}_1 = \mathsf{wr}) \vee (\mathsf{idx}_1 = t_1 + 2 \wedge \mathsf{m}_1 = \mathsf{rd}))$$
$$\wedge ((\mathsf{idx}_2 = t_2 + 1 \wedge \mathsf{m}_2 = \mathsf{wr}) \vee (\mathsf{idx}_2 = t_2 + 2 \wedge \mathsf{m}_2 = \mathsf{rd})) \wedge \mathsf{idx}_1 \neq \mathsf{idx}_2$$

where each symbolic access is translated to a conjunction representing its index (idx) and access mode (m). Observe that the formula enforces that indices idx_1 and idx_2 (executed by distinct threads) are different.

For multi-dimensional arrays, we generate one pair of indices per dimension, and check that at least one pair is distinct.

6   Experimental Evaluation

We evaluate Faial over several datasets and show how it fares against existing approaches. We structure this evaluation in three claims.

Claim 1: Correctness. We claim that our approach finds more bugs and raises fewer false alarms than existing tools. To evaluate this claim, we compare Faial against four state-of-the-art kernel verification tools over 10 kernels that are known to be tricky to analyze.

Claim 2: Scalability. We claim that our approach scales better to larger programs. To evaluate this claim, we compare Faial against other tools over a set of synthetic benchmarks designed to test the limits of each tool, in terms of run time and memory usage.

Claim 3: Real-world usability. We claim that our approach is more usable than existing static verification tools on real-world CUDA programs. To evaluate this claim, we use a varied dataset of real-world DRF kernels and measure the false alarm rate, run time, and memory usage of Faial, GPUVerify, and PUG.

Benchmarking Environment. To make our evaluation reproducible, we developed a benchmarking framework to automate our experiments over the different tools and datasets. For Claim 1 and Claim 3, we designed a tool-agnostic file format for kernel functions and associated metadata (*e.g.,* expected result of DRF analysis,

Table 1. Results for Claim 1. DRF indicates that a (static analysis) tool reported a test case as DRF. NRR indicates that a (symbolic execution) tool did not report any data-race. Label x/y indicates that the tool reported y data-races, x of which are actual races. Label *timeout* indicates that the tool did not terminate within 90s. A test passes if the tool returns the expected result and all reported races are valid.

Test	Expected	Faial	GPUVerify	PUG	GKLEE	SESA
1 transposeDiagonal	Racy	**1/1**	*0/2*	*DRF*	*timeout*	*timeout*
	DRF	**DRF**	*0/1*	**DRF**	*timeout*	*timeout*
2 first-iter	Racy	**1/1**	*0/1*	**1/1**	*timeout*	*timeout*
	DRF	**DRF**	*0/1*	*0/1*	*timeout*	*timeout*
3 last-iter	Racy	**1/1**	**1/1**	*0/1*	*timeout*	*timeout*
	DRF	**DRF**	*0/1*	**DRF**	*timeout*	*timeout*
4 last-iter-first-iter	Racy	**1/1**	*0/1*	*0/1*	*timeout*	*timeout*
	DRF	**DRF**	*0/1*	*0/1*	*timeout*	*timeout*
5 read-index	Racy	*0/1*	**1/1**	*0/1*	*NRR*	*NRR*
	DRF	*0/1*	**DRF**	*0/1*	**NRR**	**NRR**
Number of tests passed (of 5):		4	1	0	0	0

grid and block dimensions, and include directives). And for Claim 2, we created a tool that generates kernels according to given templates, *e.g.*, see Figure 7.

We evaluate Faial against the following verification tools: GPUVerify [5] v2018-03-22; PUG [24] v0.2; and, GKLEE [26] and SESA [27] v3.0. Experiments for Claim 1 use an Intel i5-6500 CPU, 7.7 GB RAM, and Fedora 33 OS, while Claim 2 and Claim 3 use an Intel i7-10510U CPU, 16 GB RAM, and Pop! OS.

Excluded Tools. We excluded ESBMC-GPU [33] and Simulee [37] from the evaluation because we were unable to get them to run satisfactorily. Both tools have rudimentary support for verifying arbitrary CUDA kernels. ESBMC-GPU did not find a single data-race in our benchmarks, while Simulee produced false alarms for every DRF-kernel given.

Claim 1: Correctness

We have selected a set of tricky kernels to expose false alarms and missed data-races in Faial, GPUVerify, PUG, GKLEE, and SESA. Our results are reported in Table 1. The dataset consists of 5 tests, each consisting of two variations of the same kernel: one racy and one DRF. The racy version of Test 1 (*c.f.*, Listing 2.1) contains an inter-iteration data-races. The DRF version adds a sync after the second inner loop. Tests 2 to 4 expose various loop-related data-races. Their protocols are given in Figure 5. In the racy version of Test 2 wr[tid + 1] conflicts with wr[tid] of the first iteration. Similarly, in the racy version of Test 3, wr[tid + 1] of the last iteration races with wr[tid]. In the racy version of Test 4 the last iteration of a nested loop races with the first iteration of the following loop. Test 5 exposes the abstraction gap between kernel and access memory protocols (which abstract away array elements), see Figure 6.

Faial passes more tests than any other tool. Failed Test 5 is caused by access memory protocols abstracting away from *what* data is being read from/written

// first-iter
wr[tid + 1];
for^s x in 0..N {
   if (x > 0)
     { wr[tid] } ;
   sync}
	// last-iter
	for^s x in 0..N {
	   sync;
	   if (tid < |T|-1)
	     { wr[tid+1] } };
	wr[tid + |T|]
		// last-iter-first-iter
		for^s x in 1..N+1 {
		   for^s y in 1..x+1 {
		     sync; wr[tid+x+y]}};
		for^s z in N*2..N*3 {
		   wr[tid+z +1]; sync}

Fig. 5. Protocols for Tests 2 to 4, *c.f.*, Claim 1, where N is a free thread-global variable. Yellow shaded code only appears in the DRF version of first-iter and last-iter. Red shaded code only appears in the racy version of last-iter-first-iter (Color figure online).

// Racy kernel
A[tid] = tid ;
int x = A[tid];
A[x+1] = 0;
	// Protocol A
	wr[tid];
	rd[tid];
	wr[x+1]
		// DRF kernel
		A[tid] = tid ;
		int x = A[tid];
		A[x] = 0;
			// Protocol A
			wr[tid];
			rd[tid];
			wr[x]

Fig. 6. Kernels and protocols for Test 5 (read-index), *c.f.*, Claim 1; x becomes a free thread-local variable as protocols do not model array elements.

to arrays, *i.e.*, array elements. In each case, Faial reports one spurious data race *(0/1)*. We report on performance trade-offs wrt. tracking array elements in Claim 2.

GPUVerify passes Test 5 because it tracks array elements, but fails the remaining 4 tests. Some reported false alarms are ill-formed, *e.g.*, on the racy component of Test 2, the report $(0 : wr[tid]; 16 : wr[tid])$ has disjoint indices.

PUG obtains the worst score amongst static tools. Notably, the tool misses a data-race in Test 1, demonstrating its unsoundness, *c.f.*, Sect. 2.1.

GKLEE and SESA timeout for tests that include loops, as the loop bounds are unknown.Both tools miss the data-race in Test 5. Symbolic tools may be able to report data-races when the bound is known, *e.g.*, timeouts start in Test 1 when the bound is at least 2, in Test 2 when the bound is at least 23, 000.

Claim 2: Scalability

We evaluate the scalability of our approach with a synthetic dataset that aims at demonstrating how different kernel constructs affect run time and memory usage of Faial, GKLEE, GPUVerify, PUG, and SESA. Our dataset is divided into five categories, one per syntactical construct in the language of access memory protocols, as well as conditionals, which are supported by our inference step, *c.f.*, Sect. 5. Figure 7 shows the protocols of the kernel patterns we generate in each category: (*i*) repeated accesses (read then write), (*ii*) repeated barrier synchronizations separated by writes, (*iii*) repeated conditionals, (*iv*) increasingly nested unsynchronized loops, and (*v*) increasingly nested synchronized loops. In each category, we vary the problem size by repeating a pattern from 1 to 50 times. Note that all kernels generated this way are DRF.

// accesses	// barriers	// conditionals	// unsynchronized loops	// synchronized loops

rd[tid + n_1*|T |];
 wr[tid + 1*|T |];
 rd[tid + n_2*|T |];
 wr[tid + 2*|T |];
 // ···
	wr[tid];
	 sync;
	 wr[tid];
	 sync;
	 // ···
		if tid==0
		 {wr[tid]};
		 if tid==1
		 {wr[tid]};
		 // ···
			for^U i_1 in 0..N {
			 wr[tid];
			 for^U i_2 in 0..N {
			 wr[tid];
			 // ··· }}
				for^S i_1 in 0..N {
				 wr[tid]; sync;
				 for^S i_2 in 0..N {
				 wr[tid]; sync;
				 // ··· }}

Fig. 7. Synthetic protocols generated for Claim 2. N is a free thread-global variable, and n_1, n_2... are positive integer literals.

Figure 8 shows the average run time and memory usage over five runs on logarithmic and linear scales, respectively. For each run, we set a timeout of 90s and we exclude any run that times out or reports a false alarm. Cutoffs in the memory plots are determined by the cutoffs in the run time plots.

Overall Faial is the most scalable tool. In 4 out of 5 categories, Faial has the slowest growth for all experiments, and verifies all tests within 0.46 s. In the largest problem sizes, our tool is the fastest in 3 categories (access, conditional, unsynchronized loop), 2nd for barriers, and 3rd for synchronized loops. Overall, the memory usage of Faial is competitive with other tools. Faial is the only tool with a near constant time/memory for up to 50 unsynchronized loops, indicating the scalability of reducing unsynchronized loops to universally quantified formulas. Faial only times out for kernels which consists of >17 nested synchronized loops. However such kernels are uncommon, e.g., the levels of nested synchronized loops in the real-word kernels studied in Claim 3 are at most 3.

GPUVerify remains stable in the barrier and conditional categories but is affected negatively by loops and accesses. Loops are a known bottleneck in GPUVerify [2]. In the access category there is an exponential slowdown due to GPUVerify keeping track of what data is being written to/read from array.

PUG tool remains stable with the number of barrier synchronizations but is affected negatively by the number of conditionals and loops. PUG is the fastest tool with smaller inputs, but it raises false alarms in the access category, hence these measurements are omitted from the corresponding plots.

We discuss GKLEE and SESA together since SESA processes GKLEE's NVCC byte code output by concretizing variables, before passing it to GKLEE itself. There are two main factors that affect negatively these symbolic execution tools: (i) the number of loops, since they unroll each loop; and (ii) the amount of bookkeeping required to keep track of what is read from/written to memory. Figure 8 shows clear exponential curves for the access and barrier synchronization categories. Observe that these tools timeout immediately in the loop categories.

Claim 3: Real-World Usability

We evaluate the usability of our approach by comparing Faial with other static verification tools (GPUVerify and PUG) on real-world kernels wrt. rate of false alarm and run time. We curated a set of CUDA kernels from [2], which consists of 3 benchmark suites (totaling 227 CUDA kernels): NVIDIA GPU Computing

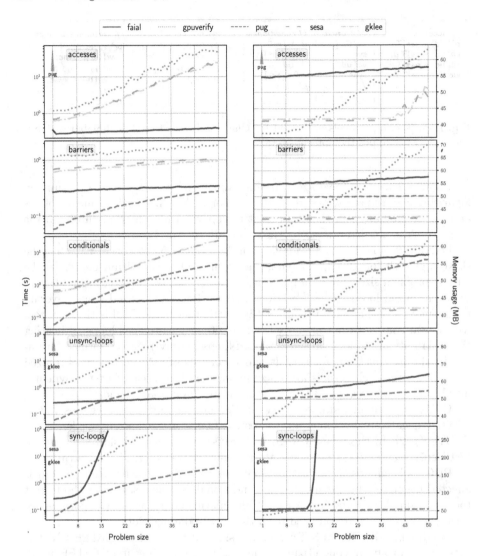

Fig. 8. Results for Claim 2. Run time (left plots) are given on a logarithmic scale, and memory (right plots) are given on a linear scale. Flatter and lower curve is better. Tools annotated with a triangle are excluded due to timeouts or errors.

SDK v2.0 (8 CUDA kernels); NVIDIA GPU Computing SDK v5.0 (166 CUDA kernels); Microsoft C++ AMP Sample Projects (20 kernels); gpgpu-sim benchmarks (33 kernels). All kernels are DRF and have been pre-processed by the authors of [2] to facilitate verification. Each kernel is in a distinct file, all dependencies are available, and kernels are annotated with minimal pre-conditions to allow for automatic analysis (*e.g.*, thread count is given).

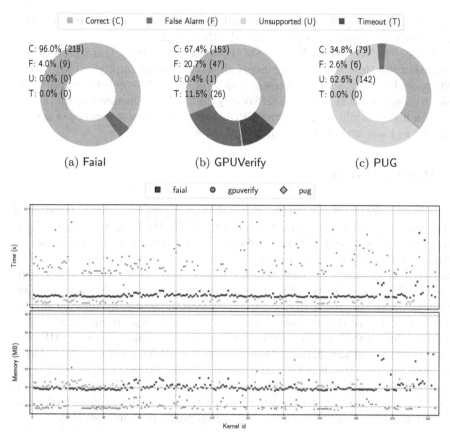

(d) Run time (top) and memory usage (bottom) of true-positives. Time (resp. memory) is cropped at 10s (resp. 100MB) and plotted on a logarithmic (resp. linear) scale.

Fig. 9. Results for Claim 3, on a set of 227 DRF CUDA kernels.

As we aim to evaluate fully automatic verification of three tools, we removed code annotations (pre-conditions and loop invariants) specific to GPUVerify. Additionally, we made minor changes to some kernels to meet the limitations of the front-end of Faial and PUG. For instance we converted nested array lookups to use temporary variables and inlined functions calls that operate on arrays in 22 kernels. Another 8 kernels were modified to simplify their control flows. Our curated dataset will be included in our artifact submission.

Figures 9a, b, and c give the correctness results of Faial, GPUVerify, and PUG, respectively. Correct refers to the true-positive rate, *i.e.*, when the tool correctly identifies the kernel as DRF. False Alarm refers to the false alarm rate, *i.e.*, when the tool incorrectly identifies the kernel as racy. A kernel is Unsupported if it makes the tool crash. A Timeout occurs when the tool exceeds the limit of 60s to verify a kernel. The values shown are an average calculated over five runs.

Figure 9d shows the average run time and memory usage of every true-positive report (we omit invalid reports) across the three tools.

Overall Faial has the highest rate of true-positives at 96%. Our tool is second in terms of run time and memory usage, showing a good compromise w.r.t. time and space. Faial verifies most kernels within 1s, and all kernels that need more time are only verified by Faial. GPUVerify shows lower memory usage at the cost of a higher verification run time. PUG verifies the lowest number of kernels (34.8%), as most kernels are unsupported (62.6%).

7   Related Work

SMT-Based DRF Analyses. Li and Gopalakrishnan propose a direct encoding of DRF analysis of GPU programs in SMT, with PUG [24,25]. Both PUG and Faial follow a similar approach of barrier splitting: having a symbolic representation of a canonical interleaving, and dividing up the analysis over barrier intervals. The two major distinctions are that (1) PUG misses inter-thread data-races in synchronized loops, *e.g.*, Listing 2.1, and (2) the algorithms of PUG are unspecified and lack soundness proofs. In [24, Sect. 6.3] the authors identify the challenge of detecting inter-thread data-races, but do not elaborate a solution. Ma *et al.* [30] present a similar technique to detect data-races and deadlocks in OpenMP programs (CPU-based parallelism). However, their work does not guarantee DRF, and they do not formalize their algorithms. In [8], Prasanth *et al.* propose a polyhedral encoding of DRF for OpenMP programs, which is only applicable to programs with affine array accesses. However the prevalence of linearized array expressions in GPU kernels is known to stump polyhedral analysis [16].

Hoare-Logic-Based DRF Analyses. The main drawback of Hoare-logic based tools is their high rate of false alarms. They also require code annotations from a concurrency expert to handle loops. GPUVerify [2,3,5,6,12] can verify CUDA and OpenCL kernels using Boogie [4] as a backend. GPUVerify also relies on a two-thread abstraction (pen and paper proof)—in this paper, we present the first *machine-checked* proof of the two-thread abstraction idea. VeriCUDA [20,21] focuses on reasoning about the functional correctness of GPU programs using Hoare-logic. In [22] the authors extend VeriCUDA to proving DRF. In a similar vein, VerCors [7] uses separation logic to prove the functional correctness and DRF of GPU kernels. Both VeriCUDA and VerCors expect a tool-specific language, hence cannot handle real-world kernels directly.

Data-Race Finders. These include dynamic data-race detection, symbolic-execution, and model-checking. Such techniques are better suited for highly detailed analysis in smaller kernels, and typically are unable to prove DRF. Dynamic data-race detection executes a kernel to find data-races on a fixed input, *e.g.*, [14,18,19,28,32,38,39]. This technique only reports real data-races, but suffers from a slowdown of at least 10× compared to the non-instrumented program, and requires the kernel input data, which might be unavailable or unknown. Symbolic execution and model checking have been extended to detect data-races [10,11,26,33,37]. These techniques do without the kernel input data and can detect more data-races than dynamic data-race detection.

Miscellaneous. Ferrel *et al.* introduce a machine-checked formalism to reason about the semantics of CUDA assembly [15]. Dabrowski *et al.* mechanize the DRF-analysis of multithreaded programs [13]. Muller and Hoffmann present a logic to reason about the evaluation cost of CUDA kernels [31].

Other behavioral types have been used to verify parallel and multithreaded systems that communicate via message-passing [29,35,36]. However these do not capture shared memory (only message-passing), thus cannot address data-races.

8   Conclusion

We tackle the problem of statically checking DRF in GPU kernels, with a new family of behavioral types, *i.e.*, access memory protocols. We provide a novel compositional analysis of access memory protocols, along with fully mechanized proofs and an implementation. Our evaluation explores challenging and diverse benchmarks (229 real-world and 258 synthetic kernels) to demonstrate that our approach is more precise (false alarms and missed alarms), scalable (time/memory growth), and usable (real-world kernels correctly verified) than other tools.

Acknowledgements. We thank Rumyana Neykova, Stephen Chang, and the anonymous reviewers for their insightful feedback on earlier versions of this work.

References

1. Ancona, D., et al.: Behavioral types in programming languages. Found. Trends Program. Lang. **3**(2–3), 95–230 (2016). https://doi.org/10.1561/2500000031
2. Bardsley, E., et al.: Engineering a static verification tool for GPU kernels. In: Biere, A., Bloem, R. (eds.) CAV 2014. LNCS, vol. 8559, pp. 226–242. Springer, Cham (2014). https://doi.org/10.1007/978-3-319-08867-9_15
3. Bardsley, E., Donaldson, A.F., Wickerson, J.: KernelInterceptor: automating GPU kernel verification by intercepting kernels and their parameters. In: Proceedings of IWOCL, pp. 1–5 (May 2014). https://doi.org/10.1145/2664666.2664673
4. Barnett, M., Chang, B.-Y.E., DeLine, R., Jacobs, B., Leino, K.R.M.: Boogie: a modular reusable verifier for object-oriented programs. In: de Boer, F.S., Bonsangue, M.M., Graf, S., de Roever, W.-P. (eds.) FMCO 2005. LNCS, vol. 4111, pp. 364–387. Springer, Heidelberg (2006). https://doi.org/10.1007/11804192_17
5. Betts, A., et al.: The design and implementation of a verification technique for GPU kernels. Trans. Program. Lang. Syst. **37**(3), 1–49 (2015). https://doi.org/10.1145/2743017
6. Betts, A., Chong, N., Donaldson, A.F., Qadeer, S., Thomson, P.: GPUVerify: a verifier for GPU kernels. In: Proceedings of OOPSLA, pp. 113–132. ACM (2012). https://doi.org/10.1145/2384616.2384625
7. Blom, S., Huisman, M., Mihelčić, M.: Specification and verification of GPGPU programs. Sci. Comput. Program. **95**(P3), 376–388 (2014). https://doi.org/10.1016/j.scico.2014.03.013

8. Chatarasi, P., Shirako, J., Kong, M., Sarkar, V.: An extended polyhedral model for SPMD programs and its use in static data race detection. In: Ding, C., Criswell, J., Wu, P. (eds.) LCPC 2016. LNCS, vol. 10136, pp. 106–120. Springer, Cham (2017). https://doi.org/10.1007/978-3-319-52709-3_10

9. Cogumbreiro, T., Lange, J., Liew Zhen Rong, D., Zicarelli, H.: Checking Data-Race Freedom of GPU Kernels, Compositionally (Artifact) (2021). https://doi.org/10.5281/zenodo.4726300

10. Collingbourne, P., Cadar, C., Kelly, P.H.J.: Symbolic testing of OpenCL code. In: Eder, K., Lourenço, J., Shehory, O. (eds.) HVC 2011. LNCS, vol. 7261, pp. 203–218. Springer, Heidelberg (2012). https://doi.org/10.1007/978-3-642-34188-5_18

11. Collingbourne, P., Cadar, C., Kelly, P.H.: Symbolic crosschecking of floating-point and SIMD code. In: Proceedings of EuroSys, pp. 315–328. ACM (2011). https://doi.org/10.1145/1966445.1966475

12. Collingbourne, P., Donaldson, A.F., Ketema, J., Qadeer, S.: Interleaving and lock-step semantics for analysis and verification of GPU kernels. In: Felleisen, M., Gardner, P. (eds.) ESOP 2013. LNCS, vol. 7792, pp. 270–289. Springer, Heidelberg (2013). https://doi.org/10.1007/978-3-642-37036-6_16

13. Dabrowski, F., Pichardie, D.: A certified data race analysis for a Java-like language. In: Berghofer, S., Nipkow, T., Urban, C., Wenzel, M. (eds.) TPHOLs 2009. LNCS, vol. 5674, pp. 212–227. Springer, Heidelberg (2009). https://doi.org/10.1007/978-3-642-03359-9_16

14. Eizenberg, A., Peng, Y., Pigli, T., Mansky, W., Devietti, J.: BARRACUDA: binary-level analysis of runtime RAces in CUDA programs. In: Proceedings of PLDI, pp. 126–140. ACM (2017). https://doi.org/10.1145/3062341.3062342

15. Ferrell, B., Duan, J., Hamlen, K.W.: CUDA au Coq: a framework for machine-validating GPU assembly programs. In: Proceedings of DATE, pp. 474–479 (2019). https://doi.org/10.23919/DATE.2019.8715160

16. Grosser, T., Ramanujam, J., Pouchet, L.N., Sadayappan, P., Pop, S.: Optimistic delinearization of parametrically sized arrays. In: Proceedings of ICS, pp. 351–360. ACM (2015). https://doi.org/10.1145/2751205.2751248

17. ul Hassan Khan Khan, A., Al-Mouhamed, M., Fatayer, A., Almousa, A., Baqais, A., Assayony, M.: Padding free bank conflict resolution for CUDA-based matrix transpose algorithm. In: Proceedings of SNPD, pp. 1–6 (2014). https://doi.org/10.1109/SNPD.2014.6888709

18. Holey, A., Mekkat, V., Zhai, A.: HAccRG: hardware-accelerated data race detection in GPUs. In: Proceedings of ICPP, pp. 60–69 (2013). https://doi.org/10.1109/ICPP.2013.15

19. Kamath, A.K., George, A.A., Basu, A.: ScoRD: a scoped race detector for GPUs. In: Proceedings of ISCA, pp. 1036–1049. IEEE (2020). https://doi.org/10.1109/ISCA45697.2020.00088

20. Kojima, K., Igarashi, A.: A hoare logic for SIMT programs. In: Shan, C. (ed.) APLAS 2013. LNCS, vol. 8301, pp. 58–73. Springer, Cham (2013). https://doi.org/10.1007/978-3-319-03542-0_5

21. Kojima, K., Igarashi, A.: A hoare logic for GPU kernels. Trans. Comput. Logic 18(1), 1–43 (2017). https://doi.org/10.1145/3001834

22. Kojima, K., Imanishi, A., Igarashi, A.: Automated verification of functional correctness of race-free GPU programs. J. Autom. Reason. 60(3), 279–298 (2017). https://doi.org/10.1007/s10817-017-9428-2

23. Lattner, C., Adve, V.: LLVM: a compilation framework for lifelong program analysis & transformation. In: Proceedings of CGO, pp. 75–88. IEEE (2004). https://doi.org/10.1109/CGO.2004.1281665

24. Li, G., Gopalakrishnan, G.: Scalable SMT-based verification of GPU kernel functions. In: Proceedings of FSE, pp. 187–196. ACM (2010). https://doi.org/10.1145/1882291.1882320
25. Li, G., Gopalakrishnan, G.: Parameterized verification of GPU kernel programs. In: Proceedings of IPDPSW, pp. 2450–2459 (2012). https://doi.org/10.1109/IPDPSW.2012.302
26. Li, G., Li, P., Sawaya, G., Gopalakrishnan, G., Ghosh, I., Rajan, S.P.: GKLEE: concolic verification and test generation for GPUs. In: Proceedings of PPoPP, vol. 47, pp. 215–224. ACM (2012). https://doi.org/10.1145/2370036.2145844
27. Li, P., Li, G., Gopalakrishnan, G.: Practical symbolic race checking of GPU programs. In: Proceedings of SC, pp. 179–190. IEEE (2014). https://doi.org/10.1109/SC.2014.20
28. Li, P., et al.: LD: low-overhead GPU race detection without access monitoring. Trans. Archit. Code Optim. 14(1), 1–25 (2017). https://doi.org/10.1145/3046678
29. López, H.A., et al.: Protocol-based verification of message-passing parallel programs. In: Proceedings of OOPSLA, pp. 280–298. ACM (2015). https://doi.org/10.1145/2814270.2814302
30. Ma, H., Diersen, S.R., Wang, L., Liao, C., Quinlan, D., Yang, Z.: Symbolic analysis of concurrency errors in OpenMP programs. In: Proceedings of ICPP, pp. 510–516. IEEE (2013). https://doi.org/10.1109/ICPP.2013.63
31. Muller, S.K., Hoffmann, J.: Modeling and analyzing evaluation cost of CUDA kernels. In: Proceedings of the ACM on Programming Languages 5(POPL) (2021). https://doi.org/10.1145/3434306
32. Peng, Y., Grover, V., Devietti, J.: CURD: a dynamic CUDA race detector. In: Proceedings of PLDI, pp. 390–403. ACM (2018). https://doi.org/10.1145/3192366.3192368
33. Pereira, P., et al.: Verifying CUDA programs using SMT-based context-bounded model checking. In: Proceedings of SAC, pp. 1648–1653. ACM (2016). https://doi.org/10.1145/2851613.2851830
34. Ruetsch, G., Micikevicius, P.: Optimizing matrix transpose in CUDA. NVIDIA CUDA SDK Application Note 18 (2009). https://www.cs.colostate.edu/~cs675/MatrixTranspose.pdf
35. Vasconcelos, V.T.: Session types for linear multithreaded functional programming. In: Proceedings of PPDP, pp. 1–6. ACM (2009). https://doi.org/10.1145/1599410.1599411
36. Vasconcelos, V., Ravara, A., Gay, S.: Session types for functional multithreading. In: Gardner, P., Yoshida, N. (eds.) CONCUR 2004. LNCS, vol. 3170, pp. 497–511. Springer, Heidelberg (2004). https://doi.org/10.1007/978-3-540-28644-8_32
37. Wu, M., Ouyang, Y., Zhou, H., Zhang, L., Liu, C., Zhang, Y.: Simulee: detecting CUDA synchronization bugs via memory-access modeling. In: Proceedings of ICSE, pp. 937–948. ACM (2020). https://doi.org/10.1145/3377811.3380358
38. Zheng, M., Ravi, V.T., Qin, F., Agrawal, G.: GRace: a low-overhead mechanism for detecting data races in GPU programs. In: Proceedings of PPoPP, pp. 135–146. ACM (2011). https://doi.org/10.1145/1941553.1941574
39. Zheng, M., Ravi, V.T., Qin, F., Agrawal, G.: GMRace: detecting data races in GPU programs via a low-overhead scheme. Trans. Parallel Distrib. Syst. 25(1), 104–115 (2014). https://doi.org/10.1109/TPDS.2013.44

426   T. Cogumbreiro et al.

GenMC: A Model Checker for Weak Memory Models

Michalis Kokologiannakis$^{(\boxtimes)}$ and Viktor Vafeiadis

MPI-SWS, Kaiserslautern, Germany
{michalis,viktor}@mpi-sws.org

Abstract. GenMC is an LLVM-based state-of-the-art stateless model checker for concurrent C/C++ programs. Its modular infrastructure allows it to support complex memory models, such as RC11 and IMM, and makes it easy to extend to support further axiomatic memory models.

In this paper, we discuss the overall architecture of the tool and how it can be extended to support additional memory models, programming languages, and/or synchronization primitives. To demonstrate the point, we have extended the tool with support for the Linux kernel memory model (LKMM), synchronization barriers, POSIX I/O system calls, and better error detection capabilities.

1 Introduction

For any software developer or verification engineer, it is no news that concurrent programming is difficult, that concurrent software is often buggy, and that therefore verification of concurrent programs has attracted a lot of research interest. Within the verification community at least, it is also common knowledge that verification of concurrent programs is challenging because of the huge number of interleavings of the threads comprising a concurrent program.

What has changed in the last decade, however, is the importance of *weak memory consistency* [6,11,13,14,21,25,32,36,40,41] as a key factor contributing to the complexity of concurrent programming. Weak memory models do not simply increase the number of thread interleavings; they also confound programmers, who typically have little intuition about how to reason about the behaviors induced by these additional interleavings.

GenMC is a fully automatic verification tool meant for such programmers. It is a *stateless model checker* (SMC) [23] that can be used to verify bounded clients of intricate concurrent algorithms, such as implementations of synchronization primitives and shared data structures (e.g., queues, sets, and maps). It accepts as input a C/C++ program using C/C++11 atomics and/or the concurrency primitives from the pthread library, and reports any data races, assertion violations, or other errors encountered. By default, verification is performed with respect to the RC11 memory model [32], but there are command line options for selecting other models, such as IMM [41] and LKMM [10].

© The Author(s) 2021
A. Silva and K. R. M. Leino (Eds.) CAV 2021, LNCS 12759, pp. 427–440, 2021.
https://doi.org/10.1007/978-3-030-81685-8_20

Since the theory underlying GENMC has already been published elsewhere [28,29,31], this paper focuses on the overall design of the tool and on various enhancements implemented in it. Our main design goals of GENMC were:

Generality: The tool should be able to verify programs written in a variety of programming languages with respect to a variety of memory models.

Efficiency: The tool should implement a state-of-the-art SMC algorithm and incorporate further optimizations for common programming patterns.

Usability: The tool should provide useful and readable error messages.

Extensibility: The tool should be easily adaptable to support additional models and synchronization primitives, and to tweak its performance. Extensibility is key to achieving the other goals, since it allows gradual improvements to the tool in terms of coverage, performance, and error detection/reporting.

These goals are achieved by a combination of techniques:

GENMC's core SMC algorithm [29,31] is parametric in the choice of the memory model—subject to a few minimal constraints (see Sect. 2).

The implementation is based on LLVM, a versatile intermediate language for multiple programming languages.

GENMC follows a modular architecture minimizing dependencies across components (see Sect. 3), which makes it easy to extend with support for additional memory models (Sect. 4) and synchronization primitives (Sect. 5).

Its architecture contains hooks to provide fast approximate consistency checks, which are exploited by the memory model implementations (see Sect. 4).

GENMC contains a number of optimizations that provide noticeable performance benefits on common workloads (Sect. 7).

GENMC keeps additional metadata so as to present error messages in terms of variables names appearing in the source code (Sect. 6).

GENMC has been applied to a few industrial settings, where it has found bugs and/or verified bounded correctness of concurrent libraries [39].

Related Work. There has been extensive work on SMC, with most tools focusing on sequential consistency [7,8,15,23,37]. Tools that support weak memory models include CDSCHECKER [38] that verifies C/C++11 programs under the original C11 memory model, TRACER [5] that verifies C/C++11 programs under the RA model, RCMC [27] that verifies C programs under RC11 [32], and NIDHUGG [1,2,4,12,13] that supports SC, TSO, PSO and provides limited support for the POWER and ARMv7 memory models. In contrast to GENMC, which uses the same core algorithm for all memory models, NIDHUGG uses multiple different algorithms depending on the memory model.

There has also been work on adapting SAT/SMT-based bounded model checking (BMC) techniques for weak memory models [9,17,22]. DARTAGNAN [22] is a BMC tool that is parametric in the choice of the memory model, as it accepts the memory model as input in the litmus format [11].

2   Memory Model Requirements

GENMC's core algorithm is parametric in the choice of the memory model provided that it can be expressed in an axiomatic way and satisfies a few basic requirements that we describe below.

Axiomatic memory models represent the executions of a concurrent program as *execution graphs* [11] that satisfy a certain consistency predicate. Execution graphs comprise a set of *events* (nodes) that represent the individual memory accesses performed by the program, and some relations on these events (edges). Example relations included in all memory models are the *preserved program order* (ppo) and *reads-from* (rf) relations: ppo relates events in the same thread that are ordered (e.g., by a chain of dependencies or a fence), while rf relates writes to reads reading from them.

GENMC can be used to verify programs under such a model as long as the model's consistency predicate fulfills the following requirements:

No-Thin-Air: In consistent graphs, ppo∪rf should be acyclic. This intuitively means that an event cannot circularly depend on itself.

Prefix-Closedness: Restricting a consistent graph to any (ppo ∪ rf)-prefix-closed subset of its events yields a consistent graph. Prefix-closedness enables the algorithm to construct a consistent graph incrementally.

Extensibility: Adding a (ppo ∪ rf)-maximal event to a consistent graph for some choice of an incoming rf-edge preserves consistency. This captures the intuitive idea that executing a program should never get stuck if a thread has more statements to execute. In particular, a read of x should always be able to return the value written by the most recent write to x.

These requirements are satisfied by almost all axiomatic memory models (e.g., TSO [40], PSO [42], Power [11], ARMv7 [11], ARMv8 [21], RC11 [32], IMM [41], LKMM [10]). The only known axiomatic memory model that does not satisfy these requirements is the original formulation of the C/C++11 model [13], which has been criticized for its flaws [32, 43].

Although these requirements cannot be satisfied by more advanced memory models that cannot be defined in an axiomatic fashion (e.g., [14, 24, 25, 33]), there is ongoing work to support such a model.

3   Tool Architecture

Verification with GENMC comprises three stages (cf. Fig. 1, left).

The first stage invokes `clang` to compile the source C/C++ program to LLVM-IR. To accommodate programs written in different languages, GENMC also accepts LLVM-IR as its input, provided that it adheres to certain conventions about thread creation.

The second stage transforms the LLVM-IR code to make verification more effective by replacing spinloops by `assume` statements, bounding infinite loops,

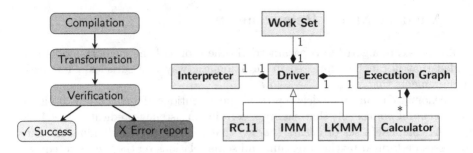

Fig. 1. Overal architecture (left) and dynamic components (right).

and performing sound optimizations, such as dead allocation elimination. It also collects additional debugging information to enable better error reporting.

The third stage invokes the verification procedure, which explores all the executions of the program. If an error is found during this stage, the execution is halted and an error report is produced (see Sect. 6).

The architectural subcomponents of this stage are depicted in Fig. 1 (right). At the center lies the verification *driver*, which owns three independent components: an execution graph, a work set, and an interpreter.

The *execution graph* records the visited execution trace, and has routines for calculating various relation on the graph, such as the happens-before relation. As each memory model comprises different relations, the execution graph contains multiple calculators that are dynamically populated when the graph is created, and the consistency predicate is calculated as a fixpoint of all the selected relations, whenever this is requested by the driver.

The *work set* records alternate options for later exploration, the precise definition of which can depend on the memory model.

The *interpreter* merely executes the user program, notifying the driver each time a "visible" action (e.g., a load/store to shared memory) is encountered. It is directly based on the LLVM interpreter lli [35], and is the only part of our code base that heavily depends on LLVM. In turn, the driver modifies accordingly the execution graph, possibly pushes some items to the work set, and returns control back to the interpreter, along with a value that will be used by the interpreter, if necessary (e.g., in the case of a load). In effect, the driver and the interpreter can be thought of as *coroutines* [18]. The interpreter calls the driver whenever it encounters a visible action or finishes running a thread, while the driver monitors execution consistency, schedules the program threads, and discovers alternative exploration options, which are pushed to the work set.

The aforementioned components are all parameterized by the user's configuration options. The most important of these options is the memory model, which also determines whether dependencies between instructions should be tracked by the interpreter and stored in the execution graph. Another important option is when and how consistency is to be calculated. Since checking consistency at each step can be expensive for some memory models, it is possible to provide an approximate consistency check to be applied at each step and only perform the full consistency check once an error is detected.

To facilitate memory-model-specific optimizations, the driver is overridden for each memory model. Each instance sets up the (approximate) consistency checks and can provide specialized methods for crucial verification components.

4 Supporting New Memory Models

Adding support for a new memory model entails three basic steps.

First, one has to provide definitions for any memory model primitives that the interpreter should intercept beyond those already supported (i.e., plain memory accesses and C/C++11 atomics). One can either provide a header file mapping these primitives to LLVM-IR instructions or create special event types for them.

Second, one has to provide calculators for the memory model's relations that are not already supported by GenMC. Depending on the memory model, this step may require a variable amount of effort, but it effectively boils down to translating relational calculations into matrix operations.

Third, one can also provide approximations for the consistency checks. Such approximations entail storing crucial information about a memory model's relations as vector clocks (e.g., causally preceding events, for some notion of causality), but deciding what to store is up to the user to decide and encode. Importantly, GenMC's performance depends not only on the calculators provided in the previous step, but also on the effectiveness of the approximations, which quickly filter out inconsistent exploration options. For instance, GenMC's current RC11 driver treats SC accesses as release-acquire (RA) accesses (the consistency of which can be quickly determined), and only checks for full RC11 consistency when an error has been triggered, a heuristic that seems to work well in practice for programs that have both SC and non-SC accesses.

All in all, adding support for a memory model largely depends on the complexity of the model. Adding support for models like SC or RA is trivial, since such accesses are already supported as part of RC11 and IMM. In contrast, adding support for LKMM involved much more work, as we describe below.

4.1 Supporting the Linux Kernel Memory Model (LKMM)

LKMM [10] is a memory model that encompasses a variety of different architectures supported by the Linux kernel. As LKMM differs substantially from RC11 and IMM, supporting it required all steps described above as well as a few other engineering decisions, the most important of which are discussed below.

First, LKMM uses complex constraints for checking consistency of an execution graph. As repeatedly calculating these constraints can be expensive, we designed approximations for them. Unlike most other memory models, LKMM does not define a suitable happens-before relation for checking coherence and detecting races. (Its hb relation cannot be used for this purpose.) We thus defined a custom happens-before relation that can rule out inconsistent executions very quickly, and use it to approximate coherence and race detection checks.

Second, although LKMM dictates that non-atomic accesses (called plain in LKMM's jargon) only conditionally contribute to ppo, we incorporate such accesses in GenMC's ppo (thus arriving at a stronger notion of ppo), mostly for technical reasons. Specifically, the calculation of dependencies between only non-plain accesses is difficult because each non-plain access in the source-code level may map to several plain and non-plain accesses in LLVM-IR level.

To increase confidence in our implementation, we ran all litmus tests distributed along with LKMM as part of the Linux kernel (32 tests in total), and compared our results with the results of the Herd [11] memory model simulator. Both tools explored the same number of executions for all tests.

In addition, we extracted some manually written tests from LKMM's supplementary repository [34] (categories `atomic` and `kernel`). We picked these categories as they contain tests written in C pseudocode (thus easily translatable to C) and do not contain tests with plain accesses, which, as described, GenMC treats slightly differently from what LKMM dictates. In total, these categories amount to another 84 tests, from which we excluded two tests containing unsupported primitives, one test for which Herd did not terminate within 42 h, and three tests that cannot be cleanly translated to C. Out of the remaining 78 tests, GenMC explores the same number of executions for 75 tests. The discrepancies observed in the three remaining tests are due to the different way the two tools produce and calculate dependencies. (In GenMC, control dependencies extend to all subsequent memory accesses of the same thread, whereas in Herd they extend only to the merge point of a conditional statement.)

We note that Herd took about 18 min to run all the above tests, while GenMC needed less than 2 s.

5   Supporting New Languages and Libraries

Supporting additional programming languages is straightforward as long as they can be compiled to LLVM. This was, for example, the case when we extended GenMC to accept C++ (the initial version accepted only C input). All we had to do was to create stub header files for the C++ library, and to extend the interpreter to recognize the memory (de)allocation calls generated by `clang`.

Supporting different runtime environments (e.g., JVM bytecode) requires constructing a new interpreter for the desired runtime system that calls the driver whenever a visible action is encountered. In addition, since the driver and the interpreter communicate using the LLVM type information, it may be necessary to add a translation layer between the interpreter(s) and the driver.

Supporting new concurrency libraries requires localized changes. If the library's semantics can be implemented in terms of memory accesses, one has to construct an appropriate header file or extend the interpreter to provide the mapping from library calls to the relevant memory access events. If this is not possible and/or if native support for a library is desirable (e.g., for performance reasons), then the execution graph has to be extended with new kinds of events and the consistency checks have to be adapted accordingly.

Next, we present two such library extensions, one mapping its calls to individual memory accesses, and the other creating new kinds of events.

System Calls. As part of [26], we extended GenMC with support for system calls, such as `open()`, `close()`, `read()` and `write()`, which can be modeled by making multiple primitive calls (reads and writes) to a different address space.

There are two ways one could implement these system calls: either by providing an actual implementation (which would then be compiled to LLVM-IR) or by adding support in the interpreter to internally implement those calls and communicating multiple times with the driver.

We preferred the latter solution because it is more portable. An external implementation would have to be manually ported whenever support for more languages is added. In contrast, the internal implementation needs no change. Further, even if a new interpreter for a different runtime system is added, it should be simple to decouple the system calls from the interpreter, and have the different runtime systems share the infrastructure that handles system calls.

Barriers. N-way barriers are a widely-used synchronization primitive. They have two functions: `barrier_init` and `barrier_wait`. The former initializes a barrier object with the number of threads that will rendezvous at the barrier, while the latter is called every time a thread reaches the barrier. A thread that is calling `barrier_wait` blocks until the initially specified number of threads reaches the barrier, at which point all threads will be simultaneously unblocked, and the barrier value will reset to the one specified with `barrier_init`.

Barriers can be straightforwardly implemented with a shared variable counting the number of threads that have called `barrier_wait`. But doing so yields poor model checking performance. For N threads calling `barrier_wait`, there are $N!$ possible orders in which they can update the shared counter, thus crippling the performance of the tool. Tracking the order of these updates is not only expensive but also completely unnecessary. For many real-world use cases of barriers (e.g., scatter-gather workloads), the order in which different threads reached the barrier is irrelevant, and the thread that reached last unimportant.

We leverage this intuition and provide built-in support for `barrier_init` and `barrier_wait` calls that does not track the relative ordering among `barrier_wait` calls synchronizing with one another, thereby achieving an exponential reduction in verification time. Concretely, in the simple program below where N threads execute `barrier_wait` concurrently, GenMC explores only one execution instead of $N!$ executions:

$$\texttt{barrier\_wait(); } \| \ ... \ \| \ \texttt{barrier\_wait();}$$

Our extension is called BAM (Barrier-Aware Model-checking) and is detailed and evaluated in a companion paper [30].

6   Error Detection and Reporting

GENMC detects a number of different kinds of errors: violations of user-supplied regular and persistency assertions, data races, memory errors and simple cases of termination errors. It reports errors by printing an offending execution graph and highlighting the event(s) that caused the violation. Upon request, GENMC can also print a total ordering of the instructions that lead to the violation, or produce the offending execution in the DOT graph description language.

Persistency Errors. To verify persistency properties of programs performing file I/O, we allow user programs to contain a special *recovery routine* [26], which would typically check some invariant over the persisted state.

When such a routine is present, GENMC simulates all possible ways in which the program could have crashed because of a power failure, executing the recovery routine at the end of every such execution. Of course, to avoid the obvious state-space explosion, the simulation of all the possible failures is done in an optimized fashion, driven by the memory accesses of the recovery routine.

The performance of GENMC when verifying persistency properties of programs under the `ext4` filesystem has been evaluated at [26].

Memory Errors. Memory errors refers to accessing uninitialized, unallocated or deallocated memory. In models like RC11 [32], reasoning about memory safety can be tricky at times, as demonstrated by the example below:

$$
\begin{array}{l|l}
p := \mathsf{alloc}(); & \textbf{if } x = 1 \textbf{ then} \\
{*}p :=_{\mathtt{rlx}} 42; & \quad a :=_{\mathtt{rlx}} p; \\
x :=_{\mathtt{rlx}} 1; & \quad b :=_{\mathtt{rlx}} {*}a;
\end{array}
$$

This example is erroneous under RC11 because the allocation of p is not guaranteed to have propagated to the second thread by the time it is dereferenced. (Since all accesses are relaxed, there is no synchronization between the threads.)

GENMC also accounts for more complicated scenarios such as p being concurrently freed when accessed, p being freed twice, or p being the address of a local (stack) variable that might not be alive when accessed.

Refining Error Reports. It is often useful to refine the error reporting. For example, in memory models that treat data races as errors (such as RC11), GENMC by default detects data races and reports them as errors. This, however, can be costly in terms of verification time or even prohibit the verification of programs that use compiler/custom primitives to access shared memory, as such programs would almost certainly be considered racy.

To deal with such cases, GENMC provides switches that disable race detection and refine the range of errors that will be reported to the user. Switches of the latter kind are especially useful when dealing with programs that contain system calls. By default, when such system calls fail, GENMC reports an error, which is inconvenient for programs that contain proper error handling, as some system errors are rather benign (e.g., a file not existing). With the appropriate switch, in case of system errors, an appropriate value is written in `errno`, as dictated by the POSIX standard.

Case Study. We demonstrate the error reporting capabilities of GenMC with a real use case. We consider a flat-combining queue [19] that has been proposed to be ported in Rust's `crossbeam` library.

This queue serves as a nice case study for a couple of reasons. First, it contains loops that can diverge, and so its verification requires loop bounding, which GenMC can do automatically. Second, it is implemented using compiler primitives for concurrent accesses, and so its verification requires disabling race detection. Third, while experimenting with it, we found it to be buggy.

The error report produced by GenMC can be seen in Fig. 2. The error is quite intricate: it requires three threads to manifest, each of which executes a large number of instructions. The error is due to an ordering bug (relaxed accesses are used instead of release/acquire), which demonstrates the need for model checking tools that handle weak memory models.

```
Error detected: Attempt to read from uninitialized memory!
Event (3, 63) in graph:
<-1, 0> main:

<0, 1> thread_n:

  (1, 18): Urel (cmb.queue, 0) [(0, 36)] L.169: combiner.c
  (1, 19): Urel (cmb.queue, 2565579352) L.169: combiner.c

  (1, 96): Racq (m.msg._meta.next, 2565579416) [(2, 26)] L.228: combiner.c

  (1, 112): Wrlx (cmb.takeover, 2565579416) L.158: combiner.c
<0, 2> thread_n:

  (2, 26): Wrel (m.msg._meta.next, 94798317999592) L.167: combiner.c
<0, 3> thread_n:

  (3, 18): Urel (cmb.queue, 2565579352) [(1, 19)] L.169: combiner.c
  (3, 19): Urel (cmb.queue, 2565579480) L.169: combiner.c

  (3, 50): Rrlx (cmb.takeover, 2565579416) [(1, 112)] L.87: combiner.c

  (3, 63): Racq (m.msg._meta.next, 0) [BOTTOM] L.187: combiner.c
Number of complete executions explored: 2795
Number of blocked executions seen: 6001
Total wall-clock time: 2.12s
```

Fig. 2. An error report by GenMC after removing irrelevant lines.

We note that the error report contains helpful debugging information, such as the names of variables accessed (e.g., `m.msg._meta.next`) and the values read/written. To display this information, GenMC maintains a mapping from addresses to program variables using the additional debugging information collected in the "Transformation" phase.

7   Other Performance Enhancements to GENMC

In this section, we briefly discuss two recent changes to the driver to optimize its performance for certain kinds of programs.

Symmetry Reduction. Many programs, such as the flat-combining queue of Sect. 6, have a symmetric structure: each thread runs the same code. In such cases, many execution graphs are equivalent up to some thread relabeling—a property that is exploited by *symmetry reduction* (SR) [16,20].

We implemented a simple SR algorithm that detects whether multiple threads with the same code are spawned with no intervening memory accesses, and avoids exploring executions for which a symmetric one (by relabeling such threads) has already been explored. This can yield exponential improvements. For example, a program with N threads incrementing a shared variable atomically has $N!$ executions; employing SR yields only one execution. With SR, the verification time of the corrected flat-combining queue drops from 15 s to 2.5 s.

To further demonstrate the benefits of SR, we measured the performance of GENMC with and without SR on some realistic lock implementations adapted from the literature. The results can be seen in Table 1. All reported times are in seconds, unless mentioned otherwise. We ran both GENMC versions three times for each benchmark, with an increasing number of threads each time (the initial thread number for each benchmark is provided in the second column). As it can be seen, SR leads to a significant performance improvement in all cases.

Table 1. Testing lock implementations (1 h timeout; 4 GB memory limit)

	N	Without SR			With SR		
		N	$N+1$	$N+2$	N	$N+1$	$N+2$
mutex	2	0.02	0.40	41 min	0.03	0.08	164.66
mutex_musl	2	0.01	34.47	OOM	0.01	5.92	OOM
rwlock	2	0.02	0.18	47.34	0.04	0.05	1.94
spinlock	3	0.03	0.08	1.19	0.02	0.03	0.18
ticketlock	4	0.02	0.13	2.35	0.01	0.01	0.01
ttaslock	3	0.06	2.05	38 min	0.08	0.11	33.87
twalock	3	0.03	0.49	79.68	0.03	0.04	0.36

Lock-Aware Partial Order Reduction. A common problem with locking is that of false sharing, where N threads contend to acquire the same lock even if it is unnecessary for correctness. In such cases, GENMC's partial order reduction algorithm [29] will explore all $N!$ orders in which the lock can be acquired even though they all lead to the same outcome.

We have implemented *lock-aware partial order reduction* (LAPOR) [28], an enhancement to partial order reduction that does not track ordering among locks unless their critical regions have conflicting accesses, in which case the lock ordering is induced from the ordering among those accesses. With LAPOR, GenMC achieves exponential improvements in lock-based implementations of concurrent libraries that have false sharing, such as search trees with coarse-grained or hand-over-hand locking. LAPOR has been evaluated at [28].

8   Conclusion

We presented GenMC, a state-of-the-art stateless model checker that can be used to verify consistency and persistency properties of C/C++ programs. We described its architecture, and how its modular design can be leveraged to account for new features and memory models. To widen the applicability of GenMC, we have extended it with support for LKMM, basic system calls and additional synchronization primitives. We have also improved its performance with optimizations, such as symmetry reduction and lock-aware partial order reduction that can exponentially decrease its search space.

In the future, we plan to implement a DSL for memory models, so as to make it easier to extend GenMC with new models and quickly tweak their approximation strategies. We are also planning to incorporate further optimizations into the tool to enable more effective verification of lock-free algorithms.

Acknowledgements. We thank the anonymous reviewers for their feedback. This work was supported by a European Research Council (ERC) Consolidator Grant for the project "PERSIST" under the European Union's Horizon 2020 research and innovation programme (grant agreement No. 101003349).

References

1. Abdulla, P.A., Aronis, S., Atig, M.F., Jonsson, B., Leonardsson, C., Sagonas, K.: Stateless model checking for TSO and PSO. In: Baier, C., Tinelli, C. (eds.) TACAS 2015. LNCS, vol. 9035, pp. 353–367. Springer, Heidelberg (2015). https://doi.org/10.1007/978-3-662-46681-0_28
2. Abdulla, P.A., Aronis, S., Jonsson, B., Sagonas, K.: Optimal dynamic partial order reduction. In: POPL 2014, pp. 373–384. ACM, New York (2014). https://doi.org/10.1145/2535838.2535845
3. Abdulla, P.A., Atig, M.F., Jonsson, B., Lång, M., Ngo, T.P., Sagonas, K.: Optimal stateless model checking for reads-from equivalence under sequential consistency. Proc. ACM Program. Lang. **3**, 150:1–150:29 (2019) https://doi.org/10.1145/3360576
4. Abdulla, P.A., Atig, M.F., Jonsson, B., Leonardsson, C.: Stateless model checking for power. In: Chaudhuri, S., Farzan, A. (eds.) CAV 2016. LNCS, vol. 9780, pp. 134–156. Springer, Cham (2016). https://doi.org/10.1007/978-3-319-41540-6_8
5. Abdulla, P.A., Atig, M.F., Jonsson, B., Ngo, T.P.: Optimal stateless model checking under the release-acquire semantics. Proc. ACM Program. Lang. **2**(OOPSLA), 135:1–135:29 (2018) https://doi.org/10.1145/3276505

6. Adve, S.V., Gharachorloo, K.: Shared memory consistency models: A tutorial. IEEE Comput. **29**(12), 66–76 (1996)
7. Albert, E., Arenas, P., de la Banda, M.G., Gómez-Zamalloa, M., Stuckey, P.J.: Context-sensitive dynamic partial order reduction. In: Majumdar, R., Kunčak, V. (eds.) CAV 2017. LNCS, vol. 10426, pp. 526–543. Springer, Cham (2017). https://doi.org/10.1007/978-3-319-63387-9_26
8. Albert, E., Gómez-Zamalloa, M., Isabel, M., Rubio, A.: Constrained dynamic partial order reduction. In: Chockler, H., Weissenbacher, G. (eds.) CAV 2018. LNCS, vol. 10982, pp. 392–410. Springer, Cham (2018). https://doi.org/10.1007/978-3-319-96142-2_24
9. Alglave, J., Kroening, D., Tautschnig, M.: Partial orders for efficient bounded model checking of concurrent software. In: Sharygina, N., Veith, H. (eds.) CAV 2013. LNCS, vol. 8044, pp. 141–157. Springer, Heidelberg (2013). https://doi.org/10.1007/978-3-642-39799-8_9
10. Alglave, J., Maranget, L., McKenney, P.E., Parri, A., Stern, A.: Frightening small children and disconcerting grown-ups: concurrency in the Linux kernel. In: ASPLOS 2018, pp. 405–418. ACM, Williamsburg, VA, USA (2018). https://doi.org/10.1145/3173162.3177156
11. Alglave, J., Maranget, L., Tautschnig, M.: Herding cats: Modelling, simulation, testing, and data mining for weak memory. ACM Trans. Program. Lang. Syst. **36**(2), 7:1–7:74 (2014) https://doi.org/10.1145/2627752
12. Aronis, S., Jonsson, B., Lång, M., Sagonas, K.: Optimal dynamic partial order reduction with observers. In: Beyer, D., Huisman, M. (eds.) TACAS 2018. LNCS, vol. 10806, pp. 229–248. Springer, Cham (2018). https://doi.org/10.1007/978-3-319-89963-3_14
13. Batty, M., Owens, S., Sarkar, S., Sewell, P., Weber, T.: Mathematizing C++ concurrency. In: POPL 2011, pp. 55–66. ACM, Austin, Texas, USA (2011). https://doi.org/10.1145/1926385.1926394
14. Chakraborty, S., Vafeiadis, V.: Grounding thin-air reads with event structures. Proc. ACM Program. Lang. **3**(POPL), 70:1–70:28 (2019) https://doi.org/10.1145/3290383
15. Chalupa, M., Chatterjee, K., Pavlogiannis, A., Sinha, N., Vaidya, K.: Data-centric dynamic partial order reduction. Proc. ACM Program. Lang. **2**(POPL), 31:1–31:30 (2017) https://doi.org/10.1145/3158119
16. Clarke, E.M., Jha, S., Enders, R., Filkorn, T.: Exploiting symmetry in temporal logic model checking. Form. Meth. Syst. Des. **9**(1/2), 77–104 (1996) https://doi.org/10.1007/BF00625969
17. Clarke, E., Kroening, D., Lerda, F.: A tool for checking ANSI-C programs. In: Jensen, K., Podelski, A. (eds.) TACAS 2004. LNCS, vol. 2988, pp. 168–176. Springer, Heidelberg (2004). https://doi.org/10.1007/978-3-540-24730-2_15
18. Conway, M.E.: Design of a separable transition-diagram compiler. Commun. ACM **6**(7), 396–408 (1963) https://doi.org/10.1145/366663.366704
19. Crossbeam: Flat combining #63. https://github.com/crossbeam-rs/crossbeam/issues/63. Accessed 29 Jan 2021
20. Emerson, E.A., Wahl, T.: Dynamic symmetry reduction. In: Halbwachs, N., Zuck, L.D. (eds.) TACAS 2005. LNCS, vol. 3440, pp. 382–396. Springer, Heidelberg (2005). https://doi.org/10.1007/978-3-540-31980-1_25
21. Flur, S., et al.: Modelling the ARMv8 architecture, operationally: concurrency and ISA. In: POPL 2016, pp. 608–621. ACM, St. Petersburg, FL, USA (2016). https://doi.org/10.1145/2837614.2837615

22. Gavrilenko, N., Ponce-de-León, H., Furbach, F., Heljanko, K., Meyer, R.: BMC for weak memory models: relation analysis for compact SMT encodings. In: Dillig, I., Tasiran, S. (eds.) CAV 2019. LNCS, vol. 11561, pp. 355–365. Springer, Cham (2019). https://doi.org/10.1007/978-3-030-25540-4_19
23. Godefroid, P.: Model checking for programming languages using VeriSoft. In: POPL 1997, pp. 174–186. ACM, Paris, France (1997). https://doi.org/10.1145/263699.263717
24. Jagadeesan, R., Jeffrey, A., Riely, J.: Pomsets with preconditions: a simple model of relaxed memory. Proc. ACM Program. Lang. 4(OOPSLA) (2020) https://doi.org/10.1145/3428262
25. Kang, J., Hur, C.-K., Lahav, O., Vafeiadis, V., Dreyer, D.: A promising semantics for relaxed-memory concurrency. In: POPL 2017, pp. 175–189. ACM, Paris, France (2017). https://doi.org/10.1145/3009837.3009850
26. Kokologiannakis, M., Kaysin, I., Raad, A., Vafeiadis, V.: PerSeVerE: persistency semantics for verification under ext4. Proc. ACM Program. Lang. 5(POPL) (2021) https://doi.org/10.1145/3434324
27. Kokologiannakis, M., Lahav, O., Sagonas, K., Vafeiadis, V.: Effective stateless model checking for C/C++ concurrency. Proc. ACM Program. Lang. 2(POPL), 17:1–17:32 (2017). https://doi.org/10.1145/3158105
28. Kokologiannakis, M., Raad, A., Vafeiadis, V.: Effective lock handling in stateless model checking. Proc. ACM Program. Lang. 3(OOPSLA) (2019). https://doi.org/10.1145/3360599
29. Kokologiannakis, M., Raad, A., Vafeiadis, V.: Model checking for weakly consistent libraries. In: PLDI 2019, ACM, New York (2019). https://doi.org/10.1145/3314221.3314609
30. Kokologiannakis, M., Vafeiadis, V.: BAM: Efficient Model Checking for Barriers. In: NETYS 2021, LNCS, Springer, Heidelberg (2021). https://plv.mpi-sws.org/genmc
31. Kokologiannakis, M., Vafeiadis, V.: HMC: Model checking for hardware memory models. In: ASPLOS 2020, pp. 1157–1171. ACM, Lausanne, Switzerland (2020). https://doi.org/10.1145/3373376.3378480
32. Lahav, O., Vafeiadis, V., Kang, J., Hur, C.-K., Dreyer, D.: Repairing sequential consistency in C/C++11. In: PLDI 2017, pp. 618–632. ACM, Barcelona, Spain (2017). https://doi.org/10.1145/3062341.3062352
33. Lee, S.-H., Cho, M., Podkopaev, A., Chakraborty, S., Hur, C.-K., Lahav, O., Vafeiadis, V.: Promising 2.0: Global optimizations in relaxed memory concurrency. In: Donaldson, A.F., Torlak, E. (eds.) PLDI 2020, pp. 362–376. ACM (2020). https://doi.org/10.1145/3385412.3386010
34. McKenney, P.E.: *Automatically generated litmus tests for validation LISA-language Linux-kernel memory models*(2021). https://github.com/paulmckrcu/litmus. Accessed: 28 Apr 2021
35. lli - directly execute programs from LLVM bitcode (2003). https://llvm.org/docs/CommandGuide/lli.html. Accessed 29 Jan 2021
36. Manson, J., Pugh, W., Adve, S.V.: The Java memory model. In: POPL 2005, pp. 378–391. ACM (2005). https://doi.org/10.1145/1040305.1040336
37. Musuvathi, M., Qadeer, S., Ball, T., Basler, G., Nainar, P.A., Neamtiu, I.: Finding and reproducing Heisenbugs in concurrent programs. In: OSDI 2008, pp. 267–280. USENIX Association (2008). https://www.usenix.org/legacy/events/osdi08/tech/full_papers/musuvathi/musuvathi.pdf

38. Norris, B., Demsky, B.: CDSChecker: Checking concurrent data structures written with C/C++ atomics. In: OOPSLA 2013, pp. 131–150. ACM (2013). https://doi.org/10.1145/2509136.2509514
39. Oberhauser, J., et al.: VSync: Push-Button Verification and Optimization for Synchronization Primitives on Weak Memory Models. In: ASPLOS 2021, pp. 530–545. ACM, Virtual, USA (2021). https://doi.org/10.1145/3445814.3446748
40. Owens, S., Sarkar, S., Sewell, P.: A better x86 memory model: x86-TSO. In: Berghofer, S., Nipkow, T., Urban, C., Wenzel, M. (eds.) TPHOLs 2009. LNCS, vol. 5674, pp. 391–407. Springer, Heidelberg (2009). https://doi.org/10.1007/978-3-642-03359-9_27
41. Podkopaev, A., Lahav, O., Vafeiadis, V.: Bridging the gap between programming languages and hardware weak memory models. Proc. ACM Program. Lang. 3(POPL), 69:1–69:31 (2019). https://doi.org/10.1145/3290382
42. SPARC International Inc., The SPARC architecture manual (version 9). Prentice-Hall (1994)
43. Vafeiadis, V., Balabonski, T., Chakraborty, S., Morisset, R., Zappa Nardelli, F.: Common compiler optimisations are invalid in the C11 memory model and what we can do about it. In: POPL 2015, pp. 209–220. ACM, Mumbai, India (2015). https://doi.org/10.1145/2676726.2676995

Hybrid and Cyber-Physical Systems

Synthesizing Invariant Barrier Certificates via Difference-of-Convex Programming

Qiuye Wang$^{1,2(\boxtimes)}$ ⓘ, Mingshuai Chen$^{3(\boxtimes)}$ ⓘ, Bai Xue$^{1,2(\boxtimes)}$ ⓘ,
Naijun Zhan$^{1,2(\boxtimes)}$ ⓘ, and Joost-Pieter Katoen$^{3(\boxtimes)}$ ⓘ

^{1} SKLCS, Institute of Software, CAS, Beijing, China
^{2} University of Chinese Academy of Sciences, Beijing, China
{wangqye,xuebai,znj}@ios.ac.cn
^{3} RWTH Aachen University, Aachen, Germany
{chenms,katoen}@cs.rwth-aachen.de

Abstract. A barrier certificate often serves as an inductive invariant that isolates an unsafe region from the reachable set of states, and hence is widely used in proving safety of hybrid systems possibly over the infinite time horizon. We present a novel condition on barrier certificates, termed the *invariant barrier-certificate condition*, that witnesses unbounded-time safety of differential dynamical systems. The proposed condition is by far the least conservative one on barrier certificates, and can be shown as the weakest possible one to attain inductive invariance. We show that discharging the invariant barrier-certificate condition—thereby synthesizing invariant barrier certificates—can be encoded as solving an *optimization problem subject to bilinear matrix inequalities* (BMIs). We further propose a synthesis algorithm based on difference-of-convex programming, which approaches a local optimum of the BMI problem via solving *a series of convex optimization problems*. This algorithm is incorporated in a branch-and-bound framework that searches for the global optimum in a divide-and-conquer fashion. We present a weak completeness result of our method, in the sense that a barrier certificate is guaranteed to be found (under some mild assumptions) whenever there exists an inductive invariant (in the form of a given template) that suffices to certify safety of the system. Experimental results on benchmark examples demonstrate the effectiveness and efficiency of our approach.

1 Introduction

Hybrid systems are mathematical models that capture the interaction between continuous physical dynamics and discrete switching behaviors, and hence are widely used in modelling cyber-physical systems (CPS). These CPS may be

This work has been partially funded by the NSFC under grant No. 61625206, 61732001, 61872341, and 61836005, by the ERC Advanced Project FRAPPANT under grant No. 787914, and by the CAS Pioneer Hundred Talents Program.

A. Silva and K. R. M. Leino (Eds.) CAV 2021, LNCS 12759, pp. 443–466, 2021.
https://doi.org/10.1007/978-3-030-81685-8_21

complex and safety-critical, with sensitive variables of the environment in its sphere of control. Everyday examples include process control at all scales, ranging from household appliances to nuclear power plants, or embedded systems in transportation domain, such as autonomous driving maneuvers in automotive, aircraft collision-avoidance protocols in avionics, or automatic train control applications, as well as a broad range of devices in health technologies, such as cardiac pacemakers.

The safety-critical feature of these CPS, with increasingly complex behaviors, has initiated automatic safety or, dually, reachability verification of hybrid systems [1,15]. The problem of reachability verification is undecidable in general [1], albeit with decidable families of sub-classes (see, e.g., [2,16–18,31]) identified in the literature. The hard core of the verification problem lies in reasoning about the continuous dynamics, which are often characterized by ordinary differential equations (ODEs). In particular, when nonlinearity arises in the ODEs, the explicit computation of the exact reachable set is usually intractable even for purely continuous dynamics [49].

Therefore in the literature, a plethora of approximation schemes, as surveyed in [15], for reachability analysis of hybrid systems has been developed, including an invariant-style reasoning scheme known as *barrier certificate* [41]. A barrier certificate often serves as an inductive invariant that isolates an unsafe region from the reachable set, thereby witnessing safety of hybrid systems possibly over the infinite time horizon. A common way to synthesize barrier certificates is to reduce the condition defining barrier certificates to a numerical optimization or constraint solving problem. There is, however, a trade-off between the expressiveness of the barrier-certificate condition and the efficiency in discharging the reduced constraints. Hence, to enable efficient algorithmic synthesis of barrier certificates via, e.g., linear programming (LP), second-order cone programming (SOCP), semidefinite programming (SDP) and interval analysis [11,30], the general condition on inductive invariance (that a barrier certificate defines an invariant, see [8,51]) has been strengthened into a spectrum of different shapes, e.g., [8,29,51,60,62]. It has been, nevertheless, a long-standing challenge *to find a barrier-certificate condition that is as weak as possible while admitting efficient synthesis algorithms*.

In this paper, we present a new condition on barrier certificates, termed the *invariant barrier-certificate condition*, based on the sufficient and necessary condition on being an inductive invariant [36]. Our invariant barrier-certificate condition is by far, to the best of our knowledge, the least conservative one on barrier certificates, and can be shown as the weakest possible one to attain inductive invariance. We show, by leveraging Putinar's Positivstellensatz [32], that discharging the invariant barrier-certificate condition —thereby synthesizing invariant barrier certificates— can be encoded as solving an optimization problem subject to *bilinear matrix inequalities* (BMIs). We further show that general bilinear matrix-valued functions can be decomposed as a difference of two psd-convex (extension of convexity to matrix-valued functions) functions using eigendecomposition, thus resulting in a synthesis algorithm as per *difference-of-convex programming* (DCP) [33,52], which solves a series of convex sub-problems (in the form of *linear matrix inequalities* (LMIs)) that approaches (arbitrarily close to) a local optimum of the BMI problem. This algorithm is incorporated in a branch-and-bound framework that searches for the global optimum in a divide-and-conquer fashion. We present a weak completeness result of our method, in the sense that a barrier certificate is guaranteed to be found (under some mild assumptions) whenever there exists an inductive invariant (in the form of a given template) that suffices to certify the system's safety. A similar result on completeness is previously provided only by symbolic approaches, yet to the best of our knowledge, not by methods base on numerical constraint solving, e.g., [4,60,61]. Experiments on a collection of examples suggested that our invariant barrier-certificate condition recognizes more barrier certificates than existing conditions, and that our DCP-based algorithm is more efficient than directly solving the BMIs via off-the-shelf solvers.

Due to space restrictions, proofs and benchmark details have been omitted; they are found in an extended version of this paper [57].

2   A Bird's-Eye Perspective

We use the following example to give a bird's-eye view of our approach.

*Example 1 (*overview [11]*).* Consider the following continuous-time dynamical system modelled by an ordinary differential equation:

$$\dot{\mathbf{x}} = \begin{pmatrix} \dot{x}_1 \\ \dot{x}_2 \end{pmatrix} = \begin{pmatrix} x_1 + x_2 \\ x_1 x_2 - 0.5 x_2^2 + 0.1 \end{pmatrix}.$$

The verification obligation is to show that the system trajectory originating from any state in the initial set $\mathcal{X}_0 = \{\mathbf{x} \mid \mathcal{I}(\mathbf{x}) \leq 0\}$ with $\mathcal{I}(\mathbf{x}) = x_1^2 + (x_2 - 2)^2 - 1$ will never enter the unsafe set $\mathcal{X}_u = \{\mathbf{x} \mid \mathcal{U}(\mathbf{x}) \leq 0\}$ with $\mathcal{U}(\mathbf{x}) = x_2 + 1$.   ◁

A barrier certificate satisfying our condition in Definition 4 serves as an inductive invariant that suffices to isolate the unsafe region $\mathcal{X}_u$ from the set of reachable states from $\mathcal{X}_0$, thereby proving safety of the system over the infinite time horizon. To this end, we proceed in the following steps.

1) Encode as Sum-of-Squares (SOS) Constraints. We set a (polynomial) barrier-certificate template $B(\mathbf{a}, \mathbf{x}) = a x_2$ with unknown coefficient $a \in \mathbb{R}$. According to Theorem 1, we only need to consider Lie derivatives up to order $N_{B,f} = 1$, i.e., $\mathcal{L}_f^0 B(\mathbf{a}, \mathbf{x}) = a x_2$ and $\mathcal{L}_f^1 B(\mathbf{a}, \mathbf{x}) = a(x_1 x_2 - 0.5 x_2^2 + 0.1)$.

By Theorem 5, $B(\mathbf{a}, \mathbf{x})$ is an invariant barrier certificate if there exists a polynomial $v(\mathbf{x})$, SOS polynomials $\sigma(\mathbf{x}), \sigma'(\mathbf{x})$ and a constant $\epsilon > 0$ such that

$$- \underbrace{a x_2}_{B} + \sigma(\mathbf{x}) \underbrace{(x_1^2 + (x_2 - 2)^2 - 1)}_{\mathcal{I}}, \qquad (1.1, \text{initial})$$

$$- a \underbrace{(x_1 x_2 - 0.5 x_2^2 + 0.1)}_{\mathcal{L}_f^1 B} + v(\mathbf{x}) \underbrace{a x_2}_{\mathcal{L}_f^0 B}, \qquad (1.2, \text{Lieconsecution})$$

$$\underbrace{a x_2}_{B} + \sigma'(\mathbf{x}) \underbrace{(x_2 + 1)}_{\mathcal{U}} - \epsilon \qquad (1.3, \text{separation})$$

are SOS polynomials. We set $\epsilon = 0.01$ in this example.

2) Reduce to a BMI Optimization Problem. Observe that the above SOS constraints can be formulated as BMI constraints. For instance, let us assume that (1.2) is an SOS polynomial of degree at most 2 and $v(\mathbf{s}, \mathbf{x}) = s_0 + s_1 x_1 + s_2 x_2$ is a template polynomial with unknown coefficients $\mathbf{s}$. Then constraint (1.2) is equivalent to the BMI constraint

$$\mathcal{F}_2(\mathbf{a}, \mathbf{s}) = - \begin{pmatrix} -0.1a & 0 & 0.5as_0 \\ 0 & 0 & 0.5(as_1 - a) \\ 0.5as_0 & 0.5(as_1 - a) & as_2 + 0.5a \end{pmatrix} \preceq 0$$

meaning that the bilinear matrix (LHS of $\preceq$) is negative semidefinite. Note that the bilinearity arises due to the coupling of the unknown coefficients $\mathbf{a}$ and $\mathbf{s}$.

Constraints (1.1) and (1.3) can be reduced to BMI constraints in an analogous way[1], yielding $\mathcal{F}_1$ and $\mathcal{F}_3$. It then follows that, to solve the SOS constraints, we need to find a feasible solution $(\mathbf{a}, \mathbf{s})$ such that[2]

$$\mathcal{F}_1(\mathbf{a}, \mathbf{s}) \preceq 0 \wedge \mathcal{F}_2(\mathbf{a}, \mathbf{s}) \preceq 0 \wedge \mathcal{F}_3(\mathbf{a}, \mathbf{s}) \preceq 0. \tag{2}$$

To exploit well-developed optimization techniques, the feasibility problem (2) is transformed to an optimization problem subject to BMI constraints:

$$\begin{aligned} \underset{\lambda, \mathbf{a}, \mathbf{s}}{\text{maximize}} \quad & \lambda \\ \text{subject to} \quad & \mathcal{B}_i(\lambda, \mathbf{a}, \mathbf{s}) \mathrel{\hat{=}} \mathcal{F}_i(\mathbf{a}, \mathbf{s}) + \lambda I \preceq 0, \quad i = 1, 2, 3 \end{aligned} \tag{3}$$

where I is the identity matrix with compatible dimensions. Note that problem (2) has a feasible solution if and only if the optimal value λ^* in (3) is non-negative.

3) Decompose as Difference-of-Convex Problems. The problem (3) contains non-convex constraints and hence does not admit efficient (polynomial-time) algorithms tailored for convex optimizations. However, by our technique presented in Sect. 5, a non-convex function $\mathcal{B}_i(\lambda, \mathbf{a}, \mathbf{s})$ can be decomposed as the difference of two psd-convex (defined later) matrix-valued functions:

$$\mathcal{B}_i(\lambda, \mathbf{a}, \mathbf{s}) = \mathcal{B}_i^+(\lambda, \mathbf{a}, \mathbf{s}) - \mathcal{B}_i^-(\lambda, \mathbf{a}, \mathbf{s}). \tag{4}$$

The decomposition of $\mathcal{B}_2(\lambda, \mathbf{a}, \mathbf{s})$, for instance, gives

$\mathcal{B}_2^+(\lambda, \mathbf{a}, \mathbf{s}) =$

$$\frac{1}{8} \begin{pmatrix} 8\lambda + 0.08a + a^2 + 0.408s_0^2 & 0.408s_0s_1 & -2as_0 + 0.816s_0s_2 \\ 0.408s_0s_1 & 8\lambda + a^2 + 0.408s_1^2 & 4a - 2as_1 + 0.816s_1s_2 \\ -2as_0 + 0.816s_0s_2 & 4a - 2as_1 + 0.816s_1s_2 & 8\lambda - 4a + 2.449a^2 - 4as_2 + s_0^2 + s_1^2 + 1.632s_2^2 \end{pmatrix}$$

$\mathcal{B}_2^-(\lambda, \mathbf{a}, \mathbf{s}) =$

$$\frac{1}{8} \begin{pmatrix} a^2 + 0.408s_0^2 & 0.408s_0s_1 & 2as_0 + 0.816s_0s_2 \\ 0.408s_0s_1 & a^2 + 0.408s_1^2 & 2as_1 + 0.816s_1s_2 \\ 2as_0 + 0.816s_0s_2 & 2as_1 + 0.816s_1s_2 & 2.449a^2 + 4as_2 + s_0^2 + s_1^2 + 1.632s_2^2 \end{pmatrix}.$$

---

[1] Despite that no bilinearity is involved in constraints (1.1) and (1.3), they can be processed in the same way as (1.2), yielding LMI constraints.

[2] Extra constraints on $\sigma(\mathbf{x})$ and $\sigma'(\mathbf{x})$ being SOS polynomials can be encoded analogously in the feasibility problem, yet are omitted here for the sake of simplicity.

4) Solve a Series of Convex Sub-problems. Now, we apply a standard iterative procedure in difference-of-convex programming [10] as follows. Given a feasible solution $\mathbf{z}^k = (\lambda^k, \mathbf{a}^k, \mathbf{s}^k)$ to the BMI optimization problem (3), the concave part $-\mathcal{B}_i^-(\lambda, \mathbf{a}, \mathbf{s})$ in (4) is linearized around $\mathbf{z}^k$, thus yielding a series of convex programs ($k = 0, 1, \ldots$):

$$\begin{aligned} \underset{\lambda, \mathbf{a}, \mathbf{s}}{\text{maximize}} \quad & \lambda \\ \text{subject to} \quad & \mathcal{B}_i^+(\mathbf{z}) - \mathcal{B}_i^-\left(\mathbf{z}^k\right) - \mathcal{D}\mathcal{B}_i^-\left(\mathbf{z}^k\right)\left(\mathbf{z} - \mathbf{z}^k\right) \preceq 0, \quad i = 1, 2, 3 \quad (5) \end{aligned}$$

where $\mathcal{D}\mathcal{B}_i^-$ denotes the derivative of the matrix-valued function $\mathcal{B}_i^-$.

The soundness of our approach asserts that the feasible set of the linearized program (5) under-approximates the feasible set of the original BMI program (3). Therefore, if $\lambda^k \geq 0$ after iteration k, we can safely claim that $(\mathbf{a}^k, \mathbf{s}^k)$ is a feasible solution to (2). A barrier certificate $B(\mathbf{x})$ is then obtained by substituting $\mathbf{a}^k$ in $B(\mathbf{a}, \mathbf{x})$. Moreover, if we take the optimum $\mathbf{z}^{*,k}$ of (5) to be the next linearization point $\mathbf{z}^{k+1}$, the solution sequence $\{\mathbf{z}^k\}_{k \in \mathbb{N}}$ converges to a local optimum of (3).

We show that the linearized program (5) is equivalent to an LMI optimization problem admitting polynomial-time algorithms, say the well-known *interior-point methods* supported by most off-the-shelf SDP solvers. Our iterative procedure starts with a strictly feasible initial solution $\mathbf{z}^0$ to program (3) and terminates with $\lambda^2 \geq 0$ (subject to numerical round-off) and $a^2 = -0.00363421$, yielding the barrier certificate

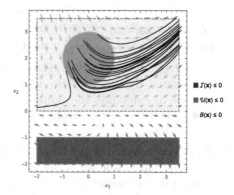

$$B(\mathbf{a}^2, \mathbf{x}) = -0.00363421x_2 \leq 0.$$

Figure 1 depicts the system dynamics and the synthesized barrier certificate.

We remark that the aforementioned

Fig. 1. Phase portrait of the system in Example 1. The arrows indicate the vector field and the solid curves are randomly sampled trajectories.

iterative procedure on solving a series of convex optimizations converges only to a local optimum of the BMI problem (3). This means that, in some cases, it may miss the global optimum that induces a non-negative λ^*. We will present in Sect. 6 a solution to this problem by incorporating our iterative procedure into a branch-and-bound framework that searches for the global optimum in a divide-and-conquer fashion.

3   Mathematical Foundations

Notations. Let $\mathbb{N}, \mathbb{N}^+, \mathbb{R}, \mathbb{R}^+$ and $\mathbb{R}_0^+$ be respectively the set of natural, positive natural, real, positive real and non-negative real numbers. For a vector $\mathbf{x} \in \mathbb{R}^n$, x_i refers to its i-th component and $\|\mathbf{x}\|$ denotes the ℓ^2-norm; for a matrix $A \in$

$\mathbb{R}^{n \times m}$, $A(i, j)$ refers to its (i, j)-th element. Let $\mathbb{R}[\mathbf{x}]$ be the polynomial ring in $\mathbf{x}$ over the field $\mathbb{R}$. A polynomial $h \in \mathbb{R}[\mathbf{x}]$ is *sum-of-squares* (SOS) iff there exist polynomials $g_1, \ldots, g_k \in \mathbb{R}[\mathbf{x}]$ such that $h = \sum_{i=1}^{k} g_i^2$. We denote by $\Sigma[\mathbf{x}] \subset \mathbb{R}[\mathbf{x}]$ the set of SOS polynomials over $\mathbf{x}x$. $\mathcal{S}^n$ denotes the space of $n \times n$ real, symmetric matrices. For $A \in \mathcal{S}^n$, $A \succeq 0$ means that A is *positive semidefinite* (psd, for short)[3], i.e., $\forall \mathbf{x} \in \mathbb{R}^n \colon \mathbf{x}^{\mathsf{T}} A \mathbf{x} \geq 0$. A matrix-valued function $\mathcal{B} \colon \mathbb{R}^n \to \mathcal{S}^m$ is *psd-convex* on a convex set $\mathcal{C} \subseteq \mathbb{R}^n$ if $\forall \mathbf{x}_1, \mathbf{x}_2 \in \mathcal{C}. \forall \mu \in (0, 1) \colon \mathcal{B}(\mu \mathbf{x}_1 + (1 - \mu) \mathbf{x}_2) \preceq \mu \mathcal{B}(\mathbf{x}_1) + (1 - \mu) \mathcal{B}(\mathbf{x}_2)$.

Differential Dynamical Systems. We consider a class of continuous dynamical systems modelled by ordinary differential equations of the autonomous type:

$$\dot{\mathbf{x}} = \boldsymbol{f}(\mathbf{x}) \tag{6}$$

where $\mathbf{x} \in \mathbb{R}^n$ is the *state* vector, $\dot{\mathbf{x}}$ denotes its temporal derivative $d\mathbf{x}/dt$, with $t \in \mathbb{R}_0^+$ modelling time, and $\boldsymbol{f} \colon \mathbb{R}^n \to \mathbb{R}^n$ is a polynomial *flow field* (or *vector field*) that governs the evolution of the system. A polynomial vector field is local Lipschitz, and hence for some $T \in \mathbb{R}^+ \cup \{\infty\}$, there exists a unique *solution* (or *trajectory*) $\boldsymbol{\zeta}_{\mathbf{x}_0} \colon [0, T) \to \mathbb{R}^n$ originating from any initial state $\mathbf{x}_0 \in \mathbb{R}^n$ such that (1) $\boldsymbol{\zeta}_{\mathbf{x}_0}(0) = \mathbf{x}_0$, and (2) $\forall \tau \in [0, T) \colon \frac{d\boldsymbol{\zeta}_{\mathbf{x}_0}}{dt}\big|_{t=\tau} = \boldsymbol{f}(\boldsymbol{\zeta}_{\mathbf{x}_0}(\tau))$. We assume in the sequel that T is the maximal instant up to which $\boldsymbol{\zeta}_{\mathbf{x}_0}$ exists for all $\mathbf{x}_0$.

Remark 1. Our techniques on synthesizing barrier certificates in this paper focus on differential dynamics of the form (6). However, we foresee no substantial difficulties in extending the results to multi-mode hybrid systems where extra constraints on the system evolution, e.g., guards, are present.

Safety Verification Problem. Given a domain set $\mathcal{X} \subseteq \mathbb{R}^n$, an initial set $\mathcal{X}_0 \subseteq \mathcal{X}$ and an unsafe set $\mathcal{X}_u \subseteq \mathcal{X}$, the *reachable set* of a dynamical system of the form (6) at time instant $t \in [0, T)$ is defined as $\mathcal{R}_{\mathcal{X}_0}(t) \triangleq \{\boldsymbol{\zeta}_{\mathbf{x}_0}(t) \mid \mathbf{x}_0 \in \mathcal{X}_0\}$. We denote by $\mathcal{R}_{\mathcal{X}_0}$ the aggregated reachable set, i.e., the union of $\mathcal{R}_{\mathcal{X}_0}(t)$ over $t \in [0, T)$[4]. The system is said to be *safe* iff $\mathcal{R}_{\mathcal{X}_0} \cap \mathcal{X}_u = \emptyset$, and *unsafe* otherwise. For simplicity, we consider $\mathcal{X} = \mathbb{R}^n$ throughout this paper.

To avoid the explicit computation of the exact reachable set, which is usually intractable for nonlinear hybrid systems (cf., e.g., [15]), barrier-certificate methods make use of a partial differential operator, termed the *Lie derivative*, to capture the evolution of a barrier function along the vector field:

Definition 1 (Lie Derivative [28]). *Given a vector field $\boldsymbol{f} \colon \mathbb{R}^n \to \mathbb{R}^n$ over $\mathbf{x}$, the Lie derivative of a polynomial function $B(\mathbf{x})$ along $\boldsymbol{f}$, $\mathcal{L}_{\boldsymbol{f}}^k B \colon \mathbb{R}^n \to \mathbb{R}$ of order $k \in \mathbb{N}$, is*

$$\mathcal{L}_{\boldsymbol{f}}^k B(\mathbf{x}) \triangleq \begin{cases} B(\mathbf{x}), & k = 0, \\ \left\langle \frac{\partial}{\partial \mathbf{x}} \mathcal{L}_{\boldsymbol{f}}^{k-1} B(\mathbf{x}), \boldsymbol{f}(\mathbf{x}) \right\rangle, & k > 0 \end{cases}$$

---

[3] More generally, for $A, B \in \mathcal{S}^n$, $A \preceq B$ indicates that $B - A$ is positive semidefinite.
[4] This subsumes the problem of unbounded-time safety verification where a unique solution exists over the infinite time horizon $[0, \infty)$.

where $\langle \cdot, \cdot \rangle$ is the inner product of vectors, i.e., $\langle \mathbf{u}, \mathbf{v} \rangle \triangleq \sum_{i=1}^{n} u_i v_i$ for $\mathbf{u}, \mathbf{v} \in \mathbb{R}^n$.

The Lie derivative $\mathcal{L}_f^k B(\mathbf{x})$ is essentially the k-th temporal derivative of the (barrier) function $B(\mathbf{x})$, and thus captures the change of $B(\mathbf{x})$ over time.

An *inductive invariant* $\Psi \subseteq \mathbb{R}^n$ of a dynamical system is a set of states such that all the trajectories starting from within Ψ remain in Ψ:

Definition 2 (Inductive Iinvariant [40]). *Given a system (6), a set $\Psi \subseteq \mathbb{R}^n$ is an* inductive invariant *of system (6) if and only if*

$$\forall \mathbf{x}_0 \in \Psi. \forall t \in [0, T): \boldsymbol{\zeta}_{\mathbf{x}_0}(t) \in \Psi. \tag{7}$$

In the sequel, we refer to inductive invariants simply as invariants. In [36], a sufficient and necessary condition on being a polynomial invariant is proposed:

Theorem 1 (Invariant condition [36]). *Given a polynomial $B \in \mathbb{R}[\mathbf{x}]$, its zero sub-level set $\{\mathbf{x} \mid B(\mathbf{x}) \leq 0\}$ is an invariant of system (6) if and only if [5]*

$$B \leq 0 \implies \bigvee_{i=0}^{N_{B,f}} \left(\left(\bigwedge_{j=0}^{i-1} \mathcal{L}_f^j B = 0 \right) \wedge \mathcal{L}_f^i B < 0 \right) \vee \bigwedge_{i=0}^{N_{B,f}} \mathcal{L}_f^i B = 0 \tag{8}$$

where $N_{B,f} \in \mathbb{N}^+$ is a completeness threshold, i.e., a finite positive integer that bounds the order of Lie derivatives, which can be computed using Gröbner bases[6].

In contrast, a *barrier certificate* is a function whose zero sub-level set isolates an unsafe region $\mathcal{X}_u$ from the reachable set $\mathcal{R}_{\mathcal{X}_0}$ w.r.t. some initial set $\mathcal{X}_0$:

Definition 3 (Semantic Barrier Certificate [51]). *Given a system (6), an initial set $\mathcal{X}_0$ and an unsafe set $\mathcal{X}_u$, a* barrier certificate *of (6) is a differentiable function $B: \mathbb{R}^n \to \mathbb{R}$ satisfying*

$$\forall \mathbf{x}_0 \in \mathcal{X}_0. \forall t \in [0, T): B(\boldsymbol{\zeta}_{\mathbf{x}_0}(t)) \leq 0 \quad \text{and} \quad \forall \mathbf{x} \in \mathcal{X}_u: B(\mathbf{x}) > 0. \tag{9}$$

The existence of such a barrier certificate trivially implies safety of the system. Moreover, one may readily verify that if some set $\Psi = \{\mathbf{x} \mid B(\mathbf{x}) \leq 0\}$ is an invariant and satisfies $(\mathcal{X}_0 \subseteq \Psi) \wedge (\Psi \cap \mathcal{X}_u = \emptyset)$, then $B(\mathbf{x})$ is a barrier certificate.

As observed in [51], however, the semantic statement in Definition 3 encodes merely the general *principle of barrier certificates* [8], yet in itself is not that useful for safety verification because it explicitly involves the system solutions. Therefore, in order to enable efficient synthesis, the semantic condition on barrier certificates has been strengthened into a handful of different shapes (see, e.g., [8, 29,41,60], which all imply inductive invariance). It has been yet a long-standing challenge *to find a barrier-certificate condition that is as weak as possible while admitting efficient synthesis algorithms.*

Our BMI encoding of the invariant barrier-certificate condition (cf. Sect. 4) roots in Putinar's Positivstellensatz, which characterizes positivity of polynomials on a semi-algebraic set defined by a system of polynomial inequalities:

---

[5] In (8), $\bigwedge_{j=0}^{i-1} \mathcal{L}_f^j B = 0$ is true for $i = 0$ by default. This applies in the sequel.

[6] $N_{B,f}$ is the minimal i such that $\mathcal{L}_f^{i+1} B$ is in the polynomial ideal generated by $\mathcal{L}_f^0 B, \mathcal{L}_f^1 B, \dots, \mathcal{L}_f^i B$. The ideal membership can be decided via Gröbner basis.

Theorem 2 (Putinar's Positivstellensatz [32]). *Let* $\mathcal{K} = \{\mathbf{x} \mid \bigwedge_{i=1}^{m} g_i(\mathbf{x}) \geq 0\}$ *be a compact semi-algebraic set defined by* $g_1, \ldots, g_m \in \mathbb{R}[\mathbf{x}]$. *Assume the Archimedean condition holds[7], i.e., there exists* $L \in \mathbb{R}^+$ *such that* $L - \|\mathbf{x}\|^2 = \sigma_0(\mathbf{x}) + \sum_{i=1}^{m} \sigma_i(\mathbf{x}) g_i(\mathbf{x})$ *for some* $\sigma_0, \ldots, \sigma_m \in \Sigma[\mathbf{x}]$. *If* $h \in \mathbb{R}[\mathbf{x}]$ *is strictly positive on* $\mathcal{K}$, *then*

$$h(\mathbf{x}) = \sigma_0(\mathbf{x}) + \sum_{i=1}^{m} \sigma_i(\mathbf{x}) g_i(\mathbf{x})$$

holds for some SOS polynomials $\sigma_0, \ldots, \sigma_m \in \Sigma[\mathbf{x}]$.

We now recall a key technique used in our reduction to semidefinite optimizations. Given a symmetric matrix $X \in \mathcal{S}^n$ partitioned as $X = \begin{pmatrix} A & C \\ C^\mathsf{T} & D \end{pmatrix}$ with invertible A, the *Schur complement* of A in X is defined as $X/A \triangleq D - C^\mathsf{T} A^{-1} C$. An important property of the Schur complement X/A is that it characterizes the positive semidefiniteness of the block matrix X:

Theorem 3 (Schur Complement [3]). *If* $A \succ 0$, *then* $X \succeq 0$ *iff* $X/A \succeq 0$.

We apply the Schur complement in Sect. 5 to transform nonlinear convex constraints into linear constraints.

4 Invariant Barrier-Certificate Condition as BMIs

In this section, we present our *invariant barrier-certificate condition* (see Definition 4) based on the necessary and sufficient condition on being an inductive invariant (cf. Theorem 1), and show how to encode it as BMI constraints.

4.1 Invariant Barrier-Certificate Condition

Definition 4 (Invariant Barrier Certificate). *Given a system* (6), *an initial set* $\mathcal{X}_0$ *and an unsafe set* $\mathcal{X}_u$, *a polynomial function* $B \colon \mathbb{R}^n \to \mathbb{R}$ *is an invariant barrier certificate of system* (6) *if and only if*

1. *(initial):* $\forall \mathbf{x} \in \mathcal{X}_0 \colon B(\mathbf{x}) \leq 0$;
2. *(consecution):* $\forall \mathbf{x} \in \mathbb{R}^n \colon \bigwedge_{i=1}^{N_{B,f}} \left(\left(\bigwedge_{j=0}^{i-1} \mathcal{L}_f^j B(\mathbf{x}) = 0 \right) \implies \mathcal{L}_f^i B(\mathbf{x}) \leq 0 \right)$;
3. *(separation):* $\forall \mathbf{x} \in \mathcal{X}_u \colon B(\mathbf{x}) > 0$.

Notice that the consecution constraint in Definition 4 involves Lie derivatives of orders up to $N_{B,f} \in \mathbb{N}^+$, as is the case in Theorem 1. Our invariant barrier-certificate condition hence generalizes existing conditions on barrier certificates, e.g., [4,60,63], which consider Lie derivatives only up to the first order.

The consecution condition in Definition 4 is in fact equivalent to the invariant condition (8) in Theorem 1 (cf. [57, Lemma 2]), thereby revealing the relation between an inductive invariant and an invariant barrier certificate:

---

[7] This condition can be met by adding a (redundant) constraint $g_{m+1}(\mathbf{x}) = L_0 - \|\mathbf{x}\|^2 \leq 0$, provided that a bound $L_0 \in \mathbb{R}^+$ is known such that $\forall \mathbf{x} \in \mathcal{K} \colon L_0 - \|\mathbf{x}\|^2 \geq 0$.

Theorem 4 (Inductive Invariance). *Given a system* (6), *an initial set* $\mathcal{X}_0$ *and an unsafe set* $\mathcal{X}_u$. *If* $B(\mathbf{x})$ *is an invariant barrier certificate, then* $\Psi = \{\mathbf{x} \mid B(\mathbf{x}) \leq 0\}$ *is an invariant. Conversely, if* $\Psi = \{\mathbf{x} \mid B(\mathbf{x}) \leq 0\}$ *is an invariant satisfying* $\mathcal{X}_0 \subseteq \Psi$ *and* $\Psi \cap \mathcal{X}_u = \emptyset$, *then* $B(\mathbf{x})$ *is an invariant barrier certificate.*

It follows from Theorem 4 that our invariant barrier-certificate condition is the least conservative one on barrier certificates to attain inductive invariance.

Remark 2. We do not employ the invariant condition (8) in Theorem 1 as the constraint on the consecution of Lie derivatives. This is because our consecution condition in Definition 4 is simpler, and in particular, amenable to more straightforward transformations to SOS constraints via Putinar's Positivstellensatz, as shown later in Subsect. 4.2.

Remark 3. For a fixed $0 < \mathfrak{N} < N_{B,f}$, the consecution condition in Definition 4 can be strengthened in the following way while preserving inductive invariance:

$$\forall \mathbf{x} \in \mathbb{R}^n : \bigwedge_{i=1}^{\mathfrak{N}-1} \left(\left(\bigwedge_{j=0}^{i-1} \mathcal{L}_f^j B(\mathbf{x}) = 0 \right) \implies \mathcal{L}_f^i B(\mathbf{x}) \leq 0 \right) \wedge$$
$$\left(\left(\bigwedge_{j=0}^{\mathfrak{N}-1} \mathcal{L}_f^j B(\mathbf{x}) = 0 \right) \implies \mathcal{L}_f^{\mathfrak{N}} B(\mathbf{x}) < 0 \right)$$

where for the $\mathfrak{N}$-th Lie derivative, one needs $\mathcal{L}_f^{\mathfrak{N}} B(\mathbf{x}) < 0$ (rather than $\mathcal{L}_f^{\mathfrak{N}} B(\mathbf{x}) \leq 0$). In practice, using such a strengthened consecution condition —with less subconstraints to solve— may yield more efficient synthesis.

4.2 Encoding as BMI Optimizations

Next, we show how to encode synthesizing an invariant barrier certificate (cf. Definition 4) as an optimization problem subject to BMIs. To this end, we first recast the invariant barrier-certificate condition into a collection of SOS constraints[8].

Theorem 5 (Sufficient Condition for Invariant Barrier Certificate). *Given a system* (6), *an initial set* $\mathcal{X}_0 = \{\mathbf{x} \mid \mathcal{I}(\mathbf{x}) \leq 0\}$ *and an unsafe set* $\mathcal{X}_u = \{\mathbf{x} \mid \mathcal{U}(\mathbf{x}) \leq 0\}$. *A polynomial* $B \in \mathbb{R}[\mathbf{x}]$ *is an invariant barrier certificate of* (6) *if for some* $\epsilon \in \mathbb{R}^+$, *there exist* $v_{i,j} \in \mathbb{R}[\mathbf{x}]$ *and SOS polynomials* $\sigma(\mathbf{x}), \sigma'(\mathbf{x})$ *s.t.*

1. $-B(\mathbf{x}) + \sigma(\mathbf{x})\mathcal{I}(\mathbf{x})$,
2. *for all* $1 \leq i \leq N_{B,f}$, $-\mathcal{L}_f^i B(\mathbf{x}) + \sum_{j=0}^{i-1} v_{i,j}(\mathbf{x})\mathcal{L}_f^j B(\mathbf{x})$,
3. $B(\mathbf{x}) + \sigma'(\mathbf{x})\mathcal{U}(\mathbf{x}) - \epsilon$

are SOS polynomials.

By enforcing the Archimedean condition and applying Putinar's Positivstellensatz, we further derive a necessary condition of invariant barrier certificate:

---

[8] For simplicity, we assume that $\mathcal{X}_0$ and $\mathcal{X}_u$ are both captured by a single polynomial. Our formulations, however, apply also to cases with basic semi-algebraic $\mathcal{X}_0$ or $\mathcal{X}_u$.

Theorem 6 (Necessary Condition for Invariant Barrier Certificate).
Given a system (6), *an initial set* $\mathcal{X}_0 = \{\mathbf{x} \mid \mathcal{I}(\mathbf{x}) \leq 0\}$ *and an unsafe set* $\mathcal{X}_u = \{\mathbf{x} \mid \mathcal{U}(\mathbf{x}) \leq 0\}$. *If* $B \in \mathbb{R}[\mathbf{x}]$ *is an invariant barrier certificate of* (6), *then for some* $\epsilon \in \mathbb{R}^+$, *there exist* $v_{i,j} \in \mathbb{R}[\mathbf{x}]$ *and SOS polynomials* $\sigma(\mathbf{x}), \sigma'(\mathbf{x}), \rho(\mathbf{x}), \rho'(\mathbf{x}), \rho_i''(\mathbf{x})$ *s.t. for any* $L \in \mathbb{R}^+$,

1. $-B(\mathbf{x}) + \rho(\mathbf{x})(\|\mathbf{x}\|^2 - L) + \sigma(\mathbf{x})\mathcal{I}(\mathbf{x}) + \epsilon$,
2. *for all* $1 \leq i \leq N_{B,f}$, $-\mathcal{L}_f^i B(\mathbf{x}) + \rho_i''(\mathbf{x})(\|\mathbf{x}\|^2 - L) + \sum_{j=0}^{i-1} v_{i,j}(\mathbf{x})\mathcal{L}_f^j B(\mathbf{x}) + \epsilon$,
3. $B(\mathbf{x}) + \rho'(\mathbf{x})(\|\mathbf{x}\|^2 - L) + \sigma'(\mathbf{x})\mathcal{U}(\mathbf{x})$

are SOS polynomials.

Notice that a polynomial $B(\mathbf{x})$ satisfying the sufficient condition in Theorem 5 suffices as an invariant barrier certificate that witnesses safety of the system. In contrast, a polynomial $B(\mathbf{x})$ satisfying the necessary condition in Theorem 6 may serve as a candidate invariant barrier certificate, and safety of the system can be concluded via a posterior check[9] of $B(\mathbf{x})$ per Definition 4.

Next we show how to encode an SOS constraint of the shape "$h(\mathbf{x}) \in \Sigma[\mathbf{x}]$" in Theorems 5 and 6 as a BMI constraint. To this end, we first set a *template polynomial*[10] $B(\mathbf{a}, \mathbf{x})$ parameterized by unknown real coefficients $\mathbf{a}$ as the barrier certificate. We then proceed by setting templates for the remaining unknown polynomials (e.g., $v_{i,j}(\mathbf{x})$) and SOS polynomials (e.g., $\sigma(\mathbf{x})$ and $\rho(\mathbf{x})$) in $h(\mathbf{x})$, with all the parameters in these templates grouped into $\mathbf{s}$. Observe that the parameterized SOS polynomial $h(\mathbf{a}, \mathbf{s}, \mathbf{x})$ is of a bilinear form on the parameter spaces, i.e., $h(\mathbf{a}, \mathbf{s}, \mathbf{x})$ is linear in $\mathbf{a}$ and $\mathbf{s}$ separately. However, nonlinearity arises in the combined parameter space $(\mathbf{a}, \mathbf{s})$ due to the product couplings of $\mathbf{a}$ and $\mathbf{s}$, i.e., $v_{i,j}(\mathbf{s}_{i,j}, \mathbf{x})\mathcal{L}_f^j B(\mathbf{a}, \mathbf{x})$ in the consecution constraint.

Now the problem of synthesizing an invariant barrier certificate boils down to searching for an instantiation of the parameters $\mathbf{a}$ and $\mathbf{s}$ such that the sufficient condition in Theorem 5 holds (or alternatively, the necessary condition in Theorem 6 holds and the posterior check passed). Such an instantiation of $\mathbf{a}$ (making $B(\mathbf{a}, \mathbf{x})$ an invariant barrier certificate) will be called *valid* in the sequel.

Suppose that a parameterized SOS polynomial $h(\mathbf{a}, \mathbf{s}, \mathbf{x})$ is of degree at most $2d$, with user-specified $d \in \mathbb{N}$. Then $h(\mathbf{a}, \mathbf{s}, \mathbf{x})$ can always be written in *quadratic form* as $h(\mathbf{a}, \mathbf{s}, \mathbf{x}) = \mathbf{b}^\mathsf{T} Q(\mathbf{a}, \mathbf{s})\mathbf{b}$, where $\mathbf{b} = (1, x_1, x_2, x_1 x_2, \ldots, x_n^d)$ is the *basis vector* of size $p = \binom{n+d}{n}$ containing all monomials of degree up to d, and $Q(\mathbf{a}, \mathbf{s}) \in \mathcal{S}^p$ is a parameterized real symmetric matrix known as the *Gram matrix* [6][11]. An important fact states that $h(\mathbf{a}, \mathbf{s}, \mathbf{x})$ is SOS if and only if $Q(\mathbf{a}, \mathbf{s}) \succeq 0$.

Let $\mathcal{F}(\mathbf{a}, \mathbf{s}) = -Q(\mathbf{a}, \mathbf{s})$. As per $h(\mathbf{a}, \mathbf{s}, \mathbf{x})$, the matrix-valued function $\mathcal{F}(\mathbf{a}, \mathbf{s})$ is bilinear in $(\mathbf{a}, \mathbf{s})$. Observe that $h(\mathbf{a}, \mathbf{s}, \mathbf{x})$ *is SOS if and only if the BMI constraint* $\mathcal{F}(\mathbf{a}, \mathbf{s}) \preceq 0$ *holds.* See Example 1 for an illustration of this BMI encoding.

---

[9] Such a check inherits decidability of the first-order theory of real-closed fields [53].

[10] A template polynomial $g(\mathbf{a}, \mathbf{x})$ is required to be linear in its parameters $\mathbf{a}$.

[11] Extracting the Gram matrix amounts to solving a system of linear equations resulting from coefficient matching. The derived Gram matrix may contain extra unknowns if the system of linear equations admits multiple solutions, which nevertheless can be encoded in our subsequent workflow by enumerating the basis of its null space.

In general, $\mathcal{F}(\mathbf{a}, \mathbf{s})$ can be flattened in an expanded bilinear form as

$$\mathcal{F}(\mathbf{a}, \mathbf{s}) = F + \sum_{i=1}^{m} a_i H_i + \sum_{j=1}^{n} s_j G_j + \sum_{i=1}^{m} \sum_{j=1}^{n} a_i s_j F_{i,j}$$

where m and n are the size of $\mathbf{a}$ and $\mathbf{s}$, respectively; $F, H_i, G_j, F_{i,j} \in \mathcal{S}^p$ are constant matrices. Discharging the conditions of invariant barrier certificates hence amounts to solving the BMI feasibility problem of finding $\mathbf{a}$ and $\mathbf{s}$ s.t.

$$\mathcal{F}_\iota(\mathbf{a}, \mathbf{s}) \preceq 0, \quad \iota = 1, 2, \ldots, l. \tag{10}$$

Here $\mathcal{F}(\mathbf{a}, \mathbf{s})$ is indexed by ι and l is the number of SOS constraints involved.

To exploit well-developed techniques in optimization, the feasibility problem (10) is transformed to an optimization problem subject to BMI constraints:

$$\begin{aligned} \underset{\lambda, \mathbf{a}, \mathbf{s}}{\text{maximize}} \quad & \lambda \\ \text{subject to} \quad & \mathcal{F}_\iota(\mathbf{a}, \mathbf{s}) + \lambda I \preceq 0, \quad \iota = 1, 2, \ldots, l. \end{aligned} \tag{11}$$

A solution $(\lambda, \mathbf{a}, \mathbf{s})$ to (11) is *feasible* if it satisfies the BMIs in (11), and *strictly feasible* if all the BMIs are satisfied with strict inequalities. We sometimes drop the λ component in the solution when it is clear from the context. Notice that *problem (10) has a feasible solution if and only if the optimal value λ^* in the BMI optimization problem (11) is non-negative.*

To achieve (weak) completeness of our method in subsequent sections on solving the BMI optimization problem, we make the following assumption on the boundedness of the search space $(\mathbf{a}, \mathbf{s})$ of the optimization.

Assumption 1 (Boundedness on the Parameters). *Every feasible solution* $(\mathbf{a}, \mathbf{s})$ *to the BMI problem (11) is in a compact set with non-empty interior, i.e.,*

$$(\mathbf{a}, \mathbf{s}) \in \mathcal{C}_\mathbf{a} \times \mathcal{C}_\mathbf{s} = \left\{ (\mathbf{a}, \mathbf{s}) \mid \|\mathbf{a}\|^2 \leq L_\mathbf{a}, \|\mathbf{s}\|^2 \leq L_\mathbf{s} \right\}$$

for some known bounds $L_\mathbf{a}, L_\mathbf{s} \in \mathbb{R}^+$.

Remark 4. The boundedness on $\mathbf{a}$ in Assumption 1 makes sense in practice since we usually prefer barrier certificates with bounded coefficients. Moreover, when the bilinear functions $\mathcal{F}_\iota(\mathbf{a}, \mathbf{s})$ in (11) are affine in $\mathbf{a}$ and $\mathbf{s}$, i.e., with a zero constant matrix F, the parameters $\mathbf{a}$ and $\mathbf{s}$ can be scaled independently by any positive factor. Therefore in this case, w.l.o.g, one may simply set $L_\mathbf{a} = L_\mathbf{s} = 1$.

5 Solving BMI Optimizations via DCP

The BMI optimization problem (11), derived from the synthesis problem, is known to be NP-hard and contains non-convex constraints [55], and hence is not amenable to efficient (polynomial-time) algorithms committed to solving convex optimizations. In this section, we present an algorithm for solving general BMI optimizations via difference-of-convex programming [33,52], which solves a series of convex sub-problems that approaches a local optimum of (11).

For brevity, we consider optimization problems with a single BMI constraint[12]:

$$\underset{\mathbf{z}=(\mathbf{x},\mathbf{y})}{\text{maximize}} \quad g(\mathbf{z})$$

$$\text{subject to} \quad \mathcal{B}(\mathbf{x},\mathbf{y}) \hat{=} F + \sum_{i=1}^{m} x_i H_i + \sum_{j=1}^{n} y_j G_j + \sum_{i=1}^{m}\sum_{j=1}^{n} x_i y_j F_{i,j} \preceq 0 \quad (12)$$

where the objective function $g \colon \mathbb{R}^{m+n} \to \mathbb{R}$ is linear in $\mathbf{z} = (\mathbf{x}, \mathbf{y})$; $F, H_i, G_j, F_{i,j} \in \mathcal{S}^p$ are constant symmetric matrices.

5.1 Difference-of-Convex Decomposition

The key challenge in solving the BMI problem (12) is its non-convexity, that is, the matrix-valued function $\mathcal{B}(\mathbf{x},\mathbf{y})$ is, in general, not psd-convex.

There have been attempts, most pertinently in [10], to decompose a bilinear function as a difference between two psd-convex functions, known as the *difference-of-convex* (DC) *decomposition*, such that the optimization in its decomposed form enjoys well-established techniques in difference-of-convex programming [33,52]. The DC decomposition in [10], however, is confined to BMIs of a specific structure, namely, $X^\mathsf{T}Y + Y^\mathsf{T}X \preceq 0$, where X and Y are matrix variables containing variables x_i and y_j, respectively. The more general bilinear function $\mathcal{B}(\mathbf{x},\mathbf{y})$ in (12) does unfortunately not admit straightforward forms of decomposition such as those in [10, Lemma 3.1].

In what follows, we present a difference-of-convex decomposition of the matrix-valued function $\mathcal{B}(\mathbf{x},\mathbf{y})$, inspired by [58], using eigendecomposition. First, observe that the function $\mathcal{B}(\mathbf{x},\mathbf{y})$ can be written as

$$\mathcal{B}(\mathbf{x},\mathbf{y}) = \begin{pmatrix} \mathbf{x}\otimes I \\ \mathbf{y}\otimes I \end{pmatrix}^\mathsf{T} \begin{pmatrix} 0 & \Gamma \\ \Gamma^\mathsf{T} & 0 \end{pmatrix} \begin{pmatrix} \mathbf{x}\otimes I \\ \mathbf{y}\otimes I \end{pmatrix} + \begin{pmatrix} \Omega_1 & \Omega_2 \end{pmatrix} \begin{pmatrix} \mathbf{x}\otimes I \\ \mathbf{y}\otimes I \end{pmatrix} + F \quad (13)$$

where $\otimes$ denotes the Kronecker product: for two matrices $A \in \mathbb{R}^{a\times b}$ and $B \in \mathbb{R}^{c\times d}$, $A \otimes B \hat{=} [A(1,1)B,\dots,A(1,b)B; \cdots; A(a,1)B,\dots,A(a,b)B] \in \mathbb{R}^{ac\times bd}$, 0 represents the zero matrices with compatible dimensions, and

$$\Gamma = \frac{1}{2} \begin{pmatrix} F_{1,1} & \cdots & F_{1,n} \\ \vdots & \ddots & \vdots \\ F_{m,1} & \cdots & F_{m,n} \end{pmatrix}, \quad \Omega_1 = \begin{pmatrix} H_1 \dots H_m \end{pmatrix}, \quad \Omega_2 = \begin{pmatrix} G_1 \dots G_n \end{pmatrix}.$$

The form of (13) implies that $\mathcal{B}(\mathbf{x},\mathbf{y})$ is psd-convex if the matrix $M = \begin{pmatrix} 0 & \Gamma \\ \Gamma^\mathsf{T} & 0 \end{pmatrix}$ is positive semidefinite. Unfortunately, as [58, Theorem 1] points out, for a non-trivial bilinear function $\mathcal{B}(\mathbf{x},\mathbf{y})$, M may not be positive semidefinite.

---

[12] Multiple BMI constraints can be joined as a single BMI in a block-diagonal fashion.

Nevertheless, the matrix M can always be decomposed as $M = M_1 - M_2$ with $M_1, M_2 \succeq 0$, i.e., a difference between two psd-matrices. One way to do so is to use the *eigendecomposition* of the (real symmetric[13]) matrix $M \in \mathcal{S}^{(m+n)p}$. That is, $M = V^{\mathsf{T}} D V$, where the orthogonal matrix V contains the eigenvectors of M; D is a diagonal matrix whose diagonal elements are the eigenvalues of M.

Let D^+ be the matrix obtained by setting all negative elements of D to zero and $D^- = D^+ - D$. We have

$$M = \underbrace{V^{\mathsf{T}} D^+ V}_{M_1} - \underbrace{V^{\mathsf{T}} D^- V}_{M_2}.$$

It follows that $M_1, M_2 \succeq 0$ and therefore we find a DC decomposition of $\mathcal{B}(\mathbf{x}, \mathbf{y})$:

Theorem 7 (Difference-of-Convex Decomposition). *The following form*

$$\mathcal{B}(\mathbf{x}, \mathbf{y}) = \mathcal{B}^+(\mathbf{x}, \mathbf{y}) - \mathcal{B}^-(\mathbf{x}, \mathbf{y}) \tag{14}$$

where

$$\mathcal{B}^+(\mathbf{x}, \mathbf{y}) = \begin{pmatrix} \mathbf{x} \otimes I \\ \mathbf{y} \otimes I \end{pmatrix}^{\mathsf{T}} M_1 \begin{pmatrix} \mathbf{x} \otimes I \\ \mathbf{y} \otimes I \end{pmatrix} + (\Omega_1 \ \Omega_2) \begin{pmatrix} \mathbf{x} \otimes I \\ \mathbf{y} \otimes I \end{pmatrix} + F$$

$$\mathcal{B}^-(\mathbf{x}, \mathbf{y}) = \begin{pmatrix} \mathbf{x} \otimes I \\ \mathbf{y} \otimes I \end{pmatrix}^{\mathsf{T}} M_2 \begin{pmatrix} \mathbf{x} \otimes I \\ \mathbf{y} \otimes I \end{pmatrix}$$

is a difference-of-convex decomposition of $\mathcal{B}(\mathbf{x}, \mathbf{y})$. Namely, the matrix-valued functions $\mathcal{B}^+(\mathbf{x}, \mathbf{y})$ and $\mathcal{B}^-(\mathbf{x}, \mathbf{y})$ are psd-convex on $\mathbb{R}^{m+n}$.

Remark 5. In practice, the aforementioned matrices M, M_1 and M_2 induced by eigendecomposition are often highly sparse. One can hence exploit the sparsity to improve the algorithmic performance of the DCP-based synthesis approach.

5.2   Reduction to LMIs

On top of the DC decomposition (cf. Theorem 7), we can now apply a standard iterative procedure in difference-of-convex programming [10] to solve the BMIs.

The core idea of the procedure is to iteratively solve a series of convex sub-problems. More specifically, given a feasible solution $\mathbf{z}^k = (\mathbf{x}^k, \mathbf{y}^k)$ to the BMI optimization problem (12), the "concave part" $-\mathcal{B}^-(\mathbf{x}, \mathbf{y})$ in (14) is linearized around $\mathbf{z}^k$, thereby yielding a series of convex programs ($k = 0, 1, \dots$):

$$\underset{\mathbf{z}=(\mathbf{x},\mathbf{y})}{\text{maximize}} \quad g(\mathbf{z}) + \frac{1}{2}\delta \left\| \mathbf{z} - \mathbf{z}^k \right\|^2$$

$$\text{subject to} \quad \mathcal{B}^+(\mathbf{z}) - \mathcal{B}^-\left(\mathbf{z}^k\right) - \mathcal{D}\mathcal{B}^-\left(\mathbf{z}^k\right)\left(\mathbf{z} - \mathbf{z}^k\right) \preceq 0 \tag{15}$$

where $\mathcal{D}\mathcal{B}^-(\mathbf{z}) \colon \mathbb{R}^{m+n} \to \mathcal{S}^p$ is the derivative of the matrix-valued function $\mathcal{B}^-$ at $\mathbf{z}$, i.e., a linear mapping from a vector $\mathbf{u} \in \mathbb{R}^{m+n}$ to a matrix in $\mathcal{S}^p$:

$$\mathcal{D}\mathcal{B}^-(\mathbf{z})(\mathbf{u}) \hat{=} \sum_{i=1}^{n+m} u_i \frac{\partial \mathcal{B}^-}{\partial z_i}(\mathbf{z}).$$

---

[13] M thus only has real eigenvalues.

Algorithm 1: BMI-DC: Solving BMIs based on DC decomposition

---

input: A BMI optimization problem (12) with a strictly feasible initial solution $\mathbf{z}^0$.
output: A sequence of feasible solutions $S = \{\mathbf{z}^0, \ldots, \mathbf{z}^k\}$ to the BMI optimization.

1 $k \leftarrow 0$; $S \leftarrow \{\mathbf{z}^0\}$;
2 $M \leftarrow$ reformulation of (12) as (13);
3 $(M_1, M_2) \leftarrow$ DC decomposition of M as in (14);
4 **repeat**
5 $\quad$ Construct the convex sub-problem (15) out of (M_1, M_2) linearized around $\mathbf{z}^k$;
6 $\quad$ $\mathbf{z}^{k+1} \leftarrow$ optimum of the program (15);
7 $\quad$ $S \leftarrow S \cup \{\mathbf{z}^{k+1}\}$;   ▷ S keeps track of visited points
8 $\quad$ $k \leftarrow k + 1$;
9 **until** $\|\mathbf{z}^k - \mathbf{z}^{k-1}\| < \varepsilon$ for a given tolerance $\varepsilon \in \mathbb{R}_0^+$;
10 **return** S;

An extra regularization term $\frac{1}{2}\delta\|\mathbf{z} - \mathbf{z}^k\|^2$ with $\delta < 0$ is added in (15) to enforce that $g(\mathbf{z})$ strictly increases after each iteration until it stabilizes, which can be encoded as a second-order cone constraint and embedded in SDP solving.

Note that the linearized problem (15) is convex and therefore can be solved efficiently[14] via methods including, among others, augmented Lagrangian methods [35] and gradient descent methods [3]. Furthermore, the Schur complement in Theorem 3 implies that (15) can be reformulated as an LMI problem:

Theorem 8. *The quadratic matrix inequality (QMI) constraint*

$$\mathcal{B}^+(\mathbf{z}) - \mathcal{B}^-\left(\mathbf{z}^k\right) - \mathcal{D}\mathcal{B}^-\left(\mathbf{z}^k\right)\left(\mathbf{z} - \mathbf{z}^k\right) \preceq 0$$

in (15) *is equivalent to the LMI constraint*[15]

$$\begin{pmatrix} -I & N(\mathbf{z} \otimes I) \\ (\mathbf{z} \otimes I)^\mathsf{T} N^\mathsf{T} & -\mathcal{B}^-\left(\mathbf{z}^k\right) - \mathcal{D}\mathcal{B}^-\left(\mathbf{z}^k\right)\left(\mathbf{z} - \mathbf{z}^k\right) + \Omega(\mathbf{z} \otimes I) + F \end{pmatrix} \preceq 0$$

where N is the square root matrix of M_1, i.e., $M_1 = N^\mathsf{T} N$, and $\Omega = \left(\Omega_1 \ \Omega_2\right)$.

Theorem 8 entails that the series of linearized convex sub-problems of the form (15) can be solved alternatively by most off-the-shelf SDP solvers designated for discharging LMIs via polynomial-time algorithms, say the interior-point methods. Furthermore, by taking the optimum of the k-th sub-problem to be the next linearization point $\mathbf{z}^{k+1}$, we obtain an iterative procedure for solving general BMIs, as depicted in Algorithm 1.

Algorithm 1 falls into the DCP framework [10] and thus enjoys useful properties, e.g., soundness, termination and convergence as follows.

---

[14] The global optimum of (15) is attainable under standard assumptions, e.g., Slater's condition and the second-order sufficient KKT conditions [3].
[15] This transforms a QMI with matrices in $\mathcal{S}^p$ to an LMI with matrices in $\mathcal{S}^{(m+n+1)p}$.

Theorem 9 (Soundness). *Every solution* $\mathbf{z}^i = (\mathbf{x}^i, \mathbf{y}^i) \in S$ *with* $i = 0, \ldots, k$ *returned by Algorithm 1 is a feasible solution to the original BMI problem* (12).

The result below states termination and convergence of Algorithm 1 in terms of *KKT points* of (12), i.e., solutions fulfilling the KKT conditions [3] of (12)[16].

Theorem 10 (Termination and convergence). *If* (12) *has finitely many KKT points, then (1) for* $\varepsilon \in \mathbb{R}^+$, *Algorithm 1 terminates; (2) for* $\varepsilon = 0$, *Algorithm 1 visits an infinite sequence of solutions converging to a KKT point.*

We remark that, under some sufficient KKT conditions and regularity conditions [3], a KKT point suffices as a local optimum. In this case, the infinite sequence $\{\mathbf{z}^i\}_{i \in \mathbb{N}}$ of points visited by Algorithm 1 (for $\varepsilon = 0$) converges to a local optimum of (12).

5.3   Finding the Initial Solution

The iterative procedure in Algorithm 1 starts with a fed-by-oracle strictly feasible initial solution $\mathbf{z}^0$ to the BMI problem (12). Finding such an initial solution, however, is non-trivial in general due to the non-convexity of (12). We argue though, that a strictly feasible initial solution can be obtained for the BMI problem of the form (11) induced by the barrier-certificate synthesis problem.

Recall that in the BMI problem (11), bilinearity arises from the multiplication of $B(\mathbf{a}, \mathbf{x})$ with some unknown multiplier polynomials parameterized by $\mathbf{s}$. One way to reduce the BMI constraints to LMIs is to fix every multiplier polynomial to be a non-negative constant, thereby yielding a linear program:

$$\underset{\lambda, \mathbf{a}}{\text{maximize}} \quad \lambda$$

$$\text{subject to} \quad \mathcal{F}_\iota(\mathbf{a}, \mathbf{s})\big|_{\mathbf{s}=(c_\iota, 0, \ldots, 0)} + \lambda I \preceq 0, \quad \iota = 1, 2, \ldots, l \qquad (16)$$

where $\mathbf{s}$ in $\mathcal{F}_\iota(\mathbf{a}, \mathbf{s})$ is substituted by $(c_\iota, 0, \ldots, 0)$ with $c_\iota \in \mathbb{R}_0^+$, which encodes a non-negative constant multiplier polynomial. Observe that no $\mathbf{s}$-variable is involved in (16) and the constraints therein are linear in $\mathbf{a}$.

Apparently, a strictly feasible solution $(\lambda, \mathbf{a})$ to (16) induces a strictly feasible solution $(\lambda, \mathbf{a}, (c_\iota, 0, \ldots, 0))$ to (11) as well. Moreover, we have

Lemma 1. *The LMI program* (16) *always has a strictly feasible solution.*

As a consequence, a strictly feasible solution to the BMI problem (11) can be obtained by solving the LMI problem (16). In fact, when considering Lie derivatives only up to the first order, solving (the feasibility counterpart of) (16) is exactly the procedure to synthesize either an *exponential barrier certificate* [29] (with $c_\iota \in \mathbb{R}^+$) or a *convex barrier certificate* [41] (with $c_\iota = 0$). Algorithm 1 therefore subsumes existing synthesis techniques in the sense that any valid barrier certificate synthesized by methods in [29,41] can also be discovered by Algorithm 1. Moreover, an alternative way to reduce the BMI constraints to LMIs is to fix the multipliers to be some given non-trivial (SOS) polynomials [62].

---

[16] Addressing the KKT conditions in detail falls outside the scope of this paper.

Algorithm 2: Branch-and-Bound: Searching for a valid parameter $\bar{a}$

---

input: A BMI optimization problem of the form (11) with $\mathcal{C}_a = \{a \mid \|a\|^2 \leq L_a\}$.
output: A valid parameter $\bar{a}$, or otherwise $\perp$ indicating a failure.

1 **if** $L_a < \eta$ **then return** $\perp$;   ▷ abort on fine-enough partitions ($\eta \in \mathbb{R}^+$)
    /* sample-and-check is not necessary if Theorem 6 is used */
2 $\bar{a} \leftarrow$ a randomly-sampled point in $\mathcal{C}_a$;
3 **if** $\bar{a}$ is valid **then return** $\bar{a}$;   ▷ check validity (inductive invariance)
4 **if** $proj_a(S_{glb}) \cap \mathcal{C}_a = \emptyset$ **then**   ▷ S_{glb} contains a global set of visited points
5      $S \leftarrow$ apply BMI-DC in Algorithm 1 to (11) with initial solution in $(\mathcal{C}_a, \mathcal{C}_s)$;
6      $S_{glb} \leftarrow S_{glb} \cup S$;
        /* checking validity is not necessary if Theorem 5 is used */
7   **if** a valid parameter $\bar{a} \in proj_a(S)$ is found **then return** $\bar{a}$;
8 $(\mathcal{C}_a^1, \mathcal{C}_a^2) \leftarrow bisect(\mathcal{C}_a)$;   ▷ partition the parameter space
9 $\bar{a} \leftarrow$ Branch-and-Bound$(\mathcal{C}_a^1)$;
10 **if** $\bar{a} \neq \perp$ **then return** $\bar{a}$;
11 **else return** Branch-and-Bound$(\mathcal{C}_a^2)$;

Remark 6. Different choices of the multiplier constants c_ι in (16) may lead to different initial solutions fed to Algorithm 1, thereby considerably different number of iterations until termination. In practice, techniques like randomization are worth exploring when choosing these multiplier constants.

6   Incorporating in a Branch-and-Bound Framework

The aforementioned iterative procedure on solving a series of convex optimizations converges only to a local optimum of the BMI problem (11) (or more generally, (12)). This means that, in some cases, it may miss the global optimum that induces a non-negative λ^*. We present in this section a solution to this problem by incorporating the iterative procedure into a branch-and-bound framework that searches for the global optimum in a divide-and-conquer fashion, as is a common technique in non-convex optimizations.

The basic idea is as follows. We first try to solve the BMI problem (11) by Algorithm 1 over the compact parameter space $(\mathcal{C}_a, \mathcal{C}_s)$. If a valid solution, (i.e., a solution that contains a valid parameter $\bar{a} \in \mathcal{C}_a$ such that $B(\bar{a}, x)$ is an invariant barrier certificate) is found, then the corresponding barrier certificate can be obtained. Otherwise, we keep bisecting $\mathcal{C}_a$ and apply Algorithm 1 over each bisection[17]. The procedure, as depicted in Algorithm 2 in a recursive manner, terminates when a valid parameter is found or the partition is fine enough.

Algorithm 2 takes as input a BMI problem of the form (11) that encodes either the sufficient condition in Theorem 5 or the necessary condition in Theorem 6 for invariant barrier certificates. In the former case, a sample-and-check process (Line 2–3) is necessary to attain (weak) completeness (see Theorem 11). The conditional statement in Line 4 rules out parameter (sub-)spaces that have

---

[17] The validity of $\bar{a} \in \mathcal{C}_a$ does not depend on s, thus we do not partition $\mathcal{C}_s$.

already been explored, which is the case when the projection of some visited point in S_{glb} (a global set that keeps track of visited points by Algorithm 1, initialized as $\emptyset$) onto $\mathbf{a}$ is in the current parameter space.

The following theorem claims a weak completeness result: our method guarantees to find a barrier certificate when there exists an inductive invariant (in the form of a given template) that suffices to certify safety of the system.

Theorem 11 (Weak Completeness). *Algorithm 2 returns a valid parameter* $\bar{\mathbf{a}} \in \mathcal{C}_\mathbf{a}$, *if (1) the partition granularity is fine enough (i.e., small enough $\eta \in \mathbb{R}^+$), (2) the degrees of multiplier polynomials and SOS polynomials used to form* (11) *are large enough, and (3) there exists, for the given template $B(\mathbf{a}, \mathbf{x})$, a strictly valid parameter $\hat{\mathbf{a}} \in \mathcal{C}_\mathbf{a}$ (i.e., any parameter in some neighborhood of $\hat{\mathbf{a}}$ is valid).*

Remark 7. The bisection operation in Algorithm 2 induces —in the worst case— an exponential blow-up in the number of branches. In practice, one can prune branches inducing only negative objective values, via, e.g., convex relaxation [26].

7   Experimental Results

We have carried out a prototypical implementation[18] of our synthesis techniques in Wolfram MATHEMATICA, which was selected due to its built-in primitives for SDP, polynomial algebra and matrix operations. Given a safety verification problem as input, our implementation works toward discovering an invariant barrier certificate (in the form of a given template) that witnesses unbounded-time safety of the system. A collection of benchmark examples (detailed in [57, Appendix B]) has been evaluated on a 2.10 GHz Intel Xeon processor with 376 GB RAM running 64-bit CentOS Linux 7.

Table 1 reports the empirical results. BMI-DC concerns our locally-convergent Algorithm 1 for solving BMIs (encoding the sufficient condition in Theorem 5) based on DC decomposition. We compare our approach with PENLAB [14]—an off-the-shelf solver in MATLAB for directly discharging the same BMI problems (with no guarantee on convergence)—and SOSTOOLS [39]—for solving LMIs derived from Prajna and Jadbabaie's original barrier-certificate condition [41]. The comparison is performed under the same problem configurations[19]. Due to numerical errors caused by floating-point computations and the fact that reaching the local/global optimum does not necessarily yield a valid barrier certificate, we additionally perform a posterior check, via both the quantifier-elimination procedure in MATHEMATICA and the SMT solver Z3 [37], of the synthesized candidate barrier certificate per Definition 4.

Table 1 shows that BMI-DC suffices to synthesize valid barrier certificates in most of the examples within a reasonable number of iterations (i.e., the number of convex sub-problems solved by SDP). This however does not cover all the cases:

---

[18] Available at ⏾ https://github.com/Chenms404/BMI-DC.

[19] For PENLAB and SOSTOOLS, we use their optimized, built-in criteria for termination and methods for finding the initial solutions.

Table 1. Empirical results on benchmark examples (time in seconds)

Example name	n_{sys}	d_{flow}	d_{BC}	BMI-DC			PENLAB		SOSTOOLS	
				#iter.	Time	Verified	Time	Verified	Time	Verified
overview [11]	2	2	1	2	**0.03**	✓	0.31	✓	0.07	✓
contrived	2	1	2	0	**0.01**	✓	0.48	✓	0.75	✓
lie-der [36]	2	2	1	0	**0.01**	✓	0.22	✓	0.04	✓
lorenz [11]	3	2	2	8	**2.37**	✓	75.11	✗	1.47	✗
lti-stable [19]	2	1	2	0	**0.01**	✓	0.23	✓	0.14	✓
lotka-volterra [21]	3	2	1	3	**0.07**	✓	0.36	✓	0.21	✓
clock [43]	2	3	1	0	**0.01**	✓	0.88	✗	0.18	✗
lyapunov [44]	3	3	2	4	1.25	✓	56.98	✗	**0.35**	✓
arch1 [50]	2	5	2	0	**0.01**	✓	33.76	✗	0.31	✓
arch2 [50]	2	2	2	5	**0.37**	✓	0.38	✗	0.17	✗
arch3 [50]	2	3	2	1	**0.07**	✓	0.54	✓	0.18	✓
arch4 [50]	2	2	1	2	0.09	✓	0.49	✗	**0.06**	✓
barr-cert1 [41]	2	3	2	12	**0.85**	✓	2.53	✗	0.09	✗
barr-cert2 [11]	2	2	2	6	1.57	✓	1.16	✗	0.15	✓
barr-cert3 [63]	2	2	1	0	**0.01**	✓	0.20	✓	0.11	✗
barr-cert4 [63]	2	3	2	13	**0.96**	✓	0.89	✗	0.23	✗
fitzhugh-nagumo [47]	2	3	2	2	**0.16**	✓	1.24	✓	0.25	✗
stabilization [48]	3	2	2	9	2.88	✓	55.22	✓	**0.11**	✓
lie-high-order	2	1	2	32	**4.12**	✓	1.56	✗	0.25	✗
raychaudhuri [13]	4	2	2	34	**9.51**	✓	33.64	✗	0.14	✗
focus [42]	2	1	4	100	54.89	✗	0.95	✗	0.48	✗
sys-bio1 [27]	7	2	2	2	73.22	?	101.95	?	1.35	?
sys-bio2 [27]	9	2	1	1	1.03	?	15.54	?	0.16	?
quadcopter [19]	12	1	1	0	0.03	?	65.42	?	0.36	?

n_{sys}: system dimension; d_{flow}: maximal flow-field degree; d_{BC}: degree of the template barrier certificate.
#iter.: number of iterations. 0 means that the initial solution (cf. Subsect. 5.3) is valid.
verified: the synthesized barrier certificate is valid (✓), invalid (✗) or inconclusive (?, beyond the capability of quantifier elimination in MATHEMATICA and nonlinear reasoning in Z3).
time: CPU-time, excluding that for casting the BMIs/LMIs. Boldface marks the winner among ✓'s.

for the focus example, the solution is close enough to a local optimum (after 100 iterations) but yields still an invalid barrier certificate. This problem can be solved (if there exists an invariant barrier certificate as specified) by enforcing the branch-and-bound framework as presented in Sect. 6. The phase portraits of a selected set of examples and the synthesized invariant barrier certificates are depicted in Fig. 2 (see more in [57, Appendix B]).

The comparison in Table 1 suggests that (1) Our invariant barrier-certificate condition recognizes more barrier certificates than the original (more conservative) condition as implemented in SOSTOOLS. In particular, the lie-high-order example does admit an inductive invariant in the form of the given template, but none of the existing barrier-certificate conditions [4,60,63] —concerning Lie derivatives only up to the first order— recognizes it, since we have $\mathcal{L}_f^1 B(\mathbf{x}) = 0$

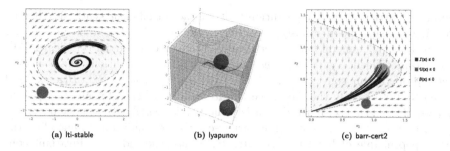

| (a) lti-stable | (b) lyapunov | (c) barr-cert2 |

Fig. 2. Phase portraits of a selected set of examples with the synthesized invariant barrier certificates. The arrows indicate the vector field (hidden in 3D-graphics for a clear presentation) and the solid curves are randomly sampled trajectories.

for some **x** on the boundary of B and hence it requires to exploit the second-order Lie derivative $\mathcal{L}_f^2 B$; (2) Our DCP-based synthesis algorithm finds more barrier certificates in less time than directly solving the BMI problems via non-convex optimization techniques as implemented in PENLAB.

We remark that symbolic methods based on, e.g., quantifier elimination [36], can hardly deal with any of the examples listed in Table 1 due to the prohibitively high computation complexity. Moreover, it would be desirable to pursue a comparison with the augmented Lagrangian method for solving BMIs as proposed in [4], which unfortunately is not yet possible due to the unavailability of the implementation thereof. We will discuss crucial differences to [4] in Sect. 8.

8   Related Work

As surveyed in [15], the research community has, over the past three decades, extensively addressed the automatic verification of safety-critical hybrid systems. The almost universal undecidability of the unbounded-time reachability problem [1], however, confines the sound key-press routines to either semi-decision procedures or approximation schemes, most of which address bounded-time verification by, e.g., computing the finite-time image of a set of initial states.

Invariant generation [36,41], amongst others, is a well-established approximation scheme that provides a reliable witness for safety (or equivalently, unreachability) of dynamical systems over the infinite time horizon. Invariants can be constructed in various forms, e.g., barrier certificates [41,51] and differential invariants [36,40]. With a priori specified templates, the invariant synthesis problem can be reduced to numerical optimizations or constraint solving, as in, e.g., [22,25,46,54].

Most pertinently, Prajna and Jadbabaie proposed in their seminal work [41] a concept coined *barrier certificate* to encode invariants. To enable efficient synthesis via semidefinite programming, the barrier-certificate condition in [41] strengthens the general condition encoding inductive invariance. Since then, significant efforts have been investigated in developing more relaxed (i.e., weaker) forms of barrier-certificate condition that still admit efficient synthesis, thereby leading to, e.g., exponential-type barrier certificates [29], Darboux-type barrier certificates [62], general barrier certificates [8] and vector barrier certificates [51]. To attain efficient synthesis, these barrier-certificate conditions share a common property on convexity. That is, if for some $\mathbf{a}_1, \mathbf{a}_2 \in \mathbb{R}^m$, $B(\mathbf{a}_1, \mathbf{x})$ and $B(\mathbf{a}_2, \mathbf{x})$ both satisfy the barrier-certificate condition, then for any $0 < \mu < 1$, $B(\mu \mathbf{a}_1 + (1 - \mu)\mathbf{a}_2, \mathbf{x})$ must also satisfy the barrier-certificate condition.

However, neither the semantic barrier-certificate condition (9) encoding the general principle of barrier certificates [8,51] nor the inductive invariant condition (8) is convex. This means, when resorting to convex barrier-certificate conditions, one may miss some potential barrier certificates that suffice as inductive invariants witnessing safety. Therefore, non-convex conditions were suggested [60], for which the synthesis problem can be reduced to BMI problems solvable via customized schemes, e.g., the augmented Lagrangian method [4] and the alternating minimization algorithm [63]. Our synthesis techniques also exploit a BMI reduction, with three crucial differences: (1) our invariant barrier-certificate condition is equivalent to the inductive invariant condition in the sense of Theorem 4, and thus is less conservative than all the aforementioned conditions which consider Lie derivatives only up to the first order; (2) our DCP-based techniques for solving BMIs naturally inherit appealing results on convergence and (weak) completeness, which are not (and can hardly be) provided by the approaches in [4,60,63]; (3) our DCP-based iterative procedure visits only feasible solutions to the original BMI problem, and hence whenever a solution that induces a non-negative objective value is found, we can safely terminate the algorithm and claim a feasible solution to the original BMI problem, which may yield a valid barrier certificate. This is not the case for the approaches in [4,60,63].

Beyond barrier certificates, Wang and Rajamani [58] investigated the feasibility problem of general BMI problems with an application to multi-objective nonlinear observer design. The technique of eigendecomposition was also used therein to conduct the DC decomposition. The decomposed concave part, however, is simply ignored and no iterative procedure that exhibits convergence to a local optimum can be provided.

The idea of augmenting a locally-convergent algorithm with a branch-and-bound framework to find the global optimum has been exploited in the realm of optimization [20] and control [56]. In contrast, our method is designed for the specific problem of barrier-certificate synthesis, and hence our branch-and-bound algorithm concerns only the parameter space of $\mathbf{a}$, i.e., coefficients of the template barrier certificate.

Finally, we refer interested readers to other approaches to solving BMI problems, e.g., rank minimization [23,38,45], sequential SDP [7,12], as well as methods committed to general non-convex optimizations, e.g., interior point trust-region [5,9,34], successive linearization [24] and primal-dual interior point [59].

9 Conclusion

Barrier certificates are powerful tools to prove time-unbounded safety of hybrid systems. We have presented a new condition on barrier certificates—the invariant barrier-certificate condition. This condition is by far the least conservative one on barrier certificates, and can be shown as the weakest possible one to attain inductive invariance. We showed that our invariant barrier-certificate condition can be reformulated as an optimization problem subject to bilinear matrix inequalities, which can be solved by our locally-convergent algorithm based on difference-of-convex programming. By incorporating this algorithm into a branch-and-bound framework, we obtained a weak completeness result. Experiments on benchmark examples suggested that our invariant barrier-certificate condition recognizes more barrier certificates than existing conditions, and that our DCP-based algorithm is more efficient than directly solving the BMIs via off-the-shelf solvers.

We stress that our techniques for solving BMIs are of a general nature rather than being confined to barrier-certificate synthesis. Interesting future directions include to extend our method to other synthesis problems, e.g., discovering invariants and/or termination proofs of deterministic/probabilistic programs.

Acknowledgements. The authors would like to thank Hengjun Zhao for the fruitful discussion on differential dynamics requiring high-order Lie derivatives.

References

1. Alur, R., et al.: The algorithmic analysis of hybrid systems. Theor. Comput. Sci. **138**(1), 3–34 (1995)
2. Anai, H., Weispfenning, V.: Reach set computations using real quantifier elimination. In: HSCC (2001)
3. Boyd, S., Vandenberghe, L.: Convex Optimization (2004)
4. Chen, X., et al.: A novel approach for solving the BMI problem in barrier certificates generation. In: CAV (2020)
5. Chiu, W.Y.: Method of reduction of variables for bilinear matrix inequality problems in system and control designs. IEEE SMC **47**(7), 1241–1256 (2016)
6. Choi, M.D., Lam, T.Y., Reznick, B.: Sums of squares of real polynomials. In: Proceedings of Symposia in Pure Mathematics (1995)
7. Correa, R.: A global algorithm for nonlinear semidefinite programming. SIOPT **15**(1), 303–318 (2004)
8. Dai, L., et al.: Barrier certificates revisited. J. Symb. Comput. **80**, 62–86 (2017)
9. Dennis, J., Heinkenschloss, M., Vicente, L.N.: Trust-region interior-point SQP algorithms for a class of nonlinear programming problems. SICON **36**(5), 1750–1794 (1998)
10. Dinh, Q.T., et al.: Combining convex-concave decompositions and linearization approaches for solving BMIs, with application to static output feedback. IEEE TAC **57**(6), 1377–1390 (2011)

11. Djaballah, A., et al.: Construction of parametric barrier functions for dynamical systems using interval analysis. Automatica **78**, 287–290 (2017)
12. Eggers, A., et al.: Improving the SAT modulo ODE approach to hybrid systems analysis by combining different enclosure methods. In: SoSyM (2012)
13. Ferragut, A., Gasull, A.: Seeking Darboux polynomials. Acta Applicandae Mathematicae **139**(1), 167–186 (2015)
14. Fiala, J., Kočvara, M., Stingl, M.: PENLAB: A MATLAB solver for nonlinear semidefinite optimization. CoRR abs/1311.5240 (2013)
15. Fränzle, M., Chen, M., Kröger, P.: In memory of Oded Maler: automatic reachability analysis of hybrid-state automata. ACM SIGLOG News **6**(1), 19–39 (2019)
16. Gan, T., et al.: Decidability of the reachability for a family of linear vector fields. In: ATVA (2015)
17. Gan, T., et al.: Computing reachable sets of linear vector fields revisited. In: ECC (2016)
18. Gan, T., et al.: Reachability analysis for solvable dynamical systems. IEEE TAC **63**(7), 2003–2018 (2018)
19. Gao, S., et al.: Numerically-robust inductive proof rules for continuous dynamical systems. In: CAV (2019)
20. Goh, K.C., Safonov, M.G., Papavassilopoulos, G.P.: Global optimization for the biaffine matrix inequality problem. J. Glob. Optim. **7**(4), 365–380 (1995)
21. Goubault, E., et al.: Finding non-polynomial positive invariants and Lyapunov functions for polynomial systems through Darboux polynomials. In: ACC (2014)
22. Gulwani, S., Tiwari, A.: Constraint-based approach for analysis of hybrid systems. In: CAV (2008)
23. Ibaraki, S., Tomizuka, M.: Rank minimization approach for solving BMI problems with random search. In: ACC (2001)
24. Kanzow, C., et al.: Successive linearization methods for nonlinear semidefinite programs. Comput. Optim. Appl. **31**(3), 252–273 (2005)
25. Kapinski, J., et al.: Simulation-guided Lyapunov analysis for hybrid dynamical systems. In: HSCC (2014)
26. Kheirandishfard, M., Zohrizadeh, F., Madani, R.: Convex relaxation of bilinear matrix inequalities Part I: Theoretical results. In: CDC (2018)
27. Klipp, E., et al.: Systems Biology in Practice: Concepts, Implementation and Application (2008)
28. Kolář I., Michor, P.W., Slovák, J.: Natural Operations in Differential Geometry (1993)
29. Kong, H., et al.: Exponential-condition-based barrier certificate generation for safety verification of hybrid systems. In: CAV (2013)
30. Kong, S., Solar-Lezama, A., Gao, S.: Delta-decision procedures for exists-forall problems over the reals. In: CAV (2018)
31. Lafferriere, G., Pappas, G.J., Yovine, S.: Symbolic reachability computation for families of linear vector fields. J. Symb. Comput. **32**(3), 23–253 (2001)
32. Lasserre, J.B.: Moments, Positive Polynomials and Their Applications (2010)
33. Le Thi, H.A., Dinh, T.P.: DC programming and DCA: thirty years of developments. Math. Program. **169**(1), 5–68 (2018)
34. Leibfritz, F., Mostafa, E.: An interior point constrained trust region method for a special class of nonlinear semidefinite programming problems. SIOPT **12**(4), 1048–1071 (2002)
35. Li, X., Sun, D., Toh, K.C.: QSDPNAL: a two-phase augmented Lagrangian method for convex quadratic semidefinite programming. Math. Program. Comput. **10**(4), 703–743 (2018)

36. Liu, J., Zhan, N., Zhao, H.: Computing semi-algebraic invariants for polynomial dynamical systems. In: EMSOFT (2011)
37. de Moura, L.M., Bjørner, N.: Z3: an efficient SMT solver. In: TACAS (2008)
38. Orsi, R., Helmke, U., Moore, J.B.: A Newton-like method for solving rank constrained linear matrix inequalities. Automatica $42(11)$, 1875–1882 (2006)
39. Papachristodoulou, A., et al.: SOSTOOLS version 3.00 sum of squares optimization toolbox for MATLAB. CoRR abs/1310.4716 (2013)
40. Platzer, A., Clarke, E.M.: Computing differential invariants of hybrid systems as fixedpoints. In: CAV (2008)
41. Prajna, S., Jadbabaie, A.: Safety verification of hybrid systems using barrier certificates. In: HSCC (2004)
42. Ratschan, S., She, Z.: Constraints for continuous reachability in the verification of hybrid systems. In: AISC (2006)
43. Ratschan, S., She, Z.: Safety verification of hybrid systems by constraint propagation-based abstraction refinement. ACM TECS $6(1)$, 8-es (2007)
44. Ratschan, S., She, Z.: Providing a basin of attraction to a target region of polynomial systems by computation of Lyapunov-like functions. SICON $48(7)$, 4377–4394 (2010)
45. Recht, B., Fazel, M., Parrilo, P.A.: Guaranteed minimum-rank solutions of linear matrix equations via nuclear norm minimization. SIAM Rev. $52(3)$, 471–501 (2010)
46. Sankaranarayanan, S., Sipma, H.B., Manna, Z.: Constructing invariants for hybrid systems. In: HSCC (2004)
47. Sassi, M.A.B., Girard, A., Sankaranarayanan, S.: Iterative computation of polyhedral invariants sets for polynomial dynamical systems. In: CDC (2014)
48. Sassi, M.A.B., Sankaranarayanan, S.: Stability and stabilization of polynomial dynamical systems using Bernstein polynomials. In: HSCC (2015)
49. Smith, W.D.: Church's thesis meets the n-body problem. Appl. Math. Comput. $178(1)$, 154–183 (2006)
50. Sogokon, A., Ghorbal, K., Johnson, T.T.: Non-linear continuous systems for safety verification (benchmark proposal). In: ARCH @ CPSWeek (2016)
51. Sogokon, A., et al.: Vector barrier certificates and comparison systems. In: FM (2018)
52. Tao, P.D., Souad, E.B.: Algorithms for solving a class of nonconvex optimization problems. North-Holland Mathematics Studies, Methods of subgradients (1986)
53. Tarski, A.: A Decision Method for Elementary Algebra and Geometry (1951)
54. Tiwari, A.: Approximate reachability for linear systems. In: HSCC (2003)
55. Toker, O., Ozbay, H.: On the NP-hardness of solving bilinear matrix inequalities and simultaneous stabilization with static output feedback. In: ACC (1995)
56. Tuan, H.D., Apkarian, P., Nakashima, Y.: A new Lagrangian dual global optimization algorithm for solving bilinear matrix inequalities. Int. J. Rob. Nonlinear Control IFAC-Affiliat. J. $10(7)$, 561–578 (2000)
57. Wang, Q., et al.: Synthesizing invariant barrier certificates via difference-of-convex programming (extended version). arXiv abs/2105.14311 (2021)
58. Wang, Y., Rajamani, R.: Feasibility analysis of the bilinear matrix inequalities with an application to multi-objective nonlinear observer design. In: CDC (2016)
59. Yamashita, H., Yabe, H.: Local and superlinear convergence of a primal-dual interior point method for nonlinear semidefinite programming. Math. Program. $132(1–2)$, 1–30 (2012)
60. Yang, Z., Lin, W., Wu, M.: Exact safety verification of hybrid systems based on bilinear SOS representation. ACM TECS $14(1)$, 1–19 (2015)

61. Yang, Z., et al.: A linear programming relaxation based approach for generating barrier certificates of hybrid systems. In: FM (2016)
62. Zeng, X., et al.: Darboux-type barrier certificates for safety verification of nonlinear hybrid systems. In: EMSOFT (2016)
63. Zhang, Y., et al.: Safety verification of nonlinear hybrid systems based on bilinear programming. IEEE TCAD **37**(11),(2018)

An Iterative Scheme of Safe Reinforcement Learning for Nonlinear Systems via Barrier Certificate Generation

Zhengfeng Yang[1], Yidan Zhang[1], Wang Lin[2(✉)], Xia Zeng[3], Xiaochao Tang[1], Zhenbing Zeng[4], and Zhiming Liu[3,5]

[1] Shanghai Key Lab of Trustworthy Computing, East China Normal University, Shanghai, China
zfyang@sei.ecnu.edu.cn, {ydzhang,xctang}@stu.ecnu.edu.cn
[2] School of Information Science and Technology, Zhejiang Sci-Tech University, Hangzhou, China
linwang@zstu.edu.cn
[3] School of Computer and Information Science, Southwest University, Chongqing, China
xzeng0712@swu.edu.cn
[4] Department of Mathematics, Shanghai University, Shanghai, China
zbzeng@shu.edu.cn
[5] Centre for Intelligent and Embedded Software, Northwestern Polytechnical University, Suzhou, China
zliu@nwpu.edu.cn

Abstract. In this paper, we propose a safe reinforcement learning approach to synthesize deep neural network (DNN) controllers for nonlinear systems subject to safety constraints. The proposed approach employs an iterative scheme where a *learner* and a *verifier* interact to synthesize safe DNN controllers. The *learner* trains a DNN controller via deep reinforcement learning, and the *verifier* certifies the learned controller through computing a maximal safe initial region and its corresponding barrier certificate, based on polynomial abstraction and bilinear matrix inequalities solving. Compared with the existing verification-in-the-loop synthesis methods, our iterative framework is a sequential synthesis scheme of controllers and barrier certificates, which can learn safe controllers with adaptive barrier certificates rather than user-defined ones. We implement the tool SRLBC and evaluate its performance over a set of benchmark examples. The experimental results demonstrate that our approach efficiently synthesizes safe DNN controllers even for a nonlinear system with dimension up to 12.

This work was partially supported by the Scientific and Technological Innovation 2030 Major Projects under Grant 2018AAA0100902, the National Natural Science Foundation of China under Grant 61772203, 61902325, 62032019, 61732019, the Zhejiang Provincial Natural Science Foundation of China under Grant LY20F020020, the Capacity Development Grant of Southwest University under Grant SWU116007, the Fundamental Research Funds for the Central Universities under Grant SWU117058.

A. Silva and K. R. M. Leino (Eds.) CAV 2021, LNCS 12759, pp. 467–490, 2021.
https://doi.org/10.1007/978-3-030-81685-8_22

Keywords: Formal verification · Safe reinforcement learning · Barrier certificates · Continuous dynamical systems

1   Introduction

The design and synthesis of controllers for dynamical systems is a fundamental problem in the field of control. In recent years, with the boom of deep learning, there has been considerable research activities in the use of deep neural networks (DNNs) for control of cyber-physical systems such as unmanned aerial vehicles, self-driving cars, etc. [33]. For these safety-critical systems, one of the most important and challenging problems is safe controller synthesis, that is, to synthesize a controller guaranteeing that the system's trajectory will never intersect with an undesired region.

A number of techniques included under the umbrella of Deep Reinforcement Learning (DRL) have been used to effectively learn controllers from user-defined reward functions encoding desired system behavior [17,36]. A majority of these works lack formal reasoning about the safety of such DNN-controlled dynamical systems from such learning process. To guarantee the safety property of synthesized DNN controllers, considerable works focus on the safety verification of DNN-controlled closed-loop systems, which is a really hard problem because it is tangled with highly nonlinear DNN expressions. The main research on this topic is through reachable set estimation of DNN-controlled systems, which can only deal with time bounded safety property [11,12,18,19,37]. On the other hand, other than formally verifying synthesized DNN controllers, more recent works have been proposed to learn DNN controllers for dynamical systems with safety guarantees [8,39,40]. For example, a verification-in-the-loop DNN controller training algorithm is presented in [8], which integrates RL framework with user-provided control barrier functions (CBFs) for reward function encoding, combined with SMT based formal CBF checking; a correctness-by-design method is proposed in [39] that first learns DNN controllers and barrier certificates simultaneously using supervised learning, and then performs posterior formal verification of barrier certificates via SMT solvers.

In this paper, we propose a safe reinforcement learning approach to synthesize DNN controller for nonlinear systems subject to safety constraints via barrier certificate generation. The proposed approach employs an iterative scheme where a *learner* and a *verifier* interact to synthesize safe DNN controllers. Firstly, the *learner* applies DRL method to train a DNN controller by encoding the safety requirement (and the barrier certificate requirement, if applicable) into reward function. For the learned controller, the *verifier* computes a Maximal Safe Input Region (MSIR) and the corresponding barrier certificate. Once the MSIR is a superset of the prescribed initial set Θ, it is easy to see that the safety of the closed-loop system under the learned controller with Θ is verified. Otherwise, the computed barrier certificate needs to be adjusted and fed to guide the *learner* to retrain a new controller. The above inductive loop repeats until an MSIR enclosing Θ is computed.

Compared with [8], a user-provided barrier certificate is adopted for reward function encoding and the barrier certificate is fixed through the learning process, whereas in this paper the controllers and the barrier certificates are synthesized simultaneously and yielded in a larger state space, which increases the diversity and flexibility of barrier certificates. Meanwhile, the barrier certificates in our approach are computed by numerical optimization method, which is more efficient than the SMT based method in [8]. Compared with [39], our method is based on RL framework and thus has better data sampling efficiency than the meshing-based data set generation in [39] for supervised learning. Besides, our method is iterative so that can utilize intermediate learned results to guide learning in the next iteration, rather than restarting from scratch as in [39] when a learned barrier certificate failed formal checking. Thanks to these advantages, our method has really good performance in efficiency and scalability even for problems with dimension up to 12.

The main contributions of this paper are summarized as follows:

- We propose a safe reinforcement learning via barrier certificate generation to synthesize DNN controller, which can guarantee the unbounded-time safety of the closed-loop systems.
- Our synthesis approach employs a sequential iterative scheme, where DNN controllers and the corresponding barrier certificates are synthesized alternatively, and in each iteration, barrier certificates are slightly adjusted to guide retraining safe DNN controllers quickly.
- We provide a detailed experimental evaluation on a set of benchmarks, which shows the efficiency and effectiveness of our approach.

The paper is organized as follows. Section 2 gives a brief introduction to the safe controller synthesis problem. Section 3 describes an iterative scheme of safe reinforcement learning for safe DNN controller synthesis. In Sect. 4, we provide an overall algorithm with a detailed example attached to depict how the algorithm works. In Sect. 5, we present an experimental evaluation of our algorithm over a set of benchmark examples. We compare with related works in Sect. 6 before concluding in Sect. 7.

2   Preliminaries

Notations. Let $\mathbb{R}$ and $\mathbb{N}$ be the field of real number and natural number, respectively. $\mathbb{R}[\mathbf{x}]$ denotes the ring of polynomials with coefficients in $\mathbb{R}$ over variables $\mathbf{x} = [x_1, x_2, \ldots, x_n]^T$, and $\mathbb{R}[\mathbf{x}]^n$ denotes the n-dimensional polynomial ring vector. Let $R[\mathbf{x}]_d \subset \mathbb{R}[\mathbf{x}]$ be the vector space of polynomials of degree at most d. Let $\mathbb{N}_d^n := \{\alpha \in \mathbb{N}^n : \sum_i \alpha_i \leq d\}$. Denote by $\Sigma[\mathbf{x}] \subset \mathbb{R}[\mathbf{x}]$ (resp. $\Sigma[\mathbf{x}]_d \subset \mathbb{R}[\mathbf{x}]_{2d}$) the space of sums of squares (SOS) polynomials.

Consider a continuous dynamical system of the form

$$\dot{\mathbf{x}} = \mathbf{f}(\mathbf{x}), \tag{1}$$

where $\mathbf{x} = (x_1, \ldots, x_n)^T \in \mathbb{R}^n$ and $\mathbf{f} = (f_1, \ldots, f_n)^T \in \mathbb{R}[\mathbf{x}]^n$ is the vector field defined on the state space $D \subset \mathbb{R}^n$. We assume that $\mathbf{f}$ satisfies the local Lipschitz condition, so that (1) has a unique solution $\mathbf{x}(t, \mathbf{x}_0)$ in D for every initial state $\mathbf{x}_0 \in D$ at time $t = 0$.

In many contexts, a dynamical system is equipped with a domain $\Psi \subset D$ and an initial set $\Theta \subset \Psi$, represented as a triple $\mathcal{C} \doteq (\mathbf{f}, \Theta, \Psi)$. Given a prespecified unsafe region $X_u \subset D$, we say that the system $\mathcal{C}$ is *safe* if all system trajectories starting from Θ can not evolve into any state specified by X_u, which has been widely investigated in safety critical applications.

Definition 1 (Safety). *For a constrained continuous dynamical system (CCDS) $\mathcal{C} \doteq (\mathbf{f}, \Psi, \Theta)$ and a given unsafe region X_u, the system is safe if for all $\mathbf{x}_0 \in \Theta$, there does not exist $t_1 > 0$ such that*

$$\forall t \in [0, t_1].\mathbf{x}(t, \mathbf{x}_0) \in \Psi \quad \text{and } \mathbf{x}(t_1, \mathbf{x}_0) \in X_u,$$

that is, the system's trajectory never reaches X_u from Θ as long as it remains in Ψ.

Remark 1. If the trajectory $\mathbf{x}(t, \mathbf{x}_0)$ first leaves Ψ and then enters Ψ again, then by Definition 1, the part of the trajectory from the first exit point is excluded from our concern and is not relevant to the safety of the considered CCDS.

In this paper, we consider a *controlled CCDS* $\mathcal{C} = (\mathbf{f}, \Psi, \Theta)$ with continuous dynamics defined by

$$\begin{cases} \dot{\mathbf{x}} = \mathbf{f}(\mathbf{x}, \mathbf{u}) \\ \mathbf{u} = \mathbf{k}(\mathbf{x}), \end{cases} \tag{2}$$

where $\mathbf{x} \in \Psi \subseteq \mathbb{R}^n$ are the system states, $\mathbf{u} \in U \subseteq \mathbb{R}^m$ are the control inputs, and $\mathbf{f} : \Psi \times U \to \mathbb{R}^n$ and $\mathbf{k} : \Psi \to U$ are the locally Lipschitz continuous vector field and feedback controller function, respectively. The problem we considered in this paper is defined as follows.

Definition 2 (Safe Controller Synthesis). *For a controlled CCDS $\mathcal{C} = (\mathbf{f}, \Psi, \Theta)$ with $\mathbf{f}$ defined by (2) and a given unsafe region X_u, design a locally Lipschitz continuous feedback control law $\mathbf{k}$ such that the closed-loop system $\mathcal{C}$ with $\mathbf{f} = \mathbf{f}(\mathbf{x}, \mathbf{k}(\mathbf{x}))$ is safe as per Definition 1.*

The concept of *barrier certificates* plays an important role in safety verification of continuous systems. The essential idea is to use the zero level set of a barrier certificate $B(\mathbf{x})$ as a barrier to separate all the reachable states from the unsafe region. The following theorem states the conditions that must be satisfied by a barrier certificate.

Theorem 1 [26]. *Given a continuous system $\mathcal{C} = (\mathbf{f}, \Psi, \Theta)$, and the unsafe region X_u. Suppose there exists a real-valued function $B : \Psi \to \mathbb{R}$ satisfying the following conditions:*

(i) $B(\mathbf{x}) \geq 0 \quad \forall \mathbf{x} \in \Theta,$

(ii) $B(\mathbf{x}) < 0 \quad \forall \mathbf{x} \in X_u$,

(iii) $B(\mathbf{x}) = 0 \Rightarrow \mathcal{L}_f B(\mathbf{x}) > 0 \quad \forall \mathbf{x} \in \Psi$,

where $\mathcal{L}_f B(\mathbf{x})$ denotes the Lie-derivative of $B(\mathbf{x})$ along the vector field $\mathbf{f}(\mathbf{x})$, i.e., $\mathcal{L}_f B(\mathbf{x}) = \sum_{i=1}^n \frac{\partial B}{\partial x_i} \cdot f_i(\mathbf{x})$, then $B(\mathbf{x})$ is a barrier certificate, and the safety of system $\mathcal{C}$ is guaranteed.

Corollary 1. *For a controlled CCDS $\mathcal{C} = (\mathbf{f}, \Psi, \Theta)$ with $\mathbf{f}$ defined by (2), a feedback control law $u = \mathbf{k}(\mathbf{x})$ can be used to ensure the safety control of $\mathcal{C}$, if there exists a barrier certificate for the closed-loop system under the control law $\mathbf{k}(\mathbf{x})$.*

Throughout this paper, we assume that the initial set Θ, the domain Ψ and the unsafe set X_u are compact semi-algebraic sets, defined by polynomial equations and inequalities. Concretely, the semi-algebraic sets Θ, Ψ and X_u are represented as follows:

$$\left\{ \begin{array}{l} \Theta := \{\mathbf{x} \in \mathbb{R}^n \mid g_i(\mathbf{x}) \geq 0, i = 1, \ldots, m_1\}, \\ \Psi := \{\mathbf{x} \in \mathbb{R}^n \mid h_j(\mathbf{x}) \geq 0, j = 1, \ldots, m_2\}, \\ X_u := \{\mathbf{x} \in \mathbb{R}^n \mid q_k(\mathbf{x}) \geq 0, k = 1, \ldots, m_3\}, \end{array} \right.$$

for some polynomials $g_i, h_j, q_k \in \mathbb{R}[\mathbf{x}]$.

3 Synthesis of Safe Controller via Learning and Verification

In this section, we introduce an iterative framework for synthesizing a deep neural network (DNN) controller for a CCDS subject to safety constraints. As shown in Fig. 1, the procedure is structured as an inductive loop between a *learner* and a *verifier*. The *learner* trains a DNN controller using reinforcement learning. The trained DNN controller is passed to the *verifier*, which checks the safety of the closed-loop system under the trained controller via barrier certificate generation.

Observing Fig. 1, we first apply the reinforcement learning method to train a neural network controller $u = k(\mathbf{x})$ in terms of the target of the safety satisfiability, and then try to yield a barrier certificate $B(\mathbf{x})$ based on the bilinear matrix inequalities (BMI) solving, to guarantee the safety of the closed-loop system with the controller $k(\mathbf{x})$.

However, for the system with the controller $k(\mathbf{x})$, such barrier certificate $B(\mathbf{x})$ may not exist. The reasons are twofold: (i) the controller $k(\mathbf{x})$ is trained through the trajectories starting from finite points in the initial set Θ; (ii) the existence of the barrier certificate is just a sufficient condition of the safety of the given system.

In this situation, for the learned controller $k(\mathbf{x})$, one may compute a Maximal Safe Input Region (MSIR) Θ_γ and the corresponding barrier certificate $B(\mathbf{x})$, which can guarantee the safety of the continuous system with respect to the initial set Θ_γ. Once Θ_γ is a superset of the prescribed initial set Θ, i.e., $\Theta \subseteq \Theta_\gamma$,

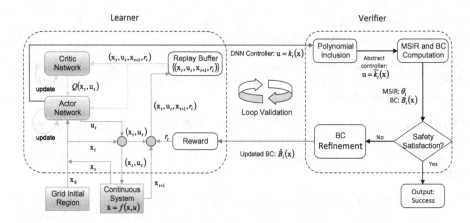

Fig. 1. The framework of safe neural network controller synthesis.

it is easy to see that the safety of the system with Θ is verified. Otherwise, we need adjust the barrier certificate $B(\mathbf{x})$ and the controller $k(\mathbf{x})$ sequentially. This operation is able to build an iterative framework, wherein each iteration proceeds in two stages:

– **Update the neural network controller.** We apply deep reinforcement learning method to obtain the updated controller $k_i(\mathbf{x})$ by feeding $\hat{B}_{i-1}(\mathbf{x})$, which is the barrier certificate yielded from the above iteration (See the *learner* in Fig. 1).
– **Compute the barrier certificate with the maximal safe input region.** With the updated controller $k_i(\mathbf{x})$, we transfer the problem of barrier certificate generation into a bilinear matrix inequalities (BMI) solving, and then compute the maximal region Θ_i with the corresponding barrier certificate $B_i(\mathbf{x})$. Namely, the existence of $B_i(\mathbf{x})$ suffices to prove the safety of the system with respect to the initial set Θ_i. Once Θ_i encloses the original initial set Θ, i.e., $\Theta \subseteq \Theta_i$, the current controller $k_i(\mathbf{x})$ is the desired safe one. Otherwise, we need refine $B_i(\mathbf{x})$, and then go to the next iteration (See the *verifier* in Fig. 1).

3.1 Training of Safe Controller

In the following, we focus on the *learner* component of Fig. 1 and show how to train a safe controller using deep deterministic policy gradient (DDPG) [23], which is a popular reinforcement learning approach suited for continuous control applications. The DDPG combines the value-based and policy-based method, and is made up of two parts: actor and critic. The critic uses the off-policy data to learn the action-value function, which evaluates how good the action k taken is in the given state $\mathbf{x}$. The actor can learn the continuous action policy by using the action-value function. In practice, it is difficult to obtain the exact action-value function and policy function. Thus, two deep neural networks are introduced to solve this problem, i.e. the critic network $Q(\mathbf{x}, \mathbf{u}|\beta^Q)$ and actor network $k(\mathbf{x}|\beta^k)$ with weights β^Q and β^k, respectively.

The reward function should be appropriately designed to achieve the goal of safety controller synthesis via reinforcement learning. For safe controller synthesis, the task is to synthesize a DNN controller such that all the trajectories of the closed-loop system starting from Θ can not evolve into the unsafe region X_u. Thus, the reward function is preliminarily defined as

$$\hat{r}_t = \beta_1 \cdot \text{dist}(X_u, \mathbf{x}_t)$$

where $\beta_1 > 0$ is the scale factor, and $\text{dist}(X_u, \mathbf{x}_t)$ denotes the distance between the state $\mathbf{x}_t$ and the unsafe region X_u. In addition, according to the third condition of Theorem 1, once the trajectory hit the zero level set of barrier certificate it must satisfy $\mathcal{L}_f B(\mathbf{x}_t) > 0$; otherwise, the system behavior should be penalized. For this purpose, the reward function is updated as

$$r_t = \begin{cases} \hat{r}_t - \min(\beta_2|\mathcal{L}_f B(\mathbf{x}_t)|, \Delta r_{\min}), & |B(\mathbf{x}_t)| < \delta \text{ and } \mathcal{L}_f B(\mathbf{x}_t) \leq 0 \\ \hat{r}_t, & \text{otherwise} \end{cases} \quad (3)$$

where $\mathcal{L}_f B(\mathbf{x}_t) = \sum_{i=1}^n \frac{\partial B(\mathbf{x}_t)}{\partial x_i} f_i(\mathbf{x}_t, u)$, $\beta_2 > 0$ is the scale factor, δ is a small positive value characterizing the zero-level set of B, and $\Delta r_{\min} > 0$ is the threshold avoiding too large fluctuations of reward value. In this work, we set $\beta_1 = 1.0$, $\beta_2 = 1.0$, $\delta = 0.1$, $\Delta r_{\min}$ denotes the size of Ψ. Since $0 \leq \hat{r}_t \leq \Delta r_{\min}$, the setting r_t (3) can be kept within a certain range, making the convergence effect better.

Algorithm 1. Barrier Certificate Guided Reinforcement Learning

---

Input: CCDS $\mathcal{C}$; unsafe region X_u; barrier certificate $B(\mathbf{x})$
Output: DNN Controller k
1: Initialize critic Q and actor k, corresponding target networks $Q' = Q$ and $k' = k$
2: Initialize barrier certificate $B(\mathbf{x}) = \perp$ and replay buffer $R = \emptyset$
3: Sample initial states from Θ and store them to Ω_Θ
4: **for** $\mathbf{x}_0 \in \Omega_\Theta$ **do**
5:     **for** $t = 1, \cdots, T$ **do**
6:         calculate $\mathbf{u}_t = k(\mathbf{x}_t)$
7:         calculate $\mathbf{x}_{t+1} = \mathbf{x}_t + \mathbf{f}(\mathbf{x}_t, \mathbf{u}_t)$
8:         calculate $r_t = r(\mathbf{x}_{t+1}, X_u, B(\mathbf{x}))$
9:         store $(\mathbf{x}_t, \mathbf{x}_{t+1}, u_t, r_t)$ to R
10:        Sample random minibatch of transitions from R
11:        Update critic Q and actor k
12:     **end for**
13:     Update the target networks Q' and k'
14: **end for**
15: **return** k

To synthesize the safety controller using reinforcement learning, a dataset of sampled trajectories is needed. To sample trajectories, we first generate a set of initial states from Θ. Let $\mathbf{l}, \mathbf{u} \in \mathbb{R}^n$ be the vectors of the lower and upper bounds of Θ, i.e., $\Theta \subseteq [\mathbf{l}, \mathbf{u}]$. We first sample from each dimension of $[\mathbf{l}, \mathbf{u}]$ equidistantly with a fixed mesh size. For a sampled initial state $\mathbf{x}_0$, its trajectory is generated, and the transition tuples $(\mathbf{x}_t, \mathbf{x}_{t+1}, \mathbf{u}_t, r_t)$ are collected to form a replay buffer to update the action and critic networks. Concretely, the action network receives a state $\mathbf{x}_t$ in time step t as input, and directly outputs a continuous action $\mathbf{u}_t = k(\mathbf{x}_t | \beta^k)$. The critic network takes the state $\mathbf{x}_t$ and the action $\mathbf{u}_t$ as input, and outputs a scalar Q-value $Q(\mathbf{x}_t, \mathbf{u}_t | \beta^Q)$. For every m simulated time steps, we sample a batch of tuples from the buffer as the training data to update the actor and critic networks, until a certain prescribed termination condition is met for the learning process. The resulting actor network is the synthesized controller. All training related parameters, such as smoothing factor, are set as default. Our DDPG implementation is based on an open-source package DDPG [23]. The algorithm is outlined in Algorithm 1.

Remark 2. The barrier certificate is initialized to be $\perp$, which means that the *learner* initially trains a DNN controller via standard reinforcement learning, without the aid of barrier certificates.

3.2 Safety Verification with Barrier Certificates

In the following, we focus on the *verifier* component of the proposed safe DNN synthesis framework, as described in Fig. 2, and show how to verify the safety of the closed-loop system under the DNN controller yielded from the *learner*.

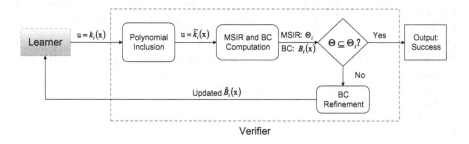

Fig. 2. The framework of the *verifier*.

Shown in Fig. 2, the *learner* produces a DNN controller $k_i(\mathbf{x})$. In order to make the problem of generating barrier certificates amenable to polynomial optimization problem, the *verifier* first employs Bernstein polynomial approximation to abstract the learned DNN controller as a polynomial one $\widetilde{k}_i(\mathbf{x})$, with the associated abstract error ϵ modeled as a bounded parameter, that is, $\mathbf{u} = \widetilde{k}_i(\mathbf{x}) + \epsilon$.

By doing it, the safety of the closed-loop system under the DNN controller can be guaranteed via the existence of barrier certificates for the closed-loop system under the abstract controller. The *verifier* then performs bilinear matrix inequalities (BMI) solving technique, to obtain a maximal safe initial region (MSIR) Θ_i and the corresponding barrier certificate $B_i(\mathbf{x})$. Once the computed MSIR Θ_i contains the given initial set Θ, then the safety of the closed-loop system under the DNN controller $\mathbf{u} = k_i(\mathbf{x})$ is verified. Otherwise, the *verifier* slightly adjusts the barrier certificate $B_i(\mathbf{x})$, based on quadratic programming solving, to gain an updated one $\widetilde{B}_i(\mathbf{x})$, which can separate the unsafe region from the initial set. Then, the refined BC is fed to guide the *learner* to retrain a new DNN controller.

Polynomial Abstraction of DNN Controllers. In the following, we consider the DNN controller with a single output, and for multiple-output cases, an extension is to approximate each output respectively. Formally, for a DNN controller $k(\mathbf{x})$, we seek to compute an approximate polynomial $p(\mathbf{x}) \in \mathbb{R}[\mathbf{x}]$ with a verified bound $\mu \in \mathbb{R}_+$, such that

$$|k(\mathbf{x}) - p(\mathbf{x})| < \mu, \forall \mathbf{x} \in \Psi,$$

and the bound μ is as small as possible.

Weierstrass approximation theorem [7] asserts that a continuous function on a closed and bounded interval can be uniformly approximated on the interval by polynomials to any degree of accuracy. In this paper, we will compute the approximate polynomial based on the theory of Bernstein polynomials [9]. Let $\mathbf{d} = (d_1, \cdots, d_n) \in \mathbb{N}^n$ and $f : [0,1]^n \to \mathbb{R}$. The polynomial

$$B_{f,\mathbf{d}}(\mathbf{x}) = \sum_{\substack{0 \le c_j \le d_j \\ j \in \{1,\cdots,n\}}} f\left(\frac{c_1}{d_1}, \cdots, \frac{c_n}{d_n}\right) \prod_{j=1}^{n} \binom{d_j}{c_j} x_j^{c_j} (1 - x_j)^{d_j - c_j}$$

is called the multivariate Bernstein polynomial of f. Theoretically, the Bernstein polynomial $B_{f,\mathbf{d}}(\mathbf{x})$ converges uniformly to f for $d_1, \cdots, d_n \to \infty$. In practice, the estimation of the approximation error bound is needed. As stated in [9], assume f is a Lipschitz continuous function over $I : [0,1]^n$ with a Lipschitz constant L, then we have

$$\|B_{f,\mathbf{d}}(\mathbf{x}) - f(\mathbf{x})\| \le \frac{L}{2}\left(\sum_{j=1}^{n}(\frac{1}{d_j})\right)^{\frac{1}{2}}, \forall \mathbf{x} \in I.$$

Now, for the DNN controller $k(\mathbf{x})$ over a domain Ψ, we can apply the above method to obtain a Bernstein polynomial with a valid approximate error bound as its abstraction. Concretely, we first construct an interval enclosure for Ψ, and apply a linear transformation to map the interval enclosure onto the unit box I, then utilize Bernstein polynomial approximation to obtain an abstract polynomial controller $\widetilde{k}(\mathbf{x}) + \epsilon$ with $\epsilon \in [-\mu, \mu]$, where $\widetilde{k}(\mathbf{x})$ is a Bernstein polynomial of $k(\mathbf{x})$ and μ is its valid approximate error bound. Note that the fully-connected neural networks with sigmoid and tanh activation functions are Lipschitz continuous, and the estimation of Lipschitz constants for deep neural networks has been studied in [14,31,34].

Maximal Safe Initial Region Computation. Since $\widetilde{k}(\mathbf{x}) + \epsilon$ enclosures $k(\mathbf{x})$, the safety of the closed-loop system under the DNN controller $k(\mathbf{x})$ can be guaranteed via the existence of barrier certificates for the closed-loop system under the abstract controller $\widetilde{k}(\mathbf{x}) + \epsilon$. From this observation, we try to compute an MSIR Θ_γ and its corresponding barrier certificate $B_\gamma(\mathbf{x})$, which can guarantee the safety of the closed-loop system under the abstract controller $\widetilde{k}(\mathbf{x}) + \epsilon$ with respect to Θ_γ.

Firstly, we consider how to predefine a suitable initial state set template Θ_γ from the given initial set Θ. In what follows, we provide some parametric initial state sets for two typical representations: Boxes and Euclidean ellipsoids (balls).

Box Template. Suppose that the box initial set Θ is represented as

$$\Theta = \{\mathbf{x} \in \mathbb{R}^n | |x_i - c_i| \le b_i\},$$

where $\mathbf{x}_c = (c_1, \cdots, c_n)^T$ is the center of the box, and $b_i \in \mathbb{R}_{>0}$. Then, the parametric initial set can be expressed as

$$\Theta_\gamma = \{\mathbf{x} \in \mathbb{R}^n | \|D^{-1}(\mathbf{x} - \mathbf{x}_c)\|_\infty \le \gamma\},$$

where $D = \mathrm{diag}(b_1, \cdots, b_n)$ is a diagonal matrix.

Ellipsoid Template. Suppose that the ellipsoid initial set Θ is expressed as a common representation:

$$\Theta = \{\mathbf{x} \in \mathbb{R}^n | \mathbf{x} = \mathbf{x}_c + A\mathbf{v}, \ \|\mathbf{v}\|_2 \le 1\},$$

where $\mathbf{x}_c$ is the center of the ellipsoid, and the matrix A is nonsingular. Then the parametric initial set can be expressed as

$$\begin{aligned}
\Theta_\gamma &= \{\mathbf{x} \in \mathbb{R}^n | \mathbf{x} = \mathbf{x}_0 + \gamma\, A\,\mathbf{v}, \|\mathbf{v}\|_2 \le 1\} \\
&= \{\mathbf{x} \in \mathbb{R}^n | \|A^{-1}(\mathbf{x} - \mathbf{x}_0)\|_2 \le \gamma\}.
\end{aligned}$$

Without loss of generality, we can select the template of the parametric initial sets by taking the form $\Theta_\gamma := \{\mathbf{x} \in \mathbb{R}^n | g(\mathbf{x}) \le \gamma, i = 1, \ldots, m_1\}$ with $\gamma \in \mathbb{R}_{>0}$, where $g(\mathbf{x})$ is the polynomial used to defined the prescribed initial set Θ.

In order to enlarge the safe initial region by choice of Θ_γ, we maximize γ while imposing the constraints for the existence of barrier certificates. Assume that the barrier certificate $B(\mathbf{x})$ is a polynomial of degree at most d, whose coefficients form a vector space of dimension $s(d) = \binom{n+d}{d}$ with the canonical basis $(\mathbf{x}^\alpha)$ of monomials. Suppose the coefficients are unknown, and denote by $\mathbf{b} = (b_\alpha) \in \mathbb{R}^{s(d)}$ the coefficient vector of $B(\mathbf{x})$, and write

$$B(\mathbf{x}, \mathbf{b}) = \sum_{\alpha \in \mathbb{N}_d^n} b_\alpha \mathbf{x}^\alpha = \sum_{\alpha \in \mathbb{N}_d^n} b_\alpha\, x_1^{\alpha_1} x_2^{\alpha_2} \cdots x_n^{\alpha_n},$$

in the canonical basis. Thus, the problem of computing an MSIR Θ_γ of the closed-loop system under the abstract controller $\widetilde{k}(\mathbf{x}) + \epsilon$ can be represented as an optimization problem

$$
\left.
\begin{aligned}
\gamma_{opt}^* &= \max_{\mathbf{b},\gamma} \gamma \\
\text{s.t. } & B(\mathbf{x},\mathbf{b}) \geq 0, \ \forall \mathbf{x} \in \Theta_\gamma, \\
& \mathcal{L}_{\mathbf{f}} B(\mathbf{x},\mathbf{b}) > 0, \ \forall \mathbf{x} \in \Psi \text{ and } B(\mathbf{x},\mathbf{b}) = 0, \\
& B(\mathbf{x},\mathbf{b}) < 0, \ \forall \mathbf{x} \in X_u.
\end{aligned}
\right\} \tag{4}
$$

Then, Sum-of-Squares (SOS) relaxation technique is applied to encode the optimization problem (4) as a SOS program. In fact, given a basic semi-algebraic set $\mathbb{K}$ defined by:

$$
\mathbb{K} = \{\mathbf{x} \in \mathbb{R}^n \mid p_1(\mathbf{x}) \geq 0, \ldots, p_s(\mathbf{x}) \geq 0\},
$$

where $p_j \in \mathbb{R}[\mathbf{x}], 1 \leq j \leq s$, a sufficient condition for the nonnegativity of the given polynomial $f(\mathbf{x})$ on the semi-algebraic set $\mathbb{K}$ is provided as

$$
f(\mathbf{x}) = \sigma_0(\mathbf{x}) + \sum_{i=1}^{s} \sigma_i(\mathbf{x}) p_i(\mathbf{x}), \tag{5}
$$

where $\sigma_i \in \Sigma[\mathbf{x}]_d$, $1 \leq i \leq s$. Thus, the representation (5) ensures that the polynomial $f(\mathbf{x})$ is nonnegative on the given semi-algebraic set $\mathbb{K}$.

Observing (4), the polynomial $\mathcal{L}_{\mathbf{f}} B(\mathbf{x},\mathbf{b})$ is involved with the uncertain variable ϵ in the range $[-\mu, \mu]$, which can be written as the constraint, $\hat{h}(\epsilon) \geq 0$ with

$$
\hat{h}(\epsilon) := (\epsilon + \mu)(\mu - \epsilon).
$$

Thus, the problem (4) can be transformed into the following optimization problem

$$
\left.
\begin{aligned}
\gamma^* &= \max_{\mathbf{b},\gamma} \gamma \\
\text{s.t. } & B(\mathbf{x},\mathbf{b}) - \sigma(\mathbf{x})(\gamma - g(\mathbf{x})) \in \Sigma[\mathbf{x}], \\
& \mathcal{L}_{\mathbf{f}} B(\mathbf{x},\mathbf{b}) - \lambda(\mathbf{x}) B(\mathbf{x},\mathbf{b}) - \sum_j \phi_j(\mathbf{x}) h_j(\mathbf{x}) - \nu(\mathbf{x},\varepsilon)\hat{h}(\varepsilon) - \epsilon_1 \in \Sigma[\mathbf{x}], \\
& -B(\mathbf{x},\mathbf{b}) - \epsilon_2 - \sum_j \kappa_j(\mathbf{x}) q_j(\mathbf{x}) \in \Sigma[\mathbf{x}],
\end{aligned}
\right\} \tag{6}
$$

where $\epsilon_1, \epsilon_2 > 0$, the entries of $\sigma(\mathbf{x})$, $\phi_j(\mathbf{x})$ $\kappa(\mathbf{x}) \in \Sigma[\mathbf{x}]$, and $\nu(\mathbf{x},\varepsilon) \in \Sigma[\mathbf{x},\varepsilon]$, and $\lambda(\mathbf{x}) \in \mathbb{R}[\mathbf{x}]$. Note that ϵ_1, ϵ_2 are needed to ensure positivity of polynomials as required in the second and third constraints in (4). Clearly, the feasibility of the constraints in (6) is sufficient to imply the feasibility of the constraints in (4), thus the optimum of (6) is a lower bound of the optimum of (4), i.e., $\gamma^* \leq \gamma_{opt}^*$.

The SOS program (6) is bilinear due to the product of the unknown coefficients of $(B(\mathbf{x},\mathbf{b}), \lambda(\mathbf{x}))$ and $(\sigma(\mathbf{x}), \gamma)$, yielding a non-convex bilinear matrix inequalities (BMI) problem. Fortunately, a Matlab package PENBMI solver [22], which combines the (exterior) penalty and (interior) barrier method with the augmented Lagrangian method, can be applied directly to obtain a numerical solution of the problem (6). The solution $\gamma^*, \mathbf{b}^*$ to problem (6) yields an MSIR Θ_{γ^*} and its corresponding barrier certificate $B(\mathbf{x}, \mathbf{b}^*)$. It means that the closed-loop system under the abstract controller $\widetilde{k}(\mathbf{x}) + \epsilon$ is safe, with respect to Θ_{γ^*}. Moreover, if the given initial set Θ is a subset of Θ_{γ^*}, then the safety of the closed-loop system under the DNN controller $k(\mathbf{x})$ with respect to Θ is verified. Otherwise, $B(\mathbf{x}, \mathbf{b}^*)$ will be further refined via quadratic programming method.

Remark 3. The gap between the optima of problems (4) and (6) decreases as increasing of degrees for the multiplier polynomials. The degree bound for the multiplier polynomials is exponential with the number of variables $\mathbf{x}$ and the degrees of the polynomials appearing in the semi-algebraic sets. In practice, we set up a truncated SOS programming for (6) by fixing a *priori* (much smaller) degree bound of all the unknown multiplier polynomials, to avoid high computational complexity.

Barrier Certificate Refinement. Consider the case in which the initial set Θ is not a subset of the MSIR Θ_{γ^*}. In this case, the barrier certificate $B(\mathbf{x}, \mathbf{b}^*)$ can succeed to separate the unsafe region X_u from Θ_{γ^*}, but it may fail to separate from Θ. In other words, $B(\mathbf{x}, \mathbf{b}^*)$ can not be regarded as a truly candidate barrier certificate with respect to Θ and X_u. Therefore, we will utilize the information of $B(\mathbf{x}, \mathbf{b}^*)$ to refine it, in order to obtain a new candidate barrier certificate that can separate Θ from X_u. Consider the change in $B(\mathbf{x}, \mathbf{b}^*)$ is expected as small as possible, the step of the barrier certificate refinement can be represented as

$$\left.\begin{aligned} \min \|\hat{\mathbf{b}} - \mathbf{b}^*\|_2^2 \\ \text{s.t.} \quad B(\mathbf{x}, \hat{\mathbf{b}}) \geq 0 \ \forall \mathbf{x} \in \Theta, \\ B(\mathbf{x}, \hat{\mathbf{b}}) < 0 \ \forall \mathbf{x} \in X_u. \end{aligned}\right\} \tag{7}$$

By investigating (7), the constraints are the ones involving universal quantifiers. To avoid eliminating universal quantifiers directly, here we provide a relaxation technique to deal with (7), which is based on selecting sampling points. For Θ and X_u, let us first construct rectangular meshes in Θ and X_u respectively, with a mesh spacing $r \in \mathbb{R}_+$ (say $r = 0.05$). The resulting mesh point sets are denoted as Ω_Θ and Ω_{X_u}, respectively.

It is known that for a continuously differentiable function $\phi(\mathbf{x})$ over a compact domain D, the mean value theorem yields that

$$|\phi(\mathbf{x} + \Delta\mathbf{x}) - \phi(\mathbf{x})| \leq n\eta \|\Delta\mathbf{x}\|_\infty,$$

where $\mathbf{x}, \mathbf{x} + \Delta \in \Omega$ are chosen randomly, and $\eta = \sup_{\mathbf{x} \in D} \|\nabla\phi(\mathbf{x})\|_\infty$. Based on the above observation, the following implications are satisfied:

$$\left.\begin{aligned} B(\mathbf{x}_j, \hat{\mathbf{b}}) - \delta_1 \geq 0, \ \forall \mathbf{x}_j \in \Omega_\Theta \Longrightarrow B(\mathbf{x}, \hat{\mathbf{b}}) \geq 0 \ \forall \mathbf{x} \in \Theta, \\ B(\mathbf{x}_j, \hat{\mathbf{b}}) + \delta_2 < 0, \ \forall \mathbf{x}_j \in \Omega_{X_u} \Longrightarrow B(\mathbf{x}, \hat{\mathbf{b}}) < 0 \ \forall \mathbf{x} \in X_u. \end{aligned}\right\}$$

where $\delta_i = n\eta_i r \in \mathbb{R}_{>0}, i = 1, 2$ with $\eta_1 = \sup_{\mathbf{x} \in \Theta} \|\nabla B(\mathbf{x}, \mathbf{b}^*)\|_\infty$ and $\eta_2 = \sup_{\mathbf{x} \in X_u} \|\nabla B(\mathbf{x}, \mathbf{b}^*)\|_\infty$.

By using the above relaxation technique based on sampling points, (7) can be relaxed as the following problem

$$\left.\begin{aligned} \min \|\hat{\mathbf{b}} - \mathbf{b}^*\|_2^2 \\ \text{s.t.} \quad B(\mathbf{x}_j, \hat{\mathbf{b}}) - \delta \geq 0, \ \forall \mathbf{x}_j \in \Omega_\Theta, \\ B(\mathbf{x}_j, \hat{\mathbf{b}}) + \delta < 0, \ \forall \mathbf{x}_j \in \Omega_{X_u}, \end{aligned}\right\} \tag{8}$$

which is a typical quadratic programming problem and can be solved by state-of-the-art solvers with great efficiency.

Now, the refined $\widehat{B}(\mathbf{x}) = B(\mathbf{x}, \hat{\mathbf{b}})$ can separate Θ from X_u, but may still not satisfy the Lie derivative condition for barrier certificates. According to Theorem 1, $\widehat{B}(\mathbf{x})$ is not a truly barrier certificate for the closed-loop system under the abstract controller $\widetilde{k}(\mathbf{x}) + \epsilon$ with respect to Θ and X_u. Next, the refined $\widehat{B}(\mathbf{x})$ will be further fed to guide the *learner* to retrain a new controller. To do it, we first consider the additional constraint for the Lie derivative of $\widehat{B}(\mathbf{x})$, and apply barrier certificate guided reinforcement learning to compute a new DNN controller.

4 Algorithm

In Sect. 3, we have elaborated on the iteration-based safe controller synthesis method that iteratively co-synthesizes a DNN controller within the RL framework and a polynomial barrier certificate via BMI solving. Briefly, we describe the main implementation steps of our approach in the following Algorithm 2.

Algorithm 2. SRLBC: Safe Reinforcement Learning with Barrier Certificate

---

Input: The CCDS $\mathcal{C}$; unsafe region X_u; maximum number of iterations *maxIter*
Output: Safe DNN Controller k

1: $iter \leftarrow 0$
2: $B \leftarrow \bot$
3: **while** $iter < maxIter$ **do**
4:　　$k \leftarrow$ Learning(f, Θ, X_u, B)
5:　　$\widehat{k}, \mu \leftarrow$ PolyInclusion(k)
6:　　$\Theta_\gamma^*, B(\mathbf{x}, \mathbf{b}^*) \leftarrow$ MaxSafeSet$(f, \widehat{k}, \mu, \Theta, X_u)$
7:　　**if** $\Theta \subseteq \Theta_\gamma^*$ **then**
8:　　　　**return** k
9:　　**end if**
10:　　$B \leftarrow$ RefineBarrier$(B(\mathbf{x}, \mathbf{b}^*), \Theta, X_u)$
11: **end while**

Algorithm 2 shows the iteration scheme of our safe controller synthesis, which guides the experiment implementation. The procedure takes as inputs a CCDS $\mathcal{C}$, an unsafe region X_u, a maximum number of iterations *maxIter*, and returns a safe DNN controller of a given architecture. In a pass of the iteration, the implementation process has four steps as follows.

(i) Apply the RL method to train a DNN controller. The *learner* introduced in Sect. 3.1 is implemented by Line 4 in Algorithm 2, and the barrier certificate is initialized to be $\bot$, which means that the *learner* trains a DNN controller via classical reinforcement learning, without the aid of barrier certificates in the initial pass;

(ii) For the closed-loop system under the DNN controller learned in Step (i), compute a maximal safe initial region (MSIR), with which a barrier certificate exists. We use Bernstein polynomial approximation to compute a polynomial abstraction for the learned DNN controller by Line 5, and then compute an MSIR Θ_{γ^*} and the corresponding barrier certificate $B(\mathbf{x}, \mathbf{b}^*)$ by Line 6;

(iii) Check the condition wether the MSIR Θ_{γ^*} in Step (ii) contains the given initial set Θ. If $\Theta \subseteq \Theta_{\gamma^*}$, then we terminate the loop with a verified safe DNN controller; otherwise go to Step (iv). This process refers to Lines 7–9;

(iv) Slightly modify the barrier certificate from Step (iii) so that it separates the initial set and the unsafe region, and then go to Step (i) to learn a new controller by encoding the refined barrier certificate into the reward function. For this task, the barrier certificate B is refined via quadratic programming by Line 10.

This inductive loop repeats until an MSIR enclosing Θ_γ and its corresponding barrier certificate are computed or until a timeout is reached.

Remark 4. Our procedure is sound, i.e. a valid output from the *verifier* is provably correct. However, we cannot claim any completeness, since our procedure might in general not terminate because the existence of the barrier certificate is just a sufficient condition of the safety of the system, and such a barrier certificate may not exist indeed. Once the procedure fails, we may improve the relaxation precision and then increase the possibility to find the barrier certificate by increasing the degree bound for the multiplier polynomials in the SOS program (6).

Furthermore, an example is used to depict how our safe controller synthesis algorithm works.

Example 1. Consider the Van der Pol system

$$\begin{bmatrix} \dot{x}_1 \\ \dot{x}_2 \end{bmatrix} = \begin{bmatrix} x_2 \\ -x_1 + \frac{1}{3}x_1^3 - x_2 + u \end{bmatrix}$$

with the domain $\Psi = \{\mathbf{x} \in \mathbb{R}^2 \mid -3 \leq x_1, x_2 \leq 3\}$. Our goal is to design a control law k such that all trajectories of the system under $u = k(x_1, x_2)$ starting from the initial set

$$\Theta = \{\mathbf{x} \in \mathbb{R}^2 \mid (x_1 - 1.5)^2 + x_2^2 \leq 1.1^2\}$$

will never enter the unsafe set

$$X_u = \{\mathbf{x} \in \mathbb{R}^2 \mid (x_1 + 1)^2 + (x_2 + 1)^2 \leq 1\}.$$

We complete our goal by Algorithm 2, and provide the details here. At first, we apply the reinforcement learning method to train the initial neural network controller $u = k_0(\mathbf{x})$ in terms of the target of safety satisfiability, which is Step

(i) and refers to Line 4 in Algorithm 2, and then try to yield the barrier certificate $B(\mathbf{x})$. We compute polynomial abstraction of DNN Controller $k_0(\mathbf{x})$ via Bernstein polynomials which is Step (ii), where

$$
\begin{aligned}
\tilde{k}_0(\mathbf{x}) = {} & 0.0142x_1 + 0.0092x_2 - 0.0205x_1^2 + 0.0077x_1x_2 + 0.0340x_2^2 \\
& + 0.0246x_1^3 + 0.0018x_1^2x_2 - 0.0820x_1x_2^2 + 0.0435x_2^3 + \epsilon.
\end{aligned}
\tag{9}
$$

with $\epsilon \in [-0.05, 0.05]$, which is implemented by Line 5. Thus, the polynomial abstraction technique can yield an abstract polynomial system.

Go on Step (ii) to compute a maximal safety region Θ_γ and the corresponding barrier certificate $B(\mathbf{x})$. In this case, we parameterize the initial set:

$$
\Theta_\gamma = \{\mathbf{x} \in \mathbb{R}^2 \mid (x_1 - 1.5)^2 + x_2^2 \le \gamma\}.
$$

For the given abstract polynomial system with the parameterized initial set Θ_γ, our goal is to maximize the radius γ subject to the existence of a barrier certificate. By calling the PENBMI solver [22] we can obtain a barrier certificate $B_0(\mathbf{x})$ with the maximal safe initial region Θ_0 (Line 6 in our Algorithm 2), i.e.,

$$
\begin{aligned}
\Theta_0 &= \{\mathbf{x} \in \mathbb{R}^2 \mid (x_1 - 1.5)^2 + x_2^2 \le 0.8132\}, \\
B_0(\mathbf{x}) &= 11.716 + 22.8064x_1 + 21.5368x_2 - 4.5273x_1^2 + 13.8084x_1x_2 + 3.0453x_2^2.
\end{aligned}
\tag{10}
$$

Thus, the safety of the system with the controller $k_0(\mathbf{x})$ with respect to the set Θ_0 is guaranteed. Now the present controller $k_0(\mathbf{x})$ can not be safe for whole initial set Θ, we continue to update controller and barrier certificate (Line 7–9).

Let $k_0(\mathbf{x})$ and $B_0(\mathbf{x})$ be the initial controller and the initial barrier certificate, we perform the iterative framework to synthesize the controller subject to the safety constraint. As shown in Fig. 3(a), the zero level set of $B_0(\mathbf{x})$ is the blue dashed line. Observing Fig. 3(a), $B_0(\mathbf{x})$ can succeed to separate the unsafe region X_u (the red circle) from Θ_0 (the green dashed circle), but not separate from the initial set Θ, which means that $B_0(\mathbf{x})$ can not be regarded as the truly barrier certificate. Therefore, one may perturb the coefficients of $B_0(\mathbf{x})$ to obtain $\hat{B}_0(\mathbf{x})$ which can separate Θ and X_u. And this process corresponds to Step (iv) and Line 10 of our Algorithm 2. The perturbed polynomial is represented as

$$
\hat{B}_0(\mathbf{x}) = 10.5590 + 22.9401x_1 + 18.2448x_2 - 0.8954x_1^2 + 14.4971x_1x_2 + 1.1060x_2^2.
$$

As shown in Fig. 1(b), the zero level set of the barrier $\hat{B}_0(\mathbf{x})$ (the blue dash) separates X_u (the red circle) from Θ (the green circle). According to the concept of barrier certificate and Theorem 1, $\hat{B}_0(\mathbf{x})$ is not a truly barrier certificate, since the condition of the Lie derivative of the barrier certificate is not satisfied. Accordingly, by using the $\hat{B}_0(\mathbf{x})$ and the initial controller $k_0(\mathbf{x})$, we then try to retrain a control law with an additional constraint of the lie derivative for the barrier certificate $\hat{B}_0(\mathbf{x})$. Calling the *learner* module (Line 4), we update a new control law $k_1(\mathbf{x})$ represented as a two-hidden layer sigmoid-based DNN with 20 neurons per layer by RL approach.

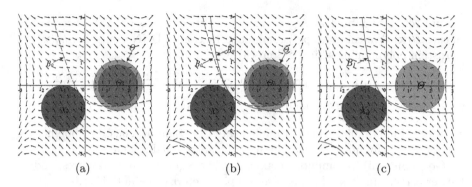

(a)   (b)   (c)

Fig. 3. This picture shows the iteration process of barrier certificate updating when we learn the safe controller. The red circles stand for unsafe regions, the blue curves stand for the zero level set of barrier certificates, and the green circles stand for the initial sets and safe initial sets. Subfigure (a) describes the intermediate results of maximal safe initial set Θ_0 (the green dashed circle) with its associate barrier certificate B_0 obtained from Line 6 in Algorithm 2 at the first iteration. We slightly modify the barrier function B_0 to separate Θ and X_u by Line 10 and obtain $\hat{B}_0$ which is the blue solid curve shown in Subfigure (b). Using $\hat{B}_0$ as a guide, a new controller is learned, from which a barrier certificate B_1 is generated as shown in Subfigure (c). It can be shown that B_1 is the real barrier certificate of the system. (Color figure online)

Repeating the above abstraction technique and solving the BMI problem for finding the maximal safety initial set Θ_1, we obtain the barrier certificate $B_1(\mathbf{x})$ with respect to Θ_1, i.e.,

$$\begin{aligned}
\Theta_1 &= \{\mathbf{x} \in \mathbb{R}^2 \mid (x_1 - 1.5)^2 + x_2^2 \le 1.2201\}, \\
B_1(\mathbf{x}) &= 10.3661 + 22.6569x_1 + 17.7852x_2 - 0.9037x_1^2 + 14.1832x_1x_2 + 0.9471x_2^2.
\end{aligned} \tag{11}$$

It is easy to check that the original initial set Θ is now a subset of Θ_1, which means that $B_1(\mathbf{x})$ is a truly barrier certificate.

5   Experiments

In this section, we first depict an example of three dimension nonlinear continuous system to show our algorithm by synthesizing a safe DNN controller for it, and then present an experimental evaluation of our algorithm over a set of benchmark examples by comparing with a DNN controller learning framework called *nncontroller* in [39].

Example 2. Consider the continuous dynamical system

$$\begin{bmatrix} \dot{x_1} \\ \dot{x_2} \\ \dot{x_3} \end{bmatrix} = \begin{bmatrix} x_3 + 8x_2 \\ -x_2 + x_3 \\ -x_3 - x_1^2 + u \end{bmatrix}$$

with the domain

$$\Psi = \{\mathbf{x} \in \mathbb{R}^3 \mid x_1^2 + x_2^2 + x_3^2 \le 16\}.$$

Our goal is to design a control law k such that all trajectories of the closed-loop system under $u = k(x_1, x_2, x_3)$ starting from the initial set

$$\Theta = \{\mathbf{x} \in \mathbb{R}^3 \mid x_1^2 + x_2^2 + x_3^2 \leq 1\}$$

will never enter the unsafe set

$$X_u = \{\mathbf{x} \in \mathbb{R}^3 \mid (x_1 - 2.1)^2 + (x_2 - 2.1)^2 + (x_3^2 - 2.1) \leq 1.8^2\}.$$

It suffices to synthesize a control law k and a barrier certificate $B(\mathbf{x})$ with the maximal safe initial region Θ_γ such that $\Theta \subseteq \Theta_\gamma$. Suppose that the DNN controller k is represented as a five-hidden layer sigmoid activated DNN with 30 neurons per layer. We first call the *learner* to train a DNN controller, and then call the *verifier* to compute the maximal safe initial region Θ_γ and its corresponding barrier certificate $B(\mathbf{x})$. After two iterations, we successfully obtain a safe DNN controller, and the following barrier certificate

$$\begin{aligned} B(\mathbf{x}) = {} & 220.1981 - 45.7322x_1 - 40.2831x_2 - 218.4765x_3 + 4.9575x_1^2 \\ & + 38.7288x_1x_2 - 9.8224x_1x_3 - 66.8398x_2^2 + 17.2562x_2x_3 + 18.3967x_3^2. \end{aligned}$$
(12)

As shown in Fig. 4, the zero level set of the barrier certificate $B(\mathbf{x})$ (the blue surface) separates X_u (the red ball) from all trajectories starting from Θ (the green ball). Therefore, the safety of the above system is verified.

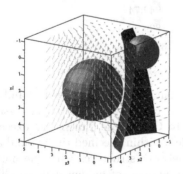 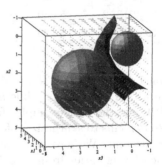

Fig. 4. Phase portrait of the system in Example 2. The zero level set of the barrier certificate $B(\mathbf{x})$ (the blue surface) separates X_u (the red ball) from all trajectories starting from Θ (the green ball). (Color figure online)

We have implemented a safe controller synthesis tool called *SRLBC* based on Algorithm 2, with Tensorflow 1.14 for the DNN controller synthesis and a Matlab package PENBMI [22] for barrier certificate generation. Table 1 shows the performance evaluation of our *SRLBC* and *nncontroller* in [39] on 12 continuous systems. All experiments are conducted on a machine running Windows 10 with 16 GB RAM, a 3.20 GHz AMD Ryzen 7 3700X CPU, and an NVIDIA GeForce GTX 1650 super GPU.

In Table 1, the origins of these 12 examples are provided in the first column; d_f denotes the maximal degree of the polynomials in the vector fields; n_x denotes the number of the state variables; L and N refer to the numbers of hidden layers and the neurons per each hidden layer, respectively; t_1 and t_2 denote the time spent by $SRLBC$ and $nncontroller$ in seconds, respectively; the symbol $'-'$ means that $nncontroller$ was unable to return a safe DNN controller within 10,000 s.

Table 1. Performance evaluation

Examples	d_f	n_x	NNstructure		$SRLBC$		$nncontroller$	
			L	N	$\deg B(\mathbf{x})$	t(s)	NN-type BC	t(s)
C1 [28]	2	2	4	20	2	54.77	2-10-1	20.52
C2 [6]	3	2	4	20	2	37.54	2-10-1	8.46
C3 [6]	3	2	4	20	2	35.99	2-10-1	6.77
C4 [27]	3	2	4	20	4	38.68	2-10-1	6.88
C5 [39]	3	3	5	30	2	56.21	3-10-1	32.19
C6 [20]	3	4	5	30	2	45.54	4-10-1	78.52
C7 [6]	3	4	5	30	4	40.82	4-10-1	184.85
C8 [32]	2	5	5	30	2	423.11	5-20-1	2217.41
C9 [38]	2	6	5	30	2	383.26	–	–
C10 [4]	3	6	5	30	4	942.74	–	–
C11 [21]	2	7	5	30	2	1829.46	–	–
C12 [21]	2	9	5	30	2	6208.79	–	–

Table 1 shows that for the 12 examples, our $SRLBC$ manages to handle all of them within 3 iterations, while $nncontroller$ can only deal with 8 successfully. Especially for the four examples from C9 to C12 whose dimensions exceed 5, $nncontroller$ fails to synthesize safe controllers within specified time bound after various attempt. We have tried different network structures with the number of hidden layers varies from 1 to 5 and the number of hidden neurons chosen among $\{10, 20, 30, 40\}$, the $nncontroller$ fails to train candidate DNN controllers and barrier certificates within the time limit, whereas our $SRLBC$ can yield safe controllers, represented as five-layer sigmoid activated neural networks.

Consider the efficiency of our $SRLBC$ and $nncontroller$ in terms of the time spent in synthesizing safe DNN controllers for shared examples. On average, our $SRLBC$ takes 91.58 s to synthesize a safe DNN controller while $nncontroller$ needs 323.2 s, which is about 3.53 times slower than our $SRLBC$. Despite the network structures used for $SRLBC$ is more complex than that for $nncontroller$, and the number of neural network neurons of $SRLBC$ is much more than that of $nncontroller$, we could synthesize more efficiently.

Obviously, our *SRLBC* scales better than *nncontroller* for the considered examples. Although our *SRLBC* consumes a little more time than *nncontroller* for the systems with dimension 2 or 3, our tool shows its advantage on time consuming when handling the systems with dimension higher than 3 (C6-C8) and its ability on examples C9-C12. Comparing with *nncontroller* which is also a data driven approach, *SRLBC* inherits the advantage in learning efficiency of reinforcement learning, whereas the size of the training data for *nncontroller* increases exponentially with the dimension of the considered systems, which greatly limits the scale of the problem to deal with. Beyond Table 1, we have tried an example of nonlinear polynomial system [16] with dimension up to 12, and *SRLBC* yields successfully a result in 54,314 s while *nncontroller* fails. It is clear that our approach is able to attack large-scale problems.

During the experiment, we have observed that *SRLBC* obtains the near-safe controllers at the first iteration for most examples, and the remaining work is to refine barrier certificates slightly and use them to guide and adjust the controllers. In fact, the numbers of the iterations in our experiments on the benchmarks did not exceed 3 for all cases. These observations show that our iterative scheme of safe reinforcement learning converges well in practice, because the refinement of the controllers could utilize the intermediate learned results before we get the final results. In addition, *SRLBC* could easily generalize to deal with non-polynomial systems and it has successfully solved the classical continuous Cartpole system [3], which would be presented in the future work.

6 Related Work

Our work on synthesizing DNN controllers for safety control of nonlinear systems is mainly related to two categories of research, i.e. *formal verification of nonlinear systems with DNN controller* and *safe DNN controller synthesis*. There has been considerable research conducted in these areas because of the applications in safety critical systems in recent years.

Formal Verification of Nonlinear Systems with DNN Controller. One of the mainstream methodologies is through constructing over-approximations to the reachable sets of the system trajectories under DNN controllers. And the core technique first focuses on output range analysis of the neural network components, then combines the output range with reachability analysis on the dynamical systems. For instance, based on the output range analysis in [13], Dutta et al. verified the feedback control systems with DNN controllers using mixed-integer linear programming [12]. And they implemented the prototype tool for the neural rule generation inside the tool termed as Sherlock, and used it together with Flow* for computing the reach sets of the systems [10].

The difference of works on this direction lies in what kind of abstract domains is adopted for output range analysis of the neural network components. A recent attempt involves the work of Xiang et al. that computes the output ranges as a union of convex polytopes [37]. For the piecewise linear systems with ReLU neural network as the controller, they compute the output range of ReLU neural network by a layer-by-layer approach. Dutta et al. propose an approach to abstract the DNN by a local polynomial approximation along with rigorous error bound, and then integrate it with a Taylor model-based flow pipe construction scheme for continuous differential equations to derive the over-approximation of the real reachable set [11]. Likely, Huang et al. present an approach to constructing a polynomial approximation for a DNN controller using Bernstein polynomials, and then integrate result with the plant to get the over-approximated reachable set [18]. There is a different route for reachability of systems with neural network components proposed by Ivanov et al. and termed as Verisig [19]. It transforms the problem of verifying neural network controlled system into a hybrid system verification problem by first transforming a sigmoid-based neural network into an equivalent hybrid system and then composing it with the plant.

Instead of computing reachable sets, a different approach for verifying neural network controlled systems is through barrier certificate synthesis. Tuncali et al. synthesize candidate barrier certificates using simulation-guided techniques, and then verify the overall system safety by checking the validity of the barrier certificate conditions for the candidate [35]. The safety property was proofed, or a counterexample was returned to updated candidate barrier certificates.

Safety Critical Controller Generation. Research works in this category differ in: (1) the overall learning framework, e.g. reinforcement learning (RL) or supervised learning; (2) the kind of safety certificate, e.g., control Lyapunov function (CLF) or control barrier function (CBF) [2].

For CLFs or CBFs synthesis, a demonstrator-learner-verifier framework was proposed in [29] to learn polynomial CLFs for polynomial nonlinear dynamical systems; a special type of neural network was designed in [30] as candidates for learning Lyapunov functions; a supervised learning approach was proposed in [5] to learn neural network Lyapunov functions and linear control policies; data-driven model predictive control (MPC) exploiting neural Lyapunov function and neural network dynamics model was proposed in [12,25]. For multi-agent systems, barrier function has recently been applied for safe policy synthesis on POMDP models [1]. The computer science community has dealt with the issue of safe controller learning in different ways from above: for example, a logical-proof based approach was proposed in [15] towards safe RL; a synthesis framework capable of synthesizing deterministic programs from neural network policies was proposed in [41] and so formal verification techniques for traditional software systems can be applied. Compared with these works, [39] learn controllers based on neural networks. To certify the safety property they utilize barrier certificates, which are represented by DNNs as well. In this way, they train DNN controllers and DNN barrier certificates simultaneously, achieving a verification-in-the-loop synthesis. Liu et al. proposed a Recurrent Neural Network (RNN) framework to synthesize feedback control policies for a system under STL specifications [24]. The CBF was used to modify the control policies predicted by the RNN to guarantee safety.

7   Conclusion

In this paper, we have developed a novel scheme for synthesizing safe controllers of nonlinear systems with control against safety constraints. It employs an iterative architecture, where a *learner* trains DNN controllers using reinforcement learning and a *verifier* checks them via computation of maximal safe initial regions and the corresponding barrier certificates, based on polynomial abstraction and bilinear matrix inequalities solving. The key idea in this paper is to use an alternating co-synthesis scheme of controllers and barrier certificates to generate safe controllers, which could refine barrier certificates during iteration. On the one hand, this synthesis scheme has inherited the higher learning efficiency from RL technique than other data driven methods. On the other hand, this iterative architecture could modify barrier certificates to obtain an adaptive one along with DNN controller retraining, and other verification-in-the-loop synthesis methods are usually based on user-defined barrier functions. Furthermore, our BMI solving based barrier certificate generation is more efficient than SMT based verification. The experimental results demonstrate that our method is more scalable and effective than the existing DNN controller synthesis method *nncontroller*.

References

1. Ahmadi, M., Singletary, A., Burdick, J.W., Ames, A.D.: Safe policy synthesis in multi-agent POMDPs via discrete-time barrier functions. In: Proceedings of the IEEE 58th Conference on Decision and Control (CDC), pp. 4797–4803. IEEE (2019)
2. Ames, A.D., Coogan, S., Egerstedt, M., Notomista, G., Sreenath, K., Tabuada, P.: Control barrier functions: theory and applications. In: Proceedings of the 17th European Control Conference, (ECC), pp. 3420–3431 (2019)
3. Barto, A.G., Sutton, R.S., Anderson, C.W.: Neuronlike adaptive elements that can solve difficult learning control problems. IEEE Trans. Syst. Man Cybern. **13**(5), 834–846 (1983)
4. Bouissou, O., Chapoutot, A., Djaballah, A., Kieffer, M.: Computation of parametric barrier functions for dynamical systems using interval analysis. In: Proceedings of the 53rd IEEE Conference on Decision and Control (CDC), pp. 753–758. IEEE (2014)
5. Chang, Y.C., Roohi, N., Gao, S.: Neural Lyapunov control. In: Proceedings of the Annual Conference on Advances in Neural Information Processing Systems (NeurIPS), pp. 3245–3254 (2019)
6. Chesi, G.: Computing output feedback controllers to enlarge the domain of attraction in polynomial systems. IEEE Trans. Autom. Control **49**(10), 1846–1853 (2004)
7. Davis, P.J.: Interpolation and Approximation. Dover Books on Mathematics. Dover Publications, New York (1975)
8. Deshmukh, J.V., Kapinski, J., Yamaguchi, T., Prokhorov, D.: Learning deep neural network controllers for dynamical systems with safety guarantees: Invited paper. In: Proceedings of the IEEE/ACM International Conference on Computer-Aided Design (ICCAD), pp. 1–7 (2019)

9. Duchoň, M.: A generalized bernstein approximation theorem. Tatra Mt. Math. Publ. **49**(1), 99–109 (2011)
10. Dutta, S., Chen, X., Jha, S., Sankaranarayanan, S., Tiwari, A.: Sherlock - a tool for verification of neural network feedback systems: demo abstract. In: Proceedings of the 22nd ACM International Conference on Hybrid Systems: Computation and Control (HSCC), pp. 262–263 (2019)
11. Dutta, S., Chen, X., Sankaranarayanan, S.: Reachability analysis for neural feedback systems using regressive polynomial rule inference. In: Proceedings of the 22nd ACM International Conference on Hybrid Systems: Computation and Control (HSCC), pp. 157–168 (2019)
12. Dutta, S., Jha, S., Sankaranarayanan, S., Tiwari, A.: Learning and verification of feedback control systems using feedforward neural networks. IFAC-PapersOnLine **51**(16), 151–156 (2018)
13. Dutta, S., Jha, S., Sankaranarayanan, S., Tiwari, A.: Output range analysis for deep feedforward neural networks. In: Dutle, A., Muñoz, C., Narkawicz, A. (eds.) NFM 2018. LNCS, vol. 10811, pp. 121–138. Springer, Cham (2018). https://doi.org/10.1007/978-3-319-77935-5_9
14. Fazlyab, M., Robey, A., Hassani, H., Morari, M., Pappas, G.J.: Efficient and accurate estimation of lipschitz constants for deep neural networks. arXiv preprint arXiv:1906.04893 (2019)
15. Fulton, N., Platzer, A.: Safe reinforcement learning via formal methods: toward safe control through proof and learning. In: Proceedings of the Thirty-Second AAAI Conference on Artificial Intelligence (AAAI), pp. 6485–6492 (2018)
16. Gao, S.: Quadcopter model. https://github.com/dreal/benchmarks
17. García, J., o Fernández, F., et al.: A comprehensive survey on safe reinforcement learning. J. Mach. Learn. Res. **16**(42), 1437–1480 (2015)
18. Huang, C., Fan, J., Li, W., Chen, X., Zhu, Q.: ReachNN: reachability analysis of neural-network controlled systems. ACM Trans. Embedded Comput. Syst. **18**(5s), 106:1-106:22 (2019)
19. Ivanov, R., Weimer, J., Alur, R., Pappas, G.J., Lee, I.: Verisig: verifying safety properties of hybrid systems with neural network controllers. In: Proceedings of the 22nd ACM International Conference on Hybrid Systems: Computation and Control (HSCC), pp. 169–178 (2019)
20. Jarvis-Wloszek, Z.: Lyapunov based analysis and controller synthesis for polynomial systems using sum-of-squares optimization. Ph.D. thesis, University of California (2003)
21. Klipp, E., Herwig, R., Kowald, A., Wierling, C., Lehrach, H.: Systems Biology in Practice: Concepts. Implementation and Application, Wiley-Blackwell (2005)
22. Kočvara, M., Stingl, M.: PENBMI user's guide (version 2.0) (2005). http://www.penopt.com
23. Lillicrap, T.P., et al.: Continuous control with deep reinforcement learning. In: Proceedings of the 4th International Conference on Learning Representations (ICLR) (2016)
24. Liu, W., Mehdipour, N., Belta, C.: Recurrent neural network controllers for signal temporal logic specifications subject to safety constraints (2020). https://arxiv.org/abs/2009.11468
25. Mittal, M., Gallieri, M., Quaglino, A., Salehian, S.S.M., Koutník, J.: Neural Lyapunov model predictive control (2020). https://arxiv.org/abs/2002.10451
26. Prajna, S., Jadbabaie, A., Pappas, G.J.: A framework for worst-case and stochastic safety verification using barrier certificates. IEEE Trans. Autom. Control **52**(8), 1415–1429 (2007)

27. Prajna, S., Parrilo, P.A., Rantzer, A.: Nonlinear control synthesis by convex optimization. IEEE Trans. Autom. Control **49**(2), 310–314 (2004)
28. Pylorof, D., Bakolas, E.: Analysis and synthesis of nonlinear controllers for input constrained systems using semidefinite programming optimization. In: Proceedings of the 2016 American Control Conference (ACC), pp. 6959–6964 (2016)
29. Ravanbakhsh, H., Sankaranarayanan, S.: Learning control Lyapunov functions from counterexamples and demonstrations. Auton. Rob. **43**(2), 275–307 (2019)
30. Richards, S.M., Berkenkamp, F., Krause, A.: The Lyapunov neural network: adaptive stability certification for safe learning of dynamic systems (2018). http://arxiv.org/abs/1808.00924
31. Ruan, W., Huang, X., Kwiatkowska, M.: Reachability analysis of deep neural networks with provable guarantees. In: Proceedings of the Twenty-Seventh International Joint Conference on Artificial Intelligence (IJCAI), pp. 2651–2659 (2018)
32. Sassi, M.A.B., Sankaranarayanan, S.: Stabilization of polynomial dynamical systems using linear programming based on bernstein polynomials (2015). arXiv preprint arXiv:1501.04578
33. Squires, E., Pierpaoli, P., Egerstedt, M.: Constructive barrier certificates with applications to fixed-wing aircraft collision avoidance. In: Proceedings of the IEEE Conference on Control Technology and Applications (CCTA), pp. 1656–1661 (2018)
34. Szegedy, C., et al.: Intriguing properties of neural networks. In: Proceedings of the 2nd International Conference on Learning Representations (ICLR) (2014)
35. Tuncali, C.E., Kapinski, J., Ito, H., Deshmukh, J.V.: Reasoning about safety of learning-enabled components in autonomous cyber-physical systems. In: Proceedings of the 55th Annual Design Automation Conference (DAC), pp. 30:1–30:6 (2018)
36. Turchetta, M., Kolobov, A., Shah, S., Krause, A., Agarwal, A.: Safe reinforcement learning via curriculum induction. In: Proceedings of the Annual Conference on Advances in Neural Information Processing Systems (NeurIPS), pp. 12151–12162 (2020)
37. Xiang, W., Tran, H.D., Rosenfeld, J.A., Johnson, T.T.: Reachable set estimation and safety verification for piecewise linear systems with neural network controllers. In: Proceedings of the Annual American Control Conference (ACC), pp. 1574–1579 (2018)
38. Zeng, X., Lin, W., Yang, Z., Chen, X., Wang, L.: Darboux-type barrier certificates for safety verification of nonlinear hybrid systems. In: Proceedings of the 2016 International Conference on Embedded Software (EMSOFT), pp. 1–10 (2016)
39. Zhao, H., Zeng, X., Chen, T., Liu, Z., Woodcock, J.: Learning safe neural network controllers with barrier certificates. In: Proceedings of the International Symposium on the Dependable Software Engineering. Theories, Tools, and Applications (SETTA), pp. 177–185 (2020)
40. Zhao, H., Zeng, X., Chen, T. Liu, Z., Woodcock, J.: Learning safe neural network controllers with barrier certificates. Formal Aspects Comput., 1–19 (2021). https://doi.org/10.1007/s00165-021-00544-5
41. Zhu, H., Xiong, Z., Magill, S., Jagannathan, S.: An inductive synthesis framework for verifiable reinforcement learning. In: Proceedings of the 40th ACM SIGPLAN Conference on Programming Language Design and Implementation (PLDI), pp. 686–701 (2019)

HYBRIDSYNCHAADL: Modeling and Formal Analysis of Virtually Synchronous CPSs in AADL

Jaehun Lee[1], Sharon Kim[1], Kyungmin Bae[1(✉)] ,
and Peter Csaba Ölveczky[2]

[1] Pohang University of Science and Technology, Pohang, Korea
kmbae@postech.ac.kr
[2] University of Oslo, Oslo, Norway

Abstract. We present the HYBRIDSYNCHAADL modeling language and formal analysis tool for virtually synchronous cyber-physical systems with complex control programs, continuous behaviors, bounded clock skews, network delays, and execution times. We leverage the Hybrid PALS equivalence, so that it is sufficient to model and verify the simpler underlying synchronous designs. We define the HYBRIDSYNCHAADL language as a sublanguage of the avionics modeling standard AADL for modeling such designs in AADL, and demonstrate the effectiveness of HYBRIDSYNCHAADL on a number of applications.

1 Introduction

Many cyber-physical systems (CPSs) are *virtually synchronous* networks of hybrid components with continuous behaviors combined with sophisticated controllers. They should logically behave as if they were synchronous—in each iteration of the system, all components, in lockstep, read inputs and perform transitions which generate outputs for the next iteration—but have to be realized in a distributed setting, with clock skews and message passing communication. Examples of such CPSs include avionics and automotive systems [34,42], networked medical devices [5,30], and other distributed control systems such as the steam-boiler benchmark [1], where the underlying infrastructure often guarantees bounds on clock skews, network delays, and local execution times.

The uptake of automated formal analysis of such CPSs is challenging, since:

1. The combination of large "discrete" state spaces, caused by interleavings due to asynchronous communication, and continuous behaviors, taking into account clock skews, network delays, and sampling/actuation times (based on imprecise clocks) makes direct automatic model checking analysis infeasible.
2. To enable formal analysis to a large user base, the modeling language for such CPSs, with complex control programs, should be well-known for CPS developers, and should be integrated into mature modeling environments.

To confront these challenges, we present in this paper the HYBRIDSYNCH-AADL modeling language and analysis tool, which address them as follows:

© The Author(s) 2021
A. Silva and K. R. M. Leino (Eds.) CAV 2021, LNCS 12759, pp. 491–504, 2021.
https://doi.org/10.1007/978-3-030-81685-8_23

1. To dramatically reduce both the modeling complexity and the state space caused by asynchronous communication, we use the Hybrid PALS equivalence [8], which says that the underlying synchronous design—where all components execute in lockstep, and there is no asynchronous message passing—satisfies the same properties as the asynchronous distributed system.

2. The HYBRIDSYNCHAADL modeling language is a subset of the avionics modeling standard AADL [22] and its behavioral annex to model control programs, and captures a synchronous subset of AADL with continuous behaviors. We have also integrated modeling and formal analysis of HYBRID-SYNCHAADL models into the OSATE modeling environment for AADL.

Providing formal semantics and analysis for HYBRIDSYNCHAADL, with its expressive control program formalism, continuous behaviors, and clock skews, and having to cover all possible continuous behaviors based on imprecise clocks, is challenging. We combine Maude [19] and the SMT solver Yices [21] to provide such a semantics, as well as symbolic reachability analysis of bounded invariant properties. To make the analysis feasible, our tool also implements a state-space reduction method that merges symbolic states for Maude-with-SMT to significantly improve the performance of symbolic reachability analysis. We illustrate the use of the HYBRIDSYNCHAADL language and tool—and compare its effectiveness with other state-of-the-art CPS analysis tools—on a number of hybrid CPS applications, including distributed drones that communicate to reach the "same" location, or fly in formation, without crashing into each other.

Our tool extends the SynchAADL tool [7,9,10] for distributed *real-time* systems without continuous behaviors, where the time when an event takes place can be abstracted away, so there is no need to consider clock skews, and any (sufficiently expressive) explicit-state model checker can be applied. In contrast, HYBRIDSYNCHAADL must model continuous behaviors and clock skews, and must analyze all possible behaviors based on when the continuous components are sampled and actuated, which depend on the imprecise local clocks. The tool is available at https://hybridsynchaadl.github.io.

2   Preliminaries

PALS and Hybrid PALS. When the infrastructure guarantees bounds Γ on clock skews, network delays, and execution times, the PALS pattern [4,36] reduces the problems of designing and verifying virtually synchronous distributed real-time systems to the much simpler problems of designing and verifying their underlying synchronous designs: Given a synchronous system design SD, bounds Γ, and a period p of each round, the PALS transformation gives the asynchronous distributed real-time system $PALS(SD, \Gamma, p)$, which is stuttering bisimilar to SD.

The synchronous design SD is formalized as the synchronous composition of state machines with input and output ports [36]. In each iteration, all machines simultaneously perform a transition, which includes reading inputs, changing the local state, and generating outputs (for the next iteration).

Hybrid PALS [8] extends PALS to virtually synchronous CPSs with physical environments that exhibit continuous behaviors. The *physical environment* E_M of a machine M has real-valued parameters $\vec{x} = (x_1, \ldots, x_l)$. The continuous behaviors of $\vec{x}$ are modeled by ordinary differential equations (ODEs) that specify different *trajectories* on $\vec{x}$. E_M also defines *which* trajectory the environment follows, as a function of the last *control command* received by E_M.

The local clock of a machine M can be seen as a function $c_M : \mathbb{R}_{\geq 0} \to \mathbb{R}_{\geq 0}$, where $c_M(t)$ is the value of the local clock at time t, with $\forall t \in \mathbb{R}_{\geq 0}$, $|c_M(t) - t| < \epsilon$ for $\epsilon > 0$ the maximal clock skew [36]. In its ith iteration, a controller M samples the values of its environment at time $c_M(i \cdot p) + t_s$, where t_s is the *sampling time*, and then executes a transition. As a result, the new control command is received by the environment at time $c_M(i \cdot p) + t_a$, where t_a is the *actuating time*.

AADL. The *Architecture Analysis & Design Language* (AADL) [22] is an industrial modeling standard used in avionics, aerospace, automotive, medical devices, and robotics to describe an embedded real-time system. In AADL, a component *type* specifies the component's *interface* (e.g., ports) and *properties* (e.g., periods), and a component *implementation* specifies its internal structure as a set of *subcomponents* and a set of *connections* linking their ports. An AADL construct may have *properties* describing its parameters, declared in *property sets*. The OSATE modeling environment provides a set of Eclipse plug-ins for AADL.

An AADL model describes a system of hardware and software components. Software components include *threads* that model the application software and *data* components representing data types. *System* components are the top-level components. A port is a *data* port, an *event* port, or an *event data* port. A component can have different *modes* and mode-specific property values, subcomponents, etc. Mode transitions are triggered by events.

Thread behavior is modeled as a guarded transition system with local variables using AADL's *Behavior Annex* [23]. When a thread is activated, transitions are applied until a *complete* state is reached. The *dispatch protocol* determines when a thread is executed. A *periodic* thread is activated at fixed time intervals.

Maude with SMT. Maude [19] is a language and tool for formally specifying and analyzing distributed systems in rewriting logic. System states are specified as elements of algebraic data types, and transitions are specified using rewrite rules. In addition to its explicit-state analysis methods for concrete states, Maude provides SMT solving and *symbolic reachability analysis* for *constrained terms* $\phi \parallel t$, which symbolically represent all instances of the term $t(x_1, \ldots, x_n)$ satisfying the constraint $\phi(x_1, \ldots, x_n)$ [40], using connections to Yices2 [21] and CVC4 [14].

3   The HYBRIDSYNCHAADL Modeling Language

This section presents the HYBRIDSYNCHAADL language for modeling virtually synchronous CPSs in AADL. HYBRIDSYNCHAADL can specify environments with continuous dynamics, synchronous designs of distributed controllers, and nontrivial interactions between controllers and environments with respect to imprecise local clocks and sampling and actuation times.

The HYBRIDSYNCHAADL language is a subset of AADL extended with property set Hybrid_SynchAADL. We use a subset of AADL without changing the meaning of AADL constructs or adding a new annex—the subset has the same meaning for synchronous models and distributed implementations—so that AADL experts can easily develop and understand HYBRIDSYNCHAADL models.

```
property set Hybrid_SynchAADL is
  Synchronous: inherit aadlboolean applies to (system);
  isEnvironment: inherit aadlboolean applies to (system);
  ContinuousDynamics: aadlstring applies to (system);
  Max_Clock_Deviation: inherit Time applies to (system);
  Sampling_Time: inherit Time_Range applies to (system);
  Response_Time: inherit Time_Range applies to (system);
end Hybrid_SynchAADL;
```

Environment Components. An *environment component* models real-valued state variables that continuously change over time. State variables are specified using data subcomponents of type Base_Types::Float. Each environment component declares the property Hybrid_SynchAADL::isEnvironment => true.

An environment component can have different *modes* to specify different continuous behaviors (trajectories). A controller command may change the mode of the environment or the value of a variable. The continuous dynamics in each mode is specified using either ODEs or continuous real functions as follows:

```
Hybrid_SynchAADL::ContinuousDynamics =>
    "dynamics₁" in modes (mode₁), ..., "dynamicsₙ" in modes (modeₙ);
```

In HYBRIDSYNCHAADL, a set of ODEs over n variables $x_1, \ldots, x_n$, say, $\frac{dx_i}{dt} = e_i(x_1, \ldots, x_n)$ for $i = 1, \ldots, n$, is written as a semicolon-separated string:

```
d/dt(x₁) = e₁(x₁,...,xₙ); ... ; d/dt(xₙ) = eₙ(x₁,...,xₙ);
```

If a closed-form solution of ODEs is known, we can directly specify concrete continuous functions, which are parameterized by a time parameter t and the initial values $x_1(0), \ldots, x_n(0)$ of the variables $x_1, \ldots, x_n$:

```
x₁(t) = e₁(t,x₁(0),...,xₙ(0)); ... ; xₙ(t) = eₙ(t,x₁(0),...,xₙ(0));
```

An environment component interacts with discrete controllers by sending its state values, and by receiving actuator commands that may update state variables or trigger mode (and hence trajectory) changes. This behavior is specified in HYBRIDSYNCHAADL using *connections between ports and data subcomponents*. A connection from a data subcomponent d inside the environment to an output data port o declares that the value of d is "sampled" by a controller. A connection from an environment's input port i to d declares that a controller command arrived at i updates the value of the data subcomponent d.

Controller Components. Discrete controllers are usual software components in the Synchronous AADL subset [7,9]. A controller component is specified using the behavioral and structural subset of AADL: hierarchical system, process, thread components, and thread behaviors defined by the Behavior Annex [23].

A controller receives the state of the environment at some *sampling time*, and sends a controller command to the environment at some *actuation time*. Sampling and actuation take place according to the local clock of the controller.

```
Hybrid_SynchAADL::Max_Clock_Deviation => time;
Hybrid_SynchAADL::Sampling_Time => lower bound .. upper bound;
Hybrid_SynchAADL::Response_Time => lower bound .. upper bound;
```

The top-level system component declares the following properties to state that the entire model is a synchronous design with a period T:

```
Hybrid_SynchAADL::Synchronous => true;     Period => T;
```

Communication. In HYBRIDSYNCHAADL, connections are constrained for synchronous behaviors: no connection is allowed between environments, or between environments and the enclosing system components.

All (non-actuator) outputs of controller components generated in an iteration are available to the receiving *controller* components at the beginning of the *next* iteration. As explained in [7,9], *delayed connections between data ports* meet this requirement. Therefore, two controller components can be connected only by data ports with delayed connections: `Timing => Delayed`.

Interactions between a controller and an environment occur *instantaneously* at the sampling and actuating times of the controller. Because an environment does not "actively" send data for sampling, every output port of an environment must be a *data* port, whereas its input ports could be of any kind.

4   The HYBRIDSYNCHAADL Tool

This section introduces the HYBRIDSYNCHAADL tool supporting the modeling and formal analysis of HYBRIDSYNCHAADL models. The tool is an OSATE plugin which: (i) provides an intuitive language to specify properties of models, (ii) synthesizes a rewriting logic model from a HYBRIDSYNCHAADL model, and (iii) performs various formal analyses using Maude combined with SMT solving.

Specifying Properties. The tool's *property specification language* allows the user to specify time-bounded invariant and reachability properties as propositional formulas whose atomic propositions are AADL Boolean expressions.

A "named" atomic proposition can be declared in HYBRIDSYNCHAADL as follows, where each identifier is fully qualified with its component path:

```
proposition [id]: AADL Boolean Expression
```

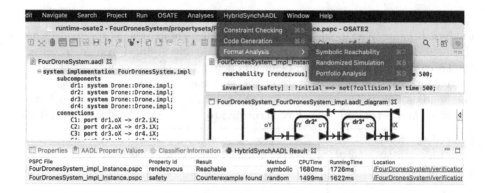

Fig. 1. Interface of the HYBRIDSYNCHAADL tool.

The following *named invariant property* holds if, for every (initial) state satisfying the initial condition φ_{init}, all states reachable within the time bound τ_{bound} satisfy the invariant condition φ_{inv}.

> **invariant** [*name*]: φ_{init} ==> φ_{inv} **in time** τ_{bound}

A *reachability property* (the dual of an invariant) holds if a state satisfying φ_{goal} is reachable from some state satisfying φ_{init} within the time bound τ_{bound}.

> **reachability** [*name*]: φ_{init} ==> φ_{goal} **in time** τ_{bound}

Tool Interface. The tool first statically checks whether a given model is a valid model that satisfies the syntactic constraints of HYBRIDSYNCHAADL.

HYBRIDSYNCHAADL provides two analysis methods. *Symbolic reachability analysis* can verify that all possible behaviors satisfy a given requirement;[1] if not, a counterexample is generated. *Randomized simulation* repeatedly executes the model until a counterexample is found, by randomly choosing concrete sampling and actuating times, nondeterministic transitions, etc.

Our tool also provides *portfolio analysis* that combines symbolic reachability analysis and randomized simulation. HYBRIDSYNCHAADL runs both methods in parallel using multithreading, and displays the result of the analysis that terminates first. Symbolic analysis can guarantee the absence of a counterexample, whereas randomized simulation is effective for finding "obvious" bugs.

Figure 1 shows the interface of our tool that is fully integrated into OSATE. The left editor shows the code of FourDronesSystem in Sect. 5, the bottom right editor shows its graphical representation, and the top right editor shows two properties in the property specification language. The HYBRIDSYNCHAADL menu contains three items for constraint checking, code generation, and formal analysis. The Portfolio Analysis item has already been clicked, and the Result view at the bottom displays the analysis results in a readable format.

---

[1] Symbolic analysis currently only supports polynomial continuous dynamics, since the Yices2 SMT solver does not support general classes of ODEs.

Tool Implementation. We have (in our report [33]) developed a Maude-with-SMT semantics for HYBRIDSYNCHAADL that formalizes our modeling language and implements our tool's analysis commands. Maude is suitable to capture the expressive control program language, the hierarchical structure of systems, and communication. Symbolic rewriting with SMT allows us to analyze infinite states and all possible behaviors caused by sampling and actuation times with imprecise clocks, where continuous dynamics can be encoded in SMT [18,26].

Nontrivial control programs with many conditional branches and guarded transitions typically involve a large number of symbolic states; to reduce the number of results of executing one iteration of the system, we have implemented a *state merging* optimization technique [11] that merges two symbolic states into one using disjunction and generalization. As shown in the report [33], this state merging dramatically improves the performance of symbolic analysis and makes the formal analysis feasible for such distributed hybrid systems.

The HYBRIDSYNCHAADL tool uses OSATE's code generation facilities to synthesize a Maude model from the HYBRIDSYNCHAADL model. It then invokes Maude and an SMT solver to check whether the model satisfies given invariant and reachability requirements. Our tool is implemented in around 6,200 lines of Maude code and around 8,600 lines of Java and Xtend code.

5   Case Study: Collaborating Autonomous Drones

This section shows how virtually synchronous CPSs for controlling distributed drones—which collaborate to achieve common goals, such as rendezvous and formation control—can be modeled and analyzed in HYBRIDSYNCHAADL.

Rendezvous of Multiple Drones. Consider N drones, where vectors $\vec{x}_i$ and $\vec{v}_i$, for $1 \leq i \leq N$, denote the position and velocity of the i-th drone. The continuous dynamics of the i-th drone is specified by the ordinary differential equation $\dot{\vec{x}}_i = \vec{v}_i$. The controller samples the drone's position and velocity, and gives the new velocity value to the environment as a control command. The goal of rendezvous is for all drones to arrive near a common location simultaneously.

Figure 2 shows the AADL architecture of our rendezvous model for four drones. Each drone is connected to two other drones to exchange positions. A drone component consists of an environment (with the drone's position and velocity) and its controller. Figure 3 shows the implementation of the top-level component, a Drone system component, an Environment system component, and a thread component for a drone controller in HYBRIDSYNCHAADL.

In each round, the controller obtains the position $\vec{x}$ from its environment at its sampling time. The position of the connected drone was sent in the previous round. The controller determines a new velocity to synchronize its movement with the other drones using a distributed consensus algorithm [39]. The environment changes its position according to the velocity indicated by its controller, where the new velocity $\vec{v}$ becomes effective at its actuation time.

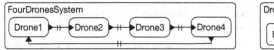 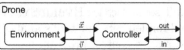

Fig. 2. The AADL architecture of four drones (left), and a drone component (right).

```
system implementation FourDronesSystem.impl
 subcomponents
  dr1: system Drone::Drone.impl;
  dr2: system Drone::Drone.impl;
  dr3: system Drone::Drone.impl;
  dr4: system Drone::Drone.impl;
 connections
  C1: port dr1.oX -> dr2.iX {Timing => Delayed;};
  C2: port dr1.oY -> dr2.iY {Timing => Delayed;};
  C3: port dr2.oX -> dr3.iX {Timing => Delayed;};
  C4: port dr2.oY -> dr3.iY {Timing => Delayed;};
  C5: port dr3.oX -> dr4.iX {Timing => Delayed;};
  C6: port dr3.oY -> dr4.iY {Timing => Delayed;};
  C7: port dr4.oX -> dr1.iX {Timing => Delayed;};
  C8: port dr4.oY -> dr1.iY {Timing => Delayed;};
 properties
  Hybrid_SynchAADL::Synchronous => true;
  Hybrid_SynchAADL::Max_Clock_Deviation => 10ms;
  Period => 100ms;
end FourDrones.impl;

system Drone
 features
  iX: in data port Base_Types::Float;
  iY: in data port Base_Types::Float;
  oX: out data port Base_Types::Float;
  oY: out data port Base_Types::Float;
end Drone;

system implementation Drone.impl
 subcomponents
  ctl: system DroneControl::DroneControl.impl;
  env: system Environment::Environment.impl;
 connections
  C1: port ctl.oX -> oX;   C2: port ctl.oY -> oY;
  C3: port iX -> ctl.iX;   C4: port iY -> ctl.iY;
  C5: port ctl.vX -> env.vX;
  C6: port ctl.vY -> env.vY;
  C7: port env.cX -> ctl.cX;
  C8: port env.cY -> ctl.cY;
 properties
  Hybrid_SynchAADL::Sampling_Time => 2ms .. 4ms;
  Hybrid_SynchAADL::Response_Time => 6ms .. 9ms;
end Drone.impl;

system Environment
 features
  cX: out data port Base_Types::Float;
  cY: out data port Base_Types::Float;
  vX: in data port Base_Types::Float;
  vY: in data port Base_Types::Float;
 properties
  Hybrid_SynchAADL::isEnvironment => true;
end Environment;
```

```
system implementation Environment.impl
 subcomponents
  x: data Base_Types::Float;
  y: data Base_Types::Float;
  velx: data Base_Types::Float;
  vely: data Base_Types::Float;
 connections
  C1: port x -> cX;      C2: port y -> cY;
  C3: port vX -> velx;   C4: port vY -> vely;
 properties
  Hybrid_SynchAADL::ContinuousDynamics =>
   "x(t) = 0.001 * velx * t + x(0);
    y(t) = 0.001 * vely * t + y(0);";
end Environment.impl;

thread DroneControlThread
 features
  iX: in data port Base_Types::Float;
  iY: in data port Base_Types::Float;
  oX: out data port Base_Types::Float;
  oY: out data port Base_Types::Float;
  cX: in data port Base_Types::Float;
  cY: in data port Base_Types::Float;
  vX: out data port Base_Types::Float;
  vY: out data port Base_Types::Float;
 properties
  Dispatch_Protocol => Periodic;
end DroneControlThread;

thread implementation DroneControlThread.impl
 subcomponents
  cls: data Base_Types::Boolean;
  annex behavior_specification {**
 variables
  nx: Base_Types::Float; ny: Base_Types::Float;
 states
  s1: initial complete state;   s2, s3: state;
 transitions
  s1 -[on dispatch]-> s2;
  s2 -[abs(cX - iX) < 0.1 and
        abs(cY - iY) < 0.1]-> s3 {
    vX := 0; vY := 0; cls := true };
  s2 -[otherwise]-> s3 {
    nx := -1 * (cX - iX); ny := -1 * (cY - iY);
    if (nx > 0.3)  vX := 2.5
    elsif (nx > 0.15)
       if (cls) vX := 1.5 else vX := 0.0 end if
    else vX := -2.5 end if;
    if (ny > 0.3) vY := 2.5
    elsif (ny > 0.15)
       if (cls) vY := 1.5 else vY := 0.0 end if
    else vY := -2.5 end if; cls := false };
  s3 -[]-> s1 { oX := cX; oY := cY }; **};
end DroneControlThread.impl;
```

Fig. 3. A HYBRIDSYNCHAADL model for four distributed drones.

Verification. We analyze the following properties up to bound 500 ms using HYBRIDSYNCHAADL portfolio analysis: (i) drones do not collide (`safety`), and (ii) all drones can eventually gather together (`rendezvous`).

```
invariant [safety]: ?initial ==> not ?collision in time 500;
reachability [rendezvous]: ?initial ==> ?gather in time 500;
```

We define three propositions: `initial`, defining the range of initial positions of the four drones `dr1`, `dr2`, `dr3`, and `dr4`; `collision`, where two drones collide if the (horizontal and vertical) distance between them is less than 0.1; and `gather`, indicating that the distance between each pair of drones is less than 1. For example, `collision` and `initial` are defined as follows.

```
proposition [initial] :
  abs(dr1.env.x - 1.1) < 0.01 and abs(dr1.env.y - 1.5) < 0.01 and
  abs(dr2.env.x + 1.5) < 0.01 and abs(dr2.env.y + 1.1) < 0.01 and
  abs(dr3.env.x - 1.5) < 0.01 and abs(dr3.env.y - 1.1) < 0.01 and
  abs(dr4.env.x + 1.1) < 0.01 and abs(dr4.env.y + 1.5) < 0.01;

proposition [collision] :
  (abs(dr1.env.x - dr2.env.x) < 0.1 and abs(dr1.env.y - dr2.env.y) < 0.1) or
  ...
  (abs(dr3.env.x - dr4.env.x) < 0.1 and abs(dr3.env.y - dr4.env.y) < 0.1);
```

The analysis result is shown in the `Result` view at the bottom of Fig. 1. There is a witness for `rendezvous`, obtained by symbolic reachability analysis in 1.7 seconds. A counterexample for `safety` is found by randomized simulation in 1.5 seconds, since `initial` does not constrain the speed of the drones. In [33], we add initial velocity constraints, and verify that `safety` holds up to the time bound by symbolic reachability analysis in 15 minutes.

6 Experimental Evaluation

We compare the performance of HYBRIDSYNCHAADL's symbolic analysis with four reachability analysis tools for hybrid automata, HyComp [18], SpaceEx [24], Flow* [17], and dReach [31], on models of rendezvous and formation control for distributed drones, and on networked thermostats (adapted from [6,29]). We use *simplified* models with less complex control; otherwise, most of the other tools time out (see [33] for results on more complex models). We use two invariant properties for each model: $Inv_\top$, which holds, and $Inv_\perp$, which does not hold.

To use the other tools, we have "encoded" the *synchronous designs* of the HYBRIDSYNCHAADL models as networks of hybrid automata. Each component is modeled as a hybrid automaton with three modes: starting a new round, sampling, and controller transition/actuation. The behavior of a controller is encoded as single jumps. We use flat hybrid automata (obtained by HYST [12]) for Flow* and dReach, which do not support networks of hybrid automata.

We measure the execution times for analyzing the invariant properties *up to* bound 500 ms, with a timeout of 60 minutes. For HYBRIDSYNCHAADL, we use

Table 1. HYBRIDSYNCHAADL vs. HyComp, SpaceEx, dReach, and Flow*.

Model	Tool	$Inv_\top$						$Inv_\perp$					
		$N=2$		$N=3$		$N=4$		$N=2$		$N=3$		$N=4$	
		Time	B	Time	B	Time	B	Time	B	Time	B	Time	B
Rend (single)	HSADDL	2.0	5	3.9	5	5.8	5	2.4	3	4.2	3	5.9	3
	HyComp	0.8	5	4.0	5	17.2	5	8.9	3	11.5	3	192.6	3
	SpaceEx	8.0	5	2230.3	3	4.5	1	5.1	3	2676.6	3	T/O	-
	dReach	1382.7	3	107.1	1	T/O	-	T/O	-	T/O	-	T/O	-
	Flow⋆	3552.8	4	2725.5	2	1205.2	1	167.3	3	380.4	2	838.0	3
Form (single)	HSAADL	3.0	5	7.3	5	7.9	5	15.5	4	2.5	2	5.2	2
	HyComp	13.3	5	41.3	5	182.1	5	T/O	-	2.6	2	20.3	2
	SpaceEx	91.9	2	2.8	1	114.8	1	T/O	-	T/O	-	T/O	-
	dReach	139.0	1	T/O	-	T/O	-	T/O	-	T/O	-	T/O	-
	Flow⋆	1464.7	2	873.4	1	T/O	-	T/O	-	45.3	1	291.3	2
Thermostat	HSAADL	2.7	5	4.7	5	7.8	5	7.6	5	15.3	5	10.7	4
	HyComp	1.6	5	8.5	5	37.9	5	2.6	5	15.5	5	43.1	4
	SpaceEx	2.3	5	696.4	3	34.5	1	2.2	5	T/O	-	T/O	-
	dReach	341.6	3	57.5	1	T/O	-	T/O	-	T/O	-	T/O	-
	Flow⋆	3196.4	5	1240.7	2	977.7	1	15.5	3	1718.1	4	T/O	-
Rend (double)	HSAADL	3.7	4	37.8	4	6.9	4	1.4	2	16.3	2	2.8	2
	SpaceEx	1147.6	3	81.1	1	T/O	-	15.2	2	T/O	-	T/O	-
	dReach	2156.2	3	274.3	1	T/O	-	T/O	-	T/O	-	T/O	-
	Flow⋆	232.5	2	230.1	1	T/O	-	2.2	2	25.4	2	2613.8	1

a specialized version of Maude with Yices 2.6 for polynomial arithmetic [44]. For SpaceEx, we use PHAVer for linear dynamics, and STC for nonlinear polynomial dynamics. For Flow*, we use adaptive steps, and TM orders 1 (for single) and 2 (for double). We use the default precision for dReach, and BMC for HyComp. We have run all experiments on Intel Xeon 2.8GHz with 256 GB memory.

The results are summarized in Table 1, as execution times (seconds) over time bounds ($B \cdot 100$ ms), with N the number of components. The results for "Rend (double)" (rendezvous with double-integrator dynamics, where control input is given by acceleration instead of velocity) do not include HyComp, which does not support nonlinear polynomial dynamics. For $Inv_\top$, Table 1 shows the largest time bound for which the tool could prove the absence of counterexamples. Often, *tools timed out when trying to verify that $Inv_\top$ holds up to time bound 500.*[2] For $Inv_\perp$, the table shows the smallest bound for which the tool found counterexamples.[3] As seen, HYBRIDSYNCHAADL outperforms the other tools in most cases, in particular for complex models with larger N.

---

[2] E.g., for "Rend (single)" with $N = 4$, HYBRIDSYNCHAADL needs 5.8 seconds for $B = 5$, whereas SpaceEx needs 4.5 seconds for $B = 1$ and timed out for $B > 1$.

[3] Flow* occasionally found (spurious) counterexamples at smaller bounds, because of over-approximation by the Taylor model flowpipe construction.

7   Related Work

Our tool can model check virtually synchronous CPSs with both complex control programs and continuous behaviors (and imprecise local clocks, etc.), whereas most formal tools are strong at analyzing either discrete or continuous behaviors. The latter includes analysis tools for hybrid automata [13,18,24], which do not deal well with the "discrete complexity" (e.g., control programs) of CPSs.

The *Hybrid Annex* [2,3] allows specifying continuous behaviors in AADL, but message delays, clock skews, etc., are not taken into account. Controllers are defined in Hybrid CSP instead of in AADL's convenient Behavioral Annex. Another hybrid annex is proposed in [38], and an AADL sublanguage, AADL+, in [35]. None of these languages support automated formal correctness analysis.

Hybrid PALS models with simple controllers are encoded as logical formulas and analyzed by dReal in [8]. However, there is no tool support, and so CPSs must be *manually* modeled as SMT formulas in [8]. In contrast, we provide a tool for modeling Hybrid PALS models using a well-known modeling standard.

Our work is also related to *almost-synchronous* systems, including approximate synchrony [20], quasi-synchrony [15,16,28,32], GALS [27,37], time-triggered architectures [41,43], etc. Our method makes it possible to verify such systems *with continuous behaviors*, which are typically not considered in related work.

8   Concluding Remarks

We have presented the HYBRIDSYNCHAADL modeling language and formal analysis tool for modeling and analyzing the *synchronous designs*—and, by the Hybrid PALS equivalence, also the corresponding *asynchronous distributed real-time system* with bounded clock skews, network delays, and execution times— of virtually synchronous networks of hybrid systems with potentially complex control programs in the modeling standard AADL. Our tool provides randomized simulation and symbolic reachability analysis, and is fully integrated into the OSATE modeling environment for AADL. We have shown that in most cases, HYBRIDSYNCHAADL's symbolic analysis outperforms state-of-the-art hybrid systems reachability analysis tools on a number of distributed hybrid systems.

Currently, HYBRIDSYNCHAADL's symbolic analysis is restricted to systems with (nonlinear) polynomial continuous dynamics, because the underlying SMT solver, Yices2, cannot deal with general classes of ODEs. We should therefore integrate Maude with ODE solvers such as dReal [25] and Flow* [17].

Acknowledgments. This work was supported in part by the National Research Foundation of Korea (NRF) grants funded by the Korea government (MSIT) (No. 2019R1C1C1002386 and No. 2017M3C4A7068175).

References

1. Abrial, J.-R., Börger, E., Langmaack, H. (eds.): Formal Methods for Industrial Applications. LNCS, vol. 1165. Springer, Heidelberg (1996). https://doi.org/10.1007/BFb0027227
2. Ahmad, E., Dong, Y., Wang, S., Zhan, N., Zou, L.: Adding formal meanings to AADL with Hybrid Annex. In: Lanese, I., Madelaine, E. (eds.) FACS 2014. LNCS, vol. 8997, pp. 228–247. Springer, Cham (2015). https://doi.org/10.1007/978-3-319-15317-9_15
3. Ahmad, E., Larson, B.R., Barrett, S.C., Zhan, N., Dong, Y.: Hybrid Annex: An AADL extension for continuous behavior and cyber-physical interaction modeling. In: Proceedings of ACM SIGAda HILT 2014. ACM (2014)
4. Al-Nayeem, A., Sun, M., Qiu, X., Sha, L., Miller, S.P., Cofer, D.D.: A formal architecture pattern for real-time distributed systems. In: Proceedings of RTSS. IEEE (2009)
5. Arney, D., Jetley, R., Jones, P., Lee, I., Sokolsky, O.: Formal methods based development of a PCA infusion pump reference model: Generic infusion pump (GIP) project. In: Proceedings of HCMDSS-MDPnP 2007. IEEE (2007)
6. Bae, K., Gao, S.: Modular SMT-based analysis of nonlinear hybrid systems. In: Proceedings of FMCAD, pp. 180–187. IEEE (2017)
7. Bae, K., Ölveczky, P.C., Al-Nayeem, A., Meseguer, J.: Synchronous AADL and its formal analysis in Real-Time Maude. In: Qin, S., Qiu, Z. (eds.) ICFEM 2011. LNCS, vol. 6991, pp. 651–667. Springer, Heidelberg (2011). https://doi.org/10.1007/978-3-642-24559-6_43
8. Bae, K., Ölveczky, P.C., Kong, S., Gao, S., Clarke, E.M.: SMT-based analysis of virtually synchronous distributed hybrid systems. In: Proceedings of HSCC. ACM (2016)
9. Bae, K., Ölveczky, P.C., Meseguer, J.: Definition, semantics, and analysis of Multirate Synchronous AADL. In: Jones, C., Pihlajasaari, P., Sun, J. (eds.) FM 2014. LNCS, vol. 8442, pp. 94–109. Springer, Cham (2014). https://doi.org/10.1007/978-3-319-06410-9_7
10. Bae, K., Ölveczky, P.C., Meseguer, J., Al-Nayeem, A.: The SynchAADL2Maude tool. In: de Lara, J., Zisman, A. (eds.) FASE 2012. LNCS, vol. 7212, pp. 59–62. Springer, Heidelberg (2012). https://doi.org/10.1007/978-3-642-28872-2_4
11. Bae, K., Rocha, C.: Symbolic state space reduction with guarded terms for rewriting modulo SMT. Sci. Comput. Program. **178**, 20–42 (2019)
12. Bak, S., Bogomolov, S., Johnson, T.T.: HYST: A source transformation and translation tool for hybrid automaton models. In: Proceedings of HSCC 2015. ACM (2015)
13. Bak, S., Duggirala, P.S.: Hylaa: A tool for computing simulation-equivalent reachability for linear systems. In: Proceedings of HSCC 2017. ACM (2017)
14. Barrett, C., Conway, C.L., Deters, M., Hadarean, L., Jovanović, D., King, T., Reynolds, A., Tinelli, C.: CVC4. In: Gopalakrishnan, G., Qadeer, S. (eds.) CAV 2011. LNCS, vol. 6806, pp. 171–177. Springer, Heidelberg (2011). https://doi.org/10.1007/978-3-642-22110-1_14
15. Baudart, G., Bourke, T., Pouzet, M.: Soundness of the quasi-synchronous abstraction. In: Proceedings of FMCAD, pp. 9–16. IEEE (2016)
16. Caspi, P., Mazuet, C., Paligot, N.R.: About the design of distributed control systems: The quasi-synchronous approach. In: Voges, U. (ed.) SAFECOMP 2001. LNCS, vol. 2187, pp. 215–226. Springer, Heidelberg (2001). https://doi.org/10.1007/3-540-45416-0_21

17. Chen, X., Ábrahám, E., Sankaranarayanan, S.: Flow*: An analyzer for non-linear hybrid systems. In: Sharygina, N., Veith, H. (eds.) CAV 2013. LNCS, vol. 8044, pp. 258–263. Springer, Heidelberg (2013). https://doi.org/10.1007/978-3-642-39799-8_18

18. Cimatti, A., Griggio, A., Mover, S., Tonetta, S.: HyComp: An SMT-based model checker for hybrid systems. In: Baier, C., Tinelli, C. (eds.) TACAS 2015. LNCS, vol. 9035, pp. 52–67. Springer, Heidelberg (2015). https://doi.org/10.1007/978-3-662-46681-0_4

19. Clavel, M., Durán, F., Eker, S., Lincoln, P., Martí-Oliet, N., Meseguer, J., Talcott, C.: All About Maude - A High-Performance Logical Framework. LNCS, vol. 4350. Springer, Heidelberg (2007). https://doi.org/10.1007/978-3-540-71999-1

20. Desai, A., Seshia, S.A., Qadeer, S., Broman, D., Eidson, J.C.: Approximate synchrony: An abstraction for distributed almost-synchronous systems. In: Kroening, D., Păsăreanu, C.S. (eds.) CAV 2015. LNCS, vol. 9207, pp. 429–448. Springer, Cham (2015). https://doi.org/10.1007/978-3-319-21668-3_25

21. Dutertre, B.: Yices 2.2. In: Biere, A., Bloem, R. (eds.) CAV 2014. LNCS, vol. 8559, pp. 737–744. Springer, Cham (2014). https://doi.org/10.1007/978-3-319-08867-9_49

22. Feiler, P.H., Gluch, D.P.: Model-Based Engineering with AADL: An Introduction to the SAE Architecture Analysis and Design Language. Addison-Wesley (2012)

23. França, R., Bodeveix, J.P., Filali, M., Rolland, J.F., Chemouil, D., Thomas, D.: The AADL Behaviour Annex - experiments and roadmap. In: ICECCS. IEEE (2007)

24. Frehse, G., Le Guernic, C., Donzé, A., Cotton, S., Ray, R., Lebeltel, O., Ripado, R., Girard, A., Dang, T., Maler, O.: SpaceEx: Scalable verification of hybrid systems. In: Gopalakrishnan, G., Qadeer, S. (eds.) CAV 2011. LNCS, vol. 6806, pp. 379–395. Springer, Heidelberg (2011). https://doi.org/10.1007/978-3-642-22110-1_30

25. Gao, S., Kong, S., Clarke, E.M.: dReal: An SMT solver for nonlinear theories over the reals. In: Bonacina, M.P. (ed.) CADE 2013. LNCS (LNAI), vol. 7898, pp. 208–214. Springer, Heidelberg (2013). https://doi.org/10.1007/978-3-642-38574-2_14

26. Gao, S., Kong, S., Clarke, E.M.: Satisfiability modulo ODEs. In: Proceedings of FMCAD. IEEE (2013)

27. Girault, A., Ménier, C.: Automatic production of globally asynchronous locally synchronous systems. In: Sangiovanni-Vincentelli, A., Sifakis, J. (eds.) EMSOFT 2002. LNCS, vol. 2491, pp. 266–281. Springer, Heidelberg (2002). https://doi.org/10.1007/3-540-45828-X_20

28. Halbwachs, N., Mandel, L.: Simulation and verification of asynchronous systems by means of a synchronous model. In: Proceedings of ACSD 2006. IEEE (2006)

29. Henzinger, T.: The theory of hybrid automata. In: Inan, M.K., Kurshan, R.P. (eds.) Verification of Digital and Hybrid Systems. NATO ASI Series, vol. 170, pp. 265–292. Springer, Heidelberg (2000). https://doi.org/10.1007/978-3-642-59615-5_13

30. Kim, C., Sun, M., Mohan, S., Yun, H., Sha, L., Abdelzaher, T.F.: A framework for the safe interoperability of medical devices in the presence of network failures. In: Proceedings of ICCPS 2010. ACM (2010)

31. Kong, S., Gao, S., Chen, W., Clarke, E.: dReach: δ-reachability analysis for hybrid systems. In: Baier, C., Tinelli, C. (eds.) TACAS 2015. LNCS, vol. 9035, pp. 200–205. Springer, Heidelberg (2015). https://doi.org/10.1007/978-3-662-46681-0_15

32. Larrieu, R., Shankar, N.: A framework for high-assurance quasi-synchronous systems. In: Proceedings of MEMOCODE 2014. IEEE (2014)

33. Lee, J., Kim, S., Bae, K., Ölveczky, P.C.: HybridSynchAADL: Modeling and formal analysis of virtually synchronous CPSs in AADL. manuscript, January 2021. https://hybridsynchaadl.github.io//docs/techrep.pdf
34. Leen, G., Heffernan, D., Dunne, A.: Digital networks in the automotive vehicle. Comput. Control Eng. J. **10**(6), 257–266 (1999)
35. Liu, J., Li, T., Ding, Z., Qian, Y., Sun, H., He, J.: AADL+: A simulation-based methodology for cyber-physical systems. Front. Comput. Sci. **13**(3), 516–538 (2018). https://doi.org/10.1007/s11704-018-7039-7
36. Meseguer, J., Ölveczky, P.C.: Formalization and correctness of the PALS architectural pattern for distributed real-time systems. Theor. Comput. Sci. **451**, 5–27 (2012)
37. Potop-Butucaru, D., Caillaud, B.: Correct-by-construction asynchronous implementation of modular synchronous specifications. Fundam. Inform. **78**(1), 131–159 (2007)
38. Qian, Y., Liu, J., Chen, X.: Hybrid AADL: A sublanguage extension to AADL. In: Proceedings of MEMOCODE 2014. ACM (2013)
39. Ren, W., Beard, R.W.: Distributed Consensus in Multi-vehicle Cooperative Control. Springer, London (2008). https://doi.org/10.1007/978-1-84800-015-5
40. Rocha, C., Meseguer, J., Muñoz, C.: Rewriting modulo SMT and open system analysis. J. Log. Algebraic Methods Program. **86**(1), 269–297 (2017)
41. Rushby, J.: Systematic formal verification for fault-tolerant time-triggered algorithms. IEEE Trans. Software Eng. **25**(5), 651–660 (1999)
42. Steiner, W., Bauer, G., Hall, B., Paulitsch, M., Varadarajan, S.: TTEthernet dataflow concept. In: 2009 Eighth IEEE International Symposium on Network Computing and Applications, pp. 319–322. IEEE (2009)
43. Tripakis, S., Pinello, C., Benveniste, A., Sangiovanni-Vincent, A., Caspi, P., Di Natale, M.: Implementing synchronous models on loosely time triggered architectures. IEEE Trans. Comput. **57**(10), 1300–1314 (2008)
44. Yu, G., Bae, K.: Maude-SE: A tight integration of Maude and SMT solvers. In: Proceedings of International Workshop on Rewriting Logic and Its Applications (2020)

Computing Bottom SCCs Symbolically Using Transition Guided Reduction

Nikola Beneš, Luboš Brim, Samuel Pastva$^{(\boxtimes)}$, and David Šafránek

Faculty of Informatics, Masaryk University, Brno,
Czech Republic
{xbenes3,brim,xpastva,safranek}@fi.muni.cz

Abstract. Detection of bottom strongly connected components (BSCC) in state-transition graphs is an important problem with many applications, such as detecting recurrent states in Markov chains or attractors in dynamical systems. However, these graphs' size is often entirely out of reach for algorithms using explicit state-space exploration, necessitating alternative approaches such as the symbolic one.

Symbolic methods for BSCC detection often show impressive performance, but can sometimes take a long time to converge in large graphs. In this paper, we provide a symbolic state-space reduction method for labelled transition systems, called *interleaved transition guided reduction* (ITGR), which aims to alleviate current problems of BSCC detection by efficiently identifying large portions of the non-BSCC states.

We evaluate the suggested heuristic on an extensive collection of 125 real-world biologically motivated systems. We show that ITGR can easily handle all these models while being either the only method to finish, or providing at least an order-of-magnitude speedup over existing state-of-the-art methods. We then use a set of synthetic benchmarks to demonstrate that the technique also consistently scales to graphs with more than 2^{1000} vertices, which was not possible using previous methods.

Keywords: Bottom SCC · Symbolic algorithm · Boolean network

1 Introduction

Finding strongly connected components (SCCs) is a basic problem in graph theory. It is impractical or even impossible for large graphs to find SCCs using explicit depth-first search, motivating the study of symbolic SCCs computation. The structure of SCCs in a graph is captured by its quotient graph, obtained by collapsing each SCC into a single node. This graph is acyclic, thus defines a partial order on the SCCs. *Bottom SCCs* (BSCCs) are SCCs corresponding to leaf nodes in the quotient graph (alternatively referred to as *Terminal SCCs*).

Detection of BSCCs is an important problem with many applications. For example, in Markov chains and Markov decision processes, the recurrent states

© The Author(s) 2021
A. Silva and K. R. M. Leino (Eds.) CAV 2021, LNCS 12759, pp. 505–528, 2021.
https://doi.org/10.1007/978-3-030-81685-8_24

belong to terminal SCCs [1,11,38]. In LTL model checking, the detection of bottom SCCs is used during the decomposition of the property automaton to speed up the model checking procedure [52]. Another example of an application where detection of BSCCs is crucial is detecting non-terminating sections of parallel programs written in C or C++ [55]. In models of dynamical systems, which are of our primary interest, BSCCs correspond to so-called *attractors* that determine the long-term behaviour of the system [43]. Identification of attractors has many important applications, including communication protocols [4,47], systems biology [31,40], mathematical physics [26], ecology [54], epidemiology [42], etc. In biology, the possibility of reaching a particular phenotype of a living cell is indicated by the presence of a specific attractor [40]. The knowledge of attractors then unlocks the path towards cell control [33], reprogramming [49] and even regenerative medicine [17]. Consequently, detection of BSCCs is a fundamental task important not only in computer-aided verification but also many other disciplines.

Our motivation to develop a new symbolic approach to find BSCCs comes from the need to handle extremely large graphs representing *labelled transition systems* that encode the behaviour of complex real-world concurrent processes. In particular, assuming we deal with finite-state systems, such large transition systems are typically generated from models encoded in a compact formalism such as process calculi, Petri nets, Boolean networks [32,57], their combinations [6] or other higher-level modelling languages. For such transition systems, the limits of general symbolic SCC algorithms also define the limits of realistic applications.

In most cases, the size of a transition system generated from a model is exponential in the number of concurrently interacting entities. For example, in the case of biological systems, the number of entities is typically ranging from several hundred to hundreds of thousands. Despite strong simplifications employed at the side of models, the size of respective transition systems rarely falls below 10^6 states and is usually much bigger [23,27,44]. Thus, the need to tackle large transition systems gives us a solid motivation to revisit the algorithmics for BSCC detection.

In general, it is possible to find all BSCCs as a part of a general SCC decomposition algorithm. There is a rich history of research on computing SCCs symbolically. An algorithm based on forward and backward reachability performing $\mathcal{O}(n^2)$ symbolic steps was presented by Xie and Beerel in [59]. Bloem et al. present an improved $\mathcal{O}(n \cdot \log n)$ algorithm in [7]. Finally, an $\mathcal{O}(n)$ algorithm was presented by Gentilini et al. in [25]. This bound has been proved to be tight in [16]. In [16], the authors argue that the algorithm from [25] is optimal even when considering more fine-grained complexity criteria, like the diameter of the graph and the diameter of the individual components. Ciardo et al. [62] use the idea of saturation [20] to speed up state exploration when computing each SCC in the Xie-Beerel algorithm and compute the transitive closure of the transition relation using a novel algorithm based on saturation.

Our approach is motivated by the fact that techniques working very well for full SCC decomposition do not help to sufficiently accelerate BSCC detection. At the same time, some heuristics, such as saturation, can provide a meaningful impact even when using simpler algorithms [62]. The key novelty of our method lies in a heuristic called *transition guided reduction* that filters the state space by reflecting the possibility of transitions to appear in BSCCs. This step allows to remove some states not belonging to any BSCC, and that way reduce the transition system under analysis to be tractable by the modified Xie-Beerel algorithm with saturation [62].

To target specific characteristics of transition systems representing dynamical systems, e.g., those generated by Boolean networks (BNs) [32,57], several specialised symbolic SCC decomposition methods have been developed. Since systems for our evaluation come primarily from BNs, we also discuss these specialised methods here. A BN consists of Boolean variables, each having a Boolean update function. Update functions change the state of the variables. The semantics of a BN is a transition system where the states are the possible valuations of the variables, and the transitions are induced by the execution of the update functions. Some of the existing algorithms utilise the synchronous update semantics (updates of all variables executed synchronously) that significantly simplifies the problem [24]. However, it is known that synchronous update can produce unrealistic behaviour [37,53]. Models with asynchronous update (concurrently executed updates of variables) are closer to reproducing the real behaviour [15]. For the evaluation of our method, we consider asynchronous BNs. Various specialised techniques of BSCC detection have been developed for asynchronous BNs, including BDDs [24,46,56,60], optimisation [34,35], algebraic-based methods [29], SAT [28], answer set programming [45], concurrency theory [14], sampling [61], or network structure decomposition [18,21]. Moreover, detection of BSCCs is also present as a necessary step in cell reprogramming [41,49] and cell control [2,33] based on BNs. To the best of our knowledge, existing methods specialised for asynchronous BNs do not satisfactorily handle huge models (hundreds of variables and beyond). The best state-of-the-art tools [21,56] are not yet able to robustly work with BNs of such size. We believe that the generally applicable heuristic we propose in this paper can significantly shift the present technology towards massive real-world applications (thousands of variables and beyond).

The main contribution of this paper is a *novel symbolic method for BSCCs detection in state-transition graphs of huge labelled transition systems* for which the problem cannot be handled by existing algorithms. We introduce a novel reduction technique, called *interleaved transition guided reduction (ITGR)*, which aims to enable the use of existing methods by removing large portions of the irrelevant non-BSCC states. The method relies on the observation that BSCCs in real-world systems rarely employ all transition labels available. Therefore, if a state s can fire a transition with a label that is not employed by some BSCC reachable from s, after applying ITGR, s is eliminated. As a result, all paths in the remaining state space only perform transitions with labels employed by their reachable BSCCs. What makes the method truly competitive is the interleaving of multiple processes, each of which performs the reduction for a different transition label. The completion of faster processes speeds up the remaining parts of the computation, which would be otherwise intractable.

To show the real-world benefits of our method, we use a wide collection of models and compare the prototype implementation of ITGR to the state-of-the-art tool CABEAN [56] as well as to our own implementation of the Xie-Beerel BSCC detection algorithm [62]. In particular, we consider a set of 125 real-world asynchronous BNs selected from publicly available Boolean network repositories, and show that ITGR can easily handle all these models, while either being the only method to finish the computation or providing at least an order-of-magnitude speedup over existing methods. Additionally, we analyse a set of 200 even larger but structurally similar synthetic BNs, which generate transition systems with approximately 2^{1000} states. We show that ITGR is the only method that can consistently handle systems of this magnitude.

2   Preliminaries

To represent a wide variety of large discrete systems, we consider the abstraction generally known as *labelled transition systems*:

Definition 1. *Let $\mathcal{L}$ be a non-empty set of labels. A labelled transition system over $\mathcal{L}$ is a pair $T = (S, \{\xrightarrow{a} \mid a \in \mathcal{L}\})$, where S is a finite non-empty set of states, and for each $a \in \mathcal{L}$, $\xrightarrow{a} \subseteq S \times S$ is a transition relation.*

When $(s, s') \in \xrightarrow{a}$, we write $s \xrightarrow{a} s'$, and when $(s, s') \in \xrightarrow{a}$ for *some* $a \in \mathcal{L}$, we simply write $s \to s'$. When there is a path $s_1 \to s_2 \to \ldots \to s_n$, we write $s_1 \to^* s_n$. Each labelled transition system T can be seen as a directed *state-transition graph* $G_T = (S, E)$, whose vertices are the states of T and whose edges are given by the transition relations, i.e. $(s, s') \in E \iff s \to s'$. This formalism can naturally describe a wide variety of modelling frameworks with built-in nondeterminism, such as Petri nets, Boolean networks, or multi-valued regulatory networks.

We assume to have a symbolic representation of a labelled transition system that allows us to perform symbolic set operations on the subsets of S (union $\cup$, intersection $\cap$, difference $\setminus$, subset test $\subseteq$, pick an element PICK, etc.) as well as apply the following operations using the associated transition relations:

$$\text{POST}(a, X) = \{s' \in S \mid \exists s \in X. s \xrightarrow{a} s'\}$$

$$\text{PRE}(a, X) = \{s \in S \mid \exists s' \in X. s \xrightarrow{a} s'\}$$

$$\text{CANPOST}(a, X) = \{s \in X \mid \exists s' \in S. s \xrightarrow{a} s'\}$$

We further assume a symbolic complexity model where the complexity of each such operation is in $\mathcal{O}(1)$. Additionally, we use the notation $\text{ALLPOST}(X) = \bigcup_{a \in \mathcal{L}} \text{POST}(a, X)$ for *all successors* and $\text{ALLPRE}(X) = \bigcup_{a \in \mathcal{L}} \text{PRE}(a, X)$ for *all predecessors.* However, the symbolic complexity of these operations is in $\mathcal{O}(|\mathcal{L}|)$. Finally, we assume that the labels in $\mathcal{L}$ are sorted based on the order in which they influence the variables in the symbolic representation (as in, for example, an ordered binary decision diagram [10]). As a consequence, we index the labels and write $\mathcal{L} = \{a_1, \ldots, a_{|\mathcal{L}|}\}$.

Now let us recall a few basic definitions from graph theory in order to define the BSCC detection problem for labelled transition systems:

Definition 2. *Let $G = (V, E)$ be a directed graph. A subset $C \subseteq V$ is a strongly connected component (SCC) of G iff it is a maximal subset such that for all pairs $v, v' \in C$, there is a path from v to v'.*

A strongly connected component C is called bottom *(or* terminal, *BSCC in the following) when there is no edge going from any $v \in C$ to any $v' \in V \setminus C$.*

For a given $s \in V$, we write $SCC(s)$ to denote the strongly connected component that contains s. Furthermore, we say that a set X is SCC-closed when $X = \bigcup_{x \in X} SCC(x)$. This means that every SCC of G is either included in X, or is completely disjoint with X. As an example, a set of all reachable vertices from any given initial set is SCC-closed. When $|SCC(x)| = 1$ and $(x, x) \notin E$, the SCC is called *trivial.*

For a set $X \subseteq V$, we sometimes use the term *the basin of X* to denote the set of all the vertices that have a path to a state in X, formally $basin(X) = \{u \mid \exists v \in X : u \to^* v\}$. Note that although the name is motivated by the notion of attractor basins in dynamical systems, we use it in a more generalised form here, i.e. we do not require X to be a BSCC.

Problem 1. *Let T be a labelled transition system and G_T its corresponding state-transition graph. The problem of* bottom strongly connected component detection (BSCC detection) *is to identify all subsets of S that correspond to the bottom strongly connected components of G_T.*

A detailed analysis of optimal symbolic asymptotic complexity of a full SCC decomposition can be found in [16]. However, the authors in [16] use a slightly different complexity model, where operations like ALLPOST and ALLPRE also assume $\mathcal{O}(1)$ complexity. However, their observations about the relationship between problem complexity and graph (or component) diameter are very relevant.

3   Basic Symbolic BSCC Detection

First, we discuss a BSCC detection algorithm from [62], which will form our baseline going forward. In [62], the authors discuss several symbolic approaches to SCC and BSCC computation, as well as fair cycle detection using various symbolic algorithms, and compare them on large systems from computer science.

In particular, the paper points out that more complex approaches, like the lock-step method [7], work well for full SCC decomposition but do not bring much benefit to the detection of BSCCs. However, the authors do highlight the benefits

---

Algorithm 1: Basic BSCC detection algorithm with saturation.

---
1 **Function** BSCC(universe ⊆ S)
2   **while** universe ≠ ∅ **do**
3   pivot ← PICK(universe);
4   basin ← BWD*({pivot}, universe);
5   forward ← {pivot};
6   **repeat**
7   (fixpoint, forward) ← FWD(forward, universe);
8   **until** fixpoint **or** forward ⊄ basin;
9   **if** forward ⊆ basin **then**
10   OUTPUT(forward);
11   universe ← universe \ basin;

12 **Function** BWD*(reachable, universe)
13   **repeat**
14   (fixpoint, reachable) ← BWD(reachable, universe);
15   **until** fixpoint;
16   **return** reachable;

17 **Function** BWD(reachable, universe)
18   **for** $i \in |\mathcal{L}| \ldots 1$ **do**
19   pre ← universe ∩ PRE(a_i, reachable);
20   **if** pre ⊄ reachable **then**
21   **return** (*false*, reachable ∪ pre);

22   **return** (*true*, reachable);

---

of basin saturation [19] as a heuristic to speed up the state space search. What we present here is therefore the Xie-Beerel algorithm [59], adapted to BSCC detection with saturation, based on the notes from [62] (we have rewritten the pseudocode to better match the presentation style and background of this paper, though).

The method is summarised in Algorithm 1, which shows the main procedure (BSCC) as well as the reachability procedures BWD and BWD*, which we also use in the later sections. We omit the pseudocode for FWD and FWD*, as they are identical to the BWD case, only swapping PRE for POST.

Reachability and Saturation. The forward and backward reachability procedures are divided into two methods each, FWD, BWD, FWD* and BWD*. Since they are functionally symmetrical, we only explicitly discuss backward reachability, with everything directly translating to forward reachability as well.

BWD performs a single backward reachability step and returns the new set of states together with an indication of whether a fixed point has been reached (i.e. whether no new states have been discovered). Note that in classical saturation, once BWD selects some a_i, it is typically applied repeatedly. However, for our primary application domain (Boolean networks), multiple subsequent applications of a single transition would not yield any benefit; we thus use this observation to simplify the pseudocode. In other cases, the recommended approach is to follow [19].

BWD* then simply wraps BWD into a cycle that actually computes the full fixed point of the `reachable` set. This separation into two sub-procedures allows us to perform reachability step-by-step or even interleave multiple reachability procedures (which will come into play later). Remember that for saturation to work well, the ordering of labels needs to follow the ordering of variables in the symbolic representation.

Xie-Beerel Algorithm. The main algorithm relies on the well-known observation that for a fixed `pivot` vertex, the SCC of this vertex can be computed as the intersection of vertices forward and backward reachable from `pivot`. When searching for BSCCs, we can easily extend this with two extra observations: First, `pivot` is in a BSCC when only the SCC itself is forward-reachable from `pivot`. Second, a vertex backward-reachable from `pivot` is either in the same SCC as `pivot` (in which case it is in a BSCC iff `pivot` is in a BSCC), or it is not in a BSCC.

Based on these two extra observations, the original algorithm is modified in two ways: First, not just the SCC around `pivot`, but all backward-reachable vertices are eliminated at the end of each iteration. Second, the backward reachability from `pivot` is computed in full, as these are the vertices we can eliminate. However, the forward reachability is terminated early if it leaves the backward-reachable set, since this implies that `pivot` does not belong to a BSCC.

The asymptotic complexity of this algorithm (in terms of symbolic operations) is $\mathcal{O}(|\mathcal{L}| \cdot |S|)$, which follows from the fact that every vertex will appear in `basin` exactly once but may need $\mathcal{O}(|\mathcal{L}|)$ operations to be discovered. Note that optimal symbolic algorithms for BSCC detection are expected to have linear asymptotic complexity. That is, however, assuming a model where ALLPOST is an $\mathcal{O}(1)$ operation, not $\mathcal{O}(|\mathcal{L}|)$. This may be reasonable for some (in particular synchronous) systems, but as demonstrated in [19], saturation is typically more effective in practice, even though it is not asymptotically optimal in this model.

In [62], the authors show very impressive performance numbers for this simple algorithm. However, there are two drawbacks, which we believe can be improved significantly. And as we demonstrate in the evaluation, while powerful, this algorithm certainly has limits on some real-world models.

First, the performance of this method is directly tied to the selection of the `pivot` vertex. If the BSCCs of the graph are relatively small, the probability of picking a right pivot is also tiny (remember, even an SCC with 2^{100} vertices is only a minuscule fraction of a graph with 2^{1000} vertices). As a consequence, the algorithm may require a lot of pivots to explore the entire graph. Second, the overall complexity is limited by the diameter of the whole graph instead of the diameter of the BSCCs. Even if the `pivot` is picked perfectly, the algorithm still has to explore each BSCC's whole basin sequentially. To some extent, this is inevitable; however, as we hope to demonstrate in the next section, it is not always necessary.

Algorithm 2: Core reduction principle

---

1 **Function** REDUCE(pivots, universe)
2   forward ← FWD*(pivots, universe);
3   extendedComponent ← BWD*(pivots, forward);
4   bottom ← forward \ extendedComponent;
5   if universe ≠ forward then
6   basin ← BWD*(forward, universe);
7   universe ← universe \ (basin \ forward);
8   if bottom ≠ ∅ then
9   basin ← BWD*(bottom, universe);
10   universe ← universe \ (basin \ bottom);
11   return universe;

To sum up, Algorithm 1 is a powerful tool for the detection of BSCCs. However, it performs best in graphs where the BSCCs either form a large portion of the state space or have basins of small diameter, allowing the algorithm to converge quickly.

4   Transition Guided Reduction

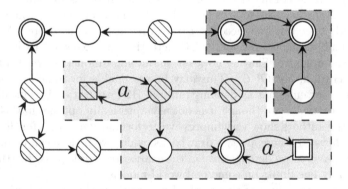

Fig. 1. Example of transition guided reduction. Square nodes show the `pivots` set used for this reduction (in this case, the states that can fire transition a). Double-drawn states are the BSCCs of the graph. The green area then shows the `extendedComponent` induced by the two a transitions, and the blue area is the `bottom` set. The striped states are the basins of the two sets, which are eliminated in this reduction. (Color figure online)

In this section, we introduce a technique that we call *transition guided reduction* (TGR) to eliminate a large portion of non-BSCC states. Algorithm 1 can then perform much better on this reduced state space.

We present the technique in two steps: First, in Algorithm 2, we present the core principle of the reduction procedure and prove its correctness. This approach is generally applicable to any directed graph. Then in Algorithm 3 we show how to apply Algorithm 2 in the context of a labelled transition system. Here, we can exploit the knowledge of the transition labels to guide the reduction.

The reduction principle is described in Algorithm 2 and illustrated in Fig. 1. Given a set of pivot states and the current universe of all considered states, the method starts by computing forward—the set of all states reachable from the pivot states. Using this forward set, we then compute the extendedComponent of the given pivot states. Formally, an extended component of set X is a subset $X' \subseteq S$ that contains all states from X, as well as all paths between the states in X. It is a superset of the union $\bigcup_{x \in X} SCC(x)$ but also contains all paths (and SCCs on these paths) that lead between the elements of this union.

We can observe the following properties:

- The forward set is SCC-closed, as it is the result of a reachability procedure. Thus any state that can reach but is not contained in forward is not a part of any BSCC.
- The set bottom (i.e. forward \ extendedComponent) is also SCC-closed (as it is the difference of two SCC-closed sets). Notice that if this set is not empty, it must contain at least one BSCC, and also that any state that can reach bottom but is not contained in it is necessarily not a part of any BSCC.

The algorithm then computes the two sets of states that definitely do not contain a BSCC according to these observations and discards these sets from the state space. This is done on lines 5–7 and 8–10, respectively.

Now we can formulate the following theorem:

Theorem 1. *If state $s \in$ universe is discarded by Algorithm 2, then it is not part of any BSCC.*

Proof. The proof follows from the two previous observations. If the state s is removed on line 7, it means s can reach a state $s' \in$ forward. Since the set forward is SCC-closed, we get $SCC(s) \neq SCC(s')$. State s therefore does not belong to a BSCC.

Similarly, if the state s is removed on line 10, then it means s can reach a state $s' \in$ bottom, and again due to the fact that bottom is SCC-closed, the state s does not belong to a BSCC.   □

However, this does not provide any guidance as to which pivots should we select for the reduction or why. This is addressed in Algorithm 3. Here, we go through all the available transitions $a \in \mathcal{L}$ and select as the pivots the set of all the states that can fire a (notice that pivots in Fig. 1 also correspond to such states). As a result, all BSCCs that use a are contained in extendedComponent and all BSCCs that do not use a, but a is performed in their basin are contained in the bottom set. This effectively separates the BSCCs based on the transitions that they use.

Algorithm 3: Transition Guided Reduction

---

1 **Function** TGR(universe ⊆ S)
2   **for** $a \in \mathcal{L}$ **do**
3   universe ← REDUCE(CANPOST(a, universe), universe);
4   **if** CANPOST(a, universe) $= \emptyset$ **then**
5              $\mathcal{L} \leftarrow \mathcal{L} \setminus a$;

6   **return** universe;

Finally, notice that if all transitions of a certain type are eliminated, we remove a from $\mathcal{L}$ completely. In large systems, this can significantly reduce the overhead of the FWD/BWD procedures that have to iterate through $\mathcal{L}$.

To better describe the cases in which this reduction works well, let us first formally define the following:

Definition 3. *Given a labelled transition system T and a state s, the* fire set *$F(s)$ is the subset of transition labels $F(s) \subseteq \mathcal{L}$ that can be fired in state s, i.e. $a \in F(s) \Leftrightarrow \exists s' \in S : s \xrightarrow{a} s'$. A* transitive fire set *$F^*(s)$ is the union of all the fire sets $F(s')$ of all the states s' reachable from s (i.e. $s \to^* s'$).*

Notice that for any two states such that $s \to^* s'$, it holds that $F^*(s') \subseteq F^*(s)$. This also means that in any SCC, the transitive fire set of all states is the same.

Theorem 2. *Let s be an arbitrary state and s' be a state of a BSCC such that $s \to^* s'$. If $F^*(s) \neq F^*(s')$, Algorithm 3 discards the state s.*

Proof. Since $s \to^* s$ and $F^*(s) \neq F^*(s')$, it follows that $F^*(s') \subset F^*(s)$. Let $a \in F^*(s) \setminus F^*(s')$ be arbitrary and let us consider the iteration of the main loop when a is selected. Assume that s has not been discarded in any of the previous iterations (otherwise, the proof is already finished). Let E be the extendedComponent computed in the current iteration. Then s is either *in* E, or s can *reach* E, because $a \in F^*(s)$.

If $s \notin E$, but s can reach E, then s is eliminated on line 7 of Algorithm 3 as part of the forward basin. When $s \in E$, it holds that $s' \in$ bottom, since $a \notin F^*(s')$. However, since $s \to^* s'$, we know that s is removed on line 10 because it belongs to the basin of the bottom set. □

However, note that the other implication does not hold. That is, these are not the *only* states that Algorithm 3 eliminates (this can be also seen in Fig. 1).

Based on this theorem, we can derive two extra observations which help to explain the effectiveness of the reduction:

Corollary 1. *If a transition system T has a trivial BSCC, then the whole basin of this SCC is discarded by Algorithm 3.*

Corollary 2. *If a state s is not discarded by Algorithm 3, then all paths starting in s in the reduced state space only use the same transitions as contained in BSCCs reachable from s.*

The first corollary follows from the fact that $F^*(s) = \emptyset$ iff s is a trivial BSCC. The second corollary is essentially a rephrasing of Theorem 2, but it highlights an important property of the reduction: if some transition label is not used by a BSCC, all states in its basin that use it will be eliminated. In our experience, real-world systems rarely use *all* available labels in *all* BSCCs (unless most of the state space is just a single large BSCC). Thus by using this pre-processing step, we can greatly simplify the work of Algorithm 1 by pruning "easily identifiable" non-BSCC states.

There is one more point to be made here: Algorithm 1 has to walk the entire depth of the BSCC basins, which can be substantial. Meanwhile, our approach can often "skip ahead" because it is not starting from a single `pivot` but rather a larger subset of states. However, this may not always be sufficient. In practice, some transitions may be much harder to reduce than others. We address this problem in the next section.

5   Interleaved Transition Guided Reduction

While TGR can significantly reduce the number of states Algorithm 1 needs to consider, TGR itself iterates transitions in an arbitrary order which can significantly influence the speed and number of steps the reduction needs to perform. Removing a transition potentially reduces the number of states which subsequent reductions need to consider. It is thus beneficial to perform the "easiest" reductions first, as this can greatly simplify the following "harder" cases.

However, determining which reductions are "easy" and which are "hard" is not a simple problem. We could try to use additional structural information about the system to determine this, but that would limit us to a specific subclass of models. Instead, we let the algorithm determine this dynamically on the fly.

Our approach is summarised in Algorithm 4. Instead of reducing one transition relation at a time, we interleave all reductions in one procedure. This is done by creating a number of *processes*, one per each $a \in \mathcal{L}$, that we run in an interleaving fashion. The processes work in two phases: FORWARD and EXTENDEDCOMPONENT. The goal of a process in the FORWARD phase is to compute the value of the `forward` set starting from the states that enable an a-transition, and then switch to the EXTENDEDCOMPONENT phase, in which the goal of the process is to compute the corresponding `extendedComponent` set. The computation proceeds using the one-reachability-step functions FWD and BWD, which we defined in Algorithm 1. Every process has its process variables that are local to each process, but their values are kept between steps: The set `reach` represents the part of `forward` that has already been discovered; the set `component` represents the part of `extendedComponent` that has already been discovered; the variable `weight` is explained below; and the variable `phase` holds the current phase of the process (FORWARD or EXTENDEDCOMPONENT).

The process selected for execution in each iteration (line 31) is the one with the smallest *weight*. The weight of a process is determined by the size of the symbolic representation of the set it is currently expanding (`reach` in the first

---

Algorithm 4: Interleaved Transition Guided Reduction

---

1 **Process** ITGRWORKER($a \in \mathcal{L}$)

    process variables: reach, component, weight, phase

    shared variables : $\mathcal{L}$, universe, processes

2   **initialisation:**

3 | reach $\leftarrow$ CANPOST(a, universe);

4 | weight $\leftarrow$ NODECOUNT(reach);

5 | phase $\leftarrow$ FORWARD;

6   **step** *if* phase *is* FORWARD:

7 | (fixpoint, reach) $\leftarrow$ FWD(reach $\cap$ universe, universe);

8 | weight $\leftarrow$ NODECOUNT(reach);

9 | **if** fixpoint **then**

10 | **if** universe $\neq$ reach **then**

11 | | basin $\leftarrow$ BWD*(reach);

12 | | universe $\leftarrow$ universe $\setminus$ (basin $\setminus$ reach);

13 | component $\leftarrow$ CANPOST(a, universe);

14 | weight $\leftarrow$ NODECOUNT(component);

15 | phase $\leftarrow$ EXTENDEDCOMPONENT;

16   **step** *if* phase *is* EXTENDEDCOMPONENT:

17 | (fixpoint, component) $\leftarrow$ BWD(component, reach $\cap$ universe);

18 | weight $\leftarrow$ NODECOUNT(component);

19 | **if** fixpoint **then**

20 | bottom $\leftarrow$ (reach $\cap$ universe) $\setminus$ component;

21 | **if** bottom $\neq \emptyset$ **then**

22 | | basin $\leftarrow$ BWD*(bottom, universe);

23 | | universe $\leftarrow$ universe $\setminus$ (basin $\setminus$ bottom);

24 | **if** CANPOST(a, universe) $= \emptyset$ **then**

25 | | $\mathcal{L} \leftarrow \mathcal{L} \setminus \{a\}$;

26 | **stop current process** (remove it from processes);

27 **Function** ITGR(universe $\subseteq S$)

28 | processes $\leftarrow \{$ITGRWORKER(a) $\mid a \in \mathcal{L}\}$;

29 | initialise all processes;

30 | **while** processes $\neq \emptyset$ **do**

31 | p $\leftarrow$ MINBYKEY(processes, weight);

32 | run one **step** of p;

33 | **return** universe;

---

phase, component in the second). For BDDs (or MDDs), this is the number of nodes in the decision diagram (NODECOUNT). The algorithm thus prioritises processes that have the potential to advance quickly because they will use fast symbolic operations.

Notice that the universe variable is shared by all processes and needs to be now taken into account in multiple places. This means that whenever one process discards some states from universe, all processes benefit from this change. This update can be performed safely because whenever Algorithm 4 discards some states, the discarded set is SCC-closed.

Because both Algorithm 3 and Algorithm 4 compute the same states for `forward` and `extendedComponent` (modulo the states eliminated by other reductions), Theorem 1 and Theorem 2 remain valid for Algorithm 4 as well. The only difference is that this approach should be much more resilient to a bad ordering of transition relations.

Finally, let us note that this approach should be quite simple to parallelise to some extent. If w parallel workers are available, the algorithm can advance w processes at a time instead of picking a single process. However, we do not pursue this approach in this paper as the other methods we use as a reference are also not parallelised.

6   Evaluation

To see how ITGR affects the performance of attractor detection for real-life systems, we implemented the method for asynchronous Boolean networks (BN), a common logical modelling framework used predominantly in systems biology.

Using this implementation, we aim to support the following claims:

1. ITGR performs significantly better than available state-of-the-art tools (for Boolean networks) on real-world models.
2. On realistic Boolean networks, ITGR easily scales to 1000 or more variables, which is not possible with other methods.
3. Interleaving plays a crucial role in making ITGR competitive.

To evaluate the first claim, we compare our implementation with the tool CABEAN [56] on a set of 125 real-world Boolean networks with up to 350 variables. We then generate a pseudo-random set of 200 networks with similar structural characteristics to our real-world benchmarks, but with up to 1100 variables. We show that ITGR can successfully deal with models of this magnitude as well. Finally, we compare the performance of ITGR with the basic attractor detection algorithm as well as with "sequential" TGR on both benchmark sets, showing that ITGR is overall faster and is the only method able to handle the large benchmarks efficiently.

The whole set of benchmarks, as well as the implementation of all the algorithms in Rust, is available as a paper artefact at Zenodo[1]. Additionally, the method is successfully employed by our tool AEON that facilitates long-term analysis of Boolean networks [3].

Before we present the actual benchmark results, let us also first briefly comment on the modelling paradigm chosen (Boolean networks) and the actual setup used to perform the measurements.

---

[1] https://doi.org/10.5281/zenodo.4709882.

6.1   Boolean Networks

A Boolean network, as the name suggests, consists of n Boolean variables, each variable having an associated update function b_i. The state space of the network consists of 2^n Boolean variable valuation vectors, $\{0,1\}^n$. Each update function takes the current state of the network and produces a new value that is assigned to the associated variable, $b_i : \{0,1\}^n \to \{0,1\}$. We assume the update functions can be applied non-deterministically, resulting in an asynchronous updating scheme. This is not the only updating scheme used in practice (e.g. synchronous or generalised asynchronous can be used as well) but is generally considered to cover the possible behaviour of the biological system well.

Typically, an update function of a particular variable x only depends on a smaller subset of the system variables. In such a case, we say that these variables *regulate* x (specifically, y regulates x if the update function of x depends on the value of y). The number of such *regulations* in a Boolean network can be viewed to represent the connectedness or structural complexity of the network in general. In short, the more regulations the network has, the more complex update functions it contains, possibly resulting in more complex behaviour. Variables and regulations together form a directed *regulatory graph*.

A Boolean network with an asynchronous updating scheme fits naturally into our definition of a labelled transition system. The state space of the network variables corresponds with S, i.e. $S = \{0,1\}^n$. Each transition a_i of $\mathcal{L}$ corresponds to the application of the i-th Boolean update function b_i to the i-th Boolean variable, i.e. $(s, s') \in a_i \Leftrightarrow s' = s[i \leftarrow b_i(s)] \wedge s' \neq s$.

When dealing with Boolean networks, BSCCs are typically referred to as *attractors*. The rationale behind this term is that the BSCCs are the states where the fair runs of any system eventually converge to—the behaviour is thus *attracted* towards these states. In the following, we use these two terms interchangeably.

As a symbolic representation, the most natural choice for Boolean networks are Reduced Ordered Binary Decision Diagrams (ROBDD, or BDD) [10], as these can be easily used to represent sets of Boolean vectors. We do not make any specific optimisations with regards to variable ordering, but to enable saturation-like reachability, we assume that the ordering of transitions $a_1, \ldots, a_n$ follows that of the variables in the ROBDD that they update.

Since a Boolean network consists of n Boolean variables, a set of states of such a network can be seen as a Boolean formula (represented as a BDD) over the network variables. Here, a state belongs to such a set iff it represents a satisfying assignment of this formula – a fairly standard approach to state-space encoding using BDDs. To apply a particular update function, we must first construct a BDD describing all states where the update function should change the value of its associated variable (note that this BDD can be reused in subsequent steps). By computing an intersection of a state set with this BDD (yielding the result of the CANPOST operation) and then performing a "bit flip" of the updated variable in the result BDD, we obtain a set of successor states with respect to this one update function (i.e. POST). Similarly, we can obtain CANPRE and PRE.

6.2   Benchmark Set-Up

Real-world Models. To provide the best possible real-world evaluation of our method, we have collected all the models from publicly available Boolean network repositories that we were aware of, and that support the universally accepted SBML-qual format [12] for model transfer. Specifically, our benchmark set includes models available through GINsim [13], Cellcollective [30], Biomodels [39] and the COVID-19 disease map project [48]. Together, the benchmark set consists of 125 models, peaking at 351 variables and 1100 regulations, respectively.

Note that some of these models contain Boolean constants (also called inputs or parameters) that can be specified by the user. For such models, we performed a simple parameter sampling to determine if some of the valuations result in non-trivial attractors, as these are the main focus of this paper. If such valuation was found, we have used it in our benchmark set. However, for the vast majority of models (approximately 90%), there were either no tunable parameters or the sampling did not find any significant changes in the structure of attractors.

Environment. We ran all the benchmarks on a machine with a modest 4-core i7 4790 and 32 GB of RAM. However, none of the benchmarks used more than one core at a time, and typical memory consumption was significantly below 1 GB. Hence our evaluation should be reproducible even using a much slower machine.

We have measured the runtime for each model using the standard Unix `time` utility, with a one-hour timeout per benchmark model. We have run a large portion of the benchmarks repeatedly but have not observed any significant variance in runtime; we thus only report average runtime values.

CABEAN. In the real-world performance test, we compare our method to the tool CABEAN [56]. To the best of our knowledge, CABEAN is both the most recent and the most advanced tool that targets the detection of non-trivial attractors in asynchronous Boolean networks. Other tools that we know of (such as [14, 21, 36]) are not built for systems of the size we are dealing with (for example, due to explicit state-space representation). CABEAN focuses on Boolean network reprogramming, but as a necessary component of this process, it also provides state-of-the-art methods for attractor detection. Specifically, CABEAN uses symbolic manipulation using BDDs, just as our method, but implements advanced decomposition techniques [50] to reduce the state space of the network.

6.3   Real-World Networks

The core of our results is summarised in Fig. 2. On the left, we see a comparison of total successfully completed benchmarks by both CABEAN and ITGR, and on the right, we have relative speedup for each individual benchmark. On the right, we only show benchmarks that took CABEAN more than one second to complete (remaining models would be normally easy to compute even without any special techniques).

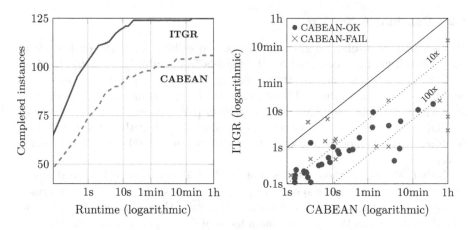

Fig. 2. The left plot shows the total number of benchmarks that each tool has completed before a certain time limit. The dashed line represents CABEAN, whereas the solid line shows our ITGR implementation. On the right, the graph displays the relative runtime between CABEAN and ITGR. The dotted lines represent 10x and 100x speedup compared to CABEAN. The solid circles are the benchmarks where CABEAN successfully computed the attractors. The crosses represent the benchmarks where CABEAN was able to finish the decomposition but failed to extract the actual attractors. Notice that we use logarithmic scaling for the time in both graphs.

In this test, ITGR completed all but one benchmark in less than 1 min. The one remaining case took almost 15 min to complete. However, the reduction process for this model was also quite fast at roughly 100 s. The rest of the computation was spent on identifying the 352 non-trivial attractors in the remaining state space (together, the attractors account for almost 2^{85} states – by far the largest we have seen in any model). Out of the 125 benchmarks, we uncovered non-trivial attractors in exactly 40 models (however, this also includes 6 models with only small 2- or 4-state attractors).

On the other hand, CABEAN failed to compute attractors for 19 of these 125 models (15.2%). Upon closer inspection, all but one of these 19 benchmarks contained non-trivial attractors, which means CABEAN failed for 45% of models with non-trivial attractors.

However, we note that on some models, CABEAN did not simply timeout but actually terminated early due to a segfault. While this behaviour does not seem to be directly linked to the total size of the attractors, it certainly appears to be more common in such networks. We have seen this happen in networks with relatively small attractors, while other networks (even one with a 2^{30}-state attractor) were completed successfully. We hypothesise that this occurs when the decomposition is (at least partially) successful but does not reduce the complexity of the network enough to continue with attractor search[2].

These failed attempts are visualised in the right plot using crosses, as they represent an interesting lower-bound approximation on the performance of this decomposition technique. Overall, the plot shows that for the vast majority of models, ITGR provides an order of magnitude (10x) speedup compared to CABEAN, with some (especially larger) models attacking or exceeding the 100x speedup threshold.

Overall, we have shown that ITGR is capable of solving all publicly available problem instances (that we know of), and it outperforms current state-of-the-art decomposition methods with the median of 16x speedup (77x average). Naturally, we also compared the actual attractors found by CABEAN and ITGR, and we are happy to report that we found no inconsistencies between the two methods.

6.4   Pseudo-random Networks

Next, we set out to test the limits of ITGR on larger models than the ones available in the public repositories today. Specifically, we wanted to test networks with 1000 or more Boolean variables. While such a number is arguably not possible to achieve in a single hand-made model, fully or semi-automated machine learning techniques [5, 8, 22, 51] are making models of this magnitude much more approachable.

Pseudo-Random BNs. To create a benchmark set of larger models, we have decided to generate pseudo-random networks structurally similar to our real-world benchmark set. Biological systems, specifically protein and gene regulatory networks, are known to follow certain properties of small-world networks [9, 58]. However, aside from other differences, they are directed and typically quite sparse (our real-world benchmark set has the average node degree of 4.3). This makes most common random network models unsuitable for this specific task. For example, the famous Watts–Strogatz model would, in this case, assume that the average degree is significantly larger than $ln(1000) \sim 7$.

We have thus first measured the relative in- and out-degree distributions in the regulatory graphs of our real-world networks and then generated random networks by sampling from this distribution to approximate the real-world dataset. Additionally, regulatory graphs of Boolean networks are essentially always weakly connected. In each model, we have thus filtered out all variables except the largest weakly connected component. Note that this makes the dataset slightly skewed towards more connected networks (i.e. more challenging), as these have a higher chance of being weakly connected when randomly generated. However, it is still well within the connectivity limits expected based on the real-world dataset.

---

[2] Developers of CABEAN have confirmed that this assumption is essentially accurate, i.e. for some structurally complex networks with large non-trivial attractors, the tool can segfault instead of timing-out.

To generate the boolean functions, we have measured that 80.7% of the regulations in the real-world dataset are positively monotonous, with the remaining being negatively monotonous (monotonicity is typically expected in biological networks). Each regulation was thus assigned monotonicity based on this distribution, and a function was generated by randomly choosing between $\wedge$ and $\vee$ when connecting the positive/negative literals. Note that this does not cover the full spectrum of possible Boolean functions, but it is well within reason for biological networks, where some techniques tend to even implicitly assume the function is just a simple conjunction/disjunction of literals.

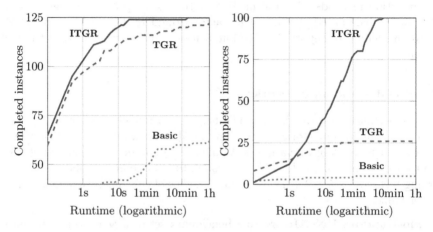

Fig. 3. Runtime comparison of ITGR, "sequential" TGR and the basic symbolic BSCC detection. The left plot shows the real-world benchmark set with up to 350 variables per model. On the right, we see the *medium* synthetic benchmark ranging from 50 to 1100 variables. Note that the *large* synthetic benchmark ($\sim$ 1000 variables only) is not shown, as ITGR was the only method capable of actually completing these models. All the time axes have a logarithmic scale.

Performance. In the end, we have obtained two benchmark sets: A *medium* set with 100 networks ranging from 50 to 1100 variables, and one *large* benchmark set, also with 100 models, but all with $\sim$ 1000 variables and ranging from 2471 to 5099 regulations. Out of these 200 models, we discovered non-trivial attractors in 61 of them.

The runtime for the *medium* benchmarks is summarised in Fig. 3 (right). Here, we see that ITGR successfully completed all instances within 10 min. For the *large* benchmark set, ITGR consistently finished 98% of the models within 5 to 10 min. The remaining two outliers took 28 and 55 min to complete. Similar to what we saw in the real-world benchmark, these models contained very large non-trivial attractors (the largest having again more than 2^{80} states) and were thus not limited by the speed of the reduction but by the diameter of the actual attractors.

Additionally, for each reduction procedure, we kept track of the actual number of reachability iterations that needed to be performed (specifically, how many times we applied line 21 of BWD as shown in Algorithm 1, or the same line in FWD). For all models, this number was well below 10 000 iterations, which is quite low considering the procedure needed to evaluate up to 1100 transition relations. In particular, this supports our hypothesis that ITGR works well due to typically short distances between states that can fire individual transitions.

6.5 Interleaving Performance Impact

Finally, we would like to evaluate the influence of smart interleaving on the performance of ITGR. For this purpose, we consider three algorithms:

1. the basic symbolic algorithm with saturation as described in Sect. 3;
2. TGR, as described in Sect. 4, applied to variables in the order in which they appear in the network declaration (that is, without any interleaving);
3. the full ITGR as described in Sect. 5.

Keep in mind that all three approaches use the same implementation of symbolic representation and differ only in the actual attractor detection. Also, TGR/ITGR use the basic algorithm to actually identify attractors once the reduction is completed. Any speedup between TGR and the basic algorithm can be thus directly attributed to the state-space reduction, while any speedup between ITGR and TGR is due to the introduction of interleaving.

For the real-world benchmarks (up to 350 variables) and medium synthetic benchmarks (50 to 1100 variables), the comparison is presented in Fig. 3. Here, we see that the basic algorithm is indeed not generally sufficient for large networks, finishing only 62 of the 125 real-world models and only 5 of the medium synthetic benchmarks (the main reason was typically poor pivot selection; however, some instances also timed out due to long reachability procedures).

The difference between TGR and ITGR is not as drastic for real-world models. TGR finished in 122/125 instances but was consistently slower than ITGR, especially on larger models (on one instance, we have even seen a 55 min vs 2.9 s speedup, i.e. more than 1000x). However, as we look into even larger graphs with the medium synthetic benchmark set, ITGR easily outperforms TGR, which completed only 26/100 instances.

Finally, for the large benchmarks, all with ~ 1000 variables, we have ITGR completing all benchmarks within the 1-h timeout (with 98% finishing within 10 min); no other method has finished any of the 100 models within this limit. This leaves ITGR as the only implementation in this comparison capable of successfully analysing networks with 1000 or more Boolean variables.

7 Conclusions

In this paper, we present a novel symbolic method for BSCC detection in state-transition graphs of labelled transition systems, called *interleaved transition guided reduction* (ITGR). The method relies on the observation that BSCCs in real-world systems rarely employ all transition labels available. Therefore, if a state *s* can fire a transition with a label that is not employed by some BSCC reachable from *s*, after applying ITGR, *s* is eliminated. As a result, all paths in the remaining state space only perform transitions with labels employed by their reachable BSCCs. If the system has only trivial BSCCs, this solves the problem completely. For non-trivial BSCCs, this may make the problem tractable using previously known techniques.

ITGR relies on smart interleaving to prioritise the elimination of "symbolically easier" transitions. Completing the reduction in this order allows ITGR to subsequently simplify the analysis of transitions which would initially be too complex to handle.

We tested the method on a large benchmark set of real-world Boolean networks (up to 350 variables) as well as randomly generated benchmarks (up to 1100 variables) with similar structural properties. Our experiments show that ITGR significantly outperforms the state-of-the-art tool CABEAN and can easily handle all models from both benchmark sets, pushing the boundary of what was previously possible in this field.

References

1. Abrahám, E., Jansen, N., Wimmer, R., Katoen, J.P., Becker, B.: DTMC model checking by SCC reduction. In: 2010 Seventh International Conference on the Quantitative Evaluation of Systems, pp. 37–46. IEEE (2010)
2. Baudin, A., Paul, S., Su, C., Pang, J.: Controlling large Boolean networks with single-step perturbations. Bioinformatics **35**(14), i558–i567 (2019)
3. Beneš, N., Brim, L., Kadlecaj, J., Pastva, S., Šafránek, D.: AEON: attractor bifurcation analysis of parametrised boolean networks. In: Lahiri, S.K., Wang, C. (eds.) CAV 2020. LNCS, vol. 12224, pp. 569–581. Springer, Cham (2020). https://doi.org/10.1007/978-3-030-53288-8_28
4. Beneš, N., Brim, L., Pastva, S., Šafránek, D.: Digital bifurcation analysis of TCP dynamics. In: Vojnar, T., Zhang, L. (eds.) TACAS 2019. LNCS, vol. 11428, pp. 339–356. Springer, Cham (2019). https://doi.org/10.1007/978-3-030-17465-1_19
5. Berestovsky, N., Nakhleh, L.: An evaluation of methods for inferring Boolean networks from time-series data. PLoS ONE **8**(6), e66031 (2013)
6. Berestovsky, N., Zhou, W., Nagrath, D., Nakhleh, L.: Modeling integrated cellular machinery using hybrid Petri-Boolean networks. PLOS Comput. Biol. **9**(11), 1–13 (2013)
7. Bloem, R., Gabow, H.N., Somenzi, F.: An algorithm for strongly connected component analysis in *nlogn* symbolic steps. In: Formal Methods in Computer-Aided Design, pp. 37–54. Springer (2000)
8. Bonnaffoux, A., et al.: WASABI: a dynamic iterative framework for gene regulatory network inference. BMC Bioinformatics **20**(1), 1–19 (2019)
9. Bork, P., Jensen, L.J., Von Mering, C., Ramani, A.K., Lee, I., Marcotte, E.M.: Protein interaction networks from yeast to human. Curr. Opin. Struct. Biol. **14**(3), 292–299 (2004)
10. Bryant, R.E.: Graph-based algorithms for Boolean function manipulation. IEEE Trans. Comput. **35**(8), 677–691 (1986)

11. Buchholz, P., Katoen, J.P., Kemper, P., Tepper, C.: Model-checking large structured Markov chains. J. Logic Algebraic Program. **56**(1), 69–97 (2003)
12. Chaouiya, C., et al.: SBML qualitative models: a model representation format and infrastructure to foster interactions between qualitative modelling formalisms and tools. BMC Syst. Biol. **7**(1), 1–15 (2013)
13. Chaouiya, C., Naldi, A., Thieffry, D.: Logical modelling of gene regulatory networks with GINsim. In: van Helden, J., Toussaint, A., Thieffry, D. (eds.) Bacterial Molecular Networks, pp. 463–479. Springer, New York (2012). https://doi.org/10.1007/978-1-61779-361-5_23
14. Chatain, T., Haar, S., Jezequel, L., Paulevé, L., Schwoon, S.: Characterization of reachable attractors using petri net unfoldings. In: Mendes, P., Dada, J.O., Smallbone, K. (eds.) CMSB 2014. LNCS, vol. 8859, pp. 129–142. Springer, Cham (2014). https://doi.org/10.1007/978-3-319-12982-2_10
15. Chatain, T., Haar, S., Kolčák, J., Paulevé, L., Thakkar, A.: Concurrency in Boolean networks. Nat. Comput. **19**(1), 91–109 (2020)
16. Chatterjee, K., Dvořák, W., Henzinger, M., Loitzenbauer, V.: Lower bounds for symbolic computation on graphs: strongly connected components, liveness, safety, and diameter. In: Proceedings of the Twenty-Ninth Annual ACM-SIAM Symposium on Discrete Algorithms, pp. 2341–2356. SIAM (2018)
17. Cherry, A.B.C., Daley, G.Q.: Reprogramming cellular identity for regenerative medicine. Cell **148**(6), 1110–1122 (2012)
18. Choo, S.M., Cho, K.H.: An efficient algorithm for identifying primary phenotype attractors of a large-scale Boolean network. BMC Syst. Biol. **10**(1), 95 (2016)
19. Ciardo, G., Lüttgen, G., Siminiceanu, R.: Saturation: an efficient iteration strategy for symbolic state—space generation. In: Tools and Algorithms for the Construction and Analysis of Systems. pp. 328–342. Springer (2001)
20. Ciardo, G., Marmorstein, R.M., Siminiceanu, R.: The saturation algorithm for symbolic state-space exploration. Int. J. Softw. Tools Technol. Transf. **8**(1), 4–25 (2006)
21. Gan, X., Albert, R.: General method to find the attractors of discrete dynamic models of biological systems. Phys. Rev. E **97**, 042308 (2018)
22. Gao, S., Sun, C., Xiang, C., Qin, K., Lee, T.H.: Learning asynchronous Boolean networks from single-cell data using multiobjective cooperative genetic programming. IEEE Transactions on Cybernetics (2020)
23. García-Gómez, M.L., Ornelas-Ayala, D., Garay-Arroyo, A., García-Ponce, B., de la Paz Sánchez, M., Álvarez-Buylla, E.R.: A system-level mechanistic explanation for asymmetric stem cell fates: arabidopsis thaliana root niche as a study system. Sci. Rep. **10**(1), 1–16 (2020)
24. Garg, A., Di Cara, A., Xenarios, I., Mendoza, L., De Micheli, G.: Synchronous versus asynchronous modeling of gene regulatory networks. Bioinformatics **24**(17), 1917–1925 (2008)
25. Gentilini, R., Piazza, C., Policriti, A.: Computing strongly connected components in a linear number of symbolic steps. In: Proceedings of the Twenty-Ninth Annual ACM-SIAM Symposium on Discrete Algorithms. vol. 3, pp. 573–582. SIAM (2003)
26. Grebogi, C., Ott, E., Yorke, J.A.: Chaos, strange attractors, and fractal basin boundaries in nonlinear dynamics. Science **238**(4827), 632–638 (1987)
27. Grieco, L., Calzone, L., Bernard-Pierrot, I., Radvanyi, F., Kahn-Perles, B., Thieffry, D.: Integrative modelling of the influence of MAPK network on cancer cell fate decision. PLOS Comput. Biol. **9**(10), 1–15 (2013)

28. Guo, W., Yang, G., Wu, W., He, L., Sun, M.I.: A parallel attractor finding algorithm based on Boolean satisfiability for genetic regulatory networks. PLOS ONE 9(4), 1–10 (2014)
29. Harvey, I., Bossomaier, T.: Time out of joint: attractors in asynchronous random Boolean networks. In: Proceedings of the Fourth European Conference on Artificial Life (ECAL97), pp. 67–75. MIT Press (1997)
30. Helikar, T., Kowal, B., McClenathan, S., Bruckner, M., Rowley, T., Madrahimov, A., et al.: The Cell Collective: toward an open and collaborative approach to systems biology. BMC Syst. Biol. 6(1), 96 (2012)
31. Huang, S., Ernberg, I., Kauffman, S.: Cancer attractors: a systems view of tumors from a gene network dynamics and developmental perspective. Seminars Cell Dev. Biol. 20(7), 869–876 (2009)
32. Kauffman, S.: Metabolic stability and epigenesis in randomly constructed genetic nets. J. Theor. Biol. 22(3), 437–467 (1969)
33. Kim, J., Park, S.M., Cho, K.H.: Discovery of a kernel for controlling biomolecular regulatory networks. Sci. Rep. 3, 2223 (2013)
34. Klarner, H., Bockmayr, A., Siebert, H.: Computing symbolic steady states of boolean networks. In: Wąs, J., Sirakoulis, G.C., Bandini, S. (eds.) ACRI 2014. LNCS, vol. 8751, pp. 561–570. Springer, Cham (2014). https://doi.org/10.1007/978-3-319-11520-7_59
35. Klarner, H., Bockmayr, A., Siebert, H.: Computing maximal and minimal trap spaces of Boolean networks. Nat. Comput. 14(4), 535–544 (2015)
36. Klarner, H., Streck, A., Siebert, H.: PyBoolNet: a python package for the generation, analysis and visualization of Boolean networks. Bioinformatics 33(5), 770–772 (2017)
37. Klemm, K., Bornholdt, S.: Stable and unstable attractors in Boolean networks. Phys. Rev. E 72(5), 055101 (2005)
38. Kučera, A., Stražovský, O.: On the Controller Synthesis for Finite-State Markov Decision Processes. In: Sarukkai, S., Sen, S. (eds.) FSTTCS 2005. LNCS, vol. 3821, pp. 541–552. Springer, Heidelberg (2005). https://doi.org/10.1007/11590156_44
39. Le Novere, N., et al.: Biomodels database: a free, centralized database of curated, published, quantitative kinetic models of biochemical and cellular systems. Nucleic Acids Res. 34(suppl_1), D689–D691 (2006)
40. MacArthur, B.D., Ma'ayan, A., Lemischka, I.R.: Systems biology of stem cell fate and cellular reprogramming. Nat. Rev. Mol. Cell Biol. 10(10), 672–681 (2009)
41. Mandon, H., Su, C., Pang, J., Paul, S., Haar, S., Paulevé, L.: Algorithms for the sequential reprogramming of Boolean networks. IEEE/ACM Trans. Comput. Biol. Bioinf. 16(5), 1610–1619 (2019)
42. Matouk, A.: Complex dynamics in susceptible-infected models for COVID-19 with multi-drug resistance. Chaos, Solitons Fractals 140, 110257 (2020)
43. Mendes, N.D., Henriques, R., Remy, E., Carneiro, J., Monteiro, P.T., Chaouiya, C.: Estimating attractor reachability in asynchronous logical models. Front. Physiol. 9, 1161 (2018)
44. Mizera, A., Pang, J., Qu, H., Yuan, Q.: Taming asynchrony for attractor detection in large Boolean networks. IEEE/ACM Trans. Comput. Biol. Bioinf. 16(1), 31–42 (2019)
45. Mushthofa, M., Schockaert, S., De Cock, M.: Computing attractors of multi-valued gene regulatory networks using fuzzy answer set programming. FUZZ-IEEE 2016, 1955–1962 (2016)

46. Naldi, A., Thieffry, D., Chaouiya, C.: Decision diagrams for the representation and analysis of logical models of genetic networks. In: Calder, M., Gilmore, S. (eds.) CMSB 2007. LNCS, vol. 4695, pp. 233–247. Springer, Heidelberg (2007). https://doi.org/10.1007/978-3-540-75140-3_16

47. Nga, J., Iu, H.H., Ling, B.W.K., Lam, H.K.: Analysis and control of bifurcation and chaos in average queue length in TCP/RED model. Int. J. Bifurcation Chaos 18(08), 2449–2459 (2008)

48. Ostaszewski, M., et al.: COVID-19 disease map, building a computational repository of SARS-CoV-2 virus-host interaction mechanisms. Sci. Data 7(1), 1–4 (2020)

49. Pardo, J., Ivanov, S., Delaplace, F.: Sequential reprogramming of biological network fate. In: Bortolussi, L., Sanguinetti, G. (eds.) CMSB 2019. LNCS, vol. 11773, pp. 20–41. Springer, Cham (2019). https://doi.org/10.1007/978-3-030-31304-3_2

50. Paul, S., Su, C., Pang, J., Mizera, A.: A decomposition-based approach towards the control of Boolean networks. In: International Conference on Bioinformatics, Computational Biology, and Health Informatics, pp. 11–20 (2018)

51. Razzaq, M., Paulevé, L., Siegel, A., Saez-Rodriguez, J., Bourdon, J., Guziolowski, C.: Computational discovery of dynamic cell line specific Boolean networks from multiplex time-course data. PLoS Comput. Biol. 14(10), e1006538 (2018)

52. Renault, E., Duret-Lutz, A., Kordon, F., Poitrenaud, D.: Strength-based decomposition of the property Büchi automaton for faster model checking. In: Tools and Algorithms for the Construction and Analysis of Systems. pp. 580–593. Springer (2013)

53. Saadatpour, A., Albert, I., Albert, R.: Attractor analysis of asynchronous Boolean models of signal transduction networks. J. Theor. Biol. 266(4), 641–656 (2010)

54. Steffen, W., et al.: Trajectories of the earth system in the anthropocene. Proc. Natl. Acad. Sci. 115(33), 8252–8259 (2018)

55. Štill, V., Barnat, J.: Local nontermination detection for parallel C++ programs. In: Software Engineering and Formal Methods. pp. 373–390. Springer, Cham (2019)

56. Su, C., Pang, J.: CABEAN: a software for the control of asynchronous Boolean networks. Bioinformatics (2020)

57. Thomas, R.: Boolean formalization of genetic control circuits. J. Theor. Biol. 42(3), 563–585 (1973)

58. Van Noort, V., Snel, B., Huynen, M.A.: The yeast coexpression network has a small-world, scale-free architecture and can be explained by a simple model. EMBO Rep. 5(3), 280–284 (2004)

59. Xie, A., Beerel, P.A.: Implicit enumeration of strongly connected components and an application to formal verification. IEEE Trans. Comput. Aided Des. Integr. Circuits Syst. 19(10), 1225–1230 (2000)

60. Yuan, Q., Mizera, A., Pang, J., Qu, H.: A new decomposition-based method for detecting attractors in synchronous Boolean networks. Sci. Comput. Program. 180, 18–35 (2019)

61. Zhang, S.Q., Hayashida, M., Akutsu, T., Ching, W.K., Ng, M.K.: Algorithms for finding small attractors in Boolean networks. EURASIP J. Bioinformatics Syst. Biol. 2007, 4–4 (2007)

62. Zhao, Y., Ciardo, G.: Symbolic computation of strongly connected components and fair cycles using saturation. Innovations Syst. Softw. Eng. 7(2), 141–150 (2011)

Implicit Semi-Algebraic Abstraction
for Polynomial Dynamical Systems

Sergio Mover[1]($\boxtimes$), Alessandro Cimatti[2],
Alberto Griggio[2], Ahmed Irfan[3], and Stefano Tonetta[2]

[1] LIX, CNRS, École Polytechnique, Institut Polytechnique de Paris,
Palaiseau, France
sergio.mover@lix.polytechnique.fr
[2] Fondazione Bruno Kessler, Trento, Italy
[3] Stanford University, Stanford, USA

Abstract. Semi-algebraic abstraction is an approach to the safety verification problem for polynomial dynamical systems where the state space is partitioned according to the sign of a set of polynomials. Similarly to predicate abstraction for discrete systems, the number of abstract states is exponential in the number of polynomials. Hence, semi-algebraic abstraction is expensive to explicitly compute and then analyze (e.g., to prove a safety property or extract invariants).

In this paper, we propose an implicit encoding of the semi-algebraic abstraction, which avoids the explicit enumeration of the abstract states: the safety verification problem for dynamical systems is reduced to a corresponding problem for infinite-state transition systems, allowing us to reuse existing model-checking tools based on Satisfiability Modulo Theory (SMT). The main challenge we solve is to express the semi-algebraic abstraction as a first-order logic formula that is linear in the number of predicates, instead of exponential, thus letting the model checker lazily explore the exponential number of abstract states with symbolic techniques. We implemented the approach and validated experimentally its potential to prove safety for polynomial dynamical systems.

1 Introduction

Non-linear dynamical systems are characterized by continuous evolution resulting from ordinary differential equations containing non-linear polynomials. Proving safety properties for non-linear dynamical systems is extremely challenging, and several approaches have been proposed. Semi-automatic deductive verification techniques based on theorem proving include proving hybrid programs using differential dynamic logic [27] or hybrid Cyber Physical System (CPS) using Hybrid Hoare Logic (HHL) [21]). Among various automatic techniques (e.g., [30]), an important line of work applies symbolic model checking to abstractions of hybrid systems, both with, using qualitative predicate abstraction [34]. Unfortunately, the problem with the above techniques is twofold. On one side, the abstractions are often unable to precisely lift important information, thus

© The Author(s) 2021
A. Silva and K. R. M. Leino (Eds.) CAV 2021, LNCS 12759, pp. 529–551, 2021.
https://doi.org/10.1007/978-3-030-81685-8_25

resulting in an abstract system that is not strong enough to prove the property. On the other side, the abstraction computation may be too expensive to compute, especially in the non-linear case.

To tackle the first problem, we consider the semi-algebraic decomposition for dynamical systems of [32]. The idea is to build an abstraction from a given set of polynomials, partitioning the concrete state space according to the sign of each polynomial. The abstraction is *exact*: there is a transition from an abstract state to another abstract state if and only if there is (at least) a concrete transition from the two concretizations of the abstract states. Semi-algebraic decomposition is also appealing because it can be made *more precise* adding new polynomials.

The abstraction can be computed by means of logical operations (by repeatedly checking the satisfiability of quantifier-free formulas interpreted over the reals). However, the second problem remains: the explicit computation of the abstraction is extremely costly, since it requires the enumeration of all possible transitions between abstract states, which are exponential in the number of considered polynomials.

Interestingly, an effective use of abstraction is at the core of the most successful verification techniques for discrete infinite-state transition systems. The technique of predicate abstraction [16] was originally adapted for symbolic verification in [9] and then optimized in [19]. This idea has been further developed in *implicit predicate abstraction* [35], which eliminates the burden of an up-front exponential blowup in the computation of the abstract states by embedding the abstraction in the symbolic encoding of the transitions. This approach has been used also in combination with IC3 [1,5,6].

In this paper, we propose a new approach to the verification of dynamical systems with non-linear polynomial dynamics based on the use of semi-algebraic decomposition. The contributions of the paper are the following:

- We cast the problem of computing and verifying properties of dynamical systems using the semi-algebraic decomposition in the framework of verification via implicit predicate abstraction (i.e., a first-order logic characterization of the semi-algebraic decomposition abstraction). Thus, we apply SMT-based model checking techniques to prove safety properties of polynomial dynamical systems.
- We define a linear symbolic encoding for the abstraction. Note that the naive formulation of the predicate abstraction problem (which follows from the explicit computation approach proposed in [32]) is not effective in practice: in fact, the number of abstract states is exponential in the total number of polynomials that define the abstraction, and the encoding requires to enumerate all the possible pairs of abstract states to check the existence of an abstract transition. We exploit the properties of the LZZ formulation to define a concise encoding that is linear in the number of the polynomials, hence making the approach feasible in practice.
- We implement and experimentally evaluate the approach. The results show how the reduction to the verification of discrete infinite-state transition systems is complementary to reachability analysis techniques and proves cases that were previously out of reach for the state-of-the-art tools.

Outline: The rest of the paper is structured as follows: Sect. 2 gives an overview of the approach with a motivating example; Sect. 3 provides the background definitions; Sect. 4 shows the naive encoding of the abstraction, while in Sect. 5 we derive the linear encoding and define the related implicit semi-algebraic abstraction; in Sect. 6, we present the experimental results; in Sect. 7, we discuss the related work and, finally, in Sect. 8, we draw some conclusions and directions for future work.

2   Overview of the Approach

Consider a verification problem (adapted from [22]) on the non-linear dynamical system with two variables x and y, and differential equations $\dot{x} = -2y, \dot{y} = x^2$. We want to prove that the system cannot reach the set of bad states $(x+2)^2 + y^2 - 1 \leq 0$ (i.e., it never leaves the safe region $(x+2)^2 + y^2 - 1 > 0$) when starting from the initial set of states $x - y - \frac{1}{2} \geq 0 \wedge x + 2 > 0$. Note that although in this example the evolution of the system is not restricted, our approach can deal with the more general case in which the evolution is constrained by an invariant condition that must always hold. The system is safe and avoids the set of bad states (see system's dynamic in Fig. 1a).

We can prove that the system is safe by first constructing and then model checking a discrete semi-algebraic abstraction [32]: given the set of polynomials $\mathbb{A} := \{x - y - \frac{1}{2}, x + y + \frac{1}{2}, x + 2\}$, the semi-algebraic abstraction partitions the state space according to the sign ($\{>, <, =\}$) of the polynomials in $\mathbb{A}$ (an example of abstract state is the state $x + 2 > 0 \wedge x - y - \frac{1}{2} < 0 \wedge x + y + \frac{1}{2} < 0$ represented as ① in Fig. 1b). There exists a transition from an abstract state to another one if the two states are neighbors and there exists at least one trajectory of the dynamical system going from one state to the other. The existence of such condition can be checked using the *LZZ* algorithm [22], which checks if a semi-algebraic set ψ is a differential invariant for a polynomial dynamical system f when its execution is restricted to the domain H (another semi-algebraic set). The algorithm reduces the invariant check to the satisfiability of the Non-Linear Real Arithmetic Theory formula $LZZ_{\psi,f,H}(Z)$, where Z is a set of real-valued variables. We can systematically check if there exists a transition from an abstract state s_1 to the abstract state s_2 proving that s_1 *is not invariant* when restricted to the domain $s_1 \vee s_2$ (i.e., checking that $LZZ_{s_1,f,s_1 \vee s_2}(Z)$ is false).

Furthermore, we can use an algorithm, called *LazyReach* [32], to compute the forward set of reachable abstract states starting from the initial states. As usual, if no abstract states intersect the set of bad states then the system is safe, and the reachable set of abstract states is a continuous invariant for the system. Figure 1b shows the state space of the dynamical system: the initial and bad states of the verification problem (represented with the green and red region respectively), the solution of the polynomials from $\mathbb{A}$ (represented as blue lines), and further superimpose the set of reachable abstract states and transitions (represented as numbered circles and arrows between the circles). The abstraction shown in Fig. 1b is the result after applying *LazyReach* to the verification problem.

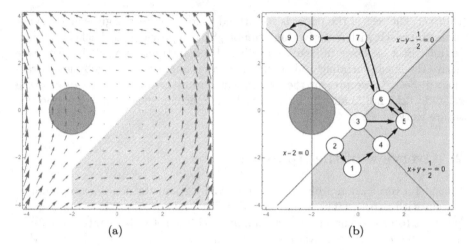

(a)   (b)

Fig. 1. Safety verification problem and reachable states of the abstraction for the non-linear dynamical system $\dot{x} = -2y, \dot{y} = x^2$, bad states $(x+2)^2 + y^2 - 1 \leq 0$ (red circle), and initial set of states $x - y - \frac{1}{2} \geq 0 \wedge x + 2 > 0$ (green region). Figure **(a)** shows the verification problem and the system's vector field. Figure **(b)** shows the reachable abstract states and the transitions of the algebraic abstraction (numbered circles and arrows) computed using *LazyReach* and the differential invariant (green and gray regions) obtained from the set of polynomials $\mathbb{A} = \{x - y - \frac{1}{2}, x + y + \frac{1}{2}, x + 2\}$ (blue lines), computed using *Implicit Abstraction*. Abstract states represent different combinations of signs for the abstraction's polynomials. Examples of abstract states are ① $x+2 > 0 \wedge x-y-\frac{1}{2} < 0 \wedge x+y+\frac{1}{2} < 0$, ② $x+2 > 0 \wedge x-y-\frac{1}{2} = 0 \wedge x+y+\frac{1}{2} < 0$, and ③ $x + 2 > 0 \wedge x - y - \frac{1}{2} = 0 \wedge x + y + \frac{1}{2} = 0$. (Color figure online)

A main challenge for the *LazyReach* algorithm is to explicitly enumerate the reachable states and transitions among them, since their number is exponential in the number of polynomials $\mathbb{A}$ (i.e., the number of total states is already $3^{|\mathbb{A}|}$). For the example above, where we have 3 polynomials, the maximum number of states would be 27, with an even bigger number of transitions (e.g., one must consider the transition between each pair of neighbouring abstract states). Even if *LazyReach* enumerates the reachable abstract states on-the-fly, the explosion in the number of states and transitions is still a bottleneck. Our implementation of *LazyReach* applied to the above example explores a total of 9 states and checks the existence of 27 transitions, taking about 12 s to complete.

A possible solution to tackle the state explosion problem is the *DWCL* algorithm, proposed in [32]. The *DWCL* algorithm[1] tries to reduce the number of abstract states by checking if the sign of a polynomial $a \in \mathbb{A}$ is invariant, that is if:

---

[1] We provide the main intuition behind the *DWCL* algorithm and we refer the reader to [32] for a detailed exposition.

- the sign of the polynomial a does not change in the initial states (i.e., the predicate $a \bowtie 0$, with $\bowtie \in \{<, >, =\}$, holds for all the initial states); and
- $a \bowtie 0$ is a continuous invariant for the dynamical system (this can be checked with $LZZ_{a\bowtie 0, f, H}(Z)$).

When a predicate $a \bowtie 0$ is a continuous invariant, the algorithm strengthens the invariant of the dynamical system (by adding $a \bowtie 0$ to the invariants), allowing to remove a from the set of polynomials $\mathbb{A}$. While the $DWCL$ algorithm may already find a strong-enough invariant to prove the safety property, the algorithm falls back to the $LazyReach$ algorithm in the general case to explore the abstract state space, hopefully with a strengthened invariant domain and a smaller set of polynomials. In practice, the state-space explosion problem of $LazyReach$ still exists in the case "not enough" polynomials are sign-invariant, as it happens in our motivating example. In the example, no polynomials are sign-invariant[2]: this means that the $DWCL$ algorithm will not remove any polynomials from the set $\mathbb{A}$ and $LazyReach$ will still suffer from the state-space explosion problem.

The semi-algebraic abstraction is a specific instance of predicate abstraction [16] of the dynamical system f. For discrete-state systems, there exist efficient algorithms to either *explicitly* compute the abstraction using Satisfiability Modulo Theory (SMT) solvers [19,20] or to *implicitly* represent the abstraction and directly verify a safety property (e.g., implicit predicate abstraction [35]). Since these algorithms work on a fully symbolic representation of the abstract state space, they can cope with the state-space explosion due to the number of predicates of the abstraction. However, applying the same symbolic-state techniques to compute or verify the semi-algebraic abstraction is still challenging, mainly because it requires to express the transition relation $T(X, X')$ of the semi-algebraic abstraction in a first-order logic formula. We notice that such transition relation T can be directly obtained from the abstraction's definition[3]:

$$\exists Z. \left(\bigvee_{(s_1, s_2) \in 3^{\mathbb{A}}} s_1(X) \wedge s_2(X') \wedge (\neg LZZ_{s_1, f, s_1 \vee s_2}(Z)) \right).$$

The above transition relation enumerates all the possible pairs of abstract states and its size is exponential in the number of polynomials in $\mathbb{A}$. The additional variables Z are copies of the state variables of the system and are used to encode the LZZ condition. Clearly, even creating such formula is not scalable and hinders the application of the standard abstraction and verification techniques used for discrete systems. Note that, while the LZZ algorithm works for semi-algebraic sets (i.e., the candidate invariant ψ and the invariant states H are both arbitrary Boolean combinations of non-linear arithmetic terms), here we apply LZZ to

---

[2] The differential-cut (DC) and the differential divide-and-conquer (DDC) proof rules used in $DWCL$ fail for all the polynomials from $\mathbb{A}$, so $DWCL$ would not remove any polynomial.

[3] For clarity, here we do not include additional constraints in the transition relation, such as the neighborhood relation, which instead we consider later in Sect. 4.

check the existence of a transition between two abstract states, hence we still have to explicitly enumerate the abstract transitions.

Our main contribution, presented in Sect. 5, is a compact formulation of the above transition relation that has a size *linear* in the number of the polynomials $\mathbb{A}$. The steps to obtain such exponentially smaller transition are:

1. We specialize the LZZ formula $\neg LZZ_{s_1,f,s_1 \vee s_2}(Z)$ to encode the existence of a transition between two abstract states s_1 and s_2. The resulting formula is a disjunction, and each disjunct encodes the necessary and sufficient condition for a continuous transition to s_2 to exist, either *inside* the set $s_1(Z)$ or *outside* the set $\neg s_1(Z)$. Intuitively, we obtain a specific encoding for checking the existence of an abstract transition, instead of reusing the LZZ as a "black box".
2. We "lift" the above disjunction to the disjunction of all the abstract states, obtaining the formula:

$$\exists Z.(InsExpl_f(X, X', Z) \vee OutExpl_f(X, X', Z)),$$

where $InsExpl_f(X, X', Z)$ encodes the "inside condition" for all the pairs of transitions (and similarly for the "outside condition" $OutExpl_f(X, X', Z)$).
3. The formula $InsExpl_f(X, X', Z)$ still contains an explicit enumeration on the pairs of abstract states. We show how we obtain an equivalent formula, $InsSymb_f(X, X', Z)$, that encodes the same condition for each polynomial $a \in \mathbb{A}$ in the abstraction, obtaining a linear, instead of exponential, encoding. We apply the same reasoning on $OutExpl_f(X, X', Z)$.

We then use the concise transition relation of T to obtain a symbolic transition system $S_{Impl,\mathbb{P}}$ that implicitly encodes the semi-algebraic abstraction for the dynamical system f with the polynomials $\mathbb{A}$ and predicates $\mathbb{P} = \{a \bowtie 0 \mid a \in \mathbb{A} \wedge \bowtie \in \{>, <, =\}\}$. Technically, instead of computing the predicate abstraction, we encode an implicit abstraction [35]. Consequently, we avoid the expensive quantifier elimination step. We can then verify the safety property on the transition system $S_{Impl,\mathbb{P}}$ using an SMT-based model checking algorithm. We use the algorithm from [4], since $S_{Impl,\mathbb{P}}$ contains non-linear arithmetic formulas. Our approach verifies the example of Fig. 1 and finds the continuous invariant:

$$(x - y < \frac{1}{2} \vee x \geq -2) \wedge (x - y \geq \frac{1}{2} \vee x + y \geq -\frac{1}{2}) \wedge (x - y \geq \frac{1}{2} \vee x + y > -\frac{1}{2}),$$

which is shown in the union of the green and gray regions in Fig. 1b.

3   Preliminaries

In this work, we consider first order logic formulas in the theory of non-linear arithmetic over the reals (NRA). We denote with $\phi(X)$ the formula ϕ containing free variables from the set $X = \{x_1, \ldots, x_n\}$. We simplify the notation of the formula $\phi(X)$ to ϕ when the set X is clear from the context.

Invariant Verification for Polynomial Dynamical Systems

Safety Verification of Dynamical Systems. Given a set of variables X we write $X = [x_1, \ldots, x_n]^T$ to specify a vector containing all the variables in X ordered lexicographically. We use the subscript X_i to access to the i-th element of the vector. We focus on *polynomial dynamical systems* of ordinary differential equations (ODEs) $\dot{X} = f(X)$, where $\dot{X}$ is the vector of first-order derivatives of the variables X and $f(X)$ is a vector of polynomials (i.e., $f_i(X)$ is a polynomial). The *safety verification problem* consists of proving that every trajectory of the dynamical system $\dot{X} = f(X)$ starting inside the initial set of states ψ and while being inside the evolution domain constraints H remains inside the safe set of states ϕ. We write the problem using the *differential dynamic logic* [27] formula:

$$\psi \to [\dot{X} = f(X) \ \& \ H]\phi, \tag{1}$$

asserting that if the system is in a state satisfying the pre-condition ϕ (the initial states) this implies ($\to$ operator) that all the trajectories evolving according to the ODE $\dot{X} = f(X)$ and evolution domain H (box modality []) will satisfy the post-condition ϕ (the safe states). Formally, the system is safe if:

$$\forall x_0 \in \psi. \forall \tau \geq 0. \forall t \in [0, \tau]. ((\varphi(x_0, t) \in H) \to \varphi(x_0, t) \in \phi),$$

were the differentiable function $\varphi : \mathbb{R}^{n+1} \to \mathbb{R}^n$, such that $\frac{d}{dt}(\varphi(x_0, t)) = f(\varphi(x_0, t))$, is the solution to the initial value problem $x_0 \in \mathbb{R}^n$ (i.e., $\varphi(x_0, t)$ describes the state the dynamical system f reaches after $t \in \mathbb{R}$ time when starting in the initial state x_0).

The problem of proving the system is safe can be reduced to find a formula $\theta(X)$ such that: i) $H \wedge \psi \to \theta$, ii) $\theta \to [\dot{X} = f(X) \ \& \ H] \theta$, and iii) $\theta \to \phi$. $\theta(X)$ is a *continuous invariant* [28] that contains the initial states and that is contained in the safe states.

LZZ Algorithm [22]. The LZZ algorithm reduces the problem of checking if θ is a continuous invariant to checking the validity of the following formula:

$$LZZ_{\theta,f,H}(X) \doteq ((\theta(X) \wedge H(X) \wedge In_{f,H}(X)) \to In_{f,\theta}(X)) \wedge \tag{2}$$
$$((\neg\theta(X) \wedge H(X) \wedge In_{-f,H}(X)) \to \neg In_{-f,\theta}(X)),$$

where the formula $In_{f,\gamma}(X)$ for the ODEs f and the formula γ represents the set of states which will evolve inside the set γ for some non-zero time in the future. Respectively, the formula $In_{-f,\gamma}(X)$ represents the set of states evolved inside the set γ for some non-zero time in the past, and $-f$ represents the dynamical system evolving in "reverse". Note that the construction of the formula $In_{f,\gamma}(X)$ assumes γ to be in disjunctive normal form (DNF):

$$\gamma = \bigvee_{d \in disj(\gamma)} \bigwedge_{a \bowtie 0 \in pred(d)} a(X) \bowtie 0,$$

where $disj(\gamma)$ are the disjuncts of a formula γ, $pred(d)$ are the predicates in the disjunct d, and $\bowtie \in \{>, \geq\}$[4]. The formula $In_{f,\gamma}(X)$ is defined as:

$$In_{f,\gamma}(X) = \bigvee_{d \in disj(\gamma)} \bigwedge_{a\bowtie 0 \in pred(d)} In_{f,a\bowtie 0}(X). \tag{3}$$

The formula $In_{f,a\bowtie 0}(X)$ encodes the set for a single predicate $a \bowtie 0$ using the Lie derivatives of the polynomial $a(X)$. The i-th *Lie derivative* $L_f^i a$ of a polynomial $a(X)$ with respect to the ODEs f is defined recursively as:

$$L_f^{(0)} a \doteq a, \qquad L_f^{(i)} a \doteq \frac{\partial}{\partial X} L_f^{(i-1)} a f.$$

$In_{f,a>0}(X)$ encodes that the first non-zero Lie derivative of a must be positive in order for the trajectories of the system to enter the set $a > 0$ and stay inside the set for a positive time[5](see [22] and [12] for a thorough explanation):

$$In_{f,a>0}(X) \doteq \bigvee_{0 \leq i \leq N_{a,f}} \left(\bigwedge_{0 \leq j < i} L_f^{(j)} a = 0 \wedge L_f^{(i)} a > 0 \right), \tag{4}$$

$$In_{f,a\geq 0}(X) \doteq In_{f,a>0}(X) \vee \bigvee_{0 \leq i \leq N_{a,f}} L_f^{(i)} a = 0, \tag{5}$$

where $N_{a,f}$ is an integer constant and is an upper bound on the minimum integer number r (called *rank*) such that $L_f^{(r)} a \neq 0$ (for all $x \in \mathbb{R}^n$). $N_{a,f}$ can be computed using Gröbner basis as explained in [22].

In the following, we will only use the fact that the formula $In_{f,\gamma}(X)$ for the DNF formula γ is the DNF formula where In_f is applied to the predicates (as shown in Formula (3)).

Semi-Algebraic Abstraction [32]. The *semi-algebraic abstraction* of the dynamical system $\dot{X} = f(X)$ partitions its state space with respect to a set of polynomials $\mathbb{A} \doteq \{a_1, \ldots, a_m\}$. The abstraction is the (explicit state) transition system $S_{\mathbb{A}} \doteq \langle 3^{\mathbb{A}}, I_{f,\mathbb{A}}, T_{f,\mathbb{A}} \rangle$ where:

- $3^{\mathbb{A}} \doteq \{s = \bigwedge_{a \in \mathbb{A}} a \bowtie 0 \mid \bowtie \in \{>, <, =\}\}$ is the set of abstract states;
- $I_{f,\mathbb{A}} \doteq \{s \in 3^{\mathbb{A}} \mid s \wedge \psi \text{ is satisfiable}\}$ is the set of abstract initial states; and
- $T_{f,\mathbb{A}} \subseteq 3^{\mathbb{A}} \times 3^{\mathbb{A}}$ is the abstract transition relation. A transition $(s_1, s_2) \in T_{f,\mathbb{A}}$ if:
  - s_1 is an abstract state *adjacent* to s_2. The abstraction exploits the continuity assumption on f and does not allow the system to transition directly from a state where a predicate is greater than 0 (e.g., $a > 0$) to a state where the same predicate is less than 0 (e.g., $a < 0$), and vice-versa.

---

[4] Later we also consider equalities (i.e., predicates of the form $a = 0$). The construction of $In_{f,a=0}(X)$ can be found in [12].

[5] In our implementation we encode $In_{f,a>0}(X)$ using the remainders of the Lie derivative, as in [12].

The abstraction does not visit two abstract states containing predicates with opposite signs, forcing instead to visit the intermediate state where the predicate is equal to 0.

- There exists a continuous trajectory from s_1 to s_2. This condition corresponds to checking that the following differential dynamic logic formula is *not valid* (i.e. s_1 is not a differential invariant when restricting the evolution domain to $s_1 \lor s_2$):

$$s_1 \rightarrow [\dot{\boldsymbol{X}} = \boldsymbol{f}(\boldsymbol{X}) \ \& \ s_1 \lor s_2]s_1,$$

which can be checked using the sound and complete LZZ algorithm, i.e. checking the satisfiability of the first-order formula $\neg LZZ_{s_1,\boldsymbol{f},s_1 \lor s_2}(Z))$.

Since the number of states $3^\mathbb{A}$ is finite we can compute the set of reachable states. The concretization of this set, θ contains the initial states and is a differential invariant. If θ further implies the safe states ψ, then we prove the safety verification problem 1. However, the computation of the abstract transition relation is exponential in the number of polynomials in $\mathbb{A}$ because we would need to enumerate all the possible pairs of transitions $(s_1, s_2) \in 3^\mathbb{A} \times 3^\mathbb{A}$.

Predicate Abstraction

A *symbolic transition system* S is a tuple $S \doteq \langle V, I, T \rangle$, where V is a set of (state) variables, $I(V)$ is a formula representing the initial states, and $T(V, V')$ is a formula representing the transition relation. A *state* s of S is an interpretation of the state variables V. A (finite) *path* π of S is a finite sequence $\pi \doteq s_0, s_1, \ldots, s_k$ of states with the same domain and interpretation of symbols in the signature Σ such that $s_0 \models I$ and for all i, $0 \leq i < k$, $s_i, s'_{i+1} \models T$. We say that a state s is *reachable* in S iff there exists a path of S ending in s. Given a formula $P(V)$ and a transition system S, the *invariant verification problem*, denoted with $S \models P$, checks if for all the finite paths $s_0, s_1, \ldots, s_k$ of S, for all i, $0 \leq i \leq k$, $s_i \models P$.

Predicate Abstraction [16] partitions the concrete system $S = \langle V, I, T \rangle$ according to a finite set of predicates $\mathbb{P} \doteq \{p_1, \ldots, p_k\}$ in a finite symbolic transition system:

$$\widehat{S}_\mathbb{P} = \langle V_\mathbb{P}, \widehat{I}_\mathbb{P}(V_\mathbb{P}), \widehat{T}_\mathbb{P}(V_\mathbb{P}, V'_\mathbb{P}) \rangle$$

using a new abstract Boolean variable v_p for each predicate p ($V_\mathbb{P} = \{v_p \mid v \in V\}$ is the set of those new variables). The abstraction relation $H_\mathbb{P}(V, V_\mathbb{P}) \doteq \bigwedge_{p \in \mathbb{P}} v_p \leftrightarrow p(V)$ defines how a set of concrete states is abstracted to the abstract states. We compute the abstraction of a formula $\psi(V)$ by existentially quantifying the concrete variables V:

$$\widehat{\psi}_\mathbb{P}(V_\mathbb{P}) \doteq \exists V.(\psi(V) \land H_\mathbb{P}(V, V_\mathbb{P})).$$

Similarly, we compute the abstract transition relation for $T(V, V')$:

$$\widehat{T}_\mathbb{P}(V_\mathbb{P}, V'_\mathbb{P}) \doteq \exists V, V'.(T(V, V') \land H_\mathbb{P}(V, V_\mathbb{P}) \land H_\mathbb{P}(V', V'_\mathbb{P})).$$

The above formulation is sufficient to compute the predicate abstraction for an infinite-state transition system $S = \langle V, I, T \rangle$ and a set of predicates $\mathbb{P}$. However, the main challenge in computing the abstraction is to eliminate the quantifiers, since quantifier elimination is expensive to compute.

Implicit Predicate Abstraction. Implicit Predicate Abstraction [35] is a model checking algorithm that avoids computing the abstract version of the initial states, safety property, and transition relation, instead it encodes the existence of a path in the abstract system. It exploits the fact that the abstraction induces an equivalence relation among concrete states of the system (i.e., two concrete states are equivalent if they belong to the same abstract state) and that this relation can be expressed as a quantifier free formula:

$$EQ_{\mathbb{P}}(V, \overline{V}) \doteq \bigwedge_{p \in \mathbb{P}} p(V) \leftrightarrow p(\overline{V}). \tag{6}$$

We use the equivalence $EQ_{\mathbb{P}}(V, \overline{V})$ to relate two sets of concrete states and we encode the problem of reaching a set of target states $\neg P$ in k steps of the transition system S as follows:

$$BMC_{\mathbb{P}}^{k} \doteq I(V^0) \wedge EQ_{\mathbb{P}}(V^0, \overline{V}^0) \wedge$$
$$\bigwedge_{1 \leq h < k} \left(T(\overline{V}^{h-1}, V^h) \wedge EQ_{\mathbb{P}}(V^h, \overline{V}^h) \right) \wedge T(\overline{V}^{k-1}, V^k) \wedge$$
$$EQ_{\mathbb{P}}(V^k, \overline{V}^k) \wedge (\neg P(\overline{V}^k)).$$

The formula $BMC_{\mathbb{P}}^{k}$ is satisfiable iff there exists a path in the abstract transition system $\widehat{S}_{\mathbb{P}}$ of length k starting from the (abstracted) initial states $\widehat{I}_{\mathbb{P}}(V_{\mathbb{P}})$ and reaching the (abstracted) bad states $\widehat{\neg P}_{\mathbb{P}}(V_{\mathbb{P}})$.

4   Explicit Computation of the Semi-Algebraic Abstraction

We frame the problem of computing the semi-algebraic abstraction as a predicate abstraction problem. This formulation allows us to use the standard techniques to compute or analyze the predicate abstraction for discrete systems.

We consider the invariant verification problem $\psi \rightarrow [\dot{\boldsymbol{X}} = \boldsymbol{f}(\boldsymbol{X}) \ \& \ H]\phi$ as in Eq. (1) and a set of polynomials $\mathbb{A} = \{a_1, \ldots, a_m\}$ for the abstraction. We construct a symbolic transition system of the semi-algebraic abstraction:

$$\widehat{S}_{\mathbb{P}} \doteq \langle V_{\mathbb{P}}, \widehat{I}_{\mathbb{P}}(V_{\mathbb{P}}), \widehat{T}_{\mathbb{P}}(V_{\mathbb{P}}, V'_{\mathbb{P}}) \rangle,$$

where the set of predicates of the abstraction is $\mathbb{P} = \{a \bowtie 0 \mid a \in \mathbb{A} \wedge \bowtie \in \{>, <, =\}\}$, and the set of abstract variables $V_{\mathbb{P}}$ is defined as in Sect. 3 (i.e., the abstraction contains a Boolean variable v_p for each predicates $p \in \mathbb{P}$). We similarly use the formula $H_{\mathbb{P}}(X, V_{\mathbb{P}})$ to describe the equivalence relation of the concrete states.

The formulas $\widehat{I}_{\mathbb{P}}(V_{\mathbb{P}})$ and $\widehat{\neg P}_{\mathbb{P}}(V_{\mathbb{P}})$ are the semi-algebraic abstraction of the initial states ψ and of the unsafe states $\neg\phi$:

$$\widehat{I}_{\mathbb{P}}(V_{\mathbb{P}}) \doteq \exists X.(\psi(X) \wedge H_{\mathbb{P}}(X, V_{\mathbb{P}})), \qquad \widehat{\neg P}_{\mathbb{P}}(V_{\mathbb{P}}) \doteq \exists X.(\neg\phi(X) \wedge H_{\mathbb{P}}(X, V_{\mathbb{P}})),$$

and we obtain the abstraction by existentially quantifying the concrete variables X. The definition of the abstract transition relation $\widehat{T}_{\mathbb{P}}(V_{\mathbb{P}}, V'_{\mathbb{P}})$, which differs from the encoding of the semi-algebraic decomposition, is:

$$\widehat{T}_{\mathbb{P}}(V_{\mathbb{P}}, V'_{\mathbb{P}}) \doteq \exists X, X'. \bigg(N(X, X') \wedge H(X) \wedge H(X') \wedge \tag{7}$$

$$H_{\mathbb{P}}(X, V_{\mathbb{P}}) \wedge H_{\mathbb{P}}(X', V'_{\mathbb{P}}) \wedge \exists Z. T_{\mathbb{A}}(X, X', Z) \bigg),$$

where $N(X, X')$ encodes the adjacent relation between abstract states:

$$N(X, X') = \bigwedge_{a \in \mathbb{A}} \Big((a(X) < 0 \rightarrow a(X') \leq 0) \wedge (a(X) > 0 \rightarrow a(X') \geq 0) \Big),$$

and $T_{\mathbb{A}}(X, X', Z)$ encodes the existence of a transition in the dynamical system f for each pair of abstract states $(s_1, s_2) \in 3^{\mathbb{A}}$:

$$T_{\mathbb{A}}(X, X', Z) \doteq \bigvee_{(s_1, s_2) \in 3^{\mathbb{A}}} \Big(s_1(X) \wedge s_2(X') \wedge \neg LZZ_{s_1, f, s_1 \vee s_2}(Z) \Big). \tag{8}$$

Theorem 1. *The transition systems $S_{\mathbb{A}}$ and $\widehat{S}_{\mathbb{P}}$ are bisimilar.*

Corollary 1. $\widehat{S}_{\mathbb{P}} \models \neg\widehat{\neg P}_{\mathbb{P}}(V_{\mathbb{P}})$ *implies* $\psi \rightarrow [\dot{X} = f(X) \ \& \ H]\phi$.

Proof (sketch). The proof follows directly from Theorem 1. $\qquad\square$

   While the encoding of the transition relation $\widehat{T}_{\mathbb{P}}(V_{\mathbb{P}}, V'_{\mathbb{P}})$ is symbolic, it (and in particular the sub-formula $T_{\mathbb{A}}(X, X', Z)$) explicitly enumerates an exponential number of abstract pairs of states. Clearly, this encoding is not practical and defeats the purpose of using symbolic techniques to compute the abstraction.

5   Linear Encoding of the Semi-Algebraic Abstraction

Specializing the LZZ Formula for Checking Abstract Transitions

The construction of the semi-algebraic abstraction uses the formula $\neg LZZ_{s_1, f, s_1 \vee s_2}(Z)$ to encode the existence of a transition from the abstract state s_1 to the abstract state s_2. We observe that here the LZZ algorithm is applied to formulas with a specific structure – the abstract states $s_1(Z)$ and $s_2(Z)$, in contrast to arbitrary semi-algebraic sets as in the general case of $LZZ_{\theta, f, H}(X)$ where the formulas θ and H are in DNF. Instead, in the case of $LZZ_{s_1, f, s_1 \vee s_2}(Z)$, each abstract state $s_i(X)$ assigns a sign to each polynomial $a \in \mathbb{A}$ and is represented as conjunctions of predicates $s_i = a_1 \bowtie_1 0 \wedge a_2 \bowtie_2 0 \wedge \ldots a_m \bowtie_m 0$, where $\bowtie_j \in \{>, <, =\}$. We will write the conjunction representing a state $s_i(X)$ as $\bigwedge_{a \bowtie 0 \in s_i} a(X) \bowtie 0$. Also note that the evolution domain constraints are also a disjunction of two abstract states $s_1 \vee s_2$.

We specialize Eq. (2) to the specific case of $LZZ_{s_1,f,s_1 \vee s_2}(Z)$. We will use such specialization to obtain a compact (linear in the number of polynomials) encoding later in the section. Instantiating the formula (2) to the case of $LZZ_{s_1,f,s_1 \vee s_2}(Z)$, we get:

$$LZZ_{s_1,f,s_1 \vee s_2}(Z) \doteq$$
$$((s_1(Z) \wedge (s_1(Z) \vee s_2(Z)) \wedge In_{f,s_1 \vee s_2}(Z)) \rightarrow In_{f,s_1}(Z)) \wedge \tag{9}$$
$$((\neg s_1(Z) \wedge (s_1(Z) \vee s_2(Z)) \wedge In_{-f,s_1 \vee s_2}(Z)) \rightarrow \neg In_{-f,s_1}(Z))$$

Applying the Boolean identities: $(\alpha \wedge (\alpha \vee \beta)) \leftrightarrow \alpha$, $(\neg \alpha \wedge (\alpha \vee \beta)) \leftrightarrow \neg \alpha \wedge \beta$

$$\Longleftrightarrow ((s_1(Z) \wedge In_{f,s_1 \vee s_2}(Z)) \rightarrow In_{f,s_1}(Z)) \wedge \tag{10}$$
$$((\neg s_1(Z) \wedge s_2(Z) \wedge In_{-f,s_1 \vee s_2}(Z)) \rightarrow \neg In_{-f,s_1}(Z))$$

Rewriting the implication and applying De Morgan's laws:

$$\Longleftrightarrow (\neg s_1(Z) \vee \neg In_{f,s_1 \vee s_2}(Z) \vee In_{f,s_1}(Z)) \wedge \tag{11}$$
$$(s_1(Z) \vee \neg s_2(Z) \vee \neg In_{-f,s_1 \vee s_2}(Z) \vee \neg In_{-f,s_1}(Z))$$

Expanding the definition of $In(Eq. (3))$: $In_{f,\alpha \vee \beta} \doteq (In_{-f,\alpha} \vee In_{f,\beta})$
$$In_{-f,\alpha \vee \beta} \doteq (In_{-f,\alpha} \vee In_{-f,\beta})$$

$$\Longleftrightarrow (\neg s_1(Z) \vee \neg(In_{f,s_1}(Z) \vee In_{f,s_2}(Z)) \vee In_{f,s_1}(Z)) \wedge \tag{12}$$
$$(s_1(Z) \vee \neg s_2(Z) \vee \neg(In_{-f,s_1}(Z) \vee In_{-f,s_2}(Z)) \vee \neg In_{-f,s_1}(Z))$$

Applying the Boolean identities: $(\neg(\alpha \vee \beta) \vee \alpha) \leftrightarrow (\neg \beta \vee \alpha), (\neg(\alpha \vee \beta) \vee \neg \alpha) \leftrightarrow \neg \alpha$

$$\Longleftrightarrow (\neg s_1(Z) \vee \neg In_{f,s_2}(Z) \vee In_{f,s_1}(Z)) \wedge \tag{13}$$
$$(s_1(Z) \vee \neg s_2(Z) \vee \neg In_{-f,s_1}(Z)).$$

Note that, while In does not distribute over arbitrary Boolean formulas (see [12]), when we expand the definition of $In_{f,s_1 \vee s_2}$ (Eq. (12)), the formula $s_1 \vee s_2$ is in DNF. Thus, Formula (13) is equivalent to the initial Formula (9) of $LZZ_{s_1,f,s_1 \vee s_2}(Z)$. We then write the negation of the Formula 13 as:

$$\neg LZZ_{s_1,f,s_1 \vee s_2}(Z) \doteq (s_1(Z) \wedge In_{f,s_2}(Z) \wedge \neg In_{f,s_1}(Z)) \vee \tag{14}$$
$$(\neg s_1(Z) \wedge s_2(Z) \wedge In_{-f,s_1}(Z)).$$

Linear Encoding of the Semi-Algebraic Transition Relation

In the following steps, we revise the formula $T_\mathbb{A}(X, X', Z)$ that encodes the existence of the transitions in the abstraction, still enumerating all possible pairs of states, using the specialized LZZ encoding from Eq. (14). We substitute the subformula $\neg LZZ_{s_1,f,s_1 \vee s_2}(Z)$ with the specialized LZZ encoding (Eq. (16)); we then distribute the conjunction $s_1(X) \wedge s_2(X')$ over the disjunction present in the definition of $\neg LZZ_{s_1,f,s_1 \vee s_2}(Z)$ (Eq. (17)), and then over possible pairs of states (Eq. (18)). We rename the two disjuncts in Eq. (18) as $InsExpl_f(X, X', Z)$ and $OutExpl_f(X, X', Z))$ (Eq. (19)). The formulas $InsExpl_f(X, X', Z)$ and $OutExpl_f(X, X', Z))$ still enumerate explicitly the abstract states. However, each of these formulas is a conjunction of predicates, application of the In_f operator to a conjunction of predicates, and negations of the application of In_f.

$$T_{\mathbb{A}}(X, X', Z) \doteq$$

$$\exists Z. \bigvee_{(s_1, s_2) \in 3^{\mathbb{A}}} (s_1(X) \wedge s_2(X') \wedge \neg LZZ_{s_1, f, s_1 \vee s_2}(Z)) \tag{15}$$

$$\iff \exists Z. \bigvee_{(s_1, s_2) \in 3^{\mathbb{A}}} \left(\begin{array}{c} s_1(X) \wedge s_2(X') \wedge ((s_1(Z) \wedge In_{f, s_2}(Z) \wedge \neg In_{f, s_1}(Z)) \vee \\ (\neg s_1(Z) \wedge s_2(Z) \wedge In_{-f, s_1}(Z))) \end{array} \right) \tag{16}$$

$$\iff \exists Z. \bigvee_{(s_1, s_2) \in 3^{\mathbb{A}}} \left(\begin{array}{c} (s_1(X) \wedge s_2(X') \wedge s_1(Z) \wedge In_{f, s_2}(Z) \wedge \neg In_{f, s_1}(Z)) \vee \\ ((s_1(X) \wedge s_2(X') \wedge \neg s_1(Z) \wedge s_2(Z) \wedge In_{-f, s_1}(Z)) \end{array} \right) \tag{17}$$

$$\iff \exists Z. \left(\begin{array}{c} \bigvee_{(s_1, s_2) \in 3^{\mathbb{A}}} (s_1(X) \wedge s_2(X') \wedge s_1 \wedge In_{f, s_2}(Z) \wedge \neg In_{f, s_1}(Z)) \vee \\ \bigvee_{(s_1, s_2) \in 3^{\mathbb{A}}} (s_1(X) \wedge s_2(X') \wedge \neg s_1 \wedge s_2 \wedge In_{-f, s_1}(Z)) \end{array} \right) \tag{18}$$

$$\iff \exists Z.(InsExpl_f(X, X', Z) \vee OutExpl_f(X, X', Z)). \tag{19}$$

We now show how we obtain a formula $InsExpl_f(X, X', Z)$ with a linear size. We expand the definition of the formula $InsExpl_f(X, X', Z)$ with respect to the predicates in s_1 and s_2. Recall that each abstract state is a conjunction of predicates obtained from the set of polynomial $\mathbb{A}$ (i.e., $s \doteq \bigwedge_{a \in \mathbb{A}} a \bowtie_a 0$, $\bowtie_a \in \{>, <, =\}$) and that we use $a \bowtie 0 \in s$ to enumerate the predicates in s.

$$InsExpl_f(X, X', Z) \doteq \bigvee_{s_1, s_2 \in 3^{\mathbb{A}}} \left(\bigwedge_{a \bowtie 0 \in s_1} a(X) \bowtie 0 \wedge \bigwedge_{a \bowtie 0 \in s_2} a(X') \bowtie 0 \wedge \tag{20} \right.$$

$$\bigwedge_{a \bowtie 0 \in s_1} a(Z) \bowtie 0 \wedge \bigwedge_{a \bowtie 0 \in s_2} In_{f, a \bowtie 0}(Z) \wedge$$

$$\left. \bigvee_{a \bowtie 0 \in s_1} \neg In_{f, a \bowtie 0}(Z) \right).$$

In the above formula, we used De Morgan rules to rewrite the formula $\neg \bigwedge_{a \bowtie 0 \in s_1} In_{f, a \bowtie 0}(Z)$ as the formula $\bigvee_{a \bowtie 0 \in s_1} \neg In_{f, a \bowtie 0}(Z)$. We express the formula $InsExpl_f(X, X', Z)$ as an enumeration of the predicates, over the variables X and X', determining the abstract states s_1 and s_2, instead of the pairs of abstract states:

$$InsSymb_f(X, X', Z) \doteq \bigwedge_{a \in \mathbb{A}, \bowtie \in \{>,<,=\}} \Big(a(X) \bowtie 0 \rightarrow a(Z) \bowtie 0\Big) \wedge \qquad (21)$$
$$\bigwedge_{a \in \mathbb{A}, \bowtie \in \{>,<,=\}} \Big(a(X') \bowtie 0 \rightarrow In_{f,a\bowtie 0}(Z)\Big) \wedge$$
$$\bigvee_{a \in \mathbb{A}, \bowtie \in \{>,<,=\}} \Big(a(X) \bowtie 0 \wedge (\neg In_{f,a\bowtie 0}(Z))\Big).$$

Lemma 1. *$InsExpl_f(X, X', Z)$ and $InsSymb_f(X, X', Z)$ are equivalent.*

Proof (sketch).
$\Rightarrow$) We show that $\mu \models InsExpl_f(X, X', Z)$ implies $\mu \models InsSymb_f(X, X', Z)$. Since $\mu \models InsExpl_f(X, X', Z)$ we have that μ is an interpretation for one of the disjuncts on the possible pairs of states of $InsExpl_f(X, X', Z)$:

$$\bigwedge_{a\bowtie 0 \in s_1} a(X) \bowtie 0 \wedge \bigwedge_{a\bowtie 0 \in s_2} a(X') \bowtie 0 \wedge \bigwedge_{a\bowtie 0 \in s_1} a(Z) \bowtie 0 \wedge$$
$$\bigwedge_{a\bowtie 0 \in s_2} In_{f,a\bowtie 0}(Z) \wedge \bigvee_{a\bowtie 0 \in s_1} \neg In_{f,a\bowtie 0}(Z).$$

Hence, there exist two (and exactly two) abstract states s_1, s_2, such that $\mu \models s_1(X)$ and $\mu \models s_2(X')$. This means that any predicate $a \bowtie 0 \notin s_1$ is such that $\mu \not\models a \bowtie (X)$ and similarly for predicates not in the state s_2 for the variables X' (recall that, given a polynomial $a \in \mathbb{A}$, the possible abstraction predicates $a > 0$, $a < 0$, and $a = 0$ are mutually exclusive). We show that μ is an interpretation for all the conjuncts in $InsSymb_f(X, X', Z)$. We have that $\mu \models \bigwedge_{a \in \mathbb{A}, \bowtie \in \{>,<,=\}} \Big(a(X) \bowtie 0 \rightarrow a(Z) \bowtie 0\Big)$ since for all $a \in \mathbb{A}$, $\mu \models a(X) \bowtie 0 \rightarrow a(Z) \bowtie 0$ (when $a \in s_1$ we have $\mu \models a(Z) \bowtie 0$, while when $a \notin s_1$ the implication trivially holds). Similarly, this happens for $\bigwedge_{a \in \mathbb{A}, \bowtie \in \{>,<,=\}} \Big(a(X) \bowtie 0 \rightarrow a(Z) \bowtie 0\Big)$. We can see the disjunction: $\bigvee_{a \in \mathbb{A}, \bowtie \in \{>,<,=\}} \Big(a(X) \bowtie 0 \wedge (\neg In_{f,a\bowtie 0}(Z))\Big)$ as:

$$\bigvee_{a\bowtie 0 \in s_1} \Big(a(X) \bowtie 0 \wedge (\neg In_{f,a\bowtie 0}(Z))\Big) \vee \bigvee_{a\bowtie 0 \notin s_1} \Big(a(X) \bowtie 0 \wedge (\neg In_{f,a\bowtie 0}(Z))\Big).$$

We have that μ satisfies the first disjunct (and hence the whole disjunction) because when $a \bowtie 0 \in s_1$ we have that $\mu \models \bigvee_{a\bowtie 0 \in s_1} \neg In_{f,a\bowtie 0}(Z)$.
$\Leftarrow$) We show that $\mu \models InsSymb_f(X, X', Z)$ implies $\mu \models InsExpl_f(X, X', Z)$. As before, we notice that are only two predicates s_1, s_2 such that $\mu \models s_1(X)$ and $\mu \models s_2(X')$ and that all the predicates not in s_1 and not in s_2 do not hold in μ. Thus, from $\mu \models InsSymb_f(X, X', Z)$ we have that

$$\mu \models \bigwedge_{a \in s_1} a(Z) \bowtie 0 \wedge \bigwedge_{a \in s_2} In_{f,a\bowtie 0}(Z) \wedge \bigvee_{a \in s_1} \neg In_{f,a\bowtie 0}(Z).$$

Hence, μ is a model for at least one of the disjuncts in $InsExpl_f(X, X', Z)$. □

We similarly define the compact encoding of $OutExpl_f(X, X', Z)$:

$$OutSymb_f(X, X', Z) \doteq \bigwedge_{a \in \mathbb{A}, \bowtie \in \{>, <, =\}} \left(a(X) \bowtie 0 \rightarrow In_{-f, a\bowtie 0}(Z) \right) \wedge \qquad (22)$$

$$\bigwedge_{a \in \mathbb{A}, \bowtie \in \{>, <, =\}} \left(a(X') \bowtie 0 \rightarrow a(Z) \bowtie 0 \right) \wedge$$

$$\bigvee_{a \in \mathbb{A}, \bowtie \in \{>, <, =\}} \left(a(X) \bowtie 0 \wedge \neg a(Z) \bowtie 0 \right).$$

Lemma 2. $OutExpl_f(X, X', Z)$ and $OutSymb_f(X, X', Z)$ are equivalent.

Proof. The proof of Lemma 2 is similar to the proof of Lemma 1.   □

We now express the transition relation from Eq. (7) in a compact form:

$$\widehat{T_{Symb\mathbb{P}}}(V_\mathbb{P}, V'_\mathbb{P}) \doteq \exists X, X'. \left(N(X, X') \wedge H(X) \wedge H(X') \wedge \right. \qquad (23)$$

$$H_\mathbb{A}(X, V_\mathbb{P}) \wedge H_\mathbb{A}(X', V'_\mathbb{P}) \wedge$$

$$\left. \exists Z. (InsSymb_f(X, X', Z) \vee OutSymb_f(X, X', Z)) \right).$$

Theorem 2. $\widehat{T_\mathbb{P}}(V_\mathbb{P}, V'_\mathbb{P})$ and $\widehat{T_{Symb\mathbb{P}}}(V_\mathbb{P}, V'_\mathbb{P})$ are equivalent.

Proof. Follows directly from Lemma 2 and Lemma 1.   □

Implicit Semi-Algebraic Abstraction

The formula $\widehat{T_{Symb\mathbb{P}}}(V_\mathbb{P}, V'_\mathbb{A})$ represents the transition relation of the semi-algebraic abstraction. Computing the finite-state transition system representing the semi-algebraic abstraction requires to eliminate the existential quantifiers from the initial states, transition relation, and safety property formulas. However, the above formula $\widehat{T_{Symb\mathbb{P}}}(V_\mathbb{P}, V'_\mathbb{A})$ contains non-linear real arithmetic terms from the polynomials and the Lie derivatives we compute in In_f, so removing the quantifiers from the formula requires to apply a quantifier elimination algorithm (e.g., Cylindrical Algebraic Decomposition [8]) that does not scale, even when the number of polynomials is small. Instead, we construct a symbolic transition system that *implicitly* encodes the abstraction:

$$S_{Impl,\mathbb{P}} \doteq \langle X \cup \overline{X} \cup Z, \psi(X) \wedge EQ_\mathbb{P}(X, \overline{X}), T_{Impl,\mathbb{P}}(\overline{X}, X', Z) \wedge EQ_\mathbb{P}(X', \overline{X'}) \rangle,$$

where

$$T_{Impl,\mathbb{P}}(\overline{X}, X', Z) \doteq N(\overline{X}, X') \wedge H(\overline{X}) \wedge H(X') \wedge$$
$$(InsSymb_f(\overline{X}, X', Z) \vee OutSymb_f(\overline{X}, X', Z)).$$

The above encoding is a an implicit predicate abstraction [35] that preserves reachability properties and is such that:

Theorem 3. $S_{Impl,\mathbb{P}} \models P(\overline{X})$ *if and only if* $\widehat{S}_{\mathbb{P}} \models \neg\neg\widehat{P}_{\mathbb{P}}(V_{\mathbb{P}})$.

Thus, we can model check the transition system $S_{Impl,\mathbb{P}} \models P(\overline{X})$ to prove a property P holds on the dynamical system. Note that, to this purpose, we can apply standard SMT-based model checking algorithms.

The transition system $S_{Impl,\mathbb{P}}$ doubles the state space introducing a copy of the state variables $\overline{X}$ and encodes the equivalence relation between pairs of concrete states in X and in $\overline{X}$ with the formula $EQ_{\mathbb{P}}(X, \overline{X})$ (c.f. Formula 6). The transition relation $T_{Impl,\mathbb{P}}(\overline{X}, X', Z)$ then encodes a transition in the semi-algebraic abstraction with the linear encoding $InsSymb_f(\overline{X}, X', Z)$ and $OutSymb_f(\overline{X}, X', Z)$. In this way, a transition in the transition system $S_{Impl,\mathbb{P}}$ corresponds to a transition in the semi-algebraic abstraction, and vice-versa.

6   Experimental Evaluation

Research Questions

We evaluate the performance of our approach (*Implicit Abstraction*) for the verification of invariant properties on the semi-algebraic abstraction of dynamical systems. *Implicit Abstraction* first encodes the semi-algebraic abstraction in a transition system (as we show in Sect. 5), and then model checks the invariant on the transition system with an off-the-shelf model checker. Our experiments aim to answer the following research questions:

RQ 1: How does *Implicit Abstraction* compare with the *LazyReach* algorithm [32], which explicitly enumerates the reachable states of the abstraction?

RQ 2: How does *Implicit Abstraction* compare with the *DWCL* algorithm [32], which applies a divide-and-conquer strategy to reduce the number of polynomials in the abstraction?

Experimental Setup

We implemented the construction of the implicit abstraction transition system in Python using *PySMT* [11] to manipulate formulas, and *SymPy* [23] for polynomial manipulation and Gröbner bases computation (i.e., to compute the Lie derivatives' ranks). We verify the implicit abstraction transition system with the model checking algorithm for symbolic transition systems with NRA constraints from [4]. The algorithm abstracts the non-linear transition system into a linear transition system, which is checked by the algorithm in [6] and is implemented using the *MathSAT* [7] SMT solver. We implemented both the *LazyReach* and the *DWCL* algorithms in the same Python tool. Our implementation of *DWCL* can use different backends to decide the satisfiability of NRA formulas, namely *MathSAT*[6], the *z3* SMT solver [25], or *Mathematica* [17].

We consider 90 invariant verification problems for dynamical systems from the *KeyMaera X* theorem prover [10]. These problems are a superset of the

---

[6] *MathSAT* uses a different decision procedure [4] than *z3* and *Mathematica* based on incremental linearization rather than cylindrical algebraic decomposition.

ones used in [32] and are used in the Applied Verification of Continuous and Hybrid Systems (ARCH) competition [24]. We obtain a total of 180 benchmark instances using, for each problem, two sets of polynomials for the semi-algebraic abstraction[7]. The first set contains all the factors of the right-hand side of the ODEs; the second set extends the first one by including also the Lie derivatives of the polynomials. The latter set induces an abstraction that is more precise but also has a larger state-space.

We evaluate the performance of the algorithms *Implicit Abstraction*, *LazyReach*, and *DWCL* to solve the above verification problems. The underlying problem requires to decide the satisfiability of NRA formulas, and the decision procedures for this problem are efficient for different subsets of problems. For this reason we further evaluate different configurations of the *LazyReach* and *DWCL* algorithms using three different solvers for NRA formulas (*MathSAT*, *z3*, and *Mathematica*). Note that, while in principle, we could use multiple SMT backends also in the model checking algorithm [4] and replace the *MathSAT* SMT solver with another SMT solver (e.g., *z3*), this change would not significantly impact the overall performance, because the algorithm abstracts the non-linear formulas with linear ones where both *MathSAT* and *z3* have comparable performance.

We run the *Implicit Abstraction*, *LazyReach*, and *DWCL* algorithm on all the 180 benchmark instances with a time out of 100 seconds, and we measure the execution times to either prove (*safe* result) or find an abstract counterexample (*unknown* result) for each instance. An archive containing the necessary to reproduce the experiments is available online at http://www.sergiomover.eu/cav2021.html.

Results

RQ 1 - Implicit Abstraction vs. LazyReach. From the cumulative plot in Fig. 2, we see that *Implicit Abstraction* almost always outperforms *LazyReach*.

From the cumulative plot in Fig. 2a we see that *Implicit Abstraction* significantly outperforms *LazyReach* on *safe* instances. For better readability, in the plot we only show the (virtual) portfolio algorithm running each configuration of *LazyReach*, *Virtual Best LazyReach*, obtained by considering the best run time among the different configurations of *LazyReach* using different backend solvers. *Virtual Best LazyReach* solves a total of 42 safe instances, while *Implicit Abstraction* solves 100 safe instances. The scatter plots shown in the first row of Fig. 3 confirms the same intuition (note that the safe instances represented as blue circles are mostly in the lower-right triangle of the plot).

Figure 2b shows the cumulative plot when verifying *unknown* instances. Note that the total number of unknown instances in the benchmarks are much smaller than the safe ones (combining the results of all the algorithms we have 123 safe instances, 19 unknown instances, and 38 still unsolved instances). From

---

[7] The benchmarks have 321 sign-invariant polynomials (c.f. Sect. 2) over a total of 1089 polynomials that *DWCL* will use to split the state space.

Fig. 2b, we see that the performance of *Implicit Abstraction* is comparable with *LazyReach*, solving a total of 8 instances and 11 instances respectively.

RQ 2 - Implicit Abstraction vs. DWCL. From the cumulative plots in Fig. 2, the *Virtual Best DWCL* solves 37 more instances than *Implicit Abstraction*. However, we also see from Fig. 2 that the global *Virtual Best* solves more instances and is faster than *Virtual Best DWCL*. In fact, *Implicit Abstraction* is *orthogonal* to *DWCL* and is comparable to *DWCL* when fixing either *Mathematica* or *z3* (*Implicit Abstraction* solves 108 instances, *DWCL Mathematica* solves 109, and *DWCL z3* solves 114).

The scatter plots in the second row of Fig. 3 compare *Implicit Abstraction* with *DWCL MathSAT*, *DWCL Mathematica*, and *DWCL z3*. From these plots, we see that there are several instances that are solved by only one of the two algorithms compared in each plot. While we see similar data when comparing *Implicit Abstraction* with *Virtual Best DWCL* (always in the scatter plots of Fig. 3), the number of instances solved uniquely by *Implicit Abstraction* seems smaller. We get a more precise picture of the complementarity of *Implicit Abstraction*, *DWCL Mathematica*, and *DWCL z3* from the diagrams in Fig. 4, where we can clearly see that *Implicit Abstraction* is orthogonal to both *DWCL Mathematica* and *DWCL z3*. From the diagram, we see that when using a different backend (i.e., *Mathematica* or *z3*) *DWCL* solves a different set of instances. This difference in performance using *Mathematica* and *z3* is not surprising since *Mathematica* and *z3* uses different algorithms to solve formulas in NRA.

We further notice that *Implicit Abstraction* uses the *MathSAT* SMT solver in the backend, and from our experiments (see again Fig. 3) *DWCL MathSAT* performs quite poorly compared to both *DWCL Mathematica* and *DWCL z3*. While naively replacing *MathSAT* in the model checking algorithm we use [4] would not provide a significant performance improvement, it is reasonable to think that investigating a tighter integration with either *z3* or *Mathematica* could improve the model checking performance. However, we believe this integration to be beyond the scope for this paper, where we enable the use of symbolic model checking techniques to analyze the semi-algebraic decomposition.

7   Related Work

In this work, we focus on the (unbounded time) safety verification problem for polynomial dynamical systems. Such problem is relevant when proving safety for hybrid programs [27] with Keymaera X [10] or for hybrid CPS with the HHL Prover [36]. Our reduction to transition systems may be used as sub-procedure in both theorem provers to automate the search of a continuous invariant.

There exist different techniques to prove safety properties for polynomial dynamical systems (see e.g., [13]): barrier certificates [18,29], first integrals [14], and Darboux Polynomials [15]. All these techniques are orthogonal to semi-algebraic abstraction, and can be used to find invariant polynomials to restrict the abstract state space. Pegasus [33] implements all the above techniques, the *LazyReach*, and *DWCL* algorithms. Our algorithm can be integrated in Pegasus.

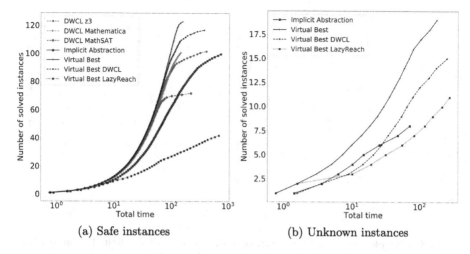

(a) Safe instances   (b) Unknown instances

Fig. 2. Plots the total number of instances (on the y axis) as a function of the cumulative time (in seconds, on the x axis) took by *Implicit Abstraction*, *LazyReach*, and *DWCL* to solve (a) *safe* and (b) *unknown* instances. The comparison includes the results of *LazyReach* and *DWCL* using different (*MathSAT*, *z3*, and *Mathematica*), as well as virtual portfolios combining the best results obtained by a given algorithm when run with multiple backends. We omit some configurations in (b) to improve readability.

The LZZ [22] procedure has been originally proposed to synthesize a continuous invariant. Instead, we use the LZZ procedure to encode the abstract transition relation, and then we prove a safety property in the abstraction. We also provide a specialized encoding of LZZ to check the existence of abstract transitions.

The semi-algebraic abstraction [32] is a qualitative abstraction [34,37]. In this work, we propose a different algorithm to verify semi-algebraic abstractions that allows us to explore the abstract state-space symbolically, in contrast to the *LazyReach* algorithm [32]. In principle, our technique is orthogonal to the *DWCL* algorithm [32], since we could replace *LazyReach*, which is used in *DWCL* as a sub-routine, with our approach (i.e., model check the implicit abstraction).

Relational abstraction [31] abstracts the dynamical system's trajectories with a discrete transition relation, reducing the verification problem on the continuous system to a verification problem on the discrete system. The implicit encoding of the semi-algebraic abstraction can be seen as an instance of relational abstraction, where a trajectory of the dynamical system is mapped to a sequence of abstract transitions (similarly to what happen with relational abstractions for time-sampled systems in [2,38]). Since relational abstractions can be composed with each other (e.g., see [26]), we can strengthen the implicit semi-algebraic abstraction encoding with a relational abstraction. This composition is useful in the case the semi-algebraic abstraction cannot easily capture the system's behavior (e.g., a precise relation of the time elapsed in a transition [26]).

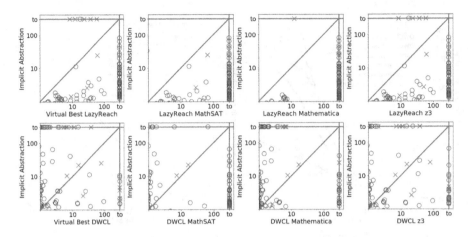

Fig. 3. Scatter plots comparing the run time (in seconds) of *Implicit Abstraction* (on the y axis) with *LazyReach* (first row, on the x axis) and *DWCL* (second row, on the x axis). Blue circles represent safe verification problems. Red crosses are instances where the algorithm found an abstract counterexample. When *Implicit Abstraction* runs for more than the 100 s time out, we plot the instance on the vertical line marked as *to*, and similarly for *LazyReach* and *DWCL* on the horizontal line.

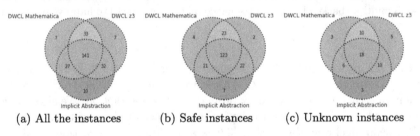

(a) All the instances   (b) Safe instances   (c) Unknown instances

Fig. 4. Diagrams representing the distribution of unique instances solved combining different algorithms (*DWCL Mathematica*, *DWCL z3*, and *Implicit Abstraction*). Each set, displayed as a dotted circle enclosed by a dotted line, represents the set of instances solved with one algorithm. The number shown in each partition is the number of instances solved uniquely by the sets forming the partition. For example, the central partition (i.e., the intersection of all the sets) of the diagram (a) shows that *DWCL Mathematica*, *DWCL z3*, and *Implicit Abstraction* solved the same set of 141 instances.

Predicate abstraction [16] is a commonly used abstraction techniques to verify infinite-state systems. Several symbolic techniques [3,19,20] focus on the efficient computation of the predicate abstraction. In principle, we can also use those technique to explicitly compute the semi-algebraic abstraction. However, the up-front, explicit computation of the abstraction is a bottleneck and can be avoided with implicit predicate abstraction [35] when the goal is to verify a safety property on the abstract system. We use implicit abstraction to obtain an implicit encoding of the semi-algebraic abstraction. The transition system of the semi-algebraic abstraction contains NRA formulas (the polynomials can be non-linear or the Lie derivative of the polynomials are non-linear). While there are few algorithms and tool that can verify such transition systems (e.g., [4]), our technique is agnostic to the underlying model checking algorithm.

8 Conclusions and Future Work

In this paper, we addressed the safety problem of polynomial dynamical systems. We built on the LZZ algorithm to define a symbolic encoding of the abstraction based on a set of polynomials. The encoding is linear in the number of polynomials and can be used to implicitly represent the abstraction without the need of enumerating the abstract states, enabling the use of SMT-based model checking techniques. The experimental evaluation showed that the approach is promising and complementary to existing techniques solving a number of new instances.

The main directions for future works are, on one side, refining the abstraction discovering new polynomials that are able to remove spurious abstract counterexamples, and, on the other side, the application of the approach to hybrid systems where the continuous dynamics depends on the discrete state of the system.

Acknowledgements. S. Mover was partially supported by the academic chair "Complex Systems Engineering", École Polytechnique-ENSTA Paris-Télécom Paris-Thalés-Dassault Aviation-Naval Group-DGA-Foundation ParisTech-FX and the AID project "Validation of Autonomous Drones and Swarms of Drones". A. Cimatti, A. Griggio, and S. Tonetta were partially supported by ECSEL JU under grant agreement No 876852. The JU receives support from EU's H2020 programme, Austria, Czech Republic, Germany, Ireland, Italy, Portugal, Spain, Sweden, Turkey.

References

1. Birgmeier, J., Bradley, A.R., Weissenbacher, G.: Counterexample to Induction-Guided Abstraction-Refinement (CTIGAR). In: CAV, pp. 831–848 (2014)
2. Chen, X., Mover, S., Sankaranarayanan, S.: Compositional relational abstraction for nonlinear hybrid systems. ACM Trans. Embedded Comput. Syst. **16**(5), 187:1–187:19 (2017)
3. Cimatti, A., Franzén, A., Griggio, A., Kalyanasundaram, K., Roveri, M.: Tighter integration of bdds and smt for predicate abstraction. In: DATE, pp. 1707–1712. IEEE (2010)
4. Cimatti, A., Griggio, A., Irfan, A., Roveri, M., Sebastiani, R.: Incremental linearization for satisfiability and verification modulo nonlinear arithmetic and transcendental functions. ACM Trans. Comput. Log. **19**(3), 19:1–19:52 (2018)
5. Cimatti, A., Griggio, A., Mover, S., Tonetta, S.: IC3 modulo theories via implicit predicate abstraction. In: TACAS, pp. 46–61 (2014)
6. Cimatti, A., Griggio, A., Mover, S., Tonetta, S.: Infinite-state invariant checking with IC3 and predicate abstraction. Formal Methods Syst. Des. **49**(3), 190–218 (2016). https://doi.org/10.1007/s10703-016-0257-4
7. Cimatti, A., Griggio, A., Schaafsma, B.J., Sebastiani, R.: The MathSAT5 SMT solver. In: TACAS, pp. 93–107 (2013)

8. Collins, G.E.: Quantifier elimination for real closed fields by cylindrical algebraic decompostion. In: Brakhage, H. (ed.) GI-Fachtagung 1975. LNCS, vol. 33, pp. 134–183. Springer, Heidelberg (1975). https://doi.org/10.1007/3-540-07407-4_17

9. Flanagan, C., Qadeer, S.: Predicate abstraction for software verification. In: POPL, pp. 191–202 (2002)

10. Fulton, N., Mitsch, S., Quesel, J., Völp, M., Platzer, A.: KeYmaera X: An axiomatic tactical theorem prover for hybrid systems. In: CADE, pp. 527–538 (2015)

11. Gario, M., Micheli, A.: PySMT: a solver-agnostic library for fast prototyping of SMT-based algorithms. In: SMT Workshop 2015 (2015)

12. Ghorbal, K., Sogokon, A.: Characterizing Positively Invariant Sets: Inductive and Topological Methods. CoRR abs/2009.09797 (2020). https://arxiv.org/abs/2009.09797

13. Ghorbal, K., Sogokon, A., Platzer, A.: A hierarchy of proof rules for checking positive invariance of algebraic and semi-algebraic sets. Comput. Lang. Syst. Struct. **47**, 19–43 (2017)

14. Goriely, A.: Integrability and nonintegrability of dynamical systems (2001)

15. Goubault, E., Jourdan, J., Putot, S., Sankaranarayanan, S.: Finding non-polynomial positive invariants and lyapunov functions for polynomial systems through darboux polynomials. In: ACC, pp. 3571–3578 (2014)

16. Graf, S., Saidi, H.: Construction of abstract state graphs with PVS. In: Grumberg, O. (ed.) CAV 1997. LNCS, vol. 1254, pp. 72–83. Springer, Heidelberg (1997). https://doi.org/10.1007/3-540-63166-6_10

17. Inc., W.R.: Mathematica, Version 12.2, https://www.wolfram.com/mathematica, champaign, IL, 2020

18. Kong, H., He, F., Song, X., Hung, W.N.N., Gu, M.: Exponential-condition-based barrier certificate generation for safety verification of hybrid systems. In: CAV, pp. 242–257 (2013)

19. Lahiri, S.K., Bryant, R.E., Cook, B.: A Symbolic Approach to Predicate Abstraction. In: CAV, pp. 141–153 (2003)

20. Lahiri, S.K., Nieuwenhuis, R., Oliveras, A.: SMT techniques for fast predicate abstraction. In: CAV, pp. 424–437 (2006)

21. Liu, J., Lv, J., Quan, Z., Zhan, N., Zhao, H., Zhou, C., Zou, L.: A calculus for hybrid CSP. In: Ueda, K. (ed.) APLAS 2010. LNCS, vol. 6461, pp. 1–15. Springer, Heidelberg (2010). https://doi.org/10.1007/978-3-642-17164-2_1

22. Liu, J., Zhan, N., Zhao, H.: Computing semi-algebraic invariants for polynomial dynamical systems. In: EMSOFT, pp. 97–106 (2011)

23. Meurer, A., et al.: Sympy: symbolic computing in python. PeerJ Comput. Sci. **3**, e103 (2017)

24. Mitsch, S., Munive, J.J.H.Y., Jin, X., Zhan, B., Wang, S., Zhan, N.: Arch-comp20 category report:hybrid systems theorem proving. In: ARCH20. EPiC Series in Computing, vol. 74, pp. 153–174. EasyChair (2020)

25. de Moura, L.M., Bjørner, N.: Z3: An efficient SMT solver. In: TACAS, pp. 337–340 (2008)

26. Mover, S., Cimatti, A., Tiwari, A., Tonetta, S.: Time-aware relational abstractions for hybrid systems. In: EMSOFT pp. 14:1–14:10 (2013)

27. Platzer, A.: Differential dynamic logic for hybrid systems. J. Autom. Reason. **41**(2), 143–189 (2008)

28. Platzer, A., Clarke, E.M.: Computing differential invariants of hybrid systems as fixedpoints. Formal Methods Syst. Design **35**(1), 98–120 (2009)

29. Prajna, S.: Barrier certificates for nonlinear model validation. Autom. **42**(1), 117–126 (2006)

30. Roohi, N., Prabhakar, P., Viswanathan, M.: HARE: a hybrid abstraction refinement engine for verifying non-linear hybrid automata. In: TACAS, pp. 573–588 (2017)
31. Sankaranarayanan, S., Tiwari, A.: Relational abstractions for continuous and hybrid systems. In: CAV, pp. 686–702 (2011)
32. Sogokon, A., Ghorbal, K., Jackson, P.B., Platzer, A.: A method for invariant generation for polynomial continuous systems. In: VMCAI, pp. 268–288 (2016)
33. Sogokon, A., Mitsch, S., Tan, Y.K., Cordwell, K., Platzer, A.: Pegasus: a framework for sound continuous invariant generation. In: FM, pp. 138–157 (2019)
34. Tiwari, A.: Abstractions for hybrid systems. Formal Methods Syst. Des. **32**(1), 57–83 (2008)
35. Tonetta, S.: Abstract model checking without computing the abstraction. In: FM, pp. 89–105 (2009)
36. Wang, S., Zhan, N., Zou, L.: An improved HHL prover: an interactive theorem prover for hybrid systems. In: ICFEM, pp. 382–399 (2015)
37. Zaki, M.H., Denman, W., Tahar, S., Bois, G.: Integrating abstraction techniques for formal verification of analog designs. J. Aerosp. Comput. Inf. Commun. **6**(5), 373–392 (2009)
38. Zutshi, A., Sankaranarayanan, S., Tiwari, A.: Timed relational abstractions for sampled data control systems. In: CAV, pp. 343–361 (2012)

IMITATOR 3: Synthesis of Timing Parameters Beyond Decidability

Étienne André[✉][iD]

Université de Lorraine, CNRS, Inria, LORIA,
54000 Nancy, France
Andre.Etienne@lipn13.fr

Abstract. Real-time systems are notoriously hard to verify due to non-determinism, concurrency and timing constraints. When timing constants are uncertain (in early the design phase, or due to slight variations of the timing bounds), timed model checking techniques may not be satisfactory. In contrast, parametric timed model checking synthesizes timing values ensuring correctness. IMITATOR takes as input an extension of parametric timed automata (PTAs), a powerful formalism to formally verify critical real-time systems. IMITATOR extends PTAs with multi-rate clocks, global rational-valued variables and a set of additional useful features. We describe here the new features and algorithms offered by IMITATOR 3, that moved along the years from a simple prototype dedicated to robustness analysis to a standalone parametric model checker for timed systems.

Keywords: Parametric timed automata · Parameter synthesis · Real-time systems

1 Introduction

Real-time systems are often used in critical environments, and may be verified using formal methods. Such systems are notoriously hard to verify due to nondeterminism, concurrency and timing constraints. Timed model checking provides designers with techniques to formally verify a real-time system. However, timed model checking may not always be fully satisfactory: First, in the early design phase, timing constants may not be known and, without them, model checking is not possible; Second, at runtime, timing constants may vary (due to uncertain bounds, or to processor clock drifts), in which case the model checking result may not hold anymore. In contrast, parametric timed model checking *synthesizes* timing values ensuring the system correctness.

Parametric timed automata (PTAs) are a powerful formalism to reason about, and formally verify critical real-time systems [5]. PTAs are finite state

This work is partially supported by the ANR-NRF French-Singaporean research program ProMiS (ANR-19-CE25-0015).

A. Silva and K. R. M. Leino (Eds.) CAV 2021, LNCS 12759, pp. 552–565, 2021.
https://doi.org/10.1007/978-3-030-81685-8_26

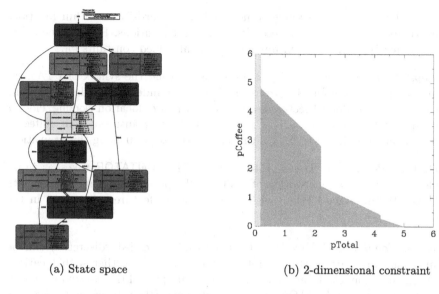

(a) State space   (b) 2-dimensional constraint

Fig. 1. Examples of graphical outputs

automata extended with clocks, i.e., real-valued variables evolving linearly, that can be compared with either integer constants or parameters in guards (constraints to take a transition) and invariants (constraints to remain in a location).

IMITATOR takes as input networks of "IMITATOR PTAs" (IPTAs) extending PTAs with several convenient features such as stopwatches, multi-rate clocks or global shared rational-valued variables.

IMITATOR answers variants of the following problem:

Parameter synthesis problem:
INPUT: A network of IPTAs $\mathcal{A}$ and a specification φ
PROBLEM: Synthesize the set of parameter valuations for which $\mathcal{A}$ satisfies φ

IMITATOR answers this problem by synthesizing sets of parameter valuations in the form of a finite disjunction of linear constraints over the parameters.

IMITATOR is a command-line only tool; its input is text-based (partially inspired by HyTech syntax [41]) and is "human-readable", different from, e.g., XML. IMITATOR produces standardized result files (that can be possibly parsed from external tools), and can produce graphical outputs, such as in Fig. 1.

The expressive power (i.e., ease to write a complicated model in a compact manner) of the tool has been largely improved since IMITATOR 2.5 [17], and IMITATOR is now a parametric timed model checker taking as inputs a model and a property, implementing various synthesis algorithms.

2   An Expressive Input Language

Parametric Timed Automata (PTAs). Timed automata (TAs) [3] extend finite-state automata with *clocks*, i.e., real-valued variables evolving at the same rate 1, that can be compared to integers along edges ("guards") or within locations ("invariants"). Clocks can be reset (to 0) along transitions. PTAs extend TAs with (timing) parameters, i.e., unknown rational-valued constants [5].

Example 1. In the model in Fig. 2 (that goes beyond the syntax of PTAs, see Example 2), there are four locations, depicted as rounded rectangles. Invariants are depicted using dotted rectangles. In the invariant of location working, clock x is compared to parameter p_{total}. The guard of the transition from coffee to working compares clock t to p_{coffee}; this clock t is reset to 0 along this transition.

IMITATOR *Parametric Timed Automata (IPTAs).* IMITATOR takes as input models described as networks of IMITATOR parametric timed automata (IPTAs). IPTAs extend PTAs with a set of useful features, described in the following.

Global Rational-Valued Variables. Global variables (called "discrete") can be defined, and are part of the discrete part of a state, together with locations (and different from clocks and parameters that are part of the *continuous* part). Global variables in IMITATOR are exact rationals, following exact arithmetics (as opposed to, e.g., floating-point arithmetic that can accumulate errors and lead to faulty assertions). Exact rationals are encoded in IMITATOR using the GNU MP library. Such discrete variables can be updated along transitions, and can also be part of the clock guards and invariants; in fact, virtually any linear expression over clocks, parameters and discrete variables can be used in guards, invariants and updates. Non-linear arithmetic expressions over sole discrete variables are allowed too.

Automata Synchronization. IPTAs can be synchronized together on shared actions, or by reading shared variables. All variables (clocks, parameters, discrete) are potentially global in IMITATOR. This allows users to define models component by component.

Arbitrary Flows. Since version 3.0, IMITATOR supports arbitrary (constant) flows for clocks; this way, clocks do not necessarily evolve at the same time, and can encode different concepts from only time: temperature, amount of completion, continuous cost... Their value can increase or decrease at any predefined rate in each location, and can become negative. In that sense, IMITATOR's clocks are closer to *continuous variables* (as in hybrid automata) rather than TAs' clocks; nevertheless, we keep the name *clock* for sake of backward-compatibility. This makes IMITATOR support a parametric extension of *multi-rate automata* [2]. This notably includes stopwatches, where clocks can have a 1- or 0-rate [36].

Additional Syntax Improvements. Beyond the aforementioned increase of the syntactic expressive power, the syntax was enhanced with accepting locations (that can be used in properties), global constants, "if... then... else" conditions in updates, and with the ability to include model fragments from different

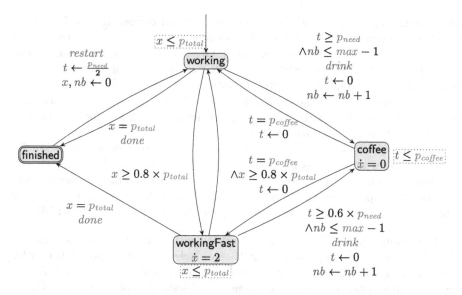

Fig. 2. An IPTA example: writing papers and drinking coffee

files (new syntax `#include(modelpart.imi)`). Several simplifications were made to the syntax to keep it "human-readable". For example, location workingFast of Fig. 2 is written in IMITATOR syntax as follows:

```
loc workingFast: invariant x <= pTotal flow{x' = 2}
```

Translations. Finally, translations of the model are available to other model checkers such as HyTech [41] and Uppaal [42] (in both cases, not all features can be translated since some of the features of IMITATOR do not exist in the target tool, e.g., Uppaal does not support parameters nor complex linear constraints over clocks (only "diagonal")). Graphical translations of the model are also available to JPEG, PDF and LATEX formats.

Example 2. Consider the IPTA in Fig. 2, modeling a researcher writing papers. The model features two clocks t (measuring the time when needing a coffee) and x (measuring the amount of work done on a given paper), both initially 0. Their rate is always 1, unless otherwise specified (e.g., in workingFast). Initially, the researcher is working (location working) on a paper, requiring an amount of work p_{total}. When the paper is completed (guard $x = p_{total}$), the IPTA moves to location finished. From there, at any time, the researcher can start working on a new paper (transition back to working, updating x and t).

Alternatively, after at least a certain time (guard $t \geq p_{need}$), the researcher may need a coffee; this action can only be taken until a maximum number of coffees have been drunk for this paper ($nb \leq max - 1$), where nb is a discrete global variable recording the number of coffees drunk while working on the current paper. When drinking a coffee (location coffee), the work is obviously not progressing ($\dot{x} = 0$). Drinking a coffee takes exactly p_{coffee} time units (guard $t = p_{coffee}$ back to location working). Observe that, from the second paper onwards (transition labeled with *restart*), the researcher is already half-way of her/his need for a coffee (parametric update $t \leftarrow 0.5 \times p_{need}$ [22]).

Also, whenever 80% of the work is done (guard $x \geq 0.8 \times p_{total}$), the researcher may work twice as fast (location workingFast, with a rate 2 for clock x). In that case, (s)he needs a coffee faster too ($0.6 \times p_{need}$).

All three durations p_{coffee}, p_{need} and p_{total} are timing parameters. We fix their parameter domains as follows: $p_{coffee}, p_{total} \in [0, \infty)$ and $p_{need} \in [1, \infty)$. The maximum number of coffees $max \in [0, \infty)$ is also a parameter; observe that it is (only) compared to the discrete variable nb, and therefore can be seen as a "discrete parameter"—which is allowed by the liberal syntax of IMITATOR.

The example in Fig. 2 could not be modeled with UPPAAL due to the presence of timing parameters, stopwatches, multi-rate clocks and non-0 update. It may be modeled using HyTech; however, most algorithms implemented in IMITATOR (even the most basic ones, such as liveness synthesis) do not exist in HyTech, as HyTech mainly focuses on basic state space computation.

3   A Variety of Synthesis Algorithms

The formalism of networks of IPTAs is "highly undecidable" for most problems. Indeed, while several problems are decidable for timed automata (notably the reachability [3]), most interesting problems become undecidable in the presence of timing parameters [5,8] , notably when such parameters are unbounded [35]. On top of this, multi-rate automata together with linear constraints over the clocks also yield undecidability [2]. Finally, the mere use of stopwatches, even without the aforementioned extensions, brings undecidability [36]. Also note that, in contrast to several existing model checkers, IMITATOR offers the use of unbounded rational variables, therefore with an infinite domain. For all these reasons, it is always possible to find examples of IPTAs for which the algorithms implemented in IMITATOR would not terminate with an exact (sound and complete) result. The rational behind IMITATOR is therefore to follow a "best-effort" approach, by:

- using aggressive optimizations and abstractions (e.g., [11,19,45]), leading to termination for most case studies in practice;
- outputting over- or under-approximated results, i.e., the set of synthesized parameter valuations may be larger or smaller than the exact result.

IMITATOR outputs a standardized result (in a text file), that contains the synthesized constraint with a set of information, and notably the *validity* of the constraint, i.e., whether the set of valuations is *exact* (sound and complete), *possibly over-approximated*, *possibly under-approximated*, or *potentially invalid* i.e., when both under-approximating and over-approximating heuristics were used.

By default, IMITATOR attempts to synthesize an exact result; only when some specific options are used (e.g., a limit on the number of states explored, or on the computation time), approximations may be used. These approximations are conservative for most algorithms; for example, if an approximation is used for safety synthesis, then the result will be under-approximated (i.e., the system is safe for all synthesized valuations—even though some more safe valuations may exist).

IMITATOR offers two main classes of synthesis: *i)* *Witness* (or counter-example), which attempts to exhibit at least one parameter valuation satisfying the property; often, IMITATOR still outputs a *symbolic* set of valuations (i.e., a linear constraint over the parameters), but stops the analysis as soon as one such set is found. *ii)* Normal *synthesis*, where IMITATOR attempts to synthesize *all* parameter valuations satisfying the property.

Properties include reachability (denoted by "EF", following the TCTL syntax), safety (denoted by "AGnot"), liveness, deadlock-freeness, robustness, and some others.

Throughout this section, we exemplify the main synthesis algorithms of IMITATOR on Example 2.[1] All the results synthesized in the following are exact (sound and complete), unless otherwise specified.

Safety. A first algorithm of IMITATOR is safety synthesis, i.e., synthesizing parameter valuations for which a discrete state (location and/or valuation of the discrete variables) is unreachable for all runs. For example, one synthesize the valuations for which it is impossible to drink any coffee, i.e., it is impossible to reach the coffee location of the "researcher" automaton of Fig. 2.

```
#synth AGnot(loc[researcher] = coffee)
```

The result is: $max \in [0, 1) \vee \left(max \geq 1 \wedge p_{total} < \dfrac{p_{need}}{10} \right)$

Let us explain this result. The first disjunct is trivial: if the researcher is not allowed to drink any coffee ($max < 1$), the transition to coffee (guarded by "$nb \leq max - 1$") can never be taken. The second disjunct is, despite the relative simplicity of this model, less trivial: assume for illustration that $p_{need} = 10$ and $p_{total} = 1$, and let us show that the researcher is still able to start drinking a coffee in this situation. After the first paper completion (action $restart$), we have $x \leftarrow 0$ and $t \leftarrow 5$. After one time unit in location working ($x = 1$ and $t = 6$), the researcher moves to workingFast, and can immediately move to coffee (guard $t \geq 0.6 \times p_{need}$ is now satisfied). This scenario, that can be seen on the parametric state space output by IMITATOR (see Fig. 1a), is also possible for larger values of p_{total}. This explains the strict inequality $p_{total} < \frac{p_{need}}{10}$.

---

[1] All finishing executions for our example using IMITATOR 3.0 "Cheese" ea560fd on a Dell XPS 13 7390 Intel® Core™ i7-10510U CPU @ 1.80 GHz running Linux Mint 20 Ulyana terminate within $< 1\,s$. All examples and results can be found at [9].

Reachability. Reachability can be seen as the opposite of safety, i.e., the goal is to synthesize parameter valuations for which a discrete state is reachable for at least one run. For example, one can ask for the valuations for which it is possible to drink at least one coffee:

```
#synth EF(loc[researcher] = coffee)
```

The result is $max \geq 1 \wedge p_{total} \geq \frac{p_{need}}{10}$, which is obviously the complement of the result synthesized for the aforementioned safety property.

One can also synthesize valuations for which it is possible to drink at least five coffees while working on some article (i.e., $nb \geq 5$).

```
#synth EF(loc[researcher] = coffee & nb >= 5)
```

The result is $max \geq 5 \wedge p_{total} \geq \frac{37}{10} \times p_{need}$.

Minimum-Time Reachability. Minimal-time synthesis [12] aims at synthesizing parameter valuations minimizing the time needed to reach a discrete state. Here, we can ask for the valuations for which it is possible to finish an article after drinking at least 2 coffees:

```
#synth EFtmin(loc[researcher] = finished & nb >= 2)
```

The result is $\frac{p_{total}}{2} + p_{need} + 2 \times p_{coffee} \leq 2 \wedge max \geq 2$ and the minimal time is 2. That is, any of these valuations guarantee the reachability of a state where the researcher has drunk 2 coffees, and the minimum time is 2 (recall that $p_{need} \in [1, \infty)$).

Optimal Parameter Reachability. One can ask here for the valuations for which the value of a given parameter is minimized or maximized when reaching a given state. Let us ask for the valuations minimizing the value of p_{total} when finishing a paper after drinking (at least) 3 coffees.

```
#synth EFpmin(loc[researcher] = finished & nb >= 3, pTotal)
```

The result is $max \geq 3 \wedge p_{total} = 2.1 \wedge p_{need} = 1$. Observe that p_{coffee} is not involved in this constraint (contrarily to minimum-time synthesis); indeed, the time spent in drinking coffee does not impact the total duration of the *work* (p_{total}), as the progress of clock x is stopped in coffee.

Parametric Deadlock Freeness. Deadlocks are states in which no discrete action can be taken, and time cannot elapse ("timelock"). Such situations may denote ill-formed models. IMITATOR offers an algorithm [7] synthesizing parameter valuations for which the model is deadlock-free. In case of "early termination" (predefined bound on the depth of the state space or on the computation time), a backward procedure synthesizes a subset of correct (deadlock-free) valuations.

```
#synth DeadlockFree
```

For this property, the analysis does not terminate, as the state space is infinite (unbounded rational-valued parameters, unbounded variable nb) and IMITATOR needs to explore it as a whole to deduce deadlock-freeness for our example.

Adding a bound on the depth of the state space (option `-depth-limit 40`) yields termination, with a *pair* of constraints: an under-approximated positive constraint (i.e., valuations that are guaranteed to be deadlock-free) $max < 16 \vee (max \geq 16 \wedge p_{total} < \frac{27}{2} p_{need})$, and an over-approximated negative constraint (i.e., valuations that *might* be deadlocked) $max \geq 16 \wedge p_{total} \geq \frac{27}{2} p_{need}$. Observe that both constraints are complementary, i.e., IMITATOR is sure that the former set is deadlock-free, and is not sure that the latter set contains deadlocks. (Note that, in fact, the model is very likely to be deadlock-free for all valuations, even though IMITATOR is not able to show it.)

Liveness Synthesis. A new feature of IMITATOR 3 is cycle synthesis, i.e., parameter valuations for which there exists an infinite run, possibly passing infinitely often by a given discrete state (Büchi condition). IMITATOR uses by default an original algorithm by Laure Petrucci and Jaco van de Pol based on NDFS extended with parametric subsumption and pruning [45] (other algorithms, such as BFS, are also available [11]). In our running example , one can ask for the valuations for which the researcher infinitely often writes papers after drinking (at least) 3 coffees for each of them.

```
#synth CycleThrough(loc[researcher] = finished & nb>=3)
```

The result is $max \geq 3 \wedge p_{total} \geq 2.1 \times p_{need}$.

Robustness. Inherited from earlier versions of IMITATOR, one can apply the *inverse method* [29] (also called trace preservation [21]) that, given a reference parameter valuation, synthesizes the set of parameter valuations for which the set of "traces" (discrete behaviors, i.e., abstracting time information away) is the same as for this reference valuation.

```
#synth TracePreservation(pTotal = 10, pNeed = 5, pCoffee = 3, max = 3)
```

The result is: $\left(3 \times p_{need} > p_{total} \geq 2 \times p_{need} \wedge max \in [2, 3)\right) \vee \left(2.1 \times p_{need} > p_{total} \geq 2 \times p_{need} \wedge max \geq 3\right)$. The synthesized constraint can be seen as a characterization of the *robustness* of the original parameter valuation.

Synthesis Using Patterns. Another way to specify properties is to use a set of pre-defined observer patterns [6,28]. Observer patterns are translated into observer automata (called reachability testing in [1]), and their correctness reduces to reachability. This procedure is transparent to the user, i.e., (s)he only needs to specify the pattern and IMITATOR takes care of the translation and synthesis. IMITATOR patterns specify the order between actions, extended with (possibly parametric) timing information. The syntax is detailed in the user manual, and the semantics is given in [6].

For example, one can synthesize the set of valuations such that, every time the researcher restarts a new article, (s)he completes it within 5 time units. That is, every occurrence of the *restart* action must be followed within (at most) 5 time units by the *done* action.

```
#synth pattern(everytime restart then eventually done within 5)
```

A part of the valuations set is: $max \geq 6 \wedge 5 - 6 \times p_{coffee} \geq p_{total} \geq 4.7 \times p_{need}$.

A graphical 2D representation projected onto p_{total} and p_{coffee} (setting $p_{need} = 2$ and $max = 3$) is given in Fig. 1b.

Other Algorithms. IMITATOR features a number of additional algorithms, including *i) non-Zeno infinite run synthesis* [27], *ii) behavioral cartography* [16] that partitions the parameter space into *tiles* where the discrete behavior is uniform, or *iii) parametric reachability preservation*, that takes as input a discrete state and a reference valuation, and synthesizes valuations for which this discrete state is reachable iff it is reachable for the reference valuation [25]. The two latter algorithms can be distributed over a cluster, showing interesting results, and can be used to perform reachability synthesis while being faster than the normal reachability synthesis algorithm for some benchmarks [14,15]. Finally, compositional verification for a subclass of IPTAs (a parametric extension of event-recording automata [4]) was proposed in [24].

4 Distribution

IMITATOR is distributed under the terms of the GNU General Public License. Its source code is therefore publicly available, and benefited from several contributors' additions. IMITATOR is available online[2], together with its documentation, and a benchmarks library [26].

IMITATOR depends on several libraries. Notably, the core engine relies on the Parma Polyhedra Library (PPL) [32] for the computation of symbolic states. As a consequence, IMITATOR can be cumbersome to compile. For this reason, standalone binaries are available for all Linux-like systems. A Docker version[3] (made by Jaime Arias) and a prototype Web service[4] are available too.

An extensive user manual, explaining all algorithms and providing users with a full description of the input syntax for models and properties, is available [10].

5 A Selection of Applications

IMITATOR was applied to a variety of both academic and industrial case studies over the last few years. These applications range within several domains, including real-time systems, testing and monitoring, cybersecurity, or hardware verification. One can cite:

---

[2] https://www.imitator.fr.
[3] https://hub.docker.com/r/imitator/imitator/.
[4] https://imitator.lipn.univ-paris13.fr/.

- the parametric verification of an asynchronous memory circuit by ST-Microelectronics (from a model described in [37]),
- verification of parametric scheduling problems by Astrium Space Transportation [40] and ArianeGroup SAS [13],
- analysis of music scores [38],
- verifying the multi-processor image processing system of an unmanned aerial aircraft with uncertain periods, as a benchmark made public by Thales [46],
- parametric pattern matching and monitoring of logs from the automative industry [20],
- synthesis of timing/cost parameters in attack-fault trees [23, 31],
- testing product lines using parametric constraints [44],
- verification of an industrial asynchronous leader election algorithm by Thales using IMITATOR combined with abstractions [18],
- performing parametric opacity analyses for timed automata [30], and
- synthesis of parameter valuations guaranteeing liveness properties for the Bounded Retransmission Protocol [11].

6   Related Tools

HyTech [41] was the first model checker for hybrid systems (a class of formalisms beyond PTAs), including parameters; it is not maintained anymore.

UPPAAL [42] is a state-of-the-art tool for modeling and verifying systems modeled as networks of timed automata and extended with variables and data structures; while UPPAAL became a major tool for model checking timed automata, it does not support parametric verification, and the use of clocks is restricted to comparing one clock with one constant or with another clock, while IMITATOR allows a liberal syntax based on polyhedra.

RoMÉo [43] performs parameter synthesis for parametric time Petri nets with inhibitor arcs [47].

While RoMÉo shares similarities with IMITATOR, it does not support (extensions of) timed automata, and notably not multi-rate clocks.

SpaceEx [39] is a tool for verifying hybrid systems. It is not specifically dedicated to parameter synthesis, and mainly targets safety and reachability, in contrast to IMITATOR that proposes multiple synthesis algorithms.

IMITATOR's input syntax also shares some similarities with that of PHAVer-Lite [33] (a fork of PHAVer and predecessor of SpaceEx, that uses PPLite [34] instead of PPL [32]), coming from the fact that both IMITATOR and PHAVerLite originate from the HyTech syntax.

7   Perspectives

To gain some further speed for models that require less expressiveness (notably no strict inequality nor rational-valued variables), offering to replace PPL [32] with PPLite [34], or using standard 32-bit integers instead of GNU MP rationals is on our agenda.

Acknowledgement. While the author has been the main developer of IMITATOR since 2008, several colleagues brought very valuable enhancements, notably Camille Coti and Sami Evangelista [14] (on distributed algorithms), Nguyễn Hoàng Gia [27] (on non-Zeno algorithms), Vincent Bloemen [12] (on minimal-time synthesis), Laure Petrucci and Jaco van de Pol [11] (on NDFS-based cycle synthesis), and Jaime Arias for multiple practical enhancements. Many thanks to Dylan Marinho for a careful rereading of this paper, and to Stephan Merz for useful suggestions.

References

1. Aceto, L., Bouyer, P., Burgueño, A., Larsen, K.G.: The power of reachability testing for timed automata. TCS **300**(1–3), 411–475 (2003). https://doi.org/10.1016/S0304-3975(02)00334-1
2. Alur, R., et al.: The algorithmic analysis of hybrid systems. TCS **138**(1), 3–34 (1995). https://doi.org/10.1016/0304-3975(94)00202-T
3. Alur, R., Dill, D.L.: A theory of timed automata. TCS **126**(2), 183–235 (1994). https://doi.org/10.1016/0304-3975(94)90010-8
4. Alur, R., Fix, L., Henzinger, T.A.: Event-clock automata: a determinizable class of timed automata. TCS **211**(1–2), 253–273 (1999). https://doi.org/10.1016/S0304-3975(97)00173-4
5. Alur, R., Henzinger, T.A., Vardi, M.Y.: Parametric real-time reasoning. In: Kosaraju, S.R., Johnson, D.S., Aggarwal, A. (eds.) STOC, pp. 592–601. ACM, New York, NY, USA (1993). https://doi.org/10.1145/167088.167242
6. André, É.: Observer patterns for real-time systems. In: Liu, Y., Martin, A. (eds.) ICECCS, pp. 125–134. IEEE Computer Society, July 2013. https://doi.org/10.1109/ICECCS.2013.26
7. André, É.: Parametric deadlock-freeness checking timed automata. In: Sampaio, A., Wang, F. (eds.) ICTAC 2016. LNCS, vol. 9965, pp. 469–478. Springer, Cham (2016). https://doi.org/10.1007/978-3-319-46750-4_27
8. André, É.: What's decidable about parametric timed automata? STTT **21**(2), 203–219 (2019). https://doi.org/10.1007/s10009-017-0467-0
9. André, É.: Artifact for IMITATOR 3.0, April 2021. https://doi.org/10.5281/zenodo.4723415
10. André, É.: IMITATOR user manual, January 2021. https://github.com/imitator-model-checker/imitator/releases/download/v3.0.0/IMITATOR-user-manual.pdf
11. André, É., Arias, J., Petrucci, L., Pol, J.: Iterative bounded synthesis for efficient cycle detection in parametric timed automata. In: TACAS 2021. LNCS, vol. 12651, pp. 311–329. Springer, Cham (2021). https://doi.org/10.1007/978-3-030-72016-2_17
12. André, É., Bloemen, V., Petrucci, L., van de Pol, J.: Minimal-time synthesis for parametric timed automata. In: Vojnar, T., Zhang, L. (eds.) TACAS 2019. LNCS, vol. 11428, pp. 211–228. Springer, Cham (2019). https://doi.org/10.1007/978-3-030-17465-1_12
13. André, É., Coquard, E., Fribourg, L., Jerray, J., Lesens, D.: Scheduling synthesis for a launcher flight control using parametric stopwatch automata. In: Keller, J., Penczek, W. (eds.) ACSD, pp. 13–22. IEEE (2019). https://doi.org/10.1109/ACSD.2019.00006
14. André, É., Coti, C., Evangelista, S.: Distributed behavioral cartography of timed automata. In: Dongarra, J., Ishikawa, Y., Atsushi, H. (eds.) EuroMPI/ASIA, pp. 109–114. ACM, September 2014. https://doi.org/10.1145/2642769.2642784

15. André, É., Coti, C., Nguyen, H.G.: Enhanced distributed behavioral cartography of parametric timed automata. In: Butler, M., Conchon, S., Zaïdi, F. (eds.) ICFEM 2015. LNCS, vol. 9407, pp. 319–335. Springer, Cham (2015). https://doi.org/10.1007/978-3-319-25423-4_21
16. André, É., Fribourg, L.: Behavioral cartography of timed automata. In: Kučera, A., Potapov, I. (eds.) RP 2010. LNCS, vol. 6227, pp. 76–90. Springer, Heidelberg (2010). https://doi.org/10.1007/978-3-642-15349-5_5
17. André, É., Fribourg, L., Kühne, U., Soulat, R.: IMITATOR 2.5: a tool for analyzing robustness in scheduling problems. In: Giannakopoulou, D., Méry, D. (eds.) FM 2012. LNCS, vol. 7436, pp. 33–36. Springer, Heidelberg (2012). https://doi.org/10.1007/978-3-642-32759-9_6
18. André, É., Fribourg, L., Mota, J.-M., Soulat, R.: Verification of an industrial asynchronous leader election algorithm using abstractions and parametric model checking. In: Enea, C., Piskac, R. (eds.) VMCAI 2019. LNCS, vol. 11388, pp. 409–424. Springer, Cham (2019). https://doi.org/10.1007/978-3-030-11245-5_19
19. André, É., Fribourg, L., Soulat, R.: Merge and conquer: state merging in parametric timed automata. In: Van Hung, D., Ogawa, M. (eds.) ATVA 2013. LNCS, vol. 8172, pp. 381–396. Springer, Cham (2013). https://doi.org/10.1007/978-3-319-02444-8_27
20. André, É., Hasuo, I., Waga, M.: Offline timed pattern matching under uncertainty. In: Lin, A.W., Sun, J. (eds.) ICECCS, pp. 10–20. IEEE Computer Society (2018). https://doi.org/10.1109/ICECCS2018.2018.00010
21. André, É., Lime, D., Markey, N.: Language preservation problems in parametric timed automata. LMCS 16, January 2020. https://doi.org/10.23638/LMCS-16(1:5)2020
22. André, É., Lime, D., Ramparison, M.: Parametric updates in parametric timed automata. In: Pérez, J.A., Yoshida, N. (eds.) FORTE 2019. LNCS, vol. 11535, pp. 39–56. Springer, Cham (2019). https://doi.org/10.1007/978-3-030-21759-4_3
23. André, É., Lime, D., Ramparison, M., Stoelinga, M.: Parametric analyses of attack-fault trees. In: Keller, J., Penczek, W. (eds.) ACSD, pp. 33–42. IEEE (2019). https://doi.org/10.1109/ACSD.2019.00008
24. André, É., Lin, S.-W.: Learning-based compositional parameter synthesis for event-recording automata. In: Bouajjani, A., Silva, A. (eds.) FORTE 2017. LNCS, vol. 10321, pp. 17–32. Springer, Cham (2017). https://doi.org/10.1007/978-3-319-60225-7_2
25. André, É., Lipari, G., Nguyen, H.G., Sun, Y.: Reachability preservation based parameter synthesis for timed automata. In: Havelund, K., Holzmann, G., Joshi, R. (eds.) NFM 2015. LNCS, vol. 9058, pp. 50–65. Springer, Cham (2015). https://doi.org/10.1007/978-3-319-17524-9_5
26. André, É., Marinho, D., van de Pol, J.: A benchmarks library for extended timed automata. In: Loulergue, F., Wotawa, F. (eds.) TAP (2021). (to appear)
27. André, É., Nguyen, H.G., Petrucci, L., Sun, J.: Parametric model checking timed automata under non-zenoness assumption. In: Barrett, C., Davies, M., Kahsai, T. (eds.) NFM 2017. LNCS, vol. 10227, pp. 35–51. Springer, Cham (2017). https://doi.org/10.1007/978-3-319-57288-8_3
28. André, É., Petrucci, L.: Unifying patterns for modelling timed relationships in systems and properties. In: Moldt, D., Rölke, H., Störrle, H. (eds.) PNSE, vol. 1372, pp. 25–40. CEUR-WS, June 2015
29. André, É., Soulat, R.: The Inverse Method. FOCUS Series in Computer Engineering and Information Technology, p. 176, ISTE Ltd and John Wiley & Sons Inc. Hoboken (2013)

30. André, É., Sun, J.: Parametric timed model checking for guaranteeing timed opacity. In: Chen, Y.-F., Cheng, C.-H., Esparza, J. (eds.) ATVA 2019. LNCS, vol. 11781, pp. 115–130. Springer, Cham (2019). https://doi.org/10.1007/978-3-030-31784-3_7

31. Arias, J., Budde, C.E., Penczek, W., Petrucci, L., Sidoruk, T., Stoelinga, M.: Hackers vs. Security: attack-defence trees as asynchronous multi-agent systems. In: Lin, S.-W., Hou, Z., Mahony, B. (eds.) ICFEM 2020. LNCS, vol. 12531, pp. 3–19. Springer, Cham (2020). https://doi.org/10.1007/978-3-030-63406-3_1

32. Bagnara, R., Hill, P.M., Zaffanella, E.: The Parma Polyhedra Library: Toward a complete set of numerical abstractions for the analysis and verification of hardware and software systems. Sci. Comput. Programm. **72**(1–2), 3–21 (2008). https://doi.org/10.1016/j.scico.2007.08.001

33. Becchi, A., Zaffanella, E.: Revisiting polyhedral analysis for hybrid systems. In: Chang, B.-Y.E. (ed.) SAS 2019. LNCS, vol. 11822, pp. 183–202. Springer, Cham (2019). https://doi.org/10.1007/978-3-030-32304-2_10

34. Becchi, A., Zaffanella, E.: PPLite: zero-overhead encoding of NNC polyhedra. Inf. Comput. **275**, 104620 (2020). https://doi.org/10.1016/j.ic.2020.104620

35. Beneš, N., Bezděk, P., Larsen, K.G., Srba, J.: Language emptiness of continuous-time parametric timed automata. In: Halldórsson, M.M., Iwama, K., Kobayashi, N., Speckmann, B. (eds.) ICALP 2015. LNCS, vol. 9135, pp. 69–81. Springer, Heidelberg (2015). https://doi.org/10.1007/978-3-662-47666-6_6

36. Cassez, F., Larsen, K.: The impressive power of stopwatches. In: Palamidessi, C. (ed.) CONCUR 2000. LNCS, vol. 1877, pp. 138–152. Springer, Heidelberg (2000). https://doi.org/10.1007/3-540-44618-4_12

37. Chevallier, R., Encrenaz-Tiphène, E., Fribourg, L., Xu, W.: Timed verification of the generic architecture of a memory circuit using parametric timed automata. FMSD **34**(1), 59–81 (2009). https://doi.org/10.1007/s10703-008-0061-x

38. Fanchon, L., Jacquemard, F.: Formal timing analysis of mixed music scores. In: ICMC. Michigan Publishing, August 2013

39. Frehse, G., et al.: SpaceEx: scalable verification of hybrid systems. In: Gopalakrishnan, G., Qadeer, S. (eds.) CAV 2011. LNCS, vol. 6806, pp. 379–395. Springer, Heidelberg (2011). https://doi.org/10.1007/978-3-642-22110-1_30

40. Fribourg, L., Lesens, D., Moro, P., Soulat, R.: Robustness analysis for scheduling problems using the inverse method. In: Reynolds, M., Terenziani, P., Moszkowski, B. (eds.) TIME, pp. 73–80. IEEE Computer Society Press, September 2012. https://doi.org/10.1109/TIME.2012.10

41. Henzinger, T.A., Ho, P.H., Wong-Toi, H.: HyTech: a model checker for hybrid systems. STTT **1**(1–2), 110–122 (1997). https://doi.org/10.1007/s100090050008

42. Larsen, K.G., Pettersson, P., Yi, W.: UPPAAL in a nutshell. STTT **1**(1–2), 134–152 (1997). https://doi.org/10.1007/s100090050010

43. Lime, D., Roux, O.H., Seidner, C., Traonouez, L.-M.: Romeo: a parametric model-checker for petri nets with stopwatches. In: Kowalewski, S., Philippou, A. (eds.) TACAS 2009. LNCS, vol. 5505, pp. 54–57. Springer, Heidelberg (2009). https://doi.org/10.1007/978-3-642-00768-2_6

44. Luthmann, L., Gerecht, T., Stephan, A., Bürdek, J., Lochau, M.: Minimum/maximum delay testing of product lines with unbounded parametric real-time constraints. J. Syst. Softw. **149**, 535–553 (2019). https://doi.org/10.1016/j.jss.2018.12.028

45. Nguyen, H.G., Petrucci, L., van de Pol, J.: Layered and collecting NDFS with subsumption for parametric timed automata. In: Lin, A.W., Sun, J. (eds.) ICECCS, pp. 1–9. IEEE Computer Society, December 2018. https://doi.org/10.1109/ICECCS2018.2018.00009
46. Sun, Y., André, É., Lipari, G.: Verification of two real-time systems using parametric timed automata. In: Quinton, S., Vardanega, T. (eds.) WATERS, July 2015
47. Traonouez, L.M., Lime, D., Roux, O.H.: Parametric model-checking of stopwatch Petri nets. J. Univ. Comput. Sci. **15**(17), 3273–3304 (2009). https://doi.org/10.3217/jucs-015-17-3273

Formally Verified Switching Logic
for Recoverability of Aircraft Controller

Ratan Lal[1]($\boxtimes$), Aaron McKinnis[2], Dustin Hauptman[2], Shawn Keshmiri[2],
and Pavithra Prabhakar[1]

[1] Kansas State University, Manhattan, KS, USA
{ratan,pprabhakar}@ksu.edu
[2] Department of Aerospace, University of Kansas, Lawrence, KS, USA
{amckinnis,dhauptman,keshmiri}@ku.edu

Abstract. In this paper, we investigate the design of a safe hybrid controller for an aircraft that switches between a classical linear quadratic regulator (LQR) controller and a more intelligent artificial neural network (ANN) controller. Our objective is to switch safely between the controllers, such that the aircraft is always recoverable within a fixed amount of time while allowing the maximum time of operation for the ANN controller. There is a *priori* known safety zone for the LQR controller operation in which the aircraft never stalls, over accelerates, or exceeds maximum structural loading, and hence, by switching to the LQR controller just before exiting this zone, one can guarantee safety. However, this *priori* known safety zone is conservative, and therefore, limits the time of operation for the ANN controller. We apply reachability analysis to expand the known safety zone, such that the LQR controller will always be able to drive the aircraft back to the safe zone from the expanded zone ("recoverable zone") within a fixed duration. The "recoverable zone" extends the time of operation of the ANN controller. We perform simulations using the hybrid controller corresponding to the recoverable zone and observe that the design is indeed safe.

1 Introduction

Different types of controller designs have been investigated for aircraft control, such as Linear Quadratic Regulators [28], Fuzzy Logic (FL) [8], and Artificial Neural Networks [26]. The LQR controllers provide an optimal controller for linear time invariant (LTI) systems that minimizes a quadratic cost function and guarantees stability and robustness. Though the LQR design is not directly applicable to non-linear systems, often non-linear systems are approximated by linear systems via linearization around the equilibrium point, thus enabling the application of the LQR based design. Although the LQR controller provides good performance for LTI systems [28], studies have shown that the ANN controllers have better performance in the presence of uncertain environments [26]. The ANN controller is especially suitable for adaptive flight control applications,

© The Author(s) 2021
A. Silva and K. R. M. Leino (Eds.) CAV 2021, LNCS 12759, pp. 566–579, 2021.
https://doi.org/10.1007/978-3-030-81685-8_27

where system dynamics are dominated by unknown nonlinearities [19]. An aircraft can experience a number of issues that may cause failures in the system. Things like over-acceleration can cause the aircraft to gain too much energy and enter into unstable modes, while rapid de-acceleration and hard maneuvers will cause increased structural loading, leading to broken lifting platforms. Another issue is that of stall, in which the airflow over the lifting section crosses a "critical angle of attack", compromising the lift generation. All of these problems can occur as a function of the control input or as external disturbances, such as high wind gust, further complicating the problem. Though ANN-based adaptive controllers are capable of handling these situations, guaranteeing safe functionality of these systems remains a challenge due to the complexity of these controllers. So, we have LQR-based controllers on one hand, that are efficient in nominal conditions, and are simple enough to be amenable to analysis, and sophisticated ANN-based controllers on the other hand that can handle difficult environmental conditions, but are, at the same time, too complex to be amenable to analysis. Our solution is a "hybrid controller" consisting of a simplex like architecture [7], wherein, we switch between the ANN and LQR controller in such a way that safety is guaranteed by the switching logic, that is, the aircraft is always recoverable from a stall within a fixed amount of time if it occurs.

Our broad objective is to find an ANN-based controller that can improve performance in uncertain environments. To achieve this goal, we need to train the ANN-controller, however, it is risky to train an ANN controller during a real flight test as it poses a safety risk. Hence, the solution we propose is to switch between a traditional LQR controller and the ANN controller in such a way that safety is guaranteed. More precisely, we allow the ANN controller to operate while the aircraft remains within a "safe zone" from which the LQR controller can guarantee that the aircraft never stalls. When the ANN controller is on the verge of leaving the safe zone, we switch to the LQR controller. However, these expert determined safe zones are often too conservative (small), thereby not providing sufficient time of operation for the ANN controller. A longer duration of operation for the ANN controller is desirable for the learning process, so we provide a method to extend the safe zone to a larger set ("recoverable zone"), which guarantees that the aircraft recovers within a fixed amount of time if a stall occurs. The recoverable zone computation is performed using formal methods based reachable set computation, thereby providing a formally verified switching component decision procedure that guarantees the safe operation of the aircraft.

We consider a dynamic model of a fixed-wing aircraft, with six-degrees-of-freedom (6-DOF), which is used as an experimental platform to employ a hybrid controller that consists of an intelligent and automatic switching between an LQR and an ANN based controller. The aircraft dynamics consists of a decoupled longitudinal and lateral linear time invariant dynamics, with a decoupled state-feedback LQR controller for each component. For our simulations, we consider an ANN controller that combines aircraft guidance and control systems and performs end-to-end mapping from error states to control surface values, in order to fly along a straight line with steady state wings-level and altitude hold.

We have performed Hardware in The Loop (HITL) simulation of the hybrid controller in conjunction with the the 6-DOF differential equations, on the aircraft avionics using the open source software, QGroundControl. Our simulations exhibit that the number of sample iterations for which ANN controller actions are performed while ensuring safe flying, increases as the learning space (recoverable zone) is expanded.

2   Related Work

Artificial Neural Networks have been widely used in many control applications, such as automatic generation control of interconnected power systems [41], irrigation scheduling [37], micro-turbine power plant [36], solar binding [4], robotics [1,6], and aircraft control [17]. ANN is popularly used in flight control [19], robot control [25] as well as for non-linear systems [42].

Verification has been extensively applied to dynamical systems, and focus on over-approximation based methods including predicate abstraction [3,22], state-space exploration based fix-point computation [14], Hamilton-Jacobi based methods [2], symbolic state space exploration based methods [16], Satisfiability Modulo Theory (SMT) based methods [20,21,23,38], and counter-example guided abstraction-refinement based methods [24,31,32].

Recent studies [40] compare several neural network verification algorithms. Formal verification of feedforward neural networks with different activation functions, such as ReLU [18] and Lipschitz-continuous functions [33], have been studied. Different verification problems have been considered including output range analysis [10], and robustness analysis [15]. Verification methods include those based on reduction to satisfiability solving [18], optimization solving [12], abstract interpretation [35], abstraction-refinement [30], and linearization [13]. Verification of ANN with feedback controllers has been explored [11].

In this paper, one of the problems we study is stall. The stall could occur due to many reasons. Researchers have developed different techniques to avoid or recover from the stall. Deep stall has been studied [27], which is an uncontrollable state at which the angle of attack (AOA) increases automatically and will be locked at a certain AOA which is far beyond the critical angle of attack. A stall due to wing has been studied [39]. The stall avoidance/recovery have been studied [9]. Here, we present a hybrid controller consisting of ANN and LQR controller similar to simplex design [7], which will not only recover, but also provide more learning space for the ANN controller to explore. Our hybrid controller is different from the simplex design [7] in many perspectives. Our hybrid controller makes the decision between ANN and LQR control input via safety checking performed based on an under-approximation reach set, which is computed off-line. However, in the work [7], the analysis is performed based on an over-approximation reach set. Also, in the work [7], an initial set is known; however, in our work, a target set ("safe zone") is known and the initial set is unknown.

3   Hybrid Controller Architecture

In this section, we provide details of the hybrid controller architecture which is shown in Fig. 1. It has mainly four components: (a) Aircraft dynamics, (b) LQR controller (c) ANN controller, and (d) Switching logic. For the aircraft dynamics, we consider a 6-DOF model of the fixed wing aircraft. The hybrid controller consists of the LQR and the ANN controller, and the switching logic; the LQR and the ANN controller each receive the state of the aircraft periodically (which is obtained from the aircraft dynamics model in the simulations) and compute the inputs to the aircraft. The switching logic decides which input is fed back to the aircraft (dynamics) at each sample time, based on the current state of the system. The state of the system (dynamics) is updated according to the input selected. We note that the details of the ANN controller is not important for the correctness of this work, since the safety is guaranteed even when the ANN control is considered as a black box. However, we adapt the ANN controller from the work [34] for the ANN component of the hybrid controller. We briefly describe the important aspects of the aircraft dynamics, LQR controller and the switching logic.

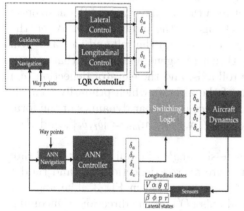

Input: : **Switch(x, τ, $\mathcal{S}$):**
    x - Current state,
    τ - Sample time interval,
    $\mathcal{S}$ - Safe zone
Output: **u** - Control input
1:   $\mathbf{u}_{ann} = \mathbf{ANN}(\mathbf{x})$
2:   $\mathbf{x}' = \mathbf{nextstate}(\mathbf{x}, \mathbf{u}_{ann}, \tau)$
3:   **if** $\mathbf{x}' \in \mathcal{S}$ **then**
4:     **return** $\mathbf{u}_{ann}$
5:   **else**
6:     $\mathbf{u}_{lqr} = \mathbf{LQR}(\mathbf{x})$
7:     **return** $\mathbf{u}_{lqr}$
8:   **end if**

Fig. 1. Hybrid controller architecture

Fig. 2. Switching Logic for LQR and ANN controller

3.1   Aircraft Dynamics

We start with a brief description of the aircraft states and motion. The aircraft has 3 axes, the roll axis (I), pitch axis (J) and yaw axis (K) as shown in Fig. 3. Motion occurs in two planes, the longitudinal, axes (I) and (K), and lateral, axes (I) and (J), which are often considered to be decoupled.

In the longitudinal plane, the states are, velocity (V), angle of attack (α), pitch angle (θ) and pitch rate (q), and control inputs are thrust (δ_t) and elevator

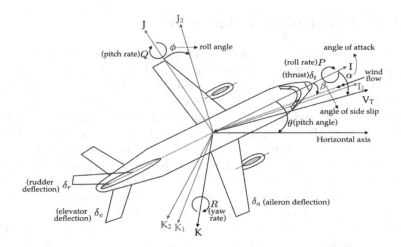

Fig. 3. Overview of aircraft

deflection δ_e. All the states and control inputs are shown in Fig. 3. The angle of attack (α) is the angle between the roll axis (I) and the direction of velocity (V). The pitch angle (θ) is the angle between the roll axis (I) and the horizontal axis. The pitch rate (q) is the rate of change in the pitch angle θ. When the pitch angle (θ) changes, the lateral plane rotates and the roll and yaw axes will change to I_1 and K_1, respectively. The thrust (δ_t) generates a force that is used to move the aircraft forward along the roll axis, and the elevator deflection (δ_e) is a control surface located at the rear of the aircraft which primarily controls the pitch angle (θ). The longitudinal dynamics is a linear dynamics of the form $\dot{\mathbf{x}}_{lon} = A_{lon}\mathbf{x}_{lon} + B_{lon}\mathbf{u}_{lon}$, where $\mathbf{x}_{lon} = [V, \alpha, \theta, q]'$, $\mathbf{u}_{lon} = [\delta_t, \delta_e]'$, and A_{lon} and B_{lon} are specific matrices.

In the lateral plane, the states are, side-slip angle (β), roll angle (ϕ), roll rate (p) and yaw rate (r), and control inputs are aileron deflection (δ_a) and rudder deflection (δ_r). The states and control inputs are shown Fig. 3. The angle of side-slip (β) is the angle between the roll axis (I) and the direction of incoming airflow. When the roll axis I rotates, the pitch axis (J) and the yaw axis (K) will change to J_2 and K_2, respectively. The roll angle (ϕ) is the angle between J and J_2. The roll rate (p) is the rate of change in the roll angle (ϕ). The yaw rate (r) is the rotational rate of change in the yaw axis (K). The aileron deflection (δ_a) is the control surface which is used to control the rotation of the roll axis (I). The rudder deflection (δ_r) is the control surface which is used to control the rotation of the yaw axis (K). The lateral dynamics is a linear dynamics of the form $\dot{\mathbf{x}}_{lat} = A_{lat}\mathbf{x}_{lat} + B_{lat}\mathbf{u}_{lat}$, where $\mathbf{x}_{lat} = [\beta, \phi, p, r]'$, $\mathbf{u}_{lat} = [\delta_a, \delta_r]'$, and A_{lat} and B_{lat} are specific matrices.

3.2   LQR Controller

Linear Quadratic Regulator (LQR) controller for a linear dynamics $\dot{x} = Ax + Bu$ is an optimal controller that minimizes a quadratic cost function (J). It is a linear state feedback controller of the form $-Kx$, where K is referred to as the gain matrix. The closed loop dynamics is given by $\dot{x} = (A - BK)\mathbf{x}$; which is the system behavior when controller by the LQR controller. Since the longitudinal and lateral dynamics of the aircraft are decoupled, we have an LQR controller for each component with gains K_{lon} and K_{lat}, resulting in corresponding closed loop systems, $\dot{\mathbf{x}}_{lon} = (A_{lon} - B_{lon}K_{lon})\mathbf{x}_{lon}$ and $\dot{\mathbf{x}}_{lat} = (A_{lat} - B_{lat}K_{lat})\mathbf{x}_{lat}$.

3.3   Switching Algorithm for the Safety of ANN Controller

Stall is one of the important issues for any aircraft. Stall is a condition in which the angle of attack surpasses a critical bound and greatly decreases lift generation. Consequently, the aircraft will start rapidly descending. Additional problems occur when the aircraft encounters large accelerations, primarily about the roll and yaw axes, which can lead the aircraft into an unstable spiral mode, a dangerous and usually unrecoverable event. Finally, rapid maneuvers can lead to large loads on the aircraft structure, causing permanent deformation or breaking the structure altogether. Generally, exact constraints for these problems cannot be found due to the complexity of aircraft motion. However, a set of safe constraints has been generated for the testbed aircraft by examining previous flight test data in which problems did not occur.

The objective of the switching logic is to arbitrate the switching between the LQR and ANN based controllers, while maintaining safety and at the same time providing ANN controller the maximum opportunity to operate, and thereby learn. Our premise is that we have some known safe zone $\mathcal{S}$ give by an expert in which LQR controller actions are safe, that is, if we apply control input $\mathbf{u} = -K\mathbf{x}$, when $\mathbf{x} \in \mathcal{S}$, to the LTI dynamics of the aircraft, then the aircraft never stalls. However, if we apply control input $\mathbf{u}'$ obtained by the ANN controller at a state $\mathbf{x} \in \mathcal{S}$, we cannot ensure that the system never stalls. Computing such a safe zone for an ANN controller would be computationally hard. Hence, the switching algorithm computes the effect of applying $\mathbf{u}'$ computed by the ANN controller, and decides to pass it on to the system, if it infers that the system will be safe in the next step. Otherwise, it outputs the input suggested by the LQR controller. In either case, it ensures that the system is in the $\mathcal{S}$ region at all times during the operation of the flight. The details of the switching algorithm are provided in Fig. 2.

The performance of the hybrid controller depends on the safe zone. The safe zone obtained by expert advice is often conservative. Hence, we provide a method to extend the safe zone ("recoverable zone") for which the switching algorithm guarantees that the system is always recoverable within the fixed duration if it occurs. Next, we provide the details of computing the recoverable zone.

4   Computation of Recoverable Zone

In this section, we provide the details of computing a recoverable zone for the fixed time $T > 0$. Our broad goal is to compute all those states from which the given safe zone S can be reached within the time $T > 0$ for an LTI dynamics of aircraft which is in the form of $\dot{\mathbf{x}} = (A - BK)\mathbf{x}$, where K is an LQR control gain matrix. This is the problem of computing the backward reach set of a linear system

$$\dot{\mathbf{x}} = C\mathbf{x} \tag{1}$$

where $C = A - BK$. The solution of a linear system $\dot{\mathbf{x}} = C\mathbf{x}$ is given by $x(t) = e^{Ct}x(0)$, where $x(t)$ is the state of the system at time t. Hence, we define the backward reach set for a given linear closed loop system as follows:

Definition 1. *[Backward Reach Set] Given a linear closed loop system $\dot{\mathbf{x}} = A\mathbf{x}$, a time horizon $T > 0$, and a final set of states $\mathcal{X}_f$, the backward reach set $Reach_B(\mathcal{X}_f, A, [0, T])$ is defined as follows:*

$$Reach_B(\mathcal{X}_f, A, [0, T]) = \{\boldsymbol{x} \mid \exists\, t \in [0, T], e^{At}\boldsymbol{x} \in \mathcal{X}_f\}.$$

Next, we formally define the recoverable zone in terms of backward reach set.

Definition 2. *[Recoverable Zone] Given system in Eq. (1), a time horizon $T > 0$, and a safe zone S, a recoverable zone S' is defined as follows:*
$S' = Reach_B(S, C, [0, T])$.

The computation of the recoverable zone S' can be alternatively tackled using a forward reachability analysis on the following transformed equation.

$$\dot{\mathbf{x}} = -C\mathbf{x} \tag{2}$$

We define forward reach set for a given linear closed loop system as follows:

Definition 3. *[Forward Reach Set] Given a linear closed loop system $\dot{\mathbf{x}} = A\mathbf{x}$, a time horizon $T > 0$, and an initial set of states $\mathcal{X}_0$, forward reach set $Reach_F(\mathcal{X}_0, A, [0, T])$ is defined as follows:*

$$Reach_F(\mathcal{X}_0, A, [0, T]) = \{e^{At}\boldsymbol{x}_0 \mid \exists\, t \in [0, T], \exists\, \boldsymbol{x}_0 \in \mathcal{X}_0\}.$$

Equation (2) is obtained from Eq. (1) by negating the right hand side. The effect of the transformation is that the system now evolves backward in time. We notice that the set of states that can reach S within time T from Equation (1) ($Reach_B(S, C, [0, T])$) is equal to the set of states reached using Equation (2) from S in a given time horizon $T > 0$ ($Reach_F(S, C, [0, T])$). Next, we formulate this equivalence of forward and backward reach sets of the two systems, namely Equations (1), (2) in Theorem 1.

Theorem 1. *Given systems in Equation (1) and Equation (2), a time horizon* $T > 0$, *a safe zone* $\mathcal{S}$, *we have* $Reach_F(\mathcal{S}, -C, [0, T]) = Reach_B(\mathcal{S}, C, [0, T])$.

The computation of the exact recoverable zone is complex because the solution of Equation (2) consists of exponential function, and there are no known algorithms for solving constraints with exponential functions, unlike solvers for linear and polynomial functions. Hence, several over-approximation methods have been investigated [5,16,20,29,31,32]. An over-approximated recoverable zone violates the property of the recoverable zone, that is, it contains point that are not guaranteed to reach the safe zone within the time bound. In this situation, the stall may not be recoverable if it occurs. Therefore, we compute an under-approximation of the exact recoverable zone $\mathcal{S}'$ which is conservative, nevertheless, ensures the safety of the switching algorithm.

4.1   Under-Approximation of Recoverable Zone

In this section, we provide a method to compute an under-approximation of the exact recoverable zone $\mathcal{S}'$. While computing under-approximations are in general hard, we use a simple idea that provides a practically viable under-approximation for our purposes. Our broad approach is based on sampling, and consists of an under-approximate reach set which is the union of the reach set at certain time points, as opposed to all the points in the given interval. We sample the time interval $[0, T]$ at sample times that are multiples of r. Then, we compute forward reach set from safe zone $\mathcal{S}$ under Equation (2) at sample times $r, 2r, \ldots, kr = T$ and take their union, that is, the under-approximation of the recoverable zone denoted $Approx(\mathcal{S})$ is $\bigcup\limits_{i=0}^{k} Reach_F(\mathcal{S}, -C, ir)$, where $Reach(\mathcal{S}, -C, ir)$ denotes the forward reach set from $\mathcal{S}$ at time ir. Next, we show that $Approx(\mathcal{S})$ is an under-approximation of the recoverable zone $\mathcal{S}'$. We formulate this in Theorem 2.

Theorem 2. *Given system in Equation (2), a time horizon* $T > 0$, *a safe zone* $\mathcal{S}$, *we have* $Approx(\mathcal{S}) \subseteq Reach_F(\mathcal{S}, -C, [0, T])$.

Note that $Approx(\mathcal{S})$ converges to the exact recoverable zone $\mathcal{S}'$ as $r \to 0$.

5   Experimental Analysis

In this section, we provide the details of our implementation of hybrid controller architecture. Then, we present the experimental results.

5.1   Experimental Setup

The experimentation method for preliminary concept testing is a Hardware in The Loop (HITL) simulation. The HITL runs the 6-DOF differential equations, on the aircraft avionics, which are then propagated using a Runge-Kutta fourth order integration method.

Fig. 4. AFS 6.0   **Fig. 5.** HITL aggressive trajectory

This technique generates all aircraft states and control inputs that are necessary to the operation of the switch. The main advantage of conducting these simulations as an HITL rather than software simulations is that all the codes will be tested on the actual hardware used for flight, showcasing any shortcomings in computation power or integration missteps, which may impact flight test success.

The current avionics, Autopilot Flight System (AFS) 6.0, consists of three main components. Sensor data and outputs are handled by the Pixhawk 2.1 cube. The onboard computer which runs the in-house designed guidance, navigation and control (GNC) algorithms, as well as handles the state emulation is the Nvidia Tegra Nano. The Tegra Nano is a low cost system, with a quad-core CPU and a 128 core GPU. The final component is a 900 MHz telemetry unit which serves as the communication between the aircraft and the ground station, where the ground station provides a visual representation of the current aircraft state as well as relevant GNC information. The ground station used for these simulations is a modified version of the open source software, QGroundControl, which is also used to generate way-points for the given area of operation. Figure 4 shows both the front and back sides of the custom avionics boards.

While in HITL, the ANN controllers are very stable due to being trained with similar dynamic models to those that are used to propagate the simulation. This makes it unlikely to see the switching logic in action as no control inputs would be deemed unsafe, especially in grid or racetrack patterns that make up the majority of flight test operations. To circumvent this, an oddly shaped trajectory, shown in Fig. 5, with multiple sharp turns is used to ensure previously un-visited states are achieved. The simulation is run for approximately one lap of the given trajectory for each value of the time horizon shown in the following section.

5.2   Experimental Results

In this section, we present the simulation results for the performance of hybrid controller. For the simulation, we consider the safe zone provided by experts, which are given in Table 1. We run the simulation for different recoverable zones, which are computed for different values of time horizon T, namely, $T = 0.05$,

$T = 0.15$, $T = 0.25$, and $T = 0.35$ with time step $\tau = 0.05$ unit. The simulation results are shown in Figs. 6 and 7. The simulation results are plotted in Fig. 6 and Fig. 7 for longitudinal velocity and lateral angle of side-slip, respectively.

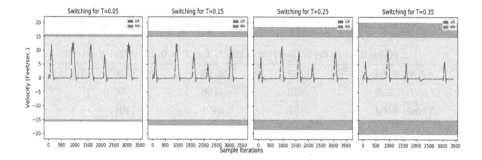

Fig. 6. Switching between ANN and LQR controller for the longitudinal velocity

Table 1. Safe zone for longitudinal and lateral state variables

Safe Zone	V (Feet/sec.)	α (Radians)	θ (Radians)	Q (Radians/sec.)	β (Radians)	ϕ (Radians)	P (Radians/sec.)	R (Radians/sec.)
Min	−15	−0.087	−0.262	−0.262	−0.122	−0.785	−0.873	−0.349
Max	15	0.087	0.262	0.262	0.122	0.785	0.873	0.349

In both Figs. 6 and 7, we observe that the recoverable zone expands when the time horizon T increases.

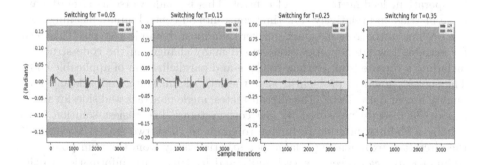

Fig. 7. Switching between ANN and LQR controller for the lateral angle of side-slip

Also, we observe that the number of sample iterations in which ANN controller actions are performed, increases when the recoverable zone is expanded. For instance, in Figs. 6 and 7, for $T = 0.35$, ANN controller actions have been performed from the sample iteration 1500 to 3000, which was not the case for $T = 0.25$. For clarity, in Table 2, we present the number of sample iterations N for both ANN and LQR controller in which their actions have been performed, for different values of time horizon T.

Table 2. Number of sample iterations for ANN and LQR controller

	N for $T = 0.05$	N for $T = 0.15$	N for $T = 0.25$	N for $T = 0.35$
ANN	3181	3269	3295	3345
LQR	220	132	106	56
Total	3401	3401	3401	3401

In Table 2, we observe that N grows for ANN controller when the time horizon T increases, that is, the recoverable zone is expanded. However, N decreases for LQR controller when T increases. This validate the fact that hybrid controller framework provides ample time for the ANN controller to learn while ensuring a safe flight.

5.3   Practical Challenges

The implementation of the hybrid controller proved to be complex in two ways. First, the timing of the switching logic was important to the overall safety of the project. When delays are introduced into the system, the current state of the aircraft and the information the switch is making the decision on can become out of sync. If the switching logic is behind the aircraft states it can make incorrect calls on whether or not the aircraft is still safe, and cause the ANN to overextend its operation, leading to a loss of control. This is made worse as aircraft have large inertias and relatively slow time constants on control inputs meaning they can become uncontrollable much quicker than most dynamic systems. This need for extreme low latency operation caused many changes in the code structure including a rewrite from Python to C++ and parallelization of applicable code. The second practical problem is that the lack of full state feedback and low-quality sensor data. Two of the aircraft states, angle of attack and sideslip angle, cannot be directly measured by low cost systems. The easiest solution is to employ a Kalman filtering technique to estimate these two states. However, if the aircraft is experiencing a large perturbation away from the trim point, the Kalman Filter can diverge very rapidly and feed incorrect information to the switch about the relevant states. On top of this, many of the measured states are taken using low-cost, off the shelf components. In a similar way, the use of these components may introduce noise or a bias which could allow the aircraft to go into the uncontrollable region without alerting the switch or the aircraft operator. Low pass filtering is applied to attempt to deal with the noise, but the imparted delay to the sensor data must also be taken into consideration.

6 Conclusions

We have developed a hybrid controller for an aircraft dynamics which provides considerable amount of time to the ANN controller to operate and learn, while at the same time guarantees the safe operation of the flight at all times. In future, we will consider more sophisticated ANN controllers and investigate methods for computing larger recoverable zones that allow for further increase of the ANN operation time. Additionally, experimentation will be done with real flight tests, moving past HITL simulations.

Acknowledgements. Pavithra Prabhakar was partially supported by NSF CAREER Grant No. 1552668, NSF Grant No. 2008957, ONR YIP Grant No. N000141712577 and USDA Grant No. 2017-67007-26153. Also, this work was partially supported with funding from National Aeronautics and Space Administration (NASA) Grant No. NNX15AJ97H and Grant No. 80NSSC19C0102.

References

1. Abdelhameed, M.M.: Adaptive neural network based controller for robots. Mechatronics **9**, 147–162 (1999)
2. Akametalu, A.K., Fisac, J.F., Gillula, J.H., Kaynama, S., Zeilinger, M.N., Tomlin, C.J.: Reachability-based safe learning with gaussian processes. In: Conference on Decision and Control (2014)
3. Alur, R., Dang, T., Ivancic, F.: Predicate abstraction for reachability analysis of hybrid systems. ACM Trans. Embedded Comput. Syst. (TECS) **5**, 152–199 (2006)
4. Argiriou, A.A., Bellas-Velidis, I., Kummert, M., André, P.: A neural network controller for hydronic heating systems of solar buildings. Neural Netw. **17**, 472–440 (2004)
5. Asarin, E., Bournez, O., Dang, T., Maler, O.: Approximate reachability analysis of piecewise-linear dynamical systems. Computation and Control. In: International Workshop on Hybrid Systems (2000)
6. Azhar, M.A.H.B., Dimond, K.R.: Design of an FPGA based adaptive neural controller for intelligent robot navigation. In: Proceedings Euromicro Symposium on Digital System Design. Architectures, Methods and Tools (2002)
7. Bak, S., Johnson, T.T., Caccamo, M., Sha, L.: Real-time reachability for verified simplex design. In: IEEE Real-Time Systems Symposium (2014)
8. Bhangal, N.S.: Design and performance of LQR and LQR based fuzzy controller for double inverted pendulum system. J. Image Graph. **1**, 143–146 (2013)
9. Brown, J.A.: Stall avoidance system for aircraft, 1986. US Patent 4,590,475 (1986)
10. Dutta, S., Chen, X., Sankaranarayanan, S.: Reachability analysis for neural feedback systems using regressive polynomial rule inference. In: International Conference on Hybrid Systems: Computation and Control, (2019)
11. Dutta, S., Jha, S., Sankaranarayanan, S., Tiwari, A.: Output range analysis for deep feedforward neural networks. In: NASA Formal Methods Symposium (2018)
12. Dvijotham, K., Stanforth, R., Gowal, S., Mann, T.A., Kohli, P.: A dual approach to scalable verification of deep networks. CoRR, abs/1803.06567 (2018)
13. Ehlers, R.: Formal verification of piece-wise linear feed-forward neural networks. In: D'Souza, D., Kumar, K.N. (eds.) Automated Technology for Verification and Analysis (2017)

14. Frehse, G., et al.: SpaceEX: scalable verification of hybrid systems. In: International Conference on Computer Aided Verification (2011)
15. Gehr, T., Mirman, M., Drachsler-Cohen, D., Tsankov, P., Chaudhuri, S., Vechev, M.T.: AI2: safety and robustness certification of neural networks with abstract interpretation. In: IEEE Symposium on Security and Privacy (2018)
16. Girard, A.: Reachability of uncertain linear systems using zonotopes. Computation and Control. In: International Workshop on Hybrid Systems (2005)
17. Julian, K.D., Kochenderfer, M.J., Owen, M.P.: Deep Neural Network Compression for Aircraft Collision Avoidance Systems. arXiv e-prints (2018)
18. Katz, G., Barrett, C.W., Dill, D.L., Julian, K., Kochenderfer, M.J.: Reluplex: an efficient SMT solver for verifying deep neural networks. CoRR (2017)
19. Khosravani, M.R.: Application of neural network on flight control. Int. J. Mach. Learn. Comput. **2**, 882–885 (2012)
20. Lal, R., Prabhakar, P.: Bounded error flowpipe computation of parameterized linear systems. In: International Conference on Embedded Software (2015)
21. Lal, R., Prabhakar, P.: Safety analysis using compositional bounded error approximations of communicating hybrid systems. In: IEEE 56th Annual Conference on Decision and Control (CDC) (2017)
22. Lal, R., Prabhakar, P.: Hierarchical abstractions for reachability analysis of probabilistic hybrid systems. In: 56th Annual Allerton Conference on Communication, Control, and Computing (Allerton) (2018)
23. Lal, R., Prabhakar, P.: Compositional construction of bounded error over-approximations of acyclic interconnected continuous dynamical systems. In: ACM-IEEE International Conference on Formal Methods and Models for System Design (2019)
24. Lal, R., Prabhakar, P.: Counterexample guided abstraction refinement for polyhedral probabilistic hybrid systems. ACM Trans. Embedded Comput. Syst. (TECS) **18**, 1–23 (2019)
25. Lewis, F.W., Jagannathan, S., Yesildirak, A.: Neural Network Control of Robot Manipulators and Non-linear Systems. CRC Press, Boca Raton (1998)
26. Mehri, M.: A comparison of neural network models, fuzzy logic, and multiple linear regression for prediction of hatchability. Poult. Sci. **92**, 1138–1142 (2013)
27. Montgomery, R.C., Moul, M.T.: Analysis of deep-stall characteristics of t-tailed aircraft configurations and some recovery procedures. J. Airc. **3**, 562–566 (1966)
28. Nair, V.G., Dileep, M.V., George, V.: Aircraft yaw control system using LQR and fuzzy logic controller. Int. J. Comput. Appl. **45**, 25–30 (2012)
29. Prabhakar, P., Viswanathan, M.: A dynamic algorithm for approximate flow computations. In: International Conference on Hybrid Systems: Computation and Control (2011)
30. Pulina, L., Tacchella, A.: An abstraction-refinement approach to verification of artificial neural networks. In: International Conference on Computer Aided Verification (2010)
31. Roohi, N., Prabhakar, P., Viswanathan, M.: HARE: A Hybrid Abstraction Refinement Engine for Verifying Non-linear Hybrid Automata. In: Legay, A., Margaria, T. (eds.) TACAS 2017. LNCS, vol. 10205, pp. 573–588. Springer, Heidelberg (2017). https://doi.org/10.1007/978-3-662-54577-5_33
32. Roohi, N., Prabhakar, P., Viswanathan, M.: Hybridization based CEGAR for hybrid automata with affine dynamics. In: International Conference on Tools and Algorithms for the Construction and Analysis of Systems (2016)
33. Ruan, W., Huang, X., Kwiatkowska, M.: Reachability analysis of deep neural networks with provable guarantees. CoRR, abs/1805.02242 (2018)

34. Shukla, D., Lal, R., Hauptman, D., Keshmiri, S.S., Prabhakar, P., Beckage, N.: Flight test validation of a safety-critical neural network based longitudinal controller for a fixed-wing UAS. In: AIAA AVIATION (2020)
35. Singh, G., Gehr, T., Püschel, M., Vechev, M.T.: An abstract domain for certifying neural networks. PACMPL 3(POPL), 41:1–41:30 (2019)
36. Sisworahardjo, N.S., El-Sharkh, M.Y., Alam, M.S.: Neural network controller for microturbine power plants. Electr. Power Syst. Res. **78**, 1378–1384 (2008)
37. Umair, S.M., Usman, R.: Automation of irrigation system using ANN based controller. Int. J. Electr. Comput. Sci. (2010)
38. Veanes, M., Bjørner, N., Raschke, A.: An SMT approach to bounded reachability analysis of model programs. In: International Conference on Formal Techniques for Networked and Distributed Systems (2008)
39. Wang, T.: Aircraft wing stall control device and method, 1987. US Patent 4,702,441 (1987)
40. Xiang, W., et al.: Verification for machine learning, autonomy, and neural networks survey. CoRR, abs/1810.01989 (2018)
41. Zeynelgil, H.L., Demiroren, A., Sengor, N.S.: The application of ANN technique to automatic generation control for multi-area power system. Int. J. Electr. Power Energy Systems (2002)
42. Zhang, T., Ge, S.S., Hang, C.C.: Adaptive neural network control for strict-feedback nonlinear systems using backstepping design. Automatica **36**, 1835–1846 (2000)

SceneChecker: Boosting Scenario Verification Using Symmetry Abstractions

Hussein Sibai[✉], Yangge Li, and Sayan Mitra

Coordinated Science Laboratory, University of Illinois
at Urbana-Champaign, Urbana, USA
{sibai2,li213,mitras}@illinois.edu

Abstract. We present SceneChecker, a tool for verifying scenarios involving vehicles executing complex plans in large cluttered workspaces. SceneChecker converts the scenario verification problem to a standard hybrid system verification problem, and solves it effectively by exploiting structural properties in the plan and the vehicle dynamics. SceneChecker uses symmetry abstractions, a novel refinement algorithm, and importantly, is built to boost the performance of any existing reachability analysis tool as a plug-in subroutine. We evaluated SceneChecker on several scenarios involving ground and aerial vehicles with nonlinear dynamics and neural network controllers, employing different kinds of symmetries, using different reachability subroutines, and following plans with hundreds of waypoints in complex workspaces. Compared to two leading tools, DryVR and Flow*, SceneChecker shows $14\times$ average speedup in verification time, even while using those very tools as reachability subroutines.

Keywords: Hybrid systems · Safety verification · Symmetry

1 Introduction

Remarkable progress has been made in safety verification of hybrid and cyber-physical systems in the last decade [2–9]. The methods and tools developed have been applied to check safety of aerospace, medical, and autonomous vehicle control systems [4,5,10,11]. The next barrier in making these techniques usable for more complex applications is to deal with what is colloquially called the *scenario verification problem*. A key part of the scenario verification problem is to check that a vehicle or an agent can execute a plan through a complex environment. A planning algorithm (e.g., probabilistic roadmaps [12] and rapidly-exploring random trees (RRTs) [13]) generates a set of possible paths avoiding obstacles, but only considering the geometry of the scenario, not the dynamics. The verification task has to ensure that the plan can indeed

---

The authors are supported by a research grant from The Boeing Company and a research grant from NSF (FMITF: 1918531). We would like to thank John L. Olson, Aaron A. Mayne, and Michael R. Abraham from The Boeing Company for valuable technical discussions.

A. Silva and K. R. M. Leino (Eds.) CAV 2021, LNCS 12759, pp. 580–594, 2021.
https://doi.org/10.1007/978-3-030-81685-8_28

be safely executed by the vehicle with all the dynamic constraints and the state estimation uncertainties. Indeed, one can view a scenario as a hybrid automaton with the modes defined by the segments of the planner, but this leads to massive models. Encoding such automata in existing tools presents some practical hurdles. More importantly, analyzing such models is challenging as the over-approximation errors and the analysis times grow rapidly with the number of transitions. At the same time, such large hybrid verification problems also have lots of repetitions and symmetries, which suggest new opportunities.

We present SceneChecker, a tool that implements a symmetry abstraction-refinement algorithm for efficient scenario verification. Symmetry abstractions significantly reduce the number of modes and edges of an automaton H by grouping all modes that share symmetric continuous dynamics [14]. SceneChecker implements a novel refinement algorithm for symmetry abstractions and is able to use any existing reachability analysis tool as a subroutine. Our current implementation comes with plug-ins for using Flow* [4] and DryVR [6]. SceneChecker's verification algorithm is sound, i.e., if it returns *safe*, then the reachset of H indeed does not intersect the unsafe set. The algorithm is lossless in the sense that if one can prove safety without using abstraction, then SceneChecker can also prove safety via abstraction-refinement, and typically a lot faster. SceneChecker can be found on figshare: https://figshare.com/articles/software/CAV2021_reduce_v6_ova/14504352 and its website: https://publish.illinois.edu/scenechecker/. An extended version of this paper is available online [1].

SceneChecker offers an easy interface to specify plans, agent dynamics, obstacles, initial uncertainty, and symmetry maps. SceneChecker checks if a fixed point has been reached after each call to the reachability subroutine, avoiding repeating computations. First, SceneChecker represents the input scenario as a hybrid automaton H where modes are defined by the plan's segments. It uses the symmetry maps provided by the user to construct an abstract automaton H_v. Automaton H_v represents another scenario with fewer segments, each representing an equivalence class of symmetric segments in H. A side effect of the abstraction is that upon reaching waypoints in H_v, the agent's state resets non-deterministically to a set of possible states. For example, in the case of rotation and translation invariance, the abstract scenario would have a single segment for any set of segments with a unique length in the original scenario. SceneChecker refines H_v by splitting one of its modes to two modes. That corresponds to representing a set of symmetric segments with one more segment in the abstract scenario, capturing more accurately the original scenario[1].

We evaluated SceneChecker on several scenarios where car and quadrotor agents with nonlinear dynamics follow plans to reach several destinations in 2D and 3D workspaces with hundreds of waypoints and polytopic obstacles. We considered different symmetries (translation and rotation invariance) and controllers (Proportional-Derivative (PD) and Neural Networks (NN)). We compared the verification time of SceneChecker with DryVR and Flow* as reachability subroutines against Flow* and DryVR as standalone tools. SceneChecker is faster than both tools in all scenarios considered, achieving an average of $14\times$ speedup in verification time (Table 1). In certain scenarios where Flow* timed out (executing for more than 120 min), SceneChecker

---

[1] A figure showing the architecture of SceneChecker can be found in the extended version [1].

is able to complete verification in as fast as 12 min using Flow* as a subroutine. SceneChecker when using abstraction-refinement achieved 13× speedup in verification time over not using abstraction-refinement in scenarios with the NN-controlled quadrotor (Sect. 7).

Related Work. The idea of using symmetries to accelerate verification has been exploited in a number of contexts such as probabilistic models [15,16], automata [17,18], distributed architectures [19], and hardware [20,21]. Some symmetry utilization algorithms are implemented in Murφ [22] and Uppaal [23].

In our context of cyber-physical systems, Bak et al. [24] suggested using symmetry maps, called *reachability reduction transformations*, to transform reachsets to symmetric reachsets for continuous dynamical systems modeling non-interacting vehicles. Maidens et al. [25] proposed a symmetry-based dimensionality reduction method for backward reachable set computations for discrete dynamical systems. Majumdar et al. [26] proposed a safe motion planning algorithm that computes a family of reachsets offline and composes them online using symmetry. Bujorianu et al. [27] presented a symmetry-based theory to reduce stochastic hybrid systems for faster reachability analysis and discussed the challenges of designing symmetry reduction techniques across mode transitions.

In a more closely related research, we presented a modified version of DryVR that utilizes symmetry to cache reachsets aiming to accelerate simulation-based safety verification of continuous dynamical systems [28]. We developed the related tool CacheReach that implements a hybrid system verification algorithm that uses symmetry to accelerate reachability analysis [29]. CacheReach caches and shares computed reachsets between different modes of non-interacting agents using symmetry. SceneChecker is based on the theory of symmetry abstractions of hybrid automata we presented in [14]. We suggested computing the reachset of the abstract automaton instead of the concrete one then transform it to the concrete reachset using symmetry maps to accelerate verification. SceneChecker is built based on this line of work with significant algorithmic and engineering improvements. In addition to the abstraction of [14], SceneChecker 1) maps the unsafe set to an abstract unsafe set and verifies the abstract automaton instead of the concrete one and 2) decreases the over-approximation error of the abstraction through refinement. SceneChecker does not cache reachsets and thus saves cache-access and reachset-transformation times and does not incur over-approximation errors due to caching that CacheReach suffers from [29]. At the implementation level, SceneChecker accepts plans that are general directed graphs and polytopic unsafe sets while CacheReach accepts only single-path plans and hyperrectangle unsafe sets. We show more than 30× speedup in verification time while having more accurate verification results when comparing SceneChecker against CacheReach (Table 1 in Sect. 7).

2   Specifying Scenarios in SceneChecker

A scenario verification problem is specified by a set of fixed obstacles, a plan, and an agent that is supposed to execute the plan without running into the obstacles (e.g., see

Fig. 1B). For ground and air vehicles, for example, the agent moves in a subset of the 2D or the 3D Euclidean space called the *workspace*. A *plan* is a directed graph $G = \langle V, S \rangle$ with vertices V in the workspace called *waypoints* and edges S called *segments*[2]. A general graph allows for nondeterministic and contingency planning.

An *agent* is a control system that can follow waypoints. Let the state space of the agent be X and $\Theta \subseteq X$ be the uncertain initial set. Let s_{init} be the initial segment in G that the agent has to follow. From any state $x \in X$, the agent follows a segment $s \in S$ by moving along a *trajectory*. A trajectory is a function $\xi : X \times S \times \mathbb{R}^{\geq 0} \to X$ that meets certain dynamical constraints of the vehicle. Dynamics are either specified by ordinary differential equations (ODE) or by a black-box simulator. For ODE models, ξ is a solution of an equation of the form: $\frac{d\xi}{dt}(x, s, t) = f(\xi(x, s, t), s)$, for any $t \in \mathbb{R}^{\geq 0}$ and $\xi(x, s, 0) = x$, where $f : X \times S \to X$ is Lipschitz continuous in the first argument. Note that the trajectories only depend on the segment the agent is following (and not on the full plan G). We denote by ξ.*fstate*, ξ.*lstate*, and ξ.*dom* the initial and last states and the time domain of the time bounded trajectory ξ, respectively.

We can view the obstacles near each segment as sets of unsafe states, $O : S \to 2^X$. The map *tbound* $: S \to \mathbb{R}^{\geq 0}$ determines the maximum time the agent should spend in following any segment. For any pair of consecutive segments (s, s'), i.e. sharing a common waypoint in G, *guard*$((s, s'))$ defines the set of states (a hyperrectangle around a waypoint) at which the agent is allowed to transition from following s to following s'.

Scenario JSON file is the first of the two user inputs. It specifies the scenario: Θ as a hyperrectangle; S as a list of lists each representing two waypoints; *guard* as a list of hyperrectangles; *tbound* as a list of floats; and O as a list of polytopes. Output of SceneChecker is the scenario verification result (*safe* or *unknown*) and a number of useful performance metrics, such as the number of mode-splits, number of reachability calls, reachsets computation time, and total time. SceneChecker can also visualize the various computed reachsets.

---

3   Transforming Scenarios to Hybrid Automata

The input scenario is first represented as a hybrid automaton by a Hybrid constructor. This constructor is a Python function that parses the Scenario file and constructs the data structures to store the scenario's hybrid automaton components. In what follows, we describe the constructed automaton informally. In our current implementation, sets are represented either as hyper-rectangles or as polytopes using the Tulip Polytope Library[3].

---

[2] We introduce this redundant nomenclature because later we will reserve the term edges to talk about mode transitions in hybrid automata. We use waypoints instead of vertices as a more natural term for points that vehicles have to follow.

[3] https://pypi.org/project/polytope/.

Scenario as a Hybrid Automaton. A hybrid automaton has a set of *modes* (or discrete states) and a set of continuous states. The evolution of the continuous states in each mode is specified by a set of trajectories and the transition across the modes are specified by *guard* and *reset* maps. The agent following a plan in a workspace can be naturally modeled as a hybrid automaton H, where s_{init} and Θ are its initial mode and set of states.

Each segment $s \in S$ of the plan G defines a *mode* of H (e.g. see Fig. 1A). The set of edges $E \subseteq S \times S$ of H is defined as pairs of consecutive segments in G. For an edge $e \in E$, $guard(e)$ is the same as that of G. The *reset* map of H is the identity map. We will see in Sect. 5 that abstract automata will have nontrivial reset maps.

Verification Problem. An *execution* of length k is a sequence $\sigma := (\xi_0, s_0), \ldots, (\xi_k, s_k)$. It models the behavior of the agent following a particular path in the plan G. An execution σ must satisfy: 1) $\xi_0.fstate \in \Theta$ and $s_0 = s_{init}$, for each $i \in \{0, \ldots, k-1\}$, 2) $(s_i, s_{i+1}) \in E$, 3) $\xi_i.lstate \in guard((s_i, s_{i+1}))$, and 4) $\xi_i.lstate = \xi_{i+1}.fstate$, and 5) for each $i \in \{0, \ldots, k\}$, $\xi_i.dom \leq tbound(s_i)$. The set of *reachable states* is $Reach_H := \{\sigma.lstate \mid \sigma$ is an execution$\}$. The restriction of $Reach_H$ to states with mode $s \in S$ (i.e., agent following segment s) is denoted by $Reach_H(s)$. Thus, the hybrid system verification problem requires us to check whether $\forall s \in S$, $Reach_H(s) \cap O(s) = \emptyset$.

4   Specifying Symmetry Maps in SceneChecker

The hybrid automaton representing a scenario, as constructed by the Hybrid constructor, is transformed into an abstract automaton. SceneChecker uses symmetry abstractions [14]. The abstraction is constructed by the abstract function (line 1 of Algorithm 1) which uses a collection of pairs of maps $\Phi = \{(\gamma_s : X \to X, \rho_s : S \to S)\}_{s \in S}$ that is provided by the user. We describe below how these maps are specified by the user in the Dynamics file. These maps should satisfy:

$$\forall t \geq 0, x_0 \in X, s \in S, \gamma_s(\xi(x_0, s, t)) = \xi(\gamma_s(x_0), \rho_s(s), t). \tag{1}$$

where $\forall s \in S$, the map γ_s is differentiable and invertible. Such maps are called *symmetries* for the agent's dynamics. They transform the agent's trajectories to other symmetric ones of its trajectories starting from symmetric initial states and following symmetric modes (or segments in our scenario verification setting). It is worth noting that (1) does not depend on whether the trajectories ξ are defined by ODEs or black-box simulators. Currently, condition (1) is not checked by SceneChecker for the maps specified by the user. However, in the following discussion, we present some ways for the user to check (1) on their own. For ODE models, a sufficient condition for (1) to be satisfied is if: $\forall x \in X, s \in S, \frac{\partial \gamma_s}{\partial x} f(x, s) = f(\gamma_s(x), \rho_s(s))$, where f is the right-hand-side of the ODE [30]. For black-box models, (1) can be checked using sampling methods. In realistic settings, dynamics might not be exactly symmetric due to unmodeled uncertainties. In the future, we plan to account for such uncertainties as part of the reachability analysis.

In scenario verification, a given workspace would have a coordinate system according to which the plan (waypoints) and the agent's state (position, velocity, heading angle, etc.) are represented. In a 2D workspace, for any segment $s \in S$, an example symmetry ρ_s would transform the two waypoints of s to a new coordinate system where the second waypoint is the origin and s is aligned with the negative side of the horizontal axis (see Fig. 1D). The corresponding γ_s would transform the agent's state to this new coordinate system (e.g. by rotating its position and velocity vectors and shifting the heading angle). For such a pair (γ_s, ρ_s) to satisfy (1), the agent's dynamics have to be invariant to such a coordinate transformation and (1) merely formalizes this requirement. Such an invariance property is expected from vehicles' dynamics–rotating or translating the lane should not change how an autonomous car behaves.

> Dynamics file is the second input provided by the user in addition to the Scenario file and it contains the following:
> polyVir(X', s): returns $\gamma_s(X')$ for any polytope $X' \subset X$ and segment $s \in S$.
> modeVir(s): returns $\rho_s(s)$ for any given segment $s \in S$.
> virPoly(X', s): returns $\gamma_s^{-1}(X')$, implementing the inverse of polyVir.
> computeReachset$(initset, s, T)$: returns a list of hyperrectangles over-approximating the agent's reachset starting from $initset$ following segment s for T time units, for any set of states $initset \subset X$, segment $s \in S$, and $T \geq 0$.

5   Symmetry Abstraction of the Scenario's Automaton

In this section, we describe how the abstract function in Algorithm 1 uses the functions in the Dynamics file to construct an abstraction of the scenario's hybrid automaton provided by the Hybrid constructor. Given the symmetry maps of Φ, the symmetry abstraction of H is another hybrid automaton H_v that aggregates many symmetric modes (segments) of H into a single mode of H_v.

Modes and Transitions. Any segment $s \in S$ of H is mapped to the segment $\rho_s(s)$ in H_v using modeVir. The set of modes S_v of H_v is the set of segments $\{\rho_s(s)\}_{s \in S}$. For any s_v, $tbound_v(s_v) = \max_{s \in S, s_v = \rho_s(s)} tbound(s)$. In the example of Sect. 4 (Fig. 1D), the segments in H_v are aligned with the horizontal axis and ending at the origin. The number of segments in H_v would be the number of segments in G with unique lengths. The agent would always be moving towards the origin of the workspace in the abstract scenario. Any edge $e = (s, s') \in E$ of H is mapped to the edge $e_v = (\rho_s(s), \rho_{s'}(s'))$ in H_v. The $guard(e)$ is mapped to $\gamma_s(guard(e))$ using polyVir which becomes part of $guard_v(e_v)$ in H_v. For any $x \in X$, $reset(x, e)$, which is equal to x, is mapped to $\gamma_{s'}(\gamma_s^{-1}(x))$ and becomes part of $reset_v(x, e_v)$ in H_v. In our example in Sect. 4, the $\gamma_s^{-1}(x)$ would represent x in the absolute coordinate system assuming it was represented in the coordinate system defined by segment s. The $\gamma_{s'}(\gamma_s^{-1}(x))$ would represent $\gamma_s^{-1}(x)$ in the new coordinate system defined by segment s'. The $guard_v(e_v)$ would be the union of rotated hyperrectangles centered at the origin that result from translating and rotating the guards of the edges represented by e_v. The initial set Θ of H is mapped to $\Theta_v = \gamma_{s_{init}}(\Theta)$, the initial set of H_v. A formal definition of symmetry abstractions can be found in [1] (or [14]).

The unsafe map O is mapped to O_v, where $\forall s_v \in S_v, O_v(s_v) = \cup_{s \in S, \rho_s(s)=s_v} \gamma_s(O(s))$. That means that the obstacles near any segment $s \in S$ in the environment will be mapped to be near its representative segment $\rho_s(s)$ in H_v.

A forward simulation relation between H and H_v can show that if H_v is safe with respect to O_v, then H is safe with respect to O. More formally, if $\forall s_v \in S_v, Reach_{H_v}(s_v) \cap O_v(s_v) = \emptyset$, then $\forall s \in S, Reach_H(s) \cap O(s) = \emptyset$ [14].

6   SceneChecker Algorithm Overview

A sketch of the core abstraction-refinement algorithm is shown in Algorithm 1. It constructs a symmetry abstraction H_v of the concrete automaton H resulting from the Hybrid constructor. SceneChecker attempts to verify the safety of H_v using traditional reachability analysis. SceneChecker uses a *cache* to store per-mode initial sets from which reachsets have been computed and thus avoids repeating computations. An example run is shown in Fig. 1.

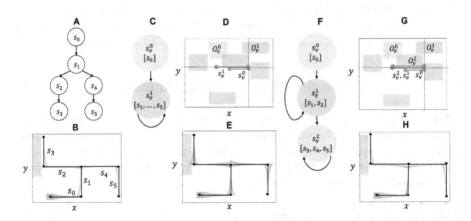

Fig. 1. A simple scenario with a car following a plan with six segments is shown in B. Set of initial positions (green square), unsafe set (grey), and the segments (black lines). The automaton (A) has one mode per segment. Translation and rotation symmetries are used to abstract A to the automaton C. The abstraction translates and rotates each segment of the original scenario to a segment aligned with the x-axis and ends at the origin resulting in the segments (i.e. modes) s_v^0 and s_v^1. The unsafe set is transformed accordingly for each mode as shown in D. SceneChecker computes the reachset of C which turns out to be unsafe; to illustrate the process this abstract reachset transformed to the original scenario is shown in E. The colors refer to a different abstract modes. The algorithm refines C to F by adding s_v^2 (same segment as s_v^1 but different guard). The reachset of F is safe and the algorithm terminates (H). (The colored figure is available in the online version of this paper)

The core algorithm verify (Algorithm 2) is called iteratively. If verify returns $(safe, \perp)$ or $(unknown, \perp)$, SceneChecker returns the same result. If verify instead results in $(refine, s_v^*)$, splitMode (check the extended version of this paper [1] for the formal definition) is called to refine H_v by splitting s_v^* into two modes s_v^1 and s_v^2. Each of

---

Algorithm 1. SceneChecker($\Phi = \{(\gamma_s, \rho_s)\}_{s \in S}, H, O$)

1: $H_v, O_v \leftarrow \text{abstract}(H, O, \Phi)$
2: $\forall s \in S, rv[s] \leftarrow \rho_s(s)$
3: **while** *True* **do**
4:     $cache \leftarrow \{s_v \mapsto \emptyset \mid s_v \in S_v\}$
5:     $result, s_v^* \leftarrow \text{verify}(rv[s_{init}], \Theta_v, cache, rv, H_v, O_v)$
6:     **if** $result = safe$ or *unknown* **then return:** *result*
7:     **else** $rv, H_v, O_v \leftarrow \text{splitMode}(s_v^*, rv, H_v, O_v, H, O)$

---

the two modes would represent part of the set of the segments of S that were originally mapped to s_v in rv. Then the edges, guards, resets, and the unsafe sets related to s_v are split according to their definitions.

The function verify executes a *depth first search* (DFS) over the mode graph of H_v. For any mode s_v being visited, computeReachset computes R_v, an over-approximation of the agent's reachset starting from *initset* following segment s_v for time $tbound_v(s_v)$. If $R_v \cap O_v(s_v) = \emptyset$, verify recursively calls s_v's children continuing the DFS in line 6. Before calling each child, its initial set is computed and the part for which a reachset has already been computed and stored in *cache* is subtracted. If all calls return *safe*, then *initset* is added to the other initial sets in $cache[s_v]$ (line 12) and verify returns *safe*. Most importantly, if verify returns $(refine, s_v^*)$ for any of s_v's children, it directly returns $(refine, s_v^*)$ for s_v as well (line 7). If any child returns *unknown* or R_v intersects $O_v(s_v)$, verify will need to split s_v. In that case, it checks if $rv^{-1}[s_v]$ is not a singleton set and thus amenable to splitting (line 10). If s_v can be split, verify returns $(refine, s_v)$. Otherwise, verify returns $(unknown, \bot)$ implicitly asking one of s_v's ancestors to be split instead.

Correctness. SceneChecker ensures that all the refined automata H_v's are abstractions of the original hybrid automaton H (a proof is given in the extended version of this paper [1]). For any mode with a reachset intersecting the unsafe set, SceneChecker keeps refining that mode and its ancestors until safety can be proven or H_v becomes H.

Theorem 1 (Soundness). *If* SceneChecker *returns safe, then H is safe.*

If verify is provided with the concrete automaton H and unsafe set O, it will be the traditional safety verification algorithm having no over-approximation error due to abstraction. If such a call to verify returns *safe*, then SceneChecker is guaranteed to return *safe*. That means that the refinement ensures that the over-approximation error of the reachset caused by the abstraction is reduced to not alter the verification result.

Counter-examples. SceneChecker currently does not find counter-examples to show that the scenario is *unsafe*. There are several sources of over-approximation errors, namely, computeReachset and guard intersections. Even after all the over-approximation errors from symmetry abstractions are eliminated, as refinement does, it still cannot infer unsafe executions or counter-examples because of the other errors. We plan to address this in the future by combining the current algorithm with systematic simulations.

Algorithm 2. verify(s_v, $initset$, $cache$, rv, H_v, O_v)

1: $R_v \leftarrow$ computeReachset($initset$, s_v)
2: **if** $R_v \cap O_v(s_v) = \emptyset$ **then**
3:     **for** $s_v' \in children(s_v)$ **do**
4:         $initset' \leftarrow reset_v(guard_v((s_v, s_v'))) \cap R_v \setminus cache[s_v']$
5:         **if** $initset' \neq \emptyset$ **then**
6:             $result, s_v^* \leftarrow$ verify(s_v', $initset'$, $cache$, rv, H_v, O_v)
7:             **if** $result = refine$ **then return:** $refine, s_v^*$
8:             **else if** $result = unknown$ **then break**
9: **if** $R_v \cap O_v(s_v) \neq \emptyset$ or $result$ is $unknown$ **then**
10:     **if** $|rv^{-1}[s_v]| > 1$ **then return:** $refine, s_v$
11:     **else return:** $unknown, \perp$
12: $cache[s_v] \leftarrow cache[s_v] \cup initset$
13: **return:** $safe, \perp$

7 Experimental Evaluation

Agents and Controllers. In our experiments, we consider two types of nonlinear agent models: a standard 3-dimensional car (C) with bicycle dynamics and 2 inputs, and a 6-dimensional quadrotor (Q) with 3 inputs. For each of these agents, we developed a PD controller and a NN controller for tracking segments. The NN controller for the quadrotor is from Verisig's paper [9] but modified to be rotation symmetric (check the extended version of this paper [1] for more details). Similarly, the NN controller for the car is made rotation symmetric. Both NN controllers are translation symmetric as they take as input the difference between the agent's state and the segment being followed. The PD controllers are translation and rotation symmetric by design.

Symmetries. We experimented with two different collections of symmetry maps Φs: 1) translation symmetry (T), where for any segment s in G, γ_s maps the states so that the coordinate system is translated by a vector that makes its origin at the end waypoint of s, and 2) rotation and translation symmetry (TR), where instead of just translating the origin, Φ rotates the xy-plane so that s is aligned with the x-axis, which we described in Sect. 4. For each agent and one of its controllers, we manually verified that condition (1) is satisfied for each of the two Φs using the sufficient condition for ODEs in Sect. 4.

Scenarios. We created four scenarios with 2D workspaces (S1-4) and one scenario with a 3D workspace (S5) with corresponding plans. We generated the plans using an RRT planner [31] after specifying a number of goal sets that should be reached. We modified S4 to have more obstacles but still have the same plan and named the new version S4.b and the original one S4.a. When the quadrotor was considered, the waypoints of the 2D scenarios (S1-4) were converted to 3D representation by setting the altitude for each waypoint to 0. Scenario S5 is the same as S2 but S5's waypoints have varying altitudes. The scenarios have different complexities ranging from few segments and obstacles to hundreds of them. All scenarios are safe when traversed by any of the two agents.

We verify these scenarios using SceneChecker and CacheReach, each with two instances, one with DryVR and the other with Flow*, implementing computeReachset.

We also use DryVR and Flow* as independent tools to verify the same scenarios. The results of experiments with tools that involve DryVR (i.e., SceneChecker+DryVR, CacheReach+DryVR, and DryVR) are stochastic and change between runs. The reason is that each time DryVR is called, it randomly samples traces of the system from which it computes the requested reachset. We fix the random seed for repeatable results in this section. We show close averaging-based results on SceneChecker's website.

SceneChecker is able to verify all scenarios with PD controllers. The results are shown in Table 1[4] and plotted for C-S1 using SceneChecker+Flow* in Fig. 1.

Observation 1: SceneChecker *offers fast scenario verification and boosts existing reachability tools* Looking at the two total time (Tt) columns for the two instances of SceneChecker with the corresponding columns for Flow* and DryVR, it becomes clear that symmetry abstractions can boost the verification performance of reachability engines. For example, in C-S4.a, SceneChecker+DR was around $20\times$ faster than DryVR. In C-S3, SceneChecker with Flow* was around $16\times$ faster than Flow*. In scenario Q-S5, SceneChecker timed out at least in part because a computeReachset call to Flow* timed out. Even when many refinements are required and thus causing several repetitions of the verification process in Algorithm 1, SceneChecker is still faster than DryVR and Flow* (C-S4.b). All three tools resulted in *safe* for all scenarios when completed executions.

Observation 2: SceneChecker *is faster and more accurate than* CacheReach Since CacheReach only handles single-path plans, we only verify the longest path in the plans of the scenarios in its experiments. CacheReach's instance with Flow* resulted in unsafe reachsets in C-S1 and C-S4.b scenarios likely because of the caching over-approximation error. In all scenarios where CacheReach completed verification besides C-S4.b, it has more Rc and longer Tt (more than $30\times$ in C-S2) while verifying simpler plans than SceneChecker using the same reachability subroutine. In all Q scenarios, both instances of CacheReach, with Flow* and DryVR, timed out.

Observation 3: *More symmetric dynamics result in faster verification time* SceneChecker usually runs slower in 3D scenarios compared to 2D ones (Q-S2 vs. Q-S5) in part because there is no rotational symmetry in the z-dimension to exploit. That leads to larger abstract automata. Therefore, many more calls to computeReachset are required.

We only used SceneChecker's instance with DryVR for agents with NN-controllers[5]. We tried different Φs. The results are shown in Table 2. When not using abstraction-refinement, SceneChecker took 10.5, 130.95, and 74.15 min for the QNN-S2, QNN-S3, and QNN-S4 scenarios, while DryVR took 5.22, 52.56, and 61.31 min for the same scenarios, respectively. Comparing these results with those in Table 2 shows

---

[4] Figures presenting the reachsets of the concrete and abstract automata for different scenarios can be found in the extended version of this paper [1] as well as the machine specifications.

[5] Check the extended version [1] for a discussion about our attempts for using other verification tools for NN-controlled systems as reachability subroutines.

Table 1. Comparison between SceneChecker, DryVR (DR), Flow* (F*), and CacheReach (CacheR). Both SceneChecker and CacheReach use reachability tools as subroutines. The subroutines used are specified after the '+' sign. Φ is TR. The table shows the number of mode-splits performed (Nrefs), the total number of calls to computeReachset (Rc), the total time spent in reachset computations (Rt), and the total computation time in minutes (Tt). In scenarios where a tool ran over 120 min, we marked the Tt column as 'Timed out' (TO) and the other ones as 'Not Available' (NA).

Sc.	|S|	SceneChecker+DR				CacheR+DR		DR	SceneChecker+F*				CacheR+F*		F*
		Nrefs	Rc	Rt	Tt	Rc	Tt	Tt	NRefs	Rc	Rt	Tt	Rc	Tt	Tt
C-S1	6	1	4	0.14	0.15	46	1.73	1.28	1	4	0.51	0.52	52	8.20	2.11
C-S2	140	0	1	0.04	0.65	424	19.92	10.57	0	1	0.18	0.79	192	30.95	17.52
C-S3	458	0	1	0.04	4.24	502	19.33	71.41	0	1	0.11	4.34	176	28.64	73.06
C-S4.a	520	2	7	0.26	4.37	404	15.84	94.62	2	7	0.80	4.96	160	25.98	61.53
C-S4.b	520	10	39	1.43	8.69	404	16.06	96.02	10	39	2.83	31.73	160	26.07	60.67
Q-S1	6	1	4	0.04	0.05	NA	TO	0.25	1	4	13.85	14.13	NA	TO	30.17
Q-S2	140	0	1	0.04	0.88	NA	TO	4.97	1	1	3.38	12.62	NA	TO	TO
Q-S3	458	0	1	0.06	5.9	NA	TO	46.34	0	1	4.98	62.66	NA	TO	TO
Q-S4.a	520	0	1	0.06	3.17	NA	TO	56.19	1	1	4.8	34.89	NA	TO	TO
Q-S5	188	0	36	0.85	3.04	NA	TO	8.03	NA	NA	NA	TO	NA	TO	TO

that the speedup in verification time of SceneChecker is caused by the abstraction-refinement algorithm, achieving more than $13\times$ in certain scenarios (QNN-S4 using $\Phi = T$). SceneChecker+DR was more than $10\times$ faster than DryVR in the same scenario.

Table 2. Comparison between Φs. In addition to the statisitics of Table 1, this table reports the number of modes and edges in the initial and final (after refinement) abstractions ($|S_v|^i$, $|E_v|^i$; $|S_v|^f$, and $|E_v|^f$, respectively)

Sc	NRef	Φ	$|S|$	$|S_v|^i$	$|E_v|^i$	$|S_v|^f$	$|E_v|^f$	Rc	Rt	Tt
CNN-S2	6	TR	140	1	1	7	17	19	1.51	3.05
CNN-S4	9	TR	520	1	1	10	28	47	3.77	11.25
QNN-S2	3	TR	140	1	1	4	9	9	0.61	3.55
QNN-S3	5	TR	458	1	1	6	16	15	1.51	12.7
QNN-S4	4	TR	520	1	1	5	13	11	1.11	7.43
QNN-S2	0	T	140	7	19	7	19	8	0.53	1.38
QNN-S3	4	T	458	7	30	11	58	29	2.92	16.88
QNN-S4	0	T	520	7	30	7	30	13	1.32	5.34

Observation 4: Choice of Φ is a trade-off between over-approximation error and number of refinements The choice of Φ affects the number of refinements performed and the total running times (e.g. QNN-S2, QNN-S3, and QNN-S4). Using TR leads to a more succinct H_v but larger over-approximation error causing more mode splits. On the other hand, using T leads to a larger H_v but less over-approximation error and thus fewer refinements. This trade-off can be seen in Table 2. For example, QNN-S4 with $\Phi = T$ resulted in zero mode splits leading to $|S_v|^i = |S_v|^f = 7$, while $\Phi = TR$ resulted in 4 mode splits, starting with $|S_v|^i = 1$ modes and ending with $|S_v|^f = 5$, and longer verification time because of refinements. On the other hand, in QNN-S3, $\Phi = TR$ resulted in Nref= 5, $|S_v|^f = 6$, and Tt= 12.7 min while $\Phi =$T resulted in Nref= 4, $|S_v|^f = 11$, and Tt= 16.88 min.

Observation 5: Complicated dynamics require more verification time Different vehicle dynamics affect the number of refinements performed and consequently the verification time (e.g. QNN-S2, QNN-S4, CNN-S2, and CNN-S4). The car appears to be less stable than the quadrotor leading to longer verification time for the same scenarios. This can also be seen by comparing the results of Tables 1 and 2. The PD controllers lead to more stable dynamics than the NN controllers requiring less total computation time for both agents. More stable dynamics lead to tighter reachsets and fewer refinements.

8 Limitations and Discussions

SceneChecker allows the choice of modes to be changed from segments to waypoints or sequences of segments as well. The waypoint-defined modes eliminate the need for segments of G to have few unique lengths, but only allow $\Phi = T$. SceneChecker splits only one mode per refinement and then repeats the computation from scratch. It has to refine many times in unsafe scenarios until reaching the result *unknown*. We plan to investigate other strategies for eliminating spurious counter-examples and returning valid ones in unsafe cases. In the future, it will be important to address other sources of uncertainty in scene verification such as moving obstacles, interactive agents, and other types of symmetries such as permutation and time scaling. Finally, it will be useful to connect a translator to generate scene files from common road simulation frameworks such as CARLA [32], commonroad [33], and Scenic [34].

References

1. Sibai, H., Li, Y., Mitra, S.: SceneChecker: boosting scenario verification using symmetry abstractions (2021). https://arxiv.org/abs/2011.10713
2. Frehse, G., et al.: SpaceEX: scalable verification of hybrid systems. In: CAV (2011)
3. Bak, S., Duggirala, P.S.: HyLAA: a tool for computing simulation-equivalent reachability for linear systems. In: Proceedings of the 20th International Conference on Hybrid Systems: Computation and Control, pp. 173–178. ACM (2017)
4. Chen, X., Ábrahám, E., Sankaranarayanan, S.: Flow*: an analyzer for non-linear hybrid systems. In: Sharygina, N., Veith, H. (eds.) CAV 2013. LNCS, vol. 8044, pp. 258–263. Springer, Heidelberg (2013). https://doi.org/10.1007/978-3-642-39799-8_18
5. Duggirala, P.S., Fan, C., Mitra, S., Viswanathan, M.: Meeting a Powertrain verification challenge. In: Kroening, D., Păsăreanu, C.S. (eds.) CAV 2015. LNCS, vol. 9206, pp. 536–543. Springer, Cham (2015). https://doi.org/10.1007/978-3-319-21690-4_37
6. Fan, C., Qi, B., Mitra, S., Viswanathan, M.: DRYVR: data-driven verification and compositional reasoning for automotive systems. In: Majumdar, R., Kunčak, V. (eds.) CAV (2017)
7. Dutta, S., Chen, X., Jha, S., Sankaranarayanan, S., Tiwari, A.: Sherlock - a tool for verification of neural network feedback systems: demo abstract, pp. 262–263. HSCC 2019. ACM, New York, USA (2019). https://doi.org/10.1145/3302504.3313351
8. Tran, H.D., et al.: NNV: the neural network verification tool for deep neural networks and learning-enabled cyber-physical systems. In: Lahiri, S.K., Wang, C. (eds.) CAV (2020)
9. Ivanov, R., Weimer, J., Alur, R., Pappas, G.J., Lee, I.: Verisig: verifying safety properties of hybrid systems with neural network controllers. In: ACM HSCC (2019)
10. Althoff, M.: An introduction to CORA 2015. In: Proceedings of the Workshop on Applied Verification for Continuous and Hybrid Systems (2015)
11. Fan, C., Qi, B., Mitra, S., Viswanathan, M., Duggirala, P.S.: Automatic reachability analysis for nonlinear hybrid models with C2E2. In: CAV (2016)
12. Kavraki, L.E., Svestka, P., Latombe, J., Overmars, M.H.: Probabilistic roadmaps for path planning in high-dimensional configuration spaces. IEEE Trans. Robot. Autom. 12(4), 566–580 (1996)
13. Lavalle, S.M.: Rapidly-exploring random trees: a new tool for path planning. Technical report (1998)
14. Sibai, H., Mitra, S.: Symmetry abstractions for hybrid systems and their applications (2020). https://arxiv.org/abs/2006.09485
15. Kwiatkowska, M.Z., Norman, G., Parker, D.: Symmetry reduction for probabilistic model checking. In: CAV (2006)
16. Antuña, L.R., Araiza-Illan, D., Campos, S., Eder, K.: Symmetry reduction enables model checking of more complex emergent behaviours of swarm navigation algorithms. In: Towards Autonomous Robotic Systems TAROS, pp. 26–37 (2015)

17. Emerson, E.A., Sistla, A.P.: Symmetry and model checking. In: Computer Aided Verification, 28 June–1 July 1993, Elounda, Greece, Proceedings, pp. 463–478 (1993)
18. Clarke, E.M., Jha, S.: Symmetry and induction in model checking. In: Computer Science Today: Recent Trends and Developments, pp. 455–470 (1995)
19. Jacobs, S., Bloem, R.: Parameterized synthesis. Logical Methods in Computer Science [electronic only] 10 (2014)
20. Mann, M., Barrett, C.: Partial order reduction for deep bug finding in synchronous hardware. In: TACAS 2020. LNCS, vol. 12078, pp. 367–386. Springer, Cham (2020). https://doi.org/10.1007/978-3-030-45190-5_20
21. Hu, Y., Shih, V., Majumdar, R., He, L.: Exploiting symmetries to speed up sat-based Boolean matching for logic synthesis of FPGAs. IEEE Trans. Comput. Aided Des. Integr. Circuits Syst. 27(10), 1751–1760 (2008). https://doi.org/10.1109/TCAD.2008.2003272
22. Ip, C.N., Dill, D.L.: Better verification through symmetry. In: Proceedings of the 11th IFIP WG10.2 International Conference, pp. 97–111. CHDL 1993, North-Holland Publishing Co., Amsterdam, The Netherlands, The Netherlands (1993)
23. Hendriks, M., Behrmann, G., Larsen, K., Niebert, P., Vaandrager, F.: Adding symmetry reduction to uppaal (2004)
24. Bak, S., Huang, Z., Abad, F.A.T., Caccamo, M.: Safety and progress for distributed cyber-physical systems with unreliable communication. ACM Trans. Embed. Comput. Syst. 14(4) (2015). https://doi.org/10.1145/2739046
25. Maidens, J., Arcak, M.: Exploiting symmetry for discrete-time reachability computations. IEEE Control Systems Letters 2(2), 213–217 (2018)
26. Majumdar, A., Tedrake, R.: Funnel libraries for real-time robust feedback motion planning. Int. J. Robot. Res. 36(8), 947–982 (2017)
27. Bujorianu, M., Katoen, J.P.: Symmetry reduction for stochastic hybrid systems. In: 2008 47th IEEE Conference on Decision and Control : CDC; Cancun, Mexico, 9–2008. - T. 1, pp. 233–238. IEEE, Piscataway, NJ (2008). https://publications.rwth-aachen.de/record/100535
28. Sibai, H., Mokhlesi, N., Mitra, S.: Using symmetry transformations in equivariant dynamical systems for their safety verification. In: Chen, Y.-F., Cheng, C.-H., Esparza, J. (eds.) ATVA 2019. LNCS, vol. 11781, pp. 98–114. Springer, Cham (2019). https://doi.org/10.1007/978-3-030-31784-3_6
29. Sibai, H., Mokhlesi, N., Fan, C., Mitra, S.: Multi-agent safety verification using symmetry transformations. In: TACAS 2020. LNCS, vol. 12078, pp. 173–190. Springer, Cham (2020). https://doi.org/10.1007/978-3-030-45190-5_10
30. Russo, G., Slotine, J.J.E.: Symmetries, stability, and control in nonlinear systems and networks. Phys. Rev. E 84(4), 041929 (2011)
31. Fan, C., Miller, K., Mitra, S.: Fast and guaranteed safe controller synthesis for nonlinear vehicle models. In: Lahiri, S.K., Wang, C. (eds.) CAV (2020)
32. Dosovitskiy, A., Ros, G., Codevilla, F., Lopez, A., Koltun, V.: CARLA: An open urban driving simulator. In: Proceedings of the 1st Annual Conference on Robot Learning, pp. 1–16 (2017)
33. Althoff, M., Koschi, M., Manzinger, S.: CommonRoad: composable benchmarks for motion planning on roads. In: Proceedings of the IEEE Intelligent Vehicles Symposium (2017)
34. Fremont, D.J., Dreossi, T., Ghosh, S., Yue, X., Sangiovanni-Vincentelli, A.L., Seshia, S.A.: Scenic: a language for scenario specification and scene generation, pp. 63–78. PLDI 2019, ACM, New York, USA (2019). https://doi.org/10.1145/3314221.3314633

594   H. Sibai et al.

Effective Hybrid System Falsification Using Monte Carlo Tree Search Guided by QB-Robustness

Zhenya Zhang[1]([✉]) [ID], Deyun Lyu[1] [ID], Paolo Arcaini[2] [ID], Lei Ma[1,3,4] [ID], Ichiro Hasuo[2] [ID], and Jianjun Zhao[1] [ID]

[1] Kyushu University, Fukuoka, Japan
zhang.zhenya.623@m.kyushu-u.ac.jp
[2] National Institute of Informatics, Tokyo, Japan
[3] University of Alberta, Edmonton, Canada
[4] Alberta Machine Intelligence Institute, Edmonton, Canada

Abstract. Hybrid system falsification is an important quality assurance method for cyber-physical systems with the advantage of scalability and feasibility in practice than exhaustive verification. Falsification, given a desired temporal specification, tries to find an input of violation instead of a proof guarantee. The state-of-the-art falsification approaches often employ stochastic hill-climbing optimization that minimizes the degree of satisfaction of the temporal specification, given by its quantitative *robust semantics*. However, it has been shown that the performance of falsification could be severely affected by the so-called *scale problem*, related to the different scales of the signals used in the specification (e.g., rpm and speed): in the robustness computation, the contribution of a signal could be *masked* by another one. In this paper, we propose a novel approach to tackle this problem. We first introduce a new robustness definition, called *QB-Robustness*, which combines classical Boolean satisfaction and quantitative robustness. We prove that QB-Robustness can be used to judge the satisfaction of the specification and avoid the scale problem in its computation. QB-Robustness is exploited by a falsification approach based on Monte Carlo Tree Search over the structure of the formal specification. First, tree traversal identifies the sub-formulas for which it is needed to compute the quantitative robustness. Then, on the leaves, numerical hill-climbing optimization is performed, aiming to falsify such sub-formulas. Our in-depth evaluation on multiple benchmarks demonstrates that our approach achieves better falsification results than the state-of-the-art falsification approaches guided by the classical quantitative robustness, and it is largely not affected by the scale problem.

Keywords: Falsification · Signal temporal logic · Scale problem · Monte carlo tree search · Robust semantics · QB-Robustness

This work is supported in part by JSPS KAKENHI Grant No. 20H04168, 19K24348, 19H04086, JST-Mirai Program Grant No. JPMJMI20B8, Japan. Lei Ma is also supported by Canada CIFAR AI Program and Natural Sciences and Engineering Research Council of Canada. Paolo Arcaini and Ichiro Hasuo are supported by ERATO HASUO Metamathematics for Systems Design Project (No. JPMJER1603), JST.

A. Silva and K. R. M. Leino (Eds.) CAV 2021, LNCS 12759, pp. 595–618, 2021.
https://doi.org/10.1007/978-3-030-81685-8_29

1   Introduction

Cyber-Physical Systems (CPS) are *hybrid systems* that combine physical systems (with continuous dynamics) and digital controllers (that are inherently discrete). Being often safety-critical, their quality assurance is of great importance and widely investigated by both academia and industry. The continuous dynamics of hybrid systems leads to infinite search spaces, making their verification often extremely difficult.

Falsification has been proposed as a more practically feasible approach that tackles the dual problem of verification: instead of exhaustively proving a property, falsification intends to uncover the existence of its violation with counterexamples. Formally, the problem is defined as follows. Given a *model* $\mathcal{M}$ taking an input signal $\mathbf{u}$ and outputting a signal $\mathcal{M}(\mathbf{u})$, and a *specification* φ (a temporal formula), the falsification problem consists in finding a *falsifying input*, i.e., an input signal $\mathbf{u}$ such that the corresponding output $\mathcal{M}(\mathbf{u})$ violates φ.

The most pursued and successful approach to the falsification problem consists in turning it into an optimization problem; we call it *optimization-based falsification*. This is possible thanks to the quantitative *robust semantics* of temporal formulas [14,19]. Robust semantics extends the classical Boolean satisfaction relation $\mathbf{v} \models \varphi$ in the following way: it assigns a value $[\![\mathbf{w}, \varphi]\!] \in \mathbb{R} \cup \{\infty, -\infty\}$ (i.e., *robustness*) that tells not only whether φ is satisfied or violated (by the sign), but also *how robustly* the formula is satisfied or violated.

Optimization-based falsification approaches adopt *hill-climbing* stochastic optimization strategies to generate inputs to decrease robustness, which terminate when they find an input with negative robustness, i.e., a *falsifying input* that triggers the violation of the specification φ. Different optimization-based falsification algorithms have been proposed (see [26] for a survey), and mature tools (e.g., Breach [13] and S-TaLiRo [4]) have also been developed.

The *scale problem* is a recognized issue in optimization-based falsification [21, 40], which could arise when multiple signals with different scales are present in the specification. Namely, it is due to the computation of robust semantics of Boolean connectives, i.e., the way in which the robustness values of different sub-formulas are compared and aggregated: such computation is problematic in the presence of signals that take values having different order of magnitudes.

Example 1. As very simple example, let us consider the formula $\varphi \equiv \Box_{[0,30]}(\varphi_1 \wedge \varphi_2)$, with $\varphi_1 \equiv gear < 6$ and $\varphi_2 \equiv speed < 130$. It is apparent that φ_1 is always satisfied (in any car model with 5 gears), and it has been added in the specification as redundant check.[1] According to robust semantics, the Boolean connective $\wedge$ is interpreted by minimum $\sqcap$, and the "always" operator $\Box_{[0,30]}$ is interpreted by infimum $\sqcap$; the robustness of an atomic formula $f(\boldsymbol{x}) < c$ is given by the margin $c - f(\boldsymbol{x})$. Therefore, the robustness of φ under the signal $(gear, speed)$, where $gear, speed \colon [0, 30] \to \mathbb{R}$, is

---

[1] Note that we built such a trivial example just to make the scale problem very easy to understand. However, in general, the scale problem frequently occurs on much less trivial specifications, as we will see in the experiments.

$[\![(gear, speed), \varphi]\!] = \bigsqcap_{t \in [0,30]} \left((6 - gear(t)) \sqcup (130 - speed(t)) \right)$. Note that the robustness of φ_1 is always in the order of units, while the robustness of φ_2 is, in general, in the order of tens. It is not difficult to see that, if both φ_1 and φ_2 are satisfied, the robustness of φ will only depend on φ_1 (because of the minimum in the robust semantics of the logical connective). In this case, we say that φ_1 *masks* φ_2. In such a case, a falsification approach relying on robustness will be misled during the search. Note that, in this particular case, the only way to falsify φ is to falsify φ_2, because φ_1 is always satisfied; therefore, falsifying this relatively simple formula could be extremely difficult for state-of-the-art optimization-based falsification approaches (as we will show and have confirmed in the experiments).

In this paper, we propose a novel approach to tackle the scale problem in optimization-based falsification. Our intuition and insights are that we should try to avoid the comparison of robustness values of different sub-formulas, so that one sub-formula does not mask the contribution of another one.

To achieve this, we first propose a new way of computing the satisfaction of a formula that combines *quantitative* robust semantics and *Boolean* semantics. We name the new semantics as QB-Robustness. QB-Robustness, for each type of formula φ, requires selecting a sub-formula φ_k among its sub-formulas $\{\varphi_1, \ldots, \varphi_K\}$. For φ_k, the quantitative robust semantics is computed, while for the other sub-formulas the Boolean semantics is computed. Therefore, the computation of QB-Robustness requires identifying a path Σ along the parse tree of the formula φ, where visited sub-formulas are those for which the quantitative robustness is computed. We prove that QB-Robustness, independently of the selected Σ, is equivalent (in terms of sign and satisfaction) to the quantitative robust semantics (and also to the Boolean one).

In general QB-Robustness is a useful tool for avoiding the scale problem of falsification. By definition, the quantitative robustness of different sub-formulas is never compared, so removing the main cause of the scale problem. It would then make sense to use it for guiding the optimization-based falsification process. However, QB-Robustness requires to choose a particular sequence Σ of sub-formulas for which to compute the quantitative robustness. It is relatively easy to show that some of them provide a better guidance than others to the falsification search. Considering the previous example, if Σ contains φ_1, we can encounter the problem that the quantitative robustness of φ_1 would not provide any guidance (i.e., no big variations in the robustness values would be observed). On the other hand, if Σ contains φ_2, the quantitative robustness would have larger variations, providing more effective guidance to the search.

Then, the key problem is how to select the *best* Σ, that enables the hill-climbing optimization used in falsification to be more effective. In general, although it is often difficult to know the best Σ in advance, it is still possible to learn it by observing sampling results using different Σ. Based on this intuition, we propose a novel falsification approach that identifies the sequences Σ that is more likely to be efficient, and uses them in the new falsification trials. Our approach could be seen as an instantiation of the classical Monte

Carlo Tree Search (MCTS) method [8,28], which is able to efficiently tackle the *exploration-exploitation* tradeoff. In our context, exploration consists in incrementally constructing the tree that represents all the possible sequences, and exploitation consists in selecting the best Σ and running optimization-based falsification in which QB-Robustness with Σ is used.

Overall, the major *Contributions* of this paper are summarized as follows:

- We propose a novel semantics (QB-Robustness) for STL formulas that combines quantitative robustness and Boolean satisfaction. We prove that QB-Robustness can be used to show the satisfiability of STL formulas;
- We define a falsification approach based on MCTS that exploits QB-Robustness to address the scale problem;
- We implement the approach in the tool `ForeSee`, based on which, we performed in-depth evaluation, demonstrating the effectiveness and advantage of our approach compared with the state of the art.

Paper Structure. In Sect. 2, we introduce the preliminaries of the optimization-based falsification. In Sect. 3, we introduce the novel STL semantics QB-Robustness, and, in Sect. 4, we describe the MCTS-based falsification approach that uses QB-Robustness. In Sect. 5, we describe the experiments and evaluation results. Finally, we discuss most relevant work to ours in Sect. 6, and conclude the paper in Sect. 7.

2 Preliminaries

In this section, we briefly review the falsification framework based on *robust semantics* of temporal logic [14].

Let $T \in \mathbb{R}_+$ be a positive real. An M-*dimensional signal* with a time horizon T is a function $\mathbf{w}\colon [0,T] \to \mathbb{R}^M$. We treat the system model as a black box, i.e., its behaviors are only observed from inputs and their corresponding outputs. Formally, a *system model*, with M-dimensional input and N-dimensional output, is a function $\mathcal{M}$ that takes an input signal $\mathbf{u}\colon [0,T] \to \mathbb{R}^M$ and returns a signal $\mathcal{M}(\mathbf{u})\colon [0,T] \to \mathbb{R}^N$. Here the common time horizon $T \in \mathbb{R}_+$ is arbitrary.

Definition 1 (STL Syntax). We fix a set **Var** of variables. In Signal Temporal Logic (STL), *atomic propositions* and *formulas* are defined as follows, respectively: $\alpha ::\equiv f(x_1, \ldots, x_N) > 0$, and $\varphi ::\equiv \alpha \mid \bot \mid \neg\varphi \mid \bigwedge \varphi \mid \bigvee \varphi \mid \Box_I \varphi \mid \Diamond_I \varphi \mid \varphi \, \mathcal{U}_I \, \varphi$ Here f is an N-ary function $f : \mathbb{R}^N \to \mathbb{R}$, $x_1, \ldots, x_N \in$ **Var**, and I is a closed non-singular interval in $\mathbb{R}_{\geq 0}$, i.e., $I = [a,b]$ or $[a,\infty)$, where $a,b \in \mathbb{R}$ and $a < b$. $\Box, \Diamond$ and $\mathcal{U}$ are temporal operators, which are usually known as *always*, *eventually* and *until* respectively. The always operator $\Box$ and eventually operator $\Diamond$ can also be considered as special cases of the until operator $\mathcal{U}$, where $\Diamond_I \varphi \equiv \top \, \mathcal{U}_I \, \varphi$ and $\Box_I \varphi \equiv \neg\Diamond_I \neg\varphi$. Other common connectives such as $\to$, $\top$ are introduced as syntactic sugar: $\top \equiv \neg\bot$, $\varphi_1 \to \varphi_2 \equiv \neg\varphi_1 \vee \varphi_2$.

Definition 2 (Quantitative Robust Semantics). Let $\mathbf{w}\colon [0,T] \to \mathbb{R}^N$ be an N-dimensional signal, and $t \in [0,T)$. The t-*shift* $\mathbf{w}^t$ of $\mathbf{w}$ is the signal

$\mathbf{w}^t \colon [0, T - t] \to \mathbb{R}^N$ defined by $\mathbf{w}^t(t') := \mathbf{w}(t + t')$. Let φ be an STL formula. We define the *robustness* $[\![\mathbf{w}, \varphi]\!] \in \mathbb{R} \cup \{\infty, -\infty\}$ as follows, by induction on the construction of formulas. $\sqcap$ and $\sqcup$ denote infimums and supremums of real numbers, respectively. $\sqcap$, the binary version of $\sqcap$, denotes minimum.

$$[\![\mathbf{w}, f(x_1, \cdots, x_N) > 0]\!] := f\big(\mathbf{w}(0)(x_1), \cdots, \mathbf{w}(0)(x_N)\big)$$

$$[\![\mathbf{w}, \bot]\!] := -\infty \qquad\qquad\qquad [\![\mathbf{w}, \neg\varphi]\!] := -[\![\mathbf{w}, \varphi]\!]$$

$$[\![\mathbf{w}, \textstyle\bigwedge_i \varphi_i]\!] := \textstyle\bigsqcap_i [\![\mathbf{w}, \varphi_i]\!] \qquad\qquad [\![\mathbf{w}, \textstyle\bigvee_i \varphi_i]\!] := \textstyle\bigsqcup_i [\![\mathbf{w}, \varphi_i]\!]$$

$$[\![\mathbf{w}, \square_I \varphi]\!] := \textstyle\bigsqcap_{t \in I \cap [0, T]} [\![\mathbf{w}^t, \varphi]\!] \qquad [\![\mathbf{w}, \lozenge_I \varphi]\!] := \textstyle\bigsqcup_{t \in I \cap [0, T]} [\![\mathbf{w}^t, \varphi]\!]$$

$$[\![\mathbf{w}, \varphi_1 \, \mathcal{U}_I \, \varphi_2]\!] := \textstyle\bigsqcup_{t \in I \cap [0, T]} \big([\![\mathbf{w}^t, \varphi_2]\!] \sqcap \textstyle\bigsqcap_{t' \in [0, t)} [\![\mathbf{w}^{t'}, \varphi_1]\!] \big)$$

The original STL semantics is Boolean, given by a binary relation $\models$ between signals and formulas. The robust semantics refines the Boolean one in the following sense: $[\![\mathbf{w}, \varphi]\!] > 0$ implies $\mathbf{w} \models \varphi$, and $[\![\mathbf{w}, \varphi]\!] < 0$ implies $\mathbf{w} \not\models \varphi$, see [19, Prop. 16].

2.1 Hill Climbing-Guided Falsification

So far, the falsification problem has received extensive industrial and academic attention. One possible approach direction by hill-climbing optimization is an established field, too: see [2–4, 10, 13–15, 17, 26, 29, 36–39, 42] and the tools Breach [13] and S-TaLiRo [4]. We formulate the problem and the methodology, for later use in describing our falsification approach.

Definition 3 (Falsifying Input). Let $\mathcal{M}$ be a system model, and φ be an STL formula. A signal $\mathbf{u} \colon [0, T] \to \mathbb{R}^{|\mathsf{Var}|}$ is a *falsifying input* if $[\![\mathcal{M}(\mathbf{u}), \varphi]\!] < 0$; the latter implies $\mathcal{M}(\mathbf{u}) \not\models \varphi$.

The use of quantitative robust semantics $[\![\mathcal{M}(\mathbf{u}), \varphi]\!] \in \mathbb{R} \cup \{\infty, -\infty\}$ in the above problem enables the use of hill-climbing optimization.

Definition 4 (Hill Climbing-Guided Falsification). Assume the setting in Definition 3, for finding a falsifying input, the methodology of *hill climbing-guided falsification* is presented in Algorithm 1. Here, the function HILL-CLIMB makes a guess of an input signal $\mathbf{u}'$, aiming at minimizing the robustness $[\![\mathcal{M}(\mathbf{u}'), \varphi]\!]$. It does so, learning from the sampling history H that contains the previous observations of input signals and their corresponding robustness values.

The HILL-CLIMB function can be designed based on various stochastic optimization algorithms. Typically, at the early phase of the optimization, the proposal of new input is usually based on random sampling; as the set of sampling history grows larger, the algorithm takes various metaheuristic-based strategies to achieve the optimization goal efficiently. Examples of such algorithms include Covariance Matrix Adaption Evolution Strategy (CMA-ES) [7] (used in our experiments), Simulated Annealing, Global Nelder Mead [32], etc.

Algorithm 1. Hill climbing-guided falsification

Require: a system model $\mathcal{M}$, an STL formula φ, and a time budget
 1: **function** HILL-CLIMB-FALSIFY$(\mathcal{M}, \varphi)$
 2:    initialize a placeholder **u** and rb $\leftarrow \infty$ ▷ the best input signal and robustness
 3:    $H \leftarrow \varnothing$ ▷ sampling history of input signals and robustness
 4:    **while** rb ≥ 0 and within the time budget **do**
 5:        $\mathbf{u}' \leftarrow$ HILL-CLIMB(H) ▷ run hill climbing based on sampling history
 6:        rb$' \leftarrow [\![\mathcal{M}(\mathbf{u}'), \varphi]\!]$ ▷ compute robustness
 7:        $H \leftarrow H \cup \{(\mathbf{u}', \text{rb}')\}$ ▷ update sampling history
 8:        **if** rb$' <$ rb **then**
 9:            rb $\leftarrow$ rb$'$, $\mathbf{u} \leftarrow \mathbf{u}'$ ▷ update the best input and robustness
10:    **return** $\begin{cases} \mathbf{u} & \text{if rb} < 0 \\ \text{Failure} & \text{otherwise, that is, no falsifying input found within the budget} \end{cases}$

---

3   QB-Robustness

The scale problem is a known important issue that negatively affects the performance of falsification, which arises when connective operators (i.e., conjunction and disjunction) with operands that predicate on different signals appear in the STL formula under falsification. According to the classic quantitative robust semantics (see Definition 2), the robustness of those formulas is calculated based on the comparison (minimum for conjunction, and maximum for disjunction) between robustness values coming from the different operand sub-formulas. However, since different signals may differ in magnitude, the comparison may be biased, such that one signal **w** may always (or often) *mask* the contribution of the others, and, therefore, the final robustness may be dominated by this signal **w**. Note that, although the scale problem affects connective operators, it is not only local to the place of their application, but it is always propagated to the robustness of the whole formula. The scale problem has been shown as a root cause of the failure of many falsification problems [21,40].

In this work, we propose a novel approach for solving the *scale problem* in falsification. Our approach consists in introducing a new semantics for STL that does not suffer from the scale problem. Such new semantics will be used in a falsification approach based on Monte Carlo Tree Search. We describe details of the new semantics in this section, and the new falsification approach in Sect. 4.

The new proposed semantics, called QB-Robustness, combines quantitative robustness and Boolean satisfaction. By construction, it never compares quantitative robustness values that come from different sub-formulas, thus avoiding the scale problem. QB-Robustness is defined for the whole STL formulas, except for the "until" operator $\varphi_1 \mathcal{U}_I \varphi_2$, when φ_1 is an arbitrary formula. We still support it as "eventually" and "always" operators[2], i.e., when $\varphi_1 = \top$. Note that this is not a major limitation, as QB-Robustness still supports the majority of specifications that are used in industry: indeed, in the experiments, we were able to

---

[2] Recall from Definition 1 that the "eventually" and "always" operators are defined in terms of the "until" operator.

handle all the specifications used in falsification competitions [18], which collect benchmarks from industrial case studies.

To better explain the computation of QB-Robustness, we introduce some definitions. Let us first define the notion of immediate sub-formula for STL.

Definition 5 (Immediate Sub-Formulas). Let φ be an STL formula (see Definition 1). We define the set $\mathsf{ISForm}(\varphi)$ of *immediate sub-formulas* of φ as follows:

$$\mathsf{ISForm}(\alpha) := \varnothing \quad \mathsf{ISForm}(\bot) := \varnothing \quad \mathsf{ISForm}(\neg\varphi) := \mathsf{ISForm}(\varphi)$$

$$\mathsf{ISForm}\left(\bigwedge_{i \in \{1,\dots,K\}} \varphi_i\right) := \{\varphi_1,\dots,\varphi_K\} \quad \mathsf{ISForm}\left(\bigvee_{i \in \{1,\dots,K\}} \varphi_i\right) := \{\varphi_1,\dots,\varphi_K\}$$

$$\mathsf{ISForm}(\Box_I\varphi) := \mathsf{ISForm}(\varphi) \quad\quad\quad \mathsf{ISForm}(\Diamond_I\varphi) := \mathsf{ISForm}(\varphi)$$

Intuitively, the immediate sub-formula set of a connective (conjunction or disjunction) contains all its operands. For the other unary operators (temporal operators, negation, etc.), its immediate sub-formula set is given by the immediate sub-formula set of its argument.

The computation of QB-Robustness requires to select some nested immediate sub-formulas. To this aim, we introduce the notion of sub-formula sequence.

Definition 6 (Sub-Formula Sequence). Let φ be an STL formula. A sub-formula sequence $\Sigma = \sigma_1 \cdot \dots \cdot \sigma_L$ w.r.t. φ is defined as follows:

$$\sigma_1 \in \mathsf{ISForm}(\varphi) \quad\quad\quad \sigma_{l+1} \in \mathsf{ISForm}(\sigma_l) \quad \text{with } l = 1,\dots,L-1$$

where the $\cdot$ is the concatenation operator in the sequence. We use Σ_k to denote the kth element of Σ. Moreover, we denote the first element by Σ_{head}, and the last element by Σ_{rear}. We use $\Sigma_{\overline{\mathsf{head}}}$ to denote Σ without Σ_{head}. We identify with ε the empty sequence; when $\mathsf{ISForm}(\varphi) = \varnothing$, we use ε as its sub-formula sequence. We identify with Σ_φ the set of all the sub-formula sequences rooted in φ.

To be specific, in a sub-formula sequence Σ, each element is one of the sub-formulas of the previous element. This means that, for Boolean connectives, only one of the operands is selected. Moreover, an atomic sub-formula predicating over a single signal can only appear as the final element of a sequence. We exploit these characteristics of Σ to define QB-Robustness, which combines the quantitative robustness of the sub-formulas related to a given signal with the Boolean satisfaction of the other sub-formulas. QB-Robustness, given a sequence Σ, decides whether to compute the quantitative robust semantics or the Boolean semantics of a sub-formula, by considering whether the sub-formula belongs to Σ or not. This implies that, in the case of conjunction and disjunction, we evaluate the quantitative robustness of the sub-formula in Σ and the Boolean satisfaction of the other sub-formulas. Based on such intuition, we define the semantics of our proposed QB-Robustness in Definition 7, and demonstrate its usefulness in Theorem 1.

Definition 7 (Semantics of QB-Robustness). Let φ be an STL formula as defined in Definition 1, and Σ be a sub-formula sequence w.r.t. φ. For $\varphi \equiv \bigwedge \varphi_i \mid \bigvee \varphi_i$, let $\varphi_k \in \mathsf{ISForm}(\varphi)$ be the first element Σ_{head} of Σ, then we can represent these two cases as $\varphi \equiv \varphi_k \wedge \varphi_{\overline{k}} \mid \varphi_k \vee \varphi_{\overline{k}}$, where $\varphi_{\overline{k}}$ is the conjunction (or disjunction, respectively) of the other formulas in $\mathsf{ISForm}(\varphi) \setminus \{\varphi_k\}$. The QB-Robustness $\mathsf{QBRob}(\mathbf{w}, \varphi, \Sigma)$ of φ w.r.t. Σ is defined as follows:

$$\mathsf{QBRob}(\mathbf{w}, \alpha, \varepsilon) := [\![\mathbf{w}, \alpha]\!] \qquad \mathsf{QBRob}(\mathbf{w}, \bot, \varepsilon) := -\infty$$

$$\mathsf{QBRob}(\mathbf{w}, \neg\varphi, \Sigma) := -\mathsf{QBRob}(\mathbf{w}, \varphi, \Sigma)$$

$$\mathsf{QBRob}(\mathbf{w}, \varphi_k \wedge \varphi_{\overline{k}}, \Sigma) := \begin{cases} \mathsf{QBRob}(\mathbf{w}, \varphi_k, \Sigma_{\overline{\mathsf{head}}}) & \text{if } \mathbf{w} \models \varphi_{\overline{k}} \\ -\infty & \text{otherwise} \end{cases}$$

$$\mathsf{QBRob}(\mathbf{w}, \varphi_k \vee \varphi_{\overline{k}}, \Sigma) := \begin{cases} \mathsf{QBRob}(\mathbf{w}, \varphi_k, \Sigma_{\overline{\mathsf{head}}}) & \text{if } \mathbf{w} \not\models \varphi_{\overline{k}} \\ \infty & \text{otherwise} \end{cases}$$

$$\mathsf{QBRob}(\mathbf{w}, \square_I \varphi, \Sigma) := \bigsqcap_{t \in I} \mathsf{QBRob}(\mathbf{w}^t, \varphi, \Sigma)$$

$$\mathsf{QBRob}(\mathbf{w}, \lozenge_I \varphi, \Sigma) := \bigsqcup_{t \in I} \mathsf{QBRob}(\mathbf{w}^t, \varphi, \Sigma)$$

We now prove that the semantics of QB-Robustness is equivalent (in the sense of satisfaction) to the Boolean semantics, and so it can be used to show violation of a specification in a falsification algorithm, as we do in this paper.

Theorem 1. *Let φ be an STL formula. Given a signal $\mathbf{w}$, for any $\Sigma \in \boldsymbol{\Sigma}_\varphi$, it holds that $\mathsf{QBRob}(\mathbf{w}, \varphi, \Sigma) > 0$ implies $\mathbf{w} \models \varphi$. Similarly, for any $\Sigma \in \boldsymbol{\Sigma}_\varphi$, it holds that $\mathsf{QBRob}(\mathbf{w}, \varphi, \Sigma) < 0$ implies $\mathbf{w} \not\models \varphi$.*

Proof. We first recall from [19, Prop. 16] that $[\![\mathbf{w}, \varphi]\!] < 0$ implies $\mathbf{w} \not\models \varphi$, and that $[\![\mathbf{w}, \varphi]\!] > 0$ implies $\mathbf{w} \models \varphi$. We prove Theorem 1 by induction on the structure of the formula.

- Case $\varphi = \alpha$. By Definition 7, $\mathsf{QBRob}(\mathbf{w}, \alpha, \varepsilon) > 0$ indicates that $[\![\mathbf{w}, \alpha]\!] > 0$ and hence $\mathbf{w} \models \alpha$, and $\mathsf{QBRob}(\mathbf{w}, \alpha, \varepsilon) < 0$ that $[\![\mathbf{w}, \alpha]\!] < 0$ and hence $\mathbf{w} \not\models \varphi$.
- For the following cases, let us assume that Theorem 1 holds for an arbitrary formula φ' and its sub-formula sequence Σ' that $\mathsf{QBRob}(\mathbf{w}, \varphi', \Sigma') > 0$ implies $[\![\mathbf{w}, \varphi']\!] > 0$, and that $\mathsf{QBRob}(\mathbf{w}, \varphi', \Sigma') < 0$ implies $[\![\mathbf{w}, \varphi']\!] < 0$. We aim to prove that Theorem 1 also holds for φ, resulting from the application of the operator in each of the following cases to φ', and Σ, the sub-formula sequence of φ.
  - Case $\varphi = \varphi' \wedge \psi$, where ψ is an arbitrary formula. Let $\Sigma = \varphi' \cdot \Sigma'$, and let us consider the two cases in which $\mathsf{QBRob}(\mathbf{w}, \varphi, \Sigma)$ is negative and positive separately:
    * If $\mathsf{QBRob}(\mathbf{w}, \varphi, \Sigma) < 0$, there are two sub-cases:
      · if $\mathsf{QBRob}(\mathbf{w}, \varphi', \Sigma') < 0$, then $[\![\mathbf{w}, \varphi']\!] < 0$ (by assumption). Then, by the robust semantics of conjunction, also $[\![\mathbf{w}, \varphi]\!] < 0$ holds, and so it does $\mathbf{w} \not\models \varphi$.

· if $\text{QBRob}(\mathbf{w}, \varphi', \Sigma') > 0$, then $[\![\mathbf{w}, \varphi']\!] > 0$ (by assumption). Then, it holds $\mathbf{w} \not\models \psi$ by Definition 7, and, therefore, it holds $\mathbf{w} \not\models \varphi$.

* If $\text{QBRob}(\mathbf{w}, \varphi, \Sigma) > 0$, it means that $\text{QBRob}(\mathbf{w}, \varphi', \Sigma') > 0$ and $\mathbf{w} \models \psi$ (by Definition 7). By assumption, if $\text{QBRob}(\mathbf{w}, \varphi', \Sigma') > 0$, then $[\![\mathbf{w}, \varphi']\!] > 0$. Therefore, $\mathbf{w} \models \varphi$.

- Case $\varphi = \square_I \varphi'$. Let $\Sigma = \Sigma'$, and let us consider the two cases in which $\text{QBRob}(\mathbf{w}, \varphi, \Sigma)$ is negative and positive separately:
  * By Definition 7, $\text{QBRob}(\mathbf{w}, \varphi, \Sigma) < 0$ indicates that there exists a $t \in I$ such that $\text{QBRob}(\mathbf{w}^t, \varphi', \Sigma) < 0$. By assumption, it holds that $\mathbf{w}^t \not\models \varphi'$. Then, by the semantics of the always operator $\square$, it holds that $\mathbf{w} \not\models \varphi$.
  * By Definition 7, $\text{QBRob}(\mathbf{w}, \varphi, \Sigma) > 0$ indicates that for all $t \in I$ it holds that $\text{QBRob}(\mathbf{w}^t, \varphi', \Sigma) > 0$. Then, by assumption, it holds that for all $t \in I$, $\mathbf{w}^t \models \varphi'$. So, by the semantics of the always operator $\square$, it holds that $\mathbf{w} \models \varphi$.
- Case $\varphi = \neg\varphi'$. Let $\Sigma = \Sigma'$, and let us consider the two cases in which $\text{QBRob}(\mathbf{w}, \varphi, \Sigma)$ is negative and positive separately:
  * By Definition 7, $\text{QBRob}(\mathbf{w}, \varphi, \Sigma) < 0$ indicates that $\text{QBRob}(\mathbf{w}, \varphi', \Sigma') > 0$. By assumption, it holds that $\mathbf{w} \models \varphi'$, and therefore, $\mathbf{w} \not\models \varphi$.
  * By Definition 7, $\text{QBRob}(\mathbf{w}, \varphi, \Sigma) > 0$ indicates that $\text{QBRob}(\mathbf{w}, \varphi', \Sigma') < 0$. By assumption, it holds that $\mathbf{w} \not\models \varphi'$, and, therefore, $\mathbf{w} \models \varphi$.
- Proofs for the cases of $\varphi = \varphi' \vee \psi$ and $\varphi = \Diamond_I \varphi'$ follow similar proof patterns, and so are left to the readers.

We use an example to illustrate how QB-Robustness is used for checking the satisfiability of an STL formula.

Example 2. Let $\mathbf{w}\colon [0, T] \to \mathbb{R}^2$ be a 2-dimensional signal and $\varphi = \square_I(\varphi_1 \vee \varphi_2)$ be an STL formula where φ_1 and φ_2 are two atomic formulas. Intuitively, to make φ falsified, there must exist $t \in I$ such that $\mathbf{w}^t \not\models \varphi_1$ and $\mathbf{w}^t \not\models \varphi_2$. Let us consider a non-trivial falsification problem in which, for most of the signals $\mathbf{w}$, sets $\{t \in I \mid \mathbf{w}^t \not\models \varphi_1\}$ and $\{t \in I \mid \mathbf{w}^t \not\models \varphi_2\}$ are non-empty and disjoint.

By Definition 7, given the sub-formula sequence $\Sigma = \varphi_1$ of φ, the corresponding QB-Robustness is $\text{QBRob}(\mathbf{w}, \varphi, \Sigma) = \bigsqcap_{t \in I} \text{QBRob}(\mathbf{w}^t, \varphi_1 \vee \varphi_2, \varphi_1)$, i.e., it takes the infimum of $\text{QBRob}(\mathbf{w}^t, \varphi_1 \vee \varphi_2, \varphi_1)$ over $t \in I$. Again, by Definition 7, for any $t' \in I$, $\text{QBRob}(\mathbf{w}^{t'}, \varphi_1 \vee \varphi_2, \varphi_1)$ is computed as follows:

- if for a $t' \in I$ it holds $\mathbf{w}^{t'} \models \varphi_2$, then $\text{QBRob}(\mathbf{w}^{t'}, \varphi_1 \vee \varphi_2, \varphi_1) = \infty$. Then, it is impossible that $\bigsqcap_{t \in I} \text{QBRob}(\mathbf{w}^t, \varphi_1 \vee \varphi_2, \varphi_1)$ is given by $\text{QBRob}(\mathbf{w}^{t'}, \varphi_1 \vee \varphi_2, \varphi_1)$;
- if for a $t' \in I$ it holds $\mathbf{w}^{t'} \not\models \varphi_2$, then $\text{QBRob}(\mathbf{w}^{t'}, \varphi_1 \vee \varphi_2, \varphi_1) = \text{QBRob}(\mathbf{w}^{t'}, \varphi_1, \varepsilon) = [\![\mathbf{w}^{t'}, \varphi_1]\!]$. In this case, $\text{QBRob}(\mathbf{w}^{t'}, \varphi_1 \vee \varphi_2, \varphi_1)$ has a chance to determine the value of $\bigsqcap_{t \in I} \text{QBRob}(\mathbf{w}^t, \varphi_1 \vee \varphi_2, \varphi_1)$.

Therefore, when $\Sigma = \varphi_1$, it holds that $\mathsf{QBRob}(\mathbf{w}, \varphi, \Sigma) = \prod_{t \in S} [\![\mathbf{w}^t, \varphi_1]\!]$, where $S = \{t \in I \mid \mathbf{w}^t \not\models \varphi_2\}$, i.e., the infimum of the quantitative robustness of φ_1 on the interval when φ_2 is violated. Indeed, once this value is negative, it means that there exists a point $t \in I$ when both φ_1 and φ_2 are violated; by the Boolean semantics of *always* and *disjunction*, φ is violated.

4   MCTS-Based Falsification Guided by QB-Robustness

QB-Robustness never compares robustness values coming from signals with different magnitudes, and, therefore, it does not suffer from the scale problem. As such, it could be used in falsification approaches instead of the classical pure quantitative robustness.

However, a sub-formula sequence Σ is required when calculating QB-Robustness, and such sequence is not unique (see Definition 7). Note that the selection of the sequence can affect the performance of the numerical optimization algorithms used in falsification. Let us consider $\varphi \equiv \Box((gear < 6) \wedge (speed < 130))$ as an example. As explained in Sect. 1, numerical optimization will perform better if guided by the robustness values coming from *speed* rather than by those coming from *gear*. Therefore, in a falsification approach using QB-Robustness, it is important to select an appropriate sub-formula sequence Σ.

By using the QB-Robustness, the problem of falsifying an STL formula φ consists in finding *both* a signal $\mathbf{w}$ and a sub-formula sequence Σ such that $\mathsf{QBRob}(\mathbf{w}, \varphi, \Sigma) < 0$. The selection of Σ is discrete, while the search for $\mathbf{w}$ is numerical. In order to combine these processes that are different in nature, we propose to adapt Monte Carlo Tree Search (MCTS) [8,28]. In the following, we firstly give a brief introduction to MCTS in Subsect. 4.1, and then present the application of MCTS to our falsification problem in Subsect. 4.2.

4.1   MCTS Background

MCTS exemplifies the "trial and error" philosophy, and has achieved a great success over the past decade, most notably in fields such as the computer Go game [35]. MCTS explores the action space given by the possible actions of the system; for example, in the Go game, these are the positions where to put the next stone. The approach builds a tree of sequences of actions, and assigns rewards to the different branches. MCTS performs the search by iteratively taking the following four steps. See Fig. 1, where the general scheme is adapted to our current setting, for illustration.

- *Selection.* It selects a node to expand or to reason about. Initially, selection has no other choice than the root. When a node has multiple expanded children, selection will be done according to the UCB1 [6] algorithm.
- *Expansion.* Child expansion happens after selection if the selected node has unexpanded children. A child will be added to the tree during expansion.
- *Playout.* After a node is just expanded or a leaf is reached, playout is performed for evaluating the node. The evaluation is given by a *reward*, which

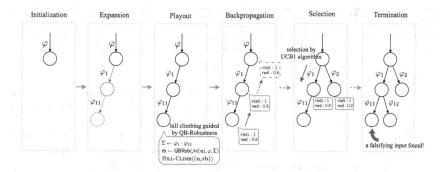

Fig. 1. The workflow of MCTS-based falsification guided by QB-Robustness. Let us consider the falsification of an STL formula $\varphi = \square_I (\varphi_1 \vee \varphi_2)$, where $\varphi_1 = \varphi_{11} \wedge \varphi_{12}$. Initially, there is only the root in the tree, so the algorithm selects it for expansion. Then, the algorithm keeps on randomly selecting a child of a non-fully expanded node, until a leaf node is reached. By reaching a leaf, a sub-formula sequence Σ has been constructed; the algorithm performs playout using Σ, by running hill-climbing optimization guided by the QB-Robustness with Σ, to estimate the reward of the path. After playout, the algorithm backpropagates the reward and the number of visits from the leaf to the root. When all the children of a node are expanded, selection is done based on the UCB1 algorithm. After many loops, the algorithm has explored all the possible sub-formula sequences in Σ_φ, and it starts allocating more resources to those branches where hill-climbing optimization progresses more smoothly. The algorithm terminates either when a falsifying input is found, or when the budget is exhausted.

is a real number in $[0, 1]$. Reward can be interpreted differently in different contexts. For example, in the Go game, the reward of a position is measured by the winning rate when a stone is positioned there; this is estimated by randomly playing the game until the end for n times, and then taking the ratio $\frac{n_w}{n}$ of the number of winning as the winning rate.

- *Backpropagation.* Backpropagation updates the number of visits and the reward of the nodes along the path from the node of playout to the root. These data are used in subsequent loops to decide the branches to explore.

At the end, the action space will be sufficiently explored in an unbalanced manner, by focusing on the most promising sub-spaces giving the highest rewards.

4.2 Proposed QB-Robustness-Guided Falsification Approach

We here propose a falsification framework based on MCTS in which, during tree construction, we synthesize and select a sub-formula sequence that facilitates the falsification progress the most, and, at the bottom layer of the tree, we run numerical optimization to search for a falsifying input and provide feedback (i.e., backpropagation) to guide the sequence selection.

We formalize our algorithm in Algorithm 2 and visualize its execution in Fig. 1. In the following, we elaborate on our approach.

Algorithm 2. MCTS-based falsification guided by QB-Robustness

---

Require: a system model $\mathcal{M}$, an STL formula φ, and the following tunable parameters: a scalar c for UCB1, an MCTS budget B_M, and a playout budget B_P.

1: **function** MCTS
2:    $\Sigma^{\text{init}} \leftarrow \varphi$ ▷ the root denoted as a sequence with φ only
3:    $\mathcal{T} \leftarrow \{\Sigma^{\text{init}}\}$ ▷ the MCTS search tree, initially root only
4:    $N \leftarrow (\Sigma^{\text{init}} \mapsto 0)$ ▷ visit count N initialized, defined only for root
5:    $R \leftarrow (\Sigma^{\text{init}} \mapsto 0)$ ▷ reward function R initialized
6:    $H \leftarrow (\Sigma^{\text{init}} \mapsto \varnothing)$ ▷ the sampling history of hill climbing
7:    **while** φ not falsified and within the MCTS budget B_M **do**
8:        MCTSSEARCH(Σ^{init})

9: **function** MCTSSEARCH(Σ)
10:    **if** $\mathsf{ISForm}(\Sigma_{\text{rear}}) \neq \varnothing$ **then**   ▷ the node has children
11:        **if** $\Sigma \cdot \varphi_k \in \mathcal{T}$ for all $\varphi_k \in \mathsf{ISForm}(\Sigma_{\text{rear}})$ **then**   ▷ all children expanded
12:          $\varphi_k \leftarrow \underset{\varphi_i \in \mathsf{ISForm}(\Sigma_{\text{rear}})}{\arg\max} \left(R(\Sigma \cdot \varphi_i) + c\sqrt{\dfrac{2\ln N(\Sigma)}{N(\Sigma \cdot \varphi_i)}} \right)$ ▷ selection by UCB1
13:        **else**   ▷ unexpanded children exist
14:          randomly select φ_k from $\{\varphi_k \in \mathsf{ISForm}(\Sigma_{\text{rear}}) \mid \Sigma \cdot \varphi_k \notin \mathcal{T}\}$
15:          $\mathcal{T} \leftarrow \mathcal{T} \cup \{\Sigma \cdot \varphi_k\}$ ▷ expand a new child
16:          $N(\Sigma \cdot \varphi_k) \leftarrow 0$
17:          $H(\Sigma \cdot \varphi_k) \leftarrow \varnothing$
18:        MCTSSEARCH($\Sigma \cdot \varphi_k$)   ▷ recursive call
19:        $R(\Sigma) \leftarrow \underset{\varphi_k \in \mathsf{ISForm}(\Sigma_{\text{rear}})}{\max} R(\Sigma \cdot \varphi_k)$ ▷ back propagation for reward
20:    **else**   ▷ a leaf node reached
21:        **while** within playout budget B_P **do** ▷ playout by hill-climbing falsification
22:          $\mathbf{u} \leftarrow \text{HILL-CLIMB}(H(\Sigma))$ ▷ hill-climbing
23:          $\mathsf{rb} \leftarrow \mathsf{QBRob}(\mathcal{M}(\mathbf{u}), \varphi, \Sigma_{\overline{\text{head}}})$
24:          **if** $\mathsf{rb} < 0$ **then**   ▷ falsifying input found
25:            **return** $(\mathbf{u}, \mathsf{rb})$
26:          $H(\Sigma) \leftarrow H(\Sigma) \cup \{(\mathbf{u}, \mathsf{rb})\}$ ▷ record sampling history
27:        $R(w) \leftarrow \mathsf{Rwd}(\mathsf{rb}, H(\Sigma))$
28:    $N(\Sigma) \leftarrow N(\Sigma) + 1$ ▷ back propagation for visit count

---

We construct the tree in this way: each node represents a sequence of formulas, and each edge of a node is a sub-formula of the last element of the sequence represented by the node. The root is initialized with a sequence holding φ only (Lines 2–3) and some other properties including the number of visits to the different nodes (Line 4), the reward (Line 5), and the history of hill-climbing sampling (Line 6). The main process of MCTS consists in calling the MCTSSEARCH function iteratively with the root as argument (Line 8), until the exhaustion of the MCTS budget or a falsifying input is found (Line 7). The MCTSSEARCH function (Line 9) goes through the four phases, namely *selection, expansion, playout* and *backpropagation,* of the original MCTS algorithm.

Selection. Selection happens when a node has children (Line 10) and these have all been expanded (Line 11). It selects a child according to the UCB1 [6] algorithm (Line 12) to take a balance between exploration and exploitation. The exploitation is embodied by the reward $R(\Sigma \cdot \varphi_i)$—the higher the reward is, the more likely a falsifying input is found following that branch. Exploration, instead, is considered via $\sqrt{\frac{2\ln N(\Sigma)}{N(\Sigma \cdot \varphi_i)}}$ that is negatively correlated to the number of visits to a child—the more the child was visited before, the less chance it will be visited again. The scalar c is a tunable parameter that balances the trade-off between exploration and exploitation. After a child $\Sigma \cdot \varphi_k$ is selected, it will be taken as the argument of the next MCTSSEARCH loop (Line 18).

Expansion. If not all the children of a node have been expanded (Line 13), a child will be expanded. Expansion consists in randomly selecting a child from the unexpanded child list (Line 14), adding it to the tree (Line 15), initilizing properties including the number of visits and history (Lines 16–17). After expansion, the newly expanded child will be taken as the argument of the recursive call to MCTSSEARCH (Line 18).

Playout. If a leaf node that has no children to expand is reached, the playout phase will start to devise a reward for evaluating the visited path. In our context, we define the reward based on the best robustness value that can be obtained with the path; specifically, playout consists in running hill-climbing guided falsification to search for a minimal robustness value (Line 22). Note that the sequence Σ represented by a leaf node is actually the concatenation between φ and a sub-formula sequence of φ. We extract the suffix of Σ, i.e., the sub-formula sequence, to compute the QB-Robustness as a guidance to the hill-climbing optimization (Line 23). If a negative QB-Robustness is found (Line 24), then the whole algorithm can be terminated and the input signal $\mathbf{u}$ that triggers the negative QB-Robustness can be returned as the falsifying input (Line 25); otherwise, the sampling history of hill climbing will be saved (Line 26) so that the future playout at the same leaf can be restored from that context. After playout, the reward of the leaf node will be updated based on the definition of the reward, which will be introduced below. *Reward* Since our goal is to find a sequence Σ with which hill-climbing optimization can minimize $\mathsf{QBRob}(\mathbf{w}, \varphi, \Sigma)$ smoothly, we connect the reward with the hill-climbing progress. Formally, given a sampling history H, our reward (Line 27) is defined as $\mathsf{Rwd}(\mathsf{rb}', H) := \frac{\max \mathsf{rb}_h - \min(\{\mathsf{rb}'\} \cup \mathsf{rb}_h)}{\max \mathsf{rb}_h}$, where rb_h is the history of robustness values in H.

Backpropagation. In MCTS, the playout result of a leaf is backpropagated to the higher layer nodes along the path, so that the future selection on the high layer is referred. Backpropagation updates two properties of each ancestor of the leaf till the root, the reward (Line 19) and the number of visits (Line 28).

Remark 1 (Approach Complexity). With respect to classical falsification, our approach introduces an exploration phase for searching the "best" sub-formula sequence to instantiate QB-Robustness. The number of these sequences corresponds to the number of atomic sub-formulas (and so the leaves of the

Table 1. Benchmarks – STL specifications

Spec. ID	Temporal specification in STL	Spec. ID	Temporal specification in STL
AT1	$\square_{[0,30]}\ (gear = 4 \rightarrow speed > 35)$	AT8	$\square_{[0,10]}\ (speed < 50) \vee \Diamond_{[0,30]}\ (rpm > 2520)$
AT2	$\square_{[0,30]}\ (gear = 4 \rightarrow \Diamond_{[0,5]}\ (rpm < 4300))$	AT9	$\Diamond_{[10,30]}(speed < 50 \vee speed > 60 \vee rpm < 1000)$
AT3	$\square_{[0,30]}\ (speed < 130 \wedge gear < 5)$	AT10	$\square_{[0,30]}\ (gear = 4 \rightarrow (speed > 35 \wedge \Diamond_{[0,5]}\ (rpm < 4000)))$
AT4	$\square_{[0,30]}\ (speed < 135 \wedge rpm < 4780)$	AT11	$\square_{[0,30]}\ (\Diamond_{[0,8]}\ (gear = 1 \rightarrow (speed < 20 \wedge rpm < 600)))$
AT5	$\square_{[0,30]}\ (rpm < 600 \rightarrow \Diamond_{[0,10]}\ (gear > 1))$	AT12	$\square_{[0,30]}\ (gear < 3) \vee \square_{[0,30]}\ (speed < 135 \wedge rpm < 4780)$
AT6	$\square_{[0,30]}\ (\Diamond_{[0,5]}(speed < 120 \vee rpm > 3500))$	AT13	$\square_{[0,30]}\ ((gear = 4 \rightarrow \Diamond_{[0,5]}\ (rpm < 4000)) \wedge gear < 5)$
AT7	$\square_{[0,30]}\ (rpm < 4750 \wedge gear < 5)$	AT14	$\square_{[0,30]}\ (throttle = 0 \vee brake = 0) \rightarrow \square_{[0,30]}\ (speed < 110)$

Spec. ID	Temporal specification in STL
AT15	$\square_{[0,30]}((rpm < 4770 \vee \square_{[0,1]}\ (rpm > 1000)) \wedge \Diamond_{[0,5]}\ (gear < 5))$
AT16	$\square_{[0,30]}\ (gear = 4 \rightarrow ((\Diamond_{[0,5]}\ (rpm < 3000) \wedge (gear = 2 \rightarrow speed < 20))))$
AT17	$\square_{[0,5]}\ (speed < 70 \wedge gear < 4) \wedge \square_{[10,20]}(rpm < 4780) \wedge \square_{[25,30]}(speed < 130)$
AT18	$\square_{[0,30]}\ ((gear = 4 \rightarrow \Diamond_{[0,5]}\ (rpm < 4250)) \wedge (gear = 3 \rightarrow \Diamond_{[0,5]}\ (rpm < 4700)) \wedge (gear = 2 \rightarrow \Diamond_{[0,5]}\ (rpm < 4800)))$
AT19	$\square_{[0,30]}\ ((gear = 1 \rightarrow speed < 80) \wedge (gear = 2 \rightarrow speed < 90) \wedge (gear = 3 \rightarrow speed > 20) \wedge (gear = 4 \rightarrow speed > 30))$
AT20	$\square_{[0,29]}\ (speed < 100) \vee \square_{[29,30]}(speed > 64) \wedge \square_{[0,30]}\ (rpm < 4770 \vee \square_{[0,1]}\ (rpm > 700))$
AT21	$\square_{[0,30]}\ (throttle > 90 \rightarrow \Diamond_{[0,10]}\ (throttle < 30)) \rightarrow \square_{[0,30]}\ (gear = 4 \rightarrow \Diamond_{[0,5]}\ (rpm < 4000))$
AT22	$\square_{[0,30]}\ (throttle > 70 \rightarrow \Diamond_{[0,10]}(brake > 50)) \rightarrow \square_{[0,30]}(gear = 4 \rightarrow speed > 35)$

Spec. ID	Temporal specification in STL
AFC1	$\square_{[11,50]}\ (mode = 1 \rightarrow \mu < 0.228)$
AFC2	$\Diamond_{[0,50]}\ (PedalAngle > 40) \rightarrow \square_{[11,50]}\ (\mu < 0.225)$
AFC3	$\Diamond_{[0,50]}\ (EngineSpeed > 1000) \rightarrow \square_{[11,50]}\ (\mu < 0.225)$
AFC4	$\square_{[0,50]}\ (EngineSpeed > 910 \vee PedalAngle > 25) \rightarrow \square_{[11,50]}\ (\mu < 0.225)$
AFC5	$\Diamond_{[0,50]}\ (PedalAngle > 40) \rightarrow \square_{[11,50]}\ (\Diamond_{[0,8]}\ (\mu < 0.06))$
AFC6	$\Diamond_{[0,50]}\ (PedalAngle > 40 \wedge EngineSpeed > 1000) \rightarrow \square_{[11,50]}\ (\Diamond_{[0,8]}\ (\mu < 0.06))$

Spec. ID	Temporal specification in STL
FFR1	$\square_{[0,5]}((u1, u3 > 0 \vee u1, u3 < 0) \wedge (u2, u4 > 0 \vee u2, u4 < 0)) \rightarrow \square_{[0,5]}(\neg(x1 > 3.9 \wedge x1 < 4.1) \wedge \neg(x3 > 3.9 \wedge x3 < 4.1))$
FFR2	$\neg(\Diamond_{[0,5]}(\square_{[0,2]}(x1 > 1.5 \wedge x1 < 1.7 \wedge x3 > 1.5 \wedge x3 < 1.7)))$

tree). Considering that most of the time is spent on playout, the complexity of our approach grows linearly with the number of atomic sub-formulas.

5 Experimental Evaluation

In this section, we present the experiments we conducted to evaluate the effectiveness of the proposed approach. We first introduce the experiment setup in Subsect. 5.1, and then we present the experimental evaluation results by answering three research questions in Subsect. 5.2.

5.1 Experiment Setup

Simulink Models and Specifications As our benchmarks, we selected three Simulink models frequently used in the falsification community (i.e., in the falsification competitions [18]), and 30 specifications defined for them. All these models are complicated hybrid systems with multiple input and output signals. The specifications are STL formulas that formalize system requirements regarding safety, performance, etc. Since we are interested in assessing the influence of the scale problem to the performance of the compared falsification approaches, all the considered specifications predicate over, at least, two signals. Table 1 reports the 30 specifications under test. The IDs of the specifications identify which models they belong to. A description of the three models and of their specifications is as follows.

- *Automatic Transmission* (AT) [24] has two input signals, *throttle* $\in [0, 100]$ and *brake* $\in [0, 325]$, and three outputs signals including *gear*, *speed* and *rpm*. Most of the specifications we used formalize safety requirements of the system. For instance, AT2 requires that when *gear* is as high as 4, *rpm* should not be larger than 4300; AT3 is an adaptation of the example we used in Sect. 1; AT10-12 reason about the relationship among the three output signals; AT17 specifies three properties for three different time intervals; AT18 specifies different properties for different values of *gear*; AT14, AT21 and AT22 impose logical constraints on input signals, in addition to the property under consideration.

- *Abstract Fuel Control* (AFC) [25] takes two input signals, *PedalAngle* $\in [8.8, 70]$ and *EngineSpeed* $\in [900, 1100]$, and outputs a ratio μ reflecting the deviation of *air-fuel-ratio* from its reference value. The basic safety requirement to this system is that μ should not be deviated from the reference value too much (AFC1); in addition to that, our specifications also reason about the resilience of the system (AFC5 and AFC6), and impose input constraints (AFC2-6).

- *Free Floating Robot* (FFR) [11] models robot moving in a 2-dimentional space. It has four input signals $u_1, u_2, u_3, u_4 \in [-10, 10]$ that are boosters for a robot, and four output signals that are the position in terms of coordinate values x, y and their one-order derivatives $\dot{x}, \dot{y}$. The specifications regulate the kinetic properties of the robot: FFR1 requires the robot to pass an area around the point $(4, 4)$ under an input constraint, and FFR2 requires the robot to stay in an area for at least 2 s.

Baseline Approach and Our Proposed Approach. In our experiments, we compare the performances of our proposed approach with the baseline `Breach` approach. We implemented our approach in the tool `ForeSee`, which stands for **FOR**mula Exploitation by **S**equence tr**EE** for falsification.

`Breach` is a state-of-the-art falsification tool that implements the classic falsification workflow we introduced in Sect. 2. The quantitative robustness calculation in `Breach` is based on the robust semantics given in Definition 2. `Breach` also encapsulates several stochastic optimization algorithms, such as CMA-ES, Simulated Annealing, etc. The implementation of our `ForeSee` approach uses `Breach` only for interfacing with the Simulink model and for the calculation of quantitative robustness; instead, the calculation of QB-Robustness, and the implementation of the MCTS algorithm are novel. Since CMA-ES has proved to be the state-of-the-art stochastic algorithm [39], we select CMA-ES as our backend optimizer for the playout phase.[3]

---

[3] `ForeSee` is available at https://github.com/choshina/ForeSee.

We apply the two approaches, `ForeSee` and `Breach`, to each benchmark specification reported in Table 1. Since both approaches are based on stochastic optimization, we repeat each experiment for 30 times, as suggested by a guideline for conducting experiments with randomized algorithms [5]. For each experiment, both approaches have been given a total timeout B_M of 900 s (see Algorithm 2).

Evaluation Metrics. As first evaluation metric, we compute the *falsification rate (FR)* as the number of runs (out of 30) in which the approach returns a falsifying input. Therefore, FR is an indicator of the *effectiveness* of an approach, i.e., it reflects the ability of an algorithm to falsify the specification. As second evaluation metric, we compute the *average time* (seconds), as average execution time of the successful falsification runs. Therefore, the average time is an indicator of the *efficiency* of the approach. We do not report the number of simulations because these are consistent with the execution time.

Experiment Platform. In our experiments, we use `Breach` [13] (ver 1.2.13) with CMA-ES (the state of the art). `Breach` accepts piece-wise constant signals as input for the Simulink models; we use the same settings used in falsification competitions [18]: we use piece-wise constant signals with five control points for AT and AFC, and with four control points for FFR. As configuration of MCTS (see Algorithm 2), we set the UCB1 scalar c to 0.2, and the playout budget B_P to 10 generations. The experiments have been executed on an Amazon EC2 c4.2xlarge instance (2.9 GHz Intel Xeon E5-2666 v3, 15 GB RAM).

5.2 Evaluation

We here analyze the experimental results using three research questions (RQs).

RQ1. *Does the proposed approach perform better than state-of-the-art falsification approaches?*

In this RQ, we aim at assessing whether the proposed approach is indeed able to tackle the scale problem in falsification and performs better than state-of-the-art approaches. Table 2 reports, for each specification benchmark, the falsification rate FR and the average execution time of our proposed approach `ForeSee` and of the baseline `Breach`. The table further reports the difference of the two metrics between the two approaches. We highlight in gray the best results in which `ForeSee` has an FR of 15 units higher than `Breach`. We observe that for 25 benchmarks out of 30, `ForeSee` has a better FR, and in 15 of these the improvement is significant (selected in gray). Note that there are notable cases, such as AT3, AT13, AT16, and AT17, in which `Breach` only finds at most two falsifying inputs, while `ForeSee` finds always at least 29 falsifying inputs. In four cases, `Breach` has a better FR: while for AT8, AFC6, and FFR2 the difference is minimal, it is quite large for AT14. We further inspected such specification and its corresponding model (see Table 1); we noticed that all the sub-formulas in AT14 must be falsified to falsify the whole specification[4], and they are all

---

[4] Note that all binary connectives of AT14 are disjunctions; indeed, $A \rightarrow B$ is the syntactic sugar for $\neg A \bigsqcup_B$.

Table 2. Falsification performance comparison between `Breach` and `ForeSee` on benchmarks. Timeout: 900 s. FR in (/30), time in secs.

	Breach		ForeSee					Breach		ForeSee			
	FR	time	FR	time	ΔFR	Δtime		FR	time	FR	time	ΔFR	Δtime
AT1	12	67.0	29	90.3	+17	+23.3	AT12	5	379.2	28	381.4	+23	+2.2
AT2	18	208.5	30	155.5	+12	-53.0	AT13	2	75.2	29	98.3	+27	+23.1
AT3	0	-	29	87.3	+29	-	AT14	24	184.9	1	601.5	-23	+416.6
AT4	8	414.0	30	376.6	+12	-37.4	AT15	1	66.1	9	331.8	+8	+265.7
AT5	13	44.7	30	159.0	+17	+114.3	AT16	1	13.0	30	6.7	+29	-6.3
AT6	14	630.5	20	545.9	+6	-84.6	AT17	0	-	30	208.8	+30	-
AT7	20	24.9	30	5.8	+10	-19.1	AT18	18	160.0	24	234.3	+6	+74.3
AT8	17	418.5	13	547.0	-4	+128.5	AT19	15	81.8	30	154.3	+15	+72.5
AT9	9	298.6	29	208.0	+20	-90.6	AT20	1	97.7	5	286.2	+4	+188.5
AT10	14	99.4	30	89.7	+16	-9.7	AT21	10	239.0	29	425.5	+19	+186.5
AT11	17	58.1	30	39.6	+13	-18.5	AT22	13	72.0	30	113.3	+17	+41.3

	Breach		ForeSee					Breach		ForeSee			
	FR	time	FR	time	ΔFR	Δtime		FR	time	FR	time	ΔFR	Δtime
AFC1	10	532.2	12	458.0	+2	-74.2	AFC4	7	634.5	22	500.3	+15	-134.2
AFC2	12	546.9	30	218.3	+18	-328.6	AFC5	8	576.9	9	322.0	+1	-254.9
AFC3	8	727.6	28	232.5	+20	-495.1	AFC6	10	518.2	6	344.2	-4	-174.0

	Breach		ForeSee					Breach		ForeSee			
	FR	time	FR	time	ΔFR	Δtime		FR	time	FR	time	ΔFR	Δtime
FFR1	7	132.1	7	399.3	+0	+267.2	FFR2	30	38.0	27	348.0	-3	+310.0

difficult to be falsified. In such a case, there is no best sub-formula sequence Σ: therefore, the time spent by `ForeSee` in exploring different Σ does not provide any improvement.

Regarding the time execution, there is no clear trend among the different results: sometimes `ForeSee` is faster, other times `Breach` is. However, even in the cases in which `ForeSee` is slower, it is still below the timeout by which it manages to find a falsifying input (so, leading to better falsification rates).

RQ2. *Does the proposed approach solve the scale problem effectively?*

The benchmarks reported in Table 1 and experimented in RQ1, predicate over signals having different scales and so they suffer from the scale problem. RQ1 showed that `ForeSee` is very efficient in falsifying them. In this RQ, we want to make a more systematic study of the effects of the scale problem; indeed, the scale problem could manifest itself in *different ways*, depending on the difference of the order of magnitudes of the different signals (e.g., speed [km/h] vs. rpm, or speed [km/h] vs. rph). To assess this, we take six specifications from Table 1 and we artificially modify their outputs: namely, we multiply by 10^k (with different k values depending on the specification) the *speed* of AT1, AT3, AT4,

Table 3. Falsification performance under different scales. Each rescaled signal is rescaled by 10^k.

(a) AT1: *speed* $\times 10^k$

k	Breach FR	Breach time	ForeSee FR	ForeSee time
-2	30	126.5	26	77.5
-1	25	64.4	29	107.9
0	12	67.0	29	90.3
1	9	92.4	28	81.8
2	9	131.9	30	94.2
min	9	64.4	26	77.5
max	30	131.9	30	107.9
mean	17	96.4	28	90.3

(b) AT3: *speed* $\times 10^k$

k	Breach FR	Breach time	ForeSee FR	ForeSee time
-3	30	124.9	30	81.2
-2	30	135.9	28	82.6
-1	1	136.7	28	101.6
0	0	-	29	87.3
1	0	-	30	103.4
min	0	124.9	28	81.2
max	30	136.7	30	103.4
mean	12	132.5	29	91.2

(c) AT4: *speed* $\times 10^k$

k	Breach FR	Breach time	ForeSee FR	ForeSee time
-2	29	247.2	29	329.4
-1	29	243.5	28	332.2
0	8	414.0	30	376.6
1	0	-	29	377.6
2	0	-	29	333.2
min	0	243.5	28	329.4
max	29	414.0	30	377.6
mean	13	301.6	29	349.8

(d) AT9: *speed* $\times 10^k$

k	Breach FR	Breach time	ForeSee FR	ForeSee time
-1	11	202.6	28	259.8
0	9	298.6	29	208.0
1	10	197.4	29	221.2
2	28	175.4	29	248.9
3	30	162.6	29	209.6
min	9	162.6	28	208.0
max	30	298.6	29	259.8
mean	18	207.3	29	229.5

(e) AT15: *rpm* $\times 10^k$

k	Breach FR	Breach time	ForeSee FR	ForeSee time
-5	20	138.3	6	222.3
-4	13	158.1	10	258.8
-3	4	144.6	5	313.6
-2	0	-	9	268.6
0	1	66.1	9	331.8
min	0	66.1	5	222.3
max	20	158.1	10	331.8
mean	10	126.8	8	279.0

(f) AFC3: *EngineSpeed* $\times 10^k$

k	Breach FR	Breach time	ForeSee FR	ForeSee time
0	8	727.6	28	232.5
-1	18	574.2	29	284.1
-2	29	401.2	29	211.5
-3	30	215.0	29	230.1
-4	29	198.2	30	236.2
min	8	198.2	28	211.5
max	30	727.7	30	284.1
mean	23	423.2	29	238.9

and AT9; the *rpm* of AT15; and the *EngineSpeed* of AFC3. For each artificial rescaling, both the Simulink model and the specification have been changed.[5] We run `ForeSee` and `Breach` on these rescaled benchmarks. Table 3 reports the experimental results for each k. The table also reports the minimum, maximum, and mean results for FR and execution time. We observe that the performance of `Breach`, in terms of FR, is very sensitive to the scale problem. Indeed, for all the specifications, FR decreases with increasing or decreasing k; notable examples are AT3 and AT4 in which `Breach` can (almost) always falsify with the minimum k, but never falsifies with the maximum two k. This is the demonstration of the effects of the scale problem on falsification approaches that only rely on quantitative robust semantics where the robustness values of different signals are compared. By looking at the results of `ForeSee`, instead, we observe that it is much more robust and its FR performance is independent of the applied rescaling. This clearly shows that our falsification approach guided by QB-Robustness is successful in avoiding the scale problem.

---

[5] Note that $k = 0$ corresponds to the experimental result in Table 2, and we report it again for reference.

Table 4. Falsification performance under different MCTS hyperparameters.

(a) Performance with varied c						(b) Performance with varied B_P					
	AT17		AT19		AT21		AT17		AT19		AT21
c	FR	time	FR	time	FR	time	B_P	FR	time	FR	time	FR	time
0	23	177.8	30	224.6	30	463.4	2	26	385.2	30	162.0	29	500.0
0.02	26	196.7	30	278.5	28	501.3	5	30	347.7	29	207.3	29	472.5
0.2	30	208.8	30	154.3	29	425.5	10	30	208.8	30	154.3	29	425.5
0.5	30	297.0	29	227.3	30	509.0	15	30	337.7	29	336.7	28	514.0
1.0	30	311.7	30	240.2	24	497.0	20	30	358.1	30	313.5	30	511.0

These results also allow us to show that the naive approach based on normalization for solving the scale problem does not work, as also reported in [41]. Indeed, one may think that a solution for tackling the scale problem could be to rescale the signals in a way to make them have the same order of magnitude. This is not a good approach. Let us consider the results in Table 3c for AT4 ($\Box_{[0,30]}$ ($speed < 135 \wedge rpm < 4780$)). In this case, $speed$ is multiplied by 10^k. We may think that the best falsification result should occur when $speed$ is multiplied by 10^2, because this would make the two signals both in the order of thousands. However, this rescaling is the one giving the worst result. The best result is actually given by the rescaling making $speed$ even smaller (i.e., $k = -2$ and $k = -1$). This means that the correct way for handling the scale problem cannot be identified in advance, but we need an approach as ours that *learns* during falsification the best strategy.

RQ3. *How do the hyperparameters of MCTS influence the performance of the proposed approach?*

Our proposed approach is an instantiation of the Monte Carlo Tree Search (MCTS) method [8,28] that can be configured with some hyperparameters, namely the scalar c used by UCB1 (Line 12 in Algorithm 2), and the playout budget B_P (Line 21 in Algorithm 2), both used for balancing between exploration and exploitation. Therefore, the performance of MCTS could be affected by the values used for these hyperparameters. In this RQ, we try to assess this. We selected three benchmarks specifications (AT17, AT19, and AT21) and varied one hyperparameter while keeping the other fixed. Namely, we experimented with $c \in \{0, 0.02, 0.2, 0.5, 1\}$ and budget $B_P = 10$ (see Table 4a), and with $B_P \in \{2, 5, 10, 15, 20\}$ and budget $c = 0.2$ (see Table 4b). Looking at the results of Table 4a for AT17 and AT21, there seems to be some influence by the scalar c. In AT17, the worst result in terms of FR is obtained when c is 0, meaning that MCTS only focuses on *exploitation*. AT17 is a specification that suffers from the scale problem, as shown by the very bad performance of Breach in Table 2; for such a specification, we need to perform some *exploration* to find the best Σ: this explain the low performance of MCTS with $c = 0$. On the other hand, the worst FR performance of AT21 is given by the highest value $c = 1$ that requires MCTS to spend a lot of time in exploration. Since AT21 is not an extremely difficult specification (indeed Breach has FR of 10 in Table 2), such very conservative approach does not pay off, while more greedy approaches (i.e., with lower c) have better performance.

Looking at the results of Table 4b related to B_P, it seems that there is no too much influence. The only difference is given in AT17 with $B_P = 2$ where the FR is slightly lower than the other cases. This means that, provided that a sufficiently large value for B_P is given, ForeSee is not too sensitive to it.

6   Related Work

Quality assurance of CPS has been actively studied, due to its great significance. Different approaches, including but not limited to model checking, theorem proving, rigorous numerics, and nonstandard analysis [9,16,20,22,23,31,33], have been proposed to solve the problem. However, due to the scalability issue and existence of black-box components, those approaches are not widely applied in the real-world systems.

The optimization-based falsification approach inherits the search-based testing methodology, and is much more scalable than pure verification-based approaches. The key issue of search-based testing is the *exploration-exploitation trade-off*. This issue has been discussed for the verification of quantitative properties (e.g., [34]). In the falsification community, there have also been a lot of works focusing on that, and these works tackle the problem from different perspectives. *Metaheuristics* refers to high-level heuristic strategies that utilize heuristics to improve the search efficiency. Several metaheuristic strategies have been applied in falsification, such as *Simulated Annealing* [1], *tabu search* [10], and so on. *Coverage-guided falsification* [2,10,15,29] aims to guide the search using some coverage metrics, so that the search space is sufficiently explored. Recently, machine learning techniques have also been applied to falsification to enhance the search ability. For instance, *Bayesian optimization* [3,11,36] utilizes an *acquisition function* to balance exploration and exploitation; *Reinforcement learning* [27,37] naturally emphasizes on exploration.

The scale problem is a recognized issue [12,21,40] that is known to severely affect the performance of falsification. In [40], we proposed a multi-armed bandit approach to solve the problem in a specific setting, that is, safety properties with Boolean connectives: $\Box_I (\varphi_1 \land \varphi_2)$ and $\Box_I (\varphi_1 \lor \varphi_2)$. The approach is not applicable to formulas having more nested sub-formulas, or even connectives having more operands; therefore many of the benchmarks we used in Subsect. 5.2 fall out of the scope of [40]. The techniques introduced in [12,21] rely on explicit declaration of *input vacuity* and *output robustness*. Compared to their approaches, our method does not need that, but we learn the significance of each signal through tree exploration and reward computation.

MCTS, as an effective search framework, has been applied in testing hybrid systems. In [30], the authors applied an adaption of MCTS in testing, namely, adaptive press testing, to detect the potential dangerous cases of airborne collision. A recent study of MCTS on hybrid system falsification is [39]. There, the authors discretized the search space to construct the search tree, and then applied MCTS to explore different sub-spaces. Compared to their approach, our work aims to tackle the scale problem and so we exploit the structure of specification formulas to construct the tree search framework.

7   Conclusion and Future Work

Optimization-based falsification is a widely used approach for quality assurance of CPS, that tries to find an input violating a Signal Temporal Logic (STL) specification. It does this by exploiting the quantitative robust semantics of the specification, trying to minimize its robustness. The performance of falsification is affected by the *scale problem* in the presence of the comparison of robustness values of sub-formulas predicating over signals having different scales. In this paper, we propose QB-Robustness, a new STL semantics that does not suffer from the scale problem, because it avoids such comparison. The computation of QB-Robustness requires to specify a sub-formula sequence telling for which sub-formulas the quantitative robustness must be computed. We then propose a Monte Carlo Tree Search (MCTS)-based falsification approach that synthesizes a sub-formula sequence for QB-Robustness, and uses this for guiding numerical optimization. Experimental results show that the proposed approach achieves better falsification results than a state-of-the-art falsification tool that uses standard quantitative robust semantics.

In the analysis of RQ1, we observed that, when the specifications have a particular structure, our approach has no advantage and, actually, it could decrease the performance by trying to find a best sub-formula sequence that does not exist for the current initial sampling. As future work, we plan to devise some heuristics that could handle these cases: for example, we could perform a better initial sampling (see Subsect. 2.1) that could provide a better initial guidance.

References

1. Abbas, H., Fainekos, G.: Convergence proofs for simulated annealing falsification of safety properties. In: 50th Annual Allerton Conference on Communication, Control, and Computing, pp. 1594–1601. IEEE (2012)
2. Adimoolam, A., Dang, T., Donzé, A., Kapinski, J., Jin, X.: Classification and coverage-based falsification for embedded control systems. In: Majumdar, R., Kunčak, V. (eds.) CAV 2017. LNCS, vol. 10426, pp. 483–503. Springer, Cham (2017). https://doi.org/10.1007/978-3-319-63387-9_24
3. Akazaki, T., Kumazawa, Y., Hasuo, I.: Causality-aided falsification. In: Proceedings First Workshop on Formal Verification of Autonomous Vehicles, FVAV@iFM 2017, Turin, Italy, 19th September 2017. EPTCS, vol. 257, pp. 3–18 (2017)
4. Annpureddy, Y., Liu, C., Fainekos, G., Sankaranarayanan, S.: S-TaLiRo: a tool for temporal logic falsification for hybrid systems. In: Abdulla, P.A., Leino, K.R.M. (eds.) TACAS 2011. LNCS, vol. 6605, pp. 254–257. Springer, Heidelberg (2011). https://doi.org/10.1007/978-3-642-19835-9_21

5. Arcuri, A., Briand, L.: A practical guide for using statistical tests to assess randomized algorithms in software engineering. In: Proceedings of the 33rd International Conference on Software Engineering, ICSE 2011, pp. 1–10. ACM New York (2011)

6. Auer, P.: Using confidence bounds for exploitation-exploration trade-offs. J. Mach. Learn. Res. **3**, 397–422 (2002)

7. Auger, A., Hansen, N.: A restart CMA evolution strategy with increasing population size. In: Proceedings of the IEEE Congress on Evolutionary Computation, CEC 2005, pp. 1769–1776. IEEE (2005)

8. Browne, C., et al.: A survey of monte carlo tree search methods. IEEE Trans. Comput. Intellig. AI Games **4**(1), 1–43 (2012)

9. Chen, X., Ábrahám, E., Sankaranarayanan, S.: Flow*: an analyzer for non-linear hybrid systems. In: Sharygina, N., Veith, H. (eds.) CAV 2013. LNCS, vol. 8044, pp. 258–263. Springer, Heidelberg (2013). https://doi.org/10.1007/978-3-642-39799-8_18

10. Deshmukh, J., Jin, X., Kapinski, J., Maler, O.: Stochastic local search for falsification of hybrid systems. In: Finkbeiner, B., Pu, G., Zhang, L. (eds.) ATVA 2015. LNCS, vol. 9364, pp. 500–517. Springer, Cham (2015). https://doi.org/10.1007/978-3-319-24953-7_35

11. Deshmukh, J.V., Horvat, M., Jin, X., Majumdar, R., Prabhu, V.S.: Testing cyber-physical systems through bayesian optimization. ACM Trans. Embedded Comput. Syst. **16**(5), 170:1–170:18 (2017)

12. Dokhanchi, A., Yaghoubi, S., Hoxha, B., Fainekos, G.E.: Vacuity aware falsification for MTL request-response specifications. In: 13th IEEE Conference on Automation Science and Engineering, CASE 2017, Xi'an, China, 20–23 August 2017, pp. 1332–1337. IEEE (2017)

13. Donzé, A.: Breach, a toolbox for verification and parameter synthesis of hybrid systems. In: Touili, T., Cook, B., Jackson, P. (eds.) CAV 2010. LNCS, vol. 6174, pp. 167–170. Springer, Heidelberg (2010). https://doi.org/10.1007/978-3-642-14295-6_17

14. Donzé, A., Maler, O.: Robust satisfaction of temporal logic over real-valued signals. In: Chatterjee, K., Henzinger, T.A. (eds.) FORMATS 2010. LNCS, vol. 6246, pp. 92–106. Springer, Heidelberg (2010). https://doi.org/10.1007/978-3-642-15297-9_9

15. Dreossi, T., Dang, T., Donzé, A., Kapinski, J., Jin, X., Deshmukh, J.V.: Efficient guiding strategies for testing of temporal properties of hybrid systems. In: Havelund, K., Holzmann, G., Joshi, R. (eds.) NFM 2015. LNCS, vol. 9058, pp. 127–142. Springer, Cham (2015). https://doi.org/10.1007/978-3-319-17524-9_10

16. Dreossi, T., Dang, T., Piazza, C.: Parallelotope bundles for polynomial reachability. In: Proceedings of the 19th International Conference on Hybrid Systems: Computation and Control, HSCC 2016 pp. 297–306. ACM, New York (2016)

17. Dreossi, T., Donzé, A., Seshia, S.A.: Compositional falsification of cyber-physical systems with machine learning components. In: Barrett, C., Davies, M., Kahsai, T. (eds.) NFM 2017. LNCS, vol. 10227, pp. 357–372. Springer, Cham (2017). https://doi.org/10.1007/978-3-319-57288-8_26

18. Ernst, G., et al.: ARCH-COMP 2020 category report: Falsification. In: ARCH20. 7th International Workshop on Applied Verification of Continuous and Hybrid Systems (ARCH20). EPiC Series in Computing, vol. 74, pp. 140–152. EasyChair (2020)

19. Fainekos, G.E., Pappas, G.J.: Robustness of temporal logic specifications for continuous-time signals. Theor. Comput. Sci. **410**(42), 4262–4291 (2009)

20. Fan, C., Qi, B., Mitra, S., Viswanathan, M., Duggirala, P.S.: Automatic reachability analysis for nonlinear hybrid models with C2E2. In: Chaudhuri, S., Farzan, A. (eds.) CAV 2016. LNCS, vol. 9779, pp. 531–538. Springer, Cham (2016). https://doi.org/10.1007/978-3-319-41528-4_29
21. Ferrère, T., Nickovic, D., Donzé, A., Ito, H., Kapinski, J.: Interface-aware signal temporal logic. In: Proceedings of the 22nd ACM International Conference on Hybrid Systems: Computation and Control, HSCC 2019, Montreal, QC, Canada, 16–18 April 2019, pp. 57–66 (2019)
22. Frehse, G., et al.: SpaceEx: scalable verification of hybrid systems. In: Gopalakrishnan, G., Qadeer, S. (eds.) CAV 2011. LNCS, vol. 6806, pp. 379–395. Springer, Heidelberg (2011). https://doi.org/10.1007/978-3-642-22110-1_30
23. Hasuo, I., Suenaga, K.: Exercises in nonstandard static analysis of hybrid systems. In: Madhusudan, P., Seshia, S.A. (eds.) CAV 2012. LNCS, vol. 7358, pp. 462–478. Springer, Heidelberg (2012). https://doi.org/10.1007/978-3-642-31424-7_34
24. Hoxha, B., Abbas, H., Fainekos, G.E.: Benchmarks for temporal logic requirements for automotive systems. In: 1st and 2nd International Workshop on Applied veRification for Continuous and Hybrid Systems, ARCH@CPSWeek 2014, Berlin, Germany, 14 April 2014/ARCH@CPSWeek 2015, Seattle, USA, 13 April 2015. EPiC Series in Computing, vol. 34, pp. 25–30. EasyChair (2014)
25. Jin, X., Deshmukh, J.V., Kapinski, J., Ueda, K., Butts, K.: Powertrain control verification benchmark. In: Proceedings of the 17th Int. Conf. on Hybrid Systems: Computation and Control, HSCC 2014, pp. 253–262. ACM, NY, USA (2014)
26. Kapinski, J., Deshmukh, J.V., Jin, X., Ito, H., Butts, K.: Simulation-based approaches for verification of embedded control systems: an overview of traditional and advanced modeling, testing, and verification techniques. IEEE Control Syst. **36**(6), 45–64 (2016)
27. Kato, K., Ishikawa, F.: Learning-based falsification for model families of cyber-physical systems. In: 2019 IEEE 24th Pacific Rim International Symposium on Dependable Computing (PRDC), pp. 236–245 (December 2019)
28. Kocsis, L., Szepesvári, C.: Bandit based monte-carlo planning. In: Fürnkranz, J., Scheffer, T., Spiliopoulou, M. (eds.) ECML 2006. LNCS (LNAI), vol. 4212, pp. 282–293. Springer, Heidelberg (2006). https://doi.org/10.1007/11871842_29
29. Kuřátko, J., Ratschan, S.: Combined global and local search for the falsification of hybrid systems. In: Legay, A., Bozga, M. (eds.) FORMATS 2014. LNCS, vol. 8711, pp. 146–160. Springer, Cham (2014). https://doi.org/10.1007/978-3-319-10512-3_11
30. Lee, R., Kochenderfer, M.J., Mengshoel, O.J., Brat, G.P., Owen, M.P.: Adaptive stress testing of airborne collision avoidance systems. In: Digital Avionics Systems Conference, 2015 IEEE/AIAA 34th, pp. 6C2-1. IEEE (2015)
31. Liebrenz, T., Herber, P., Glesner, S.: Deductive verification of hybrid control systems modeled in Simulink with KeYmaera X. In: Sun, J., Sun, M. (eds.) ICFEM 2018. LNCS, vol. 11232, pp. 89–105. Springer, Cham (2018). https://doi.org/10.1007/978-3-030-02450-5_6
32. Luersen, M.A., Le Riche, R.: Globalized Nelder-mead method for engineering optimization. Comput. Struct. **82**(23), 2251–2260 (2004)
33. Platzer, A.: Logical Foundations of Cyber-Physical Systems. Springer, Cham (2018) https://doi.org/10.1007/978-3-319-63588-0
34. Seshia, S.A., Rakhlin, A.: Quantitative analysis of systems using game-theoretic learning. ACM Trans. Embed. Comput. Syst. **11**(S2), 55:1–55:27 (2012)
35. Silver, D., et al.: Mastering the game of Go with deep neural networks and tree search. Nature **529**, 484–489 (2015)

36. Silvetti, S., Policriti, A., Bortolussi, L.: An active learning approach to the falsification of black box cyber-physical systems. In: Polikarpova, N., Schneider, S. (eds.) IFM 2017. LNCS, vol. 10510, pp. 3–17. Springer, Cham (2017). https://doi.org/10.1007/978-3-319-66845-1_1
37. Akazaki, T., Liu, S., Yamagata, Y., Duan, Y., Hao, J.: Falsification of cyber-physical systems using deep reinforcement learning. In: Havelund, K., Peleska, J., Roscoe, B., de Vink, E. (eds.) FM 2018. LNCS, vol. 10951, pp. 456–465. Springer, Cham (2018). https://doi.org/10.1007/978-3-319-95582-7_27
38. Zhang, Z., Arcaini, P., Hasuo, I.: Hybrid system falsification under (in)equality constraints via search space transformation. IEEE Trans. Comput. Aided Des. Integr. Circ. Syst. **39**(11), 3674–3685 (2020)
39. Zhang, Z., Ernst, G., Sedwards, S., Arcaini, P., Hasuo, I.: Two-layered falsification of hybrid systems guided by monte carlo tree search. IEEE Trans. Comput. Aided Des. Integr. Circuits Syst. **37**(11), 2894–2905 (2018)
40. Zhang, Z., Hasuo, I., Arcaini, P.: Multi-armed bandits for Boolean connectives in hybrid system falsification. In: Dillig, I., Tasiran, S. (eds.) CAV 2019. LNCS, vol. 11561, pp. 401–420. Springer, Cham (2019). https://doi.org/10.1007/978-3-030-25540-4_23
41. Zhang, Z., Lyu, D., Arcaini, P., Ma, L., Hasuo, I., Zhao, J.: On the effectiveness of signal rescaling in hybrid system falsification. In: Dutle, A., Moscato, M.M., Titolo, L., Muñoz, C.A., Perez, I. (eds.) NFM 2021. LNCS, vol. 12673, pp. 392–399. Springer, Cham (2021). https://doi.org/10.1007/978-3-030-76384-8_24
42. Zutshi, A., Deshmukh, J.V., Sankaranarayanan, S., Kapinski, J.: Multiple shooting, cegar-based falsification for hybrid systems. In: 2014 International Conference on Embedded Software, EMSOFT 2014, New Delhi, India, 12–17 October 2014, pp. 5:1–5:10. ACM (2014)

Fast Zone-Based Algorithms for Reachability in Pushdown Timed Automata

S. Akshay[1]($\boxtimes$) , Paul Gastin[2], and Karthik R. Prakash[1]

[1] Department of CSE, Indian Institute
of Technology Bombay, Mumbai, India
{akshayss,karthikrprakash}@cse.iitb.ac.in
[2] Université Paris-Saclay, ENS Paris-Saclay,
CNRS, LMF, 91190 Gif-sur-Yvette, France
paul.gastin@lsv.fr

Abstract. Given the versatility of timed automata a huge body of work has evolved that considers extensions of timed automata. One extension that has received a lot of interest is timed automata with a, possibly unbounded, stack, also called pushdown timed automata (PDTA). While different algorithms have been given for reachability in different variants of this model, most of these results are purely theoretical and do not give rise to efficient implementations. One main reason for this is that none of these algorithms (and the implementations that exist) use the so-called zone-based abstraction, but rely either on the region-abstraction or other approaches, which are significantly harder to implement.

In this paper, we show that a naive extension, using simulations, of the zone based reachability algorithm for the control state reachability problem of timed automata is not sound in the presence of a stack. To understand this better we give an inductive rule based view of the zone reachability algorithm for timed automata. This alternate view allows us to analyze and adapt the rules to also work for pushdown timed automata. We obtain the first zone-based algorithm for PDTA which is terminating, sound and complete. We implement our algorithm in the tool TChecker and perform experiments to show its efficacy, thus leading the way for more practical approaches to the verification of timed pushdown systems.

Keywords: Timed automata · Zone-based abstractions · Pushdown automata · Simulations · Reachability

1 Introduction

Timed automata [7] are a popular formalism for capturing real-time systems, and of use for instance, in model checking of cyber-physical systems. They extend

This work was partly supported by ReLaX CNRS IRL 2000, DST/CEFIPRA/INRIA project EQuaVE and SERB Matrices grant MTR/2018/00074.

A. Silva and K. R. M. Leino (Eds.) CAV 2021, LNCS 12759, pp. 619–642, 2021.
https://doi.org/10.1007/978-3-030-81685-8_30

finite automata with real variables called clocks whose values increase over time; transitions are guarded by constraints over these variables. The main problem of interest is the reachability problem, which asks whether a given state can be reached while satisfying the constraints imposed by the guards. This problem is known to be PSPACE-complete (already shown in [7]). The PSPACE algorithm, uses the so-called region-automaton construction, which essentially abstracts the timed automaton into an exponentially larger finite automaton of regions (collections of clock valuations), which is sound and complete for reachability.

Despite this complexity-theoretic hardness, the model of timed automata has proved to be extremely influential and versatile, resulting in an enormous body of work on its theory, variants and extensions over the past 25 years. Almost since its inception, researchers also began to develop tools to extend from theoretical algorithms to solve practical problems. Such tools range from the classical and richly featured tool UPPAAL [9,23] to the more recent open-source tool TChecker [19], which have been used on industry strength benchmarks and perform rather well on many of them. These tools use a different algorithm for reachability, where reachable sets of valuations are represented as zones and explored in a graph. While a naive exploration of zones does not terminate, the algorithms used identify different strategies [8,18,21], e.g., subsumption or simulations, extrapolations, for pruning the zone-based exploration graphs, while preserving soundness and completeness of reachability. While this does not change the worst case complexity, in practice, the zone exploration results in much better *practical* performance as it allows on-the-fly computation of reachable zones. One could even argue that the wider adoption of timed automata paradigm in the verification community has been a result of scalable implementations and tools built on this zone-based approach.

In light of this, zone-based algorithms are often looked for to improve practical performance of extensions of timed automata as well. For instance, for timed automata with diagonal constraints, classical zone-based approaches were shown to be unsound [11,12], but recently, an approach has been developed which adapts the existing construction and obtains fast zone-based algorithms [17]. In the present paper, we are interesting in adding a different feature to timed automata, namely an unbounded lifo-stack. This results in a powerful model of *pushdown timed automata (PDTA for short)*, in which the source of "infinity" is both from real-time and the unbounded stack. Unsurprisingly, this model and its variants have been widely studied over the last 20 years with several old and recent results on decidability of reachability, related problems and their complexity, including [1–5,10,13–16]. A wide variety of techniques have been employed to solve these problems, from region-based abstractions, to using atoms and systems of constraints, to encoding into different logics etc. However, except for [4,5], to the best of our knowledge, none of the others carry an implementation. In [5], the implementation uses a tree-automaton implicitly based on regions and the focus in [4] is towards multi-pushdown systems. A common factor of all these works is that none of them consider zone-based abstractions.

In this paper, we ask whether zone-based abstractions can be used to decide efficiently reachability questions in PDTA. We focus on the problem of well-nested control-state reachability of PDTA, i.e., given a PDTA, an initial and a target state, does there exist a run of the PDTA that starts at the initial state with empty stack and reaches the target state with an empty stack (in between, i.e., during the run, the stack can indeed be non-empty). As with timed automata, our goal here is towards its applicability to build powerful tools which could lead to wider adoption of the PDTA model and showcase its utility to model-checking timed recursive systems. As the first step, we examine the difficulties involved in mixing zones with stacks and point out that a naive adaptation of the zone-based algorithm would not be sound. Then we propose a new algorithm that modifies the zone-based algorithm to work for pushdown timed automata. This is done in three steps.

- First we view the zone-graph exploration at the heart of the zone-based reachability algorithm for timed automata as a least fixed point computation of two inductive rules. When applied till saturation, they compute a sound and complete finite abstraction of the set of all reachable zones.
- Next, this view allows us to generalize the approach in the presence of a stack by adding new inductive rules that correspond to push and pop transitions, and hence are specific to the stack operation. There are two main technical difficulties in this. First, we need to ensure termination of the fixed point computation, using a strong enough pruning condition of the (a priori infinite) zone graph to ensure finiteness, while being sound and not adding spurious runs. Second, we want to aggressively prune the graph as much as possible to obtain an efficient zone-exploration algorithm. We show how we can minimally change the condition of pruning in the zone exploration graph to achieve this delicate balance. Indeed, in doing so we use a judicious combination of the subsumption (or simulation) relation and an equivalence relation for obtaining a fixed point computation for PDTA that is terminating, while being sound and complete.
- Finally, we build new data structures that allow us to write an efficient algorithm that implements this fixed point computation. While getting a correct algorithm is relatively simple, to obtain an efficient one, we must again encounter and overcome several technical difficulties.

We implement our approach to build the first zone-based tool that efficiently solves well-nested control state reachability for PDTA. Our tool is built on top of existing infrastructure of TChecker [19], an open source tool and benefits from many existing optimizations. We perform experiments to show the practical performance of multiple variants of our algorithm and show how our most optimized version is vastly better in performance than other variants and of course the earlier region-based approach on a suite of example benchmarks.

We note that our PDTA model differs slightly from the model considered in [1,3], as there is no age on stack and time spent on stack cannot be compared with clocks. Hence our model is closer to [10,16]. However, in [13], it was shown that these two models are equivalent, more specifically, the stack can be untimed without loss of expressivity (albeit with an exponential blowup). Thus our approach can be applied to the other model as well by just untiming the stack. There are other more powerful extensions [14,15] studied especially in the context of binary reachability, where only theoretical results are known. We also remark that the idea of combining the subsumption relation between zones with an equivalence relation also occurs while tackling liveness, or Buchi acceptance, in timed automata. This has been studied in depth [20,22,24], where the naive zone-based algorithm does not work, forcing the authors to strengthen the simulation relation in different ways. Though these problems are quite different, there are surprising similarities in the issues faced, as explained in Sect. 3.

The structure of the paper is as follows: we start with preliminaries and move on to the difficulty in using zones and simulation relations in solving reachability in PDTA. Then, we introduce in Sect. 4 our inductive rules for timed automata and PDTA and show their correctness. In Sect. 5, we present our algorithm and helpful data-structural advancements. We show the experimental performance in Sect. 6 and end with a brief conclusion. Proofs that are missing and more experimental results can be found in the long version of the paper available at [6].

2   Preliminaries

2.1   Timed Automata

Timed automata extend finite-state automata with a set X of (non-negative) real-valued variables called *clocks*. We let $\Phi(X)$ denote the set of constraints φ that can be formed using the grammar: $\varphi ::= x \sim c \mid x - y \sim c \mid \varphi \wedge \varphi$, where $x, y \in X$, $c \in \mathbb{N}$, $\sim \in \{\leq, \geq, <, >\}$, where each $x \sim c$ is called an atomic constraint. A clock valuation is a map $v \colon X \to \mathbb{R}_{\geq 0}$ and is said to satisfy φ, denoted $v \models \varphi$, if φ evaluates to true when each clock $x \in X$ is replaced with $v(x)$. For $\delta \in \mathbb{R}^{\geq 0}$, we write $v + \delta$ to denote the valuation defined as $(v + \delta)(x) = v(x) + \delta$ for all clocks x. For $R \subseteq X$, we write $[R]v$ to denote the valuation obtained by resetting clocks in R, i.e., $([R]v)(x) = 0$ if $x \in R$, and $([R]v)(x) = v(x)$ otherwise. Finally, v_0 is the valuation that sets all clocks to 0.

A timed automaton $\mathcal{A}$ is a tuple (Q, X, q_0, Δ, F), where Q is a finite set of states, X is a finite set of clocks, $q_0 \in Q$ is an initial state, $F \subseteq Q$ is the set of final states and $\Delta \subseteq Q \times \Phi(X) \times 2^X \times Q$ is a set of transitions. A transition $t \in \Delta$ is of the form (q, g, R, q'), where q, q' are states, $g \in \Phi(X)$ is the guard of the transition and $R \subseteq X$ is the set of clocks that are reset at the transition. The semantics of a timed automaton $\mathcal{A}$ is given as a transition system $TS(\mathcal{A})$ over configurations. A configuration is a pair (q, v) where $q \in Q$ is a state and v is a valuation, with the initial configuration being (q_0, v_0). The transitions are of two types. First, for a configuration (q, v) and $\delta \in \mathbb{R}^{\geq 0}$, $(q, v) \xrightarrow{\delta} (q, v + \delta)$ is a delay transition. Second, for $t = (q, g, R, q') \in \Delta$, $(q, v) \xrightarrow{t} (q', v')$ is a discrete transition if $v \models g$ and $v' = [R](v)$. A run is an alternating sequence of delays and discrete transitions starting from the initial configuration, and is said to be accepting if the last state in the sequence is a final state.

2.2   Reachability, Zones and Simulations

The problem of control-state reachability asks whether a given timed automaton has an accepting run. This problem is known to be PSPACE-complete [7], originally shown via the so-called region abstraction. Note that, since $TS(\mathcal{A})$ is infinite, some abstraction is needed to get an algorithm. In practice however, the abstraction used to solve reachability, e.g., in tools such as UPPAAL [23] or TChecker [19] is the *zone abstraction*. A zone Z is defined as a set of valuations defined by a conjunction of atomic clock constraints. Given a guard g and reset R, we define the following operations on zones: time elapse $\overrightarrow{Z} = \{v + \delta \mid v \in Z, \delta \in \mathbb{R}^{\geq 0}\}$, guard intersection $g \cap Z = \{v \in Z \mid v \models g\}$ and reset $[R]Z = \{[R]v \mid v \in Z\}$. The resulting sets are also zones. With this, we can define the zone graph $ZG(\mathcal{A})$ as a transition system obtained as follows: the nodes are (state, zone) pairs and $(q, Z) \xrightarrow{t} (q', Z')$, if $t = (q, g, R, q')$ is a transition of $\mathcal{A}$ and $Z' = [R](\overrightarrow{g \cap Z})$. The initial node is $(q_0, Z_0 = \overrightarrow{\{v_0\}})$ and a path in the zone graph is said to be accepting if it ends at an accepting state. The zone graph is known to be sound and complete for reachability, but as the graph may still be infinite, this does not give an algorithm for solving reachability yet.

To obtain an algorithm, one resorts to different techniques such as extrapolation or simulation. Here we focus on *simulation relations* which will lead to finite abstractions. Given a timed automaton $\mathcal{A}$, a binary relation $\preceq$ on configurations is called a *simulation* if whenever $(q, v) \preceq (q', v')$, we have $q = q'$ and

- for each delay $\delta \in \mathbb{R}^{\geq 0}$, $(q, v + \delta) \preceq (q, v' + \delta)$ and
- for each $t = (q, g, R, q_1) \in \Delta$, if $v \models g$ then $v' \models g$ and $(q_1, [R]v) \preceq (q_1, [R]v')$.

We often simply write $v \preceq_q v'$ instead of $(q, v) \preceq (q, v')$. We can now lift this to sets Z, Z' of valuations as $Z \preceq_q Z'$ if for all $v \in Z$ there exists $v' \in Z'$ such that $v \preceq_q v'$. We say that node (q, Z) is subsumed by node (q, Z') when $Z \preceq_q Z'$. As a consequence we obtain the following lemma.

Lemma 1. *If $(q, Z) \xrightarrow{t} (q_1, Z_1)$ in $ZG(\mathcal{A})$ and $Z \preceq_q Z'$, then $(q, Z') \xrightarrow{t} (q_1, Z_1')$ and $Z_1 \preceq_{q_1} Z_1'$.*

Proof. Indeed, let $v_1 \in Z_1 = \overrightarrow{[R](g \cap Z)}$. We find $v \in Z$ and $\delta \geq 0$ such that $v \models g$ and $v_1 = [R]v + \delta$. Since $Z \preceq_q Z'$, we find $v' \in Z'$ with $v \preceq_q v'$. We deduce that $v' \models g$ and $[R]v \preceq_{q_1} [R]v'$, which implies $v_1 \preceq_{q_1} v_1'$ with $v_1' = [R]v' + \delta \in Z_1' = \overrightarrow{[R](g \cap Z')}$. $\square$

A simulation $\preceq$ is said to be *finite* if for every sequence of nodes (q_1, Z_1), $(q_2, Z_2), \ldots$ there exist two nodes (q_i, Z_i) and (q_j, Z_j) with $i < j$ such that $q_i = q_j$ and $Z_j \preceq_{q_i} Z_i$. The importance of the finiteness is that it allows us to stop exploration of zones along a branch of the zone graph: when a node (q_j, Z_j) is reached which is subsumed by an earlier node (q_i, Z_i), we may cut the exploration since all control states reachable from the latter are already reachable from the former. For a timed automaton $\mathcal{A}$, we call this pruned graph as $ZG_{\preceq}(A)$. Thus, if the simulation relation $\preceq$ is finite, then $ZG_{\preceq}(\mathcal{A})$ is finite, sound and complete for control state reachability. We formalize this algorithm in Sect. 4, using inductive rules.

Various finite simulations have been shown to exist in the literature, including the famous LU-abstractions [8], and more recent $\mathcal{G}$-abstractions based on sets of guards [17]. Hence this theory indeed has resulted in better implementations and is used in standard tools in this domain.

We will see that using simulation in the context of pushdown timed automata is not always sound, in some cases we need a stronger condition to stop the exploration. Towards this, we consider the equivalence relation on nodes induced by the simulation relation: $Z \sim_q Z'$ if $Z \preceq_q Z'$ and $Z' \preceq_q Z$. We say that the simulation $\preceq$ is strongly finite if the induced equivalence relation $\sim$ has finite index. Notice that strongly finite implies finite but the converse does not necessarily hold. Fortunately, the usual simulations for timed automata, in particular the LU-simulation and the $\mathcal{G}$-simulation, are strongly finite.

2.3   Pushdown Timed Automata (PDTA)

A Pushdown Timed Automaton $\mathcal{A}$ is a tuple $(Q, X, q_0, \Gamma, \Delta, F)$, where Q is a finite set of states, X is a finite set of clocks, $q_0 \in Q$ is an initial state, Γ is the stack alphabet, $F \subseteq Q$ is the set of final states and Δ is a set of transitions. A transition $t \in \Delta$ is of the form $(q, g, \mathrm{op}, R, q')$, where q, q' are states, $g \in \Phi(X)$ is the guard of the transition and $R \subseteq X$ is the set of clocks that are reset at the transition, op is one of three stack operations: nop or push_a or pop_a for some $a \in \Gamma$.

The semantics of a PDTA $\mathcal{A}$ is given as a transition system $TS(\mathcal{A})$ over configurations. A configuration here is a tuple (q, v, χ) where $q \in Q$ is a state, v is a valuation, $\chi \in \Gamma^*$ is the stack content, with the initial configuration being (q_0, v_0, ε). The transitions are of two types. First, for a configuration (q, v, χ) and $\delta \in \mathbb{R}^{\geq 0}$, $(q, v, \chi) \xrightarrow{\delta} (q, v + \delta, \chi)$ is a delay transition. Second, for $t = (q, g, \mathrm{op}, R, q') \in \Delta$, $(q, v, \chi) \xrightarrow{t} (q', v', \chi')$ is a discrete transition if $v \models g$, $v' = [R](v)$ and

- if $\mathrm{op} = \mathrm{nop}$, then $\chi' = \chi$,
- if $\mathrm{op} = \mathrm{push}_a$ then $\chi' = \chi \cdot a$,
- if $\mathrm{op} = \mathrm{pop}_a$, then $\chi = \chi' \cdot a$.

A run is an alternating sequence of delays and discrete actions starting from the initial configuration. It is accepting if the last state in the sequence is final.

Our main focus is the *well-nested control state reachability* problem for PDTA, which asks whether a configuration (q, v, ε) with $q \in F$ is reachable, where the stack is empty. Later, in Sect. 7, we remark how our solution can be extended to solve general control state reachability, i.e., asking whether a configuration (q, v, χ) with $q \in F$ is reachable, possibly with a nonempty stack χ.

Fig. 1. A simple PDTA with 2 clocks $\{x, y\}$. Note that if we ignore the push/pop actions we get a TA, say A.

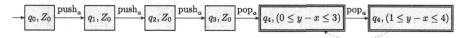

Fig. 2. Zone graph with simulation edges for finiteness. Again ignoring push/pop actions gives us a zone graph for the TA. Z_0 is the initial zone.

3 Zones in PDTA and the Problem with Simulations

As mentioned earlier, zones are collections of clock valuations defined by conjunctions of timing constraints, and exploring zones reached by a timed automaton gives a sound and complete abstraction for state reachability. To make sure that the exploration is finite we need to prune the graph and one way this is done by simulation, i.e., not exploring paths from some nodes if they are "subsumed" by earlier nodes visited in the graph. Consider Fig. 1, in which we ignore the $push_a$ and pop_a or we can think of them as internal actions. Then the usual zone-graph construction with simulation would give the graph depicted in Fig. 2. In this section, just for illustration we instantiate the simulation relation to be the well-known LU-simulation (we do not give the definition here as it is not relevant to what comes later, instead we refer to earlier work [8]). Using this, we obtain that the rightmost node is subsumed by the previous one, and hence the dotted simulation edge. If we did not do this we immediately observe that we get an infinite graph with increasing sets of zones.

Now, our first question is whether this zone exploration with simulation can be lifted to PDTA. In this example, if we were to add back the push/pop edges, we get exactly the same Zone graph with annotations, and further, the final state is indeed reachable. Hence, for this particular example we do obtain a finite, sound and complete graph exploration. However, in general it turns out that the procedure is not sound.

Consider the example in Fig. 3. In this example, again considering it as a TA (ignoring the push/pops), we would get the zone graph below, which would be finite, sound and complete for reachability in that TA. But if we consider it as a PDTA, now doing the same does not preserve soundness. In other words, in the PDTA, q_3 is no longer reachable. However, in the zone graph we would conclude that it is reachable due to the simulation edge. If, to fix this, we remove the dotted simulation edge, then we will lose finiteness.

Thus, it seems that we have a difficult situation where zones with the simulation relation, needed for termination, do not preserve soundness. This situation resembles the situation studied in [20,22,24], where the authors study liveness or Buchi-acceptance conditions in timed automata. Again in that situation, the

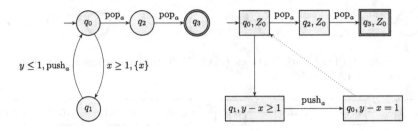

Fig. 3. A PDTA and its zone graph with simulation. With the simulation (dotted) edges, q_3 is reachable in the zone graph, but its not reachable in the PDTA.

naive algorithm with zone simulation does not work and the authors are forced to strengthen the simulation relation in different ways.

Surprisingly, it turns out, that even in our very different problem setting of reachability in PDTA, a similar solution works. That is, we replace simulation by equivalence (defined in the previous section) as the pruning criterion. However, there are two issues (i) it is not easy to prove its correctness and (ii) this is far from efficient as shown in the experimental section. Our goal to use zones in the first place was efficiency and hence we would like to prune the zone graph as much as possible, i.e., we would like to use simulation edges as much as possible. In the next two sections, we describe our fix. We first show a different view of the exploration algorithm as a fixed point rule based approach. This allows us to then describe our fix in the same language, which is much easier to understand conceptually. Also as a corollary we will be able to show that using equivalence everywhere also gives a correct algorithm. After proving the correctness of our rule-based algorithm, we then tackle the challenges in implementing it.

4 Viewing Reachability Algorithms Using Rewrite Rules

In this section, our goal is to compute a set S of nodes of the zone graph of a PDTA, as a least fixed point of a small set of inductive rules, such that a control state q occurs in S, i.e., $(q, Z) \in S$ for some Z iff q is reachable in the PDTA from its initial state. To understand the rules and their correctness it is easier to first visualize this on plain timed automata without any push-pop edges.

4.1 Rewrite Rules for Timed Automata.

Given a TA $\mathcal{A} = (Q, X, q_0, \Delta, F)$, the set S containing all reachable nodes of the zone graph, can be obtained as the least fixed point of the following inductive rules, with a natural deduction style of presentation.

$$\overline{S := \{(q_0, Z_0)\}} \; \text{start}$$

$$\frac{(q,Z) \in S \qquad q \xrightarrow{g,R} q' \qquad Z' = \overrightarrow{R(g \cap Z)} \neq \emptyset}{S := S \cup \{(q',Z')\}} \text{ Trans}$$

Let S^* denote the set at the fixed point by starting with the start rule and repeatedly applying the trans rule. It is easy to see that this computes the set of all reachable nodes of the zone graph: the start rule starts with the initial node and each application of trans rule takes a reachable node and applies a transition of the automaton and includes the resulting node reached. However, this set S^* is a priori infinite since number of zones is infinite.

To make it finite we add a condition under which we will apply the transition rule based on a finite simulation relation (let us denote it $\preceq$) for $\mathcal{A}$.

$$\frac{(q,Z) \in S \qquad q \xrightarrow{g,R} q' \qquad Z' = \overrightarrow{R(g \cap Z)} \neq \emptyset}{S := S \cup \{(q',Z')\}, \text{ unless } \exists (q',Z'') \in S, \ Z' \preceq_{q'} Z''} \text{ Trans-}\preceq$$

Thus to obtain an algorithm, we would explore all nodes in the Zone graph using a search algorithm (say DFS/BFS) and we would add a node only if it is not subsumed by an already visited node, according to the simulation relation. We explained in Sect. 2.2 that doing this preserves soundness and completeness and gives a finite exploration.

Lemma 2. *Let $S^*_{\preceq}$ denote any set obtained from the start rule and by repeatedly applying Trans-$\preceq$ till a fixed point is reached. Note that depending on the order of applications we may have different sets. Then we have:*

1. *(finiteness) $S^*_{\preceq}$ is finite.*
2. *(soundness and completeness) For all $q \in Q$, a configuration (q,v) is reachable from (q_0,v_0) in the TA $\mathcal{A}$ iff $(q,Z) \in S^*_{\preceq}$ for some zone Z.*

We do not give the proof here as (i) it is only a reformulation of known results and (ii) it will be subsumed by the much stronger theorem we prove next.

4.2   Rewrite Rules for PDTA

Let $\mathcal{A} = (Q, X, q_0, \Gamma, \Delta, F)$ be a PDTA, we will need not just a set but a tuple of sets. More precisely, we maintain a set of nodes $\mathfrak{S}$ called *root* nodes. For each root node $(q,Z) \in \mathfrak{S}$, we also maintain a set of nodes, denoted $S_{(q,Z)}$. The intuition is that root nodes are those that can be reached after pushing a symbol to the stack, whereas $S_{(q,Z)}$ will be the set of nodes that can be reached from (q,Z) with a well-nested run, i.e., starting with an empty stack and ending in an empty stack. This is to avoid storing the stack contents in our algorithm, which would be another source of infinity. Again, we use simulations to make the computation finite. So we fix a strongly finite simulation relation $\preceq$ for $\mathcal{A}$.

Our inductive rules for the control state reachability of pushdown timed automata are given in Table 1. Note that the internal rule is just the same as for timed automata above. The start rule not only starts the set of nodes computation but also the set of roots computation as described above. So the only

Table 1. Inductive rules for control state reachability of PDTA

$$\frac{}{\mathfrak{S} := \{(q_0, Z_0)\},\ S_{(q_0, Z_0)} := \{(q_0, Z_0)\}} \text{ Start}$$

$$\frac{(q, Z) \in \mathfrak{S} \qquad (q', Z') \in S_{(q,Z)} \qquad q' \xrightarrow{g, \mathrm{nop}, R} q'' \qquad Z'' = \overrightarrow{R(g \cap Z')} \neq \emptyset}{S_{(q,Z)} := S_{(q,Z)} \cup \{(q'', Z'')\},\ \text{unless } \exists (q'', Z''') \in S_{(q,Z)},\ Z'' \preceq_{q''} Z'''} \text{ Internal}$$

$$\frac{(q, Z) \in \mathfrak{S} \qquad (q', Z') \in S_{(q,Z)} \qquad q' \xrightarrow{g, \mathrm{push}_a, R} q'' \qquad Z'' = \overrightarrow{R(g \cap Z')} \neq \emptyset}{\mathfrak{S} := \mathfrak{S} \cup \{(q'', Z'')\},\ S_{(q'', Z'')} = \{(q'', Z'')\},\ \text{unless } \exists (q'', Z''') \in \mathfrak{S},\ Z'' \sim_{q''} Z'''} \text{ Push}$$

$$\frac{\begin{array}{l} (q, Z) \in \mathfrak{S} \qquad (q', Z') \in S_{(q,Z)} \qquad q' \xrightarrow{g, \mathrm{push}_a, R} q'' \qquad Z'' = \overrightarrow{R(g \cap Z')} \sim_{q''} Z_1 \\ (q'', Z_1) \in \mathfrak{S} \qquad (q_1', Z_1') \in S_{(q'', Z_1)} \qquad q_1' \xrightarrow{g_1, \mathrm{pop}_a, R_1} q_2 \qquad Z_2 = \overrightarrow{R_1(g_1 \cap Z_1')} \neq \emptyset \end{array}}{S_{(q,Z)} := S_{(q,Z)} \cup \{(q_2, Z_2)\},\ \text{unless } \exists (q_2, Z_2') \in S_{(q,Z)},\ Z_2 \preceq_{q_2} Z_2'} \text{ Pop}$$

interesting rules are the Push and Pop rules. The push rule says that when a push is encountered, then we must start exploring from a new root (i.e., context). So the only complicated rule is the Pop rule. Here the intuition is that if we see a push at a node and from a root equivalent to the root created from it, (i.e., its context) we see a matching pop reaching a new node, then this push-pop context is complete, and we can add this new node to the set of reachable nodes. This is precisely the point where we *need* equivalence rather than simulation and this will be made clear in the proof of the theorem below.

Theorem 1. *Let $\mathfrak{S}^*$ and $(S_{(q,Z)})_{(q,Z) \in \mathfrak{S}^*}$ denote any tuple of sets obtained from the start rule and by repeatedly applying the rules in Table 1 till a fixed point is reached[1]. Note that we always have $(q_0, Z_0) \in \mathfrak{S}^*$. The following statements hold:*

1. *(finiteness) $\mathfrak{S}^*$ is finite and for each $(q, Z) \in \mathfrak{S}^*$, $S_{(q,Z)}$ is finite.*
2. *(completeness) For each $(q, Z) \in \mathfrak{S}^*$, if there exists a run $(q, v, \varepsilon) \xrightarrow{*} (q', v', \varepsilon)$ of $\mathcal{A}$ with $\{v\} \preceq_q Z$, then there exists $(q', Z') \in S_{(q,Z)}$ such that $\{v'\} \preceq_{q'} Z'$.*
3. *(soundness) For each $(q, Z) \in \mathfrak{S}^*$, $(q', Z') \in S_{(q,Z)}$ and $v' \in Z'$, there exists a run in PDTA from (q, v, ε) to (q', v'', ε) with $v \in Z$ and $v' \preceq_{q'} v''$.*

Proof. **1.** Note that only the Push rule creates new root nodes and the red condition states that a new root node is added only if there isn't already an equivalent node in $\mathfrak{S}^*$. Since the simulation relation is strongly finite, the set of roots $\mathfrak{S}^*$ must be finite. Also, before adding a node to some $S_{(q,Z)}$ with the internal rule or the pop rule, we check that the node is not subsumed by an existing one. Since the simulation relation is finite, this ensures that each set $S_{(q,Z)}$ is finite.

---

[1] As before, there could be several such sets depending on the order in which the rules are applied.

$$(q,v,\varepsilon) \xrightarrow{\ast} (q_i,v_i,\varepsilon) \xrightarrow{t} (q_{i+1},v_{i+1},a) \xrightarrow{\ast} (q_{n-1},v_{n-1},a) \xrightarrow{t_1} (q_n,v_n,\varepsilon)$$

$$v \preceq_q Z \qquad v_i \preceq_{q_i} Z_i \qquad v_{i+1} \preceq_{q_{i+1}} Z_{i+1} \qquad v_{n-1} \preceq_{q_{n-1}} Z_{n-1} \qquad v_n \preceq_{q_n} Z_n$$

$$(q,Z) \in \mathfrak{S} \quad (q_i,Z_i) \in S_{(q,Z)} \quad Z_{i+1} = \overrightarrow{R(g \cap Z_i)} \quad (q_{n-1},Z_{n-1}) \in S_{(q_{i+1},Z'_{i+1})} \quad Z_n = \overrightarrow{R_1(g_1 \cap Z_{n-1})}$$

$$Z_{i+1} \sim_{q_{i+1}} Z'_{i+1} \qquad\qquad\qquad\qquad Z_n \preceq_{q_n} Z'_n$$

$$(q_{i+1},Z'_{i+1}) \in \mathfrak{S} \qquad\qquad\qquad\qquad\qquad (q_n,Z'_n) \in S_{(q,Z)}$$

Fig. 4. Construction for the completeness-push-pop last sub-case.

2. Let $(q,Z) \in \mathfrak{S}^*$ and assume that (q',v',ε) is reachable from some (q,v,ε) with $v \preceq_q Z$, i.e., there exists a run $(q,v,\varepsilon) = (q_1,v_1,\chi_1) \to \cdots \to (q_n,v_n,\chi_n) = (q',v',\varepsilon)$. We will then show that $v_n \preceq_{q_n} Z'$ for some $(q_n,Z') \in S_{(q,Z)}$. The proof is by induction on n. Base case: For $n = 1$ we have $q' = q$ and $v' = v$. The result is obtained by taking $Z' = Z$. Notice that $(q,Z) \in S_{(q,Z)}$ follows immediately from the start rule if $q = q_0$, $Z = Z_0$ or from the push-create rule.

Let us then assume that the statement holds for runs of length at most $n-1$. Consider any run of the form $(q,v,\varepsilon) = (q_1,v_1,\chi_1) \to \cdots \to (q_n,v_n,\chi_n = \varepsilon)$ with $v \preceq_q Z$. Notice that its last transition $(q_{n-1},v_{n-1},\chi_{n-1}) \to (q_n,v_n,\chi_n)$ cannot be a push transition (in the PDTA) since $\chi_n = \varepsilon$. Hence, we have three subcases, depending on the last transition.

– Time elapse. $\chi_{n-1} = \chi_n = \varepsilon$, $q_{n-1} = q_n = q'$, $v_n = v_{n-1} + \delta$ for some $\delta \in \mathbb{R}^{\geq 0}$. Applying induction hypothesis, we have $v_{n-1} \preceq_{q'} Z'$ for some $(q',Z') \in S_{(q,Z)}$. Since zones are closed under time elapse, we get $Z' = \overrightarrow{Z'}$ and by definition of the simulation relation $v_n = v_{n-1} + \delta \preceq_{q'} \overrightarrow{Z'} = Z'$. This completes the case.

– Discrete internal transition. In this case $\chi_{n-1} = \chi_n = \varepsilon$, $t = q_{n-1} \xrightarrow{g,\text{nop},R} q_n$, $v_{n-1} \models g$ and $v_n = [R]v_{n-1}$. Then applying induction hypothesis, there exists $(q_{n-1},Z') \in S_{(q,Z)}$ such that $v_{n-1} \preceq_{q_{n-1}} Z'$. Now let $Z'' = \overrightarrow{R(g \cap Z')}$. From the definition of the simulation relation we get $v_n \preceq_{q_n} Z''$. Then, applying the Internal rule, there exists $(q_n,Z''') \in S_{(q,Z)}$ such that $Z'' \preceq_{q_n} Z'''$, with possibly $Z''' = Z''$. Hence, $v_n \preceq_{q_n} Z'' \preceq_{q_n} Z'''$, which completes the case.

– Pop transition. Then there exists $1 \leq i < n-1$ such that the run has the form: $(q_1,v_1,\varepsilon) \to \cdots \to (q_i,v_i,\chi_i = \varepsilon) \xrightarrow{\text{push}_a} (q_{i+1},v_{i+1},\chi_{i+1} = a) \to \cdots \to (q_{n-1},v_{n-1},\chi_{n-1} = a) \xrightarrow{\text{pop}_a} (q_n,v_n,\chi_n = \varepsilon)$, where the push and pop are matching transitions, i.e., $|\chi_j| \geq 1$ for all $i < j < n-1$ (see Fig. 4). Then by induction hypothesis at i, we have

$$v_i \preceq_{q_i} Z_i \text{ for some } (q_i,Z_i) \in S_{(q,Z)}. \tag{1}$$

From the push transition we have

$$\exists t = q_i \xrightarrow{g,\text{push}_a,R} q_{i+1} \in \Delta \text{ with } v_i \models g \text{ and } v_{i+1} = [R]v_i. \tag{2}$$

Let $Z_{i+1} = \overrightarrow{R(g \cap Z_i)}$. By definition of the simulation relation, we deduce from $v_i \preceq_{q_i} Z_i$ that $v_{i+1} \preceq_{q_{i+1}} Z_{i+1}$. We can apply the Push rule to obtain

$$(q_{i+1},Z'_{i+1}) \in \mathfrak{S}^* \text{ for some } Z'_{i+1} \sim_{q_{i+1}} Z_{i+1} \tag{3}$$

possibly with $Z'_{i+1} = Z_{i+1}$ as a special case.

Further the segment of run $(q_{i+1}, v_{i+1}, a) \to \ldots (q_{n-1}, v_{n-1}, a)$ in the PDTA never pops the symbol a (by choice, since otherwise the push and pop would not be matching). Hence we will also have the same sequence of transitions forming a run $(q_{i+1}, v_{i+1}, \varepsilon) \to \ldots (q_{n-1}, v_{n-1}, \varepsilon)$. Using $v_{i+1} \preceq_{q_{i+1}}$ $Z_{i+1} \sim_{q_{i+1}} Z'_{i+1}$, we deduce that $v_{i+1} \preceq_{q_{i+1}} Z'_{i+1}$. By induction hypothesis,

$$v_{n-1} \preceq_{q_{n-1}} Z_{n-1} \text{ for some } (q_{n-1}, Z_{n-1}) \in S_{(q_{i+1}, Z'_{i+1})}. \tag{4}$$

Finally, we have the pop transition

$$t_1 = q_{n-1} \xrightarrow{g_1, \mathrm{pop}_a, R_1} q_n \in \Delta \text{ with } v_{n-1} \models g_1 \text{ and } v_n = [R_1]v_{n-1}. \tag{5}$$

We let $Z_n = \overrightarrow{R_1(g_1 \cap Z_{n-1})}$. From $v_{n-1} \preceq_{q_{n-1}} Z_{n-1}$ and the definition of the simulation relation we obtain $v_n \preceq_{q_n} Z_n$. Then, combining all the above equations (1–5), and applying the Pop-rule we obtain some $(q_n, Z'_n) \in S_{(q,Z)}$ with $Z_n \preceq_{q_n} Z'_n$ (possibly $Z'_n = Z_n$). Finally we get $v_n \preceq_{q_n} Z_n \preceq_{q_n} Z'_n$. This completes the proof.

3. We will show that the following property is invariant by rule applications:

$$\forall (q, Z) \in \mathfrak{S}, \ \forall (q', Z') \in S_{(q,Z)}, \forall v' \in Z', \text{ there is a run} \tag{Inv}$$

$$(q, v, \varepsilon) \xrightarrow{*} (q', v'', \varepsilon) \text{ with } v \in Z \text{ and } v' \preceq_{q'} v''$$

The invariant holds initially, i.e., after application of the start rule. Indeed, in this case we have $\mathfrak{S} = \{(q_0, Z_0)\}$ and $S_{(q_0, Z_0)} = \{(q_0, Z_0)\}$. Hence $(q', Z') = (q, Z) = (q_0, Z_0)$ and for all $v \in Z_0$ we can choose the empty run $(q_0, v, \varepsilon) \xrightarrow{0} (q_0, v, \varepsilon)$.

We show below that (Inv) is preserved by application of an internal/push/pop rule. Therefore, the invariant still holds when reaching the fixed point, which proves the soundness. Let us write $\mathfrak{S}^-$ and $S^-_{(q,Z)}$ for the sets before the application of the rule and $\mathfrak{S}$ and $S_{(q,Z)}$ for the sets after the application of the rule.

Internal Rule. Let $(q, Z) \in \mathfrak{S} = \mathfrak{S}^-$, $(q', Z') \in S_{(q,Z)}$ and $v' \in Z'$. If $(q', Z') \in S^-_{(q,Z)}$ then we get the result since (Inv) holds before applying the internal rule. Otherwise, there is some $(q_1, Z_1) \in S^-_{(q,Z)}$ and a transition $t = q_1 \xrightarrow{g, \mathrm{nop}, R} q'$ with $Z' = \overrightarrow{R(g \cap Z_1)}$.

By definition, there exists $v_1 \in Z_1$ such that $v_1 \models g$ and $v' = [R]v_1 + \delta$ for some $\delta \geq 0$. Hence we have a run $(q_1, v_1, \varepsilon) \xrightarrow{t, \delta} (q', v', \varepsilon)$. Since the invariant holds before the internal rule, there is a run $(q, v, \varepsilon) \xrightarrow{*} (q_1, v'_1, \varepsilon)$ with $v \in Z$ and $v_1 \preceq_{q_1} v'_1$. Now since $\preceq$ is a simulation we obtain that $(q_1, v'_1, \varepsilon) \xrightarrow{t, \delta} (q', v'', \varepsilon)$ with $v' \preceq_{q'} v''$ and we are done.

Push Rule. Let $(q, Z) \in \mathfrak{S}$, $(q', Z') \in S_{(q,Z)}$ and $v' \in Z'$. If $(q, Z) \in \mathfrak{S}^-$ then we get the result since (Inv) holds before applying the Push rule. Otherwise, we must have $(q', Z') = (q, Z)$ and we can choose the empty run $(q, v', \varepsilon) \xrightarrow{0} (q, v', \varepsilon)$.

$$(q_1', v_4, a) \xrightarrow{t_1} \xrightarrow{\delta'} (q_2, v', \epsilon)$$
$$|\lambda$$
$$(q'', v_3, a) \xrightarrow{*} (q_1', v_4', a)$$
$$|\lambda \qquad\qquad\qquad\qquad |\lambda$$
$$(q', v_2, \epsilon) \xrightarrow{t} \xrightarrow{\delta} (q'', v_3', a) \qquad |\lambda$$
$$|\lambda \qquad\qquad |\lambda$$
$$(q, v, \epsilon) \xrightarrow{*} (q', v_2', \epsilon) \xrightarrow{t} \xrightarrow{\delta} (q'', v_3'', a) \xrightarrow{*} (q_1', v_4'', a) \xrightarrow{t_1} \xrightarrow{\delta'} (q_2, v'', \epsilon)$$

Fig. 5. Construction for the soundness.

Pop Rule. Let $(q, Z) \in \mathfrak{S} = \mathfrak{S}^-$, $(q_2, Z_2) \in S_{(q,Z)}$ and $v' \in Z_2$. Again, if $(q_2, Z_2) \in S^-_{(q,Z)}$ then we get the result since (Inv) holds before applying the Pop rule. Otherwise, by definition of the pop rule we have:

1. some $(q', Z') \in S_{(q,Z)}$,
2. some push transition $t = q' \xrightarrow{g, \text{push}_a, R} q''$,
3. some $(q'', Z_1) \in \mathfrak{S}$ with $Z_1 \sim_{q''} Z'' = \overrightarrow{R(g \cap Z')}$,
4. some $(q_1', Z_1') \in S_{(q'', Z_1)}$,
5. some pop transition $t_1 = q_1' \xrightarrow{g_1, \text{pop}_a, R_1} q_2$,

with $Z_2 = \overrightarrow{R_1(g_1 \cap Z_1')}$. The construction below is illustrated in Fig. 5.

Since $v' \in Z_2$, we get some $v_4 \in Z_1'$ such that $v_4 \models g_1$ and $v' = [R_1]v_4 + \delta'$ for some $\delta' \geq 0$. Hence we have a run $(q_1', v_4, a) \xrightarrow{t_1} \xrightarrow{\delta'} (q_2, v', \epsilon)$.

Now, applying the invariant to $(q'', Z_1) \in \mathfrak{S}$, $(q_1', Z_1') \in S_{(q'', Z_1)}$ and $v_4 \in Z_1'$, we get a run $(q'', v_3, \epsilon) \xrightarrow{*} (q_1', v_4', \epsilon)$ with $v_3 \in Z_1$ and $v_4 \preceq_{q_1'} v_4'$. Hence, we also have a run $(q'', v_3, a) \xrightarrow{*} (q_1', v_4', a)$.

Let $v_3' \in Z'' = \overrightarrow{R(g \cap Z')} \sim_{q''} Z_1$ with $v_3 \preceq_{q''} v_3'$. we get some $v_2 \in Z'$ such that $v_2 \models g$ and $v_3' = [R]v_2 + \delta$ for some $\delta \geq 0$. Hence we have a run $(q', v_2, \epsilon) \xrightarrow{t} \xrightarrow{\delta} (q'', v_3', a)$.

Finally, we apply the invariant to $(q, Z) \in \mathfrak{S}$, $(q', Z') \in S_{(q,Z)}$ and $v_2 \in Z'$, we get a run $(q, v, \epsilon) \xrightarrow{*} (q', v_2', \epsilon)$ with $v \in Z$ and $v_2 \preceq_{q'} v_2'$.

By repeatedly applying the property of simulation $\preceq$, we may extend the run from (q', v_2', ϵ) with $(q', v_2', \epsilon) \xrightarrow{t} \xrightarrow{\delta} (q'', v_3'', a) \xrightarrow{*} (q_1', v_4'', a) \xrightarrow{t_1} \xrightarrow{\delta'} (q_2, v'', \epsilon)$ where $v_3 \preceq_{q''} v_3' \preceq_{q''} v_3''$ and $v_4 \preceq_{q_1'} v_4' \preceq_{q_1'} v_4''$. Finally $v' \preceq_{q_2} v''$. Therefore, the invariant holds after the pop rule. $\square$

5 Algorithm for PDTA Reachability via Zones

In this section, we describe Algorithm 1 implementing the fixed point computation defined by the inductive rules in Table 1. We describe the structure of the algorithm and its main data-structures.

Notice first that the sets $\mathfrak{S}$ and $S_{(q,Z)}$ for $(q,Z) \in \mathfrak{S}$ can be alternatively represented as a single set of pairs of nodes:

$$S = \{[(q,Z),(q',Z')] \mid (q,Z) \in \mathfrak{S} \text{ and } (q',Z') \in S_{(q,Z)}\}.$$

We can recover $\mathfrak{S}$ as the first projection of S and $S_{(q,Z)}$ as the second projection of S filtered by the first component being (q,Z). We use both notations below depending on which is more convenient. The start rule initializes S to $\{[(q_0, Z_0), (q_0, Z_0)]\}$.

Let us consider first the rule for internal transitions. For each already discovered pair of nodes $[(q,Z),(q',Z')] \in S$ (or $(q',Z') \in S_{(q,Z)}$ with $(q,Z) \in \mathfrak{S}$), we have to consider each possible internal transition $q' \xrightarrow{g,\text{nop},R} q''$ and check whether the node (q'', Z'') with $Z'' = \overrightarrow{R(g \cap Z')}$ should be added to $S_{(q,Z)}$ or is subsumed by an existing node. This is like a graph traversal. The set S stores the already discovered pairs of nodes, and we will use a ToDo (unordered) list to store the newly discovered nodes from which outgoing transitions should be considered. The ToDo list should also consist of pairs $[(q,Z),(q',Z')]$ so that when a new node (q'', Z'') is discovered by an internal transition from (q',Z') we know to which set $S_{(q,Z)}$ it should be added.

As we can see from Theorem 1-soundness, given $(q,Z) \in \mathfrak{S}$, the set $S_{(q,Z)}$ should consist of nodes reachable from (q,Z) via a well-nested run. Hence, when dealing with a pair $[(q,Z),(q',Z')] \in S$ and we see a push transition $q' \xrightarrow{g,\text{push}_a,R} q''$ with $Z'' = \overrightarrow{R(g \cap Z')}$, we should not try to add the pair (q'', Z'') to $S_{(q,Z)}$ since the corresponding run would not be well-nested. Instead, we should search for a matching pop transition which could be taken after a well-nested run starting from (q'', Z''). This is why the push rule adds the new root (q'', Z'') to $\mathfrak{S}$ (unless it is equivalent to an existing root). The pair of nodes $[(q'', Z''), (q'', Z'')]$ is newly discovered and added to the ToDo list for further exploration.

The push transition may be matched with several pop transitions (which could be already discovered or yet to be discovered by the algorithm). To avoid revisiting the push transition many times, it will be stored by the algorithm in an additional set S_{push}. More precisely, we will store in S_{push} the tuple $[(q,Z), a, (q'', Z'')]$ meaning that the root node (q'', Z'') may be reached from the root node (q,Z) via a well-nested run reaching some (q', Z') followed by a transition pushing a onto the stack.

Finally, assume that, when dealing with a pair $[(q_1, Z_1),(q'_1, Z'_1)] \in S$, we see a pop transition $q'_1 \xrightarrow{g_1,\text{pop}_a,R_1} q_2$ with $Z_2 = \overrightarrow{R_1(g_1 \cap Z'_1)}$. We will check whether it can be matched with an already visited push transition, stored in the set S_{push} as a pair $[(q,Z), a, (q'', Z'')]$ with $(q'', Z'') = (q_1, Z_1)$. If this is the case, the pop rule may be applied and the node (q_2, Z_2) added to $S_{(q,Z)}$ (unless it is subsumed by an existing node). The newly discovered pair of nodes $[(q,Z), (q_2, Z_2)]$ is also added to the ToDo list for further exploration. Once again, the pop transition may also be matched with push transitions that will be discovered later by the algorithm. To avoid revisiting the pop transition many times, we store the tuple $[(q_1, Z_1), a, (q_2, Z_2)]$ in a new set S_{pop}.

Data Structures. We use a data structure TLM to store the triple of sets $(\mathcal{S}, \mathcal{S}_{\text{push}}, \mathcal{S}_{\text{pop}})$ and which is accessed with the following methods.

- TLM.create() creates the data structure with the three sets empty.
- TLM.add(q, Z, q', Z') adds $[(q, Z), (q', Z')]$ to $\mathcal{S}$.
- TLM.addPush(q, Z, a, q', Z') adds $[(q, Z), a, (q', Z')]$ to $\mathcal{S}_{\text{push}}$.
- TLM.addPop(q, Z, a, q', Z') adds $[(q, Z), a, (q', Z')]$ to $\mathcal{S}_{\text{pop}}$.
- TLM.isNewRoot(q, Z) returns $[\text{false}, Z']$ if there exists some $(q, Z') \in \mathfrak{S}$ with $Z' \sim_q Z$, and returns $[\text{true}, Z]$ otherwise.
- TLM.isNewNode(q, Z, q', Z') returns false if $\exists[(q, Z), (q', Z'')] \in \mathcal{S}$ with $Z' \preceq_{q'} Z''$, and returns true otherwise.
- TLM.isNewPop(q, Z, a, q', Z') returns false if $\exists[(q, Z), a, (q', Z'')] \in \mathcal{S}_{\text{pop}}$ with $Z' \preceq_{q'} Z''$, true otherwise.
- TLM.isNewPush(q, Z, a, q', Z') returns false if $[(q, Z), a, (q', Z')] \in \mathcal{S}_{\text{push}}$, and returns true otherwise.
- TLM.iterPop(q, Z, a) returns the list of (q', Z') with $[(q, Z), a, (q', Z')] \in \mathcal{S}_{\text{pop}}$.
- TLM.iterPush(a, q', Z') returns the list of (q, Z), s.t. $[(q, Z), a, (q', Z')] \in \mathcal{S}_{\text{push}}$.

Concretely, the data structure should store sets of nodes (q, Z) and be able to search or iterate through such sets. In order to make the algorithm slightly faster, we will segregate our sets of nodes, with the name of the state. We will use a hashmap in order to accomplish this task. See Fig. 6 where the concrete data structure is depicted.

We will use a first level hashmap to store the set of roots $\mathfrak{S}$. To implement TLM.isNewNode(q, Z, q', Z'), we first search for (q, Z) in the first level map, then a pointer TLM$[q][Z][0]$ will lead to a second level hashmap for the set of nodes $S_{(q,Z)}$ and we search for (q', Z') in this second level map. See Fig. 6(b).

To implement TLM.isNewPop(q, Z, a, q', Z') and TLM.iterPop(q, Z, a), we first search the root node (q, Z) in the first level map, then a pointer TLM$[q][Z][2]$ will lead to a second level hashmap storing the set of triples (a, q', Z') such that $[(q, Z), a, (q', Z')] \in \mathcal{S}_{\text{pop}}$. To speed up the access, this second level pop map is segregated first on the key a, then on the key q' to get the list of corresponding zones Z'. See Fig. 6(c,d).

Finally, we also store the set $\mathcal{S}_{\text{push}}$ to implement TLM. isNewPush(q, Z, a, q', Z') and TLM.iterPush(a, q', Z'). Notice that $\mathcal{S}_{\text{push}}$ consists of triples $[(q, Z), a, (q', Z')]$ where both (q, Z) and (q', Z') are root nodes from $\mathfrak{S}$. Notice also that for the iteration we fix the second node (q', Z'). To get an efficient implementation, we first search the root node (q', Z') in the first level map, then a pointer TLM$[q'][Z'][1]$ will lead to a second level hashmap storing the set of triples (a, q, Z) such that $[(q, Z), a, (q', Z')] \in \mathcal{S}_{\text{push}}$. To speed up the access, this second level push map is segregated first on the key a, then on the key q to get the list of corresponding zones Z. See Fig. 6(c,d).

Algorithm 1. PDTA Reachability Using Zones.

```
 1: procedure PDTAREACH
 2:     TLM.create()
 3:     TLM.add(q₀, Z₀, q₀, Z₀)                                    ▷ Start Rule
 4:     ToDo = {[(q₀, Z₀), (q₀, Z₀)]}
 5:     while ToDo ≠ ∅ do
 6:         [(q, Z), (q′, Z′)] = ToDo.get()              ▷ (q, Z) ∈ 𝔖 ∧ (q′, Z′) ∈ S₍q,z₎
 7:         for t = q′ --g,op,R--> q″ and Z″ = R(g ∩ Z′) ≠ ∅ do
 8:             if op = nop ∧ TLM.isNewNode(q, Z, q″, Z″) then
 9:                 TLM.add(q, Z, q″, Z″)                          ▷ Internal Rule
10:                 ToDo.add([(q, Z), (q″, Z″)])
11:             else if op = pushₐ then
12:                 [isNew, Z₁] = TLM.isNewRoot(q″, Z″)
13:                 if isNew == true then
14:                     TLM.add(q″, Z″, q″, Z″)                     ▷ Push Rule
15:                     ToDo.add([(q″, Z″), (q″, Z″)])
16:                 end if
17:                 if TLM.isNewPush(q, Z, a, q″, Z₁) then
18:                     TLM.addPush(q, Z, a, q″, Z₁)
19:                     for (q₂, Z₂) in TLM.iterPop(q″, Z₁, a) do
20:                         if TLM.isNewNode(q, Z, q₂, Z₂) then
21:                             TLM.add(q, Z, q₂, Z₂)               ▷ Pop Rule
22:                             ToDo.add([(q, Z), (q₂, Z₂)])
23:                         end if
24:                     end for
25:                 end if
26:             else if op = popₐ then
27:                 if TLM.isNewPop(q, Z, a, q″, Z″) then
28:                     TLM.addPop(q, Z, a, q″, Z″)
29:                     for (q₃, Z₃) in TLM.iterPush(a, q, Z) do
30:                         if TLM.isNewNode(q₃, Z₃, q″, Z″) then
31:                             TLM.add(q₃, Z₃, q″, Z″)   ▷ Pop Rule with q = q₃, Z = Z₃
32:                             ToDo.add([(q₃, Z₃), (q″, Z″)])      ▷ q₂ = q″, Z₂ = Z″
33:                         end if
34:                     end for
35:                 end if
36:             end if
37:         end for
38:     end while
39: end procedure
```

We now show correctness of Algorithm 1. Note that TLM encodes a triple of sets $(\mathcal{S}, \mathcal{S}_{\text{push}}, \mathcal{S}_{\text{pop}})$ defined by:

$$\mathcal{S} = \{[(q, Z), (q′, Z′)] \mid (q′, Z′) \in \text{TLM}[q][Z][0]\}$$
$$\mathcal{S}_{\text{push}} = \{[(q, Z), a, (q′, Z′)] \mid (a, q, Z) \in \text{TLM}[q′][Z′][1]\}$$
$$\mathcal{S}_{\text{pop}} = \{[(q, Z), a, (q′, Z′)] \mid (a, q′, Z′) \in \text{TLM}[q][Z][2]\}$$

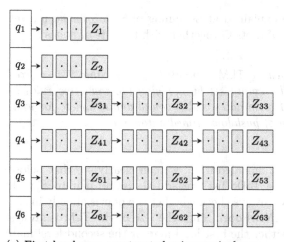

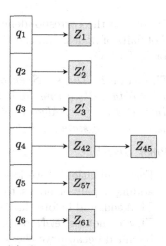

(a) First level map constructed using equivalence $\sim_q$ for controlling size. Keys will be state names, values will be lists of quadruplets, each of which has four pointers to second level maps, second level pushes maps, second level pops maps, and zones.

(b) Second level map corresponding to $S_{(q_1, Z_1)}$. Each first level map node will have its own second level map.

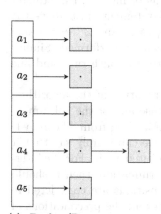

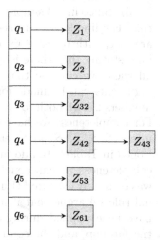

(c) Pushes/Pops map corresponding to root node (q_1, Z_1). Each pointer points to a different map where (q, Z) are stored.

(d) For pushes/pops map, this is a map corresponding to root node (q_1, Z_1), and symbol a_2 (say). The (q, Z) stored here is constructed using equivalence (pushes map), or using simulation (pops map).

Fig. 6. Two level map implementing the data structure TLM storing the sets S, S_{push}, S_{pop}.

Recall also the correspondence explained at beginning of Sect. 5 between a set $\mathcal{S}$ of pairs of nodes, and the set of roots $\mathfrak{S}$ together with the sets of nodes $S_{(q,Z)}$ for $(q, Z) \in \mathfrak{S}$.

Theorem 2. *The set $\mathcal{S}$ encoded by TLM computed by Algorithm 1 is a fixed point obtained starting from the empty set by applying the inductive rules in Table 1. Therefore, Algorithm 1 terminates and is sound and complete for well-nested control state reachability of pushdown timed automata.*

Proof (sketch).

1. For termination, if we look at our algorithm, we can clearly see that before adding a pair of nodes to the ToDo list, we add the same pair to $\mathcal{S}$ with TLM.add, and before that, we always check whether the pair is already in our TLM or not (isNewNode or isNewRoot). Since the size of the TLM is always bounded because we check either the first level map or the second level map before adding, the outer while loop will be called only a finite number of times. From this we can conclude that the algorithm will terminate.

2. For soundness we have prove that any change to the TLM is equivalent to applying one of the rewrite rules to $(\mathcal{S}, \mathcal{S}_{\text{push}}, \mathcal{S}_{\text{pop}})$, which is already known to be sound from Theorem 1. The changes to the TLM occur in lines 3, 9, 14, 21, 31. Since line 3 simply adds $[(q_0, Z_0), (q_0, Z_0)]$ to $\mathcal{S}$, it simulates the start rule. For line 9, we can see that the pre conditions of internal rule Table 1 are met, with $(q, Z) \in \mathfrak{S}$, $(q', Z') \in S_{(q,Z)}$, the *if*-statement (just above the line) stating that there is an *nop* transition from q to q', and $Z'' \neq \phi$. Using all these we can see that indeed the operation can be performed. Similar arguments can be made for line 14, which simulates the push rule, and line numbers 21, 31 both for the pop-rule.

3. For completeness we have to prove that after termination of the algorithm, using $(\mathcal{S}, \mathcal{S}_{\text{push}}, \mathcal{S}_{\text{pop}})$ to encode TLM, we cannot use any of the rules mentioned in Table 1, to add anything extra to the TLM. Then from Theorem 1-completeness we can conclude. For the start rule we can simply say that it was definitely executed (Line 3), so it cannot be executed again. For the internal rule we argue that if it can be applied after termination, then it should have been applied during execution. Since all transitions are considered in the *for*-loop, and the conditions before line 9 checks all the preconditions of the internal rule, it is certainly the case that a node (q'', Z'') could not be added because either it was already added, or $(q'', Z''') \in S_{(q,Z)}, Z'' \preceq_{q''} Z'''$. The argument for the push rule is similar. For the pop rule to be applied we argue that there must be a push transition and a pop transition satisfying the pre-conditions in the pop rule. Since both of these are already present for zones in the TLM, we say that they must have been added to $\mathcal{S}_{\text{push}}$ and $\mathcal{S}_{\text{pop}}$. We then concern ourselves with the order, arguing that if the push transition was discovered later the node either must already have been added (Line 21) or another node simulating the node must have been present in the TLM (Line 20). A similar argument is made in case the order of discovery is reversed.

For the full proof details, we refer the reader to the long version [6].   □

6 Experiments and Results

Implementation We build on the existing architecture of an open-source tool for analysis of timed automata, TChecker [19]. Our tool along with the benchmarks we used is available at https://github.com/karthik-314/PDTA_reachability and more details can be found [6]. The input for our implementation are PDTA, rather than TA so we modify TChecker in order to run our experiments. While most of the TChecker file format will remain the same, the only place where we make a change to the syntax of the input, will be the edges. TChecker uses the following format, for its transitions,

```
edge:<Process>:<src>:<tgt>:<label>{
    do:<Reset1(x=0)> ; <Reset2(y=0)> :
    provided: <guard1(x==0)> && <guard2(y>=1)>}
```

The new format in order to incorporate the pushes and pops will be,

```
edge:<Process>:<src>:<tgt>:<label>{
    do:<Reset1(x=0)> ; <Reset2(y=0)> :
    provided: <guard1(x==0)> && <guard2(y>=1)>}
    [<push/pop>:<symbol>]
```

In case the operation is nop, the square brackets are left empty.

We have implemented two variants of Algorithm 1 for PDTA and we will compare these between each other and also with a region-based approach. More precisely, we consider the following 3 algorithms:

- **Simulation Based Approach** ($\preceq_{LU}$): Direct implementation of Algorithm 1.
- **Equivalence Based Approach** ($\sim_{LU}$): This is a variation of Algorithm 1, with two methods changed,
  - TLM.isNewNode(q, Z, q', Z'): Returns **false** if $\exists[(q, Z), (q', Z'')] \in \mathcal{S}$ with $Z' \sim_{q'} Z''$, and **true** otherwise.
  - TLM.isNewPop(q, Z, a, q', Z'): Returns **false** if $\exists[(q, Z), a, (q', Z'')] \in \mathcal{S}_{pop}$ with $Z' \sim_{q'} Z''$, and **true** otherwise.

  As mentioned in Sect. 4, if instead of simulation, we just use equivalence everywhere, we do obtain a correct algorithm for reachability in PDTA. Hence it is interesting to compare it with the above approach.
- **Region Based Implementation** (RB): A previous implementation [5], uses a region based approach in order to solve the non-emptiness problem in PDTA. We note two features of the algorithm. First, it uses a tree-automaton based approach for efficiency and correctness, but underlying it is the region (rather than zone) construction. Second, it works only with closed guards, while our approach works with closed and open guards.

We note the following important points regarding our implementation:

1. The $\preceq$ used in our implementation will be $\preceq_{LU}$ [8], without extrapolation and with global clock bounds.

2. The ToDo list used currently uses LIFO (stack) ordering for popping of elements. This corresponds to a DFS exploration of the zone-graph. But we can use other data structures for this purpose as well, e.g., changing it to FIFO would give us a BFS exploration etc.

3. Both the simulation based and equivalence based approach are tested on PDTA with empty and non-empty languages, but we have ensured that both of them return an answer only after the entire exploration has been completed. In other words, we do not stop the exploration when we reach a final state. This is to make fair comparisons, where we do not terminate because of being "lucky" in encountering the final state early. Of course in practice we would not do this. In contrast, we note that the RB approach is an on the fly approach which returns non-empty as soon as the final state turns out to be reachable.

All experiments are run on Intel-i5 10th Generation processor, with an 8GB RAM, with a timeout of 120 seconds.

Benchmarks. We used a total of 10 benchmarks in our experiments, but parameterized several of them in order to test the scalability and to give us more insight into performance comparisons. The benchmark and their parameterizations are explained in [6]. We highlight only some salient points here. The benchmark B_1 is the PDTA from Fig. 1. $B_2(k)$ is directly adapted from Fig. 3 with the constant $y \leq 1$ parametrized to $y \leq k$, and $k + 1$ pops between q_0 and q_2. Note that q_3 is unreachable regardless of the value of k. Benchmarks B_3, B_4 are adapted from [5] with B_3 involving untiming of a stack age into normal clocks. B_5, B_6 involve significant interplay of push/pop edges and clocks and B_6, B_7 also have open guards. More details can be found in [6]. We also note that automata B_1, $B_3(3,4), B_5(k_1,k_2), B_8, B_9(k_1,k_2)$ accept a nonempty language, while the rest are empty. As described earlier this does not change the performance of the simulation and equivalence based approaches, but may significantly change the performance of the Region Based Approach.

Results Table 2 contains a selection of our experimental results; more can be found in [6]. From the table, we conclude first that the zone based approach is indeed faster than the Region Based Approach for all examples. Second, the simulation based approach runs faster than the equivalence based approach for all examples if the ToDo priority for removal remains the same. In fact, the performance of the simulation based approach depends mostly on the size of the PDTA, but the equivalence based approach is dependant on the constants used in guards as well, which is even more the case for the region based approach. Finally, our approach can easily handle closed and open guards.

Most of the timeouts that occurred during the experiments are due to Out of Memory (OoM) kills, especially for larger sized PDTAs. For smaller sized PDTA such as $B_2(100)$, the recorded number of nodes before timeout was 154700.

Regarding the performance, we would like to emphasize that B1, B2, B3, B4, B7 were designed to compare the Zone approach to the region (RB) approach.

Table 2. Results on the Benchmarks. Time recorded in ms, and timeout (T.O.) used is 120 s. OoM stands for Out of Memory kill. Results rounded up to 1 decimal. # nodes refers to the number of nodes in the zone/region graph explored. In case of timeout $\geq n$, refers to recorded number of nodes n before timeout occurred. NA in RB columns represents that the region based approach does not handle open guards in transitions (B_6, B_7 have open guards.)

Benchmark	$\preceq_{LU}$ Time	$\preceq_{LU}$ # nodes	$\sim_{LU}$ Time	$\sim_{LU}$ # nodes	RB Time	RB # nodes
B_1	0.2	17	0.2	17	235.6	4100
$B_2(10)$	0.8	77	0.8	77	6835.8	30200
$B_2(100)$	20.0	5252	20.7	5252	T.O	$\geq$154700
$B_3(4,3)$	0.2	6	0.2	6	1043.8	14300
$B_3(3,4)$	0.2	9	0.2	9	98.8	3400
B_4	0.2	8	0.1	8	0.3	17
$B_5(100,10)$	0.8	202	5.4	2212	OoM	OoM
$B_5(100,1000)$	0.7	202	3564.3	201202	OoM	OoM
$B_5(5000,100)$	23.2	10002	3429.3	1010102	OoM	OoM
$B_6(5,4,1000)$	0.3	30	611.8	30047	NA	NA
$B_6(5,4,10000)$	0.3	30	60271.9	300047	NA	NA
$B_6(501,500,100)$	38.2	3006	501.0	34799	NA	NA
B_7	112.4	4475	113.1	4475	NA	NA

As a consequence these models are very simple and the number of explored nodes remains almost the same regardless of whether we use $\sim$ or $\preceq$ to prune, which reflects in the times/sizes not being too different. However, the other examples B5, B6 are more complex and have nodes that get pruned during exploration (both using $\sim$ and $\preceq$). Here we can see the clear improvement of $\preceq$ over $\sim$ both in terms of time taken and also of number of explored nodes.

7 Discussion and Future Work

In this paper, we examined how an unbounded stack can be integrated seamlessly with zone-abstractions in timed automata. We would like to point out that two easy extensions of our work are possible. First, as remarked earlier, our algorithm checks for well-nested reachability, i.e., it requires to reach a final state with empty stack for acceptance. But we can generalize this to general control-state reachability by showing that a control state q is reachable in the PDTA (with possibly a non-empty stack) iff some node (q, Z) is discovered by our algorithm and added to some $S_{(q', Z')}$ (and not just to $S_{(q_0, Z_0)}$ as in the well-nested case). While this idea is simple and requires only minor edits to the existing algorithm, the proof of correctness requires more work and we leave this for future work.

Secondly, we can handle the model with ages in stack as in [1,3] with an exponential blowup (thanks to [13]). However, an open question is whether this blowup can be avoided in practice. As noted earlier, there exist extensions [14,15] studied especially in the context of binary reachability, which are expressively strictly more powerful, for which decidability results are known. It would be interesting to see how we can extend the zone-based approach to those models.

Finally, it seems interesting to examine further the link to the liveness problem, possibly allowing us to transfer ideas and obtain faster implementations. Another possibility would be to use the extrapolation operator (rather than, or in addition to, simulation), which we have not considered in this work.

References

1. Abdulla, P.A., Atig, M.F., Stenman, J.: Dense-timed pushdown automata. In: Proceedings of the 27th Annual IEEE Symposium on Logic in Computer Science, LICS 2012, Dubrovnik, Croatia, pp. 35–44 (2012)
2. Akshay, S., Gastin, P., Jugé, V., Krishna, S.N.: Timed systems through the lens of logic. In: 34th Annual ACM/IEEE Symposium on Logic in Computer Science, LICS 2019, Vancouver, BC, Canada, pp. 1–13 (2019)
3. Akshay, S., Gastin, P., Krishna, S.N.: Analyzing Timed Systems Using Tree Automata. Logical Methods Comput. Sci. **14**(2:8), 1–35 (2018)
4. Akshay, S., Gastin, P., Krishna, S., Roychowdhury, S.: Revisiting underapproximate reachability for multipushdown systems. TACAS 2020. LNCS, vol. 12078, pp. 387–404. Springer, Cham (2020). https://doi.org/10.1007/978-3-030-45190-5_21
5. Akshay, S., Gastin, P., Krishna, S.N., Sarkar, I.: Towards an efficient tree automata based technique for timed systems. In: 28th International Conference on Concurrency Theory, CONCUR 2017, 5–8 September 2017, Berlin, Germany, pp. 39:1–39:15 (2017)
6. S. Akshay, Paul Gastin, and Karthik R. Prakash. Fast zone-based algorithms for reachability in pushdown timed automata. CoRR arXiv preprint arXiv:2105.13683 (2021)
7. Alur, R., Dill, D.L.: A theory of timed automata. Theor. Comput. Sci. **126**(2), 183–235 (1994)
8. Behrmann, G., Bouyer, P., Larsen, K.G., Pelánek, R.: Lower and upper bounds in zone based abstractions of timed automata. In: Jensen, K., Podelski, A. (eds.) TACAS 2004. LNCS, vol. 2988, pp. 312–326. Springer, Heidelberg (2004). https://doi.org/10.1007/978-3-540-24730-2_25
9. Bengtsson, J., Larsen, K., Larsson, F., Pettersson, P., Yi, W.: UPPAAL — a tool suite for automatic verification of real-time systems. In: Alur, R., Henzinger, T.A., Sontag, E.D. (eds.) HS 1995. LNCS, vol. 1066, pp. 232–243. Springer, Heidelberg (1996). https://doi.org/10.1007/BFb0020949
10. Bouajjani, A., Echahed, R., Robbana, R.: On the automatic verification of systems with continuous variables and unbounded discrete data structures. In: Antsaklis, P., Kohn, W., Nerode, A., Sastry, S. (eds.) HS 1994. LNCS, vol. 999, pp. 64–85. Springer, Heidelberg (1995). https://doi.org/10.1007/3-540-60472-3_4
11. Bouyer, P.: Forward analysis of updatable timed automata. Formal Methods Syst. Des. **24**(3), 281–320 (2004)

12. Bouyer, P., Laroussinie, F., Reynier, P.-A.: Diagonal constraints in timed automata: forward analysis of timed systems. In: Pettersson, P., Yi, W. (eds.) FORMATS 2005. LNCS, vol. 3829, pp. 112–126. Springer, Heidelberg (2005). https://doi.org/10.1007/11603009_10
13. Clemente, L., Lasota, S.: Timed pushdown automata revisited. In: 30th Annual ACM/IEEE Symposium on Logic in Computer Science, LICS 2015, Kyoto, Japan, 6–10 July 2015, pp. 738–749 (2015)
14. Clemente, L., Lasota, S.: Reachability relations of timed pushdown automata. J. Comput. Syst. Sci. **117**, 202–241 (2021)
15. Clemente, L., Lasota, S., Lazić, R., Mazowiecki, F.: Timed pushdown automata and branching vector addition systems. In 32nd Annual ACM/IEEE Symposium on Logic in Computer Science, LICS 2017, Reykjavik, Iceland, 20–23 June 2017, pp. 1–12. IEEE Computer Society (2017)
16. Dang, Z.: Pushdown timed automata: a binary reachability characterization and safety verification. Theor. Comput. Sci. **1–3**, 93–121 (2003)
17. Gastin, P., Mukherjee, S., Srivathsan, B.: Fast algorithms for handling diagonal constraints in timed automata. In: Dillig, I., Tasiran, S. (eds.) CAV 2019. LNCS, vol. 11561, pp. 41–59. Springer, Cham (2019). https://doi.org/10.1007/978-3-030-25540-4_3
18. Herbreteau, F., Kini, D., Srivathsan, B., Walukiewicz, I.: Using non-convex approximations for efficient analysis of timed automata. In: IARCS Annual Conference on Foundations of Software Technology and Theoretical Computer Science, FSTTCS 2011, 12–14 December 2011, Mumbai, India, vol. 13 of LIPIcs, pp. 78–89. Schloss Dagstuhl - Leibniz-Zentrum für Informatik (2011)
19. Herbreteau, F.: Gerald Point. Tchecker. https://github.com/fredher/tchecker
20. Herbreteau, F., Srivathsan, B., Tran, T.T., Walukiewicz, I.: Why liveness for timed automata is hard, and what we can do about it. ACM Trans. Comput. Log. **21**(3), 17:1–17:28 (2020)
21. Herbreteau, F., Srivathsan, B., Walukiewicz, I.: Better abstractions for timed automata. In: Proceedings of the 27th Annual IEEE Symposium on Logic in Computer Science, LICS 2012, Dubrovnik, Croatia, 25–28 June 2012, pp. 375–384. IEEE Computer Society (2012)
22. Laarman, A., Olesen, M.C., Dalsgaard, A.E., Larsen, K.G., van de Pol, J.: Multicore emptiness checking of timed Büchi automata using inclusion abstraction. In: Sharygina, N., Veith, H. (eds.) CAV 2013. LNCS, vol. 8044, pp. 968–983. Springer, Heidelberg (2013). https://doi.org/10.1007/978-3-642-39799-8_69
23. Larsen, K.G., Pettersson, P., Yi, W.: Uppaal in a nutshell. Int. J. Softw. Tools Technol. Transf. **1**(1), 134–152 (1997). https://doi.org/10.1007/s100090050010
24. Tripakis, S.: Checking timed Büchi automata emptiness on simulation graphs. ACM Trans. Comput. Log. **10**(3), 15:1–15:19 (2009)

Security

Verified Cryptographic Code
for Everybody

Brett Boston[1], Samuel Breese[1], Joey Dodds[1(✉)], Mike Dodds[1],
Brian Huffman[1], Adam Petcher[2], and Andrei Stefanescu[1]

[1] Galois, Inc., Portland, USA
jdodds@galois.com
[2] Amazon Web Services, Seattle, USA

Abstract. We have completed machine-assisted proofs of two highly-optimized cryptographic primitives, AES-256-GCM and SHA-384. We have verified that the implementations of these primitives, written in a mix of C and x86 assembly, are memory safe and functionally correct, by which we mean input-output equivalent to their algorithmic specifications. Our proofs were completed using SAW, a bounded cryptographic verification tool which we have extended to handle embedded x86. The code we have verified comes from AWS LibCrypto. This code is identical to BoringSSL and very similar to OpenSSL, from which it ultimately derives. We believe we are the first to formally verify these implementations, which protect the security of nearly everybody on the internet.

Keywords: Cryptography · Automated reasoning · Verification

1 Introduction

Widely-used cryptographic libraries such as OpenSSL [20], BoringSSL [16], and AWS LibCrypto [2] are an enticing target for formal verification. These libraries are used, to a first approximation, by everybody—or at least the four billion or so worldwide users of the internet. Each primitive in these libraries typically consists of a modest amount of code, but these primitives loom large in both their security and performance impact. Cryptographic primitives are also unusual in that they have clearly defined specifications and very few dependencies, which removes some major challenges from general-purpose verification. As a result, in recent years many efforts have been made to verify cryptographic library code.

However, despite significant progress, widely-used cryptographic libraries have resisted verification, at least for the versions of the primitives that are used in practice. This is because these primitives are some of the most heavily optimized pieces of code in existence. For a cloud service, every packet involves a call to at least one cryptographic primitive, so even small optimizations will have large performance and cost impacts. As a result, for AES and SHA there

© The Author(s) 2021
A. Silva and K. R. M. Leino (Eds.) CAV 2021, LNCS 12759, pp. 645–668, 2021.
https://doi.org/10.1007/978-3-030-81685-8_31

is an enormous gap in complexity between simple and easily verified high-level reference implementations, and the highly optimized implementations used in production.

Optimizations create several difficulties when verifying cryptographic primitives. First, primitives are typically written in a mix of C and assembly. This means that a verification tool must model both of these languages and the manner in which they can interact. Furthermore, each optimization step inherently increases the difficulty of verification, because each requires one or more theorems showing that the optimization is sound. To add to this, many of these optimizations break the abstractions used in algorithm specifications. For example, the SHA-384 specification is defined using a function called `Sigma0` that is unfolded and rearranged during the optimisation process (see Subsect. 6.1). Solver-based automation typically struggles to recover these abstractions.

The verification of cryptographic code has seen huge advances in recent years. Purpose-built libraries such as EverCrypt [21] can now match the performance of hand-tuned OpenSSL. These correct-by-construction libraries may be the future, but as of 2021 they have not yet seen wide mainstream adoption. Our aim as formal methods practitioners is to verify the cryptographic code on which users depend. What has been missing until now is the ability to verify the legacy cryptographic code that runs in production for hundreds of millions of users. This is the problem we solve.

Approach and Results. We have formally verified the memory safety and functional correctness of two key cryptographic primitives, AES-256-GCM and SHA-384 as they currently appear in the new AWS LibCrypto library (AWS-LC) [2]. AWS-LC is a general-purpose library maintained by Amazon Web Services for use with AWS applications. We targeted these algorithms in particular because they are used within AWS and included in the Commercial National Security Algorithms Suite [18]. We chose a block cipher and a hashing algorithm in order to cover multiple algorithm types and to be representative of other algorithms in AWS-LC.

Cryptographic algorithms have fixed specifications which permit a narrow range of designs, and as a result, implementations change slowly. The AES-256-GCM and SHA-384 implementations in AWS-LC are identical to those in Google's BoringSSL library, and as a result, our proofs apply to it as well. For these primitives, there are only small differences between BoringSSL and OpenSSL, and we are confident our proofs would also apply to OpenSSL with minor modifications.

Our proofs show that the implementations of AES-256-GCM and SHA-384 are input-output equivalent to formal specifications of their expected behaviour. We write our specifications in Cryptol [11], a pre-existing high-level language designed for use by cryptographic experts. Cryptol specifications are executable, so our proofs establish that for any input, the implementation and specification produce exactly the same result. To boot, our proofs guarantee that the code is free of undefined behaviour such as memory safety errors, meaning that any remaining correctness errors are local to the code being proved and cannot affect the calling context. We do not verify side-channel properties, nor do we analyse cryptographic security properties of the AES-256-GCM and SHA-384 algorithms.

We performed these proofs using the Software Analysis Workbench (SAW) [14]. SAW is an industrial verification tool designed to prove equivalence properties between abstract specifications and lower-level, more optimized implementations. SAW is a bounded verifier: loops must be verified under preconditions that guarantee termination, and data-structures must be statically allocated with bounded sizes.

We have run our proofs on fixed sizes of input data, i.e., fixed numbers of bytes to be hashed/encrypted/decrypted. The number of loop iterations in these algorithms are strictly fixed by the input size so this also implicitly bounds the execution length. We chose these sizes so as to exercise all branches and boundary conditions in the code and specification (in this, we follow Galois and AWS's previous work: see Chudnov et al. [7]). We discuss the scope and limitations of our proof in Sect. 7.

Each proof of a cryptographic primitive in SAW has two stages. In the first, the imperative input code is converted to a functional term using bounded symbolic execution. This depends on a high-fidelity model of the input languages. SAW already had an LLVM model used for C and C++ verification. For AES-256-GCM and SHA-384 we developed a new SAW model of x86 assembly, along with an interface with SAW's existing LLVM model. As well as modeling core x86, this also included modeling special-purpose instructions used to achieve high performance. A successful conversion only occurs for well-defined programs, and implies that the program is free of undefined behavior under the given preconditions.

In the second stage of a SAW proof, the symbolic term is compared to a specification term written in Cryptol. For many applications, SAW can discharge these equivalences automatically, but this is where the optimizations in AES-256-GCM and SHA-384 made verification much more challenging. The proof steps involved cannot be discharged automatically by current solvers, so instead, our proofs make careful use of rewriting logic to massage the terms into a form that can be discharged. Some of these proof steps may be amenable to automated solving in future.

Our proofs were developed collaboratively between a team of expert verification engineers. As well as technical innovation, these proofs also required careful proof engineering. By this, we mean the analog of software engineering—a combination of proof design, tool design, and team working practices which makes it possible to execute effectively on a verification goal. We found that to a degree, proof engineering *is* software engineering; that is, successful proof engineering has similarities to the practices needed when developing a challenging software project.

Aside from proofs and tool capabilities, there is something else notable about our project: we verify code that was never intended for formal verification. This is in contrast to many other efforts, which target systems that were designed with assurance in mind. For example, Galois and AWS previously verified an Amazon TLS library that was purpose-built as a high-assurance alternative to OpenSSL's TLS support [7], while in the EverCrypt library, code and proof were developed in parallel, and even the API was designed to simplify specifications [21]. We verify legacy code because this is the code that is actually used in AWS-LC and its predecessors.

Contributions. The key contributions of this paper are as follows:

- Proofs of correctness for highly optimized versions of AES-256-GCM and SHA-384, as they appear in AWS LibCrypto and BoringSSL.
- A verifier for mixed C and x86 code which allows precise reasoning about functional correctness. This capability is built into the industrial verification tool, SAW.
- A simple system of rewrite tactics which is powerful enough to allow verification of highly optimised cryptographic algorithms.
- Lessons learned in proof engineering when applying an industry verification tool to a challenging piece of legacy cryptographic code.

All proof scripts are available online[1].

1.1 Related Work

There is a considerable amount of recent work in cryptographic verification, representing a large space of application domains and design requirements. While our work is widely applicable, we do not consider it a one-size-fits-all solution. We discuss how a developer might choose between the many verified cryptography efforts in Subsect. 7.2. Here we give an overview of projects that target C or x86, or that are closely related technically. We do not review work on verifying cryptographic security properties, which is orthogonal to the problem of verifying that code matches algorithm.

The closest work to ours in terms of technical approach is Galois and AWS's previous work verifying the HMAC and DRBG primitives in the AWS s2n TLS library [7]. Just as we do, they use SAW to verify production cryptographic code. The main difference from our current project is the complexity of the primitives verified. The HMAC and DRBG primitives are inherently simpler algorithms, and are written in C, rather than x86. Furthermore, this code was designed for verification, unlike the OpenSSL-derived code we target. In earlier work, Ye *et al.* also verified C versions of HMAC and DRBG from OpenSSL using the foundational Verified Software Toolchain (VST) [22].

The Everest project has developed verified C/x86 cryptographic library called EverCrypt [5,10,21,23]. Recent results are extremely impressive, with performance comparable to highly optimised OpenSSL code. However, EverCrypt

---

[1] https://github.com/awslabs/aws-lc-verification.

represent a different philosophy from ours, where the library and proof are co-designed, and in some cases code is synthesized. This approach looks towards a future where such libraries replace hand-written libraries like AWS-LC, BoringSSL, and OpenSSL. Our philosophy is complementary: we verify code as it currently exists while we wait for the future to arrive.

EverCrypt also differs in that they use a proof-assistant style of reasoning more similar to Coq or Isabelle. The advantage of this is that proofs are very flexible—for example, they work for unbounded input sizes. However, the cost is that proofs are relatively more verbose. Proof size is hard to estimate in Ever-Crypt, because the proof and implementation are mixed, but the earlier Vale paper [10] suggests that EverCrypt's proof of AES-GCM uses 2000 lines of proof library plus additional proof mixed in. In comparison, SAW is designed to automate reasoning where possible, and the proof of AES-256-GCM implementation takes us less than 1000 lines of proof (including white-space and comments, for attempted apples-to-apples comparison).

The CASM [17] project verifies x86-based cryptography taken from OpenSSL, including SHA-256 (we verify SHA-384). CASM's toolchain is similar to ours, based on symbolic execution and SMT solvers. However, CASM only examines functions over message blocks, rather than the whole SHA-256 algorithm. CASM also does not verify the most highly optimised versions of this algorithm. For example, it omits x86 EVP and vector operations, two of the main challenges.

Fiat Crypto [9] is a related approach, although it does not apply to the algorithms proved in this paper. It foundationally generates portable C field arithmetic implementations from a high level specification. Code synthesized by Fiat Crypto has already been added to OpenSSL. Jasmin [1] is another foundational synthesis approach. It generates high-performance vectorized x86 implementations. The Jasmin implementation of ChaCha20-Poly1305 outperforms similar hand-optimized implementations. We have not seen Jasmin implementations of SHA-2 or AES-GCM.

SAW's approach has some similarities to model checking, in that it is a bounded verification technique. However, proofs are based on symbolic execution, that is, construction of logical terms representing the program denotation, and proofs are bounded on input buffer size, not program execution length perse.

2   Project Design Constraints

Our objective in this project was to verify the cryptographic code which is actually deployed, and to ensure it stays verified as it changes over time[2]. To do this, we used *continuous reasoning*, a term due to Peter O'Hearn [19]. In continuous reasoning, there is a tight connection between code, software engineering process, and verification tools. Several recent industry projects have successfully used continuous reasoning practices. It was also important that our tools

---

[2] In fact, we do not expect AES-256-GCM and SHA-384 to change often in AWS-LC, but this work takes place in the context of a larger AWS-LC assurance project.

maintain the existing institutional trust in the original codebase—this ruled out whole-code replacements such as EverCrypt. This resulted in the following design constraints:

- Proofs had to run on the executed code, rather than a model/abstraction. This was to minimize the trusted base, and ensure that our proofs stayed in sync with the code as it evolved.
- Proofs had to run automatically with a low enough time budget to integrate with continuous integration checking. This ensures that errors are detected at the time code is changing, which increases the probability of fixes.
- Proofs had to avoid modifications to the original source code, and instead exist as separate supporting files. Our experience is that teams are typically very reluctant to modify original source code, even with non-functional annotations.
- The proof toolchain had to operate independently of the software build system. This was to avoid introducing untrusted tools into critical development pathways.

These constraints led us to use the SAW tool as our basis for verification [14]. Our project can be seen as a follow on to Galois and AWS's prior verification of AWS s2n which had many of the same design objectives [7]. Chudnov *et al.* showed that SAW can be used for continuous reasoning for a relatively simple piece of C cryptography. The difference in our current project is the inherent difficulty of verifying the code.

3   AES-256-GCM and SHA-384 Proof Structure

Conceptually, SAW's approach to proof works as follows. The tool symbolically executes C and x86 code, resulting in a collection of functional terms. A term describes every program output mathematically as a function of program inputs. Once side conditions have been discharged, completion of symbolic execution also implies that the program is safe: that is, memory safety errors cannot occur. In the final step of the proof, these functional terms are compared to specifications using a solver to determine whether they are equivalent.

Interfaces. At the top level of our proof, we verify the AWS LC primitives against OpenSSL's EVP interface[3]. OpenSSL and its descendants use this interface to make it easy to swap out algorithms without exposing their implementations. This complicates the verification task by hiding functions behind pointers and union types. It has also attempted to remain largely backwards compatible for years, resulting in an API that is not as clean as it might be otherwise. Perhaps for these reasons, previous cryptographic verification projects have not verified the EVP interface.

---

[3] https://wiki.openssl.org/index.php/EVP.

```
let EVP_CipherUpdate_spec enc gcm_len len = do {
  // ... some cipher set-up omitted (5 lines)

  cipher_data_ptr <- crucible_alloc_aligned 16 (llvm_struct "struct.EVP_AES_GCM_CTX");
  points_to_EVP_AES_GCM_CTX cipher_data_ptr ctx mres {{ 1 : [32] }} 0xffffffff;

  ctx_ptr <- crucible_alloc_readonly (llvm_struct "struct.evp_cipher_ctx_st");
  points_to_evp_cipher_ctx_st ctx_ptr cipher_ptr cipher_data_ptr enc;

  (in_, in_ptr) <- ptr_to_fresh_readonly "in" (llvm_array len (llvm_int 8));
  out_ptr <- crucible_alloc (llvm_array len (llvm_int 8));
  out_len_ptr <- crucible_alloc (llvm_int 32);

  crucible_execute_func [ctx_ptr, out_ptr, out_len_ptr, in_ptr,
                         (crucible_term {{ `len : [32] }})];

  let ctx' = {{ cipher_update enc ctx in_ }};

  // ... some cipher invariants omitted (3 lines)

  crucible_points_to out_ptr (crucible_term {{ ctr32_encrypt ctx in_ }});
  crucible_points_to out_len_ptr (crucible_term {{ `len : [32] }});
  crucible_return (crucible_term {{ 1 : [32] }});
};
```

Fig. 1. Part of the EVP interface for AES-256-GCM.

SAW-Script Specifications. The top-level EVP specifications are defined in SAW-script, the high-level control language for SAW. Figure 1 shows part of the SAW-script EVP interface for AES-256-GCM. In its form, this interface consists of a series of instructions in SAW-script, but in its effect, it is a Hoare-style pre/post specification. The interface sets up symbolic memory (the pre-condition), symbolically executes the function (`crucible_execute_func`), and then checks that the resulting symbolic memory contains the correct values (the post-condition).

For AES, the main purpose of the pre-condition is to define the layout of memory that results from the AES initialization function. Because we define post-condition for the initialization function that match the specification given here, we can end-to-end verify the common use case of initializing memory, encrypting some input, and returning the result.

The script defines the memory pre- and post-conditions for the function using points-to assertions. In SAW-script, we allocate symbolic memory at specific sizes using the `crucible_alloc` commands. We can then use the `points_to` command to specify that a pointer points to symbolic memory. The `ptr_to_fresh` command is a convenience function that allocates a pointer, and then initializes it with symbolic memory.

SAW's logic is less expressive than a full separation logic, but specifications can naturally be interpreted in terms of separation, including the property that memory cells do not overlap. To make the memory layout easier to understand, consider the following separation logic triple, which roughly corresponds to the layout defined in the SAW-script:

$$\{\text{cipher\_data\_ptr} \mapsto \text{ctx}... \; * \; \text{in\_ptr} \mapsto in \; * \; \text{out\_ptr} \mapsto (\_ : [len])\}$$

EVP_CipherUpdate(ctx_ptr, out_ptr, out_len_ptr, in_ptr, len)

$$\left\{ \begin{array}{c} \text{cipher\_data\_ptr} \mapsto \text{cipher\_update}(\text{ctx}...) \; * \\ \text{in\_ptr} \mapsto in \; * \; \text{out\_ptr} \mapsto \text{ctr32\_encrypt}(\text{ctx}, \text{in}) \end{array} \right\}$$

Rather than syntactically divide the pre-condition and post-condition, as in a Hoare triple, the two are divided by the call to `crucible_execute_func`, which indicates symbolic execution of the target C or x86 function. Crucible is the intermediate language for symbolic execution used by SAW. Internally, the semantics of LLVM, x86, and other SAW input languages are defined by translation to Crucible.

One reason for the complexity of these specification is that SAW differentiates between data that is allocated and initialized and data that is just initialized. Other verification tools tend to treat all allocated data as initialized (for example, this is true of CBMC [8]). This is generally a sound approximation because C compilers tend to behave predictably, but our approach is more accurate to the specification of C.

Functional Specifications. The other role of SAW-script is to verify the connection between the implementation and algorithmic specification. In SAW, specification are written in Cryptol, a domain-specific language designed for cryptographic specifications [11]. In the postcondition of the script, we use references to Cryptol functions to map the outputs of running the program to the outputs of our specification programs, `ctr32_encrypt` and `cipher_update`. The final lines of the specification assert that the memory cells resulting from the program must match the required values, i.e., those that would result from executing the Cryptol specification.

We show `ctr32encrypt` in Fig. 2. This function defines the top-level behavior of the CTR mode of encryption, which repeatedly increments an initialization vector, encrypts the incremented value with the secret key, and performs an XOR of that encryption with the plaintext.

The first line of the specification defines the type of the function, parameterized by type variable n. `AES_GCM_Ctx` is a structure used to maintain state for the incremental interface to AES, which allows for data to be encrypted and decrypted as it becomes available, rather than all at once. The [n] [8] arguments are sequences of bytes with length n.

The function body consists of a sequence comprehension. This takes input bytes one at a time, and labels them with i, which draws from the sequence counting up from `ctx.len`. The separate function `EKij` performs the encryption step using the initialization vector and the key contained in the context. The `take` and `drop` functions are used to convert the 64-bit length contained in the context to a 32-bit number required by the `EKij` function.

```
1  ctr32_encrypt : {n} (fin n) => AES_GCM_Ctx -> [n][8] -> [n][8]
2  ctr32_encrypt ctx in = out
3    where
4      out = [ byte ^ (EKij ctx ((take`{32} (drop`{28} i)) + 1) (drop`{60} i)) |
5                     byte <- in | i <- [ctx.len ...] ]
```

Fig. 2. Top-level Cryptol specification for AES update.

Another example of a functional specification is the following line describing the `Sigma0` function:

```
S0 x = (x >>> 28) ^ (x >>> 34) ^ (x >>> 39)
```

In the SHA-384 code, this function is implemented by the Perl code given in Fig. 3. This does not execute directly, but rather generates assembly code, which is what we verify. The instructions `ror` and `xor` correspond to the cryptol operations `>>>` and `^` respectively.

In order to include the implementation here, some constants have been substituted, and we have extracted the relevant lines from around 20 other lines calculating other parts of SHA. Those lines are mixed in with even more lines of non-interfering SHA calculations, presumably in order to keep the processor saturated. Symbolic execution allows us to reason just about these lines of code, because interleaved instructions that don't change the result of the computation in a relevant way will not be included when reasoning about the results of individual computations.

```
1      '&ror      ($a1,39-34)',
2      '&xor      ($a1,$a)',
3      '&ror      ($a1,34-28)',
4      '&xor      ($a1,$a)',
5      '&ror      ($a1,28)',              # Sigma0(a)
```

Fig. 3. Perl implementation of internal SHA computation.

Notice also that the shift amounts are different between the functional specification and the code. In Cryptol, the shift amounts are 28, 34, and 39, but in the implementation, we see shifts by $39 - 34$, $34 - 28$, and 28. This is a performance optimisation, but it makes the proof effort more difficult. To close this gap, we use a system of verified rewrites (see Sect. 6).

Verification Process. Once a specification has been defined, it must be verified. SAW divides verification into two phases: symbolic execution, and verification of equivalence. Symbolic execution converts an imperative operation into a functional term suitable for automated reasoning. Even without specifying the expected high-level behaviour of the AES function, the memory layout defined in the pre-condition is enough for symbolic execution to complete, which has the effect of proving the imperative code memory safe. We typically verify memory safety in this way before developing a specification. This lets us separate concerns between functional and safety properties.

The final task once symbolic term has been generated is to compare it to a specification term. SAW uses SMT solving to discharge these proofs, and in most use cases, these can be completed automatically. However, the complexity of the optimization stages in AES-256-GCM and SHA-384 makes the gap between specification and implementation too large to be completely automated. SAW solves this with a small tactic language embedded into SAW-script that supports term rewriting. Each of these rewrites Sect. 6.

Modular Reasoning. Symbolic execution is a precise technique with hard limits on its scalability. The AES-256-GCM and SHA-384 functions are too large to be symbolically executed in their entirety. SAW solves this problem through using a modular reasoning system called *overrides*. SAW treats specifications as executable code that can be freely substituted for implementation functions. When a function is verified equivalent to a Cryptol specification, calls to that function can be overridden (i.e., replaced) during symbolic execution. As Cryptol specifications are typically much less complex than implementations, this massively increases the tractability of the verification task.

As a result, a typical SAW proof consists of a hierarchy of equivalence proofs. The proof begins at the leaf functions, which are verified by symbolic execution. The functions at the next level are then symbolically executed with the leaf functions replaced by their specifications. These are then also added to the library of verified functions. This proceeds until the top-level function is verified. One of the main tasks when developing a SAW proof is defining these internal specifications (our proof is unusual in that we also needed a significant number of rewrite rules).

We also use the override mechanism at the interface between C and x86 code. Functions in x86 are proved equivalent to Cryptol specifications, and these specifications can then be used as overrides in the surrounding C context. This approach works because we have defined a compatible memory model that works for both C and x86 code—see Sect. 5 for more.

Finally, the override functionality can be used to assume specifications for functionality that has been assumed, not verified. This is useful for library calls that might be out of scope for a particular project, but that might be verified in the future. For example, Chudnov *et al.*'s SAW proofs for s2n [7] use this approach to parameterize the proofs of HMAC and DRBG over different primitives[4]. In our proofs, the only assumptions we make are that OPENSSL_malloc and OPENSSL_free behave correctly.

4   SAW's Verification Pipeline

SAW is structured as a pipeline of linked verification stages. The inputs to the pipeline are, firstly, executable mathematical specifications for the top-level function, and selected sub-functions; secondly, the compiled code, made up of LLVM and embedded x86 binary code; and thirdly, a proof script which sets up memory, identifies the mapping between Cryptol specifications and function interfaces, and contains the rewrites that are applied to the resulting logical terms. The verification pipeline then works as follows:

1. The x86 binary is extracted from the LLVM and decompiled into a CFG representation that recovers the x86 instructions and control-flow structure. This relies on a SAW sibling project called Macaw [12].
2. The x86 control-flow graph and LLVM code are divided into functions at the interfaces identified in the SAW-script file.
3. Beginning at the leaves of the call-graph, each x86 and LLVM function is symbolically executed, resulting in a term written in a intermediate language called SAW-core. At this stage, any already-verified functions are substituted for Cryptol overrides.
4. If a function has an associated Cryptol specification, it too is symbolically executed, resulting in a specification term in SAW-core.
5. The function term and specification term are rewritten using the rewrites defined in SAW-script.
6. The rewritten function and specification terms are proved equivalent through a generic solver interface library called What4 [15].

Verification proceeds with functions progressively higher on the call-graph, until the top-level equivalence is proved between code and specification.

While the structure of this pipeline is simple, making it work for real code requires a significant amount of tool sophistication. SAW is the product of many years of refinement and development, and we used many of the components in this pipeline without modification.

Our C support is based on SAW's LLVM support, which is mature, and has been used in many other industry and government verification projects—for example, Chudnov et al. [7]. While we do not claim complete coverage of the standard, in practice we rarely need to add new C language features to SAW. Likewise, Cryptol support is built into SAW and is designed to be symbolically executed, so this part of the tool required no modifications. The Macaw and What4 tools similarly functioned without modification.

---

[4] In fact, we have now verified some of the primitives that were only assumed in this previous work, meaning it should be possible to stitch these proofs together end-to-end.

Therefore, in this paper we focus on the new capabilities of the tool: our symbolic execution of x86 instructions, and verified rewrites. For a more detailed treatment of the SAW suite as a whole, readers should look at the SAW documentation and tutorial [13,14].

5 New Capability: x86 Semantics

The first SAW capability we developed for this project was symbolic execution for x86 assembly code, including support for mixed C/x86 code. Doing this required us to solve two problems. First, decompiling the binary into a series of x86 instructions, and second, defining the semantics of instructions, which mainly involves defining the model of memory.

To decompile we use Macaw, a SAW sibling project which is able to parse Elf binaries and output a control-flow graph complete with the representation of the x86 instructions [12]. We treat Macaw as a black box, and in fact any decompiler with similar capabilities could serve in its place.

Once the CFG has been constructed, we apply our x86 semantics. For the behaviour of individual instructions, we consulted the Intel manual. We note that processor manuals contain errors, and hand-encoding the semantics could also introduce errors. However, we have reasonable confidence in this encoding because, in practice, most conceivable errors would immediately cause the proof to fail. This is because cryptographic functions are very sensitive to small changes: most small value errors would result in a dramatically different output.

Much more important and subtle is the memory model, which describes under what conditions reads and writes to memory can occur, as well as describing how reads and writes can be combined to store and retrieve values. Unlike C, there are almost no accepted memory usage rules for assembly programming, aside from the conventions used in a particular program and the Application Binary Interface (ABI) for functions that can be called externally. Fortunately, AES and SHA implementations are designed to be called by C programs. They therefore must follow C-like conventions and respect the ABI. Memory is used to get inputs and define outputs, read global constants, and maintain a stack for storing temporary results. Functions always respect the boundaries of data as provided. Because of this, we were able to adapt SAW's well-tested model used for LLVM support.

In SAW's memory model, addresses are represented by a pair of integers: the first integer is a base address, identifying an allocated memory region, while the second is an offset into the region. Memory operations, such as pointer arithmetic and pointer comparisons, are only well-defined for addresses in the same region.

Even after defining this model, we had to decide how to apply it within the proof. There were two options: (i) modeling the entire memory as a single region, and (ii) representing different objects as separate regions. The former is the more flexible because it does not enforce any invariants on the way that memory is used. Any read or write within the entire memory region is valid at any time. This comes at an increased cost of manually specifying necessary invariants. For example, each function would have to manually encode the memory region it might write to so that its calling function can predict all of the side effects of calling it.

Instead, we take the second approach: automatically specifying such memory invariants as part of the way that memory can be used. This means that some valid assembly will be impossible to verify. It could be completely safe and correct, but because it violates the strict memory model we've chosen, our tool will be unable to reason about it. On the other hand, the memory model we chose works for all of the cryptographic assembly code we've run into, and implementing the memory model in this way saves us a substantial amount of specification and proof work.

It is not surprising that this approach works; The models and abstractions C uses for memory are useful in assembly as well. Furthermore, the ABI and the C memory model have heavily co-evolved, making the C memory model a natural fit for assembly functions that match the ABI.

The memory model is applied by symbolic execution of the CFG that results from Macaw. This symbolic execution has two main functions: efficiently update a symbolic representation of memory, and discharge side conditions that must hold in order for symbolic execution to continue. The result is a SAW-core term representing the input-output behaviour of the x86 binary code.

6   New Capability: Verified Rewrites

The second SAW capability we developed was a simple language of term rewrites for use in proofs.

After symbolic terms have been constructed from C, x86, or Cryptol, we must prove equivalences between these terms. The design goal with SAW is that these proofs are completed mostly automatically using SMT solvers. While this has worked well in previous, less-complicated proofs, the functional terms that result from AES-256-GCM and SHA-384 often proved to be intractable for the solvers without preprocessing. This is exactly because these algorithms are so heavily optimised, as we have discussed above.

In order to solve this, we introduce a language of equivalences between terms that are themselves verified by the solver. By applying these rewrites, we can close the gap between the more abstract Cryptol term and the optimized C/x86 term. These rewrites serve as a small tactic language for controlling the proof, while preserving the principle that SAW proofs are mostly automatic.

To illustrate how this works, we consider an example rewrite from our SHA-384 proof. In the Cryptol portion of our proof, we define the following function, S0 (shortened for convenience from `Sigma0`):

```
S0 x = (x >>> 28) ^ (x >>> 34) ^ (x >>> 39)
```

In Cryptol, >>> and <<< are right and left rotation respectively, while ^ is XOR. In order to complete the proof, we need to be able to rewrite occurrences of this function. To do this, we define the following rewrite, `Sigma0_thm`:

```
Sigma0_thm <- prove_folding_theorem
           {{ \x -> (x ^ ((x ^ (x <<< 59)) <<< 58)) <<< 36 == S0 x }};
```

The left hand side of this equation is how symbolic execution interprets the code in Fig. 3. The rotate-rights have been swapped to rotate-lefts, which allows our semantics to model both types of instruction by rotate-left. In order to swap the rotates, we subtract the rotate amount from 64, which is why we have a different set of constants than we see in either the specification or the implementation.

The solver verifies this equivalence for all possible values of x and saves it with the name Sigma0_thm. In this case, we verify the equality using the ABC solver [6] through What4, but different solvers can be applied as needed to provide different equivalences.

Consider the following SAWscript command, which verifies an x86 function matches its specification:

```
sha512_block_data_order_spec <-
  crucible_llvm_verify_x86 m "<filename>" "sha512_block_data_order"
    [ ("K512", 5120) ] // Initialize global for round constants
    true
    sha512_block_data_order_spec
    (do {
      simplify (cryptol_ss ());                    // std simplifications
      simplify (addsimps thms empty_ss);           // folding theorems
      simplify (addsimp concat_assoc_thm empty_ss); // final theorem
      w4_unint_yices ["S0", "S1", "s0", "s1", "Ch"]; // uninterpreted fns
    });
```

Here, the do-block defines the order in which the simplification rewrite rules are applied. The folding theorems thms contains 30 rewrite rules, including the Sigma0_thm presented above. The concat_assoc_thm theorem normalizes the concatenations that result from other proof rules. The final line of this script instructs the Yices solver to treat certain functions as uninterpreted, including the S0 function. This illustrates the usefulness of the rewriting support. Rather than reasoning about the S0 function directly, we rely on the verified rewrites. This allows us to abstract away from complexity that previously made the proof infeasible for the solver.

Overall, the tactics we use for SAW proofs constitute a very simple decision procedure, made up almost exclusively of user-supplied rewrites. The other main mechanism we have for guiding proofs is the modular override system described in Sect. 3, which allows us to decompose proof tasks into lemmas, at least at the granularity of functions. In practice, we have found that these capabilities are sufficient to meet the needs of proving cryptographic implementations correct with respect to specifications.

Ultimately, we may find ourselves limited by the tools available in SAW for controlling the proof process, particularly if we attempt to prove higher degrees of abstraction between specification and implementation. These more manual proofs largely fall outside of the scope of what SAW aims to do well. An ideal solution would be to export proof goals to Coq, Lean, or F*, all of which already have highly-usable better tools for manual proof. Chudnov *et al.* have previously demonstrated that SAW proofs about code and more abstract Coq proofs can be connected in this way.

6.1 Role of Rewrites in AES-256-GCM and SHA-384 Proofs

Rewrites in SAW can be seen as a small tactic language, serving a similar purpose to proof tactics in Coq or Isabelle. However, SAW occupies a very different point in design space, because it is designed to maximize proof automation. Heavy use of SMT-backed automation is the reason our proofs were feasible, but if the automation makes poor choices, it can also obstruct the proofs. We use rewrites along with appropriate choices of abstraction boundaries, to recover abstractions that automation would not discover itself.

For example, consider the `Sigma0_thm` rewrite defined above. The solver can verify the rewrite when supplied in isolation. However in the context of SHA, the solver fails to identify this as a valuable fact. One reason is that `S0` is a function that is present in the Cryptol specification, but this abstraction is lost when we symbolically execute an x86 function. The rewrites replace occurrences of `S0` with an uninterpreted function, pruning the proof space dramatically.

However, there is the trade-off in reintroducing such an abstraction. Even if the abstraction holds locally, the functionality that calls that abstraction might depend on the internal functionality. In that case, swapping out the code for an uninterpreted function could actually turn a solvable goal into an unsolvable one. The answer is to choose these rewrites carefully: this is one of the main intellectual challenges in completing a proof. In general, this problem is undecidable. For example the rewrite rules inferred may not terminate, this means that at best it might be a guided special-purpose mode of solvers, rather than a general purpose approach.

Our rewrites plug into SAW late in the pipeline, after many of SAW's optimizations. This means that rewrites sometimes have to compensate for earlier optimizations. SAW is designed to aggressively optimize terms into a form suitable for the solver, and in some cases, this means breaking up abstractions that would be useful in completing the proof. In these cases, our rewrites must operate on the post-optimization proof term.

For example, in one case, it would have been desirable for our proof to use the term:

```
{{ \x -> (slice_59_5_0 x) # (slice_0_59_5 x) == x <<< 59 }};
```

However, SAW discovered that it could drop off the operation on the final byte of x, but to do so, it had to break up x into its constituent bytes. This is a desirable optimization if the term is passed to the solver directly, because the solver itself will reason at the level of bytes. However, this made writing an appropriate rewrite for our proof much more challenging. We include the eventual rewrite rule in Fig. 4. Again, a large amount of the intellectual challenge with our proof rested in finding appropriate rewrites that integrated with SAW's existing automation.

```
rotate59_slice_add_thm <- prove_folding_theorem
    {{ \x0 x1 x2 x3 x4 x5 x6 x7 x8 x9 x10 x11 x12 x13 x14 x15 x16 x17 x18
          x19 x20 x21 x22 x23 x24 x25 x26 x27 x28 x29 x30 x31 x32 x33 x34
          x35 x36 x37 x38 x39 x40 x41 x42 x43 x44 x45 x46 x47 x48 x49 x50 ->
      (slice_59_5_0 (x0 + x2 + x3 + x4 + x5 + x6 + x7 +x8 + x9 + x10 + x11
                  + x12 + x13 + x14 + x15 + x16 + x17 + x18 + x19 + x20
                  + x21 + x22 + x23 + x24 + x25 + x26 + x27 + x28 + x29
                  + x30 + x31 + x32 + x33 + x34 + x35 + x36 + x37 + x38
                  + x39 + x40 + x41 + x42 + x43 + x44 + x45 + x46 + x47
                  + x48 + x49 + x50))
      # (slice_0_59_5 (x0 + (64 * x1) + x2 + x3 + x4 + x5 + x6 + x7 +x8
                  + x9 + x10 + x11 + x12 + x13 + x14 + x15 + x16 + x17
                  + x18 + x19 + x20 + x21 + x22 + x23 + x24 + x25 + x26
                  + x27 + x28 + x29 + x30 + x31 + x32 + x33 + x34 + x35
                  + x36 + x37 + x38 + x39 + x40 + x41 + x42 + x43 + x44
                  + x45 + x46 + x47 + x48 + x49 + x50))
      == (x0 + (64 * x1) + x2 + x3 + x4 + x5 + x6 + x7 +x8 + x9 + x10 + x11
              + x12 + x13 + x14 + x15 + x16 + x17 + x18 + x19 + x20 + x21 + x22
              + x23 + x24 + x25 + x26 + x27 + x28 + x29 + x30 + x31 + x32 + x33
              + x34 + x35 + x36 + x37 + x38 + x39 + x40 + x41 + x42 + x43 + x44
              + x45 + x46 + x47 + x48 + x49 + x50) <<< 59 }};
```

Fig. 4. Example rewrite rule. This rule is made much more complex by the fact it happens after SAW's existing term optimization phases.

7   Results and Lessons Learned

Our proofs run on the current version of AWS-LC [2] as of January 2021, built using the default compiler flags. We verify the AVX implementation of SHA-384, which is the current fastest implementation. Our AES-256-GCM proof uses the code path for AESNI, CLMUL, and AVX instructions.

Proof Size and Composition. Our code can be broken down into top-level functional specifications, top-level interface specifications, and proof scripts. The top-level specifications are what must be understood in order to understand the results of our proofs.

We have 168 lines of top-level interface specifications, which define the 8 interface functions that we've proved correct. Those functions specify memory layouts for the interface functions and link them to the top-level functional specification. We have 435 lines of top-level functional specifications, which were only slightly modified from specifications that we and others have used in previous cryptographic verification projects. These are almost completely free of implementation details, and live in a specifications only repository, separate from the code. If the functional specifications were made any shorter, they would likely also be less readable, so we believe they are close to optimal for their purpose.

The proof scripts consist of 1286 lines of intermediate function specifications, rewrite rules, tactics, and proof running logic. These intermediate functions are both proved and checked each time they're called. As a result, they do not need to be understood or trusted in order to believe the top level results.

Following continuous reasoning practice [19], our proofs are integrated into the CI process for AWS-LC. We do not expect this code to change, but we have adopted this practice as part of a larger AWS-LC assurance effort, including code which does change more often. Quickcheck versions of our proofs run as GitHub actions that take around 25 min[5]. The complete version runs on private systems in 30 min, but using more cores and memory. A significant part of our proof and tool development effort was dedicated to making sure proofs could run within a time budget acceptable for CI (typically 1 h). For example, this sometimes required introducing overrides to break the proof into smaller segments.

Achieving Trust in the Proof. SAW is designed to increase confidence in software, but it cannot supply total certainty. A key question is therefore what parts of the toolchain and proof must be trusted. For our proofs, the Trusted Code Base (TCB) consists of:

- The top-level functional and interface specifications in the proof scripts.
- Library behavior that is assumed and then used in overrides. In our case, that OPENSSL_malloc and OPENSSL_free behave correctly.
- The SAW and Cryptol toolchain, the tools themselves, the language models of x86 and LLVM, the back-end SMT solvers, and ultimately the Haskell runtime and other downstream infrastructure.
- Correctness of the compilation chain from LLVM to executable (for C code), and correct execution of compiled code by the hardware.
- Any behaviours of code not covered by proofs at the fixed sizes we have verified.

Although this TCB is significant, it is comparable in scale to similar verification projects like EverCrypt [21]. The highest impact improvement would likely proving the algorithms at arbitrary sizes. While we could throw computation at running the proofs at a wide range of fixed input sizes, this would spend computation and developer wait time with fairly little benefit. We believe an inductive approach is achievable in future work and would allow us to verify the algorithms once and for all.

In the mean time, we have covered some of the most-used block sizes, as well as all code paths. Given we have verified the algorithm at fixed sizes, and the code does not branch on input size, the only place that bugs could remain is in the looping behaviour at other sizes. We have inspected the dynamically bounded loops in the code carefully to mitigate this possibility.

---

[5] https://github.com/awslabs/aws-lc-verification/actions.

We could also shrink the TCB by applying foundational techniques such as used in the Verified Software Toolchain project [3]. This would remove much of the need to trust the tool itself. However, we believe doing this would make it infeasibly expensive to develop a tool as complex as SAW, at least given current foundational techniques.

Another important question is whether a correctness failure in the toolchain could result in a proof that does not establish the result we expect. We believe the probability of this is quite low. Our current best defense against this failure of TCB is thorough testing and code review. SAW itself is a well-tested tool that has been used for many projects. The language models have also been tested, and it is unlikely that a behavioural bug could cause an incorrect specification to be verified. For this to occur, several failures would need to occur at once.

As an aside, the intent of the people doing the proof, and the precise nature of any external review should be considered when answering this question. A tool bug is unlikely to result in a proof that falsely appears correct, *assuming that the proof effort is done in good faith*. On the other hand, all tools have bugs, and in most logic-based tools, bugs can allow the construction of false proofs that appears superficially correct. In other words, for most current tools, trust in verified code requires trust in the team and process producing the proof.

We believe the highest risk of accidental error lies in the specifications. It is quite common for draft specifications to contain subtle discrepancies between what users intends and the specification's formal meaning. We mitigate this with extensive manual audit. Every line of code we write is reviewed at least once within the verification team, and once by AWS-LC domain experts. The internal review ensures that our specifications are correct and that our style is consistent with our guidelines. The external review allows us to ensure that we have explained our proofs correctly, and that we have correctly specified the functions in the context that they are being used.

Proof Engineering Process. The proofs were completed over six calendar months, using approximately nine person-months engineering effort total. We consider this to be an upper bound estimate as the proof effort was mixed in with tool improvements, in particular for the less-mature x86 tooling. The core team consisted of four engineers, with additional contributions from verification tooling experts and AWS-LC domain experts. This project represented a significant engineering effort, but for our project, this represented a good use of resources to achieve a high level of confidence in the AWS-LC code. Proofs were completed alongside more traditional assurance approaches, e.g., testing, fuzzing, and code audits.

New proof techniques and tooling were a factor in our success, but there is no single technical breakthrough that made these proofs possible. While combined x86 and C verification is challenging, it would likely be possible (although not easy) to add such a capability to a number of existing tools. Rather, a series of tool extensions, design choices, and engineering working practices combined to make the project feasible.

Using SAW, we automated most of the trivial reasoning, which meant that a majority of proof engineering was spent on legitimately difficult verification problems. These mainly involved understanding the code being verified and using rewrites to manually rearrange verification terms to make them amenable to automated proving. Many of these steps could in principle be automated, but in practice engineers sometimes needed to resort to clunky debugging measures. We find it unsurprising that highly specialized code such as AWS-LC would generate edge cases that challenge generic proof automation. For proofs of this type, for now we believe completely automated proving is out of reach.

We take several steps to try to minimise engineer effort when building proofs. The most important of these is to lean on automation wherever possible. One example is that we try to avoid internal specifications, which are often the most challenging part of the proof. Because SAW is a bounded verifier, internal specifications are just a performance optimization—given sufficient compute resources, we could in principle symbolically execute the entire code-base. Of course, in practice, internal specifications are needed to make the proof tractable. Our practice is to prove functions at the largest scope which fits within our time budget. By doing this, we are sometimes able to avoid specifying internal functions that do relatively little computationally.

Another important strategy for us is to separate memory-safety proofs from functional correctness proofs. We have found that much of the technical risk in a verification project can be eliminated at the memory-safety stage. This is where the verification tools are most likely to run into show-stopping bugs that will put success of the project in jeopardy. Separating these concerns results in proof terms that are smaller and easier to understand, so bugs are easier to diagnose. Then, if we run into challenges during the correctness proving phase, we can limit the cause to correctness properties, eliminating a large fraction of the proof from consideration.

An important factor that enabled us to carry out these proofs is a team of expert proof engineers who have built their skills over years. This project was undertaken by a team which has worked continuously on verification projects for four years. This expertise has given us a better understanding of what we can attempt, and a far wider toolkit to dip into when things go wrong. We have seen, anecdotally, similar evidence of improved verification capabilities from other long-standing teams—for example, for the Project Everest, SeL4, and CompCert projects. Long-standing teams of proof experts are still unusual, but we believe they will be necessary to achieve the most ambitious proof engineering tasks, just as they are in software and tool development.

A significant lesson that we have learned about proof engineering is that a tool's behaviour when it fails is more important than success. This is a critical aspect of verification tools often overlooked in research papers. Many tools show a demo where everything works, but in a proof engineering effort, the vast majority of time is spent with a proof that does not work. In that sense, one of the most critical aspects of a verification tool is what it does when the proofs are not working. SAW provides some support for diagnosing errors, but there is a lot of room for improvement. It lacks tooling to allow proof engineers to easily inspect and modify proof terms that are not successfully proving. Furthermore, it has inefficiencies that can make repeatedly running and modifying proofs slow and painful, increasing the pain of developing proofs and reducing the time that engineers can spend on the real challenges of verification.

7.1   Trade-Offs When Building on Existing Verification Tools

As we saw in Sect. 6, rewriting is an example where SAW's existing tooling made some parts of our proof more awkward. It is reasonable to wonder whether we could have modified SAW to allow more control of the rewriting pipeline. This highlights an interesting trade-off that exists when developing proofs using a more mature tool like SAW.

SAW has existed for a decade, and has been developed and improved itera- tively over this time. Design decisions such as the order in which optimizations occur can sometimes be baked deeply into the tool. This stands in contrast to more experimental tools which often have short histories and a relatively clean design that can be torn down and refactored easily. SAW also has an active user community which relies on it for different verification and assurance tasks. The main users are at Galois, Amazon Web Services, and in the US government. This means that tool changes need wider approval from a community. Again, this stands in contrast to research tools which often have a single designer who is also the main user. The effect of this is that changes such as the introduction of rewriting must be carefully designed to fit with SAW's existing architecture.

The pay-off for these restrictions is an enormous increase in the power and scope of what we can achieve with the tool. In the large, we have benefited from many features that were developed by independent research teams. For example, we rely on the Macaw decompiler, which we used off-the-shelf without modification. The SAW LLVM semantics is likewise a product of many years of research, which did not require any further work from us. In the small, SAW embodies many, many clever tricks and pieces of good design that together make verification of challenging problems more feasible. Sometimes working with a mature tool imposes costs, but overall we believe it raises the bar for our work in a way that easily justifies the cost.

An open question for us is how we can make such collaboration possible across the verification community. Boogie [4] is a good example of a verifica- tion technology that has seen use across different teams and institutions. Proof assistants and SMT solvers are also widely used as a basis for new tools. How- ever, there are still very few software verification tools that have seen significant adoption. We believe such tools will be necessary in the future if we collectively are to tackle larger and more complex verification problems.

7.2   Verified Code Generation Versus Verifying Existing Code

While the approach in this paper results in an artifact that may appear externally similar to other state-of-the art verified cryptography efforts, there are some engineering factors that might influence which approach is most appropriate for a particular cryptographic use-case. The approach of EverCrypt, Jasmin, Fiat, and similar efforts require the user to produce code or a model in a language that is specific to the verification system. While these systems have demonstrated ability to produce efficient verified implementations, they cannot directly verify existing code. Our approach verifies existing code without modification, and there are several engineering benefits to this.

The most significant reason to verify existing code is that producing new code or modifying existing code introduces risk. Modifying optimized cryptographic code is particularly risky because it is complex, and because an error could have a devastating impact on the security of the system. A software project may be unwilling to accept the risk of modifying mature code, even if the new code is formally verified. For example, OpenSSL and its variants have been tested and audited over more than a decade, and this maturity is appealing to many software projects. In our approach, the code is verified without any modification. Zero new risk is introduced, and the verification process only increases trust in the system. A related benefit is that the verified code maintains any existing certifications, such as FIPS 140-2.

Another benefit of verifying existing code is that the verification works on the programming languages that are already used in the project, and the build pipeline does not require additional compilers or other tooling to support the language of the verification system. Having the build depend on this tooling can be risky because it is less familiar and less mature compared to the compilers and build systems that are typically utilized. There is a risk that a build pipeline could break or produce incorrect machine code due to a bug or lack of understanding of the verification system. In contrast, our approach produces a verification pipeline that is parallel to the build pipeline, and a failure in this pipeline does not have any impact on the main build pipeline.

Many cryptographic applications do not have any legacy concerns and never plan on maintaining or improving cryptographic code by hand. In those cases, EverCrypt, Jasmin, and Fiat all produce trustworthy, high-performance implementations that might prove easier to use and understand than what is provided by OpenSSL and its variants. Long-term support might be a concern, given these are research tools. However the slow-moving nature of cryptographic code makes it less likely that the implementations would need modification in the future.

8 Conclusion and Future Work

The purpose of formal verification is to allow users to be confident in the software on which they depend. This is the reason that AWS-LC, BoringSSL, and OpenSSL are excellent targets for formal verification. Nearly everyone who uses the internet relies on this code for security, either through end-user software, or through a cloud provider's infrastructure. Our proofs show for the first time that this kind of highly optimised, hand-written code matches its mathematical specification. More importantly, we show that such code can be verified for a reasonable amount of proof engineering effort.

We do not consider our proofs the last word on this code—there are several ways in which our work can be improved. Most importantly, we have not yet verified the OpenSSL version of AES-256-GCM and SHA-384. Based on inspection of the code, we believe the proofs would only need small changes to the term rewrites, but this is currently not a high priority in comparison to further AWS-LC assurance work.

There are also several ways we could improve the proofs themselves. We have verified this code at fixed input sizes. We believe we have covered all edge cases, so the probability that bugs remain is low, but a size-agnostic proof would be more complete. Our proofs also rely on term rewriting tactics to close the gap between implementation and specification. These rewrites are specialized to our application and are therefore the most fragile part of the proof. We believe that, with further research, automated solvers could solve many of these logical queries without the need for manual tactics (this would also make our proofs less fragile against code change). Finally, our proofs say nothing about non-functional security properties, such as timing or architectural side channels, nor do they connect to cryptographic security proofs.

We are at an exciting moment for cryptographic verification. It is now possible to deploy verified cryptography without compromising on performance. We are tantalisingly close to a world where most cryptographic traffic originates from verified code, and where new cryptographic primitives are verified as a matter of course. For our part, we consider AES-256-GCM and SHA-384 a stepping stone to the real prize: a fully verified library of production-grade cryptographic primitives. Stay tuned!

References

1. Almeida, J.B., et al.: The last mile: high-assurance and high-speed cryptographic implementations. In: 2020 IEEE Symposium on Security and Privacy, SP 2020, San Francisco, CA, USA, 18–21 May 2020, pp. 965–982. IEEE (2020). https://doi.org/10.1109/SP40000.2020.00028
2. Amazon Web Services: AWS libcrypto (AWS-LC) public preview. https://github.com/awslabs/aws-lc
3. Appel, A.W.: Verified software toolchain. In: Goodloe, A.E., Person, S. (eds.) NFM 2012. LNCS, vol. 7226, p. 2. Springer, Heidelberg (2012). https://doi.org/10.1007/978-3-642-28891-3_2
4. Barnett, M., Chang, B.-Y.E., DeLine, R., Jacobs, B., Leino, K.R.M.: Boogie: a modular reusable verifier for object-oriented programs. In: de Boer, F.S., Bonsangue, M.M., Graf, S., de Roever, W.-P. (eds.) FMCO 2005. LNCS, vol. 4111, pp. 364–387. Springer, Heidelberg (2006). https://doi.org/10.1007/11804192_17
5. Bond, B., et al.: Vale: verifying high-performance cryptographic assembly code. In: 26th USENIX Security Symposium, USENIX Security 2017, Vancouver, BC, pp. 917–934. USENIX Association (August 2017)
6. Brayton, R., Mishchenko, A.: ABC: an academic industrial-strength verification tool. In: Touili, T., Cook, B., Jackson, P. (eds.) CAV 2010. LNCS, vol. 6174, pp. 24–40. Springer, Heidelberg (2010). https://doi.org/10.1007/978-3-642-14295-6_5

7. Chudnov, A., et al.: Continuous formal verification of Amazon s2n. In: Chockler, H., Weissenbacher, G. (eds.) CAV 2018. LNCS, vol. 10982, pp. 430–446. Springer, Cham (2018). https://doi.org/10.1007/978-3-319-96142-2_26

8. Clarke, E., Kroening, D., Lerda, F.: A tool for checking ANSI-C programs. In: Jensen, K., Podelski, A. (eds.) TACAS 2004. LNCS, vol. 2988, pp. 168–176. Springer, Heidelberg (2004). https://doi.org/10.1007/978-3-540-24730-2_15

9. Erbsen, A., Philipoom, J., Gross, J., Sloan, R., Chlipala, A.: Simple high-level code for cryptographic arithmetic - with proofs, without compromises. In: Proceedings of the 40th IEEE Symposium on Security and Privacy, S&P 2019 (May 2019)

10. Fromherz, A., Giannarakis, N., Hawblitzel, C., Parno, B., Rastogi, A., Swamy, N.: A verified, efficient embedding of a verifiable assembly language. Proc. ACM Program. Lang. 3(POPL), 63:1-63:30 (2019). https://doi.org/10.1145/3290376

11. Galois Inc.: Cryptol: the language of cryptography. https://cryptol.net/files/ProgrammingCryptol.pdf

12. Galois Inc.: Macaw binary analysis framework. https://github.com/GaloisInc/macaw

13. Galois Inc.: SAW tutorial. https://saw.galois.com/tutorial.html

14. Galois Inc.: Software analysis workbench (SAW). https://saw.galois.com/

15. Galois Inc.: What4 symbolic formula representation and solver interaction library. https://github.com/GaloisInc/what4

16. Google: boringssl. https://boringssl.googlesource.com/boringssl

17. Lim, J.P., Nagarakatte, S.: Automatic equivalence checking for assembly implementations of cryptography libraries. In: Kandemir, M.T., Jimborean, A., Moseley, T. (eds.) IEEE/ACM International Symposium on Code Generation and Optimization, CGO 2019, Washington, DC, USA, 16–20 February 2019, pp. 37–49. IEEE (2019). https://doi.org/10.1109/CGO.2019.8661180

18. National Security Agency: Commercial national security algorithm suite. https://apps.nsa.gov/iad/programs/iad-initiatives/cnsa-suite.cfm

19. O'Hearn, P.W.: Continuous reasoning: scaling the impact of formal methods. In: Dawar, A., Grädel, E. (eds.) Proceedings of the 33rd Annual ACM/IEEE Symposium on Logic in Computer Science, LICS 2018, Oxford, UK, 9–12 July 2018, pp. 13–25. ACM (2018). https://doi.org/10.1145/3209108.3209109

20. OpenSSL cryptography and SSL/TLS toolkit. https://www.openssl.org

21. Protzenko, J., et al.: Evercrypt: a fast, verified, cross-platform cryptographic provider. In: 2020 IEEE Symposium on Security and Privacy, SP 2020, San Francisco, CA, USA, 18–21 May 2020, pp. 983–1002. IEEE (2020). https://doi.org/10.1109/SP40000.2020.00114

22. Ye, K.Q., Green, M., Sanguansin, N., Beringer, L., Petcher, A., Appel, A.W.: Verified correctness and security of mbedtls HMAC-DRBG. In: Thuraisingham, B.M., Evans, D., Malkin, T., Xu, D. (eds.) Proceedings of the 2017 ACM SIGSAC Conference on Computer and Communications Security, CCS 2017, Dallas, TX, USA, 30 October–03 November 2017, pp. 2007–2020. ACM (2017). https://doi.org/10.1145/3133956.3133974

23. Zinzindohoué, J.K., Bhargavan, K., Protzenko, J., Beurdouche, B.: HACL*: a verified modern cryptographic library. In: Thuraisingham, B.M., Evans, D., Malkin, T., Xu, D. (eds.) Proceedings of the 2017 ACM SIGSAC Conference on Computer and Communications Security, CCS 2017, Dallas, TX, USA, 30 October–03 November 2017, pp. 1789–1806. ACM (2017). https://doi.org/10.1145/3133956.3134043

Not All Bugs Are Created Equal, But Robust Reachability Can Tell the Difference

Guillaume Girol[1]($\boxtimes$), Benjamin Farinier[2],
and Sébastien Bardin[1]

[1] Université Paris-Saclay, CEA, List,
Gif-sur-Yvette, France
{guillaume.girol,sebastien.bardin}@cea.fr
[2] TU Wien, Vienna, Austria
benjamin.farinier@tuwien.ac.at

Abstract. This paper introduces a new property called *robust reachability* which refines the standard notion of reachability in order to take replicability into account. A bug is robustly reachable if a *controlled input* can make it so the bug is reached whatever the value of *uncontrolled input*. Robust reachability is better suited than standard reachability in many realistic situations related to security (e.g., criticality assessment or bug prioritization) or software engineering (e.g., replicable test suites and flakiness). We propose a formal treatment of the concept, and we revisit existing symbolic bug finding methods through this new lens. Remarkably, robust reachability allows differentiating bounded model checking from symbolic execution while they have the same deductive power in the standard case. Finally, we propose the first symbolic verifier dedicated to robust reachability: we use it for criticality assessment of 4 existing vulnerabilities, and compare it with standard symbolic execution.

1 Introduction

Context. Many problems in software verification are encoded as *reachability* queries of some undesired condition—a bug, the exploitation of a vulnerability, *etc.* When a verification engine establishes that a certain buggy location in the program is reachable, an input triggering the bug is reported to the developer so that it can be fixed. In the case of techniques based on an under-approximation of program behaviors, like Symbolic Execution (SE) [9] or Bounded Model Checking (BMC) [13], we even have *in principle* the guarantee that the reported issue is real (*correctness*): there are no false positives.

Problem. Yet, things are more subtle in practice, as some bugs can be triggered reliably whereas others only happen in very specific and highly improbable initial

This work has been partially supported by ANR (grant ANR-20-CE25-0009-TAVA) and ERC (grant agreement 771527-BROWSEC).

© The Author(s) 2021
A. Silva and K. R. M. Leino (Eds.) CAV 2021, LNCS 12759, pp. 669–693, 2021.
https://doi.org/10.1007/978-3-030-81685-8_32

conditions. While standard reachability cannot tell the difference, this distinction is crucial in many real-life scenarios related to security (bug triage, bug prioritization, criticality assessment) or software engineering (test suite replicability and the problem of flaky tests [42]). For example, fuzzers are able to detect so many bugs [38] that they can lead to "bug triage issues" [30]. If each *replicable* (reliably-triggered) bug is hidden by dozens of more *fragile* ones in the reports of a verification engine, it is hard to focus development effort efficiently. Also, if one is only interested in vulnerability reports, bugs which cannot be reliably triggered may even be dismissed as "not exploitable" altogether.

Goal and Challenges. *Our goal is to develop a formal framework able to distinguish replicable bugs from fragile bugs, and amenable to automatic software verification—precisely, we want to be able in practice to find such replicable bugs.* This is challenging as we need to avoid any quantitative [37] or probabilistic reasoning [2,34], insofar as they would hinder automation on real examples—these techniques are often either restricted to finite-state systems [2,34] or rely on highly expensive model counting solvers [11,39].

Proposal. Our approach consists in partitioning inputs of the program into *controlled inputs* and *uncontrolled inputs*. This lets us refine the concept of reachability into *robust reachability*: a (buggy) location of a program is robustly reachable if there exist controlled inputs, such that for all uncontrolled inputs, this location is reached. In other words, with adequate input we do not need luck.

We typically focus on *security* scenarios where an *attacker* provides controlled input in one go, without knowledge of uncontrolled input – typically sending a malicious crafted file to obtain remote code execution or privilege escalation. We *deliberately* exclude interactive attack scenarios and weaker interpretations like "bugs replicable *most of the time*" in order to keep proof methods *tractable*.

Proving robust reachability is harder than standard reachability. While we show that robust reachability is expressible in formalisms like branching temporal logics [14], hyperproperties [16] or hyper temporal logic [15], there exist no efficient automated analysis methods for these formalisms at the software level (for Turing-complete languages). Therefore, we investigate dedicated verification techniques, revisiting standard methods (SE, BMC) for standard reachability as well as some of their standard companion optimizations.

Our prototype of Robust Symbolic Execution (RSE) relies on the ability of state of the art Satisfiability Modulo Theory (SMT) solvers [4] to generate models for *universally* quantified formulas [25,27,44], which comes with a performance and completeness cost—yet we report promising results.

Contributions. We claim the following contributions.

- We formally introduce the concept of robust reachability (Sect. 4) and motivate its use (Sect. 2), giving practical examples where standard reachability leads to false positives in practice (whatever the underlying verification technology). We also characterize robust reachability in terms of temporal logic and hyperproperties, and compare it with *non-interference* (Sect. 4);

- We revisit Symbolic Execution (SE) [9] and Bounded Model Checking (BMC) [13] and show how they can be lifted to the robust case (Sect. 5). While they both have the same deductive power in the standard case, they do not anymore in the robust setting—yet, *path merging* allows Robust SE to pace up with Robust BMC. Finally, we show how to adapt standard optimizations for Symbolic Execution and Bounded Model Checking;
- We implement and evaluate[1] (Sect. 6) the *first* symbolic execution engine dedicated to robust reachability, namely BINSEC/RSE. We show how to use it for criticality assessment of 4 existing vulnerabilities (CVEs), and compare it with standard symbolic execution. RSE appears to be tractable with reasonable overhead, yielding false-positive-free symbolic reasoning.

We believe robust reachability is an important sweet spot in terms of expressiveness and tractability, allowing to highlight serious bugs in practical situations. We hope this first step will pave the way to more refinements and applications of robust reachability.

2 Motivation

In this section we show why standard reachability is not always a good fit for bug finding, as it cannot distinguish between *replicable* bugs and *fragile* bugs.

```
                                          1    void victim() {
void fill(unsigned n, char* ptr) {        2      /* stack variables, top to bottom */
  for (unsigned i = 0; i < n; i++) {      3      // return address goes here
    ptr[i] = 0x61;                        4      int canary = global_random_value;
  }                                       5      char buffer[8];
}                                         6      /* end stack variables */
void victim() {                           7
  unsigned n = controlled_input;          8      register unsigned n = controlled_input;
  char buffer[8];                         9      fill(n, buffer);
  fill(n, buffer);                        10     if (canary != global_random_value)
}                                         11       fail_and_dont_return_at_all();
void main() {                             12     /* everything is ok */
  victim();                               13   }
}
      (a) C-like code, for simplicity          (b) Explanation of compiler instrumenta-
                                                tion with Stack Smashing Protection (SSP)
```

Fig. 1. Simple stack buffer overflow

Stack Canaries. Consider the program presented in Fig. 1. It suffers from a stack buffer overflow: if variable n is greater than 8 (the size of buffer), then 0x61 will be written to stack memory above buffer. For high enough n, this will overwrite the return address (Fig. 1b, line 3) of function victim and make the program jump to an unexpected program location when victim returns.

---

[1] The tool, benchmark and data are available at https://github.com/binsec/cav2021-artifacts and https://zenodo.org/record/4721753.

Mitigations for such programming errors exist, like Stack Smashing Protection (SSP) [18]. This technique consists in pushing a randomly-chosen constant value called a *canary* at the top of the stack in the prologue of each function, and checking that this value is intact before returning. If the canary has been tampered with, the program exits to prevent exploitation (Fig. 1b, line 11). Here, SSP prevents the attacker from overwriting the return address of `victim`, as doing so also overwrites the canary with `0x61616161`. This will be detected at line 10 of Fig. 1b with probability $1 - 2^{-32}$ on a 32-bit architecture: the only way to pass through it is to have the canary value equal to `0x61616161`. *Hence, the buffer overflow in this program is not exploitable anymore.*

Table 1. Standard reachability is not a good criterion to measure the protection of SSP on the program of Fig. 1.

Prog. Fig. 1	Ground truth	Standard reachability	BINSEC [23]	Angr [46]	Robust reachability	BINSEC/RSE
No SSP	Vulnerable	Vulnerable ✓	Vulnerable ✓	Vulnerable ✓	Vulnerable ✓	Vulnerable ✓
SSP	Protected	Vulnerable ✗	Vulnerable ✗	Vulnerable ✗	Protected ✓	Protected ✓

The Problem with Standard Reachability. Can the attacker hijack the control flow without triggering SSP? We can model this security question as a *standard reachability query* over inputs `controlled_input` and `global_random_value`. The attacker succeeds if line 12 is reachable with the additional condition that the return address of `victim` is overwritten with an unexpected address.

Unfortunately, this standard reachability query is satisfiable with the canary `global_random_value` equal to `0x61616161` and `controlled_input` equal to *e.g.*, 42. And indeed, binary-level SE tools Angr [46] or BINSEC [23] do report the bug as reachable (cf. Table 1). Yet, this answer is unsatisfying as this only happens with a very low probability: it may not be considered a plausible attack. *Hence, it turns out that SE can yield false positives in practice—especially in a security context.*

Proposal: Robust Reachability. We label `controlled_input` as a *controlled input* and `global_random_value` as an *uncontrolled input*. There exists no value of `controlled_input` such that `victim` returns to an address tampered with independently of the value of `global_random_value`. We thus say that our exploitation condition (line 12) is not *robustly reachable*. We can automatically verify this intuition. We adapted the SE engine of BINSEC to robust reachability: our tool finds the vulnerability when we disable the protection (by labelling the canary as *controlled input*) and does not find it anymore when the protection is present. This shows that robust reachability can model the protection provided by SSP, while standard reachability cannot.

This phenomenon is not restricted to stack protectors. We identify in Table 2 several situations where standard reachability may lead to false positives, unlike robust reachability. Note that some cases (randomisation based protections, uninitialized reads) concern binary-level issues, and cannot be observed from a source-level analysis.

Discussion. Consider the slightly different problem of reaching line 11 in Fig. 1b. It is reachable for all values of the canary *except* `0x61616161`, hence it is not considered robustly reachable – *all* values of uncontrolled input should lead to line 11. This restriction is *deliberate*. A more quantitative approach would hinder automation. For similar reasons, we limit ourselves to non-interactive scenarios, where the attacker input is chosen before uncontrolled input are known. We will further motivate these choices in Sects. 4.1 and 6.4.

Despite these deliberate restrictions, our case studies (Sect. 6.2) show the versatility of robust reachability. In the example above, we distinguish inputs controlled by an attacker (a bad guy) from inputs which he cannot influence (see also *e.g.*libvncserver in Sect. 6.2). But with `doas` (Sect. 6.2), we distinguish inputs controlled by the system administrator (the good guy) from those which vary on each execution. Other situations are possible, for instance deterministic inputs versus non-deterministic ones like in the case of flaky tests [42]—where there are neither good nor bad guys. Robust reachability can help in all these situations either assessing the "quality" of a given trigger or test suite (criticality, replicability), generating "good" triggers or test suites, or proving their absence.

Table 2. Program constructs for which standard reachability yields fragile input

Randomisation based protections	Standard reachability models randomized or arbitrary values like canaries or ASLR as attacker-chosen values. This voids such protections. See also Fig. 1 and `libvncserver` in Sect. 6.2
Uninitialized reads	With standard reachability, the attacker can choose the initial content of uninitialized memory. For example he can choose it to contain a password or a secret. See also `doas` in Sect. 6.2
Underspecified initial state	A bug which is unreachable in normal operating conditions can become reachable if, *e.g.*, one leaves the stack location completely free. Then the bug only happens with pathological initial state
Undefined behavior	A bug in a branch depending on undefined behavior is still *technically* reachable, but not robustly reachable. Note that even machine code has some undefined behaviors
Interactions with the environment	Contrary to robust reachability, standard reachability lets the attacker use system calls and interactions by *e.g.*letting him choose the date to nanosecond precision, as if the environment helped him
Opaque functions	One can abstract complex functions (crypto functions, `malloc`) as black boxes returning a fresh, symbolic value. Standard reachability allows the attacker to choose these values, yielding fragile triggers

3   Background

Consider a program P and $\mathcal{S}$ the set of its possible states. Each state $s \in \mathcal{S}$ is labeled by a program location $\lambda(s) \in \mathcal{L}$. Execution of the program is represented by a (one-step) successor relation $\to \in \mathcal{S} \times \mathcal{S}$; its transitive reflexive closure is denoted by $\to^*$. For a finite trace $t \in \mathcal{S}^*$ and $s, s' \in \mathcal{S}$ two states, we write $s \to_t^* s'$ if t starts with s, ends with s' and follows $\to$. The initial state $s_0(y)$ depends on the program input y. For a location $\ell \in \mathcal{L}$ and input y we write $y \vdash \ell$ if $s_0(y) \to^* s$ where $\lambda(s) = \ell$. Additionally, for a trace $t \in \mathcal{S}^*$, we write $y \vdash_t \ell$ if $s_0(y) \to_t^* s$ where $\lambda(s) = \ell$. We use *trace* for successions of states and *path* for successions of locations. By abuse of notation, the path corresponding to a trace $t \in \mathcal{S}^*$ is $\lambda(t) \in \mathcal{L}^*$. For a path π, we denote its length $|\pi|$ and we write $y \vdash \pi$ if $\exists t \in \mathcal{S}^*. \lambda(t) = \pi \wedge y \vdash_t \ell$ where ℓ is the final location of π.

Definition 1 (standard reachability). *Given a program P, a location $\ell \in \mathcal{L}$ is reachable if $\exists y. y \vdash \ell$.*

It is often useful to consider the case of reaching a location ℓ with a state s satisfying some predicate ϕ. This can be reduced to standard reachability by adding if (ϕ) /*new target*/ at the target location.

Definition 2 (correctness, completeness). *Let $\mathcal{V} : (P, l) \mapsto \{1, 0\}$ be a verifier taking as input a program P and a location ℓ:*

- *$\mathcal{V}$ is correct when for all P, ℓ, if $\mathcal{V}(P, \ell) = 1$ then ℓ is reachable in P;*
- *$\mathcal{V}$ is complete when for all P, ℓ, if ℓ is reachable then $\mathcal{V}(P, \ell) = 1$;*
- *If $\mathcal{V}$ also takes an integer bound as input, $\mathcal{V}$ is k-complete when for all integers k and P, ℓ, if $\exists y. \exists t \in \mathcal{S}^*. |t| \leq k \wedge y \vdash_t \ell$ then $\mathcal{V}(P, \ell, k) = 1$.*

In general, verifying reachability is undecidable, so verifiers cannot be both correct and complete. Correct verifiers can still be k-complete as k-completeness can be thought of as completeness for finite-path systems.

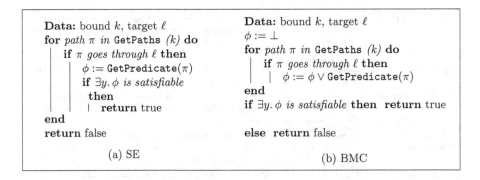

Fig. 2. Reachability of ℓ with SE and BMC

Symbolic Execution (SE) and Bounded Model Checking (BMC). SE [9] incrementally explores all paths in the program (up to, say, a bound k) and when an explored path reaches the target location ℓ, checks that this path is indeed executable. This is performed by converting a path π to an SMT formula pc_π, called *path constraint*, which has input y as its only free variable and is equivalent to $y \vdash \pi$, i.e., a path is executable if and only if its path constraint is satisfiable. Conversely, BMC [13] considers the program as a whole and builds a SMT formula expressing that one of the paths of length at most k leads to ℓ. It is equivalent to the disjunction of the path constraints of these paths. The target is reachable in k steps at most if and only if this formula is satisfiable.

These algorithms are detailed in Fig. 2, where `GetPredicate` turns a path into its path constraint and `GetPaths`(k) yields all paths below size bound k.

Proposition 1. *SE and BMC have the same expressive power: both are correct and k-complete.*

Interestingly, we show in Sect. 5 this is not true anymore with robust reachability.

Solvers. SE and BMC commonly discharge their satisfiability queries to SMT solvers [4] which take formulas as input, and output whether they are satisfiable (along with a model) or not. Typical queries are expressed in the quantifier-free fragments of well known theories (linear integer arithmetic, bitvectors, arrays, *etc.*) where SMT solvers perform well in practice. In case of an undecidable theory, we can use incomplete solvers (possibly answering UNKNOWN), at the price of k-completeness.

4 Robust Reachability

4.1 Definition

We introduce the new notion of *robust reachability*. We partition the input y into the *controlled input* a and the *uncontrolled input* x—we denote $y \triangleq (a, x)$. Let $\mathcal{A}$ and $\mathcal{X}$ be the sets of possible controlled and uncontrolled inputs respectively. A location is *robustly reachable* when the attacker can choose controlled input $a \in \mathcal{A}$ without having to rely on specific values of the uncontrolled input $x \in \mathcal{X}$ to reach his target. Input a is then called a *robust trigger*—otherwise it is a *fragile trigger*.

Definition 3 (Robust reachability). *A location $\ell \in \mathcal{L}$ is robustly reachable if $\exists a. \forall x. (a, x) \vdash \ell$. This definition depends on the partition of inputs.*

Proposition 2. *Robust reachability implies standard reachability. The converse implication does not hold.*

Discussion. As already mentioned at the end of Sect. 2, our definition of robust reachability specifically targets a threat model where the attacker speaks first, unaware of uncontrolled inputs. It deliberately excludes interactive systems where the attacker can choose some input, then receive some program output possibly leaking uncontrolled input, and then choose some more input *depending on what was received*. Modeling such situations requires additional quantifier alternations, which deeply impact the performance of proof methods and cripple automation, as shown in Sect. 6.4.

Likewise, a bug triggered for all uncontrolled inputs but one is not robustly reachable according to Definition 3. A quantitative definition of robust reachability could take into account the *proportion of uncontrolled inputs* triggering a bug. This hints at works about model counting [11,39], but the problem at hand is actually harder. Consider the following alternative definition: *(i)* find $a_{max} \in \mathcal{A}$ such that a maximal proportion of uncontrolled inputs x lead to ℓ: $(a_{max}, x) \vdash \ell$; *(ii)* measure how robustly ℓ can be reached by computing the proportion of uncontrolled inputs x such that $(a_{max}, x) \vdash \ell$. Current model counting algorithms can only tackle problem *(ii)* along one path, and we argue in Sect. 6.4 that even *(ii)* alone is considerably more expensive than our SMT-based approach.

In other words, Definition 3 is a tradeoff to keep robust reachability amenable to automated verification. This does not prevent it from meeting its main goal: drawing the attention on more serious bugs. Some may of course be missed, but, as our case studies will show (Sect. 6), a good number will be found.

In the rest of this section, we review a few related properties and see how much they overlap with, but do not remove the need of, robust reachability.

4.2   Relation with Non-interference

We partition inputs and outputs of a system into either *high* (highly classified) or *low* (public, e.g. observable). A system satisfies *non-interference* [31] when low outputs do not depend on high inputs, implying that secrets cannot leak. Robust reachability can be reformulated in a very non-interference-sounding phrasing: uncontrolled inputs (call them high) must not interfere with the attacker reaching the target location (the low output). Let us clarify this link.

Formally, let high input be uncontrolled input x, and low input be controlled input a. Let low output be whether control flow reached location ℓ. Non interference of the resulting system means that $\forall a, x, x'. ((a, x) \vdash \ell \iff (a, x') \vdash \ell)$.

Proposition 3. *If ℓ is (standardly) reachable and the system satisfies non-interference with the high/low partition described above, then ℓ is robustly reachable. The converse is false.*

Robust reachability requires a single value of the controlled input a for which reachability of ℓ is guaranteed but says nothing for other values of a, whereas non-interference constrains the system to behave much more independently of uncontrolled input than robust reachability but says nothing of reachability.

4.3   Interpretation in Terms of Hyperproperty

Robust reachability and its negation are not trace properties: the observation of a single trace is never enough to prove or disprove them. For example, observing a single trace reaching target ℓ with input (a, x) is both compatible with ℓ being robustly reachable (if all other inputs $(a, x'), x' \in \mathcal{X}$ also reach ℓ), and with ℓ not being robustly reachable (if some other x' is such that (a, x') does not reach ℓ). Robust reachability and its negation thus belong to the more general class of *hyperproperties* [16], i.e. statements relating several traces.

More specifically, Clarkson et al. [16] show that any hyperproperty is the intersection of a hypersafety hyperproperty (*i.e.*something bad cannot happen) and a hyperliveness hyperproperty (something good will eventually happen). Hypersafety is generally thought as easier to prove, notably with self-composition [6]. Unfortunately, robust reachability and its negation are pure hyperliveness in the general case: no finite set of finite traces can falsify them. However, in some conditions, they degenerate partly into hypersafety:

Proposition 4. *If the domain $\mathcal{X}$ of uncontrolled inputs is finite, then the negation of robust reachability is not pure hyperliveness (i.e., it has a non-trivial hypersafety component).*

Proof. Robust reachability of ℓ can be proved by finding controlled input $a \in \mathcal{A}$ such that for all uncontrolled input $x \in \mathcal{X}$ one observes a trace starting with input (a, x) and reaching ℓ. When $\mathcal{X}$ is finite, this means that a finite observation can disprove non-(robust reachability). This is the definition of hypersafety.

This idea—trying to observe a hopefully small set of traces which together prove robust reachability—is crucial for algorithms and leads to our use of path merging in Sect. 5.3.

4.4   Interpretation in Terms of Temporal Logic

Computational Tree Logic (CTL). CTL [14] is a temporal logic over the tree of possible traces. Let L be a labeling which maps states to the set of (atomic) predicates they satisfy. If ℓ is a predicate, the CTL formula ℓ is satisfied by all systems whose initial state s_0 verifies $\ell \in L(s_0)$. If ϕ is a CTL formula and s a state, then $\mathbf{EX}\phi$ expresses that ϕ holds in at least one (direct) successor of s, and $\mathbf{AF}\phi$ that all traces arising from s eventually reach a state from which ϕ holds. CTL introduces other operators, not needed here.

Proposition 5. *It is possible to express robust reachability with CTL.*

Proof. Let $\mathcal{S}' \triangleq \mathcal{S} \cup \mathcal{A} \cup \{s_i\}$ where s_i is a new state, let $\rightarrow' \triangleq \rightarrow \cup \{(s_i, a) \mid a \in \mathcal{A}\} \cup \{(a, s_0(a, x)) \mid a \in \mathcal{A}, x \in \mathcal{X}\}$, and let $L'(s)$ be equal to $L(s)$ if $s \in \mathcal{S}$ and $\varnothing$ otherwise. Then ℓ is robustly reachable if, and only if $\mathbf{EXAF}\ell$ is true in the new extended system $(\mathcal{S}', \rightarrow', L')$ with s_i as initial state.

HyperLTL. It is also possible to express robust reachability in the temporal logic HyperLTL [15], which allows to reason over sets of traces π, assuming we have an atomic predicate $\equiv_v$ stating that the first states of two traces have the same value for variable v. Robust reachability of ℓ can then be expressed as $\exists \pi. \forall \pi'. \mathbf{F}\ell_\pi \wedge (\pi \equiv_a \pi' \rightarrow \mathbf{F}\ell_{\pi'})$, where $\mathbf{F}\ell_\pi$ denotes that trace π goes through ℓ. In other words, there exists a trace π reaching ℓ s.t. all traces sharing the same controlled input also reach ℓ.

4.5 Robust Reachability and Automatic Verification

The previous classification does not help us find an efficient *software verification method* for robust reachability. Indeed, while efficient CTL model checkers exists for the finite case [12] or very specific formalisms such as pushdown systems [47], most efforts in (general) software verification have been directed towards the verification of safety temporal formulas or simple termination [17] (formulas of the form $\mathbf{AF}\varphi$). Moreover, temporal logics like HyperLTL [15] suffer the same limitations, and checking for both reachability and non-interference is probably too strong a requirement in practice. Finally, one can prove the *absence* of robust reachability by proving the absence of standard reachability. It is thus possible to use existing algorithms for unreachability, based *e.g.* on invariant computation, at the price of even larger over-approximation than when they are used for their original purpose. This kind of approach is not our focus. In this paper we look for *correct verifiers* able to prove robust reachability (and report robust triggers) rather than to disprove it.

5   Automatically Proving Robust Reachability

We now extend SE and BMC to the robust case.

5.1 Robust Bounded Model Checking

As mentioned in Sect. 3, BMC determines the reachability of a location ℓ by building a family of SMT formulas $\varphi_k(a, x)$ equivalent to $\exists t \in \mathcal{S}^\star. |t| \leq k \land (a, x) \vdash_t \ell$. φ_k expresses that ℓ is reachable in less that k steps. Then one proves that ℓ is reachable if and only if $\exists k. \exists a. \exists x. \varphi_k(a, x)$. This extends to robust reachability:

Proposition 6. *If the domain of uncontrolled input $\mathcal{X}$ is finite or the system has finitely many paths, then ℓ is robustly reachable if and only if $\exists k. \exists a. \forall x. \varphi_k(a, x)$.*

Proof. ($\Longleftarrow$) comes directly from the definition of φ_k. ($\Longrightarrow$). If ℓ is robustly reachable, let a_0 be a robust trigger. The set of paths P arising from inputs in $\{a_0\} \times \mathcal{X}$ is finite (bounded either by $\mathcal{X}$ or the number of paths in the system), and $\forall x. \bigvee_{\pi \in P} \mathrm{pc}_\pi(a_0, x)$ holds. Let $k = 1 + \max_{\pi \in P} |\pi|$. All paths in P are unrolled in φ_k so $\bigvee_{\pi \in P} \mathrm{pc}_\pi(a_0, x) \Longrightarrow \varphi_k(a_0, x)$ and thus $\forall x. \varphi_k(a_0, x)$.

As a result, it is enough to replace the condition "$\exists y. \phi$ is satisfiable" by "$\exists a. \forall x. \phi$ is satisfiable" in Fig. 2b.

Corollary 1. *The resulting algorithm, robust BMC, is correct w.r.t. robust reachability. If the domain of uncontrolled input $\mathcal{X}$ is finite or the system has finitely many paths, then robust BMC is also k-complete.*

The finiteness hypothesis is required: if a program reaches a location after having executed a loop an unbounded, uncontrolled number of times, then robust BMC has to unroll an unbounded number of paths to prove robust reachability.

5.2   Robust Symbolic Execution

Similarly to BMC, we check that a path π robustly reaches the target by checking the satisfiability of $\exists a. \forall x. \mathrm{pc}_\pi(a, x)$, instead of $\exists a. \exists x. \mathrm{pc}_\pi(a, x)$. This means replacing "$\exists y. \phi$ is satisfiable" by "$\exists a. \forall x. \phi$ is satisfiable" in Fig. 2a. Unfortunately the resulting algorithm, robust SE, is not exactly what we want, as it proves a stronger property.

Definition 4 (Single-path robust reachability). *A location $\ell \in \mathcal{L}$ is single-path robustly reachable if $\exists \pi \in \mathcal{L}^\star. \exists a. \forall x. \exists t \in \mathcal{S}^\star. \lambda(t) = \pi \wedge (a, x) \vdash_t \ell$. In other words, the path used to reach ℓ is the same regardless of the uncontrolled input.*

Proposition 7. *Single-path robust reachability implies robust reachability. The converse implication does not hold.*

Proposition 8. *Robust SE is correct and k-complete w.r.t. single-path robust reachability.*

Proof. By construction, $\mathrm{pc}_\pi(a, x)$ is equivalent to $(a, x) \vdash \pi$ so $\exists \pi. \exists a. \forall x. \mathrm{pc}_\pi(a, x)$ is equivalent to single-path robust reachability of the last location of π.

Corollary 2. *Robust SE is correct but incomplete for robust reachability.*

Interestingly, the expressive powers of SE and BMC, which are the same for standard reachability, diverge when extended to robust reachability.

5.3   Path Merging

Path merging [33] (a.k.a. state joining) consists in identifying "close" paths leading to the same location and replacing them by a *merged* path (summary). With original path constraints pc_{π_1} and pc_{π_2}, the merged path constraint is $\mathrm{pc}_{\pi_1} \vee \mathrm{pc}_{\pi_2}$. This is only an optimization in the standard setting, with no impact on k-completeness. The situation is different in the robust setting.

```
   Data: bound k, target ℓ
 1  φ := ⊥
 2  for path π in GetPaths (k) do
 3      if π goes through ℓ then
 4          φ := φ ∨ GetPredicate(π)
 5          if ∃a. ∀x. φ is satisfiable then
 6              return true
 7  end
 8  return false
```

Algorithm 1: RSE+: Robust SE with systematic path merging

```
1  void main(a, x) {
2      if (x) x++; // π₁
3      else x--;   // π₂
4
5      if (!a) bug();
6  }
```

Fig. 3. An example where path merging is required

Consider the program in Fig. 3: the bug is robustly reachable with controlled input $a = 0$, but the control flow takes one of two paths π_1 and π_2 depending on the value x of uncontrolled input. This bug will not be found by robust SE as defined previously, as neither π_1 nor π_2 fulfills the satisfiability criterion $\exists a. \forall x. \mathrm{pc}_{\pi_i}(a, x)$. However, if π_1 and π_2 are merged, then the bug is found because $\exists a. \forall x. \mathrm{pc}_{\pi_1}(a, x) \vee \mathrm{pc}_{\pi_2}(a, x)$ is satisfiable. This leads us to robust SE with systematic path merging (RSE+, Algorithm 1), better fit to robust reachability.

Proposition 9. *Robust SE with systematic path merging (RSE+) is correct for robust reachability. If the domain of uncontrolled input $\mathcal{X}$ is finite or the system has finitely many paths, then it is also k-complete.*

Proof. For k-completeness: If ℓ is robustly reachable, let a_0 be a robust trigger. The set of paths P arising from inputs in $\{a_0\} \times \mathcal{X}$ is finite (bounded either by $\mathcal{X}$ or the number of paths in the system). Let $k = 1 + \max_{\pi \in P} |\pi|$. For bound k, when GetPaths has output all paths in P, $\bigvee_{\pi \in P} \mathrm{pc}_\pi \implies \phi$ so $\exists a. \forall x. \phi$ is satisfiable.

In conclusion, *path merging improves the completeness of robust SE.* This is surprising because path merging is merely optional in standard SE.

5.4   Revisiting Standard Optimizations and Constructs

Some optimizations commonly used in SE are not correct nor complete anymore in a robust setting. We show here how to adapt them.

Data: program entrypoint ℓ_0, bound k
1 $P := \{\ell_0\}$
2 **while** $P \neq \emptyset$ **do**
3   Take a path π out of P
4   **if** $|\pi| > k$ **then continue**
5   **if** $\exists a, x. \mathrm{pc}_\pi$ unsat **then**
      continue
6   **yield** π
7      $P := P \cup \{$children paths of $\pi\}$
8 **end**

Algorithm 2: Implementation of GetPaths with path pruning

```
uncontrolled int x;
if (x<10)      { /* a */ }
else           { /* b */ }
/* c */
if (x>20) {
    /* d */
    if (x>30) { /* e */ }
    else      { /* f */ }
}
```

Fig. 4. Failure case for universal path pruning

Incremental Path Pruning [3,48]. When a path has an unsatisfiable path constraint, all its descendent paths are also infeasible. For example, the path acd in Fig. 4 has path constraint $x < 10 \wedge x > 20$, which is unsatisfiable. One can prune this path, *i.e.* stop exploring it and its children acde and acdf.

Data: entrypoint ℓ_0, bound k
$P := \{\ell_0\}$
while $P \neq \varnothing$ **do**
  Take a path π out of P
  if $|\pi| > k$ **then continue**
  if $\exists a. \forall x. \mathrm{pc}_\pi$ unsat **then**
    /* Skip MaybeMerge to
       disable path
       merging   */
    $P := \texttt{MaybeMerge}(\pi, P)$
    continue
  end
  yield π
  $P :=$
    $P \cup \{$children paths of $\pi\}$
end

Algorithm 3: `GetPaths` with universal path pruning

---

1 **Function** `MaybeMerge`(π, P)
2 | Choose u a transitive child of the last location of π *(ideally, a strict postdominator of the second to last location of π)*
3 | Let π' the longest strict prefix of π.
4 | Let U the set of paths from π' to u.
5 | **if** $\exists a. \forall x. \bigvee_{\pi'' \in U} \pi''$ is SAT **then**
6 | | Merge paths in U and add the result to P
7 | **end**
8 | **return** P

Algorithm 4: Incomplete path merging for universal path pruning

---

In Fig. 2a this would be an optimization of `GetPaths`: as shown in Algorithm 2, one checks that the path constraint of currently explored paths are satisfiable, and if not, the paths at fault are *pruned*, and their children paths are not explored. As a result, we now issue satisfiability queries in two occasions: during `GetPaths` to *prune* paths (Algorithm 2, line 5), and when *validating* a candidate reaching path (Fig. 2a, line 5). Pruning queries and validation queries must be treated differently.

Robust SE is obtained from SE by adding a universal quantifier to *validation queries* but not *pruning queries*. The path constraint for path a in Fig. 4 is $\mathrm{pc}_a = x < 10$ but $\exists a. \forall x. \mathrm{pc}_a$ is false. Same applies for b. If we added a universal quantifier to pruning queries—which we call *universal path pruning*, see Algorithm 3—we would prune a and b, and incorrectly conclude that c is not robustly reachable. In other words, Symbolic Execution with universal path pruning (denoted $RSE_\forall$) is correct but not complete.

Universal path pruning, however, conveys an interesting intuition: the full if branch below acd in Fig. 4 is not robustly reachable, because $\forall x. x > 20$ is false. With normal path pruning and RSE+, we would needlessly explore these paths. To take advantage of this, we keep $RSE_\forall$ but improve its completeness with path merging, as depicted in Algorithm 4.

The main idea is that when a set of paths are to be pruned, they may pass the universal pruning test $\exists a. \forall x. \mathrm{pc}$ when merged together. One way to find such sets of paths is the use the Control Flow Graph (CFG) of the program. For example when trying to prune $\pi = $ a in Fig. 4, we know by invariant of the set P of paths to be explored that $\pi' = \epsilon$ the empty path passes the universal test. We compute the strict postdominator $u = $ c of π': when the paths from π' to c join again, they pass the pruning test again. We then replace π by this merged path in the set P of paths to be explored.

Note that computing a postdominator is not required for correction. In our implementation, we cannot compute the exact CFG at the binary level so the chosen u may be wrong. In line 5 of Algorithm 4 we check that we picked correctly, and otherwise, merging failed and we prune π. Despite the heuristic approach, the technique proves useful, as we will see in Sect. 6.

We denote Robust SE with universal path pruning and path merging as $RSE_\forall+$. It is correct and less incomplete than $RSE_\forall$.

Assumptions. It is common to model complex parts of the system by introducing their result as a symbolic input z and then *assume* that z satisfies the required properties. For example, Address Space Layout Randomisation (ASLR) for the stack pointer could be modeled by adding an *assumption* that $esp \in [m, M]$ where m and M are inlined constant values. In standard SE this would be translated to an *assertion*

```
controlled unsigned int a;
uncontrolled unsigned int x;
assume(x < a);
if (false) bug();
```

Fig. 5. Unsound assumption, in pseudo-C.

$esp_0 \in [m, M]$ conjoined to the path constraint pc_π, where esp_0 is the initial value of esp. *Actually, in standard SE and BMC, assertions and assumptions are dealt with identically.*

In a robust setting, to the contrary, adding an *assumption* ψ to a path constraint yields $\psi \implies pc_\pi$, while adding an *assertion* ϕ yields $pc_\pi \wedge \phi$. Additionally, assumptions which mix controlled and uncontrolled inputs can make the algorithms above unsound without adaptation: in Fig. 5, reachability of bug maps to the SMT query $\exists a. \forall x. x < a \implies \bot$. It is satisfiable, with $a = 0$, which makes the premise false. However, this does not correspond to an executable path. Actually, formalizing robust reachability assuming $\psi(a, x)$ naively by $\exists a. \forall x. (\psi(a, x) \implies a, x \vdash \ell)$ does not imply standard reachability anymore. A slight adaptation is needed:

Definition 5 (Robust reachability under assumption). *A location ℓ is robustly reachable under the assumption of ψ when*

$$\exists a. ((\exists x. \psi(a, x)) \wedge (\forall x. (\psi(a, x) \implies (a, x) \vdash \ell)))$$

This definition preserves the implication from robust to standard reachability. The algorithms we presented are easily adapted to take it into account.

Interestingly, in the robust case, SE and BMC cannot handle assertions and assumptions in the same way anymore.

Concretisation and Other Optimizations. When path constraints along a path become too complex, some variables can be *concretized*: their symbolic value can be replaced by a concrete one [21,29,45]. Formally, concretizing a variable u to value 42 corresponds to adding an *assertion* $u = 42$. This sacrifices k-completeness for tractability. Actually, any additional constraint can be added, and several common optimizations (e.g., domain shrinking, path filtering) can be seen through this lens. These optimizations must be taken with care in the robust setting. First, considering them as assumptions instead of assertions would be incorrect. Second, if the value of the concretized variable ultimately depends semantically on uncontrolled input, the path does not pass universal validation anymore: for example, when concretizing x to 42, $\exists a.\forall x.\mathrm{pc}(a, x) \wedge x = 42$ is unsatisfiable because $\forall x.\, x = 42$ is false. As a result, locations visited further on this path become robustly unreachable. *In other words, concretisation only works on controlled or constant values.*

5.5 About Constraint Solving

Adaptations to robust reachability require solvers to deal with one alternation of quantifiers. Most theories become undecidable with quantifiers. Dedicated algorithms exist for a few decidable quantified theories, *e.g.* the array property fragment [7] or Presburger arithmetic [8]. For other theories, generic methods like E-matching [40] and MBQI [27] have proven rather efficient, although not complete. Sound approximations [25] also have been proposed to reduce quantified formulas to quantifier-free ones. In our experiments, the newly introduced quantifier associates to an increase in the frequency of time-outs and memory-outs, as seen in Sect. 6.3 and specifically Table 4.

6 Proof-of-Concept of a Robust Symbolic Execution Engine

6.1 Implementation

We propose BINSEC/RSE, the *first* symbolic execution engine dedicated to robust reachability. We base our proof-of-concept on BINSEC [23], a binary executable formal analysis engine written in OCaml and already used in several significant case studies [19,20,43]. For the sake of experimental evaluation (Sect. 6.3) we actually implement five variants of robust reachability: **RSE** (basic approach in Sect. 5.2 with existential path pruning Sect. 5.4), **RSE+** (the same plus systematic path merging, Sect. 5.3), **RSE∀** (RSE with universal path pruning, Algorithm 3), **RSE∀+** (same, with path merging during path pruning, Algorithm 4), and **RBMC** (Sect. 5.1). BINSEC/RSE emits quantified formulas in the theory of bitvectors and arrays (arrays are used to model memory) which are then solved by the quantified solver Z3 [22]. We reuse the recent ROW simplification [26] to reduces the number of array indexations. The source code of BINSEC/RSE, the test suite and the case studies of this section are available for reproduction at https://github.com/binsec/cav2021-artifacts and https://zenodo.org/record/4721753.

6.2 Case Studies: Exploitability Assessment for Vulnerabilities

We show here how BINSEC/RSE (unless otherwise specified, the RSE+ variant) can help in vulnerability assessment. Especially, we demonstrate that robust reachability allows deeper insights into a bug than standard reachability, by replaying 4 existing vulnerabilities.

CVE-2019-15900 in doas. doas is a utility granting higher privileges to users specified in a configuration file. User IDs are sometimes parsed incorrectly and left uninitialized. We look for a *vulnerable configuration file* denying root access to the attacker such that the (flawed) executable reliably grants root access to the attacker. For simplicity we assume that the system has no named users and groups and the configuration file has two lines.

BINSEC/RSE with standard reachability reports that root access is granted with a configuration file containing `permit :("@@@@@` when the initial memory address `0xffefffff` contains the group ID of the attacker and the stack starts at `0xfff0001f`. *This is a typical "false positive in practice": these conditions may vary unpredictably across executions so we cannot conclude regarding the exploitability of the flaw.*

With robust reachability where the configuration file is controlled but the initial state of memory is not, BINSEC/RSE reports in less than 10 s that root access is granted reliably to the attacker when the configuration file contains `deny :4` and `permit b%@)@@(`. This is more useful, but `b%@)@@(` We test therefore if any other given user name is also affected by running the analysis with this user name concretized in the initial state. By this method, we proved that the flaw is also robustly reachable for `wwww`, a possible typo of a usual user name, as well as all two-letter lowercase user names.

In other words, if the system administrator grants privileges to a non existing user by mistake, he may unknowingly grant them to the attacker instead. *Here, robust reachability provides us with invaluable insight about the severity of a bug where standard reachability fails.*

CVE-2019-20839 in libvncserver. An attacker-chosen null-terminated string is copied by an unbounded `strcpy` into a 108-bytes buffer, leading to a stack buffer overflow. Exploitability is not guaranteed: null bytes cannot be copied, the executable is protected by SSP, *etc.*. Starting from the vulnerable function, we ask whether it is possible to return to the address `0xdeadbeef`, chosen arbitrarily.

BINSEC/RSE reports that for standard reachability, the bug can be reached when: *(1)* the stack starts at `0xfff00000`; *(2)* the initial value of the return address of the function is 0; *(3)* the `gs` segment starts at `0xf7f00000`; *(4)* the stack canary is `0x01010180`; *(5)* neither system call in the function fails; *(6)* file descriptor 0 is free; *(7)* the input path has a specific value. *The attacker cannot prepare such a state, so this is another false positive in practice.*

With robust reachability, when only the input buffer is controlled and not the stack canary, BINSEC/RSE fails to prove or disprove exploitability in 24 h. However, if we mark the canary as controlled, BINSEC/RSE finds an exploit in about 15 min. This suggests the canary brings a real protection against exploitation.

CVE-2019-14192 in U-boot. U-boot is an open-source boot-loader, popular for embedded boards. When booting over Network File System (NFS), U-boot does not validate the length field of some network packets. This length is subtracted 16 and used as a size to be copied. If a malicious packet declares a length of less than 16, computation underflows and leads to a buffer overflow.

We encode the situation as follows: the input network packet is controlled, the IP address of the victim is constant, the NFS state machine is initialized to expect the appropriate packet type and all other values are uncontrolled. BINSEC/RSE with the RSE$_\forall$+ variant (RSE+ times out here) proves in about 2 min that a memory copy of more than 4GB is robustly reachable, which is a strong indication of the criticality of this denial-of-service vulnerability.

CVE-2019-19307 in Mongoose. Mongoose is an embedded networking library. When receiving large MQTT packets, the length of the parsed packet can be computed as 0. The parsing loop does not advance and is thus infinite. We look for network packets whose length is parsed as 0 but are accepted as valid. BINSEC/RSE proves in less than a second that such situations are robustly reachable when only the network packet is controlled, confirming exploitability.

6.3 Experimental Evaluation

Research Questions. We now seek to investigate in a more systematic way the following research questions:

Table 3. The 46 reachability problems selected for our evaluation

Type	Description		Controlled variable
Real	Vulnerability	CVE-2019-14192 (U-boot)	Network packet
		CVE-2019-20839 (libvncserver)	Socket path
		CVE-2019-19307 (mongoose)	Network packet
		CVE-2019-15900 (doas)	Configuration file
		CVE-2015-8370 (grub, simplified)	Password entry
	CTF	Flare-on 2015 1 & 2	Text entry
		Nintendo Coding Game	Input to hash function to invert
		Manticore	Text entry
	Function inversion	musl (strptime, strverscmp, atoi, strtol)	Preimage
		busybox (chmod mode and ip parsing)	
		μclibc (fnmatch)	
		openssl (base64 decoding)	
Synthetic	Motivating example of [25] and variants		Coefficients to affine function
	Motivating example of [24, Figure 2.2]		Text entry
	SSP bypass	See Sect. 2	Overflowing buffer
	ASLR bypass	2 examples	Various
	Undefined behavior	Overflow flag after 3-bit shl in x86	None
	Other	Various	Various

RQ1 **Precision**: What is the best algorithm for robust reachability in terms of correctness and completeness?

RQ2 **Gain associated to robustness**: Is standard SE subject to false positives and does robust reachability avoid them in practice?

RQ3 **Path pruning**: Does universal path pruning (Sect. 5.4) help explore less paths than normal path pruning?

RQ4 **Performance**: What is the overhead of robust reachability?

Protocol. We base our analysis on a set of 46 reachability problems on binary executables from various architectures (i686-windows-pc, i686-linux-gnu and armv7-linux-gnu) presented in Table 3. The average trace length for reachable problem instances is 809 instruction-long, with a maximum of 18k instructions. The problems fall into two categories: real code and synthetic examples (*e.g.* code designed to be analysed). For each executable, BINSEC/RSE determines if a certain location is robustly reachable from a certain initial state. If this is the case a model is output by BINSEC/RSE, and compared to a ground truth obtained by manual analysis. Tests were run on Intel Xeon E-2176M(12)@4.4 GHz and we use Z3 4.8.7. Results are classified as follows:

Correct BINSEC/RSE proves the expected result, i.e. it either reports a robust trigger or rightfully proves the absence of such a trigger;

False positive a fragile trigger is reported;

Inconclusive BINSEC/RSE reports no trigger but search was incomplete or the solver returned UNKNOWN at some point;

Resource exhaustion timeout is an hour and memory usage is capped to 7 GB.

Table 4. Comparison of standard and robust algorithms over our 46 test cases

	SE	BMC	RSE$_\forall$	RSE$_\forall$+	RSE	RSE+	RBMC
Correct	30	22	30	34	37	44	32
False positive	16	14					
Inconclusive			16	11	7		1
Resource exhaustion		10		1	2	2	13
Total time (s)	2725	36911	3947	4374	13590	11534	47784
... w/o resource exhaustion	2725	911	3947	3589	6390	4334	984

Precision (RQ1). As expected, robust variants do not report any false positives, and path merging increases completeness. RSE variants with universal path pruning (RSE$_\forall$, RSE$_\forall$+) are less complete than those with existential path pruning, but they are less prone to timeouts. This is the case of CVE-2019-14192 in U-boot (Sect. 6.2), for example. RBMC suffers from path explosion (time out) much more often than RSE variants. *Overall, Robust SE with path merging and* *existential path pruning is the most promising method among those presented here, with 44/46 correct answers. RSE∀+ is less complete but terminates more often.*

Note that two interesting test cases in the "real" category of Table 3 need path merging to prove robust reachability: one where a pointer with uncontrolled alignment is passed to memcpy, and one where a branch depends on the result of IO. These situations are common programming idioms, demonstrating the importance of path merging.

Gain Associated to Robustness (RQ2). We compare standard SE with RSE+, the most precise algorithm of RQ1. *Standard reachability has about 30% false positives while robust reachability has none, at the cost of slightly more timeouts.*

There are no false positives in code in the "real" category, except in CVE replays. Our interpretation is that well-functioning programs are designed to behave the same regardless of the uncontrolled environment: concrete memory layout, stack canaries, *etc.*. Robust reachability becomes decisive on buggy code, notably with undefined behavior. This is also illustrated by case studies (Sect. 6.2).

Path Pruning (RQ3). We compare RSE∀, which features universal path pruning, to RSE, which features usual path pruning. Comparison is limited to test runs of more than a second which succeed with both methods. This is to prevent comparing a run where BINSEC/RSE proves that the target is reachable and stops, to a run where BINSEC/RSE does not find the target and explores the whole program. *RSE∀ explores 17% less paths and interprets 21% less instructions than RSE.* This comes at the price of more universally quantified SMT queries: the average time per SMT query goes up by 25%. Overall the run time of both methods is very close.

With path merging, the difference in paths explored disappears: RSE∀+ explores 1% less paths and instructions than RSE+. This is due to the fact that for some tests, path merging "unlocks" some new paths. Overall, RSE∀+ is 6% slower than RSE+ on successful, terminating tests.

Performance (RQ4). In this question, we compare the run time of robust algorithms to SE. Comparison is done on the same basis as before, except that we count timeouts. RSE+ is 74% slower than standard SE on geometric average. This is mostly due to newly introduced time-outs (up to 260× slower) since median slowdown is only 15%. RSE∀ is more consistently slower with about 30% slowdown in both geomean and median. This is mainly explain by increased solver time (universal path pruning queries). RSE∀+ is close in median slowdown, but path merging introduces new timeouts and drives the average slowdown up to 62%. *RSE+ has a low overhead compared to standard SE, except for a few time-outs (2/46).*

6.4   Additional Considerations

We excluded interactive systems and quantitative approaches from our definition of robustness (Definition 3, Sect. 4.1) to keep automated proof methods tractable. We motivate this choice by experimentally showing that these alternatives yield significant overhead. Technical details are provided in Appendix A.

Quantitative Reasoning and Model Counting. We could imagine refining our definition of robust reachability, looking for some controlled input for which the number of uncontrolled inputs allowing to reach the intended target is maximal (or, above a certain threshold). Although we have already observed that model counters do not directly solve this problem (Sect. 4.1), we can lower bound its runtime cost by the cost of determining the number of uncontrolled x satisfying a path constraint for some given controlled input a_0. We experimentally measured it with SearchMC [39] and SMTApproxMC [11], two of the few model counters supporting the SMTlib2 format and the QF_BV theory. We compare this to our "all-or-nothing" qualitative approach on our 4 CVE case-studies: *the quantitative approach is here several orders of magnitude slower than our qualitative method*—SMTApproxMC always times out while SearchMC is at least 400× slower.

Interactive Systems and Quantifier Alternations. We estimate the cost of adding more quantifier alternations in order to deal with interactive systems (Sect. 4.1), by modifying queries on the two of our case studies where interactive input makes sense (libvncserver and doas, *cf.* Sect. 6.2). *RSE+ in this setting does not terminate within 24 h*, highlighting the fact that current SMT solvers have a very hard time generating models for quantified formulas beyond $\exists\forall$. It seems to be a fundamental issue as none of Z3 [22], Boolector [41] and CVC4 [5] is able to prove in less than 1 h that $\forall z.\exists a.\, a\ \text{XOR}\ 1 = z$ holds over 32-bit bitvectors.

7   Related Work

Broadly speaking, we are interested in defining a subclass of *comparatively more interesting bugs* amenable to automation. We review related prior attempts.

Automatic Exploit Generation (AEG). These approaches seek to demonstrate the *impact* of a bug by automatically generating an exploit from it [1,10,36]. *This is complementary to robustness*, which focuses on replicability. Actually, both techniques could be advantageously combined, as a replicable exploit is clearly more threatening than a fragile one. Current AEG methods being based on symbolic methods, adapting them for robustness looks feasible.

Quantitative Reasoning and Model Counting. Several approaches rely on probabilities or counting to distinguish important issues from minor ones—for example (quantitative) *probabilistic model checking* [2,34] or *quantitative information flow analysis* [37]. Robust reachability could be refined in such a way. Yet, current quantitative approaches do not scale on software, as they often rely either on the finite-state hypothesis, or on *model counting* solvers [32], which are only at their beginning (see Sects. 4.1 and 6.4).

Flakiness. The opposition between *flaky* tests and *sturdy* tests [42, section 6.3] is close to that between robustly reachable bugs and normally reachable bugs. A test is flaky when it is reachable, but not robustly reachable under the partition of inputs where controlled inputs are deterministic inputs and uncontrolled inputs are non-deterministic inputs. *Flakiness is thus a particular case of (non-) robustness.* Especially, our tool can help find non-flaky tests.

Fairness. *Fairness assumptions* in model checking [35] aim at discarding traces considered as unrealistic and avoiding false alarms from the user point of view. While the goal is rather similar to ours, the two techniques are very different: fairness assumptions typically require certain sets of states to be visited infinitely often along a trace, while robust reachability requires that a trace cannot be influenced by uncontrolled input w.r.t.a given reachability property.

Symbolic Execution and Quantifiers. Finally, while symbolic execution is commonly performed with quantifier-free constraints, a notable exception is *higher-order test generation* [28], where Godefroid proposes to rely on universally quantified uninterpreted functions ($\forall \exists$ queries) in order to soundly approximate opaque code constructs. Higher-order test generation and robust reachability are complementary as they serve two different purposes: robust reachability can only be used in a modest way for opaque code constructs (finding controlled inputs for which their value does not matter), while higher-order test generation is inadequate for robust reachability, as it would be as if the attacker could choose the controlled inputs knowing the uncontrolled ones.

8 Conclusion

We introduce the novel concept of robust reachability, that we argue is better suited than standard reachability in several important scenarios for both security (e.g., criticality assessment, bug prioritization) and software engineering (e.g., replicable test suites). We formally define and study robust reachability, discuss how standard symbolic methods to prove reachability can be revisited to deal with the robust case, design and implement the first robust symbolic execution engine and demonstrate its abilities in criticality assessment over 4 CVEs. We believe robust reachability is an important sweet spot in terms of expressiveness and tractability. We hope this first step will pave the way to more refinements and applications of robust reachability.

A Details on the Experiments Supporting Sect. 6.4

We reuse the notations of the discussion in Sect. 4.1.

Model Counting. For simplicity, consider single-path robust reachability of ℓ along a path with path constraint $\mathrm{pc}(a, x)$. It is equivalent to $\exists a. \forall x. \mathrm{pc}(a, x)$.

A more quantitative approach would be to consider a_{max} s.t. the ratio $r(a_{max})$ of x satisfying $pc(a_{max}, x)$ is maximal. The larger $r(a_{max})$, the more robustly reachable ℓ. We try to experimentally get an idea of the cost of computing this. Determining a_{max} is an open problem, but we can lower bound the full computation time by the time to compute $r(a_{max})$ from a_{max}. As the algorithms below are randomized, we can measure the time to compute $r(a_0)$ for any a_0.

We collect the path constraint of the first path standardly reaching the target in our 4 case studies of Sect. 6.2. We arbitrarily choose a_0 satisfying $\exists x.\, pc(a_0, x)$, and compare the time to (dis)prove $\forall x.\, pc(a_0, x)$ with Z3 to the time to approximate $r(a_0)$ with two of the few model counters supporting SMTlib2 input in the QF_BV theory: SearchMC [39] (with tolerance $\varepsilon = 0.8$ and confidence $1 - \delta = 0.95$) and SMTApproxMC [11] (with tolerance $\varepsilon = 0.8$ and 1 iteration). We found no tool supporting arrays, so arrays were blasted. As shown in Table 5, the quantitative approach is orders of magnitude slower in all cases, and especially in the one case where it is indeed significantly more precise than our qualitative approach (u-boot).

Table 5. All-or-nothing (Z3) *vs* quantitative (SearchMC, SMTApproxMC) approaches: runtime and lower bound on $r(a_0)$. Timeout (TO) is 2,400 s.

	doas		libvncserver		u-boot		mongoose	
Z3	0.02 s	0%	0.01 s	0%	0.07 s	0%	0.04 s	100%
SearchMC	9.4 s	10^{-13}	4.8 s	10^{-12}	190.6 s	25%	35.1 s	59%
SMTApproxMC	TO	–	TO	–	TO	–	TO	–

Quantifier Alternations. We want to model a leak in ASLR in libvncserver (Sect. 6.2): the attacker knows about an address z and wants to use the bug to jump to z. The corresponding property is: for all values[2] of z, there exists an attacker input a such that for all other uncontrolled inputs x, control flow is diverted to z. This uses another universal quantifier, which we exclude in our definition of robust reachability to keep satisfiability queries tractable. We implemented this for libvncserver (additional quantification on the target jump address) and doas (additional quantification on the user and group ID of the attacker, and the typoed user name): RSE+ does not terminate within 24 h.

References

1. Avgerinos, T., Cha, S.K., Rebert, A., Schwartz, E.J., Woo, M., Brumley, D.: Automatic exploit generation. Commun. ACM **57**(2), 74–84 (2014)
2. Aziz, A., Sanwal, K., Singhal, V., Brayton, R.: Verifying continuous time Markov chains. In: Alur, R., Henzinger, T.A. (eds.) CAV 1996. LNCS, vol. 1102, pp. 269–276. Springer, Heidelberg (1996). https://doi.org/10.1007/3-540-61474-5_75

---

[2] Without a null byte, but we ignore this detail for the sake of simplicity.

3. Baldoni, R., Coppa, E., D'elia, D.C., Demetrescu, C., Finocchi, I.: A Survey of symbolic execution techniques. ACM Comput. Surv. **51**(3), 1–39 (2018)
4. Barret, C.W., Sebastiani, R., Seshia, S.A., Tinelli, C.: Satisfiability modulo theories. In: Handbook of Satisfiability. IOS Press (2009)
5. Barrett, C., et al.: CVC4. In: Gopalakrishnan, G., Qadeer, S. (eds.) CAV 2011. LNCS, vol. 6806, pp. 171–177. Springer, Heidelberg (2011). https://doi.org/10.1007/978-3-642-22110-1_14
6. Barthe, G., D'Argenio, P., Rezk, T.: Secure information flow by self-composition. In: CSF 2004 Workshop (2004)
7. Jaffar, J., Santosa, A.E., Voicu, R.: A CLP method for compositional and intermittent predicate abstraction. In: Emerson, E.A., Namjoshi, K.S. (eds.) VMCAI 2006. LNCS, vol. 3855, pp. 17–32. Springer, Heidelberg (2005). https://doi.org/10.1007/11609773_2
8. Brillout, A., Kroening, D., Rümmer, P., Wahl, T.: Beyond quantifier-free interpolation in extensions of Presburger arithmetic. In: Jhala, R., Schmidt, D. (eds.) VMCAI 2011. LNCS, vol. 6538, pp. 88–102. Springer, Heidelberg (2011). https://doi.org/10.1007/978-3-642-18275-4_8
9. Cadar, C., Sen, K.: Symbolic execution for software testing: three decades later. Commun. ACM **56**(2), 82–90 (2013)
10. Cha, S.K., Avgerinos, T., Rebert, A., Brumley, D.: Unleashing Mayhem on binary code. In: S&P 2012 (2012)
11. Chakraborty, S., Meel, K., Mistry, R., Vardi, M.: Approximate probabilistic inference via word-level counting. In: AAAI, vol. 30, no. 1 (2016)
12. Cimatti, A., Clarke, E., Giunchiglia, F., Roveri, M.: NuSMV: a new symbolic model verifier. In: Halbwachs, N., Peled, D. (eds.) CAV 1999. LNCS, vol. 1633, pp. 495–499. Springer, Heidelberg (1999). https://doi.org/10.1007/3-540-48683-6_44
13. Clarke, E., Kroening, D., Lerda, F.: A tool for checking ANSI-C programs. In: Jensen, K., Podelski, A. (eds.) TACAS 2004. LNCS, vol. 2988, pp. 168–176. Springer, Heidelberg (2004). https://doi.org/10.1007/978-3-540-24730-2_15
14. Clarke, E.M., Emerson, E.A.: Design and synthesis of synchronization skeletons using branching time temporal logic. In: Kozen, D. (ed.) Logic of Programs 1981. LNCS, vol. 131, pp. 52–71. Springer, Heidelberg (1982). https://doi.org/10.1007/BFb0025774
15. Clarkson, M.R., Finkbeiner, B., Koleini, M., Micinski, K.K., Rabe, M.N., Sánchez, C.: Temporal logics for hyperproperties. In: Abadi, M., Kremer, S. (eds.) POST 2014. LNCS, vol. 8414, pp. 265–284. Springer, Heidelberg (2014). https://doi.org/10.1007/978-3-642-54792-8_15
16. Clarkson, M.R., Schneider, F.B.: Hyperproperties. J. Comput. Secur. **18**(6), 1157–1210 (2010)
17. Cook, B., Podelski, A., Rybalchenko, A.: TERMINATOR: beyond safety. In: Ball, T., Jones, R.B. (eds.) CAV 2006. LNCS, vol. 4144, pp. 415–418. Springer, Heidelberg (2006). https://doi.org/10.1007/11817963_37
18. Cowan, C., et al.: StackGuard: automatic adaptive detection and prevention of buffer-overflow attacks (1998)
19. Daniel, L.A., Bardin, S., Rezk, T.: Binsec/Rel: efficient relational symbolic execution for constant-time at binary-level. In: S&P 2020. IEEE (2020)
20. David, R., et al.: BINSEC/SE: a dynamic symbolic execution toolkit for binary-level analysis. In: SANER 2016. IEEE (2016)
21. David, R., et al.: Specification of concretization and symbolization policies in symbolic execution. In: ISSTA 2016. ACM (2016)

22. de Moura, L., Bjørner, N.: Z3: an efficient SMT solver. In: Ramakrishnan, C.R., Rehof, J. (eds.) TACAS 2008. LNCS, vol. 4963, pp. 337–340. Springer, Heidelberg (2008). https://doi.org/10.1007/978-3-540-78800-3_24

23. Djoudi, A., Bardin, S.: BINSEC: binary code analysis with low-level regions. In: Baier, C., Tinelli, C. (eds.) TACAS 2015. LNCS, vol. 9035, pp. 212–217. Springer, Heidelberg (2015). https://doi.org/10.1007/978-3-662-46681-0_17

24. Farinier, B.: Decision procedures for vulnerability analysis. Ph.D. thesis, Université Grenoble-Alpes (2020)

25. Farinier, B., Bardin, S., Bonichon, R., Potet, M.-L.: Model generation for quantified formulas: a taint-based approach. In: Chockler, H., Weissenbacher, G. (eds.) CAV 2018. LNCS, vol. 10982, pp. 294–313. Springer, Cham (2018). https://doi.org/10.1007/978-3-319-96142-2_19

26. Farinier, B., David, R., Bardin, S., Lemerre, M.: Arrays made simpler: an efficient, scalable and thorough preprocessing. In: LPAR-22 (2018)

27. Ge, Y., de Moura, L.: Complete instantiation for quantified formulas in satisfiabiliby modulo theories. In: Bouajjani, A., Maler, O. (eds.) CAV 2009. LNCS, vol. 5643, pp. 306–320. Springer, Heidelberg (2009). https://doi.org/10.1007/978-3-642-02658-4_25

28. Godefroid, P.: Higher-order test generation. In: PLDI 2011. ACM (2011)

29. Godefroid, P., Klarlund, N., Sen, K.: DART: directed automated random testing. In: PLDI 2005. ACM (2005)

30. Godefroid, P., Levin, M.Y., Molnar, D.: SAGE: whitebox fuzzing for security testing: SAGE has had a remarkable impact at Microsoft. Queue 10(1), 20–27 (2012)

31. Goguen, J.A., Meseguer, J.: Security policies and security models. In: S&P 1982. IEEE (1982)

32. Gomes, C.P., Sabharwal, A., Selman, B.: Model counting. In: Handbook of Satisfiability. IOS Press (2008)

33. Hansen, T., Schachte, P., Søndergaard, H.: State joining and splitting for the symbolic execution of binaries. In: Bensalem, S., Peled, D.A. (eds.) RV 2009. LNCS, vol. 5779, pp. 76–92. Springer, Heidelberg (2009). https://doi.org/10.1007/978-3-642-04694-0_6

34. Hansson, H., Jonsson, B.: A logic for reasoning about time and reliability. Formal Aspects Comput. 6, 512–535 (1994). https://doi.org/10.1007/BF01211866

35. Hart, S., Sharir, M., Pnueli, A.: Termination of probabilistic concurrent program. ACM Trans. Program. Lang. Syst. 5(3), 356–380 (1983)

36. Heelan, S.: Automatic generation of control flow hijacking exploits for software vulnerabilities. Master's thesis, University of Oxford (2009)

37. Heusser, J., Malacaria, P.: Quantifying information leaks in software. In: ACSAC 2010. ACM Press (2010)

38. Holler, C., Herzig, K., Zeller, A.: Fuzzing with code fragments. In: 21st USENIX Security Symposium. USENIX Association (2012)

39. Kim, S., McCamant, S.: Bit-vector model counting using statistical estimation. In: Beyer, D., Huisman, M. (eds.) TACAS 2018. LNCS, vol. 10805, pp. 133–151. Springer, Cham (2018). https://doi.org/10.1007/978-3-319-89960-2_8

40. de Moura, L., Bjørner, N.: Efficient E-matching for SMT solvers. In: Pfenning, F. (ed.) CADE 2007. LNCS (LNAI), vol. 4603, pp. 183–198. Springer, Heidelberg (2007). https://doi.org/10.1007/978-3-540-73595-3_13

41. Niemetz, A., Preiner, M., Biere, A.: Boolector 2.0: system description. J. Satisfiability Boolean Model. Comput. 9(1), 53–58 (2015)

42. O'Hearn, P.W.: Incorrectness logic. In: POPL (2020)

43. Recoules, F., Bardin, S., Bonichon, R., Mounier, L., Potet, M.L.: Get rid of inline assembly through verification-oriented lifting. In: ASE 2019. IEEE (2019)
44. Reynolds, A., Tinelli, C., Goel, A., Krstić, S.: Finite model finding in SMT. In: Sharygina, N., Veith, H. (eds.) CAV 2013. LNCS, vol. 8044, pp. 640–655. Springer, Heidelberg (2013). https://doi.org/10.1007/978-3-642-39799-8_42
45. Sen, K., Marinov, D., Agha, G.: CUTE: a concolic unit testing engine for C. In: ESEC/FSE-13. ACM (2005)
46. Shoshitaishvili, Y., et al.: SOK: (state of) the art of war: offensive techniques in binary analysis. In: SP 2016 (2016)
47. Song, F., Touili, T.: Efficient CTL model-checking for pushdown systems. Theor. Comput. Sci. **549**, 127–145 (2014)
48. Williams, N., Marre, B., Mouy, P., Roger, M.: PathCrawler: automatic generation of path tests by combining static and dynamic analysis. In: Dal Cin, M., Kaâniche, M., Pataricza, A. (eds.) EDCC 2005. LNCS, vol. 3463, pp. 281–292. Springer, Heidelberg (2005). https://doi.org/10.1007/11408901_21

A Temporal Logic for Asynchronous Hyperproperties

Jan Baumeister[1], Norine Coenen[1], Borzoo Bonakdarpour[2],
Bernd Finkbeiner[1], and César Sánchez[3]

[1] CISPA Helmholtz Center for Information Security,
Saarbrücken, Germany
[2] Michigan State University, East Lansing, USA
[3] IMDEA Software Institute, Madrid, Spain
cesar.sanchez@imdea.org

Abstract. *Hyperproperties* are properties of computational systems
that require more than one trace to evaluate, e.g., many information-flow
security and concurrency requirements. Where a trace property defines
a set of traces, a hyperproperty defines a set of sets of traces. The temporal logics HyperLTL and HyperCTL* have been proposed to express
hyperproperties. However, their semantics are *synchronous* in the sense
that all traces proceed at the same speed and are evaluated at the same
position. This precludes the use of these logics to analyze systems whose
traces can proceed at different speeds and allow that different traces take
stuttering steps independently. To solve this problem in this paper, we
propose an *asynchronous* variant of HyperLTL. On the negative side,
we show that the model-checking problem for this variant is undecidable. On the positive side, we identify a decidable fragment which covers
a rich set of formulas with practical applications. We also propose two
model-checking algorithms that reduce our problem to the HyperLTL
model-checking problem in the synchronous semantics.

1 Introduction

Hyperproperties [8] extend the conventional notion of trace properties [1] from a
set of traces to a set of sets of traces. In other words, a hyperproperty stipulates a
system property and not the property of just individual traces. Many interesting
requirements in computing systems are hyperproperties and cannot be expressed
by trace properties. Examples include (1) a wide range of information-flow security policies such as *noninterference* [14] and *observational determinism* [28],

This work was funded in part by Madrid Regional Government under project
"S2018/TCS-4339 (BLOQUES-CM)", by Spanish National Project "BOSCO
(PGC2018-102210-B-100)", by the German Research Foundation (DFG) as part of
the Collaborative Research Center "Foundations of Perspicuous Software Systems"
(TRR 248, 389792660), by the European Research Council (ERC) Grant OSARES
(No. 683300), and by the United Stated NSF SaTC Award 2100989.

A. Silva and K. R. M. Leino (Eds.) CAV 2021, LNCS 12759, pp. 694–717, 2021.
https://doi.org/10.1007/978-3-030-81685-8_33

```
ℓ₁   int 1 = 0;
ℓ₂
ℓ₃   if (h = 0)
ℓ₄       1 := 1 + 1;
ℓ₅   else
ℓ₆       1 := 1;
```

```
ℓ₁   int 1 = 0;
ℓ₂
ℓ₃   if (h = 0)
ℓ₄       reg:= 1 + 1;
ℓ₅       1 := reg;
ℓ₆   else
ℓ₇       1 := 1;
```

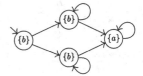

Fig. 1. Program P_1 **Fig. 2.** Program P_2 **Fig. 3.** $\mathcal{K}$ with a self-loop

(2) sensitivity and robustness requirements in cyber-physical systems [27], and (3) consistency conditions such as *linearizability* in concurrent data structures [5].

HyperLTL [7] is a temporal logic for hyperproperties that enriches LTL with quantifiers allowing explicit and simultaneous quantification over multiple execution traces. For example, the observational determinism security policy [28] stipulates that any two executions that start in two *low-equivalent* states (i.e., states whose value of publicly observable variables are the same), should remain in low-equivalent states. This property can be expressed in HyperLTL as the following formula, called $\varphi_{\mathsf{OD}}, \forall\pi.\forall\pi'.(l_\pi \leftrightarrow l_{\pi'}) \rightarrow \Box(l_\pi \leftrightarrow l_{\pi'})$. However, the semantics of HyperLTL (and other formal languages for hyperproperties) is *synchronous*, meaning that they completely abstract away the notion of time passage. In HyperLTL, all traces proceed at the same speed, as all temporal operators move the position on all traces simultaneously. Consider the program P_1 in Fig. 1, where input values 0 and 1 are possible for *high-secret* variable h. This renders two possible traces shown in Fig. 4a that satisfy φ_{OD}.

The synchronous semantics of HyperLTL has a shortcoming which has practical implications as well: formulas are not invariant under *stuttering*. Note that, contrary to LTL, disallowing the use of ○ does not make the formula invariant under stuttering, as traces can still stutter independently. This limits the scope of application of HyperLTL to only those settings where different traces can be perfectly aligned. For example, consider program P_2 in Fig. 2, where line ℓ_4 in P_1 is refined to its intermediate code using a register that stores the value $1 + 1$ and then stores this value in memory location 1 in lines ℓ_4 and ℓ_5, respectively. Applying the synchronous semantics of HyperLTL results in declaring a violation of φ_{OD} in the second position. This, however, is not an accurate interpretation of φ_{OD} (assuming that an attacker only has access to the memory footprint and not the CPU registers or a timing channel), as the two traces are stutter equivalent with respect to the state of variable 1. In fact, the synchronous semantics of HyperLTL may incorrectly identify good programs as bad because it ignores the notion of relative time between traces. This problem is generally amplified in Kripke structures where self-loops correspond to non-deterministic choices that model that the system may remain in a state for some arbitrary time. For instance, consider $\mathcal{K}$ in Fig. 3 and HyperLTL formula $\forall\pi.\forall\pi'.((b_\pi \leftrightarrow b_{\pi'}) \ \mathcal{U} \ \Box(a_\pi \leftrightarrow a_{\pi'}))$. Only pairs of traces that take the self-loop the same number of times satisfy this formula. However, since the goal of employing a self-loop is typically to make the duration of staying in a state irrelevant, this semantics is too restrictive.

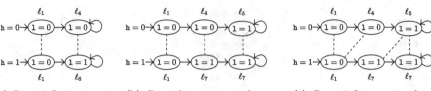

(a) P_1 satisfies φ_{OD} under synchronous sems.

(b) P_2 violates φ_{OD} under synchronous semantics

(c) P_2 satisfies φ_{OD} under asynchronous semantics.

Fig. 4. Synchronous vs. asynchronous semantics for HyperLTL.

Besides HyperLTL, other logics have been proposed that allow trace quantification, for example, H_μ [15], which extends the linear time μ-calculus [3] with path quantifiers and indexed next operators. For H_μ, the model-checking problem is in general undecidable, but two fragments, the k-synchronous, k-context bounded fragments, have been identified for which model checking remains decidable [15].

In this paper, we propose an asynchronous temporal logic for hyperproperties. Our main motivation is to be able to reason about execution traces according to the relative order of the sequences of actions in each trace but not about the duration of each action. Software is inherently asynchronous, and so is hardware in many cases if one abstracts the execution platform or many features of the execution platform like pipelines, caches, memory contention, etc. We call our temporal logic *Asynchronous HyperLTL* or in short, A-HLTL. The key addition is the notion of *trajectory* that controls the relative speed at which traces progress by chosing at each instant which traces move and which traces stutter. For example, the trajectory shown in Fig. 4c for the two traces of the program in Fig. 2 allows the lower trace to stutter in the first position while the upper trace advances. On the contrary, in the third position, the upper trace stutters while the lower trace moves from the second to the third position. This trajectory enables identification of stutter equivalence of the two traces with respect to state variable 1 and, hence, successful verification of observational determinism. In order to reflect the notion of trajectories in our logic, we lift the syntax of HyperLTL by allowing a trajectory modality. This way, the corresponding formula for observational determinism in A-HLTL is the following:

$$\varphi_{\mathsf{OD}} \stackrel{\text{def}}{=} \forall\pi.\forall\pi'.\mathsf{E}.(li_\pi \leftrightarrow li_{\pi'}) \rightarrow \square(lo_\pi \leftrightarrow lo_{\pi'})$$

where E denotes the *existence* of a trajectory for temporal operator $\square$. The A-HLTL formula for the Kripke structure in Fig. 3 is $\forall\pi.\forall\pi'.\mathsf{E}.((b_\pi \leftrightarrow b_{\pi'})\ \mathcal{U}\ \square(a_\pi \leftrightarrow a_{\pi'}))$. A-HLTL allows us to reason about relational properties between two different systems that differ on timing, like for example, translation validation [22], which relates executions of the target code with the source code with respect to a (trace or hyper) property.

We show an encoding of the PCP problem into model-checking a formula of the shape $\forall\pi.\forall\pi'.\mathsf{E}.(\square\psi_1(\pi,\pi')\wedge\Diamond\psi_2(\pi,\pi'))$, which implies that model-checking A-HLTL is undecidable, even for the universal fragment. On the positive side, we show two decidable fragments of A-HLTL. The first algorithm is based on a *stuttering construction* in which we modify the Kripke structure to accept all stuttering expansions of the original paths. This algorithm can handle fragment $\forall \pi_1 \ldots \pi_n.\mathsf{E}.\psi$, where the ψ is a *phase formula*, a class of safety formulas that appear in many hyperproperties and are the building block of expressing trace equivalence. Our second algorithm uses an *acceleration construction* to convert a finite sequence of transitions that do not change phase, into a single transition. This algorithm is able to handle formulas with arbitrary quantification but a simpler kind of phase formulas. A-HLTL is, thus, the first logic for hyperproperties that can express the major asynchronous hyperproperties of interest within decidable fragments. Moreover, A-HLTL is the first logic for asynchronous hyperproperties with a practical model checking algorithm. Both algorithms use internally HyperLTL model-checking as a building block. However, the reduction from A-HLTL model-checking into HyperLTL requires modifying both the formula and the model in a highly non-trivial way, to encode the exitence of trajectories. The choice of using HyperLTL model-checking as a building block is based on the existence of tools, but it does not imply that asynchronous properties of interest can be expressed in HyperLTL directly.

We have evaluated the stuttering construction on two sets of cases studies: a range of compiler optimizations and an SPI bus protocol. In both case studies, we were able to prove system correctness using our reduction from A-HLTL to synchronous HyperLTL.

Organization. The rest of the paper is structured as follows. Section 2 contains the preliminaries, and Sect. 3 introduces A-HLTL and presents examples of properties expressible in A-HLTL. Section 4 describes the decidable fragments and present procedures for the model-checking problem. Section 5 shows that the model-checking problem for general A-HLTL formulas is undecidable and present the lower-bound complexity. Experimental results are presented in Sect. 6. Finally, Sect. 7 discusses the related work, while Sect. 8 concludes. Detailed proofs appear in the longer version of this paper in [4].

2 Preliminaries

Let AP be a set of *atomic propositions* and $\Sigma = 2^{\mathsf{AP}}$ be the *alphabet*, where we call each element of Σ a *letter*. A *trace* is an infinite sequence $\sigma = a_0 a_1 \cdots$ of letters from Σ. We denote the set of all infinite traces by Σ^ω. We use $\sigma(i)$ for a_i and σ^i for the suffix $a_i a_{i+1} \cdots$. A *pointed trace* is a pair (σ, p), where $p \in \mathbb{N}_0$ is a natural number (called the *pointer*). Pointed traces allow to traverse a trace by moving the pointer. Given a pointed trace (σ, p) and $n > 0$, we use $(\sigma, p) + n$ as a short for $(\sigma, p + n)$. We denote the set of all pointed traces by $\mathsf{PTR} = \{(\sigma, p) \mid \sigma \in \Sigma^\omega \text{ and } p \in \mathbb{N}_0\}$.

Two pointed traces (σ, p) and (σ', p') are *stuttering equivalent* if there are two infinite sequences of indices $p = i_0 < i_1 \ldots$ and $p' = j_0 < j_1 \ldots$ such that for all $k \geq 0$ and for all $l \in [i_k, i_{k+1})$ and $l' \in [j_k, j_{k+1})$, $\sigma(l) = \sigma'(l')$. A pointed trace

(σ', p') is a *stuttering expansion* of (σ, p) if there is a sequence $p' = j_0 < j_1 < \cdots$ such that for all $k \geq 0$ and for all $l \in [j_k, j_{k+1})$, $\sigma(p + k) = \sigma'(l)$. We say that σ is stuttering equivalent to σ' if $(\sigma, 0)$ is stuttering equivalent to $(\sigma', 0)$, and that σ' is a stuttering expansion of σ if $(\sigma', 0)$ is a stuttering expansion of $(\sigma, 0)$.

A *Kripke structure* is a tuple $\mathcal{K} = \langle S, S_{init}, \delta, L \rangle$, where S is a set of states, $S_{init} \subseteq S$ is the set of initial states, $\delta \subseteq S \times S$ is a transition relation, and $L : S \to \Sigma$ is a labeling function on the states of $\mathcal{K}$. We require that for each $s \in S$, there exists $s' \in S$, such that $(s, s') \in \delta$.

A *path* of a Kripke structure is an infinite sequence of states $s(0)s(1) \cdots \in S^\omega$, such that $s(0) \in S_{init}$ and $(s(i), s(i + 1)) \in \delta$, for all $i \geq 0$. A *trace* of a Kripke structure is a trace $\sigma(0)\sigma(1)\sigma(2) \cdots \in \Sigma^\omega$, such that there exists a path $s(0)s(1) \cdots \in S^\omega$ with $\sigma(i) = L(s(i))$ for all $i \geq 0$. Abusing notation we use $\sigma = L(\rho)$ to denote that σ is the trace corresponding to path ρ. We denote by $\mathsf{Traces}(\mathcal{K}, s)$ the set of all traces of $\mathcal{K}$ with paths that start in state $s \in S$, We denote by $\mathsf{Traces}(\mathcal{K}, A)$ the set of all traces that start from some state in $A \subseteq S$ and $\mathsf{Traces}(\mathcal{K})$ as a short for $\mathsf{Traces}(\mathcal{K}, S_{init})$.

HyperLTL. HyperLTL [7] is a temporal logic that extends LTL [19,21] for hyperproperties, which allows reasoning about multiple execution traces simultaneously. The syntax of HyperLTL is:

$$\varphi ::= \exists \pi.\varphi \mid \forall \pi.\varphi \mid \psi$$
$$\psi ::= a_\pi \mid \psi \vee \psi \mid \neg \psi \mid \bigcirc \psi \mid \psi \, \mathcal{U} \, \psi$$

where π is a *trace variable* from an infinite supply of trace variables. The intended meaning of a_π is that proposition $a \in \Sigma$ holds in the current time in trace π. Trace quantifiers $\exists \pi$ and $\forall \pi$ allow reasoning simultaneously about different traces of the computation. Atomic predicates a_π refer to a single trace π. Given a HyperLTL formula φ, we use $\mathsf{Vars}(\varphi)$ for the set of trace variables quantified in φ. A formula φ is well-formed if for all atoms a_π in φ, π is quantified in φ (i.e., $\pi \in \mathsf{Vars}(\varphi)$) and if no trace variable is quantified twice in φ. Given a set of traces T, the semantics of a HyperLTL formula φ is defined in terms of trace assignments, which is a (partial) map from trace variables to indexed traces $\Pi : \mathsf{Vars}(\varphi) \rightharpoonup \mathsf{PTR}$. The trace assignment with empty domain is denoted by $\Pi_\emptyset$. We use $Dom(\Pi)$ for the subset of $\mathsf{Vars}(\varphi)$ for which Π is defined. Given a trace assignment Π, a trace variable π, a trace σ and a pointer p, we denote by $\Pi[\pi \mapsto (\sigma, p)]$ the assignment that coincides with Π for every trace variable except for π, which is mapped to (σ, p). Also, we use $\Pi + n$ to denote the trace assignment Π' such that $\Pi'(\pi) = \Pi(\pi) + n$ for all $\pi \in Dom(\Pi) = Dom(\Pi')$. The semantics of HyperLTL is:

$\Pi \models_T \exists \pi.\varphi$	iff	for some $\sigma \in T$, $\Pi[\pi \mapsto (\sigma, 0)] \models_T \varphi$
$\Pi \models_T \forall \pi.\varphi$	iff	for all $\sigma \in T$, $\Pi[\pi \mapsto (\sigma, 0)] \models_T \varphi$
$\Pi \models_T \psi$	iff	$\Pi \models \psi$
$\Pi \models a_\pi$	iff	$a \in \sigma(p)$, where $(\sigma, p) = \Pi(\pi)$

$$\Pi \models_T \psi_1 \vee \psi_2 \qquad \text{iff} \qquad \Pi \models_T \psi_1 \text{ or } \Pi \models_T \psi_2$$
$$\Pi \models \neg \psi \qquad \text{iff} \qquad \Pi \not\models \psi$$
$$\Pi \models \bigcirc \psi \qquad \text{iff} \qquad (\Pi + 1) \models \psi$$
$$\Pi \models \psi_1 \, \mathcal{U} \, \psi_2 \qquad \text{iff} \qquad \text{for some } j \geq 0 \ (\Pi + j) \models \psi_2$$
$$\text{and for all } 0 \leq i < j, (\Pi + i) \models \psi_1$$

Note that quantifiers assign traces to trace variables and set the pointer to the initial position 0. We say that a set of traces T is a model of a HyperLTL formula φ, denoted $T \models \varphi$ whenever $\Pi_\emptyset \models_T \varphi$. A Kripke structure $\mathcal{K}$ is a model of a HyperLTL formula φ, denoted by $\mathcal{K} \models \varphi$, whenever $\mathsf{Traces}(\mathcal{K}) \models \varphi$.

3 Asynchronous HyperLTL

We introduce a temporal logic A-HLTL as an extension of HyperLTL to express asynchronous hyperproperties.

Trajectories. To model the asynchronous passage of time, we now introduce the notion of a trajectory, which chooses when traces move and when they stutter. Let $\mathcal{V}$ be a set of trace variables and let $I \subseteq \mathcal{V}$. The I-successor of a trace assignment Π, denoted by $\Pi + I$, is the trace assignment Π' such that $\Pi'(\pi) = \Pi(\pi) + 1$ if $\pi \in I$ and $\Pi'(\pi) = \Pi(\pi)$ otherwise. That is, the pointers of indices in I advance by one step, while the others remain the same. A *trajectory* t : $t(0)t(1)t(2)\cdots$ for a formula φ is an infinite sequence of non-empty subsets of $\mathsf{Vars}(\varphi)$. Essentially, in each step of the trajectory one or more of the traces make progress. A trajectory is fair for a trace variable $\pi \in \mathsf{Vars}(\varphi)$ if there are infinitely many positions j such that $\pi \in t(j)$. A trajectory is fair if it is fair for all trace variables in $\mathsf{Vars}(\varphi)$. Given a trajectory t, by t^i, we mean the suffix $t(i)t(i+1)\cdots$. Furthermore, for a set of trace variables $\mathcal{V}$, we use $\mathsf{TRJ}_\mathcal{V}$ for set of all trajectories for indices from $\mathcal{V}$.

3.1 Syntax and Semantics of Asynchronous HyperLTL

The syntax of Asynchornous HyperLTL is:

$$\varphi ::= \exists \pi.\varphi \mid \forall \pi.\varphi \mid \mathsf{E}\psi \mid \mathsf{A}\psi$$
$$\psi ::= a_\pi \quad \mid \neg \psi \quad \mid \psi_1 \vee \psi_2 \mid \psi_1 \, \mathcal{U} \, \psi_2 \mid \bigcirc \psi$$

where $a \in \mathsf{AP}$, π is a trace variable from an infinite supply $\mathcal{V}$ of trace variables, E is the existential trajectory modality and A is the universal trajectory modality. The intended meaning of E is that there is a trajectory that gives an interpretation of the relative passage of time between the traces for which the temporal formula that relates the traces is satisfied. Dualy, A means that for all trajectories, the resulting alignment makes the inner formula true. It is important to note that there is no nesting of trajectory modalities and that all temporal operators in a formula are interpreted with respect to a single modality.

We use the usual syntactic sugar for Boolean operators $true \overset{\text{def}}{=} a_\pi \vee \neg a_\pi$, $false \overset{\text{def}}{=} \neg true$, $\varphi_1 \wedge \varphi_2 \overset{\text{def}}{=} \neg(\neg\varphi_1 \vee \neg\varphi_2)$, and the syntactic sugar for temporal operators $\Diamond\varphi \overset{\text{def}}{=} true\,\mathcal{U}\,\varphi$, $\varphi_1 \rightarrow \varphi_2 \overset{\text{def}}{=} \neg\varphi_1 \vee \varphi_2$, and $\Box\varphi \overset{\text{def}}{=} \neg\Diamond\neg\varphi$, etc.

As before, we use trace assignments for the semantics of A-HLTL. Given (Π, t) where Π is a trace assignment and t a trajectory, we use $(\Pi, t) + 1$ for the successor of (Π, t) defined as (Π', t') where $t' = t^1$, and $\Pi'(\pi) = \Pi(\pi) + 1$ if $\pi \in t(0)$ and $\Pi'(\pi) = \Pi(\pi)$ otherwise. We use $(\Pi, t) + k$ as the k-th successor of (Π, t).

The satisfaction of an asynchronous HyperLTL formula φ over a trace assignment Π and a set of traces T, denoted by $\Pi \models_T \varphi$ is defined as follows:

$\Pi \models_T \exists\pi.\varphi$	iff	for some $\sigma \in T : \Pi[\pi \mapsto (\sigma, 0)] \models_T \varphi$
$\Pi \models_T \forall\pi.\varphi$	iff	for all $\sigma \in T : \Pi[\pi \mapsto (\sigma, 0)] \models_T \varphi$
$\Pi \models_T \mathsf{E}\psi$	iff	for some $t \in \mathsf{TRJ}_{Dom(\Pi)}.(\Pi, t) \models \psi$
$\Pi \models_T \mathsf{A}\psi$	iff	for all $t \in \mathsf{TRJ}_{Dom(\Pi)}.(\Pi, t) \models \psi$
$(\Pi, t) \models a_\pi$	iff	$a \in \Pi(\pi)(0)$
$(\Pi, t) \models \neg\psi$	iff	$(\Pi, t) \not\models \psi$
$(\Pi, t) \models \psi_1 \vee \psi_2$	iff	$(\Pi, t) \models \psi_1$ or $(\Pi, t) \models \psi_2$
$(\Pi, t) \models \bigcirc\psi$	iff	$(\Pi, t) + 1 \models \psi$
$(\Pi, t) \models \psi_1 \mathcal{U} \psi_2$	iff	for some $i \geq 0 : (\Pi, t) + i \models \psi_2$ and for all $j < i : (\Pi, t) + j \models \psi_1$

We say that a set T of traces satisfies a closed sentence φ, denoted by $T \models \varphi$, if $\Pi_\emptyset \models_T \varphi$. We say that a Kripke structure $\mathcal{K}$ satisfies an A-HLTL formula φ (and write $\mathcal{K} \models \varphi$) if and only if we have $\mathsf{Traces}(\mathcal{K}, S_{init}) \models \varphi$.

3.2   Examples of A-HLTL

We illustrate the expressive power of A-HLTL by introducing the asynchronous version of well-known properties.

Linearizability. [16] requires that any history of execution of a concurrent data structure (i.e., sequence of invocation and response by different threads) matches some sequential order of invocations and responses:

$$\varphi_{\mathsf{LNZ}} \overset{\text{def}}{=} \forall\pi.\exists\pi'.\mathsf{E}.\Box(\mathsf{history}_\pi \leftrightarrow \mathsf{history}_{\pi'})$$

where history denotes method invocations (and not the actual execution of the internal instructions of the concurrent library) by the different threads and the response observed, trace π ranges over the concurrent data structure and π' ranges over its sequential counterpart.

Goguen and Meseguer's Noninterference (GMNI). [14] stipulates that, for all traces, the low-observable output must not change when all high inputs are removed:

$$\varphi_{\mathsf{GMNI}} \stackrel{\text{def}}{=} \forall \pi.\exists \pi'.\mathsf{E}.(\Box \lambda_{\pi'}) \wedge \Box(lo_\pi \leftrightarrow lo_{\pi'})$$

where $\lambda_{\pi'}$ expresses that all of the high inputs in the current state of π' have dummy value λ, and denotes low-observable output proposition.

Not never Terminates. [18] requires that for every initial state, there is a terminating trace and a non-terminating trace:

$$\varphi_{\mathsf{NNT}} \stackrel{\text{def}}{=} \forall \pi.\exists \pi'.\exists \pi''.\mathsf{E}.(\pi[0] = \pi'[0] = \pi''[0]) \ \rightarrow \ (\Diamond\, \mathsf{term}_{\pi'} \wedge \Box \neg \mathsf{term}_{\pi''})$$

Termination-Insensitive Noninterference. [25] requires that for two executions that start from a low-observable states, information leaks are permitted if they are transmitted purely by the program's termination behavior. That is, the program may diverge on some high inputs and terminate on others:

$$\varphi_{\mathsf{TIN}} \stackrel{\text{def}}{=} \forall \pi.\forall \pi'.\mathsf{E}.\left(l_\pi \leftrightarrow l_{\pi'}\right) \ \rightarrow \ \left(\begin{array}{l} (\Box \neg \mathsf{term}_\pi \vee \Box \neg \mathsf{term}_{\pi'}) \vee \\ \Diamond(\mathsf{term}_\pi \wedge \mathsf{term}_{\pi'} \wedge l_\pi \leftrightarrow l_{\pi'}) \end{array} \right)$$

Termination-Sensitive Noninterference. [2] Termination-sensitive noninterference is the same as termination insensitive, except that it forbids one trace to diverge and the other to terminate:

$$\varphi_{\mathsf{TSN}} \stackrel{\text{def}}{=} \forall \pi.\forall \pi'.\mathsf{E}.\left(l_\pi \leftrightarrow l_{\pi'}\right) \ \rightarrow \ \left(\begin{array}{l} (\Box \neg \mathsf{term}_\pi \wedge \Box \neg \mathsf{term}_{\pi'}) \vee \\ \Diamond(\mathsf{term}_\pi \wedge \mathsf{term}_{\pi'} \wedge l_\pi \leftrightarrow l_{\pi'}) \end{array} \right)$$

4 Model-Checking A-HLTL

In this section, we show the decidability of the model-checking problem for two classes of A-HLTL formulas using two different algorithms:

(1) a *stuttering* construction in which we modify the Kripke structure $\mathcal{K}$ to accept all stuttering expansions of paths in $\mathcal{K}$; and
(2) an *acceleration* construction in which the modified Kripke structure accelerates jumping directly to the synchronization points.

In both cases the problem is reduced to model-checking HyperLTL formulas, which is known to be decidable [7,12]. We describe each construction separately.

4.1   The Stuttering Construction

We consider first A-HLTL formulas of the form $\forall \pi_1 \ldots \pi_n.\mathsf{E}.\psi$. We will then extend our results to the $\exists^*$ fragment, to handle the A trajectory modality and to a larger collection of predicates. The class of temporal formulas ψ that we handle are called *admissible* formulas, and are defined as the Boolean combination of:

1. any number of state formulas, which may relate propositions p_{π_i} of different traces arbitrarily;
2. any number temporal formulas (called *monadic temporal formulas*), each of which only uses one trace variable and is invariant under stuttering (guaranteed for example by forbidding the use of $\bigcirc$), and
3. one *phase formula*, which is an invariant that can relate different traces in a restricted way (see below).

Given an admissible formula ψ, we use ψ_{ph} for its phase formula, and we use $\psi[\psi_{ph} \lhd \xi]$ for the formula that results from ψ by replacing ψ_{ph} with ξ. Since ψ_{ph} occurs only once in ψ, we use the fact that ψ_{ph} appears with a single polarity. We present here the construction for positive polarity which is the case in all practical formulas (the case for negative polarity is analogous).

   The algorithm has two parts. First, we generate the *stuttering* Kripke structure $\mathcal{K}^{st}$ whose paths are the stuttering expansions of paths in the original Kripke structure $\mathcal{K}$. Then, we modify the admissible formula ψ into ψ_{sync} such that $\mathcal{K} \models \forall \pi_1 \ldots \pi_n.\mathsf{E}.\psi$ if and only if $\mathcal{K}^{st} \models \forall \pi_1 \ldots \pi_n.\psi_{sync}$. We describe each of the concepts separately.

Phase Formulas. We first define *atomic phase formulas* ($\bigwedge_{p \in P} p_{\pi_i} \leftrightarrow p_{\pi_j}$) which are characterized by (π_i, π_j, P), where $P \subseteq \mathsf{AP}$ and π_i and π_j are two different trace variables. We use *color* to refer to a valuation of the variables in P. Essentially, an atomic phase formula asserts that all propositions in P coincide in both traces at all points in time, that is, both traces exhibit the same sequence of colors. Since the passage of time proceeds at different speeds in the different traces—according to the trajectory—atomic phase formulas state the traces for π_i and π_j are sequences of phases of the same color, where corresponding phases may have different lengths. A phase formula is formed from atomic formulas as follows:

$$\Box \Big(\bigwedge_{p \in P^1} p_{\pi_i^1} \leftrightarrow p_{\pi_j^1} \wedge \cdots \wedge \bigwedge_{p \in P^k} p_{\pi_i^k} \leftrightarrow p_{\pi_j^k} \Big)$$

We use $\mathcal{P} : \{(\pi_i^1, \pi_j^1, P^1), \ldots, (\pi_i^k, \pi_j^k, P^k)\}$ for the collection of predicates and trace variables that characterize a phase formula.

Stuttering Kripke Structure. We start from $\mathcal{K}$ and create $\mathcal{K}^{st}$ that accepts the stuttering expansions of traces in $\mathcal{K}$. First, the alphabet of atomic propositions is enriched with a fresh proposition st, that is $\mathsf{AP}^{st} = \mathsf{AP} \cup \{st\}$, to encode whether the state represents a real move or a stuttering move. Given $\mathcal{K} = \langle S, S_{init}, \delta, L \rangle$, the stuttering Kripke structure is $\mathcal{K}^{st} = \langle S^{st}, S_{init}, \delta^{st}, L^{st} \rangle$ where:

- $S^{st} = S \cup \{s^{st} \mid s \in S\}$ contains two copies of each state in S, where we use s^{st} to denote the stuttering state that corresponds to s;
- $\delta^{st} = \delta \cup \{(s, s^{st})\} \cup \{(s^{st}, s^{st})\} \cup \{(s^{st}, s') \mid$ for every $(s, s') \in \delta\}$.
- $L^{st}(s) = L(s)$ for $s \in S$, and $L^{st}(s^{st}) = L(s) \cup \{st\}$.

The construction generates a Kripke structure $\mathcal{K}^{st}$ which is linear in the size of the original Kripke structure $\mathcal{K}$. It is easy to see that every stuttering expansion of a path of $\mathcal{K}$ has a corresponding path in $\mathcal{K}^{st}$, where the repeated version of state s is captured by state s^{st}. Conversely every path ρ' in $\mathcal{K}^{st}$ whose trace satisfies $\square\lozenge\neg st$ can be turned into its "stuttering compression" by removing all stuttering states, which is a path of $\mathcal{K}$. Note that the constraint $\square\lozenge\neg st$ guarantees that there are infinitely many non-stuttering positions in ρ', so ρ is well-defined. Hence, this constructions provides a one-to-one correspondence between a trajectory toguether with a tuple of traces of $\mathcal{K}$, and the corresponding tuple of traces of $\mathcal{K}^{st}$.

State and Monadic Formulas are not Affected by Trajectories. State formulas are relational formulas that are evaluated at the beginning of the computation. Temporal monadic formulas only refer to one trace variable and are stuttering invariant by definition. Therefore, none of these formulas are affected by the stuttering induced by a trajectory, as the relative stuttering among traces does not affect their truth valuation. We first note that given a trace assigned for each of the trace variables in $\mathsf{Vars}(\varphi)$ the truth value of state formulas and monadic formulas does not depend on the trajectory chosen.

Phase Alignment of Asynchronous Sequences. We use the stuttering in $\mathcal{K}^{st}$ to encode the relative progress of traces as dictated by a trajectory. We will now introduce synchronous HyperLTL formulas to reason in $\mathcal{K}^{st}$ about the corresponding states during the asynchronous evaluation in $\mathcal{K}$. The important concept is that of "phase changes", which are the points in a trace σ at which the valuation of the predicates P in an atomic phase formula (π_i, π_j, P) change. Let Π be a trace assignment for traces in $\mathcal{K}$ that maps π_i to a pointed trace (σ, l). We say that in assignment Π, trace variable π_i is *about to change phase* with respect to (π_i, π_j, P) if for some $p \in P$ either $p \in \sigma(l)$ but $p \notin \sigma(l+1)$ or $p \notin \sigma(l)$ but $p \in \sigma(l+1)$. Note that in $\mathcal{K}^{st}$ the next relevant letter (the one corresponding to $\sigma(l+1)$ is the first letter that is not a stuttering letter). Formula $change_P(\pi_i)$ captures that the next non-stuttering step of π_i is a phase change (with respect to predicates in P and therefore with respect to atomic phase formula α):

$$change_P(\pi_i) \overset{\text{def}}{=} \bigvee_{p \in P} p_{\pi_i} \not\leftrightarrow \bigcirc(st_{\pi_i} \, \mathcal{U} \, p_{\pi_i})$$

A phase change for π_i in atomic phase formula (π_i, π_j, P) implies that π_j must also proceed to change phase. The second observation is that when π_i and π_j are not changing phases, any choice that the trajectory makes will preserve the valuation of the atomic phase formula.

We now capture formally this intuition as formulas. Predicate $move(\pi_i) \overset{\text{def}}{=}$ $\bigcirc(\neg st_{\pi_i})$ indicates whether trace variable π_i will move (and not stutter) at a given instant of the computation. The following temporal formula captures the consistency criteria of phase changes as a synchronized decision for moving traces π_i and π_j related by an atomic phase formula (π_i, π_j, P):

$$align_{(\pi_i,\pi_j,P)} \overset{\text{def}}{=}$$
$$\left(\begin{array}{l} (move(\pi_i) \wedge \quad move(\pi_j)) \rightarrow (change_P(\pi_i) \leftrightarrow change_P(\pi_j)) \wedge \\ (move(\pi_i) \wedge \neg move(\pi_j)) \rightarrow \neg change_P(\pi_i) \qquad\qquad\qquad \wedge \\ (\neg move(\pi_i) \wedge \quad move(\pi_j)) \rightarrow \neg change_P(\pi_j) \end{array} \right)$$

We will reduce the model-checking problem in A-HLTL to checking in $\mathcal{K}^{st}$ that tuples of traces that align phase changes—for all atomic phase formulas— satisfy all sub-formulas of the specification ψ. The following two formulas express that all atomic phase formulas align, and that all traces are fair (all traces eventually move):

$$phase \overset{\text{def}}{=} \bigwedge_{(\pi_i,\pi_j,P)\in\mathcal{P}} align_{(\pi_i,\pi_j,P)} \qquad\qquad fair \overset{\text{def}}{=} \bigwedge_{\pi_i\in\{\pi_1...\pi_n\}} \Box\Diamond\neg st_i$$

We will then check in $\mathcal{K}^{st}$ that all stuttering traces that align phases and are fair satisfy the desired formula ψ, that is $(\Box phase \wedge fair) \rightarrow \psi$. Note that all those tuples of traces that do not align phases are ruled out in the antecedent.

A final technical detail in the construction is that we must guarantee that for all tuples of paths of $\mathcal{K}$ there are stuttering expansions that are fair and align phases, and that they have the same number of phases. Otherwise, there are paths of $\mathcal{K}$ that cannot be aligned, which inevitably leads to a violation of ψ_{ph}. It could be the case that some tuple of traces of $\mathcal{K}$ cannot possibly align the phase changes corresponding to all atomic phase formulas. This can happen in two cases: (1) when two traces have different number of phases, and (2) when there is a circular dependency between the atomic formulas that force the trajectory to synchronize the traces in incompatible orders. The first case is captured by:

$$missalign \overset{\text{def}}{=} \bigvee_{(\pi_i,\pi_j,P)} \left(\Box\neg change_P(\pi_i)\right) \not\leftrightarrow \left(\Box\neg change_P(\pi_j)\right)$$

The second case is captured by the following formula, where $cycles(\psi_{ph})$ are the sequences of atomic formulas that form a simple cycle, that is $[(\pi^0, \pi^1, P^0), (\pi^1, \pi^2, P^1) \ldots (\pi^k, \pi^0, P^k)]$ such that the second trace variable is the first trace variable of the next atomic phase formula, circularly (see Ex. 1 below):

$$block \overset{\text{def}}{=} \bigvee_{C\in cycles(\psi_{ph})} \left(\bigwedge_{(\pi_i,\pi_j,P)\in C} change_P(\pi_i) \wedge \neg change_P(\pi_j) \right)$$

Essentially, *block* encodes whether the set of traces involved cannot proceed without violating *phase*, because *align* forbids all traces involved to move. Hence, the formula *phase* $\mathcal{U}$ (*missalign* $\vee$ *block*) captures to those traces of $\mathcal{K}^{st}$ that contain an aligned prefix of computation that lead to a miss-alignment or a block. The proof of correctness shows that given a tuple of traces of $\mathcal{K}$, if there is a trajectory that aligns the phase changes (which must exist if there is a trajectory that makes ψ_{ph} true), then all trajectories that respect $\square phase$ will also align the phase changes (and also satisfy ψ_{ph}).

We are finally ready to describe the synchronous phase formula ψ_{sync}. First, this formula is only evaluated against tuples of fair traces, which correspond to the stuttering extensions of paths of $\mathcal{K}$. Then, the phase formula ψ_{ph} is translated into a formula that captures (1) that following a phase alignment cannot lead to a block or to two traces changing phases a different number of times, and (2) that if phases are aligned then ψ_{ph} holds. Formally,

$$\psi_{sync} \stackrel{\text{def}}{=} fair \rightarrow \psi[\psi_{ph} \lhd \psi'], \quad \text{where } \psi' = \begin{pmatrix} \neg(phase \ \mathcal{U} \ (missalign \vee block)) \ \wedge \\ \square phase \rightarrow \psi_{ph} \end{pmatrix}$$

Example 1. We illustrate the previous definitions with the Kripke structures $\mathcal{K}_1$, $\mathcal{K}_2$ and $\mathcal{K}_3$ in Fig. 5 and their stuttering variants $\mathcal{K}_1^{st}$, $\mathcal{K}_2^{st}$ and $\mathcal{K}_3^{st}$ Consider formula $\forall \pi_1. \forall \pi_2. \mathsf{E}.\square(a_{\pi_1} \leftrightarrow a_{\pi_2})$. Consider the following trace assignments:

$\Pi^1(\pi_1) \mapsto \{\} \{st\} \{a\} \dots$	$\Pi^2(\pi_1) \mapsto \{\} \{a\} \{a\} \dots$	$\Pi^3(\pi_1) \mapsto \{a\} \{\} \{\} \ \dots$
$\Pi^1(\pi_2) \mapsto \{\} \{\} \ \ \{a\} \dots$	$\Pi^2(\pi_2) \mapsto \{\} \{\} \ \ \{a\} \dots$	$\Pi^3(\pi_2) \mapsto \{a\} \{\} \{a\} \dots$

Consider the trace assignment Π^1 on the left, where π_1 is a trace of $\mathcal{K}_1^{st}$ corresponding to the path of $\mathcal{K}_1$ that visits s_1, and π_2 corresponds to the path that visits s_2. This trace assignment aligns the atomic phase formula $(\pi_1, \pi_2, \{a\})$ at all positions. In particular, at position 0, we have $change_{\{a\}}(\pi_1)$, but $\neg change_{\{a\}}(\pi_2)$, and $\neg move(\pi_1)$ and $move(\pi_2)$, as $align_{\{a\}}$ requires.

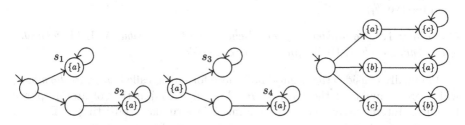

Fig. 5. Kripke structure $\mathcal{K}_1$ (left), $\mathcal{K}_2$ (middle) and $\mathcal{K}_3$ (right).

$$\Pi(\pi_1) \mapsto \{\} \{\} \{a\} \{c\} \dots$$
$$\Pi(\pi_2) \mapsto \{\} \{\} \{b\} \{a\} \dots$$
$$\Pi(\pi_3) \mapsto \{\} \{\} \{c\} \{b\} \dots$$

Consider now the trace assignment Π^2 in the middle, where again π_1 corresponds to the path in $\mathcal{K}_1^{st}$ that visits s_1 and π_2 the path that visits s_2. In this case, we have $\neg align_{\{a\}}$ at position 0 because $change_{\{a\}}(\pi_1)$ and $\neg change_{\{a\}}(\pi_2)$ hold, and both $move(\pi_1)$ and $move(\pi_2)$. Consider now Π^3 on the right, where π_1 corresponds to the path of $\mathcal{K}_2^{st}$ that visits s_3 and π_2 to the path of $\mathcal{K}_2^{st}$ that visits s_4. In this case $align_{\{a\}}$ holds at 0 and $missalign$ holds at 1 because at 1, $\Box\neg change_{\{a\}}(\pi_1)$ holds, but not $\Box\neg change_{\{a\}}(\pi_2)$. Therefore, $phase\,\mathcal{U}\,(missalign \vee block)$ holds for Π^3. Finally, consider $\forall\pi_1.\forall\pi_2.\forall\pi_3.\mathsf{E}.\Box(a_{\pi_1} \leftrightarrow a_{\pi_2} \wedge b_{\pi_2} \leftrightarrow b_{\pi_3} \wedge c_{\pi_3} \leftrightarrow c_{\pi_2})$ and the trace assignment Π of $\mathcal{K}_3^{st}$ shown below on the left. In this case $phase$ holds at position 0 and $block$ holds at position 1. This is because $change_{\{a\}}(\pi_1)$ and $\neg change_{\{a\}}(\pi_2)$, $change_{\{b\}}(\pi_2)$ and $\neg change_{\{b\}}(\pi_3)$, and $change_{\{c\}}(\pi_3)$ and also $\neg change_{\{c\}}(\pi_1)$. This illustrates that it will not be possible to align all three atomic phase formulas.

We are now ready to state the main result of this section.

Theorem 1. *Let $\mathcal{K}$ be a Kripke structure and ψ an admissible formula. Then, $\mathcal{K} \models \forall\pi_1 \dots \pi_n.\mathsf{E}.\psi$ if and only if $\mathcal{K}^{st} \models \forall\pi_1 \dots \pi_n.\psi_{sync}$.*

Dually, to show that the $\exists^*$ fragment is decidable, we consider replacing ψ_{ph} by the formula

$$\psi_{esync} \overset{\text{def}}{=} fair \wedge \psi[\psi_{ph} \triangleleft (\Box phase \wedge \psi_{ph})]$$

Theorem 2. *Let $\mathcal{K}$ be a Kripke structure and ψ an admissible formula. Then $\mathcal{K} \models \exists\pi_1 \dots \pi_n.\mathsf{E}.\psi$ if and only if $\mathcal{K}^{st} \models \exists\pi_1 \dots \pi_n.\psi_{esync}$.*

The proof of Theorem 2 takes a witness tuple and trajectory in $\mathcal{K}$ and shows that the induced tuple in $\mathcal{K}^{st}$ is *fair*, satisfies $\Box phase$ and that the valuation of ψ_{ph} is preserved. Similarly, as before, tuples of traces of $\mathcal{K}^{st}$ that are fair and follow phase alignments induce a trajectory on their stuttering compression that also preserve ψ_{ph}.

Corollary 1. *The problems of model-checking $\forall^*$ admissible A-HLTL formulas and $\exists^*$ admissible A-HLTL formulas is decidable.*

We finally consider the negation of phase formulas, called *co-phase formulas*, which are formulas of the form $\Diamond\neg R$ where R a conjunction of atomic phase formulas. Interestingly, deciding co-admissible formulas (consisting of Boolean combinations of state-formulas, monadic temporal formulas and one co-phase formula in positive polarity) is easier than before, as one can turn the co-phase formula into a monadic formula enumerating all the violations of the atomic phase formulas ($p \in P$ such that $p_{\pi_i} \not\leftrightarrow p_{\pi_j}$) turns the atomic phase formula into $(\Diamond p_{\pi_i} \wedge \Diamond\neg p_{\pi_j}) \vee (\Diamond\neg p_{\pi_i} \wedge \Diamond p_{\pi_j})$. It follows that model-checking co-admissible formulas is also decidable (for both $\forall^*$ and $\exists^*$). Note that an admissible formula in negative polarity is a co-admissible formula in positive polarity (and vice versa). Finally, since $\mathcal{K} \models \forall \pi_1 \ldots \forall \pi_n.\mathsf{A}.\psi$ if and only if $\mathcal{K} \not\models \exists \pi_1 \ldots \exists \pi_n.\mathsf{E}.\neg\psi$, it follows that model-checking is also decidable for the A modality for both admissible and co-admissible formulas (in both polarities), and for both the $\forall^*$ and $\exists^*$ fragments.

Theorem 3. *Model-checking $\forall^*$ or $\exists^*$ admissible and co-admissible formulas is decidable both for formulas with E and formulas with A.*

4.2   The Accelerating Construction

The admissible formula in the stuttering construction can express many formulas of interest, but the quantifier structure admits no quantifier alternation. We now consider a second decidable fragment for A-HLTL formulas consisting of formulas with arbitrary quantification $\mathbb{Q}_1\pi_1.\mathbb{Q}_2\pi_2.\ldots.\mathbb{Q}_n\pi_n\mathsf{E}.\psi$ such that $\mathbb{Q}_i \in \{\forall, \exists\}$, but where ψ is an admissible formula where all atomic phase formulas use the same atomic predicates $P \subseteq \mathsf{AP}$. We call these admissible formulas *simple admissible formulas*. The proof of decidability proceeds this time by creating the *accelerated* Kripke structure $\mathcal{K}^{acc}$, where paths jump in one step to the next phase change, and reducing to a HyperLTL model-checking problem on $\mathcal{K}^{acc}$.

Accelerated Kripke Structure. The main idea of the acceleration construction is to convert a finite sequence of transitions in $\mathcal{K}$ that only change phase in the last transition into a single transition in $\mathcal{K}^{acc}$. Also, an infinite sequence of transitions with no phase change is transformed into a self-loop around a sink state. The alphabet remains the same, AP. Given $\mathcal{K} = \langle S, S_{init}, \delta, L \rangle$, the accelerated Kripke structure is $\mathcal{K}^{acc} = \langle S^{acc}, S_{init}, \delta^{acc}, L^{acc} \rangle$ where:

- $S^{acc} = S \cup \{s_\perp \mid s \in S\}$ contains two copies of each state in S, where we use $s_\perp$ to denote the sink state associated with s. We use $color(s)$ for the phase of s, that is, the concrete valuation in s of the Boolean predicates in P of the atomic phase formula.
- For every states $s, s' \in S$ such that $color(s) \neq color(s')$, if there is a finite path $s s_2 s_3 \ldots s_n s'$ in $\mathcal{K}$ such that $color(s) = color(s_2) = \cdots = color(s_n)$, then we add a transition (s, s') to δ^{acc}. These transitions model the jump at the frontier of phase changes. Additionally, if s can be a sink we add a transition $(s, s_\perp)$ and a self-loop from $s_\perp$ to itself.
- $L^{acc}(s) = L(s)$ for $s \in S$, and $L^{acc}(s_\perp) = L(s)$.

This construction can, with standard techniques, be enriched to encode the satisfaction of the temporal monadic formulas along paths of $\mathcal{K}$, and then also accelerate the fairness conditions (annotating the accepting states reached along the accelerated paths) into $\mathcal{K}^{acc}$.

Relating Paths to Accelerated Paths. We now define two auxiliary functions to aid in the proof.

- The first function, acc, maps paths in $\mathcal{K}$ into paths in $\mathcal{K}^{acc}$. Let s be an arbitrary state of $\mathcal{K}$ and $\rho : ss_1s_2s_3\ldots$ an outgoing path from s. Either there are infinitely many phase changes in ρ or only finitely many changes. We create the path $\rho' = acc(\rho)$ as follows. The initial state of ρ, that is, s, is preserved. The states s_{i_j} in σ that are color changes (that is $color(s_{i_j-1}) \neq color(s_{i_j})$ are also preserved, while the states s_k with $color(s_{k-1}) = color(s_k)$ are removed from ρ. If there are only finitely many color changes in ρ, with r being the last state preserved, then we pad the path with $r_\perp^\omega$, so ρ' is also an infinite path. It is easy to see that ρ' is a path of $\mathcal{K}^{acc}$ outgoing s. It is also easy to see that the phase changes in ρ and ρ' are the same.
- The second map, dec, takes a path $\rho' : ss_1's_2'\ldots$ of $\mathcal{K}^{acc}$ and maps it to a path of $\mathcal{K}$ as follows. For every transition (s_i', s_{i+1}') in ρ such that s_{i+1}' is not of the form $r_\perp$, there is a finite path $r_1r_2\ldots r_m$ in $\mathcal{K}$ from s_i' into s_{i+1}' that visits only states with the same color as s_i', except s_{i+1} that is a color change. In ρ, we insert $r_1r_2\ldots r_m$ between s_i' and s_{i+1}'. Now, if for some j, s_j' is of the form $r_\perp$ then $s_k' = r_\perp$ for all $k > j$. In $\mathcal{K}$ there must an infinite path from s_j' that only visits the same color as s_j'. We remove all successor states after the first such $r_\perp$ state and replace it with one such infinite path.

Given a trace assignment Π for formula $\mathbb{Q}_1\pi_1.\ldots.\mathbb{Q}_n\pi_n.\mathsf{E}.\psi$ that assigns $\Pi(\pi_i) = (\sigma_i, 0)$ for every i and a path assignment Π' for formula $\mathbb{Q}_1\pi_1.\ldots.\mathbb{Q}_n\pi_n.\psi$ that assigns $\Pi'(\pi)i = (\sigma_i', 0)$, we write $acc(\Pi) = \Pi'$ if the paths that generate the corresponding traces are related by acc. Similarly we defined $dec(\Pi') = \Pi$. It is easy to show from the construction above that if $\Pi \models \mathsf{E}\psi$ then $acc(\Pi) \models \psi$, and if $\Pi' \models \psi$ then $dec(\Pi') \models \mathsf{E}\psi$.

The main result for the accelerating construction follows immediately from this observation and allows to reduce the model-checking problem to HyperLTL.

Theorem 4. *Let $\mathcal{K}$ be an arbitrary Kripke structure, $\mathbb{Q}_1\pi_1.\ldots.\mathbb{Q}_n\pi_n.\mathsf{E}.\psi$ such that ψ is a simple admissible formula. Then $\mathcal{K} \models \mathbb{Q}_1\pi_1.\ldots.\mathbb{Q}_n\pi_n\mathsf{E}.\psi$ if and only if $\mathcal{K}^{acc} \models \mathbb{Q}_1\pi_1.\ldots.\mathbb{Q}_n\pi_n.\psi$.*

4.3   Decidable Practical A-HLTL Formulas

We revisit the properties expressed in Sect. 3.2.

- *Linearizability.* The property φ_{LNZ} is of the form $\forall\pi.\exists\pi'.\mathsf{E}.\square(\text{history}_\pi \leftrightarrow \text{history}_{\pi'})$ where the temporal formula is a simple admissible formula. Therefore φ_{LNZ} is decidable by the accelerating construction.
- *Goguen and Meseguer's non-interference.* The property φ_{GMNI} is expressed by $\forall\pi.\exists\pi'.\mathsf{E}.(\square\lambda_{\pi'}) \wedge \square(lo_\pi \leftrightarrow lo_{\pi'})$, that is, a Boolean combination of a monadic temporal formula and a simple admissible formula. Therefore, φ_{GMNI} is decidable by the acceleration algorithm.
- *Not never terminates.* Formula φ_{NNT} is simply a Boolean combination of state formulas and monadic temporal formulas: $\forall\pi.\exists\pi'.\exists\pi''.\mathsf{E}.(\pi[0] = \pi'[0] = \pi''[0]) \rightarrow (\Diamond\,\text{term}_{\pi'} \wedge \square\neg\text{term}_{\pi''})$, so it is again decidable by the acceleration construction.

- *Termination-insensitive noninterference.* To handle φ_{TIN} we rewrite the formula as follows

$$\varphi_{\mathsf{TIN}} \stackrel{\text{def}}{=} \forall\pi.\forall\pi'.\mathsf{E}.\left(l_\pi \leftrightarrow l_{\pi'}\right) \rightarrow \left(\begin{array}{c}(\Box\neg\mathsf{term}_\pi \vee \Box\neg\mathsf{term}_{\pi'}) \vee \\ \Box((l_\pi \wedge \mathsf{term}_\pi) \leftrightarrow (l_{\pi'} \wedge \mathsf{term}_{\pi'}))\end{array}\right)$$

Note that $(l_\pi \wedge \mathsf{term}_\pi)$ can be turned into a state predicate of π. This formula is equivalent because the last case is evaluates precisely to $l_\pi \leftrightarrow l_{\pi'}$ when both traces terminate. This formula can be handled by the stuttering construction.

- *Termination-sensitive noninterference.* Similarly, to handle φ_{TSN} we rewrite the formula as

$$\varphi_{\mathsf{TSN}} \stackrel{\text{def}}{=} \forall\pi.\forall\pi'.\mathsf{E}.\left(l_\pi \leftrightarrow l_{\pi'}\right) \rightarrow \left(\begin{array}{c}(\Box\neg\mathsf{term}_\pi \wedge \Box\neg\mathsf{term}_{\pi'}) \vee \\ \Box((l_\pi \wedge \mathsf{term}_\pi) \leftrightarrow (l_{\pi'} \wedge \mathsf{term}_{\pi'}))\end{array}\right)$$

This is again equivalent because the last case again is the only relevant case when both paths terminate. Again, this case is covered by the stuttering construction.

5 Undecidability and Lower-Bound Complexity

In this section, we show that the general problem of model-checking A-HLTL is undecidable. Then, we show a polynomial reduction from the synchronous HyperLTL model-checking into A-HLTL model-checking, which shows that even for those A-HLTL formulas for which the model-checking is decidable, this problem is no easier than the corresponding problem for HyperLTL, which is known to be PSPACE-hard in the size of the Kripke structure.

Theorem 5. *Let $\mathcal{K}$ be a Kripke structure and φ be an asynchronous HyperLTL formula. The problem of determining whether or not $\mathcal{K} \models \varphi$ is undecidable.*

Proof (sketch). We reduce the complement of the *post correspondence problem (PCP)* [23,26] to the A-HLTL model checking problem. PCP consists of a set of dominos, for example, of the form $[\frac{w}{v}] = \{[\frac{b}{ca}], [\frac{a}{ab}], [\frac{ca}{a}], [\frac{abc}{c}]\}$ and the problem is to decide whether there is a sequence of dominos (with possible repetitions), such that the upper and lower finite strings of the dominos are equal. A solution to the above set of dominos is the sequence $[\frac{a}{ab}][\frac{b}{ca}][\frac{ca}{a}][\frac{a}{ab}][\frac{abc}{c}]$. We map a given set of dominos to a Kripke structure that allows arranging the dominos in a sequence (see Fig. 6 for an example), where v and w indicate lower and upper words, respectively, dom^i is for each domino $[\frac{w_i}{v_i}]$, and proposition lc marks whether or not a new letter is processed. The A-HLTL formula in our reduction is the following such that $dom_{\pi_w} \stackrel{\text{def}}{=} \bigvee_{i\in[1..k]} dom^i_{\pi_w}$:

$$\varphi_{\overline{pcp}} \stackrel{\text{def}}{=} \forall\pi_w \forall\pi_v.\mathsf{E}.\left(\varphi_{type} \rightarrow (\varphi_{domino} \vee \varphi_{word})\right)$$

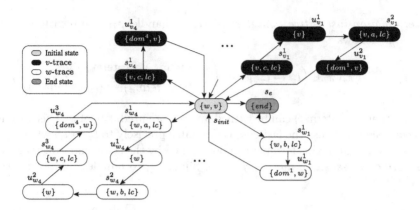

Fig. 6. Mapping from PCP to model checking A-HLTL (only construction for dominos $[\frac{w_1}{v_1}] = [\frac{b}{ca}]$ and $[\frac{w_4}{v_4}] = [\frac{abc}{c}]$ are shown).

where $\quad \varphi_{type} \stackrel{\text{def}}{=} \left((w_{\pi_w} \wedge \neg v_{\pi_w}) \, \mathcal{U} \, end_{\pi_w} \right) \wedge \left((\neg w_{\pi_v} \wedge v_{\pi_v}) \, \mathcal{U} \, end_{\pi_v} \right)$

$$\varphi_{domino} \stackrel{\text{def}}{=} \Box(dom_{\pi_w} \leftrightarrow dom_{\pi_v}) \wedge \Diamond \bigvee_{i=1}^{k} dom^i_{\pi_w} \not\leftrightarrow dom^i_{\pi_v}$$

$$\varphi_{word} \stackrel{\text{def}}{=} \Box(lc_{\pi_w} \leftrightarrow lc_{\pi_v}) \wedge \Diamond \bigvee_{l \in \Sigma_{pcp}} (l_{\pi_w} \not\leftrightarrow l_{\pi_v})$$

The intention of formula $\varphi_{\overline{pcp}}$ is that the Kripke structure is a model of the formula if and only if the original PCP problem has *no* solution. Intuitively, formula φ_{type} forces trace π_w (respectively, π_v) to traverse only the traces labeled by w (respectively, v) to build a w-word (respectively, v-word). Formula φ_{domino} establishes that the trajectory aligns the positions at which the domino indices are checked and at last once the index is different. Finally, formula φ_{word} captures if π_w and π_v are aligned to compare the letters, at least one pair of the letters prescribed by the existential trajectory are different. In the detailed proof in [4], we show that the constructed Kripke structure satisfies formula $\varphi_{\overline{pcp}}$ if and only if the answer to deciding PCP is negative. □

Theorem 5 above implies that there is no algorithm to decide the model-checking problem correctly for every formula and every system. However, as we saw in Sect. 4 for some formulas the model-checking problem is decidable. We now show that in these cases the problem is at least as hard as model-checking HyperLTL, which is known to be PSPACE-hard [7,24].

Theorem 6. *Given a HyperLTL formula φ and a Kripke structure $\mathcal{K}$ there is a A-HLTL formula φ' and a Kripke structure $\mathcal{K}'$ such that $\mathcal{K}'$ is linear in the size of $\mathcal{K}$, φ' is polynomial on the size of φ and $\mathcal{K} \models \varphi$ if and only if $\mathcal{K}' \models \varphi'$.*

The proof proceeds as follow. Giving $\mathcal{K}$ we build a Kripke structure $\mathcal{K}'$ that alternates between real states in $\mathcal{K}$ and synchronization states. Then the formula is transformed to force alternations at every other step, therefore forcing the trajectory to synchronize (see [4] for details). Since the model-checking problem for HyperLTL is PSPACE-hard on the size of the Kripke structure, the same follows for A-HLTL.

Corollary 2. *For asynchronous HyperLTL formulas, the model checking problem is PSPACE-hard in the size of the system.*

6 Case Studies and Evaluation

We applied our algorithm for the $\forall_\pi^* E$ A-HLTL fragment to several examples. After manually reducing the asynchronous model checking problem to a synchronous one, we use MCHYPER [10,11] to check our property. MCHYPER is a model checker for synchronous HyperLTL that can handle formulas with up to one quantifier alternation. It computes the self composition of the system and composes it with the formula automaton. ABC [6] is then used as the backend tool checking the reachability of a violation.

Our reduction from the asynchronous to the synchronous semantics follows the stuttering construction described in Sect. 4.1. To model check a system against an A-HLTL formula, we first add a stuttering input to the system that forces the system to stutter in the current state. The transformed formula ensures that the stuttering guarantees synchronous phase changes. In future work, we will fully automate our reduction resulting in a verification tool for asynchronous hyperproperties from the decidable fragment. We now describe the various case studies[1]. All our experiments were performed on a MacBook Pro with a 3.3 GHz processor and 16 GB of RAM running MacOS 11.1.

6.1 Compiler Optimizations

We modeled the source and target programs of different compiler optimization techniques (from [20]) as finite state machines encoded as circuits, and used asynchronous hyperproperties to prove the correspondence between both programs. We analyzed the following optimizations:

- Common Branch Factorization (CBF), where expressions occurring in both branches of a conditional are factored out;
- Loop Peeling (LP), which consists in unrolling of a loop that is executed at least once;
- Dead Branch Elimination (DBE), that is, removing conditional checks and their branches that are unreachable; and
- Expression Flatting (EF), which splits complex computations into several explicit steps.

---

[1] The experimental data is publicly available at https://github.com/reactive-systems/ MCHyper in `case-studies/asynchronous-hyperltl_2021`.

Table 1. Verification times of MCHYPER and system sizes in number of latches (#LS) and AND-gates (#ANDS) for the case studies.

Optimizations	System Size		Time (s)
	#LS	#ANDS	
EF	12	64	0.6
DBE	16	128	0.8
CBF	16	145	2.7
LP	28	514	365.9
CBF+DBE	16	137	11.4
CBF+DBE+EF	20	175	10.0
CBF+EF	20	180	1.7
EF+LP	41	8642	1315.2

(a) Compiler Optimizations

Propery	System Size		Time (s)
	#LS	#ANDS	
SPI-correct	30	175	65.7
SPI-term	33	296	155.8

(b) SPI

Besides evaluating each optimization individually, we also examined several combinations of these optimizations. Each optimization affects the alignment between source and target program, so synchronous hyperproperties fail to recognize the correspondence between both programs. Using asynchronous hyperproperties instead allows us to compensate for this misalignment by stuttering the programs accordingly. Essentially, each optimization is checked against the following A-HLTL formula in which π represents traces from the source program and π' traces from the target program:

$$\forall \pi. \forall \pi'. \mathsf{E}. (\bigwedge_{i \in I} i_\pi \leftrightarrow i_{\pi'}) \rightarrow (\Box \bigwedge_{o \in O} o_\pi \leftrightarrow o_{\pi'})$$

This formula states that for all pairs of traces that initially agree on the inputs from the set I there exists a trajectory that aligns the phase changes of the outputs in set O. We use the stuttering construction and MCHYPER to verify that in all cases the source and target programs go through the same phases of possibly different length. The results of this case study are summarized in Table 1(a). We note that A-HLTL model-checking subsumes the approach in [20] based on construction of a *buffer automaton* to reason about the alignment of executions.

6.2   SPI Bus Protocol

The Serial Peripheral Interface (SPI) is a bus protocol that supports a single main component's communication with multiple secondary components. Each secondary can be selected individually by the main via the secondary's own *ss* ("secondary select") input signal. If a secondary is enabled (that is, if $\neg ss$ holds as the secondary select is "active low"), it reads the *mosi* (main out, secondary in) signal and writes to the *miso* (main in, secondary out) wire.

We verify the behavior of a single SPI secondary component that receives an input which it sends to the main component upon request. This behavior should always be the same, independent of when the secondary is enabled or how fast the bus protocol's "serial clock" (*sclk*) set by the main component ticks compared to the secondary's internal clock. The A-HLTL formula we check is the following (see observational determinism in Sect. 1):

$$
\forall \pi. \forall \pi'. \mathrm{E}. \left(\begin{array}{c} \bigwedge\limits_{i \in \{in, init\}} i_\pi \leftrightarrow i_{\pi'} \\ \wedge \\ SPI \ input \ assumptions \end{array} \right) \rightarrow \Box \left(\begin{array}{c} (miso_\pi \wedge \neg sclk_\pi \wedge \neg ss_\pi) \\ \leftrightarrow \\ (miso_{\pi'} \wedge \neg sclk_{\pi'} \wedge \neg ss_{\pi'}) \end{array} \right)
$$

This formula (called SPI-correct in Table 1(b)) ensures that for all pairs of traces π and π' that agree on the initial configuration, on the input, and additional *SPI input assumptions*, there is a trajectory that aligns their relevant behavior. We consider it relevant that both secondaries agree on their *miso* output whenever they are enabled and the *sclk* is low. Checking *miso* only when the *sclk* is low is sufficient as changes on *miso* only occur at falling edges of the *sclk*. The *SPI input assumptions* are required to guarantee the implicit assumptions of the protocol, for example, that the *sclk* behaves as an infinitely ticking clock. By introducing additional variables and applying logical transformations, we obtain an equivalent formula that syntactically lies in the fragment of the stuttering construction. Again, we reduce this model checking problem to the synchronous semantics and use MCHYPER to perform the verification.

In a second experiment, we modified the system to send the value only once and checked it for termination insensitive noninterference SPI-term (see Sects. 3.2 and 4.3). In our setup, we use the variable *term* to flag that the secondary has sent the full value. In the premise of the formula, we require that the input value is equal on both traces and again assume that the inputs conform to the SPI protocol. The conclusion checks if both secondaries have sent the same values by using additional variables that are set together with *term*. The results of this case study are summarized in Table 1(b).

7   Related Work

The study of specific hyperproperties, such as noninterference, dates back to the seminal work by Goguen and Meseguer [14] in the 1980s. The first systematic study of hyperproperties is due to Clarkson and Schneider [8].

It is well-known that classic specification languages like LTL cannot express hyperproperties. There are two principal methods with which the standard logics have been extended to express hyperproperties:

- The first method is the quantification over variables that identify specific paths or traces. The temporal logics LTL, CTL* have been extended with quantification over traces and paths, resulting in the temporal logics Hyper-LTL and HyperCTL* [7]. There are also extensions of the μ-calculus, most

recently, the temporal fixpoint calculus H_μ [15], which extends the linear time μ-calculus [3] with path quantifiers and indexed next operators.
- The second method is the addition of the equal-level predicate E to first-order and second-order logics, like MPL, MSO, FOL, and S1S, which results in the logics FOL[E], S1S[E], MPL[E], MSO[E] [9,13].

HyperCTL*, MPL[E], and MSO[E] are branching-time logics, we therefore focus in the following on the linear-time logics HyperLTL, H_μ, FOL[E], and S1S[E]. Among these logics, HyperLTL is the only logic for which practical model-checking algorithms are known [10,11,17]. For HyperLTL, the algorithms have been implemented in the model checkers MCHyper and bounded model checker HyperQube. As discussed in this paper, HyperLTL is limited to synchronous hyperproperties.

FOL[E] can express a limited form of asynchronous hyperproperties. As shown in [9], FOL[E] is subsumed by HyperLTL with additional quantification over predicates. Using such predicates as "markers," one can relate different positions in different traces. However, only a finite number of such predicates is available in each formula. S1S[E] is known to be strictly more expressive than FOL[E] [9], and conjectured to subsume H_μ [15]. For $S1S[E]$ and H_μ, the model checking problem is in general undecidable; for H_μ, two fragments, the k-synchronous, k-context bounded fragments, have been identified for which model checking remains decidable [15]. Even though some asynchronous properties can be expressed in these decidable fragments of H_μ, there is no systematic study to characterize practical properties that can be encoded. Like S1S[E] and H_μ, asynchronous HyperLTL has an (in general) undecidable model checking problem. However, in this paper we have identified decidable fragments of asynchronous HyperLTL that can express observational determinism, noninterference, and linearizability. A-HLTL is thus the first logic for hyperproperties that can express the major asynchronous hyperproperties of interest within decidable fragments. Furthermore, asynchronous HyperLTL is the first logic for asynchronous hyperproperties with a practical model checking algorithm.

8   Conclusion

We have introduced A-HLTL, a temporal logic to describe asynchronous hyperproperties. This logic extends HyperLTL with *trajectory* modalities, which control when a trace proceeds and when it stutters. Synchronous HyperLTL corresponds to a trajectory that always moves all paths in a lock-step manner. This notion of trajectory allows to define formulas that are invariant under stuttering, paving the way for relevant model-checking optimizations such a partial order reduction and abstraction-refinement techniques in the context of hyperproperties. We show that model-checking A-HLTL formulas is in general undecidable, and identify two fragments of A-HLTL formulas, which cover a rich set of security requirements and can be decided by a reduction to HyperLTL model-checking. This in turn has allowed us to the reuse the existing model-checker MCHYPER.

Future work includes the study of larger decidable fragments (that encompass both fragments studied here), extending the logic allowing several trajectory modalities, as well as their implementation in practical tools. Extending bounded model-checking [17] to A-HLTL is another interesting research problem. Asynchronous hyperproperties are important for applying a logic-based verification approach to verify hyperproperties for *software* programs, because the relative speed of the execution of programs depends on many factors like the compiler, hardware, execution platform and concurrent running programs, that the analysis must tolerate. Therefore, future work includes adapting techniques for infinite-state software model-checking, like deductive methods, abstraction, etc. to verify A-HLTL properties of software systems.

References

1. Alpern, B., Schneider, F.B.: Defining liveness. Inf. Process. Lett. **21**, 181–185 (1985)
2. Askarov, A., Hunt, S., Sabelfeld, A., Sands, D.: Termination-insensitive noninterference leaks more than just a bit. In: Jajodia, S., Lopez, J. (eds.) ESORICS 2008. LNCS, vol. 5283, pp. 333–348. Springer, Heidelberg (2008). https://doi.org/10.1007/978-3-540-88313-5_22
3. Barringer, H., Kuiper, R., Pnueli, A.: A really abstract concurrent model and its temporal logic. In: Proceedings of the 13th Annual ACM Symposium on Principles of Programming Languages (POPL 1986), pp. 173–183. ACM (1986)
4. Baumeister, J., Coenen, N., Bonakdarpour, B., Finkbeiner, B., Sánchez, C.: A temporal logic for asynchronous hyperproperties. CoRR, abs/2104.14025 (2021)
5. Bonakdarpour, B., Sanchez, C., Schneider, G.: Monitoring hyperproperties by combining static analysis and runtime verification. In: Margaria, T., Steffen, B. (eds.) ISoLA 2018, Part II. LNCS, vol. 11245, pp. 8–27. Springer, Cham (2018). https://doi.org/10.1007/978-3-030-03421-4_2
6. Brayton, R., Mishchenko, A.: ABC: an academic industrial-strength verification tool. In: Touili, T., Cook, B., Jackson, P. (eds.) CAV 2010. LNCS, vol. 6174, pp. 24–40. Springer, Heidelberg (2010). https://doi.org/10.1007/978-3-642-14295-6_5
7. Clarkson, M.R., Finkbeiner, B., Koleini, M., Micinski, K.K., Rabe, M.N., Sánchez, C.: Temporal logics for hyperproperties. In: Abadi, M., Kremer, S. (eds.) POST 2014. LNCS, vol. 8414, pp. 265–284. Springer, Heidelberg (2014). https://doi.org/10.1007/978-3-642-54792-8_15
8. Clarkson, M.R., Schneider, F.B.: Hyperproperties. J. Comput. Secur. **18**(6), 1157–1210 (2010)
9. Coenen, N., Finkbeiner, B., Hahn, C., Hofmann, J.: The hierarchy of hyperlogics. In: Proceedings of the 34th Annual ACM/IEEE Symposium on Logic in Computer Science (LICS 2019), pp. 1–13. IEEE (2019)
10. Coenen, N., Finkbeiner, B., Sánchez, C., Tentrup, L.: Verifying hyperliveness. In: Dillig, I., Tasiran, S. (eds.) CAV 2019, Part I. LNCS, vol. 11561, pp. 121–139. Springer, Cham (2019). https://doi.org/10.1007/978-3-030-25540-4_7
11. Finkbeiner, B., Rabe, M.N., Sánchez, C.: Algorithms for model checking HyperLTL and HyperCTL*. In: Kroening, D., Păsăreanu, C.S. (eds.) CAV 2015, Part I. LNCS, vol. 9206, pp. 30–48. Springer, Cham (2015). https://doi.org/10.1007/978-3-319-21690-4_3

12. Finkbeiner, B., Rabe, M.N., Sánchez, C.: A temporal logic for hyperproperties. CoRR, abs/1306.6657 (2013)
13. Finkbeiner, B., Zimmermann, M.: The first-order logic of hyperproperties. In: 34th Symposium on Theoretical Aspects of Computer Science, STACS 2017, 8–11 Mar 2017, Hannover, Germany, pp. 30:1–30:14 (2017)
14. Goguen, J.A., Meseguer, J.: Security policies and security models. In: Proceedings of the IEEE Symposium on Security and Privacy, pp. 11–20 (1982)
15. Gutsfeld, J.O., Müller-Olm, M., Ohrem, C.: Automata and fixpoints for asynchronous hyperproperties. Proc. ACM Program. Lang. 5(POPL), 1–29 (2021)
16. Herlihy, M., Wing, J.M.: Linearizability: a correctness condition for concurrent objects. ACM Trans. Program. Lang. Syst. 12(3), 463–492 (1990)
17. Hsu, T.-H., Sánchez, C., Bonakdarpour, B.: Bounded model checking for hyperproperties. In: TACAS 2021, Part I. LNCS, vol. 12651, pp. 94–112. Springer, Cham (2021). https://doi.org/10.1007/978-3-030-72016-2_6
18. Lamport, L.: "Sometime" is sometimes "not never" - on the temporal logic of programs. In: Proceedings of the Seventh Annual ACM Symposium on Principles of Programming Languages (POPL 1980), pp. 174–185. ACM Press (1980)
19. Manna, Z., Pnueli, A.: Temporal Verification of Reactive Systems. Springer-Verlag, New York (1995). https://doi.org/10.1007/978-1-4612-4222-2
20. Namjoshi, K.S., Tabajara, L.M.: Witnessing secure compilation. In: Beyer, D., Zufferey, D. (eds.) VMCAI 2020. LNCS, vol. 11990, pp. 1–22. Springer, Cham (2020). https://doi.org/10.1007/978-3-030-39322-9_1
21. Pnueli, A.: The temporal logic of programs. In: Symposium on Foundations of Computer Science (FOCS), pp. 46–57 (1977)
22. Pnueli, A., Siegel, M., Singerman, E.: Translation validation. In: Steffen, B. (ed.) TACAS 1998. LNCS, vol. 1384, pp. 151–166. Springer, Heidelberg (1998). https://doi.org/10.1007/BFb0054170
23. Post, E.L.: A variant of a recursively unsolvable problem. Bull. Am. Math. Soc. 52, 264–268 (1946)
24. Rabe, M.N.: A Temporal Logic Approach to Information-flow Control. PhD thesis, Saarland University (2016)
25. Sabelfeld, A., Sands, D.: A per model of secure information flow in sequential programs. High. Order Symb. Comput. 14(1), 59–91 (2001)
26. Sipser, M.: Introduction to the Theory of Computation. MIT Press, Boston (2012)
27. Wang, Y., Zarei, M., Bonakdarpour, B., Pajic, M.: Statistical verification of hyperproperties for cyber-physical systems. ACM Trans. Embed. Comput. Syst. (TECS) 18(5s), 92:1–92:23 (2019)
28. Zdancewic, S., Myers, A.C.: Observational determinism for concurrent program security. In: Proceedings of the 16th IEEE Computer Security Foundations Workshop (CSFW), p. 29 (2003)

Product Programs in the Wild: Retrofitting Program Verifiers to Check Information Flow Security

Marco Eilers(✉)🆔, Severin Meier, and Peter Müller🆔

Department of Computer Science, ETH Zurich,
Zurich, Switzerland
{marco.eilers,peter.mueller}@inf.ethz.ch

Abstract. Most existing program verifiers check trace properties such as functional correctness, but do not support the verification of hyperproperties, in particular, information flow security. In principle, product programs allow one to reduce the verification of hyperproperties to trace properties and, thus, apply standard verifiers to check them; in practice, product constructions are usually defined only for simple programming languages without features like dynamic method binding or concurrency and, consequently, cannot be directly applied to verify information flow security in a full-fledged language. However, many existing verifiers encode programs from source languages into simple intermediate verification languages, which opens up the possibility of constructing a product program on the intermediate language level, reusing the existing encoding and drastically reducing the effort required to develop new verification tools for information flow security.

In this paper, we explore the potential of this approach along three dimensions: (1) Soundness: We show that the combination of an encoding and a product construction that are individually sound can still be unsound, and identify a novel condition on the encoding that ensures overall soundness. (2) Concurrency: We show how sequential product programs on the intermediate language level can be used to verify information flow security of concurrent source programs. (3) Performance: We implement a product construction in Nagini, a Python verifier built upon the Viper intermediate language, and evaluate it on a number of challenging examples. We show that the resulting tool offers acceptable performance, while matching or surpassing existing tools in its combination of language feature support and expressiveness.

1 Introduction

Since computer programs increasingly handle sensitive user data and communicate using encryption, it is vital that programs do not leak secret data such as private keys to attackers, that is, that they are *information flow secure*. One way of formalizing information flow security is *noninterference*, a so-called *2-hyperproperty*, i.e., a property of pairs of executions of the program.

© The Author(s) 2021
A. Silva and K. R. M. Leino (Eds.) CAV 2021, LNCS 12759, pp. 718–741, 2021.
https://doi.org/10.1007/978-3-030-81685-8_34

Noninterference can be checked by type systems [45] and static analyses [22]. However, complex language features (such as concurrency) and noninterference properties (such as termination sensitivity) generally require the expressiveness of deductive verification. In recent years, many automated and expressive verification tools have been developed for a wide range of programming languages, but most of these tools are limited to trace properties (properties of single program traces) and cannot prove hyperproperties such as noninterference.

The problem we address in this paper is how to retrofit existing program verifiers to check noninterference. Compared to building noninterference verifiers from scratch, which can take years when targeting substantial subsets of real-world programming languages, this approach would allow us to reuse most aspects of existing verifiers, such as the semantic representation of language features and proof search algorithms. Moreover, it naturally allows one to verify combinations of correctness and noninterference properties.

In principle, existing program verifiers can be used to verify hyperproperties by reducing them to trace properties via self-composition [6] or product programs [4,5]. However, self-composition does not allow modular verification [48], and product programs have generally been defined only for simple languages without features like dynamic method binding or concurrency [4,18]. Applying product constructions to programs written in complex languages would therefore require defining and implementing new and complex product constructions for every new verifier.

We explore a more efficient approach here: We leverage the fact that most automatic deductive verifiers are organized into a custom frontend, which encodes a source program into an intermediate verification language (IVL), and a reusable backend, which verifies the IVL program using generic proof search engines. Boogie [3], Viper [35], and Why3 [21] are examples of such IVLs, which power a large number of program verifiers; for instance Boogie is used by Dafny [29], VCC [13], Spec# [30], and GPUVerify [8], Why3 [21] by Frama-C [14] and Krakatoa [20], and Viper [35] by Vercors [10], Prusti [2], and Nagini [17]. The ubiquitiy of this architecture offers a chance to retrofit existing verifiers to check noninterference by performing the product construction on the level of the IVL (an approach that is already used by SymDiff [27] for the related problem of program equivalence). The resulting architecture, which allows one to reuse both the frontend and the backend of the existing verifier, is shown in Fig. 1.

Performing the product construction on the IVL-level has three major advantages over a product construction on the source program: (1) It cleanly separates the encoding of the source language (which tends to be complex for full-fledged languages) from the product construction. (2) The product construction is much simpler since IVLs are small, sequential languages. (3) The product construction can be reused across all verifiers built on the same IVL. Overall, this architecture therefore has the potential to make existing verifiers information flow aware with substantially less effort than building a new tool from scratch.

Even though this approach has strong advantages, there are several open questions that must be addressed to make it useful and widely applicable:

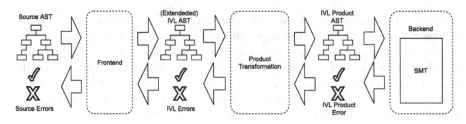

Fig. 1. Proposed architecture for information flow verifiers. The existing encoding from source to IVL (frontend) as well as the proof search (backend) can be reused. The product construction needs to support only the (relatively small) IVL and can be reused across different verifiers.

1. Soundness: Given an IVL encoding and a product construction that are individually sound, is the resulting combination always sound as well?
2. Concurrency: There is a substantial number of verifiers that verify concurrent source programs by encoding them into (sequential) IVLs. Can we soundly verify information flow security of concurrent programs based on the a product program of the sequential IVL encoding?
3. Performance: Product constructions cause a performance penalty for verification. Does this overhead prevent the construction of useful verification tools in practice?

In this paper, we answer these three questions. We focus our investigation on modular product programs [18], a kind of product program that allows modular verification and is well-suited for precise specification and verification of information flow security. We make the following contributions:

– We show that the combination of sound IVL encodings and sound product constructions can indeed be unsound in practically-relevant cases. We identify a novel condition on IVL encodings that ensures the soundness of the overall workflow. We show how to adjust existing unsound encodings on the example of a commonly-used encoding for dynamically-bound method calls (Sect. 3).
– We show for the common case of data race free programs using locks that it is possible to verify both possibilistic and probabilistic noninterference for concurrent programs using sequential product programs. Furthermore, we demonstrate that existing criteria for verifying information flow security are insufficient in this setting; we provide alternative criteria that are sound and show how to encode them in a product program (Sect. 4).
– We implement the approach for Nagini [17], an automated, modular verification tool for a large subset of Python, built on top of the Viper IVL [35]. We evaluate the performance impact of the product construction and show that, while worse than a custom-made information flow verifier, performance is acceptable for real-world use (Sect. 5). Our implementation and evaluation are available as an artifact [16].

These results demonstrate that the proposed approach can indeed be used to retrofit an existing verifier to *soundly* check information flow security, even for concurrent programs. The resulting tool, made with only a fraction of the effort required for the development of a new verifier, can compete with custom-made tools in its expressiveness at an acceptable performance cost.

2   Preliminaries

In this section, we introduce the necessary background about noninterference and product programs.

2.1   Noninterference

A common way of formalizing information flow security is *noninterference* [23]. Informally, noninterference specifies that the secret (or *high*) inputs of a program do not influence the values of its public (or *low*) outputs. We will not define a formal semantics here, but just assume that there is a steps-to relation $\langle s, \sigma \rangle \rightarrow \langle s', \sigma' \rangle$ that relates program configurations consisting of a store σ and a statement s.

We formalize noninterference as a property of pairs of program executions (that is, a *2-hyperproperty* [12]) as follows:

Definition 1. *A program s with a set of input variables I and output variables O, of which some subsets $I_l \subseteq I$ and $O_l \subseteq O$ are low, satisfies noninterference iff for all σ_1, σ_2 and σ_1', σ_2', if $\forall x \in I_l. \sigma_1(x) = \sigma_2(x)$ and $\langle s, \sigma_1 \rangle \rightarrow^* \langle \mathtt{skip}, \sigma_1' \rangle$ and $\langle s, \sigma_2 \rangle \rightarrow^* \langle \mathtt{skip}, \sigma_2' \rangle$ then $\forall x \in O_l. \sigma_1'(x) = \sigma_2'(x)$.*

Note that in this definition (and throughout this paper unless stated otherwise), we do not consider non-terminating executions, i.e., we focus on verifying termination-insensitive noninterference.

2.2   Modular Product Programs

Proving hyperproperties requires reasoning about multiple (here, two) executions of a program. However, hyperproperties can be reduced to properties of a single execution by using *self-composition* [6] or *product programs* [4]. The idea is to duplicate a program's state space by creating two renamed copies of all variables, one for each execution (we write $x^{(i)}$ for the ith renaming of variable x, and lift this notation to expressions), and to transform each statement so that it has the effect of the original statement on both copies of the state. Unlike self-composition, which achieves this effect by simply duplicating every statement, *modular product programs* [18] do not duplicate loops and method calls, and instead encode differing control flow through *activation variables*, which represent, for each execution, whether or not it is active (i.e., it executes the code) at the current point in the program. This approach results in a structural alignment

```
def bar(z): ...                   1    def bar(p1, p2, z1, z2): ...
                                  2
def foo(x):                       3    def foo(p1, p2, x1, x2):
    if x > 0:                     4        p1t = p1 and x1 > 0
        y = 1                     5        p2t = p2 and x2 > 0
    else:                         6        p1e = p1 and not (x1 > 0)
        y = 2                     7        p2e = p2 and not (x2 > 0)
    bar(y > 0)                    8        if p1t: y1 = 1
                                  9        if p2t: y2 = 1
                                 10        if p1e: y1 = 2
                                 11        if p2e: y2 = 2
                                 12        if p1 or p2:
                                 13            bar(p1, p2, y1 > 0, y2 > 0)
```

Fig. 2. A modular product program (on the right) of the program on the left.

of both program executions, which allows one to use method specifications and loop invariants that relate both executions, as we discuss below. We denote the product of statement s under activation variables $p1$ and $p2$ as $[\![s]\!]^{\dot{p}}$.

Figure 2 shows an example program and the respective product program. For both functions, the product program duplicates the parameters of the original function and adds boolean activation variables $p1$ and $p2$. Control structures like conditionals are encoded by creating a set of new activation variables (lines 4–7). For example, $p1t$ represents whether the first execution is active in the then-branch of the conditional, which is the case if it was active at the beginning of the function and the if-condition is true for the first execution. Conversely, $p2e$ represents whether the second execution is active in the else-branch. Primitive statements like assignments are then executed under the condition that their execution is active at the current point in the execution (lines 8–11). Crucially, the method call to bar is *not* duplicated; it is executed if at least one execution is active at the call site, and the values of the current activation variables are passed to the function, meaning that if an execution is inactive at the call site, no state changes will be performed for that execution in the called method.

Because a single method call in the product represents the calls from both executions, one can reason about method calls modularly in terms of *relational* specifications, i.e., specifications that relate behavior of two executions of the method, as opposed to *unary* specifications that describe only a single execution. Relational specifications are encoded as ordinary specifications in the product program that relate parameters from the two different executions.

As an example, assume that bar prints the value of its input z, which must therefore be low. We can express this as a (relational) precondition $low(z)$, which can be encoded as the precondition $p1 \wedge p2 \Rightarrow z1 = z2$ in the product of bar.

Events the attacker can observe (such as I/O) must not happen depending on a secret, to avoid leaking secret data. It is, thus, useful to express in specifications that the control flow at the current program point is low, i.e., whether the current statement is executed does not depend on secret data. This property is denoted in specifications as *lowEvent*. We generally write $\lceil P \rceil^{\dot{p}}$ for the encoding of assertion P under activation variables $p1$ and $p2$; $\lceil lowEvent \rceil^{\dot{p}}$ is then defined as $p1 = p2$.

A unary (that is, non-relational) predicate Q, such as a standard method pre- or postcondition, is encoded in the product program as applying to each active execution, i.e., $\lceil Q \rceil^{\mathring{p}}$ is defined as $\mathsf{p1} \Rightarrow Q^{(1)} \land \mathsf{p2} \Rightarrow Q^{(2)}$.

Compared to type systems and taint analyses, verification based on product programs allows for much more precise reasoning. Assume for example that foo's parameter x is high. Nonetheless, we can show that the example does not leak information, since the precondition of bar, $low(\mathsf{z})$, will always be fulfilled ($\mathsf{y} > 0$ is true independently of the value of x). In contrast, security type systems would flag y as high, since it is assigned to under a high guard, leading to imprecision.

In addition to ordinary noninterference, modular product programs can also be used to encode more advanced security properties, including termination-sensitive noninterference, value-dependent sensitivity [36], and a form of declassification [18].

3 Sound Products of IVL Encodings

In this section, we address the first question from the introduction, namely, whether we can soundly combine an existing encoding into an IVL with a product construction. We first describe the proposed architecture in greater detail. Then we show a potential soundness issue and define a sufficient criterion on the IVL encoding for the entire approach to be sound. Finally, we discuss an example of a common encoding pattern that violates the criterion, show that it is indeed unsound, and propose an alternative sound encoding.

3.1 Proposed Architecture

The architecture proposed in the introduction (Fig. 1) enables the construction of information flow aware verifiers with relatively little effort, by reusing most of the frontend encoding of the source language to an IVL as well as the entire backend proof search. The only major change that is necessary is that the frontend and potentially the IVL have to be extended to allow for the use of information flow assertions in specifications. Crucially, the frontend does not have to know their meaning; it can treat relational source-level assertions like $low(e)$ like ordinary unary predicates and simply translate them to their counterparts on the IVL level. IVL-level relational assertions will then be translated to ordinary assertions during the product transformation.

In the remainder of this paper, we will generally assume that the existing IVL encoding is used unchanged, and point out when changes need to be made.

3.2 Soundness Issue

Surprisingly, combining a sound encoding from source language to IVL with a sound IVL-level product construction may result in a verification technique that is *unsound* in the presence of relational specifications. Consider the source program in Fig. 3 (left), where P is some predicate.

```
def foo(x):                          def foo(x):
  if x > 7:                            assert x > 7 ? P(5) : P(7)
    y = 5
  else:
    y = 7
  assert P(y)
```

Fig. 3. Example of an encoding that is unsound in our setting. The program on the left can be encoded into a conditional statement (identical to the source program, modulo language syntax) or to the program on the right; the latter leads to unsoundness if P is a relational predicate.

A frontend could encode the body of foo into an identical (modulo syntax) conditional statement on the IVL level (assuming the IVL provides conditionals, assignments, and assert statements). Alternatively, it could produce the encoding shown in Fig. 3 (right), which directly asserts a sufficient precondition of the source program. If P is a unary predicate, both encodings are sound: If they verify, the original program is correct. However, if $P(y)$ is a relational predicate, for instance, $low(y)$, then the encoding on the right is *unsound*: $low(5)$ and $low(7)$ are trivially true (since $5 = 5$ and $7 = 7$), so the assertion in the encoded program trivially passes, yet the original program is clearly incorrect: If x is greater than 7 in one execution but less in the other, y will have different values in both executions, and will therefore not be low.

The underlying reason is that the encoding on the right does not encode the exact behavior of the source program; it encodes a verification condition computed by the frontend that is sound if assertions are unary, but may not be sound for relational assertions.

We will now (1) formalize this intuition and derive a sufficient condition for the soundness of an encoding in this approach, and (2) show an example of this problem occurring in real frontends, and describe how it can be solved.

3.3 Soundness Criterion

We write Σ and S for states and statements of the source language, and σ and s for states and statements of the IVL. States may contain, for example, a mutable heap and a variable store. For simplicity, we assume that both source and IVL statements contain a statement skip that represents a finished computation. We also assume that there is a small-step transition relation $\rightarrow$ for both languages, and that the standard notion of Hoare triple validity $\vDash \{P\}s\{Q\}$ is defined for the IVL. We let P and Q range over (source and IVL level) assertions from a standard assertion language extended with $low(e)$ and $lowEvent$, and assume a standard definition of assertion validity for pairs of states.

We define an encoding to be a triple $\langle \alpha, \cong, \beta \rangle$, where $\alpha : S \rightarrow s$ is an encoding from source statements to statements of the target language (i.e., the IVL), β similarly encodes assertions to the target language, and $\cong$ relates source language states to corresponding target language states.

We first define the desired relational soundness property, which expresses that if an encoded Hoare triple holds for the encoded program, then the original property holds for all pairs of executions of the source program:

Definition 2. $\langle \alpha, \cong, \beta \rangle$ *is relationally sound iff, for all* $S, \Sigma_1, \Sigma_2, \Sigma_1', \Sigma_2', P, Q,$ *if* $\vDash \{ \lceil \beta(P) \rceil^{\mathring{p}} \} \llbracket \alpha(S) \rrbracket^{\mathring{p}} \{ \lceil \beta(Q) \rceil^{\mathring{p}} \}$ *and* $\Sigma_1, \Sigma_2 \vDash P$ *and* $\langle S, \Sigma_1 \rangle \to^* \langle \mathtt{skip}, \Sigma_1' \rangle$ *and* $\langle S, \Sigma_2 \rangle \to^* \langle \mathtt{skip}, \Sigma_2' \rangle,$ *then* $\Sigma_1', \Sigma_2' \vDash Q.$

Product programs represent the operational behavior of two program executions by the operational behavior of a single product program execution. The unsoundness shown before is caused by the fact that the encoding into the IVL does not reflect the operational behavior of the conditional statement (replacing it by an assertion of a sufficient precondition) and, thus, the resulting product does not soundly reflect two executions of the source program.

We call an encoding that preserves the operational behavior of the source program *operational*: It encodes every step of the source program into some number of steps of the target program so that c initial states result in matching end states. Similarly, it encodes specifications from the source level into target-level specifications that hold in matching states. We can formalize this intuition by requiring that the source and target programs are connected by the simulation relation $\cong$:

Definition 3. $\langle \alpha, \cong, \beta \rangle$ *is an* operational *encoding if: (1) for all* $\Sigma, \Sigma', \sigma, S, S',$ *if* $\langle S, \Sigma \rangle \to \langle S', \Sigma' \rangle$ *and* $\Sigma \cong \sigma,$ *then* $\langle \alpha(S), \sigma \rangle \to^* \langle \alpha(S'), \sigma' \rangle$ *for some* σ' *s.t.* $\Sigma' \cong \sigma',$ *and* (2) *if* $\Sigma \cong \sigma$ *then* $\Sigma \vDash P$ *iff* $\sigma \vDash \beta(P).$

Note that this notion allows the encoding to overapproximate the behaviors of the source program, i.e., admit steps that are not possible on the source level, but not vice versa.

For the example in Fig. 3, it is easy to see that this criterion is fulfilled by the left encoding: the source and IVL programs are identical (modulo syntax), matching states are identical states (modulo state encodings), and the behavior of both programs is identical. The encoding on the right, however, is *not* operational: While the left program modifies the state, the right program never performs any state modification.

We now show that operationality is sufficient for relational soundness:

Theorem 1. *If* $\langle \alpha, \cong, \beta \rangle$ *is operational then it is relationally sound.*

Note that operationality is a sufficient but not necessary condition; encodings of verification conditions may be sound for relational verification as well. The main advantage of applying the operationality criterion instead of directly reasoning about relational soundness is that, since operationality represents the simple notion that the IVL program performs equivalent steps and equivalent state changes to the source program, it is intuitive and easy to check whether a given encoding is operational. Additionally, some encodings (like the one Vercors uses for parallel blocks) are not operational, but can be seen as simplified versions of a possible operational encoding that generate the same proof obligations; these can also be quickly identified as relationally sound.

3.4 Practical Relevance

In most existing frontends, the encoding of virtually all source language constructs is operational; the main appeal of IVLs is, after all, that frontends *do not* have to compute verification conditions, but can instead "compile" input programs into an IVL without worrying about the verification process itself. However, many frontends still use non-operational encodings at least for *some* language constructs. Examples for this are VCC's encoding of local blocks, Dafny's encoding of calls on traits, Prusti's encoding for loops, and Nagini's encoding of dynamically-bound calls, which we will discuss in detail in the next subsection. Additionally, as we will discuss in Sect. 4, all encodings of concurrent source languages into sequential IVLs necessarily have some non-operational elements.

Where non-operational encodings are used, this is often intentional to enable modular verification, since operational encodings for some language constructs are inherently non-modular (see the example in the next subsection). In practice, one can therefore use the operationality criterion to quickly check that the existing encoding is sound for the vast majority of source language statements, and subsequently check the few remaining ones for relational soundness in detail.

3.5 Example: Dynamically-Bound Calls

In this section, we show a real example of an unsound encoding of dynamically-bound calls that violates the operationality criterion, and show how to derive a sound alternative.

Statically-bound method calls, i.e., calls whose exact target is fixed at compile time, can be encoded as procedure calls on the IVL level, which yields an operational encoding if the operational semantics of the IVL treats calls analogously to the source semantics. The IVL verifier might later reason about calls in terms of pre- and postconditions instead of actually performing a call, but this transformation is not relevant here as long as the product program is constructed *before* such a desugaring step.

However, the same approach does not work for dynamically-bound calls, i.e., calls whose target is chosen at runtime based on the type of the call's receiver. Since the implementation to be executed is generally not known during modular verification, it is not possible to encode dynamically-bound calls as procedure calls with the usual operational semantics (and existing IVLs do not offer dynamically-bound calls). Therefore, dynamically-bound calls are typically (e.g., in Dafny and Nagini) directly encoded using the method specification. Additional, separate proof obligations enforce that all overrides of a method respect *behavioral subtyping* [33], i.e., live up to the specification of the overridden method.

Consider method A.foo in Fig. 4 (left), which returns a constant integer and guarantees in its postcondition that the result is low. A dynamically-bound call a.foo(), where a has the static type A, will be encoded as an assertion of the (here, trivial) precondition of A.foo, followed by an assumption of the postcondition (we ignore side effects here for simplicity).

```
class A:                              class B(A):
   def foo(self) -> int:                 def foo(self) -> int:
      # ensures low(result)                 # ensures low(result)
      return 0                              return 1
```

Fig. 4. Example of a problematic method override. B.foo overrides A.foo and has a compatible specification, but the implementations return different values.

This encoding is sound if foo has a purely unary specification, without any relational parts. However, it does *not* fulfill our operationality criterion: The semantics of the source program performs a call to an implementation of foo (selected based on the dynamic type of a), whereas the IVL encoding directly encodes the proof obligations (similarly to the example from Fig. 3).

Since the encoding is not operational, we have to check whether it is still relationally sound. Method B.foo in Fig. 4 (right), which overrides A.foo, shows that it is not. B.foo's contract is identical with that of A.foo, so behavioral subtyping holds trivially. B.foo's implementation satisfies the contract because it also returns a constant (but, importantly, a different one). Now, if a client calls a.foo() and, depending on a secret, the dynamic type of a is either A or B, then, depending on the secret, the result will be either 0 or 1. With the standard encoding of dynamically-bound calls outlined above, however, the client will assume the postcondition of A.foo and will therefore incorrectly conclude that the returned result is low.

To avoid this unsoundness while retaining the ability to use relational specifications[1], the problematic encoding must be replaced, either with an operational one, or with a different non-operational encoding that is sound for relational specifications. The former option is not applicable here: An operational encoding for dynamically-bound calls would essentially have to case split on the dynamic type of the receiver and invoke the appropriate override. Since such an encoding is inherently non-modular (all possible overrides need to be known), we follow the alternative option: we give an example of a non-operational, but sound encoding.

For our new encoding we exploit the fact that the standard encoding is unsound only if the two executions of the program resolve the dynamically-bound call to two different implementations, that is, if the dynamic types of the receiver differ in the two executions. We reflect this observation by adjusting the encoding of pre- and postconditions as follows: (1) If the postcondition of a method guarantees that an expression is low, we assume this at the call site *only if* the dynamic type of the receiver is also low, that is, the calls in the two program executions are resolved to the same implementation. (2) Similarly, if a precondition requires that the call is a low event, we enforce that the receiver type is low in addition to the usual criterion for low events. Low events typically perform observable behavior such as I/O; it is therefore important that the *same* observable behavior is produced, independent of the receiver type. The meaning of low-assertions in preconditions remains unchanged, because the requirement of

---

[1] One could, of course, forbid the use of relational specifications in some places to trivially avoid the unsoundness; this, however, is typically not useful in practice.

a method to receive low arguments is independent of the invoked implementation and must, thus, not be weakened. *lowEvent*-assertions are generally not allowed in postconditions, where they add no expressiveness.

We encode this adjustment as follows:

$$\lceil low(e) \rceil^{\mathring{p}}_{post_r} = (p^{(1)} = p^{(2)} \wedge type(r^{(1)}) = type(r^{(2)})) \Rightarrow e^{(1)} = e^{(2)}$$

$$\lceil lowEvent \rceil^{\mathring{p}}_{pre_r} = p^{(1)} = p^{(2)} \wedge type(r^{(1)}) = type(r^{(2)})$$

where $type(e)$ represents the dynamic type of expression e, $\lceil P \rceil^{\mathring{p}}_{post_r}$ is the encoding of P in the postcondition of a call with receiver r, and $\lceil P \rceil^{\mathring{p}}_{pre_r}$ represents the same for the precondition. We leave the remaining encoding untouched, meaning that we can summarize the resulting encoding as follows:

1. We keep the existing check for behavioral subtyping for all overrides; this prevents, for example, that A.foo is overridden with a method that simply returns a secret value and therefore leaks information into the result.
2. We keep the existing encoding of dynamically-bound calls as an assert followed by an assume, but interpret $low(e)$ in preconditions and *lowEvent* in postconditions as shown above.

In the example above, this encoding lets the caller assume that the result is low only if it can prove that the dynamic type of a is low.

The adjusted encoding is indeed sound:

Theorem 2. *Let S_c be of the form $x{:=}r.m()$, where r has static type A, and let $pre_{A.m}$ and $post_{A.m}$ be the pre- and postcondition of A.m. Assume that the implementation of A.m and its overrides fulfill their specifications and satisfy behavioral subtyping. Then the described encoding of S_c is relationally sound.*

Note that this encoding is incomplete, since it is not aware that two different receiver types can lead to the same implementation being called (e.g., if one type inherits from the second and does not override the called method). Alternative encodings could explicitly represent this possibility. Conversely, one could approximate further (while remaining sound) by requiring the receiver *values* to be low, not just their types, in encodings that do not model dynamic types.

4   Product Programs and Concurrency

Automated verification of information flow security for concurrent programs is challenging because one needs to reason about a pair of executions that may have different thread interleavings. In fact, we are aware of only one tool that currently allows this, SecC, which automates SecCSL, a concurrent separation logic for information flow security proofs [19]. A product construction applied directly to concurrent programs would have to faithfully represent all combinations of potential thread interleavings, which makes verification infeasible. Consequently, to the best of our knowledge, no such product construction exists.

For trace properties, many existing verifiers avoid reasoning about all possible thread interleaving by employing a program logic (such as concurrent separation logic [38]) that essentially reduces verification to sequential reasoning and allows concurrent verification problems to be encoded into sequential IVLs. Examples for such verifiers include Vercors and Nagini (using the Viper IVL), as well as Chalice [32], VCC, and Spec# (using the Boogie IVL).

In this section, we show how to use IVL-level product programs to extend such verifiers to handle information flow. We first describe how existing IVL encodings for concurrent languages work, and subsequently show how we can use similar principles to apply an IVL-based product construction, and which additional proof obligations we must fulfill to ensure that no flows exist as a result of concurrency. We will do this for two different notions of information flow security for concurrent programs, *possibilistic* and *probabilistic* noninterference; however, the principles behind the approach may also extend to alternative notions of information flow security such as observational determinism [49].

Our goal is to describe a technique that applies to a wide range of source languages, IVLs, proof techniques, and encodings. Therefore, we focus on the high-level concepts, instead of formalizing them for one specific setting.

4.1 Concurrent IVL Encodings

Since all IVLs we are aware of are sequential languages, encodings from concurrent source languages to IVLs do not model the exact behavior of the original language, in particular, the aforementioned thread interleavings (i.e., these encodings are non-operational). Instead, they encode a verification condition that ensures that the original program is correct for *every possible* thread interleaving.

While the exact proof techniques differ between frontends, and can be based for example on Concurrent Separation Logic (CSL) [38] or ownership [13,24,26], they generally follow a common pattern [31]: They prove that the source program is data race free, which ensures that thread interactions need to be considered *only* at well-defined synchronization points, for instance, upon acquiring or releasing a lock. The code between such interaction points can be considered to execute without interference from other threads, and thus can be reasoned about as if it were sequential.

We focus on locks here, but other synchronization primitives are handled analogously. Program logics based on CSL or ownership systems formally connect a lock and the heap locations it protects, such that these locations may be accessed only while holding the respective lock. In addition, they associate locks with an invariant that constrains the values of the heap locations it protects. When acquiring a lock, a thread may assume that this lock invariant holds, and when releasing a lock, it has to prove that the invariant is reestablished. A frontend can encode this into an IVL as depicted in Fig. 5.

Our solution for information flow verification in concurrent programs follows the same basic approach: We exploit that code between lock operations can be considered to execute without interference, and that we can therefore use

$enc(\mathsf{I}.\,\mathsf{acquire}\,()) = //$ *gain access to protected memory*;
$\qquad\qquad\qquad$ **assume** $Inv(\mathsf{I})$
$enc(\mathsf{I}.\,\mathsf{release}\,()) = $ **assert** $Inv(\mathsf{I})$;
$\qquad\qquad\qquad //$ *lose access to protected memory*

Fig. 5. Standard IVL encoding of lock operations. $Inv(\mathsf{I})$ denotes the invariant constraining the memory protected by lock I.

ordinary sequential product programs to reason about this code. To capture the thread interactions at synchronization points, we extend lock invariants to contain relational assertions (which can prescribe that some values protected by the lock are low), and add additional checks around lock operations to ensure that they do not give rise to unwanted information flow.

4.2 Possibilistic Noninterference

For concurrent programs, standard noninterference is too strict a property because concurrent programs are usually non-deterministic. One way of approaching this problem is to instead verify *possibilistic noninterference*, which enforces that high information does not influence the *possible* values of low outputs, i.e., if some combination of low output values is reachable from an initial state, then the same combination of low output values must still be reachable using *some* possible thread schedule after arbitrarily changing the high inputs. Possibilistic noninterference can be defined as follows:

Definition 4. *A program s with a set of input variables I and output variables O, of which some subsets $I_l \subseteq I$ and $O_l \subseteq O$ are low, satisfies possibilistic noninterference iff for all σ_1, σ_2 and σ_1', if $\forall x \in I_l.\,\sigma_1(x) = \sigma_2(x)$ and $\langle s, \sigma_1 \rangle \rightarrow^* \langle \mathtt{skip}, \sigma_1' \rangle$ then $\langle s, \sigma_2 \rangle \rightarrow^* \langle \mathtt{skip}, \sigma_2' \rangle$ for some σ_2' s.t. $\forall x \in O_l.\,\sigma_1'(x) = \sigma_2'(x)$.*

Note that this property allows high inputs to influence the *probability* of different outputs and may therefore not be desirable in all scenarios; we discuss a stronger notion of noninterference in the next subsection.

Since we build on a proof technique that ensures data race freedom, we can see each program trace as a sequence of local operations and lock operations by specific threads, where (1) every local operation depends only on previous (local or lock) operations of the same thread, and (2) every lock operation depends only on the previous local operations of the same thread and all previous lock operations (of arbitrary threads). As a result, we can (akin to partial order reduction) rearrange segments freely as long as we retain the overall order of lock operations and the order of operations of every specific thread; in particular, we can rearrange a trace so that it consists of a number of *segments*, such that in each segment, one thread executes any number of local operations and then one lock operation.

$poss(\text{l . acquire ()})$ $= \text{\texttt{assert} } lowEvent;$
                  $\text{\texttt{assert} } low(l);$
                  $\text{\texttt{assume} } Inv(\text{l})$
$poss(\text{l . release ()})$ $= \text{\texttt{assert} } lowEvent;$
                  $\text{\texttt{assert} } low(l);$
                  $\text{\texttt{assert} } Inv(\text{l})$
$poss(\text{\texttt{while} } (e) \text{ \texttt{do} } \{s\}) = \text{\texttt{assert} } low(e);$
                  $\text{\texttt{while} } (e) \text{ \texttt{do} } \{poss(s); \text{\texttt{assert} } low(e)\}$

Fig. 6. Statement encoding for possibilistic information flow security. For loops, we check that the loop guard is low, ensuring that termination is also low.

Based on this observation, we impose proof obligations that ensure the following property: For every program trace with some schedule and some low and high inputs, and for arbitrary different high inputs, there exists a second trace such that: (1) Both traces include the same lock operations performed by the same threads, in the same order, and (2) at each lock operation, the lock's invariant holds; in particular, the relational assertions of the lock invariant correctly relate the state protected by the lock in both traces.

To enforce this property, we devise four proof obligations that can be checked thread-locally:

1. Every lock operation o is a low event, i.e., if a thread executes o in the first execution, it will also execute o in the second execution.
2. Termination of the local code *before* the lock operation does not depend on secret data; i.e., if lock operation o is reached in the first trace, it will also be reached in the second trace.
3. o operates on the same lock in both executions, i.e., the lock is low.
4. If o releases the lock, i.e., makes a new lock state public, this lock state fulfills the relational invariant, meaning that heap operations meant to be low are indentical in both executions after the lock operation.

Note that, even though the lock operations of both traces are closely aligned, their local operations may differ. For instance, a thread may branch on a high guard as long as no lock operation is performed before the control flow re-joins.

The above checks are sufficient to satisfy Definition 4. The proof goes by induction on the number of segments of the traces and leverages the soundness of sequential verification within each segment.

Encoding. The aforementioned checks can simply be checked as part of the encoding of lock operations. We adjust the encoding from Fig. 5 for possibilistic noninterference as shown in Fig. 6. For thread acquire and release, the assertions of $lowEvent$ and $low(l)$ directly ensure properties (1) and (3). Assuming and asserting the lock invariant works as in the standard IVL encoding for concurrent programs, but now this invariant can be relational, ensuring property (4). The condition on while loops is used to ensure property (2), which can be done simply

```
def main(secret: bool) -> None:
    c = Cell()
    l = CellLock(c)
    l.acquire()
    c.val = 4
    if secret:
        l.release()
        l.acquire()
    c.val = 5
    c.release()
```

Fig. 7. Possibilistic information flow violation via a secret-dependent lock release. The Cell state 4 is visible to other threads only if secret is True.

by asserting that the loop condition is low for every loop in the program (we assume, for simplicity, that there is no infinite recursion).

Discussion. With our verification technique, the product construction on the IVL level does not need to be aware of concurrency in *any* way; applying the standard sequential product construction to the updated encoding is sufficient to ensure possibilistic noninterference in concurrent programs.

To the best of our knowledge, we are the first to consider possibilistic information flow in a setting with locks, and therefore the first to propose that the order of lock operations must be constrained. The example in Fig. 7 demonstrates that this requirement is indeed necessary to prevent unwanted information flow: The CellLock protects the val field of a Cell object, which is intended to be low. The code unconditionally sets the field to two constants (first to 4, then to 5), which should be allowed since the constants are low. However, whether the lock is *released* while the cell has value 4 depends on a secret. As a result, when a different thread acquires the lock and sees that the value is 4, this leaks that the secret *must* have been true.

Another example that illustrates the requirement to ensure that high data does not influence *which* lock a lock operation accesses can be found in Fig. 8. Here, two locks are created, and thread 1 acquires the first one. Thread 2 acquires, depending on the secret, either the same lock or a different one. This influences the possible results of the program: If both threads acquire the same lock, then the **print** statements of one thread cannot be interleaved with those of the other, otherwise they can. As a result, if the attacker observes the pattern 1212 (or any other interleaving of 1s and 2s), they know with certainty that the two threads acquired different locks and secret must therefore be False.

The necessity to prevent termination differences in a concurrent setting has been recognized before in work on security type systems [45].

```
def thread1(l: Lock) -> None:          def main(secret: bool) -> None:
    # requires lowEvent                     l1 = Lock()
    l.acquire()                             l2 = Lock()
    print(1)                                if secret:
    print(1)                                    l = l1
    l.release()                             else:
                                                l = l2
def thread2(l: Lock) -> None:               fork thread1(l1)
    # requires lowEvent                     fork thread2(l)
    l.acquire()
    print(2)
    print(2)
    l.release()
```

Fig. 8. Possibilistic information flow violation through locks. If secret is true, both threads acquire the same lock, and their critical sections cannot be interleaved.

```
def thread1(l: Lock, c: Cell):         def thread2(l: Lock, c: Cell, secret: int):
    ctr = 0                                 ctr = 0
    for i in range(100):                    for i in range(secret):
        ctr += 1                                ctr += 1
    l.acquire()                             l.acquire()
    c.val = 1                               c.val = 2
    l.release()                             l.release()
```

Fig. 9. Example of probabilistic information flow. With a non-deterministic scheduler, secret does not influence the set of possible outputs, but a greater secret leads to higher probability of seeing a final cell value of 2.

4.3   Probabilistic Noninterference

Possibilistic noninterference is too imprecise for many applications. Figure 9 illustrates the problem: The final value of c.val can be either 1 or 2, that is, possibilistic noninterference holds. However, with most schedulers, a final value of 2 is much more likely for greater secret values than for lower values because the assignment of 1 is more likely to happen before the assignment of 2.

A stronger notion of noninterference that forbids such leaks is *probabilistic* noninterference, which requires that two executions from low-equivalent initial states will produce the same low outputs with the same probabilities.

Definition 5. *A program s with a set of input variables I and output variables O, of which some subsets $I_l \subseteq I$ and $O_l \subseteq O$ are low, satisfies probabilistic noninterference iff for all σ_1, σ_2 and σ_1', if $\forall x \in I_l. \sigma_1(x) = \sigma_2(x)$ and $\langle s, \sigma_1 \rangle \rightarrow^*$ $\langle \texttt{skip}, \sigma_1' \rangle$ with probability p then $\langle s, \sigma_2 \rangle \rightarrow^* \langle \texttt{skip}, \sigma_2' \rangle$ with probability p for some σ_2' s.t. $\forall x \in O_l. \sigma_1'(x) = \sigma_2'(x)$.*

The information flow in Fig. 9 is caused by secret data influencing the timing of thread 2, which in turn may affect the relative order of modifications of shared variables. To prevent secrets from influencing the timing of operations, we additionally assert that every branch condition in the program is low, meaning that the two executions will always follow the same code path, which leads to the adjusted encoding in Fig. 10. Note that the check that branch conditions are low must also be performed for any implicit branches; e.g., with the encoding of

$$
\begin{aligned}
prob(\mathsf{I.acquire}()) &= \mathtt{assert}\ low(l); \\
&\quad \mathtt{assume}\ Inv(\mathsf{I}) \\
prob(\mathsf{I.release}()) &= \mathtt{assert}\ low(l); \\
&\quad \mathtt{assert}\ Inv(\mathsf{I}) \\
prob(\mathtt{while}\ (e)\ \mathtt{do}\ \{s\}) &= \mathtt{assert}\ low(e); \\
&\quad \mathtt{while}\ (e)\ \mathtt{do}\ \{prob(s); \mathtt{assert}\ low(e)\} \\
prob(\mathtt{if}\ (e)\ \mathtt{then}\ \{s_1\}\ \mathtt{else}\ \{s_2\}) &= \mathtt{assert}\ low(e); \\
&\quad \mathtt{if}\ (e)\ \mathtt{then}\ \{prob(s_1)\}\ \mathtt{else}\ \{prob(s_2)\} \\
prob(r.m()) &= \mathtt{assert}\ low(type(r)); \\
&\quad r.m()
\end{aligned}
$$

Fig. 10. Statement encoding for probabilistic information flow security.

dynamically-bound calls shown before, we must now assert that the type of the receiver of every such call is low. Also note that since we enforce that branches are low, the *lowEvent* conditions we showed in the possibilistic encoding will be trivially fulfilled and can be omitted here. However, we still need to assert that acquired and released lock references are low. This last requirement has not been discussed in previous work (whereas forbidding high branches is standard practice in type systems and program logics [36]).

With this adjusted encoding, probabilistic noninterference can be verified using simple assertions in the IVL encoding and subsequently performing a standard product construction on the IVL level. So, in summary, this approach lets us extend existing verifiers for concurrent programs to verify both possibilistic and probabilistic noninterference with very small changes in the frontend, and without requiring any changes on the level of the IVL (except the ability to write relational specifications) and the product construction.

5   Implementation and Evaluation

In this section, we evaluate the performance of the proposed architecture, by extending the previously information flow unaware Nagini verifier for Python [17] according to our design. We will first briefly describe Nagini and the adaptations we needed to make, then evaluate the performance overhead generated by the product transformation, and subsequently evaluate the implementation on a number of information flow examples, comparing it to SecC [19] in the process.

5.1   Nagini

Nagini is an automated verifier for statically-typed Python 3 programs. It supports a large subset of the Python language, comprising features like exception handling, polymorphism, dynamic field creation, and concurrency. Reasoning about some of these features is quite intricate even without the overhead of a product construction, so we believe that Nagini is a good target to evaluate the performance of the proposed architecture for verifiers for complex languages.

Nagini encodes Python programs and their specifications into the Viper IVL [35], and then uses Viper's backend verifiers to automatically verify those programs using the Z3 SMT solver [34]. For concurrent programs, Nagini uses an encoding similar to the one described in Sect. 4, using implicit dynamic frames [44] (a flavor of separation logic [38,40]) to prove data race freedom; as a result, we could modify its existing encoding as shown in Sect. 4 to prove both possibilistic and probabilistic noninterference for concurrent programs. Nagini's existing encoding from Python to Viper is almost entirely operational, we only adapted the encoding of dynamically-bound calls as shown in Sect. 3.5.

We extended Nagini's existing specification language to include information flow specifications and implemented the modular product program transformation for 2-hyperproperties for the existing Viper AST (enriched, again, with new AST nodes for information flow specifications). For convenience, we also slightly extended the Viper-based product transformation to directly transform statements that Nagini previously encoded using gotos, such as **break** and **continue** statements. The Viper extension for product programs[2] and the extended version of Nagini[3] are open source and available online.

5.2   Performance Overhead of the Product Construction

Our first goal is to evaluate the performance overhead generated by the product construction. We compared the verification times of Nagini's entire functional test suite with and without the product transformation enabled. The test cases range from small programs targeting specific language or specification constructs, to realistic code examples taken from programming tutorials. We ran each test five times on a warmed up JVM with the information flow extension enabled and disabled, without adding any information flow specifications. Our test system was a 12 core AMD Ryzen 3900X with 32 GB of RAM running Ubuntu 20.04.1.

All tests report the same results with and without the product transformation, meaning that completeness is not impacted by the extension, and that we can indeed still reason about the entire language subset supported by Nagini. Without the product transformation, each test case takes between 3 and 9 s, with the majority taking between 3 and 5. For most cases, enabling the product construction leads to an increase in verification time that is clearly acceptable (less than 11% for half the tests, less than 30% for three quarters, and less than 100% for 90% of the tests). For five test cases, the slowdown is a factor between 5 and 12, and a single outlier (a quicksort implementation) has a slowdown factor of 17.5 and a resulting verification time of two minutes. We believe that the main reason for the large slowdown for these particular test cases is the use of quantifiers in their specifications (e.g., to specify properties of all elements in a list). Quantifier handling is difficult for automated verification in general, because unbounded chains of quantifier instantiations can occur during the proof search [15], and this problem seems to be exacerbated when using the product encoding.

---

[2] https://github.com/viperproject/silver-sif-extension.
[3] https://github.com/marcoeilers/nagini.

Table 1. Programs evaluated for proving information flow security. We show the total lines of code (LOC) including implementation and specification but excluding whitespace, lines of specification and proof annotation (Ann.), the property we proved (Prop., where NI = noninterference, TNI = termination sensitive noninterference, PS = possibilistic noninterference) and the verification time in seconds (T), averaged over five runs.

	LOC	Ann.	Prop.	T
banerjee	77	21	NI	5.19
constanzo	21	12	NI	5.39
darvas	38	18	NI	4.20
example	27	12	NI	5.39
Example-decl	27	12	NI	5.76
Example-term	8	4	TNI	3.59
joana-1-tl	22	7	NI	3.87
joana-2-bl	13	5	NI	3.64
joana-2-t	12	4	NI	3.72
joana-3-bl	36	15	TNI	3.55
joana-3-br	33	14	TNI	4.60
joana-3-tl	23	9	TNI	4.50
joana-3-tr	25	10	TNI	4.19
joana-13-l	11	2	NI	4.54

	LOC	Ann.	Prop.	T
kusters	28	12	NI	4.35
naumann	27	17	NI	8.46
product	39	18	NI	11.35
smith	39	21	NI	6.81
terauchi1	10	3	NI	3.59
terauchi3	19	6	NI	3.69
terauchi4	18	8	NI	3.97
Fig. 4	19	6	NI	3.82
loop leak [45]	53	17	PS	4.92
high loop	24	11	PS	4.19
Fig. 7	23	8	PS	4.37
Fig. 8	36	15	PS	4.40
Fig. 9	34	15	PS	4.57

We conclude that the performance impact of the product transformation is acceptable for most examples, but can be significant for programs with complex functional specifications.

5.3   Expressiveness and Comparison with SecC

In a second step, we evaluated the expressiveness and performance of our implementation on a number of challenging examples from the literature. In particular, we use the examples from the original paper about modular product programs [18] (sequential examples collected from various previous papers, translated to Python) and from this paper, both shown in Table 1, as well as examples taken from SecC [19], the only other automated verification tool for concurrent programs we are aware of, shown in Table 2. The latter table includes the CDDC case study [36], which models an embedded device that interacts simultaneously with multiple users and classified networks. Our examples represent the state of the art in automated information flow verification, requiring semantic reasoning that would not be possible in a type system, and using complex information flow specifications including declassification, termination-sensitive noninterference, and value-dependent sensitivity [36]. As mentioned before, these features can be easily encoded into modular product programs using existing techniques [18].

Nagini was able to verify all examples, which demonstrates that our approach can handle concurrent implementations and express complex noninterference properties. For the examples from Table 1, Nagini takes only between 3 and 12 s each. As for the tests from SecC, Nagini takes around five seconds for three

Table 2. Comparison with SecC. We show the total lines of code and lines of specification for Nagini (LOC_N, Ann_N) and SecC (LOC_S, Ann_S), the property we proved (Prop., where NI = noninterference, PR = probabilistic noninterference) and the verification time in seconds in both tools (T_N and T_S) and in Nagini *without* the product construction (T_{NP}), averaged over five runs.

	LOC_N	Ann_N	LOC_S	Ann_S	Prop.	T_S	T_N	T_{NP}
SecC CAV	40	13	50	11	PR	1.33	4.21	3.56
SecC CDDC	278	105	214	47	PR	21.20	52.20	8.60
SecC CT	64	35	211	159	PR	1.87	5.41	3.97
SecC DB	100	48	256	167	NI	2.75	182.60	6.23
SecC Encrypt	29	12	49	18	NI	1.45	4.76	3.66

of them, 52 s for the CDDC case study, and 183 s for an example involving a large number of quantifiers. We believe that 52 s for a complex case study is still acceptable, whereas the slowest example demonstrates that extensive use of quantifiers will lead to problematic performance in practice.

Table 2 shows that SecC is much faster than our implementation. However, SecC was designed and implemented for information flow verification from scratch, without being able to reuse code from an existing verifier, whereas our extended Nagini implementation could be implemented with minimal effort. Besides this crucial difference, Nagini and SecC differ in many other ways, e.g., in their supported language features, automation (see the table for required annotations), and specification styles. As a result, direct performance comparisons between the two are difficult; in fact, the unmodified version of Nagini *without* the product construction already takes more time than SecC on four out of five examples, likely as a result of the overhead required for modeling more complex language features.

6   Related Work

There are various existing type systems (e.g., [37,45]) and static analyses (e.g., [11,22]) for proving information flow security. Compared to verification based on product programs, these are more automated, but less precise. Moreover, there are dedicated program logics for information flow verification, such as SecCSL [19], Covern [36], and Veronica [42], all of which allow proving probabilistic noninterference for concurrent programs based on different reasoning techniques. The implementation of the former in SecC is the only existing tool that automates information flow verification for concurrent programs, see Sect. 5.

Relational logics, such as Relational Hoare Logic [7] and Cartesian Hoare Logic [46], allow proving general relational program properties, which includes noninterference. However, while they tackle a more general problem, they generally work only for sequential programs. Some tools automate information flow verification using self-composition, e.g., for C [9] and for Java [41]. Compared to modular product programs, this approach generally does not allow for modular proofs of information flow security [18,48].

Modular product programs were presented by Eilers et al. [18]. Other forms of product programs differ in the way executions are interleaved. While some keep executions in lock step [4], like modular product programs, others do not describe a deterministic product construction and allow for arbitrary interleavings [5]. In particular, Shemer et al. [43] propose property-directed self-composition, which dynamically determines how to compose and interleave different executions based on the property to be verified. Similarly, Strichman and Veitsman [47] propose a product-like construction that interleaves recursive functions whose executions are not in lock step. Recently, Pick et al. [39] showed how to automatically infer information flow specifications on modular product programs, which can likely be combined with the approach examined in this paper.

To the best of our knowledge, SymDiff [27] for the Boogie IVL is the only existing tool that constructs product programs on an IVL-level. SymDiff is a tool for differential program verification, which requires reasoning about pairs of executions of two different (but related) programs and is thus similar to hyperproperty verification; in fact, SymDiff has also been used to verify noninterference in the past [1]. The authors of SymDiff have proposed different techniques for modularly proving mutual function summaries, similar to relational specifications, one of which uses a kind of product construction [25,28]. However, they do not examine potential soundness problems arising from this approach, nor do they discuss if it can be applied to concurrent source programs.

7   Conclusion

We presented an approach for retrofitting existing IVL-based program verifiers to check information flow security using product programs. This approach allows reusing existing frontends to reduce the required implementation effort. We have shown when this technique is sound, that it can incorporate concurrency, and that it can be implemented in an existing verifier with acceptable performance.

References

1. Almeida, J.B., Barbosa, M., Barthe, G., Dupressoir, F., Emmi, M.: Verifying constant-time implementations. In: USENIX Security Symposium, pp. 53–70. USENIX Association (2016)
2. Astrauskas, V., Müller, P., Poli, F., Summers, A.J.: Leveraging Rust types for modular specification and verification. Proc. ACM Program. Lang. 3(OOPSLA), 147:1–147:30 (2019)
3. Barnett, M., Chang, B.-Y.E., DeLine, R., Jacobs, B., Leino, K.R.M.: Boogie: a modular reusable verifier for object-oriented programs. In: de Boer, F.S., Bonsangue, M.M., Graf, S., de Roever, W.-P. (eds.) FMCO 2005. LNCS, vol. 4111, pp. 364–387. Springer, Heidelberg (2006). https://doi.org/10.1007/11804192_17

4. Barthe, G., Crespo, J.M., Kunz, C.: Relational verification using product programs. In: Butler, M., Schulte, W. (eds.) FM 2011. LNCS, vol. 6664, pp. 200–214. Springer, Heidelberg (2011). https://doi.org/10.1007/978-3-642-21437-0_17
5. Barthe, G., Crespo, J.M., Kunz, C.: Beyond 2-safety: asymmetric product programs for relational program verification. In: Artemov, S., Nerode, A. (eds.) LFCS 2013. LNCS, vol. 7734, pp. 29–43. Springer, Heidelberg (2013). https://doi.org/10.1007/978-3-642-35722-0_3
6. Barthe, G., D'Argenio, P.R., Rezk, T.: Secure information flow by self-composition. Math. Struct. Comput. Sci. **21**(6), 1207–1252 (2011)
7. Benton, N.: Simple relational correctness proofs for static analyses and program transformations. In: POPL, pp. 14–25. ACM (2004)
8. Betts, A., Chong, N., Donaldson, A.F., Qadeer, S., Thomson, P.: GPUVerify: a verifier for GPU kernels. In: OOPSLA, pp. 113–132. ACM (2012)
9. Blatter, L., Kosmatov, N., Le Gall, P., Prevosto, V., Petiot, G.: Static and dynamic verification of relational properties on self-composed C code. In: Dubois, C., Wolff, B. (eds.) TAP 2018. LNCS, vol. 10889, pp. 44–62. Springer, Cham (2018). https://doi.org/10.1007/978-3-319-92994-1_3
10. Blom, S., Huisman, M.: The VerCors tool for verification of concurrent programs. In: Jones, C., Pihlajasaari, P., Sun, J. (eds.) FM 2014. LNCS, vol. 8442, pp. 127–131. Springer, Cham (2014). https://doi.org/10.1007/978-3-319-06410-9_9
11. Chen, Z., Chen, L., Xu, B.: Hybrid information flow analysis for Python bytecode. In: IEEE WISA, pp. 95–100. IEEE Computer Society (2014)
12. Clarkson, M.R., Schneider, F.B.: Hyperproperties. J. Comput. Secur. **18**(6), 1157–1210 (2010)
13. Cohen, E., Moskal, M., Schulte, W., Tobies, S.: Local verification of global invariants in concurrent programs. In: Touili, T., Cook, B., Jackson, P. (eds.) CAV 2010. LNCS, vol. 6174, pp. 480–494. Springer, Heidelberg (2010). https://doi.org/10.1007/978-3-642-14295-6_42
14. Kirchner, F., Kosmatov, N., Prevosto, V., Signoles, J., Yakobowski, B.: Frama-C: a software analysis perspective. Formal Aspects Comput. **27**(3), 573–609 (2015). https://doi.org/10.1007/s00165-014-0326-7
15. Detlefs, D., Nelson, G., Saxe, J.B.: Simplify: a theorem prover for program checking. J. ACM **52**(3), 365–473 (2005)
16. Eilers, M., Meier, S., Müller, P.: Product Programs in the Wild: Retrofitting Program Verifiers to Check Information Flow Security (Artifact) (2021). https://doi.org/10.5281/zenodo.4724854
17. Eilers, M., Müller, P.: Nagini: a static verifier for Python. In: Chockler, H., Weissenbacher, G. (eds.) CAV 2018. LNCS, vol. 10981, pp. 596–603. Springer, Cham (2018). https://doi.org/10.1007/978-3-319-96145-3_33
18. Eilers, M., Müller, P., Hitz, S.: Modular product programs. In: Ahmed, A. (ed.) ESOP 2018. LNCS, vol. 10801, pp. 502–529. Springer, Cham (2018). https://doi.org/10.1007/978-3-319-89884-1_18
19. Ernst, G., Murray, T.: SecCSL: security concurrent separation logic. In: Dillig, I., Tasiran, S. (eds.) CAV 2019. LNCS, vol. 11562, pp. 208–230. Springer, Cham (2019). https://doi.org/10.1007/978-3-030-25543-5_13
20. Filliâtre, J.-C., Marché, C.: The Why/Krakatoa/Caduceus platform for deductive program verification. In: Damm, W., Hermanns, H. (eds.) CAV 2007. LNCS, vol. 4590, pp. 173–177. Springer, Heidelberg (2007). https://doi.org/10.1007/978-3-540-73368-3_21

21. Filliâtre, J.-C., Paskevich, A.: Why3—where programs meet provers. In: Felleisen, M., Gardner, P. (eds.) ESOP 2013. LNCS, vol. 7792, pp. 125–128. Springer, Heidelberg (2013). https://doi.org/10.1007/978-3-642-37036-6_8

22. Giffhorn, D., Snelting, G.: A new algorithm for low-deterministic security. Int. J. Inf. Secur. **14**(3), 263–287 (2014). https://doi.org/10.1007/s10207-014-0257-6

23. Goguen, J.A., Meseguer, J.: Security policies and security models. In: IEEE Symposium on Security and Privacy, pp. 11–20. IEEE Computer Society (1982)

24. Goubault, É., Ledent, J., Mimram, S.: Concurrent specifications beyond linearizability. In: OPODIS. LIPIcs, vol. 125, pp. 28:1–28:16. Schloss Dagstuhl - Leibniz-Zentrum für Informatik (2018)

25. Hawblitzel, C., Kawaguchi, M., Lahiri, S.K., Rebêlo, H.: Towards modularly comparing programs using automated theorem provers. In: Bonacina, M.P. (ed.) CADE 2013. LNCS (LNAI), vol. 7898, pp. 282–299. Springer, Heidelberg (2013). https://doi.org/10.1007/978-3-642-38574-2_20

26. Jacobs, B., Piessens, F., Leino, K.R.M., Schulte, W.: Safe concurrency for aggregate objects with invariants. In: SEFM, pp. 137–147. IEEE Computer Society (2005)

27. Lahiri, S.K., Hawblitzel, C., Kawaguchi, M., Rebêlo, H.: SYMDIFF: a language-agnostic semantic diff tool for imperative programs. In: Madhusudan, P., Seshia, S.A. (eds.) CAV 2012. LNCS, vol. 7358, pp. 712–717. Springer, Heidelberg (2012). https://doi.org/10.1007/978-3-642-31424-7_54

28. Lahiri, S.K., McMillan, K.L., Sharma, R., Hawblitzel, C.: Differential assertion checking. In: ESEC/SIGSOFT FSE, pp. 345–355. ACM (2013)

29. Leino, K.R.M.: Dafny: an automatic program verifier for functional correctness. In: Clarke, E.M., Voronkov, A. (eds.) LPAR 2010. LNCS (LNAI), vol. 6355, pp. 348–370. Springer, Heidelberg (2010). https://doi.org/10.1007/978-3-642-17511-4_20

30. Leino, K.R.M., Müller, P.: Using the Spec# language, methodology, and tools to write bug-free programs. In: Müller, P. (ed.) LASER 2007-2008. LNCS, vol. 6029, pp. 91–139. Springer, Heidelberg (2010). https://doi.org/10.1007/978-3-642-13010-6_4

31. Leino, K.R.M., Müller, P.: A basis for verifying multi-threaded programs. In: Castagna, G. (ed.) ESOP 2009. LNCS, vol. 5502, pp. 378–393. Springer, Heidelberg (2009). https://doi.org/10.1007/978-3-642-00590-9_27

32. Leino, K.R.M., Müller, P., Smans, J.: Verification of concurrent programs with Chalice. In: Aldini, A., Barthe, G., Gorrieri, R. (eds.) FOSAD 2007-2009. LNCS, vol. 5705, pp. 195–222. Springer, Heidelberg (2009). https://doi.org/10.1007/978-3-642-03829-7_7

33. Liskov, B., Wing, J.M.: A behavioral notion of subtyping. ACM Trans. Program. Lang. Syst. **16**(6), 1811–1841 (1994)

34. de Moura, L., Bjørner, N.: Z3: an efficient SMT solver. In: Ramakrishnan, C.R., Rehof, J. (eds.) TACAS 2008. LNCS, vol. 4963, pp. 337–340. Springer, Heidelberg (2008). https://doi.org/10.1007/978-3-540-78800-3_24

35. Müller, P., Schwerhoff, M., Summers, A.J.: Viper: a verification infrastructure for permission-based reasoning. In: Jobstmann, B., Leino, K.R.M. (eds.) VMCAI 2016. LNCS, vol. 9583, pp. 41–62. Springer, Heidelberg (2016). https://doi.org/10.1007/978-3-662-49122-5_2

36. Murray, T.C., Sison, R., Engelhardt, K.: COVERN: a logic for compositional verification of information flow control. In: EuroS&P, pp. 16–30. IEEE (2018)

37. Myers, A.C., Zheng, L., Zdancewic, S., Chong, S., Nystrom, N.: Jif: Java information flow. Software release (2006). http://www.cs.cornell.edu/jif

38. O'Hearn, P.W.: Resources, concurrency, and local reasoning. Theor. Comput. Sci. **375**(1–3), 271–307 (2007)
39. Pick, L., Fedyukovich, G., Gupta, A.: Automating modular verification of secure information flow. In: FMCAD, pp. 158–168. IEEE (2020)
40. Reynolds, J.C.: Separation logic: a logic for shared mutable data structures. In: LICS, pp. 55–74. IEEE Computer Society (2002)
41. Scheben, C., Schmitt, P.H.: Verification of information flow properties of JAVA programs without approximations. In: Beckert, B., Damiani, F., Gurov, D. (eds.) FoVeOOS 2011. LNCS, vol. 7421, pp. 232–249. Springer, Heidelberg (2012). https://doi.org/10.1007/978-3-642-31762-0_15
42. Schoepe, D., Murray, T., Sabelfeld, A.: VERONICA: expressive and precise concurrent information flow security. In: CSF, pp. 79–94. IEEE (2020)
43. Shemer, R., Gurfinkel, A., Shoham, S., Vizel, Y.: Property directed self composition. In: Dillig, I., Tasiran, S. (eds.) CAV 2019. LNCS, vol. 11561, pp. 161–179. Springer, Cham (2019). https://doi.org/10.1007/978-3-030-25540-4_9
44. Smans, J., Jacobs, B., Piessens, F.: Implicit dynamic frames. ACM Trans. Program. Lang. Syst. **34**(1), 2:1-2:58 (2012)
45. Smith, G.: Principles of secure information flow analysis. In: Christodorescu, M., Jha, S., Maughan, D., Song, D., Wang, C. (eds.) Malware Detection. Advances in Information Security, vol. 27. Springer, Boston (2007). https://doi.org/10.1007/978-0-387-44599-1_13
46. Sousa, M., Dillig, I.: Cartesian hoare logic for verifying k-safety properties. In: PLDI, pp. 57–69. ACM (2016)
47. Strichman, O., Veitsman, M.: Regression verification for unbalanced recursive functions. In: Fitzgerald, J., Heitmeyer, C., Gnesi, S., Philippou, A. (eds.) FM 2016. LNCS, vol. 9995, pp. 645–658. Springer, Cham (2016). https://doi.org/10.1007/978-3-319-48989-6_39
48. Terauchi, T., Aiken, A.: Secure information flow as a safety problem. In: Hankin, C., Siveroni, I. (eds.) SAS 2005. LNCS, vol. 3672, pp. 352–367. Springer, Heidelberg (2005). https://doi.org/10.1007/11547662_24
49. Zdancewic, S., Myers, A.C.: Observational determinism for concurrent program security. In: CSFW, p. 29. IEEE Computer Society (2003)

Constraint-Based Relational Verification

Hiroshi Unno[1,2]([✉]), Tachio Terauchi[3], and Eric Koskinen[4]

[1] University of Tsukuba, Ibaraki, Japan
uhiro@cs.tsukuba.ac.jp
[2] RIKEN AIP, Tokyo, Japan
[3] Waseda University, Tokyo, Japan
[4] Stevens Institute of Technology, New Jersey, USA

Abstract. In recent years they have been numerous works that aim to automate relational verification. Meanwhile, although Constrained Horn Clauses (CHCs) empower a wide range of verification techniques and tools, they lack the ability to express hyperproperties beyond k-safety such as generalized non-interference and co-termination.

This paper describes a novel and fully automated constraint-based approach to relational verification. We first introduce a new class of predicate Constraint Satisfaction Problems called pfwCSP where constraints are represented as clauses modulo first-order theories over predicate variables of three kinds: ordinary, well-founded, or functional. This generalization over CHCs permits arbitrary (i.e., possibly non-Horn) clauses, well-foundedness constraints, functionality constraints, and is capable of expressing these relational verification problems. Our approach enables us to express and automatically verify problem instances that require non-trivial (i.e., non-sequential and non-lock-step) self-composition by automatically inferring appropriate *schedulers* (or *alignment*) that dictate when and which program copies move. To solve problems in this new language, we present a constraint solving method for pfwCSP based on *stratified* CounterExample-Guided Inductive Synthesis (CEGIS) of ordinary, well-founded, and functional predicates.

We have implemented the proposed framework and obtained promising results on diverse relational verification problems that are beyond the scope of the previous verification frameworks.

Keywords: Relational verification · Constraint solving · CEGIS

1 Introduction

We describe a novel constraint-based approach to automatically solving a wide range of relational verification problems including k-safety, co-termination [6, 10], termination-sensitive non-interference (TS-NI) [63], and generalized non-interference (GNI) [40] for infinite-state programs.

© The Author(s) 2021
A. Silva and K. R. M. Leino (Eds.) CAV 2021, LNCS 12759, pp. 742–766, 2021.
https://doi.org/10.1007/978-3-030-81685-8_35

A key challenge in relational property verification is the discovery of *relational invariants* which relate the states of multiple program executions. However, whereas most prior approaches must fix the execution *schedule*[1] (e.g., lockstep or sequential) [8,20,21,42,54,57], a recent work by Shemer et al. [50] has proposed a method to automatically infer sufficient *fair* schedulers to prove the goal relational property. Importantly, the schedulers in their approach can be *semantic* in which the choice of which program to execute can depend on the *states* of the programs as opposed to the classic *syntactic* schedulers such as lock-step and sequential that can only depend on the control locations. However, their approach requires the user to provide appropriate atomic predicates and is not fully automatic. Moreover, they only support k-safety properties. A recent work has proposed a method for automatically verifying non-hypersafety relational properties but only for *finite* state systems [19].

Meanwhile, today's constraint-based frameworks are also insufficient at automating relational verification. The class of predicate constraints called Constrained Horn Clauses (CHCs) [13] has been widely adopted as a "common intermediate language" for uniformly expressing verification problems for various programming paradigms, such as functional and object-oriented languages. Example uses of the CHCs framework include safety property verification [29,30,35] and refinement type inference [33,36,53,56,66]. The separation of constraint generation and solving has facilitated the rapid development of constraint generation tools such as RCAML [56], SEAHORN [30], and JAYHORN [35] as well as efficient constraint solving tools such as SPACER [37], ELDARICA [32], and HOICE [14]. Unfortunately, CHCs lack the ingredients to sufficiently express these relational verification problems.

In this paper we introduce automated support for relational verification by generalizing CHCs and introducing a new class of predicate Constraint Satisfaction Problems called pfwCSP. This language allows constraints that are *arbitrary (i.e., possibly non-Horn)* clauses modulo first-order theories over predicate variables that can be *functional predicates, well-founded predicates* or ordinary predicates. We then show that, thanks to the enhanced predicate variables, pfwCSP can express *non-hypersafety* relational properties such as co-termination [11], termination-sensitive non-interference (TS-NI) [63], and generalized non-interference (GNI) [40]. In addition, our approach effectively quantifies over the schedule, expressing *arbitrary fair semantic scheduling* thanks to non-Horn clauses and functional predicates (functional predicates are needed to express fairness in the presence of non-termination which is needed for properties like co-termination and TS-GNI). The flexibility allows our approach to automatically discover a fair semantic schedule and verify difficult relational problem instances that require non-trivial schedules. We prove that our encodings are *sound* and *complete*. Expressing relational invariants with such flexible scheduling is not possible with CHCs. However, pfwCSP retains a key benefit of CHCs: the idea of separating constraint generation from solving.

---

[1] The notion of *schedule* is also often called an *alignment* in literature.

We next present a novel constraint solving method for pfwCSP based on *stratified* CounterExample-Guided Inductive Synthesis (CEGIS) of ordinary, well-founded, and functional predicates. In our method, ordinary predicates represent relational inductive invariants, well-founded predicates witness synchronous termination, and functional predicates represent Skolem functions witnessing existential quantifiers that encode angelic non-determinism. These witnesses for a relational property are often mutually dependent and involve many variables in a complicated way (see the extended report [58] for examples). The synthesis thus needs to use expressive templates without compromising the efficiency. Stratified CEGIS combines CEGIS [51] with stratified families of templates [55] (*i.e.*, decomposing templates into a series of increasingly expressive templates) to achieve completeness in the sense of [34,55], a theoretical guarantee of convergence, and a faster and stable convergence by avoiding the overfitting problem of expressive templates to counterexamples [44]. The constraint solving method naturally generalizes a number of previous techniques developed for CHCs solving and invariant/ranking function synthesis, addressing the challenges due to the generality of pfwCSP that is essential for relational verification.

We have implemented the above framework and have applied our tool PCSAT to a diverse collection of 20 relational verification problems and obtained promising results. The benchmark problems go beyond the capabilities of the existing related tools (such as CHCs solvers and program verification tools). PCSAT has solved 15 problems fully automatically by synthesizing complex witnesses for relational properties, and for the 5 problems that could not be solved fully automatically within the time limit, PCSAT was able to solve them semi-automatically provided that a part of an invariant is manually given as a hint.

2   Overview

2.1   Relational Verification Problems

k-**safety**. Consider the following program taken from [50] that uses a summation to calculate the square of x, and then doubles it.

```
doubleSquare(bool h, int x) {
    int z, y=0;
    if (h) { z = 2*x; } else { z = x; }
    while (z>0) { z--; y = y+x; }
    if (!h) { y = 2*y; }
    return  y;
}
```

This program also takes another input h and, if the value of h is true, calculates the result differently. The classical relational property *termination-insensitive non-interference* (TI-NI) says that, roughly, an observer cannot infer the value of high security variables (h in this case) by observing the outputs (y). This is a *2-safety property* [17,54]: it relates two executions of the same program. In this example, we ask whether two executions that initially agree on x (*i.e.*, $x_1 = x_2$) will agree on the resulting y (*i.e.*, $y_1 = y_2$). The subscripts in these relations indicate copies of the program: x_1 is variable x in the first copy of the program and x_2 is variable x in the second copy. More generally, k-safety means that if the initial states of a k-tuple of programs satisfy a pre-relation *Pre*, then when they all terminate the k-tuple of post states will satisfy post-relation *Post*.

The literature proposes many ways to reason about k-safety including methods of reducing a multi-program problem to a single-program problem, such as through self-composition [8,54,57], product programs [7], and their variants [21,46,50,52,59]. Their key challenge is that of *scheduling*: how to interleave the programs' executions so that invariants in the combined program are able to effectively describe cross-program relationships. Indeed, as proved by [50], verifying this example with the naïve lock-step scheduling is impossible with only linear arithmetic invariants while linear arithmetic invariants suffice with a more "semantic" scheduling that schedules the copy with $h_1 = \texttt{false}$ to iterate the loop twice per each iteration of the loop in the copy with $h_2 = \texttt{true}$.

In this paper, we will describe a way to pose the scheduling problem as a part of a series of constraints so that the search for an effective scheduler is relegated to the solver level. In our approach, a k-safety verification problem is encoded as a set of constraints containing (ordinary) predicate variables that represent the scheduler to be discovered and a relational invariant preserved by the scheduler. Specially, we introduce a predicate variable inv that represents a relational invariant and for each $A \subseteq \{1, \ldots, k\}$, a predicate variable $\text{sch}_A(\tilde{V}_1, \ldots, \tilde{V}_k)$ where $\tilde{V}_i$ are the variables of the ith program, and add constraints that say that if the predicate is $\texttt{true}$, then the programs whose index are in A will step forward while the rest remain still and also inv is preserved by the step. For soundness, it is important to constrain the scheduler to be *fair*, *i.e.*, at least one program that can progress must be scheduled to progress if there is a program that can progress. As we shall show in Sect. 4, non-Horn clauses are essential to expressing the fairness constraint. Roughly, the idea is to use a clause with multiple positive predicate variables (*i.e.*, *head disjunction*) to say "*if the relational invariant holds, then at least one of the unfinished programs must be scheduled to progress.*"

Our approach is similar to and is inspired by the approach of [50] that also infers a fair semantic scheduler. However, their approach requires the user to provide sufficient atomic predicates manually and is not fully automated. By contrast, our approach soundly-and-completely encodes the k-safety verification problem together with scheduler inference as a set of constraints thanks to the expressiveness of pfwCSP, and automatically solves those constraints by the stratified CEGIS algorithm (cf. Sect. 7 for further comparison).

Co-termination. Now consider the following pair of programs.

$$P_1^{cot} : \texttt{while (x>0) \{ x = x - y; \}}$$
$$P_2^{cot} : \texttt{while (x>0) \{ x = x - 2 × y; \}}$$

A (non-safety) relational question is whether these programs P_1^{cot} and P_2^{cot} agree on termination [6,10]. In general they do not: if, for example, P_1^{cot} is executed with $\mathtt{x} < 0$ and P_2^{cot} with $\mathtt{x} > 0 \wedge \mathtt{y} = 0$, the first will terminate while the second will diverge. However, under the pre-relation $Pre \equiv \mathtt{x}_1 = \mathtt{x}_2 \wedge \mathtt{y}_1 = \mathtt{y}_2$, they will *agree* on termination: the first program terminates iff the second one does. The property falls outside of the k-safety fragment as it cannot be refuted by finite execution traces. It is worth noting that *termination-sensitive non-interference* (TS-NI) is the conjunction of TI-NI and co-termination of two copies of the same target program with Pre equating the copies' low inputs.

Proving co-termination, like k-safety, can be aided by scheduler and we can again use our constraints over predicate variables. But this is not enough. We need additional constraints to ensure that whenever one of the two has terminated, the other is also guaranteed to terminate. To address this, we next introduce *well-founded predicate variables*. These predicate variables will appear in our generalized language of constraints as terms of the form $\mathsf{wfr}(\widetilde{V}_i, \widetilde{V}_i')$, where the relation wfr must be *discovered* by the constraint solving method. (In Sect. 5 we describe how to achieve this through our stratified CEGIS algorithm.) For the above example, our stratified CEGIS algorithm and our tool PCSAT automatically discovers (1) a schedule where the two programs step together when $x_1 > 0$ and $x_2 > 0$, (2) a relational invariant that implies that if the first program is terminated, then either the second program is terminated or $y_2 \geq 1$ (and vice-versa), and (3) well-founded relations that (combined with the relational invariant) witness that if the loop has terminated in the second program ($x_2 \leq 0$) but not in the first ($x_1 > 0$), then a transition in the first is well-founded (and vice-versa). In Sect. 4, we show how co-termination problems can be soundly-and-completely encoded in pfwCSP.

Generalized Non-interference. Now consider the following program.

```
gniEx(bool high, int low) {
  if (high) {
    int x = *$^int$; if (x >= low) { return x; } else { while (true) {} }
  } else {
    int x = low; while ($*^bool$) { x++; } return x;
  }
}
```

The $*^{\mathtt{int}}$ (resp. $*^{\mathtt{bool}}$) above indicates an integer (resp. a binary) non-deterministic choice. *Termination-insensitive generalized non-interference* (TI-GNI) [40] is an extension of non-interference to non-deterministic programs, and it says that for any two copies of the program with possibly different values for the high security input (`high` in this example) and with the same value for the low security input (`low` in this example), if one copy has a terminating execution that ends in some output (the final value of x in this example), then the other copy has either a terminating execution ending in the same output or a non-terminating execution. The *termination-sensitive* variant (TS-GNI) strengthens the condition by asserting that if one copy has a terminating execution then the other copy has a terminating execution that ends in the same output. Both GNI variants are ∀∃ hyperproperties and fall outside of the k-safety fragment.

Verifying GNI requires handling non-determinism. Note that non-determinism occurs both *demonically* (*i.e.*, as ∀) and *angelically* (*i.e.*, as ∃) in GNI. While handling demonic non-determinism is straightforward in a constraint-based verification since the term variables are implicitly universally quantified, handling angelic non-determinism is less straightforward.

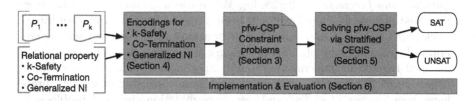

Fig. 1. Overview of the contributions and how they achieve a constraint-based strategy for relational verification.

Our approach handles finitary angelic non-determinism like $*^{\texttt{bool}}$ by adding non-Horn clauses with head disjunctions that roughly express the condition *"the relational invariant remains true in one of the finitely many next step choices"*. To handle infinitary non-determinism like $*^{\texttt{int}}$, we introduce *functional predicate variables* denoted $f(\widetilde{V}, r)$. In these terms, f is a predicate variable to be discovered but with a new wrinkle: this predicate involves a return value r and the interpretation of f is a *total function* over $\widetilde{V}$. For this example, we introduce the term $f(\widetilde{V}, r)$ where r represents the value chosen non-deterministically at $*^{\texttt{int}}$ and $\widetilde{V}$ are program variables and *prophecy variables* that represent the final return values of the demonic copy. For this example, PCSAT automatically discovers the predicate $r = \texttt{ret}_1$ where $\texttt{ret}_1$ is the prophecy variable for the return value of the demonic copy. With it, PCSAT is able to verify TS-GNI and TI-GNI of this example. We remark that functional predicates are also used to encode scheduler fairness in the presence of non-termination and is needed to ensure soundness for properties like co-termination and TS-GNI. In Sect. 4.3, we show how TI-GNI and TS-GNI can be soundly-and-completely encoded in pfwCSP.

2.2   Challenges and Contributions

There are several challenges that we face in supporting relational verification problems with a constraint-based approach. The subsequent sections of this paper are organized around addressing those challenges as follows:

– We first ask how to generalize the constraint language to go beyond CHCs to express a more general class of relational verification problems. To this end, in Sect. 3, we present a new language called *predicated constraint satisfaction problems* (pfwCSP), which incorporate non-Horn clauses, (ordinary)

predicate variables, well-founded predicate variables, and functional predicate variables.
- We next return to the above relational verification problems –k-safety, co-termination, and generalized non-interference– and describe how pfwCSP can express each of them in a sound and complete manner in Sect. 4.
- The next major contribution of our research is a novel *stratified* CEGIS algorithm for solving pfwCSP constraints. Our approach integrates advanced verification techniques: *stratified family of templates* [55] and *CEGIS of invariants/ranking functions* [14,26,28,45]. While the individual ideas have been proposed previously, they have only been designed for less expressive frameworks such as CHCs, and substantial extensions are needed to combine and apply them to the new pfwCSP framework as we shall show in Sect. 5.
- We next turn to an implementation and experimental validation on a diverse collection of 20 relational verification problems, consisting of k-safety problems from Shemer *et al.* [50] and new co-termination and GNI problems in Sect. 6. As far as we know, none of the existing *automated* tools other than our new tool called PCSAT can solve them.

In sum, Fig. 1 depicts each of these sections and how, together, they enable relational verification. For space, extra materials are deferred to the extended report [58].

3   Predicate Constraint Satisfaction Problems pfwCSP

As discussed in Sect. 2, CHCs are insufficient to express important relational verification problems. In the section we introduced a generalized language of constraints called pfwCSP. The language of constraint satisfaction problems (CSP) permits non-Horn clauses, predicate variable terms, including those for functional predicates and well-founded relations (pfw). We now define pfwCSP.

Let $\mathcal{T}$ be a (possibly many-sorted) first-order theory with the signature Σ. The syntax of $\mathcal{T}$-formulas and $\mathcal{T}$-terms is:

$$\text{(formulas) } \phi ::= X(\widetilde{t}) \mid p(\widetilde{t}) \mid \neg\phi \mid \phi_1 \vee \phi_2 \mid \phi_1 \wedge \phi_2$$
$$\text{(terms) } t ::= x \mid f(\widetilde{t})$$

Here, the meta-variables x and X respectively range over term and predicate variables. The meta-variables p and f respectively denote predicate and function symbols of Σ. We use s as a meta-variable ranging over sorts of the signature Σ. We write $\star$ for the sort of propositions and $s_1 \rightarrow s_2$ for the sort of functions from s_1 to s_2. We write $ar(o)$ and $sort(o)$ respectively for the arity and the sort of a syntactic element o. A function f represents a constant if $ar(f) = 0$. We write $ftv(\phi)$ and $fpv(\phi)$ respectively for the set of free term and predicate variables that occur in ϕ. We write $\widetilde{x}$ for a sequence of term variables, $|\widetilde{x}|$ for the length of $\widetilde{x}$, and ϵ for the empty sequence. We often abbreviate $\neg\phi_1 \vee \phi_2$ as $\phi_1 \Rightarrow \phi_2$. We henceforth consider only well-sorted formulas and terms. We use φ as a meta-variable ranging over $\mathcal{T}$-formulas without predicate variables.

We now define a pCSP $\mathcal{C}$ (with ordinary but without well-founded and functional predicate variables) to be a finite set of clauses of the form

$$\varphi \vee \left(\bigvee_{i=1}^{\ell} X_i(\widetilde{t_i})\right) \vee \left(\bigvee_{i=\ell+1}^{m} \neg X_i(\widetilde{t_i})\right) \tag{1}$$

where $0 \leq \ell \leq m$. We write $ftv(c)$ for the set of free term variables of a clause c. The set of free term variables of $\mathcal{C}$ is defined by $ftv(\mathcal{C}) = \bigcup_{c \in \mathcal{C}} ftv(c)$. We regard the variables in $ftv(c)$ as implicitly universally quantified. We write $fpv(\mathcal{C})$ for the set of free predicate variables that occur in $\mathcal{C}$. A *predicate substitution* σ is a finite map from predicate variables X to closed predicates of the form $\lambda x_1, \ldots, x_{\text{ar}(X)}.\varphi$. We write $\sigma(\mathcal{C})$ for the application of σ to $\mathcal{C}$ and $\text{dom}(\sigma)$ for the domain of σ. We call σ a *syntactic solution* for $\mathcal{C}$ if $fpv(\mathcal{C}) \subseteq \text{dom}(\sigma)$ and $\models \bigwedge \sigma(\mathcal{C})$. Similarly, we call a predicate interpretation ρ a *semantic solution* for $\mathcal{C}$ if $fpv(\mathcal{C}) \subseteq \text{dom}(\rho)$ and $\rho \models \bigwedge \mathcal{C}$.

Remark 1. The language pCSP generalizes over existing languages of constraints. CHCs can be obtained as a restriction of pCSP where $\ell \leq 1$ in (1) for all clauses. We can also define coCHCs as pCSP but with the restriction that $m \leq \ell + 1$ for all clauses. A linear CHCs is a pCSP that is both CHCs and coCHCs.

We next extend pCSP to pfwCSP by adding well-foundedness and functionness constraints. A pfwCSP $(\mathcal{C}, \mathcal{K})$ consists of

- a finite set $\mathcal{C}$ of pCSP-clauses over predicate variables and
- a kinding function $\mathcal{K}$ that maps each predicate variable $X \in fpv(\mathcal{C})$ to its kind: any one of $\bullet$, $\Downarrow$, or λ which respectively represent ordinary, well-founded, and functional predicate variables.

We write $\rho \models WF(X)$ if the interpretation $\rho(X)$ of the predicate variable X is *well-founded*, that is, $\text{sort}(X) = (\widetilde{s}, \widetilde{s}) \rightarrow \star$ for some $\widetilde{s}$ and there is no infinite sequence $\widetilde{v}_1, \widetilde{v}_2, \ldots$ of sequences $\widetilde{v}_i$ of values of the sorts $\widetilde{s}$ such that $(\widetilde{v}_i, \widetilde{v}_{i+1}) \in \rho(X)$ for all $i \geq 1$. We write $\rho \models FN(X)$ if X is *functional*, that is, $\text{sort}(X) = (\widetilde{s}, s) \rightarrow \star$ for some $\widetilde{s}$ and s, and $\rho \models \forall \widetilde{x} \colon \widetilde{s}.(\exists y \colon s.X(\widetilde{x}, y)) \wedge \forall y_1, y_2 \colon s.(X(\widetilde{x}, y_1) \wedge X(\widetilde{x}, y_2) \Rightarrow y_1 = y_2)$ holds. We call a predicate interpretation ρ a *semantic solution* for $(\mathcal{C}, \mathcal{K})$ if ρ is a semantic solution of $\mathcal{C}$, $\rho \models WF(X)$ for all X such that $\mathcal{K}(X) = \Downarrow$, and $\rho \models FN(X)$ for all X such that $\mathcal{K}(X) = \lambda$. The notion of syntactic solution can be similarly generalized to pfwCSP.

Definition 1 (Satisfiability of pfwCSP). The predicate satisfiability problem of a pfwCSP $(\mathcal{C}, \mathcal{K})$ is that of deciding whether it has a semantic solution.

Remark 2. Recall that we assume that the $\mathcal{T}$-formulas φ in pCSP clauses do not contain quantifiers. The assumption, however, is not a restriction for pfwCSP because we can Skolemize quantifiers using functional predicates.

4   Relational Verification with Constraints

We now present reductions from relational verification problems to pfwCSP, thus enabling a new route to automation of these problems. We begin with k-safety, and then move toward liveness and non-determinism, which are thorny problems in the relational setting. We first provide some basic definitions and notations.

Programs. We consider programs $P_1,\ldots,P_k$ on variables $\widetilde{V_1},\ldots,\widetilde{V_k}$, respectively. A *state* of the program P_i is a valuation of the variables $\widetilde{V_i}$. We represent such a valuation by a sequence of values $\widetilde{v}$ such that $|\widetilde{v}| = |\widetilde{V_i}|$. We assume that each P_i is defined by the predicate $T_i(\widetilde{V_i}, \widetilde{V_i}')$ denoting its one-step transition relation i.e., $T_i(\widetilde{v}, \widetilde{v}')$ implies that evaluating P_i one step from the state $\widetilde{v}$ reaches the state $\widetilde{v}'$. We also assume that there is a predicate $F_i(\widetilde{V_i})$ that represents the final states of the program such that $F_i(\widetilde{v})$ and $T_i(\widetilde{v}, \widetilde{v}')$ implies $\widetilde{v} = \widetilde{v}'$, i.e., the program self-loops when it reaches a final state. We say that a state $\widetilde{v}$ (multi-step) reaches a final state $\widetilde{v}'$ in the evaluation of P_i, written $\widetilde{v} \rightsquigarrow_i \widetilde{v}'$, if there exists a non-empty finite sequence of states π such that $\pi[1] = \widetilde{v}$, $\pi[\|\pi\|] = \widetilde{v}'$, $T_i(\pi[j-1], \pi[j])$ for all $1 < j \leq |\pi|$, and $F_i(\widetilde{v}')$. We write $\widetilde{v} \rightsquigarrow_i \bot$ if there exists a non-terminating evaluation from $\widetilde{v}$ in P_i, i.e., if there exists an infinite sequence of states ϖ such that $\varpi[1] = \widetilde{v}$, $T_i(\varpi[j-1], \varpi[j])$ for all $1 < j$, and $\neg F_i(\varpi[j])$ for all $0 < j$. We note that a program may be non-deterministic, that is, $T_i(\widetilde{v}, \widetilde{v}')$ and $T_i(\widetilde{v}, \widetilde{v}'')$ may both be true for some $\widetilde{v}' \neq \widetilde{v}''$.

4.1 k-Safety

A *k-safety property* is given by predicates $Pre(\widetilde{V})$ and $Post(\widetilde{V})$ that respectively denote the pre and the post relations across the k-tuple.

Definition 2 (k-safety). The *k-safety property verification problem* is to decide if the following holds:

$$\forall \widetilde{v} = \widetilde{v}_1,\ldots,\widetilde{v}_k.\forall \widetilde{v}' = \widetilde{v}_1',\ldots,\widetilde{v}_k'.Pre(\widetilde{v}) \wedge \bigwedge_{i \in [k]} \widetilde{v}_i \rightsquigarrow_i \widetilde{v}_i' \Rightarrow Post(\widetilde{v}')$$

That is, any k-tuple of final states reachable from a k-tuple of states satisfying the precondition satisfies the post condition. For instance, the TI-NI verification from Sect. 2.1 is a 2-safety property where P_1 and P_2 are copies of the same program, *Pre* states that the low inputs of the two programs are equal (*i.e.*, $x_1 = x_2$ in the example), and *Post* states that the low outputs of the two programs are equal (*i.e.*, $y_1 = y_2$ in the example).

    We now describe a new way to pose the k-safety relational verification problem via constraints written in pfwCSP. We write $[k]$ for the set $\{1,\ldots,k\}$. We define $\mathcal{P}^+[k] = \{S \subseteq [k] \mid S \neq \emptyset\}$. Let $\widetilde{V} = \widetilde{V_1},\ldots,\widetilde{V_k}$ be a k-tuple of vectors, corresponding to the variables of the k programs.

Definition 3 (k-safety through constraints).   We define pfwCSP constraints $\mathcal{C}_S$ be the set of following clauses:

(1) $Pre(\widetilde{V}) \Rightarrow \mathsf{inv}(\widetilde{V})$

(2) $\mathsf{inv}(\widetilde{V}) \wedge \bigwedge_{i \in [k]} F_i(\widetilde{V}_i) \Rightarrow Post(\widetilde{V})$

(3) For each $A \in \mathcal{P}^+[k]$,

$\mathsf{inv}(\widetilde{V}) \wedge \mathsf{sch}_A(\widetilde{V}) \wedge \bigwedge_{i \in A} T_i(\widetilde{V}_i, \widetilde{V}_i') \wedge \bigwedge_{i \in [k] \setminus A} \widetilde{V}_i = \widetilde{V}_i' \Rightarrow \mathsf{inv}(\widetilde{V}')$

(4) For each $A \in \mathcal{P}^+[k]$, $\mathsf{inv}(\widetilde{V}) \wedge \mathsf{sch}_A(\widetilde{V}) \wedge \bigvee_{i \in [k]} \neg F_i(\widetilde{V}_i) \Rightarrow \bigvee_{i \in A} \neg F_i(\widetilde{V}_i)$

(5) $\mathsf{inv}(\widetilde{V}) \wedge \bigvee_{i \in [k]} \neg F_i(\widetilde{V}_i) \Rightarrow \bigvee_{A \in \mathcal{P}^+[k]} \mathsf{sch}_A(\widetilde{V})$.

Here, inv and sch_A (for each $A \in \mathcal{P}^+[k]$) are ordinary predicate variables. Roughly, the predicate variables sch_A describe a *scheduler*. The scheduler stipulates that when $\mathsf{sch}_A(\widetilde{v}_1, \ldots, \widetilde{v}_k)$ is true, each P_i such that $i \in A$ takes a step from the state $\widetilde{v}_i$ while the others remain still. Note that the scheduler is *semantic* in the sense that which programs are scheduled to be executed next can depend on the current states of the programs. Clauses (1)–(3) assert that inv is an invariant sufficient to prove the given safety property with the scheduler defined by sch_A's. Clauses (4) say that if an inv-satisfying state is such that the processes in A are allowed to move and some program has not yet terminated, then at least one process in A has not yet terminated. Clause (5) says that any state satisfying inv has to satisfy some sch_A. Clauses (4) and (5) ensure the *fairness* of the scheduler, that is, at least one unfinished program is scheduled to make progress if there is an unfinished program.

Theorem 1 (Soundness and Completeness of $\mathcal{C}_S$). *The given k-tuple of programs satisfies the given k-safety property iff $\mathcal{C}_S$ is satisfiable.*

We note that the soundness direction crucially relies on scheduler fairness. The completeness is with respect to semantic solutions (cf. Definition 1) and it is only "relative" with respect to syntactic solutions: a syntactic solution only exists when the predicates of the background theory are able to express sufficient invariants and schedulers (impossible in general for any decidable theory when the class of programs is Turing-powerful as in our case when the background theory of predicates is QFLIA).

It is important to note that $\mathcal{C}_S$ is *not* CHCs because clause (5) has a head disjunction. $\mathcal{C}_S$ may be seen as a constraint-based formulation of the approach proposed in [50]. However, their approach requires the user to provide sufficient predicates manually and is not fully automated, while our approach can fully automatically solve the problems by constraint solving (cf. Sect. 5).

Example 1. The formalization allows flexible scheduling. For instance, for the TI-NI example from Sect. 2.1, our approach is able to infer the predicate substitution that maps $\mathsf{sch}_{\{1\}}$, $\mathsf{sch}_{\{2\}}$, and $\mathsf{sch}_{\{1,2\}}$ to $\lambda \widetilde{V}.\mathsf{h}_1 \wedge \neg \mathsf{h}_2 \wedge \mathsf{z}_1 = 2\mathsf{z}_2$, $\lambda \widetilde{V}.\neg \mathsf{h}_1 \wedge \mathsf{h}_2 \wedge \mathsf{z}_2 = 2\mathsf{z}_1$, and $\lambda \widetilde{V}.(\mathsf{h}_1 \wedge \neg \mathsf{h}_2 \Rightarrow \mathsf{z}_1 + 1 = 2\mathsf{z}_2) \wedge (\neg \mathsf{h}_1 \wedge \mathsf{h}_2 \wedge \mathsf{z}_2 + 1 = 2\mathsf{z}_1)$ respectively, where $\widetilde{V}$ is the list of the variables in the two program copies. The inferred predicates stipulate that the copy with $\mathsf{h} = \mathtt{true}$ is scheduled to execute the loop two times per every loop iteration of the copy with $\mathsf{h} = \mathtt{false}$. The extended report [58] shows the pfwCSP encoding of the example. A solution generated by PCSAT is also shown in [58].

4.2   Co-termination

Intuitively, co-termination means that if one program terminates, then a second program must terminate [6, 10]. This can also be thought of as a form of relational *termination problem.*[2]

Definition 4 (Co-termination). The *co-termination verification problem* is to decide if for all $\widetilde{v_1}, \widetilde{v_2}$ such that $Pre(\widetilde{v_1}, \widetilde{v_2})$, if $\widetilde{v_1} \rightsquigarrow_1 v'_1$ then $\widetilde{v_2} \not\rightsquigarrow_2 \bot$.

Roughly, the property says that from any pair of states related by Pre, if P_1 terminates, then P_2 must also terminate. Note that this is an *asymmetric* property. A symmetric version can be obtained by also asserting the property with the positions of the two programs exchanged. The symmetric version implies, assuming that there is at least one execution from any Pre-related state, that from any pair of Pre-related states, all executions from one state terminates iff all executions from the other one do as well. We now present an encoding of conditional co-termination in pfwCSP.

Definition 5 (Co-termination through constraints). Let $\widetilde{V} = \widetilde{V_1}, \widetilde{V_2}$. We define pfwCSP constraints $\mathcal{C}_{\mathrm{CoT}}$ be the set of following clauses:

(1) $Pre(\widetilde{V}) \wedge \mathsf{fnb}(\widetilde{V}, b) \Rightarrow \mathsf{inv}(0, b, \widetilde{V})$

(2) $\mathsf{inv}(d, b, \widetilde{V}) \wedge \neg F_1(\widetilde{V_1}) \wedge \neg F_2(\widetilde{V_2}) \Rightarrow (-b \leq d \wedge d \leq b \wedge b \geq 0)$

(3a) $\mathsf{inv}(d, b, \widetilde{V}) \wedge \mathsf{sch}_{\mathsf{FT}}(d, b, \widetilde{V}) \wedge T_2(\widetilde{V_2}, \widetilde{V_2}') \wedge (F_1(\widetilde{V_1}) \vee F_2(\widetilde{V_2}) \vee d' = d - 1) \Rightarrow$
$\quad \mathsf{inv}(d', b, \widetilde{V_1}, \widetilde{V_2}')$

(3b) $\mathsf{inv}(d, b, \widetilde{V}) \wedge \mathsf{sch}_{\mathsf{TF}}(d, b, \widetilde{V}) \wedge T_1(\widetilde{V_1}, \widetilde{V_1}') \wedge (F_1(\widetilde{V_1}) \vee F_2(\widetilde{V_2}) \vee d' = d + 1) \Rightarrow$
$\quad \mathsf{inv}(d', b, \widetilde{V_1}', \widetilde{V_2})$

(3c) $\mathsf{inv}(d, b, \widetilde{V}) \wedge \mathsf{sch}_{\mathsf{TT}}(d, b, \widetilde{V}) \wedge T_1(\widetilde{V_1}, \widetilde{V_1}') \wedge T_2(\widetilde{V_2}, \widetilde{V_2}') \Rightarrow \mathsf{inv}(d, b, \widetilde{V_1}', \widetilde{V_2}')$

(4a) $\mathsf{inv}(d, b, \widetilde{V}) \wedge \mathsf{sch}_{\mathsf{FT}}(d, b, \widetilde{V}) \wedge \neg F_1(\widetilde{V_1}) \Rightarrow \neg F_2(\widetilde{V_2})$

(4b) $\mathsf{inv}(d, b, \widetilde{V}) \wedge \mathsf{sch}_{\mathsf{TF}}(d, b, \widetilde{V}) \wedge \neg F_2(\widetilde{V_2}) \Rightarrow \neg F_1(\widetilde{V_1})$

(5) $\mathsf{inv}(d, b, \widetilde{V}) \wedge (\neg F_1(\widetilde{V_1}) \vee \neg F_2(\widetilde{V_2})) \Rightarrow \bigvee_{a \in \{\mathsf{TT}, \mathsf{FT}, \mathsf{TF}\}} \mathsf{sch}_a(d, b, \widetilde{V})$

(6) $\mathsf{inv}(d, b, \widetilde{V}) \wedge F_1(\widetilde{V_1}) \wedge \neg F_2(\widetilde{V_2}) \wedge T_2(\widetilde{V_2}, \widetilde{V_2}') \Rightarrow \mathsf{wfr}(\widetilde{V_2}, \widetilde{V_2}')$

Here, $\mathsf{sch}_{\mathsf{TT}}$, $\mathsf{sch}_{\mathsf{FT}}$, and $\mathsf{sch}_{\mathsf{TF}}$ are 2-specialization of the k-safety scheduler of Definition 3. Clauses (3x)'s are similar to (3) of Definition 3 and assert that inv is an invariant under the scheduler. Clauses (4x)'s and (5), like (4) and (5) of Definition 3, are used to ensure the scheduler fairness. However, they are insufficient for co-termination as a non-terminating copy can be scheduled indefinitely leaving the other copy unscheduled. Clauses (1) and (2) are added to amend the issue. In (1), fnb is a functional predicate variable that is used to select a *bound* b, and (2) asserts that the *difference* d between the numbers of steps taken by the two copies is within b in any state in inv when neither copy has terminated. Note that d is initialized to 0 by (1) and properly updated in (3x)'s. Finally, by using the well-founded predicate variable wfr, (6) asserts that if P_1 has terminated, then so must eventually P_2.

---

[2] The property has also been called *relative termination* [31].

Theorem 2 (Soundness and Completeness of $\mathcal{C}_{\mathrm{CoT}}$). *The given pair of programs co-terminate iff $\mathcal{C}_{\mathrm{CoT}}$ is satisfiable.*

As with Theorem 1, the soundness direction relies on scheduler fairness.

Example 2. Via the encoding, our PCSAT tool is able to verify the symmetric co-termination example from Sect. 2.1 by automatically inferring the solution described there. For space, the concrete constraint set and solution are given in the extended report [58].

4.3 Generalized Non-interference

We now turn to another relational property that cannot simply be captured by k-safety or co-termination. So-called *termination-insensitive (resp. -sensitive) generalized non-interference* (resp. TI-GNI, TS-GNI) are $\forall\exists$ hyperproperties: from any pre-related pair of states whenever one side can take a move to a post state, there must be a way for the other side to also move to a post state such that the post-relation holds. As remarked in Sect. 2, verifying GNI requires reasoning about both *demonic* (*i.e.*, for all) and *angelic* (*i.e.*, exists) *non-determinism.*

Definition 6 (TI/TS-GNI). The *GNI verification problem* is to decide if the following holds. If $Pre(\widetilde{v}_1, \widetilde{v}_2)$ and $\widetilde{v}_1 \leadsto_1 \widetilde{v}_1'$ then **(TI-GNI)** $(\exists \widetilde{v}_2'.\widetilde{v}_2 \leadsto_2 \widetilde{v}_2' \wedge Post(\widetilde{v}_1', \widetilde{v}_2')) \vee \widetilde{v}_2 \leadsto_2 \bot$; or **(TS-GNI)** $\exists \widetilde{v}_2'.\widetilde{v}_2 \leadsto_2 \widetilde{v}_2' \wedge Post(\widetilde{v}_1', \widetilde{v}_2')$.

Note that our definition is parameterized by *Pre* and *Post*. The standard GNI definitions [40] can be obtained by letting P_1 and P_2 be copies of the same target program and letting *Pre* be the predicate equating the low inputs of the copies and *Post* be the predicate equating the low outputs of the copies.

To formalize the pfwCSP encodings of the GNI verification problems, we define a relation U_2 to be one such that $T_2(\widetilde{v}, \widetilde{v}') \Leftrightarrow \exists r.U_2(r, \widetilde{v}, \widetilde{v}')$ and $U_2(r, \widetilde{v}, \widetilde{v}') \wedge U_2(r, \widetilde{v}, \widetilde{v}'') \Rightarrow \widetilde{v}' = \widetilde{v}''$. Roughly, U_2 is a function version of the transition relation T_2 with the extra parameter r to make the non-deterministic choices explicit.

We now show the pfwCSP encodings of TI-GNI and TS-GNI. The key idea is to augment the encodings for k-safety and/or co-termination with *functional predicate variables* and *prophecy variables* that respectively represent the non-deterministic choices of the angelic side (*i.e.*, P_2) and the final outputs of the demonic side (*i.e.*, P_1).

Definition 7 (TI-GNI through constraints). We define pfwCSP constraints $\mathcal{C}_{\mathrm{TIGNI}}$ as $\mathcal{C}_S$ in Definition 3 for $k = 2$ but with the following modifications:

(m1) The parameters representing the inputs and outputs of P_1 is extended with prophecy variables $\widetilde{p}$ where $|\widetilde{p}| = |\widetilde{V}_1|$. Accordingly, each occurrence of $\widetilde{V}_1$ is replaced by $\widetilde{p}, \widetilde{V}_1$, and each occurrence of $\widetilde{V}_1'$ is replaced by $\widetilde{p}', \widetilde{V}_1'$.

(m2) *Pre* is replaced by *Pre'* which is defined by $Pre'(\widetilde{p}, \widetilde{V}_1, \widetilde{V}_2) \Leftrightarrow Pre(\widetilde{V}_1, \widetilde{V}_2)$, *i.e.*, the prophecy values are unconstrained in the precondition.

(m3) F_1 is replaced by F_1' defined by $F_1'(\widetilde{p}, \widetilde{V_1}) \Leftrightarrow F_1(\widetilde{V_1})$.

(m4) T_1 is replaced by T_1' defined by $T_1'(\widetilde{p}, \widetilde{V_1}, \widetilde{p}', \widetilde{V_1}') \Leftrightarrow T_1(\widetilde{V_1}, \widetilde{V_1}') \wedge \widetilde{p} = \widetilde{p}'$.

(m5) $Post$ is replaced by $Post'$ defined by $Post'(\widetilde{p}, \widetilde{V_1}, \widetilde{V_2}) \Leftrightarrow (\widetilde{p} = \widetilde{V_1} \Rightarrow Post(\widetilde{V_1}, \widetilde{V_2}))$, *i.e.*, if the prophecy was correct then the original post condition must hold.

(m6) Each occurrence of $T_2(\widetilde{V_2}, \widetilde{V_2}')$ is replaced by $\mathsf{fnr}(\widetilde{p}, \widetilde{V_2}, r) \wedge U_2(r, \widetilde{V_2}, \widetilde{V_2}')$ where fnr is a functional predicate variable.

Modifications (m1)–(m5) concern prophecy variables. They are initialized arbitrarily as shown in (m2), propagated unmodified through the transitions as shown in (m4), and finally checked if they match P_1's outputs in (m5). Modification (m6) adds functional predicate variables to express the angelic nondeterministic choices of P_2. The functional predicate variables shift the onus of making the right choices to the solver's task of discovering sufficient assignments to them. Importantly, the functional predicate takes the prophecy variables as parameters, thus allowing dependence on the final outputs of the demonic side.

Definition 8 (TS-GNI through constraints). We define pfwCSP constraints $\mathcal{C}_{\mathrm{TSGNI}}$ as $\mathcal{C}_{\mathrm{CoT}}$ in Definition 5 but with modifications of Definition 7 except (m3) and (m5), and with the following modifications:

(m3') F_1 is replaced by F_1' defined by $F_1'(\widetilde{p}, \widetilde{V_1}) \Leftrightarrow F_1(\widetilde{V_1}) \wedge \widetilde{p} = \widetilde{V_1}$.

(m5') The clause $\mathsf{inv}(\widetilde{p}, \widetilde{V_1}, \widetilde{V_2}) \wedge F_1'(\widetilde{p}, \widetilde{V_1}) \wedge F_2(\widetilde{V_2}) \Rightarrow Post(\widetilde{V_1}, \widetilde{V_2})$ is added.

$\mathcal{C}_{\mathrm{TSGNI}}$ is similar to $\mathcal{C}_{\mathrm{TIGNI}}$ except that it contains the difference bound and well-foundedness constraints to handle the "co-termination" aspect of TS-GNI, *i.e.*, if P_1 terminates and makes an output then P_2 must also be able terminate and make a matching output. One subtle aspect of the encoding is that (m3') modifies the final state predicate for P_1 to enforce co-termination only when the prophecy is correct. However, it is worth noting that TS-GNI is *not* a conjunction of TI-GNI and co-termination. For instance, the GNI example from Sect. 2.1 satisfies TS-GNI but does not satisfy co-termination.

Theorem 3 (Soundess and Completeness of TI-GNI). *The given pair of programs satisfy TI-GNI iff* $\mathcal{C}_{\mathrm{TIGNI}}$ *is satisfiable.*

Theorem 4 (Soundess and Completeness of TS-GNI). *The given pair of programs satisfy TS-GNI iff* $\mathcal{C}_{\mathrm{TSGNI}}$ *is satisfiable.*

The soundness directions are proven by "determinizing" the angelic choices by solutions to the functional predicate variables and reducing the argument to those of k-safety and co-termination. The completeness directions are proven by "synthesizing" sufficient angelic choice functions from program executions.

Example 3. Via the encoding, our PCSAT tool is able to verify the TS-GNI example from Sect. 2.1 by automatically inferring not only the functional predicate described there but also relational invariants and well-founded relations given in the extended report [58]. For space, the concrete constraint set is also given in [58].

Remark 3. The angelic non-determinism encoding can be optimized by using head disjunctions when the non-determinism is finitary (*i.e.*, $\max_{\widetilde{v}}|\{\widetilde{v}' \mid T_2(\widetilde{v}, \widetilde{v}')\}|$ is finite) instead of using functional predicate variables. For this, we modify clauses (3) and (3x)'s of Definition 7 and 8 to contain multiple positive occurrences of inv where each occurrence represents one of the finitely many possible choices.

Remark 4. Recall that we allow any program to be non-deterministic. The k-safety and co-termination encodings treat non-determinism in all programs as demonic, whereas the GNI encodings treat those in one program (*i.e.*, P_1) as demonic and those in the other program (*i.e.*, P_2) as angelic. In general, an arbitrary program can be made angelic by applying the transformation done in the angelic side of GNI encodings (to factor out non-determinism).

5   Constraint Solving Method for pfwCSP

We describe a CEGIS-based method for finding a (syntactic) solution of the given pfwCSP $(\mathcal{C}, \mathcal{K})$. Our method iterates the following phases until convergence. The iteration maintains and builds a sequence σ of *candidate solutions* and a sequence $\mathcal{E}$ of *example instances* where $\mathcal{E}^{(i)}$ are ground clauses obtained from $\mathcal{C}$ by instantiating the term variables and serve as a counterexample to the candidate solution $\sigma^{(i-1)}$, for each i-th iteration. The iteration starts from $\mathcal{E}^{(1)} = \emptyset$.

Synthesis Phase: We check if $(\mathcal{E}^{(i)}, \mathcal{K})$ is unsatisfiable. If so, we stop by returning $\mathcal{E}^{(i)}$ as a genuine counterexample to the input problem $(\mathcal{C}, \mathcal{K})$. Otherwise, we use the synthesizer $\mathcal{S}_{TB}$ (cf. Sect. 5.1) to find a solution $\sigma^{(i)}$ of $(\mathcal{E}^{(i)}, \mathcal{K})$, which will be used as the next candidate solution.

Validation Phase: We check if $\sigma^{(i)}$ is a genuine solution to $(\mathcal{C}, \mathcal{K})$ by using an SMT solver. If so, we stop by returning $\sigma^{(i)}$ as a solution. Otherwise, for each clause $c \in \mathcal{C}$ not satisfied by $\sigma^{(i)}$, we obtain a term substitution θ_c such that $\mathrm{dom}(\theta_c) = ftv(c)$ and $\not\models \theta_c(\sigma^{(i)}(c))$. We then update the example set by adding a new example instance for each unsatisfied clause (i.e., $\mathcal{E}^{(i+1)} = \mathcal{E}^{(i)} \cup \{\theta_c(c) \mid c \in \mathcal{C} \wedge \not\models \sigma^{(i)}(c)\}$), and proceed to the next iteration.

The above procedure satisfies the usual *progress property* of CEGIS: discovered counterexamples and candidate solutions are not discovered again in succeeding iterations. Furthermore, as discussed in Sect. 5.1, by carefully designing the synthesizer $\mathcal{S}_{TB}$ by incorporating *stratified* CEGIS, we achieve *completeness* in the sense of [34,55]: if the given pfwCSP $(\mathcal{C}, \mathcal{K})$ has a syntactic solution expressible in the stratified families of templates, a solution of the pfwCSP is eventually found by the procedure. In Sect. 5.1, we discuss the details of the synthesis phase. There, for space, we focus on the theory of quantifier-free linear integer arithmetic (QFLIA). For space, we defer the details of the unsatisfiability checking process to the extended report [58].

Remark 5. The implementation described in Sect. 6 contains an additional phase called *resolution phase* for accelerating the convergence. There, we first apply unit propagation repeatedly to the given $\mathcal{E}^{(i)}$ to obtain positive examples $\mathcal{E}^{(i)+}$ of the form $X(\tilde{v})$ and negative examples $\mathcal{E}^{(i)-}$ of the form $\neg X(\tilde{v})$. We then repeatedly apply resolution principle to the clauses in the input clauses $\mathcal{C}$ and the clauses $\mathcal{E}^{(i)+} \cup \mathcal{E}^{(i)-}$ to obtain additional positive and negative examples.

5.1 Predicate Synthesis with Stratified Families of Templates

We describe our candidate solution synthesizer $\mathcal{S}_{TB}$. $\mathcal{S}_{TB}$ performs a template-based search for a solution to the given example instances. As we shall show, our approach allows searching for assignments to all predicate variables (of all three kinds) in the given instance which is important because satisfying assignments to different predicate variables often inter-dependent. There, however, is a trade-off between expressiveness and generalizability. With less expressive templates like intervals, we may miss actual solutions. But with very expressive templates like polyhedra, there could be many solutions, and a solution thus returned is liable to overfitting, i.e., the solution to the example instances becomes too specific to be an actual solution to the original input clauses. [44] discusses a similar overfitting issue in the context of grammar-based synthesis.

Stratified Template Family for Ordinary Predicate Variables:
$$T_X^{\bullet}(nd, nc, ac, ad) \triangleq \lambda(x_1, \ldots, x_{\mathrm{ar}(X)}). \bigvee_{i=1}^{nd} \bigwedge_{j=1}^{nc} c_{i,j,0} + \sum_{k=1}^{\mathrm{ar}(X)} c_{i,j,k} \cdot x_k \geq 0$$
$$\phi_X^{\bullet}(nd, nc, ac, ad) \triangleq \bigwedge_{i=1}^{nd} \bigwedge_{j=1}^{nc} (\sum_{k=1}^{\mathrm{ar}(X)} |c_{i,j,k}| \leq ac) \wedge |c_{i,j,0}| \leq ad$$

Stratified Template Family for Well-Founded Predicate Variables:
$$T_X^{\Downarrow}(np, nl, nc, rc, rd, dc, dd) \triangleq \lambda(\tilde{x}, \tilde{y}). \bigwedge_{i=1}^{np} \bigwedge_{k=1}^{nl} r_{i,k}(\tilde{x}) \geq 0 \wedge (\bigvee_{i=1}^{np} D_i(\tilde{x})) \wedge$$
$$(\bigvee_{j=1}^{np} D_j(\tilde{y})) \wedge (\bigvee_{i=1}^{np} D_i(\tilde{x}) \wedge \bigwedge_{j=1}^{np} (D_j(\tilde{y}) \Rightarrow DEC_{i,j}(\tilde{x}, \tilde{y})))$$
$$\phi_X^{\Downarrow}(np, nl, nc, rc, rd, dc, dd) \triangleq \bigwedge_{i=1}^{np} \bigwedge_{k=1}^{nl} (\sum_{\ell=1}^{\mathrm{ar}(X)/2} |c_{i,k,\ell}| \leq rc) \wedge |c_{i,k,0}| \leq rd \wedge$$
$$\bigwedge_{i=1}^{np} \bigwedge_{k=1}^{nc} (\sum_{\ell=1}^{\mathrm{ar}(X)/2} |c'_{i,k,\ell}| \leq dc) \wedge |c'_{i,k,0}| \leq dd$$
$$DEC_{i,j}(\tilde{x}, \tilde{y}) \triangleq \bigvee_{k=1}^{nl} (r_{i,k}(\tilde{x}) > r_{j,k}(\tilde{y}) \wedge \bigwedge_{\ell=1}^{k-1} r_{i,\ell}(\tilde{x}) \geq r_{j,\ell}(\tilde{y}))$$
$$r_{i,k}(\tilde{x}) \triangleq c_{i,k,0} + \sum_{\ell=1}^{\mathrm{ar}(X)/2} c_{i,k,\ell} \cdot x_\ell \qquad D_i(\tilde{x}) \triangleq \bigwedge_{k=1}^{nc} c'_{i,k,0} + \sum_{\ell=1}^{\mathrm{ar}(X)/2} c'_{i,k,\ell} \cdot x_\ell \geq 0$$

Stratified Template Family for Functional Predicate Variables:
$$T_X^{\lambda}(nd, nc, dc, dd, ec, ed) \triangleq \lambda(\tilde{x}, r).r = \text{if } D_1(\tilde{x}) \text{ then } e_1(\tilde{x}) \text{ else if } D_2(\tilde{x}) \text{ then } e_2(\tilde{x}) \cdots$$
$$\text{else if } D_{nd-1}(\tilde{x}) \text{ then } e_{nd-1}(\tilde{x}) \text{ else } e_{nd}(\tilde{x})$$
$$\phi_X^{\lambda}(nd, nc, ec, ed, dc, dd) \triangleq \bigwedge_{i=1}^{nd} (\sum_{j=1}^{\mathrm{ar}(X)-1} |c_{i,j}| \leq ec) \wedge |c_{i,0}| \leq ed \wedge$$
$$\bigwedge_{i=1}^{nd-1} \bigwedge_{j=1}^{nc} (\sum_{k=1}^{\mathrm{ar}(X)-1} |c'_{i,j,k}| \leq dc) \wedge |c'_{i,j,0}| \leq dd$$
$$e_i(\tilde{x}) \triangleq c_{i,0} + \sum_{j=1}^{\mathrm{ar}(X)-1} c_{i,j} \cdot x_j \qquad D_i(\tilde{x}) \triangleq \bigwedge_{j=1}^{nc} c'_{i,j,0} + \sum_{k=1}^{\mathrm{ar}(X)-1} c'_{i,j,k} \cdot x_k \geq 0$$

Fig. 2. Stratified families of templates

Our remedy to the issue is *stratified families of predicate templates*, inspired by a similar approach proposed in the context of predicate abstraction with CEGAR [34,55]. Initially, we assign each predicate variable a less expressive template and gradually refine it in a counterexample-guided manner: if no solution exists in the current template, we generate and analyze an unsat core to identify the *parameters of the families of templates* that should be updated. The stratification of templates thus automatically pushes the template to an expressive one (e.g., polyhedra) when it needs to. Importantly, with our approach, expressive templates are not always used but only when they should be used.

Stratified Families of Templates. We have designed three stratified families of templates shown in Fig. 2, respectively for ordinary ($\bullet$), well-founded ($\Downarrow$), and functional (λ) predicate variables. First, for each ordinary predicate variable X, we prepare the stratified family of templates $T_X^{\bullet}(nd, nc, ac, ad)$ with unknowns $c_{i,j,k}$'s to be inferred and its accompanying constraint $\phi_X^{\bullet}(nd, nc, ac, ad)$. The body of $T_X^{\bullet}$ is a DNF with affine inequalities as atoms. The parameter nd (resp. nc) is the number of disjuncts (resp. conjuncts). The parameter ac is the upper bound of the sum of the absolute values of coefficients $c_{i,j,k}$ ($k > 0$), and ad is the upper bound of the absolute value of $c_{i,j,0}$.

Secondly, for each functional predicate variable X, we prepare the stratified family of templates $T_X^{\Downarrow}(np, nl, nc, rc, rd, dc, dd)$ with unknowns $c_{i,j,k}$'s and $c'_{i,j,k}$'s and its accompanying constraint $\phi_X^{\Downarrow}(np, nl, nc, rc, rd, dc, dd)$. $T_X^{\Downarrow}$ represents the well-founded relation induced by a *piecewise-defined lexicographic affine ranking function* [2,39,39,60,61] where $r_{i,j}$ is the affine ranking function template for the j-th lexicographic component of the i-th region specified by the discriminator D_i. The parameter np (resp. nl) is the number of regions (resp. lexicographic components). The parameters rc, rd, dc, dd are the upper bounds of (the sums of) the absolute values of unknowns, similar to ac and ad of $T_X^{\bullet}$. The first conjunct of $T_X^{\Downarrow}$ asserts that the return value of each ranking functions is non-negative. The second and the third conjuncts assert that the discriminators cover all relevant states. Note that discriminators may overlap, and for such overlapping regions, the maximum return value of the ranking functions is used. The fourth conjunct asserts that the return value of the piecewise-defined ranking function strictly decreases from $\widetilde{x}$ to $\widetilde{y}$. Here, $DEC_{i,j}(\widetilde{x}, \widetilde{y})$ asserts that the return value of the lexicographic ranking function for the i-th region at $\widetilde{x}$ is greater than that for the j-th region at $\widetilde{y}$. It follows that for any substitution θ for the unknowns in $T_X^{\Downarrow}$, $\theta(T_X^{\Downarrow})$ represents a well-founded relation. Our implementation PCSAT uses a refined version of $T_X^{\Downarrow}$ shown in the extended report [58].

Finally, for each functional predicate variable X, we prepare the stratified family of templates $T_X^{\lambda}(nd, nc, dc, dd, ec, ed)$ with unknowns $c_{i,j}$'s and $c'_{i,j,k}$'s and its accompanying constraint $\phi_F^{\lambda}(nd, nc, dc, dd, ec, ed)$. T_X^{λ} characterizes a piecewise-defined affine function with discriminators $D_1, \ldots, D_{nd-1}$ and branch expressions $e_1, \ldots, e_{nd}$. The parameter nc is the number of conjuncts in each discriminator. The parameters dc, dd, ec, ed are the upper bounds of (the sums of) the absolute values of unknown, similar to ac and ad of $T_X^{\bullet}$. Note that for any substitution θ for the unknowns in T_X^{λ}, $\theta(T_X^{\lambda})(\widetilde{x}, r)$ expresses a total function that maps $\widetilde{x}$ to r.

Next, we give the details of the candidate solution synthesis process. Let $\widetilde{p} \in \mathbb{Z}^n$ where n is the number of parameters summed across all templates, and let $T_X^\alpha(\widetilde{p})$ and $\phi_X^\alpha(\widetilde{p})$ (for $\alpha \in \{\bullet, \Downarrow, \lambda\}$) project the corresponding parameters. Each $\widetilde{p} \in \mathbb{Z}^n$ induces a *solution space* $[\![\widetilde{p}]\!] \triangleq \{T(\widetilde{p})[\theta] \mid \theta \models Con(\widetilde{p})\}$ where $T(\widetilde{p})[\theta] \triangleq \{X \mapsto \theta(T_X^{\mathcal{K}(X)}(\widetilde{p})) \mid X \in fpv(\mathcal{C})\}$ and $Con(\widetilde{p}) \triangleq \bigwedge_{X \in fpv(\mathcal{C})} \phi_X^{\mathcal{K}(X)}(\widetilde{p})$.

Let $\widetilde{p}_1 \le \widetilde{p}_2$ be the point-wise ordering. Note that $[\![\widetilde{p}]\!]$ is a finite set for any $\widetilde{p} \in \mathbb{Z}^n$, and $\widetilde{p}_1 \le \widetilde{p}_2$ implies $[\![\widetilde{p}_1]\!] \subseteq [\![\widetilde{p}_2]\!]$. We start the CEGIS process with some small initial parameters $\widetilde{p}^{(0)}$ (the parameters will be maintained as a state of the CEGIS process). The synthesis phase of each iteration tries to find a solution $\theta \in [\![\widetilde{p}^{(i)}]\!]$ to the given example instances $(\mathcal{E}, \mathcal{K})$ where $\widetilde{p}^{(i)}$ are the current parameters. This is done by using an SMT solver for QFLIA to find θ satisfying $\bigwedge T(\widetilde{p}^{(i)})[\theta](\mathcal{E}) \wedge \theta(Con(\widetilde{p}^{(i)}))$. If such θ is found, we return $T(\widetilde{p}^{(i)})[\theta]$ as the candidate solution for the next validation phase of the CEGIS process. Note that, by construction of the templates, the solution is guaranteed to assign each well-founded (resp. functional) predicate variable a well-founded relation (resp. total function). Otherwise, no solutions to the given example instances $(\mathcal{E}, \mathcal{K})$ can be found in $[\![\widetilde{p}^{(i)}]\!]$, and we update the parameters to some $\widetilde{p}^{(i+1)} > \widetilde{p}^{(i)}$ such that $[\![\widetilde{p}^{(i+1)}]\!]$ contains a solution for $(\mathcal{E}, \mathcal{K})$. Here, it is important to do the update in a *fair manner* [34,55], that is, in any infinite series of updates $\widetilde{p}^{(0)}, \widetilde{p}^{(1)}, \ldots$, every parameter is updated infinitely often (the details are deferred to below). By the progress property and the fact that every $[\![\widetilde{p}]\!]$ is finite, this ensures that every parameter is updated infinitely often in an infinite series of CEGIS iterations. We thus obtain the following property.

Theorem 5. *Our CEGIS-procedure based on stratified families of templates is complete in the sense of [34,55]: if there is $\widetilde{p}$ and $\sigma \in [\![\widetilde{p}]\!]$ such that σ is a syntactic solution to the given* pfwCSP $(\mathcal{C}, \mathcal{K})$, *a syntactic solution to* $(\mathcal{C}, \mathcal{K})$ *is eventually found by the procedure.*

Note that, while the solution space of each stratum (*i.e.*, $[\![\widetilde{p}^{(i)}]\!]$) is finite, our procedure searches the infinite solution space obtained by taking the infinite union of the solution spaces of the template family strata (*i.e.*, $\bigcup_{i \in \omega} [\![\widetilde{p}^{(i)}]\!]$).

Remark 6. Our template-based synthesis simultaneously finds ordinary, well-founded, and functional predicates that are mutually dependent through the given $(\mathcal{E}, \mathcal{K})$. This means that templates for different kinds of predicate variables are updated in a synchronized and balanced manner, which benefits the synthesis of mutually dependent witnesses for a relational property (see the extended report [58] for examples).

Updating Parameters of Template Families via Unsat Cores. We now describe the parameter update process. We first obtain the unsat core of the unsatisfiability of $\bigwedge T(\widetilde{p}^{(i)})[\theta](\mathcal{E}) \wedge \theta(Con(\widetilde{p}^{(i)}))$ from the SMT solver. We then analyze the core to obtain the parameters of template families, such as the number of conjuncts and disjuncts, that have caused the unsatisfiability. Here, there could be a dependency between predicate variables and in such a case our unsat core analysis enumerates all the involved predicate variables from which we obtain the parameters of template families to be updated. We then increment these parameters in some fair manner, by limiting the maximum differences between different parameters to some bounded threshold, and repeatedly solve the resulting constraint until a solution is found. Thus, the parameters of stratified families of templates are grown on-the-fly guided by the reasons for unsatisfiability. We found that a careful design of parameter update strategies important for scaling the stratified CEGIS to hard relational verification problems. The manual tuning, however, is tiresome and suboptimal. We leave as future work to investigate methods for automatic tuning of parameter update strategies.

6 Evaluation

To evaluate the presented verification framework, we have implemented PCSAT, a satisfiability checking tool for pfwCSP based on stratified CEGIS. PCSAT supports the theory of Booleans and the quantifier-free theory of linear inequalities over integers and rationals. The tool is implemented in OCaml, using Z3 [41] as the backend SMT solver. We ran the tool on a diverse collection of 20 relational verification problems, consisting of k-safety, co-termination, and GNI problems. Though we have manually reduced them to pfwCSP using the presented method in Sect. 4, this process can be easily automated. The full benchmark set is provided in the extended report [58]. All experiments have been conducted on 3.1 GHz Intel Xeon Platinum 8000 CPU and 32 GB RAM with the time limit of 600 s.

The experimental results are summarized in Table 1. The columns "Time (s)" and "#Iters" respectively show elapsed wall clock time in seconds and numbers of CEGIS iterations. PCSAT solved 15 verification problems fully automatically and 5 problems labeled with the symbol † and/or ‡ semi-automatically. For the 4 problems labeled with †, we manually provided small hints for invariant synthesis (interested readers are referred to [58]). The provided hints for all but SquareSum are non-relational invariants that can be inferred prior to relational verification by using a CHCs solver or an invariant synthesizer. For the 2 problems labeled with ‡, we manually chose the initial value for the parameters of the template family for ordinary predicate variables to reduce the elapsed time. This can be automated by running PCSAT with different initial values in parallel.

The problems DoubleSquareNI_h**, HalfSquareNI, ArrayInsert, and SquareSum are k-safety verification problems obtained from [50] that require non-lock-step scheduling.[3] The problems DoubleSquareNI_h** are generated from Example 1 by a case analysis of the valuation for the boolean variables h_1 and h_2. PCSAT solved all the k-safety problems but SquareSum *fully automatically*. The tool PDSC proposed in [50] can verify them but requires the user to provide the atomic predicates for expressing relational invariants and schedulers. The problems CotermIntro1 and CotermIntro2 are asymmetric co-termination problems obtained from the symmetric problem in Example 2 and are verified by PCSAT fully automatically. The problems TS_GNI_h** are generated from Example 3 by

---

[3] We omitted ArrayIntMod from [50] because its verification requires the theory of arrays which the current version of PCSAT does not fully support.

a case analysis and are verified by PCSat with small non-relational hints. We have also tested PCSat on various TS-GNI (SimpleTS_GNI1, SimpleTS_GNI2, InfBranchTS_GNI) and TI-GNI problems (TI_GNI_h**) and obtained promising results. As far as we know, no existing tools can verify these non-k-safety relational problems.

Furthermore, manual inspection of the PCSat's output logs for the GNI problems that required hints revealed that the functional predicate synthesis appears to be the main bottleneck of the current version. In fact, we confirmed that the problems can be solved in less than 10 s if appropriate functional predicates for angelic non-determinism are manually provided. As future work, we plan to investigate methods for improved functional predicate synthesis.

7 Related Work

7.1 Relational Verification

There has been substantial work on verifying relational properties. They include program logics, type systems, or program analysis frameworks such as abstract interpretation and model checking [1,5,9,19,25,52,62], program transformation approaches such as self-composition or product programs [4,7,15,20,21,42,47, 54,57,64], and various other approaches [3,18,23,46,59]. We refer to [43] for an excellent survey. However, most prior automatic approaches address only the k-safety fragment [17,54] and cannot verify non-k-safety (actually, not even hypersafety) properties such as co-termination, TS-NI, TI-GNI, and TS-GNI [6,11,40]. The only exception that we are aware is the recent work by Coenen et al. [19] that proposes a sound method for automatically verifying $\forall\exists$ hyperproperties such as GNI for finite state systems. To our knowledge, we are the *first* to propose a sound-and-complete approach to automatically verifying these non-hypersafety properties for infinite state programs.[4]

A key task in many relational verification methods, including ours, is the discovery of *relational invariants* which relate the states of multiple program executions. While most prior approaches are limited to fixed execution schedule (or *alignment*) such as lock-step and sequential [7,8,20,21,42,54,57], a recent work by Shemer et al. [50] has proposed a k-safety property verification method that automatically infers fair schedulers sufficient to prove the goal property. Importantly, the schedulers in their approach can be *semantic* in which the choice of which program to execute can depend on the *states* of the programs as opposed to the classic *syntactic* schedulers such as lock-step and sequential that can only depend on the control locations. Our approach also infers such fair semantic schedulers, and as remarked before, they enable solving instances like doubleSquare that are difficult for previous approaches. However, [50] requires

---

[4] However, [19] can verify (relational) temporal properties, whereas we only support functional properties that are given by pre and post conditions of whole program runs. We leave as future work to investigate methods for verifying relational temporal properties of infinite state programs.

Table 1. Experimental results of PCSAT on the relational verification benchmarks

Program	Time (s)	#Iters	Program	Time (s)	#Iters
DoubleSquareNI_hFT	17.762	42	HalfSquareNI	11.853	35
DoubleSquareNI_hTF	26.495	55	ArrayInsert‡	118.671	73
DoubleSquareNI_hFF	2.944	9	SquareSum†‡	337.596	117
DoubleSquareNI_hTT	4.055	11	SimpleTS_GNI1	5.397	14
CotermIntro1	19.322	80	SimpleTS_GNI2	8.919	26
CotermIntro2	15.871	73	InfBranchTS_GNI	2.607	4
TS_GNI_hFT†	47.083	78	TI_GNI_hFT†	4.389	16
TS_GNI_hTF	5.076	17	TI_GNI_hTF	2.277	6
TS_GNI_hFF	7.174	24	TI_GNI_hFF	2.968	6
TS_GNI_hTT†	23.495	53	TI_GNI_hTT	4.148	22

the user to provide appropriate atomic predicates and is not fully automatic. By contrast, our approach soundly and completely encodes the problem as a constraint satisfaction problem and fully automatically verifies hard instances like doubleSquare by constraint solving.

Furthermore, our work extends the fair semantic scheduler synthesis to beyond k-safety problems like co-termination, TI-GNI and TS-GNI, in a sound and complete manner. We note that the extensions are non-trivial and involves delicate uses of functional predicate variables and well-founded predicate variables to ensure scheduler fairness in the presence of non-termination as well as uses of prophecy variables and functional predicate variables to handle angelic non-determinism. The higher-degree of automation and the extension to non-k-safety properties are thanks to the expressive power of our novel constraint framework pfwCSP.

7.2 Predicate Constraint Solving

Our pfwCSP solving technique builds on and generalizes a number of techniques developed for CHCs solving as well as invariant and ranking function discovery. Most closely related to our constraint solving method are CEGIS-based [51] and data-driven approaches to solving CHCs [14, 22, 24, 26, 27, 38, 44, 45, 48, 49, 65]. As remarked before, the new pfwCSP framework is strictly more expressive than CHCs and extending the prior techniques to the new framework is non-trivial.

Our stratified CEGIS is inspired by the idea of stratified languages of predicates proposed in the context of predicate abstraction with CEGAR [34, 55]. It is also similar in spirit to the work by Padhi et al. [44], but they use a stratified family of grammars. Also none of these prior works use unsat cores for updating the language/grammar stratum, synthesize well-founded relations and functional predicates, or support non-Horn clauses.

Our class of pfwCSP constraints is related to *existentially-quantified Horn clauses* (E-CHCs) introduced by Beyene et al. [12]. E-CHCs does not have non-Horn clauses or functional predicate variables. However, it has disjunctive well-foundedness constraints which are similar to our well-founded predicate variables. Also, existential quantifiers can be used to encode head disjunctions and functional predicates. We conjecture that pfwCSP and E-CHCs are inter-reducible, but it is not trivial to fill the gap. Also, inter-reducibility is a desirable feature: different formats may have different benefits. For relational verification, as we have shown, pfwCSP enables direct sound-and-complete encodings of the problems. For instance, head disjunctions allow direct encoding of scheduler fairness and finitary angelic non-determinism (cf. Remark 3). And, functional predicate variables can be explicitly given necessary-and-sufficient parameters to encode angelic non-determinism and difference bounds for ensuring scheduler fairness in the presence of non-termination. The tight encodings also lead to reduction in search space and benefited the constraint solving.

8   Conclusion

We have introduced the class pfwCSP of predicate constraint satisfaction problems that generalizes CHCs with arbitrary clauses, well-foundedness constraints, and functionality constraints. We have then established a program verification framework based on pfwCSP by showing that (1) pfwCSP can soundly-and-completely encode various classes of relational problems of infinite-state non-deterministic programs, including hard instances of k-safety, co-termination, and termination-sensitive generalized non-interference that benefit from state-dependent scheduling/alignment (Theorems 1–4), and (2) existing CHCs solving and invariants/ranking function synthesis techniques can be adopted to pfwCSP solving and further improved with the idea of stratified CEGIS for simultaneously achieving completeness (Theorem 5) and practical effectiveness.

In future work we plan to investigate ways to improve functional predicate synthesis, automatic tuning of parameter update strategies for constraint solving, and whether a constraint-based approach (and the techniques presented in the present paper) can be extended to reason about relational temporal properties such as the ones expressed in hyper temporal logics [16,25].

Acknowledgments. We thank the anonymous reviewers for their suggestions. This work was supported by ONR grant # N00014-17-1-2787, JST ERATO HASUO Meta-mathematics for Systems Design Project (No. JPMJER1603), and JSPS KAKENHI Grant Numbers 17H01720, 18K19787, 19H04084, 20H04162, 20H05703, and 20K20625.

References

1. Aguirre, A., Barthe, G., Gaboardi, M., Garg, D., Strub, P.: A relational logic for higher-order programs. J. Funct. Program. **29**, E16 (2019)

2. Alias, C., Darte, A., Feautrier, P., Gonnord, L.: Multi-dimensional rankings, program termination, and complexity bounds of flowchart programs. In: Cousot, R., Martel, M. (eds.) SAS 2010. LNCS, vol. 6337, pp. 117–133. Springer, Heidelberg (2010). https://doi.org/10.1007/978-3-642-15769-1_8

3. Antonopoulos, T., Gazzillo, P., Hicks, M., Koskinen, E., Terauchi, T., Wei, S.: Decomposition instead of self-composition for proving the absence of timing channels. In: PLDI (2017)

4. Asada, K., Sato, R., Kobayashi, N.: Verifying relational properties of functional programs by first-order refinement. In: PEPM (2015)

5. Assaf, M., Naumann, D.A., Signoles, J., Totel, E., Tronel, F.: Hypercollecting semantics and its application to static analysis of information flow. In: POPL (2017)

6. Barthe, G.: An introduction to relational program verification (2020)

7. Barthe, G., Crespo, J.M., Kunz, C.: Relational verification using product programs. In: FM (2011)

8. Barthe, G., D'Argenio, P.R., Rezk, T.: Secure information flow by self-composition. In: CSFW (2004)

9. Benton, N.: Simple relational correctness proofs for static analyses and program transformations. In: POPL (2004)

10. Beringer, L.: Relational bytecode correlations. J. Log. Alg. Meth. Pro. **79**(7), 483–514 (2010)

11. Beringer, L., Hofmann, M.: Secure information flow and program logics. Arch. Formal Proofs (2008)

12. Beyene, T.A., Popeea, C., Rybalchenko, A.: Solving existentially quantified horn clauses. In: Sharygina, N., Veith, H. (eds.) CAV 2013. LNCS, vol. 8044, pp. 869–882. Springer, Heidelberg (2013). https://doi.org/10.1007/978-3-642-39799-8_61

13. Bjørner, N., Gurfinkel, A., McMillan, K.L., Rybalchenko, A.: Horn clause solvers for program verification. In: Fields of Logic and Computation II: Essays Dedicated to Yuri Gurevich on the Occasion of His 75th Birthday (2015)

14. Champion, A., Chiba, T., Kobayashi, N., Sato, R.: ICE-based refinement type discovery for higher-order functional programs. In: Beyer, D., Huisman, M. (eds.) TACAS 2018. LNCS, vol. 10805, pp. 365–384. Springer, Cham (2018). https://doi.org/10.1007/978-3-319-89960-2_20

15. Churchill, B.R., Padon, O., Sharma, R., Aiken, A.: Semantic program alignment for equivalence checking. In: PLDI (2019)

16. Clarkson, M.R., Finkbeiner, B., Koleini, M., Micinski, K.K., Rabe, M.N., Sánchez, C.: Temporal logics for hyperproperties. In: Abadi, M., Kremer, S. (eds.) POST 2014. LNCS, vol. 8414, pp. 265–284. Springer, Heidelberg (2014). https://doi.org/10.1007/978-3-642-54792-8_15

17. Clarkson, M.R., Schneider, F.B.: Hyperproperties. In: CSF (2008)

18. Clochard, M., Marché, C., Paskevich, A.: Deductive verification with ghost monitors. In: PACMPL, vol. 4, no. POPL (2020)

19. Coenen, N., Finkbeiner, B., Sánchez, C., Tentrup, L.: Verifying hyperliveness. In: Dillig, I., Tasiran, S. (eds.) CAV 2019. LNCS, vol. 11561, pp. 121–139. Springer, Cham (2019). https://doi.org/10.1007/978-3-030-25540-4_7

20. Darvas, Á., Hähnle, R., Sands, D.: A theorem proving approach to analysis of secure information flow. In: Hutter, D., Ullmann, M. (eds.) SPC 2005. LNCS, vol. 3450, pp. 193–209. Springer, Heidelberg (2005). https://doi.org/10.1007/978-3-540-32004-3_20

21. Eilers, M., Müller, P., Hitz, S.: Modular product programs. TOPLAS **42**(1), 1–37 (2020)

22. Ezudheen, P., Neider, D., D'Souza, D., Garg, P., Madhusudan, P.: Horn-ICE learning for synthesizing invariants and contracts. PACMPL **2**(OOPSLA), 1–25 (2018)
23. Farzan, A., Vandikas, A.: Automated hypersafety verification. In: Dillig, I., Tasiran, S. (eds.) CAV 2019. LNCS, vol. 11561, pp. 200–218. Springer, Cham (2019). https://doi.org/10.1007/978-3-030-25540-4_11
24. Fedyukovich, G., Zhang, Y., Gupta, A.: Syntax-guided termination analysis. In: Chockler, H., Weissenbacher, G. (eds.) CAV 2018. LNCS, vol. 10981, pp. 124–143. Springer, Cham (2018). https://doi.org/10.1007/978-3-319-96145-3_7
25. Finkbeiner, B., Rabe, M.N., Sánchez, C.: Algorithms for model checking Hyper-LTL and HyperCTL*. In: Kroening, D., Păsăreanu, C.S. (eds.) CAV 2015. LNCS, vol. 9206, pp. 30–48. Springer, Cham (2015). https://doi.org/10.1007/978-3-319-21690-4_3
26. Garg, P., Löding, C., Madhusudan, P., Neider, D.: ICE: a robust framework for learning invariants. In: Biere, A., Bloem, R. (eds.) CAV 2014. LNCS, vol. 8559, pp. 69–87. Springer, Cham (2014). https://doi.org/10.1007/978-3-319-08867-9_5
27. Garg, P., Neider, D., Madhusudan, P., Roth, D.: Learning invariants using decision trees and implication counterexamples. In: POPL (2016)
28. Gonnord, L., Monniaux, D., Radanne, G.: Synthesis of ranking functions using extremal counterexamples. In: PLDI (2015)
29. Grebenshchikov, S., Lopes, N.P., Popeea, C., Rybalchenko, A.: Synthesizing software verifiers from proof rules. In: PLDI (2012)
30. Gurfinkel, A., Kahsai, T., Komuravelli, A., Navas, J.A.: The seahorn verification framework. In: Kroening, D., Păsăreanu, C.S. (eds.) CAV 2015. LNCS, vol. 9206, pp. 343–361. Springer, Cham (2015). https://doi.org/10.1007/978-3-319-21690-4_20
31. Hawblitzel, C., Kawaguchi, M., Lahiri, S.K., Rebêlo, H.: Towards modularly comparing programs using automated theorem provers. In: Bonacina, M.P. (ed.) CADE 2013. LNCS (LNAI), vol. 7898, pp. 282–299. Springer, Heidelberg (2013). https://doi.org/10.1007/978-3-642-38574-2_20
32. Hojjat, H., Rümmer, P.: The Eldarica horn solver. In: FMCAD (2018)
33. Jhala, R., Majumdar, R., Rybalchenko, A.: HMC: verifying functional programs using abstract interpreters. In: Gopalakrishnan, G., Qadeer, S. (eds.) CAV 2011. LNCS, vol. 6806, pp. 470–485. Springer, Heidelberg (2011). https://doi.org/10.1007/978-3-642-22110-1_38
34. Jhala, R., McMillan, K.L.: A practical and complete approach to predicate refinement. In: Hermanns, H., Palsberg, J. (eds.) TACAS 2006. LNCS, vol. 3920, pp. 459–473. Springer, Heidelberg (2006). https://doi.org/10.1007/11691372_33
35. Kahsai, T., Rümmer, P., Sanchez, H., Schäf, M.: JayHorn: a framework for verifying Java programs. In: Chaudhuri, S., Farzan, A. (eds.) CAV 2016. LNCS, vol. 9779, pp. 352–358. Springer, Cham (2016). https://doi.org/10.1007/978-3-319-41528-4_19
36. Kobayashi, N., Sato, R., Unno, H.: Predicate abstraction and CEGAR for higher-order model checking. In: PLDI (2011)
37. Komuravelli, A., Gurfinkel, A., Chaki, S.: SMT-based model checking for recursive programs. In: Biere, A., Bloem, R. (eds.) CAV 2014. LNCS, vol. 8559, pp. 17–34. Springer, Cham (2014). https://doi.org/10.1007/978-3-319-08867-9_2
38. Krishna, S., Puhrsch, C., Wies, T.: Learning invariants using decision trees. CoRR abs/1501.04725 (2015)
39. Leike, J., Heizmann, M.: Ranking templates for linear loops. LMCS **11**(1) (2015)
40. McCullough, D.: Noninterference and the composability of security properties. In: SP (1988)

41. de Moura, L., Bjørner, N.: Z3: an efficient SMT solver. In: Ramakrishnan, C.R., Rehof, J. (eds.) TACAS 2008. LNCS, vol. 4963, pp. 337–340. Springer, Heidelberg (2008). https://doi.org/10.1007/978-3-540-78800-3_24
42. Naumann, D.A.: From coupling relations to mated invariants for checking information flow. In: Gollmann, D., Meier, J., Sabelfeld, A. (eds.) ESORICS 2006. LNCS, vol. 4189, pp. 279–296. Springer, Heidelberg (2006). https://doi.org/10.1007/11863908_18
43. Naumann, D.A.: Thirty-seven years of relational hoare logic: remarks on its principles and history. CoRR abs/2007.06421 (2020)
44. Padhi, S., Millstein, T., Nori, A., Sharma, R.: Overfitting in synthesis: theory and practice. In: Dillig, I., Tasiran, S. (eds.) CAV 2019. LNCS, vol. 11561, pp. 315–334. Springer, Cham (2019). https://doi.org/10.1007/978-3-030-25540-4_17
45. Padhi, S., Sharma, R., Millstein, T.D.: Data-driven precondition inference with learned features. In: PLDI (2016)
46. Pick, L., Fedyukovich, G., Gupta, A.: Exploiting synchrony and symmetry in relational verification. In: Chockler, H., Weissenbacher, G. (eds.) CAV 2018. LNCS, vol. 10981, pp. 164–182. Springer, Cham (2018). https://doi.org/10.1007/978-3-319-96145-3_9
47. Reynolds, J.C.: The Craft of Programming. Prentice Hall (1981)
48. Sharma, R., Gupta, S., Hariharan, B., Aiken, A., Liang, P., Nori, A.V.: A data driven approach for algebraic loop invariants. In: Felleisen, M., Gardner, P. (eds.) ESOP 2013. LNCS, vol. 7792, pp. 574–592. Springer, Heidelberg (2013). https://doi.org/10.1007/978-3-642-37036-6_31
49. Sharma, R., Gupta, S., Hariharan, B., Aiken, A., Nori, A.V.: Verification as learning geometric concepts. In: Logozzo, F., Fähndrich, M. (eds.) SAS 2013. LNCS, vol. 7935, pp. 388–411. Springer, Heidelberg (2013). https://doi.org/10.1007/978-3-642-38856-9_21
50. Shemer, R., Gurfinkel, A., Shoham, S., Vizel, Y.: Property directed self composition. In: Dillig, I., Tasiran, S. (eds.) CAV 2019. LNCS, vol. 11561, pp. 161–179. Springer, Cham (2019). https://doi.org/10.1007/978-3-030-25540-4_9
51. Solar-Lezama, A., Tancau, L., Bodik, R., Seshia, S., Saraswat, V.: Combinatorial sketching for finite programs. In: ASPLOS (2006)
52. Sousa, M., Dillig, I.: Cartesian hoare logic for verifying k-safety properties. In: PLDI (2016)
53. Terauchi, T.: Dependent types from counterexamples. In: POPL (2010)
54. Terauchi, T., Aiken, A.: Secure information flow as a safety problem. In: Hankin, C., Siveroni, I. (eds.) SAS 2005. LNCS, vol. 3672, pp. 352–367. Springer, Heidelberg (2005). https://doi.org/10.1007/11547662_24
55. Terauchi, T., Unno, H.: Relaxed stratification: a new approach to practical complete predicate refinement. In: Vitek, J. (ed.) ESOP 2015. LNCS, vol. 9032, pp. 610–633. Springer, Heidelberg (2015). https://doi.org/10.1007/978-3-662-46669-8_25
56. Unno, H., Kobayashi, N.: Dependent type inference with interpolants. In: PPDP (2009)
57. Unno, H., Kobayashi, N., Yonezawa, A.: Combining type-based analysis and model checking for finding counterexamples against non-interference. In: PLAS (2006)
58. Unno, H., Terauchi, T., Koskinen, E.: Constraint-based relational verification (2021). http://www.cs.tsukuba.ac.jp/~uhiro/
59. Unno, H., Torii, S., Sakamoto, H.: Automating induction for solving horn clauses. In: Majumdar, R., Kunčak, V. (eds.) CAV 2017. LNCS, vol. 10427, pp. 571–591. Springer, Cham (2017). https://doi.org/10.1007/978-3-319-63390-9_30

60. Urban, C.: The abstract domain of segmented ranking functions. In: Logozzo, F., Fähndrich, M. (eds.) SAS 2013. LNCS, vol. 7935, pp. 43–62. Springer, Heidelberg (2013). https://doi.org/10.1007/978-3-642-38856-9_5

61. Urban, C., Miné, A.: An abstract domain to infer ordinal-valued ranking functions. In: Shao, Z. (ed.) ESOP 2014. LNCS, vol. 8410, pp. 412–431. Springer, Heidelberg (2014). https://doi.org/10.1007/978-3-642-54833-8_22

62. Volpano, D.M., Irvine, C., Smith, G.: A sound type system for secure flow analysis. J. Compt. Secr. 4(2–3), 167–187 (1996)

63. Volpano, D.M., Smith, G.: Eliminating covert flows with minimum typings. In: CSFW (1997)

64. Zaks, A., Pnueli, A.: CoVaC: compiler validation by program analysis of the cross-product. In: Cuellar, J., Maibaum, T., Sere, K. (eds.) FM 2008. LNCS, vol. 5014, pp. 35–51. Springer, Heidelberg (2008). https://doi.org/10.1007/978-3-540-68237-0_5

65. Zhu, H., Magill, S., Jagannathan, S.: A data-driven CHC solver. In: PLDI (2018)

66. Zhu, H., Nori, A.V., Jagannathan, S.: Learning refinement types. In: ICFP (2015)

Pre-deployment Security Assessment for Cloud Services Through Semantic Reasoning

Claudia Cauli[1]([✉]), Meng Li[2], Nir Piterman[1], and Oksana Tkachuk[2]

[1] University of Gothenburg, Gothenburg, Sweden
[2] Amazon Web Services, Seattle, U.S.A.

Abstract. Over the past ten years, the adoption of cloud services has grown rapidly, leading to the introduction of automated deployment tools to address the scale and complexity of the infrastructure companies and users deploy. Without the aid of automation, ensuring the security of an ever-increasing number of deployments becomes more and more challenging. To the best of our knowledge, no formal automated technique currently exists to verify cloud deployments during the design phase. In this case study, we show that Description Logic modeling and inference capabilities can be used to improve the safety of cloud configurations. We focus on the Amazon Web Services (AWS) proprietary declarative language, CloudFormation, and develop a tool to encode template files into logic. We query the resulting models with properties related to security posture and report on our findings. By extending the models with dataflow-specific knowledge, we use more comprehensive semantic reasoning to further support security reviews. When applying the developed toolchain to publicly available deployment files, we find numerous violations of widely-recognized security best practices, which suggests that streamlining the methodologies developed for this case study would be beneficial.

1 Introduction

The term *Infrastructure as Code* (*IaC*) refers to the practice of configuring, provisioning, and updating systems resources from source code files, which are compiled into atomic instructions and then executed to deploy the desired architecture [29]. The advantage of handling code, instead of manually provisioning resources, lies in the capability to use version control systems, orchestration frameworks, and automated testing tools as part of the deployment process. In addition to instructions relevant for resource creation, dependencies, and updates, IaC configuration files contain information about settings, dataflow, and access control. In a time when cloud companies provide customers with simple-to-launch, albeit extremely powerful infrastructure, it is crucial to automatically and provably verify the security of such systems.

In this study, we investigate IaC deployment frameworks and how these are formally modeled and reasoned upon. We explore the usage of description

© The Author(s) 2021
A. Silva and K. R. M. Leino (Eds.) CAV 2021, LNCS 12759, pp. 767–780, 2021.
https://doi.org/10.1007/978-3-030-81685-8_36

logics (DLs) as a conceptual-modeling formalism that is expressive, decidable, and equipped with mature tooling. We argue that formal reasoning techniques applied to deployment templates are an immensely valuable tool for developers and security engineers by substantially aiding the automation of time-consuming security reviews; helping them to detect complex logical errors at earlier stages; and, containing the costs that finding and fixing security issues at later stages would cause. As the prevalence of cloud infrastructure increases, in addition to experts, automated reasoning tools could benefit inexperienced users as well.

System Studied. We focus on the Amazon Web Services proprietary IaC tool, CloudFormation, the first to be introduced at a large scale, over ten years ago. AWS, cloud provider within Amazon, serves millions of customers worldwide. These include private businesses as well as government, education, nonprofit, and healthcare organizations. While the cloud provider is responsible for the faithful deployment of the customers' desired configurations, it is the customer's duty to make sure that these comply with the security requirements of their business context. Few management tools of this scale exist. Notable mentions are Terraform [37], Microsoft Azure's *Resource Manager* [28], Google Cloud's *Deployment Manager* [19], and the recently introduced OASIS standard TOSCA [6].

Goal of Study. Our goal is to improve the quality of the security analyses that are performed over IaC configurations pre-deployment; and by doing so, their overall security. With this study, we investigate the application of description logics to the formalization and reasoning over IaC deployments. In particular, we are interested in three aspects: *(i)* whether proposed cloud configurations comply with security best practices, *(ii)* how to aid customers in building more secure infrastructure *before* deploying it, and *(iii)* to what extent formal automated techniques can support manual pre-deployment security reviews.

Challenges. Little research has been done so far on the possibility to formalize IaC languages, and no research has been done to devise a logic that is well-suited to reason about cloud infrastructure. By nature, cloud infrastructure interacts with an open environment that is, at best, only partially known. In particular, external-facing APIs and users participate in these interactions. By design, cloud services allow for the composition of smaller components into large infrastructure, the complexity of which creates a challenge with respect to security. Our models should capture the connectivity of resources, the flow of information that spans across multiple paths, and the rich security-related data available in IaC configuration files. This is further complicated by the need for a query language for verification and falsification, able to express that mitigations must be present (vs. may be absent), and security issues must be absent (vs. may be present). Importantly, we need practical tools that support the implementation of all these parts and that can scale to real-world IaC configurations.

Our Contribution. We provide a framework to encode IaC into description logic, and investigate its effectiveness in answering configuration queries and reasoning about dataflow, trust boundaries, and potential issues within the system. Specifically, we test DLs reasoning capabilities to infer new facts about underspecified resources (such as those not included in a given deployment but used by it) and leverage DLs *open-world assumption* to perform verification and refutation, depending on the property being checked. We formalize additional security knowledge that allows for checking system-level semantic properties; i.e., properties that consider the nature of the cloud environment and more complex reachability over an *inferred* graph representation of the infrastructure.

Throughout the study, we make four novel contributions: (*i*) the formalization and logical encoding of AWS CloudFormation (Sect. 3); (*ii*) a technique to express security properties (Sect. 4); (*iii*) the experimental evaluation of encoding and query times, accounting for the most common security issues that we found over publicly available IaC templates (Sect. 5); and (*iv*) an extension that enables semantic dataflow reasoning (Sect. 6). Our tool is implemented in Scala and available online [14]. We include preliminaries in Sect. 2; discuss related work in Sect. 7; and conclude in Sect. 8.

2 Preliminaries

Description Logics. DLs are a family of logics well suited to model *relationships between entities*. They provide the logical foundation of the well-known *Web Ontology Language* [20,23,32], for which extensive tool support exists (e.g., the Protégé editor and off-the-shelf reasoners such as FaCT, HermiT, and Pellet [18,30,36,39]). We introduce the description logic $\mathcal{ALC}$ [1,24,34], *Attributive Logic with Complement*, and two additional features that are relevant for our study. $\mathcal{ALC}$ formulae are built from symbols from the alphabets N_C, of atomic concept names; N_R, of role names; and N_I, of individual names. These are the DL equivalents of FOL unary predicates, binary predicates, and constants, respectively. $\mathcal{ALC}$ concept expressions are built according to the grammar:

$$C, D ::= \bot \mid \top \mid \mathsf{A} \mid \neg C \mid C \sqcup D \mid C \sqcap D \mid \exists r.C \mid \forall r.C$$

where A is an atomic concept from the set N_C; C, D are possibly complex concepts; and r is a role from the alphabet N_R. Terminological knowledge is represented via general concept inclusion axioms $C \sqsubseteq D$. As an example, in the remainder of this paper we will refer to two standard axioms that enforce the domain and range of binary relations: $\mathsf{dom}(r, C) \equiv \exists r.\top \sqsubseteq C$ and $\mathsf{ran}(r, C) \equiv \exists r^-.\top \sqsubseteq C$. Assertional knowledge is represented via concept assertions $\mathsf{C}(a)$ and role assertions $\mathsf{r}(a, b)$. In this paper, we will use three additional operators: *inverse roles*, *functionality constraints*, and *complex role inclusions*. The first, denoted r^-, encodes the converse of the binary relationship r. The second enforces binary relationships to be functional. The third, written $r \circ s \sqsubseteq t$, establishes that the chaining of the two relationships r and s implies the relationship t, and can be used to implement transitivity (when $r = s = t$). A model of a DL knowledge base is an interpretation $\mathcal{I}$, over a domain Δ, that satisfies all the axioms and assertions contained and implied by the knowledge base. For the purpose of our application, we leverage two classical inference problems: *satisfiability* and *instance retrieval*, whose full definitions are found in standard textbooks [2,3].

AWS CloudFormation. AWS CloudFormation, cfn, provides users with a declarative programming language and a framework to provision and manage over 500 *resources* spread across 70 *services* [15].[1] Services are products such as storage, databases, and processors, and their interface is implemented through resources, which are the actual modules that users declare and deploy. Their declaration is done by writing one or more so-called *CloudFormation Templates* (JSON-formatted configuration files). Within a template, users configure settings and communication of the desired resource instances. As an example, let us consider one of the most widely known storage products within AWS: the Simple Storage Service S3 (also illustrated in Listings 1.1 and 1.2). The CloudFormation interface for S3 consists of two resources: S3::Bucket and S3::BucketPolicy. A Bucket is a single unit of storage whose properties include encryption, replication, and logging settings, which can be viewed as the bucket's own configuration parameters. They could also be *references* to other resources that are connected to the current one, e.g., the unique ID of another bucket where logs are stored. A BucketPolicy is a resource that links an access control policy to a bucket. All the properties that can be instantiated and the structure of resource-types such as S3::Bucket and S3::BucketPolicy are given in the *CloudFormation Resource Specification* [15]. The *resource specification* is a collection of files that prescribe resource properties and their allowed values. Provided that a *configuration file* is valid with respect to the specifications, an IaC deployment environment compiles it into instructions that are then executed to provision the requested resources in the correct dependency order and with the desired settings.

3   Formalization and Encoding of IaC Deployments

While setting up this case study, we found it convenient to come up with a formalization, of both IaC resource specifications and IaC configuration files, to use as an intermediate representation during the encoding process. This was also needed since we could not find suitable research in the area (although some preliminary research on IaC formalization does exist: e.g., the PhD thesis in [12]). As mentioned in Sect. 2, users consult the *resource specifications* to find out what fields and values are allowed when declaring a resource. Intuitively, these provide a sort of type-system, or JSON schema, against which *configuration files* must validate. Configuration files contain the resource declarations of the instances that the user wishes to deploy. Let us illustrate this with some examples. Listing 1.1 shows a snippet of the S3::Bucket resource-type specification. In addition to the main

```
"ResourceType":
"S3::Bucket": {
  "Properties":{
    "BucketName" : "String",
    "LoggingConfiguration":  {
      "Type": "LoggingConfiguration",
      "Required": false } ... }},

"PropertyTypes": ...,
"S3::Bucket.LoggingConfiguration":{
  "Properties": {
    "DestinationBucketName":{
      "Type": "String",
      "Required": false },
    "LogFilePrefix":{
      "Type": "String",
      "Required": false }}}
```

Listing 1.1. S3::Bucket specification

---

[1] As of August 2020, exact number is Region-dependent.

resource type, the specification includes definitions for its subproperties, their types, and whether these are required. Although the example only shows string properties, in general, allowed properties values range over objects, arrays, and primitive types such as integers, doubles, longs, strings, and booleans. Listing 1.2, on the other hand, shows a common usage scenario of the S3 storage service, where a bucket with basic configuration is used to store the desired data. The instance has logical ID `ConfigS3Bucket`, is of type S3::Bucket, and specifies two top-level properties, `BucketName` and `LoggingConfiguration`. It is easy to see that this instance declaration validates against the resource specification of Listing 1.1. This snippet is taken from one of the benchmark deployments evaluated in Sect. 5 (StackSet 15) and, incidentally, it violates a security best practice: "no bucket should store its own logs." Such formalization has been instrumental to capture infrastructure configurations, resources settings and inter-connections, and to precisely and automatically encode it into DL.

Encoding. We translate IaC specifications into DL terminological knowledge, and IaC configurations into assertional knowledge. The conceptual modeling features needed to model the former include axioms to define *domain* and *range* of properties, *requiredness*, and *functionality*. These give us enough expressivity to infer qualities of nodes that are under-

```
"ConfigS3Bucket": {
  "Type": "AWS::S3::Bucket",
  "Properties":
    "BucketName": "ConfigStore",
    "LoggingConfiguration": {
      "DestinationBucketName":
        "ConfigStore",
      "LogFilePrefix": "config-bucket-
        logs/"}}
```

Listing 1.2. S3::Bucket instance declaration

specified, such as those that are referenced by a template but not declared in it (e.g., already deployed and running elsewhere), whose configuration is unknown. To give readers an intuition of the encoding procedure, let us look at the equation below, which contains some of the axioms and assertions generated by the translation of the code in Listings 1.1 and 1.2.

$$Spec_{S3::Bucket} = \{ \text{ dom(bucketName, BUCKET), ran(bucketName, } String),$$
$$(\text{Funct bucketName}), ..., \text{dom(destinationBucket, LOGCONFIG),}$$
$$\text{ran(destinationBucket, BUCKET), ... } \}$$

$$Config = \{ \text{ BUCKET}(ConfigS3Bucket), \text{bucketName}(ConfigS3Bucket, \text{ "}ConfigStore\text{"}),$$
$$\text{loggingConfig}(ConfigS3Bucket, x), \text{destinationBucket}(x, ConfigS3Bucket),$$
$$\text{logFilePrefix}(x, \text{ "}config\text{-}bucket\text{-}logs\text{"}) \}$$

4 Security Properties Specification

We group properties into three categories that reflect their high-level meaning: *security issues*, *mitigations*, and *global protections* to security concerns. We view these in analogy to *must* and *may* specifications, which one would use to express that an issue may be present (vs. must be absent) or that a protection must be in place (vs. may be missing). Each property type is matched to a corresponding query structure, which aids the translation of security requirements into formal specifications and implements different fail/pass logics. Queries are written as description logic expressions whose outcome can be one of UNSAT, SAT with no instance found (SAT/0), and SAT with instances (SAT/+). These are achieved by running a satisfiability check, possibly followed by an instance retrieval call.

Mitigations are configurations of single resources that reduce the likelihood of a security event. In order to pass, these checks must be verified. Examples are:

M1 *"All buckets must keep logs,"*
M2 *"Only buckets that host websites can have a public preset ACL,"*   and
M3 *"Data stores must have backup or versioning enabled."*

Security Issues are configurations that potentially increase exposure to security concerns. In order to pass, these checks must be falsified. Examples are:

I1 *"There may be a bucket that is not encrypted,"*
I2 *"Encrypted bucket that sends events to a not-encrypted queue,"*   and
I3 *"There may be a networking component that opens all ports to all."*

Global Protections are more general mitigations, applied on single resources or as configuration patterns, whose presence and proper configuration ensures protection over the system as a whole. Examples are:

P1 *"There is an alarm configured to perform an action when triggered,"*   and
P2 *"There is a configuration recorder logging changes to the infrastructure."*

We refer the reader to the repository in [14] for the properties specification files.[2]

5   Application to Existing Infrastructure

We now discuss the application of our approach to real-world IaC deployments. We analyze AWS CloudFormation specification and configuration files, showing that the approach is practical, scalable, and identifies potential security issues.

Operation of the Tool. We develop a tool that performs three main tasks. First, the encoding of the cfn resource specifications into formal models (*Resource Terminologies*).[3] Second, the encoding of the actual cfn configuration files, also called *StackSet*, into formal models (*Infrastructure Model*). Third, inference and query answering for a set of predefined queries. We use the OWLApi [22] for the encoding phase, and JFact [39] as the inference engine.

---

[2] https://tiny.cc/PropertiesSpecifications.
[3] Available here: https://tiny.cc/ResourceTerminologies.

Table 1. Evaluation results (mean times in millisec).

ID	N	N_{RT}	ENC	N_α	INF	USAT	SAT0	SAT+
05	6	6	44.53	814	30.64	0.67	–	2.46
11	8	8	79.22	917	37.09	0.72	–	2.86
03	10	7	59.94	886	35.65	0.64	2.23	1.56
09	10	9	76.33	940	38.66	0.68	5.03	2.96
02	11	8	76.73	1194	49.99	0.85	2.66	2.02
01	16	7	94.95	1007	43.38	0.66	3.96	1.83
08	19	8	87.66	1051	50.93	0.78	5.40	3.23
10	30	9	89.07	1177	71.23	0.86	2.62	2.08
06	30	12	102.00	1666	108.30	1.05	–	4.91
12	31	21	185.06	2798	301.61	4.99	24.93	36.43
13	51	32	241.17	3835	608.09	7.16	38.56	47.93
14	73	31	264.56	4143	847.36	2.83	51.36	19.20
15	79	21	313.40	4596	901.18	2.86	–	17.55
04	132	33	363.58	4834	2100.85	2.94	162.95	23.21
07	508	21	1005.46	10161	15834.14	7.34	40.86	13.52

Experimental Setup. We run our tool on 15 CloudFormation StackSets openly available on GitHub. Regarding metrics, we define the infrastructure size as the numbers of both declared resources (N) and their types (N_{RT}). The latter determines which *resource terminologies* are imported into the final encoded model and thus influences its size, measured in number of logical axioms (N_α). The smallest StackSet has 6 resources and 6 resource types, the largest has 508 resources and 21 resource types. We implement 50 properties from the ScoutSuite collection [35] that are applicable at design time and, thus, over IaC deployment files. Of the 50 properties, 29 are *mitigations*, 18 are *security issues*, and 3 are *global protections*. We conduct our evaluation on an Intel Core i5 with 16 GB RAM and perform warmup runs and clear the heap before each measurement. This tuning helps to minimize the impact of just-in-time compilation and to reduce the likelihood of garbage collection during the measured benchmark runs.

Results Evaluation. The average compilation time of the entire cfn resource specifications (542 files) was 940 ms. Table 1 reports the results of our experimental evaluation. StackSets are sorted by number of resources. For each, we measure the time taken by the stackset encoding (ENC), inference (INF), and query answering task (grouped by outcome: UNSAT, SAT with no instances, and SAT with instances). As we can see from the table, the encoding time increases with the infrastructure's size, producing larger models that require longer inference times. Average query answering times increase accordingly. UNSAT queries have shorter average answering times than those evaluating to SAT/0 or SAT/+ (UNSAT proofs are found before a SAT outcome can be deduced). In addition, once a query is proved SAT, we invoke a procedure for *instances retrieval* to determine whether satisfying instances are present or not. The specific infrastructure configuration and its size are the main influencing factors of query answering times. Considering that the average template has about 50–100 resources, and templates having 100–500 resources are rare, the results suggest that our approach scales to real-world IaC templates. For example, StackSet **04** has 132 resources, is encoded in 363 ms, classified in 2.1 s, and has a max average per-query time of 162 ms. Assuming a pool of 100 checks to be run, the automated modeling and verification of such an infrastructure would take, in the worst-case, around 18 s.

5.1   Found Security Issues

Across all 15 deployments, we run $15 \times 50 = 750$ checks: 608 pass and 142 fail. Of the 142 failing checks, 73 do not return any instance and 69 return one or more instances (i.e., they fail with a SAT/+ outcome). Such a difference is due to the nature of the single check and its definition of failure. A *global protection* check fails when no instance implementing the protection is found; a *security issue* check fails whenever is possible (SAT/0 or SAT/+); and a *mitigation* check fails when no instance is found. We consider SAT/+ findings particularly important, as they do not only witness a potential security issue but also an actual misconfiguration. In particular, the 69 SAT/+-failing checks fail on 239 resource instances, with the most found issues being:

Missing or misconfigured encryption 131

Missing or misconfigured logging 46

Missing or misconfigured versioning/backup/replication 44

Missing User password reset requirement 12

Misconfigured authorization 3

Misconfigured networking configuration 3

The 73 findings returning no instances fall into two groups: the absence of any monitoring or alarming system is very frequent, as is the dependency on external resources whose security posture cannot be assessed.

Absent global monitoring/alarming/logging protection 41

Usage of external resources with unknown configuration 32

6   Semantic Reasoning About Dataflows

To conclude our study, we manually craft two proof-of-concept models of terms related to cloud security (ontologies). We use these to extend the formalization of the CloudFormation IaC specification that was automatically generated by our tool. Such domain-specific ontologies formalize several common cloud terms,

```
"CustomerData": {                          "TestData": {
  "Type": "AWS::S3::Bucket",                 "Type": "AWS::S3::Bucket",
  "Properties": {                            "Properties": {
    "LoggingConfig": {                         "LoggingConfig": {
      "DestinationBucket": "                     "DestinationBucket": "
        AccessLog" }}},                            AccessLog" }}},

"TopicSubscription":{                       "AccessLog": {
  "Type": "AWS::SNS::Subscription",          "Type": "AWS::S3::Bucket",
  "Properties": {                            "Properties": {
    "Endpoint": "devs@mail",                   "NotificationConfig" : {
    "Protocol": "email",                         "TopicConfig" : {
    "TopicArn": "AccessTopic" }}                   "Topic":"AccessTopic" }}}},

                                            "AccessTopic": {
                                             "Type": "AWS::SNS::Topic" ... }
```

Fig. 1. Sample template: accounts *prod* (left) and *test* (right).

such as account, deployment, authenticated and unauthenticated users; generic dataflow terms, such as storage, process, nodes, and flows of different kind; and service-specific dataflow terms. By adding these on top of the underlying IaC formal specification, we can reason about the higher-level business logic and reachability of the infrastructure, and we can abstract it and visualize it in a more convenient way. This is where the full inference power of description logics comes into play. Such an inference power would be hard to achieve with an alternative encoding (e.g., using a modal logic). Let us illustrate how this technique is applied to system-level analyses of interest for a security review: *dataflow* and *trust boundary* analyses. A trust boundary is a portion of a system whose components trust each other and where data can securely flow. Multiple trust boundaries may exist within one system. Dataflows that travel across boundaries may introduce security issues and should be carefully reviewed. In Fig. 1, we see an example of such a situation, where the infrastructure is deployed across two accounts, *prod* and *test*, sharing resources AccessLog and AccessTopic. In our encoding, we use the so-called DLs *inclusion* axioms to rewrite properties that (when chained) imply the existence of a more general relation and to infer additional characteristics of nodes. For example, in the following list axioms 2–7 formalize the relationships of *"logging to"* and *"sending notifications to"* a resource, which imply the existence of a *transitive dataflow* between nodes; and axioms 8–9 allow to infer that the node *devs@mail* is an external node.

$$\text{LoggingConfig} \circ \text{DestinationBucket} \sqsubseteq \text{logsTo} \tag{1}$$

$$\text{TopicArn}^- \circ \text{Endpoint} \sqsubseteq \text{sendsNotifications} \tag{2}$$

$$\text{NotificationConfig} \circ \text{TopicConfig} \circ \text{Topic} \sqsubseteq \text{sendsNotifications} \tag{3}$$

$$\text{logsTo} \sqsubseteq \text{dataflow} \tag{4}$$

$$\text{sendsNotifications} \sqsubseteq \text{dataflow} \tag{5}$$

$$\text{dataflow} \circ \text{dataflow} \sqsubseteq \text{dataflow} \tag{6}$$

$$\exists \text{Protocol.}\{\text{"email"}\} \sqsubseteq \forall \text{Endpoint.EmailAddress} \tag{7}$$

$$\text{EmailAddress} \sqsubseteq \text{ExternalNode} \tag{8}$$

This encoding enables us to compute a succinct dataflow diagram from the reasoned IaC configuration (see Fig. 2), and to formally verify properties that usually require a manual analysis of the infrastructure and its underlying graph representation. E.g., the question, *"can data flow from the customer-data bucket to the outside?"* can now be formalized as a DL formula and, using a reasoning engine, the existence of a dataflow that starts on the *customer-data* bucket and reaches the *devs@mail* node can now be inferred. We note that, due to the structure of the `TopicSubscription` resource, this dataflow could not have been detected with simple reachability analysis on a graph built without the aid of semantic reasoning. Moreover, the dataflow diagram highlights another potential

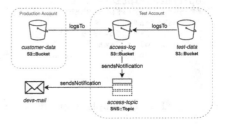

Fig. 2. Dataflow extracted from Fig. 1

source of information leakage: testers being exposed to customer access information. This needs to be mitigated by enforcing the proper trust boundaries, in particular, by adding a dedicated access log storage for *customer-data* bucket in the *prod* account.

7   Related Work

To the best of our knowledge, the problem of formally verifying the design of a cloud infrastructure in its entirety has not been addressed before. Formal reasoning techniques have been successfully applied to different aspects of the cloud, e.g. networks and access policies [4,5,7,16]. Non-formal tools exist that recommend and run checks against *already deployed* resources [13,35], or scan IaC templates [10,11,38] for syntactical patterns violating security best practices. These checks overlap considerably and can be expressed in our framework as well. The disadvantages of such tools are that checks are local to single components, can be performed only post-deployment, need complex configurations, access permissions, or even manual interaction. The CFn-Linter [10] has a rule-based component that users can extend with custom syntax checks, but none of the rules currently available focus on security. The CFn-nag linting tool [11] checks compliance to best practices only locally to the single resources; e.g., it cannot detect issues such as *"there is an events queue, receiving from a bucket with critical functionality, that may not be encrypted"* or *"there might be a user that is shared by multiple policies"* (which would go against the *least privilege* principle); as well as including in its analysis external resources that are referenced by the template being linted.

Regarding our choice of logic, large-scale configuration problems have been tackled with description logic before [26,27]. Simpler first-order logic formulas with operators to represent object-oriented interface relationships could be used to model IaC specifications. However, such an encoding would only partially solve our problem, which is more complex because our overall goal is to do formal semantic analyses (e.g., dataflow and threat modeling). Semantic-based approaches, even DL-based, are being used to do conceptual modeling of security engineers' expertise with the provable and explainable inference capabilities of logics. As an example, we refer the reader to the OWASP *"Ontology-driven Threat Modeling"* project [31] that aims at the formalization of security-related knowledge in the context of different types of computer systems by means of description logic ontologies. In contrast to logic programming languages, such as Datalog, DLs inherently support functionality axioms and the existence of anonymous individuals within a domain that is assumed to be open. These are supported out-of-the-box without the need for an additional, more complex, axiomatization or encoding. In particular, we took advantage of DL's open-world assumption to implement, in our properties encoding, verification and falsification. Another alternative to DLs as a modeling language would be to use 3-valued models with labels on states and transitions and apply model checking [8,9]. However, expressive branching-time logics [25,33] have not been studied in the context of 3-valued models and we are also not aware of tool support at the level available for DLs (cf. [17,21]).

8 Conclusion and Future Work

Throughout this case study, we investigated the usage of description logics-based semantic reasoning to evaluate the security of cloud infrastructure pre-deployment. We encoded Amazon Web Services' Infrastructure as Code specifications and configurations into description logic models and verified the presence and absence of potential security issues. We showed how this approach enables deeper system-level analyses such as dataflow analysis. All results can be generalized to other existing IaC tools. While working on this project, we interacted with developers on two occasions. First, for the benchmark templates used in our experimental evaluation, we contacted the owners, told them about the misconfigurations, and discussed potential security implications. Second, within AWS, security engineers use a technique based on this paper for security reviews of AWS products before they are launched, helping developers fix real issues pre-deployment. In the process, we received valuable feedback that we used for improving precision and reducing the number of false-positive results. We plan to continue researching for an even better-fitting description logic formalism, query language, three-valued semantics, and decision procedures for verification and falsification of properties relevant to security analyses, such as dataflows, trust boundaries, and threat modeling.

Acknowledgements. This research is supported by the ERC consolidator grant D-SynMA under the European Union's Horizon 2020 research and innovation programme (grant agreement No. 772459) and by Amazon Web Services.

References

1. Baader, F., Calvanese, D., McGuinness, D.L., Nardi, D., Patel-Schneider, P.F. (eds.): The Description Logic Handbook: Theory, Implementation, and Applications. Cambridge University Press (2003)
2. Baader, F., Horrocks, I., Lutz, C., Sattler, U.: An Introduction to Description Logic. Cambridge University Press (2017)
3. Baader, F., Horrocks, I., Sattler, U.: Description logics. In: Handbook of Knowledge Representation, Foundations of Artificial Intelligence, vol. 3, pp. 135–179. Elsevier (2008)
4. Backes, J., et al.: Reachability analysis for AWS-based networks. In: Dillig, I., Tasiran, S. (eds.) CAV 2019. LNCS, vol. 11562, pp. 231–241. Springer, Cham (2019). https://doi.org/10.1007/978-3-030-25543-5_14
5. Backes, J., et al.: Semantic-based automated reasoning for AWS access policies using SMT. In: FMCAD, pp. 1–9. IEEE (2018)
6. Binz, T., Breitenbücher, U., Kopp, O., Leymann, F.: TOSCA: portable automated deployment and management of cloud applications. In: Bouguettaya, A., Sheng, Q., Daniel, F. (eds.) Advanced Web Services, pp. 527–549. Springer, New York (2014). https://doi.org/10.1007/978-1-4614-7535-4_22
7. Bouchenak, S., Chockler, G.V., Chockler, H., Gheorghe, G., Santos, N., Shraer, A.: Verifying cloud services: present and future. Operating Syst. Rev. **47**(2), 6–19 (2013)
8. Bruns, G., Godefroid, P.: Model checking partial state spaces with 3-valued temporal logics. In: Halbwachs, N., Peled, D. (eds.) CAV 1999. LNCS, vol. 1633, pp. 274–287. Springer, Heidelberg (1999). https://doi.org/10.1007/3-540-48683-6_25
9. Bruns, G., Godefroid, P.: Model checking with multi-valued logics. In: Díaz, J., Karhumäki, J., Lepistö, A., Sannella, D. (eds.) ICALP 2004. LNCS, vol. 3142, pp. 281–293. Springer, Heidelberg (2004). https://doi.org/10.1007/978-3-540-27836-8_26
10. The AWS CloudFormation Linter (2020). https://github.com/aws-cloudformation/cfn-python-lint. Accessed 15 Oct 2020
11. The CFnNag Linting Tool (2020). https://github.com/stelligent/cfn_nag. Accessed 15 Oct 2020
12. Challita, S.: Inferring models from Cloud APIs and reasoning over them: a tooled and formal approach. (Inférer des modèles à partir d'APIs cloud et raisonner dessus: une approche outillée et formelle). Ph.D. thesis, Lille University of Science and Technology, France (2018)
13. Infrastructure Security, Compliance, and Governance (2020). http://www.cloudconformity.com/. Accessed 04 Aug 2020
14. CloudFORMAL: Prototype Implementation. http://github.com/claudiacauli/CloudFORMAL. Accessed 15 Oct 2020
15. Resource Specification (2020). https://docs.aws.amazon.com/AWSCloudFormation/latest/UserGuide/cfn-resource-specification.html. Accessed 13 Aug 2020
16. Cook, B.: Formal reasoning about the security of Amazon web services. In: Chockler, H., Weissenbacher, G. (eds.) CAV 2018. LNCS, vol. 10981, pp. 38–47. Springer, Cham (2018). https://doi.org/10.1007/978-3-319-96145-3_3
17. D'Ippolito, N., Fischbein, D., Chechik, M., Uchitel, S.: MTSA: the modal transition system analyser. In: ASE, pp. 475–476. IEEE Computer Society (2008)

18. Glimm, B., Horrocks, I., Motik, B., Stoilos, G., Wang, Z.: Hermit: An OWL 2 reasoner. J. Autom. Reason. **53**(3), 245–269 (2014)
19. Google Deployment Manager. https://cloud.google.com/deployment-manager. Accessed 28 Jan 2021
20. Grau, B.C., Horrocks, I., Motik, B., Parsia, B., Patel-Schneider, P.F., Sattler, U.: OWL 2: the next step for OWL. J. Web Semant. **6**(4), 309–322 (2008)
21. Gurfinkel, A., Wei, O., Chechik, M.: YASM: a software model-checker for verification and refutation. In: Ball, T., Jones, R.B. (eds.) CAV 2006. LNCS, vol. 4144, pp. 170–174. Springer, Heidelberg (2006). https://doi.org/10.1007/11817963_18
22. Horridge, M., Bechhofer, S.: The OWL API: a Java API for OWL ontologies. Semant. Web **2**(1), 11–21 (2011)
23. Horrocks, I., Patel-Schneider, P.F., van Harmelen, F.: From SHIQ and RDF to OWL: the making of a web ontology language. J. Web Semant. **1**(1), 7–26 (2003)
24. Krötzsch, M., Simancik, F., Horrocks, I.: A description logic primer. CoRR abs/1201.4089 (2012)
25. Kupferman, O., Grumberg, O.: Buy one, get one free!!! J. Log. Comput. **6**(4), 523–539 (1996)
26. McGuinness, D.L., Resnick, L.A., Isbell, C.L., Jr.: Description logic in practice: a classic application. In: IJCAI, pp. 2045–2046. Morgan Kaufmann (1995)
27. McGuinness, D.L., Wright, J.R.: Conceptual modelling for configuration: a description logic-based approach. AI EDAM **12**(4), 333–344 (1998)
28. Microsoft Azure Resource Manager (2020). https://azure.microsoft.com/en-us/features/resource-manager/. Accessed 28 Jan 2021
29. Morris, K.: Infrastructure as Code: Managing Servers in the Cloud. O'Reilly Media, Inc. (2016)
30. Musen, M.A.: The protégé project: a look back and a look forward. AI Matters **1**(4), 4–12 (2015)
31. OWASP Ontology-driven Threat Modeling. https://github.com/OWASP/OdTM. Accessed 14 May 2021
32. Patel-Schneider, P., Grau, B.C., Motik, B.: OWL 2 web ontology language direct semantics (second edition). W3C recommendation, W3C (December 2012). http://www.w3.org/TR/2012/REC-owl2-direct-semantics-20121211/
33. Sattler, U., Vardi, M.Y.: The hybrid μ-calculus. In: Goré, R., Leitsch, A., Nipkow, T. (eds.) IJCAR 2001. LNCS, vol. 2083, pp. 76–91. Springer, Heidelberg (2001). https://doi.org/10.1007/3-540-45744-5_7
34. Schmidt-Schauß, M., Smolka, G.: Attributive concept descriptions with complements. Artif. Intell. **48**(1), 1–26 (1991)
35. Multi-cloud Security Auditing Tool (2020). http://github.com/nccgroup/ScoutSuite. Accessed 4 Aug 2020
36. Sirin, E., Parsia, B., Grau, B.C., Kalyanpur, A., Katz, Y.: Pellet: a practical OWL-DL reasoner. J. Web Semant. **5**(2), 51–53 (2007)
37. Terraform. https://www.terraform.io/. Accessed 28 Jan 2021
38. Static Analysis Security Scanner for Terraform (2020). https://tfsec.dev/. Accessed 10 May 2021
39. Tsarkov, D., Horrocks, I.: FaCT++ description logic reasoner: system description. In: Furbach, U., Shankar, N. (eds.) IJCAR 2006. LNCS (LNAI), vol. 4130, pp. 292–297. Springer, Heidelberg (2006). https://doi.org/10.1007/11814771_26

Synthesis

Synthesis with Asymptotic Resource Bounds

Qinheping Hu[✉], John Cyphert, Loris D'Antoni,
and Thomas Reps

University of Wisconsin-Madison, Madison, USA
{qhu28,jcyphert,ldantoni,treps}@wisc.edu

Abstract. We present a method for synthesizing recursive functions that satisfy both a functional specification and an asymptotic resource bound. Prior methods for synthesis with a resource metric require the user to specify a *concrete* expression exactly describing resource usage, whereas our method uses big-O notation to specify the *asymptotic* resource usage. Our method can synthesize programs with complex resource bounds, such as a sort function that has complexity $O(n \log(n))$.

Our synthesis procedure uses a type system that is able to assign an asymptotic complexity to terms, and can track recurrence relations of functions. These typing rules are justified by theorems used in analysis of algorithms, such as the Master Theorem and the Akra-Bazzi method. We implemented our method as an extension of prior type-based synthesis work. Our tool, SYNPLEXITY, was able to synthesize complex divide-and-conquer programs that cannot be synthesized by prior solvers.

1 Introduction

Program synthesis is the task of automatically finding programs that meet a given behavioral specification, such as input-output examples or complete formal specifications. Most of the work on program synthesis has been devoted to qualitative synthesis, i.e., finding *some* correct solution. However, programmers often want more than just a correct solution—they may want the program that is smallest, most likely, or most efficient. While there are some techniques for adding a quantitative *syntactic* objective in program synthesis [12]—e.g., finding a smallest solution, or a most likely solution with respect to some distribution—little attention has been devoted to quantitative *semantic* objectives—e.g., synthesizing a program that has a certain asymptotic complexity.

Recently, Knoth et al. [16] studied the problem of resource-guided program synthesis, where the goal is to synthesize programs with limited resource usage. Their approach, which combines refinement-type-directed synthesis [18] and automatic amortized resource analysis (AARA) [9], is restricted to *concrete* resource bounds, where the user must specify the *exact* resource usage of the synthesized program as a *linear* expression. This limitation has two drawbacks: (i) the user must have insights about the coefficients to put in the supplied

© The Author(s) 2021
A. Silva and K. R. M. Leino (Eds.) CAV 2021, LNCS 12759, pp. 783–807, 2021.
https://doi.org/10.1007/978-3-030-81685-8_37

bound—which means that the user has to provide details about the complexity of code that does not yet exist; (ii) the limitation to linear bounds means that the user cannot specify resource bounds that involve logarithms, such as $O(\log n)$ and $O(n \log n)$, common in problems based on divide and conquer.

In this paper, we introduce SYNPLEXITY, a type-system paired with a type-directed synthesis technique that addresses these issues. In SYNPLEXITY, the user provides as input a refinement type that describes both the functionality and the *asymptotic* (big-O) resource usage of a program. For example, a user might ask SYNPLEXITY to synthesize an implementation of a sorting function with resource usage $O(n \log n)$, where n is the length of the input list. As in prior work, SYNPLEXITY also takes as input a set of auxiliary functions that the synthesized program can use. SYNPLEXITY then uses a type-directed synthesis algorithm to search for a program that has the desired functionality, and satisfies the asymptotic resource bound. SYNPLEXITY's synthesis algorithm uses a new type system that can reason about the asymptotic complexity of functions. To achieve this goal, this type system uses two ideas.

1. The type system uses *recurrence relations* instead of concrete resource potentials [9] to reason about the asymptotic complexity of functions. For example, the recurrence relation $T(u) \le 2T(\lfloor \frac{u}{2} \rfloor) + O(u)$ denotes that on an input of size u, the function will perform at most two recursive calls on inputs of size at most $\lfloor \frac{u}{2} \rfloor$, and will use at most $O(u)$ resources outside of the recursive calls.[1] For a given recurrence relation, our type system uses refinement types to guarantee that a function typed with this recurrence relation performs the correct number of recursive calls on parameters of the appropriate sizes.
2. These typing rules are justified by classic theorems from the field of analysis of algorithms, such as the Master Theorem [5], the Akra-Bazzi method [1], or C-finite-sequence analysis [13].

Guéneau et al. observed that reasoning with O-notation can be tricky, and exhibited a collection of plausible-sounding, but flawed, inductive proofs [8, §2]. We avoid this pitfall via SYNPLEXITY's type system, which establishes whether a term satisfies a given recurrence relation. SYNPLEXITY uses theorems that connect the form of a recurrence relation—e.g., the number of recursive calls, and the argument sizes in the subproblems—to its asymptotic complexity. In particular, the SYNPLEXITY type system does not encode inductive proofs of the kind that Guéneau et al. show can go astray.

SYNPLEXITY can synthesize functions with complexities that cannot be handled by existing type-directed tools [16,18], and compares favorably with existing tools on their benchmarks. Furthermore, for some domains, SYNPLEXITY's type system allows us to discover auxiliary functions automatically (e.g., the split function of a merge sort), instead of requiring the user to provide them.

---

[1] The recurrence relation above is one possible instantiation of the Master Theorem [5, §4.5 and §4.6]; it can also be instantiated as $T(u) \le 2T(\lceil \frac{u}{2} \rceil) + O(u)$. The type system makes use of certain templates for instantiating the algorithm-analysis theorems that we use. The use of templates means that the type system does not use all possible instantiations, but all instantiations used in the type system are valid ones.

Contributions. The contributions of our work are as follows:

- A type system that uses refinement types to check whether a program satisfies a recurrence relation over a specified resource (Sect. 3).
- A type-directed algorithm that uses our type system to synthesize functions with given resource bounds (Sect. 4, Sect. 5).
- SYNPLEXITY, an implementation of our algorithm that, unlike prior tools, can synthesize programs with desired asymptotic complexities (Sect. 6).

Complete proofs and details of the type system can be found in the technical report [11].

2   Overview

In this section, we illustrate the main components of our algorithm through an example. Consider the problem of synthesizing a function prod that implements the multiplication of two natural numbers, x and y. We want an efficient solution whose time complexity is $O(\log x)$ with respect to the value of the first argument x. In Subsect. 2.1, we show how existing type-directed synthesizers solve this problem in the absence of a complexity-bound constraint. In Subsect. 2.2, we illustrate how to specify asymptotic bounds in type-directed synthesis problems. In Subsect. 2.3, we show how the tracking of recurrence relations can be used to establish complexity bounds as well as guide the synthesis search.

2.1   Type-Directed Synthesis

We first review one of the state-of-the-art type-directed synthesizers, SYNQUID, through the aforementioned example—i.e., synthesizing a program prod that computes the product of two natural numbers. In SYNQUID, the specification is given as a refinement type that describes the desired behavior of the synthesized function. We specify the behavior of prod using the following refinement-type:

$$\texttt{prod} :: \texttt{x} : \{\texttt{Int} \mid v \geq 0\} \rightarrow \texttt{y} : \{\texttt{Int} \mid v \geq 0\} \rightarrow \{\texttt{Int} \mid v = \texttt{x} * \texttt{y}\}.$$

Here the types of the inputs x and y, as well as the return type of prod are refined with predicates. The refinement $\{\texttt{Int} \mid v \geq 0\}$ declares x and y to be non-negative, and the refinement $\{\texttt{Int} \mid v = \texttt{x} * \texttt{y}\}$ of the return type declares the output value to be an integer that is equal to the product of the inputs x and y. In addition to the specification, the synthesizer receives as input some signatures of auxiliary functions it can use. The specifications of auxiliary functions are also given as refinement types. In our example, we have the following functions:

$$\texttt{even} :: \texttt{x} : \texttt{Int} \rightarrow \{\texttt{Bool} \mid \texttt{x mod } 2 = 0\} \qquad \texttt{dec} :: \texttt{x} : \texttt{Int} \rightarrow \{\texttt{Int} \mid v = \texttt{x} - 1\}$$

$$\texttt{double} :: \texttt{x} : \texttt{Int} \rightarrow \{\texttt{Int} \mid v = \texttt{x} + \texttt{x}\} \qquad \texttt{div2} :: \texttt{x} : \texttt{Int} \rightarrow \{\texttt{Int} \mid v = \lfloor \tfrac{\texttt{x}}{2} \rfloor\}$$

$$\texttt{plus} :: \texttt{x} : \texttt{Int} \rightarrow \texttt{y} : \texttt{Int} \rightarrow \{\texttt{Int} \mid v = \texttt{x} + \texttt{y}\}$$

With the above specification and auxiliary functions, SYNQUID will output the implementation of prod shown in Eq. (1).

$$\text{prod} = \lambda\text{x}.\lambda y. \text{ if } \text{x==0 then x else plus y (prod (dec x) y)} \quad (1)$$

SYNQUID uses a sophisticated type system to guarantee that the synthesized term has the desired type. Furthermore, SYNQUID uses its type system to prune the search space by only enumerating terms that can possibly be typed, and thus meet the specification. Terms are enumerated in a top-down fashion, and appropriate specifications are propagated to sub-terms. As an example, let us see how SYNQUID synthesizes the function body—an if-then-else term—in Eq. (1), which is of refinement type $\{\text{Int} \mid v = \text{x*y}\}$. SYNQUID will first enumerate an integer term for the then branch—a variable term x. Then, with the then branch fixed, the condition guard must be refined by some predicate φ under which the then branch (the term x refined by $v = \text{x}$) fulfills the goal type $\{\text{Int} \mid v = \text{x} * \text{y}\}$, i.e., $\forall \text{x}, \text{y} \geq 0.\varphi \wedge v = \text{x} \implies v = \text{x} * \text{y}$. With this constraint, SYNQUID identifies the term $\text{x} == 0$ as the condition. Finally, SYNQUID propagates the negation of the condition to the else branch—the else branch should be a term of type $\{\text{Int} \mid v = \text{x} * \text{y}\}$ with the path condition $\text{x} \neq 0$—and enumerates the term plus y (prod (dec x) y) as the else branch, which has the desired type.

The program in Eq. (1) is correct, but inefficient. Let us count each call to an auxiliary function as one step; and let $T(x)$ denote the number of steps in which the program runs with input x. The implementation in Eq. (1) runs in $\Theta(x)$ steps because $T(x)$ satisfies the recurrence $T(x) = T(x-1)+2$, implying $T(x) \in \Theta(x)$. Because, SYNQUID does not provide a way to specify resource bounds, such as $O(\log x)$; one cannot ask SYNQUID to find a more efficient implementation.

2.2   Adding Resource Bounds

In our tool, SYNPLEXITY, one can specify a synthesis problem with an asymptotic resource bound, and can ask SYNPLEXITY to find an $O(\log x)$ implementation of prod. To express this intent, the user needs to specify (1) the asymptotic resource-usage bound the synthesized program should satisfy, (2) the cost of each provided auxiliary function, and (3) the size of the input to the program.

Asymptotic Resource Bound. We extend refinement types with resource annotations. The annotated refinement types are of the form $\langle \tau; \alpha \rangle$ where τ is a regular refinement type, and α is a resource annotation. The following example asks the synthesizer to find a solution with the resource-usage bound $O(\log u)$:

$$\text{prod} :: \langle \text{x}:\{\text{Int} \mid v \geq 0\} \to \text{y}:\{\text{Int} \mid v \geq 0\} \to \{\text{Int} \mid v = \text{x} * \text{y}\}, O(\log u)\rangle$$

Cost of Auxiliary Functions. The auxiliary functions supplied by the user serve as the API in terms of which the synthesized program is programmed. Thus, the resource usage of the synthesized program is the sum of the costs of all auxiliary calls made during execution. We allow users to assign a polynomial cost $O(u^a)$, for some constant a, or a constant cost $O(1)$ to each auxiliary function. Here, u is a free variable that represents the size of the problem on which the auxiliary function is called.

In the prod example, all auxiliary functions are assigned constant cost, e.g., we give even the signature even :: $\langle$x:Int $\rightarrow$ {Bool | x mod 2 = 0}, $O(1)\rangle$.

Size of Problems. The user needs to specify a size function, size:$\tau \rightarrow$ Int, that maps inputs to their sizes, e.g., when synthesizing the sorting function for an input of type list, the size function can be $\lambda 1.|l|$—the length of the input list. In the prod example, the size function is size $= \lambda$x.λy.x.

2.3 Checking Recurrence Relations

We extend SYNQUID's refinement-type system with resource annotations, so that the extended type system enforces the resource usage of terms. The idea of the type system is to check if the given function satisfies some recurrence relation. If so, it can infer that the function also satisfies the corresponding resource bound. For example, according to the Master Theorem [3], if a function f satisfies the recurrence relation $T(u) \leq T(\lfloor\frac{u}{2}\rfloor) + O(1)$ where u is the size of the input, then the resource usage of f is bounded by $O(\log u)$. Checking if a function satisfies a given recurrence relation can be performed by checking if the function contains appropriate recursive calls—e.g., if a function contains one recursive call to a sub-problem of half size, and consumes only a constant amount of resources in its body, then it satisfies $T(u) \leq T(\lfloor\frac{u}{2}\rfloor) + O(1)$.

The following rule is an example of how we connect recurrence annotations and resource bounds.

$$\frac{x : \tau_1, f : \tau_1 \rightarrow \tau_2, \Gamma \vdash t :: \langle\tau_2; ([1, \lfloor\frac{u}{2}\rfloor], O(1))\rangle}{\Gamma \vdash (\text{fix } f. \ \lambda x.t) :: \langle\tau_1 \rightarrow \tau_2; O(\log u)\rangle}$$

The rule instantiates the Master Theorem example above. Note that, the annotation $([1, \lfloor\frac{u}{2}\rfloor], O(1))$ states that the function body contains up to one recursive call to a problem of size $\lfloor\frac{u}{2}\rfloor$, and the resource usage in the body of t (aside from calls to f itself) is bounded by $O(1)$. The rule states that if the function body t of type τ_2 contains one recursive call to a sub-problem of size $\lfloor\frac{u}{2}\rfloor$, then the function will be bounded by $O(\log u)$.

The implementation of prod shown in Eq. (2) runs in $O(\log x)$ steps.

$$\text{prod} = \lambda\text{x. } \lambda\text{y.if x == 0 then x else} \tag{2}$$
$$\text{if even x then } \text{double (prod (div2 x) y)}$$
$$\text{else } \text{plus y (double (prod (div2 x) y))}$$

To check that, SYNPLEXITY's type system counts the number of recursive calls along any path of the function. There are three paths (two nested if-then-else terms) in the program, and at most one recursive call along each path. Also, one can check that the problem size of each recursive call is no more than $\lfloor\frac{x}{2}\rfloor$.

	Term	$t ::= e \mid b$
	E-term	$e ::= x \mid c \mid \mathtt{true} \mid \mathtt{false} \mid x\, e_1 \ldots e_n$
I-term $\Big\{$	Branching term	$b ::= \mathtt{if}\ e\ \mathtt{then}\ t\ \mathtt{else}\ t$
		$\mid \mathtt{match}\ e\ \mathtt{with}\ \mid_i C_i\ (x_i^1 \ldots x_i^n) \mapsto t_i$
	Function term	$f ::= \mathtt{fix}\ f.\lambda x_1 \ldots \lambda x_n.t$

Fig. 1. SYNPLEXITY syntax.

Logical expr.	$\varphi, \phi, \psi ::= x \mid \mathbf{m}(\psi) \mid \top \mid \bot \mid c \mid \psi \bmod \psi \mid \psi \wedge \psi \mid \psi \vee \psi$
	$\mid \neg\psi \mid \psi = \psi \mid \psi * \psi \mid \psi/\psi \mid \psi + \psi \mid \psi - \psi$
Ordinary type	$B ::= \mathtt{Bool} \mid \mathtt{Int} \mid D$
Refinement type	$\tau ::= \{B \mid \varphi\} \mid x_1{:}\tau_1 \to \ldots \to x_n{:}\tau_n \to y : \tau$
Annotated type	$\gamma ::= \langle \tau; \alpha \rangle$
Recurrence ann.	$\alpha ::= (\ [c_1, \phi_1]_\mathfrak{t}, \ldots, [c_n, \phi_n]_\mathfrak{t}; O(\psi)\ )$
Environment	$\Gamma ::= \cdot \mid x : \gamma; \Gamma \mid \varphi; \Gamma \mid \mathtt{recFun} := x; \Gamma \mid \mathtt{args} := x_1 \ldots x_n; \Gamma$

Fig. 2. SYNPLEXITY types.

For example, the recursive call `prod (div2 x) y` calls to a problem with size `div2 x`, which is consistent with $[1, \lfloor \frac{u}{2} \rfloor]$, and u is `x` because `size x y = x`. In addition, the condition that the resource usage of the body is bounded by $O(1)$ is satisfied because only auxiliary functions with constant cost are called.

3   The SYNPLEXITY Type System

In this section, we present our type system. First, we give the surface language and the types, which extend the SYNQUID liquid-types framework with resource annotations (Subsect. 3.1). Then, we show the semantics of our language (Subsect. 3.2). Finally, we present SYNPLEXITY's type system (Subsect. 3.3), which our synthesis algorithm uses to synthesize programs with desired resource bounds.

3.1   Syntax and Types

Syntax. Consider the language shown in Fig. 1. In the language, we distinguish between two kinds of terms: *elimination terms* (E-terms) and *introduction terms* (I-terms). E-terms consist of variable terms, constant values c, and application terms. Condition guards and match scrutinies can only be E-terms. I-terms are branching terms and function terms. The key property of I-terms is that if the type of any I-term is known, the types of its sub-terms are also known (which is not the case for E-terms).

Types. Our language of types, presented in Fig. 2, extends the one of SYN-QUID [18] with *recurrence annotations*, which are used to track recurrence relations on functions. To simplify the presentation, we ignore some of the features of the type system of SYNQUID [18] that do not affect our algorithm. In particular, we do not discuss polymorphic types and the enumerating strategy that ensures that only terminating programs are synthesized. However, our implementation is built on top of SYNQUID, and supports both of those features.

Logical expressions are built from variables, constants, arithmetic operators, and other user-defined logical functions. Logical expressions in our type system can be used as refinements φ, size expressions ϕ, or bound expressions ψ. Refinements φ are logical predicates used to refine ordinary types in refinement types $\{B \mid \varphi\}$. We usually use a reserved symbol v as the free variable in φ, and let v represents the inhabitants, i.e., inhabitants of the type $\{B \mid \varphi\}$ are valuations of v that satisfy φ. For example, the type $\{\texttt{Int} \mid v \bmod 2 = 0\}$ represents the even integers. Size expressions and bound expressions are used in recurrence annotations, and are explained later.

Ordinary types includes primitive types and user-defined algebraic datatypes D. Datatype constructors $\texttt{C}$ are functions of type $\tau_1 \to \ldots \to \tau_n \to D$. For example, the datatype $\texttt{List(Int)}$ has two constructors: $\texttt{Cons} : \texttt{Int} \to \texttt{List(Int)} \to \texttt{List(Int)}$, and $\texttt{Nil} : \texttt{List(Int)}$. Refinement types are ordinary types refined with some predicates ψ, or arrow types. Note that, unlike SYNQUID's type system, SYNPLEXITY's type system does not support higher-order functions[2]—i.e., arguments of functions have to be non-arrow types. All occurrences of τ_i and τ in arrow types $x_1 : \tau_1 \to \ldots \to x_n : \tau_n \to y : \tau$ have to be ordinary types or refined ordinary types. We will discuss this limitation in Sect. 7.

We use $\texttt{recFun}$ to denote the name of the function for which we are performing type-checking, and $\texttt{args}$ to denote the tuple of arguments to $\texttt{recFun}$. For example, in the function $\texttt{prod}$ shown in Eq. (1), $\texttt{recFun=prod}$ and $\texttt{args=x y}$. An environment Γ is a sequence of variable bindings $x : \gamma$, path conditions φ, and assignments for variables $\texttt{recFun}$ and $\texttt{args}$.

Recurrence Annotations. Annotated types are refinement types annotated with recurrence annotations. A recurrence annotation is a pair $([c_1, \phi_1]_\texttt{f}, \ldots, [c_n, \phi_n]_\texttt{f}; O(\psi))$ consisting of (1) a set of recursive-call costs of the form $[c_i, \phi_i]_\texttt{f}$, and (2) a resource-usage bound of the form $O(\psi)$. Intuitively, a recurrence annotation tracks the number c_i of recursive calls to $\texttt{f}$ of size ϕ_i in the first element $[c_1, \phi_1]_\texttt{f}, \ldots, [c_n, \phi_n]_\texttt{f}$ of the pair, as well as the asymptotic resource usage of the *body* of the function (the second element $O(\psi)$). Using these quantities, we can compute a recurrence relation describing the resource usage of the function $\texttt{recFun}$. For example, the recurrence annotation $([1, u-1]_\texttt{f}, [1, u-2]_\texttt{f}; O(1))$ corresponds to the recurrence relation $T_\texttt{f}(u) \leq T_\texttt{f}(u-1) + T_\texttt{f}(u-2) + O(1)$.

A *recursive-call cost* $[c, \phi]_\texttt{f}$ associated with a function $\texttt{f}$ denotes that the body of $\texttt{f}$ can contain up to c recursive calls to subproblems that have sizes up to the one specified by size expression ϕ. A size expression, ϕ, is a polynomial over a reserved variable symbol u that represents the size of the top-level problem. In our paper, a *problem* with respect to a function $g :: x_1 : \tau_1 \to \ldots \to x_n : \tau_n \to y : \tau$ is a tuple of terms $e_1 \ldots e_n$, to which g can be applied—i.e., e_i has type τ_i for all

---

[2] However, the type system can be extended to support restricted higher-order functions (Sect. 5).

i from 1 to n. For the problems of function g, the size of each problem is defined by a *size function* size_g—a user-defined logical function that has type $\tau_1 \to \ldots \to \tau_n \to \text{Int}$; i.e., it takes a problem of g as input and outputs a non-negative integer. In the body of g, we say that a recursive-call term $g\ e_1 \ldots e_n$ *satisfies* a size expression ϕ if for all $x_1, \ldots, x_n$, $\text{size}_g\ [\![e_1]\!] \ldots [\![e_n]\!] \leq [\![(\text{size}_g\ x_1 \ldots x_n)/u]\!]\phi$, where the x_i's are the arguments of g and the $[\![e_i]\!]$'s are the evaluations of e_i on input $x_1 \ldots x_n$. (See Sect. 3.2 for the formal definition of $[\![\cdot]\!]$.) Note that one annotation can contain multiple recursive-call costs, which allows the function to make recursive calls to sub-problems with different sizes. We often abbreviate $\langle \tau, (O(1)) \rangle$ as τ and omit $\mathbf{f}$ in recursive-call costs if it is clear from context.

A resource bound $O(\psi)$ of a non-arrow type specifies the bound of the resource usage strictly within the top-level-function body. A resource bound in a signature of an auxiliary function f specifies the resource usage of f. *Bound expressions* ψ in $O(\psi)$ are of the form $u^a \log^b u + c$ where a, b, and c are all non-negative constants, and u represents the size of the top-level problem.

Example 1. In the function prod (Eq. (2)), the recursive-call term $\text{prod}\ (\text{div2}\ x)\ y$ satisfies the recursive-call cost $[1, \lfloor \frac{u}{2} \rfloor]$, because $\text{size}_{\text{prod}} = \lambda z.\lambda w.z$, and

$$\text{size}_{\text{prod}}\ [\![(\text{div2}\ x)]\!]\ [\![y]\!] = [\![\text{div2}\ x]\!] = \lfloor \frac{x}{2} \rfloor = [\![(\text{size}_{\text{prod}}\ x\ y)/u]\!]\lfloor \frac{u}{2} \rfloor.$$

3.2 Semantics and Cost Model

We introduce the *concrete*-cost semantics of our language here. The semantics serves two goals: (1) it defines the evaluation of terms (i.e., how to obtain values), which can be used to compute the sizes of problems in application expressions, and (2) it defines the resource usages of terms.

Besides the syntax shown in Fig. 1, implementations of auxiliary functions can contain calls to a tick function $\text{tick}(c, t)$, which specifies that c units of a resource are used, and the overall value is the value of t. Note that in our synthesis language, we are not actually synthesizing programs with tick functions. We assume that tick functions are only called in the implementations of auxiliary functions. In the concrete-cost semantics, a configuration $\langle t, C \rangle$ consists of a term t and a nonnegative integer C denoting the resource usage so far. The evaluation judgment $\langle t, C \rangle \hookrightarrow \langle t', C + C_\Delta \rangle$ states that a term t can be evaluated in one step to a term (or a value) t', with resource usage C_Δ. We write $\langle t, C \rangle \hookrightarrow^* \langle t', C + C_\Delta \rangle$ to indicate the reduction from t to t' in zero or more steps. All of the evaluation judgments are standard. Here we show the judgment of the tick function, where resource usage happens.

$$\frac{}{\langle \text{tick}(c, t), C \rangle \hookrightarrow \langle t, C + c \rangle}\ \text{SEM-TICK}$$

For a term t, $[\![t]\!]$ denotes the evaluation result of t, i.e., $\langle t, \cdot \rangle \hookrightarrow^* \langle [\![t]\!], \cdot \rangle$.

Example 2. Consider the following function that doubles its input.

```
fix double.λx.if x = 0 then 0 else tick(1,2 + double(x-1)).
```

Let t_{body} denote the function body if x=0 then 0 else tick(1,2+double(x-1)). The result of evaluating double on input 5 is 10, with resource usage 5.

$\langle(\text{fix double}.\lambda\text{x}.t_{\text{body}})5, 0\rangle$

$\hookrightarrow \langle\text{if 5=0 then 0 else tick(1,2+double(4))}, 0\rangle$

$\hookrightarrow \langle\text{if false then 0 else tick(1,2+ double(4))}, 0\rangle$

$\hookrightarrow \langle\text{tick(1,2+double(4))}, 0\rangle \hookrightarrow \langle2+\text{double(4)}, 1\rangle$

$\hookrightarrow \langle2+(\text{fix double}.\lambda x.t_{\text{body}})4, 1\rangle \hookrightarrow^* \langle4+\text{double(3)}, 2\rangle \hookrightarrow^* \langle10+\text{double(0)}, 5\rangle$

$\hookrightarrow \langle10+(\text{if 0=0 then 0 else tick(1,2+double(0-1)))}, 5\rangle$

$\hookrightarrow \langle10+(\text{if true then 0 else tick(1,2+double(0-1)))}, 0\rangle \hookrightarrow \langle10+0, 5\rangle$

With the standard concrete semantics, the complexity of a function f is characterized by its resource usage when the function is evaluated on inputs of a given size.

Definition 1 (Complexity). *Given a function $fix\ f.\lambda\overline{y}.t$ of type* : $\tau_1 \to \tau_2$, *with size function $size_f : \tau_1 \to \mathbb{N}$, and suppose that for any possible input $\overline{x}$, the configuration $\langle(fix\ f.\lambda\overline{y}.t)\overline{x}, 0\rangle$ can be reduced to $\langle v, C_{\overline{x}}\rangle$ for some value v. Then, if $T_f : \mathbb{N} \to \mathbb{N}$ is a function such that, for all, $u \geq 0$, $T_f(u) = \sup_{\overline{x}\ s.t.\ size_f(\overline{x})=u} C_{\overline{x}}$, we say that T_f is the complexity function of f.*

Note that Definition 1 assumes that the top-level term $(fix\ f.\lambda\overline{y}.t)\overline{x}$ can be reduced to some value. Thus, Definition 1 only applies to terminating programs.

Definition 2 (Big-O notation). *Given two integer functions f and g, we say that f dominates g, i.e., $g \in O(f)$, if $\exists c, M \geq 0.\ \forall x \geq c.\ g(x) \leq Mf(x)$.*

In the rest of the paper, we use T_f to denote the complexity function of the function f, and we say the complexity of f is *bounded* by a function g if $T_f \in O(g)$. As an example, the complexity of the double function shown in Example 2 is $T_{\text{double}}(u) := u$, and hence $T_{\text{double}}(u) \in O(u)$.

Auxiliary functions. We allow users to supply signatures for auxiliary functions, instead of implementations. It is an obligation on users that such signatures be sensible; in particular, when the user gives the signature $\langle\tau_1 \to \{B \mid \varphi(v, \overline{y})\}, O(\psi(u))\rangle$ for auxiliary function f, the user asserts that there exists some implementation $fix\ f.\lambda\overline{y}.t$ of f, such that: 1) for any input $\overline{x}$, the output of f on $\overline{x}$ satisfies φ, i.e., $\varphi(\llbracket(fix\ f.\lambda\overline{y}.t)\overline{x}\rrbracket, \overline{x})$ is valid; and 2) for any input $\overline{x}$, the complexity of f is bounded by $\psi(u)$, i.e., $T_f(u) \in O(\psi(u))$. Signatures always over-approximate their implementations, as illustrated by the following example.

Example 3. The signature doubleRelaxed :: $\langle\text{x}:\text{Int} \to \{\text{Int} \mid v \leq 3*x\}, O(u^2)\rangle$ describes an auxiliary function that computes *no more* than the input times 3, and has quadratic resource usage. Note that the function double shown in Example 2 can be an implementation of this signature because $\llbracket\text{double}(\overline{x})\rrbracket = 2*x \leq 3*x$, and the complexity function $T_{\text{double}}(u) = u$ is in $O(u^2)$.

3.3   Typing Rules

The typing rules of SYNPLEXITY are inspired by bidirectional type checking [17] and type checking with cost sharing [16]. Recall that we use `recFun` to denote the name of the function for which we are performing type-checking, and `args` to denote the tuple of arguments to `recFun`.

An environment Γ is a sequence of variable bindings of the form $x : \gamma$, path conditions φ, and assignments of the form $x = \varphi$ for `recFun` and the components of `args`. SYNPLEXITY's typing rules use three judgments: 1) $\Gamma \vdash t :: \gamma$ states that t has type γ, 2) $\Gamma \vdash \gamma_1 <: \gamma_2$ states that γ_2 is a subtype of γ_1, and 3) $\Gamma \vdash \gamma \curlyvee \gamma_1|\gamma_2$ states that γ_1 and γ_2 share the costs in γ

Subtyping. The subtyping relations between refinement types are relatively standard and can be found in the technical report [11]. The subtyping relations between annotated types allow us to compare resource consumption of recurrence annotations. The following is the rule for comparing recursive-call costs.

$$\frac{c' > c \quad \Gamma \models \forall u.\ \phi' \geq \phi}{\Gamma \vdash [c, \phi] <: [c', \phi']} \text{ <:-REC}$$

For example, if one branch of some branching term has type $\langle \tau, ([1, \lfloor \frac{u}{3} \rfloor], O(\psi)) \rangle$, it can be over-approximated by a super type $\langle \tau, ([1, \lfloor \frac{u}{2} \rfloor], O(\psi)) \rangle$. The idea is that the resource usage of an application calling to a problem of size $\lfloor \frac{u}{2} \rfloor$ will be larger than the resource usage of the application calling to a smaller problem of size $\lfloor \frac{u}{3} \rfloor$ (assuming all resource usages are monotonic).

Subtyping rules also allow the type system to compare branches with a different number of recursive calls. For example, base cases of recursive procedures have no recursive calls, and thus have types of the form $\langle \tau, ([], O(\psi)) \rangle$. With subtyping, these types can be over-approximated by types of the form $\langle \tau, ([c, \phi], O(\psi)) \rangle$.

Cost Sharing. When a term has more than one sub-term in the same path, e.g., the condition guard and the `then` branch are in the same path in an `ite` term, the recursive-call costs of the term will be shared among its sub-terms. The sharing operator $\alpha \curlyvee \alpha_1|\alpha_2$ partitions the recursive-call costs of α into α_1 and α_2—i.e., the sum of the costs in α_1 and α_2 equals the cost in α. The following is the sharing rule for a single recursive-call cost:

$$\frac{c_1, c_2 \geq 0 \quad c_1 + c_2 \leq c}{\Gamma \vdash [c, \phi] \curlyvee [c_1, \phi] \mid [c_2, \phi]} \text{ S-POT}$$

Other sharing rules can be found in the technical report [11]. The idea is that a single cost c can be shared as two costs c_1 and c_2 such that their sum is no more than c. An annotation can be shared as two parts if every recursive cost $[c_i, \phi_i]$ in it can be shared as two parts $[c_i^1, \phi_1]$ and $[c_i^2, \phi_2]$. Finally, annotations can also be shared as more than two parts.

Table 1. Annotations that can be used to instantiate the rule T-ABS.

	Bound (B)	Recurrence relation	Annotation (A)
Master Theorem	$O(\log u)$	$T(u) \leq T(\lfloor \frac{u}{d} \rfloor) + O(1),\ d \geq 2$	$([1, \lfloor \frac{u}{d} \rfloor]; O(1)),\ d \geq 2$
	$O(u \log u)$	$T(u) \leq dT(\lfloor \frac{u}{d} \rfloor) + O(u),\ d \geq 2$	$([d, \lfloor \frac{u}{d} \rfloor]; O(u)),\ d \geq 2$
Akra–Bazzi	$O(u \log u)$	$T(u) \leq T(\lceil \frac{u}{2} \rceil) + T(\lfloor \frac{u}{2} \rfloor) + O(u)$	$([1, \lceil \frac{u}{2} \rceil], [1, \lfloor \frac{u}{2} \rfloor]; O(u))$
C-Finite Seq.	$O(u)$	$T(u) \leq T(u - d) + O(1),\ d \geq 1$	$([1, u - d]; O(1)),\ d \geq 1$
	$O(u^2)$	$T(u) \leq T(u - d) + O(u),\ d \geq 1$	$([1, u - d]; O(u)),\ d \geq 1$

Example 4. There are multiple ways to share the recurrence annotation $([1, \lfloor \frac{u}{2} \rfloor], [1, \lceil \frac{u}{2} \rceil]; O(u))$:

$$\Gamma \vdash ([1, \lfloor \frac{u}{2} \rfloor], [1, \lceil \frac{u}{2} \rceil]; O(u)) \curlyvee ([1, \lfloor \frac{u}{2} \rfloor], [1, \lceil \frac{u}{2} \rceil]; O(u)) \mid ([\ ], O(u)),$$

where one annotation contains both recursive-call costs $[1, \lfloor \frac{u}{2} \rfloor], [1, \lfloor \frac{u}{2} \rfloor]$; and the other contains no recursive-call cost. And

$$\Gamma \vdash ([1, \lfloor \frac{u}{2} \rfloor], [1, \lceil \frac{u}{2} \rceil]; O(u)) \curlyvee ([1, \lfloor \frac{u}{2} \rfloor]; O(u)) \mid ([1, \lceil \frac{u}{2} \rceil]; O(u)),$$

where each annotation contains one recursive-call cost.

Function Terms. The rule T-ABS shown below is really a rule-schema that is parameterized in terms of an annotation (A) for a function body t, and a resource bound (B) for the function term. If the function body t has some recurrence relation described by the annotation A, then the function f will satisfy the resource-usage bound B. Some example patterns are shown in Table 1.[3]

$$\Gamma' = [\texttt{recFun} \leftarrow \texttt{f}][\texttt{args} \leftarrow x_1 \ldots x_n]\Gamma$$
$$\gamma_f = \langle x_1 : \tau_1 \rightarrow \ldots \rightarrow x_n : \tau_n \rightarrow \tau, (B) \rangle$$
$$\frac{\Gamma'; x_1 : \langle \tau_1, O(1) \rangle; \ldots; x_n : \langle \tau_n, O(1) \rangle; \texttt{f} : \gamma_f \vdash t :: \langle \tau, (A) \rangle}{\Gamma \vdash \texttt{fix } \texttt{f}.\lambda x_1 \ldots \lambda x_n.t :: \langle x_1 : \tau_1 \rightarrow \ldots \rightarrow x_n : \tau_n \rightarrow \tau, (B) \rangle} \text{T-ABS}$$

For example, if the annotation of the function body is $([1, \lfloor \frac{u}{2} \rfloor]; O(1))$, then the resource bound in the function type will be $O(\log u)$, i.e., the resource usage of f is bounded by $O(\log(\texttt{size}_\texttt{f}\ x_1 \ldots x_n))$.

At the same time, the rule stores the name f of the recursive function into recFun, and its arguments as a tuple into args.

Example 5. We use a function $\texttt{fix bar}.\lambda x.\texttt{if } x = 1 \texttt{ then } 1 \texttt{ else } 1 + \texttt{bar}(\texttt{div2 } x)$ to illustrate the first pattern in Table 1. The body of bar has the annotated type $([1, \lfloor \frac{u}{2} \rfloor]; O(1))$ because (i) there exists only one recursive call to a sub-problem whose size is half of the top-level problem size u, and (ii) the resource usage inside the body is constant (with the assumption that all auxiliary functions

---

[3] The patterns shown in Table 1 are those we used in the implementation. Patterns capturing other recurrence relations can be added to the type system if needed.

have constant resource usage). This type appears in row 1, column 4 of Table 1. Consequently, the recurrence relation of bar is $T(u) \leq T(\lfloor \frac{u}{2} \rfloor) + O(1)$ (row 1, column 3), where $T(u)$ is the resource usage of bar on problems with size u. Finally, according to the Master Theorem, the resource usage of bar is bounded by $O(\log u)$ (row 1, column 2).

Branching Terms. In rule T-IF, the condition has type Bool with refinement φ_e. Two branches have different types—the then branch follows the path condition φ_e, and the refinement φ of the branch term, while the else branch follows the path condition $\neg\varphi_e$. By having both branches share the same recurrence annotation, T-IF can introduce some imprecision. In particular, if the branches belong to different complexity classes, the annotation of the conditional term will be the upper bound of both branches.

$$\frac{\Gamma \vdash \alpha \curlyvee \alpha_1 | \alpha_2 \quad \Gamma \vdash e :: \langle \{\texttt{Bool} \mid \varphi_e\}, \alpha_1 \rangle \quad \Gamma, \varphi_e \vdash t_1 :: \langle \{B \mid \varphi\}, \alpha_2 \rangle \quad \Gamma, \neg\varphi_e \vdash t_2 :: \langle \{B \mid \varphi\}, \alpha_2 \rangle}{\Gamma \vdash \texttt{if } e \texttt{ then } t_1 \texttt{ else } t_2 :: \langle \{B \mid \varphi\}, \alpha \rangle} \text{T-IF}$$

The rule T-MATCH is slightly different: (1) there can be more than two branches, (2) all branches have the same type $\langle \tau, \alpha_2 \rangle$, and (3) variables in each case C_i $(x_i^1 \ldots x_i^n)$ are introduced in the corresponding branch.

$$\frac{\Gamma \vdash \alpha \curlyvee \alpha_1 | \alpha_2 \quad \Gamma \vdash e :: \langle \tau_s, \alpha_1 \rangle \quad C_i = \tau_1 \to \ldots \to \tau_n \to \tau_s \quad \Gamma; x_i^1 : \tau_1; \ldots; x_i^n : \tau_n \vdash t_i :: \langle \tau, \alpha_2 \rangle}{\Gamma \vdash \texttt{match } e \texttt{ with } |_i \; C_i \; (x_i^1 \ldots x_i^n) \mapsto t_i :: \langle \tau, \alpha \rangle} \text{T-MATCH}$$

E-terms. The typing rules for E-terms are shown in Fig. 3. The two rules for application terms are the key rules of our type system. Let us first look at the E-RECAPP rule for recursive-call terms. Recall that the recursive-call annotation tracks the number of recursive calls and the sizes of sub-problems. If the term f $e_1 \ldots e_n$ is a recursive call—i.e., $\Gamma(\texttt{recFun}) = \texttt{f}$—the number of recursive calls in one of the recursive-call costs will increase by one—i.e., $[c_k, \phi_k]$ in the premise becomes $[c_k + 1, \phi_k]$ in the conclusion. Also, we want to make sure that the size of the subproblem this application term is called on satisfies the size expression ϕ_k. If each callee term is refined by the predicate φ_i, i.e., $\Gamma \vdash e_i :: \langle \{B_i \mid \varphi_i\}, \alpha_i \rangle$, then the fact that the size of the problem $e_1 \ldots e_n$ satisfies ϕ_k can be implied by the validity of the predicate $\bigwedge_{i=1}^m [y_i/v]\varphi_i \Rightarrow (\texttt{size } y_1 \ldots y_m \leq [\texttt{size } \Gamma(\texttt{args})/u]\phi_k)$. We introduce validity checking, written $\Gamma \models \varphi$, to state that a predicate expression φ is always true under any instance of the environment Γ.

Example 6. Recall Eq. (2). According to the rule T-RECAPP, the recursive call prod (div2 x) y has type $\langle \{\texttt{Int} \mid v = \lfloor \frac{x}{2} \rfloor * \texttt{y}\}, ([1, \frac{u}{2}]); O(1) \rangle$. Note that the first argument (div2 x) has type $\{\texttt{Int} \mid v = \lfloor \frac{x}{2} \rfloor\}$, the second argument y has

$$\boxed{\Gamma \vdash e :: \gamma}$$

$$\dfrac{\Gamma \vdash e :: \gamma' \qquad \Gamma \vdash \gamma' <: \gamma}{\Gamma \vdash e :: \gamma} \text{ E-SubType} \qquad\qquad \dfrac{\Gamma(x) = \gamma}{\Gamma \vdash x :: \gamma} \text{ E-Var}$$

$$\dfrac{\begin{array}{c} \Gamma \vdash \mathbf{g} : \langle x_1 : \tau_1 \to \dots \to x_m : \tau_m \to \{B \mid \varphi\}, (O(\psi_{\mathbf{g}})) \rangle \\ \Gamma(\mathbf{recFun}) \neq \mathbf{g} \qquad \Gamma \vdash ([c_1, \phi_1], \dots, \dots, [c_n, \phi_n]; O(\psi)) \;\mathcal{Y}\; \alpha_1 | \dots | \alpha_m \\ \forall 1 \leq i \leq m \qquad \Gamma \vdash e_i :: \langle \{B_i \mid \varphi_i\}, \alpha_i \rangle \qquad \Gamma \vdash \{B_i \mid \varphi_i\} <: \tau_i \\ \Gamma \models \bigwedge_{i=1}^{m} [y_i/v]\varphi_i \Rightarrow ([\mathbf{size_g}\ y_1 \dots y_m/u]\psi_{\mathbf{g}} \in O([\mathbf{size}\ \Gamma(\mathbf{args})/u]\psi)) \\ \tau = \{B \mid [z_i/x_i]\varphi \wedge \bigwedge_{i=1} [z_i/v]\varphi_i\} \; z_i \notin FV(\varphi), z_i \notin FV(\varphi_i) \end{array}}{\Gamma \vdash \mathbf{g}e_1 \dots e_m :: \langle \tau, ([c_1, \phi_1], \dots, [c_n, \phi_n]; O(\psi)) \rangle} \text{ E-App}$$

$$\dfrac{\begin{array}{c} \Gamma \vdash \mathbf{f} : \langle x_1 : \tau_1 \to \dots \to x_m : \tau_m \to \{B \mid \varphi\}, \alpha \rangle \qquad \Gamma(\mathbf{recFun}) = \mathbf{f} \\ \Gamma \vdash ([c_1, \phi_1], \dots, [c_k, \phi_k], \dots, [c_n, \phi_n]; O(\psi)) \;\mathcal{Y}\; \alpha_1 | \dots | \alpha_m \\ \forall 1 \leq i \leq m \qquad \Gamma \vdash e_i :: \langle \{B_i \mid \varphi_i\}, \alpha_i \rangle \qquad \Gamma \vdash \{B_i \mid \varphi_i\} <: \tau_i \\ \Gamma \models \bigwedge_{i=1}^{m} [y_i/v]\varphi_i \Rightarrow (\mathbf{size}\ y_1 \dots y_m \leq [\mathbf{size}\ \Gamma(\mathbf{args})/u]\phi_k) \\ \tau = \{B \mid [z_i/x_i]\varphi \wedge \bigwedge_{i=1} [z_i/v]\varphi_i\} \; z_i \notin FV(\varphi), z_i \notin FV(\varphi_i) \end{array}}{\Gamma \vdash \mathbf{f}e_1 \dots e_m :: \langle \tau, ([c_1, \phi_1], \dots [c_k + 1, \phi_k], \dots, [c_n, \phi_n]; O(\psi)) \rangle} \text{ E-RecApp}$$

Fig. 3. Typing rules of E-terms

type $\{\text{Int} \mid v = \mathbf{y}\}$, the size function is $\mathbf{size_{prod}} = \lambda z.\lambda w.z$, and the arguments in the context are $\Gamma(\mathbf{args}) = \mathbf{x}\ \mathbf{y}$. Therefore, the following predicate is valid:

$$[y_1/v](v = \lfloor \tfrac{x}{2} \rfloor) \wedge [y_2/v](v = y) \Rightarrow \mathbf{size_{prod}}\ y_1\ y_2 = [\mathbf{size_{prod}}\ \Gamma(\mathbf{args}/u)]\lfloor \tfrac{u}{2} \rfloor$$
$$\Leftrightarrow (y_1 = \lfloor \tfrac{x}{2} \rfloor) \wedge (y_2 = y) \Rightarrow y_1 = \lfloor \tfrac{x}{2} \rfloor.$$

The rule E-App states that callees have types τ_i, and the resource usage does not exceed the bound $O(\psi)$ in the annotation. Similar to the E-RecApp rule, the size of the problem $\mathbf{g}$ calls to is $[\mathbf{size_g}\ y_1 \dots y_m/u]$ with the premise $\bigwedge_{i=1}^{m}[y_i/v]\varphi_i$. The validation checking $\bigwedge_{i=1}^{m}[y_i/v]\varphi_i \Rightarrow ([\mathbf{size_g}\ y_1 \dots y_m/u]\psi_{\mathbf{g}} \in O([\mathbf{size}\ \Gamma(\mathbf{args})/u]\psi))$ in the rule states that for any instance of Γ, the size of the problem in the application term is in the big-O class $O([\mathbf{size}\ \Gamma(\mathbf{args})/u]\psi)$. Note that the membership of big-O classes can be encoded as an $\exists\forall$ query. The query is non-linear, and hence undecidable in general. However, we observed in our experiments that for many benchmarks the query stays linear. Furthermore, even when the query is non-linear, existing SMT solvers are capable of handling many such checks in practice.

3.4   Soundness

We assume that the resource-usage function ψ and the complexities T of each function are all nonnegative and monotonic integer functions—both the input and the output are integers. We show soundness of the type system with respect to the resource model. The soundness theorem states that if we derive a bound $O(\psi)$ for a function f, then the complexity of f is bounded by ψ.

Theorem 1 (Soundness of type checking). *Given a function* fix $f.\lambda x_1 \ldots \lambda x_n.t$ *and an environment* Γ, *if* $\Gamma \vdash fix\ f.\lambda x_1 \ldots \lambda x_n.t :: \langle \tau, O(\psi) \rangle$, *then the complexity of* f *is bounded by* ψ.

Our type system is incomplete with respect to resource usage. That is, there are functions in our programming language that are actually in a complexity class $O(p(x))$, but cannot be typed in our type system. The main reason why our type system is incomplete is that it ignores condition guards when building recurrence relations, and over-approximates if-then-else terms by choosing the largest complexity among all the paths including even unreachable ones.

4   The *SynPlexity* Synthesis Algorithm

In this section, we present the SynPlexity synthesis algorithm, which uses annotated types to guide the search of terms of given types.

4.1   Overview of the Synthesis Algorithm

The algorithm takes as input a goal type f : $\langle \tau, O(\psi) \rangle$, an environment Γ that includes type information of auxiliary functions, and the size functions for f and all auxiliary functions. The goal is to find a function term of type $\langle \tau, O(\psi) \rangle$.

The algorithm uses the rules of the SynPlexity type system to decompose goal types into sub-goals, and then applies itself recursively on the sub-goals to synthesize sub-terms. Concretely, given a goal γ, the algorithm tries all the typing rules, where the type in the conclusion matches γ, to construct sub-goals: for each sub-term t in the conclusion, there must be a judgment $\Gamma \vdash t :: \gamma'$ in the premise; thus, we construct the sub-goal γ'—the desired type of t. For each I-term rule, the type of each sub-term is always known, and thus a fixed set of sub-goals is generated. For each E-term rule, the algorithm enumerates E-terms up to a certain depth (the depth can be given as a parameter or it can automatically increase throughout the search). If the algorithm fails to solve some sub-goal using some E-term rule, it backtracks to an earlier choice point, and tries another rule.

Because the top-level goal is always a function type, the algorithm always starts by applying the rule T-Abs, which matches the resource bound $O(\psi)$ using Table 1 to infer a possible recurrence annotation for the type of the function body. Also T-Abs constructs a sub-goal type for the function body. In the rest of this section, we assume that goals are not function types.

Algorithm 1: GENERATEE(Γ, γ, d)

Input   : Context Γ, goal type $\gamma = \langle \{B \mid \varphi\}, \alpha \rangle$, depth bound d
1 **for** $t \leftarrow$ ENUMERATEE(Γ, d, B) **do**
2 | **if** CHECKE(t, Γ, γ) **then return** t
3 **return** $\bot$

Synthesizing E-Terms. The algorithm for synthesizing E-terms is shown in Algorithm 1. It enumerates each E-term t—with depth up to d—that satisfies the base type B in the goal $\gamma := \langle \{B \mid \varphi\}, ([c_1, \phi_1]..[c_n, \phi_n]; O(\psi)) \rangle$ from the context Γ. For each such E-term t, the algorithm checks whether t satisfies the goal type with a subroutine CHECKE, which operates as follows.

When t is a variable term, CHECKE checks the refined type of t against the goal. When t is an application term, CHECKE first checks if the total number of recursive calls in the term t exceeds the bound $\sum_i c_i$, and if it does, the term t is rejected. Otherwise, CHECKE checks the sizes of sub-problems of recursive calls in t. Formally, to check if a recursive application term $f(t_1, .., t_m)$ is consistent with some $[c_k, \phi_k]$, the algorithm queries the validity of the following predicate

$$(\bigwedge_{i=1}^{m} [y_i/v]\varphi_i \Rightarrow (\mathtt{size}_f(y_1 \,..\, y_m) = [\mathtt{size}_f(\Gamma(\mathtt{args}))/v]\phi_k)),$$

where the y_i's are fresh variables, and the φ_i's are the refinements of terms t_i's. If the sizes of sub-problems are not consistent with the recursive-call costs $[c_1, \phi_1]..[c_n, \phi_n]$, the term t is rejected. Note that one recursive call can possibly satisfy more than one $[c_k, \phi_k]$. The algorithm enumerates all possible matches. Finally, CHECKE checks the refined type of t against the goal.

Checking the validity of auxiliary application terms is similar. CHECKE needs to establish that the following predicate holds, which asserts that the resource usage of an auxiliary function does not exceed the bound $O(\psi)$.

$$\bigwedge_{i=1}^{m} [y_i/v]\varphi_i \Rightarrow ([\mathtt{size}_g \, y_1..y_m/v]\psi_g \in O([\mathtt{size} \, \Gamma(\mathtt{args})/v]\psi)).$$

Recall that the above query is undecidable in general, and is checked with best effort by an SMT solver in SYNPLEXITY.

Synthesizing I-Terms. Algorithm 2 shows the algorithm for synthesizing I-Terms. GENERATEI first tries to synthesize an E-term for the goal γ (line (1)).

If there is no E-term that satisfies the goal, and the match bound m is greater than 0, GENERATEI chooses to apply the rule T-Match lines (2)–(8). First, it enumerates candidate scrutinees s, which are E-terms of some data type. Then it generates `match` *patterns* according to the type of s (line (3)), updates the goal with a new recursive-call cost (line (4)), and generates case terms t_i for each pattern *pattern*[i] (lines (5)–(7)). The subroutine UPDATECOST is used to subtract the recursive-call cost usage from the cost in γ. Finally, if all case terms are found, the algorithm constructs the corresponding `match`-term and returns it.

If there is no `match`-term satisfying the goal, GENERATEI applies the rule T-IF to synthesize a term of the form `if` *cond* `then` t_T `else` t_F, and performs three steps to construct sub-goals for sub-terms *cond*, t_T, and t_F: (1) it enumerates the condition guard *cond* (line (10)) of type `bool`; (2) it updates the cost in the goal γ (line (11)); and (3) it propagates sub-goals to the two branches t_T and t_F with *cond* and $\neg cond$ as the path condition (lines (12) and (13)), respectively. Finally, if both t_T and t_F are found, the algorithm constructs the corresponding `if`-term and returns it as a solution (line (14)).

Optimization. Algorithm 2 discussed above is based on bidirectional type-guided synthesis with liquid types (SYNQUID [18]). Therefore, *liquid abduction* and *match abduction*, two optimizations used in SYNQUID, can also be used in SYNPLEXITY. These two techniques allow one to synthesize the branches of `if`- and `match`-terms, and then use logical abduction to infer the weakest assumption under which the branch fulfills the goal type.

Algorithm 2: GENERATEI(Γ, γ, d, m).

    Input   : Context Γ, goal type γ, depth bound d, match bound m

1   **if** $t \leftarrow$ GENERATEE(Γ, γ, d) **then** **return** t

2   **if** $m > 0$ **then** **for** $s \leftarrow$ ENUMERATEE$(\Gamma, d, dataType)$ **do**

3      $patterns \leftarrow$ GENERATEPATTERNS$(\Gamma, \text{TypeOf}(s))$

4      $\gamma' \leftarrow$ UPDATECOST(s, γ)

5   **for** $i \in [1, \text{SIZE}(patterns)]$ **do**

6          $t_i \leftarrow$ GENERATEI$(\text{UPDATECONTEXT}(\Gamma, s == patterns[i]), \gamma', d, m-1)$

7   **if** $t_i == \bot$ **then return** $\bot$

8   **return** `Match` s `with` $|_i$ $patterns[i] \rightarrow t_i$

9

10 **for** $cond \leftarrow$ ENUMERATEE$(\Gamma, d, Bool)$ **do**

11      $\gamma' \leftarrow$ UPDATECOST(s, γ)

12      $t_T \leftarrow$ GENERATEI$(\text{UPDATECONTEXT}(\Gamma, cond), \gamma', d, m)$

13      $t_F \leftarrow$ GENERATEI$(\text{UPDATECONTEXT}(\Gamma, \neg cond), \gamma', d, m)$

14   **if** $t_T \neq \bot \wedge t_F \neq \bot$ **then return** `If` $cond$ `then` t_T `else` t_F

15 **return** $\bot$

Example 7. We illustrate in Fig. 4 how the algorithm synthesizes the $O(\log x)$ implementation of `prod` presented in Eq. (2). We omit the type contexts in the example. We will use "`??`" to denote intermediate terms being synthesized (i.e., holes in the program). At the beginning, the type of $??_1$ (i.e., the term we are synthesizing) is an arrow type with resource bound $O(\log u)$ specified by the input goal. In this example, SYNPLEXITY applies to the arrow type the rule

$$\text{prod=??}_1 : \langle \texttt{x:\{Int} \mid v \geq 0\} \to \texttt{y:\{Int} \mid v \geq 0\} \to \{\texttt{Int} \mid v = \texttt{x} * \texttt{y}\}, (O(\log u)) \rangle$$

....

$$\xrightarrow{\text{T-ABS}} \quad \text{prod=}\lambda \texttt{x}.\lambda \texttt{y}.??_2 : \langle \{\texttt{Int} \mid v = \texttt{x} * \texttt{y}, ([1, \lfloor \tfrac{u}{2} \rfloor]; O(1)) \rangle$$

....

$$\xrightarrow{\text{T-IF}} \quad \text{prod=}\lambda \texttt{x}.\lambda \texttt{y}.\texttt{if } ??_3 \quad \xleftarrow{\text{E-APP}} \texttt{x==0} : \langle \{\texttt{Bool} \mid \texttt{x} = 0\}, ([0, \lfloor \tfrac{u}{2} \rfloor]; O(1)) \rangle$$
$$\texttt{then } ??_4 : \langle \{\texttt{Int} \mid v = \texttt{x} * \texttt{y} \wedge \texttt{x} = 0, ([1, \lfloor \tfrac{u}{2} \rfloor]; O(1)) \rangle$$
$$\xleftarrow{\text{E-APP}} \texttt{x} : \langle \{\texttt{Int} \mid v = 0\}, ([0, \lfloor \tfrac{u}{2} \rfloor]; O(1)) \rangle$$
$$\texttt{else } ??_5 : \langle \{\texttt{Int} \mid v = \texttt{x} * \texttt{y} \wedge \texttt{x} > 0, ([1, \lfloor \tfrac{u}{2} \rfloor]; O(1)) \rangle$$

....

$$??_5 \xrightarrow{\text{T-IF}} \texttt{if } ??_6 \quad \xleftarrow{\text{E-APP}} \texttt{even x} : \langle \{\texttt{Bool} \mid \texttt{x mod } 2 = 0\}, ([0, \lfloor \tfrac{u}{2} \rfloor]; O(1)) \rangle$$
$$\texttt{then } ??_7 : \langle \{\texttt{Int} \mid v = \texttt{x} * \texttt{y} \wedge \texttt{x mod } 2 = 0, ([1, \lfloor \tfrac{u}{2} \rfloor]; O(1)) \rangle$$
$$\xleftarrow{\text{E-APP}} \texttt{double (prod (div2 x) y)}$$
$$\texttt{else } ??_9 : \langle \{\texttt{Int} \mid v = \texttt{x} * \texttt{y} \wedge \texttt{x mod } 2 = 1, ([1, \lfloor \tfrac{u}{2} \rfloor]; O(1)) \rangle$$
$$\xleftarrow{\text{E-APP}} \texttt{plus y (double (prod (div2 x) y))}$$

Fig. 4. Trace of the synthesis of an $O(\log x)$ implementation of $\texttt{prod}$.

T-ABS, parameterized according to the first rule in Table 1. This step produces the sub-problem of synthesizing the function body $??_2$, whose annotation is $([1, \lfloor \tfrac{u}{2} \rfloor]; O(1))$—which means that $??_2$ should contain at most one recursive call to sub-problems with size $\lfloor \tfrac{u}{2} \rfloor$.

Next, SYNPLEXITY chooses to fill $??_2$ with an if-then-else term (by applying the T-IF rules) with three sub-problems: the condition guard $??_3$, the then branch $??_4$ and the else branch $??_5$. Note that here we share the number of recursive calls $[1, \tfrac{u}{2}]$ as follows: 0 recursive calls in the condition guard, and 1 in the then branch and the else branch. The left arrow E-App shows how SYNPLEXITY enumerates terms and checks them against the goal types of sub-problems. For example, to fill $??_4$, SYNPLEXITY enumerates terms of type $\langle \{\texttt{Int} \mid v = \texttt{x} * \texttt{y} \wedge \texttt{x} = 0, ([1, \tfrac{u}{2}]; O(1)) \rangle$, which are restricted to contain at most one recursive call to $\texttt{prod}$. In Fig. 4, SYNPLEXITY has picked the term $\texttt{x}$ to fill $??_4$. The refinement type of the variable term $\texttt{x}$ is $\{\texttt{Int} \mid v = \texttt{x} \wedge \texttt{x} = 0\}$ where $\texttt{x} = 0$ is the path condition. To check that $\texttt{x}$ also satisfies the type of $??_4$, the algorithm needs to apply rule E-SUBTYPE, and check that, for any v and $\texttt{x}$, $v = \texttt{x} \wedge \texttt{x} = 0$ implies $v = \texttt{x} * \texttt{y} \wedge \texttt{x} = 0$, and $[0, \lfloor \tfrac{u}{2} \rfloor]$ is approximated by $[1, \lfloor \tfrac{u}{2} \rfloor]$.

After applying another T-IF rule for $??_5$, SYNPLEXITY produces three new sub-problems $??_6$, $??_7$, and $??_8$. When enumerating terms to fill $??_7$, SYNPLEXITY finds an application term $\texttt{double (prod (div2 x) y)}$ that satisfies the goal $\langle \{\texttt{Int} \mid v = \texttt{x} * \texttt{y} \wedge \texttt{x mod } 2 = 0, ([1, \lfloor \tfrac{u}{2} \rfloor]; O(1)) \rangle$. To check that the size of the problem in the recursive call $\texttt{prod (div2 x)}$ $\texttt{y}$ satisfies the recursive-call cost $[1, \lfloor \tfrac{u}{2} \rfloor]$, the type system first checks the refinement of the callee. The refinement of the first argument $\texttt{(div2 x)}$ is $\varphi_1 := v = \lfloor \tfrac{x}{2} \rfloor$. The refinement of the second argument $\texttt{y}$ is $\varphi_2 := v = \texttt{y}$. Consequently, the size of the sub-problem $\texttt{prod (div2 x) y}$ satisfies $[1, \lfloor \tfrac{u}{2} \rfloor]$ because $[z/v]\varphi_1 \wedge [w/v]\varphi_2 \implies \texttt{size } z \ w = \lfloor (\texttt{size x y})/v \rfloor \lfloor \tfrac{u}{2} \rfloor$, which can be simplified to $z = \lfloor \frac{x}{2} \rfloor \wedge w = y \implies z = \lfloor \frac{x}{2} \rfloor$. (Recall that the size function for prod is size $:= \lambda z.\lambda w.z$.)

The algorithm is sound because it only enumerates well-typed terms.

Theorem 2 (Soundness of the synthesis algorithm). *Given a goal type* $\langle \tau, O(\psi) \rangle$ *and an environment* Γ, *if a term* $fix\ f.\lambda x_1..\lambda x_n.t$ *is synthesized by* SYNPLEXITY, *then the complexity of* f *is bounded by* ψ.

5   Extensions to the *SYNPLEXITY* Type System

In this section, we introduce two extensions to the SYNPLEXITY type system.

Recurrence Relations with Correlated Sizes. The type system shown in Sect. 3 only tracks sub-problems with independent sizes. For example, consider the recurrence relation $T(u) = T(l) + T(r) + O(1)$, where the variables l and r are correlated by the constraint $l + r < u$. This relation is needed to reason about programs that manipulate binary trees or binary heaps, where l and r represent the sizes of the two children. To support such a recurrence relation, we extend SYNPLEXITY's type system with recursive-call costs of the form $[1, l], [1, u - 1 - l]$, where l is a free variable. When correlated recurrence relations are present, the synthesis algorithm will: (1) match the first enumerated recursive-call term to $[1, l]$, and instantiate the size l with s, where s is the size of the recursive-call term (s should be smaller than the size u of the top-level function); and (2) use the size s of the recursive-call term computed in step 1 to constrain the algorithm to enumerate only recursive-call terms of sizes at most $u - 1 - s$.

Synthesis of Auxiliary Functions. Most of the existing type-directed approaches require the input to the problem to contain all needed auxiliary functions. With SYNPLEXITY, some of the auxiliary functions needed to solve synthesis problems with resource annotations can be synthesized automatically.

For example, consider the problem prod described in Sect. 2. In this problem, we observe that one of the provided auxiliary functions, div2, strongly resembles one of the elements of the recurrence relation, $T(u) \leq T(\lfloor \frac{u}{2} \rfloor) + O(1)$, needed to synthesize a program with the desired resource usage. In particular, we know that one needs an auxiliary function that can take an input of size u and produce an output of size $\lfloor \frac{u}{2} \rfloor$. In this example, the required auxiliary function div2 merely needs to divide the input by 2 (and round down), but in certain cases it might need a more precise refinement type than merely changing the size of the input. For example, the auxiliary function split used by merge sort needs to split the input list xs into two lists v1 and v2 that are half the length of the input *and* such that elems(v1) ⊎ elems(v2) = elems(xs). However, all we know from the refinement is that the output lists must be half the length of the original list.

Although we do not know what this auxiliary function should do exactly, we can use the size constraint appearing in the recurrence relation to define part of the refinement type we want the auxiliary function to satisfy. SYNPLEX-ITY builds on this idea and incorporates an (optionally enabled) algorithm, SYNAUXREF, that while trying to synthesize a solution to the top-level synthesis problem also tries in parallel to synthesize auxiliary functions that can create sub-problems with the size constraints needed in the recurrence relation. To address the problem mentioned above—i.e., that we do not know the exact refinement type the auxiliary function should satisfy—SYNAUXREF enumerates *auxiliary refinements*, which are possible specifications that the auxiliary function aux we are trying to synthesize might satisfy.

Synthesis with Higher-Order Functions. Although SYNPLEXITY does not support higher-order functions in general, it can solve restricted but practical problems with higher-order functions. The restriction supported introduces four assumptions on the synthesis problems. First, we assume that the resource usage of any function argument g is constant, i.e., $g : \langle \tau, O(1) \rangle$. Second, arrow-type arguments in recursive calls in the synthesized program are the same as the arrow-type arguments of the top-level function. For example, in the body of a higher-order function fix $f.\lambda g \lambda x \lambda y.t$, all recursive application terms must be of the form $f(g, \_, \_)$ where $\_$ can be any well-typed term. Third, we assume that the sizes of outputs of functions as arguments do not affect the asymptotic resource usage of the synthesized programs. Finally, arrow-type arguments cannot appear in size functions.

We extend the syntax and the type system of SYNPLEXITY to support the restricted problems (the detail of this extension can be found in the technical report [11]). We also modify the synthesis algorithm to prune E-terms that break the second or third restriction mentioned above.

To support the second restriction (i.e., that we need to call the same function arguments in recursive calls), the synthesis algorithm first stores the function arguments of the top-level functions. Later, when a recursive call is enumerated, the synthesizer checks whether the recursive call has the same function arguments, and rejects the candidate if it does not.

To support the third restriction (i.e., that the behavior of function arguments should not affect the resource usage), the synthesis algorithm avoids enumerating nested application terms where the resource usage of the outer application depends on the value of an inner application term that calls a function argument.

6 Evaluation

In this section, we evaluate the effectiveness and performance of SYNPLEXITY, and compare it to existing tools.[4] We implemented SYNPLEXITY in Haskell on top of SYNQUID by extending its type system with recurrence annotations as presented in Sect. 3. The detailed results can be found in the technical report [11].

---

[4] All the experiments were performed on an Intel Core i7 4.00 GHz CPU, with 8 GB of RAM. We used version 4.8.9 of Z3. The timeout for each benchmark was 10 min.

6.1   Comparison to Prior Tools

We compared SYNPLEXITY against two related tools: SYNQUID [18] and RESYN [16], which are also based on refinement types.

Benchmarks. We considered a total of 77 synthesis problems: 56 synthesis problems from RESYN (each benchmark specifies a concrete linear-time resource annotation), 16 synthesis problems from SYNQUID (which do not include resource annotations) that are not included in RESYN, and 5 new synthesis problems involving non-linear resource annotations. In these synthesis problems, synthesis specifications and auxiliary functions are all given as refinement types. For 3 of the new benchmarks, the auxiliary function required to split the input into smaller ones is not given—i.e., the synthesizer needs to identify it automatically.

The three solvers (SYNPLEXITY, SYNQUID, and RESYN) have different features, and hence not all synthesis problems can be encoded as synthesis benchmarks for a single solver. In the rest of this section, we describe what benchmarks we considered for each tool, and how we modified the benchmarks when needed.

SYNQUID: SYNQUID does not support resource bounds, so we encoded 77 synthesis problems as SYNQUID benchmarks by dropping the resource annotations. SYNQUID returns the first program that meet the synthesis specification, and cannot provide any guarantees about the resource usage of the returned program. SYNQUID can solve 75 benchmarks, and takes on average 3.3s. For 10 benchmarks SYNQUID synthesizes a non-optimal program—i.e., there exists another program with better concrete resource usage. For example, on the RESYN-triple-2 benchmark (where the input is a list xs), SYNQUID found a solution with resource usage $O(|xs|^2)$, while both SYNPLEXITY and RESYN can synthesize a more efficient implementation with resource usage $O(|xs|)$. The two benchmarks that SYNQUID failed to solve include the new benchmark SYNPLEXITY-merge-sort'. In this benchmark, the auxiliary function required to break the input into smaller inputs is not given, without which the sizes of solutions become much larger. Therefore SYNQUID times out.

RESYN: We ran RESYN on the 56 RESYN benchmarks with the corresponding concrete resource bounds. We could not encode 16 problems because RESYN does not support non-linear resources bounds—e.g., the bound $\log |y|$ in the AVL-insert SYNQUID benchmark. RESYN solved all 56 benchmarks with an average running time of 18.3 s.

SYNPLEXITY: We manually added resource usages and resource bounds to existing problems to encode them for SYNPLEXITY. For SYNQUID benchmarks without concrete resource bounds, we chose well-known time complexities as the bounds, e.g., we added the resource bound $O(u \log u)$ to the Sort-merge-sort problem. For the RESYN benchmarks, we translated the concrete resource usage and resource bounds to the corresponding asymptotic ones—e.g., for the RESYN-common' benchmark with the concrete resource bound $|ys|+|zs|$, we constructed a SYNPLEXITY variant with the asymptotic bound $O(u)$ and a size function $\lambda ys.\lambda zs.|ys| + |zs|$. We could not encode 3 synthesis problems as SYNPLEXITY benchmarks: two of them involved higher-order functions that do not satisfy the assumptions introduced in Sect. 5, and the other one has an exponential resource-usage bound $O(2^u)$ (the Tree-create-balanced problem from SYNQUID).

SYNPLEXITY solved 73 benchmarks with an average running time of 8.1s. Unlike SYNQUID, SYNPLEXITY guarantees that the synthesized program satisfies the given resource bounds. After extending the implementation to support the restrictions discussed in Sect. 5, SYNPLEXITY solved 5/6 benchmarks with higher-order functions. For 10 benchmarks, SYNPLEXITY found programs that had better resource usage than those synthesized by SYNQUID. Furthermore, SYNPLEXITY can encode and solve 9 problems that RESYN could not solve because the resource bounds involve logarithms. However, SYNPLEXITY cannot encode and solve 2 benchmarks that involve higher-order functions and do not satisfy the restrictions introduced in Sect. 5. SYNPLEXITY could solve 3 problems that required synthesizing both the main function (e.g., SYNPLEXITY-merge-sort) and its auxiliary function (e.g., a function splitting a given list into two balanced partitions). No other tool could solve the SYNPLEXITY-merge-sort' benchmark.

Finding.   SYNPLEXITY can express and solve 73/77 benchmarks. SYNPLEXITY has comparable performance to existing tools, and can synthesize programs with resource bounds that are not supported by prior tools.

6.2   Pruning the Search Space with Annotated Types

SYNPLEXITY uses recurrence annotations to guide the search and avoids enumerating terms that are guaranteed to not match the specified complexity. We compared the numbers of E-terms enumerated by SYNPLEXITY and SYNQUID for 56 benchmark on which both tool produced same solutions. SYNQUID always enumerated at least as many E-terms as SYNPLEXITY, and SYNPLEXITY enumerated strictly fewer E-terms for 26/56 benchmarks. For these 26 benchmarks, SYNPLEXITY can on average prune the search space by 6.2%. For example, in one case (BST-delete) SYNPLEXITY enumerated 2,059 E-terms, while SYNQUID enumerated 2,202.

Finding.   On average, SYNPLEXITY reduces the size of the search space by 6.2% for approximately half of the benchmarks.

---

7   Related Work

Resource-Bound Analysis. Rather than determining whether a given program satisfies a specification, a synthesizer determines whether there exists a program that inhabits a given specification. The branch of verification that we draw upon for resource-based synthesis is resource-bound analysis [20].

Within the literature on automated resource-bound analysis, there are methods that extract and solve recurrence relations for imperative code [2,4,7,15].

However, these methods are unlike the type system presented in this work because they extract concrete complexity bounds as recurrence relations, and then solve the recurrences to find a concrete upper bound on resource usage. The dominant terms of the resulting concrete bounds can then be used to state a big-O complexity bound. In contrast, we want to synthesize programs with respect to a big-O complexity directly, which is more similar to the manual reasoning of [6,8]. Thus, if we were to use these techniques for our problem, the first step in our synthesis algorithm would be to pick a concrete complexity function given a big-O complexity, and then reverse the verification problem with regards to that concrete complexity. However, for any big-O complexity, there are an infinite number of functions that satisfy that complexity, which presents a significant challenge at the outset. Our design choice also has some drawbacks. As noted in [8], reasoning compositionally with big-O complexity is challenging due to the hidden quantifier structure of big-O notation. Thus, to maintain soundness our type system has to sacrifice precision and generality in some places. For example, when a function has multiple paths, our type system over-approximates by choosing the largest complexity among all the paths.

Another set of methods to generate resource bounds are type-based [9,10,14, 19]. As we discussed throughout the paper, the complexities generated by these methods are concrete functions and not expressed with big-O notation, although [19] is sometimes able to pattern match a case of the Master Theorem. These type systems differ from ours in a few ways. The AARA line of research [9,10,14] is able to assign amortized complexity to programs, but is not able to generate logarithmic bounds. [19] is also able to perform amortized analysis; however, the technique is not fully automated, and instead requires the user to provide type annotations on terms, which are then checked by the type system.

Type- and Resource-Aware Synthesis. The SYNPLEXITY implementation is built on top of SYNQUID [18] a type-directed synthesis tool based on refinement types and polymorphism. The work that most closely resembles ours is RESYN [16]. As in our work, they combine the type-directed synthesizer SYNQUID with a type system that is able to assign complexity bounds to functional programs. The type system used in RESYN is based on one originally used in the context of verification [10]. That work uses a sophisticated type system to assign amortized resource-usage bounds to a given program. The type system of RESYN differs from the one presented in Sect. 3 in a few significant ways.

As highlighted earlier, RESYN automatically infers bounds on recursive functions using amortized analysis and is restricted to linear bounds, whereas our system is able to synthesize complexities of the form $O(n^a \log^b n + c)$.

Another difference is that RESYN synthesizes programs with a concrete complexity bound. This approach has advantages and disadvantages. For instance, it places an extra burden on the human to provide the correct bound with precise coefficient. On the other hand, the user might want an implementation that has a complexity with a small coefficient, whereas our system provides no guarantee that the complexity of an implementation will have a small coefficient in the dominant term: SYNPLEXITY only guarantees asymptotic behavior.

RESYN can synthesize programs with higher-order functions, which are supported only in a restricted manner by SYNPLEXITY. To handle higher-order functions, RESYN attaches resource units to types, which gives it *resource polymorphism*. Moreover, costs of inputs with function types can be written generally as polymorphic types (i.e., costs can be polymorphic with respect to the size of the specific input types). SYNPLEXITY does not have *asymptotic resource polymorphism* because it cannot directly compose unknown big-O functions (i.e., the complexity of higher-order inputs). We envision that with carefully crafted restrictions on the resource annotations of higher-order functions, SYNPLEXITY could handle synthesis problems involving such functions, e.g., assuming that the complexity of input functions is known and the refinements of input functions are precise enough. Detailed discussion about these restrictions can be found in Sect. 5 and the technical report [11]. Because big-O functions cannot be directly composed, developing a more general extension to SYNPLEXITY that supports higher-order functions is a challenging direction for future work.

Acknowledgments. Supported, in part, by a gift from Rajiv and Ritu Batra; by multiple Facebook Research Awards; by a Microsoft Faculty Fellowship; by NSF under grants 1420866, 1763871, and 1750965; and by ONR under grants N00014-17-1-2889 and N00014-19-1-2318. Any opinions, findings, and conclusions or recommendations expressed in this publication are those of the authors, and do not necessarily reflect the views of the sponsoring entities.

References

1. Akra, M., Bazzi, L.: On the solution of linear recurrence equations. Comput. Optim. Appl. **10**, 195–210 (1998)
2. Albert, E., Arenas, P., Genaim, S., Puebla, Germán, P.: Closed-form upper bounds in static cost analysis. J. Autom. Reasoning **46**, 161–203 (2011) https://doi.org/10.1007/s10817-010-9174-1
3. Bentley, J.L., Haken, D., Saxe, J.B.: A general method for solving divide-and-conquer recurrences. ACM SIGACT News **12**(3), 36–44 (1980)
4. Breck, J., Cyphert, J., Kincaid, Z., Reps, T.: Templates and recurrences: better together. In: Proceedings of the ACM SIGPLAN Conference on Programming Language Design and Implementation, PLDI (2020)
5. Cormen, T.H., Leiserson, C.E., Rivest, R.L., Stein, C.: Introduction to Algorithms, 3nd edn. The MIT Press, Cambridge (2009)
6. Eberl, M.: Proving divide and conquer complexities in Isabelle/HOL. J. Autom. Reasoning **58**(4), 483–508 (2016). https://doi.org/10.1007/s10817-016-9378-0
7. Flores Montoya, A.: Cost Analysis of Programs Based on the Refinement of Cost Relations. Ph.D. thesis, TU Darmstadt (2017)
8. Guéneau, A., Charguéraud, A., Pottier, F.: A fistful of dollars: formalizing asymptotic complexity claims via deductive program verification. In: Ahmed, A. (ed.) ESOP 2018. LNCS, vol. 10801, pp. 533–560. Springer, Cham (2018). https://doi.org/10.1007/978-3-319-89884-1_19
9. Hoffmann, J., Aehlig, K., Hofmann, M.: Multivariate amortized resource analysis. In: Proceedings of the 38th Annual ACM SIGPLAN-SIGACT Symposium on Principles of Programming Languages, pp. 357–370 (2011)

10. Hoffmann, J., Aehlig, K., Hofmann, M.: Resource aware ml. In: The International Conference on Computer Aided Verification, CAV (2012)
11. Hu, Q., Cyphert, J., D'Antoni, L., Reps, T.: Synthesis with asymptotic resource bounds. arXiv preprint arXiv:2103.04188 (2021)
12. Hu, Q., D'Antoni, L.: Syntax-guided synthesis with quantitative syntactic objectives. In: Chockler, H., Weissenbacher, G. (eds.) CAV 2018. LNCS, vol. 10981, pp. 386–403. Springer, Cham (2018). https://doi.org/10.1007/978-3-319-96145-3_21
13. Kauers, M., Paule, P.: The Concrete Tetrahedron: Symbolic Sums, Recurrence Equations, Generating Functions, Asymptotic Estimates. Springer, Cham (2011) https://doi.org/10.1007/978-3-7091-0445-3
14. Khan, D.M., Hoffmann, J.: Exponential automatic amortized resource analysis. In: International Conference on Foundations of Software Science and Computation Structures. FoSSaCs (2020)
15. Kincaid, Z., Cyphert, J., Breck, J., Reps, T.: Non-linear reasoning for invariant synthesis. In: ACM SIGPLAN Symposium on Principles of Programming Languages, POPL (2018)
16. Knoth, T., Wang, D., Polikarpova, N., Hoffmann, J.: Resource-guided program synthesis. In: Proceedings of the 40th ACM SIGPLAN Conference on Programming Language Design and Implementation, pp. 253–268 (2019)
17. Pierce, B.C., Turner, D.N.: Local type inference. ACM Trans. Program. Lang. Syst. (TOPLAS) 22(1), 1–44 (2000)
18. Polikarpova, N., Kuraj, I., Solar-Lezama, A.: Program synthesis from polymorphic refinement types. ACM SIGPLAN Notices 51(6), 522–538 (2016)
19. Wang, P., Wang, D., Chlipala, A.: Timl: A functional language for practical complexity analysis with invariants. Proc. ACM Program. Lang. 1(OOPSLA), 1–26 (2017)
20. Wegbreit, B.: Mechanical program analysis. In: Communications of the ACM (1975)

Program Sketching by Automatically Generating Mocks from Tests

Nate F. F. Bragg[1], Jeffrey S. Foster[1], Cody Roux[2],
and Armando Solar-Lezama[3]

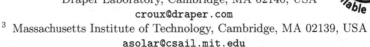

[1] Tufts University, Medford, MA 02155, USA
{nate,jfoster}@cs.tufts.edu
[2] Draper Laboratory, Cambridge, MA 02140, USA
croux@draper.com
[3] Massachusetts Institute of Technology, Cambridge, MA 02139, USA
asolar@csail.mit.edu

Abstract. Sketch is a popular program synthesis tool that solves for unknowns in a *sketch* or partial program. However, while Sketch is powerful, it does not directly support modular synthesis of dependencies, potentially limiting scalability. In this paper, we introduce Sketcham, a new technique that modularizes a regular sketch by automatically generating *mocks*—functions that approximate the behavior of complete implementations—from the sketch's test suite. For example, if the function f originally calls g, Sketcham creates a mock g_m from g's tests and augments the sketch with a version of f that calls g_m. This change allows the unknowns in f and g to be solved separately, enabling modular synthesis with no extra work from the Sketch user. We evaluated Sketcham on ten benchmarks, performing enough runs to show at a 95% confidence level that Sketcham improves median synthesis performance on six of our ten benchmarks by a factor of up to 5× compared to plain Sketch, including one benchmark that times out on Sketch, while exhibiting similar performance on the remaining four. Our results show that Sketcham can achieve modular synthesis by automatically generating mocks from tests.

Keywords: Program synthesis, mocks, Sketch

1 Introduction

Program synthesis by sketching, as embodied by the Sketch synthesis tool [30], is a popular technique that has been applied to a wide variety of problems [5,7,13,14,15,16,18,22,29]. A Sketch input (henceforth a *sketch*) is a program written in a C-like language augmented with *holes*, unknown constants, and *generators*, unknown expressions. The solution for a sketch is specified using test cases called *harnesses*, also written in the Sketch language, that make assertions about the results of to-be-synthesized code. Sketch searches for a solution using *counterexample-guided inductive synthesis (CEGIS)*, which alternately synthesizes a candidate solution and then uses a verifier to check the assertions; any counterexamples from verification feed into the next round of synthesis [27].

© The Author(s) 2021
A. Silva and K. R. M. Leino (Eds.): CAV 2021, LNCS 12759, pp. 808–831, 2021.
https://doi.org/10.1007/978-3-030-81685-8_38

One key challenge of using Sketch is that it does not specifically support modular synthesis. More precisely, even if an input sketch is divided into a number of functions that call each other, Sketch solves them all together. This approach potentially limits scalability, as SAT formulas created by Sketch can grow quite quickly as function calls are inlined. A Sketch user could potentially work around this by manually replacing calls to to-be-synthesized functions with calls to Sketch *models* [24], which are *mocks*, i.e., functions that, in place of full implementations, approximate the desired behavior with a specification in the form of assertions about individual cases. However, writing additional specifications is both time consuming and redundant with developing the original sketch.

In this paper, we introduce Sketcham (short for *Sketch and Mocks*), a novel technique that converts a regular sketch problem into a modular sketch problem by *automatically* generating mocks from harnesses. More specifically, suppose Sketcham is given a sketch in which function f calls g and g is tested by harness h. Sketcham first converts h into a mock g_m that has the same function signature as g but whose body encodes the assertions from h. Then, Sketcham augments the original sketch with new code in which f calls g_m instead of g, thereby allowing f to be synthesized separately from g. Thus, by converting tests (harnesses) to mocks (specs), Sketcham enables modular synthesis without extra work from the user. Section 2 gives an overview of Sketcham.

Sketcham generates the new, modular sketch problem using a sequence of three algorithms. First, Sketcham traverses the original sketch to build a mapping A from function names to a set of assertions in which each function is called. Note that we place some limitations of the assertions—e.g., they can contain at most one function call—to guarantee we can always translate them from harness assertions to mock assertions. Next, Sketcham traverses A, generating a mock f_m for each function $f \in dom(A)$, where f_m encodes the assertions in $A(f)$. Finally, Sketcham generates new mock harnesses that are the same as the original harnesses, except they call mocks instead of the underlying functions. Section 3 presents Sketcham's core algorithms.

We implemented Sketcham as an additional pass to Sketch, which we evaluated on ten benchmarks. We found a high variance in running time, both under Sketch and under Sketcham. To account for this difference, we used the Clopper-Pearson method [6], running each configuration (synthesis tool–benchmark combination) up to 1,487 times, reaching 95% confidence that the true median running time lies within 20% of the experimental median, excluding failures and runs exceeding a 60 minute timeout. We found that, for six of ten benchmarks, Sketcham runs up to 5× faster than Sketch; for one benchmark Sketcham is up to a factor of 0.98× slower; for the remaining three benchmarks, performance is indistinguishable. We examined one benchmark, deduplication of elements in an array, in detail. We found that the performance improvement is largely due to a mock that does a thorough job representing the function it mocks, and that the performance improvement occurs during the CEGIS synthesis phase rather than the CEGIS verification phase. Section 4 presents our evaluation.

```
1  int[n] dedup(int n, int[n] vs,
2                    ref int sz) {
3    int[n] svs=sort(n, vs); int[n] res;
4    sz = ??; // 0
5    for(int i=??; i<n; ++i) { // 0
6      int j = expr({sz,i}, {PL,MI}); // sz-1
7      if(...){//sz==0||svs[i]>res[j]
8        res[sz] = svs[i];
9        sz = expr({sz,i}, {PL,MI}); // sz+1
10   }}
11   return res;
12 }
13 int[n] sort(int n, int[n] vs) {
14   int m=..., r=..., i=..., j=...;
15   int[m] as = sort(vs[0::m]);
16   int[r] bs = sort(vs[m::r]);
17   while(exprBool({i, j, n}, {PL})) // i+j<n
18     /* add as[i++] or bs[j++] to vs */
19   return vs;
20 }
```

(a) dedup and sort (simplified).

(b) Original harnesses.

(c) Mock harnesses.

```
1  harness void h_sort(int n,
2                       int[n] vs) {
3    int[n] svs = sort(vs);
4    for(int i=0; i<n-1; ++i)
5      assert svs[i] <= svs[i+1];
6    /* also elts(vs)=elts(svs) */
7
8  }
```

⇨

```
1  model int[n] sort_mock(int n,
2                         int[n] vs) {
3    int[n] svs = sort_uf(vs);
4    for(int i=0; i<n-1; ++i)
5      assume svs[i] <= svs[i+1];
6    /* also elts(vs)=elts(svs) */
7    return svs;
8  }
```

(d) Translating sort's test harness into a mock.

Fig. 1: Sketcham applied to deduplication via sorting.

In summary, Sketcham demonstrates that modular synthesis can be achieved by automatically generating mocks from tests (specs from harnesses) without additional user effort.

2   Overview

To illustrate Sketcham, consider Figure 1a, which shows a simplified sketch whose solution deduplicates an array of integers. This sketch makes use of Sketch holes ??, which are unknown constants, and generators such as expr(vars, ops), which is an unknown expression composed of variables vars combined with operands ops, including PL for addition and MI for subtraction. The correct solutions for the holes and generators are shown in end-of-line comments.

At the top of Figure 1a, function dedup takes a length n and array vs, and it returns the deduplicated array and, by reference, the deduplicated array's length sz (in Sketch, functions can only have at most one return value, hence the return-by-reference sz). The dedup function begins by calling another function, sort, to sort the array (line 3). Then it initializes sz to a hole and loops through the array (lines 4-5). In each iteration, it computes an expression j of sz and i (line 6) used in a conditional guard (line 7; details of guard not shown). If the condition holds, the element at position i is copied into res and sz is updated; otherwise the element is ignored. Finally, dedup returns the result array res.

The sort function (line 13) takes the length and array and returns a sorted array. This particular sketch is for merge sort. Here the programmer knows that merge sort involves sorting two sub-arrays but isn't sure about the details. After some initialization (not shown), it makes two recursive calls to sort sub-arrays (lines 15 and 16). Then it loops over the sorted sub-arrays, merging the elements into array vs, which is returned. The loop guard (line 17) uses a different generator, exprBool(vars, ops), that generates arithmetic comparisons (<, <=, etc) among expressions generated by calling expr(vars, ops).

Harnesses and Mocks. To test the expected behavior of dedup and sort, the sketch also includes two harnesses, h_dedup and h_sort. Figure 1b shows the call graph of the sketch with the harnesses, and the left side of Figure 1d shows a portion of h_sort (we omit h_dedup for brevity). This harness calls sort and then makes assertions about the results, e.g., that the output array is sorted. Harnesses are distinguished from regular functions by the keyword harness, and their arguments are treated as universally quantified. Thus, h_sort tests that for all n and arrays vs of length n, the sort function is correct.

To solve this synthesis problem, Sketch converts dedup, sort, and a harness into a single SAT formula and then uses CEGIS to find a solution. This approach works, but the formula passed to the solver is large, because it contains both functions' worth of code, and complex, because reasoning about the code in dedup requires simultaneously reasoning about the code in sort. Thus, mashing together both functions into a single SAT formula potentially limits the scalability of Sketch.

The key idea of Sketcham is to observe that this sketch is actually modular—it has been divided into two functions, each with their own tests. Sketcham takes advantage of this modularity by creating a new synthesis problem that includes mock versions of functions in the sketch, which can then be used to enable separate reasoning about each function.

The right side of Figure 1d shows sort_mock, the mock version of sort. The mock has the same signature as sort, but instead of containing the actual sorting code, it contains assertions from h_sort about sort's expected behavior. In detail, in place of calling sort, the mock calls a fresh uninterpreted function sort_uf on line 3. Then it makes assumptions (rather than assertions) about the result array svs (line 5), and finally returns svs (line 7). The mock itself is a

```
int doub(int m) {
  return m * 2;
}
harness void h(int n) {
  int out = doub(n * 10);
  assert out == (n + n) * ??;
}
```

```
model int doub_mock(int m) {
  int out = doub_uf(m);
  assume (0 == m%10)  ⟹
    out == (m/10 + m/10) * ??;
  return out;
}
```

(a) Double.   (b) Mock double.

Fig. 2: The double function and its mock.

Sketch model (indicated by the model keyword), and where the mock is called, Sketch will replace the call with the assumptions in the model's body [24].

Next, Sketcham creates new code that uses the mock, as shown in Figure 1c. (Here the dashed, greyed boxes are for functions and harnesses that are generated but do not improve solving time; see Section 4.2.) In particular, dedup' is the same as dedup, except it calls sort_mock instead of sort, and h_dedup'' is the same as h_dedup but it calls dedup' instead of dedup.

The final sketch includes h_dedup'', h_dedup' (a trivial harness that calls a mocked dedup), and h_dedup—in that order—as well as the harnesses for sort. Sketcham searches for a solution for each harness in order, i.e., it tries to solve h_dedup'' first. Notice that, critically, when Sketcham solves h_dedup'', it need not consider the code of sort, but rather only its specification as encoded in the mock. In practice, this means that Sketcham can solve h_dedup'' up to 18.1× faster than Sketch solves h_dedup, a significant speedup.

Moreover, sort_mock encodes the specification of sort, so once Sketcham solves h_dedup'', it has found a solution for h_dedup as well. To preserve correctness, Sketcham keeps the original harnesses such as h_dedup, because mocks with partial specifications can lead to partially incorrect solutions to the harnesses using them. However, even in these cases, the counterexamples they generate can still help more quickly narrow the synthesis search space for the original harness, and lead to an ultimately valid solution.

Quantifier Elimination. In Figure 1d, the translation from harness to mock was straightforward: the call to the mocked function becomes a call to an uninterpreted function, and asserts become assumes. Sometimes, however, the translation is more complex. Consider the sketch in Figure 2a, which includes a function doub that doubles its input and a harness h that calls doub(n*10) and asserts the result is (n+n)*?? for some hole.

Notice this assertion only describes arguments of the form n*10 for some n, i.e., implicitly there must exist some m such that m = n*10 for the assertion to hold. Sketcham performs *quantifier elimination* [1,4] on such nested existentials, following the approach of Kuncak et al. [17]. Figure 2b shows the resulting mock.

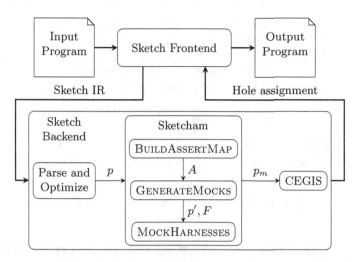

Fig. 3: Sketcham architecture

Here, in the assumption, n is replaced by witness candidate m/10. Because m is an integer, we also add a precondition that m is evenly divisible by 10.

We note that Sketcham includes quantifier elimination for completeness, and in our evaluation we consider the sketch in Figure 2a. However, we did not find quantifier elimination necessary for our other benchmarks.

3   The Sketcham Algorithm

Next we more formally describe Sketcham, which is implemented as a pass within Sketch as shown in Figure 3. The presentation that follows reflects this Sketch implementation without loss of generality of the core algorithm for converting tests to mocks. The Sketch *frontend* consumes the input sketch and transforms it into the Sketch intermediate representation (Sketch IR), which is passed to the Sketch *backend*. Sketch IR encodes first-order logic augmented with theories of arithmetic, arrays, functions, and more, as discussed below. When the backend loads the IR, it performs loop unrolling, function inlining, and other transformations that are needed by the solver [26], yielding a program p. Standard Sketch then uses CEGIS to solve the synthesis problem, outputting a hole assignment that the frontend uses to produce the solved sketch. Sketcham modifies this process by inserting, after optimization, a *mock rewriting* phase, described below, that transforms p into the augmented program p_m for CEGIS.

We formalize Sketcham on the fragment of Sketch IR shown in Figure 4. Here types are omitted, and we assume the sketch is type-correct. A program sketch p is a sequence of harness and function definitions. A harness definition h tags a function definition as a test harness. A function definition d is given named parameters[1] and a body, which is a sequence of statements. Statements s are

---

[1] For simplicity, we assume parameter names are unique across the whole program.

$$
\begin{aligned}
p &::= (h \mid d)^* \\
h &::= \textsf{harness } d \\
d &::= \textsf{def } f \, (\, x \, , \, \dots, \, x \,) \, \{ \, s^* \, \} \\
s &::= x := e \mid \textsf{return } e \mid \textsf{assert } \phi \mid \textsf{assume } \phi \\
e, \phi, \psi &::= f \, (\, e \, , \dots, \, e \,) \mid uop \; e \mid e \; bop \; e \mid n \mid x \mid \text{??} \; x \\
uop &::= \neg \mid - \\
bop &::= \wedge \mid \vee \mid \oplus \mid \implies \mid = \mid + \mid - \mid * \mid / \mid \%
\end{aligned}
$$

$x, y \in$ variable names $\qquad G \in$ graphs $\qquad A : f \to \varPhi$

$f, g \in$ function names $\qquad \varPhi \in$ set of ϕ $\qquad F : f \to f$

Fig. 4: Sketcham's fragment of Sketch IR

assignments, returns, assertions, and assumptions. The most critical expressions e in our algorithm are function calls $f \, (\, e \, , \dots, \, e \,)$ with their arguments. The detailed grammar for the remaining expressions is unimportant in the remainder of this section, but for completeness we show expressions for unary and binary logical and arithmetic operations $uop \; e$ and $e \; bop \; e$; constants n; variables x; and named holes $\text{??} \; x$. Below, we sometimes use the metavariables ϕ and ψ in place of e to indicate an expression used for Boolean-valued formulas.

Given the input Sketch IR program p as shown in Figure 3, Sketcham creates the output sketch by first calling BUILDASSERTMAP (Algorithm 1) to build mapping A from function names to assertions from tests of those functions. Next, GENERATEMOCKS (Algorithm 2) uses A to construct mocks for functions in the domain of A, yielding program p', which includes the original sketch p plus those mocks. This step also returns a mapping F from the original function names to the corresponding mock names. Finally, MOCKHARNESSES (Algorithm 3) creates the output sketch p_m, which augments p' with copies of the original sketch's harnesses, except the copies call the mocks instead of the original functions.

Critically, during this last step, holes are *not* renamed when the harnesses are copied. Moreover, the newly generated harnesses are prepended to the sketch. Thus, when CEGIS tries solving each harness in p_m in order, it will first find solutions that are consistent with the mocks. Then when it reaches the original harnesses (which must remain in case there is information in them not captured by the mocks—see discussion of GENERATEMOCKS below), CEGIS can use the information it already derived from the mocks to find the ultimate solution to the original problem.

In the remainder of this section, we describe each step of the algorithm in detail. Below, we capitalize the names of sets of a given metavariable (e.g., $\varPhi$ is a set of formulas ϕ, etc.), and we use vector notation to indicate arrays (e.g., $\vec{s}$ is an array of statements s).

Building the assertion mapping. Each mock expresses the specification of an original function as it is encoded by that function's tests. To start, Sketcham collects assertions from those tests into an assertion mapping. Algorithm 1 builds

---

Algorithm 1 Mock rewriting: building the assertion map

Input: p - the sketch
Output: A - finite map of function names to sets of assert formulas
1: **function** BUILDASSERTMAP(p)
2:      $A \leftarrow \emptyset$
3:      $\Phi \leftarrow \{\phi \mid \text{assert } \phi \in p\}$ ▷ all solver-reachable asserts in p
4:      $\Phi_0 \leftarrow \{\phi \in \Phi \mid 0 = |f(\ldots) \in \phi|\}$ ▷ asserts with 0 function calls
5:      $\Phi_1 \leftarrow \{\phi \in \Phi \mid 1 = |f(\ldots) \in \phi|\}$ ▷ asserts with 1 function call
6:      **for all** $f \in \Phi_1$ **do**
7:          $\Phi_f \leftarrow \Phi_0 \cup \{\phi \in \Phi_1 \mid f \in \phi\}$ ▷ asserts with 0 calls, or 1 call to f
8:          $\Psi \leftarrow \Phi \setminus \Phi_f$
9:          **while** $\Psi \neq \emptyset$ **do**
10:             $X \leftarrow \text{FV}(\Psi)$ ▷ inputs and holes free in Ψ
11:             $\Psi \leftarrow \{\phi \in \Phi_f \mid X \cap \text{FV}(\phi) \neq \emptyset\}$
12:             $\Phi_f \leftarrow \Phi_f \setminus \Psi$
13:         **end while**
14:         $A[f] \leftarrow \Phi_f$
15:     **end for**
16: **end function**

---

the assertion mapping A from the input sketch p. The algorithm begins by initializing A to empty and Φ to the set of all assertions from all tests in p. It then selects two subsets of Φ. The set Φ_0 contains all assertions that do not include calls to any functions, and the set Φ_1 contains all assertions that include exactly one function call. We exclude assertions with multiple function calls so that mocks are standalone, to conform to the technical requirements Sketch imposes on models. As a consequence, we exclude some terms that present no such concerns (e.g., conjunctions of otherwise unrelated terms), as translating them to assumptions may be much more complex or even impossible. We leave extending BUILDASSERTMAP to more assertion patterns to future work.

For each function f called in an assertion in Φ_1, on line 7 we next compute the set Φ_f from Φ_0 (the assertions that hold throughout each test, including at calls to f) and the subset of Φ_1 that refers to f. For example, consider the assertion in h_sort in Figure 1d. This code refers to the result of calling sort(n, vs), so $\Phi_1 = \{\phi_i(\text{sort}(\text{n},\text{vs}))\}$, where the ϕ_is capture the assertions in h_sort. Additionally, if we picked, say, a loop unrolling bound of 4, then Sketch would implicitly assert n<4, resulting in $\Phi_0 = \{\text{n<4}\}$. In general, Φ_0 might contain additional assertions that are irrelevant to the calls in Φ_1. For example, loop unrolling for harness h_dedup (not shown) might add another bound m<4 to Φ_0 for sort. However, such irrelevant assertions will not change the resulting mock.

In some cases, we cannot add assertions in Φ_f to A because other assertions on the same variables interfere. For example, suppose the sketch includes assert f(x) and assert g(x). Then Φ_f might not completely characterize f—the assertion in Φ_f is valid only if assert g(x) also holds, which puts an unknown (until the full sketch is solved) constraint on x. Thus, in this case, our algorithm discards the assertions in Φ_f. More specifically, on line 9, the loop

---

Algorithm 2 Mock rewriting: generate mocks

Input: p - the sketch
Input: A - output of Algorithm 1
Output: p' - the sketch augmented with mock definitions
Output: F - finite mapping from an original function name to its mock

1: **function** GENERATEMOCKS(p, A)
2:     $F \leftarrow \emptyset, p' \leftarrow p$
3:     **for all** $f \mapsto \Phi \in A$ **do**
4:         def $f(\vec{x})\{\ldots\} \leftarrow$ the definition of f in p
5:         $f_u \leftarrow$ FRESHNAME(f)
6:         $\vec{s} \leftarrow [\,]$
7:         $\Phi_0 \leftarrow \{\phi \in \Phi \mid 0 = |f(\ldots) \in \phi|\}$
8:         $\Phi_1 \leftarrow \{\phi \in \Phi \mid 1 = |f(\ldots) \in \phi|\}$
9:         **for all** $\phi \in \Phi_1$ **do**   ▷ convert asserts into assumes
10:             $f(\vec{e}) \leftarrow$ the lone function call in ϕ
11:             $\phi_u \leftarrow \phi[f(\vec{e}) := f_u(\vec{x})]$ ▷ substitute uninterpreted function
12:             $\Psi \leftarrow \{x_i = e_i \mid 0 \le i < |\vec{x}|\}$ ▷ equate parameters to arguments
13:             $\phi' \leftarrow (\bigwedge \Phi_0) \wedge (\bigwedge \Psi) \implies \phi_u$ ▷ the condition where ϕ holds
14:             $\phi'' \leftarrow [\![\mathrm{FV}(\phi); \Psi \vdash \phi']\!]$
15:             $\vec{s}$.append(assume ϕ'')
16:         **end for**
17:         $f_m \leftarrow$ FRESHNAME(f)
18:         $F[f] \leftarrow f_m$
19:         $d_m \leftarrow$ def $f_m(\vec{x})\{$ ▷ create the mock definition
                    $\vec{s}$

                    return $f_u(\vec{x})$
                }
20:         p'.insert(d_m)
21:     **end for**
22: **end function**

---

removes any $\phi \in \Phi_f$ whose free variables overlap with free variables outside of Φ_f. The process iterates in case free variable dependencies cascade. For example, the existence of assert g(x) would eliminate assert f(x-y), which would in turn eliminate assert f(y). The result is the transitive closure of the allowable assertions about each function.

Generate mocks. Next, Algorithm 2 iterates through each function in the domain of A, generating a corresponding mock to add to the augmented sketch p'. As it does so, it also builds a map F from function names to the names of the generated mocks.

For each $f \mapsto \Phi \in A$, GENERATEMOCKS begins by finding the definition of f and creating a corresponding freshly named uninterpreted function f_u. It then initializes $\vec{s}$, the assumptions to be inserted into the new mock body, to empty. Then, from each asserted formula $\phi \in \Phi$, the algorithm creates a formula ϕ_u by substituting the single function call $f(\vec{e})$ in ϕ with a call $f_u(\vec{x})$, where $\vec{x}$ are the formal parameters of f (line 11). Notice this call to f_u is the same no matter the

---

Algorithm 3 Mock rewriting: mock harnesses

Input: p' - the sketch from Algorithm 2
Input: F_1 - the name map from Algorithm 2
Output: p_m - the sketch augmented with mock harnesses
1: **function** MOCKHARNESSES(p', F)
2:     $G \leftarrow$ CALLGRAPH(p'), $p_m \leftarrow p'$
3:     **for** $i \leftarrow 1$, maximum mock call graph depth **do**
4:         $F_{i+1} \leftarrow \emptyset$
5:         **for all** def $g(\vec{y})\{\vec{s}\} \in$ CALLERS(G, dom F_i) **do**   ▷ similarly, harness def
6:             $g' \leftarrow$ FRESHNAME(g)
7:             $d' \leftarrow$ def $g'(\vec{y})\{$ ▷ respectively, harness def
                    $\{s[f := f' \mid f \mapsto f' \in F_i] \mid s \in \vec{s}\}$
                $\}$
8:             p_m.insert(d', before g)
9:             $F_{i+1}[g] \leftarrow g'$
10:         **end for**
11:     **end for**
12: **end function**

---

original call to f, which ensures the generated mock conforms to the technical requirements Sketch imposes on models. To encode the actual information at the call site, we next add a precondition. The algorithm constructs ϕ' (line 13), which is an implication denoting that ϕ_u holds if the ancillary asserts Φ_0, and the equalities $x_i = e_i$ from the call to f hold. One nuance we elide here is that Sketch augments all function calls with an additional explicit *path condition* parameter that captures conditional branches taken up to the point of the call, which makes it easier for Sketch to translate the IR into a SAT formula. For soundness, we include this path condition as a premise of ϕ' and assign f_u the path condition $\top$. Note that our implementation trims Φ_0 before adding it to ϕ' to the subset containing only the variables in $\vec{e}$.

Next, the algorithm performs quantifier elimination on ϕ', yielding ϕ'' (line 14). More precisely, $[\![FV(\phi); \Psi \vdash \phi']\!]$ eliminates variables in $FV(\phi)$ from ϕ', searching for witnesses in Ψ. Then, ϕ'' is added to $\vec{s}$ as an assume, and the loop continues until all mappings for f have been handled.

Finally, on lines 17-19 the algorithm computes a fresh Sketch name f_m for f, adds a mapping to F, and creates function definition d_m for f_m. The function f_m takes the same arguments as f, assumes all formulas in $\vec{s}$, and returns f_u on f_m's arguments. Thus, when f_m is called, the assertions about f from its original test suite in p are assumed on f_m's arguments, as we saw in Section 2. The definition d_m is added to p', and mock generation continues until all mappings in A have been traversed.

New mock harnesses. The last step of Sketcham adds calls to the mocks generated by GENERATEMOCKS. One naïve approach would be to simply replace each call to f with a call to f_m for all $f \mapsto f_m \in F$. However, this will not work for two reasons. First, we need a full solution for the holes in all functions, including those that are mocked. Replacing calls to f with calls to f_m would remove many constraints on the holes in f, underconstraining their solutions. Second, as we saw earlier the template for f might contain additional information excluded by BuildAssertMap, so replacing f by f_m might underconstrain f's callers.

Our solution is to create an output sketch that includes both the original sketch—including all calls to f in their original form—and duplicate sketch code that calls f_m in place of f. The duplicated code refers to the same holes as the original sketch. Hence, information derived from the duplicated code can potentially greatly speed up solving of the original code.

Algorithm 3 shows MockHarnesses, which creates this duplicate code. The algorithm begins by constructing a call graph G from the sketch p' from the previous step. Note that none of the mocks in p' are called yet, so the call graph is the same as for the original sketch. Next, the algorithm duplicates the sketch one level of the call stack at a time, starting at the mocks and working up toward the harnesses. To limit duplication, e.g., for mocks called by recursive functions whose duplication would loop infinitely, the algorithm bounds the duplication depth. For each level i, it iterates through all functions $g \in$ Callers$(G, \mathrm{dom}\, F_i)$, meaning functions g that call a function in the domain of F_i. It duplicates each such g, replacing calls to functions $f \in \mathrm{dom}\, F_i$ with calls to $F_i[f]$, and then adds the duplicated function to the sketch. Since g has now been renamed, $g \mapsto g'$ is added to a new mapping F_{i+1}, and calls to it are duplicated in the next iteration, repeating until reaching the root of the call graph or the maximum duplication depth. Note the process is the same for both regular function definitions and for functions that are harnesses.

For example, suppose harness h calls function g, which in turn calls function f, and assume GenerateMocks created f_m and g_m. Then in the first iteration, MockHarnesses creates a duplicate h' that calls g_m and a duplicate g' that calls f_m. In the next and final iteration, it creates a duplicate h'' that calls g'.

When we insert the duplicate functions, we insert them *before* the original functions. This ensures that when we insert the duplicate harnesses that call the mocks, Sketch will solve those harnesses before solving the original ones.

4   Evaluation

We evaluated Sketcham on ten benchmarks, running each from 11 to 1487 times until reaching statistically significant results. We found that, for six of ten benchmarks, Sketcham performs up to 5× faster than Sketch, for one benchmark Sketcham is slower by a factor of up to 0.9×, and for the remaining three benchmarks performance is indistinguishable. We examined the benchmark *dedup* (Figure 1) in depth and found that, as suspected, overall performance improvement is due to improved synthesis time when using `sort_mock`.

Implementation. Sketcham comprises approximately 1075 lines of C++ code within the Sketch backend. The user enables Sketcham with `-mock` and specifies the max mock duplication depth via `--bnd-mock-depth`, which defaults to 3.

Because they clone and then rearrange the input Sketch IR program, the run time of Algorithms 1-3 is approximately linear in the number of functions and the number of asserts in the sketch. Our implementation covers the features given as part of the Sketch IR fragment in Figure 4, with the modification that we explicitly depict assignment, which Sketch IR does not require because it structurally hashes expressions to yield a compact in-memory representation [26]. We also note that Sketch includes additional features that we leave to future work, such as complex harness types, and that quantifier elimination is currently restricted to arithmetic expressions.

Benchmarks. We used the following benchmarks:

- *double*, the integer doubling program given in Figure 2.
- *absval*, the absolute value function.
- *fib*, the linear-time Fibonacci function. The specification requires its output to be equivalent to the exponential time algorithm.
- *datetime*, a simplified implementation of the C strptime function. This function accepts a format that it uses to parse a date/time string.
- *boyerMoore*, which implements the Boyer Moore string search algorithm [3].
- *regex*, a regular expression matching engine and compiler.
- *spellcheck*, a program that suggests a corrected version of its input using the Levenshtein edit distance from entries in a dictionary.
- *minpair*, uses edit distance to find the closest pair out of an array of values.
- $dedup_m$, deduplication with merge sort from Figure 1, and $dedup_i$, deduplication with insertion sort.

Sketch has a multitude of configuration options that can have a large effect on performance. The middle portion of Table 1 gives values for the four options that differ across the benchmarks: *int type*, whether Sketch uses symbolic integers (in either a bit-vector encoding or a sparse encoding [26]) or native integers [28]; *int bits*, the number of bits per integer; *loop unroll*, the maximum loop unrolling depth; and *func inline*, the maximum depth of function call inlining.

We selected values for these options that reflected each benchmark's design and demonstrated pronounced run time differences from Sketch to Sketcham, as follows. *double* and *absval* use Sketch's defaults. *fib* tests recursively computing the Fibonacci sequence up to the tenth entry, so function call inlining is set accordingly. *regex* is required to reject bad matches, which requires higher unrolling and inlining. *datetime*, *boyerMoore*, *spellcheck*, and *minpair* need higher loop unrolling to iterate over long strings. These last three and both *dedups* also do much better using native integers. The *dedups* also run unreasonably slowly with more bits or higher unroll, so we reduced the amount of unrolling. In all our benchmarks, any configuration options not discussed here were left as their defaults, including the mock duplication depth, with the default of 3.

Methodology. All measurements were taken on a 3.2 GHz AMD Ryzen 5 1600 system with 32GB of RAM. We found that while most benchmarks consistently

	# lines	# holes	int type	int bits	loop unroll	func inline	Sketch runs total	failed	Sketcham runs total	failed
double	8	1	symbolic	5	8	5	17	0	17	0
absval	69	9	symbolic	5	8	5	17	0	17	0
fib	46	4	symbolic	6	8	10	20	0	65	0
datetime	177	3	symbolic	11	20	5	11	11	17	0
boyerMoore	136	16	native	7	13	5	17	0	153	19
regex	357	5604	symbolic	5	30	7	17	0	17	0
spellcheck	94	5	native	5	9	5	17	0	17	0
minpair	113	3	native	5	10	5	17	0	22	2
dedup$_i$	73	1134	native	2	4	5	1487	88	762	23
dedup$_m$	80	9008	native	2	4	5	648	281	88	16

Table 1: Benchmark config options and characteristics.

perform within half an order of magnitude under both Sketch and Sketcham, in a few cases synthesis time varies by as much as two and a half orders of magnitude. To account for this variance during our evaluation, we repeatedly ran each benchmark until achieving statistical significance, between 11 and 1487 times, as listed in the rightmost portion of Table 1. Each run was executed with the system otherwise almost totally idle to minimize interference. While most runs completed successfully, we exclude those that exceed a 60 minute timeout or fail to synthesize due to exhausting system memory or a crash within Sketch. To give an idea of the problem size, the leftmost portion of Table 1 lists the numbers of lines and holes per benchmark.

As other work has observed [9], performance evaluation methodologies that lack rigor can lead to misleading and incorrect conclusions. To avoid this problem, we collect enough data to calculate a percentile's confidence interval (CI) at a given confidence level (CL). We employ the classic Clopper-Pearson [6] (or "exact") method using the probabilities of the Binomial distribution to iteratively calculate confidence intervals for a given dataset. While other methods are often used, many of these assume an underlying Gaussian distribution. The underlying distributions for our measurements are not known and do not appear to be Gaussian, a case the exact method handles correctly.

Run time variance is not correlated across configurations, so the number of runs needed for significance can differ from Sketch to Sketcham, as reflected in the "total" columns of Table 1. We ran each configuration repeatedly until measurements met two statistical significance conditions. First, that they reach a 95% CL that the population median lies within at most a 20% CI around the sample median. For example, for a sample median of 100 s, the population median might lie between 90 s and 110 s, or between 98 s and 118 s, depending on the underlying distribution. Second, the CI must range entirely between the first and third quartiles to increase the confidence that the median measurements adequately reflect the underlying distribution. In seven out of ten benchmarks these two conditions were sufficient to yield CIs that did not overlap across Sketch

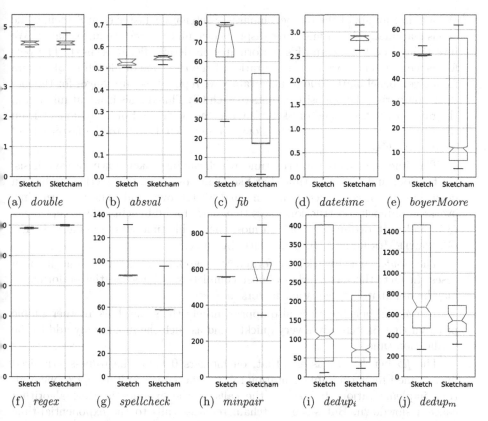

Fig. 5: Total time (s). Times are drawn as notched box plots, which give the distribution's median inside a notch indicating its confidence interval. As usual, the box extends to the first and third quartiles, and whiskers extend to the full distribution. To better focus on the data, we truncate some whiskers. Note differing y-axis scales both here and below.

and Sketcham, which allows for statistically significant performance claims about these benchmarks.

4.1 Performance

Figure 5 shows the running times of Sketch and Sketcham on our benchmarks. The distribution of times is shown as notched box plots. The boxes extend from the first to the third quartile, with the median shown as a mid-line. The CI is indicated by the notch. The whiskers extended to the minimum and maximum values (some whiskers are truncated to allow for a closer view of the median).

Following standard practice, we conclude that two configurations have a statistically significant difference in performance if their CIs do not overlap, as there is then high probability that the median times of the distributions are different.

We see that for six of the ten benchmarks, Sketcham is faster than Sketch, while one is marginally slower and three display no significant performance change. We investigated each benchmark's performance in detail, discussed next. The performance differences we report are ratios of the run time of Sketch to Sketcham for a given benchmark. Due to uncertainty we report speedup ranges for the median, comparing the opposite extents of each CI. This ranges from, at minimum, the ratio of the faster end of Sketch's CI to the slower end of Sketcham's CI, up to, at maximum, the ratio of the slower end of Sketch's CI to the faster end of Sketcham's CI.

The times shown are total run time, which can be broken down into synthesis, verification, and overhead time. For Sketcham, overhead can further be broken down into mock construction and normal Sketch overhead. The total runtime overhead of mock construction is less than 0.4% for all benchmarks except regex (3%) and both dedups (~20%). In most cases, this time was dominated by the GENERATEMOCKS and BUILDASSERTMAP phases.

The *double* benchmark's performance is approximately the same in both cases. In fact, the CIs overlap almost completely, suggesting the performance may be dominated by constant factors in Sketch.

The *absval* benchmark is also approximately the same. It is another simple program that Sketch solves very quickly, and as such the mocks only add to the verification time.

The *fib* benchmark asserts that, on integers 0 to 9, the to-be-synthesized linear-time Fibonacci implementation returns the same result as an exponential-time implementation. In Sketch, the calls to the exponential-time algorithm cause a slowdown. But since Sketcham replaces calls to the exponential-time algorithm with calls to a (constant-time) mock, Sketcham achieves a speedup of 3.8–4.5×. While it is difficult to make out in the plot, the median and CI lie immediately above the first quartile for Sketcham.

The *datetime* benchmark fails to synthesize in Sketch due to memory exhaustion, but it consistently synthesizes in just a few seconds using Sketcham. Investigating further, we found the bottleneck is a function that parses strings into integers in a loop that converts digits and adds them to a running total. For example, the digit sequence abc is converted to the integer 100*a+10*b+c. This conversion loop is unrolled to the maximum bound by Sketch, and the input strings are of varying sizes, which is encoded as a separate formula for each possible length. The SAT conversion algorithm translates symbolic arithmetic formulas according to combinations of possible values of their subformulas, which results in very large SAT formulas in this case. Later in the conversion, these are merged back together in another quadratic operation. Due to the number of formulas and overall formula size, this eventually exhausts memory. While Sketcham technically faces the same issue, it does so after decomposing the sketch into smaller formulas, and thus these limits are never approached.

The *boyerMoore* benchmark runs 4–5× faster under Sketcham than Sketch. The reason is similar to the previous case. *boyerMoore* includes a generator that constructs arithmetic expressions that add and subtract a small set of values including a hole. Sketch constructs these expressions recursively so they grow quickly, with the total number of terms determined exponentially by the degree of function inlining, and the resulting expressions have high symmetry, both factors that slow down solving, further compounded by the location of this expression deep within the sketch. Because Sketcham breaks the problem's dependencies, this expression can be synthesized separately from the rest of the program, which proceeds much more quickly.

The *regex* benchmark's overall performance using Sketcham is statistically significantly slower by a factor of $0.98\times$, which is a minimal difference in practice. The main mocked function here performs compilation of a regular expression into instructions for a virtual machine. Because compilation is recursive, it is difficult to give a specification that Sketcham can use. It is instead given by example with an exhaustive set of subproblems, which greatly increases the number of harnesses to solve. While most harnesses keep similar performance and the slowest harness is 8% faster in Sketcham, this is not enough margin to improve overall solve time.

The *spellcheck* benchmark using Sketcham sees a speedup of $1.5\times$, while *minpair* performs roughly the same (0.89–$1.04\times$). Both rely on the same Levenshtein edit distance algorithm. The harness for this algorithm, which is the most time-consuming in either sketch, runs last in both settings, which reveals the source of the performance difference between the two benchmarks. *minpair* is dominated by synthesis time and *spellcheck* by verification time, which means that harnesses for the minimum pair function are more difficult to synthesize than for the spellcheck function, and so the former accumulates more state within the solver that is compounded when solving the Levenshtein harness. This slows it down enough to decrease the overall performance. On the other hand, the improvement of *spellcheck* is distributed across all individual harnesses, and across both synthesis and verification time, more than making up for the time it takes to construct and solve the mock harnesses.

Finally, the *dedup*s show a notable performance improvement with Sketcham. In both $dedup_i$ and $dedup_m$, the problem is large and complex enough that plain Sketch struggles with it. Sketcham eliminates the interactions of holes across the deduplication and sorting functions, which speeds up synthesis by a factor of 1.3–$1.9\times$ for $dedup_i$ and 1.003–$1.5\times$ for $dedup_m$.

4.2   Case Study: Deduplication

Next, we examine the performance of $dedup_i$ and $dedup_m$ in detail, as they illustrate the strengths and weaknesses of Sketcham. We break our discussion into comparisons of solving time across harnesses and comparisons of CEGIS synthesis time to CEGIS verification time.

Time to Solve Each Harness. Both $dedup_i$ and $dedup_m$ are structured the same way, and Sketcham creates the harnesses and mocks shown in Figure 1c for both. Figure 6 breaks down the total times for $dedup_i$ and $dedup_m$, grouped by the

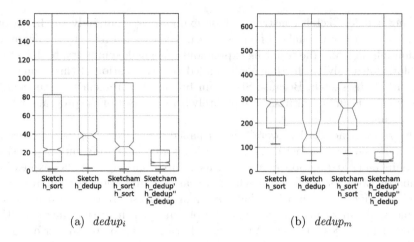

(a) $dedup_i$ (b) $dedup_m$

Fig. 6: Harness time (s)

harnesses for `sort` and for `dedup`. We exclude overheads such as time spent in mock construction, parsing the input, and reassembling the output.

We make several observations. First, comparing the first and third columns within each subfigure, we see the time for solving `h_sort` is the same for Sketch and Sketcham. This makes sense because `h_sort'` adds no information—it calls mocked `sort` and then immediately asserts the same specification as in the mock. Note that, while the trivial `h_sort'` harness could be elided here, creating an analogous harness would be useful if the harness accidentally contained a contradiction. In such a case, Sketcham would almost instantly decide the harness is unsatisfiable, whereas Sketch could spend an arbitrary amount of time reasoning about the computation in the actual called function before detecting the contradiction.

Second, comparing the second and fourth columns within each subfigure, we see that the CI of `h_dedup` using Sketcham lies well below the CI using Sketch. The speed improves by a factor of 3.2–4.7× for $dedup_i$ and 2.2–4.9× for $dedup_m$. Examining this result in detail, we find that Sketcham works exactly as intended: `h_dedup''` calls the mocked `sort`, enabling it to synthesize quickly and assign holes correctly, which are then simply verified when checking `h_dedup` (and `h_dedup'` is trivial, similarly to `h_sort'`).

Third, also comparing the second and fourth columns, we see the variance in performance for Sketch is much greater than for Sketcham. Investigating further, we found this occurs for two reasons. First, the specification in `h_sort` is weak enough[2] that sometimes an incorrect hole assignment for `sort` satisfies the verifier and is only discovered while synthesizing `h_dedup`, forcing the solver to backtrack at great cost and simultaneously consider the holes in both functions. Second, even when the solver finds a correct assignment for `sort`, it includes the

---

[2] In addition to the specification we have supplied, a complete specification of `sort` relies on the existence of a permutation function over the array's indices.

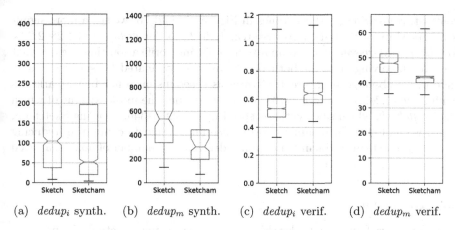

(a) $dedup_i$ synth.   (b) $dedup_m$ synth.   (c) $dedup_i$ verif.   (d) $dedup_m$ verif.

Fig. 7: Synthesis and verification time (s)

entire formula again while solving h_dedup, resulting in a much larger problem and corresponding variability. In contrast, with Sketcham, h_dedup'' is decoupled from sort, eliminating these issues.

Fourth, we observe that both Sketch and Sketcham can solve h_sort about 10× faster for $dedup_i$ than for $dedup_m$. Overall, merge sort is more challenging for Sketch than insertion sort (note that since Sketch finitizes the problem by, e.g., unrolling loops, asymptotic complexity does not play a role). More surprisingly, synthesizing h_dedup is also faster for $dedup_i$ compared to $dedup_m$. We believe this occurs because synthesis of h_dedup must sometimes recover from a bad hole assignment from h_sort, which will be quicker for $dedup_i$, and because the easier synthesis of $dedup_i$ means the solver accumulates less state, such as conflict clauses, that would otherwise slow down solving subsequent harnesses.

Finally, we begin to get a clearer picture of the divergence between $dedup_i$ and $dedup_m$. In $dedup_i$, h_dedup synthesis is the performance driver, and the improvement using Sketcham has a significant impact on total performance improvement. In $dedup_m$ it is overshadowed by h_sort, which dominates to the point that improvement elsewhere is not as significant a contributor. Combined with the overhead of mock construction, this leads to a less pronounced improvement in total performance.

Synthesis and Verification Time. Figure 7 shows the times for the CEGIS synthesis phase and verification phase for each benchmark under Sketch and Sketcham. Not shown are the overheads of mock construction, parsing, etc., which for $dedup_i$ we found took 3–4s in Sketch versus 17–19s in Sketcham, and for $dedup_m$ took 90–96s in Sketch versus 201–207s using Sketcham. We believe much of the difference between these could be eliminated with additional engineering effort.

Looking at verification times in Figures 7c and 7d, we see that while the verification times for Sketch and Sketcham are different, they are still relatively close: Sketcham is 0.81–0.86× slower for $dedup_i$ and 1.12–1.16× faster for $dedup_m$. In contrast, comparing synthesis times in Figures 7a and 7b, we see a more significant speedup for Sketcham over Sketch: 1.59–$2.55\times$ for $dedup_i$ and 1.28–$2.28\times$ for $dedup_m$. Moreover, if we compare synthesis and verification time, we see that the overall solving time for both benchmarks is dominated by synthesis time. Indeed, we observed even greater synthesis speedups on other benchmarks including fib (4.2–$5.1\times$) and $boyerMoore$ 5.2–$6.9\times$, but the most extreme of which was $spellcheck$, which saw synthesis speed up by 308.4–$345.7\times$ using Sketcham. Thus, we find that Sketcham's performance improvements come from reducing synthesis time by introducing mocks that decrease the number of holes that need to be considered at once.

4.3   Discussion

In general, we found that Sketch's performance is unpredictable in practice, which is influenced by factors such as the solver's random seed. For example, in terms of overall solving time, our experimental runs included several outliers (not shown in Figure 5) near the 60 minute timeout. In these cases, Sketch essentially makes a very poor initial guess for the holes, and verification produces counterexamples that do not add much information. Both Sketch and Sketcham exhibit this issue.

Moreover, often what seem like minor changes in the program sketch or configuration options can result in totally different solver behavior, and hence performance. One example of this was $boyerMoore$, which turned out to be non-linearly sensitive to the loop unrolling parameter. This benchmark was also extremely fickle about the problem formulation—holes in what seemed to be innocuous locations would lead to timeouts in both Sketch and Sketcham. Another example is $dedup$, which initially had a specification that omitted a requirement that the output array did not have a negative length. Without this constraint, the performance benefit of Sketcham was overwhelmed by the variability of the solver exploring ultimately impossible scenarios.

Overall, our results suggest that while Sketcham can't always outperform plain Sketch, it performs best on problems split into functions whose tests cover the behavior the sketch actually relies on while being easier to compute than the functions' actual implementations. While Sketcham affected the performance of both CEGIS phases, the best improvements were observed when the solving time of dependencies was dominated by the synthesis phase. For programs with these properties, Sketcham can exhibit a performance improvement of as much as $5\times$ overall, with synthesis time improvements alone of up to $345.7\times$. Moreover, in some cases, such as $datetime$, Sketcham can solve problems that are out of reach of plain Sketch. For programs where these properties do not hold, Sketcham performance is typically similar to plain Sketch.

5   Related Work

There are several threads of related work.

Program Synthesis with models. As discussed earlier, our work builds on work by Singh et al. [24], who propose manually created models for Sketch. While Sketcham relies on the core algorithm of that work, Sketcham frees the Sketch user from needing to write models, because we create mocks automatically from normal sketches. Mariano et al. [18] use algebraic specifications to model libraries. In contrast, our approach derives specifications from the input program's assertions, without requiring the programmer to add annotations.

Deriving mocks and specs from tests. Saff et al. [21] use the capture and replay of actual test executions to automatically generate mock dependencies with the goal of speeding up test execution. Fazzini et al. [8] further generalize this capture-and-replay technique to consistently model the environment of a mobile app under test, allowing for testing apps that use an inconsistent resource like a database or network device. Both of these target normal testing rather than synthesis. Nguyen et al. [19] leverage symbolic execution over input-output test pairs to perform program repair. However, they use these tests to model individual expressions instead of modeling entire functions. The insight underlying these approaches is similar to ours, however Sketcham is capable of both input-output pairs and general properties, and does not rely on either concrete or symbolic execution of tests.

Component-based synthesis. Gulwani et al. [10] model programs using logical input-output relations to synthesize loop-free bit-vector programs. Shi et al. [23] combine many solutions that each only partially meet a specification into one that meets the entire specification. Both approaches limit the synthesis search space by building their solutions from the bottom up, from a selection of base components. Smith and Albarghouthi [25] prune the search space using bottom up algebraic rewriting of the program into an equivalent normal form. In contrast to these, Sketcham derives its benefits from breaking apart input sketches from the top down, at function level granularity.

Modular synthesis using symbolic or actual execution. Samak et al. [22] derive specifications of class methods using symbolic execution and use them to synthesize a replacement shim class one method at a time. Van Geffen et al. [31] use symbolic execution to model abstract virtual machines to modularly synthesize a compiler one instruction at a time. In contrast, because our approach derives mocks directly from the input's assertions, we need not consider the code itself when modeling it. Hua et al. [11] modularize the synthesis of library calls through execution of actual partial programs. In contrast, we attempt to avoid called functions entirely by relying on their inferred specifications.

Other approaches. Bodík et al. [2] finalize incomplete programs using angelic nondeterminism. In contrast, Sketcham does not introduce arbitrary angelic values, but instead constrains any angelic-like behavior using a function's inferred specification. Huang et al. [12] use a divide-and-conquer strategy to iteratively split synthesis problems according to heuristics. In contrast, Sketcham splits problems structurally in a single pass. Polikarpova et al. [20] speed up synthesis through modular verification using refinement types. In contrast, our approach achieves a similar kind of modularity without being type-directed.

6   Conclusion

This paper presents Sketcham, a new technique for decomposing program sketches during synthesis by turning a function's test suite into a mock that a caller can invoke in place of that function, thereby allowing separate reasoning about callers and callees. Sketcham gathers asserts from tests into a specification for each function which it embodies as a Sketch model. We implemented Sketcham as an additional pass with Sketch and evaluated it on a set of ten benchmarks. Our rigorous evaluation strategy ensured at a confidence level of 95% that our measurements demonstrate performance gains of as much as 5×, including one benchmark that otherwise timed out on Sketch. Based on these results, we believe that automatically generating mocks from tests with Sketcham is a promising new approach for achieving modular synthesis.

Acknowledgments

We would like to thank Norman Ramsey, Milod Kazerounian, and the anonymous reviewers for their helpful comments. This research was supported in part by a Draper Fellowship.

References

1. Bjørner, N.: Linear quantifier elimination as an abstract decision procedure. In: Giesl, J., Hähnle, R. (eds.) IJCAR 2010. LNCS (LNAI), vol. 6173, pp. 316–330. Springer, Heidelberg (2010). https://doi.org/https://doi.org/10.1007/978-3-642-14203-1_27
2. Bodík, R., et al.: Programming with angelic nondeterminism. In: Proceedings of the 37th Annual ACM SIGPLAN-SIGACT Symposium on Principles of Programming Languages, POPL 2010, pp. 339–352. ACM, New York (2010). https://doi.org/https://doi.org/10.1145/1706299.1706339
3. Boyer, R.S., Moore, J.S.: A fast string searching algorithm. Commun. ACM **20**(10), 762–772 (1977). https://doi.org/https://doi.org/10.1145/359842.359859
4. Bradley, A.R., Manna, Z.: The calculus of computation: decision procedures with applications to verification. Springer, Berlin (2007), oCLC: 255687662
5. Cheung, A., Solar-Lezama, A., Madden, S.: Using program synthesis for social recommendations. In: Chen, X., Lebanon, G., Wang, H., Zaki, M.J. (eds.) 21st ACM International Conference on Information and Knowledge Management, CIKM'12, Maui, HI, USA, October 29 - November 02, 2012, pp. 1732–1736. ACM, Hawaii, USA (2012). https://doi.org/https://doi.org/10.1145/2396761.2398507, http://dl.acm.org/citation.cfm?id=2396761
6. Clopper, C.J., Pearson, E.S.: The use of confidence or fiducial limits illustrated in the case of the binomial. Biometrika **26**(4), 404–413 (1934). https://doi.org/https://doi.org/10.1093/biomet/26.4.404, publisher: Oxford Academic
7. Ellis, K., Ritchie, D., Solar-Lezama, A., Tenenbaum, J.: Learning to infer graphics programs from hand-drawn images. In: Bengio, S., Wallach, H., Larochelle, H., Grauman, K., Cesa-Bianchi, N., Garnett, R. (eds.) Advances in Neural Information Processing Systems 31, pp. 6059–6068. Curran Associates, Inc. (2018)

8. Fazzini, M., Gorla, A., Orso, A.: A framework for automated test mocking of mobile apps. In: Proceedings of the 35th IEEE/ACM International Conference on Automated Software Engineering (ASE), NIER track, pp. 1204–1208 (Sep 2020), iSSN: 2643-1572

9. Georges, A., Buytaert, D., Eeckhout, L.: Statistically rigorous Java performance evaluation. ACM SIGPLAN Notices **42**(10), 57–76 (2007). https://doi.org/https://doi.org/10.1145/1297105.1297033

10. Gulwani, S., Jha, S., Tiwari, A., Venkatesan, R.: Synthesis of loop-free programs. In: Proceedings of the 32nd ACM SIGPLAN Conference on Programming Language Design and Implementation, PLDI 2011, pp. 62–73. ACM, New York (2011). https://doi.org/https://doi.org/10.1145/1993498.1993506

11. Hua, J., Zhang, Y., Zhang, Y., Khurshid, S.: EdSketch: execution-driven sketching for Java. Int. J. Softw. Tools Technol. Transf. **21**(3), 249–265 (2019). https://doi.org/https://doi.org/10.1007/s10009-019-00512-8

12. Huang, K., Qiu, X., Shen, P., Wang, Y.: Reconciling enumerative and deductive program synthesis. In: Proceedings of the 41st ACM SIGPLAN Conference on Programming Language Design and Implementation, pp. 1159–1174. PLDI 2020, Association for Computing Machinery, New York, June 2020. https://doi.org/https://doi.org/10.1145/3385412.3386027

13. Inala, J.P., Polikarpova, N., Qiu, X., Lerner, B.S., Solar-Lezama, A.: Synthesis of recursive ADT transformations from reusable templates. In: Legay, A., Margaria, T. (eds.) TACAS 2017. LNCS, vol. 10205, pp. 247–263. Springer, Heidelberg (2017). https://doi.org/https://doi.org/10.1007/978-3-662-54577-5_14

14. Inala, J.P., Singh, R., Solar-Lezama, A.: Synthesis of domain specific CNF encoders for bit-vector solvers. In: Creignou, N., Berre, D.L. (eds.) Theory and Applications of Satisfiability Testing - SAT 2016–19th International Conference, Bordeaux, France, July 5–8, 2016, Proceedings. Lecture Notes in Computer Science, vol. 9710, pp. 302–320. Springer (2016). https://doi.org/https://doi.org/10.1007/978-3-319-40970-2_19

15. Jeon, J., Qiu, X., Fetter-Degges, J., Foster, J.S., Solar-Lezama, A.: Synthesizing framework models for symbolic execution. In: Proceedings of the 38th International Conference on Software Engineering, pp. 156–167. ICSE 2016, Association for Computing Machinery, New York, May 2016. https://doi.org/https://doi.org/10.1145/2884781.2884856

16. Jeon, J., Qiu, X., Solar-Lezama, A., Foster, J.S.: JSketch: sketching for Java. In: European Software Engineering Conference and Foundations of Software Engineering (ESEC/FSE). Tool Demo Track, pp. 934–937. ACM, Bergamo, Italy, September (2015)

17. Kuncak, V., Mayer, M., Piskac, R., Suter, P.: Complete functional synthesis. In: Proceedings of the 31st ACM SIGPLAN Conference on Programming Language Design and Implementation, pp. 316–329. PLDI 2010, ACM, New York (2010). https://doi.org/https://doi.org/10.1145/1806596.1806632

18. Mariano, B., et al.: Program synthesis with algebraic library specifications. Proc. ACM Program. Lang. **3**(OOPSLA), 132:1–132:25 (2019). https://doi.org/https://doi.org/10.1145/3360558

19. Nguyen, T.V., Weimer, W., Kapur, D., Forrest, S.: Connecting program synthesis and reachability: automatic program repair using test-input generation. In: Legay, A., Margaria, T. (eds.) TACAS 2017. LNCS, vol. 10205, pp. 301–318. Springer, Heidelberg (2017). https://doi.org/https://doi.org/10.1007/978-3-662-54577-5_17

20. Polikarpova, N., Kuraj, I., Solar-Lezama, A.: Program synthesis from polymorphic refinement types. In: Proceedings of the 37th ACM SIG-PLAN Conference on Programming Language Design and Implementation - PLDI 2016, pp. 522–538. ACM Press, Santa Barbara, CA, USA (2016). https://doi.org/https://doi.org/10.1145/2908080.2908093

21. Saff, D., Artzi, S., Perkins, J.H., Ernst, M.D.: Automatic test factoring for Java. In: Proceedings of the 20th IEEE/ACM International Conference on Automated software engineering, ASE 2005, pp. 114–123. Association for Computing Machinery, New York, November 2005. https://doi.org/https://doi.org/10.1145/1101908.1101927

22. Samak, M., Kim, D., Rinard, M.C.: Synthesizing replacement classes. Proc. ACM Programm. Lang. 4(POPL), 52:1–52:33 (2019). https://doi.org/https://doi.org/10.1145/3371120

23. Shi, K., Steinhardt, J., Liang, P.: FrAngel: component-based synthesis with control structures. Proc. ACM Programm. Lang. 3(POPL), 73:1–73:29 (2019). https://doi.org/https://doi.org/10.1145/3290386

24. Singh, R., Singh, R., Xu, Z., Krosnick, R., Solar-Lezama, A.: Modular synthesis of sketches using models. In: McMillan, K.L., Rival, X. (eds.) VMCAI 2014. LNCS, vol. 8318, pp. 395–414. Springer, Heidelberg (2014). https://doi.org/https://doi.org/10.1007/978-3-642-54013-4_22

25. Smith, C., Albarghouthi, A.: Program synthesis with equivalence reduction. In: Enea, C., Piskac, R. (eds.) VMCAI 2019. LNCS, vol. 11388, pp. 24–47. Springer, Cham (2019). https://doi.org/https://doi.org/10.1007/978-3-030-11245-5_2

26. Solar Lezama, A.: Program synthesis by sketching. Ph.D. thesis, EECS Department, University of California, Berkeley, December 2008. http://www2.eecs.berkeley.edu/Pubs/TechRpts/2008/EECS-2008-177.html

27. Solar-Lezama, A.: The sketching approach to program synthesis. In: Hu, Z. (ed.) APLAS 2009. LNCS, vol. 5904, pp. 4–13. Springer, Heidelberg (2009). https://doi.org/https://doi.org/10.1007/978-3-642-10672-9_3

28. Solar-Lezama, A.: The sketch programmers manual. Tech. rep, MIT, February 2020

29. Solar-Lezama, A., Arnold, G., Tancau, L., Bodik, R., Saraswat, V., Seshia, S.: Sketching stencils. In: Proceedings of the 28th ACM SIGPLAN Conference on Programming Language Design and Implementation, PLDI 2007, pp. 167–178. Association for Computing Machinery, San Diego, June 2007. https://doi.org/https://doi.org/10.1145/1250734.1250754

30. Solar-Lezama, A., Tancau, L., Bodík, R., Seshia, S.A., Saraswat, V.A.: Combinatorial sketching for finite programs. In: Shen, J.P., Martonosi, M. (eds.) Proceedings of the 12th International Conference on Architectural Support for Programming Languages and Operating Systems, ASPLOS 2006, San Jose, CA, USA, 21–25 October, 2006, pp. 404–415. ACM (2006). https://doi.org/https://doi.org/10.1145/1168857.1168907

31. Van Geffen, J., Nelson, L., Dillig, I., Wang, X., Torlak, E.: Synthesizing JIT compilers for in-kernel DSLs. In: Lahiri, S.K., Wang, C. (eds.) CAV 2020. LNCS, vol. 12225, pp. 564–586. Springer, Cham (2020). https://doi.org/https://doi.org/10.1007/978-3-030-53291-8_29

Counterexample-Guided Partial Bounding for Recursive Function Synthesis

Azadeh Farzan and Victor Nicolet[✉]

University of Toronto, Toronto, Canada
{azadeh,victorn}@cs.toronto.edu

Abstract. Quantifier bounding is a standard approach in inductive program synthesis in dealing with unbounded domains. In this paper, we propose one such bounding method for the synthesis of recursive functions over recursive input data types. The synthesis problem is specified by an input reference (recursive) function and a *recursion skeleton*. The goal is to synthesize a recursive function equivalent to the input function whose recursion strategy is specified by the recursion skeleton. In this context, we illustrate that it is possible to *selectively* bound a *subset* of the (recursively typed) parameters, each by a suitable bound. The choices are guided by counterexamples. The evaluation of our strategy on a broad set of benchmarks shows that it succeeds in efficiently synthesizing non-trivial recursive functions where standard across-the-board bounding would fail.

1 Introduction

Most computational tasks can be broken into logical units, many of which involve evaluating a function over a data collection. Recursively defined data types are broadly used to implement these collections. In functional languages, recursive functions implement computations over these recursive data types. Consider a typical scenario where a programmer has implemented a function f over a collection C by defining a recursive data type A and implementing f as a recursive function foo_A. Later, the programmer may need a different implementation foo_B of f over a different data type B; perhaps B is better suited for an optimized implementation of f, or the programmer now needs an implementation of a new function g (in addition to f) over the collection C and the data type B is a much better choice than A for implementing g efficiently. Ideally, the programmer should not have to start from scratch implementing foo_B.

In this paper, we propose a generic and efficient algorithm for synthesizing recursive functions in such contexts. Our synthesis problem is specified by the following three components: (1) a recursive *reference implementation* that precisely defines the functionality, (2) a high level *recursion skeleton* that specifies a recursion strategy (i.e. a traversal plan over the new recursive data type) for

© The Author(s) 2021
A. Silva and K. R. M. Leino (Eds.) CAV 2021, LNCS 12759, pp. 832–855, 2021.
https://doi.org/10.1007/978-3-030-81685-8_39

the target code, and (3) a mapping, called *representation function*, that converts an instance of the new data type to one of the old data type (of the reference implementation), and establishes that the two are different implementations of the same concept.

Let us illustrate our problem setup with the aid of an example. Consider the standard A-labelled binary trees, recursively defined as $T \rightarrow Nil \mid Node(A, T, T)$ for an arbitrary type A, and the maximum in-order prefix sum (mips) function depicted on the right. mips maintains a pair of values: sum, which keeps track of the sum of the elements it has traversed so far, and mps, which maintains the maximum value over all such sums. This reference implementation precisely defines the functional specification for a function f.

```
let mips t = aux (0, 0) t
and aux s t =
    match t with
    | Nil -> sum, mps
    | Node(a,l,r) ->
        let sum, mps = aux s l in
        aux (sum + a, max (sum + a) mps) r
```

Fig. 1. Maximum in-order prefix sum

Suppose that the programmer needs an alternative implementation that can be efficiently parallelized, and therefore, opts for the divide-and-conquer *recursion skeleton* depicted on the right. The *partially defined* code specifies that the tree should be traversed in a manner that each subtree is processed separately, and then the results should be combined by a function join. It does not, however, specify what computation is performed; the implementation of join and the initial value for s0 are *unknown*. In this example, labeled binary trees are the recursive data type for both the reference implementation and the target of synthesis. In cases like this, the representation function simply becomes the identity function.

```
let h t =
    match t with
    | Nil -> s0
    | Node(a,l,r) -> join a (h l) (h r)
```

Our algorithm reduces the problem to a set of recursion-free synthesis problems, which are solved using existing synthesis tools. It synthesizes the unknown computations for join and s0, and therefore produces the divide-and-conquer implementation of mips on binary trees:

```
let s0 = (0, 0)
let join a (s1, m1) (s2, m2) = a + s1 + s2, max m1 (m2 + a + s1)
```

At the high level, the problem of synthesizing a new recursive function can be framed as checking the validity of formulas of the type $\exists f \forall x : \theta . \phi(f, x, \dots)$ where θ is a recursive data type (i.e. x ranges over a set of inductively defined terms), f is the target recursive function, and the ellipses stand in for all the relevant components of our specific problem statement as outlined before. Elements of type θ are unbounded in two different dimensions: the recursive structure can be of arbitrary size and each element of it belongs to an unbounded (data) domain. A straightforward way of under-approximating the unbounded specification is to bound the universal quantifier $\forall x : \theta$ in both dimensions. The synthesis problem is reformulated to synthesize the function from a bounded set of examples which are concrete bounded elements of the data type with concrete elements in them. This can be done by applying a counterexample-guided inductive synthesis (CEGIS) [34] algorithm in the straightforward way.

Alternatively, one can attempt to tackle the two dimensions independently. The quantifier $\forall x : \theta$ can be bounded in one dimension, i.e. recursive structures of bounded size can be considered, and yet the elements of these bounded structures can range over unbounded domains. More formally, the universal quantification is instantiated over a finite set of bounded-depth terms, denoted by set T, and the resulting specification becomes $\exists f.\forall a \in D. \bigwedge_{t \in T} \phi(f, t)$ where a are the free variables of the terms in T and of non-recursive type D. This bounding reduces the original problem to a standard functional synthesis problem (over unbounded data domains) that can be discharged to one of the many known solvers, employing a variety of techniques for it. The set of terms in T can still be discovered in a counterexample guided loop in the spirit of CEGIS, and therefore this algorithm can be viewed as a *symbolic* CEGIS variant.

The thesis of this paper is that forcing bounds on all recursively typed variables is unnecessary and can be avoided algorithmically. A subset of variables can retain their unbounded quantification and yet the problem can be reduced to a recursion-free functional synthesis instance. Recall the mips example. The join function takes two trees, l and r, and a value a as an input. The recursion-free specification for join can retain a universal quantifier on all trees for l and limit its bounded exploration to r. In other words, one can successfully synthesize the join function from examples enumerating a few small candidate trees for r and treating h(l) (i.e. the result of the computation on l) and not l itself for the inductive enumeration of examples for synthesis. We discuss in the paper how this information can be algorithmically derived from the specific components of our synthesis problem: the reference implementation, the recursion skeleton, and the representation function.

Beyond the decision on what quantifiers should be bounded, the synthesis algorithm also needs to determine a set of terms that are used to bound these quantifiers. We propose an algorithm that discovers these bounds guided by counterexamples in a refinement-style loop. We show that this algorithm is sound, satisfies the expected weak-progress property that other CEGIS instances have, and is *parsimonious* in a precise sense. We have implemented this algorithm as a prototype synthesis tool SYNDUCE and demonstrate that SYNDUCE can efficiently synthesize recursive functions from specifications.

2   Background and Notation

The notation introduced in this section is used for formalizing the result of applying recursive functions to symbolic inputs.

Terms. We make use of a set of *symbols* that are partitioned into *terminal symbols* Σ, *non-terminal symbols* $\mathcal{N}$, and an infinite set of typed *variables* $\mathcal{V}$. There is a unique symbol $\circ_?$ that stands for a *hole*. Terms are defined by the grammar $T \to x \mid T\,T$ where x is a symbol, and $T\,T$ is a function application. These are the relevant classes of terms:

- *Concrete terms* $T(\Sigma)$ are those containing only terminal symbols. Every concrete term can be interpreted and has a concrete value.
- *Symbolic terms* $T(\Sigma, \mathcal{V})$ are those containing terminal symbols or variables.
- *Closed terms* $T(\Sigma, \mathcal{N})$ are those containing terminal or non-terminal symbols, but no variables.
- *Applicative terms* $T(\Sigma, \mathcal{N}, \mathcal{V})$ are those containing any symbol except the hole symbol.
- *Contexts* $T(\Sigma, \mathcal{N}, \mathcal{V}, \circ_?)$ are those with at least one hole. A *one-hole context* $C[\,]$ is a context with a single occurrence of $\circ_?$, and $C[t]$ stands for the term formed by replacing the single hole in $C[\,]$ with the term t.

Two terms are equal, denoted by $t =_\alpha t'$ (standard alpha conversion), iff there exists two injective substitutions $\sigma : FV(t) \to \mathcal{V} \setminus (FV(t) \cup FV(t'))$ and $\sigma' : FV(t') \to \mathcal{V} \setminus (FV(t) \cup FV(t'))$ such that $\sigma t = \sigma' t'$ (i.e. syntactically equal).

A symbolic term t can be **expanded** into a term t' iff there exists a substitution $\sigma : FV(t) \to T(FV(t') \cup \Sigma)$ that substitutes the free variables of t for symbolic terms with the free variables of t' such that $t' = \sigma t$. The relation $\succeq$ over symbolic terms, is a partial order defined as, $t \succeq t'$ iff t can be expanded into t'. A single variable is the maximal element according to this partial order and concrete terms (of any depth) are minimal elements.

Recursive Functions. This paper focuses on recursive functions $f : \tau \to D$ with terms of a recursive type (τ or θ) as input, and an output of type D. These functions can be executed on concrete or symbolic input terms of type τ. We assume all functions can be translated to *recursion schemes* as defined below:

Definition 1 ([26]). *A* recursion scheme *is a tuple* $\mathcal{P} = \langle \Sigma, \mathcal{N}, \mathcal{R}, \Lambda \rangle$ *where:*

- Σ *is a ranked alphabet of* terminals
- $\mathcal{N}$ *is a finite set of typed non-terminals.*
- $\mathcal{R}$ *is a finite set of rewrite rules, each in one of the following shapes* ($m \geq 0$):

$$\textit{(pure)} \qquad F\ x_1\ \ldots\ x_m \to t$$
$$\textit{(pattern matching)}\quad F\ x_1\ \ldots\ x_m\ p \to t$$

  where the x_i *are variables, p is a symbolic term, t is an applicative term in* $T(\Sigma \cup \mathcal{N} \cup \{x_1, \ldots, x_n\})$, *and F is a non-terminal.*
- $\Lambda : \tau \to D$ *is a distinguished non-terminal symbol whose defining rules are always pattern-matching rules.*

We associate with each recursion scheme $\mathcal{P}$ a notion of reduction. A *redex* is an applicative term of the form $F\ \sigma x_1\ \ldots\ \sigma x_m\ \sigma p$ for a substitution $\sigma : \mathcal{V} \to T(\Sigma, \mathcal{N}, \mathcal{V})$ and rule $F\ x_1\ \ldots\ x_m\ p \to t$ in $\mathcal{R}$. The *contractum* of the redex is σt. The one-step reduction relation $\mapsto\, \subseteq T(\Sigma, \mathcal{N}, \mathcal{V}) \times T(\Sigma, \mathcal{N}, \mathcal{V})$ is defined by $C[s] \mapsto C[t]$ whenever s is a redex, t is a contractum and $C[\,]$ is a one-hole context. A recursion scheme is *deterministic* iff for any redex $F\ s_1\ \ldots\ s_m$ there is exactly one rule $l \rightarrow r$ (in $\mathcal{R}$) which *matches* that redex, i.e. there exists a substitution θ such that $F\ s_1\ \dots\ s_m = \theta\ l$.

Given a recursion scheme $\mathcal{P} = \langle \Sigma, \mathcal{N}, \mathcal{R}, \Lambda \rangle$ and a term $s \in T(\Sigma, \mathcal{N}, \mathcal{V})$, $\mathcal{L}(\mathcal{P}, s)$ denotes the language of $(\Sigma \cup \mathcal{N} \cup FV(s))$-labelled trees resulted from the maximal rewriting of the term s with the one-step reduction relation associated to $\mathcal{P}$. If $\mathcal{P}$ is deterministic, then $\mathcal{L}(\mathcal{P}, s)$ is a singleton (the term s reduces to only one possible term), and $[\![s]\!]_{\mathcal{P}}$ denotes the unique resulting term. This notion of reduction is slightly different from the one used in [26], in that we do not require the substitution to be closed.

Symbolic Evaluation. For any function f that can be defined as a recursion scheme, the symbolic evaluation of f on input s is simply $[\![s]\!]_f$. In other words, $f(s) = [\![s]\!]_f$. In this view, recursive functions and the corresponding recursion schemes are interchangeable. For a recursion scheme $\langle \Sigma, \mathcal{N}, \mathcal{R}, \Lambda \rangle$ representing a function f and a variable x, $f(x)$ and $\Lambda\ x$ become two different ways of referencing the same concept. In this paper, we assume that all recursion schemes to be deterministic total functions. Specifically, they terminate on all inputs; symbolic evaluation (or the equivalent reduction) of a symbolic term always terminates.

Types Notation. We use capital letters A, B, C, and D to refer to base types, which are scalar types (int, bool, char, ...) or unlabeled products of scalar types (e.g. int × int). Our focus is on functions that take as input elements of recursive variant (or sum) types denoted by $\tau, \theta, \dots$. We denote by $\kappa_1, \dots, \kappa_n$ the constructors of a variant type τ with n variants. Each constructor is assimilated to a terminal symbol $\tau_1 \times \dots \times \tau_k \rightarrow \tau$, where $k \geq 0$. We assume that all recursive types define finite structures, that is, one can always construct a term of type τ with a finite number of constructors and elements of base type. $x : \tau$ denotes the judgement x is of type τ, and $\forall x : \tau$ denotes the universal quantification of all variables x of type τ.

In this setting, where we distinguish base types and recursive types, we differentiate **bounded terms**, which are symbolic terms where all free variables are of base type (in $\mathcal{V}_B$), and **unbounded terms** where some variables can be of recursive type. An unbounded term t is a symbolic term of finite size, but there are infinitely many bounded terms that are expansions of t.

3   Formal Definition of the Synthesis Problem

The synthesis problem solved in this paper is defined by three components: a reference recursive function $f : \tau \rightarrow D$, a representation function $r : \theta \rightarrow \tau$ that maps inputs of the target function to those of f, and a recursion skeleton for the target function. All three components are formally modelled by recursion schemes (Definition 1). f and r are standard recursive functions representable by deterministic recursion schemes. The recursion scheme for the recursion skeleton $\mathcal{S}[\Xi] : \theta \rightarrow D$ includes a special set Ξ of symbols as a subset of its terminal symbols, which correspond to the unknown components for synthesis. These unknowns stand for constants or functions that have to be synthesized.

At the high level, the solution to the synthesis problem is the definition of a new recursive function. At the low level, each of the unknowns in Ξ need to be given a definition. In each problem instance, it is assumed that f and $\mathcal{S}[\Xi]$ use a common set of terminal symbols Σ that belong to a background theory $\mathcal{T}$ (e.g. linear integer arithmetic). Formally, the solution is identified by a mapping Z from the unknowns Ξ to function definitions $\lambda x_1. \ldots . \lambda x_n.t$ where $n \geq 0$ and t is a symbolic term in $T(\Sigma, \{x_1, \ldots, x_n\})$ (a concrete term if $n = 0$). Let $\mathcal{S}[\Xi/Z]$ be the recursion scheme obtained by replacing the unknowns Ξ by their definition in Z. Any solution Z that satisfies the following specification is a valid solution:

$$\Psi \equiv \forall x : \theta, \mathcal{S}[\Xi/Z](x) = (f \circ r)(x)$$

Example 1. We use a problem instance with the goal of synthesizing a recursive function on *tree paths* as a running example of this paper. Recall the `mips` function given in Fig. 1. Suppose that we want to transform it to a function on *tree paths*[1] as an alternative data type to labelled binary trees. For an A-labelled tree (of type *Tree*), *Path* is a datatype defined by the following grammar:

$$Path \rightarrow Top \mid Zip((\top|\bot), A, Tree, Path)$$

Intuitively, a path decomposes a tree as shown on the right. The path $Zip(\top, a, t_a, Zip(\bot, b, t_b, Zip(\top, c, t_c, x)))$, from the root to a leaf decomposes the tree into the subtrees t_a, t_b, and t_c.

The synthesis problem is specified by three recursion schemes. The recursion scheme f, on the right, models the function `mips` from Fig. 1. Λ_f is

$$f : \begin{cases} \Lambda_f\ t & \rightarrow G\ (0,0)\ t \\ G\ s\ Nil & \rightarrow s \\ G\ s\ Node(a,l,r) & \rightarrow G\ (L\ a\ (G\ s\ l))\ r \\ L\ a\ (s,m) & \rightarrow (s+a, max(s+a,m)) \end{cases}$$

the non-terminal corresponding to the main function `mips` and G is an auxiliary function. An additional non-terminal L is used to mirror the tuple decomposition done by the let-binding in the code of `mips`.

The second recursion scheme is the representation function r from paths to trees. The input path is recursively decomposed by the

$$r : \begin{cases} \Lambda_r\ Top & \rightarrow Nil \\ \Lambda_r\ Zip(\top, a, t, z) & \rightarrow Node(a, t, \Lambda_r\ z) \\ \Lambda_r\ Zip(\bot, a, t, z) & \rightarrow Node(a, \Lambda_r\ z, t) \end{cases}$$

rewrite rules, and *Node* is constructed recursively on the right or on the left depending on the first value contained in the *Zip* constructor.

The last recursion scheme specifies the recursion skeleton of the target function with un-

$$\mathcal{S}[s_0, g_l, g_r] : \begin{cases} \Lambda_\mathcal{S}\ Top & \rightarrow s_0 \\ \Lambda_\mathcal{S}\ Zip(\top, a, t, z) & \rightarrow g_l\ a\ (\Lambda_f\ t)\ (\Lambda_\mathcal{S}\ z) \\ \Lambda_\mathcal{S}\ Zip(\bot, a, t, z) & \rightarrow g_r\ a\ (\Lambda_f\ t)\ (\Lambda_\mathcal{S}\ z) \end{cases}$$

knowns s_0, g_l and g_r. It traverses the input path, making recursive calls $(\Lambda_\mathcal{S}\ z)$ on paths, and calling the reference function on subtrees $(\Lambda_f\ t)$. The goal is then to synthesize implementations of s_0, g_l and g_r such that $\mathcal{S}[s_0, g_l, g_r]$ is equivalent to $f \circ r$.

---

[1] This example is from [24], which calls this data type *zipper*.

4   Recursion-Free Approximations

A *system of recursion-free equations* models an approximation of the full functional specification Ψ for a recursive synthesis problem instance.

Definition 2. *Given two sets of terminals Σ and Ξ, a system of recursion-free
equations is a finite set of constraints $\{e_i = e'_i\}$ where $e, e' \in T(\Sigma \cup \Xi, \mathcal{V}_B)$.*

We denote by $\{e_i = e'_i\}_{i \in I}$ the set of constraints of the system, and $\{x_j\}_{1 \leq j \leq n} \equiv \bigcup_{i \in I} FV(e_i) \cup FV(e'_i)$ are the free variables in the system. The above system
defines a synthesis problem where Σ is the signature of some theory T and Ξ is
the set of unknowns to be synthesized. A solution Z to this synthesis problem
is a mapping from Ξ to function definitions. Z is valid iff the following formula
is *valid*:

$$\forall x_1 : D_1. \ldots. \forall x_n : D_n. \bigwedge_{i \in I} (e_i = e'_i)[\Xi/Z]$$

where $(e_i = e'_i)[\Xi/Z]$ denotes the term in which the unknowns Ξ have been
replaced by their definition in Z. In the rest of the paper, we consider systems of
recursion-free equations where the set of terminals Σ and the set of unknowns Ξ
are fixed and the same as in the main synthesis problem of Sect. 3. We say that
a system $\mathcal{E}'$ is a sound approximation of a system $\mathcal{E}$ ($\mathcal{E}' \gtrsim \mathcal{E}$) (or the synthesis
problem Ψ) when any solution of $\mathcal{E}$ (or Ψ) is also a solution of $\mathcal{E}'$.

4.1   Partially Bounded Quantification

Consider the formal definition of the synthesis problem in Sect. 3. Bounding the
quantifiers consists in expressing the problem on a finite set of bounded terms.
This bounding effectively eliminates recursion; recursive calls can be inlined a
bounded number of times. Yet, since the free variables of the bounded term are
universally quantified over an infinite base domain, a bounded term t of type θ
represents an infinite set of concrete inputs (of bounded size).

We propose a different strategy for bounding the quantifiers: we aim to
instantiate the quantifier on a finite set of bounded and *unbounded* terms such
that the resulting specification is not recursive. To start, we instantiate the universal quantifier by a finite set of arbitrary symbolic terms T. Our first approximation then becomes the set of constraints:

$$E(T) = \{\mathcal{S}[\Xi](t) = (f \circ r)(t) \mid t \in T\} \tag{1}$$

The set of constraints $E(T)$ can be seen as a synthesis problem where free
variables are universally quantified and the unknowns in Ξ are to be synthesized.
$E(T)$ is not guaranteed to be a system of recursion-free equations for all choices
of T. For an arbitrary symbolic term t, calls to recursive functions may appear in
subterms of $\mathcal{S}[\Xi](t)$ and $(f \circ r)(t)$. Restricting T to bounded terms would yield
a recursion-free system after symbolic evaluation of both sides of the equation.

This, however, is too restrictive. There may exist unbounded terms t where the equation $\mathcal{S}[\varXi](t) = (f \circ r)(t)$ can be *rewritten* to an equivalent recursion-free equation. Intuitively, in an applicative term (resulting from the symbolic evaluation of a recursive function f) the simple subterms of the form $f(x)$ where x is a variable can be eliminated by replacing $f(x)$ with a single variable a of type D which now stands for the result of the invocation of f on any x.

Definition 3. *A symbolic term t is maximally reducible (t is a MR-term) by a recursion scheme $\mathcal{P} = (\varSigma, \mathcal{N}, \mathcal{R}, \varLambda)$ iff $[\![t]\!]_{\mathcal{P}}$ is an applicative term in $T(\varSigma, \mathcal{N}, \mathcal{V})$ such that replacing all subterms of the form $(\varLambda\ x)$ (where $x \in \mathcal{V}$) by a fresh variable $x' \notin FV(t)$ yields a symbolic term.*

Example 2. The term $z = Zip(\top, a, t, Top)$ where a is an integer and t is of type *Tree* is maximally reducible by $f \circ r$ and $\mathcal{S}[s_0, g_l, g_r]$ (cf. Example 1). First we have $r(z) = [\![z]\!]_r = Node(a, t, Nil)$ and $(f \circ r)(z) = G\ (L\ a\ (\varLambda_f\ t))\ Nil$. If $\varLambda_f\ t$ is replaced by (a_1, a_2) (of type int $\times$ int), then the term can be reduced further to $(a_1 + a, max(a_1 + a, a_2))$. For the other function, we have $\mathcal{S}[s_0, g_l, g_r](z) = g_l\ a\ (\varLambda_f\ t)\ s_0$. If $\varLambda_f\ t$ is also replaced by (a_1, a_2), then the term reduces to the symbolic term $g_l\ a\ (a_1, a_2)\ s_0$. Note that z is an unbounded term, since t is a variable representing a tree of arbitrary depth.

If every term in T is maximally reducible by both $(f \circ r)$ and $\mathcal{S}[\varXi]$, then every call to a recursive function can be eliminated in $E(T)$. Note that this new *sufficient* condition for $E(T)$ to be recursion free is strictly weaker than the condition of having the terms in T to be bounded; a maximally reducible term need not be a bounded term.

Definition 4. *A set of constraints $E(T) = \{\mathcal{S}[\varXi](t) = (f \circ r)(t)\ |\, t \in T\}$ is well-formed iff every $t \in T$ is maximally reducible by $f \circ r$ and $\mathcal{S}[\varXi]$.*

A well-formed set of constraints $E(T)$ can be transformed to a system of recursion-free equations. For each free variable $x : \theta$ in $E(T)$, a fresh variable $a : D$ is added and the subterms $(f \circ r)(x)$ and $\mathcal{S}[\varXi](x)$ are replaced by a in every constraint. We call this rewriting step *recursion elimination* over D. Note that the calls to $f \circ r$ and $\mathcal{S}[\varXi]$ are both replaced by the same variable, since their equivalence is part of the specification of the synthesis problem.

The transformation described above produces a recursion-free system of equations, but it does not always yield a *sound abstraction*, specifically when $f \circ r$ is *not onto* D. There may exist a solution of $\varPsi$ that is not a solution of the resulting system of equations. This can be fixed by having additional constraints (invariants) on the fresh variables. Let $Im_f : D \to$ bool a predicate such that $f \circ r$ is onto $\{c\ |\ c : D \wedge Im_f(c)\}$. Then, the abstraction is sound if the choices for $a : D$ are limited to when $Im_f(a)$ holds.

Example 3. Recall Example 1. The maximum in-order prefix sum is not onto int $\times$ int, since the second element of the pair is always a positive integer. The constraint $Im_f(x, y) = y \geq 0$ is required to make the function onto. In Example 2, a_2 must be a positive integer.

Definition 5. *Let T be a set of maximally reducible terms by $f \circ r$ and $\mathcal{S}[\Xi]$, and Im_f a predicate such that $f \circ r$ is onto $\{c \mid c : D \wedge Im_f(c)\}$. We denote by $\mathcal{E}(T)$ the equation system obtained by rewriting each constraint in $E(T)$ to a recursion free equation, through recursion elimination over $\{c \mid c : D \wedge Im_f(c)\}$.*

In the synthesis problem defined by $\mathcal{E}(T)$, the variables introduced by recursion elimination are universally quantified over their restricted range. The exact encoding of the range restriction by Im_f depends on the implementation of a synthesis oracle.

Proposition 1. *Z is a solution of $\mathcal{E}(T)$ iff Z is a solution of $E(T)$.*

The proof follows from the construction of $\mathcal{E}(T)$ based on $E(T)$. Combining this with the fact that $E(T)$ results from bounding the universal quantifications in Ψ, we can conclude that $\mathcal{E}(T)$ approximates Ψ.

Theorem 1 (Sound approximation). *If T is a set of maximally reducible terms by $f \circ r$ and $\mathcal{S}[\Xi]$, $\mathcal{E}(T)$ is a sound approximation of Ψ.*

By construction, any solution of the functional specification Ψ is a solution of the system of equations $\mathcal{E}(T)$.

Example 4. Let $T = \{Top, Zip(\top, a, t, Top), Zip(\bot, a, Nil, z)\}$ be a set of terms, where $a : int$, $t : Tree$ and $z : Path$. Top is a concrete term, therefore maximally reducible. We saw in Example 2 that $Zip(\top, a, t, Top)$ is a MR-term. With a similar reasoning, one can conclude that $Zip(\bot, a, Nil, z)$ is a MR-term; note how the term differs in which subterm is unbounded depending on the first component of the Zip. Therefore, $E(T)$ is a well-formed set of constraints and by substituting $\Lambda_f\, t$ and $\Lambda_S\, z$ for (a_1, a_2) (where $a_1 : int$ and $a_2 \in \{v : int | v \geq 0\}$), we obtain the following recursion-free system of equations:

$$\mathcal{E}(T) = \begin{cases} 0, 0 = s_0, \\ a_1 + a, max(a_1 + a, a_2) = g_l\ a\ (a_1, a_2)\ s_0 \\ a_1 + a, max(a_1 + a, a_2) = g_r\ a\ s_0\ (a_1, a_2) \end{cases}$$

with free variables $a : int$, $a_1 : int$ and $a_2 \in \{v : int | v \geq 0\}$.

In contrast to a canonical CEGIS setting, where the approximation is the specification projected over a finite set of concrete terms, our abstraction is over an infinite set of concrete terms represented by a finite set of symbolic terms. In the original functional specification, the equational constraint $(f \circ r)(x) = \mathcal{S}[\Xi](x)$ ranges over all possible terms x of type θ. In the abstraction

$\mathcal{E}(T)$, the universally quantified variables are the free variables of the terms in the equations, which correspond to the variable symbols of scalar type used in the symbolic terms of T, modulo the introduction of fresh variables during the rewriting of the set of constraints $E(T)$ to the system of equations $\mathcal{E}(T)$.

4.2   Refining Systems of Equations

Our approximation, the system of equations $\mathcal{E}(T)$, is parametric on a set of maximally reducible terms T. This approximation can be refined by adding terms to T, since for any two set of terms R and T such that $R \subseteq T$, $\mathcal{E}(R) \gtrsim \mathcal{E}(T)$.

The convergence of the refinement process depends on the terms added at each step. We present our refinement algorithm in the next section, but the main insights behind it, not tied to specific algorithmic choices, are captured by Propositions 2 and 3.

Proposition 2. *Let T be a set of MR-terms and Z be a solution of $\mathcal{E}(T)$. Then for any term t' such that there exists $t \in T$ s.t $t \succeq t'$, Z is a solution of $\mathcal{E}(T \cup \{t'\})$.*

This proposition implies that if Z is a spurious solution, then a counterexample term showing that it is not a solution of Ψ is necessarily not expanded from a term in T. We also learn that T should ideally be an antichain of $\succeq$ at every refinement round, since adding expanded terms does not strengthen the approximation.

Proposition 3. *Given two terms t and t' such that $t \succeq t'$ (i.e. t' is an expansion of t) and a set of MR-terms T such that $\forall x \in T, \neg(x \succeq t \land t \succeq x)$, we have $\mathcal{E}(T \cup \{t\}) \precsim \mathcal{E}(T \cup \{t'\})$.*

Adding the less expanded term (i.e. t) yields both a more general approximation and a more compact one. In other words, given a choice, always choose the least expanded term as the counterexample for refinement.

5   Synthesis Algorithm

Our synthesis algorithm computes a sequence of approximations of the functional specification Ψ from Sect. 3. Each approximation is a system of equations of the form $\mathcal{E}(T)$ (Definition 5). The approximations are incrementally refined until the synthesis solution for one is also a valid solution for the synthesis problem specified by Ψ.

Figure 2 illustrates the work flow of our algorithm. At the beginning of each iteration, a solution of the system of recursion-free equations $\mathcal{E}(T)$ is synthesized. If no solution is found, then there is no solution for the original synthesis problem, since the $\mathcal{E}(T)$ is guaranteed to be a sound approximation (Theorem 1). If a solution Z is found, then Z is verified against Ψ and if it passes, then it is returned as a solution. Otherwise, the

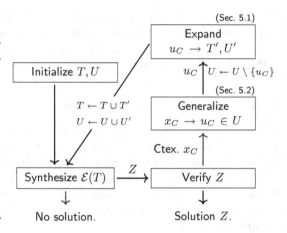

Fig. 2. Approximation refinement algorithm.

verifier returns a counterexample term x_C. By Proposition 2, x_C cannot be an expansion of any term in T, and new terms related to x_C have to be added to T in the spirit of refinement.

The algorithm additionally keeps track of a set U of non-maximally reducible terms, which intuitively represents the set of inputs not *covered* by the current approximation. The sets T and U are *complementary* in a precise sense: $T \cup U$ is always a *boundary of* $\succeq$. A boundary (of a partial order) is an antichain C such that for any bounded term t, there is some c in C such that $c \succeq t$.

The counterexample x_C is necessarily an expansion of some term $u_C \in U$. But since u_C is by definition not maximally reducible, one cannot just remove it from U and add it to T. The Expand step takes u_C as an input and produces two sets T' and U' to update the current sets T and U and repair the boundary before the loop restarts.

The figure on the right is a graphical representation of the boundary repair. The sets T (in blue) and U (in red) initially form a boundary. This boundary is updated by removing the term u_C and adding U' and T' (the results of the Expand step) to form a new boundary. The fact that $T \cup U$ always forms a boundary is a required invariant of this refinement loop: (i) T, as a parameter of $\mathcal{E}(T)$, is required to be an antichain (as discussed

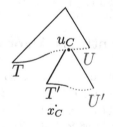

in Sect. 4.2), and (ii) the Generalize step relies on the assumption that U is an antichain containing all the terms not yet sufficiently expanded to be in T.

We rely on existing tools/techniques for the steps Synthesize and Verify of Fig. 2. In the following, we describe the Initialize, Expand, and Generalize steps of the algorithm.

Initialization. There is a straightforward way to initialize T and U: apply the Expand component to a single variable x of type θ and take the resulting sets T of maximally reducible terms and U of non-maximally reducible terms. The Expand step is described in the next section. For Example 1, a variable x of type *Path* is expanded to produce $T = \{Top\}$ and $U = \{Zip(\bot, a, t, z), Zip(\top, a, t, z)\}$ with variables a, t, and z of the appropriate types.

5.1 Expand : **Producing Maximally Reducible Terms**

Given an input term u_C, Expand generates two sets T' and U' such that the terms in T' are maximally reducible by both $f \circ r$ and $\mathcal{S}[\Xi]$. The computation of these terms is done by expanding the input term u_C until a set of maximally reducible terms is found. The algorithm on the right illustrates the process. At each step, a term u_0 is picked from the set of non-maximally reducible terms U'. This term is expanded once, by a call to EXPANDONCE (which is described later). The resulting set of terms is then partitioned into a set of maximally reducible terms T' and a set of non-maximally reducible terms U''; the latter is used to update U'.

$$
\begin{array}{|l|}
\hline
T' = \emptyset, U' = \{u_C\}; \\
\textbf{while } T' = \emptyset \textbf{ do} \\
\quad \text{Pick } u_0 \text{ in } U'; \\
\quad S = \mathsf{ExpandOnce}(u_0); \\
\quad T', U'' = \mathsf{Partition}(S); \\
\quad U' = (U' \setminus u_0) \cup U''; \\
\textbf{end} \\
\textbf{return } T', U' \\
\hline
\end{array}
$$

The choice of u_0 at the first line of the loop is important for the termination of the algorithm. There may be an infinite sequence of expansions if the u_0's are adversarially chosen. There always exists a finite sequence of expansions yielding bounded terms which are by definition maximally reducible. A breadth-first exploration of all expansions is one such strategy that ensures the termination of the algorithm.

ExpandOnce. The input of ExpandOnce is a term u_0 that is not maximally reducible. The following proposition characterizes u_0 and the reason for its non-reducibility:

Proposition 4. *Let $u_0 \in T(\Sigma, \mathcal{V})$ and $g = (\Sigma, \mathcal{N}, \mathcal{R}, \Lambda)$ a recursion scheme. u_0 is not maximally reducible by g iff there exists a subterm of $[\![u_0]\!]_g$ of the form $s = F \, t_1 \ldots t_n \, x$, where $F \in \mathcal{N}$ and $F \neq \Lambda$, the terms $t_1 \ldots t_n$ are applicative terms, and $x \in FV(u_0)$.*

The proof by cases on the subterms of u_0 is given in the extended version of this paper [7]. In order to take a step towards making u_0 maximally reducible, the variable x needs to be expanded. Expanding x into a term guarantees some rule $F \, x_1 \ldots x_n \, p \to t \in \mathcal{R}$ can be used to reduce u_0 further. Such a rule is guaranteed to exist for a recursion scheme representing a total function.

Next, we define how u_0 is expanded at a variable x identified by Proposition 4. u_0 can be written as $C[x]$ for some one-hole context $C[\ ]$. Assume the type β of x has constructors $\kappa_1, \ldots \kappa_n$ where each κ_i has type $\gamma_i \to \beta$. The *pointwise expansion* of u_0 at x is the set of terms $\{C[\kappa_1(x_1)], \ldots, C[\kappa_n(x_n)]\}$ where each x_i is a variable (or a tuple) of variables of type γ_i.

In summary, ExpandOnce first identifies a variable x in u_0 (Proposition 4) that needs to be expanded and then performs the *pointwise expansion* of u_0 at x and returns the resulting set of terms.

One important feature of ExpandOnce is that terms are expanded only where needed. Proposition 4 identifies the precise location (i.e. x) where expanding is necessary and ignores locations where it is not.

Example 5. Recall Example 1. Suppose $u_0 = Zip(\top, a, t, \underline{z})$ is a (symbolic) path and an input to ExpandOnce, where a is an integer, t is of type $Tree$, and z is of type $Path$. u_0 is not maximally reducible and has to be expanded. Note that $r(u_0) = Node(a, t, \Lambda_r \underline{z})$ and therefore $(f \circ r)(u_0) = G\ (L\ a\ (\Lambda_f\ t))\ (\Lambda_r\ \underline{z})$. The subterm $(\Lambda_r\ \underline{z})$ blocks the reduction of the term starting with G, because $\underline{z}$ blocks the reduction of $\Lambda_r\ \underline{z}$ and therefore, u_0 has to be expanded at $\underline{z}$. The pointwise expansion of u_0 at $\underline{z}$ yields the terms $u_1 = Zip(\top, a, t, \underline{Top})$, $u_2 = Zip(\top, a, t, \underline{Zip(\top, a', t', z')})$, and $u_3 = Zip(\top, a, t, \underline{Zip(\bot, a', t', z')})\}$. Note that the tree element t need not be expanded; we showed in Example 2 that u_1 is maximally reducible and therefore, the expansion loop stops and returns $T' = \{u_1\}$ and $U' = \{u_2, u_3\}$.

Consider the symmetric term $Zip(\bot, a, \underline{t}, z)$ acquired by replacing the $\top$ in u_0 with $\bot$. The expansion of this term yields $T' = Zip(\bot, a, \underline{Nil}, z)$ and $U' = \{Zi(\bot, a, \underline{Node(a', l, r)}, z)\}$. Note that unlike the case for u_0, the tree element of the path has to be expanded and the path element need not be expanded.

5.2   Counterexample Generalization

The generalization of the counterexample x_C is the unique term $u_C \in U$ such that $u_C \succeq x_C$. The term u_C is guaranteed to exist because the algorithm maintains the invariant that $T \cup U$ is a *boundary*, and it is unique since U is always an antichain.

Example 6. After initialization, the synthesis solver attempts to find a solution for the system of equations given in Example 4. One possible solution is

$$s_0 = (0, 0) \qquad g_l(a, (s_1, m_1), (s_2, m_2)) = a + s_1, max(m_1, a + s_1)$$

together with a similar solution for g_r. But the solution for g_l is incorrect; the first component should be $a + s_1 + s_2$ (i.e. the sum of both partial sums and the label of the node). The verifier returns a counterexample of the form $x_c = Zip(\top, 1, Node(?), Zip(\top, -2, Node(?), ?))$ where the question marks stand for concrete subterms of the appropriate type. These subterms are ignored. The counterexample is generalized by selecting $u_2 = Zip(\top, a, t, Zip(\top, a', t', z'))$ (where $u_2 \succeq x_C$), the term that was stored in U after the expansion described in Example 5. This determines where the algorithm must unfold the path one more time to build a stronger approximation.

We report in Sect. 7 that SYNDUCE succeeds in finding a solution for this example with 3 refinement rounds in 1.57 s, whereas the symbolic CEGIS (described in Sect. 1) times out after 10 min over 6 refinement rounds.

5.3   Algorithm Properties

Soundness. Under the assumption that the steps Synthesize and Verify are soundly implemented, the overall algorithm is sound. By construction, T is always a set of maximally reducible terms. Therefore, $\mathcal{E}(T)$ is a guaranteed to be a sound approximation of Ψ by Theorem 1. The soundness of the verification oracle guarantees that any returned solution is in fact a solution of the synthesis problem specified by Ψ.

Weak Progress. Consider the naive algorithm that would expand T by simply adding the counterexample x_C to it; x_C is a maximally reducible term after all. This naive algorithm satisfies a weak progress property, namely that, the spurious solution Z from any round will not be a solution in any future round. Our algorithm does something more sophisticated and therefore it has to be argued that the same weak progress property holds. First, Expand satisfies the following property that guarantees $T \cup U$ to always be a boundary:

Proposition 5. *Let t be some symbolic term and T', U' be the results of the call to $Expand(t)$. Then $T' \cup U'$ is a boundary of the set $\{t' | t \succeq t'\}$.*

Let u_C be the generalization of x_C. Proposition 5 guarantees that Expand computes and adds all possible expansions of u_C to T. This in turn implies that there always exists a term $t \succeq x_C$ in the updated set T (after the call to Expand), which rules x_C out as a spurious solution in all future rounds. Note that the algorithm relies on the existence of u_C in U. For this, it requires $T \cup U$ to be a boundary.

Parsimony. Finally, we can show that our algorithm is parsimonious with the selection of the terms for T in the following precise way:

Theorem 2. *[Parsimony] Let us assume (T, U) is a boundary that our algorithm reaches in some round, then (T, U) is optimal in the following two senses:*

- *for every $t \in T \cup U$ there is no MR-term t' such that $t' \succeq t$.*
- *there is no non-empty subset T' of T and set U' such that $(T \setminus T') \cup U'$ is a boundary and $\mathcal{E}(T \setminus T') \precsim \mathcal{E}(T)$.*

Intuitively, all the terms in T are expanded to the extent necessary and no proper subset of T can form a boundary that maintains the same precise approximation that $T \cup U$ induces. The full proof appears in [7].

6   Implementation

Our approach is implemented in SYNDUCE [36], a tool written in OCaml [22], and the inputs are recursive functions and datatypes written in Caml.

6.1   Verification and Synthesis Oracles

SYNDUCE uses bounded model checking to implement Verify from Fig. 2. A bounded check for the validity of a synthesis solution Z is encoded as the validity of the formula $\wedge_{t \in T} \forall a \in FV(t).\mathcal{S}[\Xi/Z](t) = (f \circ r)(t)$ for a set of *bounded* terms T. Z3 [25] is used as the backend SMT solver, which produces a counterexample in the form of a term for which at least one equality constraint is invalid.

SYNDUCE spends most of its time in the Synthesize box of Fig. 2. Since the input to Synthesize is guaranteed to be a recursion-free synthesis specification, any off-the-shelf syntax-guided synthesis (SyGuS) [4] solver that supports the standard language [29] can be used to implement Synthesize. We use CVC4 [5] for the results presented in this section.

A SyGuS problem is specified by a grammar describing the space of programs to be synthesized and a set of constraints. In this case, the grammar is generated from the type of the functions to be synthesized (the unknowns in Ξ), which can be inferred from the constraints where they appear. Instances of generic grammars for integers and booleans can be found in the SyGuS language specification [29], and these grammars for base types can be combined into tuples in a straightforward manner. The constraints are the equations of the system, with the addition of the predicates constraining the domain of the variables, i.e. Im_f from Definition 5. Each recursion-free equation $e = e'$ is translated to a constraint of the form $\neg(\bigwedge_{v \in FV(e) \cup FV(e')} Im_f(v)) \vee e = e'$ where $Im_f(v)$ is the predicate associated to the variable v.

6.2   Baseline Method

The goal of our experimentation is to evaluate the efficiency and efficacy of the proposed partial quantifier bounding approach for synthesis of recursive programs. Since there is no available (automated) tool that solves the specific problem posed in this paper, we implemented the symbolic CEGIS technique (as outlined in Sect. 1) to serve as a *baseline*. To be precise, the algorithm of Fig. 2 is modified by removing the Generalize and Expand steps; the symbolic counterexample returned by the verification at each step is added directly to the set of terms instead of being generalized. The set T is also initialized as a set of bounded terms of some minimal depth, depending on the particular definition of the data type. Note that since the baseline method is counterexample-guided, it is better than the more straightforward finitization techniques, for example, manual finitization by a preset bound.

We also implemented the concrete CEGIS method (outlined in Sect. 1) to confirm that the symbolic CEGIS is the better choice. Symbolic CEGIS solves 6 more benchmarks than concrete CEGIS, and does better time-wise in the vast majority of the rest. Detailed results are given in the extended version of this paper [7].

6.3 Optimizations

We implemented a few simple, straightforward and generic (i.e. they can be incorporated in any SyGuS solver) optimizations. These aim to compensate for the brittleness of the SyGuS solvers, which can fail for very simple constraints for no good reason. Here is a brief overview of these optimizations, which are applicable to any system of equations (baseline's and ours):

- *Syntactic definitions*, which are those that define an unknown function ξ unequivocally in the form of $\xi(x_1, \ldots, x_n) = t$, can be identified quickly and eliminated from the synthesis task to simplify it.
- A system of equations can be split into *independent subsystems* by identifying an independent subsets of equations. A subset of equations is independent if it constrains a subset of the unknowns that does not appear in the rest of the set of equations. Identification of independent subsystems generates simpler subproblems.
- Instead of starting from a default initial state, we can start from a set of terms that makes for an interesting first round and consequently saves a few refinement rounds from the solution. We form a set of initial terms by using the Expand routine to expand enough terms such that each unknown appears in at least one constraint in the approximation for the first round.

These optimizations are applied to both the baseline method and our algorithm for the purpose of evaluation. The extended version of this paper [7] includes more detailed evaluation of them and experimental results illustrating their precise impact on each algorithm.

7 Evaluation

We evaluate SYNDUCE on a broad set of benchmarks. Our benchmarks are grouped into six categories. Table 1 lists all the benchmarks, grouped accordingly. Each category, shares the same representation function and *polymorphic* recursion skeleton, but a different reference implementation is used to specify the synthesis problem. The recursion skeletons (and the representation functions) are polymorphic and therefore reusable. Only 9 different skeletons and 4 different representation functions were used across our 43 benchmarks. More details about the benchmarks, including the simple 9 utilized skeletons, appear in the extended version of this paper [7].

7.1 Case Studies

Changing Tree Traversals. An example of this category is the mips example used in the introduction. The reference function is a natural implementation of a function with a post- or in-order traversal of a binary tree. The target is an equivalent implementation corresponding to the divide-and-conquer tree homomorphism style recursion.

From Trees to Paths. A tree path (zipper in [24]) is a data structure used to represent a tree together with a subtree that is the focus of attention. Our running example belongs in this category. The other benchmarks in this category are from [24].

Enforcing Tail Recursion. In this category, the reference implementation is a direct-style recursion on the data structure, while the recursion skeleton specifies that an accumulator should be used to make the function tail-recursive. Tail recursive functions generally compile to more efficient code.

Combining Traversals. Suppose a collection of existing implementations computes different functions with different traversals of the same data structure. If in some larger context all of these functions need to be computed, *combining* them can lower the amortized cost. In this set of benchmarks, we synthesize automatically the implementation that corresponds to traversing the data structure with a single recursion strategy, combining the computations into one.

Tree Flattening. These benchmarks target the synthesis of an implementation on the more complex *plane tree* data structure from a reference implementation on the simpler binary tree data structure.

Parallelizing Functions on Lists. Parallelizing a function on lists can be seen as the translation of a recursive function on cons-lists to a homomorphic function on lists built with the concatenation operator. These benchmarks are from [8,9,23].

7.2   Experimental Results

To best of our knowledge, there are no available tools that can be directly compared against SYNDUCE. We can transform our specification to a format that can be accepted by LEON [18]. However, the latter does not succeed in solving even the simplest of our benchmarks (e.g. *sum* in the list function parallelization category), likely due to the fact that the required deductive rules are missing. We comment on the rest of the available tools in Sect. 8.

Table 1 presents the results of comparing SYNDUCE against the baseline method. Both techniques use symbolic counterexamples, and therefore, the comparison can highlight the performance impact of our partial bounding algorithm. The most important point of comparison is the overall synthesis time. In 9 out of 43 benchmarks, the baseline method times out. In another 5 cases, it outperforms the baseline by two orders of magnitude. In the easiest of the benchmarks, i.e. when the overall synthesis time of the baseline is in tens of milliseconds, the two methods are equally good within a small margin of error. The bold number in each row highlights the fastest synthesis time.

Amongst the 9 benchmarks for which the baseline algorithm times out, 7 are cases where SYNDUCE takes advantage of partial bounding by leaving some quantifiers unbounded. The baseline algorithm in these cases requires more terms and terms of higher complexity in the finite approximations. Two of the 9 benchmarks (*post-order mps* and *sum + mts + mps*) are cases where the set of maximally

Table 1. Experimental Results. Benchmarks are grouped by categories introduced in Sect. 7.1. # steps indicates the number of refinement rounds. T_{last} is the elapsed time before the last call to the SyGuS solver in the last refinement step before timeout. All times are in seconds. The best time is highlighted in bold font. A '-' indicates timeout (> 10 min). The "Inv" column indicates if codomain constraints were required. Experiments are run on a laptop with 16G memory and an i7-8750H 6-core CPU at 2.20 GHz running Ubuntu 19.10.

Class	Benchmark	Inv.	SYNDUCE			Baseline Method		
			time	# steps	T_{last}	time	# steps	T_{last}
Changing Tree Traversals	sum	no	**0.03**	2	0.01	0.04	3	0.02
	max	no	**0.33**	1	0.00	0.34	2	0.01
	max 2	no	**0.25**	1	0.00	0.34	2	0.01
	min	no	**0.23**	1	0.00	0.32	2	0.01
	min-max	no	**0.85**	3	0.15	73.16	3	0.06
	max weighted path	no	0.09	3	0.03	**0.07**	3	0.02
	sorted in-order	no	**0.01**	1	0.00	43.97	4	1.98
	pre-order poly.	no	**16.09**	2	0.06	-	4	0.97
	mips	yes	**0.29**	2	0.04	-	4	2.70
	in-order mts	yes	**0.41**	2	0.04	-	4	4.84
	post-order mps	yes	**132.14**	4	82.56	-	6	39.29
From Tree to Path	sum	no	0.07	2	0.02	**0.06**	3	0.02
	height	no	**0.90**	1	0.00	1.24	5	0.43
	max weighted path	no	0.15	2	0.03	**0.12**	3	0.03
	max w. path (hom)	no	**0.01**	1	0.00	1.42	4	0.69
	leftmost odd	no	**0.01**	1	0.00	-	4	0.27
	mips	yes	**1.57**	3	0.50	-	7	322.45
Enforcing Tail Recursion	sum	no	**0.02**	2	0.01	0.03	3	0.02
	mts	no	**5.86**	2	0.02	115.58	3	0.06
	mps	no	1.68	2	0.02	**0.34**	3	0.03
Combining Traversals	mts + sum	no	9.71	2	0.02	**5.42**	3	0.03
	sum + mts + mps	yes	**0.26**	3	0.12	-	3	0.04
Tree Flattening	sum	no	**0.07**	3	0.04	0.07	2	0.01
	product	no	**0.07**	2	0.01	0.16	2	0.01
	max of heads	no	0.21	2	0.02	**0.18**	3	0.03
	max of lasts	no	**0.21**	2	0.02	0.33	3	0.03
	max sibling sum	no	5.26	2	0.03	**2.72**	3	0.04
Parallelizing Functions on Lists	sum	no	**0.08**	1	0.00	0.30	3	0.04
	sum of even elts.	no	**0.10**	1	0.00	0.39	3	0.04
	length	no	**0.07**	1	0.00	0.22	4	0.05
	last	no	**0.01**	1	0.00	0.03	2	0.01
	product	no	**0.07**	1	0.00	0.31	3	0.04
	polynomial	no	**0.07**	1	0.00	0.71	5	0.10
	hamming	no	**0.10**	1	0.00	0.46	3	0.04
	min	no	**0.02**	1	0.00	0.08	2	0.01
	is sorted	no	3.45	2	0.11	**3.12**	4	0.14
	linear search	no	**0.08**	1	0.00	0.35	3	0.04
	line of sight	no	**0.86**	2	0.09	7.67	4	0.34
	mts	yes	**0.10**	1	0.00	4.80	4	0.08
	mps	yes	**0.09**	1	0.00	4.73	4	0.08
	mts and mps combined	yes	**0.38**	2	0.11	210.84	6	36.77
	mss	yes	**4.82**	3	1.53	-	6	24.23
	count max elements	no	**138.20**	1	0.00	-	3	0.46

reducible terms is exactly the set of bounded terms (i.e. one cannot take advantage of partial bounding), but SYNDUCE still outperforms the baseline because it adds smaller terms to the abstraction through generalization and produces less complex problems for the backend synthesis oracle. In summary, both counterexample generalization and the partial bounding yield big practical advantages in comparison with the baseline symbolic CEGIS algorithm.

It is noteworthy that whenever an instance is hard, the majority of the time is spent in the Synthesize step. This becomes nearly 100% of the time for the baseline algorithm whenever it times out. The weakness of the baseline method lies in the fact that the recursion-free instances generated by it are too difficult to solve by the backend solver. The timeout occurs within a few refinement rounds (at most 7) when the baseline algorithm gets stuck in the Synthesize step attempting to solve a prohibitively difficult recursion-free synthesis instance.

Across all benchmarks, our algorithm generally requires fewer refinement rounds than the baseline method. The few exceptions are the cases where the synthesis oracle gets lucky in producing a good solution when the target programs are very simple, for example in the case of the *sum* and *product* benchmarks of the flat tree category.

Finally, to isolate the precise contribution of the partial bounding idea, we evaluated the effect of each optimization on each algorithm. The applicability of a particular optimization highly depends on the particular set of constraints, which in turn depends on the specific benchmark and the algorithm (ours vs baseline) producing the constraints. Our synthesis algorithm yields more general and more succinct constraints, to which the optimizations are more often applicable. Of the 9 cases where Synduce succeeds and the baseline method times out, 7 are due to the inapplicability of these (simple) optimizations. SYNDUCE outperforms the baseline algorithm with all optimizations turned off for both. The detailed results are given in the extended version of this paper [7].

8   Related Work

Synthesizing recursive programs is a challenging task, and several automated techniques have tackled the problem with different specifications of the problem and different approaches to the solution.

Finitization, for example by bounding the depth of unbounded inputs or the number of recursive calls or loop iterations, is a straightforward way of dealing with unboundedness in synthesis [4,37] and verification [10]. In [32,33], high-level synthesis techniques use domain specific knowledge to finitize input programs. Quantifier instantiation, i.e. replacing quantified terms with ground terms, is commonly used in theorem proving and verification, and has also been useful in synthesis [31]. Our proposed algorithm can be viewed in the spirit of quantifier instantiation, with the major difference that (universally) quantified terms are replaced with other (universally) quantified terms which are still over an unbounded domain, yet with fewer degrees of freedom in unboundedness.

Synthesis through Program Transformation. Our precise problem statement is inspired by the transformation system developed by Burstall and Darlington [6]. They set to automate the task of transforming an initial program specified as a set of first-order recursion equations into a more efficient program, by altering the recursive structure. Their approach is based on transformation rules and semi-automatic. They use specific rules, e.g. *associativity* of a data operation, to perform the transformations and such rules do not generalize well. We defer the reasoning about the operations on the data to an SMT solver, and therefore need not rely on such rules. Techniques based on program transformation have been applied to the synthesis of special classes of recursive programs before [13, 15]. For example, the work in [1] focuses on tail recursion and a lot of attention has been given to producing divide-and-conquer recursions in the way of automated parallelization [2, 8, 23].

Synthesizing Recursive Functional Programs. Inductive techniques were developed to construct recursive programs from input/output examples [35], and this approach has been extended in more recent work [16, 17]. The latter two are examples of an analytical approach to program synthesis in which programs are constructed from the analysis of examples. Other recent approaches are search-based methods. ESCHER [3] synthesizes recursive functions from user-provided components by interactively asking for more examples from the user. λ^2 [11] synthesizes data structure transformations from input/output examples using higher-order functions.

Tools like λ^2 and ESCHER can be complementary to SYNDUCE in a more general context of recursion synthesis. The user can try to synthesize an implementation of a recursive function over a *simple* data type using λ^2 or ESCHER using input/output examples with a higher chance of success. This then serves as the reference implementation input to SYNDUCE which can aim for a more sophisticated implementation over a more complex recursive datatype.

MYTH [27], MYTH2 [12] and SYNQUID [28] use type information to direct the search for a program satisfying a specification. In MYTH, this specification is a set of input/output examples. MYTH2 generalizes this approach by treating examples as limited types. The specification for SYNQUID is a polymorphic refinement type, and the tool synthesizes an implementation of the given type using components provided by the user. Type-based approaches work well within the expressivity of refinement-types as specifications, but refinement types cannot express constraints for all desired synthesis tasks. Our specification is strictly stronger than both input/output examples and refinement types.

In SYNTREC [14], reusable templates are used to facilitate the synthesis of algebraic data type (ADT) transformations. The reusable templates are meant to lessen the burden of the user in specifying the search space of the programs to be synthesized every time. The recursion skeletons in our framework are effectively (reusable) polymorphic recursion templates. The user can be provided with a library of common recursive datatypes with representation functions mapping between these types, and useful recursion skeletons on these datatypes. SYNTREC [14] synthesizes ADT transformations from a functional specification. In contrast, our tool takes this transformation as input (the representation function) and synthesizes a function from ADT to a base type.

LEON [18], a deductive verification and synthesis framework, can synthesize recursive functions from first-order specifications with recursive predicates. In Sect. 7, we commented on a comparison of LEON against SYNDUCE.

Higher-Order Recursion Schemes. We use recursion schemes as a model for our programs, but our contribution has very little to do with the original work introducing this model. Higher-order recursion schemes have been introduced for model checking functional programs [19–21,30]. Pattern matching recursion schemes, introduced in [26], provide a model for functional programs that manipulate ADTs. We use them as an accurate description of a class of functions on ADTs and the notion of reduction associated with them as a crisp way of formulating symbolic evaluation.

9   Discussion and Future Work

We have demonstrated that partial bounding of quantifiers can be a powerful tool for the synthesis of recursive programs. Circumventing the unnecessary bounding of some quantifiers leads to simpler instances of recursion-free synthesis subtasks that can be handled by the current tools. Moreover, our counterexample generalization also yields simpler terms for bounding the quantifiers that have to be bounded. This is the result of our focus being on a class of recursive functions that perform structural recursion (i.e. recursion that deconstructs its inputs). This, together with our specific problem setup, takes the guesswork out of counterexample generalization and provides the means for a *constructive* counterexample generalization scheme which is demonstrably effective.

The reliance on structural recursion, therefore, limits the class of reference implementations and recursion skeletons that can define an acceptable synthesis instance in our framework. Another limitation tied to the input model is that the output of the recursive functions has to belong to the base (non-recursive) types to accommodate the reduction of the problem to one that can be solved by a backend solver. Consequently, the unknowns in a target recursion scheme have to all be functions from base types to base types.

In our problem setup, the recursion strategy (given by the recursion skeleton) is an integral part of the specification since it is used to communicate programmer intent. Expecting a *complete* recursion skeleton may be viewed as another limitation of our technique. For example, the mts (maximal tail sum) function can be computed as function on a list maintaining only one integer value (i.e. the current value of the maximum tail sum), yet, to implement mts in a divide-and-conquer strategy, another computation, the sum of the elements of the list, has to be performed alongside this one. It would be great if the user can ask for a divide-and-conquer recursion strategy without having to know that the additional computation of sum is required as well.

Ideally, the user should be permitted to provide an *incomplete* recursion skeleton which sufficiently communicates the intent and leave the recursion skeleton to be completed automatically by the synthesis procedure. This is a tricky problem. There are not only many recursion strategies to choose from, but each choice also leads to unboundedly many ways to organize the computation on data. This adds yet another dimension of unboundedness to the synthesis problem beyond the two already tackled in this paper. Note that in other recursion synthesis work such as [3,12,14,28], new operations on data are not synthesized, and in contrast drawn from an existing pool of operations. Therefore, this particular problem does not apply in those contexts.

Finally, our method currently does not take into account invariants over recursive data types, e.g. an invariant that specifies that a tree is a binary search tree. Some properties of the datatypes can be encoded through the representation function, e.g. the associativity of the concatenation operator in the category of list parallelization benchmarks. Incorporating the more general invariants in future work will broaden the expressivity of the framework in handling more interesting problems.

References

1. Abrahamsson, O., Myreen, M.O.: Automatically introducing tail recursion in CakeML. In: Wang, M., Owens, S. (eds.) TFP 2017. LNCS, vol. 10788, pp. 118–134. Springer, Cham (2018). https://doi.org/10.1007/978-3-319-89719-6_7
2. Ahmad, M.B.S., Cheung, A.: Automatically leveraging MapReduce frameworks for data-intensive applications. In: Proceedings of the 2018 International Conference on Management of Data, SIGMOD 2018. ACM (2018)
3. Albarghouthi, A., Gulwani, S., Kincaid, Z.: Recursive program synthesis. In: Sharygina, N., Veith, H. (eds.) CAV 2013. LNCS, vol. 8044, pp. 934–950. Springer, Heidelberg (2013). https://doi.org/10.1007/978-3-642-39799-8_67
4. Alur, R., et al.: Syntax-guided synthesis. In: 2013 Formal Methods in Computer-Aided Design, pp. 1–8. IEEE (2013)
5. Barrett, C., et al.: CVC4. In: Gopalakrishnan, G., Qadeer, S. (eds.) CAV 2011. LNCS, vol. 6806, pp. 171–177. Springer, Heidelberg (2011). https://doi.org/10.1007/978-3-642-22110-1_14
6. Burstall, R.M., Darlington, J.: A transformation system for developing recursive programs. J. ACM **24**(1), 44–67 (1977)
7. Farzan, A., Nicolet, V.: Counterexample-guided partial bounding for recursive function synthesis (Extended Version). https://www.cs.toronto.edu/~azadeh/resources/papers/cav21-extended.pdf
8. Farzan, A., Nicolet, V.: Synthesis of divide and conquer parallelism for loops. In: Proceedings of the 38th ACM Conference on Programming Language Design and Implementation, PLDI 2017 (2017)
9. Fedyukovich, G., Ahmad, M.B.S., Bodik, R.: Gradual synthesis for static parallelization of single-pass array-processing programs. In: Proceedings of the 38th ACM Conference on Programming Language Design and Implementation, PLDI 2017 (2017)
10. Feldman, Y.M.Y., Padon, O., Immerman, N., Sagiv, M., Shoham, S.: Bounded quantifier instantiation for checking inductive invariants. In: Legay, A., Margaria, T. (eds.) TACAS 2017. LNCS, vol. 10205, pp. 76–95. Springer, Heidelberg (2017). https://doi.org/10.1007/978-3-662-54577-5_5

11. Feser, J.K., Chaudhuri, S., Dillig, I.: Synthesizing data structure transformations from input-output examples. In: Proceedings of the 36th ACM Conference on Programming Language Design and Implementation, PLDI 2015 (2015)
12. Frankle, J., Osera, P.M., Walker, D., Zdancewic, S.: Example-directed synthesis: a type-theoretic interpretation. In: Proceedings of the 43rd ACM Symposium on Principles of Programming Languages, POPL 2016 (2016)
13. Hamilton, G.W., Jones, N.D.: Distillation with labelled transition systems. In: Proceedings of the ACM 2012 Workshop on Partial Evaluation and Program Manipulation, pp. 15–24. PEPM 2012. ACM (2012)
14. Inala, J.P., Polikarpova, N., Qiu, X., Lerner, B.S., Solar-Lezama, A.: Synthesis of recursive ADT transformations from reusable templates. In: Legay, A., Margaria, T. (eds.) TACAS 2017. LNCS, vol. 10205, pp. 247–263. Springer, Heidelberg (2017). https://doi.org/10.1007/978-3-662-54577-5_14
15. Itzhaky, S., et al.: Deriving divide-and-conquer dynamic programming algorithms using solver-aided transformations. In: Proceedings of the 2016 ACM Conference on Object-Oriented Programming, Systems, Languages, and Applications, pp. 145–164. ACM (2016)
16. Katayama, S.: An analytical inductive functional programming system that avoids unintended programs. In: Proceedings of the 2012 Workshop on Partial Evaluation and Program Manipulation, PEPM 2012 (2012)
17. Kitzelmann, E., Schmid, U.: Inductive synthesis of functional programs: an explanation based generalization approach. J. Mach. Learn. Res. 7(15), 429–454 (2006)
18. Kneuss, E., Kuraj, I., Kuncak, V., Suter, P.: Synthesis modulo recursive functions. In: Proceedings of the 2013 International Conference on Object Oriented Programming Systems Languages & Applications, OOPSLA 2013 (2013)
19. Kobayashi, N.: Types and higher-order recursion schemes for verification of higher-order programs. In: Proceedings of the 36th ACM Symposium on Principles of Programming Languages, POPL 2009 (2009)
20. Kobayashi, N., Sato, R., Unno, H.: Predicate abstraction and CEGAR for higher-order model checking. In: Proceedings of the 32nd ACM Conference on Programming Language Design and Implementation, pp. 222–233, PLDI 2011 (2011)
21. Kobayashi, N., Tabuchi, N., Unno, H.: Higher-order multi-parameter tree transducers and recursion schemes for program verification. In: Proceedings of the 37th ACM Symposium on Principles of Programming Languages, POPL 2010 (2010)
22. Leroy, X., Doligez, D., Frisch, A., Garrigue, J., Rémy, D., Vouillon, J.: The OCaml system release 4.11: Documentation and user's manual, p. 823 (2019)
23. Morihata, A., Matsuzaki, K.: Automatic parallelization of recursive functions using quantifier elimination. In: Proceedings of the 10th International Conference on Functional and Logic Programming, FLOPS 2010 (2010)
24. Morihata, A., Matsuzaki, K., Hu, Z., Takeichi, M.: The third homomorphism theorem on trees: downward & upward lead to divide-and-conquer. In: Proceedings of the 36th ACM Symposium on Principles of Programming Languages, POPL 2009 (2009)
25. de Moura, L., Bjørner, N.: Z3: an efficient SMT solver. In: Ramakrishnan, C.R., Rehof, J. (eds.) TACAS 2008. LNCS, vol. 4963, pp. 337–340. Springer, Heidelberg (2008). https://doi.org/10.1007/978-3-540-78800-3_24
26. Ong, C.H.L., Ramsay, S.J.: Verifying higher-order functional programs with pattern-matching algebraic data types. In: Proceedings of the 38th ACM Symposium on Principles of Programming Languages, POPL 2011 (2011)

27. Osera, P.M., Zdancewic, S.: Type-and-example-directed Program Synthesis. In: Proceedings of the 36th ACM Conference on Programming Language Design and Implementation, PLDI 2015 (2015)
28. Polikarpova, N., Kuraj, I., Solar-Lezama, A.: Program synthesis from polymorphic refinement types. In: Proceedings of the 37th ACM Conference on Programming Language Design and Implementation, PLDI 2016 (2016)
29. Raghothaman, M., Reynolds, A., Udupa, A.: The SyGuS Language Standard Version 2.0, p. 22 (2019)
30. Ramsay, S.J., Neatherway, R.P., Ong, C.H.L.: A type-directed abstraction refinement approach to higher-order model checking. In: Proceedings of the 41st ACM Symposium on Principles of Programming Languages, POPL 2014 (2014)
31. Reynolds, A., Deters, M., Kuncak, V., Tinelli, C., Barrett, C.: Counterexample-guided quantifier instantiation for synthesis in SMT. In: Kroening, D., Păsăreanu, C.S. (eds.) CAV 2015. LNCS, vol. 9207, pp. 198–216. Springer, Cham (2015). https://doi.org/10.1007/978-3-319-21668-3_12
32. Solar-Lezama, A., Arnold, G., Tancau, L., Bodik, R., Saraswat, V., Seshia, S.: Sketching stencils. In: Proceedings of the 28th ACM Conference on Programming Language Design and Implementation, PLDI 2007 (2007)
33. Solar-Lezama, A., Jones, C.G., Bodik, R.: Sketching concurrent data structures. In: Proceedings of the 29th ACM Conference on Programming Language Design and Implementation, PLDI 2008 (2008)
34. Solar-Lezama, A., Tancau, L., Bodik, R., Seshia, S., Saraswat, V.: Combinatorial sketching for finite programs. In: Proceedings of the 12th International Conference on Architectural Support for Programming Languages and Operating Systems, pp. 404–415, ASPLOS XII (2006)
35. Summers, P.D.: A methodology for LISP program construction from examples. J. ACM **24**(1), 161–175 (1977)
36. Victor, N.: Synduce. https://github.com/victornicolet/Synduce
37. Yang, W., Fedyukovich, G., Gupta, A.: Lemma synthesis for automating induction over algebraic data types. In: Schiex, T., de Givry, S. (eds.) CP 2019. LNCS, vol. 11802, pp. 600–617. Springer, Cham (2019). https://doi.org/10.1007/978-3-030-30048-7_35

PAYNT: A Tool for Inductive Synthesis of Probabilistic Programs

Roman Andriushchenko[1], Milan Češka[1(✉)], Sebastian Junges[2],
Joost-Pieter Katoen[3], and Šimon Stupinský[1]

[1] Brno University of Technology, Brno, Czech Republic
ceskam@fit.vutbr.cz
[2] University of California, Berkeley, USA
[3] RWTH Aachen University, Aachen, Germany

Abstract. This paper presents PAYNT, a tool to automatically synthesise probabilistic programs. PAYNT enables the synthesis of finite-state probabilistic programs from a program sketch representing a finite family of program candidates. A tight interaction between inductive oracle-guided methods with state-of-the-art probabilistic model checking is at the heart of PAYNT. These oracle-guided methods effectively reason about all possible candidates and synthesise programs that meet a given specification formulated as a conjunction of temporal logic constraints and possibly including an optimising objective. We demonstrate the performance and usefulness of PAYNT using several case studies from different application domains; e.g., we find the optimal randomized protocol for network stabilisation among 3M potential programs within minutes, whereas alternative approaches would need days to do so.

1 Introduction

Probabilistic programs are a powerful modelling language to describe systems containing probabilistic uncertainty. Their correctness and efficiency can be described as a set of declarative temporal constraints. Various verification tools cater for automating their a posterior verification: does a program satisfy a specification? Here, we focus on finite-state programs and consider specifications given as (conjunction of) temporal logic constraints. The automated verification of such constraints is supported by probabilistic model checkers such as STORM [19], PRISM [35] or MODEST [27].

These model checkers typically require a fixed program or a fixed model. This is not always in line with their intended usage: To keep development costs manageable and development cycles fast, system designs are preferably verified as

This work has been partially supported by the Czech Science Foundation grant GJ20-02328Y and the ERC AdG Grant 787914 FRAPPANT, NSF grants 1545126, 1646208 and 1837132, DARPA contracts FA8750-18-C-0101 (AA), FA8750-20-C-0156 (SDCPS), by Berkeley Deep Drive, and by Toyota under the iCyPhy center.

A. Silva and K. R. M. Leino (Eds.) CAV 2021, LNCS 12759, pp. 856–869, 2021.
https://doi.org/10.1007/978-3-030-81685-8_40

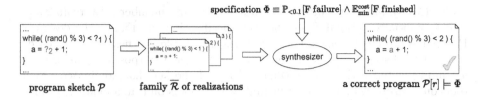

Fig. 1. The workflow of the synthesis process.

early as possible. However, at early design stages not all system details are known or they are deliberately left out, and systems or their models are incomplete—they contain holes. A hole may e.g., reflect a partially implemented controller for a complex system or an unspecified component for wireless communication.

A key aspect of the design cycle is to explore these designs, i.e., to do *design space exploration*. The verification challenge now is to analyze all combinations of fixing the hole with a concrete behavior/subsystem and reveal (Pareto-)optimal designs. Alternatively, designs should be robust for engineering choices made downstream, e.g., a system should ideally not depend on the specific characteristics of a single communication interface. Verifying that every combination of options satisfies the specification ensures that changes in available components do not need to trigger a redesign.

The application areas above require to reason about the presence and absence of designs (aka: realizations) satisfying a specification in a family of designs. To allow for efficient reasoning it is crucial that this family is concisely represented. A convenient way to describe such a family is to use *sketching* [2,45]. A sketch can be thought of as a program (or model) with holes, naturally fitting the use case outlined above.

Clearly, enumerating single realizations is unfeasible in the light of the combinatorial *design space explosion*. Instead, the prevalent approach connected with sketching is based on inductive synthesis. The idea is to analyze a single realization and generalize the analysis results to a set of realizations, often using the notion of counterexamples. In probabilistic programs, such a notion is challenging, as counterexamples are typically complex objects [1].

Driven by a range of applications, there has been significant algorithmic progress in the analysis of probabilistic program sketches and temporal logic constraints over the last years. Baier *et al.* [14] explored the use of symbolic model-checking methods so as to consider sets of realizations at once. Češka *et al.* [12] used abstraction-refinement on sets of realizations and complemented this with a counterexample-guided inductive synthesis approach [11]. The latter two approaches have recently been integrated [3] and yield a speed up of multiple orders of magnitude over a baseline that enumerates all realizations.

This paper presents PAYNT[1] (Probabilistic progrAm sYNThesizer) that takes a program sketch, concisely describing a finite family of finite Markov

---

[1] Available at https://github.com/gargantophob/synthesis.

chains (MCs), and a specification, and finds a family member (aka: realization) that (potentially optimally) satisfies the specification, see Fig. 1. The design of PAYNT is rooted in oracle-guided synthesis and enables the flexible combination of a variety of state-of-the-art algorithms. For efficiency purposes, key algorithms are implemented within the STORM [19] model checker that dominated recent tool comparisons [24]. To deliver flexibility, the tool is built in a modular fashion on top of a python API. To ease the learning curve, the tool takes a conservative extension to the widespread PRISM language as input.

PAYNT aims at two user groups: First, it provides a development platform for alternative algorithmic approaches, e.g. exploiting recent neurosymbolic approaches to find good designs. The tool provides the interface to define sketches and all baseline algorithms under one roof. Secondly, the analysis of sets of realizations is a valuable backend for automatic engines, e.g., when synthesizing finite-state controllers for partially observable MDPs (POMDPs) [33].

Related work. The synthesis problems for parametric probabilistic systems can be divided into two categories.

Topology synthesis, akin to aim of PAYNT, assumes a finite set of parameters affecting the MC topology. Finding a realization satisfying a given reachability property is NP-complete in the number of parameters [13], and can be naively solved by analysing all individual family members. An alternative [14] is to model the MC family by a Markov decision process (MDP) and use off-the-shelf MDP model-checking algorithms. The ProFeat [14] and QFLan [47] tool take this approach to quantitatively analyze alternative designs of software product lines [23,36]. These tools are limited to small families. To improve the scalability, inductive methods based on *abstraction-refinement* over the MDP representation [12], and *counter-example guided inductive synthesis* (CEGIS) for MCs [11] have been proposed. As shown by the *Maze* model in Sect. 5, the topology synthesis is closely linked to controller synthesis for POMDPs, a popular model for planning in AI under uncertainty. Other recent approaches to POMDP controller synthesis include the use of neural network oracles (obtained by reinforcement learning) to guide the search [48] and adaptive learning schemes based on imitation learning [30]. Note that the problem of sketching probabilistic programs that fit given data as studied, e.g., in [39,44], is different.

Parameter synthesis considers models with a fixed topology but with uncertain parameters associated to transition probabilities (or rates). It aims to analyze how the MC (or MDP) behaviour depends on the parameter values. Scalable approximate parameter synthesis techniques treat identical parameters in different transitions independently [10,42] and have been implemented in STORM [19] and PRISM [35]. Exact approaches construct rational functions for symbolic reachability probabilities [16] and were improved in [18,25,29]. This approach has been also applied to problems such as model repair [4,40].

Both synthesis problems can be attacked by *search-based techniques* that do not ensure an exhaustive exploration of the parameter space. These include evolutionary techniques [26,38] and genetic algorithms [22]. Their combination

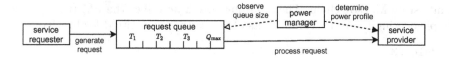

Fig. 2. The server for request processing.

with parameter synthesis has been pursued in [8] and is implemented in the tool RODES [9] to synthesize robust systems.

2 Using PAYNT

We exemplify the usage of PAYNT by the following synthesis problem.

Consider a server for request processing depicted in Fig. 2. Requests are generated (externally) in random intervals and upon arrival stored in a request queue of capacity $Q_{\max}$. When the queue is full, the request is lost. The server has three profiles – *sleeping*, *idle* and *active* – that differ in their power consumption. The requests are processed by the server only when it is in the *active* state. Switching from a low-energy state into the active state requires additional energy as well as an additional random latency before the request can be processed. We further assume that the power consumption of request processing depends on the current queue size. The operation time of the server is random but finite.

The server is controlled by a power manager (PM) that observes the current queue size and then sets the desired power profile. More precisely, the PM distinguishes between four queue occupancy levels determined by the threshold levels T_1, T_2, and T_3. These values are controllable parameters that denote *which fraction of the queue capacity is occupied*. In other words, the PM observes the queue occupancy of the intervals: $[0, T_1], (T_1, T_2]$ etc. For each occupancy level, the PM changes to the associated power profile $P_1, \ldots, P_4 \in \{0, 1, 2\}$, where numbers 0 through 2 encode the profiles *sleeping*, *idle* and *active*, respectively.

PAYNT takes as an input a *sketch* – a program description in the PRISM (or JANI) language containing some undefined parameters (holes) with associated options from domains. A PRISM program consists of one or more reactive modules that may interact with each other using synchronization. A module has a set of (bounded) variables that span its state space. Possible transitions between states of a module are described by a set of guarded commands of the form:

[action] guard $\rightarrow$ $p_1 : \text{update}_1 \ldots \ldots + p_n : \text{update}_n$

If the guard evaluates to true, an update of the variables is chosen according to the probability distribution given by expressions p_1 through p_n. The actions are used to force two or more modules to make the command simultaneously (i.e. to synchronize). The holes can appear in guards and updates. Replacing each hole with one of its options yields a complete program with the semantics given by a finite-state Markov chain. The following sketch describes the PM (the modules implementing the other components of the server are omitted for brevity).

```
module PM
    pm  :  [0..2] init 0; // 0 - sleep, 1 - idle, 2 - active
    [sync0] q <= T1*QMAX -> (pm'=P1);
    [sync0] q > T1*QMAX & q <= T2*QMAX -> (pm'=P2);
    [sync0] q > T2*QMAX & q <= T3*QMAX -> (pm'=P3);
    [sync0] q > T3*QMAX -> (pm'=P4);
endmodule
```

In our example, we consider the following holes and domains describing: the thresholds $T_1 \in \{0, 0.1, 0.2, 0.3, 0.4\}, T_2 \in \{0.5\}, T_3 \in \{0.6, 0.7, 0.8, 0.9\}^2$, the corresponding power profiles $P_1, \ldots, P_4 \in \{0, 1, 2\}$, and the queue capacity $Q_{max} \in \{1, \ldots, 10\}$. The resulting sketch describes a *design space* of $10 \cdot 5 \cdot 4 \cdot 3^4 = 16,200$ different power managers where the average size of the underlying MC (of the complete system) is around 900 states.

The goal is to find the concrete power manager, i.e., the instantiation of the holes, that minimizes power consumption while the expected number of lost requests during the operation time of the server is below 1. Such specification Φ is formalized as a list of temporal logic formulae in the PRISM syntax:

```
R{"lost"}<= 1 [ F "finished" ]   R{"power"}min=? [ F "finished" ]
```

Using the sketch and the specification Φ, PAYNT effectively explores the design space and finds a hole assignment inducing a program that satisfies Φ, provided such assignment exists. Otherwise, it reports that such design does not exist. For the example, PAYNT produces the following output containing the hole assignment and the quality wrt. Φ of the corresponding program:

```
hole assignment: QMAX=5,T1=0,T2=0.5,T3=0.7,P1=1,P2=2,P3=2,P4=2
R[exp]{"lost"}=0.6822759696 [F "finished"]
R[exp]{"power"}min=9100.064246 [F "finished"]
```

The obtained optimal power manager has queue capacity 5 with thresholds (after rounding) at 0, $2 = \lfloor 5 \cdot 0.5 \rfloor$ and $3 = \lfloor 5 \cdot 0.7 \rfloor$. In addition, the power manager always maintains an active profile unless the request queue is empty, in which case the device is put into an idle state. This solution leads to the expected number of lost requests of $\approx 0.68 < 1$ and the power consumption of 9,100 units. PAYNT computes this *optimal* solution in one minute. This is three times faster than a naive enumeration of all solutions.

Let us consider a more complex variant of the synthesis problem inspired by the well-studied model of a dynamical power manger for complex electronic systems [5,21]. The corresponding sketch describes around 43M available solutions with an the average MC size of 3.6k states. While enumeration needs more than 1 month to find the optimal power manager, PAYNT solves it within 10 h.

---

[2] Note that this simply ensures that $T_1 < T_2 < T_3$. PAYNT further supports *restrictions*—additional constraints on parameter combinations.

3   Synthesis of Probabilistic Programs

We formalize the synthesis problems supported by PAYNT and briefly present state-of-the-art synthesis algorithms; more details can be found in [3,11,12].

Problem Statement

Sketch. PAYNT uses sketches to define the set of designs. Let $\mathcal{P}$ be a sketch containing holes from the set $\mathcal{H} = \{H_k\}_k$ with R_k being the set of options available for hole H_k. Let $\overline{\mathcal{R}} = \prod_k R_k$ denote the set of all hole assignments (realizations), $\mathcal{P}[r]$ denote the program induced by a substitution $r \in \overline{\mathcal{R}}$ and $\mathcal{D}_r$ denote the underlying MC. Note that the size of the set $\overline{\mathcal{R}}$ is exponential in $|\mathcal{H}|$.

Specification. PAYNT supports conjunctions of specifications with reachability and expected rewards. For a set T of target states, *reachability* properties $\varphi \equiv \mathbb{P}_{\bowtie\lambda}[\mathrm{F}\ T]$ with $\lambda \in [0,1]$ and $\bowtie \in \{<, \leq, >, \geq\}$ express that the probability to reach T relates to $\lambda \in [0,1]$ according to $\bowtie$. *Expected reward* properties $\varphi \equiv \mathbb{E}_{\bowtie\lambda}[\mathrm{F}\ T]$ express that the expected reward accumulated before T is reached relates to $\lambda \in \mathbb{R}^+$ according to $\bowtie \in \{<, \leq\}$. Let $\mathcal{P}[r] \models \varphi$ denote that the program $\mathcal{P}[r]$ induced by the realisation r satisfies φ. For a specification $\Phi = \{\varphi_i\}_{i \in I}$ given by a finite set of properties, we write $\mathcal{P}[r] \models \Phi$ to denote $\forall i \in I : \mathcal{P}[r] \models \varphi_i$.

Synthesis problems. PAYNT is able to answer two types of synthesis questions for a PRISM sketch $\mathcal{P}$ with a set $\overline{\mathcal{R}}$ of realizations and a specification Φ:

Feasibility: Find a realization $r \in \overline{\mathcal{R}}$ such that $\mathcal{P}[r] \models \Phi$.

Maximality: For property $\varphi_{\max}$, find a realization $r^* \in \overline{\mathcal{R}}$ such that

$$r^* \in \arg\max_{r \in \overline{\mathcal{R}}} \{\mathbb{P}[\mathcal{P}[r] \models \varphi_{\max}] \mid \mathcal{P}[r] \models \Phi\}.$$

Variants of the maximal synthesis problem for expected rewards and minimization are defined analogously. PAYNT also supports a relaxed variant of maximal synthesis, ε-*maximal synthesis*: find a realization r^* such that $\mathcal{P}[r^*] \models \Phi$ and $\mathbb{P}[\mathcal{P}[r^*] \models \varphi_{\max}] \geq (1-\varepsilon) \cdot \max_{r \in \overline{\mathcal{R}}} \{\mathbb{P}[\mathcal{P}[r] \models \varphi_{\max}] \mid \mathcal{P}[r] \models \Phi\}$ for a given $\varepsilon \in (0,1]$.

Existing Synthesis Methods

Synthesis methods can be classified into two orthogonal groups: i) *complete* methods allowing to prove non-existence or optimally of the given problem, and ii) *incomplete* methods leveraging various smart search strategies and evolutionary algorithms [22,26,38]. While its architecture is flexible, the current

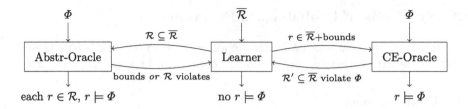

Fig. 3. Oracle-guided synthesis (adapted from [3]).

release of PAYNT is built around state-of-the-art *complete* methods. As a base-line and reference algorithm, the tool implements the so-called *one-by-one app-roach* [15] which simply enumerates through each realization $r \in \overline{\mathcal{R}}$. The design-space explosion renders this approach unusable for large problems, necessitating the usage of advanced techniques that exploit any structure of the family of MCs.

Oracle-guided synthesis. At the heart of PAYNT is an oracle-guided induc-tive synthesis approach [31,32,46]. A *learner* selects a realization r and passes it to an *oracle*. The oracle answers whether r satisfies Φ and, crucially, gives additional information, usually a counter-example (CE), whenever this is not the case. PAYNT implements two orthogonal different oracles: (a) an *inductive* oracle CE examines single realizations to infer statements about other realiza-tions [11]. (b) a *deductive* oracle AR (Abstraction Refinement) argues about sets of realizations by considering (an aggregation of) these realizations at once [12]. PAYNT supports the combined use of these two oracles as a hybrid synthesis method [3].

Figure 3 [3] illustrates the communication between the learner and the two oracles. The Abstr-Oracle analyzes a sub-family $\mathcal{R}$ with 3 possible outcomes: 1) it proves that all its realizations satisfy Φ, i.e., that the synthesis problem is feasible, or 2) it proves that all its realizations violate Φ, i.e., the learner can safely discard $\mathcal{R}$, or 3) the analysis is inconclusive and it returns safe bounds on the best- and worst-case behavior of all realizations in $\mathcal{R}$ wrt. Φ. The CE-Oracle analyzes a realization r and either proves that r satisfies Φ or it generalizes r into a subfamily $\mathcal{R}'$. The learner can discard $\mathcal{R}'$ since it is guaranteed that all its realizations violate Φ. In the hybrid approach, the CE-Oracle exploits the bounds in order to compute smaller CEs allowing a better generalization. The learner maintains a queue of subfamilies $\mathcal{R}' \subseteq \overline{\mathcal{R}}$ that has to be further processed and also controls which oracle is used based on their previous performance.

4   Tool Architecture of PAYNT

PAYNT is implemented on top of the probabilistic model checker Storm [19]. While the high-performance parts were implemented in C++, we use a python API to flexibly construct the overall synthesis loop. For SMT-solving, we use

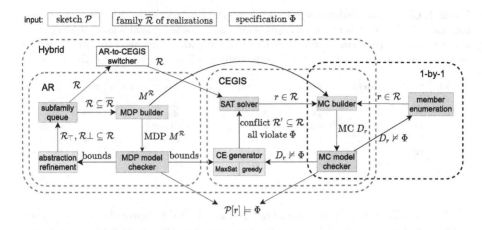

Fig. 4. The tool architecture (Color figure online)

Z3 [37]. PAYNT takes a PRISM [35] or JANI [7] sketch and a set of temporal properties, and returns a satisfying realization, if such exists. Otherwise, it reports that no such realization exists.

Figure 4 depicts a high-level view on the tool architecture, which primarily consists of components for family handling (purple), chain building (green) and model checkers (**red**).

The *family handlers* are used to store information about the previously covered design space: Member enumeration simply iterates over all realizations. The SAT representation stores a SAT-formula describing unexplored realizations and uses the SMT solver Z3 for linear (bounded) integer arithmetic to retrieve the next candidate realization. The subfamily queue stores a collection of unexplored subfamilies and refines these subfamilies as hyper-rectangles. The *chain builders* take as input a single assignment $r \in \mathcal{R}$ or a set $\mathcal{R}' \subseteq \mathcal{R}$ of realizations, and produce an representation of the MC or a quotient MDP, respectively in the internal memory model of the model checkers. The *model checkers* are then used to verify these chains. They either output yes/no or, in the case of MDPs, provide lower and upper bounds on satisfiability probabilities. PAYNT includes a module for counterexample generation by using either a MaxSat [17,49] or a greedy state-expansion [3] approach.

Figure 4 also illustrates three analysis loops that mirror the behaviour of 1-by-1 enumeration (the baseline), CEGIS and AR. The 1-by-1 approach simply iterates over all possible realizations until a satisfying one is obtained. The CEGIS loop additionally constructs counterexamples to each unsatisfying realization $r \in \mathcal{R}$, yielding a whole subset $\mathcal{R}' \subseteq \mathcal{R}$ of realizations that are pruned from the family. In contrast to this enumeration, the AR loop constructs and model checks MDPs from the subfamily queue and subsequently refines these subfamilies if the obtained bounds on satisfiability yield inconclusive results.

Table 1. Case study statistics and PAYNT synthesis times versus the naive 1-by-1 enumeration. Two problems per model are considered: an optimal synthesis problem (hard) and a feasibility problem (easy). In both cases, all realizations need to be explored to prove optimality and unsatisfiability, resp. Values indicated with * are estimates.

Model	Number of parameters	Family size	Average MC size	1-by-1 enumeration	Tool performance	
					Hard	Easy
DPM	16	43M	3.6k	35 days *	9.3 h	1.1 h
Maze	22	9.4M	0.2k	1.8 days*	1 h	54 min
Herman	7	3.1M	1.1k	1.5 days *	17 min	1.1 min
Pole	17	1.3M	5.6k	1 day *	8.5 min	5 s
Grid	8	65k	1.2k	32 min	37 s	21 s

The hybrid approach combines both AR and CEGIS approaches and switches between the two loops mid-execution. In particular, the integrated method executes the abstraction-refinement loop and, whenever it encounters an undecidable family that needs to be split, CEGIS takes a chance at analyzing it for a limited time period. If some family members are excluded based on a counterexample, the CEGIS engine updates the corresponding SAT representation to ensure it does not analyze the same member twice. There are two additional links that couple the AR and CEGIS loops and enable efficient integrated analysis. First is the use of bounds from MDP model checking during the greedy CE generation to allow the construction of larger family-aware conflicts. Since these bounds are associated with the states of the quotient MDP $M^{\mathcal{R}}$ for the (sub-)family and counterexamples are constructed as sub-MCs of the MC $\mathcal{D}_r$, $r \in \mathcal{R}$, in the integrated setting we construct $\mathcal{D}_r$ directly from $M^{\mathcal{R}}$, to save time on converting bound values between the two chains.

The implementation of PAYNT is composed of *30* Python modules containing *7k* source lines of code. These metrics consider only our implementation and do not include the extensions contributed to STORM and its Python API, invoked by PAYNT. All modules adhere to coding conventions for the Python code *PEP 8* [41, 43] and are documented with *Sphinx* for automatic generation of documentation. The specific logic components are tested with unit tests to maintain their correct functionality. Regression tests verify the accuracy and correctness of the synthesis results. Our tests currently cover more than *90%* of the source code lines.

5   Performance Evaluation and Applicability

Table 1 lists the results of PAYNT on two variants (hard and easy) of five different case studies from various domains taken from [11,12]. Further on, we demonstrate the applicability of PAYNT and interpret the synthesis results for two of these case studies. All experiments are run on an Ubuntu 19.04 machine with Intel i5-8300H (4 cores at 2.3 GHz) and using up to 8 GB RAM, with all the algorithms being executed single-threaded. The artefact allowing to reproduce the experiments is avaiable at https://doi.org/10.5281/zenodo.4726056.

Maze. This synthesis problem can be seen as an instance of POMDP controller synthesis. A robot is deployed at a random location inside a known maze, see Fig. 5. The robot is only equipped with a simple wall sensor, and cannot distinguish maze cells with identical sets of surrounding walls such as cells 1 and 3, and cells 11 through 13. Observation-equivalent cells are indicated by the same color in Fig. 5. Possible actions are movements in the four cardinal directions. Movements are subject to a random error: e.g., upon moving east, with a small probability the robot actually moves west. We sketch a robot controller that helps it to reach the exit of the maze (cell 12). The controller may use a single bit of memory initially having the value 0. The holes in this sketch are taken actions (where to steer, how to change the memory bit) based on the current observation (detected walls, current memory state). This sketch describes a family of 9.4M candidate programs. Our goal is to find a realization that minimizes the expected number of steps to reach the exit.

Using the inductive synthesis techniques, PAYNT explores the set of candidate realizations in an hour (1-by-1 enumeration takes more than one day) and synthesizes the controller depicted in Fig. 5. Here arrows represent the steering direction based on the current memory value (number at the base of an arrow), as well as the corresponding memory update (number at the tip of an arrow). For instance, a robot in cell 1 goes west if the memory value is 0 and goes east otherwise, without changing the memory in either case. A robot at cell 0 always goes east and sets its memory bit to 1. The synthesized controller is optimal. If a robot reaches a cell with a unique set of enclosing walls (cells 0,

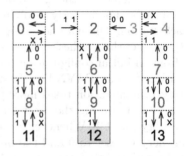

Fig. 5. The spatial structure of *Maze*. Cells with identical sets of surrounding walls are depicted with similar colors. The arrows depict the synthesized controller. (Color figure online)

2 and 4), then it knows its precise position within the maze and can navigate to the exit. Similarly, navigating north from cells 11 or 13 ensures to eventually reach cells 0 or 4. If the robot is deployed in an orange or purple cell, then it has to 'try' one possible direction in order to recognize its position within the maze. For example, a robot deployed at cells 5–10 will first go north (recall that the initial memory value is 0), from where it can determine its cell. Note that in this observation group it is indeed more beneficial to first explore north since the robot is twice as likely to be initially deployed at locations 5/7/8/10, as compared to locations 6 and 9. The expected time to reach the exit for this policy is ≈9.8 steps. Note that this cannot be improved by adding more memory to the controller.

Herman. This case study considers a token ring with an odd number of stations that are connected by a unidirectional ring. Each station has a Boolean flag, observable by itself and by its successor in the ring. A station has a token when the two flags it observes are identical. A good configuration is a situation in which only one station has a token. All other configurations are faulty. A token protocol is self-stabilizing, if the ring gets from a faulty configuration into a good configuration. The performance can be measured as stabilization time, i.e., the expected number of rounds to reach a good configuration.

We sketch a variant of *Herman's randomized self-stabilization protocol* [6,28, 34]. In this protocol, all stations behave the same[3]. The protocol is synchronized, and in every round a station without token flips its flag. Every station that has a token must *choose* whether to pass a token (by setting its flag accordingly). In the original protocol this choice is the resolved on a single (biased) coin flip. We are interested in the synthesis of alternatives. We give each station an additional single bit of memory and the choice between 25 different coin biases. The parameters in the sketch are the choice of a coin based on the memory value as well as the memory updates. By resolving the choices, we obtain the same protocol for each station. The parameter combinations yield a family of 3.1M programs and the goal of the synthesizer is to identify the one that minimizes stabilization time from an initial configuration (all flags true). For a sketch describing a system with 5 stations, PAYNT finds the optimal protocol in around 18 min, while the 1-by-1 enumeration takes more than a day. The obtained optimal strategy relies on initially using the most fair coins available (bias ≈ 0.25) and keeping the memory bit at 1. Whenever a process eventually decides to keep the token, the memory is reset to 0 and the process starts using highly unfair coins (bias ≈ 0.07), implying that the process is more likely to keep its token for a long time until it is eventually passed further. Using this strategy, the system can on average stabilize in four rounds.

References

1. Ábrahám, E., Becker, B., Dehnert, C., Jansen, N., Katoen, J.-P., Wimmer, R.: Counterexample generation for discrete-time Markov models: an introductory survey. In: Bernardo, M., Damiani, F., Hähnle, R., Johnsen, E.B., Schaefer, I. (eds.) SFM 2014. LNCS, vol. 8483, pp. 65–121. Springer, Cham (2014). https://doi.org/10.1007/978-3-319-07317-0_3

2. Alur, R., et al.: Syntax-guided synthesis. In: Proceedings of the IEEE International Conference on Formal Methods in Computer-Aided Design (FMCAD), pp. 1–17, October 2013

3. Andriushchenko, R., Češka, M., Junges, S., Katoen, J.-P.: Inductive synthesis for probabilistic programs reaches new horizons. In: TACAS 2021. LNCS, vol. 12651, pp. 191–209. Springer, Cham (2021). https://doi.org/10.1007/978-3-030-72016-2_11

---

[3] In such anonymous networks, stabilization cannot be solved in a deterministic way [20].

4. Bartocci, E., Grosu, R., Katsaros, P., Ramakrishnan, C.R., Smolka, S.A.: Model repair for probabilistic systems. In: Abdulla, P.A., Leino, K.R.M. (eds.) TACAS 2011. LNCS, vol. 6605, pp. 326–340. Springer, Heidelberg (2011). https://doi.org/10.1007/978-3-642-19835-9_30
5. Benini, L., Bogliolo, A., Paleologo, G.A., Micheli, G.D.: Policy optimization for dynamic power management. IEEE Trans. CAD Integr. Circ. Syst. **18**(6), 813–833 (1999)
6. Bruna, M., Grigore, R., Kiefer, S., Ouaknine, J., Worrell, J.: Proving the Herman-protocol conjecture. In: ICALP, LIPIcs, vol. 55, pp. 104:1–104:12. Schloss Dagstuhl - Leibniz-Zentrum für Informatik (2016)
7. Budde, C.E., Dehnert, C., Hahn, E.M., Hartmanns, A., Junges, S., Turrini, A.: JANI: quantitative model and tool interaction. In: Legay, A., Margaria, T. (eds.) TACAS 2017. LNCS, vol. 10206, pp. 151–168. Springer, Heidelberg (2017). https://doi.org/10.1007/978-3-662-54580-5_9
8. Calinescu, R., Češka, M., Gerasimou, S., Kwiatkowska, M., Paoletti, N.: Efficient synthesis of robust models for stochastic systems. J. Syst. Softw. **143**, 140–158 (2018)
9. Calinescu, R., Češka, M., Gerasimou, S., Kwiatkowska, M., Paoletti, N.: RODES: a robust-design synthesis tool for probabilistic systems. In: Bertrand, N., Bortolussi, L. (eds.) QEST 2017. LNCS, vol. 10503, pp. 304–308. Springer, Cham (2017). https://doi.org/10.1007/978-3-319-66335-7_20
10. Češka, M., Dannenberg, F., Paoletti, N., Kwiatkowska, M., Brim, L.: Precise parameter synthesis for stochastic biochemical systems. Acta Inf. **54**(6), 589–623 (2017)
11. Češka, M., Hensel, C., Junges, S., Katoen, J.-P.: Counterexample-driven synthesis for probabilistic program sketches. In: ter Beek, M.H., McIver, A., Oliveira, J.N. (eds.) FM 2019. LNCS, vol. 11800, pp. 101–120. Springer, Cham (2019). https://doi.org/10.1007/978-3-030-30942-8_8
12. Češka, M., Jansen, N., Junges, S., Katoen, J.-P.: Shepherding hordes of Markov chains. In: Vojnar, T., Zhang, L. (eds.) TACAS 2019. LNCS, vol. 11428, pp. 172–190. Springer, Cham (2019). https://doi.org/10.1007/978-3-030-17465-1_10
13. Chonev, V.: Reachability in augmented interval Markov chains. In: Filiot, E., Jungers, R., Potapov, I. (eds.) RP 2019. LNCS, vol. 11674, pp. 79–92. Springer, Cham (2019). https://doi.org/10.1007/978-3-030-30806-3_7
14. Chrszon, P., Dubslaff, C., Klüppelholz, S., Baier, C.: ProFeat: feature-oriented engineering for family-based probabilistic model checking. Formal Asp. Comput. **30**(1), 45–75 (2018)
15. Classen, A., Cordy, M., Heymans, P., Legay, A., Schobbens, P.Y.: Model checking software product lines with SNIP. Int. J. Softw. Tools Technol. Transf. **14**, 589–612 (2012)
16. Daws, C.: Symbolic and parametric model checking of discrete-time Markov chains. In: Liu, Z., Araki, K. (eds.) ICTAC 2004. LNCS, vol. 3407, pp. 280–294. Springer, Heidelberg (2005). https://doi.org/10.1007/978-3-540-31862-0_21
17. Dehnert, C., Jansen, N., Wimmer, R., Ábrahám, E., Katoen, J.-P.: Fast debugging of PRISM models. In: Cassez, F., Raskin, J.-F. (eds.) ATVA 2014. LNCS, vol. 8837, pp. 146–162. Springer, Cham (2014). https://doi.org/10.1007/978-3-319-11936-6_11
18. Dehnert, C., et al.: PROPhESY: a probabilistic parameter synthesis tool. In: Kroening, D., Păsăreanu, C.S. (eds.) CAV 2015. LNCS, vol. 9206, pp. 214–231. Springer, Cham (2015). https://doi.org/10.1007/978-3-319-21690-4_13

19. Dehnert, C., Junges, S., Katoen, J.-P., Volk, M.: A storm is coming: a modern probabilistic model checker. In: Majumdar, R., Kunčak, V. (eds.) CAV 2017. LNCS, vol. 10427, pp. 592–600. Springer, Cham (2017). https://doi.org/10.1007/978-3-319-63390-9_31

20. Dijkstra, E.W.: Self-stabilizing systems in spite of distributed control. Commun. ACM **17**(11), 643–644 (1974)

21. Gerasimou, S., Tamburrelli, G., Calinescu, R.: Search-based synthesis of probabilistic models for quality-of-service software engineering (t). In: 2015 30th IEEE/ACM International Conference on Automated Software Engineering (ASE), pp. 319–330, November 2015

22. Gerasimou, S., Calinescu, R., Tamburrelli, G.: Synthesis of probabilistic models for quality-of-service software engineering. Autom. Softw. Eng. **25**(4), 785–831 (2018)

23. Ghezzi, C., Sharifloo, A.M.: Model-based verification of quantitative non-functional properties for software product lines. Inf. Softw. Technol. **55**(3), 508–524 (2013)

24. Hahn, E.M., et al.: The 2019 comparison of tools for the analysis of quantitative formal models. In: Beyer, D., Huisman, M., Kordon, F., Steffen, B. (eds.) TACAS 2019. LNCS, vol. 11429, pp. 69–92. Springer, Cham (2019). https://doi.org/10.1007/978-3-030-17502-3_5

25. Hahn, E.M., Hermanns, H., Zhang, L.: Probabilistic reachability for parametric Markov models. Int. J. Softw. Tools Technol. Transf. **13**(1), 3–19 (2011)

26. Harman, M., Mansouri, S.A., Zhang, Y.: Search-based software engineering: Trends, techniques and applications. ACM Comp. Surv. **45**(1), 11:1–11:61 (2012)

27. Hartmanns, A., Hermanns, H.: The modest toolset: an integrated environment for quantitative modelling and verification. In: Ábrahám, E., Havelund, K. (eds.) TACAS 2014. LNCS, vol. 8413, pp. 593–598. Springer, Heidelberg (2014). https://doi.org/10.1007/978-3-642-54862-8_51

28. Herman, T.: Probabilistic self-stabilization. Inf. Process. Lett. **35**(2), 63–67 (1990)

29. Hutschenreiter, L., Baier, C., Klein, J.: Parametric markov chains: PCTL complexity and fraction-free Gaussian elimination. GandALF. EPTCS **256**, 16–30 (2017)

30. Inala, J.P., Bastani, O., Tavares, Z., Solar-Lezama, A.: Synthesizing programmatic policies that inductively generalize. In: ICLR (2020)

31. Jha, S., Gulwani, S., Seshia, S.A., Tiwari, A.: Oracle-guided component-based program synthesis. In: ICSE, pp. 215–224. ACM (2010)

32. Jha, S., Seshia, S.A.: A theory of formal synthesis via inductive learning. Acta Informatica **54**(7), 693–726 (2017)

33. Kaelbling, L.P., Littman, M.L., Cassandra, A.R.: Planning and acting in partially observable stochastic domains. Artif. Intell. **101**(1–2), 99–134 (1998)

34. Kwiatkowska, M., Norman, G., Parker, D.: Probabilistic verification of Herman's self-stabilisation algorithm. Formal Aspects Comput. **24**(4), 661–670 (2012)

35. Kwiatkowska, M., Norman, G., Parker, D.: PRISM 4.0: verification of probabilistic real-time systems. In: Gopalakrishnan, G., Qadeer, S. (eds.) CAV 2011. LNCS, vol. 6806, pp. 585–591. Springer, Heidelberg (2011). https://doi.org/10.1007/978-3-642-22110-1_47

36. Lanna, A., Castro, T., Alves, V., Rodrigues, G., Schobbens, P.Y., Apel, S.: Feature-family-based reliability analysis of software product lines. Inf. Softw. Technol. **94**, 59–81 (2018)

37. Lindemann, C.: Performance modelling with deterministic and stochastic Petri nets. SIGMETRICS Perform. Eval. Rev. **26**(2), 3 (1998)

38. Martens, A., Koziolek, H., Becker, S., Reussner, R.: Automatically improve software architecture models for performance, reliability, and cost using evolutionary algorithms. In: WOSP/SIPEW, pp. 105–116. ACM (2010)

39. Nori, A.V., Ozair, S., Rajamani, S.K., Vijaykeerthy, D.: Efficient synthesis of probabilistic programs. In: PLDI, pp. 208–217. ACM (2015)
40. Pathak, S., Ábrahám, E., Jansen, N., Tacchella, A., Katoen, J.-P.: A greedy approach for the efficient repair of stochastic models. In: Havelund, K., Holzmann, G., Joshi, R. (eds.) NFM 2015. LNCS, vol. 9058, pp. 295–309. Springer, Cham (2015). https://doi.org/10.1007/978-3-319-17524-9_21
41. Peters, T.: The Zen of Python. PEP 20 (2004). https://www.python.org/dev/peps/pep-0020/
42. Quatmann, T., Dehnert, C., Jansen, N., Junges, S., Katoen, J.-P.: Parameter synthesis for Markov models: faster than ever. In: Artho, C., Legay, A., Peled, D. (eds.) ATVA 2016. LNCS, vol. 9938, pp. 50–67. Springer, Cham (2016). https://doi.org/10.1007/978-3-319-46520-3_4
43. van Rossum, G., Warsaw, B., Coghlan, N.: Style guide for Python code. PEP 8 (2001). https://www.python.org/dev/peps/pep-0008/
44. Saad, F.A., Cusumano-Towner, M.F., Schaechtle, U., Rinard, M.C., Mansinghka, V.K.: Bayesian synthesis of probabilistic programs for automatic data modeling. In: Proceedings of the ACM on Programming Languages, vol. 3(POPL), pp. 1–32 (2019)
45. Solar-Lezama, A.: Program synthesis by sketching. Ph.D. thesis, USA (2008)
46. Solar-Lezama, A., Rabbah, R., Bodík, R., Ebcioğlu, K.: Programming by sketching for bit-streaming programs. In: PLDI, pp. 281–294. ACM (2005)
47. Vandin, A., ter Beek, M.H., Legay, A., Lluch Lafuente, A.: QFLan: a tool for the quantitative analysis of highly reconfigurable systems. In: Havelund, K., Peleska, J., Roscoe, B., de Vink, E. (eds.) FM 2018. LNCS, vol. 10951, pp. 329–337. Springer, Cham (2018). https://doi.org/10.1007/978-3-319-95582-7_19
48. Verma, A., Murali, V., Singh, R., Kohli, P., Chaudhuri, S.: Programmatically interpretable reinforcement learning. In: International Conference on Machine Learning, pp. 5045–5054. PMLR (2018)
49. Wimmer, R., Jansen, N., Vorpahl, A., Ábrahám, E., Katoen, J.P., Becker, B.: High-level counterexamples for probabilistic automata. Logical Meth. Comput. Sci. **11**(1) (2015)

Adapting Behaviors via Reactive Synthesis

Gal Amram[1], Suguman Bansal[2], Dror Fried[3(✉)], Lucas Martinelli Tabajara[4],
Moshe Y. Vardi[4], and Gera Weiss[5]

[1] Tel-Aviv University, Tel Aviv-Yafo, Israel
[2] University of Pennsylvania, Philadelphia, USA
suguman@seas.upenn.edu
[3] The Open University of Israel, Ra'anana, Israel
dfried@openu.ac.il
[4] Rice University, Houston, USA
{lucasmt,vardi}@rice.edu
[5] Ben-Gurion University of the Negev, Beersheba, Israel
geraw@bgu.ac.il

Abstract. In the *Adapter Design Pattern*, a programmer implements a *Target* interface by constructing an *Adapter* that accesses an existing *Adaptee* code. In this work, we present a reactive synthesis interpretation to the adapter design pattern, wherein an algorithm takes an *Adaptee* and a *Target* transducers, and the aim is to synthesize an *Adapter* transducer that, when composed with the *Adaptee*, generates a behavior that is equivalent to the behavior of the *Target*. One use of such an algorithm is to synthesize controllers that achieve similar goals on different hardware platforms. While this problem can be solved with existing synthesis algorithms, current state-of-the-art tools fail to scale. To cope with the computational complexity of the problem, we introduce a special form of specification format, called *Separated GR(k)*, which can be solved with a scalable synthesis algorithm but still allows for a large set of realistic specifications. We solve the realizability and the synthesis problems for Separated GR(k), and show how to exploit the separated nature of our specification to construct better algorithms, in terms of time complexity, than known algorithms for GR(k) synthesis. We then describe a tool, called SGR(k), that we have implemented based on the above approach and show, by experimental evaluation, how our tool outperforms current state-of-the-art tools on various benchmarks and test-cases.

1 Introduction

Inspired by the well known adapter design pattern [18], we study the use of reactive synthesis for generating adapters that translate inputs meant for a target transducer to inputs of an adaptee transducer. Consider, as one motivating example, the practice of adding code to an operating system that mitigates the risk posed by newly discovered hardware vulnerabilities like Spectre and Meltdown [23,26]. While the discovery of such vulnerabilities puts constraints on how

© The Author(s) 2021
A. Silva and K. R. M. Leino (Eds.) CAV 2021, LNCS 12759, pp. 870–893, 2021.
https://doi.org/10.1007/978-3-030-81685-8_41

the hardware can be used, the patch of the operating system (called adapter in this paper) takes upon itself to take care of running all applications without change [25]. It does so by allowing applications of the existing interface, while adapting their operation in way that ensures that the system is not exposed to the new threat.

Formally, we propose the following synthesis problem: given two finite-state transducers called *Target* and *Adaptee*, synthesize a finite-state transducer called *Adapter* such that

$$Adaptee \circ Adapter \approx Target.$$

The symbol $\circ$ stands for standard transducer composition and the symbol $\approx$ stands for an equivalence relation, a generalization of sequential equality, which we explain below. In words, we want an *Adapter* that stands between an *Adaptee* and its inputs and guarantees, such that the composition *Adaptee* $\circ$ *Adapter* is equivalent to *Target*. In the vulnerability patching example, *Adaptee* is a model of the constrained hardware and *Target* is a model of the hardware as used before the discovery of the vulnerability, without the new constraints. The *Adapter* that we generate models the patch that mediates between the vulnerable hardware and applications that are not aware of the vulnerability.

In our setting, an input to the synthesis algorithm is the equivalence relation along with the specification of the adaptee and of the target. While the problem of synthesizing an adapter such that *Adaptee* $\circ$ *Adapter* is sequentially equal to *Target* may be useful in some cases [32], we study here a more general problem. This is called for by applications such as the vulnerability covering patches described above. Specifically, we allow our users to specify an equivalence relation between *Adaptee* $\circ$ *Adapter* and *Target* that is not necessarily sequential equality. In this paper, we propose to use ω-regular properties [20] for specifying this equivalence relation, as follows. We assume, without loss of generality, that the outputs of both the *Target* and the *Adaptee* are assignments to disjoint sets of atomic propositions. We then consider sequences of pairs of such assignments that correspond to zipped runs of *Adaptee* $\circ$ *Adapter* and of *Target* over the same input. Having this set of sequences in mind, the user specifies a set of temporal properties using an ω-regular formalism such as LTL or Büchi automata. The transducer *Adaptee* $\circ$ *Adapter* is considered equivalent to *Target* if all the properties that the user specified are satisfied for each sequence in the set [19]. Note that the equivalence relation can be very different than sequential equality, it can, for example, say that *Adaptee* $\circ$ *Adapter* must be, in a way, a "mirror image" of *Target*, as demonstrated by the cleaning robots example in Sect. 4.1, where *Target* is a robot that cleans some rooms and *Adaptee* $\circ$ *Adapter* is a robot that clean all the rooms that *Target* did not clean.

The solution that we propose in this paper consists of two phases: we first transform the transducers to transition systems and arrive at a game structure that is more amenable for game-based techniques. Then we make use of the specific form of the resulting game and some simplifying assumptions about the form of the equivalence properties to solve the game efficiently. The game structures that we analyze consist of pairs of transition systems called *Input* and *Output*, accompanied by a set of ω-regular properties that specify equivalence relation between the two, as described above. The game that we solve is, then, to find a controller that reads the assignments to the variables of the *Input* and produces a valid sequence of assignments to the variables of the *Output* such that all the properties are satisfied. The translation of the transducers to this game structure is rather direct, as elaborated in Sect. 4. The *Input* transition system is generated from the *Target* transducer and the *Output* transition system is generated from the *Adaptee* transducer. This is because we want the *Adapter*, which we generate from the controller as described below, to consider the behavior of the *Target* and to translate it to a command that generates an equivalent behaviour of *Adaptee*. Once we find a controller that solves the game, we can transform it to an *Adapter* as we detail in Sect. 4.

The synthesis problem that we defined so far is as hard computationally as general LTL synthesis and is thus double exponential in the worst case [37]. To cope with this difficulty, we propose to use a well known fragment of LTL called GR(k). GR(k) generalizes the GR(1) subset of LTL [9], a practical fragment of LTL for which a feasible reactive synthesis algorithm exists (see, e.g., [8,28, 33]). Furthermore, GR(k) formulas are known to be highly expressive, as they can encode most commonly appearing LTL industrial patterns [15,29,30] and DBA properties (see related works for details). In addition to using GR(k), since the *Input* and *Output* in our model are separated transition systems, with separated sets of atomic propositions, we focus on properties that separate input and output variables. That is, our specification has the form $\bigwedge_{i=1}^{k}(\phi_i \rightarrow \psi_i)$, where the ϕ_i and ψ_i are conjunctions of LTL GF (Globally in the Future) formulas over *Input* variables only and *Output* variables only respectively. We call this model *Separated GR(k)*. We show through several case-studies that this fragment of LTL suffices to specify a range of useful equivalence relations.

We study the problems of realizability and synthesis on Separated GR(k) game. For that, we first consider a sub-problem of solving a *weak Büchi* game. Then we identify and make use of a property of separated games that we call *delay property*: the system can delay its response to the environment indefinitely as long as it remains in the same connected component of the game graph. This allows us to decide the realizability of Separated GR(k) in $O(|\varphi| + N)$ symbolic operations, and to synthesize a controller for a realizable specification in $O(|\varphi|N)$ symbolic operations, where φ is the Separated GR(k) specification, and N is the size of the state-space. Thus, Separated GR(k) games are easier to solve that solving GR(k) games which require $O(N^{k+1}k!)$ operations [35]. This demonstrates the efficiency of our framework, since $|\varphi|$ tends to be smaller than N and in most practical cases, $|\varphi| \in O(log(N))$.

The benefits of the complexity-theoretic improvement are reflected in empirical evaluations on our case studies of separated GR(k) formulas. We demonstrate that while separated GR(k) formulas are challenging for state-of-the-art synthesis tools, a symbolic BDD-based implementation of our algorithm solves them scalably and efficiently.

The rest of the paper is organized as follows: Sect. 2 introduces necessary preliminaries. Separated GR(k) games are introduced and formulated in Sect. 3.

In Sect. 4 we describe how to use Separated GR(k) games synthesis to generate the adapter transducer, and introduce several use-cases. Next, we turn to solving separated GR(k) games. An overview of our solution approach and a necessary property for correctness of algorithm, called the delay property, is given in Sect. 5. A complete symbolic algorithm is presented in Sect. 6. An empirical evaluation on case-studies is presented in Sect. 7. Finally, in Sects. 8 and 9 respectively, we give related work and conclude. Detailed proofs appear in the full version of the paper [3].

2   Preliminaries

General Definitions. Given a set of Boolean variables $\mathcal{V}$, a *state over $\mathcal{V}$* is an assignment s to the variables in $\mathcal{V}$. We describe s as the subset of $\mathcal{V}$ that is assigned True in s. The set of *primed variables of $\mathcal{V}$* is $\mathcal{V}' = \{v' \mid v \in \mathcal{V}\}$. Then $s' = \{v' \mid v \in s\}$ is the primed state s' over $\mathcal{V}'$. An *assertion over $\mathcal{V}$* is a Boolean formula over variables $\mathcal{V}$. A state s satisfies an assertion ρ over the same variables, denoted $s \models \rho$, if ρ evaluates to True by assigning *true* to the elements of s. We define the *projection* of a state s on a subset $\mathcal{U} \subseteq \mathcal{V}$ as denoted by $s|_{\mathcal{U}} = s \cap \mathcal{U}$. We extend the notion of projection to a set of states $S \subseteq 2^{\mathcal{V}}$ by defining $S|_{\mathcal{U}} = \{s|_{\mathcal{U}} \mid s \in S\}$.

Our specification is a special form of *Linear Temporal Logic* (LTL). LTL [36] extends propositional logic with infinite-horizon temporal operators. The syntax of an LTL formula over a finite set of Boolean variables $\mathcal{V}$ is defined as follows: $\varphi :: = v \in \mathcal{V} \mid \neg\varphi \mid \varphi \wedge \varphi \mid \varphi \vee \varphi \mid \mathsf{X}\varphi \mid \varphi\mathsf{U}\varphi \mid \mathsf{F}\varphi \mid \mathsf{G}\varphi$. Here X (Next), U (Until), F (Eventually), G (Always) are temporal operators. The semantics of LTL can be found in [5, Chapter 5].

We model the adapters as transducers. A *transducer* is a deterministic finite-state machine with no accepting states, but with additional output alphabet and an additional function from the set of states to the output alphabet. A formal definition of a transducer is not required for this paper.

The algorithms developed in this paper are symbolic, i.e. manipulate implicit representations of sets of states. To this end, we use *Binary Decision Diagrams (BDDs)* [10] to represent assertions. For a BDD B and sets of variables $\mathcal{V}_1, \cdots \mathcal{V}_n$, we write $\mathsf{B}(\mathcal{V}_1, \ldots, \mathcal{V}_n)$ to denote that B represents an assertion over $\mathcal{V}_1 \cup \cdots \cup \mathcal{V}_n$. For a state s over $\mathcal{V}$, we write $s \models B(\mathcal{V})$ to denote that the assertion that B represents is satisfied by the state s. BDDs support several *symbolic operations*: conjunction ($\vee$), disjunction ($\wedge$), negation ($\neg$), and extraction of variables using the $\exists$ and $\forall$ operators. We measure time complexity of a symbolic algorithm by a worst case #symbolic-operations it performs. A discussion on a rigorous treatment of BDD operations can be found in the paper's full version [3].

Game Structures and Games. We follow the notations of [9]. A game structure $GS = (\mathcal{I}, \mathcal{O}, \theta_{\mathcal{I}}, \theta_{\mathcal{O}}, \rho_{\mathcal{I}}, \rho_{\mathcal{O}})$ defines a turn-based interaction between an *environment* and a *system* players. The input variables $\mathcal{I}$ and output variables $\mathcal{O}$ are two disjoint sets of Boolean variables that are controlled by the environment and system, respectively. The environment's *initial assumption* $\theta_{\mathcal{I}}$ is an assertion over $\mathcal{I}$, and the system's *initial guarantee* $\theta_{\mathcal{O}}$ is an assertion over $\mathcal{I} \cup \mathcal{O}$. The environment's *safety assumption* $\rho_{\mathcal{I}}$ is an assertion over $\mathcal{I} \cup \mathcal{O} \cup \mathcal{I}'$, where the interpretation of $(i_0, o_0, i_1') \models \rho_{\mathcal{I}}$ is that from state (i_0, o_0) the environment can assign i_1 to the input variables. W.l.o.g, we assume that $\rho_{\mathcal{I}}$ is deadlock free, i.e., for all (i_0, o_0) there exists an i_1 s.t. $(i_0, o_0, i_1') \models \rho_{\mathcal{I}}$. Similarly, the system's *safety guarantee* $\rho_{\mathcal{O}}$ is an assertion over $\mathcal{I} \cup \mathcal{O} \cup \mathcal{I}' \cup \mathcal{O}'$, where the interpretation of $(i_0, o_0, i_1', o_1') \models \rho_{\mathcal{O}}$ is that from state (i_0, o_0) when the environment assigns i_1 to the input variables, the system can assign o_1 to the output variables. Again, w.l.o.g, we assume that $\rho_{\mathcal{O}}$ is deadlock free, i.e., for all (i_0, o_0, i_1') there exists an o_1 s.t. $(i_0, o_0, i_1', o_1') \models \rho_{\mathcal{O}}$.

A play over GS progresses by the players taking turns to assign values to their own variables ad infinitum, where the players must satisfy the initial conditions at the start and the safety conditions thereafter. Formally, a *play* $\pi = s_0, s_1, \ldots$ is an infinite sequence of states over $\mathcal{I} \cup \mathcal{O}$ such that $s_0 \models \theta_{\mathcal{I}} \wedge \theta_{\mathcal{O}}$ and $(s_j, s_{j+1}') \models \rho_{\mathcal{I}} \wedge \rho_{\mathcal{O}}$ for all $j \geq 0$. A *play prefix* is either a play or a finite sequence of states that can be extended to a play. Then a *strategy* is a function $f : (2^{\mathcal{I} \cup \mathcal{O}})^+ \times 2^{\mathcal{I}} \to 2^{\mathcal{O}}$ such that if $s_0, \ldots, s_m$ is a play prefix, $(s_m, i') \models \rho_{\mathcal{I}}$ and $f(s_0, \ldots, s_m, i) = o$, then $(s_m, i', o') \models \rho_{\mathcal{O}}$. Intuitively, a strategy directs the system on what to assign to the output variables, depending on the history of a play and the most recent assignment by the environment to the input variables. A play prefix is said to be *consistent with a strategy* f if for all states $s_j = (i_j, o_j)$ in that prefix, $f(s_0, \ldots, s_{j-1}, i_j) = o_j$ for all $j \geq 0$. A strategy is memoryless if it only depends on the last state and the most recent assignment to the input variables. Formally, a *memoryless strategy* is a function $f : (2^{\mathcal{I} \cup \mathcal{O}}) \times 2^{\mathcal{I}} \to 2^{\mathcal{O}}$ such that if $(s_m, i') \models \rho_{\mathcal{I}}$ and $f(s_m, i') = o$, then $(s_m, i', o') \models \rho_{\mathcal{O}}$.

A *game* is a tuple (GS, φ) where GS is a game structure over inputs $\mathcal{I}$ and outputs $\mathcal{O}$ and φ is an LTL formula over $\mathcal{I} \cup \mathcal{O}$ called a *winning condition*. A play π is *winning* for the system if $\pi \models \varphi$. A strategy f *wins from state* s if every play π from s that is consistent with f is winning for the system. A strategy f *wins from* S, where S is an assertion over $\mathcal{I} \cup \mathcal{O}$, if it wins from every state $s \models S$. The *winning region* of the system is the set of states from which it has a winning strategy. A strategy f is *winning* if for every state $i \models \theta_{\mathcal{I}}$ there exists a state $o \in 2^{\mathcal{O}}$ such that $(i, o) \models \theta_{\mathcal{O}}$ and f wins from (i, o). In this paper, we have the following games that are defined over the following winning conditions.

- *Reachability games*: $\mathsf{F}(\varphi)$ where φ is an assertion over $\mathcal{I} \cup \mathcal{O}$.
- *Safety games*: $\mathsf{G}(\varphi)$ where φ is an assertion over $\mathcal{I} \cup \mathcal{O}$.
- *Büchi games*: $\mathsf{GF}(\varphi)$ where φ is an assertion over $\mathcal{I} \cup \mathcal{O}$.
- *GR(k) games*: $\bigwedge_{l=1}^{k}(\bigwedge_{i=1}^{n_l} \mathsf{GF}(\varphi_{l,i}) \to \bigwedge_{j=1}^{m_l} \mathsf{GF}(\psi_{l,j}))$ where all $\varphi_{l,i}$ and $\psi_{l,j}$ are assertions over $\mathcal{I} \cup \mathcal{O}$.

Given a game (GS, φ), *realizability* is the problem of deciding whether a winning strategy for the system exists, and *synthesis* is the problem of constructing a winning strategy if one exists. We note that a realizability check can be reduced to the identification of the winning region, W: A winning strategy exists iff for all $i \models \theta_{\mathcal{I}}$ there exists $o \in 2^{\mathcal{O}}$ such that $(i, o) \models \theta_{\mathcal{O}}$ and $(i, o) \in W$. Hence, the synthesis problem can be solved by constructing a strategy that wins from W.

Game Graphs and Weak Büchi Games. The *game graph* for a game structure GS is the directed graph (V, E) with vertices $V = 2^{\mathcal{I} \cup \mathcal{O}}$ and edges $E = \{(s, t) \mid (s, t') \models \rho_{\mathcal{I}} \wedge \rho_{\mathcal{O}}\}$. Intuitively, vertices are states over $\mathcal{I}$ and $\mathcal{O}$, and edges represent valid transitions between states according to the safety conditions. The game graph can be useful for analyzing the structural properties of a game structure via graph-theoretical properties.

A *finite path* in a directed graph (V, E) is a sequence $v_0, \ldots, v_n \in V^+$ such that $(v_j, v_{j+1}) \in E$ for all $0 \leq j < n$. An *infinite path* $v_0, v_1, \ldots \in V^\omega$ is similarly defined. A vertex u is said to be *reachable* from another vertex v if there is a finite path from v to u. A *strongly connected component* (SCC) of a directed graph (V, E) is a maximal set of vertices within which every vertex is reachable from every other vertex. It is well known that SCCs partition the set of vertices of a directed graph, and that the set of SCCs is partially ordered with respect to reachability. Also note that every infinite path ultimately stays in an SCC.

Let $(GS, \mathsf{GF}\varphi)$ be a game with a Büchi winning condition, and let $S_0 \ldots, S_m$ be the set of SCCs that partition the game graph of GS. We say that $(GS, \mathsf{GF}\varphi)$ is a *weak Büchi game* if, given the set $\mathcal{F}$ of states that satisfy the assertion φ, for every SCC S_i, either $S_i \subseteq \mathcal{F}$ or $S_i \cap \mathcal{F} = \emptyset$. Thus, the SCCs of a weak Büchi game are either *accepting components*, meaning all of its states are contained in $\mathcal{F}$, or *non-accepting components*, meaning none of its states is present in $\mathcal{F}$. As a consequence, a play in a weak Büchi game is winning for the system if the play ultimately never exits an accepting component. Similarly, a strategy is winning for the system if it can guarantee that every play will ultimately remain inside an accepting component.

3   Separated GR(k) Games

Our framework relies on the core idea of reducing the problem of adapter generation to synthesizing a *Separated GR(k) game*, which we define in this section. At a high-level, a separated GR(k) differentiates from a regular GR(k) game in a separation between input and output variables in both the game structure and winning condition. We show in later sections that the separation of variables leads to algorithmic benefits to the synthesis problem. Formally we have the following.

Definition 1. *A game structure* $GS = (\mathcal{I}, \mathcal{O}, \theta_{\mathcal{I}}, \theta_{\mathcal{O}}, \rho_{\mathcal{I}}, \rho_{\mathcal{O}})$ *separates variables over input variables* $\mathcal{I}$ *and output variables* $\mathcal{O}$ *if:*

- *The environment's initial assumption* $\theta_{\mathcal{I}}$ *is an assertion over* $\mathcal{I}$ *only.*
- *The system's initial guarantees* $\theta_{\mathcal{O}}$ *is an assertion over* $\mathcal{O}$ *only.*
- *The environment's safety assumption* $\rho_{\mathcal{I}}$ *is an assertion over* $\mathcal{I} \cup \mathcal{I}'$ *only.*
- *The system's safety guarantee* $\rho_{\mathcal{O}}$ *is an assertion over* $\mathcal{O} \cup \mathcal{O}'$ *only.*

The interpretation of a game structure which separates variables is that the underlying game graph (V, E) is the product of two distinct directed graphs over disjoint sets of variables: $G_{\mathcal{I}}$ over the variables $\mathcal{I} \cup \mathcal{I}'$, and $G_{\mathcal{O}}$ over the variables $\mathcal{O} \cup \mathcal{O}'$. For $\mathcal{J} \in \{\mathcal{I}, \mathcal{O}\}$, the vertices of $G_{\mathcal{J}}$ correspond to states over $\mathcal{J}$ and there is an edge between states s and t if $(s, t') \models \rho_{\mathcal{J}}$.

Next, the notion of separation of variables extends to games with $GR(k)$ winning conditions as follows:

Definition 2. *A GR(k) winning condition φ over $\mathcal{I} \cup \mathcal{O}$ separates variables w.r.t. $\mathcal{I}$ and $\mathcal{O}$ if $\varphi = \bigwedge_{l=1}^{k}(\bigwedge_{i=1}^{n_l} \mathsf{GF}(\varphi_{l,i}) \to \bigwedge_{j=1}^{m_l} \mathsf{GF}(\psi_{l,j}))$ such that each $\varphi_{l,i}$ is an assertion over $\mathcal{I}$ and each $\psi_{l,j}$ is an assertion over $\mathcal{O}$.*

A *Separated GR(k) game* is a $GR(k)$ game (GS, φ) over $\mathcal{I} \cup \mathcal{O}$ in which both GS and φ separate variables w.r.t. $\mathcal{I}$ and $\mathcal{O}$.

A major observation is that in a game played over a separated game structure, the actions of the two players are independent: the environment's actions do no limit the system's actions, and vice versa. In later sections we see how this observation leads to algorithmic improvements in solving separated $GR(k)$ games over a regular $GR(k)$ game. Specifically, in Sect. 4 we see how to use Separated $GR(k)$ games to generate the adapter transducer. In Sects. 5 and 6 we discuss algorithms for realizability and synthesis of Separated $GR(k)$ games.

4   From Transducers to Separated GR(k)

We describe, using an end-to-end-example, how adapter transducer generation can be reduced to synthesis of Separated GR(k) games.

We begin with user-provided *Target* and *Adaptee* transducers. These transducers model the behavior of a system that we want to use (*Adaptee*) and the behavior of a system that we want to emulate (*Target*). For example, the transition systems in Fig. 1 formulates the following scenario. (1) *Target* is an hardware interface that we want to support, such that the U (up) and the D (down) commands send the hardware from mode s_0 to modes s_1 and s_2, respectively, from which the S (stay) command keeps the system looping at the chosen mode. (2) *Adaptee* that is a hardware that we can use that also has three modes, but which does not allow the command S after U. Instead, it allows a D command that switches the mode back to s_0.

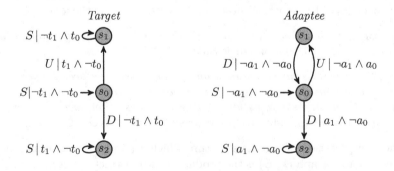

Fig. 1. An example of *Target* and *Adaptee* transducers. In this example, the t_i and a_i variables encode the binary representation of the mode being moved to.

The second step is a formulation of the equivalence relation, where we define the type of emulation that we require. In our example we want to maintain the following property: if *Target* visits a mode s_i infinitely often for a certain input sequence, then so does *Adaptee* ∘ *Adapter*. This can be expressed in LTL as:

$$\bigwedge_{i=0}^{2} \mathsf{GF}(bin_t(s_i)) \to \mathsf{GF}(bin_a(s_i))$$

where $bin_t(s_i)$ denotes the binary representation of mode s_i using variables t_1, t_0, and similarly for $bin_a(s_i)$ using variables a_1, a_0. Note that in this example we cannot just synthesize an adapter that cycles through all modes in *Adaptee* ∘ *Adapter* infinitely often, since the *Adaptee* transducer does not allow that.

As a third step, to generate a separated GR(k) game, we translate the *Target* and *Adaptee* transducers to *Input* and *Output* transition systems as depicted, for example, in Fig. 2. Since *Adaptee* and *Target* are two separate transducers, each with its own structure, it is natural to model these as two separate transition systems on distinct variables. Thus, the transition systems are produced by the well known projection construction that turns an FST into a FSA that accepts the output language of the transducers [32]. Note that in our setting *Target* is translated to *Input* and *Adaptee* is translated to *Output*. This may appear as a role inversion to readers. We propose it because the role of the controller in our setting is to translate the behavior of *Target* to an equivalent behavior of the *Adaptee*.

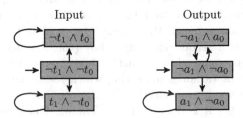

Fig. 2. A direct translation of the *Target* transducer to an *Input* transition system and of the *Adaptee* transducer to an *Output* transition system.

These separate transition systems, together with the specification described above, form a Separated GR(k) that, as a fourth step, we can feed to the Separated GR(k) synthesis algorithm. The output of the algorithm is a transducer called *Controller*, that maps runs of *Input* to runs of *Output*, as shown, in our example, in Fig. 3. This, in fact, connects the output of the *Target* to the output of the *Adaptee*.

As a final step, from the controller we can construct the *Adapter* using the formula *Adapter* = *Adaptee*$^{-1}$ ∘ *Controller* ∘ *Target*. This means that *Adapter* contains an internal model of the *Target* and of the *Adaptee*. These internal

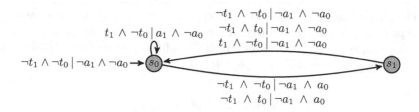

Fig. 3. A controller that reads runs of the *Input* transition system and generates runs of the *Output* transition system such that the specified Separated GR(2) formula is guaranteed to be true.

models are used to translate inputs to expected outputs of the adapter, then feed them to the controller, and then feed the output of the controller to the reverse of *Adaptee* to generate an input to *Adaptee* that emulates the behaviour of *Target*. Note that it is possible to invert transducers symbolically [21].

4.1   Additional Usages of Our Technique

We give two more examples to demonstrate uses of Separated GR(k).

Cleaning Robots. This example demonstrates how one can use our technique to fulfill tasks that have not been covered by an execution of an existing transducer. Consider a cleaning robot (the *Target* transducer) that moves along a corridor-shaped house, from room 1 to room n. The robot follows some plan and accordingly cleans some of the rooms. Our goal is to synthesize a controller that activates a second cleaning robot (the *Adaptee* transducer) that follows the first robot and cleans exactly those rooms left uncleaned. Each robot controls a set of variables indicating which room they are in and which rooms they have cleaned, and additionally the original robot controls a variable indicating whether it is done with its cleaning. Our controller is required to fulfill requirements of the form: $\mathsf{GF}(done) \wedge \mathsf{GF}(!in{:}clean_i) \to \mathsf{GF}(out{:}clean_i)$, $\mathsf{GF}(done) \wedge \mathsf{GF}(in{:}clean_i) \to \mathsf{GF}(!out{:}clean_i)$.

Railway Signalling. This example demonstrates how one can use our technique to improve the quality of an existing transducer. We consider a junction of n railways, each equipped with a signal that can be turned on (light in green) or off (light in red). Some railways overlap and thus their signals cannot be turned on simultaneously. We consider an overlapping pattern where railways 1–4 overlap, and similarly 3–6, 5–8, and so on.

An existing system (the *Target* transducer) was programmed to be strictly safe in order to avoid accidents, so it never raises two signals simultaneously. We want to improve the system's performance by synthesizing a controller that reads the assignments that the existing transducer produces and accordingly assign values to the signals in such a way as to produce both safe and *maximal* valuations: the ith signal is turned on if and only if the signal of every rail that overlaps with the ith rail is off. Furthermore, we want to maintain liveness properties of the *Target* system: (1) every signal that is turned on infinitely often by the existing system must be turned on infinitely often by the new system as well, and (2) if a signal is turned on at least once every m steps (where m is a parameter of the specification) by the existing system, then the same holds for the new system.

Note that, in terms of the GR(k) formula, this example is similar to the "hardware" example that we gave; we want to emulate the *Target*'s execution. The crux of the example lies in its *Adaptee*. Here, unlike in the explanatory example, the *Adaptee* is not a given hardware, but rather a virtual component that the user introduced to improve the *Target* performance. In this case the *Adaptee* produces safe and maximal signals.

5 Overview for Solving Separated GR(k) Games

The adapter generation framework described in Sect. 4 relies on synthesizing a controller from a separated GR(k) game. In this section and the next, we describe how to solve separated GR(k) games. This section gives an overview of the algorithm in Sect. 5.1 and describes a necessary property, called the delay property, in Sect. 5.2. The delay property is necessary to prove correctness of our synthesis algorithm. Later, Sect. 6 gives the complete algorithm and proves its correctness.

5.1 Algorithm Overview and Intuition

Following Sect. 3, we are given a Separated GR(k) game that consists of a game structure GS and a winning condition in a GR(k) form $\varphi = \bigwedge_{l=1}^{k} \varphi_l$, where $\varphi_l = \bigwedge_{i=1}^{n_l} \mathsf{GF}(a_{l,i}) \to \bigwedge_{j=1}^{m_l} \mathsf{GF}(g_{l,j})$. Let G be the game graph of GS. Consider an infinite play π in GS. Like every infinite path on a finite graph, π eventually stabilizes in an SCC S. Due to separation of variables, the game graph G can be decomposed into an input graph $G_\mathcal{I}$ and an output graph $G_\mathcal{O}$. Then the projection of S on the inputs is an SCC $S_\mathcal{I}$ in $G_\mathcal{I}$, and the projection of S on the outputs is an SCC $S_\mathcal{O}$ in $G_\mathcal{O}$. The input side of π converges to $S_\mathcal{I}$ whereas the output side π converges to $S_\mathcal{O}$.

Now, let S be an SCC with projections $S_\mathcal{I}$ on $G_\mathcal{I}$ and $S_\mathcal{O}$ on $G_\mathcal{O}$. Then we call S *accepting* if for *every* constraint φ_l, where $l \in \{1, \ldots, k\}$, one of the following holds:

All guarantees hold in S. For every $j \in \{1, \ldots, m_l\}$, there exists $o \in S_\mathcal{O}$ such that $o \models g_{l,j}$.

Some assumption cannot hold in S. There exists $j \in \{1, \ldots, n_l\}$ such that for all $i \in S_\mathcal{I}$, $i \not\models a_{l,j}$.

Then from the definition of an accepting SCC we have the following: a strategy that makes sure that every play converges to an accepting SCC, in which all the relevant guarantee states are visited, is a winning strategy for the system in (GS, φ). To synthesize such a strategy, we do the following: (i) synthesize a strategy f_B for which every play converges to an accepting SCC; (ii) synthesize a strategy f_{travel} that travels within every accepting SCC, satisfying as many of the $g_{l,j}$ guarantees as possible. (iii) construct an overall winning strategy f that works as follows: the system plays f_B until reaching an accepting SCC S, then the system switches to f_{travel} to satisfy as many of the $g_{l,j}$ guarantees in S as possible; if the environment moves the play to a non-accepting SCC, the system can start playing f_B again to reach a different accepting SCC.

The strategy f_B can be found by synthesizing the weak Büchi game $(GS, \mathsf{GF}(acc))$, where acc is the assertion that accepts exactly those states that belong to accepting SCCs (note that $(GS, \mathsf{GF}(acc))$ is a well defined weak Büchi game). f_{travel} can be constructed by simply finding a path in $S_\mathcal{O}$ that satisfies the maximum number of guarantees.

A complication arises however when switching between f_{travel} and f_B, since it is conceivable that while the system is following f_{travel}, the environment could move to a different SCC that is outside of the winning region of f_B. Thus, it is not clear that we can combine these strategies to make an overall winning strategy for the system. To show that we can indeed combine both strategies, we need the following property that we call the *delay property*: if (i_1, o_1) is a state in the winning region of f_B, and (i_2, o_0) is a state for which there is a path in $G_\mathcal{I}$ from i_1 to i_2 and a path in $G_\mathcal{O}$ from o_0 to o_1, then (i_2, o_0) is also in the winning region of f_B. We formally state and prove the delay property in Sect. 5.2. In Sect. 6 we give details of the construction of f_B, f_{travel} and the use of the delay property to prove correctness of the overall winning strategy f.

5.2   The Delay Property

The delay property essentially says that if an SCC S is contained in the winning region, and the environment moves from S unilaterally to a different SCC S', then S' is also in the winning region of the system. In this section, we prove that the Büchi game $(GS, \mathsf{GF}(acc))$ where $GS = (\mathcal{I}, \mathcal{O}, \theta_\mathcal{I}, \theta_\mathcal{O}, \rho_\mathcal{I}, \rho_\mathcal{O})$, as defined in Sect. 5.1, satisfies the delay property. Throughout this section, we write $G_\mathcal{I}$ and $G_\mathcal{O}$ to denote the graphs over $2^\mathcal{I}$ and $2^\mathcal{O}$, respectively, as in Sect. 5.1. We start with the following lemma that states that the system can still win in spite of a single step delay.

Lemma 1. *Let $i_0, i_1 \in 2^\mathcal{I}$ such that $(i_0, i_1') \models \rho_\mathcal{I}$, and assume that the system can win from (i_0, o_0). Then the system can also win from (i_1, o_0).*

Proof. Let f be a winning strategy for the system from (i_0, o_0). We construct a winning strategy f_d from (i_1, o_0). Intuitively, f_d acts from state (i_1, o_0) as if it were following f from state (i_0, o_0), with a delay of a single step: the input in the current step is used to choose the output in the next step.

We use f to define f_d inductively over play prefixes of length $m \geq 1$, by setting
$$f_d((i_1, o_0), \dots, (i_m, o_{m-1}), i_{m+1}) = f((i_0, o_0), \dots, (i_{m-1}, o_{m-1}), i_m).$$ Note that

f_d is well defined since GS separates variables: from state (i, o), the outputs that can be chosen for the successor state depend only on o, and not on i. Note that by this definition, for every play $(i_1, o_0), (i_2, o_1), \ldots, (i_{m+1}, o_m), \ldots$ consistent with f_d, the play $(i_0, o_0), (i_1, o_1), \ldots, (i_m, o_m), \ldots$ is consistent with f. We remark that we define f_d only for proving the lemma, and it is *not* part of our solution.

Next, we show that f_d is winning from (i_1, o_0). Take a play $(i_1, o_0), (i_2, o_1), \ldots$, consistent with f_d. By the construction, $(i_0, o_0), (i_1, o_1), \ldots$ is consistent with f. Since this is a play on a weak Büchi game, after some point it must remain in a single SCC S, say from state (i_j, o_j). Since f is a winning strategy, the SCC S must be accepting. Then $o_j, o_{j+1}, \ldots$ is an infinite path in the SCC $S|_{\mathcal{O}}$, and $i_j, i_{j+1}, \ldots$ is an infinite path in the SCC $S|_{\mathcal{I}}$. Consequently, $(i_1, o_0), (i_2, o_1), \ldots$ converges to an SCC $\hat{S}$ in which $\hat{S}|_{\mathcal{I}} = S|_{\mathcal{I}}$ and $\hat{S}|_{\mathcal{O}} = S|_{\mathcal{O}}$. Since the conditions for an SCC D to be accepting depend only on the relation between $D|_{\mathcal{I}}$ and $D|_{\mathcal{O}}$, we have that $\hat{S}$ is accepting since S is accepting as well. □

We can now prove the delay property, following by straightforward induction from Lemma 1.

Theorem 1 (Delay Property Theorem). *Let $i_0, \ldots, i_n \in (2^{\mathcal{I}})^+$ be a path in $G_{\mathcal{I}}$, and for $m \geq 0$, let $o_{-m}, \ldots, o_0 \in (2^{\mathcal{O}})^+$ be a path in $G_{\mathcal{O}}$. Assume that the system can win from (i_0, o_0). Then the system can also win from (i_n, o_{-m}).*

Proof. From (i_n, o_{-m}), the system can simply ignore the inputs and follow the path in $G_{\mathcal{O}}$ to o_0. Let (i_{n+m}, o_0) be the state at that point in some play. Note that there is a path between i_n and i_{n+m}, and therefore there is a path between i_0 and i_{n+m}. If the system can win from (i_0, o_0) then by using Lemma 1 in the induction steps, the system can win by induction from (i, o_0) for all i such that there is a path in between i_0 and i. Therefore, the system can win from (i_{n+m}, o_0), and by consequence from (i_n, o_{-m}). □

A corollary of Theorem 1 is the following statement about the structure of the winning region of the weak Büchi game $B = (GS, \mathsf{GF}(acc))$ as defined in Sect. 5.1.

Corollary 1. *The winning region of B is a union of SCCs.*

Proof. Let (i, o) be a state in the winning region of B, let $(\hat{i}, \hat{o})$ be a state in the same SCC S of (i, o), and let $S|_{\mathcal{I}}$ and $S|_{\mathcal{O}}$ be the projections of S on $G_{\mathcal{I}}$ and $G_{\mathcal{O}}$, respectively. Then there is a path $i_0, \ldots, i_n$ for some $n \geq 0$ in $S|_{\mathcal{I}}$ such that $i_0 = i$ and $\hat{i} = i_n$. Similarly, there is a path $o_{-m}, \ldots, o_0$ for some $m \geq 0$ in $S|_{\mathcal{O}}$ such that $\hat{o}_0 = o$ and $\hat{o} = o_{-m}$. Then by the delay property of Theorem 1, the vertex $(\hat{i}, \hat{o}) = (i_n, o_{-m})$ is also in the winning region of B. □

We use Theorem 1 and Corollary 1 in the proof of correctness of the overall winning strategy f, as described in Sect. 6.2.

6   Algorithms for Solving Separated GR(k) Games

In this section we provide the exact details of our synthesis algorithm for Separated GR(k) games, as described in Sect. 5.1. Since constructing f_B involves defining and solving a weak Büchi game, we first describe these in Sect. 6.1. We remark that our weak Büchi game synthesis algorithm works for all weak Büchi games, and not just for the special weak Büchi game defined in Sect. 5.1. Specifically, it works even when the underlying game structure does not separates variables. Next, in Sect. 6.2, we complete the algorithm construction and describe the correctness of our overall synthesis algorithm.

6.1   Realizability and Synthesis for Weak Büchi Games

We present a symbolic algorithm to solve synthesis of a weak Büchi game. When represented in explicit state-representation, weak Büchi games are known to be solved in linear-time in the size of the game [12,27]. In this section, we adapt the algorithm from [12,27] to symbolic state-space representation. For sake of exposition, we give an overview of the algorithm and then present our symbolic modification.

Overview Given a weak Büchi game, recall that each SCC in its game graph G is either an accepting SCC or a non-accepting SCC. The goal is to find the winning regions in the weak Büchi game. This can be done by backward induction on the topological ordering of the SCCs as follows. Let $(S_0, \ldots S_m)$ be a topological sort of the SCCs in G.

Base Case: Consider all *terminal partitions*, say $S_j, \ldots, S_m$; that is, every SCC from which no other SCC is reachable. In this case, plays beginning in a terminal SCC will never leave it. Therefore, all states of terminal SCCs that are accepting are in the winning region of the system and all states of terminal SCCs that are non-accepting are not in the winning region of the environment.

Induction Step: Let $\overrightarrow{S} = (S_{i+1}, \ldots, S_m)$, and suppose that the set $\bigcup \overrightarrow{S}$ has been classified into winning regions for the system W_{i+1}^s and the environment W_{i+1}^e, respectively. Let $\overrightarrow{S}_{new} = (S_j, S_{j+1}, \ldots, S_i)$ be the SCCs from which all edges leaving the SCC lead to an SCC in $\overrightarrow{S}$. Further, let A and N be the unions of all accepting SCCs and all non-accepting SCCs in $\overrightarrow{S}_{new}$, respectively. Then the basic idea is as follows: The system can win from $s \in N$ if and only if it can force $\mathsf{F}(W_{i+1}^s)$ from s. Analogously, the system can win from $s \in A$ if and only if it can force $\mathsf{G}(A \cup W_{i+1}^s)$ from s. Hence, by solving these reachability and safety games, we can update W_{i+1}^s and W_{i+1}^e into W_j^s and W_j^s that partition the larger set $\bigcup(S_j, \ldots, S_m)$ into winning regions for the system and the environment. The winning strategy can be constructed in a standard way as a side-product of the reachability and safety games in each step, see for example [40,41].

Symbolic Algorithm for Weak Büchi Games. Given a weak Büchi game $B = ((\mathcal{I}, \mathcal{O}, \theta_{\mathcal{I}}, \theta_{\mathcal{O}}, \rho_{\mathcal{I}}, \rho_{\mathcal{O}}), \mathsf{GF}(acc))$ with BDDs representing $\theta_{\mathcal{I}}$, $\theta_{\mathcal{O}}$, $\rho_{\mathcal{I}}$, $\rho_{\mathcal{O}}$ and acc, our goal is to compute a BDD for the winning region and to synthesize a memoryless winning strategy for the system. The construction follows a fixed-point computation that adapts the inductive procedure described in the overview: In the basis of the fixed point computation, the winning region is the set of accepting terminal SCCs; in the inductive step, the winning region includes winning states by examining SCCs that are higher in the topological ordering on SCCs. In what follows we describe a sequence of BDDs that we construct towards constructing the overall BDD for the winning region. We use the notation X to denote a set of variables over $\mathcal{I} \cup \mathcal{O}$. For the sake of the current construction, memoryless strategies are given in the form of BDDs over X, X', for further details on the BDDs constructions see the full version for details [3].

BDD constructions. We start by constructing a BDD for a predicate that indicates whether two states in a game structure are present in the same SCC. Let predicate $\mathsf{Reach}(s, t')$ hold if there is a path from state s over $\mathcal{I} \cup \mathcal{O}$ to state t over $\mathcal{I} \cup \mathcal{O}$ in the game structure GS. Similarly, a predicate $\mathsf{Reach}^{-1}(s, t')$ holds if and only if $\mathsf{Reach}(t, s')$ holds. BDDs for Reach and Reach^{-1} can be computed in $O(N)$ symbolic operations using the transition relation of the game structure. Then, a BDD indicating if two states share the same SCC, is constructed in $O(N)$ symbolic operations by $\mathsf{SCC}(X, X') := \mathsf{Reach}(X, X') \wedge \mathsf{Reach}^{-1}(X, X')$.

Next, we construct a BDD for the union of the terminal SCCs, required by the basis of induction for the construction of the winning region. Let predicate $\mathsf{Terminal}(s)$ hold if state s over $\mathcal{I} \cup \mathcal{O}$ is present in a terminal SCC. Then $\mathsf{Terminal}(X) := \forall X' : \mathsf{Reach}(X, X') \rightarrow \mathsf{SCC}(X, X')$. Therefore, given BDDs for Reach and SCC, the construction of $\mathsf{Terminal}$ requires $O(1)$ symbolic operations.

Computing the Winning Region. We now describe the fixed-point computation to construct a BDD for the winning region in a weak Büchi game. Let $\mathsf{Reachability}_{(M,N)}(X)$ denote a BDD generated by solving a reachability game that takes as input a set of source states M and target states N and outputs those states in M from which the system can guarantee to move into N. Similarly, let $\mathsf{Safety}_{(M,N)}(X)$ denote a BDD generated by solving a safety game that takes as input a set of source states M and target states N and outputs those states in M from which the system can guarantee that all plays remain inside the set N. These constructions are standard, details can be found in [20, Chapter 2].

Now, let $\mathsf{Win}(s)$ denote that state s over $\mathcal{I} \cup \mathcal{O}$ is in the winning region. Then, $\mathsf{Win}(X)$ is the fixed point of the BDD $\mathsf{Win\_Aux}$ defined below, where the construction essentially follows the high-level algorithm description. The BDD $\mathsf{Acc}(X)$ represents the formula acc encoding the set of accepting states. In addition, $\mathsf{DC}^i(X)$ is the union $\bigcup \overrightarrow{S}$ of the Downward-Closed set of SCCs, i.e. the SCCs that have already been classified into winning or not-winning, and $\mathsf{DC}^i_{new}(X)$ is the union $\bigcup \overrightarrow{S}_{new}$ of the SCCs in $\mathsf{DC}^i(X)$ that were not in $\mathsf{DC}^{i-1}(X)$. Finally, $\mathsf{N}^i(X)$ is the subset N of non-accepting states in $\mathsf{DC}^i_{new}(X)$, and $\mathsf{A}^i(X)$ is the subset A of accepting states in $\mathsf{DC}^i_{new}(X)$. We then define $\mathsf{Win\_Aux}$ as follows.

Base Case.

1:   $\text{Win\_Aux}^0(X) := \text{Terminal}(X) \wedge \text{Acc}(X)$

2:   $\text{DC}^0(X) := \text{Terminal}(X)$

Inductive Step.

1:   $\text{DC}^{i+1}(X) := \forall X' : \text{Reach}(X, X') \rightarrow (\text{SCC}(X, X') \vee \text{DC}^i(X'))$

2:   $\text{DC}^{i+1}_{new}(X) := \text{DC}^{i+1}(X) \setminus \text{DC}^i(X)$

3:   $\text{N}^{i+1}(X) := \text{DC}^{i+1}_{new}(X) \wedge \neg \text{Acc}(X)$

4:   $\text{A}^{i+1}(X) := \text{DC}^{i+1}_{new}(X) \wedge \text{Acc}(X)$

5:   $\text{Win\_Aux}^{i+1}(X) := \text{Win\_Aux}^i(X) \vee \text{Reachability}_{(\text{N}^{i+1}(X),\text{Win\_Aux}^i(X))}(X)$
$\qquad\qquad \vee \text{Safety}_{(\text{A}^{i+1}(X),\text{A}^{i+1}(X)\vee\text{Win\_Aux}^i(X))}(X)$

To explain the construction of Win, note that a state s in $\text{DC}^{i+1}(X)$ is winning in one of these cases: (i) s is a winning state in $\text{DC}^i(X)$. (ii) s is a non-accepting state in $\text{DC}^{i+1}(X)$ from which the system can force the play into a winning state in $\text{DC}^i(X)$. This set of states can be obtained from $\text{Reachability}_{(\text{N}^{i+1}(X),\text{Win\_Aux}^i(X))}(X)$. (iii) s is an accepting state in $\text{DC}^{i+1}(X)$ from which the system can guarantee that every play that leaves the accepting SCC moves into a winning state in $\text{DC}^i(X)$. This set of states can be obtained from $\text{Safety}_{(\text{A}^{i+1}(X),\text{A}^{i+1}(X)\vee\text{Win\_Aux}^i(X))}(X)$.

Finally, to check realizability, construct the BDD $\forall \mathcal{I}(\text{InitIn}(\mathcal{I}) \rightarrow \exists \mathcal{O}(\text{InitOut}(\mathcal{O}) \wedge \text{Win}(\mathcal{I} \cup \mathcal{O})))$, where $\text{InitIn}(\mathcal{I})$ and $\text{InitOut}(\mathcal{O})$ are BDDs representing $\theta_{\mathcal{I}}$ and $\theta_{\mathcal{O}}$, respectively. This BDD is equal to *true* iff B is realizable.

The fixed-point computation can be extended in a standard way to also compute a BDD representation $\text{Fb}(X, X')$ of the winning strategy f_B, such that $(s, (i', o')) \models \text{Fb}(X, X')$ iff $f_B(s, i) = o$, as we elaborate in the full version [3]. We then have the following theorem that follows our construction.

Theorem 2. *Realizability and synthesis for weak Büchi games can be done in $O(N)$ symbolic steps.*

Proof Outline. The proposed construction symbolically implements the inductive procedure of the explicit algorithm. Hence, it correctly identifies the system's winning region. It remains to show that the algorithm performs $O(N)$ symbolic operations. First of all, the constructions of SCC and Terminal take $O(N)$ symbolic operations collectively. It suffices to show that in the i-th induction step, solving the reachability and safety games performs $O(|\text{DC}^{i+1} \setminus \text{DC}^i|)$ operations. This can be proven by a careful analysis of the operations and the sizes of resulting BDDs using standard results on safety and reachability games. $\square$

6.2   Realizability and Synthesis for Separated GR(k) Games

We finally make use of the elements obtained so far towards solving synthesis for Separated GR(k) games. Our construction follows the overview from Sect. 5.1. To recall, we describe and construct two auxiliary strategies f_B and f_{travel} and combine them to generate the final strategy f. We use the delay property theorem from Sect. 5.2 to prove the correctness of our algorithm.

We are given a Separated GR(k) game structure $GS = (\mathcal{I}, \mathcal{O}, \theta_\mathcal{I}, \theta_\mathcal{O}, \rho_\mathcal{I}, \rho_\mathcal{O})$ and a winning condition $\varphi = \bigwedge_{l=1}^{k} \varphi_l$, where $\varphi_l = \bigwedge_{i=1}^{n_l} \mathsf{GF}(a_{l,i}) \rightarrow \bigwedge_{j=1}^{m_l} \mathsf{GF}(g_{l,j}))$. We first represent GS and φ as BDDs by standard means. We then define and construct the following.

Constructing f_B. Auxiliary strategy f_B is the winning strategy of the system player in a weak Büchi game constructed form the separated GR(k) game. To construct a weak Büchi game, we first construct, in $O(|\varphi| + N)$ symbolic operations, a BDD $\mathsf{Acc}(\mathcal{I} \cup \mathcal{O})$ that describes the set of accepting states. The construction is standard. Next, let acc be the assertion represented by Acc (the assertion defined in Sect. 5.1). Then the weak Büchi game is $B = (GS, \mathsf{GF}(acc))$. Finally, we construct f_B as the winning strategy of B, following Sect. 6.1.

Constructing f_{travel}. For the construction of f_{travel}, we arbitrarily order all guarantees that appear in our GR(k) formula: $gar_0, \ldots, gar_{m-1}$. For each guarantee gar_j, we construct a reachability strategy $f_{r(j)}$ that, when applied inside an SCC $S_\mathcal{O}$ in the output game graph $G_\mathcal{O}$, moves towards a state that satisfies gar_j without ever leaving $S_\mathcal{O}$. In case no such state exists in $S_\mathcal{O}$, $f_{r(j)}$ returns a distinguished value $\bot$. Note that this strategy can entirely ignore the inputs. We equip f_{travel} with a memory variable mem that stores values from $\{0, \ldots, m-1\}$. Then $f_{travel}(s, i)$ is operated as follows: for $mem, mem+1, \ldots$ we find the first $mem+j$ (mod m) such that the SCC of s includes a gar_j-state, and activate $f_{r(mem+j)}$ to reach such state. If no guarantees can be satisfied in S, we just return an arbitrary output to stay in $S_\mathcal{O}$. The construction of f_{travel} requires $O(|\varphi|N)$ symbolic BDD-operations as we need to construct m reachability strategies (clearly, $m \le |\varphi|$).

Constructing the overall strategy f. Finally, we interleave the strategies f_B and f_{travel} into a single strategy f as follows: given a state s and an input i, if $s \models \mathsf{Acc}(X)$ (that is, if s is an accepting state), then set $f(s, i) = f_{travel}(s, i)$; otherwise set $f(s, i) = f_B(s, i)$. Whenever f switches from f_B to f_{travel}, the memory variable mem is reset to 0. The next lemma proves that if f_B is winning then so is f.

Lemma 2. *If f_B is a winning strategy for the weak Büchi game $B = (GS, \mathsf{GF}(acc))$, then f is a winning strategy for the Separated GR(k) game (GS, φ).*

Proof. Since f_B is a winning strategy, then for every initial input $i \models \theta_\mathcal{I}$ there is an initial output $o \models \theta_\mathcal{O}$ such that (i, o) is in the winning region of GS. We show that playing f always keeps the play in the winning region of GS, and therefore the play eventually converges to an accepting SCC. Once this happens, following f_{travel} guarantees that φ is satisfied. We know that as long as the play is in the winning region of B, following f_B will keep it inside the winning region. Therefore, when we switch from f_B to f_{travel} we must be inside the winning region and, by definition of f, in some accepting SCC S. Then f_{travel} makes sure that as long as the environment remains in $S|_\mathcal{I}$, the projection of S over the inputs, the system remains in $S|_{\mathcal{O}}$, the projection of S over the output. Thus all in all the play remains in the winning region of S.

Therefore, the only way that the play can leave the winning region is if, when the system is in a state (i_0, o_0) and chooses some output o_{-m} according to f_{travel}, the environment chooses input i_n such that the play leaves S and moves to a state (i_n, o_{-m}) in a different SCC of G. Note, however, that in this case there is a path from i_0 to i_n and a path from o_{-m} to o_0 (since by construction f_{travel} remains in the same SCC in $G_{\mathcal{O}}$). Since (i_0, o_0) is in the winning region, by Theorem 1 we have that (i_n, o_{-m}) is in the winning region as well.   □

Final Results. Given Lemma 2, we can obtain our final results on synthesis and realizability of Separated GR(k) games, as follows. Given a Separated GR(k) game (GS, φ), construct acc and solve the weak Büchi game $(GS, \mathsf{GF}(acc))$. Then construct f_B, f_{travel} and f as described above. If realizable, then f_B is a winning strategy and from Lemma 2 we have that f is a winning strategy for (GS, φ). If $(GS, \mathsf{GF}(acc))$ is unrealizable, then the environment can force every play to converge to a non-accepting SCC. Since the GR(k) winning condition cannot be satisfied from a non-accepting SCC, (GS, φ) is also not realizable. Thus we have the following theorem, see [3] for full details.

Theorem 3. *Realizability for separated GR(k) games can be reduced to realizability of weak Büchi games.*

The final result on solving Separated GR(k) games is then as follows, see [3] for full details.

Theorem 4. *Let (GS, φ) be a separated GR(k) game over the input/output variables $\mathcal{I}$ and $\mathcal{O}$, respectively. Then, the realizability and synthesis problems for (GS, φ) are solved in $O(|\varphi| + N)$ and $O(|\varphi|N)$ symbolic operations, respectively, where $N = |2^{\mathcal{I} \cup \mathcal{O}}|$.*

Proof Outline. Realizability and synthesis follow Lemma 2 and Theorem 3. It is left to analyze the number of symbolic operations for constructing f_B and then f. In symbolic operations, constructing acc takes $O(|\varphi| + N)$, and computing the winning region W for $(GS, \mathsf{GF}(acc))$ takes $O(N)$. Checking realizability can be done by checking if for every initial input i there is an initial output o such that $(i, o) \in W$, which takes $O(1)$. The winning strategy f_B can be computed in the process of computing W, taking the same number of operations (see [3] for details). Finally, constructing f_{travel} takes $O((\#gars)N) \leq O(|\varphi|N)$, where $gars$ are all guarantees $\mathsf{GF}(g_{i,\ell})$ that appear in φ. Therefore, constructing f takes $O(|\varphi|N)$ symbolic operations in total.   □

Note that this result is an improvement over the complexity of synthesizing GR(k) games in general [35].

7   Implementation and Evaluation

We have implemented our Separated GR(k) framework for realizability and synthesis in a prototype tool SGR(k). The tool implements our symbolic algorithm using the CUDD [39] package for BDD manipulation. Our tool is evaluated on a suite of benchmarks created from the examples described in Sect. 4.

Benchmark Suite. We have created a suite of parametric benchmarks from the three examples described in Sect. 4. Our suite consists of 38 realizable specifications. The parametric versions of the examples are described here.

The *multi-mode hardware* example is a generalization of the example presented at the beginning of Sect. 4. It is parameterized by the number of bits n and has 2^n modes. The *Target* can move from mode 0 to any mode and stay there, while the *Adaptee* can only move from mode 0 to odd-numbered modes, and up and down between modes $2i$ and $2i + 1$. The specification consists of $2n$ variables. We generate 10 such benchmarks with $n \in \{1, \ldots, 10\}$.

The *cleaning robots* example is parameterized in the number of rooms. For a scenario with n rooms, the specification is written over $4n + 1$ variables. We create 10 such benchmarks with $n \in \{1 \ldots, 10\}$.

The *railways signalling* example consists of two parameters: a junction of n railways and the frequency parameter m. With parameters n and m, the specification consists of $(2 + 2\lceil \log m \rceil)n$ variables. We generate 18 benchmarks with $n \in \{2, \ldots, 10\}$ and $m \in \{2, 3\}$.

Experimental Setup and Methodology. We evaluate our tool against Strix [1,31], the current state-of-the-art tool for LTL synthesis and SYNTCOMP 2020 winner of 3 out of 4 tracks [2]. In order to run our benchmarks on Strix, we transform the benchmarks (a game structure and a winning condition) into an LTL formula that characterizes the same winning plays using the strict semantics from [22]. To the best of our knowledge, there is no other synthesis/realizability tool that operates on GR(k) specifications.

We compare the running time for checking realizability. For this, we compare the running time of realizability checks of each benchmark on both tools. Every benchmark is tested 10 times on both tools. We do this to account for the randomness introduced during BDD construction due to the automatic variable ordering by CUDD. For each benchmark we evaluate (a) the number of executions on which the tools terminate and (b) the mean running time over 10 executions.

All experiments were executed on a single node of a high-performance computer cluster consisting of an Intel Xeon processor running at 2.6 GHz with 32 GB of memory with a timeout of 10 mins.

Observations and Inferences. Our experiments clearly demonstrate the scalability and efficiency of our tool in solving Separated GR(k) formulas.

Figure 4 plots the mean running time for the three benchmarks. We further report the mean values in Table 1. The table rows refer to the benchmarks we

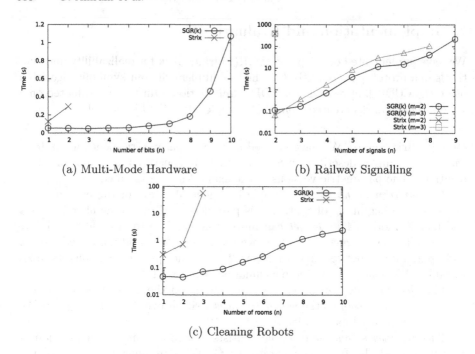

(a) Multi-Mode Hardware   (b) Railway Signalling

(c) Cleaning Robots

Fig. 4. Mean running time for different classes of benchmarks.

examine, and the columns refer to the value of the parameter n. As an example, for the specification Cleaning(3), SGR(k)'s mean running time is 0.07 s. (row titled Cleaning(n); SGR(k), column titled 3) and Strix's mean realizability check running time is 58.3 s. (row titled Cleaning(n);Strix), column titled 4). Cells reading 'TO' indicate experiments reached a timeout.

The results show that our tool solves a significantly larger number of benchmarks than Strix. On the few benchmarks which Strix solves, our tool outperforms

Table 1. Mean realizability check running times (sec.)

n		1	2	3	4	5	6	7	8	9	10
MultiMode(n)	SGR(k)	0.06	0.05	0.05	0.06	0.06	0.08	0.1	0.19	0.46	1.07
	Strix	0.13	0.29	TO	TO	TO	TO	TO	TO	TO	TO
Cleaning(n)	SGR(k)	0.05	0.05	0.07	0.09	0.16	0.26	0.63	1.16	1.78	2.43
	Strix	0.31	0.75	58.3	TO	TO	TO	TO	TO	TO	TO
Railways(n, 2)	SGR(k)	-	0.11	0.17	0.71	3.88	11.8	15.1	40.8	219	TO
	Strix	-	382	TO	TO	TO	TO	TO	TO	TO	TO
Railways(n, 3)	SGR(k)	-	0.07	0.36	1.67	8.39	29.8	50.3	102	TO	TO
	Strix	-	381	TO	TO	TO	TO	TO	TO	TO	TO

it by several orders of magnitude. Although the running time may vary depending on the automatic variable ordering chosen by CUDD, we do not believe it would vary enough to significantly change the results. Specifically, we calculated the 99% confidence interval for our results, and validated that for all data points our tool's entire interval lies below the entire interval for Strix.

Only three benchmarks were unsolvable by our tool (in the sense that the majority of the 10 executions timed out). The three benchmarks are the railway signal examples with $(n = 10, m = 2)$, $(n = 9, m = 3)$, and $(n = 10, m = 3)$. These benchmarks consist of a large number of variables (54, 40, and 60, respectively), making them particularly challenging. All executions of the remaining benchmarks were solved in less than 4 mins by our tool.

We also examined the number of solved executions per benchmark. Our tool solved all 10 executions for 35 out of 38 benchmarks. These are the 35 benchmarks that appear as solved in Fig. 4. For the railway signalling benchmark with $(n = 10, m = 2)$, our tool solved 2 out of 10 executions. In contrast, Strix was not able to solve even one execution for 31 out of 38 benchmarks. Even increasing the timeout to 8hrs only allowed Strix to solve a single additional benchmark. In total, Strix and our tool verified realizability of 7 benchmarks and 36 out of 38 benchmarks, respectively. In summary, our experiments demonstrate that our tool is able to solve specifications which are challenging for existing tools.

8 Related Work

The Adapter design pattern was introduced in [18], and has been used in many software contexts since. Our interpretation of the pattern is inspired by automata based description of the pattern proposed by Pedrazzini [34]. We reformulated the problem as synthesis of reactive controllers that compose with existing systems to achieve a temporal specification, e.g. [7,13,17]. Note that our work differs from such frameworks in its variables separation feature. A work with a concept similar to adapting behaviors is the *Shield synthesis* that studies the problem in which a synthesized controller corrects safety violations of an existing controller [24]. Note that in contrast, our problem is mostly concerned about liveness adaptation.

Reactive synthesis of LTL winning conditions is 2EXPTIME complete in the size of the formula [37], making it difficult to scale for applications. An approach to overcome the computational barrier has been to investigate fragments and variants of LTL with lower complexity for synthesis [4,14,16]. One such fragment is GR(k) [9], that offers a balance between efficiency and expressiveness. Specifically, GR(k) games are known to be efficient as they are solved in exponential time in the number of conjunctions k rather than exponential in the state-space [35]. Several studies have also shown that GR(k) specifications are highly expressive. As evidence, all properties expressed by deterministic Büchi automata (DBA) can be expressed in GR(k) [16], where a study of commonly appearing LTL patterns has shown that 52 of 55 patterns are DBA properties [15,29]. DBA properties have also been identified as common patterns in robotics applications [30].

Finally, Separated GR(k) games exhibit the *delay property*, which intuitively means that the system can win even after delaying its action for a finite amount of time while ignoring the environment before "catching up" with the environment. While this is reminiscent of asynchrony in reactive systems [6,38], a further exploration of relations between asynchrony and the delay property is required.

9   Conclusion

This paper presents a reactive systems-based model of the adapter design pattern. We model the adapters as transducers and reduce the problem of finding an *Adapter* transducer for a given *Adaptee* and *Target* systems, to the problem of synthesizing strategies for Separated GR(k) games. Through an analysis of theoretical complexity and algorithmic performance, we show that realizability and synthesis of Separated GR(k) games is efficient and scalable. Furthermore, by outperforming Strix, an existing state-of-the-art synthesis tool, we show that algorithms for the Separated GR(k) class of specifications add value to the portfolio of reactive synthesis tools.

The benefits of separation of input and output variables were previously shown in the context of Boolean Functional Synthesis [11]. Through this work, we showed that separation also leads to practically viable solutions in temporal reactive synthesis, specifically when encoding the types of equivalence relations that appear in reactive adaptation (where properties of runs of the first system are compared to properties of runs of the other). Since the systems may be loosely coupled, i.e., they may not run on the same clock, specifications that impose joint temporal constraints on the two systems may not be realizable. Thus, our proposition to use the type of equivalence that separated GR(k) formulas allow, gives users the power needed for comparing the *overall behaviors* of the systems while allowing realizability and efficient synthesis.

The results presented in this paper encourage future studies on the separation of variables in a broader context. For instance, reason about variants of the adapter design pattern that do not separate variables all the way through. That is to say, variants that translate to more general GR(k) specifications in which the separation appears in the input and output systems but not in the specification itself. One could further study the notion of separation of variables in more the general LTL specifications. Another direction is to consider systems that gets two types of input: from the input system (i.e. the *Target*) as well as from an environment. We believe that these future directions would enable the development of tools for synthesis from temporal specifications with a focus on expressing practical applications as well as ensuring scalability and efficiency.

Acknowledgements. We thank Supratik Chakraborty and Dana Fisman for useful comments. Work is supported in part by NSF grant 2030859 (CRA's CIFellows Project), NSF grants IIS-1527668, CCF-1704883, IIS-1830549, an award from the Maryland Procurement Office, ISF grant 2714/19, and by the Lynn and William Frankel Center for Computer Science.

References

1. Strix website. https://strix.model.in.tum.de/
2. The Reactive Synthesis Competition - SYNTCOMP 2020 Results. http://www.syntcomp.org/syntcomp-2020-results/
3. Amram, G., Bansal, S., Fried, D., Tabajara, L.M., Vardi, M.Y., Weiss, G.: Adapting behaviors via reactive synthesis (2021). CoRR abs/2105.13837 http://arxiv.org/abs/2105.13837
4. Amram, G., Maoz, S., Pistiner, O.: GR(1)*: GR(1) specifications extended with existential guarantees. In: ter Beek, M.H., McIver, A., Oliveira, J. (eds.) FM 2019. LNCS, vol. 11800, pp. 83–100. Springer, Cham (2019). https://doi.org/10.1007/978-3-030-30942-8_7
5. Baier, C., Katoen, J.: Principles of Model Checking. MIT Press, Cambridge (2008)
6. Bansal, S., Namjoshi, K.S., Sa'ar, Y.: Synthesis of asynchronous reactive programs from temporal specifications. In: Chockler, H., Weissenbacher, G. (eds.) CAV 2018. LNCS, vol. 10981, pp. 367–385. Springer, Cham (2018). https://doi.org/10.1007/978-3-319-96145-3_20
7. Bansal, S., Namjoshi, K.S., Sa'ar, Y.: Synthesis of coordination programs from linear temporal specifications. In: Proceedings of POPL (2019)
8. Bloem, R., Galler, S.J., Jobstmann, B., Piterman, N., Pnueli, A., Weiglhofer, M.: Interactive presentation: automatic hardware synthesis from specifications: a case study. In: Proceedings of DATE (2007)
9. Bloem, R., Jobstmann, B., Piterman, N., Pnueli, A., Sa'ar, Y.: Synthesis of reactive(1) designs. J. Comput. Syst. Sci. **78**(3), 911–938 (2012)
10. Bryant, R.E.: Graph-based algorithms for boolean function manipulation. IEEE Trans. Comput. **35**(8), 677–691 (1986)
11. Chakraborty, S., Fried, D., Tabajara, L.M., Vardi, M.Y.: Functional synthesis via input-output separation. In: Proceedings of FMCAD (2018)
12. Chatterjee, K.: Linear time algorithm for weak parity games (2008). CoRR abs/0805.1391 http://arxiv.org/abs/0805.1391
13. Ciolek, D., Braberman, V., D'Ippolito, N., Piterman, N., Uchitel, S.: Interaction models and automated control under partial observable environments. IEEE Trans. Softw. Eng. **43**(1), 19–33 (2016)
14. De Giacomo, G., Vardi, M.Y.: Linear temporal logic and linear dynamic logic on finite traces. In: Proceedings of IJCAI (2013)
15. Dwyer, M.B., Avrunin, G.S., Corbett, J.C.: Patterns in property specifications for finite-state verification. In: Proceedings of ICSE (1999)
16. Ehlers, R.: Generalized rabin(1) synthesis with applications to robust system synthesis. In: Bobaru, M., Havelund, K., Holzmann, G.J., Joshi, R. (eds.) NFM 2011. LNCS, vol. 6617, pp. 101–115. Springer, Heidelberg (2011). https://doi.org/10.1007/978-3-642-20398-5_9
17. Fried, D., Legay, A., Ouaknine, J., Vardi, M.Y.: Sequential relational decomposition. In: Proceedings of LICS (2018)
18. Gamma, E.: Design Patterns: Elements of Reusable Object-Oriented Software. Pearson Education India, Reading (1995)
19. Grabmayer, C., Endrullis, J., Hendriks, D., Klop, J.W., Moss, L.S.: Automatic sequences and zip-specifications. In: Proceedings of LICS (2012)
20. Grädel, E., Thomas, W., Wilke, T. (eds.): Automata, Logics, and Infinite Games: A Guide to Current Research (2002)

21. Hu, Q., D'Antoni, L.: Automatic program inversion using symbolic transducers. In: SIGPLAN, pp. 376–389, June 2017
22. Jacobs, S., Klein, F., Schirmer, S.: A high-level LTL synthesis format: TLSF v1.1. In: Proceedings of SYNT (2016)
23. Kocher, P., et al.: Spectre attacks: exploiting speculative execution. In: Proceedings of (S&P 2019) (2019)
24. Könighofer, B., et al.: Shield synthesis. Formal Meth. Syst. Des. **51**(2), 332–361 (2017)
25. Koruyeh, E.M., Khasawneh, K.N., Song, C., Abu-Ghazaleh, N.: Spectre returns! speculation attacks using the return stack buffer. In: Proceedings of USENIX (2018)
26. Lipp, M., et al.: Meltdown: Reading kernel memory from user space. In: Proceedings of USENIX (2018)
27. Loding, C., Thomas, W.: Alternating automata and logics over infinite words. In: van Leeuwen, J., Watanabe, O., Hagiya, M., Mosses, P.D., Ito, T. (eds.) TCS 2000. LNCS, vol. 1872, pp. 521–535. Springer, Heidelberg (2000). https://doi.org/10.1007/3-540-44929-9_36
28. Maoz, S., Ringert, J.O.: Synthesizing a lego forklift controller in GR(1): a case study. In: Proceedings of SYNT (2015)
29. Maoz, S., Ringert, J.O.: GR(1) synthesis for LTL specification patterns. In: Proceedings of ESEC/FSE (2016)
30. Menghi, C., Tsigkanos, C., Pelliccione, P., Ghezzi, C., Berger, T.: Specification patterns for robotic missions. IEEE Trans. Softw. Eng. 1 (2019)
31. Meyer, P.J., Sickert, S., Luttenberger, M.: Strix: Explicit reactive synthesis strikes back! In: Proceedings of CAV (2018)
32. Mohri, M.: Finite-state transducers in language and speech processing. Comput. Linguist. **23**(2), 269–311 (1997)
33. Ozay, N., Topcu, U., Murray, R.M.: Distributed power allocation for vehicle management systems. In: Proceedings of CDC-ECC (2011)
34. Pedrazzini, S.: The finite state automata's design patterns. In: Champarnaud, J.-M., Ziadi, D., Maurel, D. (eds.) WIA 1998. LNCS, vol. 1660, pp. 213–219. Springer, Heidelberg (1999). https://doi.org/10.1007/3-540-48057-9_19
35. Piterman, N., Pnueli, A.: Faster solutions of rabin and streett games. In: Proceedings of LICS (2006)
36. Pnueli, A.: The temporal logic of programs. In: Proceedings of FOCS (1977)
37. Pnueli, A., Rosner, R.: On the synthesis of a reactive module. In: Proceedings of POPL (1989)
38. Pnueli, A., Rosner, R.: On the synthesis of an asynchronous reactive module. In: Ausiello, G., Dezani-Ciancaglini, M., Della Rocca, S.R. (eds.) ICALP 1989. LNCS, vol. 372, pp. 652–671. Springer, Heidelberg (1989). https://doi.org/10.1007/BFb0035790
39. Somenzi, F.: CUDD: CU Decision Diagram Package Release 3.0.0 (2015). http://vlsi.colorado.edu/~fabio/CUDD/cudd.pdf
40. Zhu, S., Tabajara, L.M., Li, J., Pu, G., Vardi, M.Y.: A symbolic approach to safety LTL synthesis. In: HVC 2017. LNCS, vol. 10629, pp. 147–162. Springer, Cham (2017). https://doi.org/10.1007/978-3-319-70389-3_10
41. Zhu, S., Tabajara, L.M., Li, J., Pu, G., Vardi, M.Y.: Symbolic LTLf synthesis. In: Proceedings of IJCAI (2017)

Causality-Based Game Solving

Christel Baier[1] , Norine Coenen[2] , Bernd Finkbeiner[2] , Florian Funke[1] ,
Simon Jantsch[1] , and Julian Siber[2(✉)]

[1] Technische Universität Dresden,
Dresden, Germany
{christel.baier,florian.funke,
simon.jantsch}@tu-dresden.de
[2] CISPA Helmholtz Center for Information Security, Saarbrücken, Germany
{norine.coenen,finkbeiner,julian.siber}@cispa.de

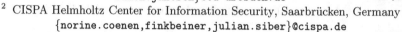

Abstract. We present a causality-based algorithm for solving two-player reachability games represented by logical constraints. These games are a useful formalism to model a wide array of problems arising, e.g., in program synthesis. Our technique for solving these games is based on the notion of *subgoals*, which are slices of the game that the reachability player necessarily needs to pass through in order to reach the goal. We use Craig interpolation to identify these necessary sets of moves and recursively slice the game along these subgoals. Our approach allows us to infer winning strategies that are structured along the subgoals. If the game is won by the reachability player, this is a strategy that progresses through the subgoals towards the final goal; if the game is won by the safety player, it is a permissive strategy that completely avoids a single subgoal. We evaluate our prototype implementation on a range of different games. On multiple benchmark families, our prototype scales dramatically better than previously available tools.

1 Introduction

Two-player games are a fundamental model in logic and verification due to their connection to a wide range of topics such as decision procedures, synthesis and control [1,2,6,7,11,21]. Algorithmic techniques for *finite-state* two-player games have been studied extensively for many acceptance conditions [20]. For *infinite-state* games most problems are directly undecidable. However, infinite state spaces occur naturally in domains like software synthesis [34] and cyber-physical systems [23], and hence handling such games is of great interest. An elegant classification of infinite-state games that can be algorithmically handled, depending

This work was partially supported by DFG grant 389792660 as part of TRR 248 – CPEC, see https://perspicuous-computing.science, the Cluster of Excellence EXC 2050/1 (CeTI, project ID 390696704, as part of Germany's Excellence Strategy), DFG-projects BA-1679/11-1 and BA-1679/12-1, the Research Training Group QuantLA (GRK 1763), and by the European Research Council (ERC) Grant OSARES (No. 683300).

A. Silva and K. R. M. Leino (Eds.) CAV 2021, LNCS 12759, pp. 894–917, 2021.
https://doi.org/10.1007/978-3-030-81685-8_42

on the acceptance condition of the game, was given in [14]. The authors assume a symbolic encoding of the game in a very general form. More recently, incomplete procedures for solving infinite-state two-player games specified using logical constraints were studied [4, 18]. While [4] is based on automated theorem-proving for Horn formulas and handles a wide class of acceptance conditions, the work in [18] focusses on reachability games specified in the theory of linear arithmetic, and uses sophisticated decision procedures for that theory.

In this paper, we present a novel technique for solving logically represented reachability games based on the notion of *subgoals*. A *necessary* subgoal is a transition predicate that is satisfied at least once on every play that reaches the overall goal. It represents an intermediate target that the reachability player must reach in order to win. Subgoals open up game solving to the study of cause-effect relationships in the form of counterfactual reasoning [28]: If a cause (the subgoal) had not occurred, then the effect (reaching the goal) would not have happened. Thus for the safety player, a necessary subgoal provides a chance to win the game based on local information: If they control all states satisfying the pre-condition of the subgoal, then any strategy that in these states picks a transition outside of the subgoal is winning. Finding such a necessary subgoal may let us conclude that the safety player wins without ever having to unroll the transition relation.

On the other hand, passing through a necessary subgoal is in general not enough for the reachability player to win. We call a subgoal *sufficient* if indeed the reachability player has a winning strategy from every state satisfying the post-condition of the subgoal. Dual to the description in the preceding paragraph, sufficient subgoals provide a chance for the reachability player to win the global game as they must merely reach this intermediate target. The two properties differ in one key aspect: While necessity of a subgoal only considers the paths of the game arena, for sufficiency the game structure is crucial.

We show how Craig interpolants can be used to compute necessary subgoals, making our methods applicable to games represented by any logic that supports interpolation. In contrast, determining whether a subgoal is sufficient requires a partial solution of the given game. This motivates the following recursive approach. We slice the game along a necessary subgoal into two parts, the pre-game and the post-game. In order to guarantee these games to be smaller, we solve the post-game under the assumption that the considered subgoal was bridged *for the last time*. We conclude that the safety player wins the overall game if they can avoid all initial states of the post-game that are winning for the reachability player. Otherwise, the pre-game is solved subject to the winning condition given by the sufficient subgoal consisting of these states. This approach does not only determine which player wins from each initial state, but also computes symbolically represented winning strategies with a causal structure. Winning safety player strategies induce necessary subgoals that the reachability player cannot pass, which constitutes a cause for their loss. Winning reachability player strategies represent a sequence of sufficient subgoals that will be passed, providing an explanation for the win. All missing proofs for our theoretical results can be found in the full version of this paper [3].

The Python-based implementation CABPY of our approach was used to compare its performance to SIMSYNTH [18], which is, to the best of our knowledge, the only other available tool for solving linear arithmetic reachability games. Our experiments demonstrate that our algorithm is competitive in many case studies. We can also confirm the expectation that our approach heavily benefits from qualitatively expressive Craig interpolants. It is noteworthy that like SIM-SYNTH our approach is fully automated and does not require any input in the form of hints or templates. Our contributions are summarized as follows:

- We introduce the concept of *necessary* and *sufficient subgoals* and show how Craig interpolation can be used to compute necessary subgoals (Sect. 4).
- We describe an algorithm for solving logically represented two-player reachability games using these concepts. We also discuss how to compute representations of winning strategies in our approach (Sect. 5).
- We evaluate our approach experimentally through our Python-based tool CABPY, demonstrating a competitive performance compared to the previously available tool SIMSYNTH on various case studies (Sect. 6).

Related Work. The problem of solving linear arithmetic games is addressed in [18] using an approach that relies on a dedicated decision procedure for quantified linear arithmetic formulas, together with a method to generalize safety strategies from truncated versions of the game that end after a prescribed number of rounds. Other approaches for solving infinite-state games include deductive methods that compute the winning regions of both players using proof rules [4], predicate abstraction where an abstract controlled predecessor operation is used on the abstract game representation [38], and symbolic BDD-based exploration of the state space [15]. Additional techniques are available for finite-state games, e.g., generalizing winning runs into a winning strategy for one of the players [31].

Our notion of subgoal is related to the concept of landmarks as used in planning [22]. Landmarks are milestones that must be true on every successful plan, and they can be used to decompose a planning task into smaller sub-tasks. Landmarks have also been used in a game setting to prevent the opponent from reaching their goal using counter-planning [32]. Whenever a planning task is unsolvable, one method to find out why is checking hierarchical abstractions for solvability and finding the components causing the problem [36].

Causality-based approaches have also been used for model checking of multi-threaded concurrent programs [24,25]. In our approach, we use Craig interpolation to compute the subgoals. Interpolation has already been used in similar contexts before, for example to extract winning strategies from game trees [16] or to compute new predicates to refine the game abstractions [10]. In [18], interpolation is used to synthesize concrete winning strategies from so called *winning strategy skeletons*, which describe a set of strategies of which at least one is winning.

2 Motivating Example

Consider the scenario that an expensive painting is displayed in a large exhibition room of a museum. It is secured with an alarm system that is controlled via a control panel on the opposite side of the room. A security guard is sleeping at the control panel and occasionally wakes up to check whether the alarm is still armed. To steal the painting, a thief first needs to disable the alarm and then reach the painting before the alarm has been reactivated. We model this scenario as a two-player game between a safety player (the guard) and a reachability player (the thief) in the theory of linear arithmetic. The moves of both players, their initial positions, and the goal condition are described by the formulas:

$$
\begin{aligned}
Init \equiv\ & \neg\mathbf{r} \wedge x = 0 \wedge y = 0 \wedge p = 0 \wedge a = 1 \wedge t = 0, \\
Guard \equiv\ & \neg\mathbf{r} \wedge \mathbf{r}' \wedge x' = x \wedge y' = y \wedge p' = p \\
& \wedge ((t' = t - 1 \wedge a' = a) \vee (t \leq 0 \wedge t' = 2)), && \text{(sleep or wake up)} \\
Thief \equiv\ & \mathbf{r} \wedge \neg\mathbf{r}' \wedge t' = t \\
& \wedge\, x + 1 \geq x' \geq x - 1 \wedge y + 1 \geq y' \geq y - 1 && \text{(move)} \\
& \wedge\, (x' \neq 0 \vee y' \neq 10 \implies a' = a) && \text{(alarm off)} \\
& \wedge\, (x' \neq 10 \vee y' \neq 5 \vee a = 1 \implies p' = p), && \text{(steal)} \\
Goal \equiv\ & \neg\mathbf{r} \wedge p = 1.
\end{aligned}
$$

The thief's position in the room is modeled by two coordinates $x, y \in \mathbb{R}$ with initial value $(0, 0)$, and with every transition the thief can move some bounded distance. Note that we use primed variables to represent the value of variables after taking a transition. The control panel is located at $(0, 10)$ and the painting at $(10, 5)$. The status of the alarm and the painting are described by two boolean variables $a, p \in \{0, 1\}$. The guard wakes up every two time units, modeled by the variable $t \in \mathbb{R}$. The variables x, y are bounded to the interval $[0, 10]$ and t to $[0, 2]$. The boolean variable $\mathbf{r}$ encodes who makes the next move. In the presented configuration, the thief needs more time to move from the control panel to the painting than the guard will sleep. It follows that there is a winning strategy for the guard, namely, to always reactivate the alarm upon waking up.

Although it is intuitively fairly easy to come up with this strategy for the guard, it is surprisingly hard for game solving tools to find it. The main obstacle is the infinite state space of this game. Our approach for solving games represented in this logical way imitates *causal reasoning*: Humans observe that in order for the thief to steal the painting (i.e., the effect $p = 1$), a transition must have been taken whose source state does not satisfy the pre-condition of (steal) while the target state does. Part of this cause is the condition $a = 0$, i.e., the alarm is off. Recursively, in order for the effect $a = 0$ to happen, a transition setting a from 1 to 0 must have occurred, and so on.

Our approach captures these cause-effect relationships through the notion of *necessary subgoals*, which are essential milestones that the reachability player has to transition through in order to achieve their goal. The first necessary subgoal corresponding to the intuitive description above is

$$C_1 = (Guard \vee Thief) \wedge p \neq 1 \wedge p' = 1.$$

In this case, it easy to see that C_1 is also a *sufficient subgoal*, meaning that all successor states of C_1 are winning for the thief. Therefore, it is enough to solve the game with the modified objective to reach those predecessor states of C_1 from which the thief can *enforce* C_1 being the next move (even if it is not their turn). Doing so recursively produces the necessary subgoal

$$C_2 = (Guard \vee Thief) \wedge a \neq 0 \wedge a' = 0,$$

meaning that some transition must have caused the effect that the alarm is disabled. However, C_2 is *not* sufficient which can be seen by recursively solving the game spanning from successor states of C_2 to C_1. This computation has an important caveat: After passing through C_2, it may happen that a is reset to 1 at a later point (in this particular case, this constitutes precisely the winning strategy of the safety player), which means that there is no canonical way to slice the game along this subgoal into smaller parts. Hence the recursive call solves the game from C_2 to C_1 *subject to* the bold assumption that any move from $a = 0$ to $a' = 1$ is winning for the guard. This generally underapproximates the winning states of the thief. Remarkably, we show that this approximation is enough to build winning strategies for *both* players from their respective winning regions. In this case, it allows us to infer that moving through C_2 is always a losing move for the thief. However, at the same time, any play reaching *Goal* has to move through C_2. It follows that the thief loses the global game.

We evaluated our method on several configurations of this game, which we call *Mona Lisa*. The results in Sect. 6 support our conjecture that the room size has little influence on the time our technique needs to solve the game.

3   Preliminaries

We consider two-player reachability games defined by formulas in a given logic $\mathcal{L}$. We let $\mathcal{L}(\mathcal{V})$ be the $\mathcal{L}$-formulas over a finite set of variables $\mathcal{V}$, also called *state predicates* in the following. We call $\mathcal{V}' = \{v' \mid v \in \mathcal{V}\}$ the set of *primed variables*, which are used to represent the value of variables after taking a transition. Transitions are expressed by formulas in the set $\mathcal{L}(\mathcal{V} \cup \mathcal{V}')$, called *transition predicates*. For some formula $\varphi \in \mathcal{L}(\mathcal{V})$, we denote the substitution of all variables by their primed variant by $\varphi[\mathcal{V}/\mathcal{V}']$. Similarly, we define $\varphi[\mathcal{V}'/\mathcal{V}]$.

For our algorithm we will require the satisfiability problem of $\mathcal{L}$-formulas to be decidable and *Craig interpolants* [13] to exist for any two mutually unsatisfiable formulas. Formally, we assume there is a function Sat : $\mathcal{L}(\mathcal{V}) \rightarrow \mathbb{B}$ that checks the satisfiability of some formula $\varphi \in \mathcal{L}(\mathcal{V})$ and an unsatisfiability check Unsat : $\mathcal{L}(\mathcal{V}) \rightarrow \mathbb{B}$. For interpolation, we assume that there is a function Interpolate : $\mathcal{L}(\mathcal{V}) \times \mathcal{L}(\mathcal{V}) \rightarrow \mathcal{L}(\mathcal{V})$ computing a *Craig interpolant* for mutually unsatisfiable formulas: If $\varphi, \psi \in \mathcal{L}(\mathcal{V})$ are such that Unsat($\varphi \wedge \psi$) holds, then $\psi \implies$ Interpolate(φ, ψ) is valid, Interpolate(φ, ψ) $\wedge \varphi$ is unsatisfiable, and Interpolate(φ, ψ) only contains variables shared by φ and ψ.

These functions are provided by many modern *Satisfiability Modulo Theories* (SMT) solvers, in particular for the theories of linear integer arithmetic and linear real arithmetic, which we will use for all our examples. Note that interpolation is usually only supported for the quantifier-free fragments of these logics, while our algorithm will introduce existential quantifiers. Therefore, we resort to quantifier elimination wherever necessary, for which there are known procedures for both linear integer arithmetic and linear real arithmetic formulas [29,33].

In order to distinguish the two players, we will assume that a Boolean variable called $\mathbf{r} \in \mathcal{V}$ exists, which holds exactly in the states controlled by the reachability player. For all other variables $v \in \mathcal{V}$, we let $\mathcal{D}(v)$ be the domain of v, and we define $\mathcal{D} = \bigcup \{\mathcal{D}(v) \mid v \in \mathcal{V}\}$. In the remainder of the paper, we consider the variables $\mathcal{V}$ and their domains to be fixed.

Definition 1 (Reachability Game). *A reachability game is defined by a tuple* $\mathcal{G} = \langle Init, Safe, Reach, Goal \rangle$, *where* $Init \in \mathcal{L}(\mathcal{V})$ *is the initial condition,* $Safe \in \mathcal{L}(\mathcal{V} \cup \mathcal{V}')$ *defines the transitions of player* **SAFE**, $Reach \in \mathcal{L}(\mathcal{V} \cup \mathcal{V}')$ *defines the transitions of player* **REACH** *and* $Goal \in \mathcal{L}(\mathcal{V})$ *is the goal condition.*
We require the formulas $(Safe \implies \neg \mathbf{r})$ *and* $(Reach \implies \mathbf{r})$ *to be valid.*

A *state* s of $\mathcal{G}$ is a valuation of the variables $\mathcal{V}$, i.e., a function $s: \mathcal{V} \to \mathcal{D}$ that satisfies $s(v) \in \mathcal{D}(v)$ for all $v \in \mathcal{V}$. We denote the set of states by S, and we let S_{SAFE} be the states s such that $s(\mathbf{r}) = \mathtt{false}$, and S_{REACH} be the states s such that $s(\mathbf{r}) = \mathtt{true}$. The variable $\mathbf{r}$ determines whether **REACH** or **SAFE** makes the move out of the current state, and in particular $Safe \wedge Reach$ is unsatisfiable.

Given a state predicate $\varphi \in \mathcal{L}(\mathcal{V})$, we denote by $\varphi(s)$ the closed formula we get by replacing each occurrence of variable $v \in \mathcal{V}$ in φ by $s(v)$. Similarly, given a transition predicate $\tau \in \mathcal{L}(\mathcal{V} \cup \mathcal{V}')$ and states s, s', we let $\tau(s, s')$ be the formula we obtain by replacing all occurrences of $v \in \mathcal{V}$ in τ by $s(v)$, and all occurrences of $v' \in \mathcal{V}'$ in τ by $s'(v)$. For replacing only $v \in \mathcal{V}$ by $s(v)$, we define $\tau(s) \in \mathcal{L}(\mathcal{V}')$. A *trap state* of $\mathcal{G}$ is a state s such that $(Safe \vee Reach)(s) \in \mathcal{L}(\mathcal{V}')$ is unsatisfiable (i.e., s has no outgoing transitions).

A *play* of $\mathcal{G}$ starting in state s_0 is a finite or infinite sequence of states $\rho = s_0 s_1 s_2 \ldots \in S^+ \cup S^\omega$ such that for all $i < \mathrm{len}(\rho)$ either $Safe(s_i, s_{i+1})$ or $Reach(s_i, s_{i+1})$ is valid, and if ρ is a finite play, then $s_{\mathrm{len}(\rho)}$ is required to be a trap state. Here, $\mathrm{len}(s_0 \ldots s_n) = n$ for finite plays, and $\mathrm{len}(\rho) = \infty$ if ρ is an infinite play. The set of plays of some game $\mathcal{G} = \langle Init, Safe, Reach, Goal \rangle$ is defined as $\mathrm{Plays}(\mathcal{G}) = \{\rho = s_0 s_1 s_2 \ldots \mid \rho \text{ is a play in } \mathcal{G} \text{ s.t. } Init(s_0) \text{ holds}\}$. **REACH** *wins* some play $\rho = s_0 s_1 \ldots$ if the play reaches a goal state, i.e., if there exists some integer $0 \leq k \leq \mathrm{len}(\rho)$ such that $Goal(s_k)$ is valid. Otherwise, **SAFE** wins play ρ. A *reachability strategy* σ_R is a function $\sigma_R : S^* S_{\mathsf{REACH}} \to S$ such that if $\sigma_R(\omega s) = s'$ and s is not a trap state, then $Reach(s, s')$ is valid. We say that a play $\rho = s_0 s_1 s_2 \ldots$ is *consistent* with σ_R if for all i such that $s_i(\mathbf{r}) = \mathtt{true}$ we have $s_{i+1} = \sigma_R(s_0 \ldots s_i)$. A reachability strategy σ_R is *winning* from some state s if **REACH** wins every play consistent with σ_R starting in s. We define *safety strategies* σ_S for **SAFE** analogously. We say that a player *wins in or from* a state s if they have a winning strategy from s. Lastly, **REACH** *wins the game* $\mathcal{G}$ if they win from some initial state. Otherwise, **SAFE** wins.

We often project a transition predicate T onto the source or target states of transitions satisfying T, which is taken care of by the formulas $\mathrm{Pre}(T) = \exists \mathcal{V}'.\, T$ and $\mathrm{Post}(T) = \exists \mathcal{V}.\, T$. The notation $\exists \mathcal{V}$ (resp. $\exists \mathcal{V}'$) represents the existential quantification over all variables in the corresponding set. Given $\varphi \in \mathcal{L}(\mathcal{V})$, we call the set of transitions in $\mathcal{G}$ that move from states not satisfying φ, to states satisfying φ, the *instantiation* of φ, formally:

$$\mathrm{Instantiate}(\varphi, \mathcal{G}) = (\mathit{Safe} \vee \mathit{Reach}) \wedge \neg\varphi \wedge \varphi'.$$

4 Subgoals

We formally define the notion of subgoals. Let $\mathcal{G} = \langle \mathit{Init}, \mathit{Safe}, \mathit{Reach}, \mathit{Goal} \rangle$ be a fixed reachability game throughout this section, where we assume that $\mathit{Init} \wedge \mathit{Goal}$ is unsatisfiable. Whenever this assumption is not satisfied in our algorithm, we will instead consider the game $\mathcal{G}' = \langle \mathit{Init} \wedge \neg \mathit{Goal}, \mathit{Safe}, \mathit{Reach}, \mathit{Goal} \rangle$ which does satisfy it. As states in $\mathit{Init} \wedge \mathit{Goal}$ are immediately winning for REACH, this is not a real restriction.

Definition 2 (Enforceable transitions). *The set of* enforceable transitions *relative to a transition predicate $T \in \mathcal{L}(\mathcal{V} \cup \mathcal{V}')$ is defined by the formula*

$$\mathrm{Enf}(T, \mathcal{G}) = (\mathit{Safe} \vee \mathit{Reach}) \wedge T \wedge \neg\exists \mathcal{V}'.\, \big(\mathit{Safe} \wedge \neg T\big).$$

The enforceable transitions operator serves a purpose similar to the *controlled predecessors* operator commonly known in the literature, which is often used in a backwards fixed point computation, called *attractor construction* [37]. For both operations, the idea is to determine controllability by REACH. The main difference is that we do not consider the whole transition relation, but only a predetermined set of transitions and check from which predecessor states the post-condition of the set can be enforced by REACH. These include all transitions in T controlled by REACH and additionally transitions in T controlled by SAFE such that *all other transitions* in the origin state of the transition also satisfy T. The similarity with the controlled predecessor is exemplified by the following lemma:

Lemma 3. *Let T be a transition predicate, and suppose that all states satisfying $\mathrm{Post}(T)[\mathcal{V}'/\mathcal{V}]$ are winning for REACH in $\mathcal{G}$. Then all states in $\mathrm{Pre}(\mathrm{Enf}(T, \mathcal{G}))$ are winning for REACH in $\mathcal{G}$.*

Proof. Clearly, all states in $\mathrm{Pre}(\mathrm{Enf}(T, \mathcal{G}))$ that are under the control of REACH are winning for REACH, as in any such state they have a transition satisfying T (observe that $\mathrm{Enf}(T, \mathcal{G}) \implies T$ is valid), which leads to a winning state by assumption.

So let s be a state satisfying $\mathrm{Pre}(\mathrm{Enf}(T, \mathcal{G}))$ that is under the control of SAFE. As $\mathrm{Pre}(\mathrm{Enf}(T, \mathcal{G}))(s)$ is valid, s has a transition that satisfies T (in particular, s is not a trap state). Furthermore, we know that there is no $s' \in S$ such that $\mathit{Safe}(s, s') \wedge \neg T(s, s')$ holds, and hence there is no transition satisfying $\neg T$ from s. Since $\mathrm{Post}(T)[\mathcal{V}'/\mathcal{V}]$ is winning for REACH, it follows that from s player SAFE cannot avoid playing into a winning state of REACH. $\qquad\square$

We now turn to a formal definition of *necessary subgoals*, which intuitively are sets of transitions that appear on every play that is winning for REACH.

Definition 4 (Necessary subgoal). *A necessary subgoal $C \in \mathcal{L}(\mathcal{V} \cup \mathcal{V}')$ for $\mathcal{G}$ is a transition predicate such that for every play $\rho = s_0 s_1 \ldots$ of $\mathcal{G}$ and $n \in \mathbb{N}$ such that $Goal(s_n)$ is valid, there exists some $k < n$ such that $C(s_k, s_{k+1})$ is valid.*

Necessary subgoals provide a means by which winning safety player strategies can be identified, as formalized in the following lemma.

Lemma 5. *A safety strategy σ_S is winning in $\mathcal{G}$ if and only if there exists a necessary subgoal C for $\mathcal{G}$ such that for all plays $\rho = s_0 s_1 \ldots$ of $\mathcal{G}$ consistent with σ_S there is no $n \in \mathbb{N}$ such that $C(s_n, s_{n+1})$ holds.*

Proof. " $\implies$ ". The transition predicate $Goal[\mathcal{V}/\mathcal{V}']$ (i.e., transitions with endpoints satisfying $Goal$) is clearly a necessary subgoal. If σ_S is winning for SAFE, then no play consistent with σ_S contains a transition in this necessary subgoal. " $\impliedby$ ". Let C be a necessary subgoal such that no play consistent with σ_S contains a transition of C. Then by Definition 4 no play consistent with σ_S contains a state satisfying $Goal$. Hence σ_S is a winning strategy for SAFE. $\square$

Of course, the question remains how to compute non-trivial subgoals. Indeed, using $Goal$ as outlined in the proof above provides no further benefit over a simple backwards exploration (see Remark 15 in the following section).

Ideally, a subgoal should represent an interesting key decision to focus the strategy search. As we show next, Craig interpolation allows to extract partial causes for the mutual unsatisfiability of $Init$ and $Goal$ and can in this way provide necessary subgoals. Recall that a Craig interpolant φ between $Init$ and $Goal$ is a state predicate that is implied by $Goal$, and unsatisfiable in conjunction with $Init$. In this sense, φ describes an observable *effect* that must occur if REACH wins, and the concrete transition that instantiates the interpolant *causes* this effect.

Proposition 6. *Let φ be a Craig interpolant for $Init$ and $Goal$. Then the transition predicate $\text{Instantiate}(\varphi, \mathcal{G})$ is a necessary subgoal.*

Proof. As φ is an interpolant, it holds that $Goal \implies \varphi$ is valid and $Init \wedge \varphi$ is unsatisfiable. Consider any play $\rho = s_0 s_1 \ldots$ of $\mathcal{G}$ such that $Goal(s_n)$ is valid for some $n \in \mathbb{N}$. It follows that $\neg\varphi(s_0)$ and $\varphi(s_n)$ are both valid. Consequently, there is some $0 \le i < n$ such that $\neg\varphi(s_i)$ and $\varphi(s_{i+1})$ are both valid. As all pairs (s_k, s_{k+1}) satisfy either $Safe$ or $Reach$, it follows that $\big(\text{Instantiate}(\varphi, \mathcal{G})\big)(s_i, s_{i+1})$ is valid. Hence, $\text{Instantiate}(\varphi, \mathcal{G})$ is a necessary subgoal. $\square$

While avoiding a necessary subgoal is a winning strategy for SAFE, reaching a necessary subgoal is in general not sufficient to guarantee a win for REACH. This is because there might be some transitions in the necessary subgoal that produce the desired effect described by the Craig interpolant, but that trap REACH in a region of the state space where they cannot enforce some other necessary effect to reach goal. For the purpose of describing a set of transitions that is guaranteed to be winning for the reachability player, we introduce *sufficient subgoals*.

Definition 7 (Sufficient subgoal). *A transition predicate $F \in \mathcal{L}(\mathcal{V} \cup \mathcal{V}')$ is called a* sufficient subgoal *if REACH wins from every state satisfying $\mathrm{Post}(F)[\mathcal{V}'/\mathcal{V}]$.*

Example 8. Consider the Mona Lisa game $\mathcal{G}$ described in Sect. 2.

$$C_1 = (Guard \lor Thief) \land p \neq 1 \land p' = 1$$

qualifies as sufficient subgoal, because REACH wins from every successor state as all those states satisfy *Goal*. Also, every play reaching *Goal* eventually passes C_1, and hence C_1 is also necessary. On the other hand,

$$C_2 = (Guard \lor Thief) \land a \neq 0 \land a' = 0$$

is only a necessary subgoal in $\mathcal{G}$, because SAFE wins from some (in fact all) states satisfying $\mathrm{Post}(C_2)$.

If the set of transitions in the necessary subgoal C that lead to winning states of REACH is definable in $\mathcal{L}$ then we call the transition predicate F that defines it the *largest sufficient subgoal* included in C. It is characterized by the properties (1) $F \implies C$ is valid, and (2) if F' is such that $F \implies F'$ is valid, then either $F \equiv F'$, or F' is not a sufficient subgoal. Since C is a necessary subgoal and F is maximal with the properties above, REACH needs to see a transition in F eventually in order to win. This balance of necessity and sufficiency allows us to partition the game along F into a game that happens after the subgoal and one that happens before.

Proposition 9. *Let C be a necessary subgoal, and F be the largest sufficient subgoal included in C. Then REACH wins from an initial state s in $\mathcal{G}$ if and only if REACH wins from s in the pre-game*

$$\mathcal{G}_{pre} = \langle Init, Safe \land \neg F, Reach \land \neg F, \mathrm{Pre}(\mathrm{Enf}(F, \mathcal{G})) \rangle.$$

Proof. " $\implies$ ". Suppose that REACH wins in $\mathcal{G}$ from s using strategy σ_R. Assume for a contradiction that SAFE wins in $\mathcal{G}_{pre}$ from s using strategy σ_S. Consider strategy σ'_S such that $\sigma'_S(\omega s') = \sigma_S(\omega s')$ if $(Safe \land \neg F)(s')$ is satisfiable, and else $\sigma'_S(\omega s') = \sigma''_S(\omega s')$, where σ''_S is an arbitrary safety player strategy in $\mathcal{G}$. Let $\rho = s_0 s_1 \ldots$ be the (unique) play of $\mathcal{G}$ consistent with both σ_R and σ'_S, where $s_0 = s$. Since σ_R is winning in $\mathcal{G}$ and C is a necessary subgoal in $\mathcal{G}$, there must exist some $m \in \mathbb{N}$ such that $C(s_m, s_{m+1})$ is valid. Let m be the smallest such index. Since $F \implies C$, we know for all $0 \leq k < m$ that $\neg F(s_k, s_{k+1})$ holds. Hence, there is the play $\rho' = s_0 s_1 \ldots s_m \ldots$ in $\mathcal{G}_{pre}$ consistent with σ_S. The state s_{m+1} is winning for REACH in $\mathcal{G}$, as it is reached on a play consistent with the winning strategy σ_R. Hence, we know that $F(s_m, s_{m+1})$ holds, because F is the largest sufficient subgoal included in C. If $(Reach \wedge F)(s_m, s_{m+1})$ held, we would have that $\mathrm{Pre}(\mathrm{Enf}(F, \mathcal{G})(s_m)$ holds: a contradiction with ρ' being consistent with σ_S, which we assumed to be winning in $\mathcal{G}_{pre}$. It follows that $(Safe \wedge F)(s_m, s_{m+1})$ holds. We can conclude that $(Safe \wedge \neg F)(s_m)$ is unsatisfiable (i.e., s_m is a trap state in $\mathcal{G}_{pre}$), because in all other cases SAFE plays according to σ_S, which cannot choose a transition satisfying F. However, this implies that $\mathrm{Pre}(\mathrm{Enf}(F, \mathcal{G})(s_m)$ holds, again a contradiction with ρ' being consistent with winning strategy σ_S. "$\Longleftarrow$". If REACH wins in $\mathcal{G}_{pre}$ they have a strategy σ_R such that every play consistent with σ_R reaches the set $\mathrm{Pre}(\mathrm{Enf}(F, \mathcal{G}))$. As F is a sufficient subgoal, the states $\mathrm{Post}(F)$ are winning for REACH by definition. It follows by Lemma 3 that all states satisfying $\mathrm{Pre}(\mathrm{Enf}(F, \mathcal{G}))$ are winning in $\mathcal{G}$. Combining σ_R with a strategy that wins in all these states yields a winning strategy for REACH in $\mathcal{G}$. $\square$

5 Causality-Based Game Solving

Lemma 9 in the preceding section foreshadows how subgoals can be employed in building a recursive approach for the solution of reachability games. Before turning to our actual algorithm, we describe a way to symbolically represent nondeterministic memoryless strategies. As discussed in [18], there is no ideal strategy description language for the class of games we consider. Our approach allows us to describe sets of concrete strategies as defined in Sect. 3 with linear arithmetic formulas. This framework will prove convenient for *strategy synthesis*, i.e., the computation of winning strategies instead of simply determining the winner of the game.

5.1 Symbolically Represented Strategies

We will represent strategies for both players using transition predicates $\mathfrak{S} \in \mathcal{L}(\mathcal{V} \cup \mathcal{V}')$, henceforth called *symbolic strategies*, where we only require that $(\mathfrak{S} \implies (Safe \vee Reach))$ is valid. A sequence $s_0 \ldots s_n \in S^+$ is called a *play prefix* if it is a prefix of some play in $\mathcal{G}$, $(\neg Goal)(s_j)$ holds for all $0 \le j \le n$, and s_n is not a trap state. We say that a play prefix $\rho = s_0 \ldots s_n$ *conforms to* a symbolic reachability strategy $\mathfrak{S}$ if for all $j < n$ we have that $\mathfrak{S}(s_j, s_{j+1})$ holds whenever $s_j \in S_{\text{REACH}}$ (and analogously for safety strategies). A play conforms to $\mathfrak{S}$ if all its play prefixes conform to $\mathfrak{S}$. We say that $\mathfrak{S}$ is winning for REACH in s if all plays from s that conform to $\mathfrak{S}$ are winning for REACH and all play prefixes $s_0 \ldots s_n \in S^* S_{\text{REACH}}$ from s that conform to $\mathfrak{S}$ are such that $(\mathfrak{S} \wedge Reach)(s_n)$ is satisfiable (and analogously for SAFE). The second condition ensures that the player cannot be forced to play a transition outside of $\mathfrak{S}$ by their opponent while the play has not reached a trap state or *Goal*, and in particular guarantees the existence of a concrete strategy (as defined in Sect. 3) conforming to $\mathfrak{S}$.

Lemma 10. *If REACH (SAFE) has a winning symbolic strategy in s, then REACH (SAFE) has a concrete winning strategy in s.*

Proof. Let $\mathfrak{S}$ by a symbolic winning strategy for REACH. Let σ_R be any reachability strategy such that for all play prefixes $\omega s \in S^* S_{\text{REACH}}$ that conform to $\mathfrak{S}$ the formula $\mathfrak{S}(s, \sigma_R(\omega s))$ is valid. Such a function is guaranteed to exist, as $(\mathfrak{S} \wedge \text{Reach})(s)$ is satisfiable for all such play prefixes by definition. Furthermore, σ_R is winning as all play prefixes of plays consistent with σ_R conform to $\mathfrak{S}$, and hence all these plays are winning by assumption. The proof for SAFE is analogous. $\square$

This representation allows us to specify nondeterministic strategies, but classical memoryless strategies on finite arenas (specified as a function $\sigma \colon S_{\text{REACH}} \to S$ or $S_{\text{SAFE}} \to S$) can also be represented in this form using a disjunction over formulas $\bigwedge_{v \in \mathcal{V}}(v = s(v) \wedge v' = \sigma(s)(v))$ for varying $s \in S$.

The following lemma shows that a necessary subgoal directly yields a symbolic strategy for SAFE if the subgoal is, in a certain sense, *locally avoidable* by SAFE. It will be our main tool for synthesizing safety player strategies.

Lemma 11. *Let C be a necessary subgoal for $\mathcal{G}$ and suppose that $\text{Unsat}(\text{Enf}(C, \mathcal{G}))$ holds. Then, $\text{Safe} \wedge \neg C$ is a winning symbolic strategy for SAFE in $\mathcal{G}$.*

5.2 A Recursive Algorithm

We now describe our algorithm which utilizes necessary subgoals to decompose and solve two-player reachability games (Algorithm 1). It is incomplete in the sense that it does not return on every input (Sect. 5.3 discusses special cases with guaranteed termination). If the algorithm returns on input $\mathcal{G}$, it returns a triple $(R, \mathfrak{S}_{\text{REACH}}, \mathfrak{S}_{\text{SAFE}})$, where (1) R is a state predicate characterizing the initial states that are winning for REACH in $\mathcal{G}$, (2) $\mathfrak{S}_{\text{REACH}}$ is a symbolic strategy for REACH that wins in all initial states satisfying R, and (3) $\mathfrak{S}_{\text{SAFE}}$ is a symbolic strategy for SAFE that wins in all initial states satisfying $\text{Init} \wedge \neg R$. The returned safety strategy $\mathfrak{S}_{\text{SAFE}}$ is such that $\neg \mathfrak{S}_{\text{SAFE}}$ is a necessary subgoal that SAFE can avoid locally in the game $\mathcal{G}$ restricted to intial states $\text{Init} \wedge \neg R$ (see Lemma 11).

Algorithm 1 works as follows. States satisfying Init and Goal are immediately winning for REACH and thus always part of the returned formula R. Following the discussion at the beginning of Sect. 4, further analysis considers the game starting in the remaining initial states $I = \text{Init} \wedge \neg \text{Goal}$. If there is no such state, we may return that all initial states are winning (line 5). Here, REACH wins from R without playing any move, and hence $\mathfrak{S}_{\text{REACH}} = \text{false}$ is a valid winning symbolic strategy (winning symbolic strategies are only required to provide moves in prefixes that have not seen Goal so far). We may choose $\mathfrak{S}_{\text{SAFE}}$ arbitrarily as there is no initial state winning for SAFE.

If the algorithm does not return in line 5, a necessary subgoal C between I and Goal is computed by instantiating a Craig interpolant φ for the two predicates (lines 6 and 7, see also Proposition 6). We break up the remaining description of the algorithm into three parts, which correspond to the main cases that occur when splitting the game along the subgoal C.

Algorithm 1: Reach($\mathcal{G}$)

In : reachability game $\mathcal{G} = \langle Init, Safe, Reach, Goal \rangle$

Out: triple $(R, \mathfrak{S}_{\text{REACH}}, \mathfrak{S}_{\text{SAFE}})$ s.t.

- $R \in \mathcal{L}(\mathcal{V})$ represents the set of initial states winning for **REACH**;
- $\mathfrak{S}_{\text{REACH}}$ is a winning symbolic reachability strategy for states in R;
- $\mathfrak{S}_{\text{SAFE}}$ is a winning symbolic safety strategy for states in $Init \wedge \neg R$.

```
1  begin
2  │  R ← Init ∧ Goal
3  │  I ← Init ∧ ¬Goal
4  │  if Unsat(I) then
5  │  └  return R, false, false
6  │  φ ← Interpolate(I, Goal)
7  │  C ← Instantiate(φ, 𝒢)
8  │  if Unsat(Enf(C, 𝒢)) then
9  │  └  return R, false, Safe ∧ ¬C
10 │  𝒢_post ← ⟨Post(C)[𝒱'/𝒱], Safe ∧ φ, Reach ∧ φ, Goal⟩
11 │  R_post, 𝔖_REACH^post, 𝔖_SAFE^post ← Reach (𝒢_post)
12 │  F ← C ∧ R_post[𝒱/𝒱']
13 │  if Unsat(Enf(F, 𝒢)) then
14 │  └  return R, false, Safe ∧ ¬F ∧ (φ ⟹ 𝔖_SAFE^post)
15 │  if Sat((Reach ∨ Safe) ∧ φ ∧ ¬φ' ∧ ¬Goal) then
16 │  │  F ← F ∨ Goal[𝒱/𝒱']
17 │  └  φ ← false
18 │  𝒢_pre ← ⟨I, Safe ∧ ¬F, Reach ∧ ¬F, Pre(Enf(F, 𝒢))⟩
19 │  R_pre, 𝔖_REACH^pre, 𝔖_SAFE^pre ← Reach (𝒢_pre)
20 │  return R ∨ R_pre,
21 │         combine(𝔖_REACH^pre, F, 𝔖_REACH^post),
22 └         (¬φ ⟹ 𝔖_SAFE^pre) ∧ (φ ⟹ 𝔖_SAFE^post)
```

Case 1: SAFE can avoid the subgoal C. If the necessary subgoal C qualifies for Lemma 11, we can immediately conclude that **SAFE** is winning for all states statisfying I (lines 8 and 9). An instance of this case occurs if the interpolant describes a bottleneck in the game which is fully controlled by **SAFE**. The winning symbolic reachability strategy is $Safe \wedge \neg C$ in this case (line 9), and we will assume that safety strategies returned by recursive calls of the algorithm are essentially negations of necessary subgoals that can be avoided by **SAFE**.

If Lemma 11 is not applicable, we next find those transitions in C that move into a winning state for the safety player. This is achieved by analyzing the *post-game* (line 10):

$$\mathcal{G}_{post} = \langle \text{Post}(C)[\mathcal{V}'/\mathcal{V}], \text{Safe} \wedge \varphi, \text{Reach} \wedge \varphi, \text{Goal} \rangle.$$

Its initial states are exactly the states one sees after bridging the subgoal C. In order to make sure that $\mathcal{G}_{post}$ is, in some sense, easier to solve than $\mathcal{G}$, we restrict both *Safe* and *Reach* to φ, which is the interpolant used to compute the subgoal C. This has the effect of removing all transitions in states *not* satisfying φ, making them trap states. For the safety player this makes $\mathcal{G}_{post}$ easier to win than $\mathcal{G}$ as all plays ending in such a trap state without seeing *Goal* before are winning for SAFE in $\mathcal{G}_{post}$. Hence we formally have:

Lemma 12. *If $\mathfrak{S}$ is a winning symbolic reachability strategy from s in $\mathcal{G}_{post}$, then $\mathfrak{S}$ is also winning from s in $\mathcal{G}$.*

Due to the restriction to φ, intuitively REACH wins from a state s in $\mathcal{G}_{post}$ if they can win from s in $\mathcal{G}$ *while staying inside the interpolant* φ. In other words, REACH must guarantee that the necessary subgoal C is not visited again in the play. Still, the set R_{post}, as returned in line 11 by the recursive call to Algorithm 1 on $\mathcal{G}_{post}$, is a sufficient subgoal in $\mathcal{G}$, by the above lemma. Furthermore, if SAFE can avoid all states satisfying R_{post} (see line 13), then this also implies a winning strategy from all initial states in I. The reason is that REACH can only win by eventually visiting a state from which they can win without leaving φ again, as *(Goal $\implies \varphi$)* is valid. This is not possible if SAFE can avoid all states in R_{post}.

In this case we construct $\mathfrak{S}_{\text{SAFE}}$ as follows. We assume that $\neg\mathfrak{S}_{\text{SAFE}}^{post}$ is a necessary subgoal that can be locally avoided in $\mathcal{G}_{post}$ from all states satisfying $\text{Post}(C)[\mathcal{V}'/\mathcal{V}] \wedge \neg R_{post}$, and furthermore, we know that $F := C \wedge R_{post}[\mathcal{V}/\mathcal{V}']$ can be locally avoided in $\mathcal{G}$ (line 13). Intuitively, playing according to $\mathfrak{S}_{\text{SAFE}}^{post}$ in $\mathcal{G}_{post}$ yields a strategy for SAFE which avoids *Goal* and may move back into a state satisfying $\neg\varphi$, which forces REACH to bridge the subgoal C again in order to win. It follows that $F \vee (\varphi \wedge \neg\mathfrak{S}_{\text{SAFE}}^{post})$ is a necessary subgoal from I that can be locally avoided by SAFE in $\mathcal{G}$, and the corresponding symbolic strategy is $\text{Safe} \wedge \neg F \wedge (\varphi \implies \mathfrak{S}_{\text{SAFE}}^{post})$ (we additionally intersect the negated necessary subgoal with *Safe* to ensure that the symbolic strategy only includes legal transitions).

So far, the subgoal was such that SAFE could avoid it entirely, or at least avoid all states from which REACH would win when forced to remain inside the post-game. If this is not the case, then we also need to consider the *pre-game* (line 18):

$$\mathcal{G}_{pre} = \langle I, \text{Safe} \wedge \neg F, \text{Reach} \wedge \neg F, \text{Pre}(\text{Enf}(F, \mathcal{G})) \rangle.$$

which intuitively describes the game before bridging the interpolant C for the last time. The exact definition of F will depend on whether C *perfectly partitions* the game or not. In both cases F will be the largest sufficient subgoal contained in a necessary subgoal, which lets us apply Proposition 9 to conclude that the initial winning regions of $\mathcal{G}$ and $\mathcal{G}_{pre}$ coincide.

Case 2: The Subgoal Perfectly Partitions $\mathcal{G}$. We say that φ *perfectly partitions* $\mathcal{G}$ if $(\text{Reach} \vee \text{Safe}) \wedge \varphi \wedge \neg\varphi' \wedge \neg\text{Goal}$ is unsatisfiable (cf. line 15). Intuitively, this means that there is no transition that "undoes" the effect of the subgoal C. If this holds, then the restriction of $\mathcal{G}_{post}$ to states satisfying φ is *de facto* no longer a restriction, as no play can reach such a state anyway after passing through the subgoal. This intuition is formalized by the following lemma.

Lemma 13. *Assume that φ perfectly partitions $\mathcal{G}$, and let s be a state satisfying* $Post(C)[\mathcal{V}'/\mathcal{V}]$. *Then REACH wins from s in $\mathcal{G}_{post}$ if and only if REACH wins from s in $\mathcal{G}$.*

It follows that $F = C \wedge R_{post}[\mathcal{V}/\mathcal{V}']$ is the largest sufficient subgoal included in C. By Proposition 9, the same initial states are winning for REACH in $\mathcal{G}_{pre}$ and in $\mathcal{G}$. In this case, we construct the desired safety strategy (line 22) as

$$\mathfrak{S}_{\text{SAFE}} = (\neg\varphi \implies \mathfrak{S}_{\text{SAFE}}^{pre}) \wedge (\varphi \implies \mathfrak{S}_{\text{SAFE}}^{post}),$$

where $\neg\mathfrak{S}_{\text{SAFE}}^{pre/post}$ are assumed to be necessary subgoals avoidable by SAFE in the corresponding subgames. Intuitively, the combined strategy consists of following $\mathfrak{S}_{\text{SAFE}}^{pre}$ as long as one remains in the pre-game, which, by induction hypothesis, allows SAFE to avoid all transitions from F if starting in R_{pre}. If the play crosses $C \wedge \neg F$, the strategy is to play according to the winning strategy of the post-game.

A symbolic strategy for REACH can be given by combining pre- and post-strategies as follows (line 21):

$$\begin{aligned}
\text{combine}(\mathfrak{S}_{\text{REACH}}^{pre}, F, \mathfrak{S}_{\text{REACH}}^{post}) := \ &(\text{Pre}(\mathfrak{S}_{\text{REACH}}^{post}) \implies \mathfrak{S}_{\text{REACH}}^{post}) \\
\wedge \ &((\neg\text{Pre}(\mathfrak{S}_{\text{REACH}}^{post}) \wedge \text{Pre}(F)) \implies F) \\
\wedge \ &((\neg\text{Pre}(\mathfrak{S}_{\text{REACH}}^{post}) \wedge \neg\text{Pre}(F)) \implies \mathfrak{S}_{\text{REACH}}^{pre}) \\
\wedge \ &(\text{Pre}(\mathfrak{S}_{\text{REACH}}^{post}) \vee \text{Pre}(F) \vee \text{Pre}(\mathfrak{S}_{\text{REACH}}^{pre})).
\end{aligned}$$

This represents a nested conditional strategy that prefers the strategies of the subgames in the priority order $\mathfrak{S}_{\text{REACH}}^{post}, F$, and finally $\mathfrak{S}_{\text{REACH}}^{pre}$. The reason for this order is that the winning condition in the post-game coincides with the global winning objective (to reach *Goal*), while in the pre-game REACH tries to reach a winning state in the post-game. The set F is exactly the bridge between these two. The last condition makes sure that the strategy only includes transitions of states in which it is winning.

Case 3: The subgoal does not perfectly partition $\mathcal{G}$. If Sat$((Reach \vee Safe) \wedge \varphi \wedge \neg\varphi' \wedge \neg Goal)$ is true in line 15, we can no longer assume that F is the largest sufficient subgoal in C. The reason is that SAFE may win in $\mathcal{G}_{post}$ by moving out of the subgame, but if this move leads to a winning state for REACH in $\mathcal{G}$, then such a strategy is winning in $\mathcal{G}_{post}$, but not in $\mathcal{G}$. So we can only assume that F is sufficient (this follows by Lemma 12). In order to apply Proposition 9 we extend F by all transitions that move directly into *Goal* (line 16). This immediately yields a necessary and sufficient subgoal, and so again Proposition 9 applies to $\mathcal{G}_{pre}$ (line 18). We could have also added *Goal*-states to F in Case

2, but we have observed that not doing so improves the performance of our procedure considerably.

The reachability strategy is composed of $\mathfrak{S}_{\mathtt{REACH}}^{pre}$, F, and $\mathfrak{S}_{\mathtt{REACH}}^{post}$ exactly as in Case 2 (line 21). As all transitions in F are losing for $\mathtt{SAFE}$, and these are the only ones that are removed in $\mathcal{G}_{pre}$, essentially $\mathtt{SAFE}$ can play using the same strategies in $\mathcal{G}$ and $\mathcal{G}_{pre}$. We implement this by setting φ to $\mathtt{false}$ (line 17), in which case $\mathfrak{S}_{\mathtt{SAFE}}$ (line 22) equals $(\mathtt{true} \implies \mathfrak{S}_{\mathtt{SAFE}}^{pre}) \wedge (\mathtt{false} \implies \mathfrak{S}_{\mathtt{SAFE}}^{post}) \equiv \mathfrak{S}_{\mathtt{SAFE}}^{pre}$.

Finally, we formally state the partial correctness of the algorithm, using the ideas from above.

Theorem 14 (Partial correctness). *If* $\mathrm{Reach}(\mathcal{G})$ *returns* $(R, \mathfrak{S}_{REACH}, \mathfrak{S}_{SAFE})$, *then*

- *R characterizes the set of initial states that are winning for $\mathtt{REACH}$ in $\mathcal{G}$,*
- *$\mathfrak{S}_{REACH}$ is a winning symbolic reachability strategy from R,*
- *$\mathfrak{S}_{SAFE}$ is a winning symbolic safety strategy from $Init \wedge \neg R$.*

Remark 15 (Simulating the attractor). Note that Craig interpolants are by no means unique. If we choose the interpolation function so that $\mathrm{Interpolate}(I, Goal)$ always returns $Goal$ (this is a valid interpolant), Algorithm 1 essentially simulates the attractor. In this case the subgoal C (line 7) contains exactly the transitions that move directly into $Goal$. All states in $\mathrm{Post}(C)[\mathcal{V}'/\mathcal{V}]$ are then winning for $\mathtt{REACH}$ and hence R_{post} would be equivalent to $\mathrm{Post}(C)[\mathcal{V}'/\mathcal{V}]$, which implies that $C \equiv F$ holds in this case. The new goal states in $\mathcal{G}_{pre}$ are set to $\mathrm{Pre}(\mathrm{Enf}(F, \mathcal{G}))$, which are exactly the states in $\mathrm{Pre}(C)$ that either are controlled by $\mathtt{REACH}$, or such that all their transitions are included in F. Hence the set $\mathrm{Pre}(\mathrm{Enf}(F, \mathcal{G}))$ is exactly the classical controlled predecessor.

One effect of slicing the game along general subgoals is that the initial predicate of the post-game (which describes all states satisfying the post-condition of the subgoal) may be satisfied by many states that do not necessarily need to be considered in order to decide who wins from the initial states of $\mathcal{G}$ (for example, because they are not reachable from any initial state, or cannot reach $Goal$). This can be a drawback if the (superfluous) size of the subgames makes them hard to solve. Notably, this is in general less of an issue for approaches based on unrolling of the transition relation: The method of solving increasingly large step-bounded games [18] will only consider states that are reachable from $Init$, while backwards fixpoint computations will not explore states that do not reach $Goal$. A way of coping with this is to provide additional information on the domains of variables, whenever this is available (we discuss the effect of bounding variable domains in Sect. 6). Indeed, in the case where all variable domains are finite, Algorithm 1 is guaranteed to terminate, as shown in the next subsection.

5.3   Special Cases with Guaranteed Termination

Deciding the winner in the types of games we consider is generally undecidable (see [18] for the case that $\mathcal{L}$ is linear real arithmetic). Since Algorithm 1 returns a correct result whenever it terminates, this implies that it cannot always terminate. In this section, we give two important cases in which we can prove termination.

Theorem 16. *If the domains of all variables in $\mathcal{G}$ are finite, then* Reach($\mathcal{G}$) *terminates.*

Remark 17 (Time complexity). The termination argument in the proof yields a single-exponential upper bound on the runtime of the algorithm, where the input size is measured in the number of concrete transitions of the game. This is because in both recursive calls the subgames may be "almost" as large as the input – they are only guaranteed to have at least one concrete transition less.

We now show that, under certain assumptions, our algorithm also terminates for games that have a finite bisimulation quotient. To this end, we first clarify what bisimilarity means in our setting. A relation $R \subseteq S \times S$ over the states of $\mathcal{G}$ is called a *bisimulation* on $\mathcal{G}$, if

- for all $(s_1, s_2) \in R$ the formulas $Goal(s_1) \iff Goal(s_2)$, $Init(s_1) \iff Init(s_2)$ and $\mathbf{r}(s_1) \iff \mathbf{r}(s_2)$ are valid (recall that $\mathbf{r}$ holds exactly in states controlled by REACH).
- for all $(s_1, s_2) \in R$ and $s_1' \in S$ such that $(Safe \vee Reach)(s_1, s_1')$ holds, there exists $s_2' \in S$ such that $(Safe \vee Reach)(s_2, s_2')$ holds, and $(s_1', s_2') \in R$.
- for all $(s_1, s_2) \in R$ and $s_2' \in S$ such that $(Safe \vee Reach)(s_2, s_2')$ holds, there exists $s_1' \in S$ such that $(Safe \vee Reach)(s_1, s_1')$ holds, and $(s_1', s_2') \in R$.

We say that s_1 and s_2 are *bisimilar* (denoted by $s_1 \sim s_2$) if there exists a bisimulation R such that $(s_1, s_2) \in R$. Bisimilarity is an equivalence relation, and it is the coarsest bisimulation on $\mathcal{G}$. The equivalence classes are called *bisimulation classes*. As the winning region of any player can be expressed in the μ-calculus [39] and the μ-calculus is invariant under bisimulation [9], it follows that bisimilar states are won by the same player.

Lemma 18. *Let R be a bisimulation on $\mathcal{G}$. If $(s_1, s_2) \in R$, then* REACH *wins from s_1 in $\mathcal{G}$ if and only if* REACH *wins from s_2 in $\mathcal{G}$.*

We will assume that for each bisimulation class S_i there exists a formula $\psi_i \in \mathcal{L}(V)$ that *defines* S_i, formally: For all $s \in S$, $\psi_i(s)$ holds if and only if $s \in S_i$. Furthermore, we will assume that the interpolation procedure *respects* $\sim$, formally: Interpolate(φ, ψ) is equivalent to a disjunction of formulas ψ_i. Such an interpolant exists if ψ or φ already satisfy this assumption.

Theorem 19. *Let $\mathcal{G}$ be a reachability game with finite bisimulation quotient under $\sim$ and assume that all bisimulation classes of $\mathcal{G}$ are definable in $\mathcal{L}$. Furthermore, assume that* Interpolate *respects $\sim$. Then,* Reach($\mathcal{G}$) *terminates.*

6 Case Studies

In this section we evaluate our approach on a number of case studies. Our prototype CABPY[2] is written in Python and implements the game solving part of the presented algorithm. Extending it to returning a symbolic strategy using the ideas outlined above is straightforward. We compared our prototype with SIMSYNTH [18], the only other readily available tool for solving linear arithmetic games. The evaluation was carried out with Ubuntu 20.04, a 4-core Intel® Core™ i5 2.30 GHz processor, as well as 8 GB of memory. CABPY uses the PySMT [19] library as an interface to the MathSAT5 [12] and Z3 [30] SMT solvers. On all benchmarks, the timeout was set to 10 min. In addition to the winner, we report the runtime and the number of subgames our algorithm visits. Both may vary with different SMT solvers or in different environments.

6.1 Game of Nim

Game of Nim is a classic game from the literature [8] and played on a number of heaps of stones. Both players take turns of choosing a single heap and removing at least one stone from it. We consider the version where the player that removes the last stone wins. Our results are shown in Fig. 1. In instances with three heaps or more we bounded the domains of the variables in the instance description, by specifying that no heap exceeds its initial size and does not go below zero.

Following the discussion in Sect. 5.3, we need to bound the domains to ensure the termination of our tool on these instances. Remarkably, bounding the variables was not necessary for instances with only two heaps, where our tool CABPY scales to considerably larger instances than SIMSYNTH. We did not add the same constraints to the input of SIMSYNTH, as for SIMSYNTH this resulted in longer runtimes rather than shorter. In Game of Nim, there are no natural necessary subgoals that the safety player can locally control.

The results (see Fig. 1) demonstrate that our approach is not completely dependent on finding the right interpolants and is in particular also competitive when the reachability player wins the game. We suspect that SIMSYNTH performs worse in these cases because the safety player has a large range of possible moves in most states, and inferring the win of the reachability player requires the tool to backtrack and try our all of them.

6.2 Corridor

We now consider an example that demonstrates the potential of our method in case the game structure contains natural bottlenecks. Consider a corridor of 100 rooms arranged in sequence, i.e., each room i with $0 \leq i < 100$ is connected to room $i + 1$ with a door. The objective of the reachability player is to reach

---

[2] The source code of CABPY and our experimental data are both available at https://github.com/reactive-systems/cabpy. We provide a virtual machine image with CABPY already installed for reproducing our evaluation [35].

| Heaps | CABPY | | SIMSYNTH | |
	Subgames	Time(s)	Time(s)	Winner
(4,4)	19	1.50	10.44	REACH
(4,5)	23	1.92	12.74	SAFE
(5,5)	23	1.99	85.75	REACH
(5,6)	27	2.90	91.66	SAFE
(6,6)	28	3.04	Timeout	REACH
(6,7)	31	3.76	Timeout	SAFE
(20,20)	88	94.85	Timeout	REACH
(20,21)	94	113.04	Timeout	SAFE
(30,30)	128	364.13	Timeout	REACH
(30,31)	135	404.02	Timeout	SAFE
(3,3,3)b	23	13.63	2.85	SAFE
(1,4,5)b	32	7.00	289.85	REACH
(4,4,4)b	33	50.55	24.39	SAFE
(2,4,6)b	38	19.77	Timeout	REACH
(5,5,5)b	33	127.89	162.50	SAFE
(3,5,6)b	40	86.56	Timeout	REACH
(2,2,2,2)b	39	84.79	213.79	REACH
(2,2,2,3)b	41	102.01	Timeout	SAFE

Fig. 1. Experimental results for the Game of Nim. The notation $(h_1, \ldots, h_n)$ denotes the instance played on n heaps, each of which consists of h_i stones. Instances marked with b indicate that the variable domains were explicitly bounded in the input for CABPY.

| r | CABPY | | SIMSYNTH | |
	Subgames	Time(s)	Time(s)	Winner
10	10	0.57	3.93	SAFE
20	20	1.23	20.48	SAFE
40	40	3.42	121.96	SAFE
60	60	7.36	Timeout	SAFE
80	80	17.72	Timeout	SAFE
100	100	26.36	Timeout	SAFE

Fig. 2. Experimental results for the Corridor game. The safety player controls the door between rooms $r - 1$ and r.

room 100 and they are free to choose valid values from $\mathbb{R}^2$ for the position in each room at every other turn. The safety player controls some door to a room $r \leq 100$. Naturally, a winning strategy is to prevent the reachability player from passing that door, which is a natural bottleneck and necessary subgoal on the way to the last room.

The experimental results are summarized in Fig. 2. We evaluated several versions of this game, increasing the length from the start to the controlled door.

The results confirm that our causal synthesis algorithm finds the trivial strategy of closing the door quickly. This is because Craig interpolation focuses the subgoals on the room number variable while ignoring the movement in the rooms in between, as can be seen by the number of considered subgames. SIMSYNTH, which tries to generalize a strategy obtained from a step-bounded game, struggles because the tool solves the games that happen between each of the doors before reaching the controlled one.

6.3   Mona Lisa

The game described in Sect. 2 between a thief and a security guard is very well suited to further assess the strength and limitations of both our approach as well as of SIMSYNTH. We ran several experiments with this scenario, scaling the size of the room and the sleep time of the guard, as well as trying a scenario where the guard does not sleep at all. Scaling the size of the room makes it harder for SIMSYNTH to solve this game with a forward unrolling approach, while our approach extracts the necessary subgoals irrespective of the room size. However, scaling the guard's sleep time makes it harder to solve the subgame between the two necessary subgoals, while it only has a minor effect on the length of the unrolling needed to stabilize the play in a safe region, as done by SIMSYNTH.

The results in Fig. 3 support this conjecture. The size of the room has *almost no effect at all* on both the runtime of CABPY and the number of considered subgames. However, as the results for a sleep value of 4 show, the employed combination of quantifier elimination and interpolation introduces some instability in the produced formulas. This means we may get different Craig interpolants and slice the game with more or less subgoals. Therefore, we see a lot of potential in optimizing the interplay between the employed tools for quantifier elimination and interpolation. The phenomenon of the runtime being sensitive to these small changes in values is also seen with SIMSYNTH, where a longer sleep time sometimes means a faster execution.

6.4   Program Synthesis

Lastly, we study two benchmarks that are directly related to program synthesis. The first problem is to synthesize a controller for a thermostat by filling out an incomplete program, as described in [4]. A range of possible initial values of the room temperature c is given, e.g., $20.8 \leq c \leq 23.5$, together with the temperature dynamics which depend on whether the heater is on (variable $o \in \mathbb{B}$). The objective for SAFE is to control the value of o in every round such that c stays between 20 and 25. This is a common benchmark for program synthesis tools and both CABPY and SIMSYNTH solve it quickly (see Fig. 4). The other problem relates to Lamport's bakery algorithm [26]. We consider two processes using this protocol to ensure mutually exclusive access to a shared resource. The game describes the task of synthesizing a scheduler that violates the mutual exclusion. This essentially is a model checking problem, and we study it to see how well the tools can infer a safety invariant that is out of control of the safety player.

		CabPy		SimSynth	
Size	Sleep	Subgames	Time(s)	Time(s)	Winner
10×10	-	7	0.61	4.79	SAFE
20×20	-	7	0.60	25.26	SAFE
40×40	-	7	0.61	157.62	SAFE
10×10	1	10	4.22	20.31	SAFE
20×20	1	11	4.34	36.44	SAFE
40×40	1	11	4.65	226.14	SAFE
10×10	2	13	5.88	7.40	SAFE
20×20	2	14	5.98	60.00	SAFE
40×40	2	13	5.92	270.48	SAFE
10×10	3	18	26.58	13.94	SAFE
20×20	3	17	26.19	115.53	SAFE
40×40	3	18	27.85	290.12	SAFE
10×10	4	30	175.27	13.96	SAFE
20×20	4	22	204.79	60.08	SAFE
40×40	4	27	123.95	319.47	SAFE

Fig. 3. Experimental results for the Mona Lisa game.

	CabPy		SimSynth	
Name	Subgames	Time(s)	Time(s)	Winner
Thermostat	6	0.44	0.39	SAFE
Bakery	46	18.25	Timeout	SAFE

Fig. 4. Experimental results for program synthesis problems.

For our approach, this makes no difference, as both players may play through a subgoal and the framework is well suited to find a safety invariant. The forward unrolling approach of SimSynth, however, seems to explore the whole state space before inferring safety, and fails to find an invariant before a timeout.

7   Conclusion

Our work is a step towards the fully automated synthesis of software. It targets symbolically represented reachability games which are expressive enough to model a variety of problems, from common game benchmarks to program synthesis problems. The presented approach exploits causal information in the form of *subgoals*, which are parts of the game that the reachability player needs to pass through in order to win. Having computed a subgoal, which can be done using Craig interpolation, the game is split along the subgoal and solved recursively. At the same time, the algorithm infers a structured symbolic strategy for the winning player. The evaluation of our prototype implementation CabPy shows that our approach is practically applicable and scales much better than previously available tools on several benchmarks. While termination is only guaranteed for games with finite bisimulation quotient, the experiments demonstrate that several infinite games can be solved as well.

This work opens up several interesting questions for further research. One concerns the quality of the returned strategies. Due to its compositional nature, at first sight it seems that our approach is not well-suited to handle global optimization criteria, such as reaching the goal in fewest possible steps. On the other hand, the returned strategies often involve only a few key decisions and we believe that therefore the strategies are often very sparse, although this has to be further investigated. We also plan to automatically extract deterministic strategies from the symbolic ones [5,17] we currently consider.

Another question regards the computation of subgoals. The performance of our algorithm is highly influenced by which interpolant is returned by the solver. In particular this affects the number of subgames that have to be solved, and how complex they are. We believe that template-based interpolation [27] is a promising candidate to explore for computing good interpolants. This could be combined with the possibility for the user to provide templates or expressive interpolants directly, thereby benefiting from the user's domain knowledge.

References

1. Alur, R., Moarref, S., Topcu, U.: Pattern-based refinement of assume-guarantee specifications in reactive synthesis. In: Baier, C., Tinelli, C. (eds.) TACAS 2015. LNCS, vol. 9035, pp. 501–516. Springer, Heidelberg (2015). https://doi.org/10.1007/978-3-662-46681-0_49
2. Alur, R., Moarref, S., Topcu, U.: Compositional synthesis of reactive controllers for multi-agent systems. In: Chaudhuri, S., Farzan, A. (eds.) CAV 2016. LNCS, vol. 9780, pp. 251–269. Springer, Cham (2016). https://doi.org/10.1007/978-3-319-41540-6_14
3. Baier, C., Coenen, N., Finkbeiner, B., Funke, F., Jantsch, S., Siber, J.: Causality-based game solving. CoRR (2021). https://arxiv.org/abs/2105.14247, long version with appendix
4. Beyene, T., Chaudhuri, S., Popeea, C., Rybalchenko, A.: A constraint-based approach to solving games on infinite graphs. In: Principles of Programming Languages (POPL). ACM, New York (2014). https://doi.org/10.1145/2535838.2535860
5. Bloem, R., Egly, U., Klampfl, P., Könighofer, R., Lonsing, F.: SAT-based methods for circuit synthesis. In: Formal Methods in Computer-Aided Design (FMCAD). IEEE (2014). https://doi.org/10.1109/FMCAD.2014.6987592
6. Bloem, R., Galler, S., Jobstmann, B., Piterman, N., Pnueli, A., Weiglhofer, M.: Specify, compile, run: hardware from PSL. Electron. Notes Theor. Comput. Sci. 190(4), 3–16 (2007). https://doi.org/10.1016/j.entcs.2007.09.004
7. Bloem, R., Jobstmann, B., Piterman, N., Pnueli, A., Sa'ar, Y.: Synthesis of reactive(1) designs. J. Comput. Syst. Sci. 78(3), 911–938 (2012). https://doi.org/10.1016/j.jcss.2011.08.007. In Commemoration of Amir Pnueli
8. Bouton, C.L.: Nim, a game with a complete mathematical theory. Ann. Math. 3(1/4), 35–39 (1901). https://doi.org/10.2307/1967631

9. Bradfield, J.C., Stirling, C.: Modal mu-calculi. In: Blackburn, P., van Benthem, J.F.A.K., Wolter, F. (eds.) Handbook of Modal Logic, Studies in Logic and Practical Reasoning, vol. 3, pp. 721–756, North-Holland (2007). https://doi.org/10.1016/s1570-2464(07)80015-2

10. Brückner, I., Dräger, K., Finkbeiner, B., Wehrheim, H.: Slicing abstractions. In: Arbab, F., Sirjani, M. (eds.) FSEN 2007. LNCS, vol. 4767, pp. 17–32. Springer, Heidelberg (2007). https://doi.org/10.1007/978-3-540-75698-9_2

11. Chen, Y., Tåmovů, J., Belta, C.: LTL Robot Motion Control based on Automata Learning of Environmental Dynamics. In: International Conference on Robotics and Automation. IEEE (2012). https://doi.org/10.1109/ICRA.2012.6225075

12. Cimatti, A., Griggio, A., Schaafsma, B.J., Sebastiani, R.: The MathSAT5 SMT solver. In: Piterman, N., Smolka, S.A. (eds.) TACAS 2013. LNCS, vol. 7795, pp. 93–107. Springer, Heidelberg (2013). https://doi.org/10.1007/978-3-642-36742-7_7

13. Craig, W.: Three uses of the Herbrand-Gentzen theorem in relating model theory and proof theory. J. Symbolic Logic 22(3), 269–285 (1957). https://doi.org/10.2307/2963594

14. de Alfaro, L., Henzinger, T.A., Majumdar, R.: Symbolic algorithms for infinite-state games. In: Larsen, K.G., Nielsen, M. (eds.) CONCUR 2001. LNCS, vol. 2154, pp. 536–550. Springer, Heidelberg (2001). https://doi.org/10.1007/3-540-44685-0_36

15. Edelkamp, S.: Symbolic exploration in two-player games: preliminary results. In: The International Conference on AI Planning & Scheduling (AIPS), Workshop on Model Checking (2002)

16. Eén, N., Legg, A., Narodytska, N., Ryzhyk, L.: SAT-based strategy extraction in reachability games. In: Conference on Artificial Intelligence (AAAI) (2015). https://ojs.aaai.org/index.php/AAAI/article/view/9752

17. Ehlers, R., Moldovan, D.: Sparse positional strategies for safety games. In: Workshop on Synthesis (SYNT), EPTCS (2012). https://doi.org/10.4204/EPTCS.84.1

18. Farzan, A., Kincaid, Z.: Strategy synthesis for linear arithmetic games. Proc. ACM Program. Lang. 2(POPL) (2017). https://doi.org/10.1145/3158149

19. Gario, M., Micheli, A.: PySMT: a solver-agnostic library for fast prototyping of SMT-based algorithms. In: SMT Workshop 2015 (2015)

20. Grädel, E., Thomas, W., Wilke, T. (eds.): Automata Logics, and Infinite Games. LNCS, vol. 2500. Springer, Heidelberg (2002). https://doi.org/10.1007/3-540-36387-4

21. Harding, A., Ryan, M., Schobbens, P.-Y.: A new algorithm for strategy synthesis in LTL games. In: Halbwachs, N., Zuck, L.D. (eds.) TACAS 2005. LNCS, vol. 3440, pp. 477–492. Springer, Heidelberg (2005). https://doi.org/10.1007/978-3-540-31980-1_31

22. Hoffmann, J., Porteous, J., Sebastia, L.: Ordered landmarks in planning. J. Artif. Intell. Res. 22(1), 215–278 (2004)

23. Jessen, J.J., Rasmussen, J.I., Larsen, K.G., David, A.: Guided controller synthesis for climate controller using UPPAAL TIGA. In: Raskin, J.-F., Thiagarajan, P.S. (eds.) FORMATS 2007. LNCS, vol. 4763, pp. 227–240. Springer, Heidelberg (2007). https://doi.org/10.1007/978-3-540-75454-1_17

24. Kupriyanov, A., Finkbeiner, B.: Causality-based verification of multi-threaded programs. Concur. Theory (CONCUR) (2013). https://doi.org/10.1007/978-3-642-40184-8_19

25. Kupriyanov, A., Finkbeiner, B.: Causal termination of multi-threaded programs. Comput. Aided Verification (CAV) (2014). https://doi.org/10.1007/978-3-319-08867-9_54

26. Lamport, L.: A new solution of Dijkstra's concurrent programming problem. Commun. ACM **17**(8), 453–455 (1974). https://doi.org/10.1145/361082.361093

27. Leroux, J., Rümmer, P., Subotić, P.: Guiding Craig interpolation with domain-specific abstractions. Acta Informatica **53**(4), 387–424 (2016). https://doi.org/10.1007/s00236-015-0236-z

28. Menzies, P., Beebee, H.: Counterfactual theories of causation. In: Zalta, E.N. (ed.) The Stanford Encyclopedia of Philosophy. Stanford University, Metaphysics Research Lab (2020)

29. Monniaux, D.: A quantifier elimination algorithm for linear real arithmetic. In: Cervesato, I., Veith, H., Voronkov, A. (eds.) LPAR 2008. LNCS (LNAI), vol. 5330, pp. 243–257. Springer, Heidelberg (2008). https://doi.org/10.1007/978-3-540-89439-1_18

30. de Moura, L., Bjørner, N.: Z3: an efficient SMT solver. In: Ramakrishnan, C.R., Rehof, J. (eds.) TACAS 2008. LNCS, vol. 4963, pp. 337–340. Springer, Heidelberg (2008). https://doi.org/10.1007/978-3-540-78800-3_24

31. Narodytska, N., Legg, A., Bacchus, F., Ryzhyk, L., Walker, A.: Solving games without controllable predecessor. In: Biere, A., Bloem, R. (eds.) CAV 2014. LNCS, vol. 8559, pp. 533–540. Springer, Cham (2014). https://doi.org/10.1007/978-3-319-08867-9_35

32. Pozanco, A., E-Martín, Y., Fernández, S., Borrajo, D.: Counterplanning using goal recognition and landmarks. In: International Joint Conference on Artificial Intelligence (IJCAI) (2018). https://doi.org/10.24963/ijcai.2018/668

33. Presburger, M.: Über die Vollständigkeit eines gewissen Systems der Arithmetik ganzer Zahlen, in welchem die Addition als einzige Operation hervortritt. Comptes Rendus du I congres de Mathématiciens des Pays Slaves (1929)

34. Ryzhyk, L., Chubb, P., Kuz, I., Le Sueur, E., Heiser, G.: Automatic device driver synthesis with termite. In: Symposium on Operating Systems Principles (SOSP). Association for Computing Machinery (ACM) (2009). https://doi.org/10.1145/1629575.1629583

35. Siber, J.: The Virtual Machine containing CabPy (2021). https://doi.org/10.6084/m9.figshare.14493804.v3

36. Sreedharan, S., Srivastava, S., Smith, D.E., Kambhampati, S.: Why can't you do that HAL? Explaining unsolvability of planning tasks. In: International Joint Conference on Artificial Intelligence (IJCAI) (2019). https://doi.org/10.24963/ijcai.2019/197

37. Thomas, W.: On the synthesis of strategies in infinite games. In: Mayr, E.W., Puech, C. (eds.) STACS 1995. LNCS, vol. 900, pp. 1–13. Springer, Heidelberg (1995). https://doi.org/10.1007/3-540-59042-0_57

38. Walker, A., Ryzhyk, L.: Predicate abstraction for reactive synthesis. Formal Meth. Comput. Aided Des. (FMCAD) (2014). https://doi.org/10.1109/FMCAD.2014.6987617

39. Zappe, J.: Modal μ-calculus and alternating tree automata. In: Grädel, E., Thomas, W., Wilke, T. (eds.) Automata Logics, and Infinite Games. LNCS, vol. 2500, pp. 171–184. Springer, Heidelberg (2002). https://doi.org/10.1007/3-540-36387-4_10

Author Index

Abate, Alessandro II-3
Agarwal, Pratyush I-341
Akshay, S. I-619
Albert, Elvira II-863
Alur, Rajeev I-249
Amram, Gal I-870
André, Étienne I-552
Andriushchenko, Roman I-856
Arcaini, Paolo I-595
Armstrong, Alasdair I-303
Arquint, Linard I-367
Ayoun, Sacha-Élie II-827

Backes, J. II-851
Bae, Kyungmin I-491
Baier, Christel I-894
Baier, Daniel II-195
Bak, Stanley I-263
Balunovic, Mislav I-225
Bansal, Suguman I-870
Bardin, Sébastien I-669
Barrett, Clark II-461
Batz, Kevin II-524
Baumeister, Jan I-694
Bayless, S. II-851
Bendík, Jaroslav II-313
Beneš, Nikola I-505
Berzish, Murphy II-289
Beyer, Dirk II-195
Biere, Armin II-363
Bodeveix, Jean-Paul II-337
Bonakdarpour, Borzoo I-694
Boston, Brett I-645
Bozzano, Marco II-209
Bragg, Nate F. F. I-808
Breese, Samuel I-645
Brim, Luboš I-505
Brown, Kristopher II-461
Brunel, Julien II-337

Campbell, Brian I-303
Carpenter, Taylor I-249
Cauli, Claudia I-767

Češka, Milan I-856
Chakraborty, Supratik II-911
Chalupa, Marek II-887
Chatterjee, Krishnendu I-341
Chemouil, David II-337
Chen, Guangke I-175
Chen, Jiayu I-225
Chen, Mingshuai I-443, II-524
Chen, Taolue I-175
Chen, Xiaohong II-477
Chiari, Michele II-387
Christakis, Maria I-201, II-777
Cimatti, Alessandro I-529, II-209
Clochard, Martin I-367
Coenen, Norine I-694, I-894
Cogumbreiro, Tiago I-403
Constantinides, George II-626
Cyphert, John I-46, I-783

D'Antoni, Loris I-84, I-783
DaCosta, D. II-851
Dahlqvist, Fredrik II-626
Dan, Andrei I-225
Day, Joel D. II-289
Dodds, Joey I-645
Dodds, Mike I-645
Dutertre, Bruno II-266
Dwyer, Matthew B. I-137

Eilers, Marco I-718
Eisenhut, Jan II-411
Elad, Neta I-317
Elbaum, Sebastian I-137
Eniser, Hasan Ferit I-201

Fang, Wang I-151
Farinier, Benjamin I-669
Farzan, Azadeh I-832
Ferlez, James I-287
Fernandes Pires, Anthony II-209
Finkbeiner, Bernd I-694, I-894
Foster, Jeffrey S. I-808
Fried, Dror I-870
Friedberger, Karlheinz II-195

Fu, Yu-Fu   II-149
Funke, Florian   I-894

Ganesh, Vijay   II-289
Gardner, Philippa   II-827
Gastin, Paul   I-619
Genaim, Samir   II-863
Giacobbe, Mirco   II-3
Girol, Guillaume   I-669
Gnad, Daniel   II-411
Goel, Shilpi   I-26
Gopinath, Divya   I-3
Griggio, Alberto   I-529, II-209
Guan, Ji   I-151
Gupta, Aarti   II-461
Gupta, Ashutosh   II-911

Hahn, Ernst Moritz   II-651
Hallé, Sylvain   II-500
Hamilton, Nathaniel   I-263
Hasuo, Ichiro   I-595, II-75
Hauptman, Dustin   I-566
Heljanko, Keijo   II-363
Hermanns, Holger   I-201
Hobor, Aquinas   II-801
Hoffmann, Jörg   I-201, II-411
Holtzen, Steven   II-577
Hu, Qinheping   I-84, I-783
Huffman, Brian   I-645
Hur, Chung-Kil   II-752

Immerman, Neil   I-317
Irfan, Ahmed   I-529, II-461
Itzhaky, Shachar   I-110, II-125
Ivanov, Radoslav   I-249

Jacobs, Bart   II-27
Jacobs, Swen   II-435
Jansen, Nils   II-602
Jantsch, Simon   I-894
Jewell, K.   II-851
Johnson, Andrew   I-380
Johnson, Taylor T.   I-263
Jonáš, Martin   II-209
Jones, B. F.   II-851
Joshi, S.   II-851
Jovanović, Dejan   II-266
Junges, Sebastian   I-856, II-553, II-577,
    II-602

Kaminski, Benjamin Lucien   II-524
Katoen, Joost-Pieter   I-443, I-856, II-524
Keshmiri, Shawn   I-566
Khedr, Haitham   I-287
Kim, Dongjoo   II-752
Kim, Jinwoo   I-84
Kim, Sharon   I-491
Kimberly, Greg   II-209
Kincaid, Zachary   I-46, II-51
Klaška, David   II-887
Kokologiannakis, Michalis   I-427
Koskinen, Eric   I-742
Kothari, Yugesh   I-201
Kovács, Laura   I-317
Kremer, Gereon   II-231
Kulczynski, Mitja   II-289
Kura, Satoshi   II-75

Lal, Ratan   I-566
Lange, Julien   I-403
Launchbury, N.   II-851
Lee, Insup   I-249
Lee, Jaehun   I-491
Lee, Juneyoung   II-752
Lefaucheux, Engel   II-172
Leow, Wei Xiang   II-801
Leutgeb, Lorenz   II-99
Li, Jianlin   I-201
Li, Meng   I-767
Li, Pengfei   II-728
Li, Yangge   I-580
Lin, Anthony W.   II-243
Lin, Wang   I-467
Lin, Zhengyao   II-477
Liu, Jiaxiang   II-149
Liu, Zhiming   I-467
Lluch Lafuente, Alberto   II-411
Lonsing, Florian   II-461
Lopes, Nuno P.   II-752
Lopez, Diego Manzanas   I-263
Lyu, Deyun   I-595

Ma, Lei   I-595
Maksimović, Petar   II-827
Mandrioli, Dino   II-387
Manea, Florin   II-289
Mann, Makai   II-461
Mansur, Muhammad Numair   II-777
Mariano, Benjamin   II-777
Markgraf, Oliver   II-243

Martin-Martin, Enrique   II-863
Matheja, Christoph   II-524
Mathews, N.   II-851
McKinnis, Aaron   I-566
Meel, Kuldeep S.   II-313
Meier, Severin   I-718
Merayo, Alicia   II-863
Millstein, Todd   II-577
Mitra, Sayan   I-580
Mohan, Anshuman   II-801
Mora, Federico   II-289
Moser, Georg   II-99
Mover, Sergio   I-529
Müller, Peter   I-367, I-718, II-704
Musau, Patrick   I-263

Navas, Jorge A.   I-201, II-777
Nicolet, Victor   I-832
Niemetz, Aina   II-231
Noller, Yannic   I-3
Nowotka, Dirk   II-289

Ölveczky, Peter Csaba   I-491
Oortwijn, Wytse   I-367
Osama, Muhammad   II-447
Ouaknine, Joël   II-172

Pal, Neelanjana   I-263
Pappas, George   I-249
Parthasarathy, Gaurav   II-704
Păsăreanu, Corina S.   I-3
Pastva, Samuel   I-505
Pathak, Shreya   I-341
Pavlogiannis, Andreas   I-341
Peleg, Hila   I-110
Pereira, João C.   I-367
Pereira, Mário   II-677
Perez, Mateo   II-651
Petcher, Adam   I-645
Peyras, Quentin   II-337
Piterman, Nir   I-767
Polikarpova, Nadia   I-110
Prabhakar, Pavithra   I-566
Pradella, Matteo   II-387
Prakash, Karthik R.   I-619
Preiner, Mathias   II-231
Pulte, Christopher   I-303
Purser, David   II-172

Rain, Sophie   I-317
Rakamarić, Zvonimir   II-626
Ravara, António   II-677
Reinhard, Tobias   II-27
Reps, Thomas   I-46, I-84, I-783
Rong, Dennis Liew Zhen   I-403
Roşu, Grigore   II-477
Roux, Cody   I-808
Rowe, Reuben N. S.   I-110
Roy, Diptarko   II-3
Rubio, Albert   II-863
Ryou, Wonryong   I-225

Šafránek, David   I-505
Sagiv, Mooly   I-317
Sakr, Mouhammad   II-435
Salvia, Rocco   II-626
Sánchez, César   I-694
Santos, José Fragoso   II-827
Schewe, Sven   II-651
Schröer, Philipp   II-524
Sergey, Ilya   I-110
Seshia, Sanjit A.   II-553, II-577, II-602
Sewell, Peter   I-303
Shi, Xiaomu   II-149
Shoukry, Yasser   I-287
Shriver, David   I-137
Sibai, Hussein   I-580
Siber, Julian   I-894
Simner, Ben   I-303
Singh, Gagandeep   I-225
Singher, Eytan   II-125
Slobodova, Anna   I-26
Solar-Lezama, Armando   I-808
Somenzi, Fabio   II-651
Song, Fu   I-175
Stan, Daniel   II-243
Stefanescu, Andrei   I-645
Strejček, Jan   II-887
Stupinský, Šimon   I-856
Summers, Alexander J.   II-704
Sumners, Rob   I-26
Sun, Youcheng   I-3
Swords, Sol   I-26

Tabajara, Lucas Martinelli   I-870
Tang, Xiaochao   I-467
Terauchi, Tachio   I-742
Tkachuk, Oksana   I-767
Toman, Viktor   I-341

Tomovič, Lukáš   II-887
Tonetta, Stefano   I-529
Torfah, Hazem   II-553
Tran, Hoang-Dung   I-263
Tremblay, Hugo   II-500
Trentin, P.   II-851
Trinh, Minh-Thai   II-477
Trivedi, Ashutosh   II-651
Tsai, Ming-Hsien   II-149

Unadkat, Divyesh   II-911
Unno, Hiroshi   I-742, II-75
Usman, Muhammad   I-3

Vafeiadis, Viktor   I-427
Van den Broeck, Guy   II-577
van der Berg, Freark I.   II-690
Vardi, Moshe Y.   I-870
Vazquez-Chanlatte, Marcell   II-577
Vechev, Martin   I-225

Wahl, Thomas   I-380
Wang, Bow-Yaw   II-149
Wang, Qiuye   I-443
Wang, Yuting   II-728
Weimer, James   I-249
Weiss, Gera   I-870
Wijs, Anton   II-447
Wojtczak, Dominik   II-651

Wolf, Felix A.   I-367
Worrell, James   II-172
Wu, Jinhua   II-728
Wüstholz, Valentin   I-201, II-777

Xu, Xiangzhe   II-728
Xue, Bai   I-443

Yang, Bo-Yin   II-149
Yang, Xiaodong   I-263
Yang, Yahan   II-461
Yang, Zhengfeng   I-467
Yin, Zhenguo   II-728
Ying, Mingsheng   I-151
Yu, Emily   II-363

Zeng, M. Q.   II-851
Zeng, Xia   I-467
Zeng, Zhenbing   I-467
Zhan, Naijun   I-443
Zhang, Hongce   II-461
Zhang, Yedi   I-175
Zhang, Yidan   I-467
Zhang, Zhenya   I-595
Zhao, Jianjun   I-595
Zhao, Zhe   I-175
Zhu, Shaowei   II-51
Zicarelli, Hannah   I-403
Zuleger, Florian   II-99

Printed in the United States
by Baker & Taylor Publisher Services

Printed in the United States
by Baker & Taylor Publisher Services